Prealgebra

SENIOR CONTRIBUTING AUTHORS
LYNN MARECEK, SANTA ANA COLLEGE
MARYANNE ANTHONY-SMITH, FORMERLY OF SANTA ANA COLLEGE

OpenStax

Rice University

6100 Main Street MS-375

Houston, Texas 77005

To learn more about OpenStax, visit https://openstax.org.

Individual print copies and bulk orders can be purchased through our website.

PRINT BOOK ISBN-10	1-938168-99-2
PRINT BOOK ISBN-13	978-1-938168-99-4
PDF VERSION ISBN-10	1-947172-00-X
PDF VERSION ISBN-13	978-1-947172-00-5
Revision Number	PA-2016-003(03/17)-LC
Original Publication Year	2016

OPENSTAX

OpenStax provides free, peer-reviewed, openly licensed textbooks for introductory college and Advanced Placement® courses and low-cost, personalized courseware that helps students learn. A nonprofit ed tech initiative based at Rice University, we're committed to helping students access the tools they need to complete their courses and meet their educational goals.

RICE UNIVERSITY

OpenStax, OpenStax CNX, and OpenStax Tutor are initiatives of Rice University. As a leading research university with a distinctive commitment to undergraduate education, Rice University aspires to path-breaking research, unsurpassed teaching, and contributions to the betterment of our world. It seeks to fulfill this mission by cultivating a diverse community of learning and discovery that produces leaders across the spectrum of human endeavor.

FOUNDATION SUPPORT

OpenStax is grateful for the tremendous support of our sponsors. Without their strong engagement, the goal of free access to high-quality textbooks would remain just a dream.

Laura and John Arnold Foundation (LJAF) actively seeks opportunities to invest in organizations and thought leaders that have a sincere interest in implementing fundamental changes that not only yield immediate gains, but also repair broken systems for future generations. LJAF currently focuses its strategic investments on education, criminal justice, research integrity, and public accountability.

The William and Flora Hewlett Foundation has been making grants since 1967 to help solve social and environmental problems at home and around the world. The Foundation concentrates its resources on activities in education, the environment, global development and population, performing arts, and philanthropy, and makes grants to support disadvantaged communities in the San Francisco Bay Area.

Calvin K. Kazanjian was the founder and president of Peter Paul (Almond Joy), Inc. He firmly believed that the more people understood about basic economics the happier and more prosperous they would be. Accordingly, he established the Calvin K. Kazanjian Economics Foundation Inc, in 1949 as a philanthropic, nonpolitical educational organization to support efforts that enhanced economic understanding.

Guided by the belief that every life has equal value, the Bill & Melinda Gates Foundation works to help all people lead healthy, productive lives. In developing countries, it focuses on improving people's health with vaccines and other life-saving tools and giving them the chance to lift themselves out of hunger and extreme poverty. In the United States, it seeks to significantly improve education so that all young people have the opportunity to reach their full potential. Based in Seattle, Washington, the foundation is led by CEO Jeff Raikes and Co-chair William H. Gates Sr., under the direction of Bill and Melinda Gates and Warren Buffett.

The Maxfield Foundation supports projects with potential for high impact in science, education, sustainability, and other areas of social importance.

Our mission at The Michelson 20MM Foundation is to grow access and success by eliminating unnecessary hurdles to affordability. We support the creation, sharing, and proliferation of more effective, more affordable educational content by leveraging disruptive technologies, open educational resources, and new models for collaboration between for-profit, nonprofit, and public entities.

The Bill and Stephanie Sick Fund supports innovative projects in the areas of Education, Art, Science and Engineering.

⊟ Table of Contents

This OpenStax book is available for free at http://cnx.org/content/col11756/1.9

PREFACE

Welcome to *Prealgebra*, an OpenStax resource. This textbook was written to increase student access to high-quality learning materials, maintaining highest standards of academic rigor at little to no cost.

About OpenStax

OpenStax is a nonprofit based at Rice University, and it's our mission to improve student access to education. Our first openly licensed college textbook was published in 2012, and our library has since scaled to over 20 books for college and AP® Courses used by hundreds of thousands of students. Our adaptive learning technology, designed to improve learning outcomes through personalized educational paths, is being piloted in college courses throughout the country. Through our partnerships with philanthropic foundations and our alliance with other educational resource organizations, OpenStax is breaking down the most common barriers to learning and empowering students and instructors to succeed.

About OpenStax Resources

Customization

Prealgebra is licensed under a Creative Commons Attribution 4.0 International (CC BY) license, which means that you can distribute, remix, and build upon the content, as long as you provide attribution to OpenStax and its content contributors.

Because our books are openly licensed, you are free to use the entire book or pick and choose the sections that are most relevant to the needs of your course. Feel free to remix the content by assigning your students certain chapters and sections in your syllabus, in the order that you prefer. You can even provide a direct link in your syllabus to the sections in the web view of your book.

Instructors also have the option of creating a customized version of their OpenStax book. The custom version can be made available to students in low-cost print or digital form through their campus bookstore. Visit your book page on openstax.org for more information.

Errata

All OpenStax textbooks undergo a rigorous review process. However, like any professional-grade textbook, errors sometimes occur. Since our books are web based, we can make updates periodically when deemed pedagogically necessary. If you have a correction to suggest, submit it through the link on your book page on openstax.org. Subject matter experts review all errata suggestions. OpenStax is committed to remaining transparent about all updates, so you will also find a list of past errata changes on your book page on openstax.org.

Format

You can access this textbook for free in web view or PDF through openstax.org.

About *Prealgebra*

Prealgebra is designed to meet scope and sequence requirements for a one-semester prealgebra course. The text introduces the fundamental concepts of algebra while addressing the needs of students with diverse backgrounds and learning styles. Each topic builds upon previously developed material to demonstrate the cohesiveness and structure of mathematics.

Students who are taking *Basic Mathematics* and *Prealgebra* classes in college present a unique set of challenges. Many students in these classes have been unsuccessful in their prior math classes. They may think they know some math, but their core knowledge is full of holes. Furthermore, these students need to learn much more than the course content. They need to learn study skills, time management, and how to deal with math anxiety. Some students lack basic reading and arithmetic skills. The organization of *Prealgebra* makes it easy to adapt the book to suit a variety of course syllabi.

Coverage and Scope

Prealgebra follows a nontraditional approach in its presentation of content. The beginning, in particular, is presented as a sequence of small steps so that students gain confidence in their ability to succeed in the course. The order of topics was carefully planned to emphasize the logical progression throughout the course and to facilitate a thorough understanding of each concept. As new ideas are presented, they are explicitly related to previous topics.

Chapter 1: Whole Numbers
Each of the four basic operations with whole numbers—addition, subtraction, multiplication, and division—is modeled and explained. As each operation is covered, discussions of algebraic notation and operation signs, translation of algebraic expressions into word phrases, and the use the operation in applications are included.

Chapter 2: The Language of Algebra
Mathematical vocabulary as it applies to the whole numbers is presented. The use of variables, which distinguishes algebra from arithmetic, is introduced early in the chapter, and the development of and practice with arithmetic concepts use variables as well as numeric expressions. In addition, the difference between expressions and equations is discussed, word problems are introduced, and the process for solving one-step equations is modeled.

Chapter 3: Integers
While introducing the basic operations with negative numbers, students continue to practice simplifying, evaluating, and translating algebraic expressions. The Division Property of Equality is introduced and used to solve one-step equations.

Chapter 4: Fractions
Fraction circles and bars are used to help make fractions real and to develop operations on them. Students continue simplifying and evaluating algebraic expressions with fractions, and learn to use the Multiplication Property of Equality to solve equations involving fractions.

Chapter 5: Decimals
Basic operations with decimals are presented, as well as methods for converting fractions to decimals and vice versa. Averages and probability, unit rates and unit prices, and square roots are included to provide opportunities to use and round decimals.

Chapter 6: Percents
Conversions among percents, fractions, and decimals are explored. Applications of percent include calculating sales tax, commission, and simple interest. Proportions and solving percent equations as proportions are addressed as well.

Chapter 7: The Properties of Real Numbers
The properties of real numbers are introduced and applied as a culmination of the work done thus far, and to prepare students for the upcoming chapters on equations, polynomials, and graphing.

Chapter 8: Solving Linear Equations
A gradual build-up to solving multi-step equations is presented. Problems involve solving equations with constants on both sides, variables on both sides, variables and constants on both sides, and fraction and decimal coefficients.

Chapter 9: Math Models and Geometry
The chapter begins with opportunities to solve "traditional" number, coin, and mixture problems. Geometry sections cover the properties of triangles, rectangles, trapezoids, circles, irregular figures, the Pythagorean Theorem, and volumes and surface areas of solids. Distance-rate-time problems and formulas are included as well.

Chapter 10: Polynomials
Adding and subtracting polynomials is presented as an extension of prior work on combining like terms. Integer exponents are defined and then applied to scientific notation. The chapter concludes with a brief introduction to factoring polynomials.

Chapter 11: Graphs
This chapter is placed last so that all of the algebra with one variable is completed before working with linear equations in two variables. Examples progress from plotting points to graphing lines by making a table of solutions to an equation. Properties of vertical and horizontal lines and intercepts are included. Graphing linear equations at the end of the course gives students a good opportunity to review evaluating expressions and solving equations.

All chapters are broken down into multiple sections, the titles of which can be viewed in the Table of Contents.

Accuracy of Content

We have taken great pains to ensure the validity and accuracy of this text. Each chapter's manuscript underwent rounds of review and revision by a panel of active instructors. Then, prior to publication, a separate team of experts checked all text, examples, and graphics for mathematical accuracy. A third team of experts was responsible for the accuracy of the Answer Key, dutifully re-working every solution to eradicate any lingering errors. Finally, the editorial team conducted a multi-round post-production review to ensure the integrity of the content in its final form.

Pedagogical Foundation and Features
Learning Objectives

Each chapter is divided into multiple sections (or modules), each of which is organized around a set of learning objectives. The learning objectives are listed explicitly at the beginning of each section and are the focal point of every instructional element.

Narrative text

Narrative text is used to introduce key concepts, terms, and definitions, to provide real-world context, and to provide transitions between topics and examples. An informal voice was used to make the content accessible to students.

Throughout this book, we rely on a few basic conventions to highlight the most important ideas:

Key terms are boldfaced, typically when first introduced and/or when formally defined.

Key concepts and definitions are called out in a blue box for easy reference.

Examples

Each learning objective is supported by one or more worked examples, which demonstrate the problem-solving approaches that students must master. Typically, we include multiple Examples for each learning objective in order to model different approaches to the same type of problem, or to introduce similar problems of increasing complexity.

All Examples follow a simple two- or three-part format. First, we pose a problem or question. Next, we demonstrate the Solution, spelling out the steps along the way. Finally (for select Examples), we show students how to check the solution. Most examples are written in a two-column format, with explanation on the left and math on the right to mimic the way that instructors "talk through" examples as they write on the board in class.

Figures

Prealgebra contains many figures and illustrations. Art throughout the text adheres to a clear, understated style, drawing the eye to the most important information in each figure while minimizing visual distractions.

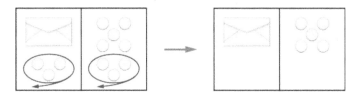

Supporting Features

Four small but important features serve to support Examples:

Be Prepared!

Each section, beginning with Section 1.2, starts with a few "Be Prepared!" exercises so that students can determine if they have mastered the prerequisite skills for the section. Reference is made to specific Examples from previous sections so students who need further review can easily find explanations. Answers to these exercises can be found in the supplemental resources that accompany this title.

How To

 A "How To" is a list of steps necessary to solve a certain type of problem. A "How To" typically precedes an Example.

Try It

 A "Try It" exercise immediately follows an Example, providing the student with an immediate opportunity to solve a similar problem. In the web view version of the text, students can click an Answer link directly below the question to check their understanding. In the PDF, answers to the Try It exercises are located in the Answer Key.

Media

[▶] The "Media" icon appears at the conclusion of each section, just prior to the Section Exercises. This icon marks a list of links to online video tutorials that reinforce the concepts and skills introduced in the section.

Disclaimer: While we have selected tutorials that closely align to our learning objectives, we did not produce these tutorials, nor were they specifically produced or tailored to accompany *Prealgebra*.

Section Exercises

Each section of every chapter concludes with a well-rounded set of exercises that can be assigned as homework or used selectively for guided practice. Exercise sets are named Practice Makes Perfect to encourage completion of homework assignments.

Exercises correlate to the learning objectives. This facilitates assignment of personalized study plans based on individual student needs.

Exercises are carefully sequenced to promote building of skills.

Values for constants and coefficients were chosen to practice and reinforce arithmetic facts.

Even and odd-numbered exercises are paired.

Exercises parallel and extend the text examples and use the same instructions as the examples to help students easily recognize the connection.

Applications are drawn from many everyday experiences, as well as those traditionally found in college math texts.

Everyday Math highlights practical situations using the math concepts from that particular section.

Writing Exercises are included in every Exercise Set to encourage conceptual understanding, critical thinking, and literacy.

Chapter Review Features

The end of each chapter includes a review of the most important takeaways, as well as additional practice problems that students can use to prepare for exams.

Key Terms provides a formal definition for each bold-faced term in the chapter.

Key Concepts summarizes the most important ideas introduced in each section, linking back to the relevant Example(s) in case students need to review.

Chapter Review Exercises includes practice problems that recall the most important concepts from each section.

Practice Test includes additional problems assessing the most important learning objectives from the chapter.

Answer Key includes the answers to all Try It exercises and every other exercise from the Section Exercises, Chapter Review Exercises, and Practice Test.

Additional Resources
Student and Instructor Resources

We've compiled additional resources for both students and instructors, including Getting Started Guides, manipulative mathematics worksheets, Links to Literacy assignments, and an answer key to Be Prepared Exercises. Instructor resources require a verified instructor account, which can be requested on your openstax.org log-in. Take advantage of these resources to supplement your OpenStax book.

Partner Resources

OpenStax Partners are our allies in the mission to make high-quality learning materials affordable and accessible to students and instructors everywhere. Their tools integrate seamlessly with our OpenStax titles at a low cost. To access the partner resources for your text, visit your book page on openstax.org.

About the Authors
Senior Contributing Authors

Lynn Marecek and MaryAnne Anthony-Smith have been teaching mathematics at Santa Ana College for many years and have worked together on several projects aimed at improving student learning in developmental math courses. They are the authors of *Strategies for Success: Study Skills for the College Math Student,* published by Pearson HigherEd.

Lynn Marecek, Santa Ana College
Lynn Marecek has focused her career on meeting the needs of developmental math students. At Santa Ana College she has been awarded the Distinguished Faculty Award, Innovation Award, and the Curriculum Development Award four times. She is a Coordinator of Freshman Experience Program, the Department Facilitator for Redesign, and a member of the Student Success and Equity Committee and the Basic Skills Initiative Task Force. Lynn holds a bachelor's degree from Valparaiso University and master's degrees from Purdue University and National University.

MaryAnne Anthony-Smith, Santa Ana College
MaryAnne has served as department chair, acting dean, chair of the professional development committee, institutional researcher, and faculty coordinator on several state and federally-funded grants and was a member of AMATYC's Placement and Assessment Committee. She is the community college coordinator of California's Mathematics Diagnostic Testing Project.

Reviewers

Tony Ayers, Collin College Preston Ridge Campus
David Behrman, Somerset Community College
Brandie Biddy, Cecil College
Bryan Blount, Kentucky Wesleyan College
Steven Boettcher, Estrella Mountain Community College
Kimberlyn Brooks, Cuyahoga Community College
Pamela Burleson, Lone Star College University Park
Tamara Carter, Texas A&M University
Phil Clark, Scottsdale Community College
Christina Cornejo, Erie Community College
Denise Cutler, Bay de Noc Community College
Richard Darnell, Eastern Wyoming College
Robert Diaz, Fullerton College
Karen Dillon, Thomas Nelson Community College
Valeree Falduto, Palm Beach State
Bryan Faulkner, Ferrum College
David French, Tidewater Community College
Stephanie Gable, Columbus State University
Heather Gallacher, Cleveland State University
Rachel Gross, Towson University

Dianne Hendrickson, Becker College
Linda Hunt, Shawnee State University
Betty Ivory, Cuyahoga Community College
Joanne Kendall, Lone Star College System
Kevin Kennedy, Athens Technical College
Stephanie Krehl, Mid-South Community College
Allyn Leon, Imperial Valley College
Gerald LePage, Bristol Community College
Laurie Lindstrom, Bay de Noc Community College
Jonathan Lopez, Niagara University
Yixia Lu, South Suburban College
Mikal McDowell, Cedar Valley College
Kim McHale, Columbia College of Missouri
Allen Miller, Northeast Lakeview College
Michelle Moravec, Baylor University TX/McLennan Community College
Jennifer Nohai-Seaman, Housatonic Community College
Rick Norwood, East Tennessee State University
Linda Padilla, Joliet Junior College
Kelly Proffitt, Patrick Henry Community College
Teresa Richards, Butte-Glenn Community College
Christian Roldan-Johnson, College of Lake County Community College
Patricia C. Rome, Delgado Community College, City Park Campus
Kegan Samuel, Naugatuck Valley Community College
Bruny Santiago, Tarrant College Southeast Campus
Sutandra Sarkar, Georgia State University
Richard Sgarlotti, Bay Mills Community College
Chuang Shao, Rose State College
Carla VanDeSande, Arizona State University
Shannon Vinson, Wake Technical Community College
Maryam Vulis, Norwalk Community College
Toby Wagner, Chemeketa Community College
Libby Watts, Tidewater Community College
Becky Wheelock, San Diego City College

Figure 1.1 Purchasing pounds of fruit at a fruit market requires a basic understanding of numbers. (credit: Dr. Karl-Heinz Hochhaus, Wikimedia Commons)

Chapter Outline

Introduction

Even though counting is first taught at a young age, mastering mathematics, which is the study of numbers, requires constant attention. If it has been a while since you have studied math, it can be helpful to review basic topics. In this chapter, we will focus on numbers used for counting as well as four arithmetic operations—addition, subtraction, multiplication, and division. We will also discuss some vocabulary that we will use throughout this book.

1.1 Introduction to Whole Numbers

Learning Objectives

By the end of this section, you will be able to:

- Identify counting numbers and whole numbers
- Model whole numbers
- Identify the place value of a digit
- Use place value to name whole numbers
- Use place value to write whole numbers
- Round whole numbers

Identify Counting Numbers and Whole Numbers

Learning algebra is similar to learning a language. You start with a basic vocabulary and then add to it as you go along. You need to practice often until the vocabulary becomes easy to you. The more you use the vocabulary, the more familiar it becomes.

Algebra uses numbers and symbols to represent words and ideas. Let's look at the numbers first. The most basic numbers used in algebra are those we use to count objects: $1, 2, 3, 4, 5, \ldots$ and so on. These are called the **counting numbers**.

The notation "..." is called an ellipsis, which is another way to show "and so on", or that the pattern continues endlessly. Counting numbers are also called natural numbers.

MANIPULATIVE MATHEMATICS

Doing the Manipulative Mathematics activity Number Line-Part 1 will help you develop a better understanding of the counting numbers and the whole numbers.

Counting Numbers

The counting numbers start with 1 and continue.

$$1, 2, 3, 4, 5\ldots$$

Counting numbers and whole numbers can be visualized on a **number line** as shown in Figure 1.2.

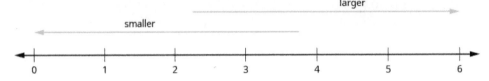

Figure 1.2 The numbers on the number line increase from left to right, and decrease from right to left.

The point labeled 0 is called the **origin**. The points are equally spaced to the right of 0 and labeled with the counting numbers. When a number is paired with a point, it is called the **coordinate** of the point.

The discovery of the number zero was a big step in the history of mathematics. Including zero with the counting numbers gives a new set of numbers called the **whole numbers**.

Whole Numbers

The whole numbers are the counting numbers and zero.

$$0, 1, 2, 3, 4, 5\ldots$$

We stopped at 5 when listing the first few counting numbers and whole numbers. We could have written more numbers if they were needed to make the patterns clear.

EXAMPLE 1.1

Which of the following are ⓐ counting numbers? ⓑ whole numbers?

$0, \frac{1}{4}, 3, 5.2, 15, 105$

⊘ Solution

ⓐ The counting numbers start at 1, so 0 is not a counting number. The numbers 3, 15, and 105 are all counting numbers.

ⓑ Whole numbers are counting numbers and 0. The numbers 0, 3, 15, and 105 are whole numbers.

The numbers $\frac{1}{4}$ and 5.2 are neither counting numbers nor whole numbers. We will discuss these numbers later.

> **TRY IT : : 1.1**   Which of the following are ⓐ counting numbers ⓑ whole numbers?
>
> $0, \frac{2}{3}, 2, 9, 11.8, 241, 376$

> **TRY IT : : 1.2**   Which of the following are ⓐ counting numbers ⓑ whole numbers?

$0, \frac{5}{3}, 7, 8.8, 13, 201$

Model Whole Numbers

Our number system is called a **place value system** because the value of a digit depends on its position, or place, in a number. The number 537 has a different value than the number 735. Even though they use the same digits, their value is different because of the different placement of the 3 and the 7 and the 5.

Money gives us a familiar model of place value. Suppose a wallet contains three $100 bills, seven $10 bills, and four $1 bills. The amounts are summarized in Figure 1.3. How much money is in the wallet?

Three $100 bills	Seven $10 bills	Four $1 bills
3 × $100	7 × $10	4 × $1
$300	$70	$4

Figure 1.3

Find the total value of each kind of bill, and then add to find the total. The wallet contains $374.

$300 + $70 + $4

$374

Base-10 blocks provide another way to model place value, as shown in Figure 1.4. The blocks can be used to represent hundreds, tens, and ones. Notice that the tens rod is made up of 10 ones, and the hundreds square is made of 10 tens, or 100 ones.

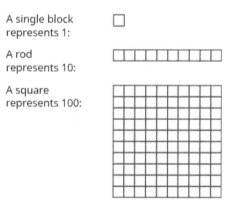

A single block represents 1:

A rod represents 10:

A square represents 100:

Figure 1.4

Figure 1.5 shows the number 138 modeled with base-10 blocks.

Figure 1.5 We use place value notation to show the value of the number $138.$

Digit	Place value	Number	Value	Total value
1	hundreds	1	100	100
3	tens	3	10	30
8	ones	8	1	+8
				Sum $=138$

EXAMPLE 1.2

Use place value notation to find the value of the number modeled by the base-10 blocks shown.

⊘ **Solution**

There are 2 hundreds squares, which is $200.$

There is 1 tens rod, which is $10.$

There are 5 ones blocks, which is $5.$

Digit	Place value	Number	Value	Total value
2	hundreds	2	100	200
1	tens	1	10	10
5	ones	5	1	+5
				215

The base-10 blocks model the number 215.

> **TRY IT : :** 1.3

Use place value notation to find the value of the number modeled by the base-10 blocks shown.

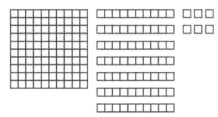

> **TRY IT : :** 1.4

Use place value notation to find the value of the number modeled by the base-10 blocks shown.

 MANIPULATIVE MATHEMATICS

Doing the Manipulative Mathematics activity "Model Whole Numbers" will help you develop a better understanding of place value of whole numbers.

Identify the Place Value of a Digit

By looking at money and base-10 blocks, we saw that each place in a number has a different value. A place value chart is a useful way to summarize this information. The place values are separated into groups of three, called periods. The periods are *ones, thousands, millions, billions, trillions*, and so on. In a written number, commas separate the periods.

Just as with the base-10 blocks, where the value of the tens rod is ten times the value of the ones block and the value of the hundreds square is ten times the tens rod, the value of each place in the place-value chart is ten times the value of the place to the right of it.

Figure 1.6 shows how the number 5,278,194 is written in a place value chart.

Place Value														
Trillions			Billions			Millions			Thousands			Ones		
Hundred trillions	Ten trillions	Trillions	Hundred billions	Ten billions	Billions	Hundred millions	Ten millions	Millions	Hundred thousands	Ten thousands	Thousands	Hundreds	Tens	Ones
								5	2	7	8	1	9	4

Figure 1.6

- The digit 5 is in the millions place. Its value is 5,000,000.

- The digit 2 is in the hundred thousands place. Its value is $200,000.$
- The digit 7 is in the ten thousands place. Its value is $70,000.$
- The digit 8 is in the thousands place. Its value is $8,000.$
- The digit 1 is in the hundreds place. Its value is $100.$
- The digit 9 is in the tens place. Its value is $90.$
- The digit 4 is in the ones place. Its value is $4.$

EXAMPLE 1.3

In the number $63,407,218;$ find the place value of each of the following digits:

ⓐ 7 ⓑ 0 ⓒ 1 ⓓ 6 ⓔ 3

⊘ Solution

Write the number in a place value chart, starting at the right.

Trillions			Billions			Millions			Thousands			Ones		
Hundred trillions	Ten trillions	Trillions	Hundred billions	Ten billions	Billions	Hundred millions	Ten millions	Millions	Hundred thousands	Ten thousands	Thousands	Hundreds	Tens	Ones
						6	3	4	0	7	2	1	8	

ⓐ The 7 is in the thousands place.

ⓑ The 0 is in the ten thousands place.

ⓒ The 1 is in the tens place.

ⓓ The 6 is in the ten millions place.

ⓔ The 3 is in the millions place.

> | **TRY IT ::** 1.5   For each number, find the place value of digits listed: $27,493,615$

ⓐ 2 ⓑ 1 ⓒ 4 ⓓ 7 ⓔ 5

> | **TRY IT ::** 1.6   For each number, find the place value of digits listed: $519,711,641,328$

ⓐ 9 ⓑ 4 ⓒ 2 ⓓ 6 ⓔ 7

Use Place Value to Name Whole Numbers

When you write a check, you write out the number in words as well as in digits. To write a number in words, write the number in each period followed by the name of the period without the 's' at the end. Start with the digit at the left, which has the largest place value. The commas separate the periods, so wherever there is a comma in the number, write a comma between the words. The ones period, which has the smallest place value, is not named.

So the number 37,519,248 is written thirty-seven million, five hundred nineteen thousand, two hundred forty-eight.

Notice that the word *and* is not used when naming a whole number.

HOW TO : : NAME A WHOLE NUMBER IN WORDS.

Step 1. Starting at the digit on the left, name the number in each period, followed by the period name. Do not include the period name for the ones.

Step 2. Use commas in the number to separate the periods.

EXAMPLE 1.4

Name the number 8,165,432,098,710 in words.

Solution

Begin with the leftmost digit, which is 8. It is in the trillions place.	eight trillion
The next period to the right is billions.	one hundred sixty-five billion
The next period to the right is millions.	four hundred thirty-two million
The next period to the right is thousands.	ninety-eight thousand
The rightmost period shows the ones.	seven hundred ten

8 , 165 , 432 , 098 , 710

trillions   billions   millions   thousands   ones

8 ⟶ Eight trillion,
165 ⟶ One hundred sixty-five billion,
432 ⟶ Four hundred thirty-two million,
098 ⟶ Ninety-eight thousand,
710 ⟶ Seven hundred ten

Putting all of the words together, we write 8,165,432,098,710 as eight trillion, one hundred sixty-five billion, four hundred thirty-two million, ninety-eight thousand, seven hundred ten.

> **TRY IT : :** 1.7   Name each number in words: 9,258,137,904,061

> **TRY IT : :** 1.8   Name each number in words: 17,864,325,619,004

EXAMPLE 1.5

A student conducted research and found that the number of mobile phone users in the United States during one month in 2014 was **327,577,529**. Name that number in words.

⊘ Solution

Identify the periods associated with the number.

$$\underbrace{327}_{millions} \, , \, \underbrace{577}_{thousands} \, , \, \underbrace{529}_{ones}$$

Name the number in each period, followed by the period name. Put the commas in to separate the periods.

Millions period: three hundred twenty-seven million

Thousands period: five hundred seventy-seven thousand

Ones period: five hundred twenty-nine

So the number of mobile phone users in the Unites States during the month of April was three hundred twenty-seven million, five hundred seventy-seven thousand, five hundred twenty-nine.

> **TRY IT ::** 1.9   The population in a country is $316,128,839$. Name that number.

> **TRY IT ::** 1.10   One year is $31,536,000$ seconds. Name that number.

Use Place Value to Write Whole Numbers

We will now reverse the process and write a number given in words as digits.

  HOW TO :: USE PLACE VALUE TO WRITE A WHOLE NUMBER.

Step 1.   Identify the words that indicate periods. (Remember the ones period is never named.)

Step 2.   Draw three blanks to indicate the number of places needed in each period. Separate the periods by commas.

Step 3.   Name the number in each period and place the digits in the correct place value position.

EXAMPLE 1.6

Write the following numbers using digits.

ⓐ fifty-three million, four hundred one thousand, seven hundred forty-two

ⓑ nine billion, two hundred forty-six million, seventy-three thousand, one hundred eighty-nine

⊘ Solution

ⓐ Identify the words that indicate periods.

Except for the first period, all other periods must have three places. Draw three blanks to indicate the number of places needed in each period. Separate the periods by commas.

Then write the digits in each period.

Put the numbers together, including the commas. The number is $53,401,742$.

ⓑ Identify the words that indicate periods.

Except for the first period, all other periods must have three places. Draw three blanks to indicate the number of places

needed in each period. Separate the periods by commas.
Then write the digits in each period.

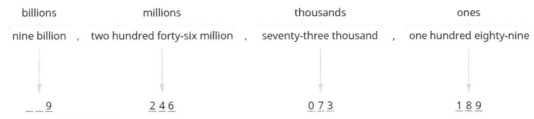

The number is 9,246,073,189.

Notice that in part ⓑ, a zero was needed as a place-holder in the hundred thousands place. Be sure to write zeros as needed to make sure that each period, except possibly the first, has three places.

> **TRY IT :: 1.11**   Write each number in standard form:

fifty-three million, eight hundred nine thousand, fifty-one.

> **TRY IT :: 1.12**   Write each number in standard form:

two billion, twenty-two million, seven hundred fourteen thousand, four hundred sixty-six.

EXAMPLE 1.7

A state budget was about $77 billion. Write the budget in standard form.

⊘ **Solution**

Identify the periods. In this case, only two digits are given and they are in the billions period. To write the entire number, write zeros for all of the other periods.

So the budget was about $77,000,000,000.

> **TRY IT :: 1.13**   Write each number in standard form:

The closest distance from Earth to Mars is about 34 million miles.

> **TRY IT :: 1.14**   Write each number in standard form:

The total weight of an aircraft carrier is 204 million pounds.

Round Whole Numbers

In 2013, the U.S. Census Bureau reported the population of the state of New York as 19,651,127 people. It might be enough to say that the population is approximately 20 million. The word *approximately* means that 20 million is not the exact population, but is close to the exact value.

The process of approximating a number is called **rounding**. Numbers are rounded to a specific place value depending on how much accuracy is needed. Saying that the population of New York is approximately 20 million means we rounded to the millions place. The place value to which we round to depends on how we need to use the number.

Using the number line can help you visualize and understand the rounding process. Look at the number line in Figure

1.7. Suppose we want to round the number 76 to the nearest ten. Is 76 closer to 70 or 80 on the number line?

Figure 1.7 We can see that 76 is closer to 80 than to 70. So 76 rounded to the nearest ten is 80.

Now consider the number 72. Find 72 in Figure 1.8.

Figure 1.8 We can see that 72 is closer to 70, so 72 rounded to the nearest ten is 70.

How do we round 75 to the nearest ten. Find 75 in Figure 1.9.

Figure 1.9 The number 75 is exactly midway between 70 and 80.

So that everyone rounds the same way in cases like this, mathematicians have agreed to round to the higher number, 80. So, 75 rounded to the nearest ten is 80.

Now that we have looked at this process on the number line, we can introduce a more general procedure. To round a number to a specific place, look at the number to the right of that place. If the number is less than 5, round down. If it is greater than or equal to 5, round up.

So, for example, to round 76 to the nearest ten, we look at the digit in the ones place.

The digit in the ones place is a 6. Because 6 is greater than or equal to 5, we increase the digit in the tens place by one. So the 7 in the tens place becomes an 8. Now, replace any digits to the right of the 8 with zeros. So, 76 rounds to 80.

$$7 \not{6}$$
add 1   8 0   replace with 0

76 rounded to the nearest ten is 80.

Let's look again at rounding 72 to the nearest 10. Again, we look to the ones place.

The digit in the ones place is 2. Because 2 is less than 5, we keep the digit in the tens place the same and replace the digits to the right of it with zero. So 72 rounded to the nearest ten is 70.

$$7 \not{2}$$
do not add 1   7 0   replace with 0

HOW TO :: ROUND A WHOLE NUMBER TO A SPECIFIC PLACE VALUE.

Step 1. Locate the given place value. All digits to the left of that place value do not change.

Step 2. Underline the digit to the right of the given place value.

Step 3. Determine if this digit is greater than or equal to 5.

- Yes—add 1 to the digit in the given place value.

- No—do not change the digit in the given place value.

Step 4. Replace all digits to the right of the given place value with zeros.

EXAMPLE 1.8

Round 843 to the nearest ten.

⊘ **Solution**

	tens place
Locate the tens place.	843
Underline the digit to the right of the tens place.	84<u>3</u>
Since 3 is less than 5, do not change the digit in the tens place.	84<u>3</u>
Replace all digits to the right of the tens place with zeros.	84<u>0</u>

Rounding 843 to the nearest ten gives 840.

> **TRY IT :: 1.15**   Round to the nearest ten: 157.

> **TRY IT :: 1.16**   Round to the nearest ten: 884.

EXAMPLE 1.9

Round each number to the nearest hundred:

ⓐ 23,658   ⓑ 3,978

⊘ **Solution**

ⓐ

Locate the hundreds place.	hundreds place ↓ 23,658
The digit of the right of the hundreds place is 5. Underline the digit to the right of the hundreds place.	23,6<u>5</u>8
Since 5 is greater than or equal to 5, round up by adding 1 to the digit in the hundreds place. Then replace all digits to the right of the hundreds place with zeros.	23,658 add 1 ↗ ↘ replace with 0s ↓ 23,700 So 23,658 rounded to the nearest hundred is 23,700.

ⓑ

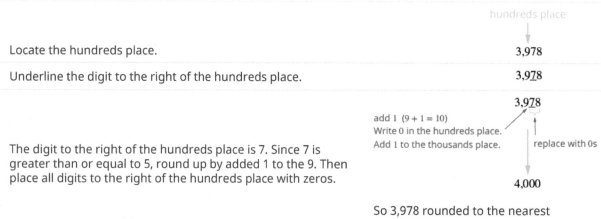

Locate the hundreds place.	hundreds place ↓ 3,978
Underline the digit to the right of the hundreds place.	3,9<u>7</u>8
The digit to the right of the hundreds place is 7. Since 7 is greater than or equal to 5, round up by added 1 to the 9. Then place all digits to the right of the hundreds place with zeros.	3,978 add 1 (9 + 1 = 10) Write 0 in the hundreds place. Add 1 to the thousands place. ↗ replace with 0s ↓ 4,000 So 3,978 rounded to the nearest hundred is 4,000.

> **TRY IT : : 1.17**   Round to the nearest hundred: 17,852.

> **TRY IT : : 1.18**   Round to the nearest hundred: 4,951.

EXAMPLE 1.10

Round each number to the nearest thousand:

　　　ⓐ 147,032   ⓑ 29,504

Solution

 ⓐ

Locate the thousands place. Underline the digit to the right of the thousands place.

thousands place

147,032

The digit to the right of the thousands place is 0. Since 0 is less than 5, we do not change the digit in the thousands place.

147,032

147,000

We then replace all digits to the right of the thousands pace with zeros.

So 147,032 rounded to the nearest thousand is 147,000.

ⓑ

Locate the thousands place.

thousands place

29,504

Underline the digit to the right of the thousands place.

29,504

29,504

add 1 (9 + 1 = 10)
Write 0 in the thousands place.
Add 1 to the ten thousands place. | replace with 0s

The digit to the right of the thousands place is 5. Since 5 is greater than or equal to 5, round up by adding 1 to the 9. Then replace all digits to the right of the thousands place with zeros.

30,000

So 29,504 rounded to the nearest thousand is 30,000.

Notice that in part ⓑ, when we add 1 thousand to the 9 thousands, the total is 10 thousands. We regroup this as 1 ten thousand and 0 thousands. We add the 1 ten thousand to the 3 ten thousands and put a 0 in the thousands place.

> **TRY IT : : 1.19**   Round to the nearest thousand: 63,921.

> **TRY IT : : 1.20**   Round to the nearest thousand: 156,437.

▶ **MEDIA : :** ACCESS ADDITIONAL ONLINE RESOURCES
 • Determine Place Value (http://www.openstaxcollege.org/l/24detplaceval)
 • Write a Whole Number in Digits from Words (http://www.openstaxcollege.org/l/24numdigword)

1.1 EXERCISES

Practice Makes Perfect

Identify Counting Numbers and Whole Numbers

In the following exercises, determine which of the following numbers are ⓐ counting numbers ⓑ whole numbers.

1. $0, \frac{2}{3}, 5, 8.1, 125$ **2.** $0, \frac{7}{10}, 3, 20.5, 300$ **3.** $0, \frac{4}{9}, 3.9, 50, 221$

4. $0, \frac{3}{5}, 10, 303, 422.6$

Model Whole Numbers

In the following exercises, use place value notation to find the value of the number modeled by the base-10 blocks.

5.

6.

7.

8.

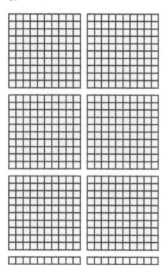

Identify the Place Value of a Digit

In the following exercises, find the place value of the given digits.

9. 579,601

ⓐ 9 ⓑ 6 ⓒ 0 ⓓ 7

ⓔ 5

10. 398,127

ⓐ 9 ⓑ 3 ⓒ 2 ⓓ 8

ⓔ 7

11. 56,804,379

ⓐ 8 ⓑ 6 ⓒ 4 ⓓ 7

ⓔ 0

12. 78,320,465

ⓐ 8 ⓑ 4 ⓒ 2 ⓓ 6

ⓔ 7

Use Place Value to Name Whole Numbers

In the following exercises, name each number in words.

13. 1,078

14. 5,902

15. 364,510

16. 146,023

17. 5,846,103

18. 1,458,398

19. 37,889,005

20. 62,008,465

21. The height of Mount Ranier is 14,410 feet.

22. The height of Mount Adams is 12,276 feet.

23. Seventy years is 613,200 hours.

24. One year is 525,600 minutes.

25. The U.S. Census estimate of the population of Miami-Dade county was 2,617,176.

26. The population of Chicago was 2,718,782.

27. There are projected to be 23,867,000 college and university students in the US in five years.

28. About twelve years ago there were 20,665,415 registered automobiles in California.

29. The population of China is expected to reach 1,377,583,156 in 2016.

30. The population of India is estimated at 1,267,401,849 as of July 1, 2014.

Use Place Value to Write Whole Numbers

In the following exercises, write each number as a whole number using digits.

31. four hundred twelve

32. two hundred fifty-three

33. thirty-five thousand, nine hundred seventy-five

34. sixty-one thousand, four hundred fifteen

35. eleven million, forty-four thousand, one hundred sixty-seven

36. eighteen million, one hundred two thousand, seven hundred eighty-three

37. three billion, two hundred twenty-six million, five hundred twelve thousand, seventeen

38. eleven billion, four hundred seventy-one million, thirty-six thousand, one hundred six

39. The population of the world was estimated to be seven billion, one hundred seventy-three million people.

40. The age of the solar system is estimated to be four billion, five hundred sixty-eight million years.

41. Lake Tahoe has a capacity of thirty-nine trillion gallons of water.

42. The federal government budget was three trillion, five hundred billion dollars.

Round Whole Numbers

In the following exercises, round to the indicated place value.

43. Round to the nearest ten:

   ⓐ 386   ⓑ 2,931

44. Round to the nearest ten:

   ⓐ 792   ⓑ 5,647

45. Round to the nearest hundred:

   ⓐ 13,748   ⓑ 391,794

46. Round to the nearest hundred:

   ⓐ 28,166   ⓑ 481,628

47. Round to the nearest ten:

   ⓐ 1,492   ⓑ 1,497

48. Round to the nearest thousand:

   ⓐ 2,391   ⓑ 2,795

49. Round to the nearest hundred:

   ⓐ 63,994   ⓑ 63,949

50. Round to the nearest thousand:

   ⓐ 163,584   ⓑ 163,246

Everyday Math

51. Writing a Check Jorge bought a car for $24,493. He paid for the car with a check. Write the purchase price in words.

52. Writing a Check Marissa's kitchen remodeling cost $18,549. She wrote a check to the contractor. Write the amount paid in words.

53. Buying a Car Jorge bought a car for $24,493. Round the price to the nearest:

   ⓐ ten dollars   ⓑ hundred dollars

   ⓒ thousand dollars   ⓓ ten-thousand dollars

54. Remodeling a Kitchen Marissa's kitchen remodeling cost $18,549. Round the cost to the nearest:

   ⓐ ten dollars   ⓑ hundred dollars

   ⓒ thousand dollars   ⓓ ten-thousand dollars

55. Population The population of China was 1,355,692,544 in 2014. Round the population to the nearest:

   ⓐ billion people   ⓑ hundred-million people

   ⓒ million people

56. Astronomy The average distance between Earth and the sun is 149,597,888 kilometers. Round the distance to the nearest:

   ⓐ hundred-million kilometers

   ⓑ ten-million kilometers   ⓒ million kilometers

Writing Exercises

57. In your own words, explain the difference between the counting numbers and the whole numbers.

58. Give an example from your everyday life where it helps to round numbers.

Self Check

ⓐ *After completing the exercises, use this checklist to evaluate your mastery of the objectives of this section.*

I can...	Confidently	With some help	No-I don't get it!
identify counting numbers and whole numbers.			
model whole numbers.			
identify the place value of a digit.			
use place value to name whole numbers.			
use place value to write whole numbers.			
round whole numbers.			

ⓑ *If most of your checks were...*

...confidently. Congratulations! You have achieved the objectives in this section. Reflect on the study skills you used so that you

can continue to use them. What did you do to become confident of your ability to do these things? Be specific.

...with some help. This must be addressed quickly because topics you do not master become potholes in your road to success. In math, every topic builds upon previous work. It is important to make sure you have a strong foundation before you move on. Who can you ask for help? Your fellow classmates and instructor are good resources. Is there a place on campus where math tutors are available? Can your study skills be improved?

...no—I don't get it! This is a warning sign and you must not ignore it. You should get help right away or you will quickly be overwhelmed. See your instructor as soon as you can to discuss your situation. Together you can come up with a plan to get you the help you need.

1.2 | Add Whole Numbers

Learning Objectives

By the end of this section, you will be able to:

- Use addition notation
- Model addition of whole numbers
- Add whole numbers without models
- Translate word phrases to math notation
- Add whole numbers in applications

Be Prepared!

Before you get started, take this readiness quiz.

1. What is the number modeled by the base-10 blocks?

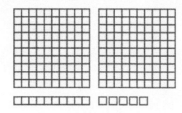

If you missed this problem, review Example 1.2.

2. Write the number three hundred forty-two thousand six using digits?
   If you missed this problem, review Example 1.6.

Use Addition Notation

A college student has a part-time job. Last week he worked 3 hours on Monday and 4 hours on Friday. To find the total number of hours he worked last week, he added 3 and 4.

The operation of addition combines numbers to get a **sum**. The notation we use to find the sum of 3 and 4 is:

$$3 + 4$$

We read this as *three plus four* and the result is the sum of three and four. The numbers 3 and 4 are called the addends. A math statement that includes numbers and operations is called an expression.

Addition Notation

To describe addition, we can use symbols and words.

Operation	Notation	Expression	Read as	Result
Addition	+	3 + 4	three plus four	the sum of 3 and 4

EXAMPLE 1.11

Translate from math notation to words:

ⓐ 7 + 1   ⓑ 12 + 14

⊘ **Solution**

ⓐ The expression consists of a plus symbol connecting the addends 7 and 1. We read this as *seven plus one*. The result is *the sum of seven and one*.

ⓑ The expression consists of a plus symbol connecting the addends 12 and 14. We read this as *twelve plus fourteen*.

The result is the *sum of twelve and fourteen*.

> **TRY IT : : 1.21**   Translate from math notation to words:

ⓐ $8 + 4$ ⓑ $18 + 11$

> **TRY IT : : 1.22**   Translate from math notation to words:

ⓐ $21 + 16$ ⓑ $100 + 200$

Model Addition of Whole Numbers

Addition is really just counting. We will model addition with base-10 blocks. Remember, a block represents 1 and a rod represents 10. Let's start by modeling the addition expression we just considered, $3 + 4$.

Each addend is less than 10, so we can use ones blocks.

We start by modeling the first number with 3 blocks.	☐☐☐ 3
Then we model the second number with 4 blocks.	☐☐☐ ☐☐☐☐ 3 4
Count the total number of blocks.	☐☐☐☐☐☐☐ 7

There are 7 blocks in all. We use an equal sign $(=)$ to show the sum. A math sentence that shows that two expressions are equal is called an equation. We have shown that. $3 + 4 = 7$.

 MANIPULATIVE MATHEMATICS

Doing the Manipulative Mathematics activity "Model Addition of Whole Numbers" will help you develop a better understanding of adding whole numbers.

EXAMPLE 1.12

Model the addition $2 + 6$.

⊘ **Solution**

$2 + 6$ means the sum of 2 and 6

Each addend is less than 10, so we can use ones blocks.

Model the first number with 2 blocks.	☐☐ 2
Model the second number with 6 blocks.	☐☐ ☐☐☐☐☐☐ 2 6
Count the total number of blocks	☐☐☐☐☐☐☐☐ 8

There are 8 blocks in all, so $2 + 6 = 8$.

> **TRY IT :: 1.23**   Model: $3 + 6$.

> **TRY IT :: 1.24**   Model: $5 + 1$.

When the result is 10 or more ones blocks, we will exchange the 10 blocks for one rod.

EXAMPLE 1.13

Model the addition $5 + 8$.

⊘ **Solution**

$5 + 8$ means the sum of 5 and 8.

Each addend is less than 10, se we can use ones blocks.

Model the first number with 5 blocks.	☐☐☐☐☐ 5
Model the second number with 8 blocks.	☐☐☐☐☐ ☐☐☐☐☐☐☐☐ 5 8
Count the result. There are more than 10 blocks so we exchange 10 ones blocks for 1 tens rod.	(☐☐☐☐☐ ☐☐☐☐☐) ☐☐☐ / ▨▨▨▨▨▨▨▨▨▨ ☐☐☐
Now we have 1 ten and 3 ones, which is 13.	$5 + 8 = 13$

Notice that we can describe the models as ones blocks and tens rods, or we can simply say *ones* and *tens*. From now on, we will use the shorter version but keep in mind that they mean the same thing.

> **TRY IT :: 1.25**   Model the addition: $5 + 7$.

> **TRY IT :: 1.26**   Model the addition: $6 + 8$.

Next we will model adding two digit numbers.

EXAMPLE 1.14

Model the addition: $17 + 26$.

⊘ **Solution**

$17 + 26$ means the sum of 17 and 26.

Model the 17.	1 ten and 7 ones	
Model the 26.	2 tens and 6 ones	
Combine.	3 tens and 13 ones	
Exchange 10 ones for 1 ten.	4 tens and 3 ones $40 + 3 = 43$	

We have shown that $17 + 26 = 43$

> **TRY IT : : 1.27**   Model each addition: $15 + 27$.

> **TRY IT : : 1.28**   Model each addition: $16 + 29$.

Add Whole Numbers Without Models

Now that we have used models to add numbers, we can move on to adding without models. Before we do that, make sure you know all the one digit addition facts. You will need to use these number facts when you add larger numbers.

Imagine filling in Table 1.11 by adding each row number along the left side to each column number across the top. Make sure that you get each sum shown. If you have trouble, model it. It is important that you memorize any number facts you do not already know so that you can quickly and reliably use the number facts when you add larger numbers.

+	0	1	2	3	4	5	6	7	8	9
0	0	1	2	3	4	5	6	7	8	9
1	1	2	3	4	5	6	7	8	9	10
2	2	3	4	5	6	7	8	9	10	11
3	3	4	5	6	7	8	9	10	11	12
4	4	5	6	7	8	9	10	11	12	13
5	5	6	7	8	9	10	11	12	13	14
6	6	7	8	9	10	11	12	13	14	15
7	7	8	9	10	11	12	13	14	15	16
8	8	9	10	11	12	13	14	15	16	17
9	9	10	11	12	13	14	15	16	17	18

Table 1.11

Did you notice what happens when you add zero to a number? The sum of any number and zero is the number itself. We call this the Identity Property of Addition. Zero is called the additive identity.

Identity Property of Addition

The sum of any number a and 0 is the number.

$$a + 0 = a$$
$$0 + a = a$$

EXAMPLE 1.15

Find each sum:

ⓐ $0 + 11$ ⓑ $42 + 0$

✓ **Solution**

ⓐ The first addend is zero. The sum of any number and zero is the number. $0 + 11 = 11$

ⓑ The second addend is zero. The sum of any number and zero is the number. $42 + 0 = 42$

> **TRY IT : : 1.29**   Find each sum:

ⓐ $0 + 19$ ⓑ $39 + 0$

> **TRY IT : : 1.30**   Find each sum:

ⓐ $0 + 24$ ⓑ $57 + 0$

Look at the pairs of sums.

$2 + 3 = 5$ $3 + 2 = 5$

$4 + 7 = 11$ $7 + 4 = 11$

$8 + 9 = 17$ $9 + 8 = 17$

Notice that when the order of the addends is reversed, the sum does not change. This property is called the Commutative Property of Addition, which states that changing the order of the addends does not change their sum.

Commutative Property of Addition

Changing the order of the addends a and b does not change their sum.

$$a + b = b + a$$

EXAMPLE 1.16

Add:

ⓐ $8 + 7$ ⓑ $7 + 8$

✓ **Solution**

ⓐ

Add. $8 + 7$

15

ⓑ

Add. $7 + 8$

           15

Did you notice that changing the order of the addends did not change their sum? We could have immediately known the sum from part ⓑ just by recognizing that the addends were the same as in part ⓑ, but in the reverse order. As a result, both sums are the same.

> **TRY IT : :** 1.31   Add: $9 + 7$ and $7 + 9$.

> **TRY IT : :** 1.32   Add: $8 + 6$ and $6 + 8$.

EXAMPLE 1.17

Add: $28 + 61$.

⊘ **Solution**

To add numbers with more than one digit, it is often easier to write the numbers vertically in columns.

Write the numbers so the ones and tens digits line up vertically.	$\begin{array}{r} 28 \\ +61 \\ \hline \end{array}$

Then add the digits in each place value. Add the ones: $8 + 1 = 9$ Add the tens: $2 + 6 = 8$	$\begin{array}{r} 28 \\ +61 \\ \hline 89 \end{array}$

> **TRY IT : :** 1.33   Add: $32 + 54$.

> **TRY IT : :** 1.34   Add: $25 + 74$.

In the previous example, the sum of the ones and the sum of the tens were both less than 10. But what happens if the sum is 10 or more? Let's use our base-10 model to find out. Figure 1.10 shows the addition of 17 and 26 again.

Figure 1.10

When we add the ones, $7 + 6$, we get 13 ones. Because we have more than 10 ones, we can exchange 10 of the ones for 1 ten. Now we have 4 tens and 3 ones. Without using the model, we show this as a small red 1 above the digits in the tens place.

When the sum in a place value column is greater than 9, we carry over to the next column to the left. Carrying is the same as regrouping by exchanging. For example, 10 ones for 1 ten or 10 tens for 1 hundred.

HOW TO :: ADD WHOLE NUMBERS.

Step 1.   Write the numbers so each place value lines up vertically.

Step 2.   Add the digits in each place value. Work from right to left starting with the ones place. If a sum in a place value is more than $9,$ carry to the next place value.

Step 3.   Continue adding each place value from right to left, adding each place value and carrying if needed.

EXAMPLE 1.18

Add: $43 + 69$.

⊘ **Solution**

Write the numbers so the digits line up vertically.
$$\begin{array}{r} 43 \\ +69 \\ \hline \end{array}$$

Add the digits in each place.
Add the ones: $3 + 9 = 12$

Write the 2 in the ones place in the sum.
Add the 1 ten to the tens place.
$$\begin{array}{r} \overset{1}{4}3 \\ +69 \\ \hline 2 \end{array}$$

Now add the tens: $1 + 4 + 6 = 11$
Write the 11 in the sum.
$$\begin{array}{r} \overset{1}{4}3 \\ +69 \\ \hline 112 \end{array}$$

> **TRY IT :: 1.35**   Add: $35 + 98$.

> **TRY IT :: 1.36**   Add: $72 + 89$.

EXAMPLE 1.19

Add: $324 + 586$.

⊘ **Solution**

Write the numbers so the digits line up vertically.	$\begin{array}{r} 3\,2\,4 \\ +\ 5\,8\,6 \\ \hline \end{array}$
Add the digits in each place value. Add the ones: $4 + 6 = 10$ Write the 0 in the ones place in the sum and carry the 1 ten to the tens place.	$\begin{array}{r} \overset{1}{3}\,2\,4 \\ +\ 5\,8\,6 \\ \hline 0 \end{array}$
Add the tens: $1 + 2 + 8 = 11$ Write the 1 in the tens place in the sum and carry the 1 hundred to the hundreds	$\begin{array}{r} \overset{1}{3}\,\overset{1}{2}\,4 \\ +\ 5\,8\,6 \\ \hline 1\,0 \end{array}$
Add the hundreds: $1 + 3 + 5 = 9$ Write the 9 in the hundreds place.	$\begin{array}{r} \overset{1}{3}\,\overset{1}{2}\,4 \\ +\ 5\,8\,6 \\ \hline 9\,1\,0 \end{array}$

> ❯ **TRY IT : : 1.37**   Add: $456 + 376$.

> ❯ **TRY IT : : 1.38**   Add: $269 + 578$.

EXAMPLE 1.20

Add: $1{,}683 + 479$.

⊘ **Solution**

Write the numbers so the digits line up vertically.	$\begin{array}{r} 1{,}683 \\ +\ 479 \\ \hline \end{array}$
Add the digits in each place value.	
Add the ones: $3 + 9 = 12$. Write the 2 in the ones place of the sum and carry the 1 ten to the tens place.	$\begin{array}{r} 1{,}6\overset{1}{8}3 \\ +\ 479 \\ \hline 2 \end{array}$
Add the tens: $1 + 7 + 8 = 16$ Write the 6 in the tens place and carry the 1 hundred to the hundreds place.	$\begin{array}{r} \overset{11}{1{,}683} \\ +\ 479 \\ \hline 62 \end{array}$
Add the hundreds: $1 + 6 + 4 = 11$ Write the 1 in the hundreds place and carry the 1 thousand to the thousands place.	$\begin{array}{r} \overset{11}{1{,}683} \\ +\ 479 \\ \hline 162 \end{array}$
Add the thousands $1 + 1 = 2$. Write the 2 in the thousands place of the sum.	$\begin{array}{r} \overset{11}{1{,}683} \\ +\ 479 \\ \hline 2{,}162 \end{array}$

When the addends have different numbers of digits, be careful to line up the corresponding place values starting with the ones and moving toward the left.

> | **TRY IT : :** 1.39   Add: $4,597 + 685$.

> | **TRY IT : :** 1.40   Add: $5,837 + 695$.

EXAMPLE 1.21

Add: $21,357 + 861 + 8,596$.

⊘ **Solution**

Write the numbers so the place values line up vertically.

$$
\begin{array}{r}
21,357 \\
861 \\
+\ 8,596 \\
\end{array}
$$

Add the digits in each place value.

Add the ones: $7 + 1 + 6 = 14$
Write the 4 in the ones place of the sum and carry the 1 to the tens place.

$$
\begin{array}{r}
\overset{1}{}7 \\
21,357 \\
861 \\
+\ 8,596 \\
\hline
4
\end{array}
$$

Add the tens: $1 + 5 + 6 + 9 = 21$
Write the 1 in the tens place and carry the 2 to the hundreds place.

$$
\begin{array}{r}
\overset{21}{21,357} \\
861 \\
+\ 8,596 \\
\hline
14
\end{array}
$$

Add the hundreds: $2 + 3 + 8 + 5 = 18$
Write the 8 in the hundreds place and carry the 1 to the thousands place.

$$
\begin{array}{r}
\overset{1\,21}{21,357} \\
861 \\
+\ 8,596 \\
\hline
814
\end{array}
$$

Add the thousands $1 + 1 + 8 = 10$.
Write the 0 in the thousands place and carry the 1 to the ten thousands place.

$$
\begin{array}{r}
\overset{1\,1\,21}{21,357} \\
861 \\
+\ 8,596 \\
\hline
0814
\end{array}
$$

Add the ten-thousands $1 + 2 = 3$.
Write the 3 in the ten thousands place in the sum.

$$
\begin{array}{r}
\overset{1\,1\,21}{21,357} \\
861 \\
+\ 8,596 \\
\hline
30,814
\end{array}
$$

This example had three addends. We can add any number of addends using the same process as long as we are careful to line up the place values correctly.

> | **TRY IT : :** 1.41   Add: $46,195 + 397 + 6,281$.

> **TRY IT :: 1.42**   Add: $53,762 + 196 + 7,458$.

Translate Word Phrases to Math Notation

Earlier in this section, we translated math notation into words. Now we'll reverse the process. We'll translate word phrases into math notation. Some of the word phrases that indicate addition are listed in Table 1.20.

Operation	Words	Example	Expression
Addition	plus sum increased by more than total of added to	1 plus 2 the sum of 3 and 4 5 increased by 6 8 more than 7 the total of 9 and 5 6 added to 4	$1 + 2$ $3 + 4$ $5 + 6$ $7 + 8$ $9 + 5$ $4 + 6$

Table 1.20

EXAMPLE 1.22

Translate and simplify: the sum of 19 and 23.

⊘ **Solution**

The word *sum* tells us to add. The words *of* 19 *and* 23 tell us the addends.

The sum of 19 and 23

Translate. $19 + 23$

Add.   42

The sum of 19 and 23 is 42.

> **TRY IT :: 1.43**   Translate and simplify: the sum of 17 and 26.

> **TRY IT :: 1.44**   Translate and simplify: the sum of 28 and 14.

EXAMPLE 1.23

Translate and simplify: 28 increased by 31.

⊘ **Solution**

The words *increased by* tell us to add. The numbers given are the addends.

28 increased by 31.

Translate. $28 + 31$

Add.   59

So 28 increased by 31 is 59.

> **TRY IT ::** 1.45   Translate and simplify: 29 increased by 76.

> **TRY IT ::** 1.46   Translate and simplify: 37 increased by 69.

Add Whole Numbers in Applications

Now that we have practiced adding whole numbers, let's use what we've learned to solve real-world problems. We'll start by outlining a plan. First, we need to read the problem to determine what we are looking for. Then we write a word phrase that gives the information to find it. Next we translate the word phrase into math notation and then simplify. Finally, we write a sentence to answer the question.

EXAMPLE 1.24

Hao earned grades of 87, 93, 68, 95, and 89 on the five tests of the semester. What is the total number of points he earned on the five tests?

Solution

We are asked to find the total number of points on the tests.

Write a phrase.	the sum of points on the tests
Translate to math notation.	$87 + 93 + 68 + 95 + 89$
Then we simplify by adding.	
Since there are several numbers, we will write them vertically.	$\overset{3}{8}7$ 93 68 95 $+89$ 432
Write a sentence to answer the question.	Hao earned a total of 432 points.

Notice that we added *points*, so the sum is 432 *points*. It is important to include the appropriate units in all answers to applications problems.

> **TRY IT ::** 1.47
>
> Mark is training for a bicycle race. Last week he rode 18 miles on Monday, 15 miles on Wednesday, 26 miles on Friday, 49 miles on Saturday, and 32 miles on Sunday. What is the total number of miles he rode last week?

> **TRY IT ::** 1.48
>
> Lincoln Middle School has three grades. The number of students in each grade is 230, 165, and 325. What is the total number of students?

Some application problems involve shapes. For example, a person might need to know the distance around a garden to put up a fence or around a picture to frame it. The perimeter is the distance around a geometric figure. The perimeter of a figure is the sum of the lengths of its sides.

EXAMPLE 1.25

Find the perimeter of the patio shown.

Solution

We are asked to find the perimeter.

Write a phrase.	the sum of the sides
Translate to math notation.	$4 + 6 + 2 + 3 + 2 + 9$
Simplify by adding.	26
Write a sentence to answer the question.	
We added feet, so the sum is 26 feet.	The perimeter of the patio is 26 feet.

> **TRY IT : : 1.49**   Find the perimeter of each figure. All lengths are in inches.

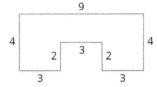

> **TRY IT : : 1.50**   Find the perimeter of each figure. All lengths are in inches.

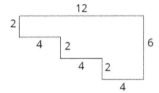

▶ **MEDIA : :** ACCESS ADDITIONAL ONLINE RESOURCES

- Adding Two-Digit Numbers with base-10 blocks (http://www.openstaxcollege.org/l/24add2blocks)
- Adding Three-Digit Numbers with base-10 blocks (http://www.openstaxcollege.org/l/24add3blocks)
- Adding Whole Numbers (http://www.openstaxcollege.org/l/24addwhlnumb)

1.2 EXERCISES

Practice Makes Perfect

Use Addition Notation

In the following exercises, translate the following from math expressions to words.

59. $5 + 2$

60. $6 + 3$

61. $13 + 18$

62. $15 + 16$

63. $214 + 642$

64. $438 + 113$

Model Addition of Whole Numbers

In the following exercises, model the addition.

65. $2 + 4$

66. $5 + 3$

67. $8 + 4$

68. $5 + 9$

69. $14 + 75$

70. $15 + 63$

71. $16 + 25$

72. $14 + 27$

Add Whole Numbers

In the following exercises, fill in the missing values in each chart.

73.

+	0	1	2	3	4	5	6	7	8	9
0	0	1	2		4	5	6	7		9
1	1	2	3	4			7	8	9	
2		3	4	5	6		8			11
3	3		5		7	8		10		12
4	4	5			8	9		11	12	
5	5	6	7	8			11		13	
6	6	7	8		10			13		15
7			9	10		12			15	16
8	8	9		11			14		16	
9	9	10	11		13	14			17	

74.

+	0	1	2	3	4	5	6	7	8	9
0	0	1	2	3	4		6		8	9
1	1	2	3		5	6		8		10
2	2		4		6	7		9	10	
3		4		6		9		11		
4	4	5	6	7			10	11		13
5	5	6		8	9		11	12	13	
6			8	9			12	13		15
7	7	8		10		12			15	16
8	8	9	10		12		14		16	17
9			11	12	13			16		

75.

+	3	4	5	6	7	8	9
6							
7							
8							
9							

76.

+	6	7	8	9
3				
4				
5				
6				
7				
8				
9				

77.

+	5	6	7	8	9
5					
6					
7					
8					
9					

78.

+	6	7	8	9
6				
7				
8				
9				

In the following exercises, add.

79.
   ⓐ $0 + 13$ ⓑ $13 + 0$

80.
   ⓐ $0 + 5,280$

   ⓑ $5,280 + 0$

81.
   ⓐ $8 + 3$ ⓑ $3 + 8$

82.
   ⓐ $7 + 5$ ⓑ $5 + 7$

83. $45 + 33$

84. $37 + 22$

85. $71 + 28$

86. $43 + 53$

87. $26 + 59$

88. $38 + 17$

89. $64 + 78$

90. $92 + 39$

91. $168 + 325$

92. $247 + 149$

93. $584 + 277$

94. $175 + 648$

95. $832 + 199$

96. $775 + 369$

97. $6,358 + 492$

98. $9,184 + 578$

99. $3,740 + 18,593$

100. $6,118 + 15,990$

101. $485,012 + 619,848$

102. $368,911 + 857,289$

103. $24,731 + 592 + 3,868$

104. $28,925 + 817 + 4,593$

105. $8,015 + 76,946 + 16,570$

106. $6,291 + 54,107 + 28,635$

Translate Word Phrases to Math Notation

In the following exercises, translate each phrase into math notation and then simplify.

107. the sum of 13 and 18

108. the sum of 12 and 19

109. the sum of 90 and 65

110. the sum of 70 and 38

111. 33 increased by 49

112. 68 increased by 25

113. 250 more than 599

114. 115 more than 286

115. the total of 628 and 77

116. the total of 593 and 79

117. $1,482$ added to 915

118. $2,719$ added to 682

Add Whole Numbers in Applications

In the following exercises, solve the problem.

119. Home remodeling Sophia remodeled her kitchen and bought a new range, microwave, and dishwasher. The range cost $1,100, the microwave cost $250, and the dishwasher cost $525. What was the total cost of these three appliances?

120. Sports equipment Aiden bought a baseball bat, helmet, and glove. The bat cost $299, the helmet cost $35, and the glove cost $68. What was the total cost of Aiden's sports equipment?

121. Bike riding Ethan rode his bike 14 miles on Monday, 19 miles on Tuesday, 12 miles on Wednesday, 25 miles on Friday, and 68 miles on Saturday. What was the total number of miles Ethan rode?

122. Business Chloe has a flower shop. Last week she made 19 floral arrangements on Monday, 12 on Tuesday, 23 on Wednesday, 29 on Thursday, and 44 on Friday. What was the total number of floral arrangements Chloe made?

123. Apartment size Jackson lives in a 7 room apartment. The number of square feet in each room is 238, 120, 156, 196, 100, 132, and 225. What is the total number of square feet in all 7 rooms?

124. Weight Seven men rented a fishing boat. The weights of the men were 175, 192, 148, 169, 205, 181, and 225 pounds. What was the total weight of the seven men?

125. Salary Last year Natalie's salary was $82,572. Two years ago, her salary was $79,316, and three years ago it was $75,298. What is the total amount of Natalie's salary for the past three years?

126. Home sales Emma is a realtor. Last month, she sold three houses. The selling prices of the houses were $292,540, $505,875, and $423,699. What was the total of the three selling prices?

In the following exercises, find the perimeter of each figure.

127.

128.

129.

130.

131.

132.

133.

134.

Everyday Math

135. Calories Paulette had a grilled chicken salad, ranch dressing, and a 16-ounce drink for lunch. On the restaurant's nutrition chart, she saw that each item had the following number of calories:

Grilled chicken salad – 320 calories

Ranch dressing – 170 calories

16-ounce drink – 150 calories

What was the total number of calories of Paulette's lunch?

136. Calories Fred had a grilled chicken sandwich, a small order of fries, and a 12-oz chocolate shake for dinner. The restaurant's nutrition chart lists the following calories for each item:

Grilled chicken sandwich – 420 calories

Small fries – 230 calories

12-oz chocolate shake – 580 calories

What was the total number of calories of Fred's dinner?

137. Test scores A students needs a total of 400 points on five tests to pass a course. The student scored $82, 91, 75, 88,$ and $70.$ Did the student pass the course?

138. Elevators The maximum weight capacity of an elevator is 1150 pounds. Six men are in the elevator. Their weights are $210, 145, 183, 230, 159,$ and 164 pounds. Is the total weight below the elevators' maximum capacity?

Writing Exercises

139. How confident do you feel about your knowledge of the addition facts? If you are not fully confident, what will you do to improve your skills?

140. How have you used models to help you learn the addition facts?

Self Check

ⓐ *After completing the exercises, use this checklist to evaluate your mastery of the objectives of this section.*

I can...	Confidently	With some help	No-I don't get it!
use addition notation.			
model addition of whole numbers.			
add whole numbers without models.			
translate word phrases to math notation.			
add whole numbers in applications.			

ⓑ *After reviewing this checklist, what will you do to become confident for all objectives?*

1.3 Subtract Whole Numbers

Learning Objectives

By the end of this section, you will be able to:
- Use subtraction notation
- Model subtraction of whole numbers
- Subtract whole numbers
- Translate word phrases to math notation
- Subtract whole numbers in applications

Be Prepared!

Before you get started, take this readiness quiz.

1. Model $3 + 4$ using base-ten blocks.
   If you missed this problem, review Example 1.12.
2. Add: $324 + 586$.
   If you missed this problem, review Example 1.20.

Use Subtraction Notation

Suppose there are seven bananas in a bowl. Elana uses three of them to make a smoothie. How many bananas are left in the bowl? To answer the question, we subtract three from seven. When we subtract, we take one number away from another to find the **difference**. The notation we use to subtract 3 from 7 is

$$7 - 3$$

We read $7 - 3$ as *seven minus three* and the result is *the difference of seven and three*.

Subtraction Notation

To describe subtraction, we can use symbols and words.

Operation	Notation	Expression	Read as	Result
Subtraction	−	$7 - 3$	seven minus three	the difference of 7 and 3

EXAMPLE 1.26

Translate from math notation to words: ⓐ $8 - 1$ ⓑ $26 - 14$.

Solution

ⓐ We read this as *eight minus one*. The result is *the difference of eight and one*.

ⓑ We read this as *twenty-six minus fourteen*. The resuilt is *the difference of twenty-six and fourteen*.

> **TRY IT :: 1.51** Translate from math notation to words:
> ⓐ $12 - 4$ ⓑ $29 - 11$

> **TRY IT :: 1.52** Translate from math notation to words:
> ⓐ $11 - 2$ ⓑ $29 - 12$

Model Subtraction of Whole Numbers

A model can help us visualize the process of subtraction much as it did with addition. Again, we will use base-10 blocks.

Remember a block represents 1 and a rod represents 10. Let's start by modeling the subtraction expression we just considered, $7 - 3$.

We start by modeling the first number, 7.

7

Now take away the second number, 3. We'll circle 3 blocks to show that we are taking them away.

Count the number of blocks remaining.

There are 4 ones blocks left.

We have shown that $7 - 3 = 4$.

MANIPULATIVE MATHEMATICS

Doing the Manipulative Mathematics activity Model Subtraction of Whole Numbers will help you develop a better understanding of subtracting whole numbers.

EXAMPLE 1.27

Model the subtraction: $8 - 2$.

⊘ **Solution**

$8 - 2$ means the difference of 8 and 2.

Model the first, 8.

8

Take away the second number, 2.

Count the number of blocks remaining.

There are 6 ones blocks left.

We have shown that $8 - 2 = 6$.

> **TRY IT : :** 1.53   Model: $9 - 6$.

> **TRY IT : :** 1.54   Model: $6 - 1$.

EXAMPLE 1.28

Model the subtraction: $13 - 8$.

Solution

Model the first number, 13. We use 1 ten and 3 ones.

Take away the second number, 8. However, there are not 8 ones, so we will exchange the 1 ten for 10 ones.

Now we can take away 8 ones.

Count the blocks remaining.

There are five ones left.   We have shown that $13 - 8 = 5$.

As we did with addition, we can describe the models as ones blocks and tens rods, or we can simply say ones and tens.

> **TRY IT : : 1.55**   Model the subtraction: $12 - 7$.

> **TRY IT : : 1.56**   Model the subtraction: $14 - 8$.

EXAMPLE 1.29

Model the subtraction: $43 - 26$.

Solution

Because $43 - 26$ means 43 take away 26, we begin by modeling the 43.

Now, we need to take away 26, which is 2 tens and 6 ones. We cannot take away 6 ones from 3 ones. So, we exchange 1 ten for 10 ones.

Now we can take away 2 tens and 6 ones.

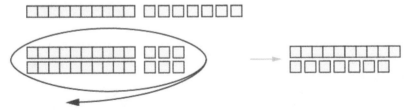

Count the number of blocks remaining. There is 1 ten and 7 ones, which is 17.

$43 - 26 = 17$

> | **TRY IT : :** 1.57   Model the subtraction: $42 - 27$.

> | **TRY IT : :** 1.58   Model the subtraction: $45 - 29$.

Subtract Whole Numbers

Addition and subtraction are inverse operations. Addition undoes subtraction, and subtraction undoes addition.

We know $7 - 3 = 4$ because $4 + 3 = 7$. Knowing all the addition number facts will help with subtraction. Then we can check subtraction by adding. In the examples above, our subtractions can be checked by addition.

$$7 - 3 = 4 \qquad \text{because} \qquad 4 + 3 = 7$$
$$13 - 8 = 5 \qquad \text{because} \qquad 5 + 8 = 13$$
$$43 - 26 = 17 \qquad \text{because} \qquad 17 + 26 = 43$$

EXAMPLE 1.30

Subtract and then check by adding:

ⓐ $9 - 7$ ⓑ $8 - 3$.

Solution

ⓐ

$$9 - 7$$

Subtract 7 from 9.   2

Check with addition.
$2 + 7 = 9$ ✓

ⓑ

$$8 - 3$$

Subtract 3 from 8.   5

Check with addition.
$5 + 3 = 8$ ✓

> | **TRY IT : :** 1.59   Subtract and then check by adding:
$7 - 0$

> | **TRY IT : :** 1.60   Subtract and then check by adding:
$6 - 2$

To subtract numbers with more than one digit, it is usually easier to write the numbers vertically in columns just as we did for addition. Align the digits by place value, and then subtract each column starting with the ones and then working to the left.

EXAMPLE 1.31

Subtract and then check by adding: $89 - 61$.

⊘ **Solution**

Write the numbers so the ones and tens digits line up vertically.	89 -61

Subtract the digits in each place value.	89
	-61
Subtract the ones: $9 - 1 = 8$	28
Subtract the tens: $8 - 6 = 2$	

Check using addition.

  28
$+61$
  89

Our answer is correct.

> **TRY IT : :** 1.61   Subtract and then check by adding: $86 - 54$.

> **TRY IT : :** 1.62   Subtract and then check by adding: $99 - 74$.

When we modeled subtracting 26 from 43, we exchanged 1 ten for 10 ones. When we do this without the model, we say we borrow 1 from the tens place and add 10 to the ones place.

HOW TO : : FIND THE DIFFERENCE OF WHOLE NUMBERS.

Step 1.   Write the numbers so each place value lines up vertically.

Step 2.   Subtract the digits in each place value. Work from right to left starting with the ones place. If the digit on top is less than the digit below, borrow as needed.

Step 3.   Continue subtracting each place value from right to left, borrowing if needed.

Step 4.   Check by adding.

EXAMPLE 1.32

Subtract: $43 - 26$.

✓ **Solution**

Write the numbers so each place value lines up vertically.	$\begin{array}{r} 4\,3 \\ -\,2\,6 \\ \hline \end{array}$
Subtract the ones. We cannot subtract 6 from 3, so we borrow 1 ten. This makes 3 tens and 13 ones. We write these numbers above each place and cross out the original digits.	$\begin{array}{r} \overset{3\ \ 13}{\cancel{4}\,\cancel{3}} \\ -\,2\,6 \\ \hline \end{array}$
Now we can subtract the ones. $13 - 6 = 7$. We write the 7 in the ones place in the difference.	$\begin{array}{r} \overset{3\ \ 13}{\cancel{4}\,\cancel{3}} \\ -\,2\,6 \\ \hline 7 \end{array}$
Now we subtract the tens. $3 - 2 = 1$. We write the 1 in the tens place in the difference.	$\begin{array}{r} \overset{3\ \ 13}{\cancel{4}\,\cancel{3}} \\ -\,2\,6 \\ \hline 1\,7 \end{array}$

Check by adding.

$$\begin{array}{r} 1\,7 \\ +\,2\,6 \\ \hline 4\,3\ \checkmark \end{array}$$

Our answer is correct.

> **TRY IT : : 1.63**   Subtract and then check by adding: $93 - 58$.

> **TRY IT : : 1.64**   Subtract and then check by adding: $81 - 39$.

EXAMPLE 1.33

Subtract and then check by adding: $207 - 64$.

⊘ **Solution**

Write the numbers so each place value lines up vertically.	$\begin{array}{r} 2\,0\,7 \\ -\ \ 6\,4 \\ \hline \end{array}$
Subtract the ones. $7 - 4 = 3$. Write the 3 in the ones place in the difference. Write the 3 in the ones place in the difference.	$\begin{array}{r} 2\,0\,7 \\ -\ \ 6\,4 \\ \hline 3 \end{array}$
Subtract the tens. We cannot subtract 6 from 0 so we borrow 1 hundred and add 10 tens to the 0 tens we had. This makes a total of 10 tens. We write 10 above the tens place and cross out the 0. Then we cross out the 2 in the hundreds place and write 1 above it.	$\begin{array}{r} {\scriptstyle 1\ \ 10} \\ \cancel{2}\,\cancel{0}\,7 \\ -\ \ 6\,4 \\ \hline 3 \end{array}$
Now we subtract the tens. $10 - 6 = 4$. We write the 4 in the tens place in the difference.	$\begin{array}{r} {\scriptstyle 1\ \ 10} \\ \cancel{2}\,\cancel{0}\,7 \\ -\ \ 6\,4 \\ \hline 4\,3 \end{array}$
Finally, subtract the hundreds. There is no digit in the hundreds place in the bottom number so we can imagine a 0 in that place. Since $1 - 0 = 1$, we write 1 in the hundreds place in the difference.	$\begin{array}{r} {\scriptstyle 1\ \ 10} \\ \cancel{2}\,\cancel{0}\,7 \\ -\ \ 6\,4 \\ \hline 1\,4\,3 \end{array}$

Check by adding.

$$\begin{array}{r} {\scriptstyle 1} \\ 1\,4\,3 \\ +\ \ 6\,4 \\ \hline 2\,0\,7\ \checkmark \end{array}$$

Our answer is correct.

> **TRY IT : : 1.65**   Subtract and then check by adding: $439 - 52$.

> **TRY IT : : 1.66**   Subtract and then check by adding: $318 - 75$.

EXAMPLE 1.34

Subtract and then check by adding: $910 - 586$.

⊘ **Solution**

Write the numbers so each place value lines up vertically.	$\begin{array}{r} 9\,1\,0 \\ -\ \ 5\,8\,6 \\ \hline \end{array}$

Subtract the ones. We cannot subtract 6 from 0, so we borrow 1 ten and add 10 ones to the 10 ones we had. This makes 10 ones. We write a 0 above the tens place and cross out the 1. We write the 10 above the ones place and cross out the 0. Now we can subtract the ones. $10 - 6 = 4$.

$$\begin{array}{r} {}^{0}\ {}^{10} \\ 9\,\cancel{1}\,\cancel{0} \\ -\ \ 5\,8\,6 \\ \hline \end{array}$$

Write the 4 in the ones place of the difference.

$$\begin{array}{r} {}^{0}\ {}^{10} \\ 9\,\cancel{1}\,\cancel{0} \\ -\ \ 5\,8\,6 \\ \hline 4 \end{array}$$

Subtract the tens. We cannot subtract 8 from 0, so we borrow 1 hundred and add 10 tens to the 0 tens we had, which gives us 10 tens. Write 8 above the hundreds place and cross out the 9. Write 10 above the tens place.

$$\begin{array}{r} {}^{8}\ {}^{10}\ {}^{10} \\ \cancel{9}\,\cancel{1}\,\cancel{0} \\ -\ \ 5\,8\,6 \\ \hline 4 \end{array}$$

Now we can subtract the tens. $10 - 8 = 2$.

$$\begin{array}{r} {}^{8}\ {}^{10}\ {}^{10} \\ \cancel{9}\,\cancel{1}\,\cancel{0} \\ -\ \ 5\,8\,6 \\ \hline 2\,4 \end{array}$$

Subtract the hundreds place. $8 - 5 = 3$ Write the 3 in the hundreds place in the difference.

$$\begin{array}{r} {}^{8}\ {}^{10}\ {}^{10} \\ \cancel{9}\,\cancel{1}\,\cancel{0} \\ -\ \ 5\,8\,6 \\ \hline 3\,2\,4 \end{array}$$

Check by adding.

$$\begin{array}{r} {}^{1}\ {}^{1} \\ 3\,2\,4 \\ +\ \ 5\,8\,6 \\ \hline 9\,1\,0\ \checkmark \end{array}$$

Our answer is correct.

> | **TRY IT : : 1.67**   Subtract and then check by adding: $832 - 376$.

> | **TRY IT : : 1.68**   Subtract and then check by adding: $847 - 578$.

EXAMPLE 1.35

Subtract and then check by adding: $2,162 - 479$.

⊘ **Solution**

Write the numbers so each place values line up vertically.	$\begin{array}{r} 2,162 \\ -\ 479 \end{array}$
Subtract the ones. Since we cannot subtract 9 from 2, borrow 1 ten and add 10 ones to the 2 ones to make 12 ones. Write 5 above the tens place and cross out the 6. Write 12 above the ones place and cross out the 2.	$\begin{array}{r} {\scriptstyle 5\ 12} \\ 2,1\,\cancel{6}\,\cancel{2} \\ -\ 479 \end{array}$
Now we can subtract the ones.	$12 - 9 = 3$
Write 3 in the ones place in the difference.	$\begin{array}{r} {\scriptstyle 5\ 12} \\ 2,1\,\cancel{6}\,\cancel{2} \\ -\ 479 \\ \hline 3 \end{array}$
Subtract the tens. Since we cannot subtract 7 from 5, borrow 1 hundred and add 10 tens to the 5 tens to make 15 tens. Write 0 above the hundreds place and cross out the 1. Write 15 above the tens place.	$\begin{array}{r} {\scriptstyle\ \ 15} \\ {\scriptstyle 0\ \cancel{5}\ 12} \\ 2,\cancel{1}\,\cancel{6}\,\cancel{2} \\ -\ 479 \\ \hline 3 \end{array}$
Now we can subtract the tens.	$15 - 7 = 8$
Write 8 in the tens place in the difference.	$\begin{array}{r} {\scriptstyle 0\ \ 15\ 12} \\ 2,\cancel{1}\,\cancel{6}\,\cancel{2} \\ -\ 479 \\ \hline 8\ 3 \end{array}$
Now we can subtract the hundreds.	$\begin{array}{r} {\scriptstyle\ \ \ \ \ 10} \\ {\scriptstyle 1\ \ \cancel{0}\ 15\ 12} \\ \cancel{2},\cancel{1}\,\cancel{6}\,\cancel{2} \\ -\ 479 \\ \hline 8\ 3 \end{array}$
Write 6 in the hundreds place in the difference.	$\begin{array}{r} {\scriptstyle 1\ \ 10\ 15\ 12} \\ \cancel{2},\cancel{1}\,\cancel{6}\,\cancel{2} \\ -\ 479 \\ \hline 6\ 8\ 3 \end{array}$
Subtract the thousands. There is no digit in the thousands place of the bottom number, so we imagine a 0. $1 - 0 = 1$. Write 1 in the thousands place of the difference.	$\begin{array}{r} {\scriptstyle 1\ \ 10\ \cancel{15}\ \cancel{12}} \\ \cancel{2},\cancel{1}\,\cancel{6}\,\cancel{2} \\ -\ 479 \\ \hline 1,6\ 8\ 3 \end{array}$

Check by adding.

$\begin{array}{r} 1,683 \\ +\ 479 \\ \hline 2,162\ \checkmark \end{array}$

Our answer is correct.

⟩ **TRY IT : : 1.69**   Subtract and then check by adding: $4,585 - 697$.

⟩ **TRY IT : : 1.70**   Subtract and then check by adding: $5,637 - 899$.

Translate Word Phrases to Math Notation

As with addition, word phrases can tell us to operate on two numbers using subtraction. To translate from a word phrase to math notation, we look for key words that indicate subtraction. Some of the words that indicate subtraction are listed in Table 1.34.

Operation	Word Phrase	Example	Expression
Subtraction	minus	5 minus 1	$5 - 1$
	difference	the difference of 9 and 4	$9 - 4$
	decreased by	7 decreased by 3	$7 - 3$
	less than	5 less than 8	$8 - 5$
	subtracted from	1 subtracted from 6	$6 - 1$

Table 1.34

EXAMPLE 1.36

Translate and then simplify:

ⓐ the difference of 13 and 8   ⓑ subtract 24 from 43

⊘ Solution

ⓐ

The word *difference* tells us to subtract the two numbers. The numbers stay in the same order as in the phrase.

the difference of 13 and 8

Translate.	$13 - 8$
Simplify.	5

ⓑ

The words *subtract from* tells us to take the second number away from the first. We must be careful to get the order correct.

subtract 24 from 43

Translate.	$43 - 24$
Simplify.	19

> **TRY IT : : 1.71**   Translate and simplify:

ⓐ the difference of 14 and 9   ⓑ subtract 21 from 37

> **TRY IT : : 1.72**   Translate and simplify:

ⓐ 11 decreased by 6   ⓑ 18 less than 67

Subtract Whole Numbers in Applications

To solve applications with subtraction, we will use the same plan that we used with addition. First, we need to determine what we are asked to find. Then we write a phrase that gives the information to find it. We translate the phrase into math notation and then simplify to get the answer. Finally, we write a sentence to answer the question, using the appropriate units.

EXAMPLE 1.37

The temperature in Chicago one morning was 73 degrees Fahrenheit. A cold front arrived and by noon the temperature was 27 degrees Fahrenheit. What was the difference between the temperature in the morning and the temperature at noon?

⊘ **Solution**

We are asked to find the difference between the morning temperature and the noon temperature.

Write a phrase.	the difference of 73 and 27
Translate to math notation. *Difference* tells us to subtract.	$73 - 27$
Then we do the subtraction.	$\begin{array}{r} {}^{6}\;{}^{13}\\ \not{7}\not{3} \\ -\;2\,7 \\ \hline 4\,6 \end{array}$
Write a sentence to answer the question.	The difference in temperatures was 46 degrees Fahrenheit.

> **TRY IT : : 1.73**
>
> The high temperature on June 1st in Boston was 77 degrees Fahrenheit, and the low temperature was 58 degrees Fahrenheit. What was the difference between the high and low temperatures?

> **TRY IT : : 1.74**
>
> The weather forecast for June 2 in St Louis predicts a high temperature of 90 degrees Fahrenheit and a low of 73 degrees Fahrenheit. What is the difference between the predicted high and low temperatures?

EXAMPLE 1.38

A washing machine is on sale for $399. Its regular price is $588. What is the difference between the regular price and the sale price?

⊘ **Solution**

We are asked to find the difference between the regular price and the sale price.

Write a phrase.	the difference between 588 and 399
Translate to math notation.	$588 - 399$
Subtract.	$\begin{array}{r} {}^{4}\;{}^{17}\;{}^{18}\\ \not{5}\not{8}\not{8} \\ -\;3\,9\,9 \\ \hline 1\,8\,9 \end{array}$
Write a sentence to answer the question.	The difference between the regular price and the sale price is $189.

> **TRY IT : : 1.75**
>
> A television set is on sale for $499. Its regular price is $648. What is the difference between the regular price and the sale price?

> **TRY IT : :** 1.76

A patio set is on sale for $149. Its regular price is $285. What is the difference between the regular price and the sale price?

▶ **MEDIA : :** ACCESS ADDITIONAL ONLINE RESOURCES

- Model subtraction of two-digit whole numbers (http://www.openstaxcollege.org/l/24sub2dignum)
- Model subtraction of three-digit whole numbers (http://www.openstaxcollege.org/l/24sub3dignum)
- Subtract Whole Numbers (http://www.openstaxcollege.org/l/24subwholenum)

1.3 EXERCISES

Practice Makes Perfect

Use Subtraction Notation

In the following exercises, translate from math notation to words.

141. $15 - 9$

142. $18 - 16$

143. $42 - 35$

144. $83 - 64$

145. $675 - 350$

146. $790 - 525$

Model Subtraction of Whole Numbers

In the following exercises, model the subtraction.

147. $5 - 2$

148. $8 - 4$

149. $6 - 3$

150. $7 - 5$

151. $18 - 5$

152. $19 - 8$

153. $17 - 8$

154. $17 - 9$

155. $35 - 13$

156. $32 - 11$

157. $61 - 47$

158. $55 - 36$

Subtract Whole Numbers

In the following exercises, subtract and then check by adding.

159. $9 - 4$

160. $9 - 3$

161. $8 - 0$

162. $2 - 0$

163. $38 - 16$

164. $45 - 21$

165. $85 - 52$

166. $99 - 47$

167. $493 - 370$

168. $268 - 106$

169. $5,946 - 4,625$

170. $7,775 - 3,251$

171. $75 - 47$

172. $63 - 59$

173. $461 - 239$

174. $486 - 257$

175. $525 - 179$

176. $542 - 288$

177. $6,318 - 2,799$

178. $8,153 - 3,978$

179. $2,150 - 964$

180. $4,245 - 899$

181. $43,650 - 8,982$

182. $35,162 - 7,885$

Translate Word Phrases to Algebraic Expressions

In the following exercises, translate and simplify.

183. The difference of 10 and 3

184. The difference of 12 and 8

185. The difference of 15 and 4

186. The difference of 18 and 7

187. Subtract 6 from 9

188. Subtract 8 from 9

189. Subtract 28 from 75

190. Subtract 59 from 81

191. 45 decreased by 20

192. 37 decreased by 24

193. 92 decreased by 67

194. 75 decreased by 49

195. 12 less than 16

196. 15 less than 19

197. 38 less than 61

198. 47 less than 62

In the following exercises, simplify.

199. $76 - 47$

200. $91 - 53$

201. $256 - 184$

202. $305 - 262$

203. $719 + 341$

204. $647 + 528$

205. $2,015 - 1,993$

206. $2,020 - 1,984$

In the following exercises, translate and simplify.

207. Seventy more than thirty-five

208. Sixty more than ninety-three

209. 13 less than 41

210. 28 less than 36

211. The difference of 100 and 76

212. The difference of 1,000 and 945

Subtract Whole Numbers in Applications

In the following exercises, solve.

213. Temperature The high temperature on June 2 in Las Vegas was 80 degrees and the low temperature was 63 degrees. What was the difference between the high and low temperatures?

214. Temperature The high temperature on June 1 in Phoenix was 97 degrees and the low was 73 degrees. What was the difference between the high and low temperatures?

215. Class size Olivia's third grade class has 35 children. Last year, her second grade class had 22 children. What is the difference between the number of children in Olivia's third grade class and her second grade class?

216. Class size There are 82 students in the school band and 46 in the school orchestra. What is the difference between the number of students in the band and the orchestra?

217. Shopping A mountain bike is on sale for $399. Its regular price is $650. What is the difference between the regular price and the sale price?

218. Shopping A mattress set is on sale for $755. Its regular price is $1,600. What is the difference between the regular price and the sale price?

219. Savings John wants to buy a laptop that costs $840. He has $685 in his savings account. How much more does he need to save in order to buy the laptop?

220. Banking Mason had $1,125 in his checking account. He spent $892. How much money does he have left?

Everyday Math

221. Road trip Noah was driving from Philadelphia to Cincinnati, a distance of 502 miles. He drove 115 miles, stopped for gas, and then drove another 230 miles before lunch. How many more miles did he have to travel?

222. Test Scores Sara needs 350 points to pass her course. She scored 75, 50, 70, and 80 on her first four tests. How many more points does Sara need to pass the course?

Writing Exercises

223. Explain how subtraction and addition are related.

224. How does knowing addition facts help you to subtract numbers?

Self Check

ⓐ *After completing the exercises, use this checklist to evaluate your mastery of the objectives of this section.*

I can...	Confidently	With some help	No-I don't get it!
use subtraction notation.			
model subtraction of whole numbers.			
subtract whole numbers.			
translate word phrases to math notation.			
subtract whole numbers in applications.			

ⓑ *What does this checklist tell you about your mastery of this section? What steps will you take to improve?*

1.4 | Multiply Whole Numbers

Learning Objectives

By the end of this section, you will be able to:

- Use multiplication notation
- Model multiplication of whole numbers
- Multiply whole numbers
- Translate word phrases to math notation
- Multiply whole numbers in applications

Be Prepared!

Before you get started, take this readiness quiz.

1. Add: $1,683 + 479$.
   If you missed this problem, review Example 1.21.

2. Subtract: $605 - 321$.
   If you missed this problem, review Example 1.33.

Use Multiplication Notation

Suppose you were asked to count all these pennies shown in Figure 1.11.

Figure 1.11

Would you count the pennies individually? Or would you count the number of pennies in each row and add that number 3 times.

$$8 + 8 + 8$$

Multiplication is a way to represent repeated addition. So instead of adding 8 three times, we could write a multiplication expression.

$$3 \times 8$$

We call each number being multiplied a factor and the result the **product**. We read 3×8 as *three times eight*, and the result as *the product of three and eight*.

There are several symbols that represent multiplication. These include the symbol $\times$ as well as the dot, $\cdot$, and parentheses ( ).

Operation Symbols for Multiplication

To describe multiplication, we can use symbols and words.

Operation	Notation	Expression	Read as	Result
Multiplication	$\times$	3×8	three times eight	the product of 3 and 8
	$\cdot$	$3 \cdot 8$		
	( )	$3(8)$		

EXAMPLE 1.39

Translate from math notation to words:

      ⓐ 7×6 ⓑ $12 \cdot 14$ ⓒ $6(13)$

⊘ **Solution**

ⓐ We read this as *seven times six* and the result is *the product of seven and six*.

ⓑ We read this as *twelve times fourteen* and the result is *the product of twelve and fourteen*.

ⓒ We read this as *six times thirteen* and the result is *the product of six and thirteen*.

> **TRY IT : : 1.77**   Translate from math notation to words:
>
>   ⓐ 8×7 ⓑ $18 \cdot 11$

> **TRY IT : : 1.78**   Translate from math notation to words:
>
>   ⓐ $(13)(7)$ ⓑ $5(16)$

Model Multiplication of Whole Numbers

There are many ways to model multiplication. Unlike in the previous sections where we used base-10 blocks, here we will use counters to help us understand the meaning of multiplication. A counter is any object that can be used for counting. We will use round blue counters.

EXAMPLE 1.40

Model: 3×8.

⊘ **Solution**

To model the product 3×8, we'll start with a row of 8 counters.

The other factor is 3, so we'll make 3 rows of 8 counters.

Now we can count the result. There are 24 counters in all.

$3 \times 8 = 24$

If you look at the counters sideways, you'll see that we could have also made 8 rows of 3 counters. The product would have been the same. We'll get back to this idea later.

> **TRY IT : : 1.79**   Model each multiplication: 4×6.

> **TRY IT : : 1.80**   Model each multiplication: 5×7.

Multiply Whole Numbers

In order to multiply without using models, you need to know all the one digit multiplication facts. Make sure you know them fluently before proceeding in this section.

Table 1.39 shows the multiplication facts. Each box shows the product of the number down the left column and the number across the top row. If you are unsure about a product, model it. It is important that you memorize any number facts you do not already know so you will be ready to multiply larger numbers.

×	0	1	2	3	4	5	6	7	8	9
0	0	0	0	0	0	0	0	0	0	0
1	0	1	2	3	4	5	6	7	8	9
2	0	2	4	6	8	10	12	14	16	18
3	0	3	6	9	12	15	18	21	24	27
4	0	4	8	12	16	20	24	28	32	36
5	0	5	10	15	20	25	30	35	40	45
6	0	6	12	18	24	30	36	42	48	54
7	0	7	14	21	28	35	42	49	56	63
8	0	8	16	24	32	40	48	56	64	72
9	0	9	18	27	36	45	54	63	72	81

Table 1.39

What happens when you multiply a number by zero? You can see that the product of any number and zero is zero. This is called the Multiplication Property of Zero.

Multiplication Property of Zero

The product of any number and 0 is 0.

$$a \cdot 0 = 0$$
$$0 \cdot a = 0$$

EXAMPLE 1.41

Multiply:

ⓐ $0 \cdot 11$ ⓑ $(42)0$

⊘ Solution

ⓐ $0 \cdot 11$

The product of any number and zero is zero. 0

ⓑ $(42)0$

Multiplying by zero results in zero. 0

> | **TRY IT : :** 1.81   Find each product:
>
> ⓐ $0 \cdot 19$ ⓑ $(39)0$

> | **TRY IT : :** 1.82   Find each product:
>
> ⓐ $0 \cdot 24$ ⓑ $(57)0$

What happens when you multiply a number by one? Multiplying a number by one does not change its value. We call this fact the Identity Property of Multiplication, and 1 is called the multiplicative identity.

Identity Property of Multiplication

The product of any number and 1 is the number.

$$1 \cdot a = a$$
$$a \cdot 1 = a$$

EXAMPLE 1.42

Multiply:

ⓐ $(11)1$ ⓑ $1 \cdot 42$

⊘ **Solution**

ⓐ | | $(11)1$
---|---
The product of any number and one is the number. | 11
ⓑ | $1 \cdot 42$
Multiplying by one does not change the value. | 42

> **TRY IT ::** 1.83   Find each product:

ⓐ $(19)1$ ⓑ $1 \cdot 39$

> **TRY IT ::** 1.84   Find each product:

ⓐ $(24)(1)$ ⓑ 1×57

Earlier in this chapter, we learned that the Commutative Property of Addition states that changing the order of addition does not change the sum. We saw that $8 + 9 = 17$ is the same as $9 + 8 = 17$.

Is this also true for multiplication? Let's look at a few pairs of factors.

$$4 \cdot 7 = 28 \quad 7 \cdot 4 = 28$$
$$9 \cdot 7 = 63 \quad 7 \cdot 9 = 63$$
$$8 \cdot 9 = 72 \quad 9 \cdot 8 = 72$$

When the order of the factors is reversed, the product does not change. This is called the Commutative Property of Multiplication.

Commutative Property of Multiplication

Changing the order of the factors does not change their product.

$$a \cdot b = b \cdot a$$

EXAMPLE 1.43

Multiply:

ⓐ $8 \cdot 7$ ⓑ $7 \cdot 8$

Solution

ⓐ $8 \cdot 7$

Multiply.   56

ⓑ $7 \cdot 8$

Multiply.   56

Changing the order of the factors does not change the product.

> **TRY IT : : 1.85**   Multiply:
>
>   ⓐ $9 \cdot 6$ ⓑ $6 \cdot 9$

> **TRY IT : : 1.86**   Multiply:
>
>   ⓐ $8 \cdot 6$ ⓑ $6 \cdot 8$

To multiply numbers with more than one digit, it is usually easier to write the numbers vertically in columns just as we did for addition and subtraction.

$$\begin{array}{r} 27 \\ \times 3 \\ \hline \end{array}$$

We start by multiplying 3 by 7.

$$3 \times 7 = 21$$

We write the 1 in the ones place of the product. We carry the 2 tens by writing 2 above the tens place.

Then we multiply the 3 by the 2, and add the 2 above the tens place to the product. So $3 \times 2 = 6$, and $6 + 2 = 8$. Write the 8 in the tens place of the product.

$$\begin{array}{r} 2 \\ 27 \\ \times 3 \\ \hline 81 \end{array}$$ ← This comes from 3×2 plus the 2 we carried.

The product is 81.

When we multiply two numbers with a different number of digits, it's usually easier to write the smaller number on the bottom. You could write it the other way, too, but this way is easier to work with.

EXAMPLE 1.44

Multiply: $15 \cdot 4$.

⊘ **Solution**

Write the numbers so the digits 5 and 4 line up vertically.	$\begin{array}{r} 15 \\ \times\,4 \\ \hline \end{array}$
Multiply 4 by the digit in the ones place of 15. $4 \cdot 5 = 20$.	
Write 0 in the ones place of the product and carry the 2 tens.	$\begin{array}{r} \overset{2}{1}5 \\ \times\,4 \\ \hline 0 \end{array}$
Multiply 4 by the digit in the tens place of 15. $4 \cdot 1 = 4$. Add the 2 tens we carried. $4 + 2 = 6$.	
Write the 6 in the tens place of the product.	$\begin{array}{r} \overset{2}{1}5 \\ \times\,4 \\ \hline 60 \end{array}$

> **TRY IT ::** 1.87   Multiply: $64 \cdot 8$.

> **TRY IT ::** 1.88   Multiply: $57 \cdot 6$.

EXAMPLE 1.45

Multiply: $286 \cdot 5$.

⊘ **Solution**

Write the numbers so the digits 5 and 6 line up vertically.	$\begin{array}{r} 286 \\ \times\,5 \\ \hline \end{array}$
Multiply 5 by the digit in the ones place of 286. $5 \cdot 6 = 30$.	
Write the 0 in the ones place of the product and carry the 3 to the tens place. Multiply 5 by the digit in the tens place of 286. $5 \cdot 8 = 40$.	$\begin{array}{r} \overset{3}{2}86 \\ \times\,5 \\ \hline 0 \end{array}$
Add the 3 tens we carried to get $40 + 3 = 43$. Write the 3 in the tens place of the product and carry the 4 to the hundreds place.	$\begin{array}{r} \overset{43}{2}86 \\ \times\,5 \\ \hline 30 \end{array}$
Multiply 5 by the digit in the hundreds place of 286. $5 \cdot 2 = 10$. Add the 4 hundreds we carried to get $10 + 4 = 14$. Write the 4 in the hundreds place of the product and the 1 to the thousands place.	$\begin{array}{r} \overset{43}{2}86 \\ \times\,5 \\ \hline 1{,}430 \end{array}$

> **TRY IT ::** 1.89   Multiply: $347 \cdot 5$.

> **TRY IT ::** 1.90   Multiply: $462 \cdot 7$.

When we multiply by a number with two or more digits, we multiply by each of the digits separately, working from right to left. Each separate product of the digits is called a partial product. When we write partial products, we must make sure to line up the place values.

HOW TO : : MULTIPLY TWO WHOLE NUMBERS TO FIND THE PRODUCT.

Step 1.   Write the numbers so each place value lines up vertically.

Step 2.   Multiply the digits in each place value.

- Work from right to left, starting with the ones place in the bottom number.
  - Multiply the bottom number by the ones digit in the top number, then by the tens digit, and so on.
  - If a product in a place value is more than 9, carry to the next place value.
  - Write the partial products, lining up the digits in the place values with the numbers above.
- Repeat for the tens place in the bottom number, the hundreds place, and so on.
- Insert a zero as a placeholder with each additional partial product.

Step 3.   Add the partial products.

EXAMPLE 1.46

Multiply: 62(87).

⊘ **Solution**

Write the numbers so each place lines up vertically.	$\begin{array}{r} 62 \\ \times\,87 \end{array}$

Start by multiplying 7 by 62. Multiply 7 by the digit in the ones place of 62. $7 \cdot 2 = 14$. Write the 4 in the ones place of the product and carry the 1 to the tens place.

$$\begin{array}{r} {\scriptstyle 1} \\ 62 \\ \times\,87 \\ \hline 4 \end{array}$$

Multiply 7 by the digit in the tens place of 62. $7 \cdot 6 = 42$. Add the 1 ten we carried. $42 + 1 = 43$. Write the 3 in the tens place of the product and the 4 in the hundreds place.

$$\begin{array}{r} {\scriptstyle 1} \\ 62 \\ \times\,87 \\ \hline 434 \end{array}$$

The first partial product is 434.

Now, write a 0 under the 4 in the ones place of the next partial product as a placeholder since we now multiply the digit in the tens place of 87 by 62. Multiply 8 by the digit in the ones place of 62. $8 \cdot 2 = 16$. Write the 6 in the next place of the product, which is the tens place. Carry the 1 to the tens place.

$$\begin{array}{r} {\scriptstyle 1} \\ \cancel{1} \\ 62 \\ \times\,87 \\ \hline 434 \\ 60 \end{array}$$

Multiply 8 by 6, the digit in the tens place of 62, then add the 1 ten we carried to get 49. Write the 9 in the hundreds place of the product and the 4 in the thousands place.

$$\begin{array}{r} {\scriptstyle 1} \\ \cancel{1} \\ 62 \\ \times\,87 \\ \hline 434 \\ 4960 \end{array}$$

The second partial product is 4960. Add the partial products.

$$\begin{array}{r} {\scriptstyle 1} \\ \cancel{1} \\ 62 \\ \times\,87 \\ \hline 434 \\ 4960 \\ \hline 5394 \end{array}$$

The product is $5,394$.

>	**TRY IT :: 1.91**	Multiply: $43(78)$.

>	**TRY IT :: 1.92**	Multiply: $64(59)$.

EXAMPLE 1.47

Multiply:

ⓐ $47 \cdot 10$ ⓑ $47 \cdot 100$.

⊘ Solution

(a) $47 \cdot 10$.

$$
\begin{array}{r}
47 \\
\times 10 \\
\hline
00 \\
470 \\
\hline
470
\end{array}
$$

(b) $47 \cdot 100$

$$
\begin{array}{r}
47 \\
\times 100 \\
\hline
00 \\
000 \\
4700 \\
\hline
4{,}700
\end{array}
$$

When we multiplied 47 times 10, the product was 470. Notice that 10 has one zero, and we put one zero after 47 to get the product. When we multiplied 47 times 100, the product was $4{,}700$. Notice that 100 has two zeros and we put two zeros after 47 to get the product.

Do you see the pattern? If we multiplied 47 times $10{,}000$, which has four zeros, we would put four zeros after 47 to get the product $470{,}000$.

> **TRY IT : : 1.93**   Multiply:
>
> (a) $54 \cdot 10$ (b) $54 \cdot 100$.

> **TRY IT : : 1.94**   Multiply:
>
> (a) $75 \cdot 10$ (b) $75 \cdot 100$.

EXAMPLE 1.48

Multiply: $(354)(438)$.

⊘ Solution

There are three digits in the factors so there will be 3 partial products. We do not have to write the 0 as a placeholder as long as we write each partial product in the correct place.

Multiply 8(354)	354
	$\times\ 438$
Multiply 3(354)	2832
Multiply 4(354)	1062
	1416
Add the partial products	$155{,}052$

> **TRY IT : : 1.95**   Multiply: $(265)(483)$.

> **TRY IT : : 1.96**   Multiply: $(823)(794)$.

EXAMPLE 1.49

Multiply: $(896)201$.

⊘ **Solution**

There should be 3 partial products. The second partial product will be the result of multiplying 896 by 0.

Multiply 1(896)	896
	× 201
Multiply 0(896)	896
	000
Multiply 200(896)	1792
Add the partial products	180,096

Notice that the second partial product of all zeros doesn't really affect the result. We can place a zero as a placeholder in the tens place and then proceed directly to multiplying by the 2 in the hundreds place, as shown.

Multiply by 10, but insert only one zero as a placeholder in the tens place. Multiply by 200, putting the 2 from the 12. $2 \cdot 6 = 12$ in the hundreds place.

$$
\begin{array}{r}
896 \\
\times 201 \\
\hline
896 \\
17920 \\
\hline
180,096
\end{array}
$$

> ⟩ **TRY IT :: 1.97**   Multiply: (718)509.

> ⟩ **TRY IT :: 1.98**   Multiply: (627)804.

When there are three or more factors, we multiply the first two and then multiply their product by the next factor. For example:

to multiply	$8 \cdot 3 \cdot 2$
first multiply $8 \cdot 3$	$24 \cdot 2$
then multiply $24 \cdot 2$.	48

Translate Word Phrases to Math Notation

Earlier in this section, we translated math notation into words. Now we'll reverse the process and translate word phrases into math notation. Some of the words that indicate multiplication are given in Table 1.47.

Operation	Word Phrase	Example	Expression
Multiplication	times product twice	3 times 8 the product of 3 and 8 twice 4	$3 \times 8, 3 \cdot 8, (3)(8),$ $(3)8,$ or $3(8)$ $2 \cdot 4$

Table 1.47

EXAMPLE 1.50

Translate and simplify: the product of 12 and 27.

⊘ **Solution**

The word *product* tells us to multiply. The words *of* 12 *and* 27 tell us the two factors.

the product of 12 and 27

Translate. $12 \cdot 27$

Multiply.   324

TRY IT :: 1.99   Translate and simplify the product of 13 and 28.

TRY IT :: 1.100   Translate and simplify the product of 47 and 14.

EXAMPLE 1.51

Translate and simplify: twice two hundred eleven.

⊘ **Solution**

The word *twice* tells us to multiply by 2.

twice two hundred eleven

Translate.   2(211)

Multiply.   422

TRY IT :: 1.101   Translate and simplify: twice one hundred sixty-seven.

TRY IT :: 1.102   Translate and simplify: twice two hundred fifty-eight.

Multiply Whole Numbers in Applications

We will use the same strategy we used previously to solve applications of multiplication. First, we need to determine what we are looking for. Then we write a phrase that gives the information to find it. We then translate the phrase into math notation and simplify to get the answer. Finally, we write a sentence to answer the question.

EXAMPLE 1.52

Humberto bought 4 sheets of stamps. Each sheet had 20 stamps. How many stamps did Humberto buy?

⊘ **Solution**

We are asked to find the total number of stamps.

Write a phrase for the total.	the product of 4 and 20
Translate to math notation.	$4 \cdot 20$
Multiply.	$\begin{array}{r} 20 \\ \times\,4 \\ \hline 80 \end{array}$
Write a sentence to answer the question.	Humberto bought 80 stamps.

> **TRY IT :: 1.103**

  Valia donated water for the snack bar at her son's baseball game. She brought 6 cases of water bottles. Each case had 24 water bottles. How many water bottles did Valia donate?

> **TRY IT :: 1.104**

  Vanessa brought 8 packs of hot dogs to a family reunion. Each pack has 10 hot dogs. How many hot dogs did Vanessa bring?

EXAMPLE 1.53

When Rena cooks rice, she uses twice as much water as rice. How much water does she need to cook 4 cups of rice?

⊘ **Solution**

We are asked to find how much water Rena needs.

Write as a phrase.	twice as much as 4 cups
Translate to math notation.	$2 \cdot 4$
Multiply to simplify.	8
Write a sentence to answer the question.	Rena needs 8 cups of water for cups of rice.

> **TRY IT :: 1.105**

  Erin is planning her flower garden. She wants to plant twice as many dahlias as sunflowers. If she plants 14 sunflowers, how many dahlias does she need?

> **TRY IT :: 1.106**

  A college choir has twice as many women as men. There are 18 men in the choir. How many women are in the choir?

EXAMPLE 1.54

Van is planning to build a patio. He will have 8 rows of tiles, with 14 tiles in each row. How many tiles does he need for the patio?

⊘ **Solution**

We are asked to find the total number of tiles.

Write a phrase.	the product of 8 and 14
Translate to math notation.	$8 \cdot 14$
Multiply to simplify.	$\begin{array}{r} 14 \\ \times 8 \\ \hline 112 \end{array}$
Write a sentence to answer the question.	Van needs 112 tiles for his patio.

> **TRY IT : :** 1.107

Jane is tiling her living room floor. She will need 16 rows of tile, with 20 tiles in each row. How many tiles does she need for the living room floor?

> **TRY IT : :** 1.108

Yousef is putting shingles on his garage roof. He will need 24 rows of shingles, with 45 shingles in each row. How many shingles does he need for the garage roof?

If we want to know the size of a wall that needs to be painted or a floor that needs to be carpeted, we will need to find its **area**. The area is a measure of the amount of surface that is covered by the shape. Area is measured in square units. We often use square inches, square feet, square centimeters, or square miles to measure area. A square centimeter is a square that is one centimeter (cm.) on a side. A square inch is a square that is one inch on each side, and so on.

For a rectangular figure, the area is the product of the length and the width. Figure 1.12 shows a rectangular rug with a length of 2 feet and a width of 3 feet. Each square is 1 foot wide by 1 foot long, or 1 square foot. The rug is made of 6 squares. The area of the rug is 6 square feet.

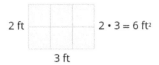

Figure 1.12 The area of a rectangle is the product of its length and its width, or 6 square feet.

EXAMPLE 1.55

Jen's kitchen ceiling is a rectangle that measures 9 feet long by 12 feet wide. What is the area of Jen's kitchen ceiling?

⊘ **Solution**

We are asked to find the area of the kitchen ceiling.

Write a phrase for the area.	the product of 9 and 12
Translate to math notation.	$9 \cdot 12$
Multiply.	$\begin{array}{r} 12 \\ \times 9 \\ \hline 108 \end{array}$
Answer with a sentence.	The area of Jen's kitchen ceiling is 108 square feet.

> **TRY IT : :** 1.109

Zoila bought a rectangular rug. The rug is 8 feet long by 5 feet wide. What is the area of the rug?

> **TRY IT : :** 1.110

Rene's driveway is a rectangle 45 feet long by 20 feet wide. What is the area of the driveway?

1.4 EXERCISES

Practice Makes Perfect

Use Multiplication Notation

In the following exercises, translate from math notation to words.

225. 4×7

226. 8×6

227. $5 \cdot 12$

228. $3 \cdot 9$

229. $(10)(25)$

230. $(20)(15)$

231. $42(33)$

232. $39(64)$

Model Multiplication of Whole Numbers

In the following exercises, model the multiplication.

233. 3×6

234. 4×5

235. 5×9

236. 3×9

Multiply Whole Numbers

In the following exercises, fill in the missing values in each chart.

237.

×	0	1	2	3	4	5	6	7	8	9
0	0	0	0		0	0	0	0		0
1	0	1	2	3			6	7	8	
2		2	4	6	8		12			18
3	0		6		12	15		21		27
4	0	4			16	20		28	32	
5	0	5	10	15			30		40	
6	0	6	12		24			42		54
7			14	21		35			56	63
8	0	8		24			48		64	
9	0	9	18		36	45			72	

238.

×	0	1	2	3	4	5	6	7	8	9
0	0	0	0	0	0		0		0	0
1	0	1	2		4	5		7		9
2	0		4		8	10		14	16	
3		3		9			18		24	
4	0	4	8	12			24	28		36
5	0	5		15	20		30	35	40	
6			12	18			36	42		54
7	0	7		21		35			56	63
8	0	8	16		32		48		64	72
9			18	27	36			63		

239.

×	3	4	5	6	7	8	9
4							
5							
6							
7							
8							
9							

240.

×	4	5	6	7	8	9
3						
4						
5						
6						
7						
8						
9						

241.

×	3	4	5	6	7	8	9
6							
7							
8							
9							

242.

×	6	7	8	9
3				
4				
5				
6				
7				
8				
9				

243.

×	5	6	7	8	9
5					
6					
7					
8					
9					

244.

×	6	7	8	9
6				
7				
8				
9				

In the following exercises, multiply.

245. $0 \cdot 15$

246. $0 \cdot 41$

247. $(99)0$

248. $(77)0$

249. $1 \cdot 43$

250. $1 \cdot 34$

251. $(28)1$

252. $(65)1$

253. $1(240,055)$

254. $1(189,206)$

255.
ⓐ $7 \cdot 6$ ⓑ $6 \cdot 7$

256.
ⓐ 8×9 ⓑ 9×8

257. $(79)(5)$

258. $(58)(4)$

259. $275 \cdot 6$

260. $638 \cdot 5$

261. $3,421 \times 7$

262. $9,143 \times 3$

263. $52(38)$

264. $37(45)$

265. $96 \cdot 73$

266. $89 \cdot 56$

267. 27×85

268. 53×98

269. $23 \cdot 10$

270. $19 \cdot 10$

271. $(100)(36)$

272. $(100)(25)$

273. $1,000(88)$

274. $1,000(46)$

275. $50 \times 1,000,000$

276. $30 \times 1,000,000$

277. 247×139

278. 156×328

279. $586(721)$

280. $472(855)$

281. $915 \cdot 879$

282. $968 \cdot 926$

283. $(104)(256)$

284. $(103)(497)$

285. $348(705)$

286. $485(602)$

287. $2,719 \times 543$

288. $3,581 \times 724$

Translate Word Phrases to Math Notation

In the following exercises, translate and simplify.

289. the product of 18 and 33

290. the product of 15 and 22

291. fifty-one times sixty-seven

292. forty-eight times seventy-one

293. twice 249

294. twice 589

295. ten times three hundred seventy-five

296. ten times two hundred fifty-five

Mixed Practice

In the following exercises, simplify.

297. 38×37

298. 86×29

299. $415 - 267$

300. $341 - 285$

301. $6,251 + 4,749$

302. $3,816 + 8,184$

303. $(56)(204)$

304. $(77)(801)$

305. $947 \cdot 0$

306. $947 + 0$

307. $15,382 + 1$

308. $15,382 \cdot 1$

In the following exercises, translate and simplify.

309. the difference of 50 and 18

310. the difference of 90 and 66

311. twice 35

312. twice 140

313. 20 more than 980

314. 65 more than 325

315. the product of 12 and 875

316. the product of 15 and 905

317. subtract 74 from 89

318. subtract 45 from 99

319. the sum of 3,075 and 95

320. the sum of 6,308 and 724

321. 366 less than 814

322. 388 less than 925

Multiply Whole Numbers in Applications

In the following exercises, solve.

323. Party supplies Tim brought 9 six-packs of soda to a club party. How many cans of soda did Tim bring?

324. Sewing Kanisha is making a quilt. She bought 6 cards of buttons. Each card had four buttons on it. How many buttons did Kanisha buy?

325. Field trip Seven school busses let off their students in front of a museum in Washington, DC. Each school bus had 44 students. How many students were there?

326. Gardening Kathryn bought 8 flats of impatiens for her flower bed. Each flat has 24 flowers. How many flowers did Kathryn buy?

327. Charity Rey donated 15 twelve-packs of t-shirts to a homeless shelter. How many t-shirts did he donate?

328. School There are 28 classrooms at Anna C. Scott elementary school. Each classroom has 26 student desks. What is the total number of student desks?

329. Recipe Stephanie is making punch for a party. The recipe calls for twice as much fruit juice as club soda. If she uses 10 cups of club soda, how much fruit juice should she use?

330. Gardening Hiroko is putting in a vegetable garden. He wants to have twice as many lettuce plants as tomato plants. If he buys 12 tomato plants, how many lettuce plants should he get?

331. Government The United States Senate has twice as many senators as there are states in the United States. There are 50 states. How many senators are there in the United States Senate?

332. Recipe Andrea is making potato salad for a buffet luncheon. The recipe says the number of servings of potato salad will be twice the number of pounds of potatoes. If she buys 30 pounds of potatoes, how many servings of potato salad will there be?

333. Painting Jane is painting one wall of her living room. The wall is rectangular, 13 feet wide by 9 feet high. What is the area of the wall?

334. Home décor Shawnte bought a rug for the hall of her apartment. The rug is 3 feet wide by 18 feet long. What is the area of the rug?

335. Room size The meeting room in a senior center is rectangular, with length 42 feet and width 34 feet. What is the area of the meeting room?

336. Gardening June has a vegetable garden in her yard. The garden is rectangular, with length 23 feet and width 28 feet. What is the area of the garden?

337. NCAA basketball According to NCAA regulations, the dimensions of a rectangular basketball court must be 94 feet by 50 feet. What is the area of the basketball court?

338. NCAA football According to NCAA regulations, the dimensions of a rectangular football field must be 360 feet by 160 feet. What is the area of the football field?

Everyday Math

339. Stock market Javier owns 300 shares of stock in one company. On Tuesday, the stock price rose $12 per share. How much money did Javier's portfolio gain?

340. Salary Carlton got a $200 raise in each paycheck. He gets paid 24 times a year. How much higher is his new annual salary?

Writing Exercises

341. How confident do you feel about your knowledge of the multiplication facts? If you are not fully confident, what will you do to improve your skills?

342. How have you used models to help you learn the multiplication facts?

Self Check

ⓐ After completing the exercises, use this checklist to evaluate your mastery of the objectives of this section.

I can...	Confidently	With some help	No-I don't get it!
use multiplication notation.			
model multiplication of whole numbers.			
multiply whole numbers.			
translate word phrases to math notation.			
multiply whole numbers in applications.			

ⓑ On a scale of 1–10, how would you rate your mastery of this section in light of your responses on the checklist? How can you improve this?

1.5 Divide Whole Numbers

Learning Objectives

By the end of this section, you will be able to:

- Use division notation
- Model division of whole numbers
- Divide whole numbers
- Translate word phrases to math notation
- Divide whole numbers in applications

Be Prepared!

Before you get started, take this readiness quiz.

1. Multiply: $27 \cdot 3$.
   If you missed this problem, review Example 1.44.

2. Subtract: $43 - 26$.
   If you missed this problem, review Example 1.32

3. Multiply: $62(87)$.
   If you missed this problem, review Example 1.45.

Use Division Notation

So far we have explored addition, subtraction, and multiplication. Now let's consider division. Suppose you have the 12 cookies in Figure 1.13 and want to package them in bags with 4 cookies in each bag. How many bags would we need?

Figure 1.13

You might put 4 cookies in first bag, 4 in the second bag, and so on until you run out of cookies. Doing it this way, you would fill 3 bags.

In other words, starting with the 12 cookies, you would take away, or subtract, 4 cookies at a time. Division is a way to represent repeated subtraction just as multiplication represents repeated addition.

Instead of subtracting 4 repeatedly, we can write

$$12 \div 4$$

We read this as *twelve divided by four* and the result is the **quotient** of 12 and 4. The quotient is 3 because we can subtract 4 from 12 exactly 3 times. We call the number being divided the **dividend** and the number dividing it the **divisor**. In this case, the dividend is 12 and the divisor is 4.

In the past you may have used the notation $4\overline{)12}$, but this division also can be written as $12 \div 4$, $12/4$, $\frac{12}{4}$. In each case the 12 is the dividend and the 4 is the divisor.

Operation Symbols for Division

To represent and describe division, we can use symbols and words.

Operation	Notation	Expression	Read as	Result
Division	$\div$ $\dfrac{a}{b}$ $b\overline{)a}$ a/b	$12 \div 4$ $\dfrac{12}{4}$ $4\overline{)12}$ $12/4$	Twelve divided by four	the quotient of 12 and 4

Division is performed on two numbers at a time. When translating from math notation to English words, or English words to math notation, look for the words *of* and *and* to identify the numbers.

EXAMPLE 1.56

Translate from math notation to words.

ⓐ $64 \div 8$ ⓑ $\dfrac{42}{7}$ ⓒ $4\overline{)28}$

⊘ Solution

ⓐ We read this as *sixty-four divided by eight* and the result is *the quotient of sixty-four and eight.*

ⓑ We read this as *forty-two divided by seven* and the result is *the quotient of forty-two and seven.*

ⓒ We read this as *twenty-eight divided by four* and the result is *the quotient of twenty-eight and four.*

> **TRY IT :: 1.111**   Translate from math notation to words:
>
> ⓐ $84 \div 7$ ⓑ $\dfrac{18}{6}$ ⓒ $8\overline{)24}$

> **TRY IT :: 1.112**   Translate from math notation to words:
>
> ⓐ $72 \div 9$ ⓑ $\dfrac{21}{3}$ ⓒ $6\overline{)54}$

Model Division of Whole Numbers

As we did with multiplication, we will model division using counters. The operation of division helps us organize items into equal groups as we start with the number of items in the dividend and subtract the number in the divisor repeatedly.

 MANIPULATIVE MATHEMATICS

Doing the Manipulative Mathematics activity Model Division of Whole Numbers will help you develop a better understanding of dividing whole numbers.

EXAMPLE 1.57

Model the division: $24 \div 8$.

⊘ Solution

To find the quotient $24 \div 8$, we want to know how many groups of 8 are in 24.

Model the dividend. Start with 24 counters.

The divisor tell us the number of counters we want in each group. Form groups of 8 counters.

Count the number of groups. There are 3 groups.

$24 \div 8 = 3$

> | **TRY IT :: 1.113**   Model: $24 \div 6$.

> | **TRY IT :: 1.114**   Model: $42 \div 7$.

Divide Whole Numbers

We said that addition and subtraction are inverse operations because one undoes the other. Similarly, division is the inverse operation of multiplication. We know $12 \div 4 = 3$ because $3 \cdot 4 = 12$. Knowing all the multiplication number facts is very important when doing division.

We check our answer to division by multiplying the quotient by the divisor to determine if it equals the dividend. In Example 1.57, we know $24 \div 8 = 3$ is correct because $3 \cdot 8 = 24$.

EXAMPLE 1.58

Divide. Then check by multiplying. ⓐ $42 \div 6$ ⓑ $\dfrac{72}{9}$ ⓒ $7\overline{)63}$

⊘ **Solution**

ⓐ

$$42 \div 6$$

Divide 42 by 6.   7

Check by multiplying.
$7 \cdot 6$

$42 \checkmark$

ⓑ

$$\frac{72}{9}$$

| Divide 72 by 9. | 8 |

Check by multiplying.
$8 \cdot 9$

$72 \checkmark$

ⓒ

$$7\overline{)63}$$

| Divide 63 by 7. | 9 |

Check by multiplying.
$9 \cdot 7$

$63 \checkmark$

> **TRY IT : : 1.115**   Divide. Then check by multiplying:

ⓐ $54 \div 6$ ⓑ $\frac{27}{9}$

> **TRY IT : : 1.116**   Divide. Then check by multiplying:

ⓐ $\frac{36}{9}$ ⓑ $8\overline{)40}$

What is the quotient when you divide a number by itself?

$$\frac{15}{15} = 1 \text{ because } 1 \cdot 15 = 15$$

Dividing any number (except 0) by itself produces a quotient of 1. Also, any number divided by 1 produces a quotient of the number. These two ideas are stated in the Division Properties of One.

Division Properties of One

| Any number (except 0) divided by itself is one. | $a \div a = 1$ |
| Any number divided by one is the same number. | $a \div 1 = a$ |

Table 1.57

EXAMPLE 1.59

Divide. Then check by multiplying:

ⓐ $11 \div 11$ ⓑ $\frac{19}{1}$ ⓒ $1\overline{)7}$

✓ **Solution**

ⓐ

$$11 \div 11$$

A number divided by itself is 1.   1

Check by multiplying.
$1 \cdot 11$

11 ✓

ⓑ

$$\frac{19}{1}$$

A number divided by 1 equals itself.   19

Check by multiplying.
$19 \cdot 1$

19 ✓

ⓒ

$$1\overline{)7}$$

A number divided by 1 equals itself.   7

Check by multiplying.
$7 \cdot 1$

7 ✓

> **TRY IT :: 1.117**   Divide. Then check by multiplying:

ⓐ $14 \div 14$ ⓑ $\frac{27}{1}$

> **TRY IT :: 1.118**   Divide. Then check by multiplying:

ⓐ $\frac{16}{1}$ ⓑ $1\overline{)4}$

Suppose we have $\$0$, and want to divide it among 3 people. How much would each person get? Each person would get $\$0$. Zero divided by any number is 0.

Now suppose that we want to divide $\$10$ by 0. That means we would want to find a number that we multiply by 0 to get 10. This cannot happen because 0 times any number is 0. Division by zero is said to be *undefined*.

These two ideas make up the Division Properties of Zero.

Division Properties of Zero

Zero divided by any number is 0.	$0 \div a = 0$
Dividing a number by zero is undefined.	$a \div 0$ undefined

Table 1.61

Another way to explain why division by zero is undefined is to remember that division is really repeated subtraction. How many times can we take away 0 from 10? Because subtracting 0 will never change the total, we will never get an answer. So we cannot divide a number by 0.

EXAMPLE 1.60

Divide. Check by multiplying: ⓐ $0 \div 3$ ⓑ $10/0$.

✓ **Solution**

ⓐ

	$0 \div 3$
Zero divided by any number is zero.	0
Check by multiplying. $0 \cdot 3$	
$0 \checkmark$	

ⓑ

	$10/0$
Division by zero is undefined.	undefined

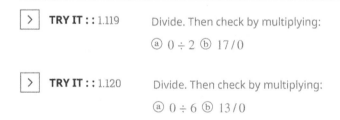

> **TRY IT : : 1.119**   Divide. Then check by multiplying:

   ⓐ $0 \div 2$ ⓑ $17/0$

> **TRY IT : : 1.120**   Divide. Then check by multiplying:

   ⓐ $0 \div 6$ ⓑ $13/0$

When the divisor or the dividend has more than one digit, it is usually easier to use the $4\overline{)12}$ notation. This process is called long division. Let's work through the process by dividing 78 by 3.

79

Divide the first digit of the dividend, 7, by the divisor, 3.

The divisor 3 can go into 7 two times since $2 \times 3 = 6$. Write the 2 above the 7 in the quotient.

$$\begin{array}{r} 2 \\ 3\overline{)78} \end{array}$$

Multiply the 2 in the quotient by 2 and write the product, 6, under the 7.

$$\begin{array}{r} 2 \\ 3\overline{)78} \\ \underline{6} \end{array}$$

Subtract that product from the first digit in the dividend. Subtract $7 - 6$. Write the difference, 1, under the first digit in the dividend.

$$\begin{array}{r} 2 \\ 3\overline{)78} \\ \underline{6} \\ 1 \end{array}$$

Bring down the next digit of the dividend. Bring down the 8.

$$\begin{array}{r} 2 \\ 3\overline{)78} \\ \underline{6} \\ 18 \end{array}$$

Divide 18 by the divisor, 3. The divisor 3 goes into 18 six times.

$$\begin{array}{r} 26 \\ 3\overline{)78} \\ \underline{6} \\ 18 \end{array}$$

Write 6 in the quotient above the 8.

Multiply the 6 in the quotient by the divisor and write the product, 18, under the dividend. Subtract 18 from 18.

$$\begin{array}{r} 26 \\ 3\overline{)78} \\ \underline{6} \\ 18 \\ \underline{18} \\ 0 \end{array}$$

We would repeat the process until there are no more digits in the dividend to bring down. In this problem, there are no more digits to bring down, so the division is finished.

$$\text{So } 78 \div 3 = 26.$$

Check by multiplying the quotient times the divisor to get the dividend. Multiply 26×3 to make sure that product equals the dividend, 78.

$$\begin{array}{r} \overset{1}{2}6 \\ \underline{\times 3} \\ 78 \checkmark \end{array}$$

It does, so our answer is correct.

 HOW TO :: DIVIDE WHOLE NUMBERS.

Step 1.　Divide the first digit of the dividend by the divisor.
　　　　　If the divisor is larger than the first digit of the dividend, divide the first two digits of the dividend by the divisor, and so on.

Step 2.　Write the quotient above the dividend.

Step 3.　Multiply the quotient by the divisor and write the product under the dividend.

Step 4.　Subtract that product from the dividend.

Step 5.　Bring down the next digit of the dividend.

Step 6.　Repeat from Step 1 until there are no more digits in the dividend to bring down.

Step 7.　Check by multiplying the quotient times the divisor.

EXAMPLE 1.61

Divide $2,596 \div 4$. Check by multiplying:

◯ **Solution**

Let's rewrite the problem to set it up for long division.	$4\overline{)2596}$
Divide the first digit of the dividend, 2, by the divisor, 4.	$4\overline{)2596}$
Since 4 does not go into 2, we use the first two digits of the dividend and divide 25 by 4. The divisor 4 goes into 25 six times.	
We write the 6 in the quotient above the 5.	$\begin{array}{r} 6 \\ 4\overline{)2596} \end{array}$
Multiply the 6 in the quotient by the divisor 4 and write the product, 24, under the first two digits in the dividend.	$\begin{array}{r} 6 \\ 4\overline{)2596} \\ \underline{24} \end{array}$
Subtract that product from the first two digits in the dividend. Subtract $25 - 24$. Write the difference, 1, under the second digit in the dividend.	$\begin{array}{r} 6 \\ 4\overline{)2596} \\ \underline{24} \\ 1 \end{array}$
Now bring down the 9 and repeat these steps. There are 4 fours in 19. Write the 4 over the 9. Multiply the 4 by 4 and subtract this product from 19.	$\begin{array}{r} 64 \\ 4\overline{)2596} \\ \underline{24} \\ 19 \\ \underline{16} \\ 3 \end{array}$
Bring down the 6 and repeat these steps. There are 9 fours in 36. Write the 9 over the 6. Multiply the 9 by 4 and subtract this product from 36.	$\begin{array}{r} 649 \\ 4\overline{)2596} \\ \underline{24} \\ 19 \\ \underline{16} \\ 36 \\ \underline{36} \\ 0 \end{array}$

So $2,596 \div 4 = 649$.

Check by multiplying.

$$\begin{array}{r} \overset{1\ 3}{649} \\ \times\quad 4 \\ \hline 2,596\ \checkmark \end{array}$$

It equals the dividend, so our answer is correct.

> | **TRY IT : : 1.121**   Divide. Then check by multiplying: $2,636 \div 4$

> | **TRY IT : : 1.122**   Divide. Then check by multiplying: $2,716 \div 4$

EXAMPLE 1.62

Divide $4,506 \div 6$. Check by multiplying:

⊘ **Solution**

Let's rewrite the problem to set it up for long division.	$6\overline{)4506}$
First we try to divide 6 into 4.	$6\overline{)4506}$
Since that won't work, we try 6 into 45. There are 7 sixes in 45. We write the 7 over the 5.	$\begin{array}{r} 7 \\ 6\overline{)4506} \end{array}$
Multiply the 7 by 6 and subtract this product from 45.	$\begin{array}{r} 7 \\ 6\overline{)4506} \\ \underline{42} \\ 3 \end{array}$
Now bring down the 0 and repeat these steps. There are 5 sixes in 30. Write the 5 over the 0. Multiply the 5 by 6 and subtract this product from 30.	$\begin{array}{r} 75 \\ 6\overline{)4506} \\ \underline{42} \\ 30 \\ \underline{30} \\ 0 \end{array}$
Now bring down the 6 and repeat these steps. There is 1 six in 6. Write the 1 over the 6. Multiply 1 by 6 and subtract this product from 6.	$\begin{array}{r} 751 \\ 6\overline{)4506} \\ \underline{42} \\ 30 \\ \underline{30} \\ 06 \\ \underline{6} \\ 0 \end{array}$

Check by multiplying.

$$\begin{array}{r} \overset{3}{7}51 \\ \times 6 \\ \hline 4{,}506 \checkmark \end{array}$$

It equals the dividend, so our answer is correct.

$>$	**TRY IT : : 1.123**	Divide. Then check by multiplying: $4{,}305 \div 5$.

$>$	**TRY IT : : 1.124**	Divide. Then check by multiplying: $3{,}906 \div 6$.

EXAMPLE 1.63

Divide $7{,}263 \div 9$. Check by multiplying.

⊘ **Solution**

Let's rewrite the problem to set it up for long division.	$9\overline{)7263}$
First we try to divide 9 into 7.	$9\overline{)7263}$
Since that won't work, we try 9 into 72. There are 8 nines in 72. We write the 8 over the 2.	$\begin{array}{r} 8 \\ 9\overline{)7263} \end{array}$
Multiply the 8 by 9 and subtract this product from 72.	$\begin{array}{r} 8 \\ 9\overline{)7263} \\ \underline{72} \\ 0 \end{array}$
Now bring down the 6 and repeat these steps. There are 0 nines in 6. Write the 0 over the 6. Multiply the 0 by 9 and subtract this product from 6.	$\begin{array}{r} 80 \\ 9\overline{)7263} \\ \underline{72} \\ 06 \\ \underline{0} \\ 6 \end{array}$
Now bring down the 3 and repeat these steps. There are 7 nines in 63. Write the 7 over the 3. Multiply the 7 by 9 and subtract this product from 63.	$\begin{array}{r} 807 \\ 9\overline{)7263} \\ \underline{72} \\ 06 \\ \underline{0} \\ 63 \\ \underline{63} \\ 0 \end{array}$

Check by multiplying.

$$\begin{array}{r} \overset{6}{8}07 \\ \times 9 \\ \hline 7{,}263\ \checkmark \end{array}$$

It equals the dividend, so our answer is correct.

> **TRY IT :: 1.125**   Divide. Then check by multiplying: $4{,}928 \div 7$.

> **TRY IT :: 1.126**   Divide. Then check by multiplying: $5{,}663 \div 7$.

So far all the division problems have worked out evenly. For example, if we had 24 cookies and wanted to make bags of 8 cookies, we would have 3 bags. But what if there were 28 cookies and we wanted to make bags of 8? Start with the 28 cookies as shown in Figure 1.14.

Figure 1.14

Try to put the cookies in groups of eight as in Figure 1.15.

Figure 1.15

There are 3 groups of eight cookies, and 4 cookies left over. We call the 4 cookies that are left over the remainder and show it by writing R4 next to the 3. (The R stands for remainder.)

To check this division we multiply 3 times 8 to get 24, and then add the remainder of 4.

$$
\begin{array}{r}
3 \\
\times 8 \\
\hline
24 \\
+4 \\
\hline
28
\end{array}
$$

EXAMPLE 1.64

Divide $1,439 \div 4$. Check by multiplying.

⊘ **Solution**

Let's rewrite the problem to set it up for long division.

$$4\overline{)1439}$$

First we try to divide 4 into 1. Since that won't work, we try 4 into 14. There are 3 fours in 14. We write the 3 over the 4.

$$
\begin{array}{r}
3 \\
4\overline{)1439}
\end{array}
$$

Multiply the 3 by 4 and subtract this product from 14.

$$
\begin{array}{r}
3 \\
4\overline{)1439} \\
12 \\
\hline
2
\end{array}
$$

Now bring down the 3 and repeat these steps. There are 5 fours in 23. Write the 5 over the 3. Multiply the 5 by 4 and subtract this product from 23.

$$
\begin{array}{r}
35 \\
4\overline{)1439} \\
12\!\downarrow \\
\hline
23 \\
20 \\
\hline
3
\end{array}
$$

Now bring down the 9 and repeat these steps. There are 9 fours in 39. Write the 9 over the 9. Multiply the 9 by 4 and subtract this product from 39. There are no more numbers to bring down, so we are done. The remainder is 3.

$$
\begin{array}{r}
359\text{R}3 \\
4\overline{)1439} \\
12 \\
\hline
23 \\
20\!\downarrow \\
\hline
39 \\
36 \\
\hline
3
\end{array}
$$

Check by multiplying.

$$
\begin{array}{rl}
\overset{2\ 3}{359} & \text{quotient} \\
\times \quad 4 & \text{divisor} \\
\hline
1,436 & \\
+\quad 3 & \text{remainder} \\
\hline
1,439\ \checkmark &
\end{array}
$$

So $1,439 \div 4$ is 359 with a remainder of 3. Our answer is correct.

> **TRY IT :: 1.127**   Divide. Then check by multiplying: $3,812 \div 8$.

> **TRY IT :: 1.128**   Divide. Then check by multiplying: $4,319 \div 8$.

EXAMPLE 1.65

Divide and then check by multiplying: $1,461 \div 13$.

⊘ **Solution**

Let's rewrite the problem to set it up for long division.	$13\overline{)1,461}$
First we try to divide 13 into 1. Since that won't work, we try 13 into 14. There is 1 thirteen in 14. We write the 1 over the 4.	$\begin{array}{r} 1 \\ 13\overline{)1461} \end{array}$
Multiply the 1 by 13 and subtract this product from 14.	$\begin{array}{r} 1 \\ 13\overline{)1461} \\ \underline{13} \\ 1 \end{array}$
Now bring down the 6 and repeat these steps. There is 1 thirteen in 16. Write the 1 over the 6. Multiply the 1 by 13 and subtract this product from 16.	$\begin{array}{r} 11 \\ 13\overline{)1461} \\ \underline{13}\downarrow \\ 16 \\ \underline{13} \\ 3 \end{array}$
Now bring down the 1 and repeat these steps. There are 2 thirteens in 31. Write the 2 over the 1. Multiply the 2 by 13 and subtract this product from 31. There are no more numbers to bring down, so we are done. The remainder is 5. $1,462 \div 13$ is 112 with a remainder of 5.	$\begin{array}{r} 112R5 \\ 13\overline{)1461} \\ \underline{13} \\ 16 \\ \underline{13}\downarrow \\ 31 \\ \underline{26} \\ 5 \end{array}$

Check by multiplying.

$$\begin{array}{r} 112 \quad \text{quotient} \\ \times\ 13 \quad \text{divisor} \\ \hline 336 \\ 1,120 \\ \underline{+\quad 5} \quad \text{remainder} \\ 1,461 \quad \checkmark \end{array}$$

Our answer is correct.

> **TRY IT :: 1.129**   Divide. Then check by multiplying: $1,493 \div 13$.

> **TRY IT :: 1.130**   Divide. Then check by multiplying: $1,461 \div 12$.

EXAMPLE 1.66

Divide and check by multiplying: $74,521 \div 241$.

⊘ Solution

Let's rewrite the problem to set it up for long division.

$$241 \overline{)74{,}521}$$

First we try to divide 241 into 7. Since that won't work, we try 241 into 74. That still won't work, so we try 241 into 745. Since 2 divides into 7 three times, we try 3. Since $3 \times 241 = 723$, we write the 3 over the 5 in 745.

Note that 4 would be too large because $4 \times 241 = 964$, which is greater than 745.

Multiply the 3 by 241 and subtract this product from 745.

$$\begin{array}{r} 3 \\ 241 \overline{)74521} \\ 723 \\ \hline 22 \end{array}$$

Now bring down the 2 and repeat these steps. 241 does not divide into 222. We write a 0 over the 2 as a placeholder and then continue.

$$\begin{array}{r} 30 \\ 241 \overline{)74521} \\ 723 \\ \hline 222 \end{array}$$

Now bring down the 1 and repeat these steps. Try 9. Since $9 \times 241 = 2{,}169$,

we write the 9 over the 1. Multiply the 9 by 241 and subtract this product from 2,221.

$$\begin{array}{r} 309 \ R\,52 \\ 241 \overline{)74521} \\ 723 \\ \hline 2221 \\ 2169 \\ \hline 52 \end{array}$$

There are no more numbers to bring down, so we are finished. The remainder is 52. So $74{,}521 \div 241$

is 309 with a remainder of 52.

Check by multiplying.

$$\begin{array}{r} {}^{3} \\ 309 \quad \text{quotient} \\ \times\ 241 \quad \text{divisor} \\ \hline 309 \\ 12{,}360 \\ 61{,}800 \\ \hline 72{,}469 \\ +\ \ 52 \quad \text{remainder} \\ \hline 74{,}521 \quad \checkmark \end{array}$$

Sometimes it might not be obvious how many times the divisor goes into digits of the dividend. We will have to guess and check numbers to find the greatest number that goes into the digits without exceeding them.

> **TRY IT :: 1.131**   Divide. Then check by multiplying: $78{,}641 \div 256$.

> **TRY IT :: 1.132**   Divide. Then check by multiplying: $76{,}461 \div 248$.

Translate Word Phrases to Math Notation

Earlier in this section, we translated math notation for division into words. Now we'll translate word phrases into math notation. Some of the words that indicate division are given in Table 1.70.

Operation	Word Phrase	Example	Expression
Division	divided by quotient of divided into	12 divided by 4 the quotient of 12 and 4 4 divided into 12	$12 \div 4$ $\dfrac{12}{4}$ $12/4$ $4\overline{)12}$

Table 1.70

EXAMPLE 1.67

Translate and simplify: the quotient of 51 and 17.

⊘ Solution

The word *quotient* tells us to divide.

the quotient of 51 and 17

Translate. $51 \div 17$
Divide.   3

We could just as correctly have translated *the quotient of 51 and 17* using the notation

$17\overline{)51}$ or $\dfrac{51}{17}$.

> **TRY IT : : 1.133**   Translate and simplify: the quotient of 91 and 13.

> **TRY IT : : 1.134**   Translate and simplify: the quotient of 52 and 13.

Divide Whole Numbers in Applications

We will use the same strategy we used in previous sections to solve applications. First, we determine what we are looking for. Then we write a phrase that gives the information to find it. We then translate the phrase into math notation and simplify it to get the answer. Finally, we write a sentence to answer the question.

EXAMPLE 1.68

Cecelia bought a 160-ounce box of oatmeal at the big box store. She wants to divide the 160 ounces of oatmeal into 8-ounce servings. She will put each serving into a plastic bag so she can take one bag to work each day. How many servings will she get from the big box?

⊘ Solution

We are asked to find the how many servings she will get from the big box.

Write a phrase.	160 ounces divided by 8 ounces
Translate to math notation.	$160 \div 8$
Simplify by dividing.	20
Write a sentence to answer the question.	Cecelia will get 20 servings from the big box.

> **TRY IT : : 1.135**
>
> Marcus is setting out animal crackers for snacks at the preschool. He wants to put 9 crackers in each cup. One box of animal crackers contains 135 crackers. How many cups can he fill from one box of crackers?

> **TRY IT : :** 1.136

Andrea is making bows for the girls in her dance class to wear at the recital. Each bow takes 4 feet of ribbon, and 36 feet of ribbon are on one spool. How many bows can Andrea make from one spool of ribbon?

▶ **MEDIA : :** ACCESS ADDITIONAL ONLINE RESOURCES
- Dividing Whole Numbers (http://www.openstaxcollege.org/l/24divwhlnum)
- Dividing Whole Numbers No Remainder (http://www.openstaxcollege.org/l/24divnumnorem)
- Dividing Whole Numbers With Remainder (http://www.openstaxcollege.org/l/24divnumwrem)

1.5 EXERCISES

Practice Makes Perfect

Use Division Notation

In the following exercises, translate from math notation to words.

343. $54 \div 9$

344. $\dfrac{56}{7}$

345. $\dfrac{32}{8}$

346. $6\overline{)42}$

347. $48 \div 6$

348. $\dfrac{63}{9}$

349. $7\overline{)63}$

350. $72 \div 8$

Model Division of Whole Numbers

In the following exercises, model the division.

351. $15 \div 5$

352. $10 \div 5$

353. $\dfrac{14}{7}$

354. $\dfrac{18}{6}$

355. $4\overline{)20}$

356. $3\overline{)15}$

357. $24 \div 6$

358. $16 \div 4$

Divide Whole Numbers

In the following exercises, divide. Then check by multiplying.

359. $18 \div 2$

360. $14 \div 2$

361. $\dfrac{27}{3}$

362. $\dfrac{30}{3}$

363. $4\overline{)28}$

364. $4\overline{)36}$

365. $\dfrac{45}{5}$

366. $\dfrac{35}{5}$

367. $72 / 8$

368. $8\overline{)64}$

369. $\dfrac{35}{7}$

370. $42 \div 7$

371. $15\overline{)15}$

372. $12\overline{)12}$

373. $43 \div 43$

374. $37 \div 37$

375. $\dfrac{23}{1}$

376. $\dfrac{29}{1}$

377. $19 \div 1$

378. $17 \div 1$

379. $0 \div 4$

380. $0 \div 8$

381. $\dfrac{5}{0}$

382. $\dfrac{9}{0}$

383. $\dfrac{26}{0}$

384. $\dfrac{32}{0}$

385. $12\overline{)0}$

386. $16\overline{)0}$

387. $72 \div 3$

388. $57 \div 3$

389. $\dfrac{96}{8}$

390. $\dfrac{78}{6}$

391. $5\overline{)465}$

392. $4\overline{)528}$

393. $924 \div 7$

394. $861 \div 7$

395. $\dfrac{5,226}{6}$

396. $\dfrac{3,776}{8}$

397. $4\overline{)31,324}$

398. $5\overline{)46,855}$

399. $7,209 \div 3$

400. $4,806 \div 3$

401. $5,406 \div 6$

402. $3,208 \div 4$

403. $4\overline{)2,816}$

404. $6\overline{)3,624}$

405. $\dfrac{91,881}{9}$

406. $\dfrac{83,256}{8}$

407. $2,470 \div 7$

408. $3,741 \div 7$

409. $8\overline{)55,305}$

410. $9\overline{)51,492}$

411. $\dfrac{431,174}{5}$

412. $\dfrac{297,277}{4}$

413. $130,016 \div 3$

414. $105,609 \div 2$

415. $15\overline{)5,735}$

416. $\dfrac{4,933}{21}$

417. $56,883 \div 67$

418. $43,725 / 75$

419. $\dfrac{30,144}{314}$

420. $26,145 \div 415$

421. $273\overline{)542,195}$

422. $816,243 \div 462$

Mixed Practice

In the following exercises, simplify.

423. $15(204)$

424. $74 \cdot 391$

425. $256 - 184$

426. $305 - 262$

427. $719 + 341$

428. $647 + 528$

429. $25\overline{)875}$

430. $1104 \div 23$

Translate Word Phrases to Algebraic Expressions

In the following exercises, translate and simplify.

431. the quotient of 45 and 15

432. the quotient of 64 and 16

433. the quotient of 288 and 24

434. the quotient of 256 and 32

Divide Whole Numbers in Applications

In the following exercises, solve.

435. Trail mix Ric bought 64 ounces of trail mix. He wants to divide it into small bags, with 2 ounces of trail mix in each bag. How many bags can Ric fill?

436. Crackers Evie bought a 42 ounce box of crackers. She wants to divide it into bags with 3 ounces of crackers in each bag. How many bags can Evie fill?

437. Astronomy class There are 125 students in an astronomy class. The professor assigns them into groups of 5. How many groups of students are there?

438. Flower shop Melissa's flower shop got a shipment of 152 roses. She wants to make bouquets of 8 roses each. How many bouquets can Melissa make?

439. Baking One roll of plastic wrap is 48 feet long. Marta uses 3 feet of plastic wrap to wrap each cake she bakes. How many cakes can she wrap from one roll?

440. Dental floss One package of dental floss is 54 feet long. Brian uses 2 feet of dental floss every day. How many days will one package of dental floss last Brian?

Mixed Practice

In the following exercises, solve.

441. Miles per gallon Susana's hybrid car gets 45 miles per gallon. Her son's truck gets 17 miles per gallon. What is the difference in miles per gallon between Susana's car and her son's truck?

442. Distance Mayra lives 53 miles from her mother's house and 71 miles from her mother-in-law's house. How much farther is Mayra from her mother-in-law's house than from her mother's house?

443. Field trip The 45 students in a Geology class will go on a field trip, using the college's vans. Each van can hold 9 students. How many vans will they need for the field trip?

444. Potting soil Aki bought a 128 ounce bag of potting soil. How many 4 ounce pots can he fill from the bag?

445. Hiking Bill hiked 8 miles on the first day of his backpacking trip, 14 miles the second day, 11 miles the third day, and 17 miles the fourth day. What is the total number of miles Bill hiked?

446. Reading Last night Emily read 6 pages in her Business textbook, 26 pages in her History text, 15 pages in her Psychology text, and 9 pages in her math text. What is the total number of pages Emily read?

447. Patients LaVonne treats 12 patients each day in her dental office. Last week she worked 4 days. How many patients did she treat last week?

448. Scouts There are 14 boys in Dave's scout troop. At summer camp, each boy earned 5 merit badges. What was the total number of merit badges earned by Dave's scout troop at summer camp?

Writing Exercises

449. Explain how you use the multiplication facts to help with division.

450. Oswaldo divided 300 by 8 and said his answer was 37 with a remainder of 4. How can you check to make sure he is correct?

Everyday Math

451. Contact lenses Jenna puts in a new pair of contact lenses every 14 days. How many pairs of contact lenses does she need for 365 days?

452. Cat food One bag of cat food feeds Lara's cat for 25 days. How many bags of cat food does Lara need for 365 days?

Self Check

ⓐ *After completing the exercises, use this checklist to evaluate your mastery of the objectives of this section.*

I can...	Confidently	With some help	No-I don't get it!
use division notation.			
model division of whole numbers.			
divide whole numbers.			
translate word phrases to algebraic expressions.			
divide whole numbers in applications.			

ⓑ *Overall, after looking at the checklist, do you think you are well-prepared for the next Chapter? Why or why not?*

CHAPTER 1 REVIEW

KEY TERMS

coordinate A number paired with a point on a number line is called the coordinate of the point.

counting numbers The counting numbers are the numbers 1, 2, 3, ...

difference The difference is the result of subtracting two or more numbers.

dividend When dividing two numbers, the dividend is the number being divided.

divisor When dividing two numbers, the divisor is the number dividing the dividend.

number line A number line is used to visualize numbers. The numbers on the number line get larger as they go from left to right, and smaller as they go from right to left.

origin The origin is the point labeled 0 on a number line.

place value system Our number system is called a place value system because the value of a digit depends on its position, or place, in a number.

product The product is the result of multiplying two or more numbers.

quotient The quotient is the result of dividing two numbers.

rounding The process of approximating a number is called rounding.

sum The sum is the result of adding two or more numbers.

whole numbers The whole numbers are the numbers 0, 1, 2, 3, ...

KEY CONCEPTS

1.1 Introduction to Whole Numbers

Place Value														
Trillions			Billions			Millions			Thousands			Ones		
Hundred trillions	Ten trillions	Trillions	Hundred billions	Ten billions	Billions	Hundred millions	Ten millions	Millions	Hundred thousands	Ten thousands	Thousands	Hundreds	Tens	Ones
								5	2	7	8	1	9	4

Figure 1.16

- **Name a whole number in words.**

  Step 1. Starting at the digit on the left, name the number in each period, followed by the period name. Do not include the period name for the ones.

  Step 2. Use commas in the number to separate the periods.

- **Use place value to write a whole number.**

  Step 1. Identify the words that indicate periods. (Remember the ones period is never named.)

  Step 2. Draw three blanks to indicate the number of places needed in each period.

  Step 3. Name the number in each period and place the digits in the correct place value position.

- **Round a whole number to a specific place value.**

  Step 1. Locate the given place value. All digits to the left of that place value do not change.

  Step 2. Underline the digit to the right of the given place value.

  Step 3. Determine if this digit is greater than or equal to 5. If yes—add 1 to the digit in the given place value. If no—do not change the digit in the given place value.

Step 4. Replace all digits to the right of the given place value with zeros.

1.2 Add Whole Numbers

- **Addition Notation** To describe addition, we can use symbols and words.

Operation	Notation	Expression	Read as	Result
Addition	$+$	$3+4$	three plus four	the sum of 3 and 4

- **Identity Property of Addition**
    - The sum of any number a and 0 is the number. $a+0=a$ $0+a=a$
- **Commutative Property of Addition**
    - Changing the order of the addends a and b does not change their sum. $a+b=b+a$.
- **Add whole numbers.**
  Step 1. Write the numbers so each place value lines up vertically.
  Step 2. Add the digits in each place value. Work from right to left starting with the ones place. If a sum in a place value is more than 9, carry to the next place value.
  Step 3. Continue adding each place value from right to left, adding each place value and carrying if needed.

1.3 Subtract Whole Numbers

Operation	Notation	Expression	Read as	Result
Subtraction	$-$	$7-3$	seven minus three	the difference of 7 and 3

- **Subtract whole numbers.**
  Step 1. Write the numbers so each place value lines up vertically.
  Step 2. Subtract the digits in each place value. Work from right to left starting with the ones place. If the digit on top is less than the digit below, borrow as needed.
  Step 3. Continue subtracting each place value from right to left, borrowing if needed.
  Step 4. Check by adding.

1.4 Multiply Whole Numbers

Operation	Notation	Expression	Read as	Result
Multiplication	$\times$ $\cdot$ $(\,)$	3×8 $3\cdot8$ $3(8)$	three times eight	the product of 3 and 8

- **Multiplication Property of Zero**
    - The product of any number and 0 is 0.
      $a\cdot0=0$
      $0\cdot a=0$
- **Identity Property of Multiplication**
    - The product of any number and 1 is the number.
      $1\cdot a=a$
      $a\cdot1=a$
- **Commutative Property of Multiplication**
    - Changing the order of the factors does not change their product.

$$a \cdot b = b \cdot a$$

- **Multiply two whole numbers to find the product.**

  Step 1. Write the numbers so each place value lines up vertically.

  Step 2. Multiply the digits in each place value.

  Step 3. Work from right to left, starting with the ones place in the bottom number.

  Step 4. Multiply the bottom number by the ones digit in the top number, then by the tens digit, and so on.

  Step 5. If a product in a place value is more than 9, carry to the next place value.

  Step 6. Write the partial products, lining up the digits in the place values with the numbers above. Repeat for the tens place in the bottom number, the hundreds place, and so on.

  Step 7. Insert a zero as a placeholder with each additional partial product.

  Step 8. Add the partial products.

1.5 Divide Whole Numbers

Operation	Notation	Expression	Read as	Result
Division	$\div$ $\dfrac{a}{b}$ $b\overline{)a}$ a/b	$12 \div 4$ $\dfrac{12}{4}$ $4\overline{)12}$ $12/4$	Twelve divided by four	the quotient of 12 and 4

- **Division Properties of One**

  ◦ Any number (except 0) divided by itself is one. $a \div a = 1$

  ◦ Any number divided by one is the same number. $a \div 1 = a$

- **Division Properties of Zero**

  ◦ Zero divided by any number is 0. $0 \div a = 0$

  ◦ Dividing a number by zero is undefined. $a \div 0$ undefined

- **Divide whole numbers.**

  Step 1. Divide the first digit of the dividend by the divisor.
  If the divisor is larger than the first digit of the dividend, divide the first two digits of the dividend by the divisor, and so on.

  Step 2. Write the quotient above the dividend.

  Step 3. Multiply the quotient by the divisor and write the product under the dividend.

  Step 4. Subtract that product from the dividend.

  Step 5. Bring down the next digit of the dividend.

  Step 6. Repeat from Step 1 until there are no more digits in the dividend to bring down.

  Step 7. Check by multiplying the quotient times the divisor.

REVIEW EXERCISES

1.1 Introduction to Whole Numbers

Identify Counting Numbers and Whole Numbers

In the following exercises, determine which of the following are (a) counting numbers (b) whole numbers.

453. 0, 2, 99

454. 0, 3, 25

455. 0, 4, 90

456. 0, 1, 75

Model Whole Numbers

In the following exercises, model each number using base-10 blocks and then show its value using place value notation.

457. 258

458. 104

Identify the Place Value of a Digit

In the following exercises, find the place value of the given digits.

459. 472,981

    ⓐ 8 ⓑ 4 ⓒ 1

    ⓓ 7 ⓔ 2

460. 12,403,295

    ⓐ 4 ⓑ 0 ⓒ 1

    ⓓ 9 ⓔ 3

Use Place Value to Name Whole Numbers

In the following exercises, name each number in words.

461. 5,280

462. 204,614

463. 5,012,582

464. 31,640,976

Use Place Value to Write Whole Numbers

In the following exercises, write as a whole number using digits.

465. six hundred two

466. fifteen thousand, two hundred fifty-three

467. three hundred forty million, nine hundred twelve thousand, sixty-one

468. two billion, four hundred ninety-two million, seven hundred eleven thousand, two

Round Whole Numbers

In the following exercises, round to the nearest ten.

469. 412

470. 648

471. 3,556

472. 2,734

In the following exercises, round to the nearest hundred.

473. 38,975

474. 26,849

475. 81,486

476. 75,992

1.2 Add Whole Numbers

Use Addition Notation

In the following exercises, translate the following from math notation to words.

477. $4 + 3$

478. $25 + 18$

479. $571 + 629$

480. $10,085 + 3,492$

Model Addition of Whole Numbers

In the following exercises, model the addition.

481. $6 + 7$

482. $38 + 14$

Add Whole Numbers

In the following exercises, fill in the missing values in each chart.

483.

+	0	1	2	3	4	5	6	7	8	9
0	0	1		3	4		6	7		9
1	1	2	3	4			7	8	9	
2		3	4	5	6	7	8		10	11
3	3		5		7	8		10		12
4	4	5			8	9			12	
5	5		7	8			11		13	
6	6	7	8		10			13		15
7			9		12	13		15	16	
8	8	9		11			14		16	
9	9	10	11		13	14			17	

484.

+	3	4	5	6	7	8	9
6							
7							
8							
9							

In the following exercises, add.

485. ⓐ $0 + 19$ ⓑ $19 + 0$

486. ⓐ $0 + 480$ ⓑ $480 + 0$

487. ⓐ $7 + 6$ ⓑ $6 + 7$

488. ⓐ $23 + 18$ ⓑ $18 + 23$

489. $44 + 35$

490. $63 + 29$

491. $96 + 58$

492. $375 + 591$

493. $7,281 + 12,546$

494. $5,280 + 16,324 + 9,731$

Translate Word Phrases to Math Notation

In the following exercises, translate each phrase into math notation and then simplify.

495. the sum of 30 and 12

496. 11 increased by 8

497. 25 more than 39

498. total of 15 and 50

Add Whole Numbers in Applications

In the following exercises, solve.

499. Shopping for an interview Nathan bought a new shirt, tie, and slacks to wear to a job interview. The shirt cost $24, the tie cost $14, and the slacks cost $38. What was Nathan's total cost?

500. Running Jackson ran 4 miles on Monday, 12 miles on Tuesday, 1 mile on Wednesday, 8 miles on Thursday, and 5 miles on Friday. What was the total number of miles Jackson ran?

In the following exercises, find the perimeter of each figure.

501.

502.

1.3 Subtract Whole Numbers

Use Subtraction Notation

In the following exercises, translate the following from math notation to words.

503. $14 - 5$

504. $40 - 15$

505. $351 - 249$

506. $5,724 - 2,918$

Model Subtraction of Whole Numbers

In the following exercises, model the subtraction.

507. $18 - 4$

508. $41 - 29$

Subtract Whole Numbers

In the following exercises, subtract and then check by adding.

509. $8 - 5$

510. $12 - 7$

511. $23 - 9$

512. $46 - 21$

513. $82 - 59$

514. $110 - 87$

515. $539 - 217$

516. $415 - 296$

517. $1,020 - 640$

518. $8,355 - 3,947$

519. $10,000 - 15$

520. $54,925 - 35,647$

Translate Word Phrases to Math Notation

In the following exercises, translate and simplify.

521. the difference of nineteen and thirteen

522. subtract sixty-five from one hundred

523. seventy-four decreased by eight

524. twenty-three less than forty-one

Subtract Whole Numbers in Applications

In the following exercises, solve.

525. Temperature The high temperature in Peoria one day was 86 degrees Fahrenheit and the low temperature was 28 degrees Fahrenheit. What was the difference between the high and low temperatures?

526. Savings Lynn wants to go on a cruise that costs $2,485. She has $948 in her vacation savings account. How much more does she need to save in order to pay for the cruise?

1.4 Multiply Whole Numbers

Use Multiplication Notation

In the following exercises, translate from math notation to words.

527. 8×5

528. $6 \cdot 14$

529. $(10)(95)$

530. $54(72)$

Model Multiplication of Whole Numbers

In the following exercises, model the multiplication.

531. 2×4

532. 3×8

Multiply Whole Numbers

In the following exercises, fill in the missing values in each chart.

533.

×	0	1	2	3	4	5	6	7	8	9
0	0	0	0	0	0		0		0	0
1	0	1	2		4	5	6	7		9
2	0		4		8	10		14	16	
3		3		9			18		24	
4	0	4		12		24			36	
5	0	5	10		20		30	35	40	45
6			12	18			36	42		54
7	0	7		21		35			56	63
8	0	8	16		32		48		64	
9			18	27	36			63	72	

534.

×	3	4	5	6	7	8	9
6							
7							
8							
9							

In the following exercises, multiply.

535. $0 \cdot 14$

536. $(256)0$

537. $1 \cdot 99$

538. $(4{,}789)1$

539. ⓐ $7 \cdot 4$ ⓑ $4 \cdot 7$

540. $(25)(6)$

541. $9{,}261 \times 3$

542. $48 \cdot 76$

543. $64 \cdot 10$

544. $1{,}000(22)$

545. 162×493

546. $(601)(943)$

547. $3{,}624 \times 517$

548. $10{,}538 \cdot 22$

Translate Word Phrases to Math Notation

In the following exercises, translate and simplify.

549. the product of 15 and 28

550. ninety-four times thirty-three

551. twice 575

552. ten times two hundred sixty-four

Multiply Whole Numbers in Applications

In the following exercises, solve.

553. Gardening Geniece bought 8 packs of marigolds to plant in her yard. Each pack has 6 flowers. How many marigolds did Geniece buy?

554. Cooking Ratika is making rice for a dinner party. The number of cups of water is twice the number of cups of rice. If Ratika plans to use 4 cups of rice, how many cups of water does she need?

555. Multiplex There are twelve theaters at the multiplex and each theater has 150 seats. What is the total number of seats at the multiplex?

556. Roofing Lewis needs to put new shingles on his roof. The roof is a rectangle, 30 feet by 24 feet. What is the area of the roof?

1.5 Divide Whole Numbers

Use Division Notation

Translate from math notation to words.

557. $54 \div 9$

558. $42 / 7$

559. $\dfrac{72}{8}$

560. $6\overline{)48}$

Model Division of Whole Numbers

In the following exercises, model.

561. $8 \div 2$

562. $3\overline{)12}$

Divide Whole Numbers

In the following exercises, divide. Then check by multiplying.

563. $14 \div 2$

564. $\dfrac{32}{8}$

565. $52 \div 4$

566. $26\overline{)26}$

567. $\dfrac{97}{1}$

568. $0 \div 52$

569. $100 \div 0$

570. $\dfrac{355}{5}$

571. $3828 \div 6$

572. $31\overline{)1,519}$

573. $\dfrac{7505}{25}$

574. $5,166 \div 42$

Translate Word Phrases to Math Notation

In the following exercises, translate and simplify.

575. the quotient of 64 and 16

576. the quotient of 572 and 52

Divide Whole Numbers in Applications

In the following exercises, solve.

577. Ribbon One spool of ribbon is 27 feet. Lizbeth uses 3 feet of ribbon for each gift basket that she wraps. How many gift baskets can Lizbeth wrap from one spool of ribbon?

578. Juice One carton of fruit juice is 128 ounces. How many 4 ounce cups can Shayla fill from one carton of juice?

PRACTICE TEST

579. Determine which of the following numbers are

ⓐ counting numbers

ⓑ whole numbers.

0, 4, 87

580. Find the place value of the given digits in the number 549,362.

ⓐ 9   ⓑ 6   ⓒ 2

ⓓ 5

581. Write each number as a whole number using digits.

ⓐ six hundred thirteen

ⓑ fifty-five thousand two hundred eight

582. Round 25,849 to the nearest hundred.

Simplify.

583. $45 + 23$

584. $65 - 42$

585. $85 \div 5$

586. $1,000 \times 8$

587. $90 - 58$

588. $73 + 89$

589. $(0)(12,675)$

590. $634 + 255$

591. $\dfrac{0}{9}$

592. $8\overline{)128}$

593. $145 - 79$

594. $299 + 836$

595. $7 \cdot 475$

596. $8,528 + 704$

597. $35(14)$

598. $\dfrac{26}{0}$

599. $733 - 291$

600. $4,916 - 1,538$

601. $495 \div 45$

602. 52×983

Translate each phrase to math notation and then simplify.

603. The sum of 16 and 58

604. The product of 9 and 15

605. The difference of 32 and 18

606. The quotient of 63 and 21

607. Twice 524

608. 29 more than 32

609. 50 less than 300

In the following exercises, solve.

610. LaVelle buys a jumbo bag of 84 candies to make favor bags for her son's party. If she wants to make 12 bags, how many candies should she put in each bag?

611. Last month, Stan's take-home pay was $3,816 and his expenses were $3,472. How much of his take-home pay did Stan have left after he paid his expenses?

612. Each class at Greenville School has 22 children enrolled. The school has 24 classes. How many children are enrolled at Greenville School?

613. Clayton walked 12 blocks to his mother's house, 6 blocks to the gym, and 9 blocks to the grocery store before walking the last 3 blocks home. What was the total number of blocks that Clayton walked?

Figure 2.1 Algebra has a language of its own. The picture shows just some of the words you may see and use in your study of Prealgebra.

Chapter Outline

Introduction

You may not realize it, but you already use algebra every day. Perhaps you figure out how much to tip a server in a restaurant. Maybe you calculate the amount of change you should get when you pay for something. It could even be when you compare batting averages of your favorite players. You can describe the algebra you use in specific words, and follow an orderly process. In this chapter, you will explore the words used to describe algebra and start on your path to solving algebraic problems easily, both in class and in your everyday life.

2.1 Use the Language of Algebra

Learning Objectives

By the end of this section, you will be able to:

Use variables and algebraic symbols
Identify expressions and equations
Simplify expressions with exponents
Simplify expressions using the order of operations

Be Prepared!

Before you get started, take this readiness quiz.

1. Add: $43 + 69$.
    If you missed this problem, review Example 1.19.

2. Multiply: $(896)201$.
    If you missed this problem, review Example 1.48.

3. Divide: $7{,}263 \div 9$.
    If you missed this problem, review Example 1.64.

Use Variables and Algebraic Symbols

Greg and Alex have the same birthday, but they were born in different years. This year Greg is 20 years old and Alex is 23, so Alex is 3 years older than Greg. When Greg was 12, Alex was 15. When Greg is 35, Alex will be 38. No matter what Greg's age is, Alex's age will always be 3 years more, right?

In the language of algebra, we say that Greg's age and Alex's age are variable and the three is a constant. The ages change, or vary, so age is a variable. The 3 years between them always stays the same, so the age difference is the constant.

In algebra, letters of the alphabet are used to represent variables. Suppose we call Greg's age g. Then we could use $g + 3$ to represent Alex's age. See Table 2.1.

Greg's age	Alex's age
12	15
20	23
35	38
g	$g + 3$

Table 2.1

Letters are used to represent variables. Letters often used for variables are x, y, a, b, and c.

Variables and Constants

A variable is a letter that represents a number or quantity whose value may change.

A constant is a number whose value always stays the same.

To write algebraically, we need some symbols as well as numbers and variables. There are several types of symbols we will be using. In Whole Numbers, we introduced the symbols for the four basic arithmetic operations: addition, subtraction, multiplication, and division. We will summarize them here, along with words we use for the operations and the result.

Operation	Notation	Say:	The result is...
Addition	$a + b$	a plus b	the sum of a and b
Subtraction	$a - b$	a minus b	the difference of a and b
Multiplication	$a \cdot b$, $(a)(b)$, $(a)b$, $a(b)$	a times b	The product of a and b
Division	$a \div b$, a/b, $\frac{a}{b}$, $b\overline{)a}$	a divided by b	The quotient of a and b

In algebra, the cross symbol, $\times$, is not used to show multiplication because that symbol may cause confusion. Does $3xy$ mean $3 \times y$ (three times y) or $3 \cdot x \cdot y$ (three times x times y)? To make it clear, use • or parentheses for multiplication.

We perform these operations on two numbers. When translating from symbolic form to words, or from words to symbolic form, pay attention to the words *of* or *and* to help you find the numbers.

The *sum of* 5 *and* 3 means add 5 plus 3, which we write as $5 + 3$.

The *difference of* 9 *and* 2 means subtract 9 minus 2, which we write as $9 - 2$.

The *product of* 4 *and* 8 means multiply 4 times 8, which we can write as $4 \cdot 8$.

The *quotient of* 20 *and* 5 means divide 20 by 5, which we can write as $20 \div 5$.

EXAMPLE 2.1

Translate from algebra to words:

ⓐ $12 + 14$ ⓑ $(30)(5)$ ⓒ $64 \div 8$ ⓓ $x - y$

⊘ **Solution**

ⓐ

$12 + 14$

12 plus 14

the sum of twelve and fourteen

ⓑ

$(30)(5)$

30 times 5

the product of thirty and five

ⓒ

$64 \div 8$

64 divided by 8

the quotient of sixty-four and eight

ⓓ

$x - y$

x minus y

the difference of x and y

> **TRY IT :: 2.1**   Translate from algebra to words.

ⓐ $18 + 11$ ⓑ $(27)(9)$ ⓒ $84 \div 7$ ⓓ $p - q$

> **TRY IT :: 2.2**   Translate from algebra to words.

ⓐ $47 - 19$ ⓑ $72 \div 9$ ⓒ $m + n$ ⓓ $(13)(7)$

When two quantities have the same value, we say they are equal and connect them with an *equal sign*.

Equality Symbol

$a = b$ is read a is equal to b

The symbol $=$ is called the equal sign.

An inequality is used in algebra to compare two quantities that may have different values. The number line can help you understand inequalities. Remember that on the number line the numbers get larger as they go from left to right. So if we know that b is greater than a, it means that b is to the right of a on the number line. We use the symbols "<" and ">" for inequalities.

Inequality

$a < b$ is read a is less than b

a is to the left of b on the number line

$a > b$ is read a is greater than b

a is to the right of b on the number line

The expressions $a < b$ and $a > b$ can be read from left-to-right or right-to-left, though in English we usually read from left-to-right. In general,

$a < b$ is equivalent to $b > a$.   For example, $7 < 11$ is equivalent to $11 > 7$.

$a > b$ is equivalent to $b < a$.   For example, $17 > 4$ is equivalent to $4 < 17$.

When we write an inequality symbol with a line under it, such as $a \leq b$, it means $a < b$ or $a = b$. We read this a is less than or equal to b. Also, if we put a slash through an equal sign, $\neq$, it means not equal.

We summarize the symbols of equality and inequality in Table 2.6.

Algebraic Notation	Say
$a = b$	a is equal to b
$a \neq b$	a is not equal to b
$a < b$	a is less than b
$a > b$	a is greater than b
$a \leq b$	a is less than or equal to b
$a \geq b$	a is greater than or equal to b

Table 2.6

Symbols $<$ and $>$

The symbols $<$ and $>$ each have a smaller side and a larger side.

smaller side $<$ larger side

larger side $>$ smaller side

The smaller side of the symbol faces the smaller number and the larger faces the larger number.

EXAMPLE 2.2

Translate from algebra to words:

      ⓐ $20 \leq 35$ ⓑ $11 \neq 15 - 3$ ⓒ $9 > 10 \div 2$ ⓓ $x + 2 < 10$

⊘ **Solution**

ⓐ

$20 \leq 35$

20 is less than or equal to 35

ⓑ

$11 \neq 15 - 3$

11 is not equal to 15 minus 3

ⓒ

$9 > 10 \div 2$

9 is greater than 10 divided by 2

ⓓ

$x + 2 < 10$

x plus 2 is less than 10

> **TRY IT :: 2.3**   Translate from algebra to words.

            ⓐ $14 \leq 27$ ⓑ $19 - 2 \neq 8$ ⓒ $12 > 4 \div 2$ ⓓ $x - 7 < 1$

> **TRY IT :: 2.4**   Translate from algebra to words.

            ⓐ $19 \geq 15$ ⓑ $7 = 12 - 5$ ⓒ $15 \div 3 < 8$ ⓓ $y + 3 > 6$

EXAMPLE 2.3

The information in Figure 2.2 compares the fuel economy in miles-per-gallon (mpg) of several cars. Write the appropriate symbol $=$, $<$, or $>$ in each expression to compare the fuel economy of the cars.

Car	Prius	Mini Cooper	Toyota Corolla	Versa	Honda Fit
Fuel economy (mpg)	48	27	28	26	27

Figure 2.2 (credit: modification of work by Bernard Goldbach, Wikimedia Commons)

ⓐ MPG of Prius____ MPG of Mini Cooper   ⓑ MPG of Versa____ MPG of Fit

ⓒ MPG of Mini Cooper____ MPG of Fit   ⓓ MPG of Corolla____ MPG of Versa

ⓔ MPG of Corolla____ MPG of Prius

✓ **Solution**

ⓐ

	MPG of Prius___MPG of Mini Cooper
Find the values in the chart.	48___27
Compare.	48 > 27
	MPG of Prius > MPG of Mini Cooper

ⓑ

	MPG of Versa___MPG of Fit
Find the values in the chart.	26___27
Compare.	26 < 27
	MPG of Versa < MPG of Fit

ⓒ

	MPG of Mini Cooper___MPG of Fit
Find the values in the chart.	27___27
Compare.	27 = 27
	MPG of Mini Cooper = MPG of Fit

ⓓ

	MPG of Corolla___MPG of Versa
Find the values in the chart.	28___26
Compare.	28 > 26
	MPG of Corolla > MPG of Versa

ⓔ

	MPG of Corolla___MPG of Prius
Find the values in the chart.	28___48
Compare.	28 < 48
	MPG of Corolla < MPG of Prius

> **TRY IT : : 2.5**   Use Figure 2.2 to fill in the appropriate symbol, =, <, or >.

ⓐ MPG of Prius____MPG of Versa   ⓑ MPG of Mini Cooper____ MPG of Corolla

> **TRY IT : : 2.6**   Use Figure 2.2 to fill in the appropriate symbol, =, <, or >.

ⓐ MPG of Fit____ MPG of Prius   ⓑ MPG of Corolla ____ MPG of Fit

Grouping symbols in algebra are much like the commas, colons, and other punctuation marks in written language. They indicate which expressions are to be kept together and separate from other expressions. Table 2.16 lists three of the most commonly used grouping symbols in algebra.

Common Grouping Symbols	
parentheses	( )
brackets	[ ]
braces	{ }

Table 2.16

Here are some examples of expressions that include grouping symbols. We will simplify expressions like these later in this section.

$$8(14 - 8) \qquad 21 - 3[2 + 4(9 - 8)] \qquad 24 \div \{13 - 2[1(6 - 5) + 4]\}$$

Identify Expressions and Equations

What is the difference in English between a phrase and a sentence? A phrase expresses a single thought that is incomplete by itself, but a sentence makes a complete statement. "Running very fast" is a phrase, but "The football player was running very fast" is a sentence. A sentence has a subject and a verb.

In algebra, we have *expressions* and *equations*. An expression is like a phrase. Here are some examples of expressions and how they relate to word phrases:

Expression	Words	Phrase
$3 + 5$	3 plus 5	the sum of three and five
$n - 1$	n minus one	the difference of n and one
$6 \cdot 7$	6 times 7	the product of six and seven
$\frac{x}{y}$	x divided by y	the quotient of x and y

Notice that the phrases do not form a complete sentence because the phrase does not have a verb. An equation is two expressions linked with an equal sign. When you read the words the symbols represent in an equation, you have a complete sentence in English. The equal sign gives the verb. Here are some examples of equations:

Equation	Sentence
$3 + 5 = 8$	The sum of three and five is equal to eight.
$n - 1 = 14$	n minus one equals fourteen.
$6 \cdot 7 = 42$	The product of six and seven is equal to forty-two.
$x = 53$	x is equal to fifty-three.
$y + 9 = 2y - 3$	y plus nine is equal to two y minus three.

Expressions and Equations

An **expression** is a number, a variable, or a combination of numbers and variables and operation symbols.

An **equation** is made up of two expressions connected by an equal sign.

EXAMPLE 2.4

Determine if each is an expression or an equation:

ⓐ $16 - 6 = 10$ ⓑ $4 \cdot 2 + 1$ ⓒ $x \div 25$ ⓓ $y + 8 = 40$

Solution

ⓐ $16 - 6 = 10$ This is an equation—two expressions are connected with an equal sign.

ⓑ $4 \cdot 2 + 1$ This is an expression—no equal sign.

ⓒ $x \div 25$ This is an expression—no equal sign.

ⓓ $y + 8 = 40$ This is an equation—two expressions are connected with an equal sign.

> **TRY IT :: 2.7** Determine if each is an expression or an equation:
>
> ⓐ $23 + 6 = 29$ ⓑ $7 \cdot 3 - 7$

> **TRY IT ::** 2.8   Determine if each is an expression or an equation:

$$y \div 14 \qquad x - 6 = 21$$

Simplify Expressions with Exponents

To simplify a numerical expression means to do all the math possible. For example, to simplify $4 \cdot 2 + 1$ we'd first multiply $4 \cdot 2$ to get 8 and then add the 1 to get 9. A good habit to develop is to work down the page, writing each step of the process below the previous step. The example just described would look like this:

$$4 \cdot 2 + 1$$
$$8 + 1$$
$$9$$

Suppose we have the expression $2 \cdot 2 \cdot 2 \cdot 2 \cdot 2 \cdot 2 \cdot 2 \cdot 2 \cdot 2$. We could write this more compactly using exponential notation. Exponential notation is used in algebra to represent a quantity multiplied by itself several times. We write $2 \cdot 2 \cdot 2$ as 2^3 and $2 \cdot 2 \cdot 2 \cdot 2 \cdot 2 \cdot 2 \cdot 2 \cdot 2 \cdot 2$ as 2^9. In expressions such as 2^3, the 2 is called the **base** and the 3 is called the exponent. The exponent tells us how many factors of the base we have to multiply.

$$\text{base} \longrightarrow 2^3 \longleftarrow \text{exponent}$$

$$\text{means multiply three factors of 2}$$

We say 2^3 is in exponential notation and $2 \cdot 2 \cdot 2$ is in expanded notation.

Exponential Notation

For any expression a^n, a is a factor multiplied by itself n times if n is a positive integer.

$$a^n \text{ means multiply } n \text{ factors of } a$$

$$\text{base} \longrightarrow a^n \longleftarrow \text{exponent}$$

$$a^n = a \cdot a \cdot a \cdot \ldots \cdot a$$

$$n \text{ factors}$$

The expression a^n is read a to the nth power.

For powers of $n = 2$ and $n = 3$, we have special names.

$$a^2 \text{ is read as "}a \text{ squared"}$$
$$a^3 \text{ is read as "}a \text{ cubed"}$$

Table 2.18 lists some examples of expressions written in exponential notation.

Exponential Notation	In Words
7^2	7 to the second power, or 7 squared
5^3	5 to the third power, or 5 cubed
9^4	9 to the fourth power
12^5	12 to the fifth power

Table 2.18

EXAMPLE 2.5

Write each expression in exponential form:

ⓐ $16 \cdot 16 \cdot 16 \cdot 16 \cdot 16 \cdot 16 \cdot 16$ ⓑ $9 \cdot 9 \cdot 9 \cdot 9 \cdot 9$ ⓒ $x \cdot x \cdot x \cdot x$ ⓓ $a \cdot a \cdot a \cdot a \cdot a \cdot a \cdot a \cdot a$

⊘ **Solution**

ⓐ The base 16 is a factor 7 times. 16^7

ⓑ The base 9 is a factor 5 times. 9^5

ⓒ The base x is a factor 4 times. x^4

ⓓ The base a is a factor 8 times. a^8

> **TRY IT : : 2.9**   Write each expression in exponential form:
> $41 \cdot 41 \cdot 41 \cdot 41 \cdot 41$

> **TRY IT : : 2.10**   Write each expression in exponential form:
> $7 \cdot 7 \cdot 7 \cdot 7 \cdot 7 \cdot 7 \cdot 7 \cdot 7 \cdot 7$

EXAMPLE 2.6

Write each exponential expression in expanded form:

ⓐ 8^6 ⓑ x^5

⊘ **Solution**

ⓐ The base is 8 and the exponent is 6, so 8^6 means $8 \cdot 8 \cdot 8 \cdot 8 \cdot 8 \cdot 8$

ⓑ The base is x and the exponent is 5, so x^5 means $x \cdot x \cdot x \cdot x \cdot x$

> **TRY IT : : 2.11**   Write each exponential expression in expanded form:
> ⓐ 4^8 ⓑ a^7

> **TRY IT : : 2.12**   Write each exponential expression in expanded form:
> ⓐ 8^8 ⓑ b^6

To simplify an exponential expression without using a calculator, we write it in expanded form and then multiply the factors.

EXAMPLE 2.7

Simplify: 3^4.

⊘ **Solution**

$$3^4$$

Expand the expression.	$3 \cdot 3 \cdot 3 \cdot 3$
Multiply left to right.	$9 \cdot 3 \cdot 3$
	$27 \cdot 3$
Multiply.	81

> **TRY IT ::** 2.13   Simplify:

ⓐ 5^3 ⓑ 1^7

> **TRY IT ::** 2.14   Simplify:

ⓐ 7^2 ⓑ 0^5

Simplify Expressions Using the Order of Operations

We've introduced most of the symbols and notation used in algebra, but now we need to clarify the order of operations. Otherwise, expressions may have different meanings, and they may result in different values.

For example, consider the expression:

$$4 + 3 \cdot 7$$

Some students say it simplifies to 49.		Some students say it simplifies to 25.	
	$4 + 3 \cdot 7$		$4 + 3 \cdot 7$
Since $4 + 3$ gives 7.	$7 \cdot 7$	Since $3 \cdot 7$ is 21.	$4 + 21$
And $7 \cdot 7$ is 49.	49	And $21 + 4$ makes 25.	25

Imagine the confusion that could result if every problem had several different correct answers. The same expression should give the same result. So mathematicians established some guidelines called the order of operations, which outlines the order in which parts of an expression must be simplified.

Order of Operations

When simplifying mathematical expressions perform the operations in the following order:

1. **P**arentheses and other Grouping Symbols
   - Simplify all expressions inside the parentheses or other grouping symbols, working on the innermost parentheses first.
2. **E**xponents
   - Simplify all expressions with exponents.
3. **M**ultiplication and **D**ivision
   - Perform all multiplication and division in order from left to right. These operations have equal priority.
4. **A**ddition and **S**ubtraction
   - Perform all addition and subtraction in order from left to right. These operations have equal priority.

Students often ask, "How will I remember the order?" Here is a way to help you remember: Take the first letter of each key word and substitute the silly phrase. **P**lease **E**xcuse **M**y **D**ear **A**unt **S**ally.

Order of Operations	
Please	**P**arentheses
Excuse	**E**xponents
My **D**ear	**M**ultiplication and **D**ivision
Aunt **S**ally	**A**ddition and **S**ubtraction

It's good that '**M**y **D**ear' goes together, as this reminds us that **m**ultiplication and **d**ivision have equal priority. We do not always do multiplication before division or always do division before multiplication. We do them in order from left to right.

Similarly, '**A**unt **S**ally' goes together and so reminds us that **a**ddition and **s**ubtraction also have equal priority and we do them in order from left to right.

 MANIPULATIVE MATHEMATICS

Doing the Manipulative Mathematics activity Game of 24 will give you practice using the order of operations.

EXAMPLE 2.8

Simplify the expressions:

ⓐ $4 + 3 \cdot 7$ ⓑ $(4 + 3) \cdot 7$

 Solution

ⓐ

	$4 + 3 \cdot 7$
Are there any **p**arentheses? No.	
Are there any **e**xponents? No.	
Is there any **m**ultiplication or **d**ivision? Yes.	
Multiply first.	$4 + 3 \cdot 7$
Add.	$4 + 21$
	25

ⓑ

	$(4 + 3) \cdot 7$
Are there any **p**arentheses? Yes.	$(4 + 3) \cdot 7$
Simplify inside the parentheses.	$(7)7$
Are there any **e**xponents? No.	
Is there any **m**ultiplication or **d**ivision? Yes.	
Multiply.	49

> **TRY IT : :** 2.15   Simplify the expressions:

ⓐ $12 - 5 \cdot 2$ ⓑ $(12 - 5) \cdot 2$

> **TRY IT : :** 2.16   Simplify the expressions:

ⓐ $8 + 3 \cdot 9$ ⓑ $(8 + 3) \cdot 9$

EXAMPLE 2.9

Simplify:

ⓐ $18 \div 9 \cdot 2$ ⓑ $18 \cdot 9 \div 2$

⊘ **Solution**

ⓐ

$$18 \div 9 \cdot 2$$

Are there any **p**arentheses? No.

Are there any **e**xponents? No.

Is there any **m**ultiplication or **d**ivision? Yes.

Multiply and divide from left to right. Divide. $2 \cdot 2$

Multiply. 4

ⓑ

$$18 \cdot 9 \div 2$$

Are there any **p**arentheses? No.

Are there any **e**xponents? No.

Is there any **m**ultiplication or **d**ivision? Yes.

Multiply and divide from left to right.

Multiply. $162 \div 2$

Divide. 81

> **TRY IT : :** 2.17   Simplify:
>
> $42 \div 7 \cdot 3$

> **TRY IT : :** 2.18   Simplify:
>
> $12 \cdot 3 \div 4$

EXAMPLE 2.10

Simplify: $18 \div 6 + 4(5 - 2)$.

⊘ **Solution**

	$18 \div 6 + 4(5 - 2)$
Parentheses? Yes, subtract first.	$18 \div 6 + 4(3)$
Exponents? No.	
Multiplication or division? Yes.	
Divide first because we multiply and divide left to right.	$3 + 4(3)$
Any other multiplication or division? Yes.	
Multiply.	$3 + 12$
Any other multiplication or division? No.	
Any addition or subtraction? Yes.	15

> | **TRY IT :: 2.19**   Simplify:

$$30 \div 5 + 10(3 - 2)$$

> | **TRY IT :: 2.20**   Simplify:

$$70 \div 10 + 4(6 - 2)$$

When there are multiple grouping symbols, we simplify the innermost parentheses first and work outward.

EXAMPLE 2.11

Simplify: $5 + 2^3 + 3[6 - 3(4 - 2)]$.

Solution

$$5 + 2^3 + 3[6 - 3(4 - 2)]$$

Are there any parentheses (or other grouping symbol)? Yes.	
Focus on the parentheses that are inside the brackets.	$5 + 2^3 + 3[6 - 3(4 - 2)]$
Subtract.	$5 + 2^3 + 3[6 - 3(2)]$
Continue inside the brackets and multiply.	$5 + 2^3 + 3[6 - 6]$
Continue inside the brackets and subtract.	$5 + 2^3 + 3[0]$
The expression inside the brackets requires no further simplification.	
Are there any exponents? Yes.	
Simplify exponents.	$5 + 2^3 + 3[0]$
Is there any multiplication or division? Yes.	
Multiply.	$5 + 8 + 3[0]$
Is there any addition or subtraction? Yes.	
Add.	$5 + 8 + 0$
Add.	$13 + 0$
	13

> **TRY IT : : 2.21**   Simplify:
>
> $$9 + 5^3 - [4(9 + 3)]$$

> **TRY IT : : 2.22**   Simplify:
>
> $$7^2 - 2[4(5 + 1)]$$

EXAMPLE 2.12

Simplify: $2^3 + 3^4 \div 3 - 5^2$.

Solution

$$2^3 + 3^4 \div 3 - 5^2$$

If an expression has several exponents, they may be simplified in the same step.	
Simplify exponents.	$2^3 + 3^4 \div 3 - 5^2$
Divide.	$8 + 81 \div 3 - 25$
Add.	$8 + 27 - 25$
Subtract.	$35 - 25$
	10

> | **TRY IT : :** 2.23   Simplify:

$$3^2 + 2^4 \div 2 + 4^3$$

> | **TRY IT : :** 2.24   Simplify:

$$6^2 - 5^3 \div 5 + 8^2$$

▶ | **MEDIA : :** ACCESS ADDITIONAL ONLINE RESOURCES

- Order of Operations (http://openstaxcollege.org/l/24orderoperate)
- Order of Operations – The Basics (http://openstaxcollege.org/l/24orderbasic)
- Ex: Evaluate an Expression Using the Order of Operations (http://openstaxcollege.org/l/24Evalexpress)
- Example 3: Evaluate an Expression Using The Order of Operations (http://openstaxcollege.org/l/24evalexpress3)

2.1 EXERCISES

Practice Makes Perfect

Use Variables and Algebraic Symbols

In the following exercises, translate from algebraic notation to words.

1. $16 - 9$

2. $25 - 7$

3. $5 \cdot 6$

4. $3 \cdot 9$

5. $28 \div 4$

6. $45 \div 5$

7. $x + 8$

8. $x + 11$

9. $(2)(7)$

10. $(4)(8)$

11. $14 < 21$

12. $17 < 35$

13. $36 \geq 19$

14. $42 \geq 27$

15. $3n = 24$

16. $6n = 36$

17. $y - 1 > 6$

18. $y - 4 > 8$

19. $2 \leq 18 \div 6$

20. $3 \leq 20 \div 4$

21. $a \neq 7 \cdot 4$

22. $a \neq 1 \cdot 12$

Identify Expressions and Equations

In the following exercises, determine if each is an expression or an equation.

23. $9 \cdot 6 = 54$

24. $7 \cdot 9 = 63$

25. $5 \cdot 4 + 3$

26. $6 \cdot 3 + 5$

27. $x + 7$

28. $x + 9$

29. $y - 5 = 25$

30. $y - 8 = 32$

Simplify Expressions with Exponents

In the following exercises, write in exponential form.

31. $3 \cdot 3 \cdot 3 \cdot 3 \cdot 3 \cdot 3 \cdot 3$

32. $4 \cdot 4 \cdot 4 \cdot 4 \cdot 4 \cdot 4$

33. $x \cdot x \cdot x \cdot x \cdot x$

34. $y \cdot y \cdot y \cdot y \cdot y \cdot y$

In the following exercises, write in expanded form.

35. 5^3

36. 8^3

37. 2^8

38. 10^5

Simplify Expressions Using the Order of Operations

In the following exercises, simplify.

39.
ⓐ $3 + 8 \cdot 5$
ⓑ $(3+8) \cdot 5$

40.
ⓐ $2 + 6 \cdot 3$
ⓑ $(2+6) \cdot 3$

41. $2^3 - 12 \div (9 - 5)$

42. $3^2 - 18 \div (11 - 5)$

43. $3 \cdot 8 + 5 \cdot 2$

44. $4 \cdot 7 + 3 \cdot 5$

45. $2 + 8(6 + 1)$

46. $4 + 6(3 + 6)$

47. $4 \cdot 12 / 8$

48. $2 \cdot 36 / 6$

49. $6 + 10 / 2 + 2$

50. $9 + 12 / 3 + 4$

51. $(6 + 10) \div (2 + 2)$

52. $(9 + 12) \div (3 + 4)$

53. $20 \div 4 + 6 \cdot 5$

54. $33 \div 3 + 8 \cdot 2$

55. $20 \div (4 + 6) \cdot 5$

56. $33 \div (3 + 8) \cdot 2$

57. $4^2 + 5^2$

58. $3^2 + 7^2$

59. $(4 + 5)^2$

60. $(3 + 7)^2$

61. $3(1 + 9 \cdot 6) - 4^2$

62. $5(2 + 8 \cdot 4) - 7^2$

63. $2[1 + 3(10 - 2)]$

64. $5[2 + 4(3 - 2)]$

Everyday Math

65. Basketball In the 2014 NBA playoffs, the San Antonio Spurs beat the Miami Heat. The table below shows the heights of the starters on each team. Use this table to fill in the appropriate symbol ($=$, $<$, $>$).

Spurs	Height	Heat	Height
Tim Duncan	83″	Rashard Lewis	82″
Boris Diaw	80″	LeBron James	80″
Kawhi Leonard	79″	Chris Bosh	83″
Tony Parker	74″	Dwyane Wade	76″
Danny Green	78″	Ray Allen	77″

ⓐ Height of Tim Duncan___Height of Rashard Lewis

ⓑ Height of Boris Diaw___Height of LeBron James

ⓒ Height of Kawhi Leonard___Height of Chris Bosh

ⓓ Height of Tony Parker___Height of Dwyane Wade

ⓔ Height of Danny Green___Height of Ray Allen

66. Elevation In Colorado there are more than 50 mountains with an elevation of over $14,000$ feet. The table shows the ten tallest. Use this table to fill in the appropriate inequality symbol.

Mountain	Elevation
Mt. Elbert	14,433′
Mt. Massive	14,421′
Mt. Harvard	14,420′
Blanca Peak	14,345′
La Plata Peak	14,336′
Uncompahgre Peak	14,309′
Crestone Peak	14,294′
Mt. Lincoln	14,286′
Grays Peak	14,270′
Mt. Antero	14,269′

ⓐ Elevation of La Plata Peak___Elevation of Mt. Antero

ⓑ Elevation of Blanca Peak___Elevation of Mt. Elbert

ⓒ Elevation of Gray's Peak___Elevation of Mt. Lincoln

ⓓ Elevation of Mt. Massive___Elevation of Crestone Peak

ⓔ Elevation of Mt. Harvard___Elevation of Uncompahgre Peak

Writing Exercises

67. Explain the difference between an expression and an equation.

68. Why is it important to use the order of operations to simplify an expression?

Self Check

ⓐ *After completing the exercises, use this checklist to evaluate your mastery of the objectives of this section.*

I can...	Confidently	With some help	No-I don't get it!
use variables and algebraic symbols.			
identify expressions and equations.			
simplify expressions with exponents.			
simplify expressions using the order of operations.			

ⓑ *If most of your checks were:*

...confidently. Congratulations! You have achieved the objectives in this section. Reflect on the study skills you used so that you can continue to use them. What did you do to become confident of your ability to do these things? Be specific.

...with some help. This must be addressed quickly because topics you do not master become potholes in your road to success. In math, every topic builds upon previous work. It is important to make sure you have a strong foundation before you move on. Who can you ask for help? Your fellow classmates and instructor are good resources. Is there a place on campus where math tutors are available? Can your study skills be improved?

...no—I don't get it! This is a warning sign and you must not ignore it. You should get help right away or you will quickly be overwhelmed. See your instructor as soon as you can to discuss your situation. Together you can come up with a plan to get you the help you need.

2.2 Evaluate, Simplify, and Translate Expressions

Learning Objectives

By the end of this section, you will be able to:

- Evaluate algebraic expressions
- Identify terms, coefficients, and like terms
- Simplify expressions by combining like terms
- Translate word phrases to algebraic expressions

Be Prepared!

Before you get started, take this readiness quiz.

1. Is $n \div 5$ an expression or an equation?
   If you missed this problem, review Example 2.4.

2. Simplify 4^5.
   If you missed this problem, review Example 2.7.

3. Simplify $1 + 8 \cdot 9$.
   If you missed this problem, review Example 2.8.

Evaluate Algebraic Expressions

In the last section, we simplified expressions using the order of operations. In this section, we'll evaluate expressions—again following the order of operations.

To **evaluate** an algebraic expression means to find the value of the expression when the variable is replaced by a given number. To evaluate an expression, we substitute the given number for the variable in the expression and then simplify the expression using the order of operations.

EXAMPLE 2.13

Evaluate $x + 7$ when

     ⓐ $x = 3$ ⓑ $x = 12$

⊘ Solution

ⓐ To evaluate, substitute 3 for x in the expression, and then simplify.

	$x + 7$
Substitute.	$3 + 7$
Add.	10

When $x = 3$, the expression $x + 7$ has a value of 10.

ⓑ To evaluate, substitute 12 for x in the expression, and then simplify.

	$x + 7$
Substitute.	$12 + 7$
Add.	19

When $x = 12$, the expression $x + 7$ has a value of 19.

Notice that we got different results for parts ⓐ and ⓑ even though we started with the same expression. This is because the values used for x were different. When we evaluate an expression, the value varies depending on the value used for the variable.

> **TRY IT : :** 2.25   Evaluate:

$y + 4$ when

ⓐ $y = 6$ ⓑ $y = 15$

> **TRY IT : :** 2.26   Evaluate:

$a - 5$ when

ⓐ $a = 9$ ⓑ $a = 17$

EXAMPLE 2.14

Evaluate $9x - 2$, when

ⓐ $x = 5$ ⓑ $x = 1$

⊘ **Solution**

Remember ab means a times b, so $9x$ means 9 times x.

ⓐ To evaluate the expression when $x = 5$, we substitute 5 for x, and then simplify.

	$9x - 2$
Substitute 5 for x.	$9 \cdot 5 - 2$
Multiply.	$45 - 2$
Subtract.	43

ⓑ To evaluate the expression when $x = 1$, we substitute 1 for x, and then simplify.

	$9x - 2$
Substitute 1 for x.	$9(1) - 2$
Multiply.	$9 - 2$
Subtract.	7

Notice that in part ⓐ that we wrote $9 \cdot 5$ and in part ⓑ we wrote $9(1)$. Both the dot and the parentheses tell us to multiply.

> **TRY IT : :** 2.27   Evaluate:

$8x - 3$, when

ⓐ $x = 2$ ⓑ $x = 1$

> **TRY IT ::** 2.28   Evaluate:

$4y - 4$, when

ⓐ $y = 3$ ⓑ $y = 5$

EXAMPLE 2.15

Evaluate x^2 when $x = 10$.

⊘ **Solution**

We substitute 10 for x,   and then simplify the expression.

	x^2
Substitute 10 for x.	10^2
Use the definition of exponent.	$10 \cdot 10$
Multiply.	100

When $x = 10$,   the expression x^2 has a value of 100.

> **TRY IT ::** 2.29   Evaluate:

x^2 when $x = 8$.

> **TRY IT ::** 2.30   Evaluate:

x^3 when $x = 6$.

EXAMPLE 2.16

Evaluate 2^x when $x = 5$.

⊘ **Solution**

In this expression, the variable is an exponent.

	2^x
Substitute 5 for x.	2^5
Use the definition of exponent.	$2 \cdot 2 \cdot 2 \cdot 2 \cdot 2$
Multiply.	32

When $x = 5$,   the expression 2^x has a value of 32.

> **TRY IT ::** 2.31   Evaluate:

2^x when $x = 6$.

> **TRY IT ::** 2.32   Evaluate:

3^x when $x = 4$.

EXAMPLE 2.17

Evaluate $3x + 4y - 6$ when $x = 10$ and $y = 2$.

Solution

This expression contains two variables, so we must make two substitutions.

	$3x + 4y - 6$
Substitute 10 for x and 2 for y.	$3(10) + 4(2) - 6$
Multiply.	$30 + 8 - 6$
Add and subtract left to right.	32

When $x = 10$ and $y = 2$, the expression $3x + 4y - 6$ has a value of 32.

> **TRY IT :: 2.33**   Evaluate:
>
> $2x + 5y - 4$ when $x = 11$ and $y = 3$

> **TRY IT :: 2.34**   Evaluate:
>
> $5x - 2y - 9$ when $x = 7$ and $y = 8$

EXAMPLE 2.18

Evaluate $2x^2 + 3x + 8$ when $x = 4$.

Solution

We need to be careful when an expression has a variable with an exponent. In this expression, $2x^2$ means $2 \cdot x \cdot x$ and is different from the expression $(2x)^2$, which means $2x \cdot 2x$.

	$2x^2 + 3x + 8$
Substitute 4 for each x.	$2(4)^2 + 3(4) + 8$
Simplify 4^2.	$2(16) + 3(4) + 8$
Multiply.	$32 + 12 + 8$
Add.	52

> **TRY IT :: 2.35**   Evaluate:
>
> $3x^2 + 4x + 1$ when $x = 3$.

> **TRY IT :: 2.36**   Evaluate:
>
> $6x^2 - 4x - 7$ when $x = 2$.

Identify Terms, Coefficients, and Like Terms

Algebraic expressions are made up of *terms*. A **term** is a constant or the product of a constant and one or more variables. Some examples of terms are 7, y, $5x^2$, $9a$, and $13xy$.

The constant that multiplies the variable(s) in a term is called the **coefficient**. We can think of the coefficient as the number *in front of* the variable. The coefficient of the term $3x$ is 3. When we write x, the coefficient is 1, since $x = 1 \cdot x$. Table 2.36 gives the coefficients for each of the terms in the left column.

Term	Coefficient
7	7
$9a$	9
y	1
$5x^2$	5

Table 2.36

An algebraic expression may consist of one or more terms added or subtracted. In this chapter, we will only work with terms that are added together. Table 2.37 gives some examples of algebraic expressions with various numbers of terms. Notice that we include the operation before a term with it.

Expression	Terms
7	7
y	y
$x + 7$	x, 7
$2x + 7y + 4$	$2x$, $7y$, 4
$3x^2 + 4x^2 + 5y + 3$	$3x^2$, $4x^2$, $5y$, 3

Table 2.37

EXAMPLE 2.19

Identify each term in the expression $9b + 15x^2 + a + 6$. Then identify the coefficient of each term.

⊘ **Solution**

The expression has four terms. They are $9b$, $15x^2$, a, and 6.

The coefficient of $9b$ is 9.

The coefficient of $15x^2$ is 15.

Remember that if no number is written before a variable, the coefficient is 1. So the coefficient of a is 1.

The coefficient of a constant is the constant, so the coefficient of 6 is 6.

> **TRY IT : : 2.37**   Identify all terms in the given expression, and their coefficients:
> $$4x + 3b + 2$$

> **TRY IT : : 2.38**   Identify all terms in the given expression, and their coefficients:
> $$9a + 13a^2 + a^3$$

Some terms share common traits. Look at the following terms. Which ones seem to have traits in common?

$$5x, \ 7, \ n^2, \ 4, \ 3x, \ 9n^2$$

Which of these terms are like terms?

- The terms 7 and 4 are both constant terms.

- The terms $5x$ and $3x$ are both terms with x.

- The terms n^2 and $9n^2$ both have n^2.

Terms are called **like terms** if they have the same variables and exponents. All constant terms are also like terms. So among the terms $5x, \ 7, \ n^2, \ 4, \ 3x, \ 9n^2,$

$$7 \text{ and } 4 \text{ are like terms.}$$
$$5x \text{ and } 3x \text{ are like terms.}$$
$$n^2 \text{ and } 9n^2 \text{ are like terms.}$$

Like Terms

Terms that are either constants or have the same variables with the same exponents are like terms.

EXAMPLE 2.20

Identify the like terms:

ⓐ $y^3, \ 7x^2, \ 14, \ 23, \ 4y^3, \ 9x, \ 5x^2$ ⓑ $4x^2 + 2x + 5x^2 + 6x + 40x + 8xy$

⊘ **Solution**

ⓐ $y^3, \ 7x^2, \ 14, \ 23, \ 4y^3, \ 9x, \ 5x^2$

Look at the variables and exponents. The expression contains $y^3, \ x^2, \ x,$ and constants.

The terms y^3 and $4y^3$ are like terms because they both have y^3.

The terms $7x^2$ and $5x^2$ are like terms because they both have x^2.

The terms 14 and 23 are like terms because they are both constants.

The term $9x$ does not have any like terms in this list since no other terms have the variable x raised to the power of 1.

ⓑ $4x^2 + 2x + 5x^2 + 6x + 40x + 8xy$

Look at the variables and exponents. The expression contains the terms $4x^2, \ 2x, \ 5x^2, \ 6x, \ 40x,$ and $8xy$

The terms $4x^2$ and $5x^2$ are like terms because they both have x^2.

The terms $2x, \ 6x,$ and $40x$ are like terms because they all have x.

The term $8xy$ has no like terms in the given expression because no other terms contain the two variables xy.

> **TRY IT : : 2.39**   Identify the like terms in the list or the expression:

$$9, \ 2x^3, \ y^2, \ 8x^3, \ 15, \ 9y, \ 11y^2$$

> **TRY IT : : 2.40**   Identify the like terms in the list or the expression:

$$4x^3 + 8x^2 + 19 + 3x^2 + 24 + 6x^3$$

Simplify Expressions by Combining Like Terms

We can simplify an expression by combining the like terms. What do you think $3x + 6x$ would simplify to? If you thought $9x,$ you would be right!

We can see why this works by writing both terms as addition problems.

$$3x \qquad + \qquad 6x$$
$$\overbrace{x+x+x} \quad + \quad \overbrace{x+x+x+x+x+x}$$
$$9x$$

Add the coefficients and keep the same variable. It doesn't matter what x is. If you have 3 of something and add 6 more of the same thing, the result is 9 of them. For example, 3 oranges plus 6 oranges is 9 oranges. We will discuss the mathematical properties behind this later.

The expression $3x + 6x$ has only two terms. When an expression contains more terms, it may be helpful to rearrange the terms so that like terms are together. The Commutative Property of Addition says that we can change the order of addends without changing the sum. So we could rearrange the following expression before combining like terms.

$$3x + 4y - 2x + 6y$$

$$3x - 2x + 4y + 6y$$

Now it is easier to see the like terms to be combined.

HOW TO : : COMBINE LIKE TERMS.

Step 1.   Identify like terms.

Step 2.   Rearrange the expression so like terms are together.

Step 3.   Add the coefficients of the like terms.

EXAMPLE 2.21

Simplify the expression: $3x + 7 + 4x + 5$.

⊘ **Solution**

	$3x + 7 + 4x + 5$
Identify the like terms.	$3x + 7 + 4x + 5$
Rearrange the expression, so the like terms are together.	$3x + 4x + 7 + 5$
Add the coefficients of the like terms.	$\underbrace{3x + 4x}_{7x} + \underbrace{7 + 5}_{12}$
The original expression is simplified to...	$7x + 12$

❯ **TRY IT : :** 2.41   Simplify:

$$7x + 9 + 9x + 8$$

❯ **TRY IT : :** 2.42   Simplify:

$$5y + 2 + 8y + 4y + 5$$

EXAMPLE 2.22

Simplify the expression: $7x^2 + 8x + x^2 + 4x$.

⊘ **Solution**

$$7x^2 + 8x + x^2 + 4x$$

Identify the like terms.	$7x^2 + 8x + x^2 + 4x$
Rearrange the expression so like terms are together.	$7x^2 + x^2 + 8x + 4x$
Add the coefficients of the like terms.	$8x^2 + 12x$

These are not like terms and cannot be combined. So $8x^2 + 12x$ is in simplest form.

> **TRY IT :: 2.43**   Simplify:

$$3x^2 + 9x + x^2 + 5x$$

> **TRY IT :: 2.44**   Simplify:

$$11y^2 + 8y + y^2 + 7y$$

Translate Words to Algebraic Expressions

In the previous section, we listed many operation symbols that are used in algebra, and then we translated expressions and equations into word phrases and sentences. Now we'll reverse the process and translate word phrases into algebraic expressions. The symbols and variables we've talked about will help us do that. They are summarized in Table 2.40.

Operation	Phrase	Expression
Addition	a plus b the sum of a and b a increased by b b more than a the total of a and b b added to a	$a + b$
Subtraction	a minus b the difference of a and b b subtracted from a a decreased by b b less than a	$a - b$
Multiplication	a times b the product of a and b	$a \cdot b$, ab, $a(b)$, $(a)(b)$
Division	a divided by b the quotient of a and b the ratio of a and b b divided into a	$a \div b$, a/b, $\frac{a}{b}$, $b\overline{)a}$

Table 2.40

Look closely at these phrases using the four operations:

- the sum *of a and b*

- the difference *of a and b*

- the product *of a and b*

- the quotient *of* a *and* b

Each phrase tells you to operate on two numbers. Look for the words ***of*** and ***and*** to find the numbers.

EXAMPLE 2.23

Translate each word phrase into an algebraic expression:

      ⓐ the difference of 20 and 4 ⓑ the quotient of $10x$ and 3

⊘ **Solution**

ⓐ The key word is *difference*, which tells us the operation is subtraction. Look for the words *of* and *and* to find the numbers to subtract.

the difference *of* 20 *and* 4
20 minus 4
$20 - 4$

ⓑ The key word is *quotient*, which tells us the operation is division.

the quotient of $10x$ and 3
divide $10x$ by 3
$10x \div 3$

This can also be written as $10x / 3$ or $\dfrac{10x}{3}$

>	**TRY IT : : 2.45**	Translate the given word phrase into an algebraic expression:

          ⓐ the difference of 47 and 41 ⓑ the quotient of $5x$ and 2

>	**TRY IT : : 2.46**	Translate the given word phrase into an algebraic expression:

          ⓐ the sum of 17 and 19 ⓑ the product of 7 and x

How old will you be in eight years? What age is eight more years than your age now? Did you add 8 to your present age? Eight *more than* means eight added to your present age.

How old were you seven years ago? This is seven years less than your age now. You subtract 7 from your present age. Seven *less than* means seven subtracted from your present age.

EXAMPLE 2.24

Translate each word phrase into an algebraic expression:

      ⓐ Eight more than y ⓑ Seven less than $9z$

⊘ **Solution**

ⓐ The key words are *more than*. They tell us the operation is addition. *More than* means "added to".

Eight more than y
Eight added to y
$y + 8$

ⓑ The key words are *less than*. They tell us the operation is subtraction. *Less than* means "subtracted from".

Seven less than $9z$
Seven subtracted from $9z$
$9z - 7$

> **TRY IT :: 2.47**   Translate each word phrase into an algebraic expression:

ⓐ Eleven more than x ⓑ Fourteen less than $11a$

> **TRY IT :: 2.48**   Translate each word phrase into an algebraic expression:

ⓐ 19 more than j ⓑ 21 less than $2x$

EXAMPLE 2.25

Translate each word phrase into an algebraic expression:

ⓐ five times the sum of m and n ⓑ the sum of five times m and n

⊘ **Solution**

ⓐ There are two operation words: *times* tells us to multiply and *sum* tells us to add. Because we are multiplying 5 times the sum, we need parentheses around the sum of m and n.

five times the sum of m and n

$$5(m + n)$$

ⓑ To take a sum, we look for the words *of* and *and* to see what is being added. Here we are taking the sum *of* five times m and n.

the sum of five times m and n

$$5m + n$$

Notice how the use of parentheses changes the result. In part ⓐ, we add first and in part ⓑ, we multiply first.

> **TRY IT :: 2.49**   Translate the word phrase into an algebraic expression:

ⓐ four times the sum of p and q ⓑ the sum of four times p and q

> **TRY IT :: 2.50**   Translate the word phrase into an algebraic expression:

ⓐ the difference of two times x and 8   ⓑ two times the difference of x and 8

Later in this course, we'll apply our skills in algebra to solving equations. We'll usually start by translating a word phrase to an algebraic expression. We'll need to be clear about what the expression will represent. We'll see how to do this in the next two examples.

EXAMPLE 2.26

The height of a rectangular window is 6 inches less than the width. Let w represent the width of the window. Write an expression for the height of the window.

Solution

Write a phrase about the height.	6 less than the width
Substitute w for the width.	6 less than w
Rewrite 'less than' as 'subtracted from'.	6 subtracted from w
Translate the phrase into algebra.	$w - 6$

> **TRY IT : : 2.51**
>
> The length of a rectangle is 5 inches less than the width. Let w represent the width of the rectangle. Write an expression for the length of the rectangle.

> **TRY IT : : 2.52**
>
> The width of a rectangle is 2 meters greater than the length. Let l represent the length of the rectangle. Write an expression for the width of the rectangle.

EXAMPLE 2.27

Blanca has dimes and quarters in her purse. The number of dimes is 2 less than 5 times the number of quarters. Let q represent the number of quarters. Write an expression for the number of dimes.

Solution

Write a phrase about the number of dimes.	two less than five times the number of quarters
Substitute q for the number of quarters.	2 less than five times q
Translate 5 *times* q.	2 less than $5q$
Translate the phrase into algebra.	$5q - 2$

> **TRY IT : : 2.53**
>
> Geoffrey has dimes and quarters in his pocket. The number of dimes is seven less than six times the number of quarters. Let q represent the number of quarters. Write an expression for the number of dimes.

> **TRY IT : : 2.54**
>
> Lauren has dimes and nickels in her purse. The number of dimes is eight more than four times the number of nickels. Let n represent the number of nickels. Write an expression for the number of dimes.

> **MEDIA : :** ACCESS ADDITIONAL ONLINE RESOURCES
> * Algebraic Expression Vocabulary (http://openstaxcollege.org/l/24AlgExpvocab)

2.2 EXERCISES

Practice Makes Perfect

Evaluate Algebraic Expressions

In the following exercises, evaluate the expression for the given value.

69. $7x + 8$ when $x = 2$ **70.** $9x + 7$ when $x = 3$ **71.** $5x - 4$ when $x = 6$

72. $8x - 6$ when $x = 7$ **73.** x^2 when $x = 12$ **74.** x^3 when $x = 5$

75. x^5 when $x = 2$ **76.** x^4 when $x = 3$ **77.** 3^x when $x = 3$

78. 4^x when $x = 2$ **79.** $x^2 + 3x - 7$ when $x = 4$ **80.** $x^2 + 5x - 8$ when $x = 6$

81.
$2x + 4y - 5$ when $x = 7$, $y = 8$ **82.**
$6x + 3y - 9$ when $x = 6$, $y = 9$ **83.** $(x - y)^2$ when $x = 10$, $y = 7$

84. $(x + y)^2$ when $x = 6$, $y = 9$ **85.** $a^2 + b^2$ when $a = 3$, $b = 8$ **86.** $r^2 - s^2$ when $r = 12$, $s = 5$

87.
$2l + 2w$ when $l = 15$, $w = 12$ **88.**
$2l + 2w$ when $l = 18$, $w = 14$

Identify Terms, Coefficients, and Like Terms

In the following exercises, list the terms in the given expression.

89. $15x^2 + 6x + 2$ **90.** $11x^2 + 8x + 5$ **91.** $10y^3 + y + 2$

92. $9y^3 + y + 5$

In the following exercises, identify the coefficient of the given term.

93. $8a$ **94.** $13m$ **95.** $5r^2$

96. $6x^3$

In the following exercises, identify all sets of like terms.

97. x^3, $8x$, 14, $8y$, 5, $8x^3$ **98.** $6z$, $3w^2$, 1, $6z^2$, $4z$, w^2 **99.**
$9a$, a^2, $16ab$, $16b^2$, $4ab$, $9b^2$

100. 3, $25r^2$, $10s$, $10r$, $4r^2$, $3s$

Simplify Expressions by Combining Like Terms

In the following exercises, simplify the given expression by combining like terms.

101. $10x + 3x$ **102.** $15x + 4x$ **103.** $17a + 9a$

104. $18z + 9z$ **105.** $4c + 2c + c$ **106.** $6y + 4y + y$

107. $9x + 3x + 8$ **108.** $8a + 5a + 9$ **109.** $7u + 2 + 3u + 1$

110. $8d + 6 + 2d + 5$

111. $7p + 6 + 5p + 4$

112. $8x + 7 + 4x - 5$

113. $10a + 7 + 5a - 2 + 7a - 4$

114. $7c + 4 + 6c - 3 + 9c - 1$

115.
$$3x^2 + 12x + 11 + 14x^2 + 8x + 5$$

116.
$$5b^2 + 9b + 10 + 2b^2 + 3b - 4$$

Translate English Phrases into Algebraic Expressions

In the following exercises, translate the given word phrase into an algebraic expression.

117. The sum of 8 and 12

118. The sum of 9 and 1

119. The difference of 14 and 9

120. 8 less than 19

121. The product of 9 and 7

122. The product of 8 and 7

123. The quotient of 36 and 9

124. The quotient of 42 and 7

125. The difference of x and 4

126. 3 less than x

127. The product of 6 and y

128. The product of 9 and y

129. The sum of $8x$ and $3x$

130. The sum of $13x$ and $3x$

131. The quotient of y and 3

132. The quotient of y and 8

133. Eight times the difference of y and nine

134. Seven times the difference of y and one

135. Five times the sum of x and y

136. Nine times five less than twice x

In the following exercises, write an algebraic expression.

137. Adele bought a skirt and a blouse. The skirt cost $15 more than the blouse. Let b represent the cost of the blouse. Write an expression for the cost of the skirt.

138. Eric has rock and classical CDs in his car. The number of rock CDs is 3 more than the number of classical CDs. Let c represent the number of classical CDs. Write an expression for the number of rock CDs.

139. The number of girls in a second-grade class is 4 less than the number of boys. Let b represent the number of boys. Write an expression for the number of girls.

140. Marcella has 6 fewer male cousins than female cousins. Let f represent the number of female cousins. Write an expression for the number of boy cousins.

141. Greg has nickels and pennies in his pocket. The number of pennies is seven less than twice the number of nickels. Let n represent the number of nickels. Write an expression for the number of pennies.

142. Jeannette has $5 and $10 bills in her wallet. The number of fives is three more than six times the number of tens. Let t represent the number of tens. Write an expression for the number of fives.

Everyday Math

In the following exercises, use algebraic expressions to solve the problem.

143. Car insurance Justin's car insurance has a $750 deductible per incident. This means that he pays $750 and his insurance company will pay all costs beyond $750. If Justin files a claim for $2,100, how much will he pay, and how much will his insurance company pay?

144. Home insurance Pam and Armando's home insurance has a $2,500 deductible per incident. This means that they pay $2,500 and their insurance company will pay all costs beyond $2,500. If Pam and Armando file a claim for $19,400, how much will they pay, and how much will their insurance company pay?

Writing Exercises

145. Explain why "the sum of x and y" is the same as "the sum of y and x," but "the difference of x and y" is not the same as "the difference of y and x." Try substituting two random numbers for x and y to help you explain.

146. Explain the difference between "4 times the sum of x and y" and "the sum of 4 times x and y."

Self Check

ⓐ After completing the exercises, use this checklist to evaluate your mastery of the objectives of this section.

I can...	Confidently	With some help	No-I don't get it!
evaluate algebraic expressions.			
identify terms, coefficients, and like terms.			
simplify expressions by combining like terms.			
translate word phrases to algebraic expressions.			

ⓑ After reviewing this checklist, what will you do to become confident for all objectives?

2.3 **Solving Equations Using the Subtraction and Addition Properties of Equality**

Learning Objectives

By the end of this section, you will be able to:

- Determine whether a number is a solution of an equation
- Model the Subtraction Property of Equality
- Solve equations using the Subtraction Property of Equality
- Solve equations using the Addition Property of Equality
- Translate word phrases to algebraic equations
- Translate to an equation and solve

Be Prepared!

Before you get started, take this readiness quiz.

1. Evaluate $x + 8$ when $x = 11$.
   If you missed this problem, review Example 2.13.

2. Evaluate $5x - 3$ when $x = 9$.
   If you missed this problem, review Example 2.14.

3. Translate into algebra: the difference of x and 8.
   If you missed this problem, review Example 2.24.

When some people hear the word *algebra*, they think of solving equations. The applications of solving equations are limitless and extend to all careers and fields. In this section, we will begin solving equations. We will start by solving basic equations, and then as we proceed through the course we will build up our skills to cover many different forms of equations.

Determine Whether a Number is a Solution of an Equation

Solving an equation is like discovering the answer to a puzzle. An algebraic equation states that two algebraic expressions are equal. To solve an equation is to determine the values of the variable that make the equation a true statement. Any number that makes the equation true is called a **solution** of the equation. It is the answer to the puzzle!

Solution of an Equation

A **solution to an equation** is a value of a variable that makes a true statement when substituted into the equation.

The process of finding the solution to an equation is called solving the equation.

To find the solution to an equation means to find the value of the variable that makes the equation true. Can you recognize the solution of $x + 2 = 7$? If you said 5, you're right! We say 5 is a solution to the equation $x + 2 = 7$ because when we substitute 5 for x the resulting statement is true.

$$x + 2 = 7$$
$$5 + 2 \stackrel{?}{=} 7$$
$$7 = 7 \checkmark$$

Since $5 + 2 = 7$ is a true statement, we know that 5 is indeed a solution to the equation.

The symbol $\stackrel{?}{=}$ asks whether the left side of the equation is equal to the right side. Once we know, we can change to an equal sign $(=)$ or not-equal sign $(\neq)$.

HOW TO :: DETERMINE WHETHER A NUMBER IS A SOLUTION TO AN EQUATION.

Step 1.   Substitute the number for the variable in the equation.

Step 2.   Simplify the expressions on both sides of the equation.

Step 3.   Determine whether the resulting equation is true.

○ If it is true, the number is a solution.

○ If it is not true, the number is not a solution.

EXAMPLE 2.28

Determine whether $x = 5$ is a solution of $6x - 17 = 16$.

⊘ **Solution**

$$6x - 17 = 16$$

Substitute 5 for x.	$6 \cdot 5 - 17 \overset{?}{=} 16$
Multiply.	$30 - 17 \overset{?}{=} 16$
Subtract.	$13 \neq 16$

So $x = 5$ is not a solution to the equation $6x - 17 = 16$.

> **TRY IT :: 2.55**   Is $x = 3$ a solution of $4x - 7 = 16$?

> **TRY IT :: 2.56**   Is $x = 2$ a solution of $6x - 2 = 10$?

EXAMPLE 2.29

Determine whether $y = 2$ is a solution of $6y - 4 = 5y - 2$.

⊘ **Solution**

Here, the variable appears on both sides of the equation. We must substitute 2 for each y.

$$6y - 4 = 5y - 2$$

Substitute 2 for y.	$6(2) - 4 \overset{?}{=} 5(2) - 2$
Multiply.	$12 - 4 \overset{?}{=} 10 - 2$
Subtract.	$8 = 8 ✓$

Since $y = 2$ results in a true equation, we know that 2 is a solution to the equation $6y - 4 = 5y - 2$.

> **TRY IT :: 2.57**   Is $y = 3$ a solution of $9y - 2 = 8y + 1$?

> **TRY IT :: 2.58**   Is $y = 4$ a solution of $5y - 3 = 3y + 5$?

Model the Subtraction Property of Equality

We will use a model to help you understand how the process of solving an equation is like solving a puzzle. An envelope represents the variable – since its contents are unknown – and each counter represents one.

Suppose a desk has an imaginary line dividing it in half. We place three counters and an envelope on the left side of desk, and eight counters on the right side of the desk as in Figure 2.3. Both sides of the desk have the same number of counters, but some counters are hidden in the envelope. Can you tell how many counters are in the envelope?

Figure 2.3

What steps are you taking in your mind to figure out how many counters are in the envelope? Perhaps you are thinking "I need to remove the 3 counters from the left side to get the envelope by itself. Those 3 counters on the left match with 3 on the right, so I can take them away from both sides. That leaves five counters on the right, so there must be 5 counters in the envelope." Figure 2.4 shows this process.

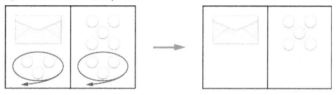

Figure 2.4

What algebraic equation is modeled by this situation? Each side of the desk represents an expression and the center line takes the place of the equal sign. We will call the contents of the envelope x, so the number of counters on the left side of the desk is $x + 3$. On the right side of the desk are 8 counters. We are told that $x + 3$ is equal to 8 so our equation is $x + 3 = 8$.

Figure 2.5

$$x + 3 = 8$$

Let's write algebraically the steps we took to discover how many counters were in the envelope.

$$x + 3 = 8$$

First, we took away three from each side.
$$x + 3 - 3 = 8 - 3$$

Then we were left with five.
$$x = 5$$

Now let's check our solution. We substitute 5 for x in the original equation and see if we get a true statement.

$$x + 3 = 8$$
$$5 + 3 \overset{?}{=} 8$$
$$8 = 8 \checkmark$$

Our solution is correct. Five counters in the envelope plus three more equals eight.

 MANIPULATIVE MATHEMATICS

Doing the Manipulative Mathematics activity, "Subtraction Property of Equality" will help you develop a better understanding of how to solve equations by using the Subtraction Property of Equality.

EXAMPLE 2.30

Write an equation modeled by the envelopes and counters, and then solve the equation:

✓ **Solution**

On the left, write x for the contents of the envelope, add the 4 counters, so we have $x + 4$. $x + 4$

On the right, there are 5 counters.   5

The two sides are equal. $x + 4 = 5$

Solve the equation by subtracting 4 counters from each side.

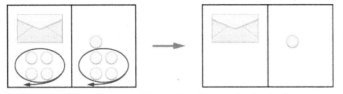

We can see that there is one counter in the envelope. This can be shown algebraically as:

$$x + 4 = 5$$
$$x + 4 - 4 = 5 - 4$$
$$x = 1$$

Substitute 1 for x in the equation to check.

$$x + 4 = 5$$
$$1 + 4 \stackrel{?}{=} 5$$
$$5 = 5 ✓$$

Since $x = 1$ makes the statement true, we know that 1 is indeed a solution.

> **TRY IT :: 2.59**   Write the equation modeled by the envelopes and counters, and then solve the equation:

> **TRY IT ::** 2.60   Write the equation modeled by the envelopes and counters, and then solve the equation:

Solve Equations Using the Subtraction Property of Equality

Our puzzle has given us an idea of what we need to do to solve an equation. The goal is to isolate the variable by itself on one side of the equations. In the previous examples, we used the Subtraction Property of Equality, which states that when we subtract the same quantity from both sides of an equation, we still have equality.

Subtraction Property of Equality

For any numbers a, b, and c, if

$$a = b$$

then

$$a - c = b - c$$

Think about twin brothers Andy and Bobby. They are 17 years old. How old was Andy 3 years ago? He was 3 years less than 17, so his age was $17 - 3$, or 14. What about Bobby's age 3 years ago? Of course, he was 14 also. Their ages are equal now, and subtracting the same quantity from both of them resulted in equal ages 3 years ago.

$$a = b$$
$$a - 3 = b - 3$$

   HOW TO :: SOLVE AN EQUATION USING THE SUBTRACTION PROPERTY OF EQUALITY.

Step 1.   Use the Subtraction Property of Equality to isolate the variable.

Step 2.   Simplify the expressions on both sides of the equation.

Step 3.   Check the solution.

EXAMPLE 2.31

Solve: $x + 8 = 17$.

⊘ Solution

We will use the Subtraction Property of Equality to isolate x.

$$x + 8 = 17$$

Subtract 8 from both sides. $x + 8 - 8 = 17 - 8$

Simplify. $x = 9$

$$x + 8 = 17$$

$$9 + 8 = 17$$

$$17 = 17 ✓$$

Since $x = 9$ makes $x + 8 = 17$ a true statement, we know 9 is the solution to the equation.

> **TRY IT : :** 2.61		Solve:
$$x + 6 = 19$$

> **TRY IT : :** 2.62		Solve:
$$x + 9 = 14$$

EXAMPLE 2.32

Solve: $100 = y + 74$.

⊘ **Solution**

To solve an equation, we must always isolate the variable—it doesn't matter which side it is on. To isolate y, we will subtract 74 from both sides.

$$100 = y + 74$$

| Subtract 74 from both sides. | $100 - 74 = y + 74 - 74$ |
| Simplify. | $26 = y$ |

Substitute 26 for y to check.
$100 = y + 74$

$100 \overset{?}{=} 26 + 74$

$100 = 100$ ✓

Since $y = 26$ makes $100 = y + 74$ a true statement, we have found the solution to this equation.

> **TRY IT : :** 2.63		Solve:
$$95 = y + 67$$

> **TRY IT : :** 2.64		Solve:
$$91 = y + 45$$

Solve Equations Using the Addition Property of Equality

In all the equations we have solved so far, a number was added to the variable on one side of the equation. We used subtraction to "undo" the addition in order to isolate the variable.

But suppose we have an equation with a number subtracted from the variable, such as $x - 5 = 8$. We want to isolate the variable, so to "undo" the subtraction we will add the number to both sides.

We use the Addition Property of Equality, which says we can add the same number to both sides of the equation without changing the equality. Notice how it mirrors the Subtraction Property of Equality.

Addition Property of Equality

For any numbers a, b, and c, if

$$a = b$$

then

$$a + c = b + c$$

Remember the **17**-year-old twins, Andy and Bobby? In ten years, Andy's age will still equal Bobby's age. They will both be **27**.

$$a = b$$
$$a + 10 = b + 10$$

We can add the same number to both sides and still keep the equality.

HOW TO :: SOLVE AN EQUATION USING THE ADDITION PROPERTY OF EQUALITY.

Step 1.   Use the Addition Property of Equality to isolate the variable.

Step 2.   Simplify the expressions on both sides of the equation.

Step 3.   Check the solution.

EXAMPLE 2.33

Solve: $x - 5 = 8$.

⊘ **Solution**

We will use the Addition Property of Equality to isolate the variable.

$$x - 5 = 8$$

Add 5 to both sides. $x - 5 + 5 = 8 + 5$

Simplify. $x = 13$

Now we can check. Let $x = 13$.

$$x - 5 = 8$$
$$13 - 5 \overset{?}{=} 8$$
$$8 = 8 \checkmark$$

> **TRY IT ::** 2.65   Solve:
> $x - 9 = 13$

> **TRY IT ::** 2.66   Solve:
> $y - 1 = 3$

EXAMPLE 2.34

Solve: $27 = a - 16$.

⊘ **Solution**

We will add 16 to each side to isolate the variable.

	$27 = a - 16$
Add 16 to each side.	$27 + 16 = a - 16 + 16$
Simplify.	$43 = a$
Now we can check. Let $a = 43$.	$27 = a - 16$
	$27 \overset{?}{=} 43 - 16$
	$27 = 27 \checkmark$

The solution to $27 = a - 16$ is $a = 43$.

> **TRY IT : :** 2.67   Solve:

$$19 = a - 18$$

> **TRY IT : :** 2.68   Solve:

$$27 = n - 14$$

Translate Word Phrases to Algebraic Equations

Remember, an equation has an equal sign between two algebraic expressions. So if we have a sentence that tells us that two phrases are equal, we can translate it into an equation. We look for clue words that mean *equals*. Some words that translate to the equal sign are:

- is equal to
- is the same as
- is
- gives
- was
- will be

It may be helpful to put a box around the *equals* word(s) in the sentence to help you focus separately on each phrase. Then translate each phrase into an expression, and write them on each side of the equal sign.

We will practice translating word sentences into algebraic equations. Some of the sentences will be basic number facts with no variables to solve for. Some sentences will translate into equations with variables. The focus right now is just to translate the words into algebra.

EXAMPLE 2.35

Translate the sentence into an algebraic equation: The sum of 6 and 9 is 15.

⊘ Solution

The word *is* tells us the equal sign goes between 9 and 15.

Locate the "equals" word(s).	The sum of 6 and 9 is 15.
Write the = sign.	The sum of 6 and 9 = 15.
Translate the words to the left of the *equals* word into an algebraic expression.	6 + 9 = ___
Translate the words to the right of the *equals* word into an algebraic expression.	6 + 9 = 15

> | **TRY IT : :** 2.69 | Translate the sentence into an algebraic equation:
> | | The sum of 7 and 6 gives 13.

> | **TRY IT : :** 2.70 | Translate the sentence into an algebraic equation:
> | | The sum of 8 and 6 is 14.

EXAMPLE 2.36

Translate the sentence into an algebraic equation: The product of 8 and 7 is 56.

⊘ **Solution**

The location of the word *is* tells us that the equal sign goes between 7 and 56.

Locate the "equals" word(s).	The product of 8 and 7 $\boxed{is}$ 56.
Write the = sign.	The product of 8 and 7 = 56.
Translate the words to the left of the *equals* word into an algebraic expression.	$8 \cdot 7 = \underline{}$
Translate the words to the right of the *equals* word into an algebraic expression.	$8 \cdot 7 = 56$

> | **TRY IT : :** 2.71 | Translate the sentence into an algebraic equation:
> | | The product of 6 and 9 is 54.

> | **TRY IT : :** 2.72 | Translate the sentence into an algebraic equation:
> | | The product of 21 and 3 gives 63.

EXAMPLE 2.37

Translate the sentence into an algebraic equation: Twice the difference of x and 3 gives 18.

⊘ **Solution**

Locate the "equals" word(s).	Twice the difference of x and 3 $\boxed{gives}$ 18.
Recognize the key words: *twice; difference of .... and ....*	*Twice* means two times.
Translate.	Twice the difference of x and 3 $\boxed{gives}$ 18.
	$2 \qquad (x-3) \qquad = \quad 18$

> | **TRY IT : :** 2.73 | Translate the given sentence into an algebraic equation:
> | | Twice the difference of x and 5 gives 30.

> | **TRY IT : :** 2.74 | Translate the given sentence into an algebraic equation:
> | | Twice the difference of y and 4 gives 16.

Translate to an Equation and Solve

Now let's practice translating sentences into algebraic equations and then solving them. We will solve the equations by using the Subtraction and Addition Properties of Equality.

EXAMPLE 2.38

Translate and solve: Three more than x is equal to 47.

Solution

	Three more than x is equal to 47.
Translate.	$x + 3 = 47$
Subtract 3 from both sides of the equation.	$x + 3 - 3 = 47 - 3$
Simplify.	$x = 44$
We can check. Let $x = 44$.	$x + 3 = 47$
	$44 + 3 \overset{?}{=} 47$
	$47 = 47$ ✓

So $x = 44$ is the solution.

TRY IT :: 2.75   Translate and solve:

Seven more than x is equal to 37.

TRY IT :: 2.76   Translate and solve:

Eleven more than y is equal to 28.

EXAMPLE 2.39

Translate and solve: The difference of y and 14 is 18.

Solution

	The difference of y and 14 is 18.
Translate.	$y - 14 = 18$
Add 14 to both sides.	$y - 14 + 14 = 18 + 14$
Simplify.	$y = 32$
We can check. Let $y = 32$.	$y - 14 = 18$
	$32 - 14 \overset{?}{=} 18$
	$18 = 18$ ✓

So $y = 32$ is the solution.

TRY IT :: 2.77   Translate and solve:

The difference of z and 17 is equal to 37.

> **TRY IT : :** 2.78   Translate and solve:

The difference of x and 19 is equal to $45.$

▶ **MEDIA : :** ACCESS ADDITIONAL ONLINE RESOURCES

- Solving One Step Equations By Addition and Subtraction (http://openstaxcollege.org/l/
  24Solveonestep)

2.3 EXERCISES

Practice Makes Perfect

Determine Whether a Number is a Solution of an Equation

In the following exercises, determine whether each given value is a solution to the equation.

147. $x + 13 = 21$
    ⓐ $x = 8$ ⓑ $x = 34$

148. $y + 18 = 25$
    ⓐ $y = 7$ ⓑ $y = 43$

149. $m - 4 = 13$
    ⓐ $m = 9$ ⓑ $m = 17$

150. $n - 9 = 6$
    ⓐ $n = 3$ ⓑ $n = 15$

151. $3p + 6 = 15$
    ⓐ $p = 3$ ⓑ $p = 7$

152. $8q + 4 = 20$
    ⓐ $q = 2$ ⓑ $q = 3$

153. $18d - 9 = 27$
    ⓐ $d = 1$ ⓑ $d = 2$

154. $24f - 12 = 60$
    ⓐ $f = 2$ ⓑ $f = 3$

155. $8u - 4 = 4u + 40$
    ⓐ $u = 3$ ⓑ $u = 11$

156. $7v - 3 = 4v + 36$
    ⓐ $v = 3$ ⓑ $v = 11$

157. $20h - 5 = 15h + 35$
    ⓐ $h = 6$ ⓑ $h = 8$

158. $18k - 3 = 12k + 33$
    ⓐ $k = 1$ ⓑ $k = 6$

Model the Subtraction Property of Equality

In the following exercises, write the equation modeled by the envelopes and counters and then solve using the subtraction property of equality.

159.

160.

161.

162.

Solve Equations using the Subtraction Property of Equality

In the following exercises, solve each equation using the subtraction property of equality.

163. $a + 2 = 18$

164. $b + 5 = 13$

165. $p + 18 = 23$

166. $q + 14 = 31$

167. $r + 76 = 100$

168. $s + 62 = 95$

169. $16 = x + 9$

170. $17 = y + 6$

171. $93 = p + 24$

172. $116 = q + 79$

173. $465 = d + 398$

174. $932 = c + 641$

Solve Equations using the Addition Property of Equality

In the following exercises, solve each equation using the addition property of equality.

175. $y - 3 = 19$

176. $x - 4 = 12$

177. $u - 6 = 24$

178. $v - 7 = 35$

179. $f - 55 = 123$

180. $g - 39 = 117$

181. $19 = n - 13$

182. $18 = m - 15$

183. $10 = p - 38$

184. $18 = q - 72$

185. $268 = y - 199$

186. $204 = z - 149$

Translate Word Phrase to Algebraic Equations

In the following exercises, translate the given sentence into an algebraic equation.

187. The sum of 8 and 9 is equal to 17.

188. The sum of 7 and 9 is equal to 16.

189. The difference of 23 and 19 is equal to 4.

190. The difference of 29 and 12 is equal to 17.

191. The product of 3 and 9 is equal to 27.

192. The product of 6 and 8 is equal to 48.

193. The quotient of 54 and 6 is equal to 9.

194. The quotient of 42 and 7 is equal to 6.

195. Twice the difference of n and 10 gives 52.

196. Twice the difference of m and 14 gives 64.

197. The sum of three times y and 10 is 100.

198. The sum of eight times x and 4 is 68.

Translate to an Equation and Solve

In the following exercises, translate the given sentence into an algebraic equation and then solve it.

199. Five more than p is equal to 21.

200. Nine more than q is equal to 40.

201. The sum of r and 18 is 73.

202. The sum of s and 13 is 68.

203. The difference of d and 30 is equal to 52.

204. The difference of c and 25 is equal to 75.

205. 12 less than u is 89.

206. 19 less than w is 56.

207. 325 less than c gives 799.

208. 299 less than d gives 850.

Everyday Math

209. Insurance Vince's car insurance has a $500 deductible. Find the amount the insurance company will pay, p, for an $1800 claim by solving the equation $500 + p = 1800$.

210. Insurance Marta's homeowner's insurance policy has a $750 deductible. The insurance company paid $5800 to repair damages caused by a storm. Find the total cost of the storm damage, d, by solving the equation $d - 750 = 5800$.

211. Sale purchase Arthur bought a suit that was on sale for $120 off. He paid $340 for the suit. Find the original price, p, of the suit by solving the equation $p - 120 = 340$.

212. Sale purchase Rita bought a sofa that was on sale for $1299. She paid a total of $1409, including sales tax. Find the amount of the sales tax, t, by solving the equation $1299 + t = 1409$.

Writing Exercises

213. Is $x = 1$ a solution to the equation $8x - 2 = 16 - 6x$? How do you know?

214. Write the equation $y - 5 = 21$ in words. Then make up a word problem for this equation.

Self Check

ⓐ *After completing the exercises, use this checklist to evaluate your mastery of the objectives of this section.*

I can...	Confidently	With some help	No-I don't get it!
determine whether a number is a solution of an equation.			
model the subtraction property of equality.			
solve equations using the subtraction property of equality.			
solve equations using the addition property of equality.			
translate word phrases to algebraic equations.			
translate to an equation and solve.			

ⓑ *What does this checklist tell you about your mastery of this section? What steps will you take to improve?*

2.4 | **Find Multiples and Factors**

Learning Objectives

By the end of this section, you will be able to:

- Identify multiples of numbers
- Use common divisibility tests
- Find all the factors of a number
- Identify prime and composite numbers

Be Prepared!

Before you get started, take this readiness quiz.

1. Which of the following numbers are counting numbers (natural numbers)?
   $0, 4, 215$
   If you missed this problem, review Example 1.1.

2. Find the sum of $3, 5,$ and $7.$
   If you missed the problem, review Example 2.1.

Identify Multiples of Numbers

Annie is counting the shoes in her closet. The shoes are matched in pairs, so she doesn't have to count each one. She counts by twos: $2, 4, 6, 8, 10, 12.$ She has 12 shoes in her closet.

The numbers $2, 4, 6, 8, 10, 12$ are called multiples of $2.$ Multiples of 2 can be written as the product of a counting number and $2.$ The first six multiples of 2 are given below.

$$1 \cdot 2 = 2$$
$$2 \cdot 2 = 4$$
$$3 \cdot 2 = 6$$
$$4 \cdot 2 = 8$$
$$5 \cdot 2 = 10$$
$$6 \cdot 2 = 12$$

A **multiple of a number** is the product of the number and a counting number. So a multiple of 3 would be the product of a counting number and $3.$ Below are the first six multiples of $3.$

$$1 \cdot 3 = 3$$
$$2 \cdot 3 = 6$$
$$3 \cdot 3 = 9$$
$$4 \cdot 3 = 12$$
$$5 \cdot 3 = 15$$
$$6 \cdot 3 = 18$$

We can find the multiples of any number by continuing this process. Table 2.55 shows the multiples of 2 through 9 for the first twelve counting numbers.

Counting Number	1	2	3	4	5	6	7	8	9	10	11	12
Multiples of 2	2	4	6	8	10	12	14	16	18	20	22	24
Multiples of 3	3	6	9	12	15	18	21	24	27	30	33	36
Multiples of 4	4	8	12	16	20	24	28	32	36	40	44	48
Multiples of 5	5	10	15	20	25	30	35	40	45	50	55	60
Multiples of 6	6	12	18	24	30	36	42	48	54	60	66	72
Multiples of 7	7	14	21	28	35	42	49	56	63	70	77	84
Multiples of 8	8	16	24	32	40	48	56	64	72	80	88	96
Multiples of 9	9	18	27	36	45	54	63	72	81	90	99	108

Table 2.55

Multiple of a Number

A number is a multiple of n if it is the product of a counting number and n.

Recognizing the patterns for multiples of 2, 5, 10, and 3 will be helpful to you as you continue in this course.

 MANIPULATIVE MATHEMATICS

Doing the Manipulative Mathematics activity "Multiples" will help you develop a better understanding of multiples.

Figure 2.6 shows the counting numbers from 1 to 50. Multiples of 2 are highlighted. Do you notice a pattern?

1	2	3	4	5	6	7	8	9	10
11	12	13	14	15	16	17	18	19	20
21	22	23	24	25	26	27	28	29	30
31	32	33	34	35	36	37	38	39	40
41	42	43	44	45	46	47	48	49	50

Figure 2.6 Multiples of 2 between 1 and 50

The last digit of each highlighted number in Figure 2.6 is either 0, 2, 4, 6, or 8. This is true for the product of 2 and any counting number. So, to tell if any number is a multiple of 2 look at the last digit. If it is 0, 2, 4, 6, or 8, then the number is a multiple of 2.

EXAMPLE 2.40

Determine whether each of the following is a multiple of 2:

ⓐ 489   ⓑ 3,714

⊘ **Solution**

ⓐ

Is 489 a multiple of 2?

Is the last digit 0, 2, 4, 6, or 8?   No.

489 is not a multiple of 2.

ⓑ

Is 3,714 a multiple of 2?

Is the last digit 0, 2, 4, 6, or 8?   Yes.

3,714 is a multiple of 2.

> **TRY IT : :** 2.79   Determine whether each number is a multiple of 2:

ⓐ 678   ⓑ 21,493

> **TRY IT : :** 2.80   Determine whether each number is a multiple of 2:

ⓐ 979   ⓑ 17,780

Now let's look at multiples of **5**. Figure 2.7 highlights all of the multiples of **5** between **1** and **50**. What do you notice about the multiples of **5**?

1	2	3	4	5	6	7	8	9	10
11	12	13	14	15	16	17	18	19	20
21	22	23	24	25	26	27	28	29	30
31	32	33	34	35	36	37	38	39	40
41	42	43	44	45	46	47	48	49	50

Figure 2.7 Multiples of 5 between 1 and 50

All multiples of 5 end with either 5 or 0. Just like we identify multiples of 2 by looking at the last digit, we can identify multiples of 5 by looking at the last digit.

EXAMPLE 2.41

Determine whether each of the following is a multiple of 5:

ⓐ 579   ⓑ 880

Solution

ⓐ

Is 579 a multiple of 5?	
Is the last digit 5 or 0?	No.
	579 is not a multiple of 5.

ⓑ

Is 880 a multiple of 5?	
Is the last digit 5 or 0?	Yes.
	880 is a multiple of 5.

> **TRY IT :: 2.81**   Determine whether each number is a multiple of 5.
>
> ⓐ 675   ⓑ 1,578

> **TRY IT :: 2.82**   Determine whether each number is a multiple of 5.
>
> ⓐ 421   ⓑ 2,690

Figure 2.8 highlights the multiples of 10 between 1 and 50. All multiples of 10 all end with a zero.

1	2	3	4	5	6	7	8	9	10
11	12	13	14	15	16	17	18	19	20
21	22	23	24	25	26	27	28	29	30
31	32	33	34	35	36	37	38	39	40
41	42	43	44	45	46	47	48	49	50

Figure 2.8 Multiples of 10 between 1 and 50

EXAMPLE 2.42

Determine whether each of the following is a multiple of 10:

ⓐ 425   ⓑ 350

Solution

ⓐ

Is 425 a multiple of 10?	
Is the last digit zero?	No.
	425 is not a multiple of 10.

ⓑ

Is 350 a multiple of 10?

Is the last digit zero?   Yes.

350 is a multiple of 10.

> **TRY IT ::** 2.83   Determine whether each number is a multiple of 10:

ⓐ 179   ⓑ 3,540

> **TRY IT ::** 2.84   Determine whether each number is a multiple of 10:

ⓐ 110   ⓑ 7,595

Figure 2.9 highlights multiples of 3. The pattern for multiples of 3 is not as obvious as the patterns for multiples of 2, 5, and 10.

1	2	3	4	5	6	7	8	9	10
11	12	13	14	15	16	17	18	19	20
21	22	23	24	25	26	27	28	29	30
31	32	33	34	35	36	37	38	39	40
41	42	43	44	45	46	47	48	49	50

Figure 2.9 Multiples of 3 between 1 and 50

Unlike the other patterns we've examined so far, this pattern does not involve the last digit. The pattern for multiples of 3 is based on the sum of the digits. If the sum of the digits of a number is a multiple of 3, then the number itself is a multiple of 3. See Table 2.62.

Multiple of 3	3	6	9	12	15	18	21	24
Sum of digits	3	6	9	$\dfrac{1+2}{3}$	$\dfrac{1+5}{6}$	$\dfrac{1+8}{9}$	$\dfrac{2+1}{3}$	$\dfrac{2+4}{6}$

Table 2.62

Consider the number 42. The digits are 4 and 2, and their sum is $4 + 2 = 6$. Since 6 is a multiple of 3, we know that 42 is also a multiple of 3.

EXAMPLE 2.43

Determine whether each of the given numbers is a multiple of 3:

ⓐ 645   ⓑ 10,519

⊘ **Solution**

ⓐ Is 645 a multiple of 3?

Find the sum of the digits.	$6 + 4 + 5 = 15$
Is 15 a multiple of 3?	Yes.
If we're not sure, we could add its digits to find out. We can check it by dividing 645 by 3.	$645 \div 3$
The quotient is 215.	$3 \cdot 215 = 645$

ⓑ Is $10{,}519$ a multiple of 3?

Find the sum of the digits.	$1 + 0 + 5 + 1 + 9 = 16$
Is 16 a multiple of 3?	No.
So 10,519 is not a multiple of 3 either..	$645 \div 3$
We can check this by dividing by 10,519 by 3.	$\begin{array}{r} 3{,}506\text{R}1 \\ 3\overline{)10{,}519} \end{array}$

When we divide $10{,}519$ by 3, we do not get a counting number, so $10{,}519$ is not the product of a counting number and 3. It is not a multiple of 3.

> **TRY IT : :** 2.85   Determine whether each number is a multiple of 3:

ⓐ 954 ⓑ $3{,}742$

> **TRY IT : :** 2.86   Determine whether each number is a multiple of 3:

ⓐ 643 ⓑ $8{,}379$

Look back at the charts where you highlighted the multiples of 2, of 5, and of 10. Notice that the multiples of 10 are the numbers that are multiples of both 2 and 5. That is because $10 = 2 \cdot 5$. Likewise, since $6 = 2 \cdot 3$, the multiples of 6 are the numbers that are multiples of both 2 and 3.

Use Common Divisibility Tests

Another way to say that 375 is a multiple of 5 is to say that 375 is divisible by 5. In fact, $375 \div 5$ is 75, so 375 is $5 \cdot 75$. Notice in Example 2.43 that $10{,}519$ is not a multiple 3. When we divided $10{,}519$ by 3 we did not get a counting number, so $10{,}519$ is not divisible by 3.

Divisibility
If a number m is a multiple of n, then we say that m is divisible by n.

Since multiplication and division are inverse operations, the patterns of multiples that we found can be used as divisibility tests. Table 2.65 summarizes divisibility tests for some of the counting numbers between one and ten.

Divisibility Tests	
A number is divisible by	
2	if the last digit is $0,\ 2,\ 4,\ 6,$ or 8
3	if the sum of the digits is divisible by 3
5	if the last digit is 5 or 0
6	if divisible by both 2 and 3
10	if the last digit is 0

Table 2.65

EXAMPLE 2.44

Determine whether $1{,}290$ is divisible by 2, 3, 5, and 10.

⊘ Solution

Table 2.66 applies the divisibility tests to $1{,}290.$ In the far right column, we check the results of the divisibility tests by seeing if the quotient is a whole number.

Divisible by...?	Test	Divisible?	Check
2	Is last digit $0,\ 2,\ 4,\ 6,$ or 8? *Yes.*	yes	$1290 \div 2 = 645$
3	Is sum of digits divisible by 3? $1 + 2 + 9 + 0 = 12$ *Yes.*	yes	$1290 \div 3 = 430$
5	Is last digit 5 or 0? *Yes.*	yes	$1290 \div 5 = 258$
10	Is last digit 0? *Yes.*	yes	$1290 \div 10 = 129$

Table 2.66

Thus, $1{,}290$ is divisible by 2, 3, 5, and 10.

>	**TRY IT : :** 2.87	Determine whether the given number is divisible by 2, 3, 5, and 10.
		6240

>	**TRY IT : :** 2.88	Determine whether the given number is divisible by 2, 3, 5, and 10.
		7248

EXAMPLE 2.45

Determine whether $5{,}625$ is divisible by 2, 3, 5, and 10.

⊘ Solution

Table 2.67 applies the divisibility tests to $5{,}625$ and tests the results by finding the quotients.

Divisible by...?	Test	Divisible?	Check
2	Is last digit 0, 2, 4, 6, or 8? *No.*	no	$5625 \div 2 = 2812.5$
3	Is sum of digits divisible by 3? $5 + 6 + 2 + 5 = 18$ *Yes.*	yes	$5625 \div 3 = 1875$
5	Is last digit is 5 or 0? *Yes.*	yes	$5625 \div 5 = 1125$
10	Is last digit 0? *No.*	no	$5625 \div 10 = 562.5$

Table 2.67

Thus, $5,625$ is divisible by 3 and 5, but not 2, or 10.

> **TRY IT : : 2.89**   Determine whether the given number is divisible by 2, 3, 5, and 10.

   4962

> **TRY IT : : 2.90**   Determine whether the given number is divisible by 2, 3, 5, and 10.

   3765

Find All the Factors of a Number

There are often several ways to talk about the same idea. So far, we've seen that if m is a multiple of n, we can say that m is divisible by n. We know that 72 is the product of 8 and 9, so we can say 72 is a multiple of 8 and 72 is a multiple of 9. We can also say 72 is divisible by 8 and by 9. Another way to talk about this is to say that 8 and 9 are factors of 72. When we write $72 = 8 \cdot 9$ we can say that we have factored 72.

$$\underbrace{8 \cdot 9}_{\text{factors}} \quad = \quad \underbrace{72}_{\text{product}}$$

Factors

If $a \cdot b = m$, then a and b are factors of m, and m is the product of a and b.

In algebra, it can be useful to determine all of the factors of a number. This is called factoring a number, and it can help us solve many kinds of problems.

 MANIPULATIVE MATHEMATICS

Doing the Manipulative Mathematics activity "Model Multiplication and Factoring" will help you develop a better understanding of multiplication and factoring.

For example, suppose a choreographer is planning a dance for a ballet recital. There are 24 dancers, and for a certain scene, the choreographer wants to arrange the dancers in groups of equal sizes on stage.

In how many ways can the dancers be put into groups of equal size? Answering this question is the same as identifying the factors of 24. Table 2.68 summarizes the different ways that the choreographer can arrange the dancers.

Number of Groups	Dancers per Group	Total Dancers
1	24	$1 \cdot 24 = 24$
2	12	$2 \cdot 12 = 24$
3	8	$3 \cdot 8 = 24$
4	6	$4 \cdot 6 = 24$
6	4	$6 \cdot 4 = 24$
8	3	$8 \cdot 3 = 24$
12	2	$12 \cdot 2 = 24$
24	1	$24 \cdot 1 = 24$

Table 2.68

What patterns do you see in Table 2.68? Did you notice that the number of groups times the number of dancers per group is always 24? This makes sense, since there are always 24 dancers.

You may notice another pattern if you look carefully at the first two columns. These two columns contain the exact same set of numbers—but in reverse order. They are mirrors of one another, and in fact, both columns list all of the factors of 24, which are:

$$1, 2, 3, 4, 6, 8, 12, 24$$

We can find all the factors of any counting number by systematically dividing the number by each counting number, starting with 1. If the quotient is also a counting number, then the divisor and the quotient are factors of the number. We can stop when the quotient becomes smaller than the divisor.

HOW TO :: FIND ALL THE FACTORS OF A COUNTING NUMBER.

Step 1.   Divide the number by each of the counting numbers, in order, until the quotient is smaller than the divisor.

      ◦ If the quotient is a counting number, the divisor and quotient are a pair of factors.

      ◦ If the quotient is not a counting number, the divisor is not a factor.

Step 2.   List all the factor pairs.

Step 3.   Write all the factors in order from smallest to largest.

EXAMPLE 2.46

Find all the factors of 72.

⊘ **Solution**

Divide 72 by each of the counting numbers starting with 1. If the quotient is a whole number, the divisor and quotient are a pair of factors.

Dividend	Divisor	Quotient	Factors
72	1	72	1, 72
72	2	36	2, 36
72	3	24	3, 24
72	4	18	4, 18
72	5	14.4	–
72	6	12	6, 12
72	7	~10.29	–
72	8	9	8, 9

The next line would have a divisor of 9 and a quotient of 8. The quotient would be smaller than the divisor, so we stop. If we continued, we would end up only listing the same factors again in reverse order. Listing all the factors from smallest to greatest, we have

1, 2, 3, 4, 6, 8, 9, 12, 18, 24, 36, and 72

> **TRY IT ::** 2.91   Find all the factors of the given number:
>
> 96

> **TRY IT ::** 2.92   Find all the factors of the given number:
>
> 80

Identify Prime and Composite Numbers

Some numbers, like 72, have many factors. Other numbers, such as 7, have only two factors: 1 and the number. A number with only two factors is called a **prime number**. A number with more than two factors is called a **composite number**. The number 1 is neither prime nor composite. It has only one factor, itself.

Prime Numbers and Composite Numbers

A prime number is a counting number greater than 1 whose only factors are 1 and itself.

A composite number is a counting number that is not prime.

Figure 2.10 lists the counting numbers from 2 through 20 along with their factors. The highlighted numbers are prime, since each has only two factors.

Number	Factors	Prime or Composite?		Number	Factors	Prime or Composite?
2	1,2	Prime		12	1,2,3,4,6,12	Composite
3	1,3	Prime		13	1,13	Prime
4	1,2,4	Composite		14	1,2,7,14	Composite
5	1,5	Prime		15	1,3,5,15	Composite
6	1,2,3,6	Composite		16	1,2,4,8,16	Composite
7	1,7	Prime		17	1,17	Prime
8	1,2,4,8	Composite		18	1,2,3,6,9,18	Composite
9	1,3,9	Composite		19	1,19	Prime
10	1,2,5,10	Composite		20	1,2,4,5,10,20	Composite
11	1,11	Prime				

Figure 2.10 Factors of the counting numbers from 2 through 20, with prime numbers highlighted

The prime numbers less than 20 are 2, 3, 5, 7, 11, 13, 17, and 19. There are many larger prime numbers too. In order to determine whether a number is prime or composite, we need to see if the number has any factors other than 1 and itself. To do this, we can test each of the smaller prime numbers in order to see if it is a factor of the number. If none of the prime numbers are factors, then that number is also prime.

HOW TO : : DETERMINE IF A NUMBER IS PRIME.

Step 1.   Test each of the primes, in order, to see if it is a factor of the number.

Step 2.   Start with 2 and stop when the quotient is smaller than the divisor or when a prime factor is found.

Step 3.   If the number has a prime factor, then it is a composite number. If it has no prime factors, then the number is prime.

EXAMPLE 2.47

Identify each number as prime or composite:

    ⓐ 83   ⓑ 77

⊘ Solution

ⓐ Test each prime, in order, to see if it is a factor of 83 , starting with 2, as shown. We will stop when the quotient is smaller than the divisor.

Prime	Test	Factor of 83?
2	Last digit of 83 is not 0, 2, 4, 6, or 8.	No.
3	$8 + 3 = 11,$ and 11 is not divisible by 3.	No.
5	The last digit of 83 is not 5 or 0.	No.
7	$83 \div 7 = 11.857\ldots$	No.
11	$83 \div 11 = 7.545\ldots$	No.

We can stop when we get to 11 because the quotient $(7.545\ldots)$ is less than the divisor.

We did not find any prime numbers that are factors of 83, so we know 83 is prime.

ⓑ Test each prime, in order, to see if it is a factor of 77.

Prime	Test	Factor of 77?
2	Last digit is not 0, 2, 4, 6, or 8.	No.
3	$7 + 7 = 14,$ and 14 is not divisible by 3.	No.
5	the last digit is not 5 or 0.	No.
7	$77 \div 11 = 7$	Yes.

Since 77 is divisible by 7, we know it is not a prime number. It is composite.

> **TRY IT : :** 2.93   Identify the number as prime or composite:

    91

TRY IT : : 2.94   Identify the number as prime or composite:

137

 LINKS TO LITERACY

The Links to Literacy activities *One Hundred Hungry Ants*, *Spunky Monkeys on Parade* and *A Remainder of One* will provide you with another view of the topics covered in this section.

▶ **MEDIA : :** ACCESS ADDITIONAL ONLINE RESOURCES

- Divisibility Rules (http://openstaxcollege.org/l/24Divisrules)
- Factors (http://openstaxcollege.org/l/24Factors)
- Ex 1: Determine Factors of a Number (http://openstaxcollege.org/l/24Factors1)
- Ex 2: Determine Factors of a Number (http://openstaxcollege.org/l/24Factors2)
- Ex 3: Determine Factors of a Number (http://openstaxcollege.org/l/24Factors3)

2.4 EXERCISES

Practice Makes Perfect

Identify Multiples of Numbers

In the following exercises, list all the multiples less than 50 for the given number.

215. 2

216. 3

217. 4

218. 5

219. 6

220. 7

221. 8

222. 9

223. 10

224. 12

Use Common Divisibility Tests

In the following exercises, use the divisibility tests to determine whether each number is divisible by 2, 3, 4, 5, 6, and 10.

225. 84

226. 96

227. 75

228. 78

229. 168

230. 264

231. 900

232. 800

233. 896

234. 942

235. 375

236. 750

237. 350

238. 550

239. 1430

240. 1080

241. 22,335

242. 39,075

Find All the Factors of a Number

In the following exercises, find all the factors of the given number.

243. 36

244. 42

245. 60

246. 48

247. 144

248. 200

249. 588

250. 576

Identify Prime and Composite Numbers

In the following exercises, determine if the given number is prime or composite.

251. 43

252. 67

253. 39

254. 53

255. 71

256. 119

257. 481

258. 221

259. 209

260. 359

261. 667

262. 1771

Everyday Math

263. Banking Frank's grandmother gave him $100 at his high school graduation. Instead of spending it, Frank opened a bank account. Every week, he added $15 to the account. The table shows how much money Frank had put in the account by the end of each week. Complete the table by filling in the blanks.

Weeks after graduation	Total number of dollars Frank put in the account	Simplified Total
0	100	100
1	100 + 15	115
2	100 + 15 · 2	130
3	100 + 15 · 3	
4	100 + 15 · [ ]	
5	100 + [ ]	
6		
20		
x		

264. Banking In March, Gina opened a Christmas club savings account at her bank. She deposited $75 to open the account. Every week, she added $20 to the account. The table shows how much money Gina had put in the account by the end of each week. Complete the table by filling in the blanks.

Weeks after opening the account	Total number of dollars Gina put in the account	Simplified Total
0	75	75
1	75 + 20	95
2	75 + 20 · 2	115
3	75 + 20 · 3	
4	75 + 20 · [ ]	
5	75 + [ ]	
6		
20		
x		

Writing Exercises

265. If a number is divisible by 2 and by 3, why is it also divisible by 6?

266. What is the difference between prime numbers and composite numbers?

Self Check

ⓐ *After completing the exercises, use this checklist to evaluate your mastery of the objectives of this section.*

I can...	Confidently	With some help	No-I don't get it!
identify multiples of numbers.			
use common divisibility tests.			
find all the factors of a number.			
identify prime and composite numbers.			

ⓑ *On a scale of 1–10, how would you rate your mastery of this section in light of your responses on the checklist? How can you improve this?*

2.5 | Prime Factorization and the Least Common Multiple

Learning Objectives

By the end of this section, you will be able to:
- Find the prime factorization of a composite number
- Find the least common multiple (LCM) of two numbers

Be Prepared!

Before you get started, take this readiness quiz.

1. Is 810 divisible by $2, 3, 5, 6,$ or 10?
   If you missed this problem, review Example 2.44.
2. Is 127 prime or composite?
   If you missed this problem, review Example 2.47.
3. Write $2 \cdot 2 \cdot 2 \cdot 2$ in exponential notation.
   If you missed this problem, review Example 2.5.

Find the Prime Factorization of a Composite Number

In the previous section, we found the factors of a number. Prime numbers have only two factors, the number 1 and the prime number itself. Composite numbers have more than two factors, and every composite number can be written as a unique product of primes. This is called the **prime factorization** of a number. When we write the prime factorization of a number, we are rewriting the number as a product of primes. Finding the prime factorization of a composite number will help you later in this course.

Prime Factorization

The prime factorization of a number is the product of prime numbers that equals the number.

 MANIPULATIVE MATHEMATICS

Doing the Manipulative Mathematics activity "Prime Numbers" will help you develop a better sense of prime numbers.

You may want to refer to the following list of prime numbers less than 50 as you work through this section.

$$2, 3, 5, 7, 11, 13, 17, 19, 23, 29, 31, 37, 41, 43, 47$$

Prime Factorization Using the Factor Tree Method

One way to find the prime factorization of a number is to make a factor tree. We start by writing the number, and then writing it as the product of two factors. We write the factors below the number and connect them to the number with a small line segment—a "branch" of the factor tree.

If a factor is prime, we circle it (like a bud on a tree), and do not factor that "branch" any further. If a factor is not prime, we repeat this process, writing it as the product of two factors and adding new branches to the tree.

We continue until all the branches end with a prime. When the factor tree is complete, the circled primes give us the prime factorization.

For example, let's find the prime factorization of $36.$ We can start with any factor pair such as 3 and $12.$ We write 3 and 12 below 36 with branches connecting them.

The factor 3 is prime, so we circle it. The factor 12 is composite, so we need to find its factors. Let's use 3 and $4.$ We write these factors on the tree under the $12.$

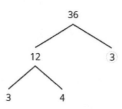

The factor 3 is prime, so we circle it. The factor 4 is composite, and it factors into $2 \cdot 2$. We write these factors under the 4. Since 2 is prime, we circle both 2s.

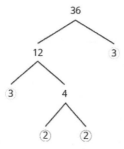

The prime factorization is the product of the circled primes. We generally write the prime factorization in order from least to greatest.

$$2 \cdot 2 \cdot 3 \cdot 3$$

In cases like this, where some of the prime factors are repeated, we can write prime factorization in exponential form.

$$2 \cdot 2 \cdot 3 \cdot 3$$

$$2^2 \cdot 3^2$$

Note that we could have started our factor tree with any factor pair of 36. We chose 12 and 3, but the same result would have been the same if we had started with 2 and 18, 4 and 9, or 6 and 6.

 HOW TO :: FIND THE PRIME FACTORIZATION OF A COMPOSITE NUMBER USING THE TREE METHOD.

Step 1.   Find any factor pair of the given number, and use these numbers to create two branches.

Step 2.   If a factor is prime, that branch is complete. Circle the prime.

Step 3.   If a factor is not prime, write it as the product of a factor pair and continue the process.

Step 4.   Write the composite number as the product of all the circled primes.

EXAMPLE 2.48

Find the prime factorization of 48 using the factor tree method.

⊘ Solution

We can start our tree using any factor pair of 48. Let's use 2 and 24.
We circle the 2 because it is prime and so that branch is complete.

Now we will factor 24. Let's use 4 and 6.

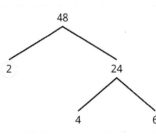

Neither factor is prime, so we do not circle either.
We factor the 4, using 2 and 2.
We factor 6, using 2 and 3.

We circle the 2s and the 3 since they are prime. Now all of the branches end in a prime.

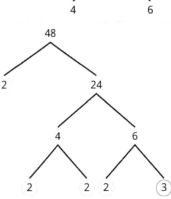

Write the product of the circled numbers. $2 \cdot 2 \cdot 2 \cdot 2 \cdot 3$

Write in exponential form. $2^4 \cdot 3$

Check this on your own by multiplying all the factors together. The result should be 48.

> **TRY IT : : 2.95**   Find the prime factorization using the factor tree method: 80

> **TRY IT : : 2.96**   Find the prime factorization using the factor tree method: 60

EXAMPLE 2.49

Find the prime factorization of 84 using the factor tree method.

⊘ **Solution**

We start with the factor pair 4 and 21.

Neither factor is prime so we factor them further.

Now the factors are all prime, so we circle them.

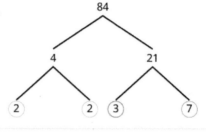

Then we write 84 as the product of all circled primes.

$$2 \cdot 2 \cdot 3 \cdot 7$$
$$2^2 \cdot 3 \cdot 7$$

Draw a factor tree of 84.

> **TRY IT : : 2.97**   Find the prime factorization using the factor tree method: 126

> **TRY IT : : 2.98**   Find the prime factorization using the factor tree method: 294

Prime Factorization Using the Ladder Method

The ladder method is another way to find the prime factors of a composite number. It leads to the same result as the factor tree method. Some people prefer the ladder method to the factor tree method, and vice versa.

To begin building the "ladder," divide the given number by its smallest prime factor. For example, to start the ladder for 36, we divide 36 by 2, the smallest prime factor of 36.

$$\begin{array}{r} 18 \\ 2\overline{)36} \end{array}$$

To add a "step" to the ladder, we continue dividing by the same prime until it no longer divides evenly.

$$\begin{array}{r} 9 \\ 2\overline{)18} \\ 2\overline{)36} \end{array}$$

Then we divide by the next prime; so we divide 9 by 3.

$$\begin{array}{r} 3 \\ 3\overline{)9} \\ 2\overline{)18} \\ 2\overline{)36} \end{array}$$

We continue dividing up the ladder in this way until the quotient is prime. Since the quotient, 3, is prime, we stop here.

Do you see why the ladder method is sometimes called stacked division?

The prime factorization is the product of all the primes on the sides and top of the ladder.

$$2 \cdot 2 \cdot 3 \cdot 3$$

$$2^2 \cdot 3^2$$

Notice that the result is the same as we obtained with the factor tree method.

HOW TO :: FIND THE PRIME FACTORIZATION OF A COMPOSITE NUMBER USING THE LADDER METHOD.

Step 1.   Divide the number by the smallest prime.

Step 2.   Continue dividing by that prime until it no longer divides evenly.

Step 3.   Divide by the next prime until it no longer divides evenly.

Step 4.   Continue until the quotient is a prime.

Step 5.   Write the composite number as the product of all the primes on the sides and top of the ladder.

EXAMPLE 2.50

Find the prime factorization of 120 using the ladder method.

 Solution

Divide the number by the smallest prime, which is 2.

$$\begin{array}{r} 60 \\ \hline 2)\,120 \end{array}$$

Continue dividing by 2 until it no longer divides evenly.

$$\begin{array}{r} 15 \\ \hline 2)\,30 \\ \hline 2)\;\;\,60 \\ \hline 2)\quad 120 \end{array}$$

Divide by the next prime, 3.

$$\begin{array}{r} 5 \\ \hline 3)\,15 \\ \hline 2)\;\;\,30 \\ \hline 2)\quad 60 \\ \hline 2)\qquad 120 \end{array}$$

The quotient, 5, is prime, so the ladder is complete. Write the prime factorization of 120.

$$2 \cdot 2 \cdot 2 \cdot 3 \cdot 5$$
$$2^3 \cdot 3 \cdot 5$$

Check this yourself by multiplying the factors. The result should be 120.

> **TRY IT :: 2.99**   Find the prime factorization using the ladder method: 80

> **TRY IT :: 2.100**   Find the prime factorization using the ladder method: 60

EXAMPLE 2.51

Find the prime factorization of 48 using the ladder method.

⊘ **Solution**

Divide the number by the smallest prime, 2.

$$2\overline{)48}^{\,24}$$

Continue dividing by 2 until it no longer divides evenly.

$$\begin{array}{r}3\\2\overline{)6}\\2\overline{)\,12}\\2\overline{)\,24}\\2\overline{)\,\ 48}\end{array}$$

The quotient, 3, is prime, so the ladder is complete. Write the prime factorization of 48.

$$2 \cdot 2 \cdot 2 \cdot 2 \cdot 3$$
$$2^4 \cdot 3$$

> **TRY IT :: 2.101**   Find the prime factorization using the ladder method. 126

> **TRY IT :: 2.102**   Find the prime factorization using the ladder method. 294

Find the Least Common Multiple (LCM) of Two Numbers

One of the reasons we look at multiples and primes is to use these techniques to find the least common multiple of two numbers. This will be useful when we add and subtract fractions with different denominators.

Listing Multiples Method

A common multiple of two numbers is a number that is a multiple of both numbers. Suppose we want to find common multiples of 10 and 25. We can list the first several multiples of each number. Then we look for multiples that are common to both lists—these are the common multiples.

$$10{:}10, 20, 30, 40, \mathbf{50}, 60, 70, 80, 90, \mathbf{100}, 110, \dots$$
$$25{:}25, \mathbf{50}, 75, \mathbf{100}, 125, \dots$$

We see that 50 and 100 appear in both lists. They are common multiples of 10 and 25. We would find more common multiples if we continued the list of multiples for each.

The smallest number that is a multiple of two numbers is called the **least common multiple** (LCM). So the least LCM of 10 and 25 is 50.

HOW TO :: FIND THE LEAST COMMON MULTIPLE (LCM) OF TWO NUMBERS BY LISTING MULTIPLES.

Step 1.   List the first several multiples of each number.

Step 2.   Look for multiples common to both lists. If there are no common multiples in the lists, write out additional multiples for each number.

Step 3.   Look for the smallest number that is common to both lists.

Step 4.   This number is the LCM.

EXAMPLE 2.52

Find the LCM of 15 and 20 by listing multiples.

⊘ **Solution**

List the first several multiples of 15 and of 20. Identify the first common multiple.

15: 15, 30, 45, **60**, 75, 90, 105, 120
20: 20, 40, **60**, 80, 100, 120, 140, 160

The smallest number to appear on both lists is $60,$ so 60 is the least common multiple of 15 and $20.$

Notice that 120 is on both lists, too. It is a common multiple, but it is not the least common multiple.

> **TRY IT : : 2.103**   Find the least common multiple (LCM) of the given numbers: 9 and 12

> **TRY IT : : 2.104**   Find the least common multiple (LCM) of the given numbers: 18 and 24

Prime Factors Method

Another way to find the least common multiple of two numbers is to use their prime factors. We'll use this method to find the LCM of 12 and $18.$

We start by finding the prime factorization of each number.
$$12 = 2 \cdot 2 \cdot 3 \qquad 18 = 2 \cdot 3 \cdot 3$$

Then we write each number as a product of primes, matching primes vertically when possible.
$$12 = 2 \cdot 2 \cdot 3$$
$$18 = 2 \cdot \quad 3 \cdot 3$$

Now we bring down the primes in each column. The LCM is the product of these factors.
$$12 = 2 \cdot 2 \cdot 3$$
$$18 = 2 \cdot \quad 3 \cdot 3$$
$$\overline{\text{LCM} = 2 \cdot 2 \cdot 3 \cdot 3}$$
$$\text{LCM} = 2 \cdot 2 \cdot 3 \cdot 3 = 36$$

Notice that the prime factors of 12 and the prime factors of 18 are included in the LCM. By matching up the common primes, each common prime factor is used only once. This ensures that 36 is the least common multiple.

 HOW TO : : FIND THE LCM USING THE PRIME FACTORS METHOD.

Step 1.   Find the prime factorization of each number.

Step 2.   Write each number as a product of primes, matching primes vertically when possible.

Step 3.   Bring down the primes in each column.

Step 4.   Multiply the factors to get the LCM.

EXAMPLE 2.53

Find the LCM of 15 and 18 using the prime factors method.

Solution

Write each number as a product of primes.	$15 = 3 \cdot 5 \qquad 18 = 2 \cdot 3 \cdot 3$
Write each number as a product of primes, matching primes vertically when possible.	$15 = \quad 3 \cdot \quad 5$ $18 = 2 \cdot 3 \cdot 3$
Bring down the primes in each column.	$15 = \quad 3 \cdot \quad 5$ $18 = 2 \cdot 3 \cdot 3$ $\overline{\text{LCM} = 2 \cdot 3 \cdot 3 \cdot 5}$
Multiply the factors to get the LCM.	$\text{LCM} = 2 \cdot 3 \cdot 3 \cdot 5$ The LCM of 15 and 18 is 90.

> | **TRY IT : :** 2.105   Find the LCM using the prime factors method. 15 and 20

> | **TRY IT : :** 2.106   Find the LCM using the prime factors method. 15 and 35

EXAMPLE 2.54

Find the LCM of 50 and 100 using the prime factors method.

⊘ **Solution**

Write the prime factorization of each number.	$50 = 2 \cdot 5 \cdot 5 \qquad 100 = 2 \cdot 2 \cdot 5 \cdot 5$
Write each number as a product of primes, matching primes vertically when possible.	$50 = 2 \cdot 5 \cdot 5$ $100 = 2 \cdot 2 \cdot 5 \cdot 5$
Bring down the primes in each column.	$50 = 2 \cdot 5 \cdot 5$ $100 = 2 \cdot 2 \cdot 5 \cdot 5$ $\overline{}$ $LCM = 2 \cdot 2 \cdot 5 \cdot 5$
Multiply the factors to get the LCM.	$LCM = 2 \cdot 2 \cdot 5 \cdot 5$ The LCM of 50 and 100 is 100.

> | **TRY IT : :** 2.107   Find the LCM using the prime factors method: 55, 88

> | **TRY IT : :** 2.108   Find the LCM using the prime factors method: 60, 72

▶ | **MEDIA : :** ACCESS ADDITIONAL ONLINE RESOURCES

- Ex 1: Prime Factorization (http://openstaxcollege.org/l/24PrimeFactor1)
- Ex 2: Prime Factorization (http://openstaxcollege.org/l/24PrimeFactor2)
- Ex 3: Prime Factorization (http://openstaxcollege.org/l/24PrimeFactor3)
- Ex 1: Prime Factorization Using Stacked Division (http://openstaxcollege.org/l/24stackeddivis)
- Ex 2: Prime Factorization Using Stacked Division (http://openstaxcollege.org/l/24stackeddivis2)
- The Least Common Multiple (http://openstaxcollege.org/l/24LCM)
- Example: Determining the Least Common Multiple Using a List of Multiples (http://openstaxcollege.org/l/24LCM2)
- Example: Determining the Least Common Multiple Using Prime Factorization (http://openstaxcollege.org/l/24LCMFactor)

2.5 EXERCISES

Practice Makes Perfect

Find the Prime Factorization of a Composite Number

In the following exercises, find the prime factorization of each number using the factor tree method.

267. 86

268. 78

269. 132

270. 455

271. 693

272. 420

273. 115

274. 225

275. 2475

276. 1560

In the following exercises, find the prime factorization of each number using the ladder method.

277. 56

278. 72

279. 168

280. 252

281. 391

282. 400

283. 432

284. 627

285. 2160

286. 2520

In the following exercises, find the prime factorization of each number using any method.

287. 150

288. 180

289. 525

290. 444

291. 36

292. 50

293. 350

294. 144

Find the Least Common Multiple (LCM) of Two Numbers

In the following exercises, find the least common multiple (LCM) by listing multiples.

295. 8, 12

296. 4, 3

297. 6, 15

298. 12, 16

299. 30, 40

300. 20, 30

301. 60, 75

302. 44, 55

In the following exercises, find the least common multiple (LCM) by using the prime factors method.

303. 8, 12

304. 12, 16

305. 24, 30

306. 28, 40

307. 70, 84

308. 84, 90

In the following exercises, find the least common multiple (LCM) using any method.

309. 6, 21

310. 9, 15

311. 24, 30

312. 32, 40

Everyday Math

313. Grocery shopping Hot dogs are sold in packages of ten, but hot dog buns come in packs of eight. What is the smallest number of hot dogs and buns that can be purchased if you want to have the same number of hot dogs and buns? (Hint: it is the LCM!)

314. Grocery shopping Paper plates are sold in packages of 12 and party cups come in packs of 8. What is the smallest number of plates and cups you can purchase if you want to have the same number of each? (Hint: it is the LCM!)

Writing Exercises

315. Do you prefer to find the prime factorization of a composite number by using the factor tree method or the ladder method? Why?

316. Do you prefer to find the LCM by listing multiples or by using the prime factors method? Why?

Self Check

ⓐ *After completing the exercises, use this checklist to evaluate your mastery of the objectives of this section.*

I can...	Confidently	With some help	No-I don't get it!
find the prime factorization of a composite number.			
find the least common multiple (LCM) of two numbers.			

ⓑ *Overall, after looking at the checklist, do you think you are well-prepared for the next Chapter? Why or why not?*

CHAPTER 2 REVIEW

KEY TERMS

coefficient The constant that multiplies the variable(s) in a term is called the coefficient.

composite number A composite number is a counting number that is not prime.

divisibility If a number m is a multiple of n, then we say that m is divisible by n.

equation An equation is made up of two expressions connected by an equal sign.

evaluate To evaluate an algebraic expression means to find the value of the expression when the variable is replaced by a given number.

expressions An expression is a number, a variable, or a combination of numbers and variables and operation symbols.

least common multiple The smallest number that is a multiple of two numbers is called the least common multiple (LCM).

like terms Terms that are either constants or have the same variables with the same exponents are like terms.

multiple of a number A number is a multiple of n if it is the product of a counting number and n.

prime factorization The prime factorization of a number is the product of prime numbers that equals the number.

prime number A prime number is a counting number greater than 1 whose only factors are 1 and itself.

solution of an equation A solution to an equation is a value of a variable that makes a true statement when substituted into the equation. The process of finding the solution to an equation is called solving the equation.

term A term is a constant or the product of a constant and one or more variables.

KEY CONCEPTS

2.1 Use the Language of Algebra

Operation	Notation	Say:	The result is...
Addition	$a + b$	a plus b	the sum of a and b
Multiplication	$a \cdot b$, $(a)(b)$, $(a)b$, $a(b)$	a times b	The product of a and b
Subtraction	$a - b$	a minus b	the difference of a and b
Division	$a \div b$, a/b, $\frac{a}{b}$, $b\overline{)a}$	a divided by b	The quotient of a and b

- **Equality Symbol**
  - $a = b$ is read as a is equal to b
  - The symbol $=$ is called the equal sign.
- **Inequality**
  - $a < b$ is read a is less than b
  - a is to the left of b on the number line

  - $a > b$ is read a is greater than b
  - a is to the right of b on the number line

Algebraic Notation	Say
$a = b$	a is equal to b
$a \neq b$	a is not equal to b
$a < b$	a is less than b
$a > b$	a is greater than b
$a \leq b$	a is less than or equal to b
$a \geq b$	a is greater than or equal to b

Table 2.77

- **Exponential Notation**
  - For any expression a^n is a factor multiplied by itself n times, if n is a positive integer.
  - a^n means multiply n factors of a

$$\text{base} \longrightarrow a^n \longleftarrow \text{exponent}$$

$$a^n = \underbrace{a \cdot a \cdot a \cdot \ldots \cdot a}_{n \text{ factors}}$$

  - The expression of a^n is read a to the nth power.

Order of Operations When simplifying mathematical expressions perform the operations in the following order:
- Parentheses and other Grouping Symbols: Simplify all expressions inside the parentheses or other grouping symbols, working on the innermost parentheses first.
- Exponents: Simplify all expressions with exponents.
- Multiplication and Division: Perform all multiplication and division in order from left to right. These operations have equal priority.
- Addition and Subtraction: Perform all addition and subtraction in order from left to right. These operations have equal priority.

2.2 Evaluate, Simplify, and Translate Expressions

- Combine like terms.
  Step 1. Identify like terms.
  Step 2. Rearrange the expression so like terms are together.
  Step 3. Add the coefficients of the like terms

2.3 Solving Equations Using the Subtraction and Addition Properties of Equality

- Determine whether a number is a solution to an equation.
  Step 1. Substitute the number for the variable in the equation.
  Step 2. Simplify the expressions on both sides of the equation.
  Step 3. Determine whether the resulting equation is true. If it is true, the number is a solution.
  If it is not true, the number is not a solution.
- Subtraction Property of Equality
  - For any numbers a, b, and c,

$$\text{if} \qquad a = b$$

$$\text{then} \qquad a - b = b - c$$

- Solve an equation using the Subtraction Property of Equality.
  Step 1. Use the Subtraction Property of Equality to isolate the variable.
  Step 2. Simplify the expressions on both sides of the equation.
  Step 3. Check the solution.
- Addition Property of Equality
  - For any numbers a, b, and c,

$$\text{if} \qquad a = b$$

$$\text{then} \qquad a + b = b + c$$

- Solve an equation using the Addition Property of Equality.
  Step 1. Use the Addition Property of Equality to isolate the variable.
  Step 2. Simplify the expressions on both sides of the equation.
  Step 3. Check the solution.

2.4 Find Multiples and Factors

Divisibility Tests	
A number is divisible by	
2	if the last digit is **0, 2, 4, 6,** or **8**
3	if the sum of the digits is divisible by **3**
5	if the last digit is **5** or **0**
6	if divisible by both **2** and **3**
10	if the last digit is **0**

- Factors If $a \cdot b = m$, then a and b are factors of m, and m is the product of a and b.
- Find all the factors of a counting number.
  Step 1. Divide the number by each of the counting numbers, in order, until the quotient is smaller than the divisor.
    a. If the quotient is a counting number, the divisor and quotient are a pair of factors.
    b. If the quotient is not a counting number, the divisor is not a factor.
  Step 2. List all the factor pairs.
  Step 3. Write all the factors in order from smallest to largest.
- Determine if a number is prime.
  Step 1. Test each of the primes, in order, to see if it is a factor of the number.
  Step 2. Start with 2 and stop when the quotient is smaller than the divisor or when a prime factor is found.
  Step 3. If the number has a prime factor, then it is a composite number. If it has no prime factors, then the number is prime.

2.5 Prime Factorization and the Least Common Multiple

- Find the prime factorization of a composite number using the tree method.

    Step 1. Find any factor pair of the given number, and use these numbers to create two branches.

    Step 2. If a factor is prime, that branch is complete. Circle the prime.

    Step 3. If a factor is not prime, write it as the product of a factor pair and continue the process.

    Step 4. Write the composite number as the product of all the circled primes.

- Find the prime factorization of a composite number using the ladder method.

    Step 1. Divide the number by the smallest prime.

    Step 2. Continue dividing by that prime until it no longer divides evenly.

    Step 3. Divide by the next prime until it no longer divides evenly.

    Step 4. Continue until the quotient is a prime.

    Step 5. Write the composite number as the product of all the primes on the sides and top of the ladder.

- Find the LCM using the prime factors method.

    Step 1. Find the prime factorization of each number.

    Step 2. Write each number as a product of primes, matching primes vertically when possible.

    Step 3. Bring down the primes in each column.

    Step 4. Multiply the factors to get the LCM.

- Find the LCM using the prime factors method.

    Step 1. Find the prime factorization of each number.

    Step 2. Write each number as a product of primes, matching primes vertically when possible.

    Step 3. Bring down the primes in each column.

    Step 4. Multiply the factors to get the LCM.

REVIEW EXERCISES

2.1 Use the Language of Algebra

Use Variables and Algebraic Symbols

In the following exercises, translate from algebra to English.

317. $3 \cdot 8$

318. $12 - x$

319. $24 \div 6$

320. $9 + 2a$

321. $50 \geq 47$

322. $3y < 15$

323. $n + 4 = 13$

324. $32 - k = 7$

Identify Expressions and Equations

In the following exercises, determine if each is an expression or equation.

325. $5 + u = 84$

326. $36 - 6s$

327. $4y - 11$

328. $10x = 120$

Simplify Expressions with Exponents

In the following exercises, write in exponential form.

329. $2 \cdot 2 \cdot 2$

330. $a \cdot a \cdot a \cdot a \cdot a$

331. $x \cdot x \cdot x \cdot x \cdot x \cdot x$

332. $10 \cdot 10 \cdot 10$

In the following exercises, write in expanded form.

333. 8^4

334. 3^6

335. y^5

336. n^4

In the following exercises, simplify each expression.

337. 3^4

338. 10^6

339. 2^7

340. 4^3

Simplify Expressions Using the Order of Operations

In the following exercises, simplify.

341. $10 + 2 \cdot 5$

342. $(10 + 2) \cdot 5$

343. $(30 + 6) \div 2$

344. $30 + 6 \div 2$

345. $7^2 + 5^2$

346. $(7 + 5)^2$

347. $4 + 3(10 - 1)$

348. $(4 + 3)(10 - 1)$

2.2 Evaluate, Simplify, and Translate Expressions

Evaluate an Expression

In the following exercises, evaluate the following expressions.

349. $9x - 5$ when $x = 7$

350. y^3 when $y = 5$

351. $3a - 4b$ when $a = 10,\ b = 1$

352. bh when $b = 7,\ h = 8$

Identify Terms, Coefficients and Like Terms

In the following exercises, identify the terms in each expression.

353. $12n^2 + 3n + 1$

354. $4x^3 + 11x + 3$

In the following exercises, identify the coefficient of each term.

355. $6y$

356. $13x^2$

In the following exercises, identify the like terms.

357. $5x^2,\ 3,\ 5y^2,\ 3x,\ x,\ 4$

358. $8,\ 8r^2,\ 8r,\ 3r,\ r^2,\ 3s$

Simplify Expressions by Combining Like Terms

In the following exercises, simplify the following expressions by combining like terms.

359. $15a + 9a$

360. $12y + 3y + y$

361. $4x + 7x + 3x$

362. $6 + 5c + 3$

363. $8n + 2 + 4n + 9$

364. $19p + 5 + 4p - 1 + 3p$

365. $7y^2 + 2y + 11 + 3y^2 - 8$

366. $13x^2 - x + 6 + 5x^2 + 9x$

Translate English Phrases to Algebraic Expressions

In the following exercises, translate the following phrases into algebraic expressions.

367. the difference of x and 6

368. the sum of 10 and twice a

369. the product of $3n$ and 9

370. the quotient of s and 4

371. 5 times the sum of y and 1

372. 10 less than the product of 5 and z

373. Jack bought a sandwich and a coffee. The cost of the sandwich was $\$3$ more than the cost of the coffee. Call the cost of the coffee c. Write an expression for the cost of the sandwich.

374. The number of poetry books on Brianna's bookshelf is 5 less than twice the number of novels. Call the number of novels n. Write an expression for the number of poetry books.

2.3 Solve Equations Using the Subtraction and Addition Properties of Equality

Determine Whether a Number is a Solution of an Equation

In the following exercises, determine whether each number is a solution to the equation.

375. $y + 16 = 40$
  ⓐ 24 ⓑ 56

376. $d - 6 = 21$
  ⓐ 15 ⓑ 27

377. $4n + 12 = 36$
  ⓐ 6 ⓑ 12

378. $20q - 10 = 70$
  ⓐ 3 ⓑ 4

379. $15x - 5 = 10x + 45$
  ⓐ 2 ⓑ 10

380. $22p - 6 = 18p + 86$
  ⓐ 4 ⓑ 23

Model the Subtraction Property of Equality

In the following exercises, write the equation modeled by the envelopes and counters and then solve the equation using the subtraction property of equality.

381.

382.

Solve Equations using the Subtraction Property of Equality

In the following exercises, solve each equation using the subtraction property of equality.

383. $c + 8 = 14$

384. $v + 8 = 150$

385. $23 = x + 12$

386. $376 = n + 265$

Solve Equations using the Addition Property of Equality

In the following exercises, solve each equation using the addition property of equality.

387. $y - 7 = 16$

388. $k - 42 = 113$

389. $19 = p - 15$

390. $501 = u - 399$

Translate English Sentences to Algebraic Equations

In the following exercises, translate each English sentence into an algebraic equation.

391. The sum of 7 and 33 is equal to 40.

392. The difference of 15 and 3 is equal to 12.

393. The product of 4 and 8 is equal to 32.

394. The quotient of 63 and 9 is equal to 7.

395. Twice the difference of n and 3 gives 76.

396. The sum of five times y and 4 is 89.

Translate to an Equation and Solve

In the following exercises, translate each English sentence into an algebraic equation and then solve it.

397. Eight more than x is equal to 35.

398. 21 less than a is 11.

399. The difference of q and 18 is 57.

400. The sum of m and 125 is 240.

Mixed Practice

In the following exercises, solve each equation.

401. $h - 15 = 27$

402. $k - 11 = 34$

403. $z + 52 = 85$

404. $x + 93 = 114$

405. $27 = q + 19$

406. $38 = p + 19$

407. $31 = v - 25$

408. $38 = u - 16$

2.4 Find Multiples and Factors

Identify Multiples of Numbers

In the following exercises, list all the multiples less than 50 for each of the following.

409. 3

410. 2

411. 8

412. 10

Use Common Divisibility Tests

In the following exercises, using the divisibility tests, determine whether each number is divisible by 2, by 3, by 5, by 6, and by 10.

413. 96

414. 250

415. 420

416. 625

Find All the Factors of a Number

In the following exercises, find all the factors of each number.

417. 30

418. 70

419. 180

420. 378

Identify Prime and Composite Numbers

In the following exercises, identify each number as prime or composite.

421. 19

422. 51

423. 121

424. 219

2.5 Prime Factorization and the Least Common Multiple

Find the Prime Factorization of a Composite Number

In the following exercises, find the prime factorization of each number.

425. 84   **426.** 165   **427.** 350

428. 572

Find the Least Common Multiple of Two Numbers

In the following exercises, find the least common multiple of each pair of numbers.

429. 9, 15   **430.** 12, 20   **431.** 25, 35

432. 18, 40

Everyday Math

433. Describe how you have used two topics from The Language of Algebra chapter in your life outside of your math class during the past month.

PRACTICE TEST

In the following exercises, translate from an algebraic equation to English phrases.

434. $6 \cdot 4$

435. $15 - x$

In the following exercises, identify each as an expression or equation.

436. $5 \cdot 8 + 10$

437. $x + 6 = 9$

438. $3 \cdot 11 = 33$

439.

ⓐ Write $n \cdot n \cdot n \cdot n \cdot n \cdot n$ in exponential form.

ⓑ Write 3^5 in expanded form and then simplify.

In the following exercises, simplify, using the order of operations.

440. $4 + 3 \cdot 5$

441. $(8 + 1) \cdot 4$

442. $1 + 6(3 - 1)$

443. $(8 + 4) \div 3 + 1$

444. $(1 + 4)^2$

445. $5[2 + 7(9 - 8)]$

In the following exercises, evaluate each expression.

446. $8x - 3$ when $x = 4$

447. y^3 when $y = 5$

448. $6a - 2b$ when $a = 5$, $b = 7$

449. hw when $h = 12$, $w = 3$

450. Simplify by combining like terms.

ⓐ $6x + 8x$

ⓑ $9m + 10 + m + 3$

In the following exercises, translate each phrase into an algebraic expression.

451. 5 more than x

452. the quotient of 12 and y

453. three times the difference of a and b

454. Caroline has 3 fewer earrings on her left ear than on her right ear. Call the number of earrings on her right ear, r. Write an expression for the number of earrings on her left ear.

In the following exercises, solve each equation.

455. $n - 6 = 25$

456. $x + 58 = 71$

In the following exercises, translate each English sentence into an algebraic equation and then solve it.

457. 15 less than y is 32.

458. the sum of a and 129 is 164.

459. List all the multiples of 4, that are less than 50.

460. Find all the factors of 90.

461. Find the prime factorization of 1080.

462. Find the LCM (Least Common Multiple) of 24 and 40.

Figure 3.1 The peak of Mount Everest. (credit: Gunther Hagleitner, Flickr)

Chapter Outline

Introduction

At over 29,000 feet, Mount Everest stands as the tallest peak on land. Located along the border of Nepal and China, Mount Everest is also known for its extreme climate. Near the summit, temperatures never rise above freezing. Every year, climbers from around the world brave the extreme conditions in an effort to scale the tremendous height. Only some are successful. Describing the drastic change in elevation the climbers experience and the change in temperatures requires using numbers that extend both above and below zero. In this chapter, we will describe these kinds of numbers and operations using them.

3.1 Introduction to Integers

Learning Objectives

By the end of this section, you will be able to:

- Locate positive and negative numbers on the number line
- Order positive and negative numbers
- Find opposites
- Simplify expressions with absolute value
- Translate word phrases to expressions with integers

Be Prepared!

Before you get started, take this readiness quiz.

1. Plot 0, 1, and 3 on a number line.
    If you missed this problem, review Example 1.1.

2. Fill in the appropriate symbol: $(=, <, \text{ or } >)$: 2___4
    If you missed this problem, review Example 2.3.

Locate Positive and Negative Numbers on the Number Line

Do you live in a place that has very cold winters? Have you ever experienced a temperature below zero? If so, you are already familiar with negative numbers. A **negative number** is a number that is less than 0. Very cold temperatures are measured in degrees below zero and can be described by negative numbers. For example, $-1°\text{F}$ (read as "negative one degree Fahrenheit") is 1 degree below 0. A minus sign is shown before a number to indicate that it is negative. Figure 3.2 shows $-20°\text{F}$, which is 20 degrees below 0.

Figure 3.2 Temperatures below zero are described by negative numbers.

Temperatures are not the only negative numbers. A bank overdraft is another example of a negative number. If a person writes a check for more than he has in his account, his balance will be negative.

Elevations can also be represented by negative numbers. The elevation at sea level is 0 feet. Elevations above sea level are positive and elevations below sea level are negative. The elevation of the Dead Sea, which borders Israel and Jordan, is about $1{,}302$ feet below sea level, so the elevation of the Dead Sea can be represented as $-1{,}302$ feet. See Figure 3.3.

Figure 3.3 The surface of the Mediterranean Sea has an elevation of 0 ft. The diagram shows that nearby mountains have higher (positive) elevations whereas the Dead Sea has a lower (negative) elevation.

Depths below the ocean surface are also described by negative numbers. A submarine, for example, might descend to a depth of 500 feet. Its position would then be -500 feet as labeled in Figure 3.4.

Figure 3.4 Depths below sea level are described by negative numbers. A submarine 500 ft below sea level is at -500 ft.

Both positive and negative numbers can be represented on a number line. Recall that the number line created in Add Whole Numbers started at 0 and showed the counting numbers increasing to the right as shown in Figure 3.5. The counting numbers $(1, 2, 3, \ldots)$ on the number line are all positive. We could write a plus sign, $+$, before a positive number such as $+2$ or $+3$, but it is customary to omit the plus sign and write only the number. If there is no sign, the number is assumed to be positive.

Figure 3.5

Now we need to extend the number line to include negative numbers. We mark several units to the left of zero, keeping the intervals the same width as those on the positive side. We label the marks with negative numbers, starting with -1 at the first mark to the left of 0, -2 at the next mark, and so on. See Figure 3.6.

Figure 3.6 On a number line, positive numbers are to the right of zero. Negative numbers are to the left of zero. What about zero? Zero is neither positive nor negative.

The arrows at either end of the line indicate that the number line extends forever in each direction. There is no greatest positive number and there is no smallest negative number.

 MANIPULATIVE MATHEMATICS

Doing the Manipulative Mathematics activity "Number Line-part 2" will help you develop a better understanding of integers.

EXAMPLE 3.1

Plot the numbers on a number line:

ⓐ 3 ⓑ -3 ⓒ -2

⊘ **Solution**

Draw a number line. Mark 0 in the center and label several units to the left and right.

ⓐ To plot 3, start at 0 and count three units to the right. Place a point as shown in Figure 3.7.

Figure 3.7

ⓑ To plot -3, start at 0 and count three units to the left. Place a point as shown in Figure 3.8.

Figure 3.8

ⓒ To plot -2, start at 0 and count two units to the left. Place a point as shown in Figure 3.9.

Figure 3.9

> | **TRY IT ::** 3.1   Plot the numbers on a number line.

ⓐ 1   ⓑ −1   ⓒ −4

> | **TRY IT ::** 3.2   Plot the numbers on a number line.

ⓐ −4   ⓑ 4   ⓐ −1

Order Positive and Negative Numbers

We can use the number line to compare and order positive and negative numbers. Going from left to right, numbers increase in value. Going from right to left, numbers decrease in value. See Figure 3.10.

Figure 3.10

Just as we did with positive numbers, we can use inequality symbols to show the ordering of positive and negative numbers. Remember that we use the notation $a < b$ (read a *is less than* b) when a is to the left of b on the number line. We write $a > b$ (read a *is greater than* b) when a is to the right of b on the number line. This is shown for the numbers 3 and 5 in Figure 3.11.

Figure 3.11 The number 3 is to the left of 5 on the number line. So 3 is less than 5, and 5 is greater than 3.

The numbers lines to follow show a few more examples.

ⓐ

4 is to the right of 1 on the number line, so $4 > 1$.

1 is to the left of 4 on the number line, so $1 < 4$.

ⓑ

−2 is to the left of 1 on the number line, so $-2 < 1$.

1 is to the right of −2 on the number line, so $1 > -2$.

ⓒ

−1 is to the right of −3 on the number line, so $-1 > -3$.

−3 is to the left of −1 on the number line, so $-3 < -1$.

EXAMPLE 3.2

Order each of the following pairs of numbers using $<$ or $>$:

    ⓐ $14\_\_6$ ⓑ $-1\_\_9$ ⓒ $-1\_\_-4$ ⓓ $2\_\_-20$

⊘ Solution

Begin by plotting the numbers on a number line as shown in Figure 3.12.

Figure 3.12

ⓐ Compare 14 and 6.

$14\_\_6$

14 is to the right of 6 on the number line.

$14 > 6$

ⓑ Compare −1 and 9.

$-1\_\_9$

−1 is to the left of 9 on the number line.

$-1 < 9$

ⓒ Compare −1 and −4.

$-1\_\_-4$

−1 is to the right of −4 on the number line.

$-1 > -4$

ⓓ Compare 2 and −20.

$-2\_\_-20$

2 is to the right of −20 on the number line.

$2 > -20$

> **TRY IT :: 3.3**   Order each of the following pairs of numbers using $<$ or $>$.
>
>   ⓐ $15\_\_7$ ⓑ $-2\_\_5$ ⓒ $-3\_\_-7$ ⓓ $5\_\_-17$

> **TRY IT :: 3.4**   Order each of the following pairs of numbers using $<$ or $>$.
>
>   ⓐ $8\_\_13$ ⓑ $3\_\_-4$ ⓒ $-5\_\_-2$ ⓓ $9\_\_-21$

Find Opposites

On the number line, the negative numbers are a mirror image of the positive numbers with zero in the middle. Because the numbers 2 and -2 are the same distance from zero, they are called **opposites**. The opposite of 2 is -2, and the opposite of -2 is 2 as shown in Figure 3.13(a). Similarly, 3 and -3 are opposites as shown in Figure 3.13(b).

The numbers –2 and 2 are opposites.

(a)

The numbers –3 and 3 are opposites.

(b)

Figure 3.13

Opposite

The opposite of a number is the number that is the same distance from zero on the number line, but on the opposite side of zero.

EXAMPLE 3.3

Find the opposite of each number:

ⓐ 7   ⓑ -10

⊘ Solution

ⓐ The number -7 is the same distance from 0 as $7,$ but on the opposite side of $0.$ So -7 is the opposite of 7 as shown in Figure 3.14.

Figure 3.14

ⓑ The number 10 is the same distance from 0 as -10, but on the opposite side of $0.$ So 10 is the opposite of -10 as shown in Figure 3.15.

Figure 3.15

> **TRY IT : : 3.5**   Find the opposite of each number:

ⓐ 4   ⓑ -3

> **TRY IT : : 3.6**   Find the opposite of each number:

ⓐ 8   ⓑ -5

Opposite Notation

Just as the same word in English can have different meanings, the same symbol in algebra can have different meanings.

The specific meaning becomes clear by looking at how it is used. You have seen the symbol "−", in three different ways.

$10 - 4$	Between two numbers, the symbol indicates the operation of subtraction. We read $10 - 4$ as 10 *minus* 4.
-8	In front of a number, the symbol indicates a negative number. We read -8 as *negative eight*.
$-x$	In front of a variable or a number, it indicates the opposite. We read $-x$ as *the opposite of* x.
$-(-2)$	Here we have two signs. The sign in the parentheses indicates that the number is negative 2. The sign outside the parentheses indicates the opposite. We read $-(-2)$ as *the opposite of* -2.

Opposite Notation

$-a$ means the opposite of the number a

The notation $-a$ is read *the opposite of* a.

EXAMPLE 3.4

Simplify: $-(-6)$.

⊘ **Solution**

$$-(-6)$$

The opposite of -6 is 6. 6

> **TRY IT :: 3.7**   Simplify:

$$-(-1)$$

> **TRY IT :: 3.8**   Simplify:

$$-(-5)$$

Integers

The set of counting numbers, their opposites, and 0 is the set of integers.

Integers

Integers are counting numbers, their opposites, and zero.

$$\dots -3, -2, -1, 0, 1, 2, 3 \dots$$

We must be very careful with the signs when evaluating the opposite of a variable.

EXAMPLE 3.5

Evaluate $-x$:

ⓐ when $x = 8$ ⓑ when $x = -8$.

⊘ **Solution**

ⓐ To evaluate $-x$ when $x = 8$, substitute 8 for x.

	$-x$
Substitute 8 for x.	$-(8)$
Simplify.	-8

ⓑ To evaluate $-x$ when $x = -8$, substitute -8 for x.

	$-x$
Substitute –8 for x.	$-(-8)$
Simplify.	8

> **TRY IT ::** 3.9   Evaluate $-n$:

ⓐ when $n = 4$ ⓑ when $n = -4$

> **TRY IT ::** 3.10   Evaluate: $-m$:

ⓐ when $m = 11$ ⓑ when $m = -11$

Simplify Expressions with Absolute Value

We saw that numbers such as 5 and -5 are opposites because they are the same distance from 0 on the number line. They are both five units from 0. The distance between 0 and any number on the number line is called the **absolute value** of that number. Because distance is never negative, the absolute value of any number is never negative.

The symbol for absolute value is two vertical lines on either side of a number. So the absolute value of 5 is written as $|5|$, and the absolute value of -5 is written as $|-5|$ as shown in Figure 3.16.

Figure 3.16

Absolute Value

The absolute value of a number is its distance from 0 on the number line.

The absolute value of a number n is written as $|n|$.

$$|n| \geq 0 \text{ for all numbers}$$

EXAMPLE 3.6

Simplify:

ⓐ |3| ⓑ |−44| ⓒ |0|

Solution

ⓐ

|3|

3 is 3 units from zero.   3

ⓑ

|−44|

−44 is 44 units from zero.   44

ⓒ

|0|

0 is already at zero.   0

> **TRY IT : :** 3.11   Simplify:

ⓐ |12| ⓑ − |−28|

> **TRY IT : :** 3.12   Simplify:

ⓐ |9| ⓑ (b) − |37|

We treat absolute value bars just like we treat parentheses in the order of operations. We simplify the expression inside first.

EXAMPLE 3.7

Evaluate:

ⓐ $|x|$ when $x = −35$ ⓑ $|−y|$ when $y = −20$ ⓒ $−|u|$ when $u = 12$ ⓓ $−|p|$ when $p = −14$

Solution

ⓐ To find $|x|$ when $x = −35$:

$|x|$

Substitute −35 for x. $|−35|$

Take the absolute value.   35

ⓑ To find $|-y|$ when $y = -20$:

	$|-y|$
Substitute –20 for *y*.	$|-(-20)|$
Simplify.	$|20|$
Take the absolute value.	20

ⓒ To find $-|u|$ when $u = 12$:

	$-|u|$
Substitute 12 for *u*.	$-|12|$
Take the absolute value.	-12

ⓓ To find $-|p|$ when $p = -14$:

	$-|p|$
Substitute –14 for *p*.	$-|-14|$
Take the absolute value.	-14

Notice that the result is negative only when there is a negative sign outside the absolute value symbol.

> **TRY IT : : 3.13**

Evaluate:

ⓐ $|x|$ when $x = -17$ ⓑ $|-y|$ when $y = -39$ ⓒ $-|m|$ when $m = 22$

ⓓ $-|p|$ when $p = -11$

> **TRY IT : : 3.14**

ⓐ $|y|$ when $y = -23$ ⓑ $|-y|$ when $y = -21$ ⓒ $-|n|$ when $n = 37$

ⓓ $-|q|$ when $q = -49$

EXAMPLE 3.8

Fill in $<$, $>$, or $=$ for each of the following:

ⓐ $|-5|$___ $-|-5|$ ⓑ 8___ $-|-8|$ ⓒ -9___ $-|-9|$ ⓓ $-|-7|$___-7

⊘ **Solution**

To compare two expressions, simplify each one first. Then compare.

ⓐ

$$|-5| \underline{\quad} - |-5|$$

Simplify. $5 \underline{\quad} -5$

Order. $5 > -5$

ⓑ

$$8 \underline{\quad} - |-8|$$

Simplify. $8 \underline{\quad} - 8$

Order. $8 > - 8$

ⓒ

$$-9 \underline{\quad} - |-9|$$

Simplify. $-9 \underline{\quad} - 9$

Order. $-9 = -9$

ⓓ

$$- |-7| \underline{\quad} -7$$

Simplify. $-7 \underline{\quad} - 7$

Order. $-7 = - 7$

> **TRY IT :: 3.15**

Fill in $<$, $>$, or $=$ for each of the following:

ⓐ $|-9| \underline{\quad} - |-9|$ ⓑ $2 \underline{\quad} - |-2|$ ⓒ $-8 \underline{\quad} |-8|$ ⓓ $- |-5| \underline{\quad} -5$

> **TRY IT :: 3.16**

Fill in $<$, $>$, or $=$ for each of the following:

ⓐ $7 \underline{\quad} - |-7|$ ⓑ $- |-11| \underline{\quad} -11$ ⓒ $|-4| \underline{\quad} - |-4|$ ⓓ $-1 \underline{\quad} |-1|$

Absolute value bars act like grouping symbols. First simplify inside the absolute value bars as much as possible. Then take the absolute value of the resulting number, and continue with any operations outside the absolute value symbols.

EXAMPLE 3.9

Simplify:

ⓐ |9−3| ⓑ 4|−2|

✓ **Solution**

For each expression, follow the order of operations. Begin inside the absolute value symbols just as with parentheses.

ⓐ

	|9−3|
Simplify inside the absolute value sign.	|6|
Take the absolute value.	6

ⓑ

	4|−2|
Take the absolute value.	4·2
Multiply.	8

> **TRY IT : : 3.17**   Simplify:

ⓐ |12 − 9| ⓑ 3|−6|

> **TRY IT : : 3.18**   Simplify:

ⓐ |27 − 16| ⓑ 9|−7|

EXAMPLE 3.10

Simplify: |8 + 7| − |5 + 6|.

✓ **Solution**

For each expression, follow the order of operations. Begin inside the absolute value symbols just as with parentheses.

	|8+7|−|5+6|
Simplify inside each absolute value sign.	|15|−|11|
Subtract.	4

> **TRY IT : : 3.19**   Simplify: |1 + 8| − |2 + 5|

> **TRY IT : : 3.20**   Simplify: |9−5| − |7 − 6|

EXAMPLE 3.11

Simplify: 24 − |19 − 3(6 − 2)|.

⊘ Solution

We use the order of operations. Remember to simplify grouping symbols first, so parentheses inside absolute value symbols would be first.

	$24 - |19 - 3(6 - 2)|$
Simplify in the parentheses first.	$24 - |19 - 3(4)|$
Multiply $3(4)$.	$24 - |19 - 12|$
Subtract inside the absolute value sign.	$24 - |7|$
Take the absolute value.	$24 - 7$
Subtract.	17

> **TRY IT : :** 3.21   Simplify: $19 - |11 - 4(3 - 1)|$

> **TRY IT : :** 3.22   Simplify: $9 - |8 - 4(7 - 5)|$

Translate Word Phrases into Expressions with Integers

Now we can translate word phrases into expressions with integers. Look for words that indicate a negative sign. For example, the word *negative* in "negative twenty" indicates -20. So does the word *opposite* in "the opposite of 20."

EXAMPLE 3.12

Translate each phrase into an expression with integers:

ⓐ the opposite of positive fourteen   ⓑ the opposite of -11 ⓒ negative sixteen

ⓓ two minus negative seven

⊘ Solution

ⓐ the opposite of fourteen	ⓑ the opposite of –11	ⓒ negative sixteen	ⓓ two minus negative seven
-14	$-(-11)$	-16	$2 - (-7)$

> **TRY IT : :** 3.23
>
> Translate each phrase into an expression with integers:
>
> ⓐ the opposite of positive nine   ⓑ the opposite of -15 ⓒ negative twenty
>
> ⓓ eleven minus negative four

> **TRY IT : :** 3.24
>
> Translate each phrase into an expression with integers:
>
> ⓐ the opposite of negative nineteen   ⓑ the opposite of twenty-two   ⓒ negative nine
>
> ⓓ negative eight minus negative five

As we saw at the start of this section, negative numbers are needed to describe many real-world situations. We'll look at some more applications of negative numbers in the next example.

EXAMPLE 3.13

Translate into an expression with integers:

    ⓐ The temperature is 12 degrees Fahrenheit below zero.   ⓑ The football team had a gain of 3 yards.

    ⓒ The elevation of the Dead Sea is 1,302 feet below sea level.

    ⓓ A checking account is overdrawn by $40.

⊘ **Solution**

Look for key phrases in each sentence. Then look for words that indicate negative signs. Don't forget to include units of measurement described in the sentence.

ⓐ	The temperature is 12 degrees Fahrenheit below zero.
Below zero tells us that 12 is a negative number.	$-12°F$

ⓑ	The football team had a gain of 3 yards.
A *gain* tells us that 3 is a positive number.	3 yards

ⓒ	The elevation of the Dead Sea is 1,302 feet below sea level.
Below sea level tells us that 1,302 is a negative number.	$-1,302$ feet

ⓓ	A checking account is overdrawn by $40.
Overdrawn tells us that 40 is a negative number.	$-\$40$

> **TRY IT :: 3.25**   Translate into an expression with integers:

        The football team had a gain of 5 yards.

> **TRY IT :: 3.26**   Translate into an expression with integers:

        The scuba diver was 30 feet below the surface of the water.

▶ **MEDIA ::** ACCESS ADDITIONAL ONLINE RESOURCES

- Introduction to Integers (http://openstaxcollege.org/l/24introinteger)
- Simplifying the Opposites of Negative Integers (http://openstaxcollege.org/l/24neginteger)
- Comparing Absolute Value of Integers (http://openstaxcollege.org/l/24abvalue)
- Comparing Integers Using Inequalities (http://openstaxcollege.org/l/24usinginequal)

3.1 EXERCISES

Practice Makes Perfect

Locate Positive and Negative Numbers on the Number Line

In the following exercises, locate and label the given points on a number line.

1.
ⓐ 2   ⓑ −2
ⓒ −5

2.
ⓐ 5   ⓑ −5
ⓒ −2

3.
ⓐ −8   ⓑ 8
ⓒ −6

4.
ⓐ −7   ⓑ 7
ⓒ −1

Order Positive and Negative Numbers on the Number Line

In the following exercises, order each of the following pairs of numbers, using < or >.

5.
ⓐ 9__4   ⓑ −3__6
ⓒ −8__−2   ⓓ 1__−10

6.
ⓐ 6__2;   ⓑ −7__4;
ⓒ −9__−1;   ⓓ 9__−3

7.
ⓐ −5__1;   ⓑ −4__−9;
ⓒ 6__10;   ⓓ 3__−8

8.
ⓐ −7__3;
ⓑ −10__−5;
ⓒ 2__−6;   ⓓ 8__9

Find Opposites

In the following exercises, find the opposite of each number.

9.
ⓐ 2   ⓑ −6

10.
ⓐ 9   ⓑ −4

11.
ⓐ −8   ⓑ 1

12.
ⓐ −2   ⓑ 6

In the following exercises, simplify.

13. $-(-4)$

14. $-(-8)$

15. $-(-15)$

16. $-(-11)$

In the following exercises, evaluate.

17. $-m$ when
ⓐ $m = 3$ ⓑ $m = -3$

18. $-p$ when
ⓐ $p = 6$ ⓑ $p = -6$

19. $-c$ when
ⓐ $c = 12$ ⓑ $c = -12$

20. $-d$ when
ⓐ $d = 21$
ⓑ $d = -21$

Simplify Expressions with Absolute Value

In the following exercises, simplify each absolute value expression.

21.
ⓐ $|7|$ ⓑ $|-25|$
ⓒ $|0|$

22.
ⓐ $|5|$ ⓑ $|20|$
ⓒ $|-19|$

23.
ⓐ $|-32|$ ⓑ $|-18|$
ⓒ $|16|$

24.
ⓐ $|-41|$ ⓑ $|-40|$
ⓒ $|22|$

In the following exercises, evaluate each absolute value expression.

25.
ⓐ $|x|$ when $x = -28$
ⓑ $|-u|$ when $u = -15$

26.
ⓐ $|y|$ when $y = -37$
ⓑ $|-z|$ when $z = -24$

27.
ⓐ $-|p|$ when $p = 19$
ⓑ $-|q|$ when $q = -33$

28.
ⓐ $-|a|$ when $a = 60$
ⓑ $-|b|$ when $b = -12$

In the following exercises, fill in $<$, $>$, or $=$ to compare each expression.

29.
ⓐ $-6 \_\_ |-6|$
ⓑ $-|-3| \_\_ -3$

30.
ⓐ $-8 \_\_ |-8|$
ⓑ $-|-2| \_\_ -2$

31.
ⓐ $|-3| \_\_ -|-3|$
ⓑ $4 \_\_ -|-4|$

32.
ⓐ $|-5| \_\_ -|-5|$
ⓑ $9 \_\_ -|-9|$

In the following exercises, simplify each expression.

33. $|8 - 4|$

34. $|9 - 6|$

35. $8|-7|$

36. $5|-5|$

37. $|15 - 7| - |14 - 6|$

38. $|17 - 8| - |13 - 4|$

39. $18 - |2(8 - 3)|$

40. $15 - |3(8 - 5)|$

41. $8(14 - 2|-2|)$

42. $6(13 - 4|-2|)$

Translate Word Phrases into Expressions with Integers

Translate each phrase into an expression with integers. Do not simplify.

43.
ⓐ the opposite of 8
ⓑ the opposite of -6
ⓒ negative three
ⓓ 4 minus negative 3

44.
ⓐ the opposite of 11
ⓑ the opposite of -4
ⓒ negative nine
ⓓ 8 minus negative 2

45.
ⓐ the opposite of 20
ⓑ the opposite of -5
ⓒ negative twelve
ⓓ 18 minus negative 7

46.
ⓐ the opposite of 15
ⓑ the opposite of -9
ⓒ negative sixty
ⓓ 12 minus 5

47. a temperature of 6 degrees below zero

48. a temperature of 14 degrees below zero

49. an elevation of 40 feet below sea level

50. an elevation of 65 feet below sea level

51. a football play loss of 12 yards

52. a football play gain of 4 yards

53. a stock gain of $\$3$

54. a stock loss of $\$5$

55. a golf score one above par

56. a golf score of 3 below par

Everyday Math

57. Elevation The highest elevation in the United States is Mount McKinley, Alaska, at $20,320$ feet above sea level. The lowest elevation is Death Valley, California, at 282 feet below sea level. Use integers to write the elevation of:
ⓐ Mount McKinley   ⓑ Death Valley

58. Extreme temperatures The highest recorded temperature on Earth is $58°$ Celsius, recorded in the Sahara Desert in 1922. The lowest recorded temperature is $90°$ below $0°$ Celsius, recorded in Antarctica in 1983. Use integers to write the:
ⓐ highest recorded temperature
ⓑ lowest recorded temperature

59. State budgets In June, 2011, the state of Pennsylvania estimated it would have a budget surplus of $\$540$ million. That same month, Texas estimated it would have a budget deficit of $\$27$ billion. Use integers to write the budget:
ⓐ surplus   ⓑ deficit

60. College enrollments Across the United States, community college enrollment grew by $1,400,000$ students from 2007 to 2010. In California, community college enrollment declined by $110,171$ students from 2009 to 2010. Use integers to write the change in enrollment:
ⓐ growth   ⓑ decline

Writing Exercises

61. Give an example of a negative number from your life experience.

62. What are the three uses of the "–" sign in algebra? Explain how they differ.

Self Check

ⓐ After completing the exercises, use this checklist to evaluate your mastery of the objectives of this section.

I can...	Confidently	With some help	No-I don't get it!
locate positive and negative numbers on the number line.			
order positive and negative numbers.			
find opposites.			
simplify expressions with absolute value.			
translate word phrases to expressions with integers.			

ⓑ *If most of your checks were:*

...confidently. Congratulations! You have achieved the objectives in this section. Reflect on the study skills you used so that you can continue to use them. What did you do to become confident of your ability to do these things? Be specific.

...with some help. This must be addressed quickly because topics you do not master become potholes in your road to success. In math, every topic builds upon previous work. It is important to make sure you have a strong foundation before you move on. Who can you ask for help? Your fellow classmates and instructor are good resources. Is there a place on campus where math tutors are available? Can your study skills be improved?

...no—I don't get it! This is a warning sign and you must not ignore it. You should get help right away or you will quickly be overwhelmed. See your instructor as soon as you can to discuss your situation. Together you can come up with a plan to get you the help you need.

3.2 Add Integers

Learning Objectives

By the end of this section, you will be able to:

- Model addition of integers
- Simplify expressions with integers
- Evaluate variable expressions with integers
- Translate word phrases to algebraic expressions
- Add integers in applications

Be Prepared!

Before you get started, take this readiness quiz.

1. Evaluate $x + 8$ when $x = 6$.
   If you missed this problem, review Example 2.13.

2. Simplify: $8 + 2(5 + 1)$.
   If you missed this problem, review Example 2.8.

3. Translate *the sum of 3 and negative 7* into an algebraic expression.
   If you missed this problem, review Table 2.40

Model Addition of Integers

Now that we have located positive and negative numbers on the number line, it is time to discuss arithmetic operations with integers.

Most students are comfortable with the addition and subtraction facts for positive numbers. But doing addition or subtraction with both positive and negative numbers may be more difficult. This difficulty relates to the way the brain learns.

The brain learns best by working with objects in the real world and then generalizing to abstract concepts. Toddlers learn quickly that if they have two cookies and their older brother steals one, they have only one left. This is a concrete example of $2 - 1$. Children learn their basic addition and subtraction facts from experiences in their everyday lives. Eventually, they know the number facts without relying on cookies.

Addition and subtraction of negative numbers have fewer real world examples that are meaningful to us. Math teachers have several different approaches, such as number lines, banking, temperatures, and so on, to make these concepts real.

We will model addition and subtraction of negatives with two color counters. We let a blue counter represent a positive and a red counter will represent a negative.

positive   negative

If we have one positive and one negative counter, the value of the pair is zero. They form a neutral pair. The value of this neutral pair is zero as summarized in Figure 3.17.

1 + (–1) = 0

Figure 3.17 A blue counter represents $+1$. A red counter represents -1. Together they add to zero.

   MANIPULATIVE MATHEMATICS

Doing the Manipulative Mathematics activity "Addition of signed Numbers" will help you develop a better understanding of adding integers.

We will model four addition facts using the numbers 5, -5 and 3, -3.

$$5+3 \quad -5+(-3) \quad -5+3 \quad 5+(-3)$$

EXAMPLE 3.14

Model: $5+3$.

⊘ **Solution**

Interpret the expression.	$5+3$ means the sum of 5 and 3.
Model the first number. Start with 5 positives.	
Model the second number. Add 3 positives.	
Count the total number of counters.	8 positives
The sum of 5 and 3 is 8.	$5+3=8$

> **TRY IT : :** 3.27   Model the expression.

$2+4$

> **TRY IT : :** 3.28   Model the expression.

$2+5$

EXAMPLE 3.15

Model: $-5+(-3)$.

⊘ **Solution**

Interpret the expression.	$-5+(-3)$ means the sum of -5 and -3.
Model the first number. Start with 5 negatives.	
Model the second number. Add 3 negatives.	
Count the total number of counters.	8 negatives
The sum of –5 and –3 is –8.	$-5+-3=-8$

> **TRY IT : :** 3.29   Model the expression.

$-2+(-4)$

> **TRY IT :: 3.30**   Model the expression.

$$-2 + (-5)$$

Example 3.14 and Example 3.15 are very similar. The first example adds 5 positives and 3 positives—both positives. The second example adds 5 negatives and 3 negatives—both negatives. In each case, we got a result of 8—either 8 positives or 8 negatives. When the signs are the same, the counters are all the same color.

Now let's see what happens when the signs are different.

EXAMPLE 3.16

Model: $-5 + 3$.

⊘ **Solution**

Interpret the expression.	$-5 + 3$ means the sum of -5 and 3.
Model the first number. Start with 5 negatives.	
Model the second number. Add 3 positives.	
Remove any neutral pairs.	
Count the result.	2 negatives
The sum of –5 and 3 is –2.	$-5 + 3 = -2$

Notice that there were more negatives than positives, so the result is negative.

> **TRY IT :: 3.31**   Model the expression, and then simplify:
>
> $$2 + (-4)$$

> **TRY IT :: 3.32**   Model the expression, and then simplify:
>
> $$2 + (-5)$$

EXAMPLE 3.17

Model: $5 + (-3)$.

⊘ Solution

Interpret the expression.	$5 + (-3)$ means the sum of 5 and -3.
Model the first number. Start with 5 positives.	
Model the second number. Add 3 negatives.	
Remove any neutral pairs.	
Count the result.	**2 positives**
The sum of 5 and –3 is 2.	$5 + (-3) = 2$

> **TRY IT :: 3.33**   Model the expression, and then simplify:

$(-2) + 4$

> **TRY IT :: 3.34**   Model the expression:

$(-2) + 5$

EXAMPLE 3.18   MODELING ADDITION OF POSITIVE AND NEGATIVE INTEGERS

Model each addition.

ⓐ 4 + 2   ⓑ –3 + 6   ⓒ 4 + (–5)   ⓓ -2 + (–3)

⊘ Solution

ⓐ

	$4 + 2$
Start with 4 positives.	
Add two positives.	
How many do you have?	6 . $4 + 2 = 6$

ⓑ

$$-3 + 6$$

Start with 3 negatives.

Add 6 positives.

Remove neutral pairs.

How many are left?

$$3 \, . \; -3 + 6 = 3$$

ⓒ

$$4 + (-5)$$

Start with 4 positives.

Add 5 negatives.

Remove neutral pairs.

How many are left?

$$-1 \, . \; 4 + (-5) = -1$$

ⓓ

$$-2 + (-3)$$

Start with 2 negatives.

Add 3 negatives.

How many do you have? $$-5 \, . \; -2 + (-3) = -5$$

Chapter 3 Integers

TRY IT :: 3.35

Model each addition.

(a) $3 + 4$ (b) $-1 + 4$ (c) $4 + (-6)$ (d) $-2 + (-2)$

> **TRY IT :: 3.36**

(a) $5 + 1$ (b) $-3 + 7$ (c) $2 + (-8)$ (d) $-3 + (-4)$

Simplify Expressions with Integers

Now that you have modeled adding small positive and negative integers, you can visualize the model in your mind to simplify expressions with any integers.

For example, if you want to add $37 + (-53)$, you don't have to count out 37 blue counters and 53 red counters.

Picture 37 blue counters with 53 red counters lined up underneath. Since there would be more negative counters than positive counters, the sum would be negative. Because $53 - 37 = 16$, there are 16 more negative counters.

$$37 + (-53) = -16$$

Let's try another one. We'll add $-74 + (-27)$. Imagine 74 red counters and 27 more red counters, so we have 101 red counters all together. This means the sum is -101.

$$-74 + (-27) = -101$$

Look again at the results of Example 3.14 - Example 3.17.

$5 + 3$	$-5 + (-3)$
both positive, sum positive	both negative, sum negative
When the signs are the same, the counters would be all the same color, so add them.	
$-5 + 3$	$5 + (-3)$
different signs, more negatives	different signs, more positives
Sum negative	sum positive
When the signs are different, some counters would make neutral pairs; subtract to see how many are left.	

Table 3.35 Addition of Positive and Negative Integers

EXAMPLE 3.19

Simplify:

(a) $19 + (-47)$ (b) $-32 + 40$

Solution

(a) Since the signs are different, we subtract 19 from 47. The answer will be negative because there are more negatives than positives.

$$19 + (-47)$$
$$-28$$

(b) The signs are different so we subtract 32 from 40. The answer will be positive because there are more positives than negatives

$$-32 + 40$$
$$8$$

This OpenStax book is available for free at http://cnx.org/content/col11756/1.9

> **TRY IT :: 3.37**   Simplify each expression:

ⓐ $15 + (-32)$ ⓑ $-19 + 76$

> **TRY IT :: 3.38**   Simplify each expression:

ⓐ $-55 + 9$ ⓑ $43 + (-17)$

EXAMPLE 3.20

Simplify: $-14 + (-36)$.

⊘ **Solution**

Since the signs are the same, we add. The answer will be negative because there are only negatives.

$$-14 + (-36)$$
$$-50$$

> **TRY IT :: 3.39**   Simplify the expression:

$-31 + (-19)$

> **TRY IT :: 3.40**   Simplify the expression:

$-42 + (-28)$

The techniques we have used up to now extend to more complicated expressions. Remember to follow the order of operations.

EXAMPLE 3.21

Simplify: $-5 + 3(-2 + 7)$.

⊘ **Solution**

	$-5 + 3(-2 + 7)$
Simplify inside the parentheses.	$-5 + 3(5)$
Multiply.	$-5 + 15$
Add left to right.	10

> **TRY IT :: 3.41**   Simplify the expression:

$-2 + 5(-4 + 7)$

> **TRY IT :: 3.42**   Simplify the expression:

$-4 + 2(-3 + 5)$

Evaluate Variable Expressions with Integers

Remember that to evaluate an expression means to substitute a number for the variable in the expression. Now we can use negative numbers as well as positive numbers when evaluating expressions.

Chapter 3 Integers

Evaluate $x + 7$ when

ⓐ $x = -2$ ⓑ $x = -11$.

✓ **Solution**

ⓐ Evaluate $x + 7$ when $x = -2$

	$-2 + 7$
Substitute –2 for x.	$-2 + 7$
Simplify.	5

ⓑ Evaluate $x + 7$ when $x = -11$

	$x + 7$
Substitute –11 for x.	$-11 + 7$
Simplify.	-4

> **TRY IT ::** 3.43   Evaluate each expression for the given values:
> $x + 5$ when
> ⓐ $x = -3$ and   ⓑ $x = -17$

> **TRY IT ::** 3.44   Evaluate each expression for the given values: $y + 7$ when
> ⓐ $y = -5$ ⓑ $y = -8$

EXAMPLE 3.23

When $n = -5$, evaluate

ⓐ $n + 1$ ⓑ $-n + 1$.

✓ **Solution**

ⓐ Evaluate $n + 1$ when $n = -5$

	$n + 1$
Substitute –5 for n.	$-5 + 1$
Simplify.	-4

This OpenStax book is available for free at http://cnx.org/content/col11756/1.9

ⓑ Evaluate $-n + 1$ when $n = -5$

$$-n + 1$$

Substitute –5 for *n*. $-(-5) + 1$

Simplify. $5 + 1$

Add.   6

> **TRY IT ::** 3.45   When $n = -8$, evaluate

ⓐ $n + 2$ ⓑ $-n + 2$

> **TRY IT ::** 3.46   When $y = -9$, evaluate

ⓐ $y + 8$ ⓑ $-y + 8$.

Next we'll evaluate an expression with two variables.

EXAMPLE 3.24

Evaluate $3a + b$ when $a = 12$ and $b = -30$.

⊘ **Solution**

$$3a + b$$

Substitute 12 for *a* and –30 for *b*. $3(12) + (-30)$

Multiply. $36 + (-30)$

Add.   6

> **TRY IT ::** 3.47   Evaluate the expression:
> $a + 2b$ when $a = -19$ and $b = 14$.

> **TRY IT ::** 3.48   Evaluate the expression:
> $5p + q$ when $p = 4$ and $q = -7$.

EXAMPLE 3.25

Evaluate $(x + y)^2$ when $x = -18$ and $y = 24$.

⊘ **Solution**

This expression has two variables. Substitute -18 for x and 24 for y.

$$(x+y)^2$$

Substitute –18 for x and 24 for y.	$(-18+24)^2$
Add inside the parentheses.	$(6)^2$
Simplify	36

> **TRY IT : : 3.49**   Evaluate:
> $(x+y)^2$ when $x=-15$ and $y=29$.

> **TRY IT : : 3.50**   Evaluate:
> $(x+y)^3$ when $x=-8$ and $y=10$.

Translate Word Phrases to Algebraic Expressions

All our earlier work translating word phrases to algebra also applies to expressions that include both positive and negative numbers. Remember that the phrase *the sum* indicates addition.

EXAMPLE 3.26

Translate and simplify: the sum of -9 and 5.

⊘ **Solution**

The sum of –9 and 5 indicates addition.	the sum of -9 and 5
Translate.	$-9+5$
Simplify.	-4

> **TRY IT : : 3.51**   Translate and simplify the expression:
> the sum of -7 and 4

> **TRY IT : : 3.52**   Translate and simplify the expression:
> the sum of -8 and -6

EXAMPLE 3.27

Translate and simplify: the sum of 8 and -12, increased by 3.

⊘ **Solution**

The phrase *increased by* indicates addition.

The sum of 8 and -12, increased by 3

Translate.	$[8 + (-12)] + 3$
Simplify.	$-4 + 3$
Add.	-1

> **TRY IT : :** 3.53

Translate and simplify:

the sum of 9 and -16, increased by 4.

> **TRY IT : :** 3.54

Translate and simplify:

the sum of -8 and -12, increased by 7.

Add Integers in Applications

Recall that we were introduced to some situations in everyday life that use positive and negative numbers, such as temperatures, banking, and sports. For example, a debt of $5 could be represented as $-$5$. Let's practice translating and solving a few applications.

Solving applications is easy if we have a plan. First, we determine what we are looking for. Then we write a phrase that gives the information to find it. We translate the phrase into math notation and then simplify to get the answer. Finally, we write a sentence to answer the question.

EXAMPLE 3.28

The temperature in Buffalo, NY, one morning started at $7\,\text{degrees}$ below zero Fahrenheit. By noon, it had warmed up $12\,\text{degrees}$. What was the temperature at noon?

Solution

We are asked to find the temperature at noon.

Write a phrase for the temperature.	The temperature warmed up 12 degrees from 7 degrees below zero.
Translate to math notation.	$-7 + 12$
Simplify.	5
Write a sentence to answer the question.	The temperature at noon was 5 degrees Fahrenheit.

> **TRY IT : :** 3.55

The temperature in Chicago at 5 A.M. was $10\,\text{degrees}$ below zero Celsius. Six hours later, it had warmed up $14\,\text{degrees Celsius}$. What is the temperature at 11 A.M.?

> **TRY IT : :** 3.56

A scuba diver was swimming $16\,\text{feet}$ below the surface and then dove down another $17\,\text{feet}$. What is her new depth?

EXAMPLE 3.29

A football team took possession of the football on their 42-yard line. In the next three plays, they lost 6 yards, gained 4 yards, and then lost 8 yards. On what yard line was the ball at the end of those three plays?

⊘ **Solution**

We are asked to find the yard line the ball was on at the end of three plays.

Write a word phrase for the position of the ball.	Start at 42, then lose 6, gain 4, lose 8.
Translate to math notation.	42 − 6 + 4 − 8
Simplify.	32
Write a sentence to answer the question.	At the end of the three plays, the ball is on the 32-yard line.

> **TRY IT ∷** 3.57

The Bears took possession of the football on their 20-yard line. In the next three plays, they lost 9 yards, gained 7 yards, then lost 4 yards. On what yard line was the ball at the end of those three plays?

> **TRY IT ∷** 3.58

The Chargers began with the football on their 25-yard line. They gained 5 yards, lost 8 yards and then gained 15 yards on the next three plays. Where was the ball at the end of these plays?

▶ **MEDIA ∷** ACCESS ADDITIONAL ONLINE RESOURCES

- Adding Integers with Same Sign Using Color Counters (http://openstaxcollege.org/l/24samesigncount)
- Adding Integers with Different Signs Using Counters (http://openstaxcollege.org/l/24diffsigncount)
- Ex1: Adding Integers (http://openstaxcollege.org/l/24Ex1Add)
- Ex2: Adding Integers (http://openstaxcollege.org/l/24Ex2Add)

3.2 EXERCISES

Practice Makes Perfect

Model Addition of Integers

In the following exercises, model the expression to simplify.

63. $7 + 4$

64. $8 + 5$

65. $-6 + (-3)$

66. $-5 + (-5)$

67. $-7 + 5$

68. $-9 + 6$

69. $8 + (-7)$

70. $9 + (-4)$

Simplify Expressions with Integers

In the following exercises, simplify each expression.

71. $-21 + (-59)$

72. $-35 + (-47)$

73. $48 + (-16)$

74. $34 + (-19)$

75. $-200 + 65$

76. $-150 + 45$

77. $2 + (-8) + 6$

78. $4 + (-9) + 7$

79. $-14 + (-12) + 4$

80. $-17 + (-18) + 6$

81. $135 + (-110) + 83$

82. $140 + (-75) + 67$

83. $-32 + 24 + (-6) + 10$

84. $-38 + 27 + (-8) + 12$

85. $19 + 2(-3 + 8)$

86. $24 + 3(-5 + 9)$

Evaluate Variable Expressions with Integers

In the following exercises, evaluate each expression.

87. $x + 8$ when
ⓐ $x = -26$ ⓑ $x = -95$

88. $y + 9$ when
ⓐ $y = -29$ ⓑ $y = -84$

89. $y + (-14)$ when
ⓐ $y = -33$ ⓑ $y = 30$

90. $x + (-21)$ when
ⓐ $x = -27$ ⓑ $x = 44$

91. When $a = -7$, evaluate:
ⓐ $a + 3$ ⓑ $-a + 3$

92. When $b = -11$, evaluate:
ⓐ $b + 6$ ⓑ $-b + 6$

93. When $c = -9$, evaluate:
ⓐ $c + (-4)$
ⓑ $-c + (-4)$

94. When $d = -8$, evaluate:
ⓐ $d + (-9)$
ⓑ $-d + (-9)$

95. $m + n$ when, $m = -15$, $n = 7$

96. $p + q$ when, $p = -9$, $q = 17$

97. $r - 3s$ when, $r = 16$, $s = 2$

98. $2t + u$ when, $t = -6$, $u = -5$

99. $(a + b)^2$ when, $a = -7$, $b = 15$

100. $(c + d)^2$ when, $c = -5$, $d = 14$

101. $(x + y)^2$ when, $x = -3$, $y = 14$

102. $(y + z)^2$ when, $y = -3$, $z = 15$

Translate Word Phrases to Algebraic Expressions

In the following exercises, translate each phrase into an algebraic expression and then simplify.

103. The sum of -14 and 5

104. The sum of -22 and 9

105. 8 more than -2

106. 5 more than -1

107. -10 added to -15

108. -6 added to -20

109. 6 more than the sum of -1 and -12

110. 3 more than the sum of -2 and -8

111. the sum of 10 and -19, increased by 4

112. the sum of 12 and -15, increased by 1

Add Integers in Applications

In the following exercises, solve.

113. **Temperature** The temperature in St. Paul, Minnesota was $-19°F$ at sunrise. By noon the temperature had risen $26°F$. What was the temperature at noon?

114. **Temperature** The temperature in Chicago was $-15°F$ at 6 am. By afternoon the temperature had risen $28°F$. What was the afternoon temperature?

115. Credit Cards Lupe owes $73 on her credit card. Then she charges $45 more. What is the new balance?

116. Credit Cards Frank owes $212 on his credit card. Then he charges $105 more. What is the new balance?

117. Weight Loss Angie lost 3 pounds the first week of her diet. Over the next three weeks, she lost 2 pounds, gained 1 pound, and then lost 4 pounds. What was the change in her weight over the four weeks?

118. Weight Loss April lost 5 pounds the first week of her diet. Over the next three weeks, she lost 3 pounds, gained 2 pounds, and then lost 1 pound. What was the change in her weight over the four weeks?

119. Football The Rams took possession of the football on their own 35-yard line. In the next three plays, they lost 12 yards, gained 8 yards, then lost 6 yards. On what yard line was the ball at the end of those three plays?

120. Football The Cowboys began with the ball on their own 20-yard line. They gained 15 yards, lost 3 yards and then gained 6 yards on the next three plays. Where was the ball at the end of these plays?

121. Calories Lisbeth walked from her house to get a frozen yogurt, and then she walked home. By walking for a total of 20 minutes, she burned 90 calories. The frozen yogurt she ate was 110 calories. What was her total calorie gain or loss?

122. Calories Ozzie rode his bike for 30 minutes, burning 168 calories. Then he had a 140-calorie iced blended mocha. Represent the change in calories as an integer.

Everyday Math

123. Stock Market The week of September 15, 2008, was one of the most volatile weeks ever for the U.S. stock market. The change in the Dow Jones Industrial Average each day was:

Monday -504 Tuesday $+142$ Wednesday -449
Thursday $+410$ Friday $+369$

What was the overall change for the week?

124. Stock Market During the week of June 22, 2009, the change in the Dow Jones Industrial Average each day was:

Monday -201 Tuesday -16 Wednesday -23
Thursday $+172$ Friday -34

What was the overall change for the week?

Writing Exercises

125. Explain why the sum of -8 and 2 is negative, but the sum of 8 and -2 and is positive.

126. Give an example from your life experience of adding two negative numbers.

Self Check

ⓐ After completing the exercises, use this checklist to evaluate your mastery of the objectives of this section.

I can...	Confidently	With some help	No-I don't get it!
model addition of integers.			
simplify expressions with integers.			
evaluate variable expressions with integers.			
translate word phrases to algebraic expressions.			
add integers in applications.			

ⓑ After reviewing this checklist, what will you do to become confident for all objectives?

3.3   Subtract Integers

Learning Objectives

By the end of this section, you will be able to:

- Model subtraction of integers
- Simplify expressions with integers
- Evaluate variable expressions with integers
- Translate words phrases to algebraic expressions
- Subtract integers in applications

Be Prepared!

Before you get started, take this readiness quiz.

1. Simplify: $12 - (8-1)$.
   If you missed this problem, review Example 2.8.

2. Translate *the difference of 20 and* -15 into an algebraic expression.
   If you missed this problem, review Example 1.36.

3. Add: $-18 + 7$.
   If you missed this problem, review Example 3.20.

Model Subtraction of Integers

Remember the story in the last section about the toddler and the cookies? Children learn how to subtract numbers through their everyday experiences. Real-life experiences serve as models for subtracting positive numbers, and in some cases, such as temperature, for adding negative as well as positive numbers. But it is difficult to relate subtracting negative numbers to common life experiences. Most people do not have an intuitive understanding of subtraction when negative numbers are involved. Math teachers use several different models to explain subtracting negative numbers.

We will continue to use counters to model subtraction. Remember, the blue counters represent positive numbers and the red counters represent negative numbers.

Perhaps when you were younger, you read $5 - 3$ as *five take away three*. When we use counters, we can think of subtraction the same way.

MANIPULATIVE MATHEMATICS

Doing the Manipulative Mathematics activity "Subtraction of Signed Numbers" will help you develop a better understanding of subtracting integers.

We will model four subtraction facts using the numbers 5 and 3.

$$5 - 3 \quad -5 - (-3) \quad -5 - 3 \quad 5 - (-3)$$

EXAMPLE 3.30

Model: $5 - 3$.

⊘ **Solution**

Interpret the expression. $5 - 3$ means 5 take away 3.

Model the first number. Start with 5 positives.

Take away the second number. So take away 3 positives.

Find the counters that are left.

$5 - 3 = 2$.
The difference between 5 and 3 is 2.

> **TRY IT : : 3.59**   Model the expression:
> $6 - 4$

> **TRY IT : : 3.60**   Model the expression:
> $7 - 4$

EXAMPLE 3.31

Model: $-5 - (-3)$.

⊘ **Solution**

Interpret the expression. $-5 - (-3)$ means -5 take away -3.

Model the first number. Start with 5 negatives.

Take away the second number. So take away 3 negatives.

Find the number of counters that are left.

$-5 - (-3) = -2$.
The difference between -5 and -3 is -2.

> **TRY IT : : 3.61**   Model the expression:
> $-6 - (-4)$

> **TRY IT : : 3.62**   Model the expression:
> $-7 - (-4)$

Notice that Example 3.30 and Example 3.31 are very much alike.

- First, we subtracted 3 positives from 5 positives to get 2 positives.

- Then we subtracted 3 negatives from 5 negatives to get 2 negatives.

Each example used counters of only one color, and the "take away" model of subtraction was easy to apply.

Now let's see what happens when we subtract one positive and one negative number. We will need to use both positive and negative counters and sometimes some neutral pairs, too. Adding a neutral pair does not change the value.

EXAMPLE 3.32

Model: $-5 - 3$.

⊘ **Solution**

Interpret the expression.	$-5 - 3$ means -5 take away 3.
Model the first number. Start with 5 negatives.	
Take away the second number. So we need to take away 3 positives.	
But there are no positives to take away. Add neutral pairs until you have 3 positives.	
Now take away 3 positives.	
Count the number of counters that are left.	8 negatives

$-5 - 3 = -8$.
The difference of -5 and 3 is -8.

> **TRY IT : : 3.63**   Model the expression:

$-6 - 4$

> **TRY IT : : 3.64**   Model the expression:

$-7 - 4$

EXAMPLE 3.33

Model: $5 - (-3)$.

⊘ Solution

Interpret the expression.

$5 - (-3)$ means 5 take away -3.

Model the first number. Start with 5 positives.

Take away the second number, so take away 3 negatives.

But there are no negatives to take away.
Add neutral pairs until you have 3 negatives.

Then take away 3 negatives.

Count the number of counters that are left.

8 positives

The difference of 5 and -3 is 8.
$5 - (-3) = 8$

> **TRY IT : :** 3.65   Model the expression:
> $6 - (-4)$

> **TRY IT : :** 3.66   Model the expression:
> $7 - (-4)$

EXAMPLE 3.34

Model each subtraction.

ⓐ $8 - 2$ ⓑ $-5 - 4$ ⓒ $6 - (-6)$ ⓓ $-8 - (-3)$

⊘ Solution

ⓐ

$8 - 2$
This means 8 take away 2.

Start with 8 positives.

Take away 2 positives.

How many are left?   6

$8 - 2 = 6$

ⓑ

$$-5 - 4$$
This means -5 take away 4.

Start with 5 negatives.

You need to take away 4 positives.
Add 4 neutral pairs to get 4 positives.

Take away 4 positives.

How many are left?

$$-9$$

$$-5 - 4 = -9$$

ⓒ

$$6 - (-6)$$
This means 6 take away -6.

Start with 6 positives.

Add 6 neutrals to get 6 negatives to take away.

Remove 6 negatives.

How many are left?

$$12$$

$$6 - (-6) = 12$$

ⓓ

$$-8 - (-3)$$
This means -8 take away -3.

Start with 8 negatives.

Take away 3 negatives.

How many are left?

$$-5$$
$$-8 - (-3) = -5$$

> **TRY IT : :** 3.67   Model each subtraction.

ⓐ 7 - (-8)   ⓑ -2 - (-2)   ⓒ 4 - 1   ⓓ -6 - 8

> **TRY IT : :** 3.68   Model each subtraction.

ⓐ 4 - (-6)   ⓑ -8 - (-1)   ⓒ 7 - 3   ⓓ -4 - 2

EXAMPLE 3.35

Model each subtraction expression:

ⓐ $2 - 8$ ⓑ $-3 - (-8)$

✓ **Solution**

ⓐ

We start with 2 positives.

We need to take away 8 positives, but we have only 2.

Add neutral pairs until there are 8 positives to take away.

Then take away eight positives.

Find the number of counters that are left.
There are 6 negatives.

6 negatives

$$2 - 8 = -6$$

ⓑ

We start with 3 negatives.

3

We need to take away 8 negatives, but we have only 3.

Add neutral pairs until there are 8 negatives to take away.

Then take away the 8 negatives.

Find the number of counters that are left.
There are 5 positives.

5 positives

$$-3 - (-8) = 5$$

> **TRY IT : :** 3.69   Model each subtraction expression.

ⓐ $7 - 9$ ⓑ $-5 - -9)$

> **TRY IT : :** 3.70   Model each subtraction expression.

ⓐ $4 - 7$ ⓑ $-7 - (-10)$

Simplify Expressions with Integers

Do you see a pattern? Are you ready to subtract integers without counters? Let's do two more subtractions. We'll think about how we would model these with counters, but we won't actually use the counters.

- Subtract $-23 - 7$.
  Think: We start with 23 negative counters.
  We have to subtract 7 positives, but there are no positives to take away.
  So we add 7 neutral pairs to get the 7 positives. Now we take away the 7 positives.
  So what's left? We have the original 23 negatives plus 7 more negatives from the neutral pair. The result is 30 negatives.

$$-23 - 7 = -30$$

  Notice, that to subtract 7, we added 7 negatives.

- Subtract $30 - (-12)$.
  Think: We start with 30 positives.
  We have to subtract 12 negatives, but there are no negatives to take away.
  So we add 12 neutral pairs to the 30 positives. Now we take away the 12 negatives.
  What's left? We have the original 30 positives plus 12 more positives from the neutral pairs. The result is 42 positives.

$$30 - (-12) = 42$$

  Notice that to subtract -12, we added 12.

While we may not always use the counters, especially when we work with large numbers, practicing with them first gave us a concrete way to apply the concept, so that we can visualize and remember how to do the subtraction without the counters.

Have you noticed that subtraction of signed numbers can be done by adding the opposite? You will often see the idea, the Subtraction Property, written as follows:

Subtraction Property

$$a - b = a + (-b)$$

Look at these two examples.

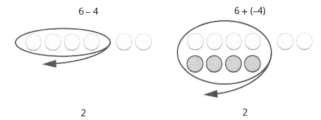

We see that $6 - 4$ gives the same answer as $6 + (-4)$.

Of course, when we have a subtraction problem that has only positive numbers, like the first example, we just do the subtraction. We already knew how to subtract $6 - 4$ long ago. But knowing that $6 - 4$ gives the same answer as $6 + (-4)$ helps when we are subtracting negative numbers.

EXAMPLE 3.36

Simplify:

      ⓐ $13 - 8$ and $13 + (-8)$ ⓑ $-17 - 9$ and $-17 + (-9)$

⊘ **Solution**

ⓐ

$$13 - 8 \text{ and } 13 + (-8)$$

Subtract to simplify. $13 - 8 = 5$

Add to simplify. $13 + (-8) = 5$

Subtracting 8 from 13 is the same as adding –8 to 13.

ⓑ

$$-17 - 9 \text{ and } -17 + (-9)$$

Subtract to simplify. $-17 - 9 = -26$

Add to simplify. $-17 + (-9) = -26$

Subtracting 9 from –17 is the same as adding –9 to –17.

> **TRY IT : :** 3.71   Simplify each expression:

          ⓐ $21 - 13$ and $21 + (-13)$ ⓑ $-11 - 7$ and $-11 + (-7)$

> **TRY IT ::** 3.72   Simplify each expression:

ⓐ $15 - 7$ and $15 + (-7)$ ⓑ $-14 - 8$ and $-14 + (-8)$

Now look what happens when we subtract a negative.

We see that $8 - (-5)$ gives the same result as $8 + 5.$ Subtracting a negative number is like adding a positive.

EXAMPLE 3.37

Simplify:

ⓐ $9 - (-15)$ and $9 + 15$ ⓑ $-7 - (-4)$ and $-7 + 4$

✓ **Solution**

ⓐ

	$9 - (-15)$ and $9 + 15$
Subtract to simplify.	$9 - (-15) = -24$
Add to simplify.	$9 + 15 = 24$
Subtracting –15 from 9 is the same as adding 15 to 9.	

ⓑ

	$-7 - (-4)$ and $-7 + 4$
Subtract to simplify.	$-7 - (-4) = -3$
Add to simplify.	$-7 + 4 = -3$
Subtracting –4 from –7 is the same as adding 4 to –7	

> **TRY IT ::** 3.73   Simplify each expression:

ⓐ $6 - (-13)$ and $6 + 13$ ⓑ $-5 - (-1)$ and $-5 + 1$

> **TRY IT ::** 3.74   Simplify each expression:

ⓐ $4 - (-19)$ and $4 + 19$ ⓐ $-4 - (-7)$ and $-4 + 7$

Look again at the results of Example 3.30 - Example 3.33.

5 – 3	–5 – (–3)
2	–2
2 positives	2 negatives

When there would be enough counters of the color to take away, subtract.

–5 – 3	5 – (–3)
–8	8
5 negatives, want to subtract 3 positives need neutral pairs	5 positives, want to subtract 3 negatives need neutral pairs

When there would not be enough of the counters to take away, add neutral pairs.

Table 3.61 Subtraction of Integers

EXAMPLE 3.38

Simplify: $-74 - (-58)$.

Solution

| We are taking 58 negatives away from 74 negatives. | $-74 - (-58)$ |
| Subtract. | -16 |

> **TRY IT : : 3.75**   Simplify the expression:
> $-67 - (-38)$

> **TRY IT : : 3.76**   Simplify the expression:
> $-83 - (-57)$

EXAMPLE 3.39

Simplify: $7 - (-4 - 3) - 9$.

Solution

We use the order of operations to simplify this expression, performing operations inside the parentheses first. Then we subtract from left to right.

Simplify inside the parentheses first.	$7 - (-4 - 3) - 9$
Subtract from left to right.	$7 - (-7) - 9$
Subtract.	$14 - 9$
	5

> **TRY IT : : 3.77**   Simplify the expression:

$$8 - (-3 - 1) - 9$$

> **TRY IT : : 3.78**   Simplify the expression:

$$12 - (-9 - 6) - 14$$

EXAMPLE 3.40

Simplify: $3 \cdot 7 - 4 \cdot 7 - 5 \cdot 8$.

⊘ **Solution**

We use the order of operations to simplify this expression. First we multiply, and then subtract from left to right.

Multiply first.	$3 \cdot 7 - 4 \cdot 7 - 5 \cdot 8$
Subtract from left to right.	$21 - 28 - 40$
Subtract.	$-7 - 40$
	-47

> **TRY IT : : 3.79**   Simplify the expression:

$$6 \cdot 2 - 9 \cdot 1 - 8 \cdot 9.$$

> **TRY IT : : 3.80**   Simplify the expression:

$$2 \cdot 5 - 3 \cdot 7 - 4 \cdot 9$$

Evaluate Variable Expressions with Integers

Now we'll practice evaluating expressions that involve subtracting negative numbers as well as positive numbers.

EXAMPLE 3.41

Evaluate $x - 4$ when

    ⓐ $x = 3$ ⓑ $x = -6$.

⊘ **Solution**

ⓐ To evaluate $x - 4$ when $x = 3$, substitute 3 for x in the expression.

	$x - 4$
Substitute 3 for x.	$3 - 4$
Subtract.	-1

ⓑ To evaluate $x - 4$ when $x = -6$, substitute -6 for x in the expression.

	$x - 4$
Substitute −6 for x.	$-6 - 4$
Subtract.	-10

> **TRY IT : :** 3.81

Evaluate each expression:

$y - 7$ when

ⓐ $y = 5$ ⓑ $y = -8$

> **TRY IT : :** 3.82

Evaluate each expression:

$m - 3$ when

ⓐ $m = 1$ ⓑ $m = -4$

EXAMPLE 3.42

Evaluate $20 - z$ when

ⓐ $z = 12$ ⓑ $z = -12$

⊘ **Solution**

ⓐ To evaluate $20 - z$ when $z = 12$, substitute 12 for z in the expression.

$$20 - z$$

| Substitute 12 for z. | $20 - 12$ |
| Subtract. | 8 |

ⓑ To evaluate $20 - z$ when $z = -12$, substitute -12 for z in the expression.

$$20 - z$$

| Substitute −12 for z. | $20 - (-12)$ |
| Subtract. | 32 |

> **TRY IT : :** 3.83

Evaluate each expression:

$17 - k$ when

ⓐ $k = 19$ ⓑ $k = -19$

> **TRY IT : :** 3.84

Evaluate each expression:

$-5 - b$ when

ⓐ $b = 14$ ⓑ $b = -14$

Translate Word Phrases to Algebraic Expressions

When we first introduced the operation symbols, we saw that the expression $a - b$ may be read in several ways as shown below.

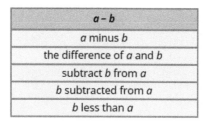

Figure 3.18

Be careful to get a and b in the right order!

EXAMPLE 3.43

Translate and then simplify:

ⓐ the difference of 13 and -21

ⓑ subtract 24 from -19

⊘ Solution

ⓐ A *difference* means subtraction. Subtract the numbers in the order they are given.

the difference of 13 and -21

Translate.	$13 - (-21)$
Simplify.	34

ⓑ *Subtract* means to take 24 away from -19.

subtract 24 from -19

Translate.	$-19 - 24$
Simplify.	-43

> **TRY IT : : 3.85** Translate and simplify:

ⓐ the difference of 14 and -23 ⓑ subtract 21 from -17

> **TRY IT : : 3.86** Translate and simplify:

ⓐ the difference of 11 and -19 ⓑ subtract 18 from -11

Subtract Integers in Applications

It's hard to find something if we don't know what we're looking for or what to call it. So when we solve an application problem, we first need to determine what we are asked to find. Then we can write a phrase that gives the information to find it. We'll translate the phrase into an expression and then simplify the expression to get the answer. Finally, we summarize the answer in a sentence to make sure it makes sense.

HOW TO :: SOLVE APPLICATION PROBLEMS.

Step 1.   Identify what you are asked to find.

Step 2.   Write a phrase that gives the information to find it.

Step 3.   Translate the phrase to an expression.

Step 4.   Simplify the expression.

Step 5.   Answer the question with a complete sentence.

EXAMPLE 3.44

The temperature in Urbana, Illinois one morning was 11 degrees Fahrenheit. By mid-afternoon, the temperature had dropped to -9 degrees Fahrenheit. What was the difference between the morning and afternoon temperatures?

⊘ Solution

Step 1. Identify what we are asked to find.	the difference between the morning and afternoon temperatures
Step 2. Write a phrase that gives the information to find it.	the difference of 11 and -9
Step 3. Translate the phrase to an expression. The word *difference* indicates subtraction.	$11 - (-9)$
Step 4. Simplify the expression.	20
Step 5. Write a complete sentence that answers the question.	The difference in temperature was 20 degrees Fahrenheit.

> **TRY IT :: 3.87**
>
> The temperature in Anchorage, Alaska one morning was 15 degrees Fahrenheit. By mid-afternoon the temperature had dropped to 30 degrees below zero. What was the difference between the morning and afternoon temperatures?

> **TRY IT :: 3.88**
>
> The temperature in Denver was -6 degrees Fahrenheit at lunchtime. By sunset the temperature had dropped to -15 degree Fahrenheit. What was the difference between the lunchtime and sunset temperatures?

Geography provides another application of negative numbers with the elevations of places below sea level.

EXAMPLE 3.45

Dinesh hiked from Mt. Whitney, the highest point in California, to Death Valley, the lowest point. The elevation of Mt. Whitney is $14,497$ feet above sea level and the elevation of Death Valley is 282 feet below sea level. What is the difference in elevation between Mt. Whitney and Death Valley?

✓ Solution

Step 1. What are we asked to find?	The difference in elevation between Mt. Whitney and Death Valley
Step 2. Write a phrase.	elevation of Mt. Whitney–elevation of Death Valley
Step 3. Translate.	$14{,}497 - (-282)$
Step 4. Simplify.	$14{,}779$
Step 5. Write a complete sentence that answers the question.	The difference in elevation is $14{,}779$ feet.

> **TRY IT ::** 3.89
>
> One day, John hiked to the $10{,}023$ foot summit of Haleakala volcano in Hawaii. The next day, while scuba diving, he dove to a cave 80 feet below sea level. What is the difference between the elevation of the summit of Haleakala and the depth of the cave?

> **TRY IT ::** 3.90
>
> The submarine Nautilus is at 340 feet below the surface of the water and the submarine Explorer is 573 feet below the surface of the water. What is the difference in the position of the Nautilus and the Explorer?

Managing your money can involve both positive and negative numbers. You might have overdraft protection on your checking account. This means the bank lets you write checks for more money than you have in your account (as long as they know they can get it back from you!)

EXAMPLE 3.46

Leslie has $25 in her checking account and she writes a check for $8.

    ⓐ What is the balance after she writes the check?

    ⓑ She writes a second check for $20. What is the new balance after this check?

    ⓒ Leslie's friend told her that she had lost a check for $10 that Leslie had given her with her birthday card. What is the balance in Leslie's checking account now?

✓ Solution

ⓐ

What are we asked to find?	The balance of the account
Write a phrase.	$25 minus $8
Translate	$25 – $8
Simplify.	$17
Write a sentence answer.	The balance is $ 17 .

ⓑ

What are we asked to find?	The new balance
Write a phrase.	$17 minus $20
Translate	$17 − $20
Simplify.	−$3
Write a sentence answer.	She is overdrawn by $3.

ⓒ

What are we asked to find?	The new balance
Write a phrase.	$10 more than −$3
Translate	−$3 + $10
Simplify.	$7
Write a sentence answer.	The balance is now $7.

> **TRY IT :: 3.91**

Araceli has $75 in her checking account and writes a check for $27.

ⓐ What is the balance after she writes the check?

ⓑ She writes a second check for $50. What is the new balance?

ⓒ The check for $20 that she sent a charity was never cashed. What is the balance in Araceli's checking account now?

> **TRY IT :: 3.92**

Genevieve's bank account was overdrawn and the balance is −$78.

ⓐ She deposits a check for $24 that she earned babysitting. What is the new balance?

ⓑ She deposits another check for $49. Is she out of debt yet? What is her new balance?

LINKS TO LITERACY

The Links to Literacy activity "Elevator Magic" will provide you with another view of the topics covered in this section.

▶ **MEDIA :** : ACCESS ADDITIONAL ONLINE RESOURCES

- Adding and Subtracting Integers (http://openstaxcollege.org/l/24AddSubtrInteg)
- Subtracting Integers with Color Counters (http://openstaxcollege.org/l/24Subtrinteger)
- Subtracting Integers Basics (http://openstaxcollege.org/l/24Subtractbasic)
- Subtracting Integers (http://openstaxcollege.org/l/24introintegerr)
- Integer Application (http://openstaxcollege.org/l/24integerappp)

3.3 EXERCISES

Practice Makes Perfect

Model Subtraction of Integers

In the following exercises, model each expression and simplify.

127. $8 - 2$

128. $9 - 3$

129. $-5 - (-1)$

130. $-6 - (-4)$

131. $-5 - 4$

132. $-7 - 2$

133. $8 - (-4)$

134. $7 - (-3)$

Simplify Expressions with Integers

In the following exercises, simplify each expression.

135.
ⓐ $15 - 6$
ⓑ $15 + (-6)$

136.
ⓐ $12 - 9$
ⓑ $12 + (-9)$

137.
ⓐ $44 - 28$
ⓑ $44 + (-28)$

138.
ⓐ $35 - 16$
ⓑ $35 + (-16)$

139.
ⓐ $8 - (-9)$ ⓑ $8 + 9$

140.
ⓐ $4 - (-4)$ ⓑ $4 + 4$

141.
ⓐ $27 - (-18)$
ⓑ $27 + 18$

142.
ⓐ $46 - (-37)$
ⓑ $46 + 37$

In the following exercises, simplify each expression.

143. $15 - (-12)$

144. $14 - (-11)$

145. $10 - (-19)$

146. $11 - (-18)$

147. $48 - 87$

148. $45 - 69$

149. $31 - 79$

150. $39 - 81$

151. $-31 - 11$

152. $-32 - 18$

153. $-17 - 42$

154. $-19 - 46$

155. $-103 - (-52)$

156. $-105 - (-68)$

157. $-45 - (-54)$

158. $-58 - (-67)$

159. $8 - 3 - 7$

160. $9 - 6 - 5$

161. $-5 - 4 + 7$

162. $-3 - 8 + 4$

163. $-14 - (-27) + 9$

164. $-15 - (-28) + 5$

165. $71 + (-10) - 8$

166. $64 + (-17) - 9$

167. $-16 - (-4 + 1) - 7$

168. $-15 - (-6 + 4) - 3$

169. $(2 - 7) - (3 - 8)$

170. $(1 - 8) - (2 - 9)$

171. $-(6 - 8) - (2 - 4)$

172. $-(4 - 5) - (7 - 8)$

173. $25 - [10 - (3 - 12)]$

174. $32 - [5 - (15 - 20)]$

175. $6 \cdot 3 - 4 \cdot 3 - 7 \cdot 2$

176. $5 \cdot 7 - 8 \cdot 2 - 4 \cdot 9$ **177.** $5^2 - 6^2$ **178.** $6^2 - 7^2$

Evaluate Variable Expressions with Integers

In the following exercises, evaluate each expression for the given values.

179. $x - 6$ when
ⓐ $x = 3$ ⓑ $x = -3$

180. $x - 4$ when
ⓐ $x = 5$ ⓑ $x = -5$

181. $5 - y$ when
ⓐ $y = 2$ ⓑ $y = -2$

182. $8 - y$ when
ⓐ $y = 3$ ⓑ $y = -3$

183. $4x^2 - 15x + 1$ when $x = 3$

184. $5x^2 - 14x + 7$ when $x = 2$

185. $-12 - 5x^2$ when $x = 6$

186. $-19 - 4x^2$ when $x = 5$

Translate Word Phrases to Algebraic Expressions

In the following exercises, translate each phrase into an algebraic expression and then simplify.

187.
ⓐ The difference of 3 and −10
ⓑ Subtract −20 from 45

188.
ⓐ The difference of 8 and −12
ⓑ Subtract −13 from 50

189.
ⓐ The difference of −6 and 9
ⓑ Subtract −12 from −16

190.
ⓐ The difference of −8 and 9
ⓑ Subtract −15 from −19

191.
ⓐ 8 less than −17
ⓑ −24 minus 37

192.
ⓐ 5 less than −14
ⓑ −13 minus 42

193.
ⓐ 21 less than 6
ⓑ 31 subtracted from −19

194.
ⓐ 34 less than 7
ⓑ 29 subtracted from −50

Subtract Integers in Applications

In the following exercises, solve the following applications.

195. Temperature One morning, the temperature in Urbana, Illinois, was 28° Fahrenheit. By evening, the temperature had dropped 38° Fahrenheit. What was the temperature that evening?

196. Temperature On Thursday, the temperature in Spincich Lake, Michigan, was 22° Fahrenheit. By Friday, the temperature had dropped 35° Fahrenheit. What was the temperature on Friday?

197. Temperature On January 15, the high temperature in Anaheim, California, was 84° Fahrenheit. That same day, the high temperature in Embarrass, Minnesota was −12° Fahrenheit. What was the difference between the temperature in Anaheim and the temperature in Embarrass?

198. Temperature On January 21, the high temperature in Palm Springs, California, was 89°, and the high temperature in Whitefield, New Hampshire was −31°. What was the difference between the temperature in Palm Springs and the temperature in Whitefield?

199. Football At the first down, the Warriors football team had the ball on their 30-yard line. On the next three downs, they gained 2 yards, lost 7 yards, and lost 4 yards. What was the yard line at the end of the third down?

200. Football At the first down, the Barons football team had the ball on their 20-yard line. On the next three downs, they lost 8 yards, gained 5 yards, and lost 6 yards. What was the yard line at the end of the third down?

201. Checking Account John has $148 in his checking account. He writes a check for $83. What is the new balance in his checking account?

202. Checking Account Ellie has $426 in her checking account. She writes a check for $152. What is the new balance in her checking account?

203. Checking Account Gina has $210 in her checking account. She writes a check for $250. What is the new balance in her checking account?

204. Checking Account Frank has $94 in his checking account. He writes a check for $110. What is the new balance in his checking account?

205. Checking Account Bill has a balance of $-\$14$ in his checking account. He deposits $40 to the account. What is the new balance?

206. Checking Account Patty has a balance of $-\$23$ in her checking account. She deposits $80 to the account. What is the new balance?

Everyday Math

207. Camping Rene is on an Alpine hike. The temperature is $-7°$. Rene's sleeping bag is rated "comfortable to $-20°$". How much can the temperature change before it is too cold for Rene's sleeping bag?

208. Scuba Diving Shelly's scuba watch is guaranteed to be watertight to -100 feet. She is diving at -45 feet on the face of an underwater canyon. By how many feet can she change her depth before her watch is no longer guaranteed?

Writing Exercises

209. Explain why the difference of 9 and -6 is 15.

210. Why is the result of subtracting $3 - (-4)$ the same as the result of adding $3 + 4$?

Self Check

ⓐ After completing the exercises, use this checklist to evaluate your mastery of the objectives of this section.

I can...	Confidently	With some help	No-I don't get it!
model subtraction of integers.			
simplify expressions with integers.			
evaluate variable expressions with integers.			
translate word phrases to algebraic expressions.			
subtract integers in applications.			

ⓑ What does this checklist tell you about your mastery of this section? What steps will you take to improve?

3.4 Multiply and Divide Integers

Learning Objectives

By the end of this section, you will be able to:

- Multiply integers
- Divide integers
- Simplify expressions with integers
- Evaluate variable expressions with integers
- Translate word phrases to algebraic expressions

Be Prepared!

Before you get started, take this readiness quiz.

1. Translate the quotient of 20 and 13 into an algebraic expression.
   If you missed this problem, review Example 1.67.
2. Add: $-5 + (-5) + (-5)$.
   If you missed this problem, review Example 3.21.
3. Evaluate $n + 4$ when $n = -7$.
   If you missed this problem, review Example 3.23.

Multiply Integers

Since multiplication is mathematical shorthand for repeated addition, our counter model can easily be applied to show multiplication of integers. Let's look at this concrete model to see what patterns we notice. We will use the same examples that we used for addition and subtraction.

We remember that $a \cdot b$ means add a, b times. Here, we are using the model shown in Figure 3.19 just to help us discover the pattern.

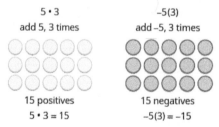

Figure 3.19

Now consider what it means to multiply 5 by -3. It means subtract 5, 3 times. Looking at subtraction as *taking away*, it means to take away 5, 3 times. But there is nothing to take away, so we start by adding neutral pairs as shown in Figure 3.20.

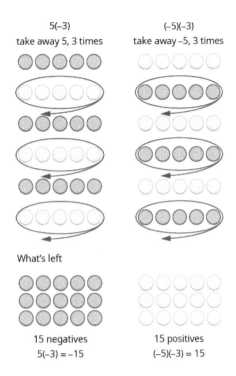

Figure 3.20

In both cases, we started with **15** neutral pairs. In the case on the left, we took away **5, 3** times and the result was **−15**. To multiply **(−5)(−3)**, we took away **−5, 3** times and the result was **15**. So we found that

$$5 \cdot 3 = 15 \qquad -5(3) = -15$$
$$5(-3) = -15 \quad (-5)(-3) = 15$$

Notice that for multiplication of two signed numbers, when the signs are the same, the product is positive, and when the signs are different, the product is negative.

Multiplication of Signed Numbers

The sign of the product of two numbers depends on their signs.

Same signs	Product
•Two positives	Positive
•Two negatives	Positive

Different signs	Product
•Positive • negative	Negative
•Negative • positive	Negative

EXAMPLE 3.47

Multiply each of the following:

ⓐ $-9 \cdot 3$ ⓑ $-2(-5)$ ⓒ $4(-8)$ ⓓ $7 \cdot 6$

⊘ **Solution**

ⓐ

	$-9 \cdot 3$
Multiply, noting that the signs are different and so the product is negative.	-27

ⓑ

	$-2(-5)$
Multiply, noting that the signs are the same and so the product is positive.	10

ⓒ

	$4(-8)$
Multiply, noting that the signs are different and so the product is negative.	-32

ⓓ

	$7 \cdot 6$
The signs are the same, so the product is positive.	42

> **TRY IT :: 3.93** Multiply:

ⓐ $-6 \cdot 8$ ⓑ $-4(-7)$ ⓒ $9(-7)$ ⓓ $5 \cdot 12$

> **TRY IT :: 3.94** Multiply:

ⓐ $-8 \cdot 7$

ⓑ $-6(-9)$

ⓒ $7(-4)$

ⓓ $3 \cdot 13$

When we multiply a number by $1,$ the result is the same number. What happens when we multiply a number by -1? Let's multiply a positive number and then a negative number by -1 to see what we get.

$$-1 \cdot 4 \qquad\qquad -1(-3)$$
$$-4 \qquad\qquad\quad 3$$

-4 is the opposite of **4**   **3** is the opposite of -3

Each time we multiply a number by $-1,$ we get its opposite.

Multiplication by -1

Multiplying a number by -1 gives its opposite.

$$-1a = -a$$

EXAMPLE 3.48

Multiply each of the following:

    ⓐ $-1 \cdot 7$ ⓑ $-1(-11)$

✓ **Solution**

ⓐ

The signs are different, so the product will be negative. $-1 \cdot 7$

Notice that –7 is the opposite of 7. -7

ⓑ

The signs are the same, so the product will be positive. $-1(-11)$

Notice that 11 is the opposite of –11. 11

> **TRY IT ::** 3.95   Multiply.
>
>   ⓐ $-1 \cdot 9$ ⓑ $-1 \cdot (-17)$

> **TRY IT ::** 3.96   Multiply.
>
>   ⓐ $-1 \cdot 8$ ⓑ $-1 \cdot (-16)$

Divide Integers

Division is the inverse operation of multiplication. So, $15 \div 3 = 5$ because $5 \cdot 3 = 15$ In words, this expression says that **15** can be divided into **3** groups of **5** each because adding five three times gives **15**. If we look at some examples of multiplying integers, we might figure out the rules for dividing integers.

$$5 \cdot 3 = 15 \text{ so } 15 \div 3 = 5 \qquad\qquad -5(3) = -15 \text{ so } -15 \div 3 = -5$$
$$(-5)(-3) = 15 \text{ so } 15 \div (-3) = -5 \qquad 5(-3) = -15 \text{ so } -15 \div -3 = 5$$

Division of signed numbers follows the same rules as multiplication. When the signs are the same, the quotient is positive, and when the signs are different, the quotient is negative.

Division of Signed Numbers

The sign of the quotient of two numbers depends on their signs.

Same signs	Quotient
•Two positives	Positive
•Two negatives	Positive

Different signs	Quotient
•Positive & negative	Negative
•Negative & positive	Negative

Remember, you can always check the answer to a division problem by multiplying.

EXAMPLE 3.49

Divide each of the following:

    ⓐ $-27 \div 3$ ⓑ $-100 \div (-4)$

⊘ **Solution**

ⓐ

	$-27 \div 3$
Divide, noting that the signs are different and so the quotient is negative.	-9

ⓑ

	$-100 \div (-4)$
Divide, noting that the signs are the same and so the quotient is positive.	25

> **TRY IT ::** 3.97   Divide:

    ⓐ $-42 \div 6$ ⓑ $-117 \div (-3)$

> **TRY IT ::** 3.98   Divide:

    ⓐ $-63 \div 7$ ⓑ $-115 \div (-5)$

Just as we saw with multiplication, when we divide a number by 1, the result is the same number. What happens when we divide a number by -1? Let's divide a positive number and then a negative number by -1 to see what we get.

$$8 \div (-1) \qquad\qquad -9 \div (-1)$$
$$-8 \qquad\qquad\qquad\qquad 9$$
$$-8 \text{ is the opposite of } 8 \qquad 9 \text{ is the opposite of } -9$$

When we divide a number by, -1 we get its opposite.

Division by -1

Dividing a number by -1 gives its opposite.

$$a \div (-1) = -a$$

EXAMPLE 3.50

Divide each of the following:

ⓐ $16 \div (-1)$ ⓑ $-20 \div (-1)$

⊘ **Solution**

ⓐ

$$16 \div (-1)$$

The dividend, 16, is being divided by –1. -16

Dividing a number by –1 gives its opposite.

Notice that the signs were different, so the result was negative.

ⓑ

$$-20 \div (-1)$$

The dividend, –20, is being divided by –1. 20

Dividing a number by –1 gives its opposite.

Notice that the signs were the same, so the quotient was positive.

> **TRY IT : : 3.99**   Divide:

ⓐ $6 \div (-1)$ ⓑ $-36 \div (-1)$

> **TRY IT : : 3.100**   Divide:

ⓐ $28 \div (-1)$ ⓑ $-52 \div (-1)$

Simplify Expressions with Integers

Now we'll simplify expressions that use all four operations–addition, subtraction, multiplication, and division–with integers. Remember to follow the order of operations.

EXAMPLE 3.51

Simplify: $7(-2) + 4(-7) - 6$.

⊘ **Solution**

We use the order of operations. Multiply first and then add and subtract from left to right.

$$7(-2) + 4(-7)-6$$

Multiply first. $-14 + (-28)-6$

Add. $-42 - 6$

Subtract. -48

> **TRY IT :: 3.101**   Simplify:

$$8(-3) + 5(-7) - 4$$

> **TRY IT :: 3.102**   Simplify:

$$9(-3) + 7(-8) - 1$$

EXAMPLE 3.52

Simplify:

ⓐ $(-2)^4$ ⓑ -2^4

✓ **Solution**

The exponent tells how many times to multiply the base.

ⓐ The exponent is 4 and the base is -2. We raise -2 to the fourth power.

$$(-2)^4$$

Write in expanded form.	$(-2)(-2)(-2)(-2)$
Multiply.	$4(-2)(-2)$
Multiply.	$-8(-2)$
Multiply.	16

ⓑ The exponent is 4 and the base is 2. We raise 2 to the fourth power and then take the opposite.

$$-2^4$$

Write in expanded form.	$-(2 \cdot 2 \cdot 2 \cdot 2)$
Multiply.	$-(4 \cdot 2 \cdot 2)$
Multiply.	$-(8 \cdot 2)$
Multiply.	-16

> **TRY IT :: 3.103**   Simplify:

ⓐ $(-3)^4$ ⓑ -3^4

> **TRY IT :: 3.104**   Simplify:

ⓐ $(-7)^2$ ⓑ -7^2

EXAMPLE 3.53

Simplify: $12 - 3(9 - 12)$.

⊘ **Solution**

According to the order of operations, we simplify inside parentheses first. Then we will multiply and finally we will subtract.

$$12 - 3(9 - 12)$$

Subtract the parentheses first.	$12 - 3(-3)$
Multiply.	$12 - (-9)$
Subtract.	21

> **TRY IT :: 3.105**   Simplify:

$$17 - 4(8 - 11)$$

> **TRY IT :: 3.106**   Simplify:

$$16 - 6(7 - 13)$$

EXAMPLE 3.54

Simplify: $8(-9) \div (-2)^3$.

⊘ **Solution**

We simplify the exponent first, then multiply and divide.

$$8(-9) \div (-2)^3$$

Simplify the exponent.	$8(-9) \div (-8)$
Multiply.	$-72 \div (-8)$
Divide.	9

> **TRY IT :: 3.107**   Simplify:

$$12(-9) \div (-3)^3$$

> **TRY IT :: 3.108**   Simplify:

$$18(-4) \div (-2)^3$$

EXAMPLE 3.55

Simplify: $-30 \div 2 + (-3)(-7)$.

⊘ **Solution**

First we will multiply and divide from left to right. Then we will add.

Solution

$$3x + 4y - 6$$

Substitute $x = -1$ and $y = 2$.	$3(-1) + 4(2) - 6$
Multiply.	$-3 + 8 - 6$
Simplify.	-1

> **TRY IT :: 3.113** Evaluate:
>
> $7x + 6y - 12$ when $x = -2$ and $y = 3$

> **TRY IT :: 3.114** Evaluate:
>
> $8x - 6y + 13$ when $x = -3$ and $y = -5$

Translate Word Phrases to Algebraic Expressions

Once again, all our prior work translating words to algebra transfers to phrases that include both multiplying and dividing integers. Remember that the key word for multiplication is *product* and for division is *quotient*.

EXAMPLE 3.58

Translate to an algebraic expression and simplify if possible: the product of -2 and 14.

Solution

The word *product* tells us to multiply.

	the product of -2 and 14
Translate.	$(-2)(14)$
Simplify.	-28

> **TRY IT :: 3.115** Translate to an algebraic expression and simplify if possible:
>
> the product of -5 and 12

> **TRY IT :: 3.116** Translate to an algebraic expression and simplify if possible:
>
> the product of 8 and -13

EXAMPLE 3.59

Translate to an algebraic expression and simplify if possible: the quotient of -56 and -7.

Solution

The word *quotient* tells us to divide.

the quotient of −56 and −7

Translate.	$-56 \div (-7)$
Simplify.	8

> **TRY IT : : 3.117**   Translate to an algebraic expression and simplify if possible:

the quotient of −63 and −9

> **TRY IT : : 3.118**   Translate to an algebraic expression and simplify if possible:

the quotient of −72 and −9

▶ **MEDIA : :** ACCESS ADDITIONAL ONLINE RESOURCES
- Multiplying Integers Using Color Counters (http://openstaxcollege.org/l/24Multiplyinteg)
- Multiplying Integers Using Color Counters With Neutral Pairs (http://openstaxcollege.org/l/24Multiplyneutr)
- Multiplying Integers Basics (http://openstaxcollege.org/l/24Multiplybasic)
- Dividing Integers Basics (http://openstaxcollege.org/l/24Dividebasic)
- Ex. Dividing Integers (http://openstaxcollege.org/l/24Divideinteger)
- Multiplying and Dividing Signed Numbers (http://openstaxcollege.org/l/24Multidivisign)

3.4 EXERCISES

Practice Makes Perfect

Multiply Integers

In the following exercises, multiply each pair of integers.

211. $-4 \cdot 8$

212. $-3 \cdot 9$

213. $-5(7)$

214. $-8(6)$

215. $-18(-2)$

216. $-10(-6)$

217. $9(-7)$

218. $13(-5)$

219. $-1 \cdot 6$

220. $-1 \cdot 3$

221. $-1(-14)$

222. $-1(-19)$

Divide Integers

In the following exercises, divide.

223. $-24 \div 6$

224. $-28 \div 7$

225. $56 \div (-7)$

226. $35 \div (-7)$

227. $-52 \div (-4)$

228. $-84 \div (-6)$

229. $-180 \div 15$

230. $-192 \div 12$

231. $49 \div (-1)$

232. $62 \div (-1)$

Simplify Expressions with Integers

In the following exercises, simplify each expression.

233. $5(-6) + 7(-2) - 3$

234. $8(-4) + 5(-4) - 6$

235. $-8(-2) - 3(-9)$

236. $-7(-4) - 5(-3)$

237. $(-5)^3$

238. $(-4)^3$

239. $(-2)^6$

240. $(-3)^5$

241. -4^2

242. -6^2

243. $-3(-5)(6)$

244. $-4(-6)(3)$

245. $-4 \cdot 2 \cdot 11$

246. $-5 \cdot 3 \cdot 10$

247. $(8 - 11)(9 - 12)$

248. $(6 - 11)(8 - 13)$

249. $26 - 3(2 - 7)$

250. $23 - 2(4 - 6)$

251. $-10(-4) \div (-8)$

252. $-8(-6) \div (-4)$

253. $65 \div (-5) + (-28) \div (-7)$

254. $52 \div (-4) + (-32) \div (-8)$

255. $9 - 2[3 - 8(-2)]$

256. $11 - 3[7 - 4(-2)]$

257. $(-3)^2 - 24 \div (8 - 2)$

258. $(-4)^2 - 32 \div (12 - 4)$

Evaluate Variable Expressions with Integers

In the following exercises, evaluate each expression.

259. $-2x + 17$ when

    ⓐ $x = 8$ ⓑ $x = -8$

260. $-5y + 14$ when

    ⓐ $y = 9$ ⓑ $y = -9$

261. $10 - 3m$ when

    ⓐ $m = 5$ ⓑ $m = -5$

262. $18 - 4n$ when

    ⓐ $n = 3$ ⓑ $n = -3$

263. $p^2 - 5p + 5$ when $p = -1$

264. $q^2 - 2q + 9$ when $q = -2$

265. $2w^2 - 3w + 7$ when $w = -2$

266. $3u^2 - 4u + 5$ when $u = -3$

267. $6x - 5y + 15$ when $x = 3$ and $y = -1$

268. $3p - 2q + 9$ when $p = 8$ and $q = -2$

269. $9a - 2b - 8$ when $a = -6$ and $b = -3$

270. $7m - 4n - 2$ when $m = -4$ and $n = -9$

Translate Word Phrases to Algebraic Expressions

In the following exercises, translate to an algebraic expression and simplify if possible.

271. The product of -3 and 15

272. The product of -4 and 16

273. The quotient of -60 and -20

274. The quotient of -40 and -20

275. The quotient of -6 and the sum of a and b

276. The quotient of -7 and the sum of m and n

277. The product of -10 and the difference of p and q

278. The product of -13 and the difference of c and d

Everyday Math

279. Stock market Javier owns 300 shares of stock in one company. On Tuesday, the stock price dropped $\$12$ per share. What was the total effect on Javier's portfolio?

280. Weight loss In the first week of a diet program, eight women lost an average of 3 pounds each. What was the total weight change for the eight women?

Writing Exercises

281. In your own words, state the rules for multiplying two integers.

282. In your own words, state the rules for dividing two integers.

283. Why is $-2^4 \neq (-2)^4$?

284. Why is $-4^2 \neq (-4)^2$?

Self Check

ⓐ *After completing the exercises, use this checklist to evaluate your mastery of the objectives of this section.*

I can...	Confidently	With some help	No-I don't get it!
multiply integers.			
divide integers.			
simplify expressions with integers.			
evaluate variable expressions with integers.			
translate word phrases to algebraic expressions.			

ⓑ *On a scale of 1–10, how would you rate your mastery of this section in light of your responses on the checklist? How can you improve this?*

3.5 | Solve Equations Using Integers; The Division Property of Equality

Learning Objectives

By the end of this section, you will be able to:
- Determine whether an integer is a solution of an equation
- Solve equations with integers using the Addition and Subtraction Properties of Equality
- Model the Division Property of Equality
- Solve equations using the Division Property of Equality
- Translate to an equation and solve

Be Prepared!

Before you get started, take this readiness quiz.

1. Evaluate $x + 4$ when $x = -4$.
   If you missed this problem, review Example 3.22.

2. Solve: $y - 6 = 10$.
   If you missed this problem, review Example 2.33.

3. Translate into an algebraic expression 5 *less than* x.
   If you missed this problem, review Table 1.34.

Determine Whether a Number is a Solution of an Equation

In Solve Equations with the Subtraction and Addition Properties of Equality, we saw that a solution of an equation is a value of a variable that makes a true statement when substituted into that equation. In that section, we found solutions that were whole numbers. Now that we've worked with integers, we'll find integer solutions to equations.

The steps we take to determine whether a number is a solution to an equation are the same whether the solution is a whole number or an integer.

HOW TO : : HOW TO DETERMINE WHETHER A NUMBER IS A SOLUTION TO AN EQUATION.

Step 1.   Substitute the number for the variable in the equation.

Step 2.   Simplify the expressions on both sides of the equation.

Step 3.   Determine whether the resulting equation is true.
- If it is true, the number is a solution.
- If it is not true, the number is not a solution.

EXAMPLE 3.60

Determine whether each of the following is a solution of $2x - 5 = -13$:

ⓐ $x = 4$ ⓑ $x = -4$ ⓒ $x = -9$.

✓ Solution

ⓐ Substitute 4 for x in the equation to determine if it is true.

$$2x - 5 = -13$$

Substitute 4 for x. $$2(4) - 5 \stackrel{?}{=} -13$$

Multiply. $$8 - 5 \stackrel{?}{=} -13$$

Subtract. $$3 \neq -13$$

Since $x = 4$ does not result in a true equation, 4 is not a solution to the equation.

ⓑ Substitute −4 for x in the equation to determine if it is true. $$2x - 5 = -13$$

Substitute −4 for x. $$2(-4) - 5 \stackrel{?}{=} -13$$

Multiply. $$-8 - 5 \stackrel{?}{=} -13$$

Subtract. $$-13 = -13 \checkmark$$

Since $x = -4$ results in a true equation, -4 is a solution to the equation.

ⓒ Substitute −9 for x in the equation to determine if it is true.

$$2x - 5 = -13$$

Substitute −9 for x. $$2(-9) - 5 \stackrel{?}{=} -13$$

Multiply. $$-18 - 5 \stackrel{?}{=} -13$$

Subtract. $$-23 \neq -13$$

Since $x = -9$ does not result in a true equation, -9 is not a solution to the equation.

> **TRY IT :: 3.119**   Determine whether each of the following is a solution of $2x - 8 = -14$:

ⓐ $x = -11$ ⓑ $x = 11$ ⓒ $x = -3$

> **TRY IT :: 3.120**   Determine whether each of the following is a solution of $2y + 3 = -11$:

ⓐ $y = 4$ ⓑ $y = -4$ ⓒ $y = -7$

Solve Equations with Integers Using the Addition and Subtraction Properties of Equality

In Solve Equations with the Subtraction and Addition Properties of Equality, we solved equations similar to the two shown here using the Subtraction and Addition Properties of Equality. Now we can use them again with integers.

$$x + 4 = 12 \qquad\qquad y - 5 = 9$$
$$x + 4 - 4 = 12 - 4 \qquad\qquad y - 5 + 5 = 9 + 5$$
$$x = 8 \qquad\qquad y = 14$$

When you add or subtract the same quantity from both sides of an equation, you still have equality.

Properties of Equalities

Subtraction Property of Equality	Addition Property of Equality
For any numbers a, b, c, if $a = b$ then $a - c = b - c$.	For any numbers a, b, c, if $a = b$ then $a + c = b + c$.

EXAMPLE 3.61

Solve: $y + 9 = 5$.

⊘ **Solution**

$$y + 9 = 5$$

Subtract 9 from each side to undo the addition.	$y + 9 - 9 = 5 - 9$
Simplify.	$y = -4$

Check the result by substituting -4 into the original equation.

$$y + 9 = 5$$

Substitute –4 for y	$-4 + 9 \overset{?}{=} 5$
	$5 = 5 \checkmark$

Since $y = -4$ makes $y + 9 = 5$ a true statement, we found the solution to this equation.

> **TRY IT : :** 3.121   Solve:
>
> $y + 11 = 7$

> **TRY IT : :** 3.122   Solve:
>
> $y + 15 = -4$

EXAMPLE 3.62

Solve: $a - 6 = -8$

⊘ **Solution**

$$a - 6 = -8$$

Add 6 to each side to undo the subtraction.

$$a - 6 + 6 = -8 + 6$$

Simplify.

$$a = -2$$

Check the result by substituting -2 into the original equation:

$$a - 6 = -8$$

Substitute -2 for a

$$-2 - 6 \overset{?}{=} -8$$

$$-8 = -8 \checkmark$$

The solution to $a - 6 = -8$ is -2.

Since $a = -2$ makes $a - 6 = -8$ a true statement, we found the solution to this equation.

> **TRY IT ∷ 3.123**   Solve:

$$a - 2 = -8$$

> **TRY IT ∷ 3.124**   Solve:

$$n - 4 = -8$$

Model the Division Property of Equality

All of the equations we have solved so far have been of the form $x + a = b$ or $x - a = b$. We were able to isolate the variable by adding or subtracting the constant term. Now we'll see how to solve equations that involve division.

We will model an equation with envelopes and counters in Figure 3.21.

Figure 3.21

Here, there are two identical envelopes that contain the same number of counters. Remember, the left side of the workspace must equal the right side, but the counters on the left side are "hidden" in the envelopes. So how many counters are in each envelope?

To determine the number, separate the counters on the right side into 2 groups of the same size. So 6 counters divided into 2 groups means there must be 3 counters in each group (since $6 \div 2 = 3$).

What equation models the situation shown in Figure 3.22? There are two envelopes, and each contains x counters. Together, the two envelopes must contain a total of 6 counters. So the equation that models the situation is $2x = 6$.

Figure 3.22

We can divide both sides of the equation by 2 as we did with the envelopes and counters.

$$\frac{2x}{2} = \frac{6}{2}$$
$$x = 3$$

We found that each envelope contains 3 counters. Does this check? We know $2 \cdot 3 = 6$, so it works. Three counters in each of two envelopes does equal six.

Figure 3.23 shows another example.

Figure 3.23

Now we have 3 identical envelopes and 12 counters. How many counters are in each envelope? We have to separate the 12 counters into 3 groups. Since $12 \div 3 = 4$, there must be 4 counters in each envelope. See Figure 3.24.

Figure 3.24

The equation that models the situation is $3x = 12$. We can divide both sides of the equation by 3.

$$\frac{3x}{3} = \frac{12}{3}$$
$$x = 4$$

Does this check? It does because $3 \cdot 4 = 12$.

 MANIPULATIVE MATHEMATICS

Doing the Manipulative Mathematics activity "Division Property of Equality" will help you develop a better understanding of how to solve equations using the Division Property of Equality.

EXAMPLE 3.63

Write an equation modeled by the envelopes and counters, and then solve it.

✓ **Solution**

There are 4 envelopes, or 4 unknown values, on the left that match the 8 counters on the right. Let's call the unknown quantity in the envelopes x.

Write the equation.	$4x = 8$
Divide both sides by 4.	$\dfrac{4x}{4} = \dfrac{8}{4}$
Simplify.	$x = 2$

There are 2 counters in each envelope.

> **TRY IT :: 3.125**   Write the equation modeled by the envelopes and counters. Then solve it.

> **TRY IT :: 3.126**   Write the equation modeled by the envelopes and counters. Then solve it.

Solve Equations Using the Division Property of Equality

The previous examples lead to the Division Property of Equality. When you divide both sides of an equation by any nonzero number, you still have equality.

Division Property of Equality

For any numbers a, b, c, and $c \neq 0$,

If $a = b$ then $\dfrac{a}{c} = \dfrac{b}{c}$.

EXAMPLE 3.64

Solve: $7x = -49$.

⊘ **Solution**

To isolate x, we need to undo multiplication.

	$7x = -49$
Divide each side by 7.	$\dfrac{7x}{7} = \dfrac{-49}{7}$
Simplify.	$x = -7$

Check the solution.

	$7x = -49$
Substitute –7 for x.	$7(-7) \overset{?}{=} -49$
	$-49 = -49\ \checkmark$

Therefore, -7 is the solution to the equation.

> **TRY IT :: 3.127**   Solve:
> $8a = 56$

> **TRY IT :: 3.128**   Solve:
> $11n = 121$

EXAMPLE 3.65

Solve: $-3y = 63$.

⊘ **Solution**

To isolate y, we need to undo the multiplication.

	$-3y = 63$
Divide each side by –3.	$\dfrac{-3y}{-3} = \dfrac{63}{-3}$
Simplify	$y = -21$

Check the solution.

	$-3y = 63$
Substitute –21 for y.	$-3(-21) \overset{?}{=} 63$
	$63 = 63\ \checkmark$

Since this is a true statement, $y = -21$ is the solution to the equation.

> | **TRY IT ::** 3.129   Solve:
>
> $$-8p = 96$$

> | **TRY IT ::** 3.130   Solve:
>
> $$-12m = 108$$

Translate to an Equation and Solve

In the past several examples, we were given an equation containing a variable. In the next few examples, we'll have to first translate word sentences into equations with variables and then we will solve the equations.

EXAMPLE 3.66

Translate and solve: five more than x is equal to -3.

⊘ Solution

five more than x is equal to -3

Translate	$x + 5 = -3$
Subtract 5 from both sides.	$x + 5 - 5 = -3 - 5$
Simplify.	$x = -8$

Check the answer by substituting it into the original equation.

$$x + 5 = -3$$
$$-8 + 5 \overset{?}{=} -3$$
$$-3 = -3 \checkmark$$

> | **TRY IT ::** 3.131   Translate and solve:
>
> Seven more than x is equal to -2.

> | **TRY IT ::** 3.132   Translate and solve:
>
> Eleven more than y is equal to 2.

EXAMPLE 3.67

Translate and solve: the difference of n and 6 is -10.

Solution

	the difference of n and 6 is -10
Translate.	$n - 6 = -10$
Add 6 to each side.	$n - 6 + 6 = -10 + 6$
Simplify.	$n = -4$

Check the answer by substituting it into the original equation.

$n - 6 = -10$

$-4 - 6 \overset{?}{=} -10$

$-10 = -10 \checkmark$

> **TRY IT : :** 3.133   Translate and solve:

The difference of p and 2 is -4.

> **TRY IT : :** 3.134   Translate and solve:

The difference of q and 7 is -3.

EXAMPLE 3.68

Translate and solve: the number 108 is the product of -9 and y.

Solution

	the number of 108 is the product of -9 and y
Translate.	$108 = -9y$
Divide by -9.	$\dfrac{108}{-9} = \dfrac{-9y}{-9}$
Simplify.	$-12 = y$

Check the answer by substituting it into the original equation.

$108 = -9y$

$108 \overset{?}{=} -9(-12)$

$108 = 108 \checkmark$

> **TRY IT : :** 3.135   Translate and solve:

The number 132 is the product of -12 and y.

> **TRY IT : :** 3.136   Translate and solve:

The number 117 is the product of -13 and z.

▶ | **MEDIA** : : ACCESS ADDITIONAL ONLINE RESOURCES

- One-Step Equations With Adding Or Subtracting (http://openstaxcollege.org/l/24onestepaddsub)
- One-Step Equations With Multiplying Or Dividing (http://openstaxcollege.org/l/24onestepmuldiv)

3.5 EXERCISES

Practice Makes Perfect

Determine Whether a Number is a Solution of an Equation

In the following exercises, determine whether each number is a solution of the given equation.

285. $4x - 2 = 6$

ⓐ $x = -2$ ⓑ $x = -1$

ⓒ $x = 2$

286. $4y - 10 = -14$

ⓐ $y = -6$ ⓑ $y = -1$

ⓒ $y = 1$

287. $9a + 27 = -63$

ⓐ $a = 6$ ⓑ $a = -6$

ⓒ $a = -10$

288. $7c + 42 = -56$

ⓐ $c = 2$ ⓑ $c = -2$

ⓒ $c = -14$

Solve Equations Using the Addition and Subtraction Properties of Equality

In the following exercises, solve for the unknown.

289. $n + 12 = 5$

290. $m + 16 = 2$

291. $p + 9 = -8$

292. $q + 5 = -6$

293. $u - 3 = -7$

294. $v - 7 = -8$

295. $h - 10 = -4$

296. $k - 9 = -5$

297. $x + (-2) = -18$

298. $y + (-3) = -10$

299. $r - (-5) = -9$

300. $s - (-2) = -11$

Model the Division Property of Equality

In the following exercises, write the equation modeled by the envelopes and counters and then solve it.

301.

302.

303.

304.

Solve Equations Using the Division Property of Equality

In the following exercises, solve each equation using the division property of equality and check the solution.

305. $5x = 45$

306. $4p = 64$

307. $-7c = 56$

308. $-9x = 54$

309. $-14p = -42$

310. $-8m = -40$

311. $-120 = 10q$

312. $-75 = 15y$

313. $24x = 480$

314. $18n = 540$

315. $-3z = 0$

316. $4u = 0$

Translate to an Equation and Solve

In the following exercises, translate and solve.

317. Four more than n is equal to 1.

318. Nine more than m is equal to 5.

319. The sum of eight and p is -3.

320. The sum of two and q is -7.

321. The difference of a and three is -14.

322. The difference of b and 5 is -2.

323. The number -42 is the product of -7 and x.

324. The number -54 is the product of -9 and y.

325. The product of f and -15 is 75.

326. The product of g and -18 is 36.

327. -6 plus c is equal to 4.

328. -2 plus d is equal to 1.

329. Nine less than n is -4.

330. Thirteen less than n is -10.

Mixed Practice

In the following exercises, solve.

331.
ⓐ $x + 2 = 10$
ⓑ $2x = 10$

332.
ⓐ $y + 6 = 12$
ⓑ $6y = 12$

333.
ⓐ $-3p = 27$
ⓑ $p - 3 = 27$

334.
ⓐ $-2q = 34$
ⓑ $q - 2 = 34$

335. $a - 4 = 16$

336. $b - 1 = 11$

337. $-8m = -56$

338. $-6n = -48$

339. $-39 = u + 13$

340. $-100 = v + 25$

341. $11r = -99$

342. $15s = -300$

343. $100 = 20d$

344. $250 = 25n$

345. $-49 = x - 7$

346. $64 = y - 4$

Everyday Math

347. Cookie packaging A package of 51 cookies has 3 equal rows of cookies. Find the number of cookies in each row, c, by solving the equation $3c = 51$.

348. Kindergarten class Connie's kindergarten class has 24 children. She wants them to get into 4 equal groups. Find the number of children in each group, g, by solving the equation $4g = 24$.

Writing Exercises

349. Is modeling the Division Property of Equality with envelopes and counters helpful to understanding how to solve the equation $3x = 15$? Explain why or why not.

350. Suppose you are using envelopes and counters to model solving the equations $x + 4 = 12$ and $4x = 12$. Explain how you would solve each equation.

351. Frida started to solve the equation $-3x = 36$ by adding 3 to both sides. Explain why Frida's method will not solve the equation.

352. Raoul started to solve the equation $4y = 40$ by subtracting 4 from both sides. Explain why Raoul's method will not solve the equation.

Self Check

ⓐ *After completing the exercises, use this checklist to evaluate your mastery of the objectives of this section.*

I can...	Confidently	With some help	No-I don't get it!
determine whether an integer is a solution of an equation.			
solve equations with integers using the addition and subtraction properties of equality.			
model division property of equality.			
solve equations using the division property of equality.			
translate to an equation and solve.			

ⓑ *Overall, after looking at the checklist, do you think you are well-prepared for the next Chapter? Why or why not?*

CHAPTER 3 REVIEW

KEY TERMS

absolute value The absolute value of a number is its distance from 0 on the number line.

integers Integers are counting numbers, their opposites, and zero … –3, –2, –1, 0, 1, 2, 3 …

negative number A negative number is less than zero.

opposites The opposite of a number is the number that is the same distance from zero on the number line, but on the opposite side of zero.

KEY CONCEPTS

3.1 Introduction to Integers

- Opposite Notation
  - $-a$ means the opposite of the number a
  - The notation $-a$ is read *the opposite of* a.
- Absolute Value Notation
  - The absolute value of a number n is written as $|n|$.
  - $|n| \geq 0$ for all numbers.

3.2 Add Integers

- **Addition of Positive and Negative Integers**

$$5 + 3 \qquad\qquad\qquad -5 + (-3)$$

both positive, sum positive   both negative, sum negative

When the signs are the same, the counters would be all the same color, so add them.

$$-5 + 3 \qquad\qquad\qquad 5 + (-3)$$

different signs, more negatives   different signs, more positives

Sum negative   sum positive

When the signs are different, some counters would make neutral pairs; subtract to see how many are left.

3.3 Subtract Integers

- **Subtraction of Integers**

$5 - 3$	$-5 - (-3)$
2	-2
2 positives	2 negatives

When there would be enough counters of the color to take away, subtract.

$-5 - 3$	$5 - (-3)$
-8	8
5 negatives, want to subtract 3 positives	5 positives, want to subtract 3 negatives
need neutral pairs	need neutral pairs

When there would not be enough of the counters to take away, add neutral pairs.

Table 3.110

- **Subtraction Property**
    - $a - b = a + (-b)$
    - $a - (-b) = a + b$

- **Solve Application Problems**
    - Step 1. Identify what you are asked to find.
    - Step 2. Write a phrase that gives the information to find it.
    - Step 3. Translate the phrase to an expression.
    - Step 4. Simplify the expression.
    - Step 5. Answer the question with a complete sentence.

3.4 Multiply and Divide Integers

- **Multiplication of Signed Numbers**
    - To determine the sign of the product of two signed numbers:

Same Signs	Product
Two positives	Positive
Two negatives	Positive

Different Signs	Product
Positive • negative	Negative
Negative • positive	Negative

- **Division of Signed Numbers**
    - To determine the sign of the quotient of two signed numbers:

Same Signs	Quotient
Two positives	Positive
Two negatives	Positive

Different Signs	Quotient
Positive • negative	Negative
Negative • Positive	Negative

- **Multiplication by -1**
  - ◦ Multiplying a number by -1 gives its opposite: $-1a = -a$
- **Division by -1**
  - ◦ Dividing a number by -1 gives its opposite: $a \div (-1) = -a$

3.5 Solve Equations Using Integers; The Division Property of Equality

- **How to determine whether a number is a solution to an equation.**
  - ◦ Step 1. Substitute the number for the variable in the equation.
  - ◦ Step 2. Simplify the expressions on both sides of the equation.
  - ◦ Step 3. Determine whether the resulting equation is true.
    - ▪ If it is true, the number is a solution.
    - ▪ If it is not true, the number is not a solution.
- **Properties of Equalities**

Subtraction Property of Equality	Addition Property of Equality
For any numbers a, b, c, if $a = b$ then $a - c = b - c$.	For any numbers a, b, c, if $a = b$ then $a + c = b + c$.

- **Division Property of Equality**
  - ◦ For any numbers $a, b, c,$ and $c \neq 0$

  If $a = b$, then $\frac{a}{c} = \frac{b}{c}$.

REVIEW EXERCISES

3.1 Introduction to Integers

Locate Positive and Negative Numbers on the Number Line

In the following exercises, locate and label the integer on the number line.

353. 5

354. -5

355. -3

356. 3

357. -8

358. -7

Order Positive and Negative Numbers

In the following exercises, order each of the following pairs of numbers, using $<$ or $>$.

359. 4__8

360. -6__3

361. -5__-10

362. -9__-4

363. 2__-7

364. -3__1

Find Opposites

In the following exercises, find the opposite of each number.

365. 6

366. -2

367. -4

368. 3

In the following exercises, simplify.

369.
  ⓐ $-(8)$ ⓑ $-(-8)$

370.
  ⓐ $-(9)$ ⓑ $-(-9)$

In the following exercises, evaluate.

371. $-x$, when
  ⓐ $x = 32$
  ⓑ $x = -32$

372. $-n$, when
  ⓐ $n = 20$
  ⓐ $n = -20$

Simplify Absolute Values

In the following exercises, simplify.

373. $|-21|$

374. $|-42|$

375. $|36|$

376. $-|15|$

377. $|0|$

378. $-|-75|$

In the following exercises, evaluate.

379. $|x|$ when $x = -14$

380. $-|r|$ when $r = 27$

381. $-|-y|$ when $y = 33$

382. $|-n|$ when $n = -4$

In the following exercises, fill in $<$, $>$, or $=$ for each of the following pairs of numbers.

383. $-|-4|\_\_4$

384. $-2\_\_|-2|$

385. $-|-6|\_\_-6$

386. $-|-9|\_\_-|-9|$

In the following exercises, simplify.

387. $-(-55)$ and $-|-55|$

388. $-(-48)$ and $-|-48|$

389. $|12 - 5|$

390. $|9 + 7|$

391. $6|-9|$

392. $|14-8| - |-2|$

393. $|9 - 3| - |5 - 12|$

394. $5 + 4|15 - 3|$

Translate Phrases to Expressions with Integers

In the following exercises, translate each of the following phrases into expressions with positive or negative numbers.

395. the opposite of 16

396. the opposite of -8

397. negative 3

398. 19 minus negative 12

399. a temperature of 10 below zero

400. an elevation of 85 feet below sea level

3.2 Add Integers

Model Addition of Integers

In the following exercises, model the following to find the sum.

401. $3 + 7$

402. $-2 + 6$

403. $5 + (-4)$

404. $-3 + (-6)$

Simplify Expressions with Integers

In the following exercises, simplify each expression.

405. $14 + 82$

406. $-33 + (-67)$

407. $-75 + 25$

408. $54 + (-28)$

409. $11 + (-15) + 3$

410. $-19 + (-42) + 12$

411. $-3 + 6(-1 + 5)$

412. $10 + 4(-3 + 7)$

Evaluate Variable Expressions with Integers

In the following exercises, evaluate each expression.

413. $n + 4$ when
    ⓐ $n = -1$
    ⓑ $n = -20$

414. $x + (-9)$ when
    ⓐ $x = 3$
    ⓑ $x = -3$

415.
$(x + y)^3$ when $x = -4$, $y = 1$

416.
$(u + v)^2$ when $u = -4$, $v = 11$

Translate Word Phrases to Algebraic Expressions

In the following exercises, translate each phrase into an algebraic expression and then simplify.

417. the sum of -8 and 2

418. 4 more than -12

419.
10 more than the sum of -5 and -6

420.
the sum of 3 and -5, increased by 18

Add Integers in Applications

In the following exercises, solve.

421. Temperature On Monday, the high temperature in Denver was -4 degrees. Tuesday's high temperature was 20 degrees more. What was the high temperature on Tuesday?

422. Credit Frida owed $75 on her credit card. Then she charged $21 more. What was her new balance?

3.3 Subtract Integers

Model Subtraction of Integers

In the following exercises, model the following.

423. $6 - 1$

424. $-4 - (-3)$

425. $2 - (-5)$

426. $-1 - 4$

Simplify Expressions with Integers

In the following exercises, simplify each expression.

427. $24 - 16$

428. $19 - (-9)$

429. $-31 - 7$

430. $-40 - (-11)$

431. $-52 - (-17) - 23$

432. $25 - (-3 - 9)$

433. $(1 - 7) - (3 - 8)$

434. $3^2 - 7^2$

Evaluate Variable Expressions with Integers

In the following exercises, evaluate each expression.

435. $x - 7$ when

ⓐ $x = 5$

ⓑ $x = -4$

436. $10 - y$ when

ⓐ $y = 15$

ⓑ $y = -16$

437. $2n^2 - n + 5$ when $n = -4$

438. $-15 - 3u^2$ when $u = -5$

Translate Phrases to Algebraic Expressions

In the following exercises, translate each phrase into an algebraic expression and then simplify.

439. the difference of -12 and 5

440. subtract 23 from -50

Subtract Integers in Applications

In the following exercises, solve the given applications.

441. Temperature One morning the temperature in Bangor, Maine was 18 degrees. By afternoon, it had dropped 20 degrees. What was the afternoon temperature?

442. Temperature On January 4, the high temperature in Laredo, Texas was 78 degrees, and the high in Houlton, Maine was -28 degrees. What was the difference in temperature of Laredo and Houlton?

3.4 Multiply and Divide Integers

Multiply Integers

In the following exercises, multiply.

443. $-9 \cdot 4$

444. $5(-7)$

445. $(-11)(-11)$

446. $-1 \cdot 6$

Divide Integers

In the following exercises, divide.

447. $56 \div (-8)$

448. $-120 \div (-6)$

449. $-96 \div 12$

450. $96 \div (-16)$

451. $45 \div (-1)$

452. $-162 \div (-1)$

Simplify Expressions with Integers

In the following exercises, simplify each expression.

453. $5(-9) - 3(-12)$

454. $(-2)^5$

455. -3^4

456. $(-3)(4)(-5)(-6)$

457. $42 - 4(6 - 9)$

458. $(8 - 15)(9 - 3)$

459. $-2(-18) \div 9$

460. $45 \div (-3) - 12$

Evaluate Variable Expressions with Integers

In the following exercises, evaluate each expression.

461. $7x - 3$ when $x = -9$

462. $16 - 2n$ when $n = -8$

463. $5a + 8b$ when $a = -2$, $b = -6$

464. $x^2 + 5x + 4$ when $x = -3$

Translate Word Phrases to Algebraic Expressions

In the following exercises, translate to an algebraic expression and simplify if possible.

465. the product of -12 and 6

466. the quotient of 3 and the sum of -7 and s

3.5 Solve Equations using Integers; The Division Property of Equality

Determine Whether a Number is a Solution of an Equation

In the following exercises, determine whether each number is a solution of the given equation.

467. $5x - 10 = -35$

   ⓐ $x = -9$

   ⓑ $x = -5$ ⓒ $x = 5$

468. $8u + 24 = -32$

   ⓐ $u = -7$

   ⓑ $u = -1$ ⓒ $u = 7$

Using the Addition and Subtraction Properties of Equality

In the following exercises, solve.

469. $a + 14 = 2$

470. $b - 9 = -15$

471. $c + (-10) = -17$

472. $d - (-6) = -26$

Model the Division Property of Equality

In the following exercises, write the equation modeled by the envelopes and counters. Then solve it.

473.

474.

Solve Equations Using the Division Property of Equality

In the following exercises, solve each equation using the division property of equality and check the solution.

475. $8p = 72$

476. $-12q = 48$

477. $-16r = -64$

478. $-5s = -100$

Translate to an Equation and Solve.

In the following exercises, translate and solve.

479.
The product of -6 and y is -42

480.
The difference of z and -13 is -18.

481. Four more than m is -48.

482.
The product of -21 and n is 63.

Everyday Math

483. Describe how you have used two topics from this chapter in your life outside of your math class during the past month.

PRACTICE TEST

484. Locate and label 0, 2, -4, and -1 on a number line.

In the following exercises, compare the numbers, using $<$ or $>$ or $=$.

485.
    ⓐ -6__3
    ⓑ -1__-4

486.
    ⓐ -5__$|-5|$
    ⓑ $-|-2|$__-2

In the following exercises, find the opposite of each number.

487.
    ⓐ -7 ⓑ 8

In the following exercises, simplify.

488. $-(-22)$

489. $|4-9|$

490. $-8+6$

491. $-15+(-12)$

492. $-7-(-3)$

493. $10-(5-6)$

494. $-3 \cdot 8$

495. $-6(-9)$

496. $70 \div (-7)$

497. $(-2)^3$

498. -4^2

499. $16-3(5-7)$

500. $|21-6|-|-8|$

In the following exercises, evaluate.

501. $35-a$ when $a=-4$

502. $(-2r)^2$ when $r=3$

503. $3m-2n$ when $m=6$, $n=-8$

504. $-|-y|$ when $y=17$

In the following exercises, translate each phrase into an algebraic expression and then simplify, if possible.

505. the difference of -7 and -4

506. the quotient of 25 and the sum of m and n.

In the following exercises, solve.

507. Early one morning, the temperature in Syracuse was $-8°F$. By noon, it had risen $12°$. What was the temperature at noon?

508. Collette owed $\$128$ on her credit card. Then she charged $\$65$. What was her new balance?

In the following exercises, solve.

509. $n+6=5$

510. $p-11=-4$

511. $-9r=-54$

In the following exercises, translate and solve.

512. The product of 15 and x is 75.

513. Eight less than y is -32.

Figure 4.1 Bakers combine ingredients to make delicious breads and pastries. (credit: Agustín Ruiz, Flickr)

Chapter Outline

Introduction

Often in life, whole amounts are not exactly what we need. A baker must use a little more than a cup of milk or part of a teaspoon of sugar. Similarly a carpenter might need less than a foot of wood and a painter might use part of a gallon of paint. In this chapter, we will learn about numbers that describe parts of a whole. These numbers, called fractions, are very useful both in algebra and in everyday life. You will discover that you are already familiar with many examples of fractions!

4.1 Visualize Fractions

Learning Objectives

By the end of this section, you will be able to:

- Understand the meaning of fractions
- Model improper fractions and mixed numbers
- Convert between improper fractions and mixed numbers
- Model equivalent fractions
- Find equivalent fractions
- Locate fractions and mixed numbers on the number line
- Order fractions and mixed numbers

Be Prepared!

Before you get started, take this readiness quiz.

1. Simplify: $5 \cdot 2 + 1$.
   If you missed this problem, review Example 2.8.

2. Fill in the blank with $<$ or $>$: $-2\_\_-5$

If you missed this problem, review Example 3.2.

Understand the Meaning of Fractions

Andy and Bobby love pizza. On Monday night, they share a pizza equally. How much of the pizza does each one get? Are you thinking that each boy gets half of the pizza? That's right. There is one whole pizza, evenly divided into two parts, so each boy gets one of the two equal parts.

In math, we write $\frac{1}{2}$ to mean one out of two parts.

On Tuesday, Andy and Bobby share a pizza with their parents, Fred and Christy, with each person getting an equal amount of the whole pizza. How much of the pizza does each person get? There is one whole pizza, divided evenly into four equal parts. Each person has one of the four equal parts, so each has $\frac{1}{4}$ of the pizza.

On Wednesday, the family invites some friends over for a pizza dinner. There are a total of 12 people. If they share the pizza equally, each person would get $\frac{1}{12}$ of the pizza.

Fractions

A fraction is written $\frac{a}{b}$, where a and b are integers and $b \neq 0$. In a fraction, a is called the numerator and b is called the denominator.

A fraction is a way to represent parts of a whole. The denominator b represents the number of equal parts the whole has been divided into, and the numerator a represents how many parts are included. The denominator, b, cannot equal zero because division by zero is undefined.

In Figure 4.2, the circle has been divided into three parts of equal size. Each part represents $\frac{1}{3}$ of the circle. This type of model is called a fraction circle. Other shapes, such as rectangles, can also be used to model fractions.

Figure 4.2

 MANIPULATIVE MATHEMATICS

Doing the Manipulative Mathematics activity Model Fractions will help you develop a better understanding of fractions, their numerators and denominators.

What does the fraction $\frac{2}{3}$ represent? The fraction $\frac{2}{3}$ means two of three equal parts.

EXAMPLE 4.1

Name the fraction of the shape that is shaded in each of the figures.

(a)

(b)

Solution

We need to ask two questions. First, how many equal parts are there? This will be the denominator. Second, of these equal parts, how many are shaded? This will be the numerator.

ⓐ

How many equal parts are there?   There are eight equal parts.
How many are shaded?   Five parts are shaded.

Five out of eight parts are shaded. Therefore, the fraction of the circle that is shaded is $\frac{5}{8}$.

ⓑ

How many equal parts are there?   There are nine equal parts.
How many are shaded?   Two parts are shaded.

Two out of nine parts are shaded. Therefore, the fraction of the square that is shaded is $\frac{2}{9}$.

> **TRY IT ::** 4.1   Name the fraction of the shape that is shaded in each figure:

(a)   (b)

> **TRY IT ::** 4.2   Name the fraction of the shape that is shaded in each figure:

(a)   (b)

EXAMPLE 4.2

Shade $\frac{3}{4}$ of the circle.

⊘ **Solution**

The denominator is 4, so we divide the circle into four equal parts ⓐ.

The numerator is 3, so we shade three of the four parts ⓑ.

(a)   (b)

$\frac{3}{4}$ of the circle is shaded.

> **TRY IT ::** 4.3   Shade $\frac{6}{8}$ of the circle.

> **TRY IT ::** 4.4   Shade $\frac{2}{5}$ of the rectangle.

In Example 4.1 and Example 4.2, we used circles and rectangles to model fractions. Fractions can also be modeled as manipulatives called fraction tiles, as shown in Figure 4.3. Here, the whole is modeled as one long, undivided rectangular tile. Beneath it are tiles of equal length divided into different numbers of equally sized parts.

1

| $\frac{1}{2}$ | $\frac{1}{2}$ |

| $\frac{1}{3}$ | $\frac{1}{3}$ | $\frac{1}{3}$ |

| $\frac{1}{4}$ | $\frac{1}{4}$ | $\frac{1}{4}$ | $\frac{1}{4}$ |

| $\frac{1}{6}$ | $\frac{1}{6}$ | $\frac{1}{6}$ | $\frac{1}{6}$ | $\frac{1}{6}$ | $\frac{1}{6}$ |

Figure 4.3

We'll be using fraction tiles to discover some basic facts about fractions. Refer to Figure 4.3 to answer the following questions:

How many $\frac{1}{2}$ tiles does it take to make one whole tile?

It takes two halves to make a whole, so two out of two is $\frac{2}{2} = 1$.

How many $\frac{1}{3}$ tiles does it take to make one whole tile?

It takes three thirds, so three out of three is $\frac{3}{3} = 1$.

How many $\frac{1}{4}$ tiles does it take to make one whole tile?

It takes four fourths, so four out of four is $\frac{4}{4} = 1$.

How many $\frac{1}{6}$ tiles does it take to make one whole tile?

It takes six sixths, so six out of six is $\frac{6}{6} = 1$.

What if the whole were divided into 24 equal parts? (We have not shown fraction tiles to represent this, but try to visualize it in your mind.) How many $\frac{1}{24}$ tiles does it take to make one whole tile?

It takes 24 twenty-fourths, so $\frac{24}{24} = 1$.

It takes 24 twenty-fourths, so $\frac{24}{24} = 1$.

This leads us to the *Property of One*.

Property of One

Any number, except zero, divided by itself is one.

$$\frac{a}{a} = 1 \qquad (a \neq 0)$$

 MANIPULATIVE MATHEMATICS

Doing the Manipulative Mathematics activity "Fractions Equivalent to One" will help you develop a better understanding of fractions that are equivalent to one

EXAMPLE 4.3

Use fraction circles to make wholes using the following pieces:

     ⓐ 4 fourths   ⓑ 5 fifths   ⓒ 6 sixths

✅ **Solution**

(a) 4 fourths   (b) 5 fifths   (c) 6 sixths

Form 1 whole   Form 1 whole   Form 1 whole

> **TRY IT : : 4.5**   Use fraction circles to make wholes with the following pieces: 3 thirds.

> **TRY IT : : 4.6**   Use fraction circles to make wholes with the following pieces: 8 eighths.

What if we have more fraction pieces than we need for 1 whole? We'll look at this in the next example.

EXAMPLE 4.4

Use fraction circles to make wholes using the following pieces:

     ⓐ 3 halves   ⓑ 8 fifths   ⓒ 7 thirds

✅ **Solution**

ⓐ 3 halves make 1 whole with 1 half left over.

1          $\frac{1}{2}$

ⓑ 8 fifths make 1 whole with 3 fifths left over.

1          $\frac{3}{5}$

ⓒ 7 thirds make 2 wholes with 1 third left over.

> **TRY IT : :** 4.7   Use fraction circles to make wholes with the following pieces: 5 thirds.

> **TRY IT : :** 4.8   Use fraction circles to make wholes with the following pieces: 5 halves.

Model Improper Fractions and Mixed Numbers

In Example 4.4 (b), you had eight equal fifth pieces. You used five of them to make one whole, and you had three fifths left over. Let us use fraction notation to show what happened. You had eight pieces, each of them one fifth, $\frac{1}{5}$, so altogether you had eight fifths, which we can write as $\frac{8}{5}$. The fraction $\frac{8}{5}$ is one whole, 1, plus three fifths, $\frac{3}{5}$, or $1\frac{3}{5}$, which is read as *one and three-fifths*.

The number $1\frac{3}{5}$ is called a mixed number. A mixed number consists of a whole number and a fraction.

Mixed Numbers

A **mixed number** consists of a whole number a and a fraction $\frac{b}{c}$ where $c \neq 0$. It is written as follows.

$$a\frac{b}{c} \qquad c \neq 0$$

Fractions such as $\frac{5}{4}, \frac{3}{2}, \frac{5}{5},$ and $\frac{7}{3}$ are called improper fractions. In an improper fraction, the numerator is greater than or equal to the denominator, so its value is greater than or equal to one. When a fraction has a numerator that is smaller than the denominator, it is called a proper fraction, and its value is less than one. Fractions such as $\frac{1}{2}, \frac{3}{7},$ and $\frac{11}{18}$ are proper fractions.

Proper and Improper Fractions

The fraction $\frac{a}{b}$ is a **proper fraction** if $a < b$ and an **improper fraction** if $a \geq b$.

 MANIPULATIVE MATHEMATICS

Doing the Manipulative Mathematics activity "Model Improper Fractions" and "Mixed Numbers" will help you develop a better understanding of how to convert between improper fractions and mixed numbers.

EXAMPLE 4.5

Name the improper fraction modeled. Then write the improper fraction as a mixed number.

⊘ **Solution**

Each circle is divided into three pieces, so each piece is $\frac{1}{3}$ of the circle. There are four pieces shaded, so there are four

thirds or $\frac{4}{3}$. The figure shows that we also have one whole circle and one third, which is $1\frac{1}{3}$. So, $\frac{4}{3} = 1\frac{1}{3}$.

⟩ **TRY IT : : 4.9**   Name the improper fraction. Then write it as a mixed number.

⟩ **TRY IT : : 4.10**   Name the improper fraction. Then write it as a mixed number.

EXAMPLE 4.6

Draw a figure to model $\frac{11}{8}$.

⊘ **Solution**

The denominator of the improper fraction is 8. Draw a circle divided into eight pieces and shade all of them. This takes care of eight eighths, but we have 11 eighths. We must shade three of the eight parts of another circle.

$\frac{8}{8}$ plus $\frac{3}{8}$

$1 + \frac{3}{8}$

So, $\frac{11}{8} = 1\frac{3}{8}$.

⟩ **TRY IT : : 4.11**   Draw a figure to model $\frac{7}{6}$.

⟩ **TRY IT : : 4.12**   Draw a figure to model $\frac{6}{5}$.

EXAMPLE 4.7

Use a model to rewrite the improper fraction $\frac{11}{6}$ as a mixed number.

⊘ **Solution**

We start with 11 sixths $\left(\frac{11}{6}\right)$. We know that six sixths makes one whole.

$$\frac{6}{6} = 1$$

That leaves us with five more sixths, which is $\frac{5}{6}$ $\left(11 \text{ sixths minus 6 sixths is 5 sixths}\right)$.

So, $\frac{11}{6} = 1\frac{5}{6}$.

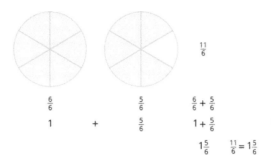

> | **TRY IT : :** 4.13   Use a model to rewrite the improper fraction as a mixed number: $\frac{9}{7}$.

> | **TRY IT : :** 4.14   Use a model to rewrite the improper fraction as a mixed number: $\frac{7}{4}$.

EXAMPLE 4.8

Use a model to rewrite the mixed number $1\frac{4}{5}$ as an improper fraction.

⊘ **Solution**

The mixed number $1\frac{4}{5}$ means one whole plus four fifths. The denominator is 5, so the whole is $\frac{5}{5}$. Together five fifths and four fifths equals nine fifths.

So, $1\frac{4}{5} = \frac{9}{5}$.

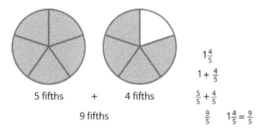

> | **TRY IT : :** 4.15   Use a model to rewrite the mixed number as an improper fraction: $1\frac{3}{8}$.

> | **TRY IT : :** 4.16   Use a model to rewrite the mixed number as an improper fraction: $1\frac{5}{6}$.

Convert between Improper Fractions and Mixed Numbers

In Example 4.7, we converted the improper fraction $\frac{11}{6}$ to the mixed number $1\frac{5}{6}$ using fraction circles. We did this by grouping six sixths together to make a whole; then we looked to see how many of the 11 pieces were left. We saw that $\frac{11}{6}$ made one whole group of six sixths plus five more sixths, showing that $\frac{11}{6} = 1\frac{5}{6}$.

The division expression $\frac{11}{6}$ (which can also be written as $6\overline{)11}$) tells us to find how many groups of 6 are in 11. To convert an improper fraction to a mixed number without fraction circles, we divide.

EXAMPLE 4.9

Convert $\frac{11}{6}$ to a mixed number.

⊘ **Solution**

$$\frac{11}{6}$$

Divide the denominator into the numerator.   Remember $\frac{11}{6}$ means $11 \div 6$.

$$\begin{array}{r} 1 \quad\leftarrow \text{quotient} \\ \text{divisor} \rightarrow 6\overline{)11} \\ \underline{6} \\ 5 \quad\leftarrow \text{remainder} \end{array}$$

Identify the quotient, remainder and divisor.

Write the mixed number as $\text{quotient}\frac{\text{remainder}}{\text{divisor}}$. $1\frac{5}{6}$

So, $\frac{11}{6} = 1\frac{5}{6}$

> **TRY IT :: 4.17**   Convert the improper fraction to a mixed number: $\frac{13}{7}$.

> **TRY IT :: 4.18**   Convert the improper fraction to a mixed number: $\frac{14}{9}$.

 HOW TO :: CONVERT AN IMPROPER FRACTION TO A MIXED NUMBER.

Step 1.   Divide the denominator into the numerator.

Step 2.   Identify the quotient, remainder, and divisor.

Step 3.   Write the mixed number as quotient $\frac{\text{remainder}}{\text{divisor}}$.

EXAMPLE 4.10

Convert the improper fraction $\frac{33}{8}$ to a mixed number.

Solution

$$\frac{33}{8}$$

Divide the denominator into the numerator.   Remember, $\frac{33}{8}$ means $8\overline{)33}$.

Identify the quotient, remainder, and divisor.

$$\text{divisor} \longrightarrow 8\overline{)33} \longleftarrow \text{quotient}$$
$$\underline{32}$$
$$1 \longleftarrow \text{remainder}$$

Write the mixed number as quotient $\frac{\text{remainder}}{\text{divisor}}$. $4\frac{1}{8}$

$$\text{So, } \frac{33}{8} = 4\frac{1}{8}$$

> **TRY IT : :** 4.19   Convert the improper fraction to a mixed number: $\frac{23}{7}$.

> **TRY IT : :** 4.20   Convert the improper fraction to a mixed number: $\frac{48}{11}$.

In Example 4.8, we changed $1\frac{4}{5}$ to an improper fraction by first seeing that the whole is a set of five fifths. So we had five fifths and four more fifths.

$$\frac{5}{5} + \frac{4}{5} = \frac{9}{5}$$

Where did the nine come from? There are nine fifths—one whole (five fifths) plus four fifths. Let us use this idea to see how to convert a mixed number to an improper fraction.

EXAMPLE 4.11

Convert the mixed number $4\frac{2}{3}$ to an improper fraction.

⊘ Solution

$$4\frac{2}{3}$$

Multiply the whole number by the denominator.	
The whole number is 4 and the denominator is 3.	$\dfrac{4 \cdot 3 + \Box}{\Box}$
Simplify.	$\dfrac{12 + \Box}{\Box}$
Add the numerator to the product.	
The numerator of the mixed number is 2.	$\dfrac{12 + 2}{\Box}$
Simplify.	$\dfrac{14}{\Box}$
Write the final sum over the original denominator.	
The denominator is 3.	$\dfrac{14}{3}$

> **TRY IT : :** 4.21   Convert the mixed number to an improper fraction: $3\frac{5}{7}$.

> **TRY IT : :** 4.22   Convert the mixed number to an improper fraction: $2\frac{7}{8}$.

HOW TO : : CONVERT A MIXED NUMBER TO AN IMPROPER FRACTION.

Step 1.   Multiply the whole number by the denominator.
Step 2.   Add the numerator to the product found in Step 1.
Step 3.   Write the final sum over the original denominator.

EXAMPLE 4.12

Convert the mixed number $10\frac{2}{7}$ to an improper fraction.

⊘ **Solution**

$$10\frac{2}{7}$$

Multiply the whole number by the denominator.

The whole number is 10 and the denominator is 7.
$$\frac{10 \cdot 7 + \square}{\square}$$

Simplify.
$$\frac{70 + \square}{\square}$$

Add the numerator to the product.

The numerator of the mixed number is 2.
$$\frac{70 + 2}{\square}$$

Simplify.
$$\frac{72}{\square}$$

Write the final sum over the original denominator.

The denominator is 7.
$$\frac{72}{7}$$

> **TRY IT :: 4.23**   Convert the mixed number to an improper fraction: $4\frac{6}{11}$.

> **TRY IT :: 4.24**   Convert the mixed number to an improper fraction: $11\frac{1}{3}$.

Model Equivalent Fractions

Let's think about Andy and Bobby and their favorite food again. If Andy eats $\frac{1}{2}$ of a pizza and Bobby eats $\frac{2}{4}$ of the pizza, have they eaten the same amount of pizza? In other words, does $\frac{1}{2} = \frac{2}{4}$? We can use fraction tiles to find out whether Andy and Bobby have eaten *equivalent* parts of the pizza.

Equivalent Fractions

Equivalent fractions are fractions that have the same value.

Fraction tiles serve as a useful model of equivalent fractions. You may want to use fraction tiles to do the following activity. Or you might make a copy of Figure 4.3 and extend it to include eighths, tenths, and twelfths.

Start with a $\frac{1}{2}$ tile. How many fourths equal one-half? How many of the $\frac{1}{4}$ tiles exactly cover the $\frac{1}{2}$ tile?

Since two $\frac{1}{4}$ tiles cover the $\frac{1}{2}$ tile, we see that $\frac{2}{4}$ is the same as $\frac{1}{2}$, or $\frac{2}{4} = \frac{1}{2}$.

How many of the $\frac{1}{6}$ tiles cover the $\frac{1}{2}$ tile?

Since three $\frac{1}{6}$ tiles cover the $\frac{1}{2}$ tile, we see that $\frac{3}{6}$ is the same as $\frac{1}{2}$.

So, $\frac{3}{6} = \frac{1}{2}$. The fractions are equivalent fractions.

 MANIPULATIVE MATHEMATICS

Doing the activity "Equivalent Fractions" will help you develop a better understanding of what it means when two fractions are equivalent.

EXAMPLE 4.13

Use fraction tiles to find equivalent fractions. Show your result with a figure.

ⓐ How many eighths equal one-half?   ⓑ How many tenths equal one-half?

ⓒ How many twelfths equal one-half?

⊘ **Solution**

ⓐ It takes four $\frac{1}{8}$ tiles to exactly cover the $\frac{1}{2}$ tile, so $\frac{4}{8} = \frac{1}{2}$.

ⓑ It takes five $\frac{1}{10}$ tiles to exactly cover the $\frac{1}{2}$ tile, so $\frac{5}{10} = \frac{1}{2}$.

ⓒ It takes six $\frac{1}{12}$ tiles to exactly cover the $\frac{1}{2}$ tile, so $\frac{6}{12} = \frac{1}{2}$.

Suppose you had tiles marked $\frac{1}{20}$. How many of them would it take to equal $\frac{1}{2}$? Are you thinking ten tiles? If you are, you're right, because $\frac{10}{20} = \frac{1}{2}$.

We have shown that $\frac{1}{2}$, $\frac{2}{4}$, $\frac{3}{6}$, $\frac{4}{8}$, $\frac{5}{10}$, $\frac{6}{12}$, and $\frac{10}{20}$ are all equivalent fractions.

> **TRY IT :: 4.25**   Use fraction tiles to find equivalent fractions: How many eighths equal one-fourth?

> **TRY IT :: 4.26**   Use fraction tiles to find equivalent fractions: How many twelfths equal one-fourth?

Find Equivalent Fractions

We used fraction tiles to show that there are many fractions equivalent to $\frac{1}{2}$. For example, $\frac{2}{4}$, $\frac{3}{6}$, and $\frac{4}{8}$ are all equivalent to $\frac{1}{2}$. When we lined up the fraction tiles, it took four of the $\frac{1}{8}$ tiles to make the same length as a $\frac{1}{2}$ tile. This showed that $\frac{4}{8} = \frac{1}{2}$. See Example 4.13.

We can show this with pizzas, too. Figure 4.4(a) shows a single pizza, cut into two equal pieces with $\frac{1}{2}$ shaded. Figure 4.4(b) shows a second pizza of the same size, cut into eight pieces with $\frac{4}{8}$ shaded.

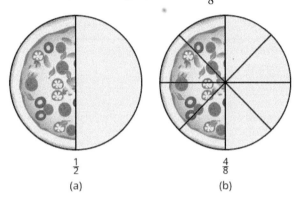

$$\frac{1}{2}$$
(a)

$$\frac{4}{8}$$
(b)

Figure 4.4

This is another way to show that $\frac{1}{2}$ is equivalent to $\frac{4}{8}$.

How can we use mathematics to change $\frac{1}{2}$ into $\frac{4}{8}$? How could you take a pizza that is cut into two pieces and cut it into eight pieces? You could cut each of the two larger pieces into four smaller pieces! The whole pizza would then be cut into eight pieces instead of just two. Mathematically, what we've described could be written as:

$$\frac{1 \cdot 4}{2 \cdot 4} = \frac{4}{8}$$

These models lead to the Equivalent Fractions Property, which states that if we multiply the numerator and denominator of a fraction by the same number, the value of the fraction does not change.

Equivalent Fractions Property

If a, b, and c are numbers where $b \neq 0$ and $c \neq 0$, then

$$\frac{a}{b} = \frac{a \cdot c}{b \cdot c}$$

When working with fractions, it is often necessary to express the same fraction in different forms. To find equivalent forms of a fraction, we can use the Equivalent Fractions Property. For example, consider the fraction one-half.

$$\frac{1 \cdot 3}{2 \cdot 3} = \frac{3}{6} \quad \text{so} \quad \frac{1}{2} = \frac{3}{6}$$

$$\frac{1 \cdot 2}{2 \cdot 2} = \frac{2}{4} \quad \text{so} \quad \frac{1}{2} = \frac{2}{4}$$

$$\frac{1 \cdot 10}{2 \cdot 10} = \frac{10}{20} \quad \text{so} \quad \frac{1}{2} = \frac{10}{20}$$

So, we say that $\frac{1}{2}, \frac{2}{4}, \frac{3}{6}$, and $\frac{10}{20}$ are equivalent fractions.

EXAMPLE 4.14

Find three fractions equivalent to $\frac{2}{5}$.

⊘ Solution

To find a fraction equivalent to $\frac{2}{5}$, we multiply the numerator and denominator by the same number (but not zero). Let us multiply them by $2,\ 3,$ and 5.

$$\frac{2 \cdot 2}{5 \cdot 2} = \frac{4}{10} \qquad \frac{2 \cdot 3}{5 \cdot 3} = \frac{6}{15} \qquad \frac{2 \cdot 5}{5 \cdot 5} = \frac{10}{25}$$

So, $\frac{4}{10},\ \frac{6}{15},$ and $\frac{10}{25}$ are equivalent to $\frac{2}{5}$.

> **TRY IT : :** 4.27   Find three fractions equivalent to $\frac{3}{5}$.

> **TRY IT : :** 4.28   Find three fractions equivalent to $\frac{4}{5}$.

EXAMPLE 4.15

Find a fraction with a denominator of 21 that is equivalent to $\frac{2}{7}$.

⊘ Solution

To find equivalent fractions, we multiply the numerator and denominator by the same number. In this case, we need to multiply the denominator by a number that will result in 21.

Since we can multiply 7 by 3 to get 21, we can find the equivalent fraction by multiplying both the numerator and denominator by 3.

$$\frac{2}{7} = \frac{2 \cdot 3}{7 \cdot 3} = \frac{6}{21}$$

> **TRY IT : :** 4.29   Find a fraction with a denominator of 21 that is equivalent to $\frac{6}{7}$.

> **TRY IT : :** 4.30   Find a fraction with a denominator of 100 that is equivalent to $\frac{3}{10}$.

Locate Fractions and Mixed Numbers on the Number Line

Now we are ready to plot fractions on a number line. This will help us visualize fractions and understand their values.

 MANIPULATIVE MATHEMATICS

Doing the Manipulative Mathematics activity "Number Line Part 3" will help you develop a better understanding of the location of fractions on the number line.

Let us locate $\frac{1}{5},\ \frac{4}{5},\ 3,\ 3\frac{1}{3},\ \frac{7}{4},\ \frac{9}{2},\ 5,$ and $\frac{8}{3}$ on the number line.

We will start with the whole numbers 3 and 5 because they are the easiest to plot.

The proper fractions listed are $\frac{1}{5}$ and $\frac{4}{5}$. We know proper fractions have values less than one, so $\frac{1}{5}$ and $\frac{4}{5}$ are located between the whole numbers 0 and 1. The denominators are both 5, so we need to divide the segment of the number line between 0 and 1 into five equal parts. We can do this by drawing four equally spaced marks on the number line, which we can then label as $\frac{1}{5}, \frac{2}{5}, \frac{3}{5},$ and $\frac{4}{5}$.

Now plot points at $\frac{1}{5}$ and $\frac{4}{5}$.

The only mixed number to plot is $3\frac{1}{3}$. Between what two whole numbers is $3\frac{1}{3}$? Remember that a mixed number is a whole number plus a proper fraction, so $3\frac{1}{3} > 3$. Since it is greater than 3, but not a whole unit greater, $3\frac{1}{3}$ is between 3 and 4. We need to divide the portion of the number line between 3 and 4 into three equal pieces (thirds) and plot $3\frac{1}{3}$ at the first mark.

Finally, look at the improper fractions $\frac{7}{4}, \frac{9}{2},$ and $\frac{8}{3}$. Locating these points will be easier if you change each of them to a mixed number.

$$\frac{7}{4} = 1\frac{3}{4}, \quad \frac{9}{2} = 4\frac{1}{2}, \quad \frac{8}{3} = 2\frac{2}{3}$$

Here is the number line with all the points plotted.

EXAMPLE 4.16

Locate and label the following on a number line: $\frac{3}{4}, \frac{4}{3}, \frac{5}{3}, 4\frac{1}{5},$ and $\frac{7}{2}$.

⊘ **Solution**

Start by locating the proper fraction $\frac{3}{4}$. It is between 0 and 1. To do this, divide the distance between 0 and 1 into four equal parts. Then plot $\frac{3}{4}$.

Next, locate the mixed number $4\frac{1}{5}$. It is between 4 and 5 on the number line. Divide the number line between 4 and 5 into five equal parts, and then plot $4\frac{1}{5}$ one-fifth of the way between 4 and 5.

Now locate the improper fractions $\frac{4}{3}$ and $\frac{5}{3}$.

It is easier to plot them if we convert them to mixed numbers first.

$$\frac{4}{3} = 1\frac{1}{3}, \quad \frac{5}{3} = 1\frac{2}{3}$$

Divide the distance between 1 and 2 into thirds.

Next let us plot $\frac{7}{2}$. We write it as a mixed number, $\frac{7}{2} = 3\frac{1}{2}$. Plot it between 3 and 4.

The number line shows all the numbers located on the number line.

> **TRY IT : : 4.31**   Locate and label the following on a number line: $\frac{1}{3}, \frac{5}{4}, \frac{7}{4}, 2\frac{3}{5}, \frac{9}{2}.$

> **TRY IT : : 4.32**   Locate and label the following on a number line: $\frac{2}{3}, \frac{5}{2}, \frac{9}{4}, \frac{11}{4}, 3\frac{2}{5}.$

In Introduction to Integers, we defined the opposite of a number. It is the number that is the same distance from zero on the number line but on the opposite side of zero. We saw, for example, that the opposite of 7 is -7 and the opposite of -7 is 7.

Fractions have opposites, too. The opposite of $\frac{3}{4}$ is $-\frac{3}{4}$. It is the same distance from 0 on the number line, but on the opposite side of 0.

Thinking of negative fractions as the opposite of positive fractions will help us locate them on the number line. To locate $-\frac{15}{8}$ on the number line, first think of where $\frac{15}{8}$ is located. It is an improper fraction, so we first convert it to the mixed number $1\frac{7}{8}$ and see that it will be between 1 and 2 on the number line. So its opposite, $-\frac{15}{8}$, will be between -1 and -2 on the number line.

EXAMPLE 4.17

Locate and label the following on the number line: $\frac{1}{4}, -\frac{1}{4}, 1\frac{1}{3}, -1\frac{1}{3}, \frac{5}{2},$ and $-\frac{5}{2}.$

⊘ Solution

Draw a number line. Mark 0 in the middle and then mark several units to the left and right.

To locate $\frac{1}{4}$, divide the interval between 0 and 1 into four equal parts. Each part represents one-quarter of the distance. So plot $\frac{1}{4}$ at the first mark.

To locate $-\frac{1}{4}$, divide the interval between 0 and -1 into four equal parts. Plot $-\frac{1}{4}$ at the first mark to the left of 0.

Since $1\frac{1}{3}$ is between 1 and 2, divide the interval between 1 and 2 into three equal parts. Plot $1\frac{1}{3}$ at the first mark to the right of 1. Then since $-1\frac{1}{3}$ is the opposite of $1\frac{1}{3}$ it is between -1 and -2. Divide the interval between -1 and -2 into three equal parts. Plot $-1\frac{1}{3}$ at the first mark to the left of -1.

To locate $\frac{5}{2}$ and $-\frac{5}{2}$, it may be helpful to rewrite them as the mixed numbers $2\frac{1}{2}$ and $-2\frac{1}{2}$.

Since $2\frac{1}{2}$ is between 2 and 3, divide the interval between 2 and 3 into two equal parts. Plot $\frac{5}{2}$ at the mark. Then since $-2\frac{1}{2}$ is between -2 and -3, divide the interval between -2 and -3 into two equal parts. Plot $-\frac{5}{2}$ at the mark.

> **TRY IT : : 4.33**   Locate and label each of the given fractions on a number line:

$$\frac{2}{3}, \; -\frac{2}{3}, \; 2\frac{1}{4}, \; -2\frac{1}{4}, \; \frac{3}{2}, \; -\frac{3}{2}$$

> **TRY IT : : 4.34**   Locate and label each of the given fractions on a number line:

$$\frac{3}{4}, \; -\frac{3}{4}, \; 1\frac{1}{2}, \; -1\frac{1}{2}, \; \frac{7}{3}, \; -\frac{7}{3}$$

Order Fractions and Mixed Numbers

We can use the inequality symbols to order fractions. Remember that $a > b$ means that a is to the right of b on the number line. As we move from left to right on a number line, the values increase.

EXAMPLE 4.18

Order each of the following pairs of numbers, using $<$ or $>$:

ⓐ $-\frac{2}{3}$____-1 ⓑ $-3\frac{1}{2}$____-3 ⓒ $-\frac{3}{7}$____$-\frac{3}{8}$ ⓓ -2____$\frac{-16}{9}$

Solution

ⓐ $-\frac{2}{3} > -1$

ⓑ $-3\frac{1}{2} < -3$

ⓒ $-\frac{3}{7} < -\frac{3}{8}$

ⓓ $-2 < \frac{-16}{9}$

> **TRY IT : :** 4.35   Order each of the following pairs of numbers, using $<$ or $>$:

ⓐ $-\frac{1}{3}\_\_ -1$ ⓑ $-1\frac{1}{2}\_\_ -2$ ⓒ $-\frac{2}{3}\_\_ -\frac{1}{3}$ ⓓ $-3\_\_ -\frac{7}{3}$

> **TRY IT : :** 4.36   Order each of the following pairs of numbers, using $<$ or $>$:

ⓐ $-3\_\_ -\frac{17}{5}$ ⓑ $-2\frac{1}{4}\_\_ -2$ ⓒ $-\frac{3}{5}\_\_ -\frac{4}{5}$ ⓓ $-4\_\_ -\frac{10}{3}$

▶ **MEDIA : :** ACCESS ADDITIONAL ONLINE RESOURCES

- **Introduction to Fractions (http://www.openstaxcollege.org/l/24Introtofract)**
- **Identify Fractions Using Pattern Blocks (http://www.openstaxcollege.org/l/24FractPattBloc)**

4.1 EXERCISES

Practice Makes Perfect

In the following exercises, name the fraction of each figure that is shaded.

1.

(a)   (b)

(c)   (d)

2.

(a)   (b)

(c)   (d)

In the following exercises, shade parts of circles or squares to model the following fractions.

3. $\frac{1}{2}$

4. $\frac{1}{3}$

5. $\frac{3}{4}$

6. $\frac{2}{5}$

7. $\frac{5}{6}$

8. $\frac{7}{8}$

9. $\frac{5}{8}$

10. $\frac{7}{10}$

In the following exercises, use fraction circles to make wholes, if possible, with the following pieces.

11. 3 thirds

12. 8 eighths

13. 7 sixths

14. 4 thirds

15. 7 fifths

16. 7 fourths

In the following exercises, name the improper fractions. Then write each improper fraction as a mixed number.

17.

(a)

(b)

(c)

18.

(a)

(b)

(c)

19.

(a)

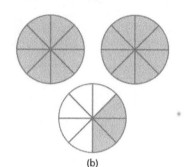

(b)

In the following exercises, draw fraction circles to model the given fraction.

20. $\frac{3}{3}$

21. $\frac{4}{4}$

22. $\frac{7}{4}$

23. $\frac{5}{3}$

24. $\frac{11}{6}$

25. $\frac{13}{8}$

26. $\frac{10}{3}$

27. $\frac{9}{4}$

In the following exercises, rewrite the improper fraction as a mixed number.

28. $\frac{3}{2}$

29. $\frac{5}{3}$

30. $\frac{11}{4}$

31. $\frac{13}{5}$

32. $\frac{25}{6}$

33. $\frac{28}{9}$

34. $\frac{42}{13}$

35. $\frac{47}{15}$

In the following exercises, rewrite the mixed number as an improper fraction.

36. $1\frac{2}{3}$

37. $1\frac{2}{5}$

38. $2\frac{1}{4}$

39. $2\frac{5}{6}$

40. $2\frac{7}{9}$

41. $2\frac{5}{7}$

42. $3\frac{4}{7}$

43. $3\frac{5}{9}$

In the following exercises, use fraction tiles or draw a figure to find equivalent fractions.

44. How many sixths equal one-third?

45. How many twelfths equal one-third?

46. How many eighths equal three-fourths?

47. How many twelfths equal three-fourths?

48. How many fourths equal three-halves?

49. How many sixths equal three-halves?

In the following exercises, find three fractions equivalent to the given fraction. Show your work, using figures or algebra.

50. $\frac{1}{4}$

51. $\frac{1}{3}$

52. $\frac{3}{8}$

53. $\frac{5}{6}$

54. $\frac{2}{7}$

55. $\frac{5}{9}$

In the following exercises, plot the numbers on a number line.

56. $\frac{2}{3}, \frac{5}{4}, \frac{12}{5}$

57. $\frac{1}{3}, \frac{7}{4}, \frac{13}{5}$

58. $\frac{1}{4}, \frac{9}{5}, \frac{11}{3}$

59. $\frac{7}{10}, \frac{5}{2}, \frac{13}{8}, 3$

60. $2\frac{1}{3}, -2\frac{1}{3}$

61. $1\frac{3}{4}, -1\frac{3}{5}$

62. $\frac{3}{4}, -\frac{3}{4}, 1\frac{2}{3}, -1\frac{2}{3}, \frac{5}{2}, -\frac{5}{2}$

63. $\frac{2}{5}, -\frac{2}{5}, 1\frac{3}{4}, -1\frac{3}{4}, \frac{8}{3}, -\frac{8}{3}$

In the following exercises, order each of the following pairs of numbers, using < or >.

64. $-1 \underline{\quad} -\frac{1}{4}$

65. $-1 \underline{\quad} -\frac{1}{3}$

66. $-2\frac{1}{2} \underline{\quad} -3$

67. $-1\frac{3}{4} \underline{\quad} -2$

68. $-\frac{5}{12} \underline{\quad} -\frac{7}{12}$

69. $-\frac{9}{10} \underline{\quad} -\frac{3}{10}$

70. $-3 \underline{\quad} -\frac{13}{5}$

71. $-4 \underline{\quad} -\frac{23}{6}$

Everyday Math

72. Music Measures A choreographed dance is broken into counts. A $\frac{1}{1}$ count has one step in a count, a $\frac{1}{2}$ count has two steps in a count and a $\frac{1}{3}$ count has three steps in a count. How many steps would be in a $\frac{1}{5}$ count? What type of count has four steps in it?

73. Music Measures Fractions are used often in music. In $\frac{4}{4}$ time, there are four quarter notes in one measure.

ⓐ How many measures would eight quarter notes make?

ⓑ The song "Happy Birthday to You" has 25 quarter notes. How many measures are there in "Happy Birthday to You?"

74. Baking Nina is making five pans of fudge to serve after a music recital. For each pan, she needs $\frac{1}{2}$ cup of walnuts.

ⓐ How many cups of walnuts does she need for five pans of fudge?

ⓑ Do you think it is easier to measure this amount when you use an improper fraction or a mixed number? Why?

Writing Exercises

75. Give an example from your life experience (outside of school) where it was important to understand fractions.

76. Explain how you locate the improper fraction $\frac{21}{4}$ on a number line on which only the whole numbers from 0 through 10 are marked.

Self Check

ⓐ *After completing the exercises, use this checklist to evaluate your mastery of the objectives of this section.*

I can...	Confidently	With some help	No-I don't get it!
understand the meaning of fractions.			
model improper fractions and mixed numbers.			
convert between improper fractions and mixed numbers.			
model equivalent fractions.			
find equivalent fractions.			
locate fractions and mixed numbers on the number line.			
order fractions and mixed numbers.			

ⓑ *If most of your checks were:*

...confidently. Congratulations! You have achieved the objectives in this section. Reflect on the study skills you used so that you can continue to use them. What did you do to become confident of your ability to do these things? Be specific.

...with some help. This must be addressed quickly because topics you do not master become potholes in your road to success. In math, every topic builds upon previous work. It is important to make sure you have a strong foundation before you move on. Who can you ask for help? Your fellow classmates and instructor are good resources. Is there a place on campus where math tutors are available? Can your study skills be improved?

...no—I don't get it! This is a warning sign and you must not ignore it. You should get help right away or you will quickly be overwhelmed. See your instructor as soon as you can to discuss your situation. Together you can come up with a plan to get you the help you need.

$\boxed{4.2}$ Multiply and Divide Fractions

Learning Objectives

By the end of this section, you will be able to:

- Simplify fractions
- Multiply fractions
- Find reciprocals
- Divide fractions

Be Prepared!

Before you get started, take this readiness quiz.

1. Find the prime factorization of 48.
    If you missed this problem, review Example 2.48.

2. Draw a model of the fraction $\frac{3}{4}$.
    If you missed this problem, review Example 4.2.

3. Find two fractions equivalent to $\frac{5}{6}$.

    Answers may vary. Acceptable answers include $\frac{10}{12}, \frac{15}{18}, \frac{50}{60},$ etc.

    If you missed this problem, review Example 4.14.

Simplify Fractions

In working with equivalent fractions, you saw that there are many ways to write fractions that have the same value, or represent the same part of the whole. How do you know which one to use? Often, we'll use the fraction that is in *simplified* form.

A fraction is considered simplified if there are no common factors, other than 1, in the numerator and denominator. If a fraction does have common factors in the numerator and denominator, we can reduce the fraction to its simplified form by removing the common factors.

Simplified Fraction

A fraction is considered simplified if there are no common factors in the numerator and denominator.

For example,

- $\frac{2}{3}$ is simplified because there are no common factors of 2 and 3.

- $\frac{10}{15}$ is not simplified because 5 is a common factor of 10 and 15.

The process of simplifying a fraction is often called *reducing the fraction*. In the previous section, we used the Equivalent Fractions Property to find equivalent fractions. We can also use the Equivalent Fractions Property in reverse to simplify fractions. We rewrite the property to show both forms together.

Equivalent Fractions Property

If a, b, c are numbers where $b \neq 0, c \neq 0,$ then

$$\frac{a}{b} = \frac{a \cdot c}{b \cdot c} \quad \text{and} \quad \frac{a \cdot c}{b \cdot c} = \frac{a}{b}.$$

Notice that c is a common factor in the numerator and denominator. Anytime we have a common factor in the numerator and denominator, it can be removed.

HOW TO :: SIMPLIFY A FRACTION.

Step 1.   Rewrite the numerator and denominator to show the common factors. If needed, factor the numerator and denominator into prime numbers.

Step 2.   Simplify, using the equivalent fractions property, by removing common factors.

Step 3.   Multiply any remaining factors.

EXAMPLE 4.19

Simplify: $\frac{10}{15}$.

⊘ **Solution**

To simplify the fraction, we look for any common factors in the numerator and the denominator.

Notice that 5 is a factor of both 10 and 15.	$\frac{10}{15}$
Factor the numerator and denominator.	$\frac{2 \cdot 5}{3 \cdot 5}$
Remove the common factors.	$\frac{2 \cdot \cancel{5}}{3 \cdot \cancel{5}}$
Simplify.	$\frac{2}{3}$

> **TRY IT :: 4.37**   Simplify: $\frac{8}{12}$.

> **TRY IT :: 4.38**   Simplify: $\frac{12}{16}$.

To simplify a negative fraction, we use the same process as in Example 4.19. Remember to keep the negative sign.

EXAMPLE 4.20

Simplify: $-\frac{18}{24}$.

⊘ **Solution**

We notice that 18 and 24 both have factors of 6.	$-\frac{18}{24}$
Rewrite the numerator and denominator showing the common factor.	$-\frac{3 \cdot 6}{4 \cdot 6}$
Remove common factors.	$-\frac{3 \cdot \cancel{6}}{4 \cdot \cancel{6}}$
Simplify.	$-\frac{3}{4}$

> TRY IT :: 4.39   Simplify: $-\dfrac{21}{28}$.

> TRY IT :: 4.40   Simplify: $-\dfrac{16}{24}$.

After simplifying a fraction, it is always important to check the result to make sure that the numerator and denominator do not have any more factors in common. Remember, the definition of a simplified fraction: *a fraction is considered simplified if there are no common factors in the numerator and denominator.*

When we simplify an improper fraction, there is no need to change it to a mixed number.

EXAMPLE 4.21

Simplify: $-\dfrac{56}{32}$.

⊘ **Solution**

	$-\dfrac{56}{32}$
Rewrite the numerator and denominator, showing the common factors, 8.	$\dfrac{7 \cdot 8}{4 \cdot 8}$
Remove common factors.	$\dfrac{7 \cdot \cancel{8}}{4 \cdot \cancel{8}}$
Simplify.	$-\dfrac{7}{4}$

> TRY IT :: 4.41   Simplify: $-\dfrac{54}{42}$.

> TRY IT :: 4.42   Simplify: $-\dfrac{81}{45}$.

 HOW TO :: SIMPLIFY A FRACTION.

Step 1.   Rewrite the numerator and denominator to show the common factors. If needed, factor the numerator and denominator into prime numbers.

Step 2.   Simplify, using the equivalent fractions property, by removing common factors.

Step 3.   Multiply any remaining factors

Sometimes it may not be easy to find common factors of the numerator and denominator. A good idea, then, is to factor the numerator and the denominator into prime numbers. (You may want to use the factor tree method to identify the prime factors.) Then divide out the common factors using the Equivalent Fractions Property.

EXAMPLE 4.22

Simplify: $\dfrac{210}{385}$.

⊘ Solution

Use factor trees to factor the numerator and denominator.	$$\frac{210}{385}$$ (factor trees)
Rewrite the numerator and denominator as the product of the primes.	$\dfrac{210}{385} = \dfrac{2 \cdot 3 \cdot 5 \cdot 7}{5 \cdot 7 \cdot 11}$
Remove the common factors.	$\dfrac{2 \cdot 3 \cdot \cancel{5} \cdot \cancel{7}}{\cancel{5} \cdot \cancel{7} \cdot 11}$
Simplify.	$\dfrac{2 \cdot 3}{11}$
Multiply any remaining factors.	$\dfrac{6}{11}$

> **TRY IT : : 4.43**   Simplify: $\dfrac{69}{120}$.

> **TRY IT : : 4.44**   Simplify: $\dfrac{120}{192}$.

We can also simplify fractions containing variables. If a variable is a common factor in the numerator and denominator, we remove it just as we do with an integer factor.

EXAMPLE 4.23

Simplify: $\dfrac{5xy}{15x}$.

⊘ **Solution**

	$\dfrac{5xy}{15x}$
Rewrite numerator and denominator showing common factors.	$\dfrac{5 \cdot x \cdot y}{3 \cdot 5 \cdot x}$
Remove common factors.	$\dfrac{\cancel{5} \cdot \cancel{x} \cdot y}{3 \cdot \cancel{5} \cdot \cancel{x}}$
Simplify.	$\dfrac{y}{3}$

> **TRY IT : : 4.45**   Simplify: $\dfrac{7x}{7y}$.

> **TRY IT :: 4.46** Simplify: $\dfrac{9a}{9b}$.

Multiply fractions

A model may help you understand multiplication of fractions. We will use fraction tiles to model $\dfrac{1}{2} \cdot \dfrac{3}{4}$. To multiply $\dfrac{1}{2}$ and $\dfrac{3}{4}$, think $\dfrac{1}{2}$ of $\dfrac{3}{4}$.

Start with fraction tiles for three-fourths. To find one-half of three-fourths, we need to divide them into two equal groups. Since we cannot divide the three $\dfrac{1}{4}$ tiles evenly into two parts, we exchange them for smaller tiles.

We see $\dfrac{6}{8}$ is equivalent to $\dfrac{3}{4}$. Taking half of the six $\dfrac{1}{8}$ tiles gives us three $\dfrac{1}{8}$ tiles, which is $\dfrac{3}{8}$.

Therefore,

$$\dfrac{1}{2} \cdot \dfrac{3}{4} = \dfrac{3}{8}$$

MANIPULATIVE MATHEMATICS

Doing the Manipulative Mathematics activity "Model Fraction Multiplication" will help you develop a better understanding of how to multiply fractions.

EXAMPLE 4.24

Use a diagram to model $\dfrac{1}{2} \cdot \dfrac{3}{4}$.

⊘ **Solution**

First shade in $\dfrac{3}{4}$ of the rectangle.

We will take $\dfrac{1}{2}$ of this $\dfrac{3}{4}$, so we heavily shade $\dfrac{1}{2}$ of the shaded region.

Notice that 3 out of the 8 pieces are heavily shaded. This means that $\dfrac{3}{8}$ of the rectangle is heavily shaded.

Therefore, $\dfrac{1}{2}$ of $\dfrac{3}{4}$ is $\dfrac{3}{8}$, or $\dfrac{1}{2} \cdot \dfrac{3}{4} = \dfrac{3}{8}$.

> **TRY IT :: 4.47** Use a diagram to model: $\dfrac{1}{2} \cdot \dfrac{3}{5}$.

> **TRY IT : : 4.48**   Use a diagram to model: $\frac{1}{2}\cdot\frac{5}{6}$.

Look at the result we got from the model in Example 4.24. We found that $\frac{1}{2}\cdot\frac{3}{4}=\frac{3}{8}$. Do you notice that we could have gotten the same answer by multiplying the numerators and multiplying the denominators?

	$\frac{1}{2}\cdot\frac{3}{4}$
Multiply the numerators, and multiply the denominators.	$\frac{1}{2}\cdot\frac{3}{4}$
Simplify.	$\frac{3}{8}$

This leads to the definition of fraction multiplication. To multiply fractions, we multiply the numerators and multiply the denominators. Then we write the fraction in simplified form.

Fraction Multiplication

If a, b, c, and d are numbers where $b\neq 0$ and $d\neq 0$, then

$$\frac{a}{b}\cdot\frac{c}{d}=\frac{ac}{bd}$$

EXAMPLE 4.25

Multiply, and write the answer in simplified form: $\frac{3}{4}\cdot\frac{1}{5}$.

⊘ **Solution**

	$\frac{3}{4}\cdot\frac{1}{5}$
Multiply the numerators; multiply the denominators.	$\frac{3\cdot 1}{4\cdot 5}$
Simplify.	$\frac{3}{20}$

There are no common factors, so the fraction is simplified.

> **TRY IT : : 4.49**   Multiply, and write the answer in simplified form: $\frac{1}{3}\cdot\frac{2}{5}$.

> **TRY IT : : 4.50**   Multiply, and write the answer in simplified form: $\frac{3}{5}\cdot\frac{7}{8}$.

When multiplying fractions, the properties of positive and negative numbers still apply. It is a good idea to determine the sign of the product as the first step. In Example 4.26 we will multiply two negatives, so the product will be positive.

EXAMPLE 4.26

Multiply, and write the answer in simplified form: $-\frac{5}{8}\left(-\frac{2}{3}\right)$.

⊘ Solution

$$-\frac{5}{8}\left(-\frac{2}{3}\right)$$

The signs are the same, so the product is positive. Multiply the numerators, multiply the denominators.	$\frac{5 \cdot 2}{8 \cdot 3}$
Simplify.	$\frac{10}{24}$
Look for common factors in the numerator and denominator. Rewrite showing common factors.	$\frac{5 \cdot \cancel{2}}{12 \cdot \cancel{2}}$
Remove common factors.	$\frac{5}{12}$

Another way to find this product involves removing common factors earlier.

$$-\frac{5}{8}\left(-\frac{2}{3}\right)$$

Determine the sign of the product. Multiply.	$\frac{5 \cdot 2}{8 \cdot 3}$
Show common factors and then remove them.	$\frac{5 \cdot \cancel{2}}{4 \cdot \cancel{2} \cdot 3}$
Multiply remaining factors.	$\frac{5}{12}$

We get the same result.

> **TRY IT : : 4.51**   Multiply, and write the answer in simplified form: $-\frac{4}{7}\left(-\frac{5}{8}\right)$.

> **TRY IT : : 4.52**   Multiply, and write the answer in simplified form: $-\frac{7}{12}\left(-\frac{8}{9}\right)$.

EXAMPLE 4.27

Multiply, and write the answer in simplified form: $-\frac{14}{15} \cdot \frac{20}{21}$.

⊘ **Solution**

	$-\dfrac{14}{15}\cdot\dfrac{20}{21}$
Determine the sign of the product; multiply.	$-\dfrac{14}{15}\cdot\dfrac{20}{21}$
Are there any common factors in the numerator and the denominator? We know that 7 is a factor of 14 and 21, and 5 is a factor of 20 and 15.	
Rewrite showing common factors.	$-\dfrac{2\cdot\cancel{7}\cdot 4\cdot\cancel{5}}{3\cdot\cancel{5}\cdot 3\cdot\cancel{7}}$
Remove the common factors.	$-\dfrac{2\cdot 4}{3\cdot 3}$
Multiply the remaining factors.	$-\dfrac{8}{9}$

> **TRY IT : : 4.53**   Multiply, and write the answer in simplified form: $-\dfrac{10}{28}\cdot\dfrac{8}{15}$.

> **TRY IT : : 4.54**   Multiply, and write the answer in simplified form: $-\dfrac{9}{20}\cdot\dfrac{5}{12}$.

When multiplying a fraction by an integer, it may be helpful to write the integer as a fraction. Any integer, a, can be written as $\dfrac{a}{1}$. So, $3 = \dfrac{3}{1}$, for example.

EXAMPLE 4.28

Multiply, and write the answer in simplified form:

ⓐ $\dfrac{1}{7}\cdot 56$

ⓑ $\dfrac{12}{5}(-20x)$

⊘ **Solution**

ⓐ

	$\dfrac{1}{7}\cdot 56$
Write 56 as a fraction.	$\dfrac{1}{7}\cdot\dfrac{56}{1}$
Determine the sign of the product; multiply.	$\dfrac{56}{7}$
Simplify.	8

ⓑ

$$\frac{12}{5}(-20x)$$

Write −20x as a fraction.

$$\frac{12}{5}\left(\frac{-20x}{1}\right)$$

Determine the sign of the product; multiply.

$$-\frac{12 \cdot 20 \cdot x}{5 \cdot 1}$$

Show common factors and then remove them.

$$-\frac{12 \cdot 4 \cdot \cancel{5}x}{\cancel{5} \cdot 1}$$

Multiply remaining factors; simplify.

$$-48x$$

> **TRY IT : : 4.55**   Multiply, and write the answer in simplified form:

ⓐ $\frac{1}{8} \cdot 72$ ⓑ $\frac{11}{3}(-9a)$

> **TRY IT : : 4.56**   Multiply, and write the answer in simplified form:

ⓐ $\frac{3}{8} \cdot 64$ ⓑ $16x \cdot \frac{11}{12}$

Find Reciprocals

The fractions $\frac{2}{3}$ and $\frac{3}{2}$ are related to each other in a special way. So are $-\frac{10}{7}$ and $-\frac{7}{10}$. Do you see how? Besides looking like upside-down versions of one another, if we were to multiply these pairs of fractions, the product would be 1.

$$\frac{2}{3} \cdot \frac{3}{2} = 1 \quad \text{and} \quad -\frac{10}{7}\left(-\frac{7}{10}\right) = 1$$

Such pairs of numbers are called reciprocals.

Reciprocal

The **reciprocal** of the fraction $\frac{a}{b}$ is $\frac{b}{a}$, where $a \neq 0$ and $b \neq 0$,

A number and its reciprocal have a product of 1.

$$\frac{a}{b} \cdot \frac{b}{a} = 1$$

To find the reciprocal of a fraction, we invert the fraction. This means that we place the numerator in the denominator and the denominator in the numerator.

To get a positive result when multiplying two numbers, the numbers must have the same sign. So reciprocals must have the same sign.

$$\frac{a}{b} \cdot \frac{b}{a} = 1 \text{ positive}$$

$$3 \cdot \frac{1}{3} = 1 \quad \text{and} \quad -3 \cdot \left(-\frac{1}{3}\right) = 1$$

both positive   both negative

To find the reciprocal, keep the same sign and invert the fraction. The number zero does not have a reciprocal. Why? A number and its reciprocal multiply to 1. Is there any number r so that $0 \cdot r = 1$? No. So, the number 0 does not have a reciprocal.

EXAMPLE 4.29

Find the reciprocal of each number. Then check that the product of each number and its reciprocal is 1.

ⓐ $\dfrac{4}{9}$ ⓑ $-\dfrac{1}{6}$ ⓒ $-\dfrac{14}{5}$ ⓓ 7

⊘ **Solution**

To find the reciprocals, we keep the sign and invert the fractions.

ⓐ

Find the reciprocal of $\dfrac{4}{9}$.	The reciprocal of $\dfrac{4}{9}$ is $\dfrac{9}{4}$.
Check:	
Multiply the number and its reciprocal.	$\dfrac{4}{9} \cdot \dfrac{9}{4}$
Multiply numerators and denominators.	$\dfrac{36}{36}$
Simplify.	$1 \checkmark$

ⓑ

Find the reciprocal of $-\dfrac{1}{6}$.	$-\dfrac{6}{1}$
Simplify.	-6
Check:	$-\dfrac{1}{6} \cdot \left(-6\right)$
	$1 \checkmark$

ⓒ

Find the reciprocal of $-\dfrac{14}{5}$.	$-\dfrac{5}{14}$
Check:	$-\dfrac{14}{5} \cdot \left(-\dfrac{5}{14}\right)$
	$\dfrac{70}{70}$
	$1 \checkmark$

(d)

Find the reciprocal of 7.

Write 7 as a fraction. $\frac{7}{1}$

Write the reciprocal of $\frac{7}{1}$. $\frac{1}{7}$

Check: $7 \cdot \left(\frac{1}{7}\right)$

1 ✓

> **TRY IT : :** 4.57   Find the reciprocal:

ⓐ $\frac{5}{7}$ ⓑ $-\frac{1}{8}$ ⓒ $-\frac{11}{4}$ ⓓ 14

> **TRY IT : :** 4.58   Find the reciprocal:

ⓐ $\frac{3}{7}$ ⓑ $-\frac{1}{12}$ ⓒ $-\frac{14}{9}$ ⓓ 21

In a previous chapter, we worked with opposites and absolute values. Table 4.20 compares opposites, absolute values, and reciprocals.

Opposite	Absolute Value	Reciprocal
has opposite sign	is never negative	has same sign, fraction inverts

Table 4.20

EXAMPLE 4.30

Fill in the chart for each fraction in the left column:

Number	Opposite	Absolute Value	Reciprocal
$-\frac{3}{8}$			
$\frac{1}{2}$			
$\frac{9}{5}$			
-5			

⊘ **Solution**

To find the opposite, change the sign. To find the absolute value, leave the positive numbers the same, but take the opposite of the negative numbers. To find the reciprocal, keep the sign the same and invert the fraction.

Number	Opposite	Absolute Value	Reciprocal
$-\dfrac{3}{8}$	$\dfrac{3}{8}$	$\dfrac{3}{8}$	$-\dfrac{8}{3}$
$\dfrac{1}{2}$	$-\dfrac{1}{2}$	$\dfrac{1}{2}$	2
$\dfrac{9}{5}$	$-\dfrac{9}{5}$	$\dfrac{9}{5}$	$\dfrac{5}{9}$
-5	5	5	$-\dfrac{1}{5}$

> **TRY IT ::** 4.59   Fill in the chart for each number given:

Number	Opposite	Absolute Value	Reciprocal
$-\dfrac{5}{8}$			
$\dfrac{1}{4}$			
$\dfrac{8}{3}$			
-8			

> **TRY IT ::** 4.60   Fill in the chart for each number given:

Number	Opposite	Absolute Value	Reciprocal
$-\dfrac{4}{7}$			
$\dfrac{1}{8}$			
$\dfrac{9}{4}$			
-1			

Divide Fractions

Why is $12 \div 3 = 4$? We previously modeled this with counters. How many groups of 3 counters can be made from a group of 12 counters?

There are 4 groups of 3 counters. In other words, there are four 3s in 12. So, $12 \div 3 = 4$.

What about dividing fractions? Suppose we want to find the quotient: $\dfrac{1}{2} \div \dfrac{1}{6}$. We need to figure out how many $\dfrac{1}{6}$s there are in $\frac{1}{2}$. We can use fraction tiles to model this division. We start by lining up the half and sixth fraction tiles as shown in Figure 4.5. Notice, there are three $\frac{1}{6}$ tiles in $\frac{1}{2}$, so $\frac{1}{2} \div \frac{1}{6} = 3$.

Figure 4.5

 MANIPULATIVE MATHEMATICS

Doing the Manipulative Mathematics activity "Model Fraction Division" will help you develop a better understanding of dividing fractions.

EXAMPLE 4.31

Model: $\frac{1}{4} \div \frac{1}{8}$.

⊘ **Solution**

We want to determine how many $\frac{1}{8}$s are in $\frac{1}{4}$. Start with one $\frac{1}{4}$ tile. Line up $\frac{1}{8}$ tiles underneath the $\frac{1}{4}$ tile.

There are two $\frac{1}{8}$s in $\frac{1}{4}$.

So, $\frac{1}{4} \div \frac{1}{8} = 2$.

> **TRY IT : : 4.61**   Model: $\frac{1}{3} \div \frac{1}{6}$.

> **TRY IT : : 4.62**   Model: $\frac{1}{2} \div \frac{1}{4}$.

EXAMPLE 4.32

Model: $2 \div \frac{1}{4}$.

⊘ **Solution**

We are trying to determine how many $\frac{1}{4}$s there are in 2. We can model this as shown.

Because there are eight $\frac{1}{4}$s in 2, $2 \div \frac{1}{4} = 8$.

> **TRY IT : : 4.63**   Model: $2 \div \frac{1}{3}$.

> **TRY IT :: 4.64**   Model: $3 \div \frac{1}{2}$

Let's use money to model $2 \div \frac{1}{4}$ in another way. We often read $\frac{1}{4}$ as a 'quarter', and we know that a quarter is one-fourth of a dollar as shown in Figure 4.6. So we can think of $2 \div \frac{1}{4}$ as, "How many quarters are there in two dollars?" One dollar is 4 quarters, so 2 dollars would be 8 quarters. So again, $2 \div \frac{1}{4} = 8$.

Figure 4.6 The U.S. coin called a quarter is worth one-fourth of a dollar.

Using fraction tiles, we showed that $\frac{1}{2} \div \frac{1}{6} = 3$. Notice that $\frac{1}{2} \cdot \frac{6}{1} = 3$ also. How are $\frac{1}{6}$ and $\frac{6}{1}$ related? They are reciprocals. This leads us to the procedure for fraction division.

Fraction Division

If a, b, c, and d are numbers where $b \neq 0$, $c \neq 0$, and $d \neq 0$, then

$$\frac{a}{b} \div \frac{c}{d} = \frac{a}{b} \cdot \frac{d}{c}$$

To divide fractions, multiply the first fraction by the reciprocal of the second.

We need to say $b \neq 0$, $c \neq 0$ and $d \neq 0$ to be sure we don't divide by zero.

EXAMPLE 4.33

Divide, and write the answer in simplified form: $\frac{2}{5} \div \left(-\frac{3}{7}\right)$.

⊘ **Solution**

$$\frac{2}{5} \div \left(-\frac{3}{7}\right)$$

Multiply the first fraction by the reciprocal of the second. $\frac{2}{5}\left(-\frac{7}{3}\right)$

Multiply. The product is negative. $-\frac{14}{15}$

> **TRY IT :: 4.65**   Divide, and write the answer in simplified form: $\frac{3}{7} \div \left(-\frac{2}{3}\right)$.

> **TRY IT :: 4.66**   Divide, and write the answer in simplified form: $\frac{2}{3} \div \left(-\frac{7}{5}\right)$.

EXAMPLE 4.34

Divide, and write the answer in simplified form: $\frac{2}{3} \div \frac{n}{5}$.

Solution

$$\frac{2}{3} \div \frac{n}{5}$$

Multiply the first fraction by the reciprocal of the second. $\frac{2}{3} \cdot \frac{5}{n}$

Multiply. $\frac{10}{3n}$

> **TRY IT :: 4.67**   Divide, and write the answer in simplified form: $\frac{3}{5} \div \frac{p}{7}$.

> **TRY IT :: 4.68**   Divide, and write the answer in simplified form: $\frac{5}{8} \div \frac{q}{3}$.

EXAMPLE 4.35

Divide, and write the answer in simplified form: $-\frac{3}{4} \div \left(-\frac{7}{8}\right)$.

Solution

$$-\frac{3}{4} \div \left(-\frac{7}{8}\right)$$

Multiply the first fraction by the reciprocal of the second. $-\frac{3}{4} \cdot \left(-\frac{8}{7}\right)$

Multiply. Remember to determine the sign first. $\frac{3 \cdot 8}{4 \cdot 7}$

Rewrite to show common factors. $\frac{3 \cdot \cancel{4} \cdot 2}{\cancel{4} \cdot 7}$

Remove common factors and simplify. $\frac{6}{7}$

> **TRY IT :: 4.69**   Divide, and write the answer in simplified form: $-\frac{2}{3} \div \left(-\frac{5}{6}\right)$.

> **TRY IT :: 4.70**   Divide, and write the answer in simplified form: $-\frac{5}{6} \div \left(-\frac{2}{3}\right)$.

EXAMPLE 4.36

Divide, and write the answer in simplified form: $\frac{7}{18} \div \frac{14}{27}$.

⊘ **Solution**

$$\frac{7}{18} \div \frac{14}{27}$$

Multiply the first fraction by the reciprocal of the second.	$\frac{7}{18} \cdot \frac{27}{14}$
Multiply.	$\frac{7 \cdot 27}{18 \cdot 14}$
Rewrite showing common factors.	$\frac{\cancel{7} \cdot \cancel{9} \cdot 3}{\cancel{9} \cdot 2 \cdot \cancel{7} \cdot 2}$
Remove common factors.	$\frac{3}{2 \cdot 2}$
Simplify.	$\frac{3}{4}$

> **TRY IT : : 4.71**   Divide, and write the answer in simplified form: $\frac{7}{27} \div \frac{35}{36}$.

> **TRY IT : : 4.72**   Divide, and write the answer in simplified form: $\frac{5}{14} \div \frac{15}{28}$.

▶ **MEDIA : :** ACCESS ADDITIONAL ONLINE RESOURCES
- Simplifying Fractions (http://www.openstaxcollege.org/l/24SimplifyFrac)
- Multiplying Fractions (Positive Only) (http://www.openstaxcollege.org/l/24MultiplyFrac)
- Multiplying Signed Fractions (http://www.openstaxcollege.org/l/24MultSigned)
- Dividing Fractions (Positive Only) (http://www.openstaxcollege.org/l/24DivideFrac)
- Dividing Signed Fractions (http://www.openstaxcollege.org/l/24DivideSign)

4.2 EXERCISES

Practice Makes Perfect

Simplify Fractions

In the following exercises, simplify each fraction. Do not convert any improper fractions to mixed numbers.

77. $\frac{7}{21}$

78. $\frac{8}{24}$

79. $\frac{15}{20}$

80. $\frac{12}{18}$

81. $-\frac{40}{88}$

82. $-\frac{63}{99}$

83. $-\frac{108}{63}$

84. $-\frac{104}{48}$

85. $\frac{120}{252}$

86. $\frac{182}{294}$

87. $-\frac{168}{192}$

88. $-\frac{140}{224}$

89. $\frac{11x}{11y}$

90. $\frac{15a}{15b}$

91. $-\frac{3x}{12y}$

92. $-\frac{4x}{32y}$

93. $\frac{14x^2}{21y}$

94. $\frac{24a}{32b^2}$

Multiply Fractions

In the following exercises, use a diagram to model.

95. $\frac{1}{2} \cdot \frac{2}{3}$

96. $\frac{1}{2} \cdot \frac{5}{8}$

97. $\frac{1}{3} \cdot \frac{5}{6}$

98. $\frac{1}{3} \cdot \frac{2}{5}$

In the following exercises, multiply, and write the answer in simplified form.

99. $\frac{2}{5} \cdot \frac{1}{3}$

100. $\frac{1}{2} \cdot \frac{3}{8}$

101. $\frac{3}{4} \cdot \frac{9}{10}$

102. $\frac{4}{5} \cdot \frac{2}{7}$

103. $-\frac{2}{3}\left(-\frac{3}{8}\right)$

104. $-\frac{3}{4}\left(-\frac{4}{9}\right)$

105. $-\frac{5}{9} \cdot \frac{3}{10}$

106. $-\frac{3}{8} \cdot \frac{4}{15}$

107. $\frac{7}{12}\left(-\frac{8}{21}\right)$

108. $\frac{5}{12}\left(-\frac{8}{15}\right)$

109. $\left(-\frac{14}{15}\right)\left(\frac{9}{20}\right)$

110. $\left(-\frac{9}{10}\right)\left(\frac{25}{33}\right)$

111. $\left(-\frac{63}{84}\right)\left(-\frac{44}{90}\right)$

112. $\left(-\frac{33}{60}\right)\left(-\frac{40}{88}\right)$

113. $4 \cdot \frac{5}{11}$

114. $5 \cdot \frac{8}{3}$

115. $\frac{3}{7} \cdot 21n$

116. $\frac{5}{6} \cdot 30m$

117. $-28p\left(-\frac{1}{4}\right)$

118. $-51q\left(-\frac{1}{3}\right)$

119. $-8\left(\frac{17}{4}\right)$

120. $\frac{14}{5}(-15)$

121. $-1\left(-\frac{3}{8}\right)$

122. $(-1)\left(-\frac{6}{7}\right)$

123. $\left(\frac{2}{3}\right)^3$

124. $\left(\frac{4}{5}\right)^2$

125. $\left(\frac{6}{5}\right)^4$

126. $\left(\frac{4}{7}\right)^4$

Find Reciprocals

In the following exercises, find the reciprocal.

127. $\frac{3}{4}$

128. $\frac{2}{3}$

129. $-\frac{5}{17}$

130. $-\frac{6}{19}$

131. $\frac{11}{8}$

132. -13

133. -19

134. -1

135. 1

136. Fill in the chart.

	Opposite	Absolute Value	Reciprocal
$-\frac{7}{11}$			
$\frac{4}{5}$			
$\frac{10}{7}$			
-8			

137. Fill in the chart.

	Opposite	Absolute Value	Reciprocal
$-\frac{3}{13}$			
$\frac{9}{14}$			
$\frac{15}{7}$			
-9			

Divide Fractions

In the following exercises, model each fraction division.

138. $\frac{1}{2} \div \frac{1}{4}$

139. $\frac{1}{2} \div \frac{1}{8}$

140. $2 \div \frac{1}{5}$

141. $3 \div \frac{1}{4}$

In the following exercises, divide, and write the answer in simplified form.

142. $\frac{1}{2} \div \frac{1}{4}$

143. $\frac{1}{2} \div \frac{1}{8}$

144. $\frac{3}{4} \div \frac{2}{3}$

145. $\frac{4}{5} \div \frac{3}{4}$

146. $-\frac{4}{5} \div \frac{4}{7}$

147. $-\frac{3}{4} \div \frac{3}{5}$

148. $-\frac{7}{9} \div \left(-\frac{7}{9}\right)$

149. $-\frac{5}{6} \div \left(-\frac{5}{6}\right)$

150. $\frac{3}{4} \div \frac{x}{11}$

151. $\frac{2}{5} \div \frac{y}{9}$

152. $\frac{5}{8} \div \frac{a}{10}$

153. $\frac{5}{6} \div \frac{c}{15}$

154. $\frac{5}{18} \div \left(-\frac{15}{24}\right)$

155. $\frac{7}{18} \div \left(-\frac{14}{27}\right)$

156. $\frac{7p}{12} \div \frac{21p}{8}$

157. $\frac{5q}{12} \div \frac{15q}{8}$

158. $\frac{8u}{15} \div \frac{12v}{25}$

159. $\frac{12r}{25} \div \frac{18s}{35}$

160. $-5 \div \frac{1}{2}$

161. $-3 \div \frac{1}{4}$

162. $\frac{3}{4} \div (-12)$

163. $\frac{2}{5} \div (-10)$

164. $-18 \div \left(-\frac{9}{2}\right)$

165. $-15 \div \left(-\frac{5}{3}\right)$

166. $\frac{1}{2} \div \left(-\frac{3}{4}\right) \div \frac{7}{8}$

167. $\frac{11}{2} \div \frac{7}{8} \cdot \frac{2}{11}$

Everyday Math

168. Baking A recipe for chocolate chip cookies calls for $\frac{3}{4}$ cup brown sugar. Imelda wants to double the recipe.

ⓐ How much brown sugar will Imelda need? Show your calculation. Write your result as an improper fraction and as a mixed number.

ⓑ Measuring cups usually come in sets of $\frac{1}{8}$, $\frac{1}{4}$, $\frac{1}{3}$, $\frac{1}{2}$, and 1 cup. Draw a diagram to show two different ways that Imelda could measure the brown sugar needed to double the recipe.

169. Baking Nina is making 4 pans of fudge to serve after a music recital. For each pan, she needs $\frac{2}{3}$ cup of condensed milk.

ⓐ How much condensed milk will Nina need? Show your calculation. Write your result as an improper fraction and as a mixed number.

ⓑ Measuring cups usually come in sets of $\frac{1}{8}$, $\frac{1}{4}$, $\frac{1}{3}$, $\frac{1}{2}$, and 1 cup. Draw a diagram to show two different ways that Nina could measure the condensed milk she needs.

170. Portions Don purchased a bulk package of candy that weighs 5 pounds. He wants to sell the candy in little bags that hold $\frac{1}{4}$ pound. How many little bags of candy can he fill from the bulk package?

171. Portions Kristen has $\frac{3}{4}$ yards of ribbon. She wants to cut it into equal parts to make hair ribbons for her daughter's 6 dolls. How long will each doll's hair ribbon be?

Writing Exercises

172. Explain how you find the reciprocal of a fraction.

173. Explain how you find the reciprocal of a negative fraction.

174. Rafael wanted to order half a medium pizza at a restaurant. The waiter told him that a medium pizza could be cut into 6 or 8 slices. Would he prefer 3 out of 6 slices or 4 out of 8 slices? Rafael replied that since he wasn't very hungry, he would prefer 3 out of 6 slices. Explain what is wrong with Rafael's reasoning.

175. Give an example from everyday life that demonstrates how $\frac{1}{2} \cdot \frac{2}{3}$ is $\frac{1}{3}$.

Self Check

ⓐ *After completing the exercises, use this checklist to evaluate your mastery of the objectives of this section.*

I can...	Confidently	With some help	No-I don't get it!
simplify fractions.			
multiply fractions.			
find reciprocals.			
divide fractions.			

ⓑ *After reviewing this checklist, what will you do to become confident for all objectives?*

4.3 Multiply and Divide Mixed Numbers and Complex Fractions

Learning Objectives

By the end of this section, you will be able to:

- Multiply and divide mixed numbers
- Translate phrases to expressions with fractions
- Simplify complex fractions
- Simplify expressions written with a fraction bar

Be Prepared!

Before you get started, take this readiness quiz.

1. Divide and reduce, if possible: $(4 + 5) \div (10 - 7)$.

   If you missed this problem, review Example 3.21.

2. Multiply and write the answer in simplified form: $\frac{1}{8} \cdot \frac{2}{3}$.

   If you missed this problem, review Example 4.25.

3. Convert $2\frac{3}{5}$ into an improper fraction.

   If you missed this problem, review Example 4.11.

Multiply and Divide Mixed Numbers

In the previous section, you learned how to multiply and divide fractions. All of the examples there used either proper or improper fractions. What happens when you are asked to multiply or divide mixed numbers? Remember that we can convert a mixed number to an improper fraction. And you learned how to do that in Visualize Fractions.

EXAMPLE 4.37

Multiply: $3\frac{1}{3} \cdot \frac{5}{8}$

Solution

$$3\frac{1}{3} \cdot \frac{5}{8}$$

Convert $3\frac{1}{3}$ to an improper fraction.	$\frac{10}{3} \cdot \frac{5}{8}$
Multiply.	$\frac{10 \cdot 5}{3 \cdot 8}$
Look for common factors.	$\frac{\cancel{2} \cdot 5 \cdot 5}{3 \cdot \cancel{2} \cdot 4}$
Remove common factors.	$\frac{5 \cdot 5}{3 \cdot 4}$
Simplify.	$\frac{25}{12}$

Notice that we left the answer as an improper fraction, $\frac{25}{12}$, and did not convert it to a mixed number. In algebra, it is preferable to write answers as improper fractions instead of mixed numbers. This avoids any possible confusion between $2\frac{1}{12}$ and $2 \cdot \frac{1}{12}$.

> **TRY IT : : 4.73**   Multiply, and write your answer in simplified form: $5\frac{2}{3} \cdot \frac{6}{17}$.

> **TRY IT : : 4.74**   Multiply, and write your answer in simplified form: $\frac{3}{7} \cdot 5\frac{1}{4}$.

 HOW TO : : MULTIPLY OR DIVIDE MIXED NUMBERS.

Step 1.   Convert the mixed numbers to improper fractions.
Step 2.   Follow the rules for fraction multiplication or division.
Step 3.   Simplify if possible.

EXAMPLE 4.38

Multiply, and write your answer in simplified form: $2\frac{4}{5}\left(-1\frac{7}{8}\right)$.

Solution

$$2\frac{4}{5}\left(-1\frac{7}{8}\right)$$

Convert mixed numbers to improper fractions.	$\frac{14}{5}\left(-\frac{15}{8}\right)$
Multiply.	$-\frac{14 \cdot 15}{5 \cdot 8}$
Look for common factors.	$-\frac{\cancel{2} \cdot 7 \cdot \cancel{5} \cdot 3}{\cancel{5} \cdot \cancel{2} \cdot 4}$
Remove common factors.	$-\frac{7 \cdot 3}{4}$
Simplify.	$-\frac{21}{4}$

> **TRY IT : : 4.75**   Multiply, and write your answer in simplified form. $5\frac{5}{7}\left(-2\frac{5}{8}\right)$.

> **TRY IT : : 4.76**   Multiply, and write your answer in simplified form. $-3\frac{2}{5} \cdot 4\frac{1}{6}$.

EXAMPLE 4.39

Divide, and write your answer in simplified form: $3\frac{4}{7} \div 5$.

⊘ **Solution**

$$3\frac{4}{7} \div 5$$

Convert mixed numbers to improper fractions.

$$\frac{25}{7} \div \frac{5}{1}$$

Multiply the first fraction by the reciprocal of the second.

$$\frac{25}{7} \cdot \frac{1}{5}$$

Multiply.

$$\frac{25 \cdot 1}{7 \cdot 5}$$

Look for common factors.

$$\frac{\cancel{5} \cdot 5 \cdot 1}{7 \cdot \cancel{5}}$$

Remove common factors.

$$\frac{5 \cdot 1}{7}$$

Simplify.

$$\frac{5}{7}$$

> **TRY IT : : 4.77**   Divide, and write your answer in simplified form: $4\frac{3}{8} \div 7$.

> **TRY IT : : 4.78**   Divide, and write your answer in simplified form: $2\frac{5}{8} \div 3$.

EXAMPLE 4.40

Divide: $2\frac{1}{2} \div 1\frac{1}{4}$.

⊘ **Solution**

$$2\frac{1}{2} \div 1\frac{1}{4}$$

Convert mixed numbers to improper fractions.

$$\frac{5}{2} \div \frac{5}{4}$$

Multiply the first fraction by the reciprocal of the second.

$$\frac{5}{2} \cdot \frac{4}{5}$$

Multiply.

$$\frac{5 \cdot 4}{2 \cdot 5}$$

Look for common factors.

$$\frac{\cancel{5} \cdot \cancel{2} \cdot 2}{\cancel{2} \cdot 1 \cdot \cancel{5}}$$

Remove common factors.

$$\frac{2}{1}$$

Simplify.

$$2$$

> **TRY IT :: 4.79**   Divide, and write your answer in simplified form: $2\frac{2}{3} \div 1\frac{1}{3}$.

> **TRY IT :: 4.80**   Divide, and write your answer in simplified form: $3\frac{3}{4} \div 1\frac{1}{2}$.

Translate Phrases to Expressions with Fractions

The words *quotient* and *ratio* are often used to describe fractions. In Subtract Whole Numbers, we defined quotient as the result of division. The quotient of a and b is the result you get from dividing a by b, or $\frac{a}{b}$. Let's practice translating some phrases into algebraic expressions using these terms.

EXAMPLE 4.41

Translate the phrase into an algebraic expression: "the quotient of $3x$ and 8."

⊘ **Solution**

The keyword is *quotient*; it tells us that the operation is division. Look for the words *of* and *and* to find the numbers to divide.

The quotient **of** $3x$ **and** 8.

This tells us that we need to divide $3x$ by 8. $\dfrac{3x}{8}$

> **TRY IT :: 4.81**   Translate the phrase into an algebraic expression: the quotient of $9s$ and 14.

> **TRY IT :: 4.82**   Translate the phrase into an algebraic expression: the quotient of $5y$ and 6.

EXAMPLE 4.42

Translate the phrase into an algebraic expression: the quotient of the difference of m and n, and p.

⊘ **Solution**

We are looking for the *quotient* of the *difference* of m and , and p. This means we want to divide the difference of m and n by p.

$$\frac{m-n}{p}$$

> **TRY IT :: 4.83**
>
> Translate the phrase into an algebraic expression: the quotient of the difference of a and b, and cd.

> **TRY IT :: 4.84**
>
> Translate the phrase into an algebraic expression: the quotient of the sum of p and q, and r.

Simplify Complex Fractions

Our work with fractions so far has included proper fractions, improper fractions, and mixed numbers. Another kind of fraction is called **complex fraction**, which is a fraction in which the numerator or the denominator contains a fraction.

Some examples of complex fractions are:

$$\frac{\frac{6}{7}}{3} \qquad \frac{\frac{3}{4}}{\frac{5}{8}} \qquad \frac{\frac{x}{2}}{\frac{5}{6}}$$

To simplify a complex fraction, remember that the fraction bar means division. So the complex fraction $\dfrac{\frac{3}{4}}{\frac{5}{8}}$ can be written as $\dfrac{3}{4} \div \dfrac{5}{8}$.

EXAMPLE 4.43

Simplify: $\dfrac{\frac{3}{4}}{\frac{5}{8}}$.

⊘ **Solution**

	$\dfrac{\frac{3}{4}}{\frac{5}{8}}$
Rewrite as division.	$\dfrac{3}{4} \div \dfrac{5}{8}$
Multiply the first fraction by the reciprocal of the second.	$\dfrac{3}{4} \cdot \dfrac{8}{5}$
Multiply.	$\dfrac{3 \cdot 8}{4 \cdot 5}$
Look for common factors.	$\dfrac{3 \cdot \cancel{4} \cdot 2}{\cancel{4} \cdot 5}$
Remove common factors and simplify.	$\dfrac{6}{5}$

> **TRY IT :: 4.85**   Simplify: $\dfrac{\frac{2}{3}}{\frac{5}{6}}$.

> **TRY IT :: 4.86**   Simplify: $\dfrac{\frac{3}{7}}{\frac{6}{11}}$.

 HOW TO :: SIMPLIFY A COMPLEX FRACTION.

Step 1.   Rewrite the complex fraction as a division problem.

Step 2.   Follow the rules for dividing fractions.

Step 3.   Simplify if possible.

EXAMPLE 4.44

Simplify: $\dfrac{-\frac{6}{7}}{3}$.

⊘ **Solution**

$$\dfrac{-\dfrac{6}{7}}{3}$$

Rewrite as division.	$-\dfrac{6}{7} \div 3$
Multiply the first fraction by the reciprocal of the second.	$-\dfrac{6}{7} \cdot \dfrac{1}{3}$
Multiply; the product will be negative.	$-\dfrac{6 \cdot 1}{7 \cdot 3}$
Look for common factors.	$-\dfrac{\cancel{3} \cdot 2 \cdot 1}{7 \cdot \cancel{3}}$
Remove common factors and simplify.	$-\dfrac{2}{7}$

> **TRY IT : :** 4.87   Simplify: $\dfrac{-\dfrac{8}{7}}{4}$.

> **TRY IT : :** 4.88   Simplify: $-\dfrac{3}{\dfrac{9}{10}}$.

EXAMPLE 4.45

Simplify: $\dfrac{\dfrac{x}{2}}{\dfrac{xy}{6}}$.

⊘ **Solution**

$$\dfrac{\dfrac{x}{2}}{\dfrac{xy}{6}}$$

Rewrite as division.	$\dfrac{x}{2} \div \dfrac{xy}{6}$
Multiply the first fraction by the reciprocal of the second.	$\dfrac{x}{2} \cdot \dfrac{6}{xy}$
Multiply.	$\dfrac{x \cdot 6}{2 \cdot xy}$
Look for common factors.	$\dfrac{\cancel{x} \cdot 3 \cdot \cancel{2}}{\cancel{2} \cdot \cancel{x} \cdot y}$
Remove common factors and simplify.	$\dfrac{3}{y}$

> **TRY IT : : 4.89**   Simplify: $\dfrac{\frac{a}{8}}{\frac{ab}{6}}$.

> **TRY IT : : 4.90**   Simplify: $\dfrac{\frac{p}{2}}{\frac{pq}{8}}$.

EXAMPLE 4.46

Simplify: $\dfrac{2\frac{3}{4}}{\frac{1}{8}}$.

⊘ **Solution**

	$\dfrac{2\frac{3}{4}}{\frac{1}{8}}$
Rewrite as division.	$2\frac{3}{4} \div \frac{1}{8}$
Change the mixed number to an improper fraction.	$\dfrac{11}{4} \div \dfrac{1}{8}$
Multiply the first fraction by the reciprocal of the second.	$\dfrac{11}{4} \cdot \dfrac{8}{1}$
Multiply.	$\dfrac{11 \cdot 8}{4 \cdot 1}$
Look for common factors.	$\dfrac{11 \cdot \cancel{4} \cdot 2}{\cancel{4} \cdot 1}$
Remove common factors and simplify.	22

> **TRY IT : : 4.91**   Simplify: $\dfrac{\frac{5}{7}}{1\frac{2}{5}}$.

> **TRY IT : : 4.92**   Simplify: $\dfrac{\frac{8}{5}}{3\frac{1}{5}}$.

Simplify Expressions with a Fraction Bar

Where does the negative sign go in a fraction? Usually, the negative sign is placed in front of the fraction, but you will sometimes see a fraction with a negative numerator or denominator. Remember that fractions represent division. The fraction $-\frac{1}{3}$ could be the result of dividing $\frac{-1}{3}$, a negative by a positive, or of dividing $\frac{1}{-3}$, a positive by a negative.

When the numerator and denominator have different signs, the quotient is negative.

$$\frac{-1}{3} = -\frac{1}{3} \qquad \frac{\text{negative}}{\text{positive}} = \text{negative} \qquad \frac{1}{-3} = -\frac{1}{3} \qquad \frac{\text{positive}}{\text{negative}} = \text{negative}$$

If *both* the numerator and denominator are negative, then the fraction itself is positive because we are dividing a negative by a negative.

$$\frac{-1}{-3} = \frac{1}{3} \qquad \frac{\text{negative}}{\text{negative}} = \text{positive}$$

Placement of Negative Sign in a Fraction

For any positive numbers a and b,

$$\frac{-a}{b} = \frac{a}{-b} = -\frac{a}{b}$$

EXAMPLE 4.47

Which of the following fractions are equivalent to $\frac{7}{-8}$?

$$\frac{-7}{-8}, \frac{-7}{8}, \frac{7}{8}, -\frac{7}{8}$$

⊘ **Solution**

The quotient of a positive and a negative is a negative, so $\frac{7}{-8}$ is negative. Of the fractions listed, $\frac{-7}{8}$ and $-\frac{7}{8}$ are also negative.

> **TRY IT ::** 4.93   Which of the following fractions are equivalent to $\frac{-3}{5}$?

$$\frac{-3}{-5}, \frac{3}{5}, -\frac{3}{5}, \frac{3}{-5}$$

> **TRY IT ::** 4.94   Which of the following fractions are equivalent to $-\frac{2}{7}$?

$$\frac{-2}{-7}, \frac{-2}{7}, \frac{2}{7}, \frac{2}{-7}$$

Fraction bars act as grouping symbols. The expressions above and below the fraction bar should be treated as if they were in parentheses. For example, $\frac{4+8}{5-3}$ means $(4+8) \div (5-3)$. The order of operations tells us to simplify the numerator and the denominator first—as if there were parentheses—before we divide.

We'll add fraction bars to our set of grouping symbols from Use the Language of Algebra to have a more complete set here.

Grouping Symbols

Parentheses	( )
Brackets	[ ]
Braces	{ }
Absolute value	| |
Fraction Bar	□/□

 HOW TO :: SIMPLIFY AN EXPRESSION WITH A FRACTION BAR.

Step 1.   Simplify the numerator.

Step 2.   Simplify the denominator.

Step 3.   Simplify the fraction.

EXAMPLE 4.48

Simplify: $\dfrac{4+8}{5-3}$.

⊘ **Solution**

$$\dfrac{4+8}{5-3}$$

Simplify the expression in the numerator. $\qquad\qquad \dfrac{12}{5-3}$

Simplify the expression in the denominator. $\qquad \dfrac{12}{2}$

Simplify the fraction. $\qquad\qquad\qquad\qquad\qquad$ 6

> **TRY IT :: 4.95** $\qquad$ Simplify: $\dfrac{4+6}{11-2}$.

> **TRY IT :: 4.96** $\qquad$ Simplify: $\dfrac{3+5}{18-2}$.

EXAMPLE 4.49

Simplify: $\dfrac{4-2(3)}{2^2+2}$.

⊘ **Solution**

$$\dfrac{4-2(3)}{2^2+2}$$

Use the order of operations. Multiply in the numerator and use the exponent in the denominator. $\qquad \dfrac{4-6}{4+2}$

Simplify the numerator and the denominator. $\qquad \dfrac{-2}{6}$

Simplify the fraction. $\qquad\qquad\qquad\qquad\qquad -\dfrac{1}{3}$

> **TRY IT :: 4.97** $\qquad$ Simplify: $\dfrac{6-3(5)}{3^2+3}$.

> **TRY IT :: 4.98** $\qquad$ Simplify: $\dfrac{4-4(6)}{3^3+3}$.

EXAMPLE 4.50

Simplify: $\dfrac{(8-4)^2}{8^2-4^2}$.

⊘ **Solution**

	$\dfrac{(8-4)^2}{8^2-4^2}$
Use the order of operations (parentheses first, then exponents).	$\dfrac{(4)^2}{64-16}$
Simplify the numerator and denominator.	$\dfrac{16}{48}$
Simplify the fraction.	$\dfrac{1}{3}$

> **TRY IT : : 4.99**   Simplify: $\dfrac{(11-7)^2}{11^2-7^2}$.

> **TRY IT : : 4.100**   Simplify: $\dfrac{(6+2)^2}{6^2+2^2}$.

EXAMPLE 4.51

Simplify: $\dfrac{4(-3)+6(-2)}{-3(2)-2}$.

⊘ **Solution**

	$\dfrac{4(-3)+6(-2)}{-3(2)-2}$
Multiply.	$\dfrac{-12+(-12)}{-6-2}$
Simplify.	$\dfrac{-24}{-8}$
Divide.	3

> **TRY IT : : 4.101**   Simplify: $\dfrac{8(-2)+4(-3)}{-5(2)+3}$.

> **TRY IT : : 4.102**   Simplify: $\dfrac{7(-1)+9(-3)}{-5(3)-2}$.

▶ **MEDIA : :** ACCESS ADDITIONAL ONLINE RESOURCES

- Division Involving Mixed Numbers (http://www.openstaxcollege.org/l/24DivisionMixed)
- Evaluate a Complex Fraction (http://www.openstaxcollege.org/l/24ComplexFrac)

4.3 EXERCISES

Practice Makes Perfect

Multiply and Divide Mixed Numbers

In the following exercises, multiply and write the answer in simplified form.

176. $4\frac{3}{8} \cdot \frac{7}{10}$

177. $2\frac{4}{9} \cdot \frac{6}{7}$

178. $\frac{15}{22} \cdot 3\frac{3}{5}$

179. $\frac{25}{36} \cdot 6\frac{3}{10}$

180. $4\frac{2}{3}\left(-1\frac{1}{8}\right)$

181. $2\frac{2}{5}\left(-2\frac{2}{9}\right)$

182. $-4\frac{4}{9} \cdot 5\frac{13}{16}$

183. $-1\frac{7}{20} \cdot 2\frac{11}{12}$

In the following exercises, divide, and write your answer in simplified form.

184. $5\frac{1}{3} \div 4$

185. $13\frac{1}{2} \div 9$

186. $-12 \div 3\frac{3}{11}$

187. $-7 \div 5\frac{1}{4}$

188. $6\frac{3}{8} \div 2\frac{1}{8}$

189. $2\frac{1}{5} \div 1\frac{1}{10}$.

190. $-9\frac{3}{5} \div \left(-1\frac{3}{5}\right)$

191. $-18\frac{3}{4} \div \left(-3\frac{3}{4}\right)$

Translate Phrases to Expressions with Fractions

In the following exercises, translate each English phrase into an algebraic expression.

192. the quotient of $5u$ and 11

193. the quotient of $7v$ and 13

194. the quotient of p and q

195. the quotient of a and b

196. the quotient of r and the sum of s and 10

197. the quotient of A and the difference of 3 and B

Simplify Complex Fractions

In the following exercises, simplify the complex fraction.

198. $\dfrac{\frac{2}{3}}{\frac{8}{9}}$

199. $\dfrac{\frac{4}{5}}{\frac{8}{15}}$

200. $\dfrac{-\frac{8}{21}}{\frac{12}{35}}$

201. $\dfrac{-\frac{9}{16}}{\frac{33}{40}}$

202. $\dfrac{-\frac{4}{5}}{2}$

203. $\dfrac{-\frac{9}{10}}{3}$

204. $\dfrac{\frac{2}{5}}{8}$

205. $\dfrac{\frac{5}{3}}{10}$

206. $\dfrac{\frac{m}{3}}{\frac{n}{2}}$

207. $\dfrac{\frac{r}{5}}{\frac{s}{3}}$

208. $\dfrac{-\frac{x}{6}}{-\frac{8}{9}}$

209. $\dfrac{-\frac{3}{8}}{-\frac{y}{12}}$

210. $\dfrac{2\frac{4}{5}}{\frac{1}{10}}$

211. $\dfrac{4\frac{2}{3}}{\frac{1}{6}}$

212. $\dfrac{\frac{7}{9}}{-2\frac{4}{5}}$

213. $\dfrac{\frac{3}{8}}{-6\frac{3}{4}}$

Simplify Expressions with a Fraction Bar

In the following exercises, identify the equivalent fractions.

214. Which of the following fractions are equivalent to $\dfrac{5}{-11}$?

$\dfrac{-5}{-11}, \dfrac{-5}{11}, \dfrac{5}{11}, -\dfrac{5}{11}$

215. Which of the following fractions are equivalent to $\dfrac{-4}{9}$?

$\dfrac{-4}{-9}, \dfrac{-4}{9}, \dfrac{4}{9}, -\dfrac{4}{9}$

216. Which of the following fractions are equivalent to $-\dfrac{11}{3}$?

$\dfrac{-11}{3}, \dfrac{11}{3}, \dfrac{-11}{-3}, \dfrac{11}{-3}$

217. Which of the following fractions are equivalent to $-\dfrac{13}{6}$?

$\dfrac{13}{6}, \dfrac{13}{-6}, \dfrac{-13}{-6}, \dfrac{-13}{6}$

In the following exercises, simplify.

218. $\dfrac{4+11}{8}$

219. $\dfrac{9+3}{7}$

220. $\dfrac{22+3}{10}$

221. $\dfrac{19-4}{6}$

222. $\dfrac{48}{24-15}$

223. $\dfrac{46}{4+4}$

224. $\dfrac{-6+6}{8+4}$

225. $\dfrac{-6+3}{17-8}$

226. $\dfrac{22-14}{19-13}$

227. $\dfrac{15+9}{18+12}$

228. $\dfrac{5\cdot 8}{-10}$

229. $\dfrac{3\cdot 4}{-24}$

230. $\dfrac{4\cdot 3}{6\cdot 6}$

231. $\dfrac{6\cdot 6}{9\cdot 2}$

232. $\dfrac{4^2-1}{25}$

233. $\dfrac{7^2+1}{60}$

234. $\dfrac{8\cdot 3+2\cdot 9}{14+3}$

235. $\dfrac{9\cdot 6-4\cdot 7}{22+3}$

236. $\dfrac{15\cdot 5-5^2}{2\cdot 10}$

237. $\dfrac{12\cdot 9-3^2}{3\cdot 18}$

238. $\dfrac{5\cdot 6-3\cdot 4}{4\cdot 5-2\cdot 3}$

239. $\dfrac{8\cdot 9-7\cdot 6}{5\cdot 6-9\cdot 2}$

240. $\dfrac{5^2-3^2}{3-5}$

241. $\dfrac{6^2-4^2}{4-6}$

242. $\dfrac{2+4(3)}{-3-2^2}$

243. $\dfrac{7+3(5)}{-2-3^2}$

244. $\dfrac{7\cdot 4-2(8-5)}{9.3-3.5}$

245. $\dfrac{9\cdot 7-3(12-8)}{8.7-6.6}$

246. $\dfrac{9(8-2)-3(15-7)}{6(7-1)-3(17-9)}$

247. $\dfrac{8(9-2)-4(14-9)}{7(8-3)-3(16-9)}$

Everyday Math

248. Baking A recipe for chocolate chip cookies calls for $2\frac{1}{4}$ cups of flour. Graciela wants to double the recipe.

1.   ⓐ How much flour will Graciela need? Show your calculation. Write your result as an improper fraction and as a mixed number.

2.   ⓑ Measuring cups usually come in sets with cups for $\frac{1}{8}$, $\frac{1}{4}$, $\frac{1}{3}$, $\frac{1}{2}$, and 1 cup. Draw a diagram to show two different ways that Graciela could measure out the flour needed to double the recipe.

249. Baking A booth at the county fair sells fudge by the pound. Their award winning "Chocolate Overdose" fudge contains $2\frac{2}{3}$ cups of chocolate chips per pound.

ⓐ How many cups of chocolate chips are in a half-pound of the fudge?

ⓑ The owners of the booth make the fudge in 10-pound batches. How many chocolate chips do they need to make a 10-pound batch? Write your results as improper fractions and as a mixed numbers.

Writing Exercises

250. Explain how to find the reciprocal of a mixed number.

251. Explain how to multiply mixed numbers.

252. Randy thinks that $3\frac{1}{2} \cdot 5\frac{1}{4}$ is $15\frac{1}{8}$. Explain what is wrong with Randy's thinking.

253. Explain why $-\frac{1}{2}$, $\frac{-1}{2}$, and $\frac{1}{-2}$ are equivalent.

Self Check

ⓐ *After completing the exercises, use this checklist to evaluate your mastery of the objectives of this section.*

I can...	Confidently	With some help	No-I don't get it!
multiply and divide mixed numbers.			
translate phrases to expressions with fractions.			
simplify complex fractions.			
simplify expressions written with a fraction bar.			

ⓑ *What does this checklist tell you about your mastery of this section? What steps will you take to improve?*

4.4 Add and Subtract Fractions with Common Denominators

Learning Objectives

By the end of this section, you will be able to:

- Model fraction addition
- Add fractions with a common denominator
- Model fraction subtraction
- Subtract fractions with a common denominator

Be Prepared!

Before you get started, take this readiness quiz.

1. Simplify: $2x + 9 + 3x - 4$.
   If you missed this problem, review Example 2.22.

2. Draw a model of the fraction $\frac{3}{4}$.
   If you missed this problem, review Example 4.2.

3. Simplify: $\frac{3 + 2}{6}$.
   If you missed this problem, review Example 4.48.

Model Fraction Addition

How many quarters are pictured? One quarter plus 2 quarters equals 3 quarters.

Remember, quarters are really fractions of a dollar. Quarters are another way to say fourths. So the picture of the coins shows that

$$\frac{1}{4} \qquad \frac{2}{4} \qquad \frac{3}{4}$$
$$\text{one quarter} \quad + \quad \text{two quarters} \quad = \quad \text{three quarters}$$

Let's use fraction circles to model the same example, $\frac{1}{4} + \frac{2}{4}$.

Start with one $\frac{1}{4}$ piece. $\frac{1}{4}$

Add two more $\frac{1}{4}$ pieces. $+$ $+\frac{2}{4}$

The result is $\frac{3}{4}$. $\frac{3}{4}$

So again, we see that

$$\frac{1}{4} + \frac{2}{4} = \frac{3}{4}$$

 MANIPULATIVE MATHEMATICS

Doing the Manipulative Mathematics activity "Model Fraction Addition" will help you develop a better understanding of adding fractions

EXAMPLE 4.52

Use a model to find the sum $\frac{3}{8} + \frac{2}{8}$.

⊘ **Solution**

Start with three $\frac{1}{8}$ pieces.   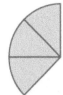 $\frac{3}{8}$

Add two $\frac{1}{8}$ pieces.   + $+\frac{2}{8}$

How many $\frac{1}{8}$ pieces are there? $\frac{5}{8}$

There are five $\frac{1}{8}$ pieces, or five-eighths. The model shows that $\frac{3}{8} + \frac{2}{8} = \frac{5}{8}$.

> **TRY IT : :** 4.103   Use a model to find each sum. Show a diagram to illustrate your model.

$\frac{1}{8} + \frac{4}{8}$

> **TRY IT : :** 4.104   Use a model to find each sum. Show a diagram to illustrate your model.

$\frac{1}{6} + \frac{4}{6}$

Add Fractions with a Common Denominator

Example 4.52 shows that to add the same-size pieces—meaning that the fractions have the same denominator—we just add the number of pieces.

Fraction Addition

If a, b, and c are numbers where $c \neq 0$, then

$$\frac{a}{c} + \frac{b}{c} = \frac{a+b}{c}$$

To add fractions with a common denominators, add the numerators and place the sum over the common denominator.

EXAMPLE 4.53

Find the sum: $\frac{3}{5} + \frac{1}{5}$.

⊘ **Solution**

$$\frac{3}{5} + \frac{1}{5}$$

Add the numerators and place the sum over the common denominator. $\frac{3+1}{5}$

Simplify. $\frac{4}{5}$

> **TRY IT : :** 4.105   Find each sum: $\frac{3}{6} + \frac{2}{6}$.

> **TRY IT : :** 4.106   Find each sum: $\frac{3}{10} + \frac{7}{10}$.

EXAMPLE 4.54

Find the sum: $\frac{x}{3} + \frac{2}{3}$.

⊘ **Solution**

$$\frac{x}{3} + \frac{2}{3}$$

Add the numerators and place the sum over the common denominator. $\frac{x+2}{3}$

Note that we cannot simplify this fraction any more. Since x and 2 are not like terms, we cannot combine them.

> **TRY IT : :** 4.107   Find the sum: $\frac{x}{4} + \frac{3}{4}$.

> **TRY IT : :** 4.108   Find the sum: $\frac{y}{8} + \frac{5}{8}$.

EXAMPLE 4.55

Find the sum: $-\frac{9}{d} + \frac{3}{d}$.

⊘ **Solution**

We will begin by rewriting the first fraction with the negative sign in the numerator.

$$-\frac{a}{b} = \frac{-a}{b}$$

$$-\frac{9}{d} + \frac{3}{d}$$

Rewrite the first fraction with the negative in the numerator.	$\frac{-9}{d} + \frac{9}{d}$
Add the numerators and place the sum over the common denominator.	$\frac{-9+3}{d}$
Simplify the numerator.	$\frac{-6}{d}$
Rewrite with negative sign in front of the fraction.	$-\frac{6}{d}$

> **TRY IT :: 4.109**   Find the sum: $-\frac{7}{d} + \frac{8}{d}$.

> **TRY IT :: 4.110**   Find the sum: $-\frac{6}{m} + \frac{9}{m}$.

EXAMPLE 4.56

Find the sum: $\frac{2n}{11} + \frac{5n}{11}$.

⊘ **Solution**

$$\frac{2n}{11} + \frac{5n}{11}$$

Add the numerators and place the sum over the common denominator.	$\frac{2n+5n}{11}$
Combine like terms.	$\frac{7n}{11}$

> **TRY IT :: 4.111**   Find the sum: $\frac{3p}{8} + \frac{6p}{8}$.

> **TRY IT :: 4.112**   Find the sum: $\frac{2q}{5} + \frac{7q}{5}$.

EXAMPLE 4.57

Find the sum: $-\frac{3}{12} + \left(-\frac{5}{12}\right)$.

Solution

$$-\frac{3}{12}+\left(-\frac{5}{12}\right)$$

Add the numerators and place the sum over the common denominator. $\frac{-3+(-5)}{12}$

Add. $\frac{-8}{12}$

Simplify the fraction. $-\frac{2}{3}$

> **TRY IT :: 4.113** Find each sum: $-\frac{4}{15}+\left(-\frac{6}{15}\right)$.

> **TRY IT :: 4.114** Find each sum: $-\frac{5}{21}+\left(-\frac{9}{21}\right)$.

Model Fraction Subtraction

Subtracting two fractions with common denominators is much like adding fractions. Think of a pizza that was cut into 12 slices. Suppose five pieces are eaten for dinner. This means that, after dinner, there are seven pieces (or $\frac{7}{12}$ of the pizza) left in the box. If Leonardo eats 2 of these remaining pieces (or $\frac{2}{12}$ of the pizza), how much is left? There would be 5 pieces left (or $\frac{5}{12}$ of the pizza).

$$\frac{7}{12}-\frac{2}{12}=\frac{5}{12}$$

Let's use fraction circles to model the same example, $\frac{7}{12}-\frac{2}{12}$.

Start with seven $\frac{1}{12}$ pieces. Take away two $\frac{1}{12}$ pieces. How many twelfths are left?

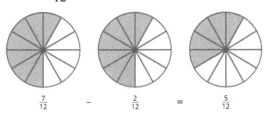

$$\frac{7}{12} \quad - \quad \frac{2}{12} \quad = \quad \frac{5}{12}$$

Again, we have five twelfths, $\frac{5}{12}$.

 MANIPULATIVE MATHEMATICS

Doing the Manipulative Mathematics activity "Model Fraction Subtraction" will help you develop a better understanding of subtracting fractions.

EXAMPLE 4.58

Use fraction circles to find the difference: $\frac{4}{5} - \frac{1}{5}$.

⊘ Solution

Start with four $\frac{1}{5}$ pieces. Take away one $\frac{1}{5}$ piece. Count how many fifths are left. There are three $\frac{1}{5}$ pieces left.

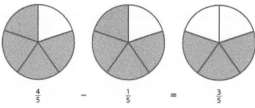

$$\frac{4}{5} \quad - \quad \frac{1}{5} \quad = \quad \frac{3}{5}$$

> **TRY IT : : 4.115**   Use a model to find each difference. Show a diagram to illustrate your model.
>
> $$\frac{7}{8} - \frac{4}{8}$$

> **TRY IT : : 4.116**   Use a model to find each difference. Show a diagram to illustrate your model.
>
> $$\frac{5}{6} - \frac{4}{6}$$

Subtract Fractions with a Common Denominator

We subtract fractions with a common denominator in much the same way as we add fractions with a common denominator.

Fraction Subtraction

If a, b, and c are numbers where $c \neq 0$, then

$$\frac{a}{c} - \frac{b}{c} = \frac{a-b}{c}$$

To subtract fractions with a common denominators, we subtract the numerators and place the difference over the common denominator.

EXAMPLE 4.59

Find the difference: $\frac{23}{24} - \frac{14}{24}$.

⊘ Solution

	$\frac{23}{24} - \frac{14}{24}$
Subtract the numerators and place the difference over the common denominator.	$\frac{23-14}{24}$
Simplify the numerator.	$\frac{9}{24}$
Simplify the fraction by removing common factors.	$\frac{3}{8}$

> **TRY IT : : 4.117**   Find the difference: $\frac{19}{28} - \frac{7}{28}$.

> **TRY IT : :** 4.118   Find the difference: $\frac{27}{32} - \frac{11}{32}$.

EXAMPLE 4.60

Find the difference: $\frac{y}{6} - \frac{1}{6}$.

⊘ **Solution**

$$\frac{y}{6} - \frac{1}{6}$$

Subtract the numerators and place the difference over the common denominator. $\frac{y-1}{6}$

The fraction is simplified because we cannot combine the terms in the numerator.

> **TRY IT : :** 4.119   Find the difference: $\frac{x}{7} - \frac{2}{7}$.

> **TRY IT : :** 4.120   Find the difference: $\frac{y}{14} - \frac{13}{14}$.

EXAMPLE 4.61

Find the difference: $-\frac{10}{x} - \frac{4}{x}$.

⊘ **Solution**

Remember, the fraction $-\frac{10}{x}$ can be written as $\frac{-10}{x}$.

$$-\frac{10}{x} - \frac{4}{x}$$

Subtract the numerators. $\frac{-10-4}{x}$

Simplify. $\frac{-14}{x}$

Rewrite with the negative sign in front of the fraction. $-\frac{14}{x}$

> **TRY IT : :** 4.121   Find the difference: $-\frac{9}{x} - \frac{7}{x}$.

> **TRY IT : :** 4.122   Find the difference: $-\frac{17}{a} - \frac{5}{a}$.

Now lets do an example that involves both addition and subtraction.

EXAMPLE 4.62

Simplify: $\frac{3}{8} + \left(-\frac{5}{8}\right) - \frac{1}{8}$.

⊘ **Solution**

$$\frac{3}{8} + \left(-\frac{5}{8}\right) - \frac{1}{8}$$

Combine the numerators over the common denominator.	$\dfrac{3 + (-5) - 1}{8}$
Simplify the numerator, working left to right.	$\dfrac{-2 - 1}{8}$
Subtract the terms in the numerator.	$\dfrac{-3}{8}$
Rewrite with the negative sign in front of the fraction.	$-\dfrac{3}{8}$

> **TRY IT ::** 4.123   Simplify: $\frac{2}{5} + \left(-\frac{4}{5}\right) - \frac{3}{5}$.

> **TRY IT ::** 4.124   Simplify: $\frac{5}{9} + \left(-\frac{4}{9}\right) - \frac{7}{9}$.

▶ **MEDIA ::** ACCESS ADDITIONAL ONLINE RESOURCES

- Adding Fractions With Pattern Blocks (http://www.openstaxcollege.org/l/24AddFraction)
- Adding Fractions With Like Denominators (http://www.openstaxcollege.org/l/24AddLikeDenom)
- Subtracting Fractions With Like Denominators (http://www.openstaxcollege.org/l/24SubtrLikeDeno)

4.4 EXERCISES

Practice Makes Perfect

Model Fraction Addition

In the following exercises, use a model to add the fractions. Show a diagram to illustrate your model.

254. $\frac{2}{5} + \frac{1}{5}$

255. $\frac{3}{10} + \frac{4}{10}$

256. $\frac{1}{6} + \frac{3}{6}$

257. $\frac{3}{8} + \frac{3}{8}$

Add Fractions with a Common Denominator

In the following exercises, find each sum.

258. $\frac{4}{9} + \frac{1}{9}$

259. $\frac{2}{9} + \frac{5}{9}$

260. $\frac{6}{13} + \frac{7}{13}$

261. $\frac{9}{15} + \frac{7}{15}$

262. $\frac{x}{4} + \frac{3}{4}$

263. $\frac{y}{3} + \frac{2}{3}$

264. $\frac{7}{p} + \frac{9}{p}$

265. $\frac{8}{q} + \frac{6}{q}$

266. $\frac{8b}{9} + \frac{3b}{9}$

267. $\frac{5a}{7} + \frac{4a}{7}$

268. $\frac{-12y}{8} + \frac{3y}{8}$

269. $\frac{-11x}{5} + \frac{7x}{5}$

270. $-\frac{1}{8} + \left(-\frac{3}{8}\right)$

271. $-\frac{1}{8} + \left(-\frac{5}{8}\right)$

272. $-\frac{3}{16} + \left(-\frac{7}{16}\right)$

273. $-\frac{5}{16} + \left(-\frac{9}{16}\right)$

274. $-\frac{8}{17} + \frac{15}{17}$

275. $-\frac{9}{19} + \frac{17}{19}$

276. $\frac{6}{13} + \left(-\frac{10}{13}\right) + \left(-\frac{12}{13}\right)$

277. $\frac{5}{12} + \left(-\frac{7}{12}\right) + \left(-\frac{11}{12}\right)$

Model Fraction Subtraction

In the following exercises, use a model to subtract the fractions. Show a diagram to illustrate your model.

278. $\frac{5}{8} - \frac{2}{8}$

279. $\frac{5}{6} - \frac{2}{6}$

Subtract Fractions with a Common Denominator

In the following exercises, find the difference.

280. $\frac{4}{5} - \frac{1}{5}$

281. $\frac{4}{5} - \frac{3}{5}$

282. $\frac{11}{15} - \frac{7}{15}$

283. $\frac{9}{13} - \frac{4}{13}$

284. $\frac{11}{12} - \frac{5}{12}$

285. $\frac{7}{12} - \frac{5}{12}$

286. $\frac{4}{21} - \frac{19}{21}$

287. $-\frac{8}{9} - \frac{16}{9}$

288. $\frac{y}{17} - \frac{9}{17}$

289. $\frac{x}{19} - \frac{8}{19}$

290. $\frac{5y}{8} - \frac{7}{8}$

291. $\frac{11z}{13} - \frac{8}{13}$

292. $-\dfrac{8}{d}-\dfrac{3}{d}$

293. $-\dfrac{7}{c}-\dfrac{7}{c}$

294. $-\dfrac{23}{u}-\dfrac{15}{u}$

295. $-\dfrac{29}{v}-\dfrac{26}{v}$

296. $\dfrac{6c}{7}-\dfrac{5c}{7}$

297. $\dfrac{12d}{11}-\dfrac{9d}{11}$

298. $\dfrac{-4r}{13}-\dfrac{5r}{13}$

299. $\dfrac{-7s}{3}-\dfrac{7s}{3}$

300. $-\dfrac{3}{5}-\left(-\dfrac{4}{5}\right)$

301. $-\dfrac{3}{7}-\left(-\dfrac{5}{7}\right)$

302. $-\dfrac{7}{9}-\left(-\dfrac{5}{9}\right)$

303. $-\dfrac{8}{11}-\left(-\dfrac{5}{11}\right)$

Mixed Practice

In the following exercises, perform the indicated operation and write your answers in simplified form.

304. $-\dfrac{5}{18}\cdot\dfrac{9}{10}$

305. $-\dfrac{3}{14}\cdot\dfrac{7}{12}$

306. $\dfrac{n}{5}-\dfrac{4}{5}$

307. $\dfrac{6}{11}-\dfrac{s}{11}$

308. $-\dfrac{7}{24}+\dfrac{2}{24}$

309. $-\dfrac{5}{18}+\dfrac{1}{18}$

310. $\dfrac{8}{15}\div\dfrac{12}{5}$

311. $\dfrac{7}{12}\div\dfrac{9}{28}$

Everyday Math

312. Trail Mix Jacob is mixing together nuts and raisins to make trail mix. He has $\dfrac{6}{10}$ of a pound of nuts and $\dfrac{3}{10}$ of a pound of raisins. How much trail mix can he make?

313. Baking Janet needs $\dfrac{5}{8}$ of a cup of flour for a recipe she is making. She only has $\dfrac{3}{8}$ of a cup of flour and will ask to borrow the rest from her next-door neighbor. How much flour does she have to borrow?

Writing Exercises

314. Greg dropped his case of drill bits and three of the bits fell out. The case has slots for the drill bits, and the slots are arranged in order from smallest to largest. Greg needs to put the bits that fell out back in the case in the empty slots. Where do the three bits go? Explain how you know.

Bits in case: $\dfrac{1}{16}, \dfrac{1}{8}, —\ —\ \dfrac{5}{16}, \dfrac{3}{8}, —\ \dfrac{1}{2}, \dfrac{9}{16}, \dfrac{5}{8}$.

Bits that fell out: $\dfrac{7}{16}, \dfrac{3}{16}, \dfrac{1}{4}$.

315. After a party, Lupe has $\dfrac{5}{12}$ of a cheese pizza, $\dfrac{4}{12}$ of a pepperoni pizza, and $\dfrac{4}{12}$ of a veggie pizza left. Will all the slices fit into 1 pizza box? Explain your reasoning.

Self Check

ⓐ *After completing the exercises, use this checklist to evaluate your mastery of the objectives of this section.*

I can...	Confidently	With some help	No-I don't get it!
model fraction addition.			
add fractions with a common denominator.			
model fraction subtraction.			
subtract fractions with a common denominator.			
find the least common denominator (LCD).			
convert fractions to equivalent fractions with the LCD.			

ⓑ *On a scale of 1–10, how would you rate your mastery of this section in light of your responses on the checklist? How can you improve this?*

4.5 Add and Subtract Fractions with Different Denominators

Learning Objectives

By the end of this section, you will be able to:

- Find the least common denominator (LCD)
- Convert fractions to equivalent fractions with the LCD
- Add and subtract fractions with different denominators
- Identify and use fraction operations
- Use the order of operations to simplify complex fractions
- Evaluate variable expressions with fractions

Be Prepared!

Before you get started, take this readiness quiz.

1. Find two fractions equivalent to $\frac{5}{6}$.

   If you missed this problem, review Example 4.14.

2. Simplify: $\frac{1 + 5 \cdot 3}{2^2 + 4}$.

   If you missed this problem, review Example 4.48.

Find the Least Common Denominator

In the previous section, we explained how to add and subtract fractions with a common denominator. But how can we add and subtract fractions with unlike denominators?

Let's think about coins again. Can you add one quarter and one dime? You could say there are two coins, but that's not very useful. To find the total value of one quarter plus one dime, you change them to the same kind of unit—cents. One quarter equals 25 cents and one dime equals 10 cents, so the sum is 35 cents. See Figure 4.7.

25¢   +   10¢

35¢

Figure 4.7 Together, a quarter and a dime are worth 35 cents, or $\frac{35}{100}$ of a dollar.

Similarly, when we add fractions with different denominators we have to convert them to equivalent fractions with a common denominator. With the coins, when we convert to cents, the denominator is 100. Since there are 100 cents in one dollar, 25 cents is $\frac{25}{100}$ and 10 cents is $\frac{10}{100}$. So we add $\frac{25}{100} + \frac{10}{100}$ to get $\frac{35}{100}$, which is 35 cents.

You have practiced adding and subtracting fractions with common denominators. Now let's see what you need to do with fractions that have different denominators.

First, we will use fraction tiles to model finding the common denominator of $\frac{1}{2}$ and $\frac{1}{3}$.

We'll start with one $\frac{1}{2}$ tile and $\frac{1}{3}$ tile. We want to find a common fraction tile that we can use to match *both* $\frac{1}{2}$ and $\frac{1}{3}$ exactly.

If we try the $\frac{1}{4}$ pieces, 2 of them exactly match the $\frac{1}{2}$ piece, but they do not exactly match the $\frac{1}{3}$ piece.

$\frac{1}{2}$	
$\frac{1}{4}$	$\frac{1}{4}$

$\frac{1}{3}$	
$\frac{1}{4}$	$\frac{1}{4}$

If we try the $\frac{1}{5}$ pieces, they do not exactly cover the $\frac{1}{2}$ piece or the $\frac{1}{3}$ piece.

If we try the $\frac{1}{6}$ pieces, we see that exactly 3 of them cover the $\frac{1}{2}$ piece, and exactly 2 of them cover the $\frac{1}{3}$ piece.

If we were to try the $\frac{1}{12}$ pieces, they would also work.

Even smaller tiles, such as $\frac{1}{24}$ and $\frac{1}{48}$, would also exactly cover the $\frac{1}{2}$ piece and the $\frac{1}{3}$ piece.

The denominator of the largest piece that covers both fractions is the **least common denominator (LCD)** of the two fractions. So, the least common denominator of $\frac{1}{2}$ and $\frac{1}{3}$ is 6.

Notice that all of the tiles that cover $\frac{1}{2}$ and $\frac{1}{3}$ have something in common: Their denominators are common multiples of 2 and 3, the denominators of $\frac{1}{2}$ and $\frac{1}{3}$. The least common multiple (LCM) of the denominators is 6, and so we say that 6 is the least common denominator (LCD) of the fractions $\frac{1}{2}$ and $\frac{1}{3}$.

 MANIPULATIVE MATHEMATICS

Doing the Manipulative Mathematics activity "Finding the Least Common Denominator" will help you develop a better understanding of the LCD.

Least Common Denominator

The **least common denominator (LCD)** of two fractions is the least common multiple (LCM) of their denominators.

To find the LCD of two fractions, we will find the LCM of their denominators. We follow the procedure we used earlier to find the LCM of two numbers. We only use the denominators of the fractions, not the numerators, when finding the LCD.

EXAMPLE 4.63

Find the LCD for the fractions $\frac{7}{12}$ and $\frac{5}{18}$.

⊘ **Solution**

Factor each denominator into its primes.

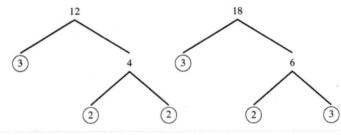

List the primes of 12 and the primes of 18 lining them up in columns when possible.

$$12 = 2 \cdot 2 \cdot 3$$
$$18 = 2 \cdot \quad 3 \cdot 3$$

Bring down the columns.

$$12 = 2 \cdot 2 \cdot 3$$
$$18 = 2 \cdot \quad 3 \cdot 3$$
$$\overline{\text{LCM} = 2 \cdot 2 \cdot 3 \cdot 3}$$

Multiply the factors. The product is the LCM.

$$\text{LCM} = 36$$

The LCM of 12 and 18 is 36, so the LCD of $\frac{7}{12}$ and $\frac{5}{18}$ is 36.

LCD of $\frac{7}{12}$ and $\frac{5}{18}$ is 36.

> **TRY IT :: 4.125**   Find the least common denominator for the fractions: $\frac{7}{12}$ and $\frac{11}{15}$.

> **TRY IT :: 4.126**   Find the least common denominator for the fractions: $\frac{13}{15}$ and $\frac{17}{5}$.

To find the LCD of two fractions, find the LCM of their denominators. Notice how the steps shown below are similar to the steps we took to find the LCM.

 HOW TO :: FIND THE LEAST COMMON DENOMINATOR (LCD) OF TWO FRACTIONS.

Step 1.   Factor each denominator into its primes.

Step 2.   List the primes, matching primes in columns when possible.

Step 3.   Bring down the columns.

Step 4.   Multiply the factors. The product is the LCM of the denominators.

Step 5.   The LCM of the denominators is the LCD of the fractions.

EXAMPLE 4.64

Find the least common denominator for the fractions $\frac{8}{15}$ and $\frac{11}{24}$.

⊘ **Solution**

To find the LCD, we find the LCM of the denominators.

Find the LCM of 15 and 24.

$$15 = \qquad\quad 3 \cdot 5$$
$$24 = 2 \cdot 2 \cdot 2 \cdot 3$$
$$\overline{}$$
$$LCD = 2 \cdot 2 \cdot 2 \cdot 3 \cdot 5$$
$$LCD = 120$$

The LCM of 15 and 24 is $120.$ So, the LCD of $\frac{8}{15}$ and $\frac{11}{24}$ is $120.$

> **TRY IT :: 4.127**   Find the least common denominator for the fractions: $\frac{13}{24}$ and $\frac{17}{32}.$

> **TRY IT :: 4.128**   Find the least common denominator for the fractions: $\frac{9}{28}$ and $\frac{21}{32}.$

Convert Fractions to Equivalent Fractions with the LCD

Earlier, we used fraction tiles to see that the LCD of $\frac{1}{4}$ and $\frac{1}{6}$ is $12.$ We saw that three $\frac{1}{12}$ pieces exactly covered $\frac{1}{4}$ and

two $\frac{1}{12}$ pieces exactly covered $\frac{1}{6},$ so

$$\frac{1}{4} = \frac{3}{12} \text{ and } \frac{1}{6} = \frac{2}{12}.$$

We say that $\frac{1}{4}$ and $\frac{3}{12}$ are equivalent fractions and also that $\frac{1}{6}$ and $\frac{2}{12}$ are equivalent fractions.

We can use the Equivalent Fractions Property to algebraically change a fraction to an equivalent one. Remember, two fractions are equivalent if they have the same value. The Equivalent Fractions Property is repeated below for reference.

Equivalent Fractions Property

If $a,\ b,\ c$ are whole numbers where $b \neq 0,\ c \neq 0,$ then

$$\frac{a}{b} = \frac{a \cdot c}{b \cdot c} \quad \text{and} \quad \frac{a \cdot c}{b \cdot c} = \frac{a}{b}$$

To add or subtract fractions with different denominators, we will first have to convert each fraction to an equivalent fraction with the LCD. Let's see how to change $\frac{1}{4}$ and $\frac{1}{6}$ to equivalent fractions with denominator 12 without using models.

EXAMPLE 4.65

Convert $\frac{1}{4}$ and $\frac{1}{6}$ to equivalent fractions with denominator $12,$ their LCD.

⊘ **Solution**

Find the LCD.	The LCD of $\frac{1}{4}$ and $\frac{1}{6}$ is 12.
Find the number to multiply 4 to get 12.	$4 \cdot 3 = 12$
Find the number to multiply 6 to get 12.	$6 \cdot 2 = 12$
Use the Equivalent Fractions Property to convert each fraction to an equivalent fraction with the LCD, multiplying both the numerator and denominator of each fraction by the same number.	$\dfrac{1}{4} \qquad \dfrac{1}{6}$ $\dfrac{1 \cdot 3}{4 \cdot 3} \qquad \dfrac{1 \cdot 2}{6 \cdot 2}$
Simplify the numerators and denominators.	$\dfrac{3}{12} \qquad \dfrac{2}{12}$

We do not reduce the resulting fractions. If we did, we would get back to our original fractions and lose the common denominator.

> **TRY IT ::** 4.129

Change to equivalent fractions with the LCD:

$\frac{3}{4}$ and $\frac{5}{6}$, $\text{LCD} = 12$

> **TRY IT ::** 4.130

Change to equivalent fractions with the LCD:

$-\frac{7}{12}$ and $\frac{11}{15}$, $\text{LCD} = 60$

 HOW TO :: CONVERT TWO FRACTIONS TO EQUIVALENT FRACTIONS WITH THEIR LCD AS THE COMMON DENOMINATOR.

Step 1. Find the LCD.

Step 2. For each fraction, determine the number needed to multiply the denominator to get the LCD.

Step 3. Use the Equivalent Fractions Property to multiply both the numerator and denominator by the number you found in Step 2.

Step 4. Simplify the numerator and denominator.

EXAMPLE 4.66

Convert $\frac{8}{15}$ and $\frac{11}{24}$ to equivalent fractions with denominator 120, their LCD.

⊘ **Solution**

	The LCD is 120. We will start at Step 2.
Find the number that must multiply 15 to get 120.	$15 \cdot 8 = 120$
Find the number that must multiply 24 to get 120.	$24 \cdot 5 = 120$
Use the Equivalent Fractions Property.	$\dfrac{8 \cdot 8}{15 \cdot 8} \qquad \dfrac{11 \cdot 5}{24 \cdot 5}$
Simplify the numerators and denominators.	$\dfrac{64}{120} \qquad \dfrac{55}{120}$

> **TRY IT :: 4.131**   Change to equivalent fractions with the LCD:

$\dfrac{13}{24}$ and $\dfrac{17}{32}$, LCD 96

> **TRY IT :: 4.132**   Change to equivalent fractions with the LCD:

$\dfrac{9}{28}$ and $\dfrac{27}{32}$, LCD 224

Add and Subtract Fractions with Different Denominators

Once we have converted two fractions to equivalent forms with common denominators, we can add or subtract them by adding or subtracting the numerators.

HOW TO :: ADD OR SUBTRACT FRACTIONS WITH DIFFERENT DENOMINATORS.

Step 1. Find the LCD.

Step 2. Convert each fraction to an equivalent form with the LCD as the denominator.

Step 3. Add or subtract the fractions.

Step 4. Write the result in simplified form.

EXAMPLE 4.67

Add: $\dfrac{1}{2} + \dfrac{1}{3}$.

⊘ Solution

$$\frac{1}{2} + \frac{1}{3}$$

Find the LCD of 2, 3.
$$2 = 2$$
$$3 = \quad 3$$
————————
$$LCD = 2 \cdot 3$$
$$LCD = 6$$

Change into equivalent fractions with the LCD 6.	$\frac{1 \cdot 3}{2 \cdot 3} + \frac{1 \cdot 2}{3 \cdot 2}$
Simplify the numerators and denominators.	$\frac{3}{6} + \frac{2}{6}$
Add.	$\frac{5}{6}$

Remember, always check to see if the answer can be simplified. Since 5 and 6 have no common factors, the fraction $\frac{5}{6}$ cannot be reduced.

> **TRY IT : :** 4.133   Add: $\frac{1}{4} + \frac{1}{3}$.

> **TRY IT : :** 4.134   Add: $\frac{1}{2} + \frac{1}{5}$.

EXAMPLE 4.68

Subtract: $\frac{1}{2} - \left(-\frac{1}{4}\right)$.

⊘ Solution

$$\frac{1}{2} - \left(-\frac{1}{4}\right)$$

Find the LCD of 2 and 4.
$$2 = 2$$
$$4 = 2 \cdot 2$$
————————
$$LCD = 2 \cdot 2$$
$$LCD = 4$$

Rewrite as equivalent fractions using the LCD 4.	$\frac{1 \cdot 2}{2 \cdot 2} - \left(-\frac{1}{4}\right)$
Simplify the first fraction.	$\frac{2}{4} - \left(-\frac{1}{4}\right)$
Subtract.	$\frac{2 - (-1)}{4}$
Simplify.	$\frac{3}{4}$

One of the fractions already had the least common denominator, so we only had to convert the other fraction.

> **TRY IT ::** 4.135   Simplify: $\frac{1}{2} - \left(-\frac{1}{8}\right)$.

> **TRY IT ::** 4.136   Simplify: $\frac{1}{3} - \left(-\frac{1}{6}\right)$.

EXAMPLE 4.69

Add: $\frac{7}{12} + \frac{5}{18}$.

⊘ **Solution**

$$\frac{7}{12} + \frac{5}{18}$$

Find the LCD of 12 and 18.
$$\begin{aligned} 12 &= 2 \cdot 2 \cdot 3 \\ 18 &= 2 \cdot 3 \cdot 3 \\ \hline \text{LCD} &= 2 \cdot 2 \cdot 3 \cdot 3 \\ \text{LCD} &= 36 \end{aligned}$$

Rewrite as equivalent fractions with the LCD. $\dfrac{7 \cdot 3}{12 \cdot 3} + \dfrac{5 \cdot 2}{18 \cdot 2}$

Simplify the numerators and denominators. $\dfrac{21}{36} + \dfrac{10}{36}$

Add. $\dfrac{31}{36}$

Because 31 is a prime number, it has no factors in common with 36. The answer is simplified.

> **TRY IT ::** 4.137   Add: $\frac{7}{12} + \frac{11}{15}$.

> **TRY IT ::** 4.138   Add: $\frac{13}{15} + \frac{17}{20}$.

When we use the Equivalent Fractions Property, there is a quick way to find the number you need to multiply by to get the LCD. Write the factors of the denominators and the LCD just as you did to find the LCD. The "missing" factors of each denominator are the numbers you need.

missing
factors

$$\begin{aligned} 12 &= 2 \cdot 2 \cdot 3 \\ 18 &= 2 \cdot 3 \cdot 3 \\ \hline \text{LCD} &= 2 \cdot 2 \cdot 3 \cdot 3 \\ \text{LCD} &= 36 \end{aligned}$$

The LCD, 36, has 2 factors of 2 and 2 factors of 3.

Twelve has two factors of 2, but only one of 3 —so it is 'missing' one 3. We multiplied the numerator and denominator of $\frac{7}{12}$ by 3 to get an equivalent fraction with denominator 36.

Eighteen is missing one factor of 2 —so you multiply the numerator and denominator $\frac{5}{18}$ by 2 to get an equivalent fraction with denominator $36.$ We will apply this method as we subtract the fractions in the next example.

EXAMPLE 4.70

Subtract: $\frac{7}{15} - \frac{19}{24}.$

⊘ **Solution**

$$\frac{7}{15} - \frac{19}{24}$$

Find the LCD.
$$
\begin{array}{rl}
15 = & 3 \cdot 5 \\
24 = & 2 \cdot 2 \cdot 2 \cdot 3 \\
\hline
\text{LCD} = & 2 \cdot 2 \cdot 2 \cdot 3 \cdot 5 \\
\text{LCD} = & 120
\end{array}
$$

15 is 'missing' three factors of 2
24 is 'missing' a factor of 5

Rewrite as equivalent fractions with the LCD.	$\frac{7 \cdot 8}{15 \cdot 8} - \frac{19 \cdot 5}{24 \cdot 5}$
Simplify each numerator and denominator.	$\frac{56}{120} - \frac{95}{120}$
Subtract.	$-\frac{39}{120}$
Rewrite showing the common factor of 3.	$-\frac{13 \cdot 3}{40 \cdot 3}$
Remove the common factor to simplify.	$-\frac{13}{40}$

> **TRY IT :: 4.139**   Subtract: $\frac{13}{24} - \frac{17}{32}.$

> **TRY IT :: 4.140**   Subtract: $\frac{21}{32} - \frac{9}{28}.$

EXAMPLE 4.71

Add: $-\frac{11}{30} + \frac{23}{42}.$

⊘ Solution

$$-\frac{11}{30} + \frac{23}{42}$$

Find the LCD.

$30 = 2 \cdot 3 \cdot 5$
$\underline{42 = 2 \cdot 3 \cdot \quad\quad 7}$
$\text{LCD} = 2 \cdot 3 \cdot 5 \cdot 7$
$\text{LCD} = 210$

Rewrite as equivalent fractions with the LCD. $\quad -\frac{11 \cdot 7}{30 \cdot 7} + \frac{23 \cdot 5}{42 \cdot 5}$

Simplify each numerator and denominator. $\quad -\frac{77}{210} + \frac{115}{210}$

Add. $\quad \frac{38}{210}$

Rewrite showing the common factor of 2. $\quad \frac{19 \cdot 2}{105 \cdot 2}$

Remove the common factor to simplify. $\quad \frac{19}{105}$

> **TRY IT : :** 4.141   Add: $-\frac{13}{42} + \frac{17}{35}$.

> **TRY IT : :** 4.142   Add: $-\frac{19}{24} + \frac{17}{32}$.

In the next example, one of the fractions has a variable in its numerator. We follow the same steps as when both numerators are numbers.

EXAMPLE 4.72

Add: $\frac{3}{5} + \frac{x}{8}$.

⊘ Solution

The fractions have different denominators.

$$\frac{3}{5}+\frac{x}{8}$$

Find the LCD. $\begin{aligned} 5 &= \qquad\quad 5 \\ 8 &= 2\cdot2\cdot2 \\ \hline \text{LCD} &= 2\cdot2\cdot2\cdot5 \\ \text{LCD} &= 40 \end{aligned}$	
Rewrite as equivalent fractions with the LCD.	$\dfrac{3\cdot8}{5\cdot8}+\dfrac{x\cdot5}{8\cdot5}$
Simplify the numerators and denominators.	$\dfrac{24}{40}+\dfrac{5x}{8}$
Add.	$\dfrac{24+5x}{40}$

We cannot add 24 and $5x$ since they are not like terms, so we cannot simplify the expression any further.

> **TRY IT : : 4.143**   Add: $\dfrac{y}{6}+\dfrac{7}{9}$.

> **TRY IT : : 4.144**   Add: $\dfrac{x}{6}+\dfrac{7}{15}$.

Identify and Use Fraction Operations

By now in this chapter, you have practiced multiplying, dividing, adding, and subtracting fractions. The following table summarizes these four fraction operations. Remember: You need a common denominator to add or subtract fractions, but not to multiply or divide fractions

Summary of Fraction Operations

Fraction multiplication: Multiply the numerators and multiply the denominators.
$$\frac{a}{b}\cdot\frac{c}{d}=\frac{ac}{bd}$$

Fraction division: Multiply the first fraction by the reciprocal of the second.
$$\frac{a}{b}\div\frac{c}{d}=\frac{a}{b}\cdot\frac{d}{c}$$

Fraction addition: Add the numerators and place the sum over the common denominator. If the fractions have different denominators, first convert them to equivalent forms with the LCD.
$$\frac{a}{c}+\frac{b}{c}=\frac{a+b}{c}$$

Fraction subtraction: Subtract the numerators and place the difference over the common denominator. If the fractions have different denominators, first convert them to equivalent forms with the LCD.
$$\frac{a}{c}-\frac{b}{c}=\frac{a-b}{c}$$

EXAMPLE 4.73

Simplify:

ⓐ $-\dfrac{1}{4}+\dfrac{1}{6}$ ⓑ $-\dfrac{1}{4}\div\dfrac{1}{6}$

⊘ **Solution**

First we ask ourselves, "What is the operation?"

ⓐThe operation is addition.

Do the fractions have a common denominator? No.

$$-\frac{1}{4}+\frac{1}{6}$$

Find the LCD.
$$
\begin{aligned}
4 &= 2 \cdot 2 \\
6 &= 2 \cdot \quad 3 \\
\hline
\text{LCD} &= 2 \cdot 2 \cdot 3 \\
\text{LCD} &= 12
\end{aligned}
$$

Rewrite each fraction as an equivalent fraction with the LCD. $\qquad -\frac{1 \cdot 3}{4 \cdot 3}+\frac{1 \cdot 2}{6 \cdot 2}$

Simplify the numerators and denominators. $\qquad -\frac{3}{12}+\frac{2}{12}$

Add the numerators and place the sum over the common denominator. $\qquad -\frac{1}{12}$

Check to see if the answer can be simplified. It cannot.

ⓑThe operation is division. We do not need a common denominator.

$$-\frac{1}{4} \div \frac{1}{6}$$

To divide fractions, multiply the first fraction by the reciprocal of the second. $\qquad -\frac{1}{4} \cdot \frac{6}{1}$

Multiply. $\qquad -\frac{6}{4}$

Simplify. $\qquad -\frac{3}{2}$

> **TRY IT : : 4.145**　　Simplify each expression:

$$\text{ⓐ} -\frac{3}{4}-\frac{1}{6} \qquad \text{ⓑ} -\frac{3}{4} \cdot \frac{1}{6}$$

> **TRY IT : : 4.146**　　Simplify each expression:

$$\text{ⓐ} \frac{5}{6} \div \left(-\frac{1}{4}\right) \qquad \text{ⓑ} \frac{5}{6}-\left(-\frac{1}{4}\right)$$

EXAMPLE 4.74

Simplify:

$$\text{ⓐ} \frac{5}{x}-\frac{3}{10} \qquad \text{ⓑ} \frac{5}{x} \cdot \frac{3}{10}$$

✓ **Solution**

ⓐ The operation is subtraction. The fractions do not have a common denominator.

$$\frac{5x}{6} - \frac{3}{10}$$

Rewrite each fraction as an equivalent fraction with the LCD, 30.	$\frac{5x \cdot 5}{6 \cdot 5} - \frac{3 \cdot 3}{10 \cdot 3}$
	$\frac{25x}{30} - \frac{9}{30}$
Subtract the numerators and place the difference over the common denominator.	$\frac{25x - 9}{30}$

ⓑ The operation is multiplication; no need for a common denominator.

$$\frac{5x}{6} \cdot \frac{3}{10}$$

To multiply fractions, multiply the numerators and multiply the denominators.	$\frac{5x \cdot 3}{6 \cdot 10}$
Rewrite, showing common factors.	$\frac{\cancel{5} \cdot x \cdot \cancel{3}}{2 \cdot \cancel{3} \cdot 2 \cdot \cancel{5}}$
Remove common factors to simplify.	$\frac{x}{4}$

> **TRY IT : : 4.147**   Simplify:

ⓐ $\frac{3a}{4} - \frac{8}{9}$ ⓑ $\frac{3a}{4} \cdot \frac{8}{9}$

> **TRY IT : : 4.148**   Simplify:

ⓐ $\frac{4k}{5} + \frac{5}{6}$ ⓑ $\frac{4k}{5} \div \frac{5}{6}$

Use the Order of Operations to Simplify Complex Fractions

In Multiply and Divide Mixed Numbers and Complex Fractions, we saw that a complex fraction is a fraction in which the numerator or denominator contains a fraction. We simplified complex fractions by rewriting them as division problems. For example,

$$\frac{\frac{3}{4}}{\frac{5}{8}} = \frac{3}{4} \div \frac{5}{8}$$

Now we will look at complex fractions in which the numerator or denominator can be simplified. To follow the order of operations, we simplify the numerator and denominator separately first. Then we divide the numerator by the denominator.

HOW TO :: SIMPLIFY COMPLEX FRACTIONS.

   Step 1.   Simplify the numerator.
   Step 2.   Simplify the denominator.
   Step 3.   Divide the numerator by the denominator.
   Step 4.   Simplify if possible.

EXAMPLE 4.75

Simplify: $\dfrac{\left(\frac{1}{2}\right)^{2}}{4+3^{2}}$.

✓ **Solution**

$$\dfrac{\left(\frac{1}{2}\right)^{2}}{4+3^{2}}$$

Simplify the numerator.	$\dfrac{\frac{1}{4}}{4+3^{2}}$
Simplify the term with the exponent in the denominator.	$\dfrac{\frac{1}{4}}{4+9}$
Add the terms in the denominator.	$\dfrac{\frac{1}{4}}{13}$
Divide the numerator by the denominator.	$\frac{1}{4}\div13$
Rewrite as multiplication by the reciprocal.	$\frac{1}{4}\cdot\frac{1}{13}$
Multiply.	$\frac{1}{52}$

> **TRY IT :: 4.149**   Simplify: $\dfrac{\left(\frac{1}{3}\right)^{2}}{2^{3}+2}$.

> **TRY IT :: 4.150**   Simplify: $\dfrac{1+4^{2}}{\left(\frac{1}{4}\right)^{2}}$.

EXAMPLE 4.76

Simplify: $\dfrac{\frac{1}{2}+\frac{2}{3}}{\frac{3}{4}-\frac{1}{6}}$.

⊘ **Solution**

	$\dfrac{\frac{1}{2}+\frac{2}{3}}{\frac{3}{4}-\frac{1}{6}}$
Rewrite numerator with the LCD of 6 and denominator with LCD of 12.	$\dfrac{\frac{3}{6}+\frac{4}{6}}{\frac{9}{12}-\frac{2}{12}}$
Add in the numerator. Subtract in the denominator.	$\dfrac{\frac{7}{6}}{\frac{7}{12}}$
Divide the numerator by the denominator.	$\dfrac{7}{6}\div\dfrac{7}{12}$
Rewrite as multiplication by the reciprocal.	$\dfrac{7}{6}\cdot\dfrac{12}{7}$
Rewrite, showing common factors.	$\dfrac{\cancel{7}\cdot\cancel{6}\cdot 2}{\cancel{6}\cdot\cancel{7}\cdot 1}$
Simplify.	2

> **TRY IT ::** 4.151   Simplify: $\dfrac{\frac{1}{3}+\frac{1}{2}}{\frac{3}{4}-\frac{1}{3}}$.

> **TRY IT ::** 4.152   Simplify: $\dfrac{\frac{2}{3}-\frac{1}{2}}{\frac{1}{4}+\frac{1}{3}}$.

Evaluate Variable Expressions with Fractions

We have evaluated expressions before, but now we can also evaluate expressions with fractions. Remember, to evaluate an expression, we substitute the value of the variable into the expression and then simplify.

EXAMPLE 4.77

Evaluate $x+\frac{1}{3}$ when

ⓐ $x=-\frac{1}{3}$ ⓑ $x=-\frac{3}{4}$.

⊘ **Solution**

ⓐ To evaluate $x+\frac{1}{3}$ when $x=-\frac{1}{3}$, substitute $-\frac{1}{3}$ for x in the expression.

	$x+\dfrac{1}{3}$
Substitute $-\frac{1}{3}$ for x.	$-\dfrac{1}{3}+\dfrac{1}{3}$
Simplify.	0

ⓑ To evaluate $x + \frac{1}{3}$ when $x = -\frac{3}{4}$, we substitute $-\frac{3}{4}$ for x in the expression.

$$x + \frac{1}{3}$$

Substitute $-\frac{3}{4}$ for x.	$-\frac{3}{4} + \frac{1}{3}$
Rewrite as equivalent fractions with the LCD, 12.	$-\frac{3 \cdot 3}{4 \cdot 3} + \frac{1 \cdot 4}{3 \cdot 4}$
Simplify the numerators and denominators.	$-\frac{9}{12} + \frac{4}{12}$
Add.	$-\frac{5}{12}$

> **TRY IT :: 4.153**   Evaluate: $x + \frac{3}{4}$ when

ⓐ $x = -\frac{7}{4}$ ⓑ $x = -\frac{5}{4}$

> **TRY IT :: 4.154**   Evaluate: $y + \frac{1}{2}$ when

ⓐ $y = \frac{2}{3}$ ⓑ $y = -\frac{3}{4}$

EXAMPLE 4.78

Evaluate $y - \frac{5}{6}$ when $y = -\frac{2}{3}$.

⊘ **Solution**

We substitute $-\frac{2}{3}$ for y in the expression.

$$y - \frac{5}{6}$$

Substitute $-\frac{2}{3}$ for y.	$-\frac{2}{3} - \frac{5}{6}$
Rewrite as equivalent fractions with the LCD, 6.	$-\frac{4}{6} - \frac{5}{6}$
Subtract.	$-\frac{9}{6}$
Simplify.	$-\frac{3}{2}$

> **TRY IT :: 4.155**   Evaluate: $y - \frac{1}{2}$ when $y = -\frac{1}{4}$.

> **TRY IT : : 4.156**   Evaluate: $x - \frac{3}{8}$ when $x = -\frac{5}{2}$.

EXAMPLE 4.79

Evaluate $2x^2 y$ when $x = \frac{1}{4}$ and $y = -\frac{2}{3}$.

⊘ **Solution**

Substitute the values into the expression. In $2x^2 y$, the exponent applies only to x.

		$2x^2y$
Substitute $\frac{1}{4}$ for x and $-\frac{2}{3}$ for y.		$2\left(\frac{1}{4}\right)^2\left(-\frac{2}{3}\right)$
Simplify exponents first.		$2\left(\frac{1}{16}\right)\left(-\frac{2}{3}\right)$
Multiply. The product will be negative.		$-\frac{2}{1} \cdot \frac{1}{16} \cdot \frac{2}{3}$
Simplify.		$-\frac{4}{48}$
Remove the common factors.		$-\frac{1 \cdot \cancel{4}}{\cancel{4} \cdot 12}$
Simplify.		$-\frac{1}{12}$

> **TRY IT : : 4.157**   Evaluate. $3ab^2$ when $a = -\frac{2}{3}$ and $b = -\frac{1}{2}$.

> **TRY IT : : 4.158**   Evaluate. $4c^3 d$ when $c = -\frac{1}{2}$ and $d = -\frac{4}{3}$.

EXAMPLE 4.80

Evaluate $\frac{p+q}{r}$ when $p = -4$, $q = -2$, and $r = 8$.

⊘ **Solution**

We substitute the values into the expression and simplify.

		$\frac{p+q}{r}$
Substitute –4 for p, –2 for q and 8 for r.		$\frac{-4 + (-2)}{8}$
Add in the numerator first.		$-\frac{6}{8}$
Simplify.		$-\frac{3}{4}$

> **TRY IT : :** 4.159

Evaluate: $\dfrac{a+b}{c}$ when $a = -8$, $b = -7$, and $c = 6$.

> **TRY IT : :** 4.160

Evaluate: $\dfrac{x+y}{z}$ when $x = 9$, $y = -18$, and $z = -6$.

4.5 EXERCISES

Practice Makes Perfect

Find the Least Common Denominator (LCD)

In the following exercises, find the least common denominator (LCD) for each set of fractions.

316. $\frac{2}{3}$ and $\frac{3}{4}$

317. $\frac{3}{4}$ and $\frac{2}{5}$

318. $\frac{7}{12}$ and $\frac{5}{8}$

319. $\frac{9}{16}$ and $\frac{7}{12}$

320. $\frac{13}{30}$ and $\frac{25}{42}$

321. $\frac{23}{30}$ and $\frac{5}{48}$

322. $\frac{21}{35}$ and $\frac{39}{56}$

323. $\frac{18}{35}$ and $\frac{33}{49}$

324. $\frac{2}{3}, \frac{1}{6},$ and $\frac{3}{4}$

325. $\frac{2}{3}, \frac{1}{4},$ and $\frac{3}{5}$

Convert Fractions to Equivalent Fractions with the LCD

In the following exercises, convert to equivalent fractions using the LCD.

326. $\frac{1}{3}$ and $\frac{1}{4}$, LCD = 12

327. $\frac{1}{4}$ and $\frac{1}{5}$, LCD = 20

328. $\frac{5}{12}$ and $\frac{7}{8}$, LCD = 24

329. $\frac{7}{12}$ and $\frac{5}{8}$, LCD = 24

330. $\frac{13}{16}$ and $-\frac{11}{12}$, LCD = 48

331. $\frac{11}{16}$ and $-\frac{5}{12}$, LCD = 48

332. $\frac{1}{3}, \frac{5}{6},$ and $\frac{3}{4}$, LCD = 12

333. $\frac{1}{3}, \frac{3}{4},$ and $\frac{3}{5}$, LCD = 60

Add and Subtract Fractions with Different Denominators

In the following exercises, add or subtract. Write the result in simplified form.

334. $\frac{1}{3} + \frac{1}{5}$

335. $\frac{1}{4} + \frac{1}{5}$

336. $\frac{1}{2} + \frac{1}{7}$

337. $\frac{1}{3} + \frac{1}{8}$

338. $\frac{1}{3} - \left(-\frac{1}{9}\right)$

339. $\frac{1}{4} - \left(-\frac{1}{8}\right)$

340. $\frac{1}{5} - \left(-\frac{1}{10}\right)$

341. $\frac{1}{2} - \left(-\frac{1}{6}\right)$

342. $\frac{2}{3} + \frac{3}{4}$

343. $\frac{3}{4} + \frac{2}{5}$

344. $\frac{7}{12} + \frac{5}{8}$

345. $\frac{5}{12} + \frac{3}{8}$

346. $\frac{7}{12} - \frac{9}{16}$

347. $\frac{7}{16} - \frac{5}{12}$

348. $\frac{11}{12} - \frac{3}{8}$

349. $\frac{5}{8} - \frac{7}{12}$

350. $\frac{2}{3} - \frac{3}{8}$

351. $\frac{5}{6} - \frac{3}{4}$

352. $-\frac{11}{30} + \frac{27}{40}$

353. $-\frac{9}{20} + \frac{17}{30}$

354. $-\frac{13}{30} + \frac{25}{42}$

355. $-\frac{23}{30} + \frac{5}{48}$

356. $-\frac{39}{56} - \frac{22}{35}$

357. $-\frac{33}{49} - \frac{18}{35}$

358. $-\dfrac{2}{3} - \left(-\dfrac{3}{4}\right)$

359. $-\dfrac{3}{4} - \left(-\dfrac{4}{5}\right)$

360. $-\dfrac{9}{16} - \left(-\dfrac{4}{5}\right)$

361. $-\dfrac{7}{20} - \left(-\dfrac{5}{8}\right)$

362. $1 + \dfrac{7}{8}$

363. $1 + \dfrac{5}{6}$

364. $1 - \dfrac{5}{9}$

365. $1 - \dfrac{3}{10}$

366. $\dfrac{x}{3} + \dfrac{1}{4}$

367. $\dfrac{y}{2} + \dfrac{2}{3}$

368. $\dfrac{y}{4} - \dfrac{3}{5}$

369. $\dfrac{x}{5} - \dfrac{1}{4}$

Identify and Use Fraction Operations

In the following exercises, perform the indicated operations. Write your answers in simplified form.

370.
ⓐ $\dfrac{3}{4} + \dfrac{1}{6}$ ⓑ $\dfrac{3}{4} \div \dfrac{1}{6}$

371.
ⓐ $\dfrac{2}{3} + \dfrac{1}{6}$ ⓑ $\dfrac{2}{3} \div \dfrac{1}{6}$

372.
ⓐ $-\dfrac{2}{5} - \dfrac{1}{8}$ ⓑ $-\dfrac{2}{5} \cdot \dfrac{1}{8}$

373.
ⓐ $-\dfrac{4}{5} - \dfrac{1}{8}$ ⓑ $-\dfrac{4}{5} \cdot \dfrac{1}{8}$

374.
ⓐ $\dfrac{5}{n} \div \dfrac{8}{15}$ ⓑ $\dfrac{5}{n} - \dfrac{8}{15}$

375.
ⓐ $\dfrac{3}{a} \div \dfrac{7}{12}$ ⓑ $\dfrac{3}{a} - \dfrac{7}{12}$

376.
ⓐ $\dfrac{9}{10} \cdot \left(-\dfrac{11}{d}\right)$
ⓑ $\dfrac{9}{10} + \left(-\dfrac{11}{d}\right)$

377.
ⓐ $\dfrac{4}{15} \cdot \left(-\dfrac{5}{q}\right)$
ⓑ $\dfrac{4}{15} + \left(-\dfrac{5}{q}\right)$

378. $-\dfrac{3}{8} \div \left(-\dfrac{3}{10}\right)$

379. $-\dfrac{5}{12} \div \left(-\dfrac{5}{9}\right)$

380. $-\dfrac{3}{8} + \dfrac{5}{12}$

381. $-\dfrac{1}{8} + \dfrac{7}{12}$

382. $\dfrac{5}{6} - \dfrac{1}{9}$

383. $\dfrac{5}{9} - \dfrac{1}{6}$

384. $\dfrac{3}{8} \cdot \left(-\dfrac{10}{21}\right)$

385. $\dfrac{7}{12} \cdot \left(-\dfrac{8}{35}\right)$

386. $-\dfrac{7}{15} - \dfrac{y}{4}$

387. $-\dfrac{3}{8} - \dfrac{x}{11}$

388. $\dfrac{11}{12a} \cdot \dfrac{9a}{16}$

389. $\dfrac{10y}{13} \cdot \dfrac{8}{15y}$

Use the Order of Operations to Simplify Complex Fractions

In the following exercises, simplify.

390. $\dfrac{\left(\frac{1}{5}\right)^2}{2 + 3^2}$

391. $\dfrac{\left(\frac{1}{3}\right)^2}{5 + 2^2}$

392. $\dfrac{2^3 + 4^2}{\left(\frac{2}{3}\right)^2}$

393. $\dfrac{3^3 - 3^2}{\left(\frac{3}{4}\right)^2}$

394. $\dfrac{\left(\frac{3}{5}\right)^2}{\left(\frac{3}{7}\right)^2}$

395. $\dfrac{\left(\frac{3}{4}\right)^2}{\left(\frac{5}{8}\right)^2}$

396. $\dfrac{2}{\frac{1}{3} + \frac{1}{5}}$

397. $\dfrac{5}{\frac{1}{4} + \frac{1}{3}}$

398. $\dfrac{\frac{2}{3} + \frac{1}{2}}{\frac{3}{4} - \frac{2}{3}}$

399. $\dfrac{\frac{3}{4}+\frac{1}{2}}{\frac{5}{6}-\frac{2}{3}}$

400. $\dfrac{\frac{7}{8}-\frac{2}{3}}{\frac{1}{2}+\frac{3}{8}}$

401. $\dfrac{\frac{3}{4}-\frac{3}{5}}{\frac{1}{4}+\frac{2}{5}}$

Mixed Practice

In the following exercises, simplify.

402. $\frac{1}{2}+\frac{2}{3}\cdot\frac{5}{12}$

403. $\frac{1}{3}+\frac{2}{5}\cdot\frac{3}{4}$

404. $1-\frac{3}{5}\div\frac{1}{10}$

405. $1-\frac{5}{6}\div\frac{1}{12}$

406. $\frac{2}{3}+\frac{1}{6}+\frac{3}{4}$

407. $\frac{2}{3}+\frac{1}{4}+\frac{3}{5}$

408. $\frac{3}{8}-\frac{1}{6}+\frac{3}{4}$

409. $\frac{2}{5}+\frac{5}{8}-\frac{3}{4}$

410. $12\left(\frac{9}{20}-\frac{4}{15}\right)$

411. $8\left(\frac{15}{16}-\frac{5}{6}\right)$

412. $\dfrac{\frac{5}{8}+\frac{1}{6}}{\frac{19}{24}}$

413. $\dfrac{\frac{1}{6}+\frac{3}{10}}{\frac{14}{30}}$

414. $\left(\frac{5}{9}+\frac{1}{6}\right)\div\left(\frac{2}{3}-\frac{1}{2}\right)$

415. $\left(\frac{3}{4}+\frac{1}{6}\right)\div\left(\frac{5}{8}-\frac{1}{3}\right)$

In the following exercises, evaluate the given expression. Express your answers in simplified form, using improper fractions if necessary.

416. $x+\frac{1}{2}$ when

ⓐ $x=-\frac{1}{8}$ ⓑ $x=-\frac{1}{2}$

417. $x+\frac{2}{3}$ when

ⓐ $x=-\frac{1}{6}$ ⓑ $x=-\frac{5}{3}$

418. $x+\left(-\frac{5}{6}\right)$ when

ⓐ $x=\frac{1}{3}$ ⓑ $x=-\frac{1}{6}$

419. $x+\left(-\frac{11}{12}\right)$ when

ⓐ $x=\frac{11}{12}$ ⓑ $x=\frac{3}{4}$

420. $x-\frac{2}{5}$ when

ⓐ $x=\frac{3}{5}$ ⓑ $x=-\frac{3}{5}$

421. $x-\frac{1}{3}$ when

ⓐ $x=\frac{2}{3}$ ⓑ $x=-\frac{2}{3}$

422. $\frac{7}{10}-w$ when

ⓐ $w=\frac{1}{2}$ ⓑ $w=-\frac{1}{2}$

423. $\frac{5}{12}-w$ when

ⓐ $w=\frac{1}{4}$ ⓑ $w=-\frac{1}{4}$

424. $4p^2q$ when

$p=-\frac{1}{2}$ and $q=\frac{5}{9}$

425.
$5m^2n$ when $m=-\frac{2}{5}$ and $n=\frac{1}{3}$

426.
$2x^2y^3$ when $x=-\frac{2}{3}$ and $y=-\frac{1}{2}$

427.
$8u^2v^3$ when $u=-\frac{3}{4}$ and $v=-\frac{1}{2}$

428.
$\frac{u+v}{w}$ when $u=-4,\ v=-8,\ w=2$

429.
$\frac{m+n}{p}$ when $m=-6,\ n=-2,\ p=4$

430. $\frac{a+b}{a-b}$ when $a=-3,\ b=8$

431. $\frac{r-s}{r+s}$ when $r=10,\ s=-5$

Everyday Math

432. Decorating Laronda is making covers for the throw pillows on her sofa. For each pillow cover, she needs $\frac{3}{16}$ yard of print fabric and $\frac{3}{8}$ yard of solid fabric. What is the total amount of fabric Laronda needs for each pillow cover?

433. Baking Vanessa is baking chocolate chip cookies and oatmeal cookies. She needs $1\frac{1}{4}$ cups of sugar for the chocolate chip cookies, and $1\frac{1}{8}$ cups for the oatmeal cookies How much sugar does she need altogether?

Writing Exercises

434. Explain why it is necessary to have a common denominator to add or subtract fractions.

435. Explain how to find the LCD of two fractions.

Self Check

ⓐ *After completing the exercises, use this checklist to evaluate your mastery of the objectives of this section.*

I can...	Confidently	With some help	No-I don't get it!
add and subtract fractions with different denominators.			
identify and use fraction operations.			
use the order of operations to simplify complex fractions.			
evaluate variable expressions with fractions.			

ⓑ *After looking at the checklist, do you think you are well prepared for the next section? Why or why not?*

4.6 Add and Subtract Mixed Numbers

Learning Objectives

By the end of this section, you will be able to:
- Model addition of mixed numbers with a common denominator
- Add mixed numbers with a common denominator
- Model subtraction of mixed numbers
- Subtract mixed numbers with a common denominator
- Add and subtract mixed numbers with different denominators

Be Prepared!

Before you get started, take this readiness quiz.

1. Draw figure to model $\frac{7}{3}$.

   If you missed this problem, review Example 4.6.

2. Change $\frac{11}{4}$ to a mixed number.

   If you missed this problem, review Example 4.9.

3. Change $3\frac{1}{2}$ to an improper fraction.

   If you missed this problem, review Example 4.11.

Model Addition of Mixed Numbers with a Common Denominator

So far, we've added and subtracted proper and improper fractions, but not mixed numbers. Let's begin by thinking about addition of mixed numbers using money.

If Ron has 1 dollar and 1 quarter, he has $1\frac{1}{4}$ dollars.

If Don has 2 dollars and 1 quarter, he has $2\frac{1}{4}$ dollars.

What if Ron and Don put their money together? They would have 3 dollars and 2 quarters. They add the dollars and add the quarters. This makes $3\frac{2}{4}$ dollars. Because two quarters is half a dollar, they would have 3 and a half dollars, or $3\frac{1}{2}$ dollars.

$$1\frac{1}{4}$$
$$+2\frac{1}{4}$$
$$\overline{}$$
$$3\frac{2}{4} = 3\frac{1}{2}$$

When you added the dollars and then added the quarters, you were adding the whole numbers and then adding the fractions.

$$1\frac{1}{4} + 2\frac{1}{4}$$

We can use fraction circles to model this same example:

$$1\frac{1}{4} + 2\frac{1}{4}$$

Start with $1\frac{1}{4}$.	one whole and one $\frac{1}{4}$ pieces		$1\frac{1}{4}$
Add $2\frac{1}{4}$ more.	two wholes and one $\frac{1}{4}$ pieces		$+ 2\frac{1}{4}$
The sum is:	three wholes and two $\frac{1}{4}$'s		$3\frac{2}{4} = 3\frac{1}{2}$

 MANIPULATIVE MATHEMATICS

Doing the Manipulative Mathematics activity "Model Mixed Number Addition/Subtraction" will help you develop a better understanding of adding and subtracting mixed numbers.

EXAMPLE 4.81

Model $2\frac{1}{3} + 1\frac{2}{3}$ and give the sum.

⊘ **Solution**

We will use fraction circles, whole circles for the whole numbers and $\frac{1}{3}$ pieces for the fractions.

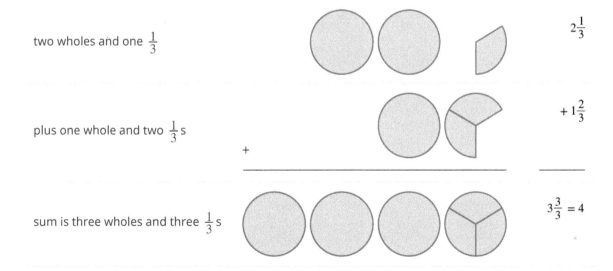

two wholes and one $\frac{1}{3}$		$2\frac{1}{3}$
plus one whole and two $\frac{1}{3}$ s		$+ 1\frac{2}{3}$
sum is three wholes and three $\frac{1}{3}$ s		$3\frac{3}{3} = 4$

This is the same as 4 wholes. So, $2\frac{1}{3} + 1\frac{2}{3} = 4$.

> **TRY IT : :** 4.161   Use a model to add the following. Draw a picture to illustrate your model.

$$1\frac{2}{5} + 3\frac{3}{5}$$

> **TRY IT : :** 4.162   Use a model to add the following. Draw a picture to illustrate your model.

$$2\frac{1}{6} + 2\frac{5}{6}$$

EXAMPLE 4.82

Model $1\frac{3}{5} + 2\frac{3}{5}$ and give the sum as a mixed number.

⊘ **Solution**

We will use fraction circles, whole circles for the whole numbers and $\frac{1}{5}$ pieces for the fractions.

one whole and three $\frac{1}{5}$s $1\frac{3}{5}$

plus two wholes and three $\frac{1}{5}$s   + $+ 2\frac{3}{5}$

sum is three wholes and six $\frac{1}{5}$s $3\frac{6}{5} = 4\frac{1}{5}$

Adding the whole circles and fifth pieces, we got a sum of $3\frac{6}{5}$. We can see that $\frac{6}{5}$ is equivalent to $1\frac{1}{5}$, so we add that to the 3 to get $4\frac{1}{5}$.

> **TRY IT : :** 4.163   Model, and give the sum as a mixed number. Draw a picture to illustrate your model.

$$2\frac{5}{6} + 1\frac{5}{6}$$

> **TRY IT : :** 4.164   Model, and give the sum as a mixed number. Draw a picture to illustrate your model.

$$1\frac{5}{8} + 1\frac{7}{8}$$

Add Mixed Numbers

Modeling with fraction circles helps illustrate the process for adding mixed numbers: We add the whole numbers and add the fractions, and then we simplify the result, if possible.

HOW TO : : ADD MIXED NUMBERS WITH A COMMON DENOMINATOR.

  Step 1. Add the whole numbers.

  Step 2. Add the fractions.

  Step 3. Simplify, if possible.

EXAMPLE 4.83

Add: $3\frac{4}{9} + 2\frac{2}{9}$.

⊘ **Solution**

$$3\frac{4}{9} + 2\frac{2}{9}$$

Add the whole numbers.

$$\begin{array}{r} 3\frac{4}{9} \\ +\, 2\frac{2}{9} \\ \hline 5 \end{array}$$

Add the fractions.

$$\begin{array}{r} 3\frac{4}{9} \\ +\, 2\frac{2}{9} \\ \hline 5\frac{6}{9} \end{array}$$

Simplify the fraction.

$$\begin{array}{r} 3\frac{4}{9} \\ +\, 2\frac{2}{9} \\ \hline 5\frac{6}{9} = 5\frac{2}{3} \end{array}$$

> **TRY IT : :** 4.165   Find the sum: $4\frac{4}{7} + 1\frac{2}{7}$.

> **TRY IT : :** 4.166   Find the sum: $2\frac{3}{11} + 5\frac{6}{11}$.

In Example 4.83, the sum of the fractions was a proper fraction. Now we will work through an example where the sum is an improper fraction.

EXAMPLE 4.84

Find the sum: $9\frac{5}{9} + 5\frac{7}{9}$.

⊘ Solution

$$9\frac{5}{9} + 5\frac{7}{9}$$

Add the whole numbers and then add the fractions.	$9\frac{5}{9}$ $+ 5\frac{7}{9}$ $\overline{14\frac{12}{9}}$
Rewrite $\frac{12}{9}$ as an improper fraction.	$14 + 1\frac{3}{9}$
Add.	$15\frac{3}{9}$
Simplify.	$15\frac{1}{3}$

> **TRY IT : :** 4.167   Find the sum: $8\frac{7}{8} + 7\frac{5}{8}$.

> **TRY IT : :** 4.168   Find the sum: $6\frac{7}{9} + 8\frac{5}{9}$.

An alternate method for adding mixed numbers is to convert the mixed numbers to improper fractions and then add the improper fractions. This method is usually written horizontally.

EXAMPLE 4.85

Add by converting the mixed numbers to improper fractions: $3\frac{7}{8} + 4\frac{3}{8}$.

⊘ Solution

$$3\frac{7}{8} + 4\frac{3}{8}$$

Convert to improper fractions.	$\frac{31}{8} + \frac{35}{8}$
Add the fractions.	$\frac{31 + 35}{8}$
Simplify the numerator.	$\frac{66}{8}$
Rewrite as a mixed number.	$8\frac{2}{8}$
Simplify the fraction.	$8\frac{1}{4}$

Since the problem was given in mixed number form, we will write the sum as a mixed number.

> **TRY IT : :** 4.169   Find the sum by converting the mixed numbers to improper fractions:

$5\frac{5}{9} + 3\frac{7}{9}.$

> **TRY IT : :** 4.170   Find the sum by converting the mixed numbers to improper fractions:

$3\frac{7}{10} + 2\frac{9}{10}.$

Table 4.74 compares the two methods of addition, using the expression $3\frac{2}{5} + 6\frac{4}{5}$ as an example. Which way do you prefer?

Mixed Numbers	Improper Fractions
$3\frac{2}{5}$	$3\frac{2}{5} + 6\frac{4}{5}$
$\dfrac{+6\frac{4}{5}}{9\frac{6}{5}}$	$\frac{17}{5} + \frac{34}{5}$
$9 + \frac{6}{5}$	$\frac{51}{5}$
$9 + 1\frac{1}{5}$	$10\frac{1}{5}$
$10\frac{1}{5}$	

Table 4.74

Model Subtraction of Mixed Numbers

Let's think of pizzas again to model subtraction of mixed numbers with a common denominator. Suppose you just baked a whole pizza and want to give your brother half of the pizza. What do you have to do to the pizza to give him half? You have to cut it into at least two pieces. Then you can give him half.

We will use fraction circles (pizzas!) to help us visualize the process.

Start with one whole.

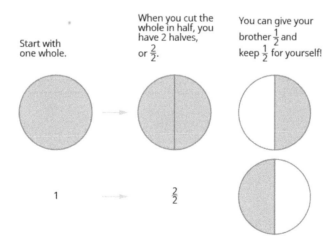

Start with one whole.

When you cut the whole in half, you have 2 halves, or $\frac{2}{2}$.

You can give your brother $\frac{1}{2}$ and keep $\frac{1}{2}$ for yourself!

1        $\frac{2}{2}$

Algebraically, you would write:

$$1 \qquad \frac{2}{2} \qquad \frac{2}{2}$$
$$\underline{-\frac{1}{2}} \rightarrow \underline{-\frac{1}{2}} \rightarrow \underline{-\frac{1}{2}}$$
$$\frac{1}{2}$$

EXAMPLE 4.86

Use a model to subtract: $1 - \frac{1}{3}$.

⊘ **Solution**

	Model	Math Notation
Rewrite vertically. Start with one whole.		$\begin{array}{r} 1 \\ -\frac{1}{3} \\ \hline \end{array}$
Since $\frac{1}{3}$ has denominator 3, cut the whole into 3 pieces. The 1 whole becomes $\frac{3}{3}$.		$\begin{array}{r} \frac{3}{3} \\ -\frac{1}{3} \\ \hline \end{array}$
Take away $\frac{1}{3}$. There are $\frac{2}{3}$ left.		$\begin{array}{r} \frac{3}{3} \\ -\frac{1}{3} \\ \hline \frac{2}{3} \end{array}$

> **TRY IT : : 4.171**   Use a model to subtract: $1 - \frac{1}{4}$.

> **TRY IT : : 4.172**   Use a model to subtract: $1 - \frac{1}{5}$.

What if we start with more than one whole? Let's find out.

EXAMPLE 4.87

Use a model to subtract: $2 - \frac{3}{4}$.

Solution

	Model	Math Notation
Rewrite vertically. Start with two wholes.		$\begin{array}{r} 2 \\ -\frac{3}{4} \\ \hline \end{array}$
Since $\frac{3}{4}$ has denominator 4, cut one of the wholes into 4 pieces. You have 1 whole and $\frac{4}{4}$.		$\begin{array}{r} 1\frac{4}{4} \\ -\frac{3}{4} \\ \hline \end{array}$
Take away $\frac{3}{4}$. There is $1\frac{1}{4}$ left.		$\begin{array}{r} 1\frac{4}{4} \\ -\frac{3}{4} \\ \hline 1\frac{1}{4} \end{array}$

> **TRY IT :: 4.173** Use a model to subtract: $2 - \frac{1}{5}$.

> **TRY IT :: 4.174** Use a model to subtract: $2 - \frac{1}{3}$.

In the next example, we'll subtract more than one whole.

EXAMPLE 4.88

Use a model to subtract: $2 - 1\frac{2}{5}$.

Solution

	Model	Math Notation
Rewrite vertically. Start with two wholes.		$\begin{array}{r} 2 \\ -1\frac{2}{5} \\ \hline \end{array}$
Since $\frac{2}{5}$ has denominator 5, cut one of the wholes into 5 pieces. You have 1 whole and $\frac{5}{5}$.		$\begin{array}{r} 1\frac{5}{5} \\ -1\frac{2}{5} \\ \hline \end{array}$
Take away $1\frac{2}{5}$. There is $\frac{3}{5}$ left.		$\begin{array}{r} 1\frac{5}{5} \\ -1\frac{2}{5} \\ \hline \frac{3}{5} \end{array}$

> **TRY IT : :** 4.175   Use a model to subtract: $2 - 1\frac{1}{3}$.

> **TRY IT : :** 4.176   Use a model to subtract: $2 - 1\frac{1}{4}$.

What if you start with a mixed number and need to subtract a fraction? Think about this situation: You need to put three quarters in a parking meter, but you have only a $1 bill and one quarter. What could you do? You could change the dollar bill into 4 quarters. The value of 4 quarters is the same as one dollar bill, but the 4 quarters are more useful for the parking meter. Now, instead of having a $1 bill and one quarter, you have 5 quarters and can put 3 quarters in the meter.

This models what happens when we subtract a fraction from a mixed number. We subtracted three quarters from one dollar and one quarter.

We can also model this using fraction circles, much like we did for addition of mixed numbers.

EXAMPLE 4.89

Use a model to subtract: $1\frac{1}{4} - \frac{3}{4}$

⊘ **Solution**

Rewrite vertically. Start with one whole and one fourth.

Since the fractions have denominator 4, cut the whole into 4 pieces. You now have $\frac{4}{4}$ and $\frac{1}{4}$ which is $\frac{5}{4}$.

Take away $\frac{3}{4}$.

There is $\frac{1}{2}$ left.

> **TRY IT : :** 4.177   Use a model to subtract. Draw a picture to illustrate your model.
>
> $1\frac{1}{3} - \frac{2}{3}$

> **TRY IT : :** 4.178   Use a model to subtract. Draw a picture to illustrate your model.
>
> $1\frac{1}{5} - \frac{4}{5}$

Subtract Mixed Numbers with a Common Denominator

Now we will subtract mixed numbers without using a model. But it may help to picture the model in your mind as you read the steps.

HOW TO ::

Subtract mixed numbers with common denominators.
Step 1. Rewrite the problem in vertical form.
Step 2. Compare the two fractions.
- If the top fraction is larger than the bottom fraction, go to Step 3.
- If not, in the top mixed number, take one whole and add it to the fraction part, making a mixed number with an improper fraction.
Step 3. Subtract the fractions.
Step 4. Subtract the whole numbers.
Step 5. Simplify, if possible.

EXAMPLE 4.90

Find the difference: $5\frac{3}{5} - 2\frac{4}{5}$.

Solution

$$5\frac{3}{5} - 2\frac{4}{5}$$

Rewrite the problem in vertical form.

$$\begin{array}{r} 5\frac{3}{5} \\ -2\frac{4}{5} \\ \hline \end{array}$$

Since $\frac{3}{5}$ is less than $\frac{4}{5}$, take 1 from the 5 and add it to the $\frac{3}{5}$: $\left(\frac{5}{5} + \frac{3}{5} = \frac{8}{5}\right)$

$$\begin{array}{r} 5\frac{3}{5} \\ -2\frac{4}{5} \\ \hline \end{array} \longrightarrow \begin{array}{r} 4\frac{8}{5} \\ -2\frac{4}{5} \\ \hline \end{array}$$

Subtract the fractions.

$$\begin{array}{r} 4\frac{8}{5} \\ -2\frac{4}{5} \\ \hline \frac{4}{5} \end{array}$$

Subtract the whole parts.
The result is in simplest form.

$$\begin{array}{r} 4\frac{8}{5} \\ -2\frac{4}{5} \\ \hline 2\frac{4}{5} \end{array}$$

Since the problem was given with mixed numbers, we leave the result as mixed numbers.

> **TRY IT :: 4.179**   Find the difference: $6\frac{4}{9} - 3\frac{7}{9}$.

> **TRY IT :: 4.180**   Find the difference: $4\frac{4}{7} - 2\frac{6}{7}$.

Just as we did with addition, we could subtract mixed numbers by converting them first to improper fractions. We should write the answer in the form it was given, so if we are given mixed numbers to subtract we will write the answer as a mixed number.

 HOW TO :: SUBTRACT MIXED NUMBERS WITH COMMON DENOMINATORS AS IMPROPER FRACTIONS.

Step 1. Rewrite the mixed numbers as improper fractions.

Step 2. Subtract the numerators.

Step 3. Write the answer as a mixed number, simplifying the fraction part, if possible.

EXAMPLE 4.91

Find the difference by converting to improper fractions:

$9\frac{6}{11} - 7\frac{10}{11}.$

⊘ **Solution**

$$9\frac{6}{11} - 7\frac{10}{11}$$

Rewrite as improper fractions.	$\frac{105}{11} - \frac{87}{11}$
Subtract the numerators.	$\frac{18}{11}$
Rewrite as a mixed number.	$1\frac{7}{11}$

> **TRY IT :: 4.181**   Find the difference by converting the mixed numbers to improper fractions:
>
> $6\frac{4}{9} - 3\frac{7}{9}.$

> **TRY IT :: 4.182**   Find the difference by converting the mixed numbers to improper fractions:
>
> $4\frac{4}{7} - 2\frac{6}{7}.$

Add and Subtract Mixed Numbers with Different Denominators

To add or subtract mixed numbers with different denominators, we first convert the fractions to equivalent fractions with the LCD. Then we can follow all the steps we used above for adding or subtracting fractions with like denominators.

EXAMPLE 4.92

Add: $2\frac{1}{2} + 5\frac{2}{3}.$

⊘ **Solution**

Since the denominators are different, we rewrite the fractions as equivalent fractions with the LCD, 6. Then we will add and simplify.

Change into
equivalent fractions

$$2\frac{1}{2} \quad \rightarrow \quad 2\frac{1\cdot 3}{2\cdot 3} \quad \rightarrow \quad 2\frac{3}{6}$$

$$+5\frac{2}{3} \qquad +5\frac{2\cdot 2}{3\cdot 2} \qquad +5\frac{4}{6}$$

$$7\frac{7}{6} \quad \rightarrow \quad 8\frac{1}{6}$$

Add.   Rewrite in
simplest form.

We write the answer as a mixed number because we were given mixed numbers in the problem.

> **TRY IT ::** 4.183   Add: $1\frac{5}{6} + 4\frac{3}{4}$.

> **TRY IT ::** 4.184   Add: $3\frac{4}{5} + 8\frac{1}{2}$.

EXAMPLE 4.93

Subtract: $4\frac{3}{4} - 2\frac{7}{8}$.

⊘ **Solution**

Since the denominators of the fractions are different, we will rewrite them as equivalent fractions with the LCD 8. Once in that form, we will subtract. But we will need to borrow 1 first.

Change into
equivalent fractions

Borrow 1 whole from the 4,
since we cannot subtract $\frac{7}{8}$ from $\frac{6}{8}$.

$$4\frac{3}{4} \quad \rightarrow \quad 4\frac{3\cdot 2}{4\cdot 2} \quad \rightarrow \quad 4\frac{6}{8} \quad \rightarrow \quad 3\frac{14}{8}$$

$$-2\frac{7}{8} \qquad -2\frac{7}{8} \qquad -2\frac{7}{8} \qquad -2\frac{7}{8}$$

$$1\frac{7}{8}$$

Subtract.

We were given mixed numbers, so we leave the answer as a mixed number.

> **TRY IT ::** 4.185   Find the difference: $8\frac{1}{2} - 3\frac{4}{5}$.

> **TRY IT ::** 4.186   Find the difference: $4\frac{3}{4} - 1\frac{5}{6}$.

EXAMPLE 4.94

Subtract: $3\frac{5}{11} - 4\frac{3}{4}$.

⊘ Solution

We can see the answer will be negative since we are subtracting 4 from 3. Generally, when we know the answer will be negative it is easier to subtract with improper fractions rather than mixed numbers.

$$3\frac{5}{11} - 4\frac{3}{4}$$

Change to equivalent fractions with the LCD.	$3\frac{5 \cdot 4}{11 \cdot 4} - 4\frac{3 \cdot 11}{4 \cdot 11}$ $3\frac{20}{44} - 4\frac{33}{44}$
Rewrite as improper fractions.	$\frac{152}{44} - \frac{209}{44}$
Subtract.	$-\frac{57}{44}$
Rewrite as a mixed number.	$-1\frac{13}{44}$

> **TRY IT :: 4.187**   Subtract: $1\frac{3}{4} - 6\frac{7}{8}$.

> **TRY IT :: 4.188**   Subtract: $10\frac{3}{7} - 22\frac{4}{9}$.

▶ **MEDIA :: ** ACCESS ADDITIONAL ONLINE RESOURCES

- Adding Mixed Numbers (http://www.openstaxcollege.org/l/24AddMixed)
- Subtracting Mixed Numbers (http://www.openstaxcollege.org/l/24SubtractMixed)

4.6 EXERCISES

Practice Makes Perfect

Model Addition of Mixed Numbers

In the following exercises, use a model to find the sum. Draw a picture to illustrate your model.

436. $1\frac{1}{5} + 3\frac{1}{5}$

437. $2\frac{1}{3} + 1\frac{1}{3}$

438. $1\frac{3}{8} + 1\frac{7}{8}$

439. $1\frac{5}{6} + 1\frac{5}{6}$

Add Mixed Numbers with a Common Denominator

In the following exercises, add.

440. $5\frac{1}{3} + 6\frac{1}{3}$

441. $2\frac{4}{9} + 5\frac{1}{9}$

442. $4\frac{5}{8} + 9\frac{3}{8}$

443. $7\frac{9}{10} + 3\frac{1}{10}$

444. $3\frac{4}{5} + 6\frac{4}{5}$

445. $9\frac{2}{3} + 1\frac{2}{3}$

446. $6\frac{9}{10} + 8\frac{3}{10}$

447. $8\frac{4}{9} + 2\frac{8}{9}$

Model Subtraction of Mixed Numbers

In the following exercises, use a model to find the difference. Draw a picture to illustrate your model.

448. $1\frac{1}{6} - \frac{5}{6}$

449. $1\frac{1}{8} - \frac{5}{8}$

Subtract Mixed Numbers with a Common Denominator

In the following exercises, find the difference.

450. $2\frac{7}{8} - 1\frac{3}{8}$

451. $2\frac{7}{12} - 1\frac{5}{12}$

452. $8\frac{17}{20} - 4\frac{9}{20}$

453. $19\frac{13}{15} - 13\frac{7}{15}$

454. $8\frac{3}{7} - 4\frac{4}{7}$

455. $5\frac{2}{9} - 3\frac{4}{9}$

456. $2\frac{5}{8} - 1\frac{7}{8}$

457. $2\frac{5}{12} - 1\frac{7}{12}$

Add and Subtract Mixed Numbers with Different Denominators

In the following exercises, write the sum or difference as a mixed number in simplified form.

458. $3\frac{1}{4} + 6\frac{1}{3}$

459. $2\frac{1}{6} + 5\frac{3}{4}$

460. $1\frac{5}{8} + 4\frac{1}{2}$

461. $7\frac{2}{3} + 8\frac{1}{2}$

462. $9\frac{7}{10} - 2\frac{1}{3}$

463. $6\frac{4}{5} - 1\frac{1}{4}$

464. $2\frac{2}{3} - 3\frac{1}{2}$

465. $2\frac{7}{8} - 4\frac{1}{3}$

Mixed Practice

In the following exercises, perform the indicated operation and write the result as a mixed number in simplified form.

466. $2\frac{5}{8} \cdot 1\frac{3}{4}$

467. $1\frac{2}{3} \cdot 4\frac{1}{6}$

468. $\frac{2}{7} + \frac{4}{7}$

469. $\frac{2}{9} + \frac{5}{9}$

470. $1\frac{5}{12} \div \frac{1}{12}$

471. $2\frac{3}{10} \div \frac{1}{10}$

472. $13\frac{5}{12} - 9\frac{7}{12}$

473. $15\frac{5}{8} - 6\frac{7}{8}$

474. $\frac{5}{9} - \frac{4}{9}$

475. $\frac{11}{15} - \frac{7}{15}$

476. $4 - \frac{3}{4}$

477. $6 - \frac{2}{5}$

478. $\frac{9}{20} \div \frac{3}{4}$

479. $\frac{7}{24} \div \frac{14}{3}$

480. $9\frac{6}{11} + 7\frac{10}{11}$

481. $8\frac{5}{13} + 4\frac{9}{13}$

482. $3\frac{2}{5} + 5\frac{3}{4}$

483. $2\frac{5}{6} + 4\frac{1}{5}$

484. $\frac{8}{15} \cdot \frac{10}{19}$

485. $\frac{5}{12} \cdot \frac{8}{9}$

486. $6\frac{7}{8} - 2\frac{1}{3}$

487. $6\frac{5}{9} - 4\frac{2}{5}$

488. $5\frac{2}{9} - 4\frac{4}{5}$

489. $4\frac{3}{8} - 3\frac{2}{3}$

Everyday Math

490. Sewing Renata is sewing matching shirts for her husband and son. According to the patterns she will use, she needs $2\frac{3}{8}$ yards of fabric for her husband's shirt and $1\frac{1}{8}$ yards of fabric for her son's shirt. How much fabric does she need to make both shirts?

491. Sewing Pauline has $3\frac{1}{4}$ yards of fabric to make a jacket. The jacket uses $2\frac{2}{3}$ yards. How much fabric will she have left after making the jacket?

492. Printing Nishant is printing invitations on his computer. The paper is $8\frac{1}{2}$ inches wide, and he sets the print area to have a $1\frac{1}{2}$-inch border on each side. How wide is the print area on the sheet of paper?

493. Framing a picture Tessa bought a picture frame for her son's graduation picture. The picture is 8 inches wide. The picture frame is $2\frac{5}{8}$ inches wide on each side. How wide will the framed picture be?

Writing Exercises

494. Draw a diagram and use it to explain how to add $1\frac{5}{8} + 2\frac{7}{8}$.

495. Edgar will have to pay $3.75 in tolls to drive to the city.

ⓐ Explain how he can make change from a $10 bill before he leaves so that he has the exact amount he needs.

ⓑ How is Edgar's situation similar to how you subtract $10 - 3\frac{3}{4}$?

496. Add $4\frac{5}{12} + 3\frac{7}{8}$ twice, first by leaving them as mixed numbers and then by rewriting as improper fractions. Which method do you prefer, and why?

497. Subtract $3\frac{7}{8} - 4\frac{5}{12}$ twice, first by leaving them as mixed numbers and then by rewriting as improper fractions. Which method do you prefer, and why?

Self Check

ⓐ *After completing the exercises, use this checklist to evaluate your mastery of the objectives of this section.*

I can...	Confidently	With some help	No-I don't get it!
model addition of mixed numbers common with a denominator.			
add mixed numbers with a common denominator.			
model subtraction of mixed numbers.			
subtract mixed numbers with a common denominator.			
add and subtract mixed numbers with different denominators.			

ⓑ *After reviewing this checklist, what will you do to become confident for all objectives?*

4.7 Solve Equations with Fractions

Learning Objectives

By the end of this section, you will be able to:
- Determine whether a fraction is a solution of an equation
- Solve equations with fractions using the Addition, Subtraction, and Division Properties of Equality
- Solve equations using the Multiplication Property of Equality
- Translate sentences to equations and solve

Be Prepared!

Before you get started, take this readiness quiz. If you miss a problem, go back to the section listed and review the material.

1. Evaluate $x + 4$ when $x = -3$
   If you missed this problem, review Example 3.23.

2. Solve: $2y - 3 = 9$.
   If you missed this problem, review Example 3.61.

3. Solve: $y - 3 = -9$
   If you missed this problem, review Example 4.28.

Determine Whether a Fraction is a Solution of an Equation

As we saw in Solve Equations with the Subtraction and Addition Properties of Equality and Solve Equations Using Integers; The Division Property of Equality, a solution of an equation is a value that makes a true statement when substituted for the variable in the equation. In those sections, we found whole number and integer solutions to equations. Now that we have worked with fractions, we are ready to find fraction solutions to equations.

The steps we take to determine whether a number is a solution to an equation are the same whether the solution is a whole number, an integer, or a fraction.

HOW TO :: DETERMINE WHETHER A NUMBER IS A SOLUTION TO AN EQUATION.

Step 1.   Substitute the number for the variable in the equation.

Step 2.   Simplify the expressions on both sides of the equation.

Step 3.   Determine whether the resulting equation is true. If it is true, the number is a solution. If it is not true, the number is not a solution.

EXAMPLE 4.95

Determine whether each of the following is a solution of $x - \frac{3}{10} = \frac{1}{2}$.

ⓐ $x = 1$ ⓑ $x = \frac{4}{5}$ ⓒ $x = -\frac{4}{5}$

✓ **Solution**

ⓐ

$$x - \frac{3}{10} = \frac{1}{2}$$

Substitute 1 for x.

$$1 - \frac{3}{10} \overset{?}{=} \frac{1}{2}$$

Change to fractions with a LCD of 10.

$$\frac{10}{10} - \frac{3}{10} \overset{?}{=} \frac{5}{10}$$

Subtract.

$$\frac{7}{10} \neq \frac{5}{10}$$

Since $x = 1$ does not result in a true equation, 1 is not a solution to the equation.

ⓑ

$$x - \frac{3}{10} = \frac{1}{2}$$

Substitute $\frac{4}{5}$ for x.

$$\frac{4}{5} - \frac{3}{10} \overset{?}{=} \frac{1}{2}$$

$$\frac{8}{10} - \frac{3}{10} \overset{?}{=} \frac{5}{10}$$

Subtract.

$$\frac{5}{10} = \frac{5}{10} \checkmark$$

Since $x = \frac{4}{5}$ results in a true equation, $\frac{4}{5}$ is a solution to the equation $x - \frac{3}{10} = \frac{1}{2}$.

ⓒ

$$x - \frac{3}{10} = \frac{1}{2}$$

Substitute $-\frac{4}{5}$ for x.

$$-\frac{4}{5} - \frac{3}{10} \overset{?}{=} \frac{1}{2}$$

$$-\frac{8}{10} - \frac{3}{10} \overset{?}{=} \frac{5}{10}$$

Subtract.

$$\frac{11}{10} \neq \frac{5}{10}$$

Since $x = -\frac{4}{5}$ does not result in a true equation, $-\frac{4}{5}$ is not a solution to the equation.

> **TRY IT : : 4.189**   Determine whether each number is a solution of the given equation.

$$x - \frac{2}{3} = \frac{1}{6}:$$

ⓐ $x = 1$ ⓑ $x = \frac{5}{6}$ ⓒ $x = -\frac{5}{6}$

> **TRY IT : : 4.190**   Determine whether each number is a solution of the given equation.

$$y - \frac{1}{4} = \frac{3}{8}:$$

ⓐ $y = 1$ ⓑ $y = -\frac{5}{8}$ ⓒ $y = \frac{5}{8}$

Solve Equations with Fractions using the Addition, Subtraction, and Division Properties of Equality

In Solve Equations with the Subtraction and Addition Properties of Equality and Solve Equations Using Integers; The Division Property of Equality, we solved equations using the Addition, Subtraction, and Division Properties of Equality. We will use these same properties to solve equations with fractions.

Addition, Subtraction, and Division Properties of Equality

For any numbers a, b, and c,

if $a = b$, then $a + c = b + c$.	Addition Property of Equality
if $a = b$, then $a - c = b - c$.	Subtraction Property of Equality
if $a = b$, then $\frac{a}{c} = \frac{b}{c}$, $c \neq 0$.	Division Property of Equality

Table 4.82

In other words, when you add or subtract the same quantity from both sides of an equation, or divide both sides by the same quantity, you still have equality.

EXAMPLE 4.96

Solve: $y + \frac{9}{16} = \frac{5}{16}$.

⊘ **Solution**

$$y + \frac{9}{16} = \frac{5}{16}$$

Subtract $\frac{9}{16}$ from each side to undo the addition.	$y + \frac{9}{16} - \frac{9}{16} = \frac{5}{16} - \frac{9}{16}$
Simplify on each side of the equation.	$y + 0 = -\frac{4}{16}$
Simplify the fraction.	$y = -\frac{1}{4}$
Check:	$y + \frac{9}{16} = \frac{5}{16}$
Substitute $y = -\frac{1}{4}$.	$-\frac{1}{4} + \frac{9}{16} \stackrel{?}{=} \frac{5}{16}$
Rewrite as fractions with the LCD.	$-\frac{4}{16} + \frac{9}{16} \stackrel{?}{=} \frac{5}{16}$
Add.	$\frac{5}{16} = \frac{5}{16}$ ✓

Since $y = -\frac{1}{4}$ makes $y + \frac{9}{16} = \frac{5}{16}$ a true statement, we know we have found the solution to this equation.

> **TRY IT :: 4.191**   Solve: $y + \frac{11}{12} = \frac{5}{12}$.

> **TRY IT :: 4.192**   Solve: $y + \frac{8}{15} = \frac{4}{15}$.

We used the Subtraction Property of Equality in Example 4.96. Now we'll use the Addition Property of Equality.

EXAMPLE 4.97

Solve: $a - \frac{5}{9} = -\frac{8}{9}$.

⊘ **Solution**

$$a - \frac{5}{9} = -\frac{8}{9}$$

Add $\frac{5}{9}$ from each side to undo the addition.

$$a - \frac{5}{9} + \frac{5}{9} = -\frac{8}{9} + \frac{5}{9}$$

Simplify on each side of the equation.

$$a + 0 = -\frac{3}{9}$$

Simplify the fraction.

$$a = -\frac{1}{3}$$

Check:

$$a - \frac{5}{9} = -\frac{8}{9}$$

Substitute $a = -\frac{1}{3}$.

$$-\frac{1}{3} - \frac{5}{9} \stackrel{?}{=} -\frac{8}{9}$$

Change to common denominator.

$$-\frac{3}{9} - \frac{5}{9} \stackrel{?}{=} -\frac{8}{9}$$

Subtract.

$$-\frac{8}{9} = -\frac{8}{9} \checkmark$$

Since $a = -\frac{1}{3}$ makes the equation true, we know that $a = -\frac{1}{3}$ is the solution to the equation.

> **TRY IT :: 4.193**   Solve: $a - \frac{3}{5} = -\frac{8}{5}$.

> **TRY IT :: 4.194**   Solve: $n - \frac{3}{7} = -\frac{9}{7}$.

The next example may not seem to have a fraction, but let's see what happens when we solve it.

EXAMPLE 4.98

Solve: $10q = 44$.

⊘ Solution

$$10q = 44$$

Divide both sides by 10 to undo the multiplication.	$\dfrac{10q}{10} = \dfrac{44}{10}$
Simplify.	$q = \dfrac{22}{5}$
Check:	
Substitute $q = \dfrac{22}{5}$ into the original equation.	$10\left(\dfrac{22}{5}\right) \overset{?}{=} 44$
Simplify.	$\overset{2}{\cancel{10}}\left(\dfrac{22}{\cancel{5}}\right) \overset{?}{=} 44$
Multiply.	$44 = 44 \checkmark$

The solution to the equation was the fraction $\dfrac{22}{5}$. We leave it as an improper fraction.

> **TRY IT :: 4.195**   Solve: $12u = -76$.

> **TRY IT :: 4.196**   Solve: $8m = 92$.

Solve Equations with Fractions Using the Multiplication Property of Equality

Consider the equation $\frac{x}{4} = 3$. We want to know what number divided by 4 gives 3. So to "undo" the division, we will need to multiply by 4. The *Multiplication Property of Equality* will allow us to do this. This property says that if we start with two equal quantities and multiply both by the same number, the results are equal.

The Multiplication Property of Equality

For any numbers a, b, and c,

$$\text{if } a = b, \text{ then } ac = bc.$$

If you multiply both sides of an equation by the same quantity, you still have equality.

Let's use the Multiplication Property of Equality to solve the equation $\frac{x}{7} = -9$.

EXAMPLE 4.99

Solve: $\frac{x}{7} = -9$.

⊘ **Solution**

$$\frac{x}{7} = -9$$

Use the Multiplication Property of Equality to multiply both sides by 7. This will isolate the variable.

$$7 \cdot \frac{x}{7} = 7(-9)$$

Multiply.

$$\frac{7x}{7} = -63$$

Simplify.

$$x = -63$$

Check.
Substitute -63 for x for in the original equation.

$$\frac{-63}{7} \overset{?}{=} -9$$

The equation is true.

$$-9 = -9 \checkmark$$

⊳ **TRY IT : : 4.197**   Solve: $\frac{f}{5} = -25$.

⊳ **TRY IT : : 4.198**   Solve: $\frac{h}{9} = -27$.

EXAMPLE 4.100

Solve: $\frac{p}{-8} = -40$.

⊘ **Solution**

Here, p is divided by -8. We must multiply by -8 to isolate p.

$$\frac{p}{-8} = -40$$

Multiply both sides by -8

$$-8\left(\frac{p}{-8}\right) = -8(-40)$$

Multiply.

$$\frac{-8p}{-8} = 320$$

Simplify.

$$p = 320$$

Check:

Substitute $p = 320$.

$$\frac{320}{-8} \overset{?}{=} -40$$

The equation is true.

$$-40 = -40 \checkmark$$

⊳ **TRY IT : : 4.199**   Solve: $\frac{c}{-7} = -35$.

⊳ **TRY IT : : 4.200**   Solve: $\frac{x}{-11} = -12$.

Solve Equations with a Coefficient of -1

Look at the equation $-y = 15$. Does it look as if y is already isolated? But there is a negative sign in front of y, so it is not isolated.

There are three different ways to isolate the variable in this type of equation. We will show all three ways in Example 4.101.

EXAMPLE 4.101

Solve: $-y = 15$.

Solution

One way to solve the equation is to rewrite $-y$ as $-1y$, and then use the Division Property of Equality to isolate y.

$$-y = 15$$

Rewrite $-y$ as $-1y$.	$-1y = 15$
Divide both sides by –1.	$\dfrac{-1y}{-1} = \dfrac{15}{-1}$
Simplify each side.	$y = -15$

Another way to solve this equation is to multiply both sides of the equation by -1.

$$y = 15$$

Multiply both sides by –1.	$-1(-y) = -1(15)$
Simplify each side.	$y = -15$

The third way to solve the equation is to read $-y$ as "the opposite of y." What number has 15 as its opposite? The opposite of 15 is -15. So $y = -15$.

For all three methods, we isolated y is isolated and solved the equation.

Check:

$$y = 15$$

Substitute $y = -15$.	$-(-15) \overset{?}{=} (15)$
Simplify. The equation is true.	$15 = 15$ ✓

> **TRY IT :: 4.201**   Solve: $-y = 48$.

> **TRY IT :: 4.202**   Solve: $-c = -23$.

Solve Equations with a Fraction Coefficient

When we have an equation with a fraction coefficient we can use the Multiplication Property of Equality to make the coefficient equal to 1.

For example, in the equation:

$$\frac{3}{4}x = 24$$

The coefficient of x is $\frac{3}{4}$. To solve for x, we need its coefficient to be 1. Since the product of a number and its reciprocal is 1, our strategy here will be to isolate x by multiplying by the reciprocal of $\frac{3}{4}$. We will do this in Example 4.102.

EXAMPLE 4.102

Solve: $\frac{3}{4}x = 24$.

⊘ **Solution**

$$\frac{3}{4}x = 24$$

Multiply both sides by the reciprocal of the coefficient.
$$\frac{4}{3} \cdot \frac{3}{4}x = \frac{4}{3} \cdot 24$$

Simplify.
$$1x = \frac{4}{3} \cdot \frac{24}{1}$$

Multiply.
$$x = 32$$

Check:
$$\frac{3}{4}x = 24$$

Substitute $x = 32$.
$$\frac{3}{4} \cdot 32 \overset{?}{=} 24$$

Rewrite 32 as a fraction.
$$\frac{3}{4} \cdot \frac{32}{1} \overset{?}{=} 24$$

Multiply. The equation is true.
$$24 = 24 \checkmark$$

Notice that in the equation $\frac{3}{4}x = 24$, we could have divided both sides by $\frac{3}{4}$ to get x by itself. Dividing is the same as multiplying by the reciprocal, so we would get the same result. But most people agree that multiplying by the reciprocal is easier.

> **TRY IT : :** 4.203   Solve: $\frac{2}{5}n = 14$.

> **TRY IT : :** 4.204   Solve: $\frac{5}{6}y = 15$.

EXAMPLE 4.103

Solve: $-\frac{3}{8}w = 72$.

⊘ **Solution**

The coefficient is a negative fraction. Remember that a number and its reciprocal have the same sign, so the reciprocal of the coefficient must also be negative.

$$\frac{3}{8}w = 72$$

Multiply both sides by the reciprocal of $-\frac{3}{8}$.	$-\frac{8}{3}\left(-\frac{3}{8}w\right) = \left(-\frac{8}{3}\right)72$
Simplify; reciprocals multiply to one.	$1w = -\frac{8}{3} \cdot \frac{72}{1}$
Multiply.	$w = -192$
Check:	$-\frac{3}{8}w = 72$
Let $w = -192$.	$-\frac{3}{8}(-192) \stackrel{?}{=} 72$
Multiply. It checks.	$72 = 72 \ \checkmark$

> **TRY IT ::** 4.205   Solve: $-\frac{4}{7}a = 52$.

> **TRY IT ::** 4.206   Solve: $-\frac{7}{9}w = 84$.

Translate Sentences to Equations and Solve

Now we have covered all four properties of equality—subtraction, addition, division, and multiplication. We'll list them all together here for easy reference.

Subtraction Property of Equality: For any real numbers a, b, and c,	**Addition Property of Equality:** For any real numbers a, b, and c,
if $a = b$, then $a - c = b - c$.	if $a = b$, then $a + c = b + c$.
Division Property of Equality: For any numbers a, b, and c, where $c \neq 0$	**Multiplication Property of Equality:** For any real numbers a, b, and c
if $a = b$, then $\frac{a}{c} = \frac{b}{c}$	if $a = b$, then $ac = bc$

When you add, subtract, multiply or divide the same quantity from both sides of an equation, you still have equality.

In the next few examples, we'll translate sentences into equations and then solve the equations. It might be helpful to review the translation table in Evaluate, Simplify, and Translate Expressions.

EXAMPLE 4.104

Translate and solve: n divided by 6 is -24.

⊘ **Solution**

		n divided by 6	is	24
Translate.

$$\frac{n}{6} = -24$$

Multiply both sides by 6.

$$6 \cdot \frac{n}{6} = 6(-24)$$

Simplify.

$$n = -144$$

Check: Is -144 divided by 6 equal to -24?

Translate. $\dfrac{-144}{6} \overset{?}{=} -24$

Simplify. It checks. $-24 = -24$ ✓

> **TRY IT :: 4.207**   Translate and solve: n divided by 7 is equal to -21.

> **TRY IT :: 4.208**   Translate and solve: n divided by 8 is equal to -56.

EXAMPLE 4.105

Translate and solve: The quotient of q and -5 is 70.

⊘ **Solution**

	The quotient of q and −5	is	70
Translate.

$$\frac{q}{-5} = 70$$

Multiply both sides by -5.

$$-5\left(\frac{q}{-5}\right) = -5(70)$$

Simplify.

$$q = -350$$

Check: Is the quotient of -350 and -5 equal to 70?

Translate. $\dfrac{-350}{-5} \overset{?}{=} 70$

Simplify. It checks. $70 = 70$ ✓

> **TRY IT :: 4.209**   Translate and solve: The quotient of q and -8 is 72.

> **TRY IT :: 4.210**   Translate and solve: The quotient of p and -9 is 81.

EXAMPLE 4.106

Translate and solve: Two-thirds of f is 18.

⊘ Solution

Translate.	$\overbrace{\text{Two-thirds of } f}$ $\overbrace{\text{is}}$ $\overbrace{18}$
	$\frac{2}{3}f \quad = \quad 18$
Multiply both sides by $\frac{3}{2}$.	$\frac{3}{2} \cdot \frac{2}{3}f = \frac{3}{2} \cdot 18$
Simplify.	$f = 27$
Check:	Is two-thirds of 27 equal to 18?
Translate.	$\frac{2}{3}(27) \overset{?}{=} 18$
Simplify. It checks.	$18 = 18$ ✓

> **TRY IT :: 4.211**   Translate and solve: Two-fifths of f is 16.

> **TRY IT :: 4.212**   Translate and solve: Three-fourths of f is 21.

EXAMPLE 4.107

Translate and solve: The quotient of m and $\frac{5}{6}$ is $\frac{3}{4}$.

⊘ **Solution**

	The quotient of m and $\frac{5}{6}$ is $\frac{3}{4}$.
Translate.	$\dfrac{m}{\frac{5}{6}} = \dfrac{3}{4}$
Multiply both sides by $\frac{5}{6}$ to isolate m.	$\dfrac{5}{6}\left(\dfrac{m}{\frac{5}{6}}\right) = \dfrac{5}{6}\left(\dfrac{3}{4}\right)$
Simplify.	$m = \dfrac{5 \cdot 3}{6 \cdot 4}$
Remove common factors and multiply.	$m = \dfrac{5}{8}$
Check:	
Is the quotient of $\frac{5}{8}$ and $\frac{5}{6}$ equal to $\frac{3}{4}$?	$\dfrac{\frac{5}{8}}{\frac{5}{6}} \overset{?}{=} \dfrac{3}{4}$
Rewrite as division.	$\dfrac{5}{8} \div \dfrac{5}{6} \overset{?}{=} \dfrac{3}{4}$
Multiply the first fraction by the reciprocal of the second.	$\dfrac{5}{8} \cdot \dfrac{6}{5} \overset{?}{=} \dfrac{3}{4}$
Simplify.	$\dfrac{3}{4} = \dfrac{3}{4}$ ✓

Our solution checks.

> **TRY IT :: 4.213**   Translate and solve. The quotient of n and $\frac{2}{3}$ is $\frac{5}{12}$.

> **TRY IT :: 4.214**   Translate and solve The quotient of c and $\frac{3}{8}$ is $\frac{4}{9}$.

EXAMPLE 4.108

Translate and solve: The sum of three-eighths and x is three and one-half.

⊘ **Solution**

	The sum of three-eighths and x is three and one-half
Translate.	$\frac{3}{8} + x = 3\frac{1}{2}$
Use the Subtraction Property of Equality to subtract $\frac{3}{8}$ from both sides.	$\frac{3}{8} + x - \frac{3}{8} = 3\frac{1}{2} - \frac{3}{8}$
Combine like terms on the left side.	$x = 3\frac{1}{2} - \frac{3}{8}$
Convert mixed number to improper fraction.	$x = \frac{7}{2} - \frac{3}{8}$
Convert to equivalent fractions with LCD of 8.	$x = \frac{28}{8} - \frac{3}{8}$
Subtract.	$x = \frac{25}{8}$
Write as a mixed number.	$x = 3\frac{1}{8}$

We write the answer as a mixed number because the original problem used a mixed number.

Check:

Is the sum of three-eighths and $3\frac{1}{8}$ equal to three and one-half?

$$\frac{3}{8} + 3\frac{1}{8} \stackrel{?}{=} 3\frac{1}{2}$$

Add.	$3\frac{4}{8} \stackrel{?}{=} 3\frac{1}{2}$
Simplify.	$3\frac{1}{2} = 3\frac{1}{2}$ ✓

The solution checks.

> **TRY IT : : 4.215**   Translate and solve: The sum of five-eighths and x is one-fourth.

> **TRY IT : : 4.216**   Translate and solve: The difference of one-and-three-fourths and x is five-sixths.

▶ **MEDIA : :** ACCESS ADDITIONAL ONLINE RESOURCES

- Solve One Step Equations With Fractions (http://www.openstaxcollege.org/l/24SolveOneStep)
- Solve One Step Equations With Fractions by Adding or Subtracting (http://www.openstaxcollege.org/l/24OneStepAdd)
- Solve One Step Equations With Fraction by Multiplying (http://www.openstaxcollege.org/l/24OneStepMulti)

4.7 EXERCISES

Practice Makes Perfect

Determine Whether a Fraction is a Solution of an Equation

In the following exercises, determine whether each number is a solution of the given equation.

498. $x - \frac{2}{5} = \frac{1}{10}$:

   ⓐ $x = 1$ ⓑ $x = \frac{1}{2}$

   ⓒ $x = -\frac{1}{2}$

499. $y - \frac{1}{3} = \frac{5}{12}$:

   ⓐ $y = 1$ ⓑ $y = \frac{3}{4}$

   ⓒ $y = -\frac{3}{4}$

500. $h + \frac{3}{4} = \frac{2}{5}$:

   ⓐ $h = 1$ ⓑ $h = \frac{7}{20}$

   ⓒ $h = -\frac{7}{20}$

501. $k + \frac{2}{5} = \frac{5}{6}$:

   ⓐ $k = 1$ ⓑ $k = \frac{13}{30}$

   ⓒ $k = -\frac{13}{30}$

Solve Equations with Fractions using the Addition, Subtraction, and Division Properties of Equality

In the following exercises, solve.

502. $y + \frac{1}{3} = \frac{4}{3}$

503. $m + \frac{3}{8} = \frac{7}{8}$

504. $f + \frac{9}{10} = \frac{2}{5}$

505. $h + \frac{5}{6} = \frac{1}{6}$

506. $a - \frac{5}{8} = -\frac{7}{8}$

507. $c - \frac{1}{4} = -\frac{5}{4}$

508. $x - \left(-\frac{3}{20}\right) = -\frac{11}{20}$

509. $z - \left(-\frac{5}{12}\right) = -\frac{7}{12}$

510. $n - \frac{1}{6} = \frac{3}{4}$

511. $p - \frac{3}{10} = \frac{5}{8}$

512. $s + \left(-\frac{1}{2}\right) = -\frac{8}{9}$

513. $k + \left(-\frac{1}{3}\right) = -\frac{4}{5}$

514. $5j = 17$

515. $7k = 18$

516. $-4w = 26$

517. $-9v = 33$

Solve Equations with Fractions Using the Multiplication Property of Equality

In the following exercises, solve.

518. $\frac{f}{4} = -20$

519. $\frac{b}{3} = -9$

520. $\frac{y}{7} = -21$

521. $\frac{x}{8} = -32$

522. $\frac{p}{-5} = -40$

523. $\frac{q}{-4} = -40$

524. $\frac{r}{-12} = -6$

525. $\frac{s}{-15} = -3$

526. $-x = 23$

527. $-y = 42$

528. $-h = -\frac{5}{12}$

529. $-k = -\frac{17}{20}$

530. $\frac{4}{5}n = 20$

531. $\frac{3}{10}p = 30$

532. $\frac{3}{8}q = -48$

533. $\frac{5}{2}m = -40$ **534.** $-\frac{2}{9}a = 16$ **535.** $-\frac{3}{7}b = 9$

536. $-\frac{6}{11}u = -24$ **537.** $-\frac{5}{12}v = -15$

Mixed Practice

In the following exercises, solve.

538. $3x = 0$ **539.** $8y = 0$ **540.** $4f = \frac{4}{5}$

541. $7g = \frac{7}{9}$ **542.** $p + \frac{2}{3} = \frac{1}{12}$ **543.** $q + \frac{5}{6} = \frac{1}{12}$

544. $\frac{7}{8}m = \frac{1}{10}$ **545.** $\frac{1}{4}n = \frac{7}{10}$ **546.** $-\frac{2}{5} = x + \frac{3}{4}$

547. $-\frac{2}{3} = y + \frac{3}{8}$ **548.** $\frac{11}{20} = -f$ **549.** $\frac{8}{15} = -d$

Translate Sentences to Equations and Solve

In the following exercises, translate to an algebraic equation and solve.

550. n divided by eight is -16.   **551.** n divided by six is -24.   **552.** m divided by -9 is -7.

553. m divided by -7 is -8.   **554.** The quotient of f and -3 is -18.   **555.** The quotient of f and -4 is -20.

556. The quotient of g and twelve is 8.   **557.** The quotient of g and nine is 14.   **558.** Three-fourths of q is 12.

559. Two-fifths of q is 20.   **560.** Seven-tenths of p is -63.   **561.** Four-ninths of p is -28.

562. m divided by 4 equals negative 6.   **563.** The quotient of h and 2 is 43.   **564.** Three-fourths of z is the same as 15.

565. The quotient of a and $\frac{2}{3}$ is $\frac{3}{4}$.   **566.** The sum of five-sixths and x is $\frac{1}{2}$.   **567.** The sum of three-fourths and x is $\frac{1}{8}$.

568. The difference of y and one-fourth is $-\frac{1}{8}$.   **569.** The difference of y and one-third is $-\frac{1}{6}$.

Everyday Math

570. Shopping Teresa bought a pair of shoes on sale for $48. The sale price was $\frac{2}{3}$ of the regular price. Find the regular price of the shoes by solving the equation $\frac{2}{3}p = 48$

571. Playhouse The table in a child's playhouse is $\frac{3}{5}$ of an adult-size table. The playhouse table is 18 inches high. Find the height of an adult-size table by solving the equation $\frac{3}{5}h = 18$.

Writing Exercises

572. Example 4.100 describes three methods to solve the equation $-y = 15$. Which method do you prefer? Why?

573. Richard thinks the solution to the equation $\frac{3}{4}x = 24$ is 16. Explain why Richard is wrong.

Self Check

ⓐ *After completing the exercises, use this checklist to evaluate your mastery of the objectives of this section.*

I can...	Confidently	With some help	No-I don't get it!
determine whether a fraction is a solution of an equation.			
solve equations with fractions using the addition, subtraction, and division properties of equality.			
solve equations using the multiplication property of equality.			
translate sentences to equations and solve.			

ⓑ *Overall, after looking at the checklist, do you think you are well-prepared for the next Chapter? Why or why not?*

CHAPTER 4 REVIEW

KEY TERMS

complex fraction A complex fraction is a fraction in which the numerator or the denominator contains a fraction.

equivalent fractions Equivalent fractions are two or more fractions that have the same value.

fraction A fraction is written $\frac{a}{b}$. in a fraction, a is the numerator and b is the denominator. A fraction represents parts of a whole. The denominator b is the number of equal parts the whole has been divided into, and the numerator a indicates how many parts are included.

least common denominator (LCD) The least common denominator (LCD) of two fractions is the least common multiple (LCM) of their denominators.

mixed number A mixed number consists of a whole number a and a fraction $\frac{b}{c}$ where $c \neq 0$. It is written as $a\frac{b}{c}$, where $c \neq 0$.

proper and improper fractions The fraction $\frac{a}{b}$ is *proper* if $a < b$ and *improper* if $a > b$.

reciprocal The reciprocal of the fraction $\frac{a}{b}$ is $\frac{b}{a}$ where $a \neq 0$ and $b \neq 0$.

simplified fraction A fraction is considered simplified if there are no common factors in the numerator and denominator.

KEY CONCEPTS

4.1 Visualize Fractions

- **Property of One**
  - Any number, except zero, divided by itself is one.
    $\frac{a}{a} = 1$, where $a \neq 0$.

- **Mixed Numbers**
  - A **mixed number** consists of a whole number a and a fraction $\frac{b}{c}$ where $c \neq 0$.

  - It is written as follows: $a\frac{b}{c} \qquad c \neq 0$

- **Proper and Improper Fractions**
  - The fraction ab is a proper fraction if $a < b$ and an improper fraction if $a \geq b$.

- **Convert an improper fraction to a mixed number.**
  Step 1. Divide the denominator into the numerator.
  Step 2. Identify the quotient, remainder, and divisor.
  Step 3. Write the mixed number as quotient $\frac{\text{remainder}}{\text{divisor}}$.

- **Convert a mixed number to an improper fraction.**
  Step 1. Multiply the whole number by the denominator.
  Step 2. Add the numerator to the product found in Step 1.
  Step 3. Write the final sum over the original denominator.

- **Equivalent Fractions Property**
  - If a, b, and c are numbers where $b \neq 0$, $c \neq 0$, then $\frac{a}{b} = \frac{a \cdot c}{b \cdot c}$.

4.2 Multiply and Divide Fractions

- **Equivalent Fractions Property**

◦ If a, b, c are numbers where $b \neq 0$, $c \neq 0$, then $\frac{a}{b} = \frac{a \cdot c}{b \cdot c}$ and $\frac{a \cdot c}{b \cdot c} = \frac{a}{b}$.

- **Simplify a fraction.**

  Step 1. Rewrite the numerator and denominator to show the common factors. If needed, factor the numerator and denominator into prime numbers.

  Step 2. Simplify, using the equivalent fractions property, by removing common factors.

  Step 3. Multiply any remaining factors.

- **Fraction Multiplication**

  ◦ If $a, b, c,$ and d are numbers where $b \neq 0$ and $d \neq 0$, then $\frac{a}{b} \cdot \frac{c}{d} = \frac{ac}{bd}$.

- **Reciprocal**

  ◦ A number and its reciprocal have a product of 1. $\frac{a}{b} \cdot \frac{b}{a} = 1$

  ◦

Opposite	Absolute Value	Reciprocal
has opposite sign	is never negative	has same sign, fraction inverts

Table 4.99

- **Fraction Division**

  ◦ If $a, b, c,$ and d are numbers where $b \neq 0$, $c \neq 0$ and $d \neq 0$, then

  $$\frac{a}{b} \div \frac{c}{d} = \frac{a}{b} \cdot \frac{d}{c}$$

  ◦ To divide fractions, multiply the first fraction by the reciprocal of the second.

4.3 Multiply and Divide Mixed Numbers and Complex Fractions

- **Multiply or divide mixed numbers.**

  Step 1. Convert the mixed numbers to improper fractions.

  Step 2. Follow the rules for fraction multiplication or division.

  Step 3. Simplify if possible.

- **Simplify a complex fraction.**

  Step 1. Rewrite the complex fraction as a division problem.

  Step 2. Follow the rules for dividing fractions.

  Step 3. Simplify if possible.

- **Placement of negative sign in a fraction.**

  ◦ For any positive numbers a and b, $\frac{-a}{b} = \frac{a}{-b} = -\frac{a}{b}$.

- **Simplify an expression with a fraction bar.**

  Step 1. Simplify the numerator.

  Step 2. Simplify the denominator.

  Step 3. Simplify the fraction.

4.4 Add and Subtract Fractions with Common Denominators

- **Fraction Addition**

  ◦ If $a, b,$ and c are numbers where $c \neq 0$, then $\frac{a}{c} + \frac{b}{c} = \frac{a+c}{c}$.

  ◦ To add fractions, add the numerators and place the sum over the common denominator.

- **Fraction Subtraction**

◦ If a, b, and c are numbers where $c \neq 0$, then $\frac{a}{c} - \frac{b}{c} = \frac{a-c}{c}$.

◦ To subtract fractions, subtract the numerators and place the difference over the common denominator.

4.5 Add and Subtract Fractions with Different Denominators

- **Find the least common denominator (LCD) of two fractions.**

  Step 1. Factor each denominator into its primes.

  Step 2. List the primes, matching primes in columns when possible.

  Step 3. Bring down the columns.

  Step 4. Multiply the factors. The product is the LCM of the denominators.

  Step 5. The LCM of the denominators is the LCD of the fractions.

- **Equivalent Fractions Property**

  ◦ If a, b, and c are whole numbers where $b \neq 0$, $c \neq 0$ then

  $\frac{a}{b} = \frac{a \cdot c}{b \cdot c}$ and $\frac{a \cdot c}{b \cdot c} = \frac{a}{b}$

- **Convert two fractions to equivalent fractions with their LCD as the common denominator.**

  Step 1. Find the LCD.

  Step 2. For each fraction, determine the number needed to multiply the denominator to get the LCD.

  Step 3. Use the Equivalent Fractions Property to multiply the numerator and denominator by the number from Step 2.

  Step 4. Simplify the numerator and denominator.

- **Add or subtract fractions with different denominators.**

  Step 1. Find the LCD.

  Step 2. Convert each fraction to an equivalent form with the LCD as the denominator.

  Step 3. Add or subtract the fractions.

  Step 4. Write the result in simplified form.

- **Summary of Fraction Operations**

  ◦ **Fraction multiplication:** Multiply the numerators and multiply the denominators.
  $$\frac{a}{b} \cdot \frac{c}{d} = \frac{ac}{bd}$$

  ◦ **Fraction division:** Multiply the first fraction by the reciprocal of the second.
  $$\frac{a}{b} + \frac{c}{d} = \frac{a}{b} \cdot \frac{d}{c}$$

  ◦ **Fraction addition:** Add the numerators and place the sum over the common denominator. If the fractions have different denominators, first convert them to equivalent forms with the LCD.
  $$\frac{a}{c} + \frac{b}{c} = \frac{a+b}{c}$$

  ◦ **Fraction subtraction:** Subtract the numerators and place the difference over the common denominator. If the fractions have different denominators, first convert them to equivalent forms with the LCD.
  $$\frac{a}{c} - \frac{b}{c} = \frac{a-b}{c}$$

- **Simplify complex fractions.**

  Step 1. Simplify the numerator.

  Step 2. Simplify the denominator.

  Step 3. Divide the numerator by the denominator.

  Step 4. Simplify if possible.

4.6 Add and Subtract Mixed Numbers

- **Add mixed numbers with a common denominator.**

  Step 1. Add the whole numbers.

  Step 2. Add the fractions.

Step 3. Simplify, if possible.

- **Subtract mixed numbers with common denominators.**

  Step 1. Rewrite the problem in vertical form.

  Step 2. Compare the two fractions.
  If the top fraction is larger than the bottom fraction, go to Step 3.
  If not, in the top mixed number, take one whole and add it to the fraction part, making a mixed number with an improper fraction.

  Step 3. Subtract the fractions.

  Step 4. Subtract the whole numbers.

  Step 5. Simplify, if possible.

- **Subtract mixed numbers with common denominators as improper fractions.**

  Step 1. Rewrite the mixed numbers as improper fractions.

  Step 2. Subtract the numerators.

  Step 3. Write the answer as a mixed number, simplifying the fraction part, if possible.

4.7 Solve Equations with Fractions

- **Determine whether a number is a solution to an equation.**

  Step 1. Substitute the number for the variable in the equation.

  Step 2. Simplify the expressions on both sides of the equation.

  Step 3. Determine whether the resulting equation is true. If it is true, the number is a solution. If it is not true, the number is not a solution.

- **Addition, Subtraction, and Division Properties of Equality**

  ○ For any numbers a, b, and c,
  if $a = b$, then $a + c = b + c$. Addition Property of Equality

  ○ if $a = b$, then $a - c = b - c$. Subtraction Property of Equality

  ○ if $a = b$, then $\frac{a}{c} = \frac{b}{c}$, $c \neq 0$. Division Property of Equality

- **The Multiplication Property of Equality**

  ○ For any numbers ab and c, $a = b$, then $ac = bc$.

  ○ If you multiply both sides of an equation by the same quantity, you still have equality.

REVIEW EXERCISES

4.1 Visualize Fractions

In the following exercises, name the fraction of each figure that is shaded.

574.

575.

In the following exercises, name the improper fractions. Then write each improper fraction as a mixed number.

576.

577.

In the following exercises, convert the improper fraction to a mixed number.

578. $\frac{58}{15}$

579. $\frac{63}{11}$

In the following exercises, convert the mixed number to an improper fraction.

580. $12\frac{1}{4}$

581. $9\frac{4}{5}$

582. Find three fractions equivalent to $\frac{2}{5}$. Show your work, using figures or algebra.

583. Find three fractions equivalent to $-\frac{4}{3}$. Show your work, using figures or algebra.

In the following exercises, locate the numbers on a number line.

584. $\frac{5}{8}, \frac{4}{3}, 3\frac{3}{4}, 4$

585. $\frac{1}{4}, -\frac{1}{4}, 1\frac{1}{3}, -1\frac{1}{3}, \frac{7}{2}, -\frac{7}{2}$

In the following exercises, order each pair of numbers, using $<$ or $>$.

586. $-1\underline{\quad}-\frac{2}{5}$

587. $-2\frac{1}{2}\underline{\quad}-3$

4.2 Multiply and Divide Fractions

In the following exercises, simplify.

588. $-\frac{63}{84}$

589. $-\frac{90}{120}$

590. $-\frac{14a}{14b}$

591. $-\frac{8x}{8y}$

In the following exercises, multiply.

592. $\frac{2}{5}\cdot\frac{8}{13}$

593. $-\frac{1}{3}\cdot\frac{12}{7}$

594. $\frac{2}{9}\cdot\left(-\frac{45}{32}\right)$

595. $6m\cdot\frac{4}{11}$

596. $-\frac{1}{4}(-32)$

597. $3\frac{1}{5}\cdot1\frac{7}{8}$

In the following exercises, find the reciprocal.

598. $\frac{2}{9}$

599. $\frac{15}{4}$

600. 3

601. $-\frac{1}{4}$

602. Fill in the chart.

	Opposite	Absolute Value	Reciprocal
$-\frac{5}{13}$			
$\frac{3}{10}$			
$\frac{9}{4}$			
-12			

In the following exercises, divide.

603. $\frac{2}{3} \div \frac{1}{6}$

604. $\left(-\frac{3x}{5}\right) \div \left(-\frac{2y}{3}\right)$

605. $\frac{4}{5} \div 3$

606. $8 \div 2\frac{2}{3}$

607. $8\frac{2}{3} \div 1\frac{1}{12}$

4.3 Multiply and Divide Mixed Numbers and Complex Fractions

In the following exercises, perform the indicated operation.

608. $3\frac{1}{5} \cdot 1\frac{7}{8}$

609. $-5\frac{7}{12} \cdot 4\frac{4}{11}$

610. $8 \div 2\frac{2}{3}$

611. $8\frac{2}{3} \div 1\frac{1}{12}$

In the following exercises, translate the English phrase into an algebraic expression.

612. the quotient of 8 and y

613. the quotient of V and the difference of h and 6

In the following exercises, simplify the complex fraction

614. $\dfrac{\frac{5}{8}}{\frac{4}{5}}$

615. $\dfrac{\frac{8}{9}}{-4}$

616. $\dfrac{\frac{n}{4}}{\frac{3}{8}}$

617. $\dfrac{-1\frac{5}{6}}{-\frac{1}{12}}$

In the following exercises, simplify.

618. $\frac{5+16}{5}$

619. $\frac{8 \cdot 4 - 5^2}{3 \cdot 12}$

620. $\frac{8 \cdot 7 + 5(8-10)}{9 \cdot 3 - 6 \cdot 4}$

4.4 Add and Subtract Fractions with Common Denominators

In the following exercises, add.

621. $\frac{3}{8} + \frac{2}{8}$

622. $\frac{4}{5} + \frac{1}{5}$

623. $\frac{2}{5} + \frac{1}{5}$

624. $\frac{15}{32} + \frac{9}{32}$

625. $\frac{x}{10} + \frac{7}{10}$

In the following exercises, subtract.

626. $\frac{8}{11} - \frac{6}{11}$

627. $\frac{11}{12} - \frac{5}{12}$

628. $\frac{4}{5} - \frac{y}{5}$

629. $-\frac{31}{30} - \frac{7}{30}$

630. $\frac{3}{2} - \left(\frac{3}{2}\right)$

631. $\frac{11}{15} - \frac{5}{15} - \left(-\frac{2}{15}\right)$

4.5 Add and Subtract Fractions with Different Denominators

In the following exercises, find the least common denominator.

632. $\frac{1}{3}$ and $\frac{1}{12}$

633. $\frac{1}{3}$ and $\frac{4}{5}$

634. $\frac{8}{15}$ and $\frac{11}{20}$

635. $\frac{3}{4}, \frac{1}{6},$ and $\frac{5}{10}$

In the following exercises, change to equivalent fractions using the given LCD.

636. $\frac{1}{3}$ and $\frac{1}{5}$, LCD = 15

637. $\frac{3}{8}$ and $\frac{5}{6}$, LCD = 24

638. $-\frac{9}{16}$ and $\frac{5}{12}$, LCD = 48

639. $\frac{1}{3}, \frac{3}{4}$ and $\frac{4}{5}$, LCD = 60

In the following exercises, perform the indicated operations and simplify.

640. $\frac{1}{5} + \frac{2}{3}$

641. $\frac{11}{12} - \frac{2}{3}$

642. $-\frac{9}{10} - \frac{3}{4}$

643. $-\frac{11}{36} - \frac{11}{20}$

644. $-\frac{22}{25} + \frac{9}{40}$

645. $\frac{y}{10} - \frac{1}{3}$

646. $\frac{2}{5} + \left(-\frac{5}{9}\right)$

647. $\frac{4}{11} \div \frac{2}{7d}$

648. $\frac{2}{5} + \left(-\frac{3n}{8}\right)\left(-\frac{2}{9n}\right)$

649. $\dfrac{\left(\frac{2}{3}\right)^2}{\left(\frac{5}{8}\right)^2}$

650. $\left(\frac{11}{12} + \frac{3}{8}\right) \div \left(\frac{5}{6} - \frac{1}{10}\right)$

In the following exercises, evaluate.

651. $y - \frac{4}{5}$ when

    ⓐ $y = -\frac{4}{5}$

    ⓑ $y = \frac{1}{4}$

652. $6mn^2$ when

$m = \frac{3}{4}$ and $n = -\frac{1}{3}$

4.6 Add and Subtract Mixed Numbers

In the following exercises, perform the indicated operation.

653. $4\frac{1}{3} + 9\frac{1}{3}$

654. $6\frac{2}{5} + 7\frac{3}{5}$

655. $5\frac{8}{11} + 2\frac{4}{11}$

656. $3\frac{5}{8} + 3\frac{7}{8}$

657. $9\frac{13}{20} - 4\frac{11}{20}$

658. $2\frac{3}{10} - 1\frac{9}{10}$

659. $2\frac{11}{12} - 1\frac{7}{12}$

660. $8\frac{6}{11} - 2\frac{9}{11}$

4.7 Solve Equations with Fractions

In the following exercises, determine whether the each number is a solution of the given equation.

661. $x - \frac{1}{2} = \frac{1}{6}$:

    ⓐ $x = 1$ ⓑ $x = \frac{2}{3}$

    ⓒ $x = -\frac{1}{3}$

662. $y + \frac{3}{5} = \frac{5}{9}$:

    ⓐ $y = \frac{1}{2}$ ⓑ $y = \frac{52}{45}$

    ⓒ $y = -\frac{2}{45}$

In the following exercises, solve the equation.

663. $n + \frac{9}{11} = \frac{4}{11}$

664. $x - \frac{1}{6} = \frac{7}{6}$

665. $h - \left(-\frac{7}{8}\right) = -\frac{2}{5}$

666. $\frac{x}{5} = -10$

667. $-z = 23$

In the following exercises, translate and solve.

668. The sum of two-thirds and n is $-\frac{3}{5}$.

669. The difference of q and one-tenth is $\frac{1}{2}$.

670. The quotient of p and -4 is -8.

671. Three-eighths of y is 24.

PRACTICE TEST

Convert the improper fraction to a mixed number.

672. $\frac{19}{5}$

Convert the mixed number to an improper fraction.

673. $3\frac{2}{7}$

Locate the numbers on a number line.

674. $\frac{1}{2}$, $1\frac{2}{3}$, $-2\frac{3}{4}$, and $\frac{9}{4}$

In the following exercises, simplify.

675. $\frac{5}{20}$

676. $\frac{18r}{27s}$

677. $\frac{1}{3}\cdot\frac{3}{4}$

678. $\frac{3}{5}\cdot 15$

679. $-36u\left(-\frac{4}{9}\right)$

680. $-5\frac{7}{12}\cdot 4\frac{4}{11}$

681. $-\frac{5}{6}\div\frac{5}{12}$

682. $\frac{7}{11}\div\left(-\frac{7}{11}\right)$

683. $\frac{9a}{10}\div\frac{15a}{8}$

684. $-6\frac{2}{5}\div 4$

685. $\left(-15\frac{5}{6}\right)\div\left(-3\frac{1}{6}\right)$

686. $\frac{-6}{\frac{6}{11}}$

687. $\frac{\frac{p}{2}}{\frac{q}{5}}$

688. $\frac{-\frac{4}{15}}{-2\frac{2}{3}}$

689. $\frac{9^2-4^2}{9-4}$

690. $\frac{2}{d}+\frac{9}{d}$

691. $-\frac{3}{13}+\left(-\frac{4}{13}\right)$

692. $-\frac{22}{25}+\frac{9}{40}$

693. $\frac{2}{5}+\left(-\frac{7}{5}\right)$

694. $-\frac{3}{10}+\left(-\frac{5}{8}\right)$

695. $-\frac{3}{4}\div\frac{x}{3}$

696. $\frac{2^3-2^2}{\left(\frac{3}{4}\right)^2}$

697. $\frac{\frac{5}{14}+\frac{1}{8}}{\frac{9}{56}}$

Evaluate.

698. $x+\frac{1}{3}$ when

ⓐ $x=\frac{2}{3}$

ⓑ $x=-\frac{5}{6}$

In the following exercises, solve the equation.

699. $y+\frac{3}{5}=\frac{7}{5}$

700. $a-\frac{3}{10}=-\frac{9}{10}$

701. $f+\left(-\frac{2}{3}\right)=\frac{5}{12}$

702. $\dfrac{m}{-2} = -16$

703. $-\dfrac{2}{3}c = 18$

704. Translate and solve: The quotient of p and -4 is -8. Solve for p.

Figure 5.1 The price of a gallon of gasoline is written as a decimal number. (credit: Mark Turnauckus, Flickr)

Chapter Outline

Introduction

Gasoline price changes all the time. They might go down for a period of time, but then they usually rise again. One thing that stays the same is that the price is not usually a whole number. Instead, it is shown using a decimal point to describe the cost in dollars and cents. We use decimal numbers all the time, especially when dealing with money. In this chapter, we will explore decimal numbers and how to perform operations using them.

5.1 Decimals

Learning Objectives

By the end of this section, you will be able to:

   Name decimals
   Write decimals
   Convert decimals to fractions or mixed numbers
   Locate decimals on the number line
   Order decimals
   Round decimals

Be Prepared!

Before you get started, take this readiness quiz.

1. Name the number $4{,}926{,}015$ in words.
   If you missed this problem, review Example 1.4.

2. Round 748 to the nearest ten.
   If you missed this problem, review Example 1.9.

3. Locate $\frac{3}{10}$ on a number line.

    If you missed this problem, review Example 4.16.

Name Decimals

You probably already know quite a bit about decimals based on your experience with money. Suppose you buy a sandwich and a bottle of water for lunch. If the sandwich costs $3.45, the bottle of water costs $1.25, and the total sales tax is $0.33, what is the total cost of your lunch?

$$
\begin{array}{ll}
\$3.45 & \text{Sandwich} \\
\$1.25 & \text{Water} \\
\underline{+\ \$0.33} & \text{Tax} \\
\$5.03 & \text{Total}
\end{array}
$$

The total is $5.03. Suppose you pay with a $5 bill and 3 pennies. Should you wait for change? No, $5 and 3 pennies is the same as $5.03.

Because 100 pennies = $1, each penny is worth $\frac{1}{100}$ of a dollar. We write the value of one penny as $0.01, since $0.01 = \frac{1}{100}$.

Writing a number with a decimal is known as decimal notation. It is a way of showing parts of a whole when the whole is a power of ten. In other words, decimals are another way of writing fractions whose denominators are powers of ten. Just as the counting numbers are based on powers of ten, decimals are based on powers of ten. Table 5.1 shows the counting numbers.

Counting number	Name
1	One
$10 = 10$	Ten
$10 \cdot 10 = 100$	One hundred
$10 \cdot 10 \cdot 10 = 1000$	One thousand
$10 \cdot 10 \cdot 10 \cdot 10 = 10{,}000$	Ten thousand

Table 5.1

How are decimals related to fractions? Table 5.2 shows the relation.

Decimal	Fraction	Name
0.1	$\frac{1}{10}$	One tenth
0.01	$\frac{1}{100}$	One hundredth
0.001	$\frac{1}{1,000}$	One thousandth
0.0001	$\frac{1}{10,000}$	One ten-thousandth

Table 5.2

When we name a whole number, the name corresponds to the place value based on the powers of ten. In Whole Numbers, we learned to read 10,000 as *ten thousand*. Likewise, the names of the decimal places correspond to their fraction values. Notice how the place value names in Figure 5.2 relate to the names of the fractions from Table 5.2.

Place Value											
Hundred thousands	Ten thousands	Thousands	Hundreds	Tens	Ones		Tenths	Hundredths	Thousandths	Ten-thousandths	Hundred-thousandths
						.					

Figure 5.2 This chart illustrates place values to the left and right of the decimal point.

Notice two important facts shown in Figure 5.2.

- The "th" at the end of the name means the number is a fraction. "One thousand" is a number larger than one, but "one thousandth" is a number smaller than one.
- The tenths place is the first place to the right of the decimal, but the tens place is two places to the left of the decimal.

Remember that 5.03 lunch? We read 5.03 as *five dollars and three cents*. Naming decimals (those that don't represent money) is done in a similar way. We read the number 5.03 as *five and three hundredths*.

We sometimes need to translate a number written in decimal notation into words. As shown in Figure 5.3, we write the amount on a check in both words and numbers.

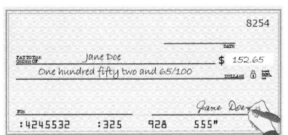

Figure 5.3 When we write a check, we write the amount as a decimal number as well as in words. The bank looks at the check to make sure both numbers match. This helps prevent errors.

Let's try naming a decimal, such as 15.68.

We start by naming the number to the left of the decimal.	fifteen_____
We use the word "and" to indicate the decimal point.	fifteen and____
Then we name the number to the right of the decimal point as if it were a whole number.	fifteen and sixty-eight____
Last, name the decimal place of the last digit.	fifteen and sixty-eight hundredths

The number 15.68 is read *fifteen and sixty-eight hundredths*.

HOW TO :: NAME A DECIMAL NUMBER.

- Name the number to the left of the decimal point.
- Write "and" for the decimal point.
- Name the "number" part to the right of the decimal point as if it were a whole number.
- Name the decimal place of the last digit.

EXAMPLE 5.1

Name each decimal: ⓐ 4.3 ⓑ 2.45 ⓒ 0.009 ⓓ −15.571.

✓ **Solution**

ⓐ

	4.3
Name the number to the left of the decimal point.	four____
Write "and" for the decimal point.	four and____
Name the number to the right of the decimal point as if it were a whole number.	four and three____
Name the decimal place of the last digit.	four and three tenths

ⓑ

	2.45
Name the number to the left of the decimal point.	two____
Write "and" for the decimal point.	two and____
Name the number to the right of the decimal point as if it were a whole number.	two and forty-five____
Name the decimal place of the last digit.	two and forty-five hundredths

ⓒ

	0.009
Name the number to the left of the decimal point.	Zero is the number to the left of the decimal; it is not included in the name.
Name the number to the right of the decimal point as if it were a whole number.	nine____
Name the decimal place of the last digit.	nine thousandths

ⓓ

	-15.571
Name the number to the left of the decimal point.	negative fifteen
Write "and" for the decimal point.	negative fifteen and____
Name the number to the right of the decimal point as if it were a whole number.	negative fifteen and five hundred seventy-one____
Name the decimal place of the last digit.	negative fifteen and five hundred seventy-one thousandths

---

> **TRY IT :: 5.1**   Name each decimal:
>
> ⓐ 6.7 ⓑ 19.58 ⓒ 0.018 ⓓ -2.053

> **TRY IT :: 5.2**   Name each decimal:
>
> ⓐ 5.8 ⓑ 3.57 ⓒ 0.005 ⓓ -13.461

Write Decimals

Now we will translate the name of a decimal number into decimal notation. We will reverse the procedure we just used. Let's start by writing the number six and seventeen hundredths:

	six and seventeen hundredths
The word *and* tells us to place a decimal point.	__.__
The word before *and* is the whole number; write it to the left of the decimal point.	6.____
The decimal part is seventeen hundredths. Mark two places to the right of the decimal point for hundredths.	6._ _
Write the numerals for seventeen in the places marked.	6.17

EXAMPLE 5.2

Write fourteen and thirty-seven hundredths as a decimal.

Solution

	fourteen and thirty-seven hundredths
Place a decimal point under the word 'and'.	____. _____
Translate the words before 'and' into the whole number and place it to the left of the decimal point.	14. _____
Mark two places to the right of the decimal point for "hundredths".	14._ _
Translate the words after "and" and write the number to the right of the decimal point.	14.37
	Fourteen and thirty-seven hundredths is written 14.37.

> **TRY IT :: 5.3**   Write as a decimal: thirteen and sixty-eight hundredths.

> **TRY IT :: 5.4**   Write as a decimal: five and eight hundred ninety-four thousandths.

HOW TO :: WRITE A DECIMAL NUMBER FROM ITS NAME.

Step 1.   Look for the word "and"—it locates the decimal point.

Step 2.   Mark the number of decimal places needed to the right of the decimal point by noting the place value indicated by the last word.

  ◦ Place a decimal point under the word "and." Translate the words before "and" into the whole number and place it to the left of the decimal point.

  ◦ If there is no "and," write a "0" with a decimal point to its right.

Step 3.   Translate the words after "and" into the number to the right of the decimal point. Write the number in the spaces—putting the final digit in the last place.

Step 4.   Fill in zeros for place holders as needed.

The second bullet in Step 1 is needed for decimals that have no whole number part, like 'nine thousandths'. We recognize them by the words that indicate the place value after the decimal – such as 'tenths' or 'hundredths.' Since there is no whole number, there is no 'and.' We start by placing a zero to the left of the decimal and continue by filling in the numbers to the right, as we did above.

EXAMPLE 5.3

Write twenty-four thousandths as a decimal.

⊘ **Solution**

	twenty-four thousandths
Look for the word "and".	There is no "and" so start with 0 0.
To the right of the decimal point, put three decimal places for thousandths.	0. __ __ __ tenths hundredths thousandths
Write the number 24 with the 4 in the thousandths place.	0. __ 2 4 tenths hundredths thousandths
Put zeros as placeholders in the remaining decimal places.	0.024
	So, twenty-four thousandths is written 0.024

> **TRY IT : : 5.5**   Write as a decimal: fifty-eight thousandths.

> **TRY IT : : 5.6**   Write as a decimal: sixty-seven thousandths.

Before we move on to our next objective, think about money again. We know that $1 is the same as $1.00. The way we write $1 (or $1.00) depends on the context. In the same way, integers can be written as decimals with as many zeros as needed to the right of the decimal.

$$5 = 5.0 \qquad -2 = -2.0$$
$$5 = 5.00 \qquad -2 = -2.00$$
$$5 = 5.000 \qquad -2 = -2.000$$
$$\text{and so on}\ldots$$

Convert Decimals to Fractions or Mixed Numbers

We often need to rewrite decimals as fractions or mixed numbers. Let's go back to our lunch order to see how we can convert decimal numbers to fractions. We know that $5.03 means 5 dollars and 3 cents. Since there are 100 cents in one dollar, 3 cents means $\frac{3}{100}$ of a dollar, so $0.03 = \frac{3}{100}$.

We convert decimals to fractions by identifying the place value of the farthest right digit. In the decimal 0.03, the 3 is in the hundredths place, so 100 is the denominator of the fraction equivalent to 0.03.

$$0.03 = \frac{3}{100}$$

For our $5.03 lunch, we can write the decimal 5.03 as a mixed number.

$$5.03 = 5\frac{3}{100}$$

Notice that when the number to the left of the decimal is zero, we get a proper fraction. When the number to the left of the decimal is not zero, we get a mixed number.

HOW TO :: CONVERT A DECIMAL NUMBER TO A FRACTION OR MIXED NUMBER.

Step 1.   Look at the number to the left of the decimal.
  ◦ If it is zero, the decimal converts to a proper fraction.
  ◦ If it is not zero, the decimal converts to a mixed number.
      ▪ Write the whole number.

Step 2.   Determine the place value of the final digit.

Step 3.   Write the fraction.
  ◦ numerator—the 'numbers' to the right of the decimal point
  ◦ denominator—the place value corresponding to the final digit

Step 4.   Simplify the fraction, if possible.

EXAMPLE 5.4

Write each of the following decimal numbers as a fraction or a mixed number:

ⓐ 4.09 ⓑ 3.7 ⓒ −0.286

✓ **Solution**

ⓐ

	4.09
There is a 4 to the left of the decimal point. Write "4" as the whole number part of the mixed number.	$4\dfrac{\square}{\square}$
Determine the place value of the final digit.	4. 0 9 tenths hundredths
Write the fraction. Write 9 in the numerator as it is the number to the right of the decimal point.	$4\dfrac{9}{\square}$
Write 100 in the denominator as the place value of the final digit, 9, is hundredth.	$4\dfrac{9}{100}$
The fraction is in simplest form.	So, $4.09 = 4\dfrac{9}{100}$

Did you notice that the number of zeros in the denominator is the same as the number of decimal places?

ⓑ

$$3.7$$

There is a 3 to the left of the decimal point. Write "3" as the whole number part of the mixed number.	$3\dfrac{\square}{\square}$

Determine the place value of the final digit.

3.   7
tenths

Write the fraction.
Write 7 in the numerator as it is the number to the right of the decimal point.

$3\dfrac{7}{\square}$

Write 10 in the denominator as the place value of the final digit, 7, is tenths.

$3\dfrac{7}{10}$

The fraction is in simplest form.

So, $3.7 = 3\dfrac{7}{10}$

ⓒ

$$-0.286$$

There is a 0 to the left of the decimal point.
Write a negative sign before the fraction.

$-\dfrac{\square}{\square}$

Determine the place value of the final digit and write it in the denominator.

−0. 2   8   6
tenths hundredths thousandths

Write the fraction.
Write 286 in the numerator as it is the number to the right of the decimal point.
Write 1,000 in the denominator as the place value of the final digit, 6, is thousandths.

$-\dfrac{286}{1000}$

We remove a common factor of 2 to simplify the fraction.

$-\dfrac{143}{500}$

> **TRY IT :: 5.7**   Write as a fraction or mixed number. Simplify the answer if possible.

ⓐ 5.3   ⓑ 6.07   ⓒ −0.234

> **TRY IT :: 5.8**   Write as a fraction or mixed number. Simplify the answer if possible.

ⓐ 8.7   ⓑ 1.03   ⓒ −0.024

Locate Decimals on the Number Line

Since decimals are forms of fractions, locating decimals on the number line is similar to locating fractions on the number line.

EXAMPLE 5.5

Locate 0.4 on a number line.

⊘ **Solution**

The decimal 0.4 is equivalent to $\frac{4}{10}$, so 0.4 is located between 0 and 1. On a number line, divide the interval between 0 and 1 into 10 equal parts and place marks to separate the parts.

Label the marks $0.1, 0.2, 0.3, 0.4, 0.5, 0.6, 0.7, 0.8, 0.9, 1.0$. We write 0 as 0.0 and 1 as 1.0, so that the numbers are consistently in tenths. Finally, mark 0.4 on the number line.

> **TRY IT :: 5.9**   Locate 0.6 on a number line.

> **TRY IT :: 5.10**   Locate 0.9 on a number line.

EXAMPLE 5.6

Locate -0.74 on a number line.

⊘ **Solution**

The decimal -0.74 is equivalent to $-\frac{74}{100}$, so it is located between 0 and -1. On a number line, mark off and label the multiples of -0.10 in the interval between 0 and -1 (-0.10, -0.20, etc.) and mark -0.74 between -0.70 and -0.80, a little closer to -0.70.

> **TRY IT :: 5.11**   Locate -0.63 on a number line.

> **TRY IT :: 5.12**   Locate -0.25 on a number line.

Order Decimals

Which is larger, 0.04 or 0.40?

If you think of this as money, you know that $\$0.40$ (forty cents) is greater than $\$0.04$ (four cents). So,

$$0.40 > 0.04$$

In previous chapters, we used the number line to order numbers.

$a < b$ 'a is less than b' when a is to the left of b on the number line
$a > b$ 'a is greater than b' when a is to the right of b on the number line

Where are 0.04 and 0.40 located on the number line?

We see that 0.40 is to the right of 0.04. So we know $0.40 > 0.04$.

How does 0.31 compare to 0.308? This doesn't translate into money to make the comparison easy. But if we convert 0.31 and 0.308 to fractions, we can tell which is larger.

	0.31	0.308
Convert to fractions.	$\dfrac{31}{100}$	$\dfrac{308}{1000}$
We need a common denominator to compare them.	$\dfrac{31 \cdot 10}{100 \cdot 10}$	$\dfrac{308}{1000}$
	$\dfrac{310}{1000}$	$\dfrac{308}{1000}$

Because $310 > 308,$ we know that $\dfrac{310}{1000} > \dfrac{308}{1000}.$ Therefore, $0.31 > 0.308.$

Notice what we did in converting 0.31 to a fraction—we started with the fraction $\dfrac{31}{100}$ and ended with the equivalent fraction $\dfrac{310}{1000}.$ Converting $\dfrac{310}{1000}$ back to a decimal gives $0.310.$ So 0.31 is equivalent to $0.310.$ Writing zeros at the end of a decimal does not change its value.

$$\frac{31}{100} = \frac{310}{1000} \text{ and } 0.31 = 0.310$$

If two decimals have the same value, they are said to be equivalent decimals.

$$0.31 = 0.310$$

We say 0.31 and 0.310 are equivalent decimals.

Equivalent Decimals

Two decimals are **equivalent decimals** if they convert to equivalent fractions.

Remember, writing zeros at the end of a decimal does not change its value.

 HOW TO :: ORDER DECIMALS.

Step 1.   Check to see if both numbers have the same number of decimal places. If not, write zeros at the end of the one with fewer digits to make them match.

Step 2.   Compare the numbers to the right of the decimal point as if they were whole numbers.

Step 3.   Order the numbers using the appropriate inequality sign.

EXAMPLE 5.7

Order the following decimals using $<$ or $>$:

ⓐ $0.64 \underline{\hspace{0.5cm}} 0.6$

ⓑ $0.83 \underline{\hspace{0.5cm}} 0.803$

⊘ **Solution**

ⓐ

	0.64 ___0.6
Check to see if both numbers have the same number of decimal places. They do not, so write one zero at the right of 0.6.	0.64 ___0.60
Compare the numbers to the right of the decimal point as if they were whole numbers.	64 > 60
Order the numbers using the appropriate inequality sign.	0.64 > 0.60 0.64 > 0.6

ⓑ

	0.83 ___0.803
Check to see if both numbers have the same number of decimal places. They do not, so write one zero at the right of 0.83.	0.830 ___0.803
Compare the numbers to the right of the decimal point as if they were whole numbers.	830 > 803
Order the numbers using the appropriate inequality sign.	0.830 > 0.803 0.83 > 0.803

> **TRY IT : : 5.13**   Order each of the following pairs of numbers, using $<$ or $>$:
>
> ⓐ 0.42___0.4 ⓑ 0.76___0.706

> **TRY IT : : 5.14**   Order each of the following pairs of numbers, using $<$ or $>$:
>
> ⓐ 0.1___0.18 ⓑ 0.305___0.35

When we order negative decimals, it is important to remember how to order negative integers. Recall that larger numbers are to the right on the number line. For example, because -2 lies to the right of -3 on the number line, we know that $-2 > -3$. Similarly, smaller numbers lie to the left on the number line. For example, because -9 lies to the left of -6 on the number line, we know that $-9 < -6$.

If we zoomed in on the interval between 0 and -1, we would see in the same way that $-0.2 > -0.3$ and $-0.9 < -0.6$.

EXAMPLE 5.8

Use $<$ or $>$ to order. -0.1___-0.8.

✓ Solution

	$-0.1\ \_\_\_\ -0.8$
Write the numbers one under the other, lining up the decimal points.	-0.1 -0.8
They have the same number of digits.	
Since $-1 > -8$, -1 tenth is greater than -8 tenths.	$-0.1 > -0.8$

> **TRY IT :: 5.15**   Order each of the following pairs of numbers, using $<$ or $>$:
>
> -0.3 _____ -0.5

> **TRY IT :: 5.16**   Order each of the following pairs of numbers, using $<$ or $>$:
>
> -0.6 _____ -0.7

Round Decimals

In the United States, gasoline prices are usually written with the decimal part as thousandths of a dollar. For example, a gas station might post the price of unleaded gas at $\$3.279$ per gallon. But if you were to buy exactly one gallon of gas at this price, you would pay $\$3.28$, because the final price would be rounded to the nearest cent. In Whole Numbers, we saw that we round numbers to get an approximate value when the exact value is not needed. Suppose we wanted to round $\$2.72$ to the nearest dollar. Is it closer to $\$2$ or to $\$3$? What if we wanted to round $\$2.72$ to the nearest ten cents; is it closer to $\$2.70$ or to $\$2.80$? The number lines in Figure 5.4 can help us answer those questions.

(a)

(b)

Figure 5.4 ⓐ We see that 2.72 is closer to 3 than to 2. So, 2.72 rounded to the nearest whole number is 3. ⓑ We see that 2.72 is closer to 2.70 than 2.80. So we say that 2.72 rounded to the nearest tenth is 2.7.

Can we round decimals without number lines? Yes! We use a method based on the one we used to round whole numbers.

HOW TO :: ROUND A DECIMAL.

Step 1.   Locate the given place value and mark it with an arrow.

Step 2.   Underline the digit to the right of the given place value.

Step 3.   Is this digit greater than or equal to 5?

  ◦ Yes - add 1 to the digit in the given place value.

  ◦ No - do not change the digit in the given place value

Step 4.   Rewrite the number, removing all digits to the right of the given place value.

EXAMPLE 5.9

Round 18.379 to the nearest hundredth.

⊘ **Solution**

	18.379
Locate the hundredths place and mark it with an arrow.	hundredths place ↓ 18.379
Underline the digit to the right of the 7.	hundredths place ↓ 18.379
Because 9 is greater than or equal to 5, add 1 to the 7.	18.379 add 1 ⟋ ↘ delete
Rewrite the number, deleting all digits to the right of the hundredths place.	18.38
	18.38 is 18.379 rounded to the nearest hundredth.

> **TRY IT :: 5.17**   Round to the nearest hundredth: 1.047.

> **TRY IT :: 5.18**   Round to the nearest hundredth: 9.173.

EXAMPLE 5.10

Round 18.379 to the nearest ⓐ tenth ⓑ whole number.

⊘ **Solution**

ⓐ Round 18.379 to the nearest tenth.

18.379

tenths place
↓
18.379

Locate the tenths place and mark it with an arrow.

tenths place
↓
18.3<u>7</u>9

Underline the digit to the right of the tenths digit.

18.379

Because 7 is greater than or equal to 5, add 1 to the 3.

delete

add 1

Rewrite the number, deleting all digits to the right of the tenths place.

18.4

So, 18.379 rounded to the nearest tenth is 18.4.

ⓑ Round 18.379 to the nearest whole number.

18.379

ones place
↓
18.379

Locate the ones place and mark it with an arrow.

ones place
↓
18.<u>3</u>79

Underline the digit to the right of the ones place.

18.379

Since 3 is not greater than or equal to 5, do not add 1 to the 8.

delete

do not add 1

Rewrite the number, deleting all digits to the right of the ones place.

18

So 18.379 rounded to the nearest whole number is 18.

> **TRY IT :: 5.19**   Round 6.582 to the nearest ⓐ hundredth ⓑ tenth ⓒ whole number.

> **TRY IT :: 5.20**   Round 15.2175 to the nearest ⓐ thousandth ⓑ hundredth ⓒ tenth.

▶ **MEDIA :** : ACCESS ADDITIONAL ONLINE RESOURCES

- Introduction to Decimal Notation (http://www.openstaxcollege.org/l/24decmlnotat)
- Write a Number in Decimal Notation from Words (http://www.openstaxcollege.org/l/24word2dcmlnot)
- Identify Decimals on the Number Line (http://www.openstaxcollege.org/l/24decmlnumline)
- Rounding Decimals (http://www.openstaxcollege.org/l/24rounddecml)
- Writing a Decimal as a Simplified Fraction (http://www.openstaxcollege.org/l/24decmlsimpfrac)

5.1 EXERCISES

Practice Makes Perfect

Name Decimals

In the following exercises, name each decimal.

1. 5.5

2. 7.8

3. 5.01

4. 14.02

5. 8.71

6. 2.64

7. 0.002

8. 0.005

9. 0.381

10. 0.479

11. −17.9

12. −31.4

Write Decimals

In the following exercises, translate the name into a decimal number.

13. Eight and three hundredths

14. Nine and seven hundredths

15. Twenty-nine and eighty-one hundredths

16. Sixty-one and seventy-four hundredths

17. Seven tenths

18. Six tenths

19. One thousandth

20. Nine thousandths

21. Twenty-nine thousandths

22. Thirty-five thousandths

23. Negative eleven and nine ten-thousandths

24. Negative fifty-nine and two ten-thousandths

25. Thirteen and three hundred ninety-five ten thousandths

26. Thirty and two hundred seventy-nine thousandths

Convert Decimals to Fractions or Mixed Numbers

In the following exercises, convert each decimal to a fraction or mixed number.

27. 1.99

28. 5.83

29. 15.7

30. 18.1

31. 0.239

32. 0.373

33. 0.13

34. 0.19

35. 0.011

36. 0.049

37. −0.00007

38. −0.00003

39. 6.4

40. 5.2

41. 7.05

42. 9.04

43. 4.006

44. 2.008

45. 10.25

46. 12.75

47. 1.324

48. 2.482

49. 14.125

50. 20.375

Locate Decimals on the Number Line

In the following exercises, locate each number on a number line.

51. 0.8

52. 0.3

53. −0.2

54. −0.9   **55.** 3.1   **56.** 2.7

57. −2.5   **58.** −1.6

Order Decimals

In the following exercises, order each of the following pairs of numbers, using < or >.

59. 0.9__0.6   **60.** 0.7__0.8   **61.** 0.37__0.63

62. 0.86__0.69   **63.** 0.6__0.59   **64.** 0.27__0.3

65. 0.91__0.901   **66.** 0.415__0.41   **67.** −0.5__−0.3

68. −0.1_−0.4   **69.** −0.62_−0.619   **70.** −7.31_−7.3

Round Decimals

In the following exercises, round each number to the nearest tenth.

71. 0.67   **72.** 0.49   **73.** 2.84

74. 4.63

In the following exercises, round each number to the nearest hundredth.

75. 0.845   **76.** 0.761   **77.** 5.7932

78. 3.6284   **79.** 0.299   **80.** 0.697

81. 4.098   **82.** 7.096

In the following exercises, round each number to the nearest ⓐ hundredth ⓑ tenth ⓒ whole number.

83. 5.781   **84.** 1.638   **85.** 63.479

86. 84.281

Everyday Math

87. Salary Increase Danny got a raise and now makes $58,965.95 a year. Round this number to the nearest:

ⓐ dollar

ⓑ thousand dollars

ⓒ ten thousand dollars.

88. New Car Purchase Selena's new car cost $23,795.95. Round this number to the nearest:

ⓐ dollar

ⓑ thousand dollars

ⓒ ten thousand dollars.

89. Sales Tax Hyo Jin lives in San Diego. She bought a refrigerator for $1624.99 and when the clerk calculated the sales tax it came out to exactly $142.186625. Round the sales tax to the nearest ⓐ penny ⓑ dollar.

90. Sales Tax Jennifer bought a $1,038.99 dining room set for her home in Cincinnati. She calculated the sales tax to be exactly $67.53435. Round the sales tax to the nearest ⓐ penny ⓑ dollar.

Writing Exercises

91. How does your knowledge of money help you learn about decimals?

92. Explain how you write "three and nine hundredths" as a decimal.

93. Jim ran a 100-meter race in 12.32 seconds. Tim ran the same race in 12.3 seconds. Who had the faster time, Jim or Tim? How do you know?

94. Gerry saw a sign advertising postcards marked for sale at "10 for $0.99¢$." What is wrong with the advertised price?

Self Check

ⓐ *After completing the exercises, use this checklist to evaluate your mastery of the objectives of this section.*

I can...	Confidently	With some help	No-I don't get it!
name decimals.			
write decimals.			
convert decimals to fractions or mixed numbers.			
locate decimals on the number line.			
order decimals.			
round decimals.			

ⓑ *If most of your checks were:*

...confidently. Congratulations! You have achieved the objectives in this section. Reflect on the study skills you used so that you can continue to use them. What did you do to become confident of your ability to do these things? Be specific.

...with some help. This must be addressed quickly because topics you do not master become potholes in your road to success. In math, every topic builds upon previous work. It is important to make sure you have a strong foundation before you move on. Who can you ask for help? Your fellow classmates and instructor are good resources. Is there a place on campus where math tutors are available? Can your study skills be improved?

...no—I don't get it! This is a warning sign and you must not ignore it. You should get help right away or you will quickly be overwhelmed. See your instructor as soon as you can to discuss your situation. Together you can come up with a plan to get you the help you need.

5.2 Decimal Operations

Learning Objectives

By the end of this section, you will be able to:

- Add and subtract decimals
- Multiply decimals
- Divide decimals
- Use decimals in money applications

Be Prepared!

Before you get started, take this readiness quiz.

Simplify $\frac{70}{100}$.

If you missed this problem, review Example 4.19.

Multiply $\frac{3}{10} \cdot \frac{9}{10}$.

If you missed this problem, review Example 4.25.

Divide $-36 \div (-9)$.

If you missed this problem, review Example 3.49.

Add and Subtract Decimals

Let's take one more look at the lunch order from the start of Decimals, this time noticing how the numbers were added together.

$$
\begin{array}{ll}
\$3.45 & \text{Sandwich} \\
\$1.25 & \text{Water} \\
+ \ \$0.33 & \text{Tax} \\
\hline
\$5.03 & \text{Total}
\end{array}
$$

All three items (sandwich, water, tax) were priced in dollars and cents, so we lined up the dollars under the dollars and the cents under the cents, with the decimal points lined up between them. Then we just added each column, as if we were adding whole numbers. By lining up decimals this way, we can add or subtract the corresponding place values just as we did with whole numbers.

 HOW TO : : ADD OR SUBTRACT DECIMALS.

Step 1. Write the numbers vertically so the decimal points line up.

Step 2. Use zeros as place holders, as needed.

Step 3. Add or subtract the numbers as if they were whole numbers. Then place the decimal in the answer under the decimal points in the given numbers.

EXAMPLE 5.11

Add: $3.7 + 12.4$.

Solution

	$3.7 + 12.4$

Write the numbers vertically so the decimal points line up.

$$\begin{array}{r} 3.7 \\ +12.4 \\ \hline \end{array}$$

Place holders are not needed since both numbers have the same number of decimal places.

Add the numbers as if they were whole numbers. Then place the decimal in the answer under the decimal points in the given numbers.

$$\begin{array}{r} \overset{1}{3.7} \\ +12.4 \\ \hline 16.1 \end{array}$$

> **TRY IT :: 5.21**   Add: $5.7 + 11.9$.

> **TRY IT :: 5.22**   Add: $18.32 + 14.79$.

EXAMPLE 5.12

Add: $23.5 + 41.38$.

Solution

	$23.5 + 41.38$

Write the numbers vertically so the decimal points line up.

$$\begin{array}{r} 23.5 \\ +41.38 \\ \hline \end{array}$$

Place 0 as a place holder after the 5 in 23.5, so that both numbers have two decimal places.

$$\begin{array}{r} 23.50 \\ +41.38 \\ \hline \end{array}$$

Add the numbers as if they were whole numbers. Then place the decimal in the answer under the decimal points in the given numbers.

$$\begin{array}{r} 23.50 \\ +41.38 \\ \hline 64.88 \end{array}$$

> **TRY IT :: 5.23**   Add: $4.8 + 11.69$.

> **TRY IT :: 5.24**   Add: $5.123 + 18.47$.

How much change would you get if you handed the cashier a $20 bill for a $14.65 purchase? We will show the steps to calculate this in the next example.

EXAMPLE 5.13

Subtract: $20 - 14.65$.

○ **Solution**

		$20 - 14.65$
Write the numbers vertically so the decimal points line up. Remember 20 is a whole number, so place the decimal point after the 0.		$\begin{array}{r} 20. \\ -\,14.65 \end{array}$
Place two zeros after the decimal point in 20, as place holders so that both numbers have two decimal places.		$\begin{array}{r} 20.00 \\ -\,14.65 \end{array}$
Subtract the numbers as if they were whole numbers. Then place the decimal in the answer under the decimal points in the given numbers.		$\begin{array}{r} \overset{1}{2}\overset{9}{\cancel{0}}.\overset{9}{\cancel{0}}\overset{10}{\cancel{0}} \\ -\,1\,4\,.\,6\,5 \\ \hline 5\,.\,3\,5 \end{array}$

> **TRY IT : : 5.25**   Subtract:

$10 - 9.58.$

> **TRY IT : : 5.26**   Subtract:

$50 - 37.42.$

EXAMPLE 5.14

Subtract: $2.51 - 7.4.$

○ **Solution**

If we subtract 7.4 from $2.51,$ the answer will be negative since $7.4 > 2.51.$ To subtract easily, we can subtract 2.51 from $7.4.$ Then we will place the negative sign in the result.

		$2.51 - 7.4$
Write the numbers vertically so the decimal points line up.		$\begin{array}{r} 7.4 \\ -\,2.51 \end{array}$
Place zero after the 4 in 7.4 as a place holder, so that both numbers have two decimal places.		$\begin{array}{r} 7.40 \\ -\,2.51 \end{array}$
Subtract and place the decimal in the answer.		$\begin{array}{r} 7.40 \\ -\,2.51 \\ \hline 4.89 \end{array}$
Remember that we are really subtracting $2.51 - 7.4$ so the answer is negative.		$2.51 - 7.4 = -4.89$

> **TRY IT : : 5.27**   Subtract: $4.77 - 6.3.$

> **TRY IT : : 5.28**   Subtract: $8.12 - 11.7.$

Multiply Decimals

Multiplying decimals is very much like multiplying whole numbers—we just have to determine where to place the decimal point. The procedure for multiplying decimals will make sense if we first review multiplying fractions.

Do you remember how to multiply fractions? To multiply fractions, you multiply the numerators and then multiply the denominators.

So let's see what we would get as the product of decimals by converting them to fractions first. We will do two examples side-by-side in Table 5.22. Look for a pattern.

	A	B
	$(0.3)(0.7)$	$(0.2)(0.46)$
Convert to fractions.	$\left(\frac{3}{10}\right)\left(\frac{7}{10}\right)$	$\left(\frac{2}{10}\right)\left(\frac{46}{100}\right)$
Multiply.	$\frac{21}{100}$	$\frac{92}{1000}$
Convert back to decimals.	0.21	0.092

Table 5.22

There is a pattern that we can use. In A, we multiplied two numbers that each had one decimal place, and the product had two decimal places. In B, we multiplied a number with one decimal place by a number with two decimal places, and the product had three decimal places.

How many decimal places would you expect for the product of $(0.01)(0.004)$? If you said "five", you recognized the pattern. When we multiply two numbers with decimals, we count all the decimal places in the factors—in this case two plus three—to get the number of decimal places in the product—in this case five.

$$(0.01)\ (0.004)\ = 0.00004$$
$$\text{2 places}\quad\text{3 places}\qquad\text{5 places}$$

$$\left(\frac{1}{100}\right)\left(\frac{4}{1000}\right) = \frac{4}{100,000}$$

Once we know how to determine the number of digits after the decimal point, we can multiply decimal numbers without converting them to fractions first. The number of decimal places in the product is the sum of the number of decimal places in the factors.

The rules for multiplying positive and negative numbers apply to decimals, too, of course.

Multiplying Two Numbers

When multiplying two numbers,

- if their signs are the same, the product is positive.
- if their signs are different, the product is negative.

When you multiply signed decimals, first determine the sign of the product and then multiply as if the numbers were both positive. Finally, write the product with the appropriate sign.

HOW TO :: MULTIPLY DECIMAL NUMBERS.

Step 1. Determine the sign of the product.

Step 2. Write the numbers in vertical format, lining up the numbers on the right.

Step 3. Multiply the numbers as if they were whole numbers, temporarily ignoring the decimal points.

Step 4. Place the decimal point. The number of decimal places in the product is the sum of the number of decimal places in the factors. If needed, use zeros as placeholders.

Step 5. Write the product with the appropriate sign.

EXAMPLE 5.15

Multiply: $(3.9)(4.075)$.

⊘ **Solution**

	$(3.9)(4.075)$
Determine the sign of the product. The signs are the same.	The product will be positive.
Write the numbers in vertical format, lining up the numbers on the right.	$\begin{array}{r} 4.075 \\ \times\, 3.9 \\ \hline \end{array}$
Multiply the numbers as if they were whole numbers, temporarily ignoring the decimal points.	$\begin{array}{r} 4.075 \\ \times\, 3.9 \\ \hline 36675 \\ 12225 \\ \hline 158925 \end{array}$
Place the decimal point. Add the number of decimal places in the factors $(1 + 3)$. Place the decimal point 4 places from the right.	$\begin{array}{r} 4.075 \quad \text{3 places} \\ \times\, 3.9 \quad \text{1 place} \\ \hline 36675 \\ 12225 \\ \hline 158925 \quad \text{4 places} \end{array}$
The product is positive.	$(3.9)(4.075) = 15.8925$

> **TRY IT : :** 5.29   Multiply: $4.5(6.107)$.

> **TRY IT : :** 5.30   Multiply: $10.79(8.12)$.

EXAMPLE 5.16

Multiply: $(-8.2)(5.19)$.

⊘ **Solution**

	$(-8.2)(5.19)$
The signs are different.	The product will be negative.
Write in vertical format, lining up the numbers on the right.	$\begin{array}{r} 5.19 \\ \times 8.2 \\ \hline \end{array}$
Multiply.	$\begin{array}{r} 5.19 \\ \times 8.2 \\ \hline 1038 \\ 4152 \\ \hline 42558 \end{array}$
Place the decimal point 3 places from the right. $(-8.2)(5.19)$ 1 place 2 places	$\begin{array}{r} 5.19 \\ \times 8.2 \\ \hline 1038 \\ 4152 \\ \hline 42.558 \end{array}$
The product is negative.	$(-8.2)(5.19) = -42.558$

> **TRY IT : : 5.31**   Multiply: $(4.63)(-2.9)$.

> **TRY IT : : 5.32**   Multiply: $(-7.78)(4.9)$.

In the next example, we'll need to add several placeholder zeros to properly place the decimal point.

EXAMPLE 5.17

Multiply: $(0.03)(0.045)$.

⊘ **Solution**

	$(0.03)(0.045)$
The product is positive.	
Write in vertical format, lining up the numbers on the right.	$\begin{array}{r} 0.045 \\ \times\, 0.03 \\ \hline \end{array}$
Multiply.	$\begin{array}{r} 0.045 \\ \times\, 0.03 \\ \hline 135 \end{array}$
The decimal point must be 5 places from the right. $(0.03)(0.045)$ 2 places 3 places	$\begin{array}{r} 0.045 \\ \times\, 0.03 \\ \hline 0.00135 \end{array}$
Add zeros as needed to get the 5 places.	
The product is positive.	$(0.03)(0.045) = 0.00135$

> **TRY IT : :** 5.33   Multiply: $(0.04)(0.087)$.

> **TRY IT : :** 5.34   Multiply: $(0.09)(0.067)$.

Multiply by Powers of 10

In many fields, especially in the sciences, it is common to multiply decimals by powers of 10. Let's see what happens when we multiply 1.9436 by some powers of 10.

$$1.9436(10) \qquad 1.9436(100) \qquad 1.9436(1000)$$

$$
\begin{array}{r} 1.9436 \\ \times 10 \\ \hline 19.4360 \end{array}
\qquad
\begin{array}{r} 1.9436 \\ \times 100 \\ \hline 194.3600 \end{array}
\qquad
\begin{array}{r} 1.9436 \\ \times 1000 \\ \hline 1943.6000 \end{array}
$$

Look at the results without the final zeros. Do you notice a pattern?

$$1.9436(10) \quad = \quad 19.436$$
$$1.9436(100) \quad = \quad 194.36$$
$$1.9436(1000) \quad = \quad 1943.6$$

The number of places that the decimal point moved is the same as the number of zeros in the power of ten. Table 5.26 summarizes the results.

Multiply by	Number of zeros	Number of places decimal point moves
10	1	1 place to the right
100	2	2 places to the right
1,000	3	3 places to the right
10,000	4	4 places to the right

Table 5.26

We can use this pattern as a shortcut to multiply by powers of ten instead of multiplying using the vertical format. We can count the zeros in the power of 10 and then move the decimal point that same of places to the right.

So, for example, to multiply 45.86 by 100, move the decimal point 2 places to the right.

$$45.86 \times 100 = 4586.$$

Sometimes when we need to move the decimal point, there are not enough decimal places. In that case, we use zeros as placeholders. For example, let's multiply 2.4 by 100. We need to move the decimal point 2 places to the right. Since there is only one digit to the right of the decimal point, we must write a 0 in the hundredths place.

$$2.4 \times 100 = 240.$$

HOW TO : : MULTIPLY A DECIMAL BY A POWER OF 10.

Step 1.   Move the decimal point to the right the same number of places as the number of zeros in the power of 10.

Step 2.   Write zeros at the end of the number as placeholders if needed.

EXAMPLE 5.18

Multiply 5.63 by factors of ⓐ 10 ⓑ 100 ⓒ 1000.

✓ **Solution**

By looking at the number of zeros in the multiple of ten, we see the number of places we need to move the decimal to the right.

ⓐ

$$56.3(10)$$

There is 1 zero in 10, so move the decimal point 1 place to the right.

5.63

$$56.3$$

ⓑ

$$5.63(100)$$

There are 2 zeros in 100, so move the decimal point 2 places to the right.

5.63

$$563$$

ⓒ

$$5.63(1000)$$

There are 3 zeros in 1000, so move the decimal point 3 places to the right.

5.63

A zero must be added at the end.

$$5,630$$

> **TRY IT : : 5.35**   Multiply 2.58 by factors of ⓐ 10 ⓑ 100 ⓒ 1000.

> **TRY IT : : 5.36**   Multiply 14.2 by factors of ⓐ 10 ⓑ 100 ⓒ 1000.

Divide Decimals

Just as with multiplication, division of decimals is very much like dividing whole numbers. We just have to figure out where the decimal point must be placed.

To understand decimal division, let's consider the multiplication problem

$$(0.2)(4) = 0.8$$

Remember, a multiplication problem can be rephrased as a division problem. So we can write

$$0.8 \div 4 = 0.2$$

We can think of this as "If we divide 8 tenths into four groups, how many are in each group?" Figure 5.5 shows that there are four groups of two-tenths in eight-tenths. So $0.8 \div 4 = 0.2$.

Figure 5.5

Using long division notation, we would write

$$\begin{array}{r} 0.2 \\ 4\overline{)0.8} \end{array}$$

Notice that the decimal point in the quotient is directly above the decimal point in the dividend.

To divide a decimal by a whole number, we place the decimal point in the quotient above the decimal point in the dividend and then divide as usual. Sometimes we need to use extra zeros at the end of the dividend to keep dividing until there is no remainder.

 HOW TO :: DIVIDE A DECIMAL BY A WHOLE NUMBER.

Step 1. Write as long division, placing the decimal point in the quotient above the decimal point in the dividend.

Step 2. Divide as usual.

EXAMPLE 5.19

Divide: $0.12 \div 3$.

⊘ **Solution**

	$0.12 \div 3$
Write as long division, placing the decimal point in the quotient above the decimal point in the dividend.	$3\overline{)0.12}$
Divide as usual. Since 3 does not go into 0 or 1 we use zeros as placeholders.	$\begin{array}{r} 0.04 \\ 3\overline{)0.12} \\ \underline{12} \\ 0 \end{array}$
	$0.12 \div 3 = 0.04$

> **TRY IT :: 5.37**   Divide: $0.28 \div 4$.

> **TRY IT :: 5.38**   Divide: $0.56 \div 7$.

In everyday life, we divide whole numbers into decimals—money—to find the price of one item. For example, suppose a case of 24 water bottles cost $\$3.99$. To find the price per water bottle, we would divide $\$3.99$ by 24, and round the answer to the nearest cent (hundredth).

EXAMPLE 5.20

Divide: $\$3.99 \div 24$.

⊘ **Solution**

$$\$3.99 \div 24$$

Place the decimal point in the quotient above the decimal point in the dividend.

$$24\overline{)3.99}$$

Divide as usual. When do we stop? Since this division involves money, we round it to the nearest cent (hundredth). To do this, we must carry the division to the thousandths place.

$$\begin{array}{r} 0.166 \\ 24\overline{)3.990} \\ \underline{24} \\ 159 \\ \underline{144} \\ 150 \\ \underline{144} \\ 6 \end{array}$$

Round to the nearest cent.

$$\$0.166 \approx \$0.17$$

$$\$3.99 \div 24 \approx \$0.17$$

This means the price per bottle is 17 cents.

> **TRY IT : : 5.39**   Divide: $\$6.99 \div 36$.

> **TRY IT : : 5.40**   Divide: $\$4.99 \div 12$.

Divide a Decimal by Another Decimal

So far, we have divided a decimal by a whole number. What happens when we divide a decimal by another decimal? Let's look at the same multiplication problem we looked at earlier, but in a different way.

$$(0.2)(4) = 0.8$$

Remember, again, that a multiplication problem can be rephrased as a division problem. This time we ask, "How many times does 0.2 go into 0.8?" Because $(0.2)(4) = 0.8$, we can say that 0.2 goes into 0.8 four times. This means that 0.8 divided by 0.2 is 4.

$$0.8 \div 0.2 = 4$$

We would get the same answer, 4, if we divide 8 by 2, both whole numbers. Why is this so? Let's think about the division problem as a fraction.

$$\frac{0.8}{0.2}$$

$$\frac{(0.8)10}{(0.2)10}$$

$$\frac{8}{2}$$

$$4$$

We multiplied the numerator and denominator by 10 and ended up just dividing 8 by 4. To divide decimals, we multiply both the numerator and denominator by the same power of 10 to make the denominator a whole number. Because of the Equivalent Fractions Property, we haven't changed the value of the fraction. The effect is to move the decimal points in the numerator and denominator the same number of places to the right.

We use the rules for dividing positive and negative numbers with decimals, too. When dividing signed decimals, first determine the sign of the quotient and then divide as if the numbers were both positive. Finally, write the quotient with the appropriate sign.

It may help to review the vocabulary for division:

$$a \div b \qquad \dfrac{a}{b} \qquad b \overline{)\,a\,}$$
$$\text{dividend} \quad \text{divisor} \qquad \text{dividend / divisor} \qquad \text{divisor} \quad \text{dividend}$$

HOW TO :: DIVIDE DECIMAL NUMBERS.

Step 1.   Determine the sign of the quotient.

Step 2.   Make the divisor a whole number by moving the decimal point all the way to the right. Move the decimal point in the dividend the same number of places to the right, writing zeros as needed.

Step 3.   Divide. Place the decimal point in the quotient above the decimal point in the dividend.

Step 4.   Write the quotient with the appropriate sign.

EXAMPLE 5.21

Divide: $-2.89 \div (3.4)$.

 Solution

Determine the sign of the quotient.	The quotient will be negative.
Make the divisor the whole number by 'moving' the decimal point all the way to the right. 'Move' the decimal point in the dividend the same number of places to the right.	$3.4\overline{)2.89}$
Divide. Place the decimal point in the quotient above the decimal point in the dividend. Add zeros as needed until the remainder is zero.	$\begin{array}{r} 0.85 \\ 34\overline{)28.90} \\ \underline{272} \\ 170 \\ \underline{170} \\ 0 \end{array}$
Write the quotient with the appropriate sign.	$-2.89 \div (3.4) = -0.85$

> **TRY IT :: 5.41**   Divide: $-1.989 \div 5.1$.

> **TRY IT :: 5.42**   Divide: $-2.04 \div 5.1$.

EXAMPLE 5.22

Divide: $-25.65 \div (-0.06)$.

⊘ **Solution**

$$-25.65 \div (-0.06)$$

The signs are the same.

The quotient is positive.

Make the divisor a whole number by 'moving' the decimal point all the way to the right.
'Move' the decimal point in the dividend the same number of places.

$$0.06\overline{)25.65}$$

Divide.
Place the decimal point in the quotient above the decimal point in the dividend.

$$
\begin{array}{r}
427.5 \\
006.\overline{)2565.0} \\
-24 \\
\hline
16 \\
-12 \\
\hline
45 \\
-42 \\
\hline
30 \\
30 \\
\hline
\end{array}
$$

Write the quotient with the appropriate sign.

$$-25.65 \div (-0.06) = 427.5$$

> **TRY IT : : 5.43**   Divide: $-23.492 \div (-0.04)$.

> **TRY IT : : 5.44**   Divide: $-4.11 \div (-0.12)$.

Now we will divide a whole number by a decimal number.

EXAMPLE 5.23

Divide: $4 \div 0.05$.

⊘ **Solution**

$$4 \div 0.05$$

The signs are the same.

The quotient is positive.

Make the divisor a whole number by 'moving' the decimal point all the way to the right.
Move the decimal point in the dividend the same number of places, adding zeros as needed.

$$0.05\overline{)4.00}$$

Divide.
Place the decimal point in the quotient above the decimal point in the dividend.

$$
\begin{array}{r}
80. \\
5\overline{)400.} \\
40 \\
\hline
00 \\
00 \\
\hline
\end{array}
$$

Write the quotient with the appropriate sign.

$$4 \div 0.05 = 80$$

We can relate this example to money. How many nickels are there in four dollars? Because $4 \div 0.05 = 80$, there are 80 nickels in $\$4$.

> **TRY IT : : 5.45**   Divide: $6 \div 0.03$.

> **TRY IT : :** 5.46   Divide: $7 \div 0.02$.

Use Decimals in Money Applications

We often apply decimals in real life, and most of the applications involving money. The Strategy for Applications we used in The Language of Algebra gives us a plan to follow to help find the answer. Take a moment to review that strategy now.

Strategy for Applications

1. Identify what you are asked to find.
2. Write a phrase that gives the information to find it.
3. Translate the phrase to an expression.
4. Simplify the expression.
5. Answer the question with a complete sentence.

EXAMPLE 5.24

Paul received $50 for his birthday. He spent $31.64 on a video game. How much of Paul's birthday money was left?

⊘ **Solution**

What are you asked to find?	How much did Paul have left?
Write a phrase.	$50 less $31.64
Translate.	$50 - 31.64$
Simplify.	18.36
Write a sentence.	Paul has $18.36 left.

> **TRY IT : :** 5.47

> Nicole earned $35 for babysitting her cousins, then went to the bookstore and spent $18.48 on books and coffee. How much of her babysitting money was left?

> **TRY IT : :** 5.48

> Amber bought a pair of shoes for $24.75 and a purse for $36.90. The sales tax was $4.32. How much did Amber spend?

EXAMPLE 5.25

Jessie put 8 gallons of gas in her car. One gallon of gas costs $3.529. How much does Jessie owe for the gas? (Round the answer to the nearest cent.)

Solution

What are you asked to find?	How much did Jessie owe for all the gas?
Write a phrase.	8 times the cost of one gallon of gas
Translate.	8($3.529)
Simplify.	$28.232
Round to the nearest cent.	$28.23
Write a sentence.	Jessie owes $28.23 for her gas purchase.

> **TRY IT ::** 5.49

Hector put 13 gallons of gas into his car. One gallon of gas costs $3.175. How much did Hector owe for the gas? Round to the nearest cent.

> **TRY IT ::** 5.50

Christopher bought 5 pizzas for the team. Each pizza cost $9.75. How much did all the pizzas cost?

EXAMPLE 5.26

Four friends went out for dinner. They shared a large pizza and a pitcher of soda. The total cost of their dinner was $31.76. If they divide the cost equally, how much should each friend pay?

Solution

What are you asked to find?	How much should each friend pay?
Write a phrase.	$31.76 divided equally among the four friends.
Translate to an expression.	$31.76 ÷ 4
Simplify.	$7.94
Write a sentence.	Each friend should pay $7.94 for his share of the dinner.

> **TRY IT ::** 5.51

Six friends went out for dinner. The total cost of their dinner was $92.82. If they divide the bill equally, how much should each friend pay?

> **TRY IT ::** 5.52

Chad worked 40 hours last week and his paycheck was $570. How much does he earn per hour?

Be careful to follow the order of operations in the next example. Remember to multiply before you add.

EXAMPLE 5.27

Marla buys 6 bananas that cost $0.22 each and 4 oranges that cost $0.49 each. How much is the total cost of the fruit?

⊘ **Solution**

What are you asked to find?	How much is the total cost of the fruit?
Write a phrase.	6 times the cost of each banana plus 4 times the cost of each orange
Translate to an expression.	$6(\$0.22) + 4(\$0.49)$
Simplify.	$\$1.32 + \$1.96$
Add.	$\$3.28$
Write a sentence.	Marla's total cost for the fruit is $3.28.

> **TRY IT : :** 5.53

Suzanne buys 3 cans of beans that cost $\$0.75$ each and 6 cans of corn that cost $\$0.62$ each. How much is the total cost of these groceries?

> **TRY IT : :** 5.54

Lydia bought movie tickets for the family. She bought two adult tickets for $\$9.50$ each and four children's tickets for $\$6.00$ each. How much did the tickets cost Lydia in all?

⊡ LINKS TO LITERACY

The *Links to Literacy* activity "Alexander Who Used to be Rich Last Sunday" will provide you with another view of the topics covered in this section.

▶ **MEDIA : :** ACCESS ADDITIONAL ONLINE RESOURCES

- Adding and Subtracting Decimals (http://www.openstaxcollege.org/l/24addsubdecmls)
- Multiplying Decimals (http://www.openstaxcollege.org/l/24multdecmls)
- Multiplying by Powers of Ten (http://www.openstaxcollege.org/l/24multpowten)
- Dividing Decimals (http://www.openstaxcollege.org/l/24divddecmls)
- Dividing by Powers of Ten (http://www.openstaxcollege.org/l/24divddecmlss)

5.2 EXERCISES

Practice Makes Perfect

Add and Subtract Decimals

In the following exercises, add or subtract.

95. $16.92 + 7.56$

96. $18.37 + 9.36$

97. $256.37 - 85.49$

98. $248.25 - 91.29$

99. $21.76 - 30.99$

100. $15.35 - 20.88$

101. $37.5 + 12.23$

102. $38.6 + 13.67$

103. $-16.53 - 24.38$

104. $-19.47 - 32.58$

105. $-38.69 + 31.47$

106. $-29.83 + 19.76$

107. $-4.2 + (-9.3)$

108. $-8.6 + (-8.6)$

109. $100 - 64.2$

110. $100 - 65.83$

111. $72.5 - 100$

112. $86.2 - 100$

113. $15 + 0.73$

114. $27 + 0.87$

115. $2.51 + 40$

116. $9.38 + 60$

117. $91.75 - (-10.462)$

118. $94.69 - (-12.678)$

119. $55.01 - 3.7$

120. $59.08 - 4.6$

121. $2.51 - 7.4$

122. $3.84 - 6.1$

Multiply Decimals

In the following exercises, multiply.

123. $(0.3)(0.4)$

124. $(0.6)(0.7)$

125. $(0.24)(0.6)$

126. $(0.81)(0.3)$

127. $(5.9)(7.12)$

128. $(2.3)(9.41)$

129. $(8.52)(3.14)$

130. $(5.32)(4.86)$

131. $(-4.3)(2.71)$

132. $(-8.5)(1.69)$

133. $(-5.18)(-65.23)$

134. $(-9.16)(-68.34)$

135. $(0.09)(24.78)$

136. $(0.04)(36.89)$

137. $(0.06)(21.75)$

138. $(0.08)(52.45)$

139. $(9.24)(10)$

140. $(6.531)(10)$

141. $(55.2)(1,000)$

142. $(99.4)(1,000)$

Divide Decimals

In the following exercises, divide.

143. $0.15 \div 5$

144. $0.27 \div 3$

145. $4.75 \div 25$

146. $12.04 \div 43$

147. $\$8.49 \div 12$

148. $\$16.99 \div 9$

149. $\$117.25 \div 48$

150. $\$109.24 \div 36$

151. $0.6 : 0.2$

152. $0.8 \div 0.4$

153. $1.44 \div (-0.3)$

154. $1.25 \div (-0.5)$

155. $-1.75 \div (-0.05)$

156. $-1.15 \div (-0.05)$

157. $5.2 \div 2.5$

158. $6.5 \div 3.25$

159. $12 \div 0.08$

160. $5 \div 0.04$

161. $11 \div 0.55$

162. $14 \div 0.35$

Mixed Practice

In the following exercises, simplify.

163. $6(12.4 - 9.2)$

164. $3(15.7 - 8.6)$

165. $24(0.5) + (0.3)^2$

166. $35(0.2) + (0.9)^2$

167. $1.15(26.83 + 1.61)$

168. $1.18(46.22 + 3.71)$

169. $\$45 + 0.08(\$45)$

170. $\$63 + 0.18(\$63)$

171. $18 \div (0.75 + 0.15)$

172. $27 \div (0.55 + 0.35)$

173. $(1.43 + 0.27) \div (0.9 - 0.05)$

174. $(1.5 - 0.06) \div (0.12 + 0.24)$

175. $[\$75.42 + 0.18(\$75.42)] \div 5$

176. $[\$56.31 + 0.22(\$56.31)] \div 4$

Use Decimals in Money Applications

In the following exercises, use the strategy for applications to solve.

177. Spending money Brenda got $40 from the ATM. She spent $15.11 on a pair of earrings. How much money did she have left?

178. Spending money Marissa found $20 in her pocket. She spent $4.82 on a smoothie. How much of the $20 did she have left?

179. Shopping Adam bought a t-shirt for $18.49 and a book for $8.92 The sales tax was $1.65. How much did Adam spend?

180. Restaurant Roberto's restaurant bill was $20.45 for the entrée and $3.15 for the drink. He left a $4.40 tip. How much did Roberto spend?

181. Coupon Emily bought a box of cereal that cost $4.29. She had a coupon for $0.55 off, and the store doubled the coupon. How much did she pay for the box of cereal?

182. Coupon Diana bought a can of coffee that cost $7.99. She had a coupon for $0.75 off, and the store doubled the coupon. How much did she pay for the can of coffee?

183. Diet Leo took part in a diet program. He weighed 190 pounds at the start of the program. During the first week, he lost 4.3 pounds. During the second week, he had lost 2.8 pounds. The third week, he gained 0.7 pounds. The fourth week, he lost 1.9 pounds. What did Leo weigh at the end of the fourth week?

184. Snowpack On April 1, the snowpack at the ski resort was 4 meters deep, but the next few days were very warm. By April 5, the snow depth was 1.6 meters less. On April 8, it snowed and added 2.1 meters of snow. What was the total depth of the snow?

185. Coffee Noriko bought 4 coffees for herself and her co-workers. Each coffee was $3.75. How much did she pay for all the coffees?

186. Subway Fare Arianna spends $4.50 per day on subway fare. Last week she rode the subway 6 days. How much did she spend for the subway fares?

187. Income Mayra earns $9.25 per hour. Last week she worked 32 hours. How much did she earn?

188. Income Peter earns $8.75 per hour. Last week he worked 19 hours. How much did he earn?

189. Hourly Wage Alan got his first paycheck from his new job. He worked 30 hours and earned $382.50. How much does he earn per hour?

190. Hourly Wage Maria got her first paycheck from her new job. She worked 25 hours and earned $362.50. How much does she earn per hour?

191. Restaurant Jeannette and her friends love to order mud pie at their favorite restaurant. They always share just one piece of pie among themselves. With tax and tip, the total cost is $6.00. How much does each girl pay if the total number sharing the mud pie is

ⓐ 2?

ⓑ 3?

ⓒ 4?

ⓓ 5?

ⓔ 6?

192. Pizza Alex and his friends go out for pizza and video games once a week. They share the cost of a $15.60 pizza equally. How much does each person pay if the total number sharing the pizza is

ⓐ 2?

ⓑ 3?

ⓒ 4?

ⓓ 5?

ⓔ 6?

193. Fast Food At their favorite fast food restaurant, the Carlson family orders 4 burgers that cost $3.29 each and 2 orders of fries at $2.74 each. What is the total cost of the order?

194. Home Goods Chelsea needs towels to take with her to college. She buys 2 bath towels that cost $9.99 each and 6 washcloths that cost $2.99 each. What is the total cost for the bath towels and washcloths?

195. Zoo The Lewis and Chousmith families are planning to go to the zoo together. Adult tickets cost $29.95 and children's tickets cost $19.95. What will the total cost be for 4 adults and 7 children?

196. Ice Skating Jasmine wants to have her birthday party at the local ice skating rink. It will cost $8.25 per child and $12.95 per adult. What will the total cost be for 12 children and 3 adults?

Everyday Math

197. Paycheck Annie has two jobs. She gets paid $14.04 per hour for tutoring at City College and $8.75 per hour at a coffee shop. Last week she tutored for 8 hours and worked at the coffee shop for 15 hours.

ⓐ How much did she earn?

ⓑ If she had worked all 23 hours as a tutor instead of working both jobs, how much more would she have earned?

198. Paycheck Jake has two jobs. He gets paid $7.95 per hour at the college cafeteria and $20.25 at the art gallery. Last week he worked 12 hours at the cafeteria and 5 hours at the art gallery.

ⓐ How much did he earn?

ⓑ If he had worked all 17 hours at the art gallery instead of working both jobs, how much more would he have earned?

Writing Exercises

199. In the 2010 winter Olympics, two skiers took the silver and bronze medals in the Men's Super-G ski event. The silver medalist's time was 1 minute 30.62 seconds and bronze medalist's time was 1 minute 30.65 seconds. Whose time was faster? Find the difference in their times and then write the name of that decimal.

200. Find the quotient of $0.12 \div 0.04$ and explain in words all the steps taken.

Self Check

ⓐ *After completing the exercises, use this checklist to evaluate your mastery of the objectives of this section.*

I can...	Confidently	With some help	No-I don't get it!
add and subtract decimals.			
multiply decimals.			
divide decimals.			
use decimals in money applications.			

ⓑ *After reviewing this checklist, what will you do to become confident for all objectives?*

5.3 Decimals and Fractions

Learning Objectives

By the end of this section, you will be able to:
- Convert fractions to decimals
- Order decimals and fractions
- Simplify expressions using the order of operations
- Find the circumference and area of circles

Be Prepared!

Before you get started, take this readiness quiz.

1. Divide: $0.24 \div 8$.
   If you missed this problem, review Example 5.19.
2. Order $0.64\_\_0.6$ using $<$ or $>$.
   If you missed this problem, review Example 5.7.
3. Order $-0.2\_\_-0.1$ using $<$ or $>$.
   If you missed this problem, review Example 5.8.

Convert Fractions to Decimals

In Decimals, we learned to convert decimals to fractions. Now we will do the reverse—convert fractions to decimals. Remember that the fraction bar indicates division. So $\frac{4}{5}$ can be written $4 \div 5$ or $5\overline{)4}$. This means that we can convert a fraction to a decimal by treating it as a division problem.

Convert a Fraction to a Decimal

To convert a fraction to a decimal, divide the numerator of the fraction by the denominator of the fraction.

EXAMPLE 5.28

Write the fraction $\frac{3}{4}$ as a decimal.

⊘ Solution

A fraction bar means division, so we can write the fraction $\frac{3}{4}$ using division.

$$4\overline{)3}$$

Divide.

$$\begin{array}{r} 0.75 \\ 4\overline{)3.00} \\ \underline{28} \\ 20 \\ \underline{20} \\ 0 \end{array}$$

So the fraction $\frac{3}{4}$ is equal to 0.75.

 TRY IT : : 5.55   Write the fraction as a decimal: $\frac{1}{4}$.

> **TRY IT : : 5.56**   Write the fraction as a decimal: $\frac{3}{8}$.

EXAMPLE 5.29

Write the fraction $-\frac{7}{2}$ as a decimal.

⊘ **Solution**

The value of this fraction is negative. After dividing, the value of the decimal will be negative. We do the division ignoring the sign, and then write the negative sign in the answer.	$-\frac{7}{2}$
Divide 7 by 2.	$\begin{array}{r} 3.5 \\ 2{\overline{)7.0}} \\ \underline{6} \\ 10 \\ \underline{10} \\ 0 \end{array}$
	So, $-\frac{7}{2} = -3.5$.

> **TRY IT : : 5.57**   Write the fraction as a decimal: $-\frac{9}{4}$.

> **TRY IT : : 5.58**   Write the fraction as a decimal: $-\frac{11}{2}$.

Repeating Decimals

So far, in all the examples converting fractions to decimals the division resulted in a remainder of zero. This is not always the case. Let's see what happens when we convert the fraction $\frac{4}{3}$ to a decimal. First, notice that $\frac{4}{3}$ is an improper fraction. Its value is greater than 1. The equivalent decimal will also be greater than 1.

We divide 4 by 3.

$$\begin{array}{r} 1.333... \\ 3{\overline{)4.000}} \\ \underline{3} \\ 10 \\ \underline{9} \\ 10 \\ \underline{9} \\ 10 \\ \underline{9} \\ 1 \end{array}$$

No matter how many more zeros we write, there will always be a remainder of 1, and the threes in the quotient will go on forever. The number $1.333\ldots$ is called a repeating decimal. Remember that the "..." means that the pattern repeats.

Repeating Decimal

A **repeating decimal** is a decimal in which the last digit or group of digits repeats endlessly.

How do you know how many 'repeats' to write? Instead of writing $1.333\ldots$ we use a shorthand notation by placing a line over the digits that repeat. The repeating decimal $1.333\ldots$ is written $1.\overline{3}$. The line above the 3 tells you that the 3 repeats endlessly. So $1.333\ldots = 1.\overline{3}$

For other decimals, two or more digits might repeat. Table 5.41 shows some more examples of repeating decimals.

$1.333... = 1.\overline{3}$	3 is the repeating digit
$4.1666... = 4.1\overline{6}$	6 is the repeating digit
$4.161616... = 4.\overline{16}$	16 is the repeating block
$0.271271271... = 0.\overline{271}$	271 is the repeating block

Table 5.41

EXAMPLE 5.30

Write $\frac{43}{22}$ as a decimal.

⊘ Solution

Divide 43 by 22.

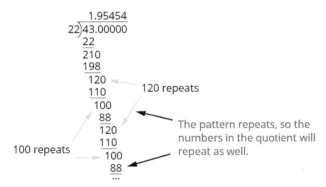

Notice that the differences of 120 and 100 repeat, so there is a repeat in the digits of the quotient; 54 will repeat endlessly. The first decimal place in the quotient, 9, is not part of the pattern. So,

$$\frac{43}{22} = 1.9\overline{54}$$

> **TRY IT : : 5.59**   Write as a decimal: $\frac{27}{11}$.

> **TRY IT : : 5.60**   Write as a decimal: $\frac{51}{22}$.

It is useful to convert between fractions and decimals when we need to add or subtract numbers in different forms. To add a fraction and a decimal, for example, we would need to either convert the fraction to a decimal or the decimal to a fraction.

EXAMPLE 5.31

Simplify: $\frac{7}{8} + 6.4$.

⊘ Solution

$$\frac{7}{8} + 6.4$$

Change $\frac{7}{8}$ to a decimal.

$$\begin{array}{r} 0.875 \\ 8\overline{)7.000} \\ \underline{64} \\ 60 \\ \underline{56} \\ 40 \\ \underline{40} \\ 0 \end{array}$$

$$0.875 + 6.4$$

Add.

$$7.275$$

> **TRY IT :: 5.61**   Simplify: $\frac{3}{8} + 4.9$.

> **TRY IT :: 5.62**   Simplify: $5.7 + \frac{13}{20}$.

Order Decimals and Fractions

In Decimals, we compared two decimals and determined which was larger. To compare a decimal to a fraction, we will first convert the fraction to a decimal and then compare the decimals.

EXAMPLE 5.32

Order $\frac{3}{8}$___0.4 using $<$ or $>$.

⊘ Solution

$$\frac{3}{8}\_\_0.4$$

Convert $\frac{3}{8}$ to a decimal.

$$0.375\_\_0.4$$

Compare 0.375 to 0.4

$$0.375 < 0.4$$

Rewrite with the original fraction.

$$\frac{3}{8} < 0.4$$

> **TRY IT :: 5.63**   Order each of the following pairs of numbers, using $<$ or $>$.
>
> $\frac{17}{20}$___0.82

> **TRY IT :: 5.64**   Order each of the following pairs of numbers, using $<$ or $>$.
>
> $\frac{3}{4}$___0.785

When ordering negative numbers, remember that larger numbers are to the right on the number line and any positive number is greater than any negative number.

EXAMPLE 5.33

Order -0.5___ $-\frac{3}{4}$ using $<$ or $>$.

Solution

$$-0.5\_\_\_ -\frac{3}{4}$$

Convert $-\frac{3}{4}$ to a decimal. $\qquad\qquad -0.5\_\_\_-0.75$

Compare -0.5 to -0.75. $\qquad\qquad -0.5 > -0.75$

Rewrite the inequality with the original fraction. $\qquad -0.5 > -\frac{3}{4}$

> **TRY IT :: 5.65**   Order each of the following pairs of numbers, using $<$ or $>$:

$$-\frac{5}{8}\_\_-0.58$$

> **TRY IT :: 5.66**   Order each of the following pairs of numbers, using $<$ or $>$:

$$-0.53\_\_ -\frac{11}{20}$$

EXAMPLE 5.34

Write the numbers $\frac{13}{20}$, 0.61, $\frac{11}{16}$ in order from smallest to largest.

Solution

$$\frac{13}{20}, 0.61, \frac{11}{16}$$

Convert the fractions to decimals. $\qquad\qquad 0.65, 0.61, 0.6875$

Write the smallest decimal number first. $\qquad\qquad 0.61, \_\_\_\_, \_\_\_\_\_$

Write the next larger decimal number in the middle place. $\qquad 0.61, 0.65, \_\_\_\_\_$

Write the last decimal number (the larger) in the third place. $\qquad 0.61, 0.65, 0.6875$

Rewrite the list with the original fractions. $\qquad\qquad 0.61, \frac{13}{20}, \frac{11}{16}$

> **TRY IT :: 5.67**   Write each set of numbers in order from smallest to largest: $\frac{7}{8}, \frac{4}{5}, 0.82$.

> **TRY IT :: 5.68**   Write each set of numbers in order from smallest to largest: $0.835, \frac{13}{16}, \frac{3}{4}$.

Simplify Expressions Using the Order of Operations

The order of operations introduced in Use the Language of Algebra also applies to decimals. Do you remember what the phrase "Please excuse my dear Aunt Sally" stands for?

EXAMPLE 5.35

Simplify the expressions:

ⓐ $7(18.3 - 21.7)$

ⓑ $\frac{2}{3}(8.3 - 3.8)$

⊘ **Solution**

ⓐ

	$7(18.3 - 21.7)$
Simplify inside parentheses.	$7(-3.4)$
Multiply.	-23.8

ⓑ

	$\frac{2}{3}(8.3 - 3.8)$
Simplify inside parentheses.	$\frac{2}{3}(4.5)$
Write 4.5 as a fraction.	$\frac{2}{3}(\frac{4.5}{1})$
Multiply.	$\frac{9}{3}$
Simplify.	3

> **TRY IT :: 5.69** Simplify: ⓐ $8(14.6 - 37.5)$ ⓑ $\frac{3}{5}(9.6 - 2.1)$.

> **TRY IT :: 5.70** Simplify: ⓐ $25(25.69 - 56.74)$ ⓑ $\frac{2}{7}(11.9 - 4.2)$.

EXAMPLE 5.36

Simplify each expression:

ⓐ $6 \div 0.6 + (0.2)4 - (0.1)^2$

ⓑ $\left(\frac{1}{10}\right)^2 + (3.5)(0.9)$

⊘ **Solution**

ⓐ

$$6 \div 0.6 + (0.2)4 - (0.1)^2$$

Simplify exponents.	$6 \div 0.6 + (0.2)4 - 0.01$
Divide.	$10 + (0.2)4 - 0.01$
Multiply.	$10 + 0.8 - 0.01$
Add.	$10.8 - 0.01$
Subtract.	10.79

ⓑ

$$\left(\frac{1}{10}\right)^2 + (3.5)(0.9)$$

Simplify exponents.	$\frac{1}{100} + (3.5)(0.9)$
Multiply.	$\frac{1}{100} + 3.15$
Convert $\frac{1}{100}$ to a decimal.	$0.01 + 3.15$
Add.	3.16

> **TRY IT : : 5.71**   Simplify: $9 \div 0.9 + (0.4)3 - (0.2)^2$.

> **TRY IT : : 5.72**   Simplify: $\left(\frac{1}{2}\right)^2 + (0.3)(4.2)$.

Find the Circumference and Area of Circles

The properties of circles have been studied for over $2,000$ years. All circles have exactly the same shape, but their sizes are affected by the length of the **radius**, a line segment from the center to any point on the circle. A line segment that passes through a circle's center connecting two points on the circle is called a **diameter**. The diameter is twice as long as the radius. See Figure 5.6.

The size of a circle can be measured in two ways. The distance around a circle is called its **circumference**.

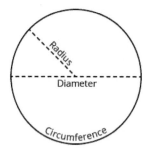

Figure 5.6

Archimedes discovered that for circles of all different sizes, dividing the circumference by the diameter always gives the same number. The value of this number is pi, symbolized by Greek letter π (pronounced pie). However, the exact value of π cannot be calculated since the decimal never ends or repeats (we will learn more about numbers like this in The Properties of Real Numbers.)

 MANIPULATIVE MATHEMATICS

Doing the Manipulative Mathematics activity Pi Lab will help you develop a better understanding of pi.

If we want the exact circumference or area of a circle, we leave the symbol π in the answer. We can get an approximate answer by substituting 3.14 as the value of π. We use the symbol $\approx$ to show that the result is approximate, not exact.

Properties of Circles

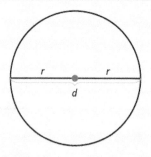

r is the length of the radius.

d is the length of the diameter.

The circumference is $2\pi r$. $C = 2\pi r$

The area is πr^2. $A = \pi r^2$

Since the diameter is twice the radius, another way to find the circumference is to use the formula $C = \pi d$.

Suppose we want to find the exact area of a circle of radius 10 inches. To calculate the area, we would evaluate the formula for the area when $r = 10$ inches and leave the answer in terms of π.

$$A = \pi r^2$$
$$A = \pi(10^2)$$
$$A = \pi \cdot 100$$

We write π after the 100. So the exact value of the area is $A = 100\pi$ square inches.

To approximate the area, we would substitute $\pi \approx 3.14$.

$$A \;=\; 100\pi$$
$$\approx\; 100 \cdot 3.14$$
$$\approx\; 314 \text{ square inches}$$

Remember to use square units, such as square inches, when you calculate the area.

EXAMPLE 5.37

A circle has radius 10 centimeters. Approximate its ⓐ circumference and ⓑ area.

✓ Solution

ⓐ Find the circumference when $r = 10$.

Write the formula for circumference.	$C = 2\pi r$
Substitute 3.14 for π and 10 for , r .	$C \approx 2(3.14)(10)$
Multiply.	$C \approx 62.8 \text{ centimeters}$

ⓑ Find the area when $r = 10$.

Write the formula for area.	$A = \pi r^2$
Substitute 3.14 for π and 10 for r .	$A \approx (3.14)(10)^2$
Multiply.	$A \approx 314 \text{ square centimeters}$

> **TRY IT : : 5.73**   A circle has radius 50 inches. Approximate its ⓐ circumference and ⓑ area.

> **TRY IT : : 5.74**   A circle has radius 100 feet. Approximate its ⓐ circumference and ⓑ area.

EXAMPLE 5.38

A circle has radius 42.5 centimeters. Approximate its ⓐ circumference and ⓑ area.

✓ Solution

ⓐ Find the circumference when $r = 42.5$.

Write the formula for circumference.	$C = 2\pi r$
Substitute 3.14 for π and 42.5 for r	$C \approx 2(3.14)(42.5)$
Multiply.	$C \approx 266.9 \text{ centimeters}$

ⓑ Find the area when $r = 42.5$.

Write the formula for area.	$A = \pi r^2$
Substitute 3.14 for π and 42.5 for r.	$A \approx (3.14)(42.5)^2$
Multiply.	$A \approx 5671.625$ square centimeters

> **TRY IT :: 5.75**   A circle has radius 51.8 centimeters. Approximate its ⓐ circumference and ⓑ area.

> **TRY IT :: 5.76**   A circle has radius 26.4 meters. Approximate its ⓐ circumference and ⓑ area.

Approximate π with a Fraction

Convert the fraction $\frac{22}{7}$ to a decimal. If you use your calculator, the decimal number will fill up the display and show 3.14285714. But if we round that number to two decimal places, we get 3.14, the decimal approximation of π. When we have a circle with radius given as a fraction, we can substitute $\frac{22}{7}$ for π instead of 3.14. And, since $\frac{22}{7}$ is also an approximation of π, we will use the $\approx$ symbol to show we have an approximate value.

EXAMPLE 5.39

A circle has radius $\frac{14}{15}$ meter. Approximate its ⓐ circumference and ⓑ area.

⊘ **Solution**

ⓐ Find the circumference when $r = \frac{14}{15}$.

Write the formula for circumference.	$C = 2\pi r$
Substitute $\frac{22}{7}$ for π and $\frac{14}{15}$ for r.	$C \approx 2(\frac{22}{7})(\frac{14}{15})$
Multiply.	$C \approx \frac{88}{15}$ meters

ⓑ Find the area when $r = \frac{14}{15}$.

Write the formula for area.	$A = \pi r^2$
Substitute $\frac{22}{7}$ for π and $\frac{14}{15}$ for r.	$A \approx (\frac{22}{7})(\frac{14}{15})^2$
Multiply.	$A \approx \frac{616}{225}$ square meters

> | TRY IT : : 5.77   A circle has radius $\frac{5}{21}$ meters. Approximate its ⓐ circumference and ⓑ area.

> | TRY IT : : 5.78   A circle has radius $\frac{10}{33}$ inches. Approximate its ⓐ circumference and ⓑ area.

▶ | MEDIA : : ACCESS ADDITIONAL ONLINE RESOURCES

- Converting a Fraction to a Decimal - Part 2 (http://www.openstaxcollege.org/l/24convfrac2dec)
- Convert a Fraction to a Decimal (repeating) (http://www.openstaxcollege.org/l/24convfr2decrep)
- Compare Fractions and Decimals using Inequality Symbols (http://www.openstaxcollege.org/l/24compfrcdec)
- Determine the Area of a Circle (http://www.openstaxcollege.org/l/24circlearea)
- Determine the Circumference of a Circle (http://www.openstaxcollege.org/l/24circlecirc)

5.3 EXERCISES

Practice Makes Perfect

Convert Fractions to Decimals

In the following exercises, convert each fraction to a decimal.

201. $\frac{2}{5}$

202. $\frac{4}{5}$

203. $-\frac{3}{8}$

204. $-\frac{5}{8}$

205. $\frac{17}{20}$

206. $\frac{13}{20}$

207. $\frac{11}{4}$

208. $\frac{17}{4}$

209. $-\frac{310}{25}$

210. $-\frac{284}{25}$

211. $\frac{5}{9}$

212. $\frac{2}{9}$

213. $\frac{15}{11}$

214. $\frac{18}{11}$

215. $\frac{15}{111}$

216. $\frac{25}{111}$

In the following exercises, simplify the expression.

217. $\frac{1}{2} + 6.5$

218. $\frac{1}{4} + 10.75$

219. $2.4 + \frac{5}{8}$

220. $3.9 + \frac{9}{20}$

221. $9.73 + \frac{17}{20}$

222. $6.29 + \frac{21}{40}$

Order Decimals and Fractions

In the following exercises, order each pair of numbers, using $<$ or $>$.

223. $\frac{1}{8}$___0.8

224. $\frac{1}{4}$___0.4

225. $\frac{2}{5}$___0.25

226. $\frac{3}{5}$___0.35

227. 0.725 ___ $\frac{3}{4}$

228. 0.92 ___ $\frac{7}{8}$

229. 0.66 ___ $\frac{2}{3}$

230. 0.83 ___ $\frac{5}{6}$

231. -0.75___ $-\frac{4}{5}$

232. -0.44___ $-\frac{9}{20}$

233. $-\frac{3}{4}$___-0.925

234. $-\frac{2}{3}$___-0.632

In the following exercises, write each set of numbers in order from least to greatest.

235. $\frac{3}{5}, \frac{9}{16}, 0.55$

236. $\frac{3}{8}, \frac{7}{20}, 0.36$

237. $0.702, \frac{13}{20}, \frac{5}{8}$

238. $0.15, \frac{3}{16}, \frac{1}{5}$

239. $-0.3, -\frac{1}{3}, -\frac{7}{20}$

240. $-0.2, -\frac{3}{20}, -\frac{1}{6}$

241. $-\frac{3}{4}, -\frac{7}{9}, -0.7$

242. $-\frac{8}{9}, -\frac{4}{5}, -0.9$

Simplify Expressions Using the Order of Operations

In the following exercises, simplify.

243. $10(25.1 - 43.8)$

244. $30(18.1 - 32.5)$

245. $62(9.75 - 4.99)$

246. $42(8.45 - 5.97)$

247. $\frac{3}{4}(12.4 - 4.2)$

248. $\frac{4}{5}(8.6 + 3.9)$

249. $\frac{5}{12}(30.58 + 17.9)$

250. $\frac{9}{16}(21.96 - 9.8)$

251. $10 \div 0.1 + (1.8)4 - (0.3)^2$

252. $5 \div 0.5 + (3.9)6 - (0.7)^2$

253. $(37.1 + 52.7) \div (12.5 \div 62.5)$

254. $(11.4 + 16.2) \div (18 \div 60)$

255. $\left(\frac{1}{5}\right)^2 + (1.4)(6.5)$

256. $\left(\frac{1}{2}\right)^2 + (2.1)(8.3)$

257. $-\frac{9}{10} \cdot \frac{8}{15} + 0.25$

258. $-\frac{3}{8} \cdot \frac{14}{15} + 0.72$

Mixed Practice

In the following exercises, simplify. Give the answer as a decimal.

259. $3\frac{1}{4} - 6.5$

260. $5\frac{2}{5} - 8.75$

261. $10.86 \div \frac{2}{3}$

262. $5.79 \div \frac{3}{4}$

263. $\frac{7}{8}(103.48) + 1\frac{1}{2}(361)$

264. $\frac{5}{16}(117.6) + 2\frac{1}{3}(699)$

265. $3.6\left(\frac{9}{8} - 2.72\right)$

266. $5.1\left(\frac{12}{5} - 3.91\right)$

Find the Circumference and Area of Circles

In the following exercises, approximate the ⓐ circumference and ⓑ area of each circle. If measurements are given in fractions, leave answers in fraction form.

267. radius $= 5$ in.

268. radius $= 20$ in.

269. radius $= 9$ ft.

270. radius $= 4$ ft.

271. radius $= 46$ cm

272. radius $= 38$ cm

273. radius $= 18.6$ m

274. radius $= 57.3$ m

275. radius $= \frac{7}{10}$ mile

276. radius $= \frac{7}{11}$ mile

277. radius $= \frac{3}{8}$ yard

278. radius $= \frac{5}{12}$ yard

279. diameter $= \frac{5}{6}$ m

280. diameter $= \frac{3}{4}$ m

Everyday Math

281. Kelly wants to buy a pair of boots that are on sale for $\frac{2}{3}$ of the original price. The original price of the boots is $84.99. What is the sale price of the shoes?

282. An architect is planning to put a circular mosaic in the entry of a new building. The mosaic will be in the shape of a circle with radius of 6 feet. How many square feet of tile will be needed for the mosaic? (Round your answer up to the next whole number.)

Writing Exercises

283. Is it easier for you to convert a decimal to a fraction or a fraction to a decimal? Explain.

284. Describe a situation in your life in which you might need to find the area or circumference of a circle.

Self Check

ⓐ *After completing the exercises, use this checklist to evaluate your mastery of the objectives of this section.*

I can...	Confidently	With some help	No-I don't get it!
convert fractions to decimals.			
order decimals and fractions.			
simplify expressions using the order of operations.			
find the circumference and area of circles.			

ⓑ *What does this checklist tell you about your mastery of this section? What steps will you take to improve?*

5.4 Solve Equations with Decimals

Learning Objectives

By the end of this section, you will be able to:

- Determine whether a decimal is a solution of an equation
- Solve equations with decimals
- Translate to an equation and solve

Be Prepared!

Before you get started, take this readiness quiz.

1. Evaluate $x + \frac{2}{3}$ when $x = -\frac{1}{4}$.

   If you missed this problem, review Example 4.77.

2. Evaluate $15 - y$ when $y = -5$.

   If you missed this problem, review Example 3.41.

3. Solve $\frac{n}{-7} = 42$.

   If you missed this problem, review Example 4.99.

Determine Whether a Decimal is a Solution of an Equation

Solving equations with decimals is important in our everyday lives because money is usually written with decimals. When applications involve money, such as shopping for yourself, making your family's budget, or planning for the future of your business, you'll be solving equations with decimals.

Now that we've worked with decimals, we are ready to find solutions to equations involving decimals. The steps we take to determine whether a number is a solution to an equation are the same whether the solution is a whole number, an integer, a fraction, or a decimal. We'll list these steps here again for easy reference.

HOW TO :: DETERMINE WHETHER A NUMBER IS A SOLUTION TO AN EQUATION.

Step 1. Substitute the number for the variable in the equation.

Step 2. Simplify the expressions on both sides of the equation.

Step 3. Determine whether the resulting equation is true.
- If so, the number is a solution.
- If not, the number is not a solution.

EXAMPLE 5.40

Determine whether each of the following is a solution of $x - 0.7 = 1.5$:

ⓐ $x = 1$ ⓑ $x = -0.8$ ⓒ $x = 2.2$

 Solution

ⓐ

$$x - 0.7 = 1.5$$

Substitute 1 for x. $\quad 1 - 0.7 \overset{?}{=} 1.5$

Subtract. $\quad\quad\quad\quad 0.3 \neq 1.5$

Since $x = 1$ does not result in a true equation, 1 is not a solution to the equation.

ⓑ

	$x - 0.7 = 1.5$
Substitute −0.8 for x.	$-0.8 - 0.7 \overset{?}{=} 1.5$
Subtract.	$-1.5 \neq 1.5$

Since $x = -0.8$ does not result in a true equation, -0.8 is not a solution to the equation.

ⓒ

	$x - 0.7 = 1.5$
Substitute 2.2 for x.	$2.2 - 0.7 \overset{?}{=} 1.5$
Subtract.	$1.5 = 1.5 \checkmark$

Since $x = 2.2$ results in a true equation, 2.2 is a solution to the equation.

> **TRY IT : : 5.79**   Determine whether each value is a solution of the given equation.
> $x - 0.6 = 1.3$: ⓐ $x = 0.7$ ⓑ $x = 1.9$ ⓒ $x = -0.7$

> **TRY IT : : 5.80**   Determine whether each value is a solution of the given equation.
> $y - 0.4 = 1.7$: ⓐ $y = 2.1$ ⓑ $y = 1.3$ ⓒ -1.3

Solve Equations with Decimals

In previous chapters, we solved equations using the Properties of Equality. We will use these same properties to solve equations with decimals.

Properties of Equality

| **Subtraction Property of Equality** For any numbers a, b, and c, If $a = b$, then $a - c = b - c$. | **Addition Property of Equality** For any numbers a, b, and c, If $a = b$, then $a + c = b + c$. |
| **The Division Property of Equality** For any numbers a, b, and c, and $c \neq 0$ If $a = b$, then $\frac{a}{c} = \frac{b}{c}$. | **The Multiplication Property of Equality** For any numbers a, b, and c, If $a = b$, then $ac = bc$ |

When you add, subtract, multiply or divide the same quantity from both sides of an equation, you still have equality.

EXAMPLE 5.41

Solve: $y + 2.3 = -4.7$.

⊘ **Solution**

We will use the Subtraction Property of Equality to isolate the variable.

$$y + 2.3 = -4.7$$

Subtract 2.3 from each side, to undo the addition.	$y + 2.3 - 2.3 = -4.7 - 2.3$
Simplify.	$y = -7$

Check: $y + 2.3 = -4.7$

Substitute $y = -7$. $-7 + 2.3 \overset{?}{=} -4.7$

Simplify. $-4.7 = -4.7$ ✓

Since $y = -7$ makes $y + 2.3 = -4.7$ a true statement, we know we have found a solution to this equation.

> **TRY IT ::** 5.81   Solve: $y + 2.7 = -5.3$.

> **TRY IT ::** 5.82   Solve: $y + 3.6 = -4.8$.

EXAMPLE 5.42

Solve: $a - 4.75 = -1.39$.

⊘ **Solution**

We will use the Addition Property of Equality.

$$a - 4.75 = -1.39$$

Add 4.75 to each side, to undo the subtraction.	$a - 4.75 + 4.75 = -1.39 + 4.75$
Simplify.	$a = 3.36$

Check: $a - 4.75 = -1.39$

Substitute $a = 3.36$. $3.36 - 4.75 \overset{?}{=} -1.39$

$-1.39 = -1.39$ ✓

Since the result is a true statement, $a = 3.36$ is a solution to the equation.

> **TRY IT ::** 5.83   Solve: $a - 3.93 = -2.86$.

> **TRY IT ::** 5.84   Solve: $n - 3.47 = -2.64$.

EXAMPLE 5.43

Solve: $-4.8 = 0.8n$.

⊘ **Solution**

We will use the Division Property of Equality.

Use the Properties of Equality to find a value for n.

$$-4.8 = 0.8n$$

We must divide both sides by 0.8 to isolate n.	$\dfrac{-4.8}{0.8} = \dfrac{0.8n}{0.8}$
Simplify.	$-6 = n$
Check:	$-4.8 = 0.8n$
Substitute $n = -6$.	$-4.8 \overset{?}{=} 0.8(-6)$
	$-4.8 = -4.8\ \checkmark$

Since $n = -6$ makes $-4.8 = 0.8n$ a true statement, we know we have a solution.

> **TRY IT : :** 5.85   Solve: $-8.4 = 0.7b$.

> **TRY IT : :** 5.86   Solve: $-5.6 = 0.7c$.

EXAMPLE 5.44

Solve: $\dfrac{p}{-1.8} = -6.5$.

⊘ **Solution**

We will use the Multiplication Property of Equality.

$$\dfrac{p}{-1.8} = -6.5$$

Here, p is divided by –1.8. We must multiply by –1.8 to isolate p	$-1.8\left(\dfrac{p}{-1.8}\right) = -1.8(-6.5)$
Multiply.	$p = 11.7$
Check:	$\dfrac{p}{-1.8} = -6.5$
Substitute $p = 11.7$.	$\dfrac{11.7}{-1.8} \overset{?}{=} -6.5$
	$-6.5 = -6.5\ \checkmark$

A solution to $\dfrac{p}{-1.8} = -6.5$ is $p = 11.7$.

> **TRY IT : :** 5.87   Solve: $\dfrac{c}{-2.6} = -4.5$.

> **TRY IT : :** 5.88   Solve: $\dfrac{b}{-1.2} = -5.4$.

Translate to an Equation and Solve

Now that we have solved equations with decimals, we are ready to translate word sentences to equations and solve. Remember to look for words and phrases that indicate the operations to use.

EXAMPLE 5.45

Translate and solve: The difference of n and 4.3 is 2.1.

⊘ **Solution**

	The difference of n and 4.3 is 2.1.
Translate.	$n - 4.3 \qquad = \quad 2.1$
Add 4.3 to both sides of the equation.	$n - 4.3 + 4.3 = 2.1 + 4.3$
Simplify.	$n = 6.4$

Check: Is the difference of n and 4.3 equal to 2.1?

Let $n = 6.4$: Is the difference of 6.4 and 4.3 equal to 2.1?

Translate. $\qquad\qquad 6.4 - 4.3 \overset{?}{=} 2.1$

Simplify. $\qquad\qquad 2.1 = 2.1 \checkmark$

> **TRY IT :: 5.89** Translate and solve: The difference of y and 4.9 is 2.8.

> **TRY IT :: 5.90** Translate and solve: The difference of z and 5.7 is 3.4.

EXAMPLE 5.46

Translate and solve: The product of -3.1 and x is 5.27.

⊘ **Solution**

	The product of 3.1 and x is 5.27.
Translate.	$-3.1x \qquad = \quad 5.27$
Divide both sides by -3.1.	$\dfrac{-3.1x}{-3.1} = \dfrac{5.27}{-3.1}$
Simplify.	$x = -1.7$

Check: Is the product of –3.1 and x equal to 5.27?

Let $x = -1.7$: Is the product of -3.1 and -1.7 equal to 5.27?

Translate. $\qquad\qquad -3.1(-1.7) \overset{?}{=} 5.27$

Simplify. $\qquad\qquad 5.27 = 5.27 \checkmark$

> **TRY IT :: 5.91** Translate and solve: The product of -4.3 and x is 12.04.

> **TRY IT :: 5.92** Translate and solve: The product of -3.1 and m is 26.66.

EXAMPLE 5.47

Translate and solve: The quotient of p and -2.4 is 6.5.

⊘ **Solution**

	The quotient of p and -2.4 is 6.5.
Translate.	$\dfrac{p}{-2.4} = 6.5$
Multiply both sides by -2.4.	$-2.4\left(\dfrac{p}{-2.4}\right) = -2.4(6.5)$
Simplify.	$p = -15.6$
Check:	Is the quotient of p and -2.4 equal to 6.5?
Let $p = -15.6$:	Is the quotient of -15.6 and -2.4 equal to 6.5?
Translate.	$\dfrac{-15.6}{-2.4} \overset{?}{=} 6.5$
Simplify.	$6.5 = 6.5$ ✓

> **TRY IT :: 5.93**   Translate and solve: The quotient of q and -3.4 is 4.5.

> **TRY IT :: 5.94**   Translate and solve: The quotient of r and -2.6 is 2.5.

EXAMPLE 5.48

Translate and solve: The sum of n and 2.9 is 1.7.

⊘ **Solution**

	The sum of n and 2.9 is 1.7.
Translate.	$n + 2.9 = 1.7$
Subtract 2.9 from each side.	$n + 2.9 - 2.9 = 1.7 - 2.9$
Simplify.	$n = -1.2$
Check:	Is the sum n and 2.9 equal to 1.7?
Let $n = -1.2$:	Is the sum -1.2 and 2.9 equal to 1.7?
Translate.	$-1.2 + 2.9 \overset{?}{=} 1.7$
Simplify.	$1.7 = 1.7$ ✓

> **TRY IT :: 5.95**   Translate and solve: The sum of j and 3.8 is 2.6.

> **TRY IT :: 5.96**   Translate and solve: The sum of k and 4.7 is 0.3.

▶ | **MEDIA : :** ACCESS ADDITIONAL ONLINE RESOURCES

- Solving One Step Equations Involving Decimals (http://openstaxcollege.org/l/24eqwithdec)
- Solve a One Step Equation With Decimals by Adding and Subtracting (http://openstaxcollege.org/l/24eqnwdecplsmin)
- Solve a One Step Equation With Decimals by Multiplying (http://openstaxcollege.org/l/24eqnwdecmult)
- Solve a One Step Equation With Decimals by Dividing (http://openstaxcollege.org/l/24eqnwdecdiv)

5.4 EXERCISES

Practice Makes Perfect

Determine Whether a Decimal is a Solution of an Equation

In the following exercises, determine whether each number is a solution of the given equation.

285. $x - 0.8 = 2.3$

ⓐ $x = 2$ ⓑ $x = -1.5$ ⓒ $x = 3.1$

286. $y + 0.6 = -3.4$

ⓐ $y = -4$ ⓑ $y = -2.8$ ⓒ $y = 2.6$

287. $\frac{h}{1.5} = -4.3$

ⓐ $h = 6.45$ ⓑ $h = -6.45$ ⓒ $h = -2.1$

288. $0.75k = -3.6$

ⓐ $k = -0.48$ ⓑ $k = -4.8$ ⓒ $k = -2.7$

Solve Equations with Decimals

In the following exercises, solve the equation.

289. $y + 2.9 = 5.7$

290. $m + 4.6 = 6.5$

291. $f + 3.45 = 2.6$

292. $h + 4.37 = 3.5$

293. $a + 6.2 = -1.7$

294. $b + 5.8 = -2.3$

295. $c + 1.15 = -3.5$

296. $d + 2.35 = -4.8$

297. $n - 2.6 = 1.8$

298. $p - 3.6 = 1.7$

299. $x - 0.4 = -3.9$

300. $y - 0.6 = -4.5$

301. $j - 1.82 = -6.5$

302. $k - 3.19 = -4.6$

303. $m - 0.25 = -1.67$

304. $q - 0.47 = -1.53$

305. $0.5x = 3.5$

306. $0.4p = 9.2$

307. $-1.7c = 8.5$

308. $-2.9x = 5.8$

309. $-1.4p = -4.2$

310. $-2.8m = -8.4$

311. $-120 = 1.5q$

312. $-75 = 1.5y$

313. $0.24x = 4.8$

314. $0.18n = 5.4$

315. $-3.4z = -9.18$

316. $-2.7u = -9.72$

317. $\frac{a}{0.4} = -20$

318. $\frac{b}{0.3} = -9$

319. $\frac{x}{0.7} = -0.4$

320. $\frac{y}{0.8} = -0.7$

321. $\frac{p}{-5} = -1.65$

322. $\frac{q}{-4} = -5.92$

323. $\frac{r}{-1.2} = -6$

324. $\frac{s}{-1.5} = -3$

Mixed Practice

In the following exercises, solve the equation. Then check your solution.

325. $x - 5 = -11$

326. $-\frac{2}{5} = x + \frac{3}{4}$

327. $p + 8 = -2$

328. $p + \frac{2}{3} = \frac{1}{12}$

329. $-4.2m = -33.6$

330. $q + 9.5 = -14$

331. $q + \frac{5}{6} = \frac{1}{12}$

332. $\frac{8.6}{15} = -d$

333. $\frac{7}{8}m = \frac{1}{10}$

334. $\frac{j}{-6.2} = -3$

335. $-\frac{2}{3} = y + \frac{3}{8}$

336. $s - 1.75 = -3.2$

337. $\frac{11}{20} = -f$

338. $-3.6b = 2.52$

339. $-4.2a = 3.36$

340. $-9.1n = -63.7$

341. $r - 1.25 = -2.7$

342. $\frac{1}{4}n = \frac{7}{10}$

343. $\frac{h}{-3} = -8$

344. $y - 7.82 = -16$

Translate to an Equation and Solve

In the following exercises, translate and solve.

345. The difference of n and 1.9 is 3.4.

346. The difference n and 1.5 is 0.8.

347. The product of -6.2 and x is -4.96.

348. The product of -4.6 and x is -3.22.

349. The quotient of y and -1.7 is -5.

350. The quotient of z and -3.6 is 3.

351. The sum of n and -7.3 is 2.4.

352. The sum of n and -5.1 is 3.8.

Everyday Math

353. Shawn bought a pair of shoes on sale for $78. Solve the equation $0.75p = 78$ to find the original price of the shoes, p.

354. Mary bought a new refrigerator. The total price including sales tax was $1,350. Find the retail price, r, of the refrigerator before tax by solving the equation $1.08r = 1,350$.

Writing Exercises

355. Think about solving the equation $1.2y = 60$, but do not actually solve it. Do you think the solution should be greater than 60 or less than 60? Explain your reasoning. Then solve the equation to see if your thinking was correct.

356. Think about solving the equation $0.8x = 200$, but do not actually solve it. Do you think the solution should be greater than 200 or less than 200? Explain your reasoning. Then solve the equation to see if your thinking was correct.

Self Check

ⓐ *After completing the exercises, use this checklist to evaluate your mastery of the objectives of this section.*

I can...	Confidently	With some help	No-I don't get it!
determine whether a decimal is a solution of an equation.			
solve equations with decimals.			
translate to an equation and solve.			

ⓑ *On a scale of 1–10, how would you rate your mastery of this section in light of your responses on the checklist? How can you improve this?*

5.5 | Averages and Probability

Learning Objectives

By the end of this section, you will be able to:

- Calculate the mean of a set of numbers
- Find the median of a set of numbers
- Find the mode of a set of numbers
- Apply the basic definition of probability

Be Prepared!

Before you get started, take this readiness quiz.

1. Simplify: $\dfrac{4+9+2}{3}$.

   If you missed this problem, review Example 4.48.

2. Simplify: $4(8) + 6(3)$.

   If you missed this problem, review Example 2.8.

3. Convert $\dfrac{5}{2}$ to a decimal.

   If you missed this problem, review Example 5.28.

One application of decimals that arises often is finding the *average* of a set of numbers. What do you think of when you hear the word *average*? Is it your grade point average, the average rent for an apartment in your city, the batting average of a player on your favorite baseball team? The average is a typical value in a set of numerical data. Calculating an average sometimes involves working with decimal numbers. In this section, we will look at three different ways to calculate an average.

Calculate the Mean of a Set of Numbers

The mean is often called the arithmetic average. It is computed by dividing the sum of the values by the number of values. Students want to know the mean of their test scores. Climatologists report that the mean temperature has, or has not, changed. City planners are interested in the mean household size.

Suppose Ethan's first three test scores were $85, 88,$ and 94. To find the mean score, he would add them and divide by 3.

$$\frac{85 + 88 + 94}{3}$$
$$\frac{267}{3}$$
$$89$$

His mean test score is 89 points.

The Mean

The **mean** of a set of n numbers is the arithmetic average of the numbers.

$$\text{mean} = \frac{\text{sum of values in data set}}{n}$$

HOW TO :: CALCULATE THE MEAN OF A SET OF NUMBERS.

Step 1.   Write the formula for the mean

$$\text{mean} = \frac{\text{sum of values in data set}}{n}$$

Step 2.   Find the sum of all the values in the set. Write the sum in the numerator.

Step 3.   Count the number, n, of values in the set. Write this number in the denominator.

Step 4.   Simplify the fraction.

Step 5.   Check to see that the mean is reasonable. It should be greater than the least number and less than the greatest number in the set.

EXAMPLE 5.49

Find the mean of the numbers 8, 12, 15, 9, and 6.

⊘ **Solution**

Write the formula for the mean:	$\text{mean} = \frac{\text{sum of all the numbers}}{n}$
Write the sum of the numbers in the numerator.	$\text{mean} = \frac{8 + 12 + 15 + 9 + 6}{n}$
Count how many numbers are in the set. There are 5 numbers in the set, so $n = 5$.	$\text{mean} = \frac{8 + 12 + 15 + 9 + 6}{5}$
Add the numbers in the numerator.	$\text{mean} = \frac{50}{5}$
Then divide.	$\text{mean} = 10$
Check to see that the mean is 'typical': 10 is neither less than 6 nor greater than 15.	The mean is 10.

> **TRY IT :: 5.97**   Find the mean of the numbers: 8, 9, 7, 12, 10; 5.

> **TRY IT :: 5.98**   Find the mean of the numbers: 9, 13, 11, 7, 5.

EXAMPLE 5.50

The ages of the members of a family who got together for a birthday celebration were 16, 26, 53, 56, 65, 70, 93, and 97 years. Find the mean age.

Solution

Write the formula for the mean:	$\text{mean} = \dfrac{\text{sum of all the numbers}}{n}$
Write the sum of the numbers in the numerator.	$\text{mean} = \dfrac{16 + 26 + 53 + 56 + 65 + 70 + 93 + 97}{n}$
Count how many numbers are in the set. Call this n and write it in the denominator.	$\text{mean} = \dfrac{16 + 26 + 53 + 56 + 65 + 70 + 93 + 97}{8}$
Simplify the fraction.	$\text{mean} = \dfrac{476}{8}$
	$\text{mean} = 59.5$

Is 59.5 'typical'? Yes, it is neither less than 16 nor greater than 97. The mean age is 59.5 years.

> **TRY IT ::** 5.99

The ages of the four students in Ben's carpool are 25, 18, 21, and 22. Find the mean age of the students.

> **TRY IT ::** 5.100

Yen counted the number of emails she received last week. The numbers were 4, 9, 15, 12, 10, 12, and 8. Find the mean number of emails.

Did you notice that in the last example, while all the numbers were whole numbers, the mean was 59.5, a number with one decimal place? It is customary to report the mean to one more decimal place than the original numbers. In the next example, all the numbers represent money, and it will make sense to report the mean in dollars and cents.

EXAMPLE 5.51

For the past four months, Daisy's cell phone bills were $42.75, $50.12, $41.54, $48.15. Find the mean cost of Daisy's cell phone bills.

Solution

Write the formula for the mean.	$\text{mean} = \dfrac{\text{sum of all the numbers}}{n}$
Count how many numbers are in the set. Call this n and write it in the denominator.	$\text{mean} = \dfrac{\text{sum of all the numbers}}{4}$
Write the sum of all the numbers in the numerator.	$\text{mean} = \dfrac{42.75 + 50.12 + 41.54 + 48.15}{4}$
Simplify the fraction.	$\text{mean} = \dfrac{182.56}{4}$
	$\text{mean} = 45.64$

Does $45.64 seem 'typical' of this set of numbers? Yes, it is neither less than $41.54 nor greater than $50.12.

The mean cost of her cell phone bill was $45.64

> **TRY IT : :** 5.101
>
> Last week Ray recorded how much he spent for lunch each workday. He spent $6.50, $7.25, $4.90, $5.30, and $12.00. Find the mean of how much he spent each day.

> **TRY IT : :** 5.102
>
> Lisa has kept the receipts from the past four trips to the gas station. The receipts show the following amounts: $34.87, $42.31, $38.04, and $43.26. Find the mean.

Find the Median of a Set of Numbers

When Ann, Bianca, Dora, Eve, and Francine sing together on stage, they line up in order of their heights. Their heights, in inches, are shown in Table 5.70.

Ann	Bianca	Dora	Eve	Francine
59	60	65	68	70

Table 5.70

Dora is in the middle of the group. Her height, $65''$, is the *median* of the girls' heights. Half of the heights are less than or equal to Dora's height, and half are greater than or equal. The median is the middle value.

Median

The **median** of a set of data values is the middle value.
- Half the data values are less than or equal to the median.
- Half the data values are greater than or equal to the median.

What if Carmen, the pianist, joins the singing group on stage? Carmen is 62 inches tall, so she fits in the height order between Bianca and Dora. Now the data set looks like this:

$$59, 60, 62, 65, 68, 70$$

There is no single middle value. The heights of the six girls can be divided into two equal parts.

59 60 62   65 68 70

Statisticians have agreed that in cases like this the median is the mean of the two values closest to the middle. So the median is the mean of 62 and 65, $\frac{62 + 65}{2}$. The median height is 63.5 inches.

Notice that when the number of girls was 5, the median was the third height, but when the number of girls was 6, the median was the mean of the third and fourth heights. In general, when the number of values is odd, the median will be the one value in the middle, but when the number is even, the median is the mean of the two middle values.

HOW TO :: FIND THE MEDIAN OF A SET OF NUMBERS.

Step 1.   List the numbers from smallest to largest.

Step 2.   Count how many numbers are in the set. Call this n.

Step 3.   Is n odd or even?

◦ If n is an odd number, the median.is the middle value.

◦ If n is an even number, the median is the mean of the two middle values.

EXAMPLE 5.52

Find the median of 12, 13, 19, 9, 11, 15, and 18.

⊘ **Solution**

List the numbers in order from smallest to largest.	9, 11, 12, 13, 15, 18, 19
Count how many numbers are in the set. Call this n.	$n = 7$
Is n odd or even?	odd
The median is the middle value.	median ↓ 9, 11, 12, **13,** 15, 18, 19 — 3 below — — 3 above —
The middle is the number in the 4th position.	So the median of the data is 13.

> **TRY IT :: 5.103**   Find the median of the data set: 43, 38, 51, 40, 46.

> **TRY IT :: 5.104**   Find the median of the data set: 15, 35, 20, 45, 50, 25, 30.

EXAMPLE 5.53

Kristen received the following scores on her weekly math quizzes:

83, 79, 85, 86, 92, 100, 76, 90, 88, and 64. Find her median score.

⊘ **Solution**

Find the median of 83, 79, 85, 86, 92, 100, 76, 90, 88, and 64.	
List the numbers in order from smallest to largest.	64, 76, 79, 83, 85, 86, 88, 90, 92, 100
Count the number of data values in the set. Call this n.	$n = 10$
Is n odd or even?	even

The median is the mean of the two middle values, the 5th and 6th numbers.

64, 76, 79, 83, **85,**   **86,** 88, 90, 92, 100

⎵⎵⎵ 5 numbers   ⎵⎵⎵ 5 numbers

Find the mean of 85 and 86.

$$\text{mean} = \frac{85 + 86}{2}$$

$$\text{mean} = 85.5$$

Kristen's median score is 85.5.

> **TRY IT : : 5.105**   Find the median of the data set: $8, 7, 5, 10, 9, 12$.

> **TRY IT : : 5.106**   Find the median of the data set: $21, 25, 19, 17, 22, 18, 20, 24$.

Identify the Mode of a Set of Numbers

The *average* is one number in a set of numbers that is somehow typical of the whole set of numbers. The mean and median are both often called the average. Yes, it can be confusing when the word average refers to two different numbers, the mean and the median! In fact, there is a third number that is also an average. This average is the **mode**. The mode of a set of numbers is the number that occurs the most. The **frequency**, is the number of times a number occurs. So the mode of a set of numbers is the number with the highest frequency.

Mode

The **mode** of a set of numbers is the number with the highest frequency.

Suppose Jolene kept track of the number of miles she ran since the start of the month, as shown in Figure 5.7.

Sunday	Monday	Tuesday	Wednesday	Thursday	Friday	Saturday
				1 2 mi New Year's day	2	3 15 mi
4 8 mi	5	6 3 mi	7 8 mi	8	9 5 mi	10 8 mi
11	12	13	14	15	16	17

Figure 5.7

If we list the numbers in order it is easier to identify the one with the highest frequency.

$$2, 3, 5, 8, 8, 8, 15$$

Jolene ran 8 miles three times, and every other distance is listed only once. So the mode of the data is 8 miles.

HOW TO :: IDENTIFY THE MODE OF A SET OF NUMBERS.

Step 1.   List the data values in numerical order.

Step 2.   Count the number of times each value appears.

Step 3.   The mode is the value with the highest frequency.

EXAMPLE 5.54

The ages of students in a college math class are listed below. Identify the mode.

18, 18, 18, 18, 19, 19, 19, 20, 20, 20, 20, 20, 20, 20, 21, 21, 22, 22, 22, 22, 22, 23, 24, 24, 25, 29, 30, 40, 44

⊘ **Solution**

The ages are already listed in order. We will make a table of frequencies to help identify the age with the highest frequency.

Age	18	19	20	21	22	23	24	25	29	30	40	44
Frequency	4	3	7	2	5	1	2	1	1	1	1	1

Now look for the highest frequency. The highest frequency is 7, which corresponds to the age 20. So the mode of the ages in this class is 20 years.

> **TRY IT :: 5.107**
>
> The number of sick days employees used last year: 3, 6, 2, 3, 7, 5, 6, 2, 4, 2. Identify the mode.

> **TRY IT :: 5.108**
>
> The number of handbags owned by women in a book club: 5, 6, 3, 1, 5, 8, 1, 5, 8, 5. Identify the mode.

EXAMPLE 5.55

The data lists the heights (in inches) of students in a statistics class. Identify the mode.

56	61	63	64	65	66	67	67
60	62	63	64	65	66	67	70
60	63	63	64	66	66	67	74
61	63	64	65	66	67	67	

⊘ **Solution**

List each number with its frequency.

Number	56	60	61	62	63	64	65	66	67	70	74
Frequency	1	2	2	1	5	4	3	5	6	1	1

Now look for the highest frequency. The highest frequency is 6, which corresponds to the height 67 inches. So the mode of this set of heights is 67 inches.

> **TRY IT : : 5.109**

> The ages of the students in a statistics class are listed here: 19, 20, 23, 23, 38, 21, 19, 21, 19, 21, 20, 43, 20, 23, 17, 21, 21, 20, 29, 18, 28. What is the mode?

> **TRY IT : : 5.110**

> Students listed the number of members in their household as follows: 6, 2, 5, 6, 3, 7, 5, 6, 5, 3, 4, 4, 5, 7, 6, 4, 5, 2, 1, 5. What is the mode?

Some data sets do not have a mode because no value appears more than any other. And some data sets have more than one mode. In a given set, if two or more data values have the same highest frequency, we say they are all modes.

Use the Basic Definition of Probability

The probability of an event tells us how likely that event is to occur. We usually write probabilities as fractions or decimals.

For example, picture a fruit bowl that contains five pieces of fruit - three bananas and two apples.

If you want to choose one piece of fruit to eat for a snack and don't care what it is, there is a $\frac{3}{5}$ probability you will choose a banana, because there are three bananas out of the total of five pieces of fruit. The probability of an event is the number of favorable outcomes divided by the total number of outcomes.

$$\text{Probability of an event} = \frac{\text{number of favorable outcomes}}{\text{total number of outcomes}}$$

$$\text{Probability of choosing a banana} = \frac{3}{5} \quad \begin{array}{l} \text{There are 3 bananas.} \\ \text{There are 5 pieces of fruit.} \end{array}$$

Probability

The **probability** of an event is the number of favorable outcomes divided by the total number of outcomes possible.

$$\text{Probability} = \frac{\text{number of favorable outcomes}}{\text{total number of outcomes}}$$

Converting the fraction $\frac{3}{5}$ to a decimal, we would say there is a 0.6 probability of choosing a banana.

$$\text{Probability of choosing a banana} = \frac{3}{5}$$

$$\text{Probability of choosing a banana} = 0.6$$

This basic definition of probability assumes that all the outcomes are equally likely to occur. If you study probabilities in a later math class, you'll learn about several other ways to calculate probabilities.

EXAMPLE 5.56

The ski club is holding a raffle to raise money. They sold 100 tickets. All of the tickets are placed in a jar. One ticket will be pulled out of the jar at random, and the winner will receive a prize. Cherie bought one raffle ticket.

ⓐ Find the probability she will win the prize.

ⓑ Convert the fraction to a decimal.

✓ Solution

ⓐ

What are you asked to find?	The probability Cherie wins the prize.
What is the number of favorable outcomes?	1, because Cherie has 1 ticket.
Use the definition of probability.	Probability of an event $= \dfrac{\text{number of favorable outcomes}}{\text{total number of outcomes}}$
Substitute into the numerator and denominator.	Probability Cherie wins $= \dfrac{1}{100}$

ⓑ

Convert the fraction to a decimal.	
Write the probability as a fraction.	Probability $= \dfrac{1}{100}$
Convert the fraction to a decimal.	Probability $= 0.01$

> **TRY IT : : 5.111**
>
> Ignaly is attending a fashion show where the guests are seated at tables of ten. One guest from each table will be selected at random to receive a door prize. ⓐ Find the probability Ignaly will win the door prize for her table. ⓑ Convert the fraction to a decimal.

> **TRY IT : : 5.112**
>
> Hoang is among 20 people available to sit on a jury. One person will be chosen at random from the 20. ⓐ Find the probability Hoang will be chosen. ⓑ Convert the fraction to a decimal.

EXAMPLE 5.57

Three women and five men interviewed for a job. One of the candidates will be offered the job.

ⓐ Find the probability the job is offered to a woman.

ⓑ Convert the fraction to a decimal.

Solution

ⓐ

What are you asked to find?	The probability the job is offered to a woman.
What is the number of favorable outcomes?	3, because there are three women.
What are the total number of outcomes?	8, because 8 people interviewed.

Use the definition of probability.

$$\text{Probability of an event} = \frac{\text{number of favorable outcomes}}{\text{total number of outcomes}}$$

Substitute into the numerator and denominator.

$$\text{Probability} = \frac{3}{8}$$

ⓑ

Convert the fraction to a decimal.

Write the probability as a fraction. $\text{Probability} = \frac{3}{8}$

Convert the fraction to a decimal. $\text{Probability} = 0.375$

> **TRY IT ::** 5.113

A bowl of Halloween candy contains 5 chocolate candies and 3 lemon candies. Tanya will choose one piece of candy at random. ⓐ Find the probability Tanya will choose a chocolate candy. ⓑ Convert the fraction to a decimal.

> **TRY IT ::** 5.114

Dan has 2 pairs of black socks and 6 pairs of blue socks. He will choose one pair at random to wear tomorrow. ⓐ Find the probability Dan will choose a pair of black socks ⓑ Convert the fraction to a decimal.

> **MEDIA ::** ACCESS ADDITIONAL ONLINE RESOURCES
> - Mean, Median, and Mode (http://www.openstaxcollege.org/l/24meanmedmode)
> - Find the Mean of a Data Set (http://www.openstaxcollege.org/l/24meandataset)
> - Find the Median of a Data Set (http://www.openstaxcollege.org/l/24meddataset)
> - Find the Mode of a Data Set (http://www.openstaxcollege.org/l/24modedataset)

5.5 EXERCISES

Practice Makes Perfect

Calculate the Mean of a Set of Numbers

In the following exercises, find the mean.

357. 3, 8, 2, 2, 5

358. 6, 1, 9, 3, 4, 7

359. 65, 13, 48, 32, 19, 33

360. 34, 45, 29, 61, and 41

361. 202, 241, 265, 274

362. 525, 532, 558, 574

363. 12.45, 12.99, 10.50, 11.25, 9.99, 12.72

364. 28.8, 32.9, 32.5, 27.9, 30.4, 32.5, 31.6, 32.7

365. Four girls leaving a mall were asked how much money they had just spent. The amounts were $0, $14.95, $35.25, and $25.16. Find the mean amount of money spent.

366. Juan bought 5 shirts to wear to his new job. The costs of the shirts were $32.95, $38.50, $30.00, $17.45, and $24.25. Find the mean cost.

367. The number of minutes it took Jim to ride his bike to school for each of the past six days was 21, 18, 16, 19, 24, and 19. Find the mean number of minutes.

368. Norris bought six books for his classes this semester. The costs of the books were $74.28, $120.95, $52.40, $10.59, $35.89, and $59.24. Find the mean cost.

369. The top eight hitters in a softball league have batting averages of .373, .360, .321, .321, .320, .312, .311, and .311. Find the mean of the batting averages. Round your answer to the nearest thousandth.

370. The monthly snowfall at a ski resort over a six-month period was 60.3, 79.7, 50.9, 28.0, 47.4, and 46.1 inches. Find the mean snowfall.

Find the Median of a Set of Numbers

In the following exercises, find the median.

371. 24, 19, 18, 29, 21

372. 48, 51, 46, 42, 50

373. 65, 56, 35, 34, 44, 39, 55, 52, 45

374. 121, 115, 135, 109, 136, 147, 127, 119, 110

375. 4, 8, 1, 5, 14, 3, 1, 12

376. 3, 9, 2, 6, 20, 3, 3, 10

377. 99.2, 101.9, 98.6, 99.5, 100.8, 99.8

378. 28.8, 32.9, 32.5, 27.9, 30.4, 32.5, 31.6, 32.7

379. Last week Ray recorded how much he spent for lunch each workday. He spent $6.50, $7.25, $4.90, $5.30, and $12.00. Find the median.

380. Michaela is in charge of 6 two-year olds at a daycare center. Their ages, in months, are 25, 24, 28, 32, 29, and 31. Find the median age.

381. Brian is teaching a swim class for 6 three-year olds. Their ages, in months, are 38, 41, 45, 36, 40, and 42. Find the median age.

382. Sal recorded the amount he spent for gas each week for the past 8 weeks. The amounts were $38.65, $32.18, $40.23, $51.50, $43.68, $30.96, $41.37, and $44.72. Find the median amount.

Identify the Mode of a Set of Numbers

In the following exercises, identify the mode.

383. 2 , 5 , 1 , 5 , 2 , 1 , 2 , 3 , 2 , 3 , 1

384. 8 , 5 , 1 , 3 , 7 , 1 , 1 , 7 , 1 , 8 , 7

385. 18 , 22 , 17 , 20 , 19 , 20 , 22 , 19 , 29 , 18 , 23 , 25 , 22 , 24 , 23 , 22 , 18 , 20 , 22 , 20

386. 42 , 28 , 32 , 35 , 24 , 32 , 48 , 32 , 32 , 24 , 35 , 28 , 30 , 35 , 45 , 32 , 28 , 32 , 42 , 42 , 30

387. The number of children per house on one block: 1 , 4 , 2 , 3 , 3 , 2 , 6 , 2 , 4 , 2 , 0 , 3 , 0.

388. The number of movies watched each month last year: 2 , 0 , 3 , 0 , 0 , 8 , 6 , 5 , 0 , 1 , 2 , 3.

389. The number of units being taken by students in one class: 12 , 5 , 11 , 10 , 10 , 11 , 5 , 11 , 11 , 11 , 10 , 12.

390. The number of hours of sleep per night for the past two weeks: 8 , 5 , 7 , 8 , 8 , 6 , 6 , 6 , 6 , 9 , 7 , 8 , 8 , 8.

Use the Basic Definition of Probability

In the following exercises, express the probability as both a fraction and a decimal. (Round to three decimal places, if necessary.)

391. Josue is in a book club with 20 members. One member is chosen at random each month to select the next month's book. Find the probability that Josue will be chosen next month.

392. Jessica is one of eight kindergarten teachers at Mandela Elementary School. One of the kindergarten teachers will be selected at random to attend a summer workshop. Find the probability that Jessica will be selected.

393. There are 24 people who work in Dane's department. Next week, one person will be selected at random to bring in doughnuts. Find the probability that Dane will be selected. Round your answer to the nearest thousandth.

394. Monica has two strawberry yogurts and six banana yogurts in her refrigerator. She will choose one yogurt at random to take to work. Find the probability Monica will choose a strawberry yogurt.

395. Michel has four rock CDs and six country CDs in his car. He will pick one CD to play on his way to work. Find the probability Michel will pick a rock CD.

396. Noah is planning his summer camping trip. He can't decide among six campgrounds at the beach and twelve campgrounds in the mountains, so he will choose one campground at random. Find the probability that Noah will choose a campground at the beach.

397. Donovan is considering transferring to a 4-year college. He is considering 10 out-of state colleges and 4 colleges in his state. He will choose one college at random to visit during spring break. Find the probability that Donovan will choose an out-of-state college.

398. There are 258,890,850 number combinations possible in the Mega Millions lottery. One winning jackpot ticket will be chosen at random. Brent chooses his favorite number combination and buys one ticket. Find the probability Brent will win the jackpot. Round the decimal to the first digit that is not zero, then write the name of the decimal.

Everyday Math

399. Joaquin gets paid every Friday. His paychecks for the past 8 Fridays were $315, $236.25, $236.25, $236.25 $315, $315, $236.25, $393.75. Find the ⓐ mean, ⓑ median, and ⓒ mode.

400. The cash register receipts each day last week at a coffee shop were $1,845, $1,520, $1,438, $1,682, $1,850, $2,721, $2,539. Find the ⓐ mean, ⓑ median, and ⓒ mode.

Writing Exercises

401. Explain in your own words the difference between the mean, median, and mode of a set of numbers.

402. Make an example of probability that relates to your life. Write your answer as a fraction and explain what the numerator and denominator represent.

Self Check

ⓐ *After completing the exercises, use this checklist to evaluate your mastery of the objectives of this section.*

I can...	Confidently	With some help	No-I don't get it!
calculate the mean of a set of numbers.			
find the median of a set of numbers.			
find the mode of a set of numbers.			
use the basic definition of probability.			

ⓑ *After looking at the checklist, do you think you are well prepared for the next section? Why or why not?*

5.6 | Ratios and Rate

Learning Objectives

By the end of this section, you will be able to:

- Write a ratio as a fraction
- Write a rate as a fraction
- Find unit rates
- Find unit price
- Translate phrases to expressions with fractions

Be Prepared!

Before you get started, take this readiness quiz.

1. Simplify: $\frac{16}{24}$.

   If you missed this problem, review Example 4.19.

2. Divide: $2.76 \div 11.5$.

   If you missed this problem, review Example 5.19.

3. Simplify: $\frac{1\frac{1}{2}}{2\frac{3}{4}}$.

   If you missed this problem, review Example 4.43.

Write a Ratio as a Fraction

When you apply for a mortgage, the loan officer will compare your total debt to your total income to decide if you qualify for the loan. This comparison is called the debt-to-income ratio. A **ratio** compares two quantities that are measured with the same unit. If we compare a and b, the ratio is written as a to b, $\frac{a}{b}$, or $a:b$.

Ratios

A **ratio** compares two numbers or two quantities that are measured with the same unit. The ratio of a to b is written

a to b, $\frac{a}{b}$, or $a:b$.

In this section, we will use the fraction notation. When a ratio is written in fraction form, the fraction should be simplified. If it is an improper fraction, we do not change it to a mixed number. Because a ratio compares two quantities, we would leave a ratio as $\frac{4}{1}$ instead of simplifying it to 4 so that we can see the two parts of the ratio.

EXAMPLE 5.58

Write each ratio as a fraction: ⓐ 15 to 27 ⓑ 45 to 18.

 Solution

ⓐ

15 to 27

Write as a fraction with the first number in the numerator and the second in the denominator. $\frac{15}{27}$

Simplify the fraction. $\frac{5}{9}$

ⓑ

	45 to 18
Write as a fraction with the first number in the numerator and the second in the denominator.	$\frac{45}{18}$
Simplify.	$\frac{5}{2}$

We leave the ratio in ⓑ as an improper fraction.

> **TRY IT ::** 5.115   Write each ratio as a fraction: ⓐ 21 to 56 ⓑ 48 to 32.

> **TRY IT ::** 5.116   Write each ratio as a fraction: ⓐ 27 to 72 ⓑ 51 to 34.

Ratios Involving Decimals

We will often work with ratios of decimals, especially when we have ratios involving money. In these cases, we can eliminate the decimals by using the Equivalent Fractions Property to convert the ratio to a fraction with whole numbers in the numerator and denominator.

For example, consider the ratio 0.8 to 0.05. We can write it as a fraction with decimals and then multiply the numerator and denominator by 100 to eliminate the decimals.

$$\frac{0.8}{0.05}$$
$$\frac{(0.8)100}{(0.05)100}$$
$$\frac{80}{5}$$

Do you see a shortcut to find the equivalent fraction? Notice that $0.8 = \frac{8}{10}$ and $0.05 = \frac{5}{100}$. The least common denominator of $\frac{8}{10}$ and $\frac{5}{100}$ is 100. By multiplying the numerator and denominator of $\frac{0.8}{0.05}$ by 100, we 'moved' the decimal two places to the right to get the equivalent fraction with no decimals. Now that we understand the math behind the process, we can find the fraction with no decimals like this:

$$\frac{0.80}{0.05}$$

"Move" the decimal 2 places.	$\frac{80}{5}$
Simplify.	$\frac{16}{1}$

You do not have to write out every step when you multiply the numerator and denominator by powers of ten. As long as you move both decimal places the same number of places, the ratio will remain the same.

EXAMPLE 5.59

Write each ratio as a fraction of whole numbers:

ⓐ 4.8 to 11.2

ⓑ 2.7 to 0.54

✓ **Solution**

ⓐ 4.8 to 11.2

Write as a fraction.	$\dfrac{4.8}{11.2}$
Rewrite as an equivalent fraction without decimals, by moving both decimal points 1 place to the right.	$\dfrac{48}{112}$
Simplify.	$\dfrac{3}{7}$

So 4.8 to 11.2 is equivalent to $\dfrac{3}{7}$.

ⓑ

The numerator has one decimal place and the denominator has 2. To clear both decimals we need to move the decimal 2 places to the right.
2.7 to 0.54

Write as a fraction.	$\dfrac{2.7}{0.54}$
Move both decimals right two places.	$\dfrac{270}{54}$
Simplify.	$\dfrac{5}{1}$

So 2.7 to 0.54 is equivalent to $\dfrac{5}{1}$.

> **TRY IT : : 5.117**   Write each ratio as a fraction: ⓐ 4.6 to 11.5 ⓑ 2.3 to 0.69.

> **TRY IT : : 5.118**   Write each ratio as a fraction: ⓐ 3.4 to 15.3 ⓑ 3.4 to 0.68.

Some ratios compare two mixed numbers. Remember that to divide mixed numbers, you first rewrite them as improper fractions.

EXAMPLE 5.60

Write the ratio of $1\frac{1}{4}$ to $2\frac{3}{8}$ as a fraction.

Solution

	$1\frac{1}{4}$ to $2\frac{3}{8}$
Write as a fraction.	$\dfrac{1\frac{1}{4}}{2\frac{3}{8}}$
Convert the numerator and denominator to improper fractions.	$\dfrac{\frac{5}{4}}{\frac{19}{8}}$
Rewrite as a division of fractions.	$\dfrac{5}{4} \div \dfrac{19}{8}$
Invert the divisor and multiply.	$\dfrac{5}{4} \cdot \dfrac{8}{19}$
Simplify.	$\dfrac{10}{19}$

> **TRY IT ::** 5.119   Write each ratio as a fraction: $1\frac{3}{4}$ to $2\frac{5}{8}$.

> **TRY IT ::** 5.120   Write each ratio as a fraction: $1\frac{1}{8}$ to $2\frac{3}{4}$.

Applications of Ratios

One real-world application of ratios that affects many people involves measuring cholesterol in blood. The ratio of total cholesterol to HDL cholesterol is one way doctors assess a person's overall health. A ratio of less than 5 to 1 is considered good.

EXAMPLE 5.61

Hector's total cholesterol is 249 mg/dl and his HDL cholesterol is 39 mg/dl. ⓐ Find the ratio of his total cholesterol to his HDL cholesterol. ⓑ Assuming that a ratio less than 5 to 1 is considered good, what would you suggest to Hector?

Solution

ⓐ First, write the words that express the ratio. We want to know the ratio of Hector's total cholesterol to his HDL cholesterol.

Write as a fraction.	$\dfrac{\text{total cholesterol}}{\text{HDL cholesterol}}$
Substitute the values.	$\dfrac{249}{39}$
Simplify.	$\dfrac{83}{13}$

ⓑ Is Hector's cholesterol ratio ok? If we divide 83 by 13 we obtain approximately 6.4, so $\dfrac{83}{13} \approx \dfrac{6.4}{1}$. Hector's cholesterol ratio is high! Hector should either lower his total cholesterol or raise his HDL cholesterol.

> **TRY IT : : 5.121**   Find the patient's ratio of total cholesterol to HDL cholesterol using the given information.

Total cholesterol is 185 mg/dL and HDL cholesterol is 40 mg/dL.

> **TRY IT : : 5.122**   Find the patient's ratio of total cholesterol to HDL cholesterol using the given information.

Total cholesterol is 204 mg/dL and HDL cholesterol is 38 mg/dL.

Ratios of Two Measurements in Different Units

To find the ratio of two measurements, we must make sure the quantities have been measured with the same unit. If the measurements are not in the same units, we must first convert them to the same units.

We know that to simplify a fraction, we divide out common factors. Similarly in a ratio of measurements, we divide out the common unit.

EXAMPLE 5.62

The Americans with Disabilities Act (ADA) Guidelines for wheel chair ramps require a maximum vertical rise of 1 inch for every 1 foot of horizontal run. What is the ratio of the rise to the run?

⊘ **Solution**

In a ratio, the measurements must be in the same units. We can change feet to inches, or inches to feet. It is usually easier to convert to the smaller unit, since this avoids introducing more fractions into the problem.

Write the words that express the ratio.

	Ratio of the rise to the run
Write the ratio as a fraction.	$\dfrac{\text{rise}}{\text{run}}$
Substitute in the given values.	$\dfrac{1 \text{ inch}}{1 \text{ foot}}$
Convert 1 foot to inches.	$\dfrac{1 \text{ inch}}{12 \text{ inches}}$
Simplify, dividing out common factors and units.	$\dfrac{1}{12}$

So the ratio of rise to run is 1 to 12. This means that the ramp should rise 1 inch for every 12 inches of horizontal run to comply with the guidelines.

> **TRY IT : : 5.123**   Find the ratio of the first length to the second length: 32 inches to 1 foot.

> **TRY IT : : 5.124**   Find the ratio of the first length to the second length: 1 foot to 54 inches.

Write a Rate as a Fraction

Frequently we want to compare two different types of measurements, such as miles to gallons. To make this comparison, we use a **rate**. Examples of rates are 120 miles in 2 hours, 160 words in 4 minutes, and 5 dollars per 64 ounces.

Rate

A **rate** compares two quantities of different units. A rate is usually written as a fraction.

When writing a fraction as a rate, we put the first given amount with its units in the numerator and the second amount with its units in the denominator. When rates are simplified, the units remain in the numerator and denominator.

EXAMPLE 5.63

Bob drove his car 525 miles in 9 hours. Write this rate as a fraction.

⊘ **Solution**

	525 miles in 9 hours
Write as a fraction, with 525 miles in the numerator and 9 hours in the denominator.	$\dfrac{525 \text{ miles}}{9 \text{ hours}}$
	$\dfrac{175 \text{ miles}}{3 \text{ hours}}$

So 525 miles in 9 hours is equivalent to $\dfrac{175 \text{ miles}}{3 \text{ hours}}$.

> **TRY IT : : 5.125**   Write the rate as a fraction: 492 miles in 8 hours.

> **TRY IT : : 5.126**   Write the rate as a fraction: 242 miles in 6 hours.

Find Unit Rates

In the last example, we calculated that Bob was driving at a rate of $\dfrac{175 \text{ miles}}{3 \text{ hours}}$. This tells us that every three hours, Bob will travel 175 miles. This is correct, but not very useful. We usually want the rate to reflect the number of miles in one hour. A rate that has a denominator of 1 unit is referred to as a **unit rate**.

> **Unit Rate**
>
> A **unit rate** is a rate with denominator of 1 unit.

Unit rates are very common in our lives. For example, when we say that we are driving at a speed of 68 miles per hour we mean that we travel 68 miles in 1 hour. We would write this rate as 68 miles/hour (read 68 miles per hour). The common abbreviation for this is 68 mph. Note that when no number is written before a unit, it is assumed to be 1.

So 68 miles/hour really means 68 miles/1 hour.

Two rates we often use when driving can be written in different forms, as shown:

Example	Rate	Write	Abbreviate	Read
68 miles in 1 hour	$\dfrac{68 \text{ miles}}{1 \text{ hour}}$	68 miles/hour	68 mph	68 miles per hour
36 miles to 1 gallon	$\dfrac{36 \text{ miles}}{1 \text{ gallon}}$	36 miles/gallon	36 mpg	36 miles per gallon

Another example of unit rate that you may already know about is hourly pay rate. It is usually expressed as the amount of money earned for one hour of work. For example, if you are paid $12.50 for each hour you work, you could write that your hourly (unit) pay rate is $12.50/hour (read $12.50 per hour.)

To convert a rate to a unit rate, we divide the numerator by the denominator. This gives us a denominator of 1.

EXAMPLE 5.64

Anita was paid $384 last week for working 32 hours. What is Anita's hourly pay rate?

⊘ **Solution**

Start with a rate of dollars to hours. Then divide.	$384 last week for 32 hours
Write as a rate.	$\dfrac{\$384}{32 \text{ hours}}$
Divide the numerator by the denominator.	$\dfrac{\$12}{1 \text{ hour}}$
Rewrite as a rate.	$12 / hour

Anita's hourly pay rate is $12 per hour.

> **TRY IT : : 5.127**   Find the unit rate: $630 for 35 hours.

> **TRY IT : : 5.128**   Find the unit rate: $684 for 36 hours.

EXAMPLE 5.65

Sven drives his car 455 miles, using 14 gallons of gasoline. How many miles per gallon does his car get?

⊘ **Solution**

Start with a rate of miles to gallons. Then divide.

	455 miles to 14 gallons of gas
Write as a rate.	$\dfrac{455 \text{ miles}}{14 \text{ gallons}}$
Divide 455 by 14 to get the unit rate.	$\dfrac{32.5 \text{ miles}}{1 \text{ gallon}}$

Sven's car gets 32.5 miles/gallon, or 32.5 mpg.

> **TRY IT : : 5.129**   Find the unit rate: 423 miles to 18 gallons of gas.

> **TRY IT : : 5.130**   Find the unit rate: 406 miles to 14.5 gallons of gas.

Find Unit Price

Sometimes we buy common household items 'in bulk', where several items are packaged together and sold for one price. To compare the prices of different sized packages, we need to find the unit price. To find the unit price, divide the total price by the number of items. A **unit price** is a unit rate for one item.

Unit price

A **unit price** is a unit rate that gives the price of one item.

EXAMPLE 5.66

The grocery store charges $3.99 for a case of 24 bottles of water. What is the unit price?

⊘ Solution

What are we asked to find? We are asked to find the unit price, which is the price per bottle.

Write as a rate.	$\dfrac{\$3.99}{24 \text{ bottles}}$
Divide to find the unit price.	$\dfrac{\$0.16625}{1 \text{ bottle}}$
Round the result to the nearest penny.	$\dfrac{\$0.17}{1 \text{ bottle}}$

The unit price is approximately $\$0.17$ per bottle. Each bottle costs about $\$0.17.$

> **TRY IT : : 5.131** Find the unit price. Round your answer to the nearest cent if necessary.

   24-pack of juice boxes for $\$6.99$

> **TRY IT : : 5.132** Find the unit price. Round your answer to the nearest cent if necessary.

   24-pack of bottles of ice tea for $\$12.72$

Unit prices are very useful if you comparison shop. The *better buy* is the item with the lower unit price. Most grocery stores list the unit price of each item on the shelves.

EXAMPLE 5.67

Paul is shopping for laundry detergent. At the grocery store, the liquid detergent is priced at $\$14.99$ for 64 loads of laundry and the same brand of powder detergent is priced at $\$15.99$ for 80 loads.

Which is the better buy, the liquid or the powder detergent?

⊘ Solution

To compare the prices, we first find the unit price for each type of detergent.

	Liquid	Powder
Write as a rate.	$\dfrac{\$14.99}{64 \text{ loads}}$	$\dfrac{\$15.99}{80 \text{ loads}}$
Find the unit price.	$\dfrac{\$0.234\ldots}{1 \text{ load}}$	$\dfrac{\$0.199\ldots}{1 \text{ load}}$
Round to the nearest cent.	$\$0.23$/load (23 cents per load.)	$\$0.20$/load (20 cents per load)

Now we compare the unit prices. The unit price of the liquid detergent is about $\$0.23$ per load and the unit price of the powder detergent is about $\$0.20$ per load. The powder is the better buy.

> **TRY IT : : 5.133**

   Find each unit price and then determine the better buy. Round to the nearest cent if necessary.

   Brand A Storage Bags, $\$4.59$ for 40 count, or Brand B Storage Bags, $\$3.99$ for 30 count

TRY IT :: 5.134

Find each unit price and then determine the better buy. Round to the nearest cent if necessary.

Brand C Chicken Noodle Soup, $1.89 for 26 ounces, or Brand D Chicken Noodle Soup, $0.95 for 10.75 ounces

Notice in Example 5.67 that we rounded the unit price to the nearest cent. Sometimes we may need to carry the division to one more place to see the difference between the unit prices.

Translate Phrases to Expressions with Fractions

Have you noticed that the examples in this section used the comparison words *ratio of, to, per, in, for, on,* and *from*? When you translate phrases that include these words, you should think either ratio or rate. If the units measure the same quantity (length, time, etc.), you have a ratio. If the units are different, you have a rate. In both cases, you write a fraction.

EXAMPLE 5.68

Translate the word phrase into an algebraic expression:

ⓐ 427 miles per h hours

ⓑ x students to 3 teachers

ⓒ y dollars for 18 hours

✓ **Solution**

ⓐ

427 miles per h hours

Write as a rate. $\dfrac{427 \text{ miles}}{h \text{ hours}}$

ⓑ

x students to 3 teachers

Write as a rate. $\dfrac{x \text{ students}}{3 \text{ teachers}}$

ⓒ

y dollars for 18 hours

Write as a rate. $\dfrac{\$\, y}{18 \text{ hours}}$

TRY IT :: 5.135   Translate the word phrase into an algebraic expression.

ⓐ 689 miles per h hours ⓑ y parents to 22 students ⓒ d dollars for 9 minutes

TRY IT :: 5.136   Translate the word phrase into an algebraic expression.

ⓐ m miles per 9 hours ⓑ x students to 8 buses ⓒ y dollars for 40 hours

▶ **MEDIA : :** ACCESS ADDITIONAL ONLINE RESOURCES

- Ratios (http://www.openstaxcollege.org/l/24ratios)
- Write Ratios as a Simplified Fractions Involving Decimals and Fractions (http://www.openstaxcollege.org/l/24ratiosimpfrac)
- Write a Ratio as a Simplified Fraction (http://www.openstaxcollege.org/l/24ratiosimp)
- Rates and Unit Rates (http://www.openstaxcollege.org/l/24rates)
- Unit Rate for Cell Phone Plan (http://www.openstaxcollege.org/l/24unitrate)

5.6 EXERCISES

Practice Makes Perfect

Write a Ratio as a Fraction

In the following exercises, write each ratio as a fraction.

403. 20 to 36

404. 20 to 32

405. 42 to 48

406. 45 to 54

407. 49 to 21

408. 56 to 16

409. 84 to 36

410. 6.4 to 0.8

411. 0.56 to 2.8

412. 1.26 to 4.2

413. $1\frac{2}{3}$ to $2\frac{5}{6}$

414. $1\frac{3}{4}$ to $2\frac{5}{8}$

415. $4\frac{1}{6}$ to $3\frac{1}{3}$

416. $5\frac{3}{5}$ to $3\frac{3}{5}$

417. $18 to $63

418. $16 to $72

419. $1.21 to $0.44

420. $1.38 to $0.69

421. 28 ounces to 84 ounces

422. 32 ounces to 128 ounces

423. 12 feet to 46 feet

424. 15 feet to 57 feet

425. 246 milligrams to 45 milligrams

426. 304 milligrams to 48 milligrams

427. total cholesterol of 175 to HDL cholesterol of 45

428. total cholesterol of 215 to HDL cholesterol of 55

429. 27 inches to 1 foot

430. 28 inches to 1 foot

Write a Rate as a Fraction

In the following exercises, write each rate as a fraction.

431. 140 calories per 12 ounces

432. 180 calories per 16 ounces

433. 8.2 pounds per 3 square inches

434. 9.5 pounds per 4 square inches

435. 488 miles in 7 hours

436. 527 miles in 9 hours

437. $595 for 40 hours

438. $798 for 40 hours

Find Unit Rates

In the following exercises, find the unit rate. Round to two decimal places, if necessary.

439. 140 calories per 12 ounces

440. 180 calories per 16 ounces

441. 8.2 pounds per 3 square inches

442. 9.5 pounds per 4 square inches

443. 488 miles in 7 hours

444. 527 miles in 9 hours

445. $595 for 40 hours

446. $798 for 40 hours

447. 576 miles on 18 gallons of gas

448. 435 miles on 15 gallons of gas

449. 43 pounds in 16 weeks

450. 57 pounds in 24 weeks

451. 46 beats in 0.5 minute

452. 54 beats in 0.5 minute

453. The bindery at a printing plant assembles 96,000 magazines in 12 hours. How many magazines are assembled in one hour?

454. The pressroom at a printing plant prints 540,000 sections in 12 hours. How many sections are printed per hour?

Find Unit Price

In the following exercises, find the unit price. Round to the nearest cent.

455. Soap bars at 8 for $8.69

456. Soap bars at 4 for $3.39

457. Women's sports socks at 6 pairs for $7.99

458. Men's dress socks at 3 pairs for $8.49

459. Snack packs of cookies at 12 for $5.79

460. Granola bars at 5 for $3.69

461. CD-RW discs at 25 for $14.99

462. CDs at 50 for $4.49

463. The grocery store has a special on macaroni and cheese. The price is $3.87 for 3 boxes. How much does each box cost?

464. The pet store has a special on cat food. The price is $4.32 for 12 cans. How much does each can cost?

In the following exercises, find each unit price and then identify the better buy. Round to three decimal places.

465. Mouthwash, 50.7-ounce size for $6.99 or 33.8-ounce size for $4.79

466. Toothpaste, 6 ounce size for $3.19 or 7.8-ounce size for $5.19

467. Breakfast cereal, 18 ounces for $3.99 or 14 ounces for $3.29

468. Breakfast Cereal, 10.7 ounces for $2.69 or 14.8 ounces for $3.69

469. Ketchup, 40-ounce regular bottle for $2.99 or 64-ounce squeeze bottle for $4.39

470. Mayonnaise 15-ounce regular bottle for $3.49 or 22-ounce squeeze bottle for $4.99

471. Cheese $6.49 for 1 lb. block or $3.39 for $\frac{1}{2}$ lb. block

472. Candy $10.99 for a 1 lb. bag or $2.89 for $\frac{1}{4}$ lb. of loose candy

Translate Phrases to Expressions with Fractions

In the following exercises, translate the English phrase into an algebraic expression.

473. 793 miles per p hours

474. 78 feet per r seconds

475. $3 for 0.5 lbs.

476. j beats in 0.5 minutes

477. 105 calories in x ounces

478. 400 minutes for m dollars

479. the ratio of y and $5x$ **480.** the ratio of $12x$ and y

Everyday Math

481. One elementary school in Ohio has 684 students and 45 teachers. Write the student-to-teacher ratio as a unit rate.

482. The average American produces about $1,600$ pounds of paper trash per year (365 days). How many pounds of paper trash does the average American produce each day? (Round to the nearest tenth of a pound.)

483. A popular fast food burger weighs 7.5 ounces and contains 540 calories, 29 grams of fat, 43 grams of carbohydrates, and 25 grams of protein. Find the unit rate of ⓐ calories per ounce ⓑ grams of fat per ounce ⓒ grams of carbohydrates per ounce ⓓ grams of protein per ounce. Round to two decimal places.

484. A 16-ounce chocolate mocha coffee with whipped cream contains 470 calories, 18 grams of fat, 63 grams of carbohydrates, and 15 grams of protein. Find the unit rate of ⓐ calories per ounce ⓑ grams of fat per ounce ⓒ grams of carbohydrates per ounce ⓓ grams of protein per ounce.

Writing Exercises

485. Would you prefer the ratio of your income to your friend's income to be $3/1$ or $1/3$? Explain your reasoning.

486. The parking lot at the airport charges $\$0.75$ for every 15 minutes. ⓐ How much does it cost to park for 1 hour? ⓑ Explain how you got your answer to part ⓐ. Was your reasoning based on the unit cost or did you use another method?

487. Kathryn ate a 4-ounce cup of frozen yogurt and then went for a swim. The frozen yogurt had 115 calories. Swimming burns 422 calories per hour. For how many minutes should Kathryn swim to burn off the calories in the frozen yogurt? Explain your reasoning.

488. Mollie had a 16-ounce cappuccino at her neighborhood coffee shop. The cappuccino had 110 calories. If Mollie walks for one hour, she burns 246 calories. For how many minutes must Mollie walk to burn off the calories in the cappuccino? Explain your reasoning.

Self Check

ⓐ After completing the exercises, use this checklist to evaluate your mastery of the objectives of this section.

I can...	Confidently	With some help	No-I don't get it!
write a ratio as a fraction.			
write a rate as a fraction.			
find unit rates.			
find unit price.			
translate phrases to expressions with fractions.			

ⓑ After reviewing this checklist, what will you do to become confident for all objectives?

5.7 | Simplify and Use Square Roots

Learning Objectives

By the end of this section, you will be able to:
- Simplify expressions with square roots
- Estimate square roots
- Approximate square roots
- Simplify variable expressions with square roots
- Use square roots in applications

Be Prepared!

Before you get started, take this readiness quiz.

1. Simplify: $(-9)^2$.
   If you missed this problem, review Example 3.52.
2. Round 3.846 to the nearest hundredth.
   If you missed this problem, review Example 5.9.
3. Evaluate $12d$ for $d = 80$.
   If you missed this problem, review Example 2.14.

Simplify Expressions with Square Roots

To start this section, we need to review some important vocabulary and notation.

Remember that when a number n is multiplied by itself, we can write this as n^2, which we read aloud as "n squared."

For example, 8^2 is read as "8 squared."

We call 64 the *square* of 8 because $8^2 = 64$. Similarly, 121 is the square of 11, because $11^2 = 121$.

Square of a Number

If $n^2 = m$, then m is the square of n.

Modeling Squares

Do you know why we use the word *square*? If we construct a square with three tiles on each side, the total number of tiles would be nine.

This is why we say that the square of three is nine.

$$3^2 = 9$$

The number 9 is called a perfect square because it is the square of a whole number.

 MANIPULATIVE MATHEMATICS

Doing the Manipulative Mathematics activity Square Numbers will help you develop a better understanding of perfect square numbers

The chart shows the squares of the counting numbers 1 through 15. You can refer to it to help you identify the perfect squares.

Number	n	1	2	3	4	5	6	7	8	9	10	11	12	13	14	15
Square	n^2	1	4	9	16	25	36	49	64	81	100	121	144	169	196	225

Perfect Squares

A **perfect square** is the square of a whole number.

What happens when you square a negative number?

$$(-8)^2 = (-8)(-8)$$
$$= 64$$

When we multiply two negative numbers, the product is always positive. So, the square of a negative number is always positive.

The chart shows the squares of the negative integers from -1 to -15.

Number	n	–1	–2	–3	–4	–5	–6	–7	–8	–9	–10	–11	–12	–13	–14	–15
Square	n^2	1	4	9	16	25	36	49	64	81	100	121	144	169	196	225

Did you notice that these squares are the same as the squares of the positive numbers?

Square Roots

Sometimes we will need to look at the relationship between numbers and their squares in reverse. Because $10^2 = 100$, we say 100 is the square of 10. We can also say that 10 is a square root of 100.

Square Root of a Number

A number whose square is m is called a square root of m.

If $n^2 = m$, then n is a **square root** of m.

Notice $(-10)^2 = 100$ also, so -10 is also a square root of 100. Therefore, both 10 and -10 are square roots of 100.

So, every positive number has two square roots: one positive and one negative.

What if we only want the positive square root of a positive number? The *radical sign*, $\sqrt{}$, stands for the positive square root. The positive square root is also called the **principal square root**.

Square Root Notation

$\sqrt{m}$ is read as "the square root of m."

If $m = n^2$, then $\sqrt{m} = n$ for n $\geq$ 0.

radical sign ——▸ $\sqrt{m}$ ◂—— radicand

We can also use the radical sign for the square root of zero. Because $0^2 = 0$, $\sqrt{0} = 0$. Notice that zero has only one square root.

The chart shows the square roots of the first 15 perfect square numbers.

$\sqrt{1}$	$\sqrt{4}$	$\sqrt{9}$	$\sqrt{16}$	$\sqrt{25}$	$\sqrt{36}$	$\sqrt{49}$	$\sqrt{64}$	$\sqrt{81}$	$\sqrt{100}$	$\sqrt{121}$	$\sqrt{144}$	$\sqrt{169}$	$\sqrt{196}$	$\sqrt{225}$
1	2	3	4	5	6	7	8	9	10	11	12	13	14	15

EXAMPLE 5.69

Simplify: ⓐ $\sqrt{25}$ ⓑ $\sqrt{121}$.

⊘ **Solution**

ⓐ

$$\sqrt{25}$$

Since $5^2 = 25$ 5

ⓑ

$$\sqrt{121}$$

Since $11^2 = 121$ -11

> **TRY IT ::** 5.137   Simplify: ⓐ $\sqrt{36}$ ⓑ $\sqrt{169}$.

> **TRY IT ::** 5.138   Simplify: ⓐ $\sqrt{16}$ ⓑ $\sqrt{196}$.

Every positive number has two square roots and the radical sign indicates the positive one. We write $\sqrt{100} = 10$. If we want to find the negative square root of a number, we place a negative in front of the radical sign. For example, $-\sqrt{100} = -10$.

EXAMPLE 5.70

Simplify. ⓐ $-\sqrt{9}$ ⓑ $-\sqrt{144}$.

⊘ **Solution**

ⓐ

$$-\sqrt{9}$$

The negative is in front of the radical sign. -3

ⓑ

$$-\sqrt{144}$$

The negative is in front of the radical sign. -12

> **TRY IT ::** 5.139   Simplify: ⓐ $-\sqrt{4}$ ⓑ $-\sqrt{225}$.

> **TRY IT ::** 5.140   Simplify: ⓐ $-\sqrt{81}$ ⓑ $-\sqrt{64}$.

Square Root of a Negative Number

Can we simplify $\sqrt{-25}$? Is there a number whose square is -25?

$$(\quad)^2 = -25 ?$$

None of the numbers that we have dealt with so far have a square that is -25. Why? Any positive number squared is positive, and any negative number squared is also positive. In the next chapter we will see that all the numbers we work with are called the real numbers. So we say there is no real number equal to $\sqrt{-25}$. If we are asked to find the square root of any negative number, we say that the solution is not a real number.

EXAMPLE 5.71

Simplify: ⓐ $\sqrt{-169}$ ⓑ $-\sqrt{121}$.

⊘ Solution

ⓐ There is no real number whose square is -169. Therefore, $\sqrt{-169}$ is not a real number.

ⓑ The negative is in front of the radical sign, so we find the opposite of the square root of 121.

$$-\sqrt{121}$$

The negative is in front of the radical. -11

| > | **TRY IT : :** 5.141 | Simplify: ⓐ $\sqrt{-196}$ ⓑ $-\sqrt{81}$. |

| > | **TRY IT : :** 5.142 | Simplify: ⓐ $\sqrt{-49}$ ⓑ $-\sqrt{121}$. |

Square Roots and the Order of Operations

When using the order of operations to simplify an expression that has square roots, we treat the radical sign as a grouping symbol. We simplify any expressions under the radical sign before performing other operations.

EXAMPLE 5.72

Simplify: ⓐ $\sqrt{25} + \sqrt{144}$ ⓑ $\sqrt{25 + 144}$.

⊘ Solution

ⓐ Use the order of operations.

$$\sqrt{25} + \sqrt{144}$$

Simplify each radical. $5 + 12$

Add. 17

ⓑ Use the order of operations.

$$\sqrt{25 + 144}$$

Add under the radical sign. $\sqrt{169}$

Simplify. 13

> | **TRY IT : :** 5.143 Simplify: ⓐ $\sqrt{9} + \sqrt{16}$ ⓑ $\sqrt{9 + 16}$.

> | **TRY IT : :** 5.144 Simplify: ⓐ $\sqrt{64 + 225}$ ⓑ $\sqrt{64} + \sqrt{225}$.

Notice the different answers in parts ⓐ and ⓑ of Example 5.72. It is important to follow the order of operations correctly. In ⓐ, we took each square root first and then added them. In ⓑ, we added under the radical sign first and then found the square root.

Estimate Square Roots

So far we have only worked with square roots of perfect squares. The square roots of other numbers are not whole numbers.

Number	Square root
4	$\sqrt{4} = 2$
5	$\sqrt{5}$
6	$\sqrt{6}$
7	$\sqrt{7}$
8	$\sqrt{8}$
9	$\sqrt{9} = 3$

We might conclude that the square roots of numbers between 4 and 9 will be between 2 and 3, and they will not be whole numbers. Based on the pattern in the table above, we could say that $\sqrt{5}$ is between 2 and 3. Using inequality symbols, we write

$$2 < \sqrt{5} < 3$$

EXAMPLE 5.73

Estimate $\sqrt{60}$ between two consecutive whole numbers.

⊘ Solution

Think of the perfect squares closest to 60. Make a small table of these perfect squares and their squares roots.

Number	Square root
36	6
49	7
64	8
81	9

60 ←→ $\sqrt{60}$

Locate 60 between two consecutive perfect squares. $49 < 60 < 64$

$\sqrt{60}$ is between their square roots. $7 < \sqrt{60} < 8$

> | **TRY IT : :** 5.145 Estimate $\sqrt{38}$ between two consecutive whole numbers.

> | **TRY IT : :** 5.146 Estimate $\sqrt{84}$ between two consecutive whole numbers.

Approximate Square Roots with a Calculator

There are mathematical methods to approximate square roots, but it is much more convenient to use a calculator to find square roots. Find the $\sqrt{}$ or $\sqrt{x}$ key on your calculator. You will to use this key to approximate square roots. When you use your calculator to find the square root of a number that is not a perfect square, the answer that you see is not the exact number. It is an approximation, to the number of digits shown on your calculator's display. The symbol for an approximation is $\approx$ and it is read *approximately*.

Suppose your calculator has a 10-digit display. Using it to find the square root of 5 will give 2.236067977. This is the approximate square root of 5. When we report the answer, we should use the "approximately equal to" sign instead of an equal sign.

$$\sqrt{5} \approx 2.236067978$$

You will seldom use this many digits for applications in algebra. So, if you wanted to round $\sqrt{5}$ to two decimal places, you would write

$$\sqrt{5} \approx 2.24$$

How do we know these values are approximations and not the exact values? Look at what happens when we square them.

$$2.236067978^2 = 5.000000002$$
$$2.24^2 = 5.0176$$

The squares are close, but not exactly equal, to 5.

EXAMPLE 5.74

Round $\sqrt{17}$ to two decimal places using a calculator.

⊘ **Solution**

$$\sqrt{17}$$

Use the calculator square root key.   4.123105626

Round to two decimal places.   4.12

$$\sqrt{17} \approx 4.12$$

> **TRY IT :: 5.147**   Round $\sqrt{11}$ to two decimal places.

> **TRY IT :: 5.148**   Round $\sqrt{13}$ to two decimal places.

Simplify Variable Expressions with Square Roots

Expressions with square root that we have looked at so far have not had any variables. What happens when we have to find a square root of a variable expression?

Consider $\sqrt{9x^2}$, where $x \geq 0$. Can you think of an expression whose square is $9x^2$?

$$(?)^2 = 9x^2$$
$$(3x)^2 = 9x^2 \qquad \text{so } \sqrt{9x^2} = 3x$$

When we use a variable in a square root expression, for our work, we will assume that the variable represents a non-negative number. In every example and exercise that follows, each variable in a square root expression is greater than or equal to zero.

EXAMPLE 5.75

Simplify: $\sqrt{x^2}$.

⊘ **Solution**

Think about what we would have to square to get x^2. Algebraically, $(?)^2 = x^2$

$$\sqrt{x^2}$$

Since $(x)^2 = x^2$ x

> **TRY IT : :** 5.149   Simplify: $\sqrt{y^2}$.

> **TRY IT : :** 5.150   Simplify: $\sqrt{m^2}$.

EXAMPLE 5.76

Simplify: $\sqrt{16x^2}$.

⊘ **Solution**

$$\sqrt{16x^2}$$

Since $(4x)^2 = 16x^2$ $4x$

> **TRY IT : :** 5.151   Simplify: $\sqrt{64x^2}$.

> **TRY IT : :** 5.152   Simplify: $\sqrt{169y^2}$.

EXAMPLE 5.77

Simplify: $-\sqrt{81y^2}$.

⊘ **Solution**

$$-\sqrt{81y^2}$$

Since $(9y)^2 = 81y^2$ $-9y$

> **TRY IT : :** 5.153   Simplify: $-\sqrt{121y^2}$.

> **TRY IT : :** 5.154   Simplify: $-\sqrt{100p^2}$.

EXAMPLE 5.78

Simplify: $\sqrt{36x^2 y^2}$.

Solution

$$\sqrt{36x^2 y^2}$$

Since $(6xy)^2 = 36x^2 y^2$ $6xy$

> **TRY IT :: 5.155**   Simplify: $\sqrt{100a^2 b^2}$.

> **TRY IT :: 5.156**   Simplify: $\sqrt{225m^2 n^2}$.

Use Square Roots in Applications

As you progress through your college courses, you'll encounter several applications of square roots. Once again, if we use our strategy for applications, it will give us a plan for finding the answer!

HOW TO :: USE A STRATEGY FOR APPLICATIONS WITH SQUARE ROOTS.

Step 1.   Identify what you are asked to find.

Step 2.   Write a phrase that gives the information to find it.

Step 3.   Translate the phrase to an expression.

Step 4.   Simplify the expression.

Step 5.   Write a complete sentence that answers the question.

Square Roots and Area

We have solved applications with area before. If we were given the length of the sides of a square, we could find its area by squaring the length of its sides. Now we can find the length of the sides of a square if we are given the area, by finding the square root of the area.

If the area of the square is A square units, the length of a side is $\sqrt{A}$ units. See Table 5.106.

Area (square units)	Length of side (units)
9	$\sqrt{9} = 3$
144	$\sqrt{144} = 12$
A	$\sqrt{A}$

Table 5.106

EXAMPLE 5.79

Mike and Lychelle want to make a square patio. They have enough concrete for an area of 200 square feet. To the nearest tenth of a foot, how long can a side of their square patio be?

Solution

We know the area of the square is 200 square feet and want to find the length of the side. If the area of the square is A square units, the length of a side is $\sqrt{A}$ units.

What are you asked to find?	The length of each side of a square patio
Write a phrase.	The length of a side
Translate to an expression.	$\sqrt{A}$
Evaluate $\sqrt{A}$ when $A = 200$.	$\sqrt{200}$
Use your calculator.	14.142135...
Round to one decimal place.	14.1 feet
Write a sentence.	Each side of the patio should be 14.1 feet.

> **TRY IT : :** 5.157

Katie wants to plant a square lawn in her front yard. She has enough sod to cover an area of 370 square feet. To the nearest tenth of a foot, how long can a side of her square lawn be?

> **TRY IT : :** 5.158

Sergio wants to make a square mosaic as an inlay for a table he is building. He has enough tile to cover an area of 2704 square centimeters. How long can a side of his mosaic be?

Square Roots and Gravity

Another application of square roots involves gravity. On Earth, if an object is dropped from a height of h feet, the time in seconds it will take to reach the ground is found by evaluating the expression $\frac{\sqrt{h}}{4}$. For example, if an object is dropped from a height of 64 feet, we can find the time it takes to reach the ground by evaluating $\frac{\sqrt{64}}{4}$.

$$\frac{\sqrt{64}}{4}$$

| Take the square root of 64. | $\frac{8}{4}$ |
| Simplify the fraction. | 2 |

It would take 2 seconds for an object dropped from a height of 64 feet to reach the ground.

EXAMPLE 5.80

Christy dropped her sunglasses from a bridge 400 feet above a river. How many seconds does it take for the sunglasses to reach the river?

Solution

What are you asked to find?	The number of seconds it takes for the sunglasses to reach the river
Write a phrase.	The time it will take to reach the river
Translate to an expression.	$\frac{\sqrt{h}}{4}$
Evaluate $\frac{\sqrt{h}}{4}$ when $h = 400$.	$\frac{\sqrt{400}}{4}$
Find the square root of 400.	$\frac{20}{4}$
Simplify.	5
Write a sentence.	It will take 5 seconds for the sunglasses to reach the river.

> **TRY IT :: 5.159**
>
> A helicopter drops a rescue package from a height of 1296 feet. How many seconds does it take for the package to reach the ground?

> **TRY IT :: 5.160**
>
> A window washer drops a squeegee from a platform 196 feet above the sidewalk. How many seconds does it take for the squeegee to reach the sidewalk?

Square Roots and Accident Investigations

Police officers investigating car accidents measure the length of the skid marks on the pavement. Then they use square roots to determine the speed, in miles per hour, a car was going before applying the brakes. According to some formulas, if the length of the skid marks is d feet, then the speed of the car can be found by evaluating $\sqrt{24d}$.

EXAMPLE 5.81

After a car accident, the skid marks for one car measured 190 feet. To the nearest tenth, what was the speed of the car (in mph) before the brakes were applied?

Solution

What are you asked to find?	The speed of the car before the brakes were applied
Write a phrase.	The speed of the car
Translate to an expression.	$\sqrt{24d}$
Evaluate $\sqrt{24d}$ when $d = 190$.	$\sqrt{24 \cdot 190}$
Multiply.	$\sqrt{4,560}$
Use your calculator.	67.527772...
Round to tenths.	67.5
Write a sentence.	The speed of the car was approximately 67.5 miles per hour.

> **TRY IT : :** 5.161

An accident investigator measured the skid marks of a car and found their length was 76 feet. To the nearest tenth, what was the speed of the car before the brakes were applied?

> **TRY IT : :** 5.162

The skid marks of a vehicle involved in an accident were 122 feet long. To the nearest tenth, how fast had the vehicle been going before the brakes were applied?

LINKS TO LITERACY

The *Links to Literacy* activity "Sea Squares" will provide you with another view of the topics covered in this section.

▶ **MEDIA : :** ACCESS ADDITIONAL ONLINE RESOURCES
   - Introduction to Square Roots (http://www.openstaxcollege.org/l/24introsqroots)
   - Estimating Square Roots with a Calculator (http://www.openstaxcollege.org/l/24estsqrtcalc)

5.7 EXERCISES

Practice Makes Perfect

Simplify Expressions with Square Roots

In the following exercises, simplify.

489. $\sqrt{36}$

490. $\sqrt{4}$

491. $\sqrt{64}$

492. $\sqrt{144}$

493. $-\sqrt{4}$

494. $-\sqrt{100}$

495. $-\sqrt{1}$

496. $-\sqrt{121}$

497. $\sqrt{-121}$

498. $\sqrt{-36}$

499. $\sqrt{-9}$

500. $\sqrt{-49}$

501. $\sqrt{9+16}$

502. $\sqrt{25+144}$

503. $\sqrt{9}+\sqrt{16}$

504. $\sqrt{25}+\sqrt{144}$

Estimate Square Roots

In the following exercises, estimate each square root between two consecutive whole numbers.

505. $\sqrt{70}$

506. $\sqrt{55}$

507. $\sqrt{200}$

508. $\sqrt{172}$

Approximate Square Roots with a Calculator

In the following exercises, use a calculator to approximate each square root and round to two decimal places.

509. $\sqrt{19}$

510. $\sqrt{21}$

511. $\sqrt{53}$

512. $\sqrt{47}$

Simplify Variable Expressions with Square Roots

In the following exercises, simplify. (Assume all variables are greater than or equal to zero.)

513. $\sqrt{y^2}$

514. $\sqrt{b^2}$

515. $\sqrt{49x^2}$

516. $\sqrt{100y^2}$

517. $-\sqrt{64a^2}$

518. $-\sqrt{25x^2}$

519. $\sqrt{144x^2y^2}$

520. $\sqrt{196a^2b^2}$

Use Square Roots in Applications

In the following exercises, solve. Round to one decimal place.

521. Landscaping Reed wants to have a square garden plot in his backyard. He has enough compost to cover an area of 75 square feet. How long can a side of his garden be?

522. Landscaping Vince wants to make a square patio in his yard. He has enough concrete to pave an area of 130 square feet. How long can a side of his patio be?

523. Gravity An airplane dropped a flare from a height of $1,024$ feet above a lake. How many seconds did it take for the flare to reach the water?

524. Gravity A hang glider dropped his cell phone from a height of 350 feet. How many seconds did it take for the cell phone to reach the ground?

525. Gravity A construction worker dropped a hammer while building the Grand Canyon skywalk, 4,000 feet above the Colorado River. How many seconds did it take for the hammer to reach the river?

526. Accident investigation The skid marks from a car involved in an accident measured 54 feet. What was the speed of the car before the brakes were applied?

527. Accident investigation The skid marks from a car involved in an accident measured 216 feet. What was the speed of the car before the brakes were applied?

528. Accident investigation An accident investigator measured the skid marks of one of the vehicles involved in an accident. The length of the skid marks was 175 feet. What was the speed of the vehicle before the brakes were applied?

529. Accident investigation An accident investigator measured the skid marks of one of the vehicles involved in an accident. The length of the skid marks was 117 feet. What was the speed of the vehicle before the brakes were applied?

Everyday Math

530. Decorating Denise wants to install a square accent of designer tiles in her new shower. She can afford to buy 625 square centimeters of the designer tiles. How long can a side of the accent be?

531. Decorating Morris wants to have a square mosaic inlaid in his new patio. His budget allows for 2,025 tiles. Each tile is square with an area of one square inch. How long can a side of the mosaic be?

Writing Exercises

532. Why is there no real number equal to $\sqrt{-64}$?

533. What is the difference between 9^2 and $\sqrt{9}$?

Self Check

ⓐ After completing the exercises, use this checklist to evaluate your mastery of the objectives of this section.

I can...	Confidently	With some help	No-I don't get it!
simplify expressions with square roots.			
estimate square roots.			
approximate square roots.			
simplify variable expressions with square roots.			
use square roots in applications.			

ⓑ Overall, after looking at the checklist, do you think you are well-prepared for the next Chapter? Why or why not?

CHAPTER 5 REVIEW

KEY TERMS

circumference of a circle The distance around a circle is called its **circumference**.

diameter of a circle A diameter of a circle is a line segment that passes through a circle's center connecting two points on the circle.

equivalent decimals Two decimals are equivalent decimals if they convert to equivalent fractions.

mean The mean of a set of n numbers is the arithmetic average of the numbers. The formula is
$$\text{mean} = \frac{\text{sum of values in data set}}{n}$$

median The median of a set of data values is the middle value.
- Half the data values are less than or equal to the median.
- Half the data values are greater than or equal to the median.

mode The mode of a set of numbers is the number with the highest frequency.

radius of a circle A radius of a circle is a line segment from the center to any point on the circle.

rate A rate compares two quantities of different units. A rate is usually written as a fraction.

ratio A ratio compares two numbers or two quantities that are measured with the same unit. The ratio of a to b is written a to b, $\frac{a}{b}$, or $a:b$.

repeating decimal A repeating decimal is a decimal in which the last digit or group of digits repeats endlessly.

unit price A **unit price** is a unit rate that gives the price of one item.

unit rate A unit rate is a rate with denominator of 1 unit.

KEY CONCEPTS

5.1 Decimals

- **Name a decimal number.**

  Step 1. Name the number to the left of the decimal point.

  Step 2. Write "and" for the decimal point.

  Step 3. Name the "number" part to the right of the decimal point as if it were a whole number.

  Step 4. Name the decimal place of the last digit.

- **Write a decimal number from its name.**

  Step 1. Look for the word "and"—it locates the decimal point.
  Place a decimal point under the word "and." Translate the words before "and" into the whole number and place it to the left of the decimal point.
  If there is no "and," write a "0" with a decimal point to its right.

  Step 2. Mark the number of decimal places needed to the right of the decimal point by noting the place value indicated by the last word.

  Step 3. Translate the words after "and" into the number to the right of the decimal point. Write the number in the spaces—putting the final digit in the last place.

  Step 4. Fill in zeros for place holders as needed.

- **Convert a decimal number to a fraction or mixed number.**

  Step 1. Look at the number to the left of the decimal.
  If it is zero, the decimal converts to a proper fraction.
  If it is not zero, the decimal converts to a mixed number.
  Write the whole number.

  Step 2. Determine the place value of the final digit.

  Step 3. Write the fraction. numerator—the 'numbers' to the right of the decimal point denominator—the place value corresponding to the final digit

  Step 4. Simplify the fraction, if possible.

- **Order decimals.**

Step 1. Check to see if both numbers have the same number of decimal places. If not, write zeros at the end of the one with fewer digits to make them match.

Step 2. Compare the numbers to the right of the decimal point as if they were whole numbers.

Step 3. Order the numbers using the appropriate inequality sign.

- **Round a decimal.**

Step 1. Locate the given place value and mark it with an arrow.

Step 2. Underline the digit to the right of the given place value.

Step 3. Is this digit greater than or equal to 5?
Yes - add 1 to the digit in the given place value.
No - do not change the digit in the given place value

Step 4. Rewrite the number, removing all digits to the right of the given place value.

5.2 Decimal Operations

- **Add or subtract decimals.**

Step 1. Write the numbers vertically so the decimal points line up.

Step 2. Use zeros as place holders, as needed.

Step 3. Add or subtract the numbers as if they were whole numbers. Then place the decimal in the answer under the decimal points in the given numbers.

- **Multiply decimal numbers.**

Step 1. Determine the sign of the product.

Step 2. Write the numbers in vertical format, lining up the numbers on the right.

Step 3. Multiply the numbers as if they were whole numbers, temporarily ignoring the decimal points.

Step 4. Place the decimal point. The number of decimal places in the product is the sum of the number of decimal places in the factors. If needed, use zeros as placeholders.

Step 5. Write the product with the appropriate sign.

- **Multiply a decimal by a power of 10.**

Step 1. Move the decimal point to the right the same number of places as the number of zeros in the power of 10.

Step 2. Write zeros at the end of the number as placeholders if needed.

- **Divide a decimal by a whole number.**

Step 1. Write as long division, placing the decimal point in the quotient above the decimal point in the dividend.

Step 2. Divide as usual.

- **Divide decimal numbers.**

Step 1. Determine the sign of the quotient.

Step 2. Make the divisor a whole number by moving the decimal point all the way to the right. Move the decimal point in the dividend the same number of places to the right, writing zeros as needed.

Step 3. Divide. Place the decimal point in the quotient above the decimal point in the dividend.

Step 4. Write the quotient with the appropriate sign.

- **Strategy for Applications**

Step 1. Identify what you are asked to find.

Step 2. Write a phrase that gives the information to find it.

Step 3. Translate the phrase to an expression.

Step 4. Simplify the expression.

Step 5. Answer the question with a complete sentence.

5.3 Decimals and Fractions

- **Convert a Fraction to a Decimal** To convert a fraction to a decimal, divide the numerator of the fraction by the denominator of the fraction.

- **Properties of Circles**

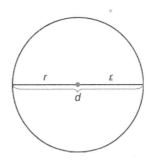

r is the length of the radius

d is the length of the diameter

The circumference is $2\pi r$.　　$C = 2\pi r$

The area is πr^2.　　　　$A = \pi r^2$

5.4 Solve Equations with Decimals

- **Determine whether a number is a solution to an equation.**
    - ◦ Substitute the number for the variable in the equation.
    - ◦ Simplify the expressions on both sides of the equation.
    - ◦ Determine whether the resulting equation is true.
      If so, the number is a solution.
      If not, the number is not a solution.
- **Properties of Equality**

Subtraction Property of Equality	**Addition Property of Equality**
For any numbers a, b, and c, 　If　　$a = b$ 　then $a - c = b - c$	For any numbers a, b, and c, 　If　　$a = b$ 　then $a + c = b + c$
Division of Property of Equality	**Multiplication Property of Equality**
For any numbers a, b, and $c \neq 0$, 　If　$a = b$ 　then $\frac{a}{c} = \frac{b}{c}$	For any numbers a, b, and c, 　If　　$a = b$ 　then $a \cdot c = b \cdot c$

Table 5.110

5.5 Averages and Probability

- **Calculate the mean of a set of numbers.**

  Step 1. Write the formula for the mean $\text{mean} = \frac{\text{sum of values in data set}}{n}$

  Step 2. Find the sum of all the values in the set. Write the sum in the numerator.

  Step 3. Count the number, n, of values in the set. Write this number in the denominator.

  Step 4. Simplify the fraction.

  Step 5. Check to see that the mean is reasonable. It should be greater than the least number and less than the greatest number in the set.

- **Find the median of a set of numbers.**

  Step 1. List the numbers from least to greatest.

  Step 2. Count how many numbers are in the set. Call this n.

Step 3. Is n odd or even?

        If n is an odd number, the median is the middle value.

        If n is an even number, the median is the mean of the two middle values

- **Identify the mode of a set of numbers.**

    Step 1. List the data values in numerical order.

    Step 2. Count the number of times each value appears.

    Step 3. The mode is the value with the highest frequency.

5.7 Simplify and Use Square Roots

- **Square Root Notation** $\sqrt{m}$ is read 'the square root of m'

    If $m = n^2$, then $\sqrt{m} = n$, for $n \geq 0$.

                radical sign $\longrightarrow \sqrt{m} \longleftarrow$ radicand

- **Use a strategy for applications with square roots.**

  - Identify what you are asked to find.
  - Write a phrase that gives the information to find it.
  - Translate the phrase to an expression.
  - Simplify the expression.
  - Write a complete sentence that answers the question.

REVIEW EXERCISES

5.1 Decimals

Name Decimals

In the following exercises, name each decimal.

534. 0.8

535. 0.375

536. 0.007

537. 5.24

538. -12.5632

539. -4.09

Write Decimals

In the following exercises, write as a decimal.

540. three tenths

541. nine hundredths

542. twenty-seven hundredths

543. ten and thirty-five thousandths

544. negative twenty and three tenths

545. negative five hundredths

Convert Decimals to Fractions or Mixed Numbers

In the following exercises, convert each decimal to a fraction. Simplify the answer if possible.

546. 0.43

547. 0.825

548. 9.7

549. 3.64

Locate Decimals on the Number Line

550. ⓐ 0.6

ⓑ -0.9

ⓒ 2.2

ⓓ -1.3

Order Decimals

In the following exercises, order each of the following pairs of numbers, using < or >.

551. 0.6___0.8

552. 0.2___0.15

553. 0.803____0.83

554. −0.56____−0.562

Round Decimals

In the following exercises, round each number to the nearest: ⓐ hundredth ⓑ tenth ⓒ whole number.

555. 12.529

556. 4.8447

557. 5.897

5.2 Decimal Operations

Add and Subtract Decimals

In the following exercises, add or subtract.

558. $5.75 + 8.46$

559. $32.89 − 8.22$

560. $24 − 19.31$

561. $10.2 + 14.631$

562. $−6.4 + (−2.9)$

563. $1.83 − 4.2$

Multiply Decimals

In the following exercises, multiply.

564. $(0.3)(0.7)$

565. $(−6.4)(0.25)$

566. $(−3.35)(−12.7)$

567. $(15.4)(1000)$

Divide Decimals

In the following exercises, divide.

568. $0.48 ÷ 6$

569. $4.32 ÷ 24$

570. $\$6.29 ÷ 12$

571. $(−0.8) ÷ (−0.2)$

572. $1.65 ÷ 0.15$

573. $9 ÷ 0.045$

Use Decimals in Money Applications

In the following exercises, use the strategy for applications to solve.

574. Miranda got $40 from her ATM. She spent $9.32 on lunch and $16.99 on a book. How much money did she have left? Round to the nearest cent if necessary.

575. Jessie put 8 gallons of gas in her car. One gallon of gas costs $3.528. How much did Jessie owe for all the gas?

576. A pack of 16 water bottles cost $6.72. How much did each bottle cost?

577. Alice bought a roll of paper towels that cost $2.49. She had a coupon for $0.35 off, and the store doubled the coupon. How much did Alice pay for the paper towels?

5.3 Decimals and Fractions

Convert Fractions to Decimals

In the following exercises, convert each fraction to a decimal.

578. $\dfrac{3}{5}$

579. $\dfrac{7}{8}$

580. $-\dfrac{19}{20}$

581. $-\dfrac{21}{4}$

582. $\dfrac{1}{3}$

583. $\dfrac{6}{11}$

Order Decimals and Fractions

In the following exercises, order each pair of numbers, using $<$ or $>$.

584. $\dfrac{1}{2}$___0.2

585. $\dfrac{3}{5}$___0.

586. $-\dfrac{7}{8}$___-0.84

587. $-\dfrac{5}{12}$___-0.42

588. 0.625___$\dfrac{13}{20}$

589. 0.33___$\dfrac{5}{16}$

In the following exercises, write each set of numbers in order from least to greatest.

590. $\dfrac{2}{3}, \dfrac{17}{20}, 0.65$

591. $\dfrac{7}{9}, 0.75, \dfrac{11}{15}$

Simplify Expressions Using the Order of Operations

In the following exercises, simplify

592. $4(10.3 - 5.8)$

593. $\dfrac{3}{4}(15.44 - 7.4)$

594. $30 \div (0.45 + 0.15)$

595. $1.6 + \dfrac{3}{8}$

596. $52(0.5) + (0.4)^2$

597. $-\dfrac{2}{5} \cdot \dfrac{9}{10} + 0.14$

Find the Circumference and Area of Circles

In the following exercises, approximate the ⓐ circumference and ⓑ area of each circle.

598. radius $= 6$ in.

599. radius $= 3.5$ ft.

600. radius $= \dfrac{7}{33}$ m

601. diameter $= 11$ cm

5.4 Solve Equations with Decimals

Determine Whether a Decimal is a Solution of an Equation

In the following exercises, determine whether the each number is a solution of the given equation.

602. $x - 0.4 = 2.1$
ⓐ $x = 1.7$ ⓑ $x = 2.5$

603. $y + 3.2 = -1.5$
ⓐ $y = 1.7$ ⓑ $y = -4.7$

604. $\dfrac{u}{2.5} = -12.5$
ⓐ $u = -5$ ⓑ $u = -31.25$

605. $0.45v = -40.5$
ⓐ $v = -18.225$ ⓑ $v = -90$

Solve Equations with Decimals

In the following exercises, solve.

606. $m + 3.8 = 7.5$

607. $h + 5.91 = 2.4$

608. $a + 2.26 = -1.1$

609. $p - 4.3 = -1.65$

610. $x - 0.24 = -8.6$

611. $j - 7.42 = -3.7$

612. $0.6p = 13.2$

613. $-8.6x = 34.4$

614. $-22.32 = -2.4z$

615. $\frac{a}{0.3} = -24$

616. $\frac{p}{-7} = -4.2$

617. $\frac{s}{-2.5} = -10$

Translate to an Equation and Solve

In the following exercises, translate and solve.

618. The difference of n and 15.2 is 4.4.

619. The product of -5.9 and x is -3.54.

620. The quotient of y and -1.8 is -9.

621. The sum of m and -4.03 is 6.8.

5.5 Averages and Probability

Find the Mean of a Set of Numbers

In the following exercises, find the mean of the numbers.

622. 2, 4, 1, 0, 1, and 1

623. $270, $310.50, $243.75, and $252.15

624. Each workday last week, Yoshie kept track of the number of minutes she had to wait for the bus. She waited 3, 0, 8, 1, and 8 minutes. Find the mean

625. In the last three months, Raul's water bills were $31.45, $48.76, and $42.60. Find the mean.

Find the Median of a Set of Numbers

In the following exercises, find the median.

626. 41, 45, 32, 60, 58

627. 25, 23, 24, 26, 29, 19, 18, 32

628. The ages of the eight men in Jerry's model train club are 52, 63, 45, 51, 55, 75, 60, and 59. Find the median age.

629. The number of clients at Miranda's beauty salon each weekday last week were 18, 7, 12, 16, and 20. Find the median number of clients.

Find the Mode of a Set of Numbers

In the following exercises, identify the mode of the numbers.

630. 6, 4, 4, 5, 6, 6, 4, 4, 4, 3, 5

631. The number of siblings of a group of students: 2, 0, 3, 2, 4, 1, 6, 5, 4, 1, 2, 3

Use the Basic Definition of Probability

In the following exercises, solve. (Round decimals to three places.)

632. The Sustainability Club sells 200 tickets to a raffle, and Albert buys one ticket. One ticket will be selected at random to win the grand prize. Find the probability Albert will win the grand prize. Express your answer as a fraction and as a decimal.

633. Luc has to read 3 novels and 12 short stories for his literature class. The professor will choose one reading at random for the final exam. Find the probability that the professor will choose a novel for the final exam. Express your answer as a fraction and as a decimal.

5.6 Ratios and Rate

Write a Ratio as a Fraction

In the following exercises, write each ratio as a fraction. Simplify the answer if possible.

634. 28 to 40

635. 56 to 32

636. 3.5 to 0.5

637. 1.2 to 1.8

638. $1\frac{3}{4}$ to $1\frac{5}{8}$

639. $2\frac{1}{3}$ to $5\frac{1}{4}$

640. 64 ounces to 30 ounces

641. 28 inches to 3 feet

Write a Rate as a Fraction

In the following exercises, write each rate as a fraction. Simplify the answer if possible.

642. 180 calories per 8 ounces

643. 90 pounds per 7.5 square inches

644. 126 miles in 4 hours

645. $612.50 for 35 hours

Find Unit Rates

In the following exercises, find the unit rate.

646. 180 calories per 8 ounces

647. 90 pounds per 7.5 square inches

648. 126 miles in 4 hours

649. $612.50 for 35 hours

Find Unit Price

In the following exercises, find the unit price.

650. t-shirts: 3 for $8.97

651. Highlighters: 6 for $2.52

652. An office supply store sells a box of pens for $11. The box contains 12 pens. How much does each pen cost?

653. Anna bought a pack of 8 kitchen towels for $13.20. How much did each towel cost? Round to the nearest cent if necessary.

In the following exercises, find each unit price and then determine the better buy.

654. Shampoo: 12 ounces for $4.29 or 22 ounces for $7.29?

655. Vitamins: 60 tablets for $6.49 or 100 for $11.99?

Translate Phrases to Expressions with Fractions

In the following exercises, translate the English phrase into an algebraic expression.

656. 535 miles per h hours

657. a adults to 45 children

658. the ratio of $4y$ and the difference of x and 10

659. the ratio of 19 and the sum of 3 and n

5.7 Simplify and Use Square Roots

Simplify Expressions with Square Roots

In the following exercises, simplify.

660. $\sqrt{64}$

661. $\sqrt{144}$

662. $-\sqrt{25}$

663. $-\sqrt{81}$

664. $\sqrt{-9}$

665. $\sqrt{-36}$

666. $\sqrt{64} + \sqrt{225}$

667. $\sqrt{64 + 225}$

Estimate Square Roots

In the following exercises, estimate each square root between two consecutive whole numbers.

668. $\sqrt{28}$

669. $\sqrt{155}$

Approximate Square Roots

In the following exercises, approximate each square root and round to two decimal places.

670. $\sqrt{15}$

671. $\sqrt{57}$

Simplify Variable Expressions with Square Roots

In the following exercises, simplify. (Assume all variables are greater than or equal to zero.)

672. $\sqrt{q^2}$

673. $\sqrt{64b^2}$

674. $-\sqrt{121a^2}$

675. $\sqrt{225m^2 n^2}$

676. $-\sqrt{100q^2}$

677. $\sqrt{49y^2}$

678. $\sqrt{4a^2 b^2}$

679. $\sqrt{121c^2 d^2}$

Use Square Roots in Applications

In the following exercises, solve. Round to one decimal place.

680. Art Diego has 225 square inch tiles. He wants to use them to make a square mosaic. How long can each side of the mosaic be?

681. Landscaping Janet wants to plant a square flower garden in her yard. She has enough topsoil to cover an area of 30 square feet. How long can a side of the flower garden be?

682. Gravity A hiker dropped a granola bar from a lookout spot 576 feet above a valley. How long did it take the granola bar to reach the valley floor?

683. Accident investigation The skid marks of a car involved in an accident were 216 feet. How fast had the car been going before applying the brakes?

PRACTICE TEST

684. Write six and thirty-four thousandths as a decimal.

685. Write 1.73 as a fraction.

686. Write $\frac{5}{8}$ as a decimal.

687. Round 16.749 to the nearest ⓐ tenth ⓑ hundredth ⓒ whole number

688. Write the numbers $\frac{4}{5}$, -0.1, 0.804, $\frac{2}{9}$, -7.4, 0.21 in order from smallest to largest.

In the following exercises, simplify each expression.

689. $15.4 + 3.02$

690. $20 - 5.71$

691. $(0.64)(0.3)$

692. $(-4.2)(100)$

693. $0.96 \div (-12)$

694. $-5 \div 0.025$

695. $-0.6 \div (-0.3)$

696. $(0.7)^2$

697. $24 \div (0.1 + 0.02)$

698. $4(10.3 - 5.8)$

699. $1.6 + \frac{3}{8}$

700. $\frac{2}{3}(14.65 - 4.6)$

In the following exercises, solve.

701. $m + 3.7 = 2.5$

702. $\frac{h}{0.5} = 4.38$

703. $-6.5y = -57.2$

704. $1.94 = a - 2.6$

705. Three friends went out to dinner and agreed to split the bill evenly. The bill was $79.35. How much should each person pay?

706. A circle has radius 12. Find the ⓐ circumference and ⓑ area. [Use 3.14 for π.]

707. The ages, in months, of 10 children in a preschool class are: 55, 55, 50, 51, 52, 50, 53, 51, 55, 49

Find the ⓐ mean ⓑ median ⓒ mode

708. Of the 16 nurses in Doreen's department, 12 are women and 4 are men. One of the nurses will be assigned at random to work an extra shift next week. ⓐ Find the probability a woman nurse will be assigned the extra shift. ⓑ Convert the fraction to a decimal.

709. Find each unit price and then the better buy.
Laundry detergent: 64 ounces for $10.99 or 48 ounces for $8.49

In the following exercises, simplify.

710. $\sqrt{36 + 64}$

711. $\sqrt{144n^2}$

712. Estimate $\sqrt{54}$ to between two whole numbers.

713. Yanet wants a square patio in her backyard. She has 225 square feet of tile. How long can a side of the patio be?

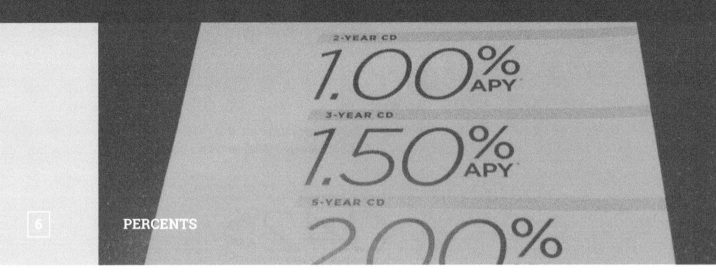

Figure 6.1 Banks provide money for savings and charge money for loans. The interest on savings and loans is usually given as a percent. (credit: Mike Mozart, Flickr)

Chapter Outline

Introduction

When you deposit money in a savings account at a bank, it earns additional money. Figuring out how your money will grow involves understanding and applying concepts of percents. In this chapter, we will find out what percents are and how we can use them to solve problems.

6.1 Understand Percent

Learning Objectives

By the end of this section, you will be able to:

Use the definition of percent
Convert percents to fractions and decimals
Convert decimals and fractions to percents

Be Prepared!

Before you get started, take this readiness quiz.

1. Translate "the ratio of 33 to 5" into an algebraic expression.
   If you missed this problem, review Table 2.40.

2. Write $\frac{3}{5}$ as a decimal.
   If you missed this problem, review Example 5.28.

3. Write 0.62 as a fraction.
   If you missed this problem, review Example 5.4.

Use the Definition of Percent

How many cents are in one dollar? There are 100 cents in a dollar. How many years are in a century? There are 100 years in a century. Does this give you a clue about what the word "percent" means? It is really two words, "per cent," and means per one hundred. A **percent** is a ratio whose denominator is 100. We use the percent symbol %, to show percent.

Percent

A percent is a ratio whose denominator is 100.

According to data from the American Association of Community Colleges (2015), about 57% of community college students are female. This means 57 out of every 100 community college students are female, as Figure 6.2 shows. Out of the 100 squares on the grid, 57 are shaded, which we write as the ratio $\frac{57}{100}$.

Figure 6.2 Among every 100 community college students, 57 are female.

Similarly, 25% means a ratio of $\frac{25}{100}$, 3% means a ratio of $\frac{3}{100}$ and 100% means a ratio of $\frac{100}{100}$. In words, "one hundred percent" means the total 100% is $\frac{100}{100}$, and since $\frac{100}{100} = 1$, we see that 100% means 1 whole.

EXAMPLE 6.1

According to the Public Policy Institute of California (2010), 44% of parents of public school children would like their youngest child to earn a graduate degree. Write this percent as a ratio.

⊘ **Solution**

The amount we want to convert is 44%.	44%
Write the percent as a ratio. Remember that *percent* means per 100.	$\frac{44}{100}$

TRY IT :: 6.1 Write the percent as a ratio.
According to a survey, 89% of college students have a smartphone.

TRY IT :: 6.2 Write the percent as a ratio.
A study found that 72% of U.S. teens send text messages regularly.

EXAMPLE 6.2

In 2007, according to a U.S. Department of Education report, 21 out of every 100 first-time freshmen college students at 4-year public institutions took at least one remedial course. Write this as a ratio and then as a percent.

Solution

The amount we want to convert is 21 out of 100.	21 out of 100
Write as a ratio.	$\dfrac{21}{100}$
Convert the 21 per 100 to percent.	21%

> **TRY IT ::** 6.3

Write as a ratio and then as a percent: The American Association of Community Colleges reported that 62 out of 100 full-time community college students balance their studies with full-time or part time employment.

> **TRY IT ::** 6.4

Write as a ratio and then as a percent: In response to a student survey, 41 out of 100 Santa Ana College students expressed a goal of earning an Associate's degree or transferring to a four-year college.

Convert Percents to Fractions and Decimals

Since percents are ratios, they can easily be expressed as fractions. Remember that percent means per $100,$ so the denominator of the fraction is $100.$

HOW TO :: CONVERT A PERCENT TO A FRACTION.

Step 1.   Write the percent as a ratio with the denominator $100.$

Step 2.   Simplify the fraction if possible.

EXAMPLE 6.3

Convert each percent to a fraction:

ⓐ 36% ⓑ 125%

Solution

ⓐ

	36%
Write as a ratio with denominator 100.	$\dfrac{36}{100}$
Simplify.	$\dfrac{9}{25}$

ⓑ

	125%
Write as a ratio with denominator 100.	$\frac{125}{100}$
Simplify.	$\frac{5}{4}$

> **TRY IT ::** 6.5   Convert each percent to a fraction:

          ⓐ 48%   ⓑ 110%

> **TRY IT ::** 6.6   Convert each percent to a fraction:

          ⓐ 64%   ⓑ 150%

The previous example shows that a percent can be greater than 1. We saw that 125% means $\frac{125}{100}$, or $\frac{5}{4}$. These are improper fractions, and their values are greater than one.

EXAMPLE 6.4

Convert each percent to a fraction:

    ⓐ 24.5%   ⓑ $33\frac{1}{3}$ %

⊘ **Solution**

ⓐ

	24.5%
Write as a ratio with denominator 100.	$\frac{24.5}{100}$
Clear the decimal by multiplying numerator and denominator by 10.	$\frac{24.5(10)}{100(10)}$
Multiply.	$\frac{245}{1000}$
Rewrite showing common factors.	$\frac{5 \cdot 49}{5 \cdot 200}$
Simplify.	$\frac{49}{200}$

ⓑ

	$33\frac{1}{3}\%$
Write as a ratio with denominator 100.	$\dfrac{33\frac{1}{3}}{100}$
Write the numerator as an improper fraction.	$\dfrac{\frac{100}{3}}{100}$
Rewrite as fraction division, replacing 100 with $\frac{100}{1}$.	$\dfrac{100}{3} \div \dfrac{100}{1}$
Multiply by the reciprocal.	$\dfrac{100}{3} \cdot \dfrac{1}{100}$
Simplify.	$\dfrac{1}{3}$

> **TRY IT ::** 6.7   Convert each percent to a fraction:

ⓐ 64.4%   ⓑ $66\frac{2}{3}\%$

> **TRY IT ::** 6.8   Convert each percent to a fraction:

ⓐ 42.5%   ⓑ $8\frac{3}{4}\%$

In Decimals, we learned how to convert fractions to decimals. To convert a percent to a decimal, we first convert it to a fraction and then change the fraction to a decimal.

HOW TO :: CONVERT A PERCENT TO A DECIMAL.

Step 1.   Write the percent as a ratio with the denominator 100.

Step 2.   Convert the fraction to a decimal by dividing the numerator by the denominator.

EXAMPLE 6.5

Convert each percent to a decimal:

ⓐ 6%   ⓑ 78%

✓ **Solution**

Because we want to change to a decimal, we will leave the fractions with denominator 100 instead of removing common factors.

ⓐ

	6%
Write as a ratio with denominator 100.	$\frac{6}{100}$
Change the fraction to a decimal by dividing the numerator by the denominator.	0.06

ⓑ

	78%
Write as a ratio with denominator 100.	$\frac{78}{100}$
Change the fraction to a decimal by dividing the numerator by the denominator.	0.78

> **TRY IT : :** 6.9   Convert each percent to a decimal:

ⓐ 9%   ⓑ 87%

> **TRY IT : :** 6.10   Convert each percent to a decimal:

ⓐ 3%   ⓑ 91%

EXAMPLE 6.6

Convert each percent to a decimal:

ⓐ 135%   ⓑ 12.5%

✓ **Solution**

ⓐ

	135%
Write as a ratio with denominator 100.	$\frac{135}{100}$
Change the fraction to a decimal by dividing the numerator by the denominator.	1.35

ⓑ

	12.5%
Write as a ratio with denominator 100.	$\frac{12.5}{100}$
Change the fraction to a decimal by dividing the numerator by the denominator.	0.125

> **TRY IT :: 6.11**   Convert each percent to a decimal:

ⓐ 115%   ⓑ 23.5%

> **TRY IT :: 6.12**   Convert each percent to a decimal:

ⓐ 123%   ⓑ 16.8%

Let's summarize the results from the previous examples in Table 6.11, and look for a pattern we could use to quickly convert a percent number to a decimal number.

Percent	Decimal
6%	0.06
78%	0.78
135%	1.35
12.5%	0.125

Table 6.11

Do you see the pattern?

To convert a percent number to a decimal number, we move the decimal point two places to the left and remove the % sign. (Sometimes the decimal point does not appear in the percent number, but just like we can think of the integer 6 as 6.0, we can think of 6% as 6.0%.) Notice that we may need to add zeros in front of the number when moving the decimal to the left.

Figure 6.3 uses the percents in Table 6.11 and shows visually how to convert them to decimals by moving the decimal point two places to the left.

Percent	Decimal
006.%	0.06
078.%	0.78
135.%	1.35
012.5%	0.125

Figure 6.3

EXAMPLE 6.7

Among a group of business leaders, 77% believe that poor math and science education in the U.S. will lead to higher unemployment rates.

Convert the percent to: ⓐ a fraction ⓑ a decimal

⊘ **Solution**

ⓐ

77%

Write as a ratio with denominator 100. $\frac{77}{100}$

ⓑ

	$\frac{77}{100}$
Change the fraction to a decimal by dividing the numerator by the denominator.	0.77

> **TRY IT : : 6.13**   Convert the percent to: ⓐ a fraction and ⓑ a decimal

Twitter's share of web traffic jumped 24% when one celebrity tweeted live on air.

> **TRY IT : : 6.14**

Convert the percent to: ⓐ a fraction and ⓑ a decimal

The U.S. Census estimated that in 2013, 44% of the population of Boston age 25 or older have a bachelor's or higher degrees.

EXAMPLE 6.8

There are four suits of cards in a deck of cards—hearts, diamonds, clubs, and spades. The probability of randomly choosing a heart from a shuffled deck of cards is 25%. Convert the percent to:

ⓐ a fraction   ⓑ a decimal

Figure 6.4   (credit: Riles32807, Wikimedia Commons)

⊘ **Solution**

ⓐ

	25%
Write as a ratio with denominator 100.	$\frac{25}{100}$
Simplify.	$\frac{1}{4}$

ⓑ $$\frac{1}{4}$$

Change the fraction to a decimal by dividing the numerator by the denominator.   0.25

> **TRY IT :: 6.15**   Convert the percent to: ⓐ a fraction, and ⓑ a decimal

                                   The probability that it will rain Monday is 30%.

> **TRY IT :: 6.16**   Convert the percent to: ⓐ a fraction, and ⓑ a decimal

                                   The probability of getting heads three times when tossing a coin three times is 12.5%.

Convert Decimals and Fractions to Percents

To convert a decimal to a percent, remember that percent means per hundred. If we change the decimal to a fraction whose denominator is 100, it is easy to change that fraction to a percent.

HOW TO :: CONVERT A DECIMAL TO A PERCENT.

Step 1.   Write the decimal as a fraction.

Step 2.   If the denominator of the fraction is not 100, rewrite it as an equivalent fraction with denominator 100.

Step 3.   Write this ratio as a percent.

EXAMPLE 6.9

Convert each decimal to a percent: ⓐ 0.05 ⓑ 0.83

✓ **Solution**

ⓐ

                                         0.05

Write as a fraction. The denominator is 100. $\frac{5}{100}$

Write this ratio as a percent.   5%

ⓑ

                                     0.83

The denominator is 100. $\frac{83}{100}$

Write this ratio as a percent.   83%

> **TRY IT : : 6.17**   Convert each decimal to a percent: ⓐ 0.01 ⓑ 0.17.

> **TRY IT : : 6.18**   Convert each decimal to a percent: ⓐ 0.04 ⓑ 0.41

To convert a mixed number to a percent, we first write it as an improper fraction.

EXAMPLE 6.10

Convert each decimal to a percent: ⓐ 1.05 ⓑ 0.075

⊘ **Solution**

ⓐ

	0.05
Write as a fraction.	$1\frac{5}{100}$
Write as an improper fraction. The denominator is 100.	$\frac{105}{100}$
Write this ratio as a percent.	105%

Notice that since $1.05 > 1$, the result is more than 100%.

ⓑ

	0.075
Write as a fraction. The denominator is 1,000.	$\frac{75}{1,000}$
Divide the numerator and denominator by 10, so that the denominator is 100.	$\frac{7.5}{100}$
Write this ratio as a percent.	7.5%

> **TRY IT : : 6.19**   Convert each decimal to a percent: ⓐ 1.75 ⓑ 0.0825

> **TRY IT : : 6.20**   Convert each decimal to a percent: ⓐ 2.25 ⓑ 0.0925

Let's summarize the results from the previous examples in Table 6.20 so we can look for a pattern.

Decimal	Percent
0.05	5%
0.83	83%
1.05	105%
0.075	7.5%

Table 6.20

Do you see the pattern? To convert a decimal to a percent, we move the decimal point two places to the right and then add the percent sign.

Figure 6.5 uses the decimal numbers in Table 6.20 and shows visually to convert them to percents by moving the decimal point two places to the right and then writing the % sign.

Percent	Decimal
006.%	0.06
078.%	0.78
135.%	1.35
012.5%	0.125

Figure 6.5

In Decimals, we learned how to convert fractions to decimals. Now we also know how to change decimals to percents. So to convert a fraction to a percent, we first change it to a decimal and then convert that decimal to a percent.

HOW TO :: CONVERT A FRACTION TO A PERCENT.

Step 1. Convert the fraction to a decimal.

Step 2. Convert the decimal to a percent.

EXAMPLE 6.11

Convert each fraction or mixed number to a percent: ⓐ $\frac{3}{4}$ ⓑ $\frac{11}{8}$ ⓒ $2\frac{1}{5}$

 Solution

To convert a fraction to a decimal, divide the numerator by the denominator.

ⓐ

Change to a decimal.	$\frac{3}{4}$
Write as a percent by moving the decimal two places.	0.75
	75%

ⓑ

Change to a decimal.	$\frac{11}{8}$
Write as a percent by moving the decimal two places.	1.375
	137.5%

ⓒ

Write as an improper fraction.	$2\frac{1}{5}$
Change to a decimal.	$\frac{11}{5}$
Write as a percent.	2.20
	220%

Notice that we needed to add zeros at the end of the number when moving the decimal two places to the right.

> **TRY IT ::** 6.21   Convert each fraction or mixed number to a percent: ⓐ $\frac{5}{8}$ ⓑ $\frac{11}{4}$ ⓒ $3\frac{2}{5}$

> **TRY IT ::** 6.22   Convert each fraction or mixed number to a percent: ⓐ $\frac{7}{8}$ ⓑ $\frac{9}{4}$ ⓒ $1\frac{3}{5}$

Sometimes when changing a fraction to a decimal, the division continues for many decimal places and we will round off the quotient. The number of decimal places we round to will depend on the situation. If the decimal involves money, we round to the hundredths place. For most other cases in this book we will round the number to the nearest thousandth, so the percent will be rounded to the nearest tenth.

EXAMPLE 6.12

Convert $\frac{5}{7}$ to a percent.

⊘ **Solution**

To change a fraction to a decimal, we divide the numerator by the denominator.

	$\frac{5}{7}$
Change to a decimal—rounding to the nearest thousandth.	0.714
Write as a percent.	71.4%

> **TRY IT ::** 6.23   Convert the fraction to a percent: $\frac{3}{7}$

> **TRY IT ::** 6.24   Convert the fraction to a percent: $\frac{4}{7}$

When we first looked at fractions and decimals, we saw that fractions converted to a repeating decimal. When we converted the fraction $\frac{4}{3}$ to a decimal, we wrote the answer as $1.\overline{3}$. We will use this same notation, as well as fraction notation, when we convert fractions to percents in the next example.

EXAMPLE 6.13

An article in a medical journal claimed that approximately $\frac{1}{3}$ of American adults are obese. Convert the fraction $\frac{1}{3}$ to a percent.

⊘ **Solution**

$$\frac{1}{3}$$

Change to a decimal.

$$\begin{array}{r} 0.33\ldots \\ 3\overline{)1.00} \\ \underline{9} \\ 10 \\ \underline{9} \\ 1 \end{array}$$

Write as a repeating decimal. $0.333\ldots$

Write as a percent. $33\frac{1}{3}\%$

We could also write the percent as $33.\overline{3}\%$.

> **TRY IT : : 6.25**

Convert the fraction to a percent:

According to the U.S. Census Bureau, about $\frac{1}{9}$ of United States housing units have just 1 bedroom.

> **TRY IT : : 6.26**

Convert the fraction to a percent:

According to the U.S. Census Bureau, about $\frac{1}{6}$ of Colorado residents speak a language other than English at home.

6.1 EXERCISES

Practice Makes Perfect

Use the Definition of Percents

In the following exercises, write each percent as a ratio.

1. In 2014, the unemployment rate for those with only a high school degree was 6.0%.

2. In 2015, among the unemployed, 29% were long-term unemployed.

3. The unemployment rate for those with Bachelor's degrees was 3.2% in 2014.

4. The unemployment rate in Michigan in 2014 was 7.3%.

In the following exercises, write as

ⓐ a ratio and   ⓑ a percent

5. 57 out of 100 nursing candidates received their degree at a community college.

6. 80 out of 100 firefighters and law enforcement officers were educated at a community college.

7. 42 out of 100 first-time freshmen students attend a community college.

8. 71 out of 100 full-time community college faculty have a master's degree.

Convert Percents to Fractions and Decimals

In the following exercises, convert each percent to a fraction and simplify all fractions.

9. 4%

10. 8%

11. 17%

12. 19%

13. 52%

14. 78%

15. 125%

16. 135%

17. 37.5%

18. 42.5%

19. 18.4%

20. 46.4%

21. $9\frac{1}{2}$ %

22. $8\frac{1}{2}$ %

23. $5\frac{1}{3}$ %

24. $6\frac{2}{3}$ %

In the following exercises, convert each percent to a decimal.

25. 5%

26. 9%

27. 1%

28. 2%

29. 63%

30. 71%

31. 40%

32. 50%

33. 115%

34. 125%

35. 150%

36. 250%

37. 21.4%

38. 39.3%

39. 7.8%

40. 6.4%

In the following exercises, convert each percent to

ⓐ a simplified fraction and   ⓑ a decimal

41. In 2010, 1.5% of home sales had owner financing. (*Source:* Bloomberg Businessweek, 5/23–29/2011)

42. In 2000, 4.2% of the United States population was of Asian descent. (*Source:* www.census.gov)

43. According to government data, in 2013 the number of cell phones in India was 70.23% of the population.

44. According to the U.S. Census Bureau, among Americans age 25 or older who had doctorate degrees in 2014, 37.1% are women.

45. A couple plans to have two children. The probability they will have two girls is 25%.

46. Javier will choose one digit at random from 0 through 9. The probability he will choose 3 is 10%.

47. According to the local weather report, the probability of thunderstorms in New York City on July 15 is 60%.

48. A club sells 50 tickets to a raffle. Osbaldo bought one ticket. The probability he will win the raffle is 2%.

Convert Decimals and Fractions to Percents

In the following exercises, convert each decimal to a percent.

49. 0.01   **50.** 0.03   **51.** 0.18

52. 0.15   **53.** 1.35   **54.** 1.56

55. 3   **56.** 4   **57.** 0.009

58. 0.008   **59.** 0.0875   **60.** 0.0625

61. 1.5   **62.** 2.2   **63.** 2.254

64. 2.317

In the following exercises, convert each fraction to a percent.

65. $\frac{1}{4}$ **66.** $\frac{1}{5}$ **67.** $\frac{3}{8}$

68. $\frac{5}{8}$ **69.** $\frac{7}{4}$ **70.** $\frac{9}{8}$

71. $6\frac{4}{5}$ **72.** $5\frac{1}{4}$ **73.** $\frac{5}{12}$

74. $\frac{11}{12}$ **75.** $2\frac{2}{3}$ **76.** $1\frac{2}{3}$

77. $\frac{3}{7}$ **78.** $\frac{6}{7}$ **79.** $\frac{5}{9}$

80. $\frac{4}{9}$

In the following exercises, convert each fraction to a percent.

81. $\frac{1}{4}$ of washing machines needed repair.

82. $\frac{1}{5}$ of dishwashers needed repair.

In the following exercises, convert each fraction to a percent.

83. According to the National Center for Health Statistics, in 2012, $\frac{7}{20}$ of American adults were obese.

84. The U.S. Census Bureau estimated that in 2013, 85% of Americans lived in the same house as they did 1 year before.

In the following exercises, complete the table.

85.

Fraction	Decimal	Percent
$\frac{1}{2}$		
	0.45	
		18 %
$\frac{1}{3}$		
	0.0008	
2		

Table 6.26

86.

Fraction	Decimal	Percent
$\frac{1}{4}$		
	0.65	
		22 %
$\frac{2}{3}$		
	0.0004	
3		

Table 6.27

Everyday Math

87. Sales tax Felipa says she has an easy way to estimate the sales tax when she makes a purchase. The sales tax in her city is 9.05%. She knows this is a little less than 10%.

ⓐ Convert 10% to a fraction.

ⓑ Use your answer from ⓐ to estimate the sales tax Felipa would pay on a $95 dress.

88. Savings Ryan has 25% of each paycheck automatically deposited in his savings account.

ⓐ Write 25% as a fraction.

ⓑ Use your answer from ⓐ to find the amount that goes to savings from Ryan's $2,400 paycheck.

89. Amelio is shopping for textbooks online. He found three sellers that are offering a book he needs for the same price, including shipping. To decide which seller to buy from he is comparing their customer satisfaction ratings. The ratings are given in the chart.

Seller	Rating
A	4/5
B	3.5/4
C	85%

90. Write seller C's rating as a fraction and a decimal.

91. Write seller B's rating as a percent and a decimal.

92. Write seller A's rating as a percent and a decimal.

93. Which seller should Amelio buy from and why?

Writing Exercises

94. Convert 25%, 50%, 75%, and 100% to fractions. Do you notice a pattern? Explain what the pattern is.

95. Convert $\frac{1}{10}$, $\frac{2}{10}$, $\frac{3}{10}$, $\frac{4}{10}$, $\frac{5}{10}$, $\frac{6}{10}$, $\frac{7}{10}$, $\frac{8}{10}$, and $\frac{9}{10}$ to percents. Do you notice a pattern? Explain what the pattern is.

96. When the Szetos sold their home, the selling price was 500% of what they had paid for the house 30 years ago. Explain what 500% means in this context.

97. According to cnn.com, cell phone use in 2008 was 600% of what it had been in 2001. Explain what 600% means in this context.

Self Check

ⓐ After completing the exercises, use this checklist to evaluate your mastery of the objectives of this section.

I can...	Confidently	With some help	No-I don't get it!
use the definition of percent.			
convert percents to fractions and decimals.			
convert decimals and fractions to percents.			

ⓑ If most of your checks were:

...confidently. Congratulations! You have achieved the objectives in this section. Reflect on the study skills you used so that you can continue to use them. What did you do to become confident of your ability to do these things? Be specific.

...with some help. This must be addressed quickly because topics you do not master become potholes in your road to success. In math, every topic builds upon previous work. It is important to make sure you have a strong foundation before you move on. Who can you ask for help? Your fellow classmates and instructor are good resources. Is there a place on campus where math tutors are available? Can your study skills be improved?

...no—I don't get it! This is a warning sign and you must not ignore it. You should get help right away or you will quickly be overwhelmed. See your instructor as soon as you can to discuss your situation. Together you can come up with a plan to get you the help you need.

6.2 | Solve General Applications of Percent

Learning Objectives

By the end of this section, you will be able to:

- Translate and solve basic percent equations
- Solve applications of percent
- Find percent increase and percent decrease

Be Prepared!

Before you get started, take this readiness quiz.

1. Translate and solve: $\frac{3}{4}$ of x is 24.

   If you missed this problem, review Example 4.105.

2. Simplify: $(4.5)(2.38)$.

   If you missed this problem, review Example 5.15.

3. Solve: $3.5 = 0.7n$.

   If you missed this problem, review Example 5.43.

Translate and Solve Basic Percent Equations

We will solve percent equations by using the methods we used to solve equations with fractions or decimals. In the past, you may have solved percent problems by setting them up as proportions. That was the best method available when you did not have the tools of algebra. Now as a prealgebra student, you can translate word sentences into algebraic equations, and then solve the equations.

We'll look at a common application of percent—tips to a server at a restaurant—to see how to set up a basic percent application.

When Aolani and her friends ate dinner at a restaurant, the bill came to $80. They wanted to leave a 20% tip. What amount would the tip be?

To solve this, we want to find what *amount* is 20% of $80. The $80 is called the *base*. The amount of the tip would be 0.20(80), or $16 See Figure 6.6. To find the amount of the tip, we multiplied the percent by the base.

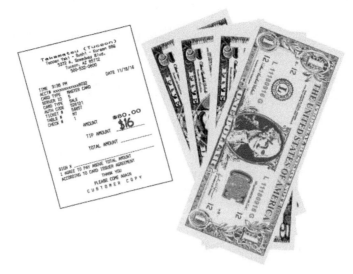

Figure 6.6 A 20% tip for an $80 restaurant bill comes out to $16.

In the next examples, we will find the amount. We must be sure to change the given percent to a decimal when we translate the words into an equation.

EXAMPLE 6.14

What number is 35% of 90?

✓ **Solution**

	What number is 35% of 90?
Translate into algebra. Let $n =$ the number.	$n = 0.35 \cdot 90$
Multiply.	$n = 31.5$
	31.5 is 35% of 90

> **TRY IT :: 6.27**   What number is 45% of 80?

> **TRY IT :: 6.28**   What number is 55% of 60?

EXAMPLE 6.15

125% of 28 is what number?

✓ **Solution**

	125% of 28 is what number?
Translate into algebra. Let $a =$ the number.	$1.25 \cdot 28 = a$
Multiply.	$35 = a$
	125% of 28 is 35.

Remember that a percent over 100 is a number greater than 1. We found that 125% of 28 is 35, which is greater than 28.

> **TRY IT :: 6.29** 150% of 78 is what number?

> **TRY IT :: 6.30** 175% of 72 is what number?

In the next examples, we are asked to find the base.

EXAMPLE 6.16

Translate and solve: 36 is 75% of what number?

Solution

Translate. Let $b =$ the number.	36 is 75% of what number? $36 = 0.75 \cdot b$
Divide both sides by 0.75.	$\dfrac{36}{0.75} = \dfrac{0.75b}{0.75}$
Simplify.	$48 = b$ 36 is 75% of 48.

> **TRY IT : :** 6.31   17 is 25% of what number?

> **TRY IT : :** 6.32   40 is 62.5% of what number?

EXAMPLE 6.17

6.5% of what number is $1.17?

Solution

Translate. Let $b =$ the number.	6.5% of what number is $1.17? $0.065 \cdot b = 1.17$
Divide both sides by 0.065.	$\dfrac{0.065n}{0.065} = \dfrac{1.17}{0.065}$
Simplify.	$n = 18$ 6.5% of $18 is $1.17.

> **TRY IT : :** 6.33   7.5% of what number is $1.95?

> **TRY IT : :** 6.34   8.5% of what number is $3.06?

In the next examples, we will solve for the percent.

EXAMPLE 6.18

What percent of 36 is 9?

⊘ Solution

	What percent of 36 is 9?
Translate into algebra. Let $p=$ the percent.	$p \cdot 36 = 9$
Divide by 36.	$\dfrac{36p}{36} = \dfrac{9}{36}$
Simplify.	$p = \dfrac{1}{4}$
Convert to decimal form.	$p = 0.25$
Convert to percent.	$p = 25\%$
	25% of 36 is 9.

> **TRY IT :: 6.35**   What percent of 76 is 57?

> **TRY IT :: 6.36**   What percent of 120 is 96?

EXAMPLE 6.19

144 is what percent of 96?

⊘ Solution

	144 is what percent of 96?
Translate into algebra. Let $p=$ the percent.	$144 = p \cdot 96$
Divide by 96.	$\dfrac{144}{96} = \dfrac{96p}{96}$
Simplify.	$1.5 = p$
Convert to percent.	$150\% = p$
	144 is 150% of 96.

> **TRY IT :: 6.37**   110 is what percent of 88?

> **TRY IT :: 6.38**   126 is what percent of 72?

Solve Applications of Percent

Many applications of percent occur in our daily lives, such as tips, sales tax, discount, and interest. To solve these applications we'll translate to a basic percent equation, just like those we solved in the previous examples in this section. Once you translate the sentence into a percent equation, you know how to solve it.

We will update the strategy we used in our earlier applications to include equations now. Notice that we will translate a sentence into an equation.

HOW TO :: SOLVE AN APPLICATION

Step 1.   Identify what you are asked to find and choose a variable to represent it.
Step 2.   Write a sentence that gives the information to find it.
Step 3.   Translate the sentence into an equation.
Step 4.   Solve the equation using good algebra techniques.
Step 5.   Check the answer in the problem and make sure it makes sense.
Step 6.   Write a complete sentence that answers the question.

Now that we have the strategy to refer to, and have practiced solving basic percent equations, we are ready to solve percent applications. Be sure to ask yourself if your final answer makes sense—since many of the applications we'll solve involve everyday situations, you can rely on your own experience.

EXAMPLE 6.20

Dezohn and his girlfriend enjoyed a dinner at a restaurant, and the bill was $68.50. They want to leave an 18% tip. If the tip will be 18% of the total bill, how much should the tip be?

⊘ **Solution**

What are you asked to find?	the amount of the tip
Choose a variable to represent it.	Let $t =$ amount of tip.
Write a sentence that give the information to find it.	The tip is 18% of the total bill.
Translate the sentence into an equation.	The tip is 18% of $68.50. $$t = 0.18 \cdot \$68.50$$
Multiply.	$t = 12.33$
Check. Is this answer reasonable?	

If we approximate the bill to $70 and the percent to 20%, we would have a tip of $14.
So a tip of $12.33 seems reasonable.

Write a complete sentence that answers the question.	The couple should leave a tip of $12.33.

> **TRY IT ::** 6.39

Cierra and her sister enjoyed a special dinner in a restaurant, and the bill was $81.50. If she wants to leave 18% of the total bill as her tip, how much should she leave?

> **TRY IT ::** 6.40

Kimngoc had lunch at her favorite restaurant. She wants to leave 15% of the total bill as her tip. If her bill was $14.40, how much will she leave for the tip?

EXAMPLE 6.21

The label on Masao's breakfast cereal said that one serving of cereal provides 85 milligrams (mg) of potassium, which is

2% of the recommended daily amount. What is the total recommended daily amount of potassium?

Nutrition Facts
Serving Size: 1 cup (47g)
Servings Per Container: About 7

Amount Per Serving	Cereal	With Milk
Calories	180	230
Calories from Fat	10	20
		% Daily Value*
Total Fat 1g	2%	2%
Saturated Fat 0g	0%	0%
Trans Fat 0g		
Polyunsaturated Fat 0.5g		
Monounsaturated Fat 0.5g		
Cholesterol 0mg	0%	0%
Sodium 190mg	8%	11%
Potassium 85mg	2%	8%
Total Carbohydrate 40g	13%	15%
Dietary Fiber 1g	4%	4%
Sugars 8g		
Protein 3g		

Solution

What are you asked to find?	the total amount of potassium recommended
Choose a variable to represent it.	Let $a =$ total amount of potassium.
Write a sentence that gives the information to find it.	85 mg is 2% of the total amount.
Translate the sentence into an equation.	85 mg is 2% of a? $85 = 0.02 \cdot a$
Divide both sides by 0.02.	$\dfrac{85}{0.02} = \dfrac{0.02a}{0.02}$
Simplify.	$4{,}250 = a$
Check: Is this answer reasonable?	
Yes. 2% is a small percent and 85 is a small part of 4,250.	
Write a complete sentence that answers the question.	The amount of potassium that is recommended is 4250 mg.

> **TRY IT ::** 6.41
>
> One serving of wheat square cereal has 7 grams of fiber, which is 29% of the recommended daily amount. What is the total recommended daily amount of fiber?

> **TRY IT ::** 6.42
>
> One serving of rice cereal has 190 mg of sodium, which is 8% of the recommended daily amount. What is the total recommended daily amount of sodium?

EXAMPLE 6.22

Mitzi received some gourmet brownies as a gift. The wrapper said each brownie was 480 calories, and had 240 calories of fat. What percent of the total calories in each brownie comes from fat?

⊘ **Solution**

What are you asked to find?	the percent of the total calories from fat
Choose a variable to represent it.	Let $p =$ percent from fat.
Write a sentence that gives the information to find it.	What percent of 480 is 240?
Translate the sentence into an equation.	What percent of 480 is 240? $$p \cdot 480 = 240$$
Divide both sides by 480.	$$\frac{p \cdot 480}{480} = \frac{240}{480}$$
Simplify.	$$p = 0.5$$
Convert to percent form.	$$p = 50\%$$
Check. Is this answer reasonable?	

Yes. 240 is half of 480, so 50% makes sense.

| Write a complete sentence that answers the question. | Of the total calories in each brownie, 50% is fat. |

> **TRY IT :: 6.43**

Veronica is planning to make muffins from a mix. The package says each muffin will be 230 calories and 60 calories will be from fat. What percent of the total calories is from fat? (Round to the nearest whole percent.)

> **TRY IT :: 6.44**

The brownie mix Ricardo plans to use says that each brownie will be 190 calories, and 70 calories are from fat. What percent of the total calories are from fat?

Find Percent Increase and Percent Decrease

People in the media often talk about how much an amount has increased or decreased over a certain period of time. They usually express this increase or decrease as a percent.

To find the **percent increase**, first we find the amount of increase, which is the difference between the new amount and the original amount. Then we find what percent the amount of increase is of the original amount.

HOW TO :: FIND PERCENT INCREASE.

Step 1. Find the amount of increase.
 • increase = new amount − original amount

Step 2. Find the percent increase as a percent of the original amount.

EXAMPLE 6.23

In 2011, the California governor proposed raising community college fees from $26 per unit to $36 per unit. Find the percent increase. (Round to the nearest tenth of a percent.)

⊘ **Solution**

What are you asked to find?	the percent increase
Choose a variable to represent it.	Let $p =$ percent.
Find the amount of increase.	$\underset{\substack{\text{new} \\ \text{amount}}}{36} - \underset{\substack{\text{original} \\ \text{amount}}}{26} = \underset{\text{increase}}{10}$
Find the percent increase.	The increase is what percent of the original amount?
Translate to an equation.	$\underset{10}{\underbrace{10}}$ $\underset{=}{\text{is}}$ $\underset{p}{\underbrace{\text{what percent}}}$ $\underset{\cdot}{\text{of}}$ $\underset{26}{\underbrace{26?}}$
Divide both sides by 26.	$\dfrac{10}{26} = \dfrac{26p}{26}$
Round to the nearest thousandth.	$0.384 = p$
Convert to percent form.	$38.4\% = P$
Write a complete sentence.	The new fees represent a 38.4% increase over the old fees.

> **TRY IT ::** 6.45

In 2011, the IRS increased the deductible mileage cost to 55.5 cents from 51 cents. Find the percent increase. (Round to the nearest tenth of a percent.)

> **TRY IT ::** 6.46

In 1995, the standard bus fare in Chicago was $1.50. In 2008, the standard bus fare was $2.25. Find the percent increase. (Round to the nearest tenth of a percent.)

Finding the **percent decrease** is very similar to finding the percent increase, but now the amount of decrease is the difference between the original amount and the final amount. Then we find what percent the amount of decrease is of the original amount.

 HOW TO :: FIND PERCENT DECREASE.

Step 1. Find the amount of decrease.

  ◦ decrease = original amount − new amount

Step 2. Find the percent decrease as a percent of the original amount.

EXAMPLE 6.24

The average price of a gallon of gas in one city in June 2014 was $3.71. The average price in that city in July was $3.64. Find the percent decrease.

⊘ **Solution**

What are you asked to find?	the percent decrease
Choose a variable to represent it.	Let $p =$ percent.
Find the amount of decrease.	$\underbrace{3.71}_{\substack{\text{original}\\\text{amount}}} - \underbrace{3.64}_{\substack{\text{new}\\\text{amount}}} = \underbrace{0.07}_{\text{increase}}$
Find the percent of decrease.	The decrease is what percent of the original amount?
Translate to an equation.	$\underbrace{0.07}\ \underbrace{\text{is}}\ \underbrace{\text{what percent}}\ \text{of}\ \underbrace{3.71}$ $0.07 = p \cdot 3.71$
Divide both sides by 3.71.	$\frac{0.07}{3.71} = \frac{3.71p}{3.71}$
Round to the nearest thousandth.	$0.019 = p$
Convert to percent form.	$1.9\% = p$
Write a complete sentence.	The price of gas decreased 1.9%.

> **TRY IT : : 6.47**

The population of one city was about 672,000 in 2010. The population of the city is projected to be about 630,000 in 2020. Find the percent decrease. (Round to the nearest tenth of a percent.)

> **TRY IT : : 6.48**

Last year Sheila's salary was $42,000. Because of furlough days, this year her salary was $37,800. Find the percent decrease. (Round to the nearest tenth of a percent.)

▶ **MEDIA : :** ACCESS ADDITIONAL ONLINE RESOURCES
- Percent Increase and Percent Decrease Visualization (http://www.openstaxcollege.org/l/24percentincdec)

6.2 EXERCISES

Practice Makes Perfect

Translate and Solve Basic Percent Equations

In the following exercises, translate and solve.

98. What number is 45% of 120?

99. What number is 65% of 100?

100. What number is 24% of 112?

101. What number is 36% of 124?

102. 250% of 65 is what number?

103. 150% of 90 is what number?

104. 800% of 2,250 is what number?

105. 600% of 1,740 is what number?

106. 28 is 25% of what number?

107. 36 is 25% of what number?

108. 81 is 75% of what number?

109. 93 is 75% of what number?

110. 8.2% of what number is $2.87?

111. 6.4% of what number is $2.88?

112. 11.5% of what number is $108.10?

113. 12.3% of what number is $92.25?

114. What percent of 260 is 78?

115. What percent of 215 is 86?

116. What percent of 1,500 is 540?

117. What percent of 1,800 is 846?

118. 30 is what percent of 20?

119. 50 is what percent of 40?

120. 840 is what percent of 480?

121. 790 is what percent of 395?

Solve Applications of Percents

In the following exercises, solve the applications of percents.

122. Geneva treated her parents to dinner at their favorite restaurant. The bill was $74.25. She wants to leave 16% of the total bill as a tip. How much should the tip be?

123. When Hiro and his co-workers had lunch at a restaurant the bill was $90.50. They want to leave 18% of the total bill as a tip. How much should the tip be?

124. Trong has 12% of each paycheck automatically deposited to his savings account. His last paycheck was $2,165. How much money was deposited to Trong's savings account?

125. Cherise deposits 8% of each paycheck into her retirement account. Her last paycheck was $1,485. How much did Cherise deposit into her retirement account?

126. One serving of oatmeal has 8 grams of fiber, which is 33% of the recommended daily amount. What is the total recommended daily amount of fiber?

127. One serving of trail mix has 67 grams of carbohydrates, which is 22% of the recommended daily amount. What is the total recommended daily amount of carbohydrates?

128. A bacon cheeseburger at a popular fast food restaurant contains 2,070 milligrams (mg) of sodium, which is 86% of the recommended daily amount. What is the total recommended daily amount of sodium?

129. A grilled chicken salad at a popular fast food restaurant contains 650 milligrams (mg) of sodium, which is 27% of the recommended daily amount. What is the total recommended daily amount of sodium?

130. The nutrition fact sheet at a fast food restaurant says the fish sandwich has 380 calories, and 171 calories are from fat. What percent of the total calories is from fat?

131. The nutrition fact sheet at a fast food restaurant says a small portion of chicken nuggets has 190 calories, and 114 calories are from fat. What percent of the total calories is from fat?

132. Emma gets paid $3,000 per month. She pays $750 a month for rent. What percent of her monthly pay goes to rent?

133. Dimple gets paid $3,200 per month. She pays $960 a month for rent. What percent of her monthly pay goes to rent?

Find Percent Increase and Percent Decrease

In the following exercises, find the percent increase or percent decrease.

134. Tamanika got a raise in her hourly pay, from $15.50 to $17.55. Find the percent increase.

135. Ayodele got a raise in her hourly pay, from $24.50 to $25.48. Find the percent increase.

136. Annual student fees at the University of California rose from about $4,000 in 2000 to about $9,000 in 2014. Find the percent increase.

137. The price of a share of one stock rose from $12.50 to $50. Find the percent increase.

138. According to Time magazine (7/19/2011) annual global seafood consumption rose from 22 pounds per person in 1960 to 38 pounds per person today. Find the percent increase. (Round to the nearest tenth of a percent.)

139. In one month, the median home price in the Northeast rose from $225,400 to $241,500. Find the percent increase. (Round to the nearest tenth of a percent.)

140. A grocery store reduced the price of a loaf of bread from $2.80 to $2.73. Find the percent decrease.

141. The price of a share of one stock fell from $8.75 to $8.54. Find the percent decrease.

142. Hernando's salary was $49,500 last year. This year his salary was cut to $44,055. Find the percent decrease.

143. From 2000 to 2010, the population of Detroit fell from about 951,000 to about 714,000. Find the percent decrease. (Round to the nearest tenth of a percent.)

144. In one month, the median home price in the West fell from $203,400 to $192,300. Find the percent decrease. (Round to the nearest tenth of a percent.)

145. Sales of video games and consoles fell from $1,150 million to $1,030 million in one year. Find the percent decrease. (Round to the nearest tenth of a percent.)

Everyday Math

146. Tipping At the campus coffee cart, a medium coffee costs $1.65. MaryAnne brings $2.00 with her when she buys a cup of coffee and leaves the change as a tip. What percent tip does she leave?

147. Late Fees Alison was late paying her credit card bill of $249. She was charged a 5% late fee. What was the amount of the late fee?

Writing Exercises

148. Without solving the problem "44 is 80% of what number", think about what the solution might be. Should it be a number that is greater than 44 or less than 44? Explain your reasoning.

149. Without solving the problem "What is 20% of 300?" think about what the solution might be. Should it be a number that is greater than 300 or less than 300? Explain your reasoning.

150. After returning from vacation, Alex said he should have packed 50% fewer shorts and 200% more shirts. Explain what Alex meant.

151. Because of road construction in one city, commuters were advised to plan their Monday morning commute to take 150% of their usual commuting time. Explain what this means.

Self Check

ⓐ *After completing the exercises, use this checklist to evaluate your mastery of the objectives of this section.*

I can...	Confidently	With some help	No-I don't get it!
translate and solve basic percent equations.			
solve applications of percent.			
find percent increase and percent decrease.			

ⓑ *After reviewing this checklist, what will you do to become confident for all objectives?*

6.3 | Solve Sales Tax, Commission, and Discount Applications

Learning Objectives

By the end of this section, you will be able to:

- Solve sales tax applications
- Solve commission applications
- Solve discount applications
- Solve mark-up applications

Be Prepared!

Before you get started, take this readiness quiz.

1. Solve $0.0875(720)$ through multiplication.
   If you missed this problem, review Example 5.17.

2. Solve $12.96 \div 0.04$ through division.
   If you missed this problem, review Example 5.22.

Solve Sales Tax Applications

Sales tax and commissions are applications of percent in our everyday lives. To solve these applications, we will follow the same strategy we used in the section on decimal operations. We show it again here for easy reference.

HOW TO ::

Solve an application

Step 1.   Identify what you are asked to find and choose a variable to represent it.

Step 2.   Write a sentence that gives the information to find it.

Step 3.   Translate the sentence into an equation.

Step 4.   Solve the equation using good algebra techniques.

Step 5.   Check the answer in the problem and make sure it makes sense.

Step 6.   Write a complete sentence that answers the question.

Remember that whatever the application, once we write the sentence with the given information (Step 2), we can translate it to a percent equation and then solve it.

Do you pay a tax when you shop in your city or state? In many parts of the United States, sales tax is added to the purchase price of an item. See Figure 6.7. The sales tax is determined by computing a percent of the purchase price.

To find the sales tax multiply the purchase price by the sales tax rate. Remember to convert the sales tax rate from a percent to a decimal number. Once the sales tax is calculated, it is added to the purchase price. The result is the total cost—this is what the customer pays.

Figure 6.7 The sales tax is calculated as a percent of the purchase price.

Sales Tax

The sales tax is a percent of the purchase price.

$$\text{Sales Tax} = \text{Tax Rate} \cdot \text{Purchase Price}$$
$$\text{Total Cost} = \text{Purchase Price} + \text{Sales Tax}$$

EXAMPLE 6.25

Cathy bought a bicycle in Washington, where the sales tax rate was 6.5% of the purchase price. What was

ⓐ the sales tax and   ⓑ the total cost of a bicycle if the purchase price of the bicycle was $\$392$?

✓ **Solution**

ⓐ

Identify what you are asked to find.	What is the sales tax?
Choose a variable to represent it.	Let $t =$ sales tax.
Write a sentence that gives the information to find it.	The sales tax is 6.5% of the purchase price.

Translate into an equation. (Remember to change the percent to a decimal).

The sales tax	is	6.5%	of	the $392 purchase price.
t	$=$	0.065	$\cdot$	392

Simplify. $t = 25.48$

Check: Is this answer reasonable?

Yes, because the sales tax amount is less than 10% of the purchase price.

Write a complete sentence that answers the question.   The sales tax is $25.48.

ⓑ

Identify what you are asked to find.	What is the total cost of the bicycle?
Choose a variable to represent it.	Let $c =$ total cost of bicycle.
Write a sentence that gives the information to find it.	The total cost is the purchase price plus the sales tax.
Translate into an equation.	The total cost is $392 plus $25.48 $c \quad = \quad 392 \quad + \quad 25.48$
Simplify.	$c = 417.48$
Check: Is this answer reasonable?	
Yes, because the total cost is a little more than the purchase price.	
Write a complete sentence that answers the question.	The total cost of the bicycle is $417.48.

> **TRY IT : :** 6.49
>
> Find ⓐ the sales tax and ⓑ the total cost: Alexandra bought a television set for $724 in Boston, where the sales tax rate was 6.25% of the purchase price.

> **TRY IT : :** 6.50
>
> Find ⓐ the sales tax and ⓑ the total cost: Kim bought a winter coat for $250 in St. Louis, where the sales tax rate was 8.2% of the purchase price.

EXAMPLE 6.26

Evelyn bought a new smartphone for $499 plus tax. She was surprised when she got the receipt and saw that the tax was $42.42. What was the sales tax rate for this purchase?

✅ **Solution**

Identify what you are asked to find.	What is the sales tax rate?
Choose a variable to represent it.	Let $r =$ sales tax.
Write a sentence that gives the information to find it.	What percent of the price is the sales tax?

Translate into an equation.

What percent	of	the \$499 price	is	the \$42.42 tax?
r	$\cdot$	499	$=$	42.42

Divide.

$$\frac{499r}{499} = \frac{42.42}{499}$$

Simplify.

$$r = 0.085$$

Check. Is this answer reasonable?

Yes, because 8.5% is close to 10%.
10% of \$500 is \$50, which is close to \$42.42.

Write a complete sentence that answers the question.   The sales tax rate is 8.5%.

> **TRY IT :: 6.51**

> Diego bought a new car for \$26,525. He was surprised that the dealer then added \$2,387.25. What was the sales tax rate for this purchase?

> **TRY IT :: 6.52**   What is the sales tax rate if a \$7,594 purchase will have \$569.55 of sales tax added to it?

Solve Commission Applications

Sales people often receive a **commission**, or percent of total sales, for their sales. Their income may be just the commission they earn, or it may be their commission added to their hourly wages or salary. The commission they earn is calculated as a certain percent of the price of each item they sell. That percent is called the **rate of commission**.

Commission

A commission is a percentage of total sales as determined by the rate of commission.

$$\text{commission} = \text{rate of commission} \cdot \text{total sales}$$

To find the commission on a sale, multiply the rate of commission by the total sales. Just as we did for computing sales tax, remember to first convert the rate of commission from a percent to a decimal.

EXAMPLE 6.27

Helene is a realtor. She receives 3% commission when she sells a house. How much commission will she receive for selling a house that costs \$260,000?

⊘ **Solution**

Identify what you are asked to find.	What is the commission?
Choose a variable to represent it.	Let $c =$ the commission.
Write a sentence that gives the information to find it.	The commission is 3% of the price.

Translate into an equation.

The commission $\underbrace{\text{The commission}}_{c}$ $\underbrace{\text{is}}{}$ $\underbrace{\text{3\%}}_{= \quad 0.03}$ $\underbrace{\text{of}}{}$ $\underbrace{\text{the \$260,000 price.}}_{260{,}000}$

Simplify.	$c = 7800$
Change to percent form.	$r = 8.5\%$
Check. Is this answer reasonable?	
Yes. 1% of \$260,000 is \$2,600, and \$7,800 is three times \$2,600.	
Write a complete sentence that answers the question.	Helene will receive a commission of \$7,800.

> **TRY IT : : 6.53**
>
> Bob is a travel agent. He receives 7% commission when he books a cruise for a customer. How much commission will he receive for booking a $\$3,900$ cruise?

> **TRY IT : : 6.54**
>
> Fernando receives 18% commission when he makes a computer sale. How much commission will he receive for selling a computer for $\$2,190$?

EXAMPLE 6.28

Rikki earned $\$87$ commission when she sold a $\$1,450$ stove. What rate of commission did she get?

✓ Solution

Identify what you are asked to find.	What is the rate of commission?
Choose a variable to represent it.	Let $r =$ the rate of commission.
Write a sentence that gives the information to find it.	The commission is what percent of the sale?

Translate into an equation.

The $87 commission	is	what percent	of	the $1450 sale?
87	$=$	0.03	.	1450

Divide.	$\dfrac{87}{1450} = \dfrac{1450r}{1450}$
Simplify.	$0.06 = r$
Change to percent form.	$r = 6\%$
Check if this answer is reasonable.	

Yes. A 10% commission would have been $145. The 6% commission, $87, is a little more than half of that.

Write a complete sentence that answers the question.	The commission was 6% of the price of the stove.

> **TRY IT : :** 6.55

Homer received $1,140 commission when he sold a car for $28,500. What rate of commission did he get?

> **TRY IT : :** 6.56

Bernice earned $451 commission when she sold an $8,200 living room set. What rate of commission did she get?

Solve Discount Applications

Applications of discount are very common in retail settings Figure 6.8. When you buy an item on sale, the **original price** of the item has been reduced by some dollar amount. The **discount rate**, usually given as a percent, is used to determine the amount of the discount. To determine the **amount of discount**, we multiply the discount rate by the original price. We summarize the discount model in the box below.

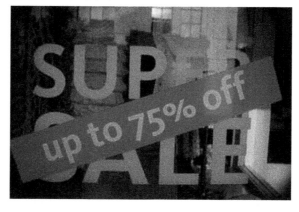

Figure 6.8 Applications of discounts are common in everyday life. (credit: Charleston's TheDigitel, Flickr)

Discount

An amount of discount is a percent off the original price.

$$\text{amount of discount} = \text{discount rate} \cdot \text{original price}$$

$$\text{sale price} = \text{original price} - \text{discount}$$

The sale price should always be less than the original price. In some cases, the amount of discount is a fixed dollar amount. Then we just find the sale price by subtracting the amount of discount from the original price.

EXAMPLE 6.29

Jason bought a pair of sunglasses that were on sale for $10 off. The original price of the sunglasses was $39. What was the sale price of the sunglasses?

⊘ **Solution**

Identify what you are asked to find.	What is the sale price?
Choose a variable to represent it.	Let $s =$ the sale price.
Write a sentence that gives the information to find it.	The sale price is the original price minus the discount.
Translate into an equation.	The sale price **is** the original $39 price **minus** the $10 discount. $s \quad = \quad 39 \quad - \quad 10$
Simplify.	$s = 29$
Check if this answer is reasonable.	
Yes. The sale price, $29, is less than the original price, $39.	
Write a complete sentence that answers the question.	The sale price of the sunglasses was $29.

> **TRY IT : : 6.57**
>
> Marta bought a dishwasher that was on sale for $75 off. The original price of the dishwasher was $525. What was the sale price of the dishwasher?

> **TRY IT : : 6.58**
>
> Orlando bought a pair of shoes that was on sale for $30 off. The original price of the shoes was $112. What was the sale price of the shoes?

In Example 6.29, the amount of discount was a set amount, $10. In Example 6.30 the discount is given as a percent of the original price.

EXAMPLE 6.30

Elise bought a dress that was discounted 35% off of the original price of $140. What was ⓐ the amount of discount and ⓑ the sale price of the dress?

⊘ **Solution**

ⓐ Before beginning, you may find it helpful to organize the information in a list.

Original price = $140

Discount rate = 35%

553

Amount of discount = ?

Identify what you are asked to find.	What is the amount of discount?
Choose a variable to represent it.	Let $d =$ the amount of discount.
Write a sentence that gives the information to find it.	The discount is 35% of the original price.
Translate into an equation.	The discount is 35% of the $140 original price. $s = 0.35 \cdot 140$
Simplify.	$d = 49$
Check if this answer is reasonable.	

Yes. A $49 discount is reasonable for a $140 dress.

| Write a complete sentence that answers the question. | The amount of discount was $49. |

ⓑ
Original price = $140
Amount of discount = $49
Sale price = ?

Identify what you are asked to find.	What is the sale price of the dress?
Choose a variable to represent it.	Let $s =$ the sale price.
Write a sentence that gives the information to find it.	The sale price is the original price minus the discount.
Translate into an equation.	The sale price is the $140 minus the $49 discount. $s = 140 - 49$
Simplify.	$s = 91$
Check if this answer is reasonable.	

Yes. The sale price, $91, is less than the original price, $140.

| Write a complete sentence that answers the question. | The sale price of the dress was $91. |

> **TRY IT : : 6.59**

 Find ⓐ the amount of discount and ⓑ the sale price: Sergio bought a belt that was discounted 40% from an original price of $29.

> **TRY IT : : 6.60**

 Find ⓐ the amount of discount and ⓑ the sale price: Oscar bought a barbecue grill that was discounted 65% from an original price of $395.

There may be times when you buy something on sale and want to know the discount rate. The next example will show this case.

EXAMPLE 6.31

Jeannette bought a swimsuit at a sale price of $13.95. The original price of the swimsuit was $31. Find the ⓐ amount of discount and ⓑ discount rate.

✓ **Solution**

ⓐ Before beginning, you may find it helpful to organize the information in a list.
Original price = $31
Amount of discount = ?
Sale price = $13.95

Identify what you are asked to find.	What is the amount of discount?
Choose a variable to represent it.	Let $d=$ the amount of discount.
Write a sentence that gives the information to find it.	The discount is the original price minus the sale price.
Translate into an equation.	The discount is the $31 original price minus the $13.95 sale price. $s = 31 - 13.95$
Simplify.	$d = 17.05$
Check if this answer is reasonable.	
Yes. The $17.05 discount is less than the original price.	
Write a complete sentence that answers the question.	The amount of discount was $17.05.

ⓑ Before beginning, you may find it helpful to organize the information in a list.
Original price = $31
Amount of discount = $17.05
Discount rate = ?

Identify what you are asked to find.	What is the discount rate?
Choose a variable to represent it.	Let $r=$ the discount rate.
Write a sentence that gives the information to find it.	The discount is what percent of the original price?
Translate into an equation.	The discount of $17.05 is what percent of the $31 original price. $s = r \cdot 31$
Divide.	$\frac{17.05}{31} = \frac{r(31)}{31}$
Simplify.	$0.55 = r$
Check if this answer is reasonable.	
The rate of discount was a little more than 50% and the amount of discount is a little more than half of $31.	
Write a complete sentence that answers the question.	The rate of discount was 55%.

> **TRY IT :: 6.61**
>
> Find ⓐ the amount of discount and ⓑ the discount rate: Lena bought a kitchen table at the sale price of $375.20. The original price of the table was $560.

> **TRY IT :: 6.62**
>
> Find ⓐ the amount of discount and ⓑ the discount rate: Nick bought a multi-room air conditioner at a sale price of $340. The original price of the air conditioner was $400.

Solve Mark-up Applications

Applications of mark-up are very common in retail settings. The price a retailer pays for an item is called the **wholesale price**. The retailer then adds a **mark-up** to the wholesale price to get the **list price**, the price he sells the item for. The mark-up is usually calculated as a percent of the wholesale price. The percent is called the **mark-up rate**. To determine the amount of mark-up, multiply the mark-up rate by the wholesale price. We summarize the mark-up model in the box below.

Mark-up

The mark-up is the amount added to the wholesale price.

$$\text{amount of mark-up} = \text{mark-up rate} \cdot \text{wholesale price}$$
$$\text{list price} = \text{wholesale price} + \text{mark up}$$

The list price should always be more than the wholesale price.

EXAMPLE 6.32

Adam's art gallery bought a photograph at the wholesale price of $250. Adam marked the price up 40%. Find the ⓐ amount of mark-up and ⓑ the list price of the photograph.

⊘ **Solution**

ⓐ

Identify what you are asked to find.	What is the amount of mark-up?
Choose a variable to represent it.	Let $m =$ the amount of each mark-up.
Write a sentence that gives the information to find it.	The mark-up is 40% of the wholesale price.
Translate into an equation.	The mark-up is 40% of the $250 wholesale price. $m = 0.40 \cdot 250$
Simplify.	$m = 100$
Check if this answer is reasonable.	
Yes. The markup rate is less than 50% and $100 is less than half of $250.	
Write a complete sentence that answers the question.	The mark-up on the photograph was $100.

ⓑ

Identify what you are asked to find.	What is the list price?
Choose a variable to represent it.	Let $p =$ the list price.
Write a sentence that gives the information to find it.	The list price is the wholesale price plus the mark-up.
Translate into an equation.	The list price is the $250 wholesale price plus the $100 mark-up. $p \quad = \quad 250 \quad + \quad 100$
Simplify.	$p = 350$
Check if this answer is reasonable.	
Yes. The list price, $350, is more than the wholesale price, $250.	
Write a complete sentence that answers the question.	The list price of the photograph was $350.

> **TRY IT : : 6.63**

  Jim's music store bought a guitar at wholesale price $1,200. Jim marked the price up 50%. Find the ⓐ amount of mark-up and ⓑ the list price.

> **TRY IT : : 6.64**

  The Auto Resale Store bought Pablo's Toyota for $8,500. They marked the price up 35%. Find the ⓐ amount of mark-up and ⓑ the list price.

6.3 EXERCISES

Practice Makes Perfect

Solve Sales Tax Applications

In the following exercises, find ⓐ the sales tax and ⓑ the total cost.

152. The cost of a pair of boots was $84. The sales tax rate is 5% of the purchase price.

153. The cost of a refrigerator was $1,242. The sales tax rate is 8% of the purchase price.

154. The cost of a microwave oven was $129. The sales tax rate is 7.5% of the purchase price.

155. The cost of a tablet computer is $350. The sales tax rate is 8.5% of the purchase price.

156. The cost of a file cabinet is $250. The sales tax rate is 6.85% of the purchase price.

157. The cost of a luggage set $400. The sales tax rate is 5.75% of the purchase price.

158. The cost of a 6-drawer dresser $1,199. The sales tax rate is 5.125% of the purchase price.

159. The cost of a sofa is $1,350. The sales tax rate is 4.225% of the purchase price.

In the following exercises, find the sales tax rate.

160. Shawna bought a mixer for $300. The sales tax on the purchase was $19.50.

161. Orphia bought a coffee table for $400. The sales tax on the purchase was $38.

162. Bopha bought a bedroom set for $3,600. The sales tax on the purchase was $246.60.

163. Ruth bought a washer and dryer set for $2,100. The sales tax on the purchase was $152.25.

Solve Commission Applications

In the following exercises, find the commission.

164. Christopher sold his dinette set for $225 through an online site, which charged him 9% of the selling price as commission. How much was the commission?

165. Michele rented a booth at a craft fair, which charged her 8% commission on her sales. One day her total sales were $193. How much was the commission?

166. Farrah works in a jewelry store and receives 12% commission when she makes a sale. How much commission will she receive for selling a $8,125 ring?

167. Jamal works at a car dealership and receives 9% commission when he sells a car. How much commission will he receive for selling a $32,575 car?

168. Hector receives 17.5% commission when he sells an insurance policy. How much commission will he receive for selling a policy for $4,910?

169. Denise receives 10.5% commission when she books a tour at the travel agency. How much commission will she receive for booking a tour with total cost $7,420?

In the following exercises, find the rate of commission.

170. Dontay is a realtor and earned $11,250 commission on the sale of a $375,000 house. What is his rate of commission?

171. Nevaeh is a cruise specialist and earned $364 commission after booking a cruise that cost $5,200. What is her rate of commission?

172. As a waitress, Emily earned $420 in tips on sales of $2,625 last Saturday night. What was her rate of commission?

173. Alejandra earned $1,393.74 commission on weekly sales of $15,486 as a salesperson at the computer store. What is her rate of commission?

174. Maureen earned $7,052.50 commission when she sold a $45,500 car. What was the rate of commission?

175. Lucas earned $4,487.50 commission when he brought a $35,900 job to his office. What was the rate of commission?

Solve Discount Applications

In the following exercises, find the sale price.

176. Perla bought a cellphone that was on sale for $50 off. The original price of the cellphone was $189.

177. Sophie saw a dress she liked on sale for $15 off. The original price of the dress was $96.

178. Rick wants to buy a tool set with original price $165. Next week the tool set will be on sale for 40% off.

179. Angelo's store is having a sale on TV sets. One set, with an original price of $859, is selling for $125 off.

In the following exercises, find ⓐ the amount of discount and ⓑ the sale price.

180. Janelle bought a beach chair on sale at 60% off. The original price was $44.95

181. Errol bought a skateboard helmet on sale at 40% off. The original price was $49.95.

182. Kathy wants to buy a camera that lists for $389. The camera is on sale with a 33% discount.

183. Colleen bought a suit that was discounted 25% from an original price of $245.

184. Erys bought a treadmill on sale at 35% off. The original price was $949.95.

185. Jay bought a guitar on sale at 45% off. The original price was $514.75.

In the following exercises, find ⓐ the amount of discount and ⓑ the discount rate. (Round to the nearest tenth of a percent if needed.)

186. Larry and Donna bought a sofa at the sale price of $1,344. The original price of the sofa was $1,920.

187. Hiroshi bought a lawnmower at the sale price of $240. The original price of the lawnmower is $300.

188. Patty bought a baby stroller on sale for $301.75. The original price of the stroller was $355.

189. Bill found a book he wanted on sale for $20.80. The original price of the book was $32.

190. Nikki bought a patio set on sale for $480. The original price was $850.

191. Stella bought a dinette set on sale for $725. The original price was $1,299.

Solve Mark-up Applications

In the following exercises, find ⓐ the amount of the mark-up and ⓑ the list price.

192. Daria bought a bracelet at wholesale cost $16 to sell in her handicraft store. She marked the price up 45%.

193. Regina bought a handmade quilt at wholesale cost $120 to sell in her quilt store. She marked the price up 55%.

194. Tom paid $0.60 a pound for tomatoes to sell at his produce store. He added a 33% mark-up.

195. Flora paid her supplier $0.74 a stem for roses to sell at her flower shop. She added an 85% mark-up.

196. Alan bought a used bicycle for $115. After re-conditioning it, he added 225% mark-up and then advertised it for sale.

197. Michael bought a classic car for $8,500. He restored it, then added 150% mark-up before advertising it for sale.

Everyday Math

198. Coupons Yvonne can use two coupons for the same purchase at her favorite department store. One coupon gives her $20 off and the other gives her 25% off. She wants to buy a bedspread that sells for $195.

ⓐ Calculate the discount price if Yvonne uses the $20 coupon first and then takes 25% off.

ⓑ Calculate the discount price if Yvonne uses the 25% off coupon first and then uses the 20% coupon.

ⓒ In which order should Yvonne use the coupons?

199. Cash Back Jason can buy a bag of dog food for $35 at two different stores. One store offers 6% cash back on the purchase plus $5 off his next purchase. The other store offers 20% cash back.

ⓐ Calculate the total savings from the first store, including the savings on the next purchase.

ⓑ Calculate the total savings from the second store.

ⓒ Which store should Jason buy the dog food from? Why?

Writing Exercises

200. Priam bought a jacket that was on sale for 40% off. The original price of the jacket was $150. While the sales clerk figured the price by calculating the amount of discount and then subtracting that amount from $150, Priam found the price faster by calculating 60% of $150.

ⓐ Explain why Priam was correct.

ⓑ Will Priam's method work for any original price?

201. Roxy bought a scarf on sale for 50% off. The original price of the scarf was $32.90. Roxy claimed that the price she paid for the scarf was the same as the amount she saved. Was Roxy correct? Explain.

Self Check

ⓐ *After completing the exercises, use this checklist to evaluate your mastery of the objectives of this section.*

I can...	Confidently	With some help	No-I don't get it!
solve sales tax applications.			
solve commission applications.			
solve discount applications.			
solve mark-up applications.			

ⓑ *What does this checklist tell you about your mastery of this section? What steps will you take to improve?*

6.4 | Solve Simple Interest Applications

Learning Objectives

By the end of this section, you will be able to:
- Use the simple interest formula
- Solve simple interest applications

Be Prepared!

Before you get started, take this readiness quiz.

1. Solve $0.6y = 45$.
   If you missed this problem, review Example 5.43.
2. Solve $\dfrac{n}{1.45} = 4.6$.
   If you missed this problem, review Example 5.44.

Use the Simple Interest Formula

Do you know that banks pay you to let them keep your money? The money you put in the bank is called the **principal**, P, and the bank pays you **interest**, I. The interest is computed as a certain percent of the principal; called the **rate of interest**, r. The rate of interest is usually expressed as a percent per year, and is calculated by using the decimal equivalent of the percent. The variable for time, t, represents the number of years the money is left in the account.

Simple Interest

If an amount of money, P, the principal, is invested for a period of t years at an annual interest rate r, the amount of interest, I, earned is

$$I = Prt$$

where

$$\begin{aligned}
I &= \text{interest} \\
P &= \text{principal} \\
r &= \text{rate} \\
t &= \text{time}
\end{aligned}$$

Interest earned according to this formula is called **simple interest**.

The formula we use to calculate simple interest is $I = Prt$. To use the simple interest formula we substitute in the values for variables that are given, and then solve for the unknown variable. It may be helpful to organize the information by listing all four variables and filling in the given information.

EXAMPLE 6.33

Find the simple interest earned after 3 years on $\$500$ at an interest rate of 6%.

⊘ Solution

Organize the given information in a list.

$$\begin{aligned}
I &= ? \\
P &= \$500 \\
r &= 6\% \\
t &= 3 \text{ years}
\end{aligned}$$

We will use the simple interest formula to find the interest.

Write the formula.	$I = Prt$
Substitute the given information. Remember to write the percent in decimal form.	$I = (500)(0.06)(3)$
Simplify.	$I = 90$

Check your answer. Is $90 a reasonable interest earned on $500 in 3 years?

In 3 years the money earned 18%. If we rounded to 20%, the interest would have been 500(0.20) or $100. Yes, $90 is reasonable.

Write a complete sentence that answers the question.	The simple interest is $90.

> **TRY IT :: 6.65**   Find the simple interest earned after 4 years on $800 at an interest rate of 5%.

> **TRY IT :: 6.66**   Find the simple interest earned after 2 years on $700 at an interest rate of 4%.

In the next example, we will use the simple interest formula to find the principal.

EXAMPLE 6.34

Find the principal invested if $178 interest was earned in 2 years at an interest rate of 4%.

⊘ **Solution**

Organize the given information in a list.

I = $178
P = ?
r = 4%
t = 2 years

We will use the simple interest formula to find the principal.

Write the formula.	$I = Prt$
Substitute the given information.	$178 = P(0.04)(2)$
Divide.	$\dfrac{178}{0.08} = \dfrac{0.08P}{0.08}$
Simplify.	$2{,}225 = P$

Check your answer. Is it reasonable that $2,225 would earn $178 in 2 years?

$I = Prt$

$178 \overset{?}{=} 2{,}225(0.04)(2)$

$178 = 178 \checkmark$

Write a complete sentence that answers the question.	The principal is $2,225.

> **TRY IT :: 6.67**   Find the principal invested if $495 interest was earned in 3 years at an interest rate of 6%.

> **TRY IT ::** 6.68

Find the principal invested if $1,246 interest was earned in 5 years at an interest rate of 7%.

Now we will solve for the rate of interest.

EXAMPLE 6.35

Find the rate if a principal of $8,200 earned $3,772 interest in 4 years.

⊘ **Solution**

Organize the given information.

$I = \$3,772$
$P = \$8,200$
$r = ?$
$t = 4 \text{ years}$

We will use the simple interest formula to find the rate.

Write the formula.	$I = Prt$
Substitute the given information.	$3,772 = 8,200r(4)$
Multiply.	$3,772 = 32,800r$
Divide.	$\dfrac{3,772}{32,800} = \dfrac{32,800r}{32,800}$
Simplify.	$0.115 = r$
Write as a percent.	$11.5\% = r$

Check your answer. Is 11.5% a reasonable rate if $3,772 was earned in 4 years?

$$I = Prt$$

$$3,772 \stackrel{?}{=} 8,200(0.115)(4)$$

$$3,772 = 3,772 \checkmark$$

Write a complete sentence that answers the question.	The rate was 11.5%.

> **TRY IT ::** 6.69   Find the rate if a principal of $5,000 earned $1,350 interest in 6 years.

> **TRY IT ::** 6.70   Find the rate if a principal of $9,000 earned $1,755 interest in 3 years.

Solve Simple Interest Applications

Applications with simple interest usually involve either investing money or borrowing money. To solve these applications, we continue to use the same strategy for applications that we have used earlier in this chapter. The only difference is that in place of translating to get an equation, we can use the simple interest formula.

We will start by solving a simple interest application to find the interest.

EXAMPLE 6.36

Nathaly deposited $12,500 in her bank account where it will earn 4% interest. How much interest will Nathaly earn in

5 years?

⊘ **Solution**

We are asked to find the Interest, I.

Organize the given information in a list.

$I = ?$
$P = \$12,500$
$r = 4\%$
$t = 5$ years

Write the formula.	$I = Prt$
Substitute the given information.	$I = (12,500)(0.04)(5)$
Simplify.	$I = 2,500$

Check your answer. Is \$2,500 a reasonable interest on \$12,500 over 5 years?

At 4% interest per year, in 5 years the interest would be 20% of the principal. Is 20% of \$12,500 equal to \$2,500? Yes.

Write a complete sentence that answers the question.	The interest is \$2,500.

> **TRY IT :: 6.71**

Areli invested a principal of \$950 in her bank account with interest rate 3%. How much interest did she earn in 5 years?

> **TRY IT :: 6.72**

Susana invested a principal of \$36,000 in her bank account with interest rate 6.5%. How much interest did she earn in 3 years?

There may be times when you know the amount of interest earned on a given principal over a certain length of time, but you don't know the rate. For instance, this might happen when family members lend or borrow money among themselves instead of dealing with a bank. In the next example, we'll show how to solve for the rate.

EXAMPLE 6.37

Loren lent his brother \$3,000 to help him buy a car. In 4 years his brother paid him back the \$3,000 plus \$660 in interest. What was the rate of interest?

⊘ **Solution**

We are asked to find the rate of interest, r.

Organize the given information.

$I = 660$
$P = \$3,000$
$r = ?$
$t = 4$ years

Write the formula.	$I = Prt$
Substitute the given information.	$660 = (3,000)r(4)$
Multiply.	$660 = (12,000)r$
Divide.	$\dfrac{660}{12,000} = \dfrac{(12,000)r}{12,000}$
Simplify.	$0.055 = r$
Change to percent form.	$5.5\% = r$

Check your answer. Is 5.5% a reasonable interest rate to pay your brother?

$$I = Prt$$

$$660 \overset{?}{=} (3,000)(0.055)(4)$$

$$660 = 660 \checkmark$$

| Write a complete sentence that answers the question. | The rate of interest was 5.5%. |

> **TRY IT ::** 6.73

Jim lent his sister $5,000 to help her buy a house. In 3 years, she paid him the $5,000, plus $900 interest. What was the rate of interest?

> **TRY IT ::** 6.74

Hang borrowed $7,500 from her parents to pay her tuition. In 5 years, she paid them $1,500 interest in addition to the $7,500 she borrowed. What was the rate of interest?

There may be times when you take a loan for a large purchase and the amount of the principal is not clear. This might happen, for instance, in making a car purchase when the dealer adds the cost of a warranty to the price of the car. In the next example, we will solve a simple interest application for the principal.

EXAMPLE 6.38

Eduardo noticed that his new car loan papers stated that with an interest rate of 7.5%, he would pay $6,596.25 in interest over 5 years. How much did he borrow to pay for his car?

⊘ **Solution**

We are asked to find the principal, P.

Organize the given information.

$I = 6,596.25$
$P = ?$
$r = 7.5\%$
$t = 5$ years

Write the formula.	$I = Prt$
Substitute the given information.	$6,596.25 = P(0.075)(5)$
Multiply.	$6,596.25 = 0.375P$
Divide.	$\dfrac{6,596.25}{0.375} = \dfrac{0.375P}{0.375}$
Simplify.	$17,590 = P$

Check your answer. Is $17,590 a reasonable amount to borrow to buy a car?

$$I = Prt$$

$$6,596.25 \overset{?}{=} (17,590)(0.075)(5)$$

$$6,596.25 = 6,596.25 \checkmark$$

| Write a complete sentence that answers the question. | The amount borrowed was $17,590. |

> **TRY IT :: 6.75**

Sean's new car loan statement said he would pay $4,866.25 in interest from an interest rate of 8.5% over 5 years. How much did he borrow to buy his new car?

> **TRY IT :: 6.76**

In 5 years, Gloria's bank account earned $2,400 interest at 5%. How much had she deposited in the account?

In the simple interest formula, the rate of interest is given as an annual rate, the rate for one year. So the units of time must be in years. If the time is given in months, we convert it to years.

EXAMPLE 6.39

Caroline got $900 as graduation gifts and invested it in a 10-month certificate of deposit that earned 2.1% interest. How much interest did this investment earn?

 Solution

We are asked to find the interest, I.

Organize the given information.

$I \ = \ ?$
$P \ = \ \$900$
$r \ = \ 2.1\%$
$t \ = \ 10 \text{ months}$

Write the formula.	$I = Prt$
Substitute the given information, converting 10 months to $\frac{10}{12}$ of a year.	$I = \$900(0.021)\left(\frac{10}{12}\right)$
Multiply.	$I = 15.75$
Check your answer. Is $15.75 a reasonable amount of interest?	
If Caroline had invested the $900 for a full year at 2% interest, the amount of interest would have been $18. Yes, $15.75 is reasonable.	
Write a complete sentence that answers the question.	The interest earned was $15.75.

> **TRY IT : :** 6.77

   Adriana invested $4,500 for 8 months in an account that paid 1.9% interest. How much interest did she earn?

> **TRY IT : :** 6.78

   Milton invested $2,460 for 20 months in an account that paid 3.5% interest How much interest did he earn?

6.4 EXERCISES

Practice Makes Perfect

Use the Simple Interest Formula

In the following exercises, use the simple interest formula to fill in the missing information.

202.

Interest	Principal	Rate	Time (years)
	$1200	3%	5

Table 6.58

203.

Interest	Principal	Rate	Time (years)
	$1500	2%	4

Table 6.59

204.

Interest	Principal	Rate	Time (years)
$4410		4.5%	7

Table 6.60

205.

Interest	Principal	Rate	Time (years)
$2212		3.2%	6

Table 6.61

206.

Interest	Principal	Rate	Time (years)
$577.08	$4580		2

Table 6.62

207.

Interest	Principal	Rate	Time (years)
$528.12	$3260		3

Table 6.63

In the following exercises, solve the problem using the simple interest formula.

208. Find the simple interest earned after 5 years on $600 at an interest rate of 3%.

209. Find the simple interest earned after 4 years on $900 at an interest rate of 6%.

210. Find the simple interest earned after 2 years on $8,950 at an interest rate of 3.24%.

211. Find the simple interest earned after 3 years on $6,510 at an interest rate of 2.85%.

212. Find the simple interest earned after 8 years on $15,500 at an interest rate of 11.425%.

213. Find the simple interest earned after 6 years on $23,900 at an interest rate of 12.175%.

214. Find the principal invested if $656 interest was earned in 5 years at an interest rate of 4%.

215. Find the principal invested if $177 interest was earned in 2 years at an interest rate of 3%.

216. Find the principal invested if $70.95 interest was earned in 3 years at an interest rate of 2.75%.

217. Find the principal invested if $636.84 interest was earned in 6 years at an interest rate of 4.35%.

218. Find the principal invested if $15,222.57 interest was earned in 6 years at an interest rate of 10.28%.

219. Find the principal invested if $10,953.70 interest was earned in 5 years at an interest rate of 11.04%.

220. Find the rate if a principal of $5,400 earned $432 interest in 2 years.

221. Find the rate if a principal of $2,600 earned $468 interest in 6 years.

222. Find the rate if a principal of $11,000 earned $1,815 interest in 3 years.

223. Find the rate if a principal of $8,500 earned $3,230 interest in 4 years.

Solve Simple Interest Applications

In the following exercises, solve the problem using the simple interest formula.

224. Casey deposited $1,450 in a bank account with interest rate 4%. How much interest was earned in 2 years?

225. Terrence deposited $5,720 in a bank account with interest rate 6%. How much interest was earned in 4 years?

226. Robin deposited $31,000 in a bank account with interest rate 5.2%. How much interest was earned in 3 years?

227. Carleen deposited $16,400 in a bank account with interest rate 3.9%. How much interest was earned in 8 years?

228. Hilaria borrowed $8,000 from her grandfather to pay for college. Five years later, she paid him back the $8,000, plus $1,200 interest. What was the rate of interest?

229. Kenneth lent his niece $1,200 to buy a computer. Two years later, she paid him back the $1,200, plus $96 interest. What was the rate of interest?

230. Lebron lent his daughter $20,000 to help her buy a condominium. When she sold the condominium four years later, she paid him the $20,000, plus $3,000 interest. What was the rate of interest?

231. Pablo borrowed $50,000 to start a business. Three years later, he repaid the $50,000, plus $9,375 interest. What was the rate of interest?

232. In 10 years, a bank account that paid 5.25% earned $18,375 interest. What was the principal of the account?

233. In 25 years, a bond that paid 4.75% earned $2,375 interest. What was the principal of the bond?

234. Joshua's computer loan statement said he would pay $1,244.34 in interest for a 3 year loan at 12.4%. How much did Joshua borrow to buy the computer?

235. Margaret's car loan statement said she would pay $7,683.20 in interest for a 5 year loan at 9.8%. How much did Margaret borrow to buy the car?

236. Caitlin invested $8,200 in an 18-month certificate of deposit paying 2.7% interest. How much interest did she earn form this investment?

237. Diego invested $6,100 in a 9-month certificate of deposit paying 1.8% interest. How much interest did he earn form this investment?

238. Airin borrowed $3,900 from her parents for the down payment on a car and promised to pay them back in 15 months at a 4% rate of interest. How much interest did she owe her parents?

239. Yuta borrowed $840 from his brother to pay for his textbooks and promised to pay him back in 5 months at a 6% rate of interest. How much interest did Yuta owe his brother?

Everyday Math

240. Interest on savings Find the interest rate your local bank pays on savings accounts.

ⓐ What is the interest rate?

ⓑ Calculate the amount of interest you would earn on a principal of $8,000 for 5 years.

241. Interest on a loan Find the interest rate your local bank charges for a car loan.

ⓐ What is the interest rate?

ⓑ Calculate the amount of interest you would pay on a loan of $8,000 for 5 years.

Writing Exercises

242. Why do banks pay interest on money deposited in savings accounts?

243. Why do banks charge interest for lending money?

Self Check

ⓐ After completing the exercises, use this checklist to evaluate your mastery of the objectives of this section.

I can...	Confidently	With some help	No-I don't get it!
use the simple interest formula.			
solve simple interest applications.			

ⓑ On a scale of 1–10, how would you rate your mastery of this section in light of your responses on the checklist? How can you improve this?

6.5 | Solve Proportions and their Applications

Learning Objectives

By the end of this section, you will be able to:

- Use the definition of proportion
- Solve proportions
- Solve applications using proportions
- Write percent equations as proportions
- Translate and solve percent proportions

Be Prepared!

Before you get started, take this readiness quiz.

1. Simplify: $\dfrac{\frac{1}{3}}{4}$.

   If you missed this problem, review Example 4.44.

2. Solve: $\frac{x}{4} = 20$.

   If you missed this problem, review Example 4.99.

3. Write as a rate: Sale rode his bike 24 miles in 2 hours.
   If you missed this problem, review Example 5.63.

Use the Definition of Proportion

In the section on Ratios and Rates we saw some ways they are used in our daily lives. When two ratios or rates are equal, the equation relating them is called a **proportion**.

Proportion

A proportion is an equation of the form $\frac{a}{b} = \frac{c}{d}$, where $b \neq 0$, $d \neq 0$.

The proportion states two ratios or rates are equal. The proportion is read "a is to b, as c is to d".

The equation $\frac{1}{2} = \frac{4}{8}$ is a proportion because the two fractions are equal. The proportion $\frac{1}{2} = \frac{4}{8}$ is read "1 is to 2 as 4 is to 8".

If we compare quantities with units, we have to be sure we are comparing them in the right order. For example, in the proportion $\frac{20 \text{ students}}{1 \text{ teacher}} = \frac{60 \text{ students}}{3 \text{ teachers}}$ we compare the number of students to the number of teachers. We put students in the numerators and teachers in the denominators.

EXAMPLE 6.40

Write each sentence as a proportion:

    ⓐ 3 is to 7 as 15 is to 35.   ⓑ 5 hits in 8 at bats is the same as 30 hits in 48 at-bats.

    ⓒ $\$1.50$ for 6 ounces is equivalent to $\$2.25$ for 9 ounces.

✓ Solution

ⓐ

3 is to 7 as 15 is to 35.

Write as a proportion. $\dfrac{3}{7} = \dfrac{15}{35}$

ⓑ

5 hits in 8 at-bats is the same as 30 hits in 48 at-bats.

Write each fraction to compare hits to at-bats. $\dfrac{\text{hits}}{\text{at-bats}} = \dfrac{\text{hits}}{\text{at-bats}}$

Write as a proportion. $\dfrac{5}{8} = \dfrac{30}{48}$

ⓒ

$1.50 for 6 ounces is equivalent to $2.25 for 9 ounces.

Write each fraction to compare dollars to ounces. $\dfrac{\$}{\text{ounces}} = \dfrac{\$}{\text{ounces}}$

Write as a proportion. $\dfrac{1.50}{6} = \dfrac{2.25}{9}$

> **TRY IT :: 6.79**

Write each sentence as a proportion:

ⓐ 5 is to 9 as 20 is to 36.   ⓑ 7 hits in 11 at-bats is the same as 28 hits in 44 at-bats.

ⓒ $2.50 for 8 ounces is equivalent to $3.75 for 12 ounces.

> **TRY IT :: 6.80**

Write each sentence as a proportion:

ⓐ 6 is to 7 as 36 is to 42.   ⓑ 8 adults for 36 children is the same as 12 adults for 54 children.

ⓒ $3.75 for 6 ounces is equivalent to $2.50 for 4 ounces.

Look at the proportions $\dfrac{1}{2} = \dfrac{4}{8}$ and $\dfrac{2}{3} = \dfrac{6}{9}$. From our work with equivalent fractions we know these equations are true.

But how do we know if an equation is a proportion with equivalent fractions if it contains fractions with larger numbers?

To determine if a proportion is true, we find the **cross products** of each proportion. To find the cross products, we multiply each denominator with the opposite numerator (diagonally across the equal sign). The results are called a cross products because of the cross formed. The cross products of a proportion are equal.

$$8 \cdot 1 = 8 \quad 2 \cdot 4 = 8 \qquad\qquad 9 \cdot 2 = 18 \quad 3 \cdot 6 = 18$$
$$\dfrac{1}{2} = \dfrac{4}{8} \qquad\qquad\qquad \dfrac{2}{3} = \dfrac{6}{9}$$

Cross Products of a Proportion

For any proportion of the form $\frac{a}{b} = \frac{c}{d}$, where $b \neq 0$, $d \neq 0$, its cross products are equal.

$$a \cdot d = b \cdot c$$
$$\frac{a}{b} \asymp \frac{c}{d}$$

Cross products can be used to test whether a proportion is true. To test whether an equation makes a proportion, we find the cross products. If they are the equal, we have a proportion.

EXAMPLE 6.41

Determine whether each equation is a proportion:

ⓐ $\frac{4}{9} = \frac{12}{28}$ ⓑ $\frac{17.5}{37.5} = \frac{7}{15}$

⊘ **Solution**

To determine if the equation is a proportion, we find the cross products. If they are equal, the equation is a proportion.

ⓐ

$$\frac{4}{9} = \frac{12}{28}$$

Find the cross products.

$$28 \cdot 4 = 112 \qquad 9 \cdot 12 = 108$$
$$\frac{4}{9} \asymp \frac{12}{28}$$

Since the cross products are not equal, $28 \cdot 4 \neq 9 \cdot 12$, the equation is not a proportion.

ⓑ

$$\frac{17.5}{37.5} = \frac{7}{15}$$

Find the cross products.

$$15 \cdot 17.5 = 262.5 \qquad 37.5 \cdot 7 = 262.5$$
$$\frac{17.5}{37.5} \asymp \frac{7}{15}$$

Since the cross products are equal, $15 \cdot 17.5 = 37.5 \cdot 7$, the equation is a proportion.

> **TRY IT : :** 6.81   Determine whether each equation is a proportion:
>
> ⓐ $\frac{7}{9} = \frac{54}{72}$ ⓑ $\frac{24.5}{45.5} = \frac{7}{13}$

> **TRY IT : :** 6.82   Determine whether each equation is a proportion:
>
> ⓐ $\frac{8}{9} = \frac{56}{73}$ ⓑ $\frac{28.5}{52.5} = \frac{8}{15}$

Solve Proportions

To solve a proportion containing a variable, we remember that the proportion is an equation. All of the techniques we have used so far to solve equations still apply. In the next example, we will solve a proportion by multiplying by the Least Common Denominator (LCD) using the Multiplication Property of Equality.

EXAMPLE 6.42

Solve: $\frac{x}{63} = \frac{4}{7}$.

⊘ **Solution**

$$\frac{x}{63} = \frac{4}{7}$$

To isolate x, multiply both sides by the LCD, 63.

$$63\left(\frac{x}{63}\right) = 63\left(\frac{4}{7}\right)$$

Simplify.

$$x = \frac{9 \cdot \cancel{7} \cdot 4}{\cancel{7}}$$

Divide the common factors.

$$x = 36$$

Check: To check our answer, we substitute into the original proportion.

$$\frac{x}{63} = \frac{4}{7}$$

Substitute $x = 36$

$$\frac{36}{63} \overset{?}{=} \frac{4}{7}$$

Show common factors.

$$\frac{4 \cdot 9}{7 \cdot 9} \overset{?}{=} \frac{4}{7}$$

Simplify.

$$\frac{4}{7} = \frac{4}{7} \checkmark$$

> **TRY IT : : 6.83**   Solve the proportion: $\frac{n}{84} = \frac{11}{12}$.

> **TRY IT : : 6.84**   Solve the proportion: $\frac{y}{96} = \frac{13}{12}$.

When the variable is in a denominator, we'll use the fact that the cross products of a proportion are equal to solve the proportions.

We can find the cross products of the proportion and then set them equal. Then we solve the resulting equation using our familiar techniques.

EXAMPLE 6.43 ⁕

Solve: $\frac{144}{a} = \frac{9}{4}$.

⊘ **Solution**

Notice that the variable is in the denominator, so we will solve by finding the cross products and setting them equal.

$$\frac{144}{a} = \frac{9}{4}$$

Find the cross products and set them equal.	$4 \cdot 144 = a \cdot 9$
Simplify.	$576 = 9a$
Divide both sides by 9.	$\frac{576}{9} = \frac{9a}{9}$
Simplify.	$64 = a$
Check your answer.	

$$\frac{144}{a} = \frac{9}{4}$$

Substitute $a = 64$	$\frac{144}{64} \overset{?}{=} \frac{9}{4}$
Show common factors..	$\frac{9 \cdot 16}{4 \cdot 16} \overset{?}{=} \frac{9}{4}$
Simplify.	$\frac{9}{4} = \frac{9}{4} \checkmark$

Another method to solve this would be to multiply both sides by the LCD, $4a$. Try it and verify that you get the same solution.

> **TRY IT : : 6.85**   Solve the proportion: $\frac{91}{b} = \frac{7}{5}$.

> **TRY IT : : 6.86**   Solve the proportion: $\frac{39}{c} = \frac{13}{8}$.

EXAMPLE 6.44

Solve: $\frac{52}{91} = \frac{-4}{y}$.

⊘ Solution

Find the cross products and set them equal.

$$\frac{52}{91} = \frac{-4}{y}$$

$$y \cdot 52 = 91(-4)$$

Simplify.

$$52y = -364$$

Divide both sides by 52.

$$\frac{52y}{52} = \frac{-364}{52}$$

Simplify.

$$y = -7$$

Check:

$$\frac{52}{91} = \frac{-4}{y}$$

Substitute $y = -7$

$$\frac{52}{91} \overset{?}{=} \frac{-4}{-7}$$

Show common factors.

$$\frac{13 \cdot 4}{13 \cdot 4} \overset{?}{=} \frac{-4}{-7}$$

Simplify.

$$\frac{4}{7} = \frac{4}{7} \checkmark$$

> **TRY IT :: 6.87** Solve the proportion: $\frac{84}{98} = \frac{-6}{x}$.

> **TRY IT :: 6.88** Solve the proportion: $\frac{-7}{y} = \frac{105}{135}$.

Solve Applications Using Proportions

The strategy for solving applications that we have used earlier in this chapter, also works for proportions, since proportions are equations. When we set up the proportion, we must make sure the units are correct—the units in the numerators match and the units in the denominators match.

EXAMPLE 6.45

When pediatricians prescribe acetaminophen to children, they prescribe 5 milliliters (ml) of acetaminophen for every 25 pounds of the child's weight. If Zoe weighs 80 pounds, how many milliliters of acetaminophen will her doctor prescribe?

⊘ **Solution**

Identify what you are asked to find.	How many ml of acetaminophen the doctor will prescribe
Choose a variable to represent it.	Let $a =$ ml of acetaminophen.
Write a sentence that gives the information to find it.	If 5 ml is prescribed for every 25 pounds, how much will be prescribed for 80 pounds?
Translate into a proportion.	$\dfrac{\text{ml}}{\text{pounds}} = \dfrac{\text{ml}}{\text{pounds}}$
Substitute given values—be careful of the units.	$\dfrac{5}{25} = \dfrac{a}{80}$
Multiply both sides by 80.	$80 \cdot \dfrac{5}{25} = 80 \cdot \dfrac{a}{80}$
Multiply and show common factors.	$\dfrac{16 \cdot 5 \cdot 5}{5 \cdot 5} = \dfrac{80a}{80}$
Simplify.	$16 = a$
Check if the answer is reasonable.	
Yes. Since 80 is about 3 times 25, the medicine should be about 3 times 5.	
Write a complete sentence.	The pediatrician would prescribe 16 ml of acetaminophen to Zoe.

You could also solve this proportion by setting the cross products equal.

> **TRY IT : : 6.89**

Pediatricians prescribe 5 milliliters (ml) of acetaminophen for every 25 pounds of a child's weight. How many milliliters of acetaminophen will the doctor prescribe for Emilia, who weighs 60 pounds?

> **TRY IT : : 6.90**

For every 1 kilogram (kg) of a child's weight, pediatricians prescribe 15 milligrams (mg) of a fever reducer. If Isabella weighs 12 kg, how many milligrams of the fever reducer will the pediatrician prescribe?

EXAMPLE 6.46

One brand of microwave popcorn has 120 calories per serving. A whole bag of this popcorn has 3.5 servings. How many calories are in a whole bag of this microwave popcorn?

⊘ Solution

Identify what you are asked to find.	How many calories are in a whole bag of microwave popcorn?
Choose a variable to represent it.	Let $c =$ number of calories.
Write a sentence that gives the information to find it.	If there are 120 calories per serving, how many calories are in a whole bag with 3.5 servings?
Translate into a proportion.	$$\frac{\text{calories}}{\text{serving}} = \frac{\text{calories}}{\text{serving}}$$
Substitute given values.	$$\frac{120}{1} = \frac{c}{3.5}$$
Multiply both sides by 3.5.	$$(3.5)\left(\frac{120}{1}\right) = (3.5)\left(\frac{c}{3.5}\right)$$
Multiply.	$$420 = c$$
Check if the answer is reasonable.	
Yes. Since 3.5 is between 3 and 4, the total calories should be between 360 (3·120) and 480 (4·120).	
Write a complete sentence.	The whole bag of microwave popcorn has 420 calories.

> **TRY IT :: 6.91**
>
> Marissa loves the Caramel Macchiato at the coffee shop. The 16 oz. medium size has 240 calories. How many calories will she get if she drinks the large 20 oz. size?

> **TRY IT :: 6.92**
>
> Yaneli loves Starburst candies, but wants to keep her snacks to 100 calories. If the candies have 160 calories for 8 pieces, how many pieces can she have in her snack?

EXAMPLE 6.47

Josiah went to Mexico for spring break and changed $325 dollars into Mexican pesos. At that time, the exchange rate had $1 U.S. is equal to 12.54 Mexican pesos. How many Mexican pesos did he get for his trip?

⊘ **Solution**

Identify what you are asked to find.	How many Mexican pesos did Josiah get?
Choose a variable to represent it.	Let $p =$ number of pesos.
Write a sentence that gives the information to find it.	If $1 U.S. is equal to 12.54 Mexican pesos, then $325 is how many pesos?
Translate into a proportion.	$\dfrac{\$}{\text{pesos}} = \dfrac{\$}{\text{pesos}}$
Substitute given values.	$\dfrac{1}{12.54} = \dfrac{325}{p}$
The variable is in the denominator, so find the cross products and set them equal.	$p \cdot 1 = 12.54(325)$
Simplify.	$c = 4{,}075.5$
Check if the answer is reasonable.	
Yes, $100 would be $1,254 pesos. $325 is a little more than 3 times this amount.	
Write a complete sentence.	Josiah has 4075.5 pesos for his spring break trip.

> **TRY IT : :** 6.93
>
> Yurianna is going to Europe and wants to change $800 dollars into Euros. At the current exchange rate, $1 US is equal to 0.738 Euro. How many Euros will she have for her trip?

> **TRY IT : :** 6.94
>
> Corey and Nicole are traveling to Japan and need to exchange $600 into Japanese yen. If each dollar is 94.1 yen, how many yen will they get?

Write Percent Equations As Proportions

Previously, we solved percent equations by applying the properties of equality we have used to solve equations throughout this text. Some people prefer to solve percent equations by using the proportion method. The proportion method for solving percent problems involves a percent proportion. A **percent proportion** is an equation where a percent is equal to an equivalent ratio.

For example, $60\% = \dfrac{60}{100}$ and we can simplify $\dfrac{60}{100} = \dfrac{3}{5}$. Since the equation $\dfrac{60}{100} = \dfrac{3}{5}$ shows a percent equal to an equivalent ratio, we call it a **percent proportion**. Using the vocabulary we used earlier:

$$\frac{\text{amount}}{\text{base}} = \frac{\text{percent}}{100}$$
$$\frac{3}{5} = \frac{60}{100}$$

Percent Proportion

The amount is to the base as the percent is to 100.

$$\frac{\text{amount}}{\text{base}} = \frac{\text{percent}}{100}$$

If we restate the problem in the words of a proportion, it may be easier to set up the proportion:

The amount is to the base as the percent is to one hundred.

We could also say:

The amount out of the base is the same as the percent out of one hundred.

First we will practice translating into a percent proportion. Later, we'll solve the proportion.

EXAMPLE 6.48

Translate to a proportion. What number is 75% of 90?

⊘ Solution

If you look for the word "of", it may help you identify the base.

Identify the parts of the percent proportion.	What number is 75% of 90? amount percent base
Restate as a proportion.	What number out of 90 is the same as 75 out of 100?
Set up the proportion. Let $n = $ number .	$\dfrac{n}{90} = \dfrac{75}{100}$

> **TRY IT :: 6.95**   Translate to a proportion: What number is 60% of 105?

> **TRY IT :: 6.96**   Translate to a proportion: What number is 40% of 85?

EXAMPLE 6.49

Translate to a proportion. 19 is 25% of what number?

⊘ Solution

Identify the parts of the percent proportion.	19 is 25% of what number ? amount percent base
Restate as a proportion.	19 out of what number is the same as 25 out of 100?
Set up the proportion. Let $n = $ number .	$\dfrac{19}{n} = \dfrac{25}{100}$

> **TRY IT :: 6.97**   Translate to a proportion: 36 is 25% of what number?

> **TRY IT :: 6.98**   Translate to a proportion: 27 is 36% of what number?

EXAMPLE 6.50

Translate to a proportion. What percent of 27 is 9?

Solution

Identify the parts of the percent proportion.	What percent of 27 is 9? percent ... base ... amount
Restate as a proportion.	9 out of 27 is the same as what number out of 100?
Set up the proportion. Let $p =$ percent .	$\dfrac{9}{27} = \dfrac{p}{100}$

> **TRY IT : :** 6.99   Translate to a proportion: What percent of 52 is 39?

> **TRY IT : :** 6.100   Translate to a proportion: What percent of 92 is 23?

Translate and Solve Percent Proportions

Now that we have written percent equations as proportions, we are ready to solve the equations.

EXAMPLE 6.51

Translate and solve using proportions: What number is 45% of 80?

Solution

Identify the parts of the percent proportion.	What number is 45% of 80? amount ... percent ... base
Restate as a proportion.	What number out of 80 is the same as 45 out of 100?
Set up the proportion. Let $n =$ number.	$\dfrac{n}{80} = \dfrac{45}{100}$
Find the cross products and set them equal.	$100 \cdot n = 80 \cdot 45$
Simplify.	$100n = 3,600$
Divide both sides by 100.	$\dfrac{100n}{100} = \dfrac{3,600}{100}$
Simplify.	$n = 36$
Check if the answer is reasonable.	
Yes. 45 is a little less than half of 100 and 36 is a little less than half 80.	
Write a complete sentence that answers the question.	36 is 45% of 80.

> **TRY IT : :** 6.101   Translate and solve using proportions: What number is 65% of 40?

> **TRY IT : :** 6.102   Translate and solve using proportions: What number is 85% of 40?

In the next example, the percent is more than $100,$ which is more than one whole. So the unknown number will be more than the base.

EXAMPLE 6.52

Translate and solve using proportions: 125% of 25 is what number?

✓ **Solution**

	125% is 25 of what number ?
Identify the parts of the percent proportion.	percent base amount
Restate as a proportion.	What number out of 25 is the same as 125 out of 100?
Set up the proportion. Let $n =$ number.	$\dfrac{n}{25} = \dfrac{125}{100}$
Find the cross products and set them equal.	$100 \cdot n = 25 \cdot 125$
Simplify.	$100n = 3{,}125$
Divide both sides by 100.	$\dfrac{100n}{100} = \dfrac{3{,}125}{100}$
Simplify.	$n = 31.25$

Check if the answer is reasonable.

Yes. 125 is more than 100 and 31.25 is more than 25.

Write a complete sentence that answers the question.   125% of 25 is 31.25.

> **TRY IT : :** 6.103   Translate and solve using proportions: 125% of 64 is what number?

> **TRY IT : :** 6.104   Translate and solve using proportions: 175% of 84 is what number?

Percents with decimals and money are also used in proportions.

EXAMPLE 6.53

Translate and solve: 6.5% of what number is $\$1.56$?

⊘ Solution

| Identify the parts of the percent proportion. | 6.5% of what number is $1.56? |
| | percent   base   amount |

Restate as a proportion.	$1.56 out of what number is the same as 6.5 out of 100?
Set up the proportion. Let $n =$ number.	$\dfrac{1.56}{n} = \dfrac{6.5}{100}$
Find the cross products and set them equal.	$100(1.56) = n \cdot 6.5$
Simplify.	$156 = 6.5n$
Divide both sides by 6.5 to isolate the variable.	$\dfrac{156}{6.5} = \dfrac{6.5n}{6.5}$
Simplify.	$24 = n$
Check if the answer is reasonable.	
Yes. 6.5% is a small amount and $1.56 is much less than $24.	
Write a complete sentence that answers the question.	6.5% of $24 is $1.56.

> **TRY IT : : 6.105**   Translate and solve using proportions: 8.5% of what number is 3.23?

> **TRY IT : : 6.106**   Translate and solve using proportions: 7.25% of what number is 4.64?

EXAMPLE 6.54

Translate and solve using proportions: What percent of 72 is 9?

✓ Solution

Identify the parts of the percent proportion.	What percent of 72 is 9? percent base amount
Restate as a proportion.	9 out of 72 is the same as what number out of 100?
Set up the proportion. Let $n =$ number.	$\dfrac{9}{72} = \dfrac{n}{100}$
Find the cross products and set them equal.	$72 \cdot n = 100 \cdot 9$
Simplify.	$72n = 900$
Divide both sides by 72.	$\dfrac{72n}{72} = \dfrac{900}{72}$
Simplify.	$n = 12.5$
Check if the answer is reasonable.	

Yes. 9 is $\dfrac{1}{8}$ of 72 and $\dfrac{1}{8}$ is 12.5%.

Write a complete sentence that answers the question.   12.5% of 72 is 9.

> **TRY IT :: 6.107**   Translate and solve using proportions: What percent of 72 is 27?

> **TRY IT :: 6.108**   Translate and solve using proportions: What percent of 92 is 23?

6.5 EXERCISES

Practice Makes Perfect

Use the Definition of Proportion

In the following exercises, write each sentence as a proportion.

244. 4 is to 15 as 36 is to 135.

245. 7 is to 9 as 35 is to 45.

246. 12 is to 5 as 96 is to 40.

247. 15 is to 8 as 75 is to 40.

248. 5 wins in 7 games is the same as 115 wins in 161 games.

249. 4 wins in 9 games is the same as 36 wins in 81 games.

250. 8 campers to 1 counselor is the same as 48 campers to 6 counselors.

251. 6 campers to 1 counselor is the same as 48 campers to 8 counselors.

252. $9.36 for 18 ounces is the same as $2.60 for 5 ounces.

253. $3.92 for 8 ounces is the same as $1.47 for 3 ounces.

254. $18.04 for 11 pounds is the same as $4.92 for 3 pounds.

255. $12.42 for 27 pounds is the same as $5.52 for 12 pounds.

In the following exercises, determine whether each equation is a proportion.

256. $\dfrac{7}{15} = \dfrac{56}{120}$

257. $\dfrac{5}{12} = \dfrac{45}{108}$

258. $\dfrac{11}{6} = \dfrac{21}{16}$

259. $\dfrac{9}{4} = \dfrac{39}{34}$

260. $\dfrac{12}{18} = \dfrac{4.99}{7.56}$

261. $\dfrac{9}{16} = \dfrac{2.16}{3.89}$

262. $\dfrac{13.5}{8.5} = \dfrac{31.05}{19.55}$

263. $\dfrac{10.1}{8.4} = \dfrac{3.03}{2.52}$

Solve Proportions

In the following exercises, solve each proportion.

264. $\dfrac{x}{56} = \dfrac{7}{8}$

265. $\dfrac{n}{91} = \dfrac{8}{13}$

266. $\dfrac{49}{63} = \dfrac{z}{9}$

267. $\dfrac{56}{72} = \dfrac{y}{9}$

268. $\dfrac{5}{a} = \dfrac{65}{117}$

269. $\dfrac{4}{b} = \dfrac{64}{144}$

270. $\dfrac{98}{154} = \dfrac{-7}{p}$

271. $\dfrac{72}{156} = \dfrac{-6}{q}$

272. $\dfrac{a}{-8} = \dfrac{-42}{48}$

273. $\dfrac{b}{-7} = \dfrac{-30}{42}$

274. $\dfrac{2.6}{3.9} = \dfrac{c}{3}$

275. $\dfrac{2.7}{3.6} = \dfrac{d}{4}$

276. $\dfrac{2.7}{j} = \dfrac{0.9}{0.2}$

277. $\dfrac{2.8}{k} = \dfrac{2.1}{1.5}$

278. $\dfrac{\frac{1}{2}}{1} = \dfrac{m}{8}$

279. $\dfrac{\frac{1}{3}}{3} = \dfrac{9}{n}$

Solve Applications Using Proportions

In the following exercises, solve the proportion problem.

280. Pediatricians prescribe 5 milliliters (ml) of acetaminophen for every 25 pounds of a child's weight. How many milliliters of acetaminophen will the doctor prescribe for Jocelyn, who weighs 45 pounds?

281. Brianna, who weighs 6 kg, just received her shots and needs a pain killer. The pain killer is prescribed for children at 15 milligrams (mg) for every 1 kilogram (kg) of the child's weight. How many milligrams will the doctor prescribe?

282. At the gym, Carol takes her pulse for 10 sec and counts 19 beats. How many beats per minute is this? Has Carol met her target heart rate of 140 beats per minute?

283. Kevin wants to keep his heart rate at 160 beats per minute while training. During his workout he counts 27 beats in 10 seconds. How many beats per minute is this? Has Kevin met his target heart rate?

284. A new energy drink advertises 106 calories for 8 ounces. How many calories are in 12 ounces of the drink?

285. One 12 ounce can of soda has 150 calories. If Josiah drinks the big 32 ounce size from the local mini-mart, how many calories does he get?

286. Karen eats $\frac{1}{2}$ cup of oatmeal that counts for 2 points on her weight loss program. Her husband, Joe, can have 3 points of oatmeal for breakfast. How much oatmeal can he have?

287. An oatmeal cookie recipe calls for $\frac{1}{2}$ cup of butter to make 4 dozen cookies. Hilda needs to make 10 dozen cookies for the bake sale. How many cups of butter will she need?

288. Janice is traveling to Canada and will change $\$250$ US dollars into Canadian dollars. At the current exchange rate, $\$1$ US is equal to $\$1.01$ Canadian. How many Canadian dollars will she get for her trip?

289. Todd is traveling to Mexico and needs to exchange $\$450$ into Mexican pesos. If each dollar is worth 12.29 pesos, how many pesos will he get for his trip?

290. Steve changed $\$600$ into 480 Euros. How many Euros did he receive per US dollar?

291. Martha changed $\$350$ US into 385 Australian dollars. How many Australian dollars did she receive per US dollar?

292. At the laundromat, Lucy changed $\$12.00$ into quarters. How many quarters did she get?

293. When she arrived at a casino, Gerty changed $\$20$ into nickels. How many nickels did she get?

294. Jesse's car gets 30 miles per gallon of gas. If Las Vegas is 285 miles away, how many gallons of gas are needed to get there and then home? If gas is $\$3.09$ per gallon, what is the total cost of the gas for the trip?

295. Danny wants to drive to Phoenix to see his grandfather. Phoenix is 370 miles from Danny's home and his car gets 18.5 miles per gallon. How many gallons of gas will Danny need to get to and from Phoenix? If gas is $\$3.19$ per gallon, what is the total cost for the gas to drive to see his grandfather?

296. Hugh leaves early one morning to drive from his home in Chicago to go to Mount Rushmore, 812 miles away. After 3 hours, he has gone 190 miles. At that rate, how long will the whole drive take?

297. Kelly leaves her home in Seattle to drive to Spokane, a distance of 280 miles. After 2 hours, she has gone 152 miles. At that rate, how long will the whole drive take?

298. Phil wants to fertilize his lawn. Each bag of fertilizer covers about 4,000 square feet of lawn. Phil's lawn is approximately 13,500 square feet. How many bags of fertilizer will he have to buy?

299. April wants to paint the exterior of her house. One gallon of paint covers about 350 square feet, and the exterior of the house measures approximately 2000 square feet. How many gallons of paint will she have to buy?

Write Percent Equations as Proportions

In the following exercises, translate to a proportion.

300. What number is 35% of 250?

301. What number is 75% of 920?

302. What number is 110% of 47?

303. What number is 150% of 64?

304. 45 is 30% of what number?

305. 25 is 80% of what number?

306. 90 is 150% of what number?

307. 77 is 110% of what number?

308. What percent of 85 is 17?

309. What percent of 92 is 46?

310. What percent of 260 is 340?

311. What percent of 180 is 220?

Translate and Solve Percent Proportions

In the following exercises, translate and solve using proportions.

312. What number is 65% of 180?

313. What number is 55% of 300?

314. 18% of 92 is what number?

315. 22% of 74 is what number?

316. 175% of 26 is what number?

317. 250% of 61 is what number?

318. What is 300% of 488?

319. What is 500% of 315?

320. 17% of what number is $7.65?

321. 19% of what number is $6.46?

322. $13.53 is 8.25% of what number?

323. $18.12 is 7.55% of what number?

324. What percent of 56 is 14?

325. What percent of 80 is 28?

326. What percent of 96 is 12?

327. What percent of 120 is 27?

Everyday Math

328. Mixing a concentrate Sam bought a large bottle of concentrated cleaning solution at the warehouse store. He must mix the concentrate with water to make a solution for washing his windows. The directions tell him to mix 3 ounces of concentrate with 5 ounces of water. If he puts 12 ounces of concentrate in a bucket, how many ounces of water should he add? How many ounces of the solution will he have altogether?

329. Mixing a concentrate Travis is going to wash his car. The directions on the bottle of car wash concentrate say to mix 2 ounces of concentrate with 15 ounces of water. If Travis puts 6 ounces of concentrate in a bucket, how much water must he mix with the concentrate?

Writing Exercises

330. To solve "what number is 45% of 350" do you prefer to use an equation like you did in the section on Decimal Operations or a proportion like you did in this section? Explain your reason.

331. To solve "what percent of 125 is 25" do you prefer to use an equation like you did in the section on Decimal Operations or a proportion like you did in this section? Explain your reason.

Self Check

ⓐ *After completing the exercises, use this checklist to evaluate your mastery of the objectives of this section.*

I can...	Confidently	With some help	No-I don't get it!
use definition of proportion.			
solve proportions.			
solve applications using proportions.			
write percent equations as proportions.			
translate and solve percent proportions.			

ⓑ *Overall, after looking at the checklist, do you think you are well-prepared for the next Chapter? Why or why not?*

CHAPTER 6 REVIEW

KEY TERMS

commission A commission is a percentage of total sales as determined by the rate of commission.

discount An amount of discount is a percent off the original price, determined by the discount rate.

mark-up The mark-up is the amount added to the wholesale price, determined by the mark-up rate.

percent A perfecnt is a ratio whose denominator is 100.

percent decrease The percent decrease is the percent the amount of decrease is of the original amount.

percent increase The percent increase is the percent the amount of increase is of the original amount.

proportion A proportion is an equation of the form $\frac{a}{b} = \frac{c}{d}$, where $b \neq 0$, $d \neq 0$. The proportion states two ratios or rates are equal. The proportion is read "a is to b, as c is to d".

sales tax The sales tax is a percent of the purchase price.

simple interest If an amount of money, P, the principal, is invested for a period of t years at an annual interest rate r, the amount of interest, I, earned is $I = Prt$. Interest earned according to this formula is called simple interest.

KEY CONCEPTS

6.1 Understand Percent

- **Convert a percent to a fraction.**

   Step 1. Write the percent as a ratio with the denominator 100.

   Step 2. Simplify the fraction if possible.

- **Convert a percent to a decimal.**

   Step 1. Write the percent as a ratio with the denominator 100.

   Step 2. Convert the fraction to a decimal by dividing the numerator by the denominator.

- **Convert a decimal to a percent.**

   Step 1. Write the decimal as a fraction.

   Step 2. If the denominator of the fraction is not 100, rewrite it as an equivalent fraction with denominator 100.

   Step 3. Write this ratio as a percent.

- **Convert a fraction to a percent.**

   Step 1. Convert the fraction to a decimal.

   Step 2. Convert the decimal to a percent.

6.2 Solve General Applications of Percent

- **Solve an application.**

   Step 1. Identify what you are asked to find and choose a variable to represent it.

   Step 2. Write a sentence that gives the information to find it.

   Step 3. Translate the sentence into an equation.

   Step 4. Solve the equation using good algebra techniques.

   Step 5. Write a complete sentence that answers the question.

   Step 6. Check the answer in the problem and make sure it makes sense.

- **Find percent increase.**

   Step 1. Find the amount of increase:
   $$\text{increase} = \text{new amount} - \text{original amount}$$

   Step 2. Find the percent increase as a percent of the original amount.

- **Find percent decrease.**

Step 1. Find the amount of decrease.
decrease = original amount − new amount

Step 2. Find the percent decrease as a percent of the original amount.

6.3 Solve Sales Tax, Commission, and Discount Applications

- **Sales Tax** The sales tax is a percent of the purchase price.
  - ◦ sales tax = tax rate · purchase price
  - ◦ total cost = purchase price + sales tax

- **Commission** A commission is a percentage of total sales as determined by the rate of commission.
  - ◦ commission = rate of commission · original price

- **Discount** An amount of discount is a percent off the original price, determined by the discount rate.
  - ◦ amount of discount = discount rate · original price
  - ◦ sale price = original price − discount

- **Mark-up** The mark-up is the amount added to the wholesale price, determined by the mark-up rate.
  - ◦ amount of mark-up = mark-up rate wholesale price
  - ◦ list price = wholesale price + mark up

6.4 Solve Simple Interest Applications

- **Simple interest**
  - ◦ If an amount of money, P, the principal, is invested for a period of t years at an annual interest rate r, the amount of interest, I, earned is $I = Prt$
  - ◦ Interest earned according to this formula is called **simple interest**.

6.5 Solve Proportions and their Applications

- **Proportion**
  - ◦ A proportion is an equation of the form $\frac{a}{b} = \frac{c}{d}$, where $b \neq 0$, $d \neq 0$. The proportion states two ratios or rates are equal. The proportion is read " a is to b, as c is to d ".

- **Cross Products of a Proportion**
  - ◦ For any proportion of the form $\frac{a}{b} = \frac{c}{d}$, where $b \neq 0$, its cross products are equal: $a \cdot d = b \cdot c$.

- **Percent Proportion**
  - ◦ The amount is to the base as the percent is to 100. $\frac{\text{amount}}{\text{base}} = \frac{\text{percent}}{100}$

REVIEW EXERCISES

6.1 Understand Percent

In the following exercises, write each percent as a ratio.

332. 32% admission rate for the university

333. 53.3% rate of college students with student loans

In the following exercises, write as a ratio and then as a percent.

334. 13 out of 100 architects are women.

335. 9 out of every 100 nurses are men.

In the following exercises, convert each percent to a fraction.

336. 48%

337. 175%

338. 64.1%

339. $8\frac{1}{4}$ %

In the following exercises, convert each percent to a decimal.

340. 6%

341. 23%

342. 128%

343. 4.9%

In the following exercises, convert each percent to ⓐ a simplified fraction and ⓑ a decimal.

344. In 2012, 13.5% of the United States population was age 65 or over. (Source: www.census.gov)

345. In 2012, 6.5% of the United States population was under 5 years old. (Source: www.census.gov)

346. When a die is tossed, the probability it will land with an even number of dots on the top side is 50%.

347. A couple plans to have three children. The probability they will all be girls is 12.5%.

In the following exercises, convert each decimal to a percent.

348. 0.04

349. 0.15

350. 2.82

351. 3

352. 0.003

353. 1.395

In the following exercises, convert each fraction to a percent.

354. $\frac{3}{4}$

355. $\frac{11}{5}$

356. $3\frac{5}{8}$

357. $\frac{2}{9}$

358. According to the Centers for Disease Control, $\frac{2}{5}$ of adults do not take a vitamin or supplement.

359. According to the Centers for Disease Control, among adults who do take a vitamin or supplement, $\frac{3}{4}$ take a multivitamin.

In the following exercises, translate and solve.

360. What number is 46% of 350?

361. 120% of 55 is what number?

362. 84 is 35% of what number?

363. 15 is 8% of what number?

364. 200% of what number is 50?

365. 7.9% of what number is $4.74?

366. What percent of 120 is 81.6?

367. What percent of 340 is 595?

6.2 Solve General Applications of Percents

In the following exercises, solve.

368. When Aurelio and his family ate dinner at a restaurant, the bill was $83.50. Aurelio wants to leave 20% of the total bill as a tip. How much should the tip be?

369. One granola bar has 2 grams of fiber, which is 8% of the recommended daily amount. What is the total recommended daily amount of fiber?

370. The nutrition label on a package of granola bars says that each granola bar has 190 calories, and 54 calories are from fat. What percent of the total calories is from fat?

371. Elsa gets paid $4,600 per month. Her car payment is $253. What percent of her monthly pay goes to her car payment?

In the following exercises, solve.

372. Jorge got a raise in his hourly pay, from $19.00 to $19.76. Find the percent increase.

373. Last year Bernard bought a new car for $30,000. This year the car is worth $24,000. Find the percent decrease.

6.3 Solve Sales Tax, Commission, and Discount Applications

In the following exercises, find ⓐ the sales tax ⓑ the total cost.

374. The cost of a lawn mower was $750. The sales tax rate is 6% of the purchase price.

375. The cost of a water heater is $577. The sales tax rate is 8.75% of the purchase price.

In the following exercises, find the sales tax rate.

376. Andy bought a piano for $4,600. The sales tax on the purchase was $333.50.

377. Nahomi bought a purse for $200. The sales tax on the purchase was $16.75.

In the following exercises, find the commission.

378. Ginny is a realtor. She receives 3% commission when she sells a house. How much commission will she receive for selling a house for $380,000?

379. Jackson receives 16.5% commission when he sells a dinette set. How much commission will he receive for selling a dinette set for $895?

In the following exercises, find the rate of commission.

380. Ruben received $675 commission when he sold a $4,500 painting at the art gallery where he works. What was the rate of commission?

381. Tori received $80.75 for selling a $950 membership at her gym. What was her rate of commission?

In the following exercises, find the sale price.

382. Aya bought a pair of shoes that was on sale for $30 off. The original price of the shoes was $75.

383. Takwanna saw a cookware set she liked on sale for $145 off. The original price of the cookware was $312.

In the following exercises, find ⓐ the amount of discount and ⓑ the sale price.

384. Nga bought a microwave for her office. The microwave was discounted 30% from an original price of $84.90.

385. Jarrett bought a tie that was discounted 65% from an original price of $45.

In the following exercises, find ⓐ the amount of discount ⓑ the discount rate. (Round to the nearest tenth of a percent if needed.)

386. Hilda bought a bedspread on sale for $37. The original price of the bedspread was $50.

387. Tyler bought a phone on sale for $49.99. The original price of the phone was $79.99.

In the following exercises, find

ⓐ the amount of the mark-up   ⓑ the list price

388. Manny paid $0.80 a pound for apples. He added 60% mark-up before selling them at his produce stand. What price did he charge for the apples?

389. It cost Noelle $17.40 for the materials she used to make a purse. She added a 325% mark-up before selling it at her friend's store. What price did she ask for the purse?

6.4 Solve Simple Interest Applications

In the following exercises, solve the simple interest problem.

390. Find the simple interest earned after 4 years on $2,250 invested at an interest rate of 5%.

391. Find the simple interest earned after 7 years on $12,000 invested at an interest rate of 8.5%.

392. Find the principal invested if $660 interest was earned in 5 years at an interest rate of 3%.

393. Find the interest rate if $2,898 interest was earned from a principal of $23,000 invested for 3 years.

394. Kazuo deposited $10,000 in a bank account with interest rate 4.5%. How much interest was earned in 2 years?

395. Brent invested $23,000 in a friend's business. In 5 years the friend paid him the $23,000 plus $9,200 interest. What was the rate of interest?

396. Fresia lent her son $5,000 for college expenses. Three years later he repaid her the $5,000 plus $375 interest. What was the rate of interest?

397. In 6 years, a bond that paid 5.5% earned $594 interest. What was the principal of the bond?

6.5 Solve Proportions and their Applications

In the following exercises, write each sentence as a proportion.

398. 3 is to 8 as 12 is to 32.

399. 95 miles to 3 gallons is the same as 475 miles to 15 gallons.

400. 1 teacher to 18 students is the same as 23 teachers to 414 students.

401. $7.35 for 15 ounces is the same as $2.94 for 6 ounces.

In the following exercises, determine whether each equation is a proportion.

402. $\dfrac{5}{13} = \dfrac{30}{78}$

403. $\dfrac{16}{7} = \dfrac{48}{23}$

404. $\dfrac{12}{18} = \dfrac{6.99}{10.99}$

405. $\dfrac{11.6}{9.2} = \dfrac{37.12}{29.44}$

In the following exercises, solve each proportion.

406. $\dfrac{x}{36} = \dfrac{5}{9}$

407. $\dfrac{7}{a} = \dfrac{-6}{84}$

408. $\dfrac{1.2}{1.8} = \dfrac{d}{6}$

409. $\dfrac{\frac{1}{2}}{2} = \dfrac{m}{20}$

In the following exercises, solve the proportion problem.

410. The children's dosage of acetaminophen is 5 milliliters (ml) for every 25 pounds of a child's weight. How many milliliters of acetaminophen will be prescribed for a 60 pound child?

411. After a workout, Dennis takes his pulse for 10 sec and counts 21 beats. How many beats per minute is this?

412. An 8 ounce serving of ice cream has 272 calories. If Lavonne eats 10 ounces of ice cream, how many calories does she get?

413. Alma is going to Europe and wants to exchange $1,200 into Euros. If each dollar is 0.75 Euros, how many Euros will Alma get?

414. Zack wants to drive from Omaha to Denver, a distance of 494 miles. If his car gets 38 miles to the gallon, how many gallons of gas will Zack need to get to Denver?

415. Teresa is planning a party for 100 people. Each gallon of punch will serve 18 people. How many gallons of punch will she need?

In the following exercises, translate to a proportion.

416. What number is 62% of 395?

417. 42 is 70% of what number?

418. What percent of 1,000 is 15?

419. What percent of 140 is 210?

In the following exercises, translate and solve using proportions.

420. What number is 85% of 900?

421. 6% of what number is $24?

422. $3.51 is 4.5% of what number?

423. What percent of 3,100 is 930?

PRACTICE TEST

In the following exercises, convert each percent to ⓐ a decimal ⓑ a simplified fraction.

424. 24%

425. 5%

426. 350%

In the following exercises, convert each fraction to a percent. (Round to 3 decimal places if needed.)

427. $\frac{7}{8}$

428. $\frac{1}{3}$

429. $\frac{11}{12}$

In the following exercises, solve the percent problem.

430. 65 is what percent of 260?

431. What number is 27% of 3,000?

432. 150% of what number is 60?

433. Yuki's monthly paycheck is $3,825. She pays $918 for rent. What percent of her paycheck goes to rent?

434. The total number of vehicles on one freeway dropped from 84,000 to 74,000. Find the percent decrease (round to the nearest tenth of a percent).

435. Kyle bought a bicycle in Denver where the sales tax was 7.72% of the purchase price. The purchase price of the bicycle was $600. What was the total cost?

436. Mara received $31.80 commission when she sold a $795 suit. What was her rate of commission?

437. Kiyoshi bought a television set on sale for $899. The original price was $1,200. Find:

ⓐ the amount of discount

ⓑ the discount rate (round to the nearest tenth of a percent)

438. Oxana bought a dresser at a garage sale for $20. She refinished it, then added a 250% markup before advertising it for sale. What price did she ask for the dresser?

439. Find the simple interest earned after 5 years on $3000 invested at an interest rate of 4.2%.

440. Brenda borrowed $400 from her brother. Two years later, she repaid the $400 plus $50 interest. What was the rate of interest?

441. Write as a proportion: 4 gallons to 144 miles is the same as 10 gallons to 360 miles.

442. Solve for a: $\frac{12}{a} = \frac{-15}{65}$

443. Vin read 10 pages of a book in 12 minutes. At that rate, how long will it take him to read 35 pages?

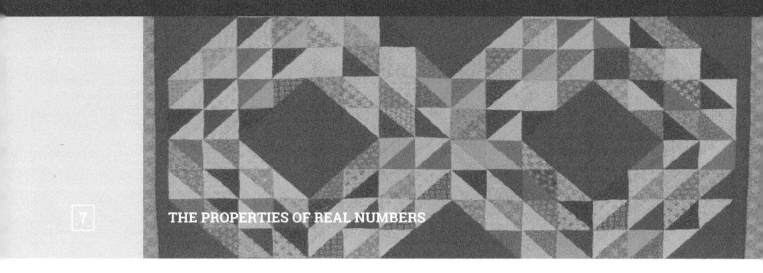

THE PROPERTIES OF REAL NUMBERS

Figure 7.1 Quiltmakers know that by rearranging the same basic blocks the resulting quilts can look very different. What happens when we rearrange the numbers in an expression? Does the resulting value change? We will answer these questions in this chapter as we will learn about the properties of numbers. (credit: Hans, Public Domain)

Chapter Outline

Introduction

A quilt is formed by sewing many different pieces of fabric together. The pieces can vary in color, size, and shape. The combinations of different kinds of pieces provide for an endless possibility of patterns. Much like the pieces of fabric, mathematicians distinguish among different types of numbers. The kinds of numbers in an expression provide for an endless possibility of outcomes. We have already described counting numbers, whole numbers, and integers. In this chapter, we will learn about other types of numbers and their properties.

7.1 Rational and Irrational Numbers

Learning Objectives

By the end of this section, you will be able to:

Identify rational numbers and irrational numbers
Classify different types of real numbers

Be Prepared!

Before you get started, take this readiness quiz.

1. Write 3.19 as an improper fraction.
   If you missed this problem, review Example 5.4.

2. Write $\frac{5}{11}$ as a decimal.
   If you missed this problem, review Example 5.30.

3. Simplify: $\sqrt{144}$.
   If you missed this problem, review Example 5.69.

Identify Rational Numbers and Irrational Numbers

Congratulations! You have completed the first six chapters of this book! It's time to take stock of what you have done so far in this course and think about what is ahead. You have learned how to add, subtract, multiply, and divide whole numbers, fractions, integers, and decimals. You have become familiar with the language and symbols of algebra, and have simplified and evaluated algebraic expressions. You have solved many different types of applications. You have established a good solid foundation that you need so you can be successful in algebra.

In this chapter, we'll make sure your skills are firmly set. We'll take another look at the kinds of numbers we have worked with in all previous chapters. We'll work with properties of numbers that will help you improve your number sense. And we'll practice using them in ways that we'll use when we solve equations and complete other procedures in algebra.

We have already described numbers as counting numbers, whole numbers, and integers. Do you remember what the difference is among these types of numbers?

counting numbers	1, 2, 3, 4...
whole numbers	0, 1, 2, 3, 4...
integers	...−3, −2, −1, 0, 1, 2, 3, 4...

Rational Numbers

What type of numbers would you get if you started with all the integers and then included all the fractions? The numbers you would have form the set of rational numbers. A **rational number** is a number that can be written as a ratio of two integers.

Rational Numbers

A rational number is a number that can be written in the form $\frac{p}{q}$, where p and q are integers and $q \neq o$.

All fractions, both positive and negative, are rational numbers. A few examples are

$$\frac{4}{5}, -\frac{7}{8}, \frac{13}{4}, \text{ and } -\frac{20}{3}$$

Each numerator and each denominator is an integer.

We need to look at all the numbers we have used so far and verify that they are rational. The definition of rational numbers tells us that all fractions are rational. We will now look at the counting numbers, whole numbers, integers, and decimals to make sure they are rational.

Are integers rational numbers? To decide if an integer is a rational number, we try to write it as a ratio of two integers. An easy way to do this is to write it as a fraction with denominator one.

$$3 = \frac{3}{1} \qquad -8 = \frac{-8}{1} \qquad 0 = \frac{0}{1}$$

Since any integer can be written as the ratio of two integers, all integers are rational numbers. Remember that all the counting numbers and all the whole numbers are also integers, and so they, too, are rational.

What about decimals? Are they rational? Let's look at a few to see if we can write each of them as the ratio of two integers. We've already seen that integers are rational numbers. The integer −8 could be written as the decimal −8.0. So, clearly, some decimals are rational.

Think about the decimal 7.3. Can we write it as a ratio of two integers? Because 7.3 means $7\frac{3}{10}$, we can write it as an improper fraction, $\frac{73}{10}$. So 7.3 is the ratio of the integers 73 and 10. It is a rational number.

In general, any decimal that ends after a number of digits (such as 7.3 or −1.2684) is a rational number. We can use the place value of the last digit as the denominator when writing the decimal as a fraction.

EXAMPLE 7.1

Write each as the ratio of two integers: ⓐ −15 ⓑ 6.81 ⓒ $-3\frac{6}{7}$.

✓ Solution

ⓐ

$$-15$$

Write the integer as a fraction with denominator 1. $\dfrac{-15}{1}$

ⓑ

$$6.81$$

Write the decimal as a mixed number. $6\dfrac{81}{100}$

Then convert it to an improper fraction. $\dfrac{681}{100}$

ⓒ

$$-3\dfrac{6}{7}$$

Convert the mixed number to an improper fraction. $-\dfrac{27}{7}$

> **TRY IT ∷ 7.1**   Write each as the ratio of two integers: ⓐ -24 ⓑ 3.57.

> **TRY IT ∷ 7.2**   Write each as the ratio of two integers: ⓐ -19 ⓑ 8.41.

Let's look at the decimal form of the numbers we know are rational. We have seen that every integer is a rational number, since $a = \frac{a}{1}$ for any integer, a. We can also change any integer to a decimal by adding a decimal point and a zero.

Integer	$-2, -1, 0, 1, 2, 3$	
Decimal	$-2.0, -1.0, 0.0, 1.0, 2.0, 3.0$	These decimal numbers stop.

We have also seen that every fraction is a rational number. Look at the decimal form of the fractions we just considered.

Ratio of Integers	$\dfrac{4}{5},$	$-\dfrac{7}{8},$	$\dfrac{13}{14},$	$-\dfrac{20}{3}$	
Decimal Forms	$0.8,$	$-0.875,$	$3.25,$	$-6.666\ldots$ $-6.\overline{66}$	These decimals either stop or repeat.

What do these examples tell you? Every rational number can be written both as a ratio of integers and as a decimal that either stops or repeats. The table below shows the numbers we looked at expressed as a ratio of integers and as a decimal.

Rational Numbers		
	Fractions	**Integers**
Number	$\frac{4}{5}$, $-\frac{7}{8}$, $\frac{13}{4}$, $\frac{-20}{3}$	$-2, -1, 0, 1, 2, 3$
Ratio of Integer	$\frac{4}{5}$, $\frac{-7}{8}$, $\frac{13}{4}$, $\frac{-20}{3}$	$\frac{-2}{1}$, $\frac{-1}{1}$, $\frac{0}{1}$, $\frac{1}{1}$, $\frac{2}{1}$, $\frac{3}{1}$
Decimal number	$0.8, -0.875, 3.25, -6.\overline{6},$	$-2.0, -1.0, 0.0, 1.0, 2.0, 3.0$

Irrational Numbers

Are there any decimals that do not stop or repeat? Yes. The number π (the Greek letter pi, pronounced 'pie'), which is very important in describing circles, has a decimal form that does not stop or repeat.

$$\pi = 3.141592654.......$$

Similarly, the decimal representations of square roots of numbers that are not perfect squares never stop and never repeat. For example,

$$\sqrt{5} = 2.236067978.....$$

A decimal that does not stop and does not repeat cannot be written as the ratio of integers. We call this kind of number an **irrational number**.

Irrational Number

An irrational number is a number that cannot be written as the ratio of two integers. Its decimal form does not stop and does not repeat.

Let's summarize a method we can use to determine whether a number is rational or irrational.

If the decimal form of a number

- stops or repeats, the number is rational.
- does not stop and does not repeat, the number is irrational.

EXAMPLE 7.2

Identify each of the following as rational or irrational:

ⓐ $0.58\overline{3}$

ⓑ 0.475

ⓒ $3.605551275...$

⊘ Solution

ⓐ $0.58\overline{3}$

The bar above the 3 indicates that it repeats. Therefore, $0.58\overline{3}$ is a repeating decimal, and is therefore a rational number.

ⓑ 0.475

This decimal stops after the 5, so it is a rational number.

ⓒ $3.605551275...$

The ellipsis $(...)$ means that this number does not stop. There is no repeating pattern of digits. Since the number doesn't stop and doesn't repeat, it is irrational.

> **TRY IT ::** 7.3   Identify each of the following as rational or irrational:
>
> ⓐ 0.29 ⓑ $0.81\overline{6}$ ⓒ $2.515115111...$

> **TRY IT : : 7.4**   Identify each of the following as rational or irrational:

ⓐ $0.\overline{23}$ ⓑ 0.125 ⓒ $0.418302...$

Let's think about square roots now. Square roots of perfect squares are always whole numbers, so they are rational. But the decimal forms of square roots of numbers that are not perfect squares never stop and never repeat, so these square roots are irrational.

EXAMPLE 7.3

Identify each of the following as rational or irrational:

ⓐ $\sqrt{36}$

ⓑ $\sqrt{44}$

⊘ Solution

ⓐ The number 36 is a perfect square, since $6^2 = 36$. So $\sqrt{36} = 6$. Therefore $\sqrt{36}$ is rational.

ⓑ Remember that $6^2 = 36$ and $7^2 = 49$, so 44 is not a perfect square.

This means $\sqrt{44}$ is irrational.

> **TRY IT : : 7.5**   Identify each of the following as rational or irrational:

ⓐ $\sqrt{81}$

ⓑ $\sqrt{17}$

> **TRY IT : : 7.6**   Identify each of the following as rational or irrational:

ⓐ $\sqrt{116}$

ⓑ $\sqrt{121}$

Classify Real Numbers

We have seen that all counting numbers are whole numbers, all whole numbers are integers, and all integers are rational numbers. Irrational numbers are a separate category of their own. When we put together the rational numbers and the irrational numbers, we get the set of **real numbers**.

Figure 7.2 illustrates how the number sets are related.

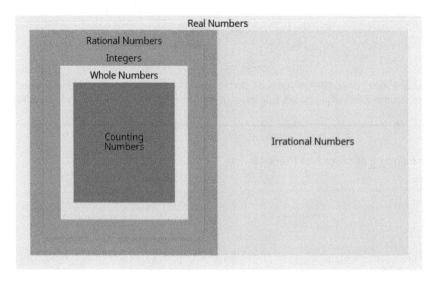

Figure 7.2 This diagram illustrates the relationships between the different types of real numbers.

Real Numbers

Real numbers are numbers that are either rational or irrational.

Does the term "real numbers" seem strange to you? Are there any numbers that are not "real", and, if so, what could they be? For centuries, the only numbers people knew about were what we now call the real numbers. Then mathematicians discovered the set of *imaginary numbers.* You won't encounter imaginary numbers in this course, but you will later on in your studies of algebra.

EXAMPLE 7.4

Determine whether each of the numbers in the following list is a ⓐ whole number, ⓑ integer, ⓒ rational number, ⓓ irrational number, and ⓔ real number.

$$-7, \frac{14}{5}, 8, \sqrt{5}, 5.9, -\sqrt{64}$$

⊘ Solution

ⓐ The whole numbers are $0, 1, 2, 3,\ldots$ The number 8 is the only whole number given.

ⓑ The integers are the whole numbers, their opposites, and 0. From the given numbers, -7 and 8 are integers. Also, notice that 64 is the square of 8 so $-\sqrt{64} = -8$. So the integers are $-7, 8, -\sqrt{64}$.

ⓒ Since all integers are rational, the numbers $-7, 8$, and $-\sqrt{64}$ are also rational. Rational numbers also include fractions and decimals that terminate or repeat, so $\frac{14}{5}$ and 5.9 are rational.

ⓓ The number 5 is not a perfect square, so $\sqrt{5}$ is irrational.

ⓔ All of the numbers listed are real.

We'll summarize the results in a table.

Number	Whole	Integer	Rational	Irrational	Real
-7		✓	✓		✓
$\frac{14}{5}$			✓		✓
8	✓	✓	✓		✓
$\sqrt{5}$				✓	✓
5.9			✓		✓
$-\sqrt{64}$		✓	✓		✓

> **TRY IT :: 7.7**
>
> Determine whether each number is a ⓐ whole number, ⓑ integer, ⓒ rational number, ⓓ irrational number, and ⓔ real number: $-3,\ -\sqrt{2},\ 0.\overline{3},\ \frac{9}{5},\ 4,\ \sqrt{49}$.

> **TRY IT :: 7.8**
>
> Determine whether each number is a ⓐ whole number, ⓑ integer, ⓒ rational number, ⓓ irrational number, and ⓔ real number: $-\sqrt{25},\ -\frac{3}{8},\ -1,\ 6,\ \sqrt{121},\ 2.041975\ldots$

▶ **MEDIA :: ACCESS ADDITIONAL ONLINE RESOURCES**
- Sets of Real Numbers (http://www.openstaxcollege.org/l/24RealNumber)
- Real Numbers (http://www.openstaxcollege.org/l/24RealNumbers)

7.1 EXERCISES

Practice Makes Perfect

Rational Numbers

In the following exercises, write as the ratio of two integers.

1.
  ⓐ 5   ⓑ 3.19

2.
  ⓐ 8   ⓑ −1.61

3.
  ⓐ −12   ⓑ 9.279

4.
  ⓐ −16   ⓑ 4.399

In the following exercises, determine which of the given numbers are rational and which are irrational.

5. 0.75, $0.22\overline{3}$, $1.39174...$

6. 0.36, $0.94729...$, $2.52\overline{8}$

7. $0.\overline{45}$, $1.919293...$, 3.59

8. $0.1\overline{3}$, $0.42982...$, 1.875

In the following exercises, identify whether each number is rational or irrational.

9.
  ⓐ $\sqrt{25}$ ⓑ $\sqrt{30}$

10.
  ⓐ $\sqrt{44}$ ⓑ $\sqrt{49}$

11.
  ⓐ $\sqrt{164}$ ⓑ $\sqrt{169}$

12.
  ⓐ $\sqrt{225}$ ⓑ $\sqrt{216}$

Classifying Real Numbers

In the following exercises, determine whether each number is whole, integer, rational, irrational, and real.

13. -8, 0, $1.95286....$, $\frac{12}{5}$, $\sqrt{36}$, 9

14. -9, $-3\frac{4}{9}$, $-\sqrt{9}$, $0.4\overline{09}$, $\frac{11}{6}$, 7

15. $-\sqrt{100}$, -7, $-\frac{8}{3}$, -1, 0.77, $3\frac{1}{4}$

Everyday Math

16. Field trip All the 5th graders at Lincoln Elementary School will go on a field trip to the science museum. Counting all the children, teachers, and chaperones, there will be 147 people. Each bus holds 44 people.

ⓐ How many buses will be needed?

ⓑ Why must the answer be a whole number?

ⓒ Why shouldn't you round the answer the usual way?

17. Child care Serena wants to open a licensed child care center. Her state requires that there be no more than 12 children for each teacher. She would like her child care center to serve 40 children.

ⓐ How many teachers will be needed?

ⓑ Why must the answer be a whole number?

ⓒ Why shouldn't you round the answer the usual way?

Writing Exercises

18. In your own words, explain the difference between a rational number and an irrational number.

19. Explain how the sets of numbers (counting, whole, integer, rational, irrationals, reals) are related to each other.

Self Check

ⓐ *After completing the exercises, use this checklist to evaluate your mastery of the objectives of this section.*

I can...	Confidently	With some help	No-I don't get it!
identify rational and irrational numbers.			
classify different types of real numbers.			

ⓑ *If most of your checks were:*

...confidently. Congratulations! You have achieved the objectives in this section. Reflect on the study skills you used so that you can continue to use them. What did you do to become confident of your ability to do these things? Be specific.

...with some help. This must be addressed quickly because topics you do not master become potholes in your road to success. In math, every topic builds upon previous work. It is important to make sure you have a strong foundation before you move on. Who can you ask for help? Your fellow classmates and instructor are good resources. Is there a place on campus where math tutors are available? Can your study skills be improved?

...no—I don't get it! This is a warning sign and you must not ignore it. You should get help right away or you will quickly be overwhelmed. See your instructor as soon as you can to discuss your situation. Together you can come up with a plan to get you the help you need.

7.2 | Commutative and Associative Properties

Learning Objectives

By the end of this section, you will be able to:
- Use the commutative and associative properties
- Evaluate expressions using the commutative and associative properties
- Simplify expressions using the commutative and associative properties

Be Prepared!

Before you get started, take this readiness quiz.

1. Simplify: $7y + 2 + y + 13$.
   If you missed this problem, review Example 2.22.

2. Multiply: $\frac{2}{3} \cdot 18$.
   If you missed this problem, review Example 4.28.

3. Find the opposite of 15.
   If you missed this problem, review Example 3.3.

In the next few sections, we will take a look at the properties of real numbers. Many of these properties will describe things you already know, but it will help to give names to the properties and define them formally. This way we'll be able to refer to them and use them as we solve equations in the next chapter.

Use the Commutative and Associative Properties

Think about adding two numbers, such as 5 and 3.

$$5 + 3 \qquad 3 + 5$$
$$8 \qquad\quad 8$$

The results are the same. $5 + 3 = 3 + 5$

Notice, the order in which we add does not matter. The same is true when multiplying 5 and 3.

$$5 \cdot 3 \qquad 3 \cdot 5$$
$$15 \qquad 15$$

Again, the results are the same! $5 \cdot 3 = 3 \cdot 5$. The order in which we multiply does not matter.

These examples illustrate the commutative properties of addition and multiplication.

Commutative Properties

Commutative Property of Addition: if a and b are real numbers, then

$$a + b = b + a$$

Commutative Property of Multiplication: if a and b are real numbers, then

$$a \cdot b = b \cdot a$$

The commutative properties have to do with order. If you change the order of the numbers when adding or multiplying, the result is the same.

EXAMPLE 7.5

Use the commutative properties to rewrite the following expressions:

ⓐ $-1 + 3 = $ _____

ⓑ $4 \cdot 9 = $ _____

✓ Solution

ⓐ

$$-1 + 3 = \underline{}$$

Use the commutative property of addition to change the order.　　$-1 + 3 = 3 + (-1)$

ⓑ

$$4 \cdot 9 = \underline{}$$

Use the commutative property of multiplication to change the order.　　$4 \cdot 9 = 9 \cdot 4$

> **TRY IT :: 7.9**　　Use the commutative properties to rewrite the following:
>
> ⓐ $-4 + 7 = \underline{}$　　ⓑ $6 \cdot 12 = \underline{}$

> **TRY IT :: 7.10**　　Use the commutative properties to rewrite the following:
>
> ⓐ $14 + (-2) = \underline{}$　　ⓑ $3(-5) = \underline{}$

What about subtraction? Does order matter when we subtract numbers? Does $7 - 3$ give the same result as $3 - 7$?

$$\begin{array}{cc} 7 - 3 & 3 - 7 \\ 4 & -4 \end{array}$$

$$4 \neq -4$$

The results are not the same. $7 - 3 \neq 3 - 7$

Since changing the order of the subtraction did not give the same result, we can say that subtraction is not commutative. Let's see what happens when we divide two numbers. Is division commutative?

$$\begin{array}{cc} 12 \div 4 & 4 \div 12 \\ \dfrac{12}{4} & \dfrac{4}{12} \\ 3 & \dfrac{1}{3} \end{array}$$

$$3 \neq \dfrac{1}{3}$$

The results are not the same. So $12 \div 4 \neq 4 \div 12$

Since changing the order of the division did not give the same result, division is not commutative.

Addition and multiplication are commutative. Subtraction and division are not commutative.

Suppose you were asked to simplify this expression.

$$7 + 8 + 2$$

How would you do it and what would your answer be?

Some people would think $7 + 8$ is 15 and then $15 + 2$ is 17. Others might start with $8 + 2$ makes 10 and then $7 + 10$ makes 17.

Both ways give the same result, as shown in Figure 7.3. (Remember that parentheses are grouping symbols that indicate which operations should be done first.)

$$(7 + 8) + 2 = 7 + (8 + 2)$$
$$15 + 2 = 7 + 10$$
$$17$$

Figure 7.3

When adding three numbers, changing the grouping of the numbers does not change the result. This is known as the Associative Property of Addition.

The same principle holds true for multiplication as well. Suppose we want to find the value of the following expression:

$$5 \cdot \frac{1}{3} \cdot 3$$

Changing the grouping of the numbers gives the same result, as shown in Figure 7.4.

$$\left(5 \cdot \frac{1}{3}\right) \cdot 3 = 5 \cdot \left(\frac{1}{3} \cdot 3\right)$$
$$\left(\frac{5}{3}\right) \cdot 3 = 5 \cdot 1$$
$$5$$

Figure 7.4

When multiplying three numbers, changing the grouping of the numbers does not change the result. This is known as the Associative Property of Multiplication.

If we multiply three numbers, changing the grouping does not affect the product.

You probably know this, but the terminology may be new to you. These examples illustrate the *Associative Properties*.

Associative Properties

Associative Property of Addition: if a, b, and c are real numbers, then

$$(a + b) + c = a + (b + c)$$

Associative Property of Multiplication: if a, b, and c are real numbers, then

$$(a \cdot b) \cdot c = a \cdot (b \cdot c)$$

EXAMPLE 7.6

Use the associative properties to rewrite the following:

ⓐ $(3 + 0.6) + 0.4 = $ _____

ⓑ $\left(-4 \cdot \frac{2}{5}\right) \cdot 15 = $ _____

⊘ **Solution**

ⓐ

$$(3 + 0.6) + 0.4 = \underline{\hspace{2cm}}$$

Change the grouping. $(3 + 0.6) + 0.4 = 3 + (0.6 + 0.4)$

Notice that $0.6 + 0.4$ is 1, so the addition will be easier if we group as shown on the right.

ⓑ

$$\left(-4 \cdot \frac{2}{5}\right) \cdot 15 = \underline{\hspace{2cm}}$$

Change the grouping. $\left(-4 \cdot \frac{2}{5}\right) \cdot 15 = -4 \cdot \left(\frac{2}{5} \cdot 15\right)$

Notice that $\frac{2}{5} \cdot 15$ is 6. The multiplication will be easier if we group as shown on the right.

> **TRY IT :: 7.11** Use the associative properties to rewrite the following:
ⓐ $(1 + 0.7) + 0.3 = \underline{\hspace{2cm}}$ ⓑ $(-9 \cdot 8) \cdot \frac{3}{4} = \underline{\hspace{2cm}}$

> **TRY IT :: 7.12** Use the associative properties to rewrite the following:
ⓐ $(4 + 0.6) + 0.4 = \underline{\hspace{2cm}}$ ⓑ $(-2 \cdot 12) \cdot \frac{5}{6} = \underline{\hspace{2cm}}$

Besides using the associative properties to make calculations easier, we will often use it to simplify expressions with variables.

EXAMPLE 7.7

Use the Associative Property of Multiplication to simplify: $6(3x)$.

⊘ **Solution**

$$6(3x)$$

Change the grouping. $(6 \cdot 3)x$

Multiply in the parentheses. $18x$

Notice that we can multiply $6 \cdot 3$, but we could not multiply $3 \cdot x$ without having a value for x.

> **TRY IT :: 7.13** Use the Associative Property of Multiplication to simplify the given expression: $8(4x)$.

> **TRY IT :: 7.14** Use the Associative Property of Multiplication to simplify the given expression: $-9(7y)$.

Evaluate Expressions using the Commutative and Associative Properties

The commutative and associative properties can make it easier to evaluate some algebraic expressions. Since order does not matter when adding or multiplying three or more terms, we can rearrange and re-group terms to make our work easier, as the next several examples illustrate.

EXAMPLE 7.8

Evaluate each expression when $x = \frac{7}{8}$.

ⓐ $x + 0.37 + (-x)$ ⓑ $x + (-x) + 0.37$

⊘ **Solution**

ⓐ

	$x + 0.37 + (-x)$
Substitute $\frac{7}{8}$ for x.	$\frac{7}{8} + 0.37 + \left(-\frac{7}{8}\right)$
Convert fractions to decimals.	$0.875 + 0.37 + (-0.875)$
Add left to right.	$1.245 - 0.875$
Subtract.	0.37

ⓑ

	$x + (-x) + 0.37$
Substitute $\frac{7}{8}$ for x.	$\frac{7}{8} + \left(-\frac{7}{8}\right) + 0.37$
Add opposites first.	0.37

What was the difference between part ⓐ and part ⓑ? Only the order changed. By the Commutative Property of Addition, $x + 0.37 + (-x) = x + (-x) + 0.37$. But wasn't part ⓑ much easier?

> **TRY IT :: 7.15**   Evaluate each expression when $y = \frac{3}{8}$: ⓐ $y + 0.84 + (-y)$ ⓑ $y + (-y) + 0.84$.

> **TRY IT :: 7.16**   Evaluate each expression when $f = \frac{17}{20}$: ⓐ $f + 0.975 + (-f)$ ⓑ $f + (-f) + 0.975$.

Let's do one more, this time with multiplication.

EXAMPLE 7.9

Evaluate each expression when $n = 17$.

ⓐ $\frac{4}{3}\left(\frac{3}{4}n\right)$

ⓑ $\left(\frac{4}{3} \cdot \frac{3}{4}\right)n$

Solution

ⓐ

$$\frac{4}{3}\left(\frac{3}{4}n\right)$$

Substitute 17 for n.	$\frac{4}{3}\left(\frac{3}{4}\cdot 17\right)$
Multiply in the parentheses first.	$\frac{4}{3}\left(\frac{51}{4}\right)$
Multiply again.	17

ⓑ

$$\left(\frac{4}{3}\cdot\frac{3}{4}\right)n$$

Substitute 17 for n.	$\left(\frac{4}{3}\cdot\frac{3}{4}\right)\cdot 17$
Multiply. The product of reciprocals is 1.	$(1)\cdot 17$
Multiply again.	17

What was the difference between part ⓐ and part ⓑ here? Only the grouping changed. By the Associative Property of Multiplication, $\frac{4}{3}\left(\frac{3}{4}n\right)=\left(\frac{4}{3}\cdot\frac{3}{4}\right)n$. By carefully choosing how to group the factors, we can make the work easier.

> **TRY IT ::** 7.17   Evaluate each expression when $p=24$: ⓐ $\frac{5}{9}\left(\frac{9}{5}p\right)$ ⓑ $\left(\frac{5}{9}\cdot\frac{9}{5}\right)p$.

> **TRY IT ::** 7.18   Evaluate each expression when $q=15$: ⓐ $\frac{7}{11}\left(\frac{11}{7}q\right)$ ⓑ $\left(\frac{7}{11}\cdot\frac{11}{7}\right)q$

Simplify Expressions Using the Commutative and Associative Properties

When we have to simplify algebraic expressions, we can often make the work easier by applying the Commutative or Associative Property first instead of automatically following the order of operations. Notice that in Example 7.8 part ⓑ was easier to simplify than part ⓐ because the opposites were next to each other and their sum is 0. Likewise, part ⓑ in Example 7.9 was easier, with the reciprocals grouped together, because their product is 1. In the next few examples, we'll use our number sense to look for ways to apply these properties to make our work easier.

EXAMPLE 7.10

Simplify: $-84n+(-73n)+84n$.

Solution

Notice the first and third terms are opposites, so we can use the commutative property of addition to reorder the terms.

$$-84n + (-73n) + 84n$$

Re-order the terms.	$-84n + 84n + (-73n)$
Add left to right.	$0 + (-73n)$
Add.	$-73n$

> **TRY IT ::** 7.19   Simplify: $-27a + (-48a) + 27a$.

> **TRY IT ::** 7.20   Simplify: $39x + (-92x) + (-39x)$.

Now we will see how recognizing reciprocals is helpful. Before multiplying left to right, look for reciprocals—their product is 1.

EXAMPLE 7.11

Simplify: $\dfrac{7}{15} \cdot \dfrac{8}{23} \cdot \dfrac{15}{7}$.

⊘ **Solution**

Notice the first and third terms are reciprocals, so we can use the Commutative Property of Multiplication to reorder the factors.

$$\dfrac{7}{15} \cdot \dfrac{8}{23} \cdot \dfrac{15}{7}$$

Re-order the terms.	$\dfrac{7}{15} \cdot \dfrac{15}{7} \cdot \dfrac{8}{23}$
Multiply left to right.	$1 \cdot \dfrac{8}{23}$
Multiply.	$\dfrac{8}{23}$

> **TRY IT ::** 7.21   Simplify: $\dfrac{9}{16} \cdot \dfrac{5}{49} \cdot \dfrac{16}{9}$.

> **TRY IT ::** 7.22   Simplify: $\dfrac{6}{17} \cdot \dfrac{11}{25} \cdot \dfrac{17}{6}$.

In expressions where we need to add or subtract three or more fractions, combine those with a common denominator first.

EXAMPLE 7.12

Simplify: $\left(\dfrac{5}{13} + \dfrac{3}{4}\right) + \dfrac{1}{4}$.

⊘ **Solution**

Notice that the second and third terms have a common denominator, so this work will be easier if we change the grouping.

$$\left(\frac{5}{13} + \frac{3}{4}\right) + \frac{1}{4}$$

Group the terms with a common denominator.	$\frac{5}{13} + \left(\frac{3}{4} + \frac{1}{4}\right)$
Add in the parentheses first.	$\frac{5}{13} + \left(\frac{4}{4}\right)$
Simplify the fraction.	$\frac{5}{13} + 1$
Add.	$1\frac{5}{13}$
Convert to an improper fraction.	$\frac{18}{13}$

> **TRY IT : : 7.23**   Simplify: $\left(\frac{7}{15} + \frac{5}{8}\right) + \frac{3}{8}$.

> **TRY IT : : 7.24**   Simplify: $\left(\frac{2}{9} + \frac{7}{12}\right) + \frac{5}{12}$.

When adding and subtracting three or more terms involving decimals, look for terms that combine to give whole numbers.

EXAMPLE 7.13

Simplify: $(6.47q + 9.99q) + 1.01q$.

⊘ **Solution**

Notice that the sum of the second and third coefficients is a whole number.

$$(6.47q + 9.99q) + 1.01q$$

Change the grouping.	$6.47q + (9.99q + 1.01q)$
Add in the parentheses first.	$6.47q + (11.00q)$
Add.	$17.47q$

Many people have good number sense when they deal with money. Think about adding 99 cents and 1 cent. Do you see how this applies to adding $9.99 + 1.01$?

> **TRY IT : : 7.25**   Simplify: $(5.58c + 8.75c) + 1.25c$.

> **TRY IT : : 7.26**   Simplify: $(8.79d + 3.55d) + 5.45d$.

No matter what you are doing, it is always a good idea to think ahead. When simplifying an expression, think about what your steps will be. The next example will show you how using the Associative Property of Multiplication can make your work easier if you plan ahead.

EXAMPLE 7.14

Simplify the expression: $[1.67(8)](0.25)$.

Solution

Notice that multiplying $(8)(0.25)$ is easier than multiplying $1.67(8)$ because it gives a whole number. (Think about having 8 quarters—that makes $2.)

	$[1.67(8)](0.25)$
Regroup.	$1.67[(8)(0.25)]$
Multiply in the brackets first.	$1.67[2]$
Multiply.	3.34

> **TRY IT :: 7.27**   Simplify: $[1.17(4)](2.25)$.

> **TRY IT :: 7.28**   Simplify: $[3.52(8)](2.5)$.

When simplifying expressions that contain variables, we can use the commutative and associative properties to re-order or regroup terms, as shown in the next pair of examples.

EXAMPLE 7.15

Simplify: $6(9x)$.

Solution

	$6(9x)$
Use the associative property of multiplication to re-group.	$(6 \cdot 9)x$
Multiply in the parentheses.	$54x$

> **TRY IT :: 7.29**   Simplify: $8(3y)$.

> **TRY IT :: 7.30**   Simplify: $12(5z)$.

In The Language of Algebra, we learned to combine like terms by rearranging an expression so the like terms were together. We simplified the expression $3x + 7 + 4x + 5$ by rewriting it as $3x + 4x + 7 + 5$ and then simplified it to $7x + 12$. We were using the Commutative Property of Addition.

EXAMPLE 7.16

Simplify: $18p + 6q + (-15p) + 5q$.

Solution

Use the Commutative Property of Addition to re-order so that like terms are together.

$$18p + 6q + (-15p) + 5q$$

Re-order terms.	$18p + (-15p) + 6q + 5q$
Combine like terms.	$3p + 11q$

> **TRY IT : :** 7.31   Simplify: $23r + 14s + 9r + (-15s)$.

> **TRY IT : :** 7.32   Simplify: $37m + 21n + 4m + (-15n)$.

LINKS TO LITERACY

The *Links to Literacy* activity, "Each Orange Had 8 Slices" will provide you with another view of the topics covered in this section.

7.2 EXERCISES

Practice Makes Perfect

Use the Commutative and Associative Properties

In the following exercises, use the commutative properties to rewrite the given expression.

20. $8 + 9 = $ ___

21. $7 + 6 = $ ___

22. $8(-12) = $ ___

23. $7(-13) = $ ___

24. $(-19)(-14) = $ ___

25. $(-12)(-18) = $ ___

26. $-11 + 8 = $ ___

27. $-15 + 7 = $ ___

28. $x + 4 = $ ___

29. $y + 1 = $ ___

30. $-2a = $ ___

31. $-3m = $ ___

In the following exercises, use the associative properties to rewrite the given expression.

32. $(11 + 9) + 14 = $ ___

33. $(21 + 14) + 9 = $ ___

34. $(12 \cdot 5) \cdot 7 = $ ___

35. $(14 \cdot 6) \cdot 9 = $ ___

36. $(-7 + 9) + 8 = $ ___

37. $(-2 + 6) + 7 = $ ___

38. $\left(16 \cdot \frac{4}{5}\right) \cdot 15 = $ ___

39. $\left(13 \cdot \frac{2}{3}\right) \cdot 18 = $ ___

40. $3(4x) = $ ___

41. $4(7x) = $ ___

42. $(12 + x) + 28 = $ ___

43. $(17 + y) + 33 = $ ___

Evaluate Expressions using the Commutative and Associative Properties

In the following exercises, evaluate each expression for the given value.

44. If $y = \frac{5}{8}$, evaluate:

  ⓐ $y + 0.49 + (-y)$

  ⓑ $y + (-y) + 0.49$

45. If $z = \frac{7}{8}$, evaluate:

  ⓐ $z + 0.97 + (-z)$

  ⓑ $z + (-z) + 0.97$

46. If $c = -\frac{11}{4}$, evaluate:

  ⓐ $c + 3.125 + (-c)$

  ⓑ $c + (-c) + 3.125$

47. If $d = -\frac{9}{4}$, evaluate:

  ⓐ $d + 2.375 + (-d)$

  ⓑ $d + (-d) + 2.375$

48. If $j = 11$, evaluate:

  ⓐ $\frac{5}{6}\left(\frac{6}{5}j\right)$ ⓑ $\left(\frac{5}{6} \cdot \frac{6}{5}\right)j$

49. If $k = 21$, evaluate:

  ⓐ $\frac{4}{13}\left(\frac{13}{4}k\right)$

  ⓑ $\left(\frac{4}{13} \cdot \frac{13}{4}\right)k$

50. If $m = -25$, evaluate:

  ⓐ $-\frac{3}{7}\left(\frac{7}{3}m\right)$

  ⓑ $\left(-\frac{3}{7} \cdot \frac{7}{3}\right)m$

51. If $n = -8$, evaluate:

  ⓐ $-\frac{5}{21}\left(\frac{21}{5}n\right)$

  ⓑ $\left(-\frac{5}{21} \cdot \frac{21}{5}\right)n$

Simplify Expressions Using the Commutative and Associative Properties

In the following exercises, simplify.

52. $-45a + 15 + 45a$

53. $9y + 23 + (-9y)$

54. $\frac{1}{2} + \frac{7}{8} + \left(-\frac{1}{2}\right)$

55. $\frac{2}{5} + \frac{5}{12} + \left(-\frac{2}{5}\right)$

56. $\frac{3}{20} \cdot \frac{49}{11} \cdot \frac{20}{3}$

57. $\frac{13}{18} \cdot \frac{25}{7} \cdot \frac{18}{13}$

58. $\frac{7}{12} \cdot \frac{9}{17} \cdot \frac{24}{7}$

59. $\frac{3}{10} \cdot \frac{13}{23} \cdot \frac{50}{3}$

60. $-24 \cdot 7 \cdot \frac{3}{8}$

61. $-36 \cdot 11 \cdot \frac{4}{9}$

62. $\left(\frac{5}{6} + \frac{8}{15}\right) + \frac{7}{15}$

63. $\left(\frac{1}{12} + \frac{4}{9}\right) + \frac{5}{9}$

64. $\frac{5}{13} + \frac{3}{4} + \frac{1}{4}$

65. $\frac{8}{15} + \frac{5}{7} + \frac{2}{7}$

66. $(4.33p + 1.09p) + 3.91p$

67. $(5.89d + 2.75d) + 1.25d$

68. $17(0.25)(4)$

69. $36(0.2)(5)$

70. $[2.48(12)](0.5)$

71. $[9.731(4)](0.75)$

72. $7(4a)$

73. $9(8w)$

74. $-15(5m)$

75. $-23(2n)$

76. $12\left(\frac{5}{6}p\right)$

77. $20\left(\frac{3}{5}q\right)$

78. $14x + 19y + 25x + 3y$

79. $15u + 11v + 27u + 19v$

80. $43m + (-12n) + (-16m) + (-9n)$

81. $-22p + 17q + (-35p) + (-27q)$

82. $\frac{3}{8}g + \frac{1}{12}h + \frac{7}{8}g + \frac{5}{12}h$

83. $\frac{5}{6}a + \frac{3}{10}b + \frac{1}{6}a + \frac{9}{10}b$

84. $6.8p + 9.14q + (-4.37p) + (-0.88q)$

85. $9.6m + 7.22n + (-2.19m) + (-0.65n)$

Everyday Math

86. Stamps Allie and Loren need to buy stamps. Allie needs four $0.49 stamps and nine $0.02 stamps. Loren needs eight $0.49 stamps and three $0.02 stamps.

ⓐ How much will Allie's stamps cost?

ⓑ How much will Loren's stamps cost?

ⓒ What is the total cost of the girls' stamps?

ⓓ How many $0.49 stamps do the girls need altogether? How much will they cost?

ⓔ How many $0.02 stamps do the girls need altogether? How much will they cost?

87. Counting Cash Grant is totaling up the cash from a fundraising dinner. In one envelope, he has twenty-three $5 bills, eighteen $10 bills, and thirty-four $20 bills. In another envelope, he has fourteen $5 bills, nine $10 bills, and twenty-seven $20 bills.

ⓐ How much money is in the first envelope?

ⓑ How much money is in the second envelope?

ⓒ What is the total value of all the cash?

ⓓ What is the value of all the $5 bills?

ⓔ What is the value of all $10 bills?

ⓕ What is the value of all $20 bills?

Writing Exercises

88. In your own words, state the Commutative Property of Addition and explain why it is useful.

89. In your own words, state the Associative Property of Multiplication and explain why it is useful.

Self Check

ⓐ *After completing the exercises, use this checklist to evaluate your mastery of the objectives of this section.*

I can...	Confidently	With some help	No-I don't get it!
use the Commutative and Associative Properties.			
evaluate expressions using the Commutative and Associative Properties.			
simplify expressions using the Commutative and Associative Properties.			

ⓑ *After reviewing this checklist, what will you do to become confident for all objectives?*

7.3 Distributive Property

Learning Objectives

By the end of this section, you will be able to:

- Simplify expressions using the distributive property
- Evaluate expressions using the distributive property

Be Prepared!

Before you get started, take this readiness quiz.

1. Multiply: $3(0.25)$.
   If you missed this problem, review Example 5.15

2. Simplify: $10 - (-2)(3)$.
   If you missed this problem, review Example 3.51

3. Combine like terms: $9y + 17 + 3y - 2$.
   If you missed this problem, review Example 2.22.

Simplify Expressions Using the Distributive Property

Suppose three friends are going to the movies. They each need $9.25; that is, 9 dollars and 1 quarter. How much money do they need all together? You can think about the dollars separately from the quarters.

$3 \times 9 = 27$

$3 \times \$0.25 = \$0.75$

They need 3 times $9, so $27, and 3 times 1 quarter, so 75 cents. In total, they need $27.75.

If you think about doing the math in this way, you are using the Distributive Property.

Distributive Property

If a, b, c are real numbers, then

$$a(b + c) = ab + ac$$

Back to our friends at the movies, we could show the math steps we take to find the total amount of money they need like this:

$$3(9.25)$$
$$3(9 \quad + \quad 0.25)$$
$$3(9) \quad + \quad 3(0.25)$$
$$27 \quad + \quad 0.75$$
$$27.75$$

In algebra, we use the Distributive Property to remove parentheses as we simplify expressions. For example, if we are asked to simplify the expression $3(x+4)$, the order of operations says to work in the parentheses first. But we cannot add x and 4, since they are not like terms. So we use the Distributive Property, as shown in Example 7.19.

EXAMPLE 7.17

Simplify: $3(x+4)$.

⊘ **Solution**

$$3(x+4)$$

Distribute.	$3\cdot x + 3\cdot 4$
Multiply.	$3x + 12$

> **TRY IT : : 7.33**   Simplify: $4(x+2)$.

> **TRY IT : : 7.34**   Simplify: $6(x+7)$.

Some students find it helpful to draw in arrows to remind them how to use the Distributive Property. Then the first step in Example 7.17 would look like this:

$$3(x+4)$$
$$3\cdot x + 3\cdot 4$$

EXAMPLE 7.18

Simplify: $6(5y+1)$.

⊘ **Solution**

$$6(5y+1)$$

Distribute.	$6\cdot 5y + 6\cdot 1$
Multiply.	$30y + 6$

> **TRY IT : : 7.35**   Simplify: $9(3y+8)$.

> **TRY IT : : 7.36**   Simplify: $5(5w+9)$.

The distributive property can be used to simplify expressions that look slightly different from $a(b+c)$. Here are two other forms.

Distributive Property

If a, b, c are real numbers, then

$$a(b+c) = ab + ac$$

Other forms

$$a(b-c) = ab - ac$$

$$(b + c)a = ba + ca$$

EXAMPLE 7.19

Simplify: $2(x - 3)$.

⊘ **Solution**

$$2(x - 3)$$

Distribute. $2 \cdot x - 2 \cdot 3$

Multiply. $2x - 6$

> **TRY IT ::** 7.37   Simplify: $7(x - 6)$.

> **TRY IT ::** 7.38   Simplify: $8(x - 5)$.

Do you remember how to multiply a fraction by a whole number? We'll need to do that in the next two examples.

EXAMPLE 7.20

Simplify: $\frac{3}{4}(n + 12)$.

⊘ **Solution**

$$\frac{3}{4}(n + 12)$$

Distribute. $\frac{3}{4} \cdot n + \frac{3}{4} \cdot 12$

Simplify. $\frac{3}{4}n + 9$

> **TRY IT ::** 7.39   Simplify: $\frac{2}{5}(p + 10)$.

> **TRY IT ::** 7.40   Simplify: $\frac{3}{7}(u + 21)$.

EXAMPLE 7.21

Simplify: $8\left(\frac{3}{8}x + \frac{1}{4}\right)$.

Solution

$$8\left(\frac{3}{8}x+\frac{1}{4}\right)$$

Distribute. $8\cdot\frac{3}{8}x+8\cdot\frac{1}{4}$

Multiply. $3x+2$

> **TRY IT :: 7.41**   Simplify: $6\left(\frac{5}{6}y+\frac{1}{2}\right)$.

> **TRY IT :: 7.42**   Simplify: $12\left(\frac{1}{3}n+\frac{3}{4}\right)$.

Using the Distributive Property as shown in the next example will be very useful when we solve money applications later.

EXAMPLE 7.22

Simplify: $100(0.3+0.25q)$.

Solution

$$100(0.3+0.25q)$$

Distribute. $100(0.3)+100(0.25q)$

Multiply. $30+25q$

> **TRY IT :: 7.43**   Simplify: $100(0.7+0.15p)$.

> **TRY IT :: 7.44**   Simplify: $100(0.04+0.35d)$.

In the next example we'll multiply by a variable. We'll need to do this in a later chapter.

EXAMPLE 7.23

Simplify: $m(n-4)$.

Solution

$$m(n-4)$$

Distribute. $m\cdot n-m\cdot4$

Multiply. $mn-4m$

Notice that we wrote $m\cdot4$ as $4m$. We can do this because of the Commutative Property of Multiplication. When a term is the product of a number and a variable, we write the number first.

> **TRY IT :: 7.45**   Simplify: $r(s-2)$.

> **TRY IT ::** 7.46   Simplify: $y(z - 8)$.

The next example will use the 'backwards' form of the Distributive Property, $(b + c)a = ba + ca$.

EXAMPLE 7.24

Simplify: $(x + 8)p$.

⊘ **Solution**

$$(x + 8)p$$

Distribute. $px + 8p$

> **TRY IT ::** 7.47   Simplify: $(x + 2)p$.

> **TRY IT ::** 7.48   Simplify: $(y + 4)q$.

When you distribute a negative number, you need to be extra careful to get the signs correct.

EXAMPLE 7.25

Simplify: $-2(4y + 1)$.

⊘ **Solution**

$$-2(4y + 1)$$

Distribute. $-2 \cdot 4y + (-2) \cdot 1$

Simplify. $-8y - 2$

> **TRY IT ::** 7.49   Simplify: $-3(6m + 5)$.

> **TRY IT ::** 7.50   Simplify: $-6(8n + 11)$.

EXAMPLE 7.26

Simplify: $-11(4 - 3a)$.

⊘ **Solution**

$$-11(4 - 3a)$$

Distribute. $-11 \cdot 4 - (-11) \cdot 3a$

Multiply. $-44 + (-33a)$

Simplify. $-44 + 33a$

You could also write the result as $33a - 44$. Do you know why?

> | **TRY IT ::** 7.51   Simplify: $-5(2 - 3a)$.

> | **TRY IT ::** 7.52   Simplify: $-7(8 - 15y)$.

In the next example, we will show how to use the Distributive Property to find the opposite of an expression. Remember, $-a = -1 \cdot a$.

EXAMPLE 7.27

Simplify: $-(y + 5)$.

⊘ **Solution**

	$-(y + 5)$
Multiplying by –1 results in the opposite.	$-1(y + 5)$
Distribute.	$-1 \cdot y + (-1) \cdot 5$
Simplify.	$-y + (-5)$
Simplify.	$-y - 5$

> | **TRY IT ::** 7.53   Simplify: $-(z - 11)$.

> | **TRY IT ::** 7.54   Simplify: $-(x - 4)$.

Sometimes we need to use the Distributive Property as part of the order of operations. Start by looking at the parentheses. If the expression inside the parentheses cannot be simplified, the next step would be multiply using the distributive property, which removes the parentheses. The next two examples will illustrate this.

EXAMPLE 7.28

Simplify: $8 - 2(x + 3)$.

⊘ **Solution**

	$8 - 2(x + 3)$
Distribute.	$8 - 2 \cdot x - 2 \cdot 3$
Multiply.	$8 - 2x - 6$
Combine like terms.	$-2x + 2$

> | **TRY IT ::** 7.55   Simplify: $9 - 3(x + 2)$.

> | **TRY IT ::** 7.56   Simplify: $7x - 5(x + 4)$.

EXAMPLE 7.29

Simplify: $4(x - 8) - (x + 3)$.

Solution

$$4(x - 8) - (x + 3)$$

Distribute. $4x - 32 - x - 3$

Combine like terms. $3x - 35$

> **TRY IT : : 7.57**   Simplify: $6(x - 9) - (x + 12)$.

> **TRY IT : : 7.58**   Simplify: $8(x - 1) - (x + 5)$.

Evaluate Expressions Using the Distributive Property

Some students need to be convinced that the Distributive Property always works.

In the examples below, we will practice evaluating some of the expressions from previous examples; in part ⓐ, we will evaluate the form with parentheses, and in part ⓑ we will evaluate the form we got after distributing. If we evaluate both expressions correctly, this will show that they are indeed equal.

EXAMPLE 7.30

When $y = 10$ evaluate: ⓐ $6(5y + 1)$ ⓑ $6 \cdot 5y + 6 \cdot 1$.

Solution

ⓐ

$$6(5y + 1)$$

Substitute 10 for y. $6(5 \cdot 10 + 1)$

Simplify in the parentheses. $6(51)$

Multiply.   306

ⓑ

$$6 \cdot 5y + 6 \cdot 1$$

Substitute 10 for y. $6 \cdot 5 \cdot 10 + 6 \cdot 1$

Simplify. $300 + 6$

Add.   306

Notice, the answers are the same. When $y = 10$,

$$6(5y + 1) = 6 \cdot 5y + 6 \cdot 1.$$

Try it yourself for a different value of y.

> **TRY IT : : 7.59**   Evaluate when $w = 3$: ⓐ $5(5w + 9)$ ⓑ $5 \cdot 5w + 5 \cdot 9$.

> **TRY IT : : 7.60**   Evaluate when $y = 2$: ⓐ $9(3y + 8)$ ⓑ $9 \cdot 3y + 9 \cdot 8$.

EXAMPLE 7.31

When $y = 3$, evaluate ⓐ $-2(4y + 1)$ ⓑ $-2 \cdot 4y + (-2) \cdot 1$.

⊘ **Solution**

ⓐ

	$-2(4y + 1)$
Substitute 3 for y.	$-2(4 \cdot 3 + 1)$
Simplify in the parentheses.	$-2(13)$
Multiply.	-26

ⓑ

	$-2 \cdot 4y + (-2) \cdot 1$
Substitute 3 for y.	$-2 \cdot 4 \cdot 3 + (-2) \cdot 1$
Multiply.	$-24 - 2$
Subtract.	-26
The answers are the same. When $y = 3$,	$-2(4y + 1) = -8y - 2$

> **TRY IT : : 7.61**   Evaluate when $n = -2$: ⓐ $-6(8n + 11)$ ⓑ $-6 \cdot 8n + (-6) \cdot 11$.

> **TRY IT : : 7.62**   Evaluate when $m = -1$: ⓐ $-3(6m + 5)$ ⓑ $-3 \cdot 6m + (-3) \cdot 5$.

EXAMPLE 7.32

When $y = 35$ evaluate ⓐ $-(y + 5)$ and ⓑ $-y - 5$ to show that $-(y + 5) = -y - 5$.

⊘ **Solution**

ⓐ

	$-(y + 5)$
Substitute 35 for y.	$-(35 + 5)$
Add in the parentheses.	$-(40)$
Simplify.	-40

ⓑ

$$-y-5$$

Substitute 35 for y. $-35-5$

Simplify. -40

The answers are the same when $y = 35$, demonstrating that $-(y+5) = -y-5$

> **TRY IT :: 7.63**   Evaluate when $x = 36$: ⓐ $-(x-4)$ ⓑ $-x+4$ to show that $-(x-4) = -x-4$.

> **TRY IT :: 7.64**   Evaluate when $z = 55$: ⓐ $-(z-10)$ ⓑ $-z+10$ to show that $-(z-10) = -z+10$.

▶ **MEDIA ::** ACCESS ADDITIONAL ONLINE RESOURCES

- Model Distribution (http://www.openstaxcollege.org/l/24ModelDist)
- The Distributive Property (http://www.openstaxcollege.org/l/24DistProp)

Chapter 7 The Properties of Real Numbers

 7.3 EXERCISES

Practice Makes Perfect

Simplify Expressions Using the Distributive Property

In the following exercises, simplify using the distributive property.

90. $4(x + 8)$

91. $3(a + 9)$

92. $8(4y + 9)$

93. $9(3w + 7)$

94. $6(c - 13)$

95. $7(y - 13)$

96. $7(3p - 8)$

97. $5(7u - 4)$

98. $\frac{1}{2}(n + 8)$

99. $\frac{1}{3}(u + 9)$

100. $\frac{1}{4}(3q + 12)$

101. $\frac{1}{5}(4m + 20)$

102. $9\left(\frac{5}{9}y - \frac{1}{3}\right)$

103. $10\left(\frac{3}{10}x - \frac{2}{5}\right)$

104. $12\left(\frac{1}{4} + \frac{2}{3}r\right)$

105. $12\left(\frac{1}{6} + \frac{3}{4}s\right)$

106. $r(s - 18)$

107. $u(v - 10)$

108. $(y + 4)p$

109. $(a + 7)x$

110. $-2(y + 13)$

111. $-3(a + 11)$

112. $-7(4p + 1)$

113. $-9(9a + 4)$

114. $-3(x - 6)$

115. $-4(q - 7)$

116. $-9(3a - 7)$

117. $-6(7x - 8)$

118. $-(r + 7)$

119. $-(q + 11)$

120. $-(3x - 7)$

121. $-(5p - 4)$

122. $5 + 9(n - 6)$

123. $12 + 8(u - 1)$

124. $16 - 3(y + 8)$

125. $18 - 4(x + 2)$

126. $4 - 11(3c - 2)$

127. $9 - 6(7n - 5)$

128. $22 - (a + 3)$

129. $8 - (r - 7)$

130. $-12 - (u + 10)$

131. $-4 - (c - 10)$

132. $(5m - 3) - (m + 7)$

133. $(4y - 1) - (y - 2)$

134. $5(2n + 9) + 12(n - 3)$

135. $9(5u + 8) + 2(u - 6)$

136. $9(8x - 3) - (-2)$

137. $4(6x - 1) - (-8)$

138. $14(c - 1) - 8(c - 6)$

139. $11(n - 7) - 5(n - 1)$

140. $6(7y + 8) - (30y - 15)$

141. $7(3n + 9) - (4n - 13)$

This OpenStax book is available for free at http://cnx.org/content/col11756/1.9

Evaluate Expressions Using the Distributive Property

In the following exercises, evaluate both expressions for the given value.

142. If $v = -2$, evaluate

ⓐ $6(4v + 7)$

ⓑ $6 \cdot 4v + 6 \cdot 7$

143. If $u = -1$, evaluate

ⓐ $8(5u + 12)$

ⓑ $8 \cdot 5u + 8 \cdot 12$

144. If $n = \frac{2}{3}$, evaluate

ⓐ $3\left(n + \frac{5}{6}\right)$

ⓑ $3 \cdot n + 3 \cdot \frac{5}{6}$

145. If $y = \frac{3}{4}$, evaluate

ⓐ $4\left(y + \frac{3}{8}\right)$

ⓑ $4 \cdot y + 4 \cdot \frac{3}{8}$

146. If $y = \frac{7}{12}$, evaluate

ⓐ $-3(4y + 15)$

ⓑ $3 \cdot 4y + (-3) \cdot 15$

147. If $p = \frac{23}{30}$, evaluate

ⓐ $-6(5p + 11)$

ⓑ $-6 \cdot 5p + (-6) \cdot 11$

148. If $m = 0.4$, evaluate

ⓐ $-10(3m - 0.9)$

ⓑ $-10 \cdot 3m - (-10)(0.9)$

149. If $n = 0.75$, evaluate

ⓐ $-100(5n + 1.5)$

ⓑ $-100 \cdot 5n + (-100)(1.5)$

150. If $y = -25$, evaluate

ⓐ $-(y - 25)$

ⓑ $-y + 25$

151. If $w = -80$, evaluate

ⓐ $-(w - 80)$

ⓑ $-w + 80$

152. If $p = 0.19$, evaluate

ⓐ $-(p + 0.72)$

ⓑ $-p - 0.72$

153. If $q = 0.55$, evaluate

ⓐ $-(q + 0.48)$

ⓑ $-q - 0.48$

Everyday Math

154. Buying by the case Joe can buy his favorite ice tea at a convenience store for $1.99 per bottle. At the grocery store, he can buy a case of 12 bottles for $23.88.

ⓐ Use the distributive property to find the cost of 12 bottles bought individually at the convenience store. (Hint: notice that $1.99 is $2 - $0.01.)

ⓑ Is it a bargain to buy the iced tea at the grocery store by the case?

155. Multi-pack purchase Adele's shampoo sells for $3.97 per bottle at the drug store. At the warehouse store, the same shampoo is sold as a 3-pack for $10.49.

ⓐ Show how you can use the distributive property to find the cost of 3 bottles bought individually at the drug store.

ⓑ How much would Adele save by buying the 3-pack at the warehouse store?

Writing Exercises

156. Simplify $8\left(x - \frac{1}{4}\right)$ using the distributive property and explain each step.

157. Explain how you can multiply $4(\$5.97)$ without paper or a calculator by thinking of $5.97 as $6 - 0.03$ and then using the distributive property.

Self Check

ⓐ *After completing the exercises, use this checklist to evaluate your mastery of the objectives of this section.*

I can...	Confidently	With some help	No-I don't get it!
simplify expressions using the Distributive Property.			
evaluate expressions using the Distributive Property.			

ⓑ *What does this checklist tell you about your mastery of this section? What steps will you take to improve?*

7.4 **Properties of Identity, Inverses, and Zero**

Learning Objectives

By the end of this section, you will be able to:

- Recognize the identity properties of addition and multiplication
- Use the inverse properties of addition and multiplication
- Use the properties of zero
- Simplify expressions using the properties of identities, inverses, and zero

Be Prepared!

Before you get started, take this readiness quiz.

1. Find the opposite of -4.
   If you missed this problem, review Example 3.3.

2. Find the reciprocal of $\frac{5}{2}$.
   If you missed this problem, review Example 4.29.

3. Multiply: $\frac{3a}{5} \cdot \frac{9}{2a}$.
   If you missed this problem, review Example 4.27.

Recognize the Identity Properties of Addition and Multiplication

What happens when we add zero to any number? Adding zero doesn't change the value. For this reason, we call 0 the **additive identity**.

For example,

$$13 + 0 \qquad -14 + 0 \qquad 0 + (-3x)$$
$$13 \qquad\qquad -14 \qquad\quad -3x$$

What happens when you multiply any number by one? Multiplying by one doesn't change the value. So we call 1 the **multiplicative identity**.

For example,

$$43 \cdot 1 \qquad -27 \cdot 1 \qquad 1 \cdot \frac{6y}{5}$$
$$43 \qquad\quad -27 \qquad\quad \frac{6y}{5}$$

Identity Properties

The **identity property of addition**: for any real number a,

$$a + 0 = a \qquad 0 + a = a$$
$$0 \text{ is called the} \qquad \textbf{additive identity}$$

The **identity property of multiplication**: for any real number a

$$a \cdot 1 = a \qquad 1 \cdot a = a$$
$$1 \text{ is called the} \qquad \textbf{multiplicative identity}$$

EXAMPLE 7.33

Identify whether each equation demonstrates the identity property of addition or multiplication.

ⓐ $7 + 0 = 7$

ⓑ $-16(1) = -16$

⊘ **Solution**

ⓐ

$$7 + 0 = 7$$

We are adding 0.   We are using the identity property of addition.

ⓑ

$$-16(1) = -16$$

We are multiplying by 1.   We are using the identity property of multiplication.

> **TRY IT : : 7.65**

Identify whether each equation demonstrates the identity property of addition or multiplication:

ⓐ $23 + 0 = 23$ ⓑ $-37(1) = -37$.

> **TRY IT : : 7.66**

Identify whether each equation demonstrates the identity property of addition or multiplication:

ⓐ $1 \cdot 29 = 29$ ⓑ $14 + 0 = 14$.

Use the Inverse Properties of Addition and Multiplication

What number added to 5 gives the additive identity, 0?

$5 + \underline{\quad} = 0$ We know $5 + (-5) = 0$

What number added to −6 gives the additive identity, 0?

$-6 + \underline{\quad} = 0$ We know $-6 + 6 = 0$

Notice that in each case, the missing number was the opposite of the number.

We call $-a$ the **additive inverse** of a. The opposite of a number is its additive inverse. A number and its opposite add to 0, which is the additive identity.

What number multiplied by $\frac{2}{3}$ gives the multiplicative identity, 1? In other words, two-thirds times what results in 1?

$\frac{2}{3} \cdot \underline{\quad} = 1$ We know $\frac{2}{3} \cdot \frac{3}{2} = 1$

What number multiplied by 2 gives the multiplicative identity, 1? In other words two times what results in 1?

$2 \cdot \underline{\quad} = 1$ We know $2 \cdot \frac{1}{2} = 1$

Notice that in each case, the missing number was the reciprocal of the number.

We call $\frac{1}{a}$ the **multiplicative inverse** of $a(a \neq 0)$. The reciprocal of a number is its multiplicative inverse. A number and its reciprocal multiply to $1,$ which is the multiplicative identity.

We'll formally state the Inverse Properties here:

Inverse Properties

Inverse Property of Addition for any real number $a,$

$$a + (-a) = 0$$

$-a$ is the **additive inverse** of a.

Inverse Property of Multiplication for any real number $a \neq 0,$

$$a \cdot \frac{1}{a} = 1$$

$\frac{1}{a}$ is the **multiplicative inverse** of a.

EXAMPLE 7.34

Find the additive inverse of each expression: ⓐ 13 ⓑ $-\frac{5}{8}$ ⓒ 0.6.

◯ **Solution**

To find the additive inverse, we find the opposite.

ⓐ The additive inverse of 13 is its opposite, -13.

ⓑ The additive inverse of $-\frac{5}{8}$ is its opposite, $\frac{5}{8}$.

ⓒ The additive inverse of 0.6 is its opposite, -0.6.

> **TRY IT :: 7.67** Find the additive inverse: ⓐ 18 ⓑ $\frac{7}{9}$ ⓒ 1.2.

> **TRY IT :: 7.68** Find the additive inverse: ⓐ 47 ⓑ $\frac{7}{13}$ ⓒ 8.4.

EXAMPLE 7.35

Find the multiplicative inverse: ⓐ 9 ⓑ $-\frac{1}{9}$ ⓒ 0.9.

◯ **Solution**

To find the multiplicative inverse, we find the reciprocal.

ⓐ The multiplicative inverse of 9 is its reciprocal, $\frac{1}{9}$.

ⓑ The multiplicative inverse of $-\frac{1}{9}$ is its reciprocal, -9.

ⓒ To find the multiplicative inverse of $0.9,$ we first convert 0.9 to a fraction, $\frac{9}{10}$. Then we find the reciprocal, $\frac{10}{9}$.

> **TRY IT :: 7.69** Find the multiplicative inverse: ⓐ 5 ⓑ $-\frac{1}{7}$ ⓒ 0.3.

> **TRY IT ::** 7.70
Find the multiplicative inverse: ⓐ 18 ⓑ $-\frac{4}{5}$ ⓒ 0.6.

Use the Properties of Zero

We have already learned that zero is the additive identity, since it can be added to any number without changing the number's identity. But zero also has some special properties when it comes to multiplication and division.

Multiplication by Zero

What happens when you multiply a number by 0? Multiplying by 0 makes the product equal zero. The product of any real number and 0 is 0.

Multiplication by Zero

For any real number a,

$$a \cdot 0 = 0 \qquad 0 \cdot a = 0$$

EXAMPLE 7.36

Simplify: ⓐ $-8 \cdot 0$ ⓑ $\frac{5}{12} \cdot 0$ ⓒ $0(2.94)$.

⊘ **Solution**

ⓐ

$$-8 \cdot 0$$

The product of any real number and 0 is 0. 0

ⓑ

$$\frac{5}{12} \cdot 0$$

The product of any real number and 0 is 0. 0

ⓒ

$$0(2.94)$$

The product of any real number and 0 is 0. 0

> **TRY IT ::** 7.71
Simplify: ⓐ $-14 \cdot 0$ ⓑ $0 \cdot \frac{2}{3}$ ⓒ $(16.5) \cdot 0$.

> **TRY IT ::** 7.72
Simplify: ⓐ $(1.95) \cdot 0$ ⓑ $0(-17)$ ⓒ $0 \cdot \frac{5}{4}$.

Dividing with Zero

What about dividing with 0? Think about a real example: if there are no cookies in the cookie jar and three people want to share them, how many cookies would each person get? There are 0 cookies to share, so each person gets 0 cookies.

$$0 \div 3 = 0$$

Remember that we can always check division with the related multiplication fact. So, we know that

$$0 \div 3 = 0 \text{ because } 0 \cdot 3 = 0.$$

Division of Zero

For any real number a, except 0, $\frac{0}{a} = 0$ and $0 \div a = 0$.

Zero divided by any real number except zero is zero.

EXAMPLE 7.37

Simplify: ⓐ $0 \div 5$ ⓑ $\frac{0}{-2}$ ⓒ $0 \div \frac{7}{8}$.

Solution

ⓐ

$$0 \div 5$$

Zero divided by any real number, except 0, is zero.　　0

ⓑ

$$\frac{0}{-2}$$

Zero divided by any real number, except 0, is zero.　　0

ⓒ

$$0 \div \frac{7}{8}$$

Zero divided by any real number, except 0, is zero.　　0

> **TRY IT :: 7.73**　　Simplify: ⓐ $0 \div 11$ ⓑ $\frac{0}{-6}$ ⓒ $0 \div \frac{3}{10}$.

> **TRY IT :: 7.74**　　Simplify: ⓐ $0 \div \frac{8}{3}$ ⓑ $0 \div (-10)$ ⓒ $0 \div 12.75$.

Now let's think about dividing a number *by* zero. What is the result of dividing 4 by 0? Think about the related multiplication fact. Is there a number that multiplied by 0 gives 4?

$$4 \div 0 = \underline{\quad} \text{ means } \underline{\quad} \cdot 0 = 4$$

Since any real number multiplied by 0 equals 0, there is no real number that can be multiplied by 0 to obtain 4. We can conclude that there is no answer to $4 \div 0$, and so we say that division by zero is undefined.

Division by Zero

For any real number a, $\frac{a}{0}$, and $a \div 0$ are undefined.

Division *by* zero is undefined.

EXAMPLE 7.38

Simplify: ⓐ $7.5 \div 0$ ⓑ $\frac{-32}{0}$ ⓒ $\frac{4}{9} \div 0$.

⊘ **Solution**

ⓐ

$$7.5 \div 0$$

| Division by zero is undefined. | undefined |

ⓑ

$$\frac{-32}{0}$$

| Division by zero is undefined. | undefined |

ⓒ

$$\frac{4}{9} \div 0$$

| Division by zero is undefined. | undefined |

> **TRY IT : : 7.75**   Simplify: ⓐ $16.4 \div 0$ ⓑ $\frac{-2}{0}$ ⓒ $\frac{1}{5} \div 0$.

> **TRY IT : : 7.76**   Simplify: ⓐ $\frac{-5}{0}$ ⓑ $96.9 \div 0$ ⓒ $\frac{4}{15} \div 0$

We summarize the properties of zero.

Properties of Zero

Multiplication by Zero: For any real number a,

$$a \cdot 0 = 0 \qquad 0 \cdot a = 0 \qquad \text{The product of any number and 0 is 0.}$$

Division by Zero: For any real number a, $a \neq 0$

$\frac{0}{a} = 0$ Zero divided by any real number, except itself, is zero.

$\frac{a}{0}$ is undefined. Division by zero is undefined.

Simplify Expressions using the Properties of Identities, Inverses, and Zero

We will now practice using the properties of identities, inverses, and zero to simplify expressions.

EXAMPLE 7.39

Simplify: $3x + 15 - 3x$.

Solution

$$3x + 15 - 3x$$

Notice the additive inverses, $3x$ and $-3x$. $\quad 0 + 15$

Add. $\quad 15$

> **TRY IT ::** 7.77   Simplify: $-12z + 9 + 12z$.

> **TRY IT ::** 7.78   Simplify: $-25u - 18 + 25u$.

EXAMPLE 7.40

Simplify: $4(0.25q)$.

Solution

$$4(0.25q)$$

Regroup, using the associative property. $\quad [4(0.25)]q$

Multiply. $\quad 1.00q$

Simplify; 1 is the multiplicative identity. $\quad q$

> **TRY IT ::** 7.79   Simplify: $2(0.5p)$.

> **TRY IT ::** 7.80   Simplify: $25(0.04r)$.

EXAMPLE 7.41

Simplify: $\dfrac{0}{n+5}$, where $n \neq -5$.

Solution

$$\dfrac{0}{n+5}$$

Zero divided by any real number except itself is zero. $\quad 0$

> **TRY IT ::** 7.81   Simplify: $\dfrac{0}{m+7}$, where $m \neq -7$.

> **TRY IT ::** 7.82   Simplify: $\dfrac{0}{d-4}$, where $d \neq 4$.

EXAMPLE 7.42

Simplify: $\dfrac{10-3p}{0}$.

⊘ **Solution**

$$\dfrac{10-3p}{0}$$

| Division by zero is undefined. | undefined |

> **TRY IT ::** 7.83   Simplify: $\dfrac{18-6c}{0}$.

> **TRY IT ::** 7.84   Simplify: $\dfrac{15-4q}{0}$.

EXAMPLE 7.43

Simplify: $\dfrac{3}{4}\cdot\dfrac{4}{3}(6x+12)$.

⊘ **Solution**

We cannot combine the terms in parentheses, so we multiply the two fractions first.

$$\dfrac{3}{4}\cdot\dfrac{4}{3}(6x+12)$$

| Multiply; the product of reciprocals is 1. | $1(6x+12)$ |
| Simplify by recognizing the multiplicative identity. | $6x+12$ |

> **TRY IT ::** 7.85   Simplify: $\dfrac{2}{5}\cdot\dfrac{5}{2}(20y+50)$.

> **TRY IT ::** 7.86   Simplify: $\dfrac{3}{8}\cdot\dfrac{8}{3}(12z+16)$.

All the properties of real numbers we have used in this chapter are summarized in Table 7.55.

Property	Of Addition	Of Multiplication
Commutative Property		
If *a* and *b* are real numbers then...	$a + b = b + a$	$a \cdot b = b \cdot a$
Associative Property		
If *a*, *b*, and *c* are real numbers then...	$(a + b) + c = a + (b + c)$	$(a \cdot b) \cdot c = a \cdot (b \cdot c)$
Identity Property	0 is the additive identity	1 is the multiplicative identity
For any real number *a*,	$a + 0 = a$ $0 + a = a$	$a \cdot 1 = a$ $1 \cdot a = a$
Inverse Property	$-a$ is the additive inverse of a	$a, \ a \neq 0$ $1a$ is the multiplicative inverse of a
For any real number *a*,	$a + (-a) = 0$	$a \cdot 1a = 1$
Distributive Property	If $a, \ b, \ c$ are real numbers, then $a(b + c) = ab + ac$	
Properties of Zero		
For any real number *a*,	$a \cdot 0 = 0$ $0 \cdot a = 0$	
For any real number $a, \ a \neq 0$	$\dfrac{0}{a} = 0$ $\dfrac{a}{0}$ is undefined	

Table 7.55 Properties of Real Numbers

▶ **MEDIA : :** ACCESS ADDITIONAL ONLINE RESOURCES

- Multiplying and Dividing Involving Zero (http://www.openstaxcollege.org/l/24MultDivZero)

7.4 EXERCISES

Practice Makes Perfect

Recognize the Identity Properties of Addition and Multiplication

In the following exercises, identify whether each example is using the identity property of addition or multiplication.

158. $101 + 0 = 101$

159. $\frac{3}{5}(1) = \frac{3}{5}$

160. $-9 \cdot 1 = -9$

161. $0 + 64 = 64$

Use the Inverse Properties of Addition and Multiplication

In the following exercises, find the multiplicative inverse.

162. 8

163. 14

164. -17

165. -19

166. $\frac{7}{12}$

167. $\frac{8}{13}$

168. $-\frac{3}{10}$

169. $-\frac{5}{12}$

170. 0.8

171. 0.4

172. -0.2

173. -0.5

Use the Properties of Zero

In the following exercises, simplify using the properties of zero.

174. $48 \cdot 0$

175. $\frac{0}{6}$

176. $\frac{3}{0}$

177. $22 \cdot 0$

178. $0 \div \frac{11}{12}$

179. $\frac{6}{0}$

180. $\frac{0}{3}$

181. $0 \div \frac{7}{15}$

182. $0 \cdot \frac{8}{15}$

183. $(-3.14)(0)$

184. $5.72 \div 0$

185. $\frac{\frac{1}{10}}{0}$

Simplify Expressions using the Properties of Identities, Inverses, and Zero

In the following exercises, simplify using the properties of identities, inverses, and zero.

186. $19a + 44 - 19a$

187. $27c + 16 - 27c$

188. $38 + 11r - 38$

189. $92 + 31s - 92$

190. $10(0.1d)$

191. $100(0.01p)$

192. $5(0.6q)$

193. $40(0.05n)$

194. $\frac{0}{r + 20}$, where $r \neq -20$

195. $\frac{0}{s + 13}$, where $s \neq -13$

196. $\frac{0}{u - 4.99}$, where $u \neq 4.99$

197. $\frac{0}{v - 65.1}$, where $v \neq 65.1$

198. $0 \div \left(x - \frac{1}{2}\right)$, where $x \neq \frac{1}{2}$

199. $0 \div \left(y - \frac{1}{6}\right)$, where $y \neq \frac{1}{6}$

200. $\frac{32 - 5a}{0}$, where $32 - 5a \neq 0$

201. $\dfrac{28 - 9b}{0}$, where $28 - 9b \neq 0$

202. $\dfrac{2.1 + 0.4c}{0}$, where $2.1 + 0.4c \neq 0$

203. $\dfrac{1.75 + 9f}{0}$, where $1.75 + 9f \neq 0$

204. $\left(\dfrac{3}{4} + \dfrac{9}{10}m\right) \div 0$, where $\dfrac{3}{4} + \dfrac{9}{10}m \neq 0$

205. $\left(\dfrac{5}{16}n - \dfrac{3}{7}\right) \div 0$, where $\dfrac{5}{16}n - \dfrac{3}{7} \neq 0$

206. $\dfrac{9}{10} \cdot \dfrac{10}{9}(18p - 21)$

207. $\dfrac{5}{7} \cdot \dfrac{7}{5}(20q - 35)$

208. $15 \cdot \dfrac{3}{5}(4d + 10)$

209. $18 \cdot \dfrac{5}{6}(15h + 24)$

Everyday Math

210. Insurance copayment Carrie had to have 5 fillings done. Each filling cost $80. Her dental insurance required her to pay 20% of the cost. Calculate Carrie's cost

ⓐ by finding her copay for each filling, then finding her total cost for 5 fillings, and

ⓑ by multiplying $5(0.20)(80)$.

ⓒ Which of the Properties of Real Numbers did you use for part (b)?

211. Cooking time Helen bought a 24-pound turkey for her family's Thanksgiving dinner and wants to know what time to put the turkey in the oven. She wants to allow 20 minutes per pound cooking time.

ⓐ Calculate the length of time needed to roast the turkey by multiplying $24 \cdot 20$ to find the number of minutes and then multiplying the product by $\dfrac{1}{60}$ to convert minutes into hours.

ⓑ Multiply $24\left(20 \cdot \dfrac{1}{60}\right)$.

ⓒ Which of the Properties of Real Numbers allows you to multiply $24\left(20 \cdot \dfrac{1}{60}\right)$ instead of $(24 \cdot 20)\dfrac{1}{60}$?

Writing Exercises

212. In your own words, describe the difference between the additive inverse and the multiplicative inverse of a number.

213. How can the use of the properties of real numbers make it easier to simplify expressions?

Self Check

ⓐ After completing the exercises, use this checklist to evaluate your mastery of the objectives of this section.

I can...	Confidently	With some help	No-I don't get it!
recognize the Identity Properties of Addition and Multiplication.			
use the Inverse Properties of Addition and Multiplication.			
use the Properties of Zero.			
simplify expressions using the properties of identities, inverses, and zero.			

ⓑ On a scale of 1–10, how would you rate your mastery of this section in light of your responses on the checklist? How can you improve this?

7.5   Systems of Measurement

Learning Objectives

By the end of this section, you will be able to:

- Make unit conversions in the U.S. system
- Use mixed units of measurement in the U.S. system
- Make unit conversions in the metric system
- Use mixed units of measurement in the metric system
- Convert between the U.S. and the metric systems of measurement
- Convert between Fahrenheit and Celsius temperatures

Be Prepared!

Before you get started, take this readiness quiz.

1. Multiply: $4.29(1000)$.

   If you missed this problem, review Example 5.18.

2. Simplify: $\dfrac{30}{54}$.

   If you missed this problem, review Example 4.20.

3. Multiply: $\dfrac{7}{15} \cdot \dfrac{25}{28}$.

   If you missed this problem, review Example 4.27.

In this section we will see how to convert among different types of units, such as feet to miles or kilograms to pounds. The basic idea in all of the unit conversions will be to use a form of 1, the multiplicative identity, to change the units but not the value of a quantity.

Make Unit Conversions in the U.S. System

There are two systems of measurement commonly used around the world. Most countries use the metric system. The United States uses a different system of measurement, usually called the U.S. system. We will look at the U.S. system first.

The U.S. system of measurement uses units of inch, foot, yard, and mile to measure length and pound and ton to measure weight. For capacity, the units used are cup, pint, quart and gallons. Both the U.S. system and the metric system measure time in seconds, minutes, or hours.

The equivalencies among the basic units of the U.S. system of measurement are listed in Table 7.56. The table also shows, in parentheses, the common abbreviations for each measurement.

U.S. System Units	
Length	**Volume**
1 foot (ft) = 12 inches (in) 1 yard (yd) = 3 feet (ft) 1 mile (mi) = 5280 feet (ft)	3 teaspoons (t) = 1 tablespoon (T) 16 Tablespoons (T) = 1 cup (C) 1 cup (C) = 8 fluid ounces (fl oz) 1 pint (pt) = 2 cups (C) 1 quart (qt) = 2 pints (pt) 1 gallon (gal) = 4 quarts (qt)
Weight	**Time**
1 pound (lb) = 16 ounces (oz) 1 ton = 2000 pounds (lb)	1 minute (min) = 60 seconds (s) 1 hour (h) = 60 minutes (min) 1 day = 24 hours (h) 1 week (wk) = 7 days 1 year (yr) = 365 days

Table 7.56

In many real-life applications, we need to convert between units of measurement. We will use the identity property of multiplication to do these conversions. We'll restate the Identity Property of Multiplication here for easy reference.

$$\text{For any real number } a, \qquad a \cdot 1 = a \qquad 1 \cdot a = a$$

To use the identity property of multiplication, we write 1 in a form that will help us convert the units. For example, suppose we want to convert inches to feet. We know that 1 foot is equal to 12 inches, so we can write 1 as the fraction $\frac{1 \text{ ft}}{12 \text{ in}}$. When we multiply by this fraction, we do not change the value but just change the units.

But $\frac{12 \text{ in}}{1 \text{ ft}}$ also equals 1. How do we decide whether to multiply by $\frac{1 \text{ ft}}{12 \text{ in}}$ or $\frac{12 \text{ in}}{1 \text{ ft}}$? We choose the fraction that will make the units we want to convert *from* divide out. For example, suppose we wanted to convert 60 inches to feet. If we choose the fraction that has inches in the denominator, we can eliminate the inches.

$$60 \ \cancel{\text{in}} \cdot \frac{1 \text{ ft}}{12 \ \cancel{\text{in}}} = 5 \text{ ft}$$

On the other hand, if we wanted to convert 5 feet to inches, we would choose the fraction that has feet in the denominator.

$$5 \text{ ft} \cdot \frac{12 \text{ in}}{1 \ \cancel{\text{ft}}} = 60 \text{ in}$$

We treat the unit words like factors and 'divide out' common units like we do common factors.

 HOW TO :: MAKE UNIT CONVERSIONS.

Step 1.   Multiply the measurement to be converted by 1; write 1 as a fraction relating the units given and the units needed.

Step 2.   Multiply.

Step 3.   Simplify the fraction, performing the indicated operations and removing the common units.

EXAMPLE 7.44

Mary Anne is 66 inches tall. What is her height in feet?

⊘ **Solution**

Convert 66 inches into feet.

Multiply the measurement to be converted by 1.	$66 \text{ inches} \cdot 1$
Write 1 as a fraction relating the units given and the units needed.	$66 \text{ inches} \cdot \dfrac{1 \text{ foot}}{12 \text{ inches}}$
Multiply.	$\dfrac{66 \text{ inches} \cdot 1 \text{ foot}}{12 \text{ inches}}$
Simplify the fraction.	$\dfrac{66 \, \cancel{\text{inches}} \cdot 1 \text{ foot}}{12 \, \cancel{\text{inches}}}$
	$\dfrac{66 \text{ feet}}{12}$
	5.5 feet

Notice that the when we simplified the fraction, we first divided out the inches.

Mary Anne is 5.5 feet tall.

> | **TRY IT ∷ 7.87**   Lexie is 30 inches tall. Convert her height to feet.

> | **TRY IT ∷ 7.88**   Rene bought a hose that is 18 yards long. Convert the length to feet.

When we use the Identity Property of Multiplication to convert units, we need to make sure the units we want to change from will divide out. Usually this means we want the conversion fraction to have those units in the denominator.

EXAMPLE 7.45

Ndula, an elephant at the San Diego Safari Park, weighs almost 3.2 tons. Convert her weight to pounds.

Figure 7.5 (credit: Guldo Da Rozze, Flickr)

⊘ **Solution**

We will convert 3.2 tons into pounds, using the equivalencies in Table 7.56. We will use the Identity Property of Multiplication, writing 1 as the fraction $\dfrac{2000 \text{ pounds}}{1 \text{ ton}}$.

	3.2 tons
Multiply the measurement to be converted by 1.	3.2 tons · 1
Write 1 as a fraction relating tons and pounds.	3.2 tons · $\frac{2000\ lbs}{1\ ton}$
Simplify.	$\frac{3.2\ \cancel{tons} \cdot 2000\ lbs}{1\ \cancel{ton}}$
Multiply.	6400 lbs
	Ndula weighs almost 6,400 pounds.

> **TRY IT :: 7.89**   Arnold's SUV weighs about 4.3 tons. Convert the weight to pounds.

> **TRY IT :: 7.90**   A cruise ship weighs 51,000 tons. Convert the weight to pounds.

Sometimes to convert from one unit to another, we may need to use several other units in between, so we will need to multiply several fractions.

EXAMPLE 7.46

Juliet is going with her family to their summer home. She will be away for 9 weeks. Convert the time to minutes.

⊘ **Solution**

To convert weeks into minutes, we will convert weeks to days, days to hours, and then hours to minutes. To do this, we will multiply by conversion factors of 1.

	9 weeks
Write 1 as $\frac{7\ days}{1\ week}$, $\frac{24\ hours}{1\ day}$, $\frac{60\ minutes}{1\ hour}$.	$\frac{9\ wk}{1} \cdot \frac{7\ days}{1\ wk} \cdot \frac{24\ hr}{1\ day} \cdot \frac{60\ min}{1\ hr}$
Cancel common units.	$\frac{9\ \cancel{wk}}{1} \cdot \frac{7\ \cancel{}}{1\ \cancel{wk}} \cdot \frac{24\ \cancel{hr}}{1\ \cancel{}} \cdot \frac{60\ min}{1\ \cancel{hr}}$
Multiply.	$\frac{9 \cdot 7 \cdot 24 \cdot 60\ min}{1 \cdot 1 \cdot 1 \cdot 1} = 90,720\ min$
	Juliet will be away for 90,720 minutes.

> **TRY IT :: 7.91**   The distance between Earth and the moon is about 250,000 miles. Convert this length to yards.

> **TRY IT :: 7.92**   A team of astronauts spends 15 weeks in space. Convert the time to minutes.

EXAMPLE 7.47

How many fluid ounces are in 1 gallon of milk?

Figure 7.6 (credit: www.bluewaikiki.com, Flickr)

⊘ Solution

Use conversion factors to get the right units: convert gallons to quarts, quarts to pints, pints to cups, and cups to fluid ounces.

	1 gallon
Multiply the measurement to be converted by 1.	$\dfrac{1\text{ gal}}{1} \cdot \dfrac{4\text{ qt}}{1\text{ gal}} \cdot \dfrac{2\text{ pt}}{1\text{ qt}} \cdot \dfrac{2\text{ C}}{1\text{ pt}} \cdot \dfrac{8\text{ fl oz}}{1\text{ C}}$
Simplify.	$\dfrac{1\ \cancel{\text{gal}}}{1} \cdot \dfrac{4\ \cancel{\text{qt}}}{1\ \cancel{\text{gal}}} \cdot \dfrac{2\ \cancel{\text{pt}}}{1\ \cancel{\text{qt}}} \cdot \dfrac{2\ \cancel{\text{C}}}{1\ \cancel{\text{pt}}} \cdot \dfrac{8\text{ fl oz}}{1\ \cancel{\text{C}}}$
Multiply.	$\dfrac{1 \cdot 4 \cdot 2 \cdot 2 \cdot 8\text{ fl oz}}{1 \cdot 1 \cdot 1 \cdot 1 \cdot 1}$
Simplify.	128 fluid ounces
	There are 128 fluid ounces in a gallon.

> **TRY IT : :** 7.93   How many cups are in 1 gallon?

> **TRY IT : :** 7.94   How many teaspoons are in 1 cup?

Use Mixed Units of Measurement in the U.S. System

Performing arithmetic operations on measurements with mixed units of measures requires care. Be sure to add or subtract like units.

EXAMPLE 7.48

Charlie bought three steaks for a barbecue. Their weights were 14 ounces, 1 pound 2 ounces, and 1 pound 6 ounces. How many total pounds of steak did he buy?

Figure 7.7 (credit: Helen Penjam, Flickr)

Solution

We will add the weights of the steaks to find the total weight of the steaks.

Add the ounces. Then add the pounds.

	14 ounces
1 pound	2 ounces
+ 1 pound	6 ounces
2 pounds	22 ounces

Convert 22 ounces to pounds and ounces.

Add the pounds.

2 pounds + 1 pound, 6 ounces
3 pounds, 6 ounces

Charlie bought 3 pounds 6 ounces of steak.

> **TRY IT : :** 7.95
>
> Laura gave birth to triplets weighing 3 pounds 12 ounces, 3 pounds 3 ounces, and 2 pounds 9 ounces. What was the total birth weight of the three babies?

> **TRY IT : :** 7.96
>
> Seymour cut two pieces of crown molding for his family room that were 8 feet 7 inches and 12 feet 11 inches. What was the total length of the molding?

EXAMPLE 7.49

Anthony bought four planks of wood that were each 6 feet 4 inches long. If the four planks are placed end-to-end, what is the total length of the wood?

Solution

We will multiply the length of one plank by 4 to find the total length.

Multiply the inches and then the feet.

	6 feet	4 inches
×		4
	24 feet	16 inches

Convert 16 inches to feet.

24 feet + 1 foot 4 inches

Add the feet.

25 feet 4 inches

Anthony bought 25 feet 4 inches of wood.

> **TRY IT : :** 7.97
>
> Henri wants to triple his spaghetti sauce recipe, which calls for 1 pound 8 ounces of ground turkey. How many pounds of ground turkey will he need?

> **TRY IT :: 7.98**

   Joellen wants to double a solution of 5 gallons 3 quarts. How many gallons of solution will she have in all?

Make Unit Conversions in the Metric System

In the metric system, units are related by powers of 10. The root words of their names reflect this relation. For example, the basic unit for measuring length is a meter. One kilometer is 1000 meters; the prefix *kilo-* means thousand. One centimeter is $\frac{1}{100}$ of a meter, because the prefix *centi-* means one one-hundredth (just like one cent is $\frac{1}{100}$ of one dollar).

The equivalencies of measurements in the metric system are shown in Table 7.63. The common abbreviations for each measurement are given in parentheses.

Metric Measurements		
Length	**Mass**	**Volume/Capacity**
1 kilometer (km) = 1000 m 1 hectometer (hm) = 100 m 1 dekameter (dam) = 10 m 1 meter (m) = 1 m 1 decimeter (dm) = 0.1 m 1 centimeter (cm) = 0.01 m 1 millimeter (mm) = 0.001 m	1 kilogram (kg) = 1000 g 1 hectogram (hg) = 100 g 1 dekagram (dag) = 10 g 1 gram (g) = 1 g 1 decigram (dg) = 0.1 g 1 centigram (cg) = 0.01 g 1 milligram (mg) = 0.001 g	1 kiloliter (kL) = 1000 L 1 hectoliter (hL) = 100 L 1 dekaliter (daL) = 10 L 1 liter (L) = 1 L 1 deciliter (dL) = 0.1 L 1 centiliter (cL) = 0.01 L 1 milliliter (mL) = 0.001 L
1 meter = 100 centimeters 1 meter = 1000 millimeters	1 gram = 100 centigrams 1 gram = 1000 milligrams	1 liter = 100 centiliters 1 liter = 1000 milliliters

Table 7.63

To make conversions in the metric system, we will use the same technique we did in the U.S. system. Using the identity property of multiplication, we will multiply by a conversion factor of one to get to the correct units.

Have you ever run a 5 k or 10 k race? The lengths of those races are measured in kilometers. The metric system is commonly used in the United States when talking about the length of a race.

EXAMPLE 7.50

Nick ran a 10-kilometer race. How many meters did he run?

Figure 7.8 (credit: William Warby, Flickr)

⊘ **Solution**

We will convert kilometers to meters using the Identity Property of Multiplication and the equivalencies in Table 7.63.

	10 kilometers
Multiply the measurement to be converted by 1.	10 km • 1
Write 1 as a fraction relating kilometers and meters.	10 km • $\dfrac{1000 \text{ m}}{1 \text{ km}}$
Simplify.	$\dfrac{10 \text{ k}\cancel{\text{m}} \cdot 1000 \text{ m}}{1 \text{ k}\cancel{\text{m}}}$
Multiply.	10,000 m
	Nick ran 10,000 meters.

> **TRY IT : :** 7.99   Sandy completed her first 5-km race. How many meters did she run?

> **TRY IT : :** 7.100   Herman bought a rug 2.5 meters in length. How many centimeters is the length?

EXAMPLE 7.51

Eleanor's newborn baby weighed 3200 grams. How many kilograms did the baby weigh?

⊘ **Solution**

We will convert grams to kilograms.

	3200 grams
Multiply the measurement to be converted by 1.	3200 g • 1
Write 1 as a fraction relating kilograms and grams.	3200 g • $\dfrac{1 \text{ kg}}{1000 \text{ g}}$
Simplify.	3200 $\cancel{g}$ • $\dfrac{1 \text{ kg}}{1000 \cancel{g}}$
Multiply.	$\dfrac{3200 \text{ kilograms}}{1000}$
Divide.	3.2 kilograms
	The baby weighed 3.2 kilograms.

> **TRY IT : :** 7.101   Kari's newborn baby weighed 2800 grams. How many kilograms did the baby weigh?

> **TRY IT : :** 7.102

> Anderson received a package that was marked 4500 grams. How many kilograms did this package weigh?

Since the metric system is based on multiples of ten, conversions involve multiplying by multiples of ten. In Decimal Operations, we learned how to simplify these calculations by just moving the decimal.

To multiply by 10, 100, or 1000, we move the decimal to the right 1, 2, or 3 places, respectively. To multiply by 0.1, 0.01, or 0.001 we move the decimal to the left 1, 2, or 3 places respectively.

We can apply this pattern when we make measurement conversions in the metric system.

In Example 7.51, we changed 3200 grams to kilograms by multiplying by $\dfrac{1}{1000}$ (or 0.001). This is the same as moving the decimal 3 places to the left.

$$3200 \cdot \frac{1}{1000} \qquad 3200.$$

$$3.2 \qquad\qquad 3.2$$

EXAMPLE 7.52

Convert: ⓐ 350 liters to kiloliters ⓑ 4.1 liters to milliliters.

✓ **Solution**

ⓐ We will convert liters to kiloliters. In Table 7.63, we see that 1 kiloliter = 1000 liters.

	350 L
Multiply by 1, writing 1 as a fraction relating liters to kiloliters.	$350 \text{ L} \cdot \frac{1 \text{ kL}}{1000 \text{ L}}$
Simplify.	$350 \cancel{\text{L}} \cdot \frac{1 \text{ kL}}{1000 \cancel{\text{L}}}$
Move the decimal 3 units to the left.	$350 \cancel{\text{L}} \cdot \frac{1 \text{ kL}}{1000 \cancel{\text{L}}}$
	0.35 kL

ⓑ We will convert liters to milliliters. In Table 7.63, we see that 1 liter = 1000 milliliters.

	4.1 L
Multiply by 1, writing 1 as a fraction relating milliliters to liters.	$4.1 \text{ L} \cdot \frac{1000 \text{ mL}}{1 \text{ L}}$
Simplify.	$4.1 \cancel{\text{L}} \cdot \frac{1000 \text{ mL}}{1 \cancel{\text{L}}}$
Move the decimal 3 units to the left.	4.100 mL
	4100 mL

> **TRY IT : : 7.103**   Convert: ⓐ 7.25 L to kL ⓑ 6.3 L to mL.

> **TRY IT : : 7.104**   Convert: ⓐ 350 hL to L ⓑ 4.1 L to cL.

Use Mixed Units of Measurement in the Metric System

Performing arithmetic operations on measurements with mixed units of measures in the metric system requires the same care we used in the U.S. system. But it may be easier because of the relation of the units to the powers of 10. We still must make sure to add or subtract like units.

EXAMPLE 7.53

Ryland is 1.6 meters tall. His younger brother is 85 centimeters tall. How much taller is Ryland than his younger brother?

Solution

We will subtract the lengths in meters. Convert 85 centimeters to meters by moving the decimal 2 places to the left; 85 cm is the same as 0.85 m.

Now that both measurements are in meters, subtract to find out how much taller Ryland is than his brother.

$$\begin{array}{r} 1.60 \text{ m} \\ -0.85 \text{ m} \\ \hline 0.75 \text{ m} \end{array}$$

Ryland is 0.75 meters taller than his brother.

> **TRY IT ::** 7.105
>
> Mariella is 1.58 meters tall. Her daughter is 75 centimeters tall. How much taller is Mariella than her daughter? Write the answer in centimeters.

> **TRY IT ::** 7.106
>
> The fence around Hank's yard is 2 meters high. Hank is 96 centimeters tall. How much shorter than the fence is Hank? Write the answer in meters.

EXAMPLE 7.54

Dena's recipe for lentil soup calls for 150 milliliters of olive oil. Dena wants to triple the recipe. How many liters of olive oil will she need?

Solution

We will find the amount of olive oil in milliliters then convert to liters.

	Triple 150 mL
Translate to algebra.	$3 \cdot 150 \text{ mL}$
Multiply.	450 mL
Convert to liters.	$450 \text{ mL} \cdot \dfrac{0.001 \text{ L}}{1 \text{ mL}}$
Simplify.	0.45 L
	Dena needs 0.45 liter of olive oil.

> **TRY IT ::** 7.107
>
> A recipe for Alfredo sauce calls for 250 milliliters of milk. Renata is making pasta with Alfredo sauce for a big party and needs to multiply the recipe amounts by 8. How many liters of milk will she need?

> **TRY IT ::** 7.108
>
> To make one pan of baklava, Dorothea needs 400 grams of filo pastry. If Dorothea plans to make 6 pans of baklava, how many kilograms of filo pastry will she need?

Convert Between U.S. and Metric Systems of Measurement

Many measurements in the United States are made in metric units. A drink may come in 2-liter bottles, calcium may come in 500-mg capsules, and we may run a 5-K race. To work easily in both systems, we need to be able to convert between the two systems.

Table 7.69 shows some of the most common conversions.

Conversion Factors Between U.S. and Metric Systems		
Length	Weight	Volume
1 in = 2.54 cm 1 ft = 0.305 m 1 yd = 0.914 m 1 mi = 1.61 km	1 lb = 0.45 kg 1 oz = 28 g	1 qt = 0.95 L 1 fl oz = 30 mL
1 m = 3.28 ft	1 kg = 2.2 lb	1 L = 1.06 qt

Table 7.69

We make conversions between the systems just as we do within the systems—by multiplying by unit conversion factors.

EXAMPLE 7.55

Lee's water bottle holds 500 mL of water. How many fluid ounces are in the bottle? Round to the nearest tenth of an ounce.

✓ Solution

	500 mL
Multiply by a unit conversion factor relating mL and ounces.	$500 \text{ mL} \cdot \dfrac{1 \text{ fl oz}}{30 \text{ mL}}$
Simplify.	$\dfrac{500 \text{ fl oz}}{30}$
Divide.	16.7 fl. oz.
	The water bottle holds 16.7 fluid ounces.

> **TRY IT ::** 7.109   How many quarts of soda are in a 2-liter bottle?

> **TRY IT ::** 7.110   How many liters are in 4 quarts of milk?

The conversion factors in Table 7.69 are not exact, but the approximations they give are close enough for everyday purposes. In Example 7.55, we rounded the number of fluid ounces to the nearest tenth.

EXAMPLE 7.56

Soleil lives in Minnesota but often travels in Canada for work. While driving on a Canadian highway, she passes a sign that says the next rest stop is in 100 kilometers. How many miles until the next rest stop? Round your answer to the nearest mile.

Solution

	100 kilometers
Multiply by a unit conversion factor relating kilometers and miles.	$100 \text{ kilometers} \cdot \dfrac{1 \text{ mile}}{1.61 \text{ kilometers}}$ $100 \cdot \dfrac{1 \text{ mi}}{1.61 \text{ km}}$
Simplify.	$\dfrac{100 \text{ mi}}{1.61}$
Divide.	62 mi
	It is about 62 miles to the next rest stop.

> **TRY IT :: 7.111**
>
> The height of Mount Kilimanjaro is $5{,}895$ meters. Convert the height to feet. Round to the nearest foot.

> **TRY IT :: 7.112**
>
> The flight distance from New York City to London is $5{,}586$ kilometers. Convert the distance to miles. Round to the nearest mile.

Convert Between Fahrenheit and Celsius Temperatures

Have you ever been in a foreign country and heard the weather forecast? If the forecast is for $22°C$. What does that mean?

The U.S. and metric systems use different scales to measure temperature. The U.S. system uses degrees Fahrenheit, written $°F$. The metric system uses degrees Celsius, written $°C$. Figure 7.9 shows the relationship between the two systems.

Figure 7.9 A temperature of $37°C$ is equivalent to $98.6°F$.

If we know the temperature in one system, we can use a formula to convert it to the other system.

Temperature Conversion

To convert from Fahrenheit temperature, $F,$ to Celsius temperature, $C,$ use the formula

$$C = \frac{5}{9}(F - 32)$$

To convert from Celsius temperature, $C,$ to Fahrenheit temperature, $F,$ use the formula

$$F = \frac{9}{5}C + 32$$

EXAMPLE 7.57

Convert $50°F$ into degrees Celsius.

⊘ **Solution**

We will substitute $50°F$ into the formula to find $C.$

Use the formula for converting °F to °C	$C = \frac{5}{9}(F - 32)$
Substitute 50 for F.	$C = \frac{5}{9}(50 - 32)$
Simplify in parentheses.	$C = \frac{5}{9}(18)$
Multiply.	$C = 10$
	A temperature of 50°F is equivalent to 10°C.

> **TRY IT : : 7.113**   Convert the Fahrenheit temperatures to degrees Celsius: $59°F.$

> **TRY IT : : 7.114**   Convert the Fahrenheit temperatures to degrees Celsius: $41°F.$

EXAMPLE 7.58

The weather forecast for Paris predicts a high of $20°C.$ Convert the temperature into degrees Fahrenheit.

⊘ **Solution**

We will substitute $20°C$ into the formula to find $F.$

Use the formula for converting °F to °C	$F = \frac{9}{5}C + 32$
Substitute 20 for C.	$F = \frac{9}{5}(20) + 32$
Multiply.	$F = 36 + 32$
Add.	$F = 68$
	So 20°C is equivalent to 68°F.

> **TRY IT : :** 7.115   Convert the Celsius temperatures to degrees Fahrenheit:

The temperature in Helsinki, Finland was $15°C$.

> **TRY IT : :** 7.116   Convert the Celsius temperatures to degrees Fahrenheit:

The temperature in Sydney, Australia was $10°C$.

▶ **MEDIA : :** ACCESS ADDITIONAL ONLINE RESOURCES

- American Unit Conversion (http://www.openstaxcollege.org/l/24USConversion)
- Time Conversions (http://www.openstaxcollege.org/l/24TimeConversio)
- Metric Unit Conversions (http://www.openstaxcollege.org/l/24MetricConvers)
- American and Metric Conversions (http://www.openstaxcollege.org/l/24UStoMetric)
- Convert from Celsius to Fahrenheit (http://www.openstaxcollege.org/l/24CtoFdegrees)
- Convert from Fahrenheit to Celsius (http://www.openstaxcollege.org/l/24FtoCdegrees)

7.5 EXERCISES

Practice Makes Perfect

Make Unit Conversions in the U.S. System

In the following exercises, convert the units.

214. A park bench is 6 feet long. Convert the length to inches.

215. A floor tile is 2 feet wide. Convert the width to inches.

216. A ribbon is 18 inches long. Convert the length to feet.

217. Carson is 45 inches tall. Convert his height to feet.

218. Jon is 6 feet 4 inches tall. Convert his height to inches.

219. Faye is 4 feet 10 inches tall. Convert her height to inches.

220. A football field is 160 feet wide. Convert the width to yards.

221. On a baseball diamond, the distance from home plate to first base is 30 yards. Convert the distance to feet.

222. Ulises lives 1.5 miles from school. Convert the distance to feet.

223. Denver, Colorado, is 5,183 feet above sea level. Convert the height to miles.

224. A killer whale weighs 4.6 tons. Convert the weight to pounds.

225. Blue whales can weigh as much as 150 tons. Convert the weight to pounds.

226. An empty bus weighs 35,000 pounds. Convert the weight to tons.

227. At take-off, an airplane weighs 220,000 pounds. Convert the weight to tons.

228. The voyage of the *Mayflower* took 2 months and 5 days. Convert the time to days.

229. Lynn's cruise lasted 6 days and 18 hours. Convert the time to hours.

230. Rocco waited $1\frac{1}{2}$ hours for his appointment. Convert the time to seconds.

231. Misty's surgery lasted $2\frac{1}{4}$ hours. Convert the time to seconds.

232. How many teaspoons are in a pint?

233. How many tablespoons are in a gallon?

234. JJ's cat, Posy, weighs 14 pounds. Convert her weight to ounces.

235. April's dog, Beans, weighs 8 pounds. Convert his weight to ounces.

236. Baby Preston weighed 7 pounds 3 ounces at birth. Convert his weight to ounces.

237. Baby Audrey weighed 6 pounds 15 ounces at birth. Convert her weight to ounces.

238. Crista will serve 20 cups of juice at her son's party. Convert the volume to gallons.

239. Lance needs 500 cups of water for the runners in a race. Convert the volume to gallons.

Use Mixed Units of Measurement in the U.S. System

In the following exercises, solve and write your answer in mixed units.

240. Eli caught three fish. The weights of the fish were 2 pounds 4 ounces, 1 pound 11 ounces, and 4 pounds 14 ounces. What was the total weight of the three fish?

241. Judy bought 1 pound 6 ounces of almonds, 2 pounds 3 ounces of walnuts, and 8 ounces of cashews. What was the total weight of the nuts?

242. One day Anya kept track of the number of minutes she spent driving. She recorded trips of 45, 10, 8, 65, 20, and 35 minutes.

How much time (in hours and minutes) did Anya spend driving?

243. Last year Eric went on 6 business trips. The number of days of each was 5, 2, 8, 12, 6, and 3. How much time (in weeks and days) did Eric spend on business trips last year?

244. Renee attached a 6-foot-6-inch extension cord to her computer's 3-foot-8-inch power cord. What was the total length of the cords?

245. Fawzi's SUV is 6 feet 4 inches tall. If he puts a 2-foot-10-inch box on top of his SUV, what is the total height of the SUV and the box?

246. Leilani wants to make 8 placemats. For each placemat she needs 18 inches of fabric. How many yards of fabric will she need for the 8 placemats?

247. Mireille needs to cut 24 inches of ribbon for each of the 12 girls in her dance class. How many yards of ribbon will she need altogether?

Make Unit Conversions in the Metric System

In the following exercises, convert the units.

248. Ghalib ran 5 kilometers. Convert the length to meters.

249. Kitaka hiked 8 kilometers. Convert the length to meters.

250. Estrella is 1.55 meters tall. Convert her height to centimeters.

251. The width of the wading pool is 2.45 meters. Convert the width to centimeters.

252. Mount Whitney is 3,072 meters tall. Convert the height to kilometers.

253. The depth of the Mariana Trench is 10,911 meters. Convert the depth to kilometers.

254. June's multivitamin contains 1,500 milligrams of calcium. Convert this to grams.

255. A typical ruby-throated hummingbird weights 3 grams. Convert this to milligrams.

256. One stick of butter contains 91.6 grams of fat. Convert this to milligrams.

257. One serving of gourmet ice cream has 25 grams of fat. Convert this to milligrams.

258. The maximum mass of an airmail letter is 2 kilograms. Convert this to grams.

259. Dimitri's daughter weighed 3.8 kilograms at birth. Convert this to grams.

260. A bottle of wine contained 750 milliliters. Convert this to liters.

261. A bottle of medicine contained 300 milliliters. Convert this to liters.

Use Mixed Units of Measurement in the Metric System

In the following exercises, solve and write your answer in mixed units.

262. Matthias is 1.8 meters tall. His son is 89 centimeters tall. How much taller, in centimeters, is Matthias than his son?

263. Stavros is 1.6 meters tall. His sister is 95 centimeters tall. How much taller, in centimeters, is Stavros than his sister?

264. A typical dove weighs 345 grams. A typical duck weighs 1.2 kilograms. What is the difference, in grams, of the weights of a duck and a dove?

265. Concetta had a 2-kilogram bag of flour. She used 180 grams of flour to make biscotti. How many kilograms of flour are left in the bag?

266. Harry mailed 5 packages that weighed 420 grams each. What was the total weight of the packages in kilograms?

267. One glass of orange juice provides 560 milligrams of potassium. Linda drinks one glass of orange juice every morning. How many grams of potassium does Linda get from her orange juice in 30 days?

268. Jonas drinks 200 milliliters of water 8 times a day. How many liters of water does Jonas drink in a day?

269. One serving of whole grain sandwich bread provides 6 grams of protein. How many milligrams of protein are provided by 7 servings of whole grain sandwich bread?

Convert Between U.S. and Metric Systems

In the following exercises, make the unit conversions. Round to the nearest tenth.

270. Bill is 75 inches tall. Convert his height to centimeters.

271. Frankie is 42 inches tall. Convert his height to centimeters.

272. Marcus passed a football 24 yards. Convert the pass length to meters.

273. Connie bought 9 yards of fabric to make drapes. Convert the fabric length to meters.

274. Each American throws out an average of $1,650$ pounds of garbage per year. Convert this weight to kilograms.

275. An average American will throw away $90,000$ pounds of trash over his or her lifetime. Convert this weight to kilograms.

276. A $5K$ run is 5 kilometers long. Convert this length to miles.

277. Kathryn is 1.6 meters tall. Convert her height to feet.

278. Dawn's suitcase weighed 20 kilograms. Convert the weight to pounds.

279. Jackson's backpack weighs 15 kilograms. Convert the weight to pounds.

280. Ozzie put 14 gallons of gas in his truck. Convert the volume to liters.

281. Bernard bought 8 gallons of paint. Convert the volume to liters.

Convert between Fahrenheit and Celsius

In the following exercises, convert the Fahrenheit temperature to degrees Celsius. Round to the nearest tenth.

282. $86°F$

283. $77°F$

284. $104°F$

285. $14°F$

286. $72°F$

287. $4°F$

288. $0°F$

289. $120°F$

In the following exercises, convert the Celsius temperatures to degrees Fahrenheit. Round to the nearest tenth.

290. $5°C$

291. $25°C$

292. $-10°C$

293. $-15°C$

294. $22°C$

295. $8°C$

296. $43°C$

297. $16°C$

Everyday Math

298. Nutrition Julian drinks one can of soda every day. Each can of soda contains 40 grams of sugar. How many kilograms of sugar does Julian get from soda in 1 year?

299. Reflectors The reflectors in each lane-marking stripe on a highway are spaced 16 yards apart. How many reflectors are needed for a one-mile-long stretch of highway?

Writing Exercises

300. Some people think that $65°$ to $75°$ Fahrenheit is the ideal temperature range.

ⓐ What is your ideal temperature range? Why do you think so?

ⓑ Convert your ideal temperatures from Fahrenheit to Celsius.

301. ⓐ Did you grow up using the U.S. customary or the metric system of measurement? ⓑ Describe two examples in your life when you had to convert between systems of measurement. ⓒ Which system do you think is easier to use? Explain.

Self Check

ⓐ *After completing the exercises, use this checklist to evaluate your mastery of the objectives of this section.*

I can...	Confidently	With some help	No-I don't get it!
make unit conversions in the U.S. system.			
use mixed units of measurement in the U.S. system.			
use mixed units of measurement in the metric system.			
convert between the U.S. and the metric systems of measurement.			
convert between Fahrenheit and Celsius temperatures.			

ⓑ *Overall, after looking at the checklist, do you think you are well-prepared for the next chapter? Why or why not?*

CHAPTER 7 REVIEW

KEY TERMS

Additive Identity The **additive identity** is 0. When zero is added to any number, it does not change the value.

Additive Inverse The opposite of a number is its **additive inverse**. The **additive inverse** of a is $-a$.

Irrational number An **irrational number** is a number that cannot be written as the ratio of two integers. Its decimal form does not stop and does not repeat.

Multiplicative Identity The **multiplicative identity** is 1. When one multiplies any number, it does not change the value.

Multiplicative Inverse The reciprocal of a number is its **multiplicative inverse**. The **multiplicative inverse** of a is $\frac{1}{a}$.

Rational number A **rational number** is a number that can be written in the form $\frac{p}{q}$, where p and q are integers and $q \neq 0$. Its decimal form stops or repeats.

Real number a **real number** is a number that is either rational or irrational.

KEY CONCEPTS

7.1 Rational and Irrational Numbers

- **Real numbers**

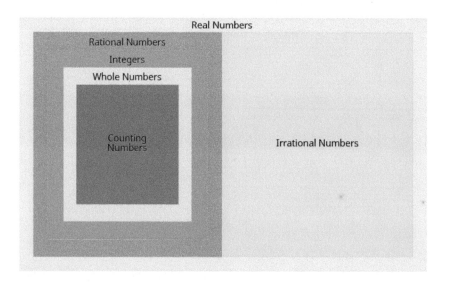

7.2 Commutative and Associative Properties

- **Commutative Properties**
    - **Commutative Property of Addition:**
        - If a, b are real numbers, then $a + b = b + a$
    - **Commutative Property of Multiplication:**
        - If a, b are real numbers, then $a \cdot b = b \cdot a$
- **Associative Properties**
    - **Associative Property of Addition:**
        - If a, b, c are real numbers then $(a + b) + c = a + (b + c)$
    - **Associative Property of Multiplication:**
        - If a, b, c are real numbers then $(a \cdot b) \cdot c = a \cdot (b \cdot c)$

7.3 Distributive Property

- **Distributive Property:**
  - If a, b, c are real numbers then
    - $a(b + c) = ab + ac$
    - $(b + c)a = ba + ca$
    - $a(b \cdot c) = ab \cdot ac$

7.4 Properties of Identity, Inverses, and Zero

- **Identity Properties**
  - **Identity Property of Addition:** For any real number a: $a + 0 = a$ $0 + a = a$ **0** is the **additive identity**
  - **Identity Property of Multiplication:** For any real number a: $a \cdot 1 = a$ $1 \cdot a = a$ **1** is the **multiplicative identity**
- **Inverse Properties**
  - **Inverse Property of Addition:** For any real number a: $a + (-a) = 0$ $-a$ is the **additive inverse** of a
  - **Inverse Property of Multiplication:** For any real number a: $\left(a \neq 0\right)$ $a \cdot \frac{1}{a} = 1$ $\frac{1}{a}$ is the **multiplicative inverse** of a
- **Properties of Zero**
  - **Multiplication by Zero:** For any real number a, $a \cdot 0 = 0$ $0 \cdot a = 0$ The product of any number and 0 is 0.
  - **Division of Zero:** For any real number a, $\frac{0}{a} = 0$ $0 + a = 0$ Zero divided by any real number, except itself, is zero.
  - **Division by Zero:** For any real number a, $\frac{0}{a}$ is undefined and $a \div 0$ is undefined. Division by zero is undefined.

REVIEW EXERCISES

7.1 Rational and Irrational Numbers

In the following exercises, write as the ratio of two integers.

302. 6

303. -5

304. 2.9

305. 1.8

In the following exercises, determine which of the numbers is rational.

306. $0.42, 0.\overline{3}, 2.56813\ldots$

307. $0.75319\ldots, 0.\overline{16}, 1.95$

In the following exercises, identify whether each given number is rational or irrational.

308. ⓐ $\sqrt{49}$ ⓑ $\sqrt{55}$

309. ⓐ $\sqrt{72}$ ⓑ $\sqrt{64}$

In the following exercises, list the ⓐ whole numbers, ⓑ integers, ⓒ rational numbers, ⓓ irrational numbers, ⓔ real numbers for each set of numbers.

310. $-9, 0, 0.361\ldots, \frac{8}{9}, \sqrt{16}, 9$

311. $-5, -2\frac{1}{4}, -\sqrt{4}, 0.\overline{25}, \frac{13}{5}, 4$

7.2 Commutative and Associative Properties

In the following exercises, use the commutative property to rewrite the given expression.

312. $6 + 4 =$ _____

313. $-14 \cdot 5 =$ _____

314. $3n =$ _____

315. $a + 8 =$ _____

In the following exercises, use the associative property to rewrite the given expression.

316. $(13 \cdot 5) \cdot 2 =$ _____

317. $(22 + 7) + 3 =$ _____

318. $(4 + 9x) + x =$ _____

319. $\frac{1}{2}(22y) =$ _____

In the following exercises, evaluate each expression for the given value.

320. If $y = \frac{11}{12}$, evaluate:

ⓐ $y + 0.7 + (-y)$

ⓑ $y + (-y) + 0.7$

321. If $z = -\frac{5}{3}$, evaluate:

ⓐ $z + 5.39 + (-z)$

ⓑ $z + (-z) + 5.39$

322. If $k = 65$, evaluate:

ⓐ $\frac{4}{9}\left(\frac{9}{4}k\right)$

ⓑ $\left(\frac{4}{9} \cdot \frac{9}{4}\right)k$

323. If $m = -13$, evaluate:

ⓐ $-\frac{2}{5}\left(\frac{5}{2}m\right)$

ⓑ $\left(-\frac{2}{5} \cdot \frac{5}{2}\right)m$

In the following exercises, simplify using the commutative and associative properties.

324. $6y + 37 + (-6y)$

325. $\frac{1}{4} + \frac{11}{15} + \left(-\frac{1}{4}\right)$

326. $\frac{14}{11} \cdot \frac{35}{9} \cdot \frac{14}{11}$

327. $-18 \cdot 15 \cdot \frac{2}{9}$

328. $\left(\frac{7}{12} + \frac{4}{5}\right) + \frac{1}{5}$

329. $(3.98d + 0.75d) + 1.25d$

330. $-12(4m)$

331. $30\left(\frac{5}{6}q\right)$

332. $11x + 8y + 16x + 15y$

333. $52m + (-20n) + (-18m) + (-5n)$

7.3 Distributive Property

In the following exercises, simplify using the distributive property.

334. $7(x + 9)$

335. $9(u - 4)$

336. $-3(6m - 1)$

337. $-8(-7a - 12)$

338. $\frac{1}{3}(15n - 6)$

339. $(y + 10) \cdot p$

340. $(a - 4) - (6a + 9)$

341. $4(x + 3) - 8(x - 7)$

In the following exercises, evaluate using the distributive property.

342. If $u = 2$, evaluate

ⓐ $3(8u + 9)$ and

ⓑ $3 \cdot 8u + 3 \cdot 9$ to show that $3(8u + 9) = 3 \cdot 8u + 3 \cdot 9$

343. If $n = \frac{7}{8}$, evaluate

ⓐ $8\left(n + \frac{1}{4}\right)$ and

ⓑ $8 \cdot n + 8 \cdot \frac{1}{4}$ to show that $8\left(n + \frac{1}{4}\right) = 8 \cdot n + 8 \cdot \frac{1}{4}$

344. If $d = 14$, evaluate

ⓐ $-100(0.1d + 0.35)$ and

ⓑ $-100 \cdot (0.1d) + (-100)(0.35)$ to show that $-100(0.1d + 0.35) = -100 \cdot (0.1d) + (-100)(0.35)$

345. If $y = -18$, evaluate

ⓐ $-(y - 18)$ and

ⓑ $-y + 18$ to show that $-(y - 18) = -y + 18$

7.4 Properties of Identities, Inverses, and Zero

In the following exercises, identify whether each example is using the identity property of addition or multiplication.

346. $-35(1) = -35$

347. $29 + 0 = 29$

348. $(6x + 0) + 4x = 6x + 4x$

349. $9 \cdot 1 + (-3) = 9 + (-3)$

In the following exercises, find the additive inverse.

350. -32

351. 19.4

352. $\frac{3}{5}$

353. $-\frac{7}{15}$

In the following exercises, find the multiplicative inverse.

354. $\frac{9}{2}$

355. -5

356. $\frac{1}{10}$

357. $-\frac{4}{9}$

In the following exercises, simplify.

358. $83 \cdot 0$

359. $\frac{0}{9}$

360. $\frac{5}{0}$

361. $0 \div \frac{2}{3}$

362. $43 + 39 + (-43)$

363. $(n + 6.75) + 0.25$

364. $\frac{5}{13} \cdot 57 \cdot \frac{13}{5}$

365. $\frac{1}{6} \cdot 17 \cdot 12$

366. $\frac{2}{3} \cdot 28 \cdot \frac{3}{7}$

367. $9(6x - 11) + 15$

7.5 Systems of Measurement

In the following exercises, convert between U.S. units. Round to the nearest tenth.

368. A floral arbor is 7 feet tall. Convert the height to inches.

369. A picture frame is 42 inches wide. Convert the width to feet.

370. Kelly is 5 feet 4 inches tall. Convert her height to inches.

371. A playground is 45 feet wide. Convert the width to yards.

372. The height of Mount Shasta is 14,179 feet. Convert the height to miles.

373. Shamu weighs 4.5 tons. Convert the weight to pounds.

374. The play lasted $1\frac{3}{4}$ hours. Convert the time to minutes.

375. How many tablespoons are in a quart?

376. Naomi's baby weighed 5 pounds 14 ounces at birth. Convert the weight to ounces.

377. Trinh needs 30 cups of paint for her class art project. Convert the volume to gallons.

In the following exercises, solve, and state your answer in mixed units.

378. John caught 4 lobsters. The weights of the lobsters were 1 pound 9 ounces, 1 pound 12 ounces, 4 pounds 2 ounces, and 2 pounds 15 ounces. What was the total weight of the lobsters?

379. Every day last week, Pedro recorded the amount of time he spent reading. He read for 50, 25, 83, 45, 32, 60, and 135 minutes. How much time, in hours and minutes, did Pedro spend reading?

380. Fouad is 6 feet 2 inches tall. If he stands on a rung of a ladder 8 feet 10 inches high, how high off the ground is the top of Fouad's head?

381. Dalila wants to make pillow covers. Each cover takes 30 inches of fabric. How many yards and inches of fabric does she need for 4 pillow covers?

In the following exercises, convert between metric units.

382. Donna is 1.7 meters tall. Convert her height to centimeters.

383. Mount Everest is 8,850 meters tall. Convert the height to kilometers.

384. One cup of yogurt contains 488 milligrams of calcium. Convert this to grams.

385. One cup of yogurt contains 13 grams of protein. Convert this to milligrams.

386. Sergio weighed 2.9 kilograms at birth. Convert this to grams.

387. A bottle of water contained 650 milliliters. Convert this to liters.

In the following exercises, solve.

388. Minh is 2 meters tall. His daughter is 88 centimeters tall. How much taller, in meters, is Minh than his daughter?

389. Selma had a 1-liter bottle of water. If she drank 145 milliliters, how much water, in milliliters, was left in the bottle?

390. One serving of cranberry juice contains 30 grams of sugar. How many kilograms of sugar are in 30 servings of cranberry juice?

391. One ounce of tofu provides 2 grams of protein. How many milligrams of protein are provided by 5 ounces of tofu?

In the following exercises, convert between U.S. and metric units. Round to the nearest tenth.

392. Majid is 69 inches tall. Convert his height to centimeters.

393. A college basketball court is 84 feet long. Convert this length to meters.

394. Caroline walked 2.5 kilometers. Convert this length to miles.

395. Lucas weighs 78 kilograms. Convert his weight to pounds.

396. Steve's car holds 55 liters of gas. Convert this to gallons.

397. A box of books weighs 25 pounds. Convert this weight to kilograms.

In the following exercises, convert the Fahrenheit temperatures to degrees Celsius. Round to the nearest tenth.

398. 95°F

399. 23°F

400. 20°F

401. 64°F

In the following exercises, convert the Celsius temperatures to degrees Fahrenheit. Round to the nearest tenth.

402. 30°C

403. −5°C

404. −12°C

405. 24°C

PRACTICE TEST

406. For the numbers $0.18349\ldots$, $0.\overline{2}$, 1.67, list the ⓐ rational numbers and ⓑ irrational numbers.

407. Is $\sqrt{144}$ rational or irrational?

408. From the numbers -4, $-1\frac{1}{2}$, 0, $\frac{5}{8}$, $\sqrt{2}$, 7, which are ⓐ integers ⓑ rational ⓒ irrational ⓓ real numbers?

409. Rewrite using the commutative property: $x \cdot 14 =$ _____

410. Rewrite the expression using the associative property: $(y+6)+3 =$ _____

411. Rewrite the expression using the associative property: $(8 \cdot 2) \cdot 5 =$ _____

412. Evaluate $\frac{3}{16}\left(\frac{16}{3}n\right)$ when $n = 42$.

413. For the number $\frac{2}{5}$ find the ⓐ additive inverse ⓑ multiplicative inverse.

In the following exercises, simplify the given expression.

414. $\frac{3}{4}(-29)\left(\frac{4}{3}\right)$

415. $-3 + 15y + 3$

416. $(1.27q + 0.25q) + 0.75q$

417. $\left(\frac{8}{15}+\frac{2}{9}\right)+\frac{7}{9}$

418. $-18\left(\frac{3}{2}n\right)$

419. $14y + (-6z) + 16y + 2z$

420. $9(q+9)$

421. $6(5x-4)$

422. $-10(0.4n + 0.7)$

423. $\frac{1}{4}(8a+12)$

424. $m(n+2)$

425. $8(6p-1)+2(9p+3)$

426. $(12a+4)-(9a+6)$

427. $\frac{0}{8}$

428. $\frac{4.5}{0}$

429. $0 \div \left(\frac{2}{3}\right)$

In the following exercises, solve using the appropriate unit conversions.

430. Azize walked $4\frac{1}{2}$ miles. Convert this distance to feet. (1 mile = 5,280 feet).

431. One cup of milk contains 276 milligrams of calcium. Convert this to grams. (1 milligram = 0.001 gram)

432. Larry had 5 phone customer phone calls yesterday. The calls lasted 28, 44, 9, 75, and 55 minutes. How much time, in hours and minutes, did Larry spend on the phone? (1 hour = 60 minutes)

433. Janice ran 15 kilometers. Convert this distance to miles. Round to the nearest hundredth of a mile. (1 mile = 1.61 kilometers)

434. Yolie is 63 inches tall. Convert her height to centimeters. Round to the nearest centimeter. (1 inch = 2.54 centimeters)

435. Use the formula $F = \frac{9}{5}C + 32$ to convert $35°C$ to degrees F

Figure 8.1 A Calder mobile is balanced and has several elements on each side. (credit: paurian, Flickr)

Chapter Outline

Introduction

Teetering high above the floor, this amazing mobile remains aloft thanks to its carefully balanced mass. Any shift in either direction could cause the mobile to become lopsided, or even crash downward. In this chapter, we will solve equations by keeping quantities on both sides of an equal sign in perfect balance.

8.1 Solve Equations Using the Subtraction and Addition Properties of Equality

Learning Objectives

By the end of this section, you will be able to:

Solve equations using the Subtraction and Addition Properties of Equality
Solve equations that need to be simplified
Translate an equation and solve
Translate and solve applications

Be Prepared!

Before you get started, take this readiness quiz.

1. Solve: $n - 12 = 16$.
   If you missed this problem, review Example 2.33.

2. Translate into algebra 'five less than x.'
   If you missed this problem, review Example 2.24.

3. Is $x = 2$ a solution to $5x - 3 = 7$?
   If you missed this problem, review Example 2.28.

We are now ready to "get to the good stuff." You have the basics down and are ready to begin one of the most important topics in algebra: solving equations. The applications are limitless and extend to all careers and fields. Also, the skills and techniques you learn here will help improve your critical thinking and problem-solving skills. This is a great benefit of studying mathematics and will be useful in your life in ways you may not see right now.

Solve Equations Using the Subtraction and Addition Properties of Equality

We began our work solving equations in previous chapters. It has been a while since we have seen an equation, so we will review some of the key concepts before we go any further.

We said that solving an equation is like discovering the answer to a puzzle. The purpose in solving an equation is to find the value or values of the variable that make each side of the equation the same. Any value of the variable that makes the equation true is called a solution to the equation. It is the answer to the puzzle.

Solution of an Equation

A **solution of an equation** is a value of a variable that makes a true statement when substituted into the equation.

In the earlier sections, we listed the steps to determine if a value is a solution. We restate them here.

HOW TO :: DETERMINE WHETHER A NUMBER IS A SOLUTION TO AN EQUATION.

Step 1.   Substitute the number for the variable in the equation.

Step 2.   Simplify the expressions on both sides of the equation.

Step 3.   Determine whether the resulting equation is true.
   ◦   If it is true, the number is a solution.
   ◦   If it is not true, the number is not a solution.

EXAMPLE 8.1

Determine whether $y = \frac{3}{4}$ is a solution for $4y + 3 = 8y$.

⊘ **Solution**

$$4y + 3 = 8y$$

Substitute $\frac{3}{4}$ for y.	$4\left(\frac{3}{4}\right) + 3 \overset{?}{=} 8\left(\frac{3}{4}\right)$
Multiply.	$3 + 3 \overset{?}{=} 6$
Add.	$6 = 6 \checkmark$

Since $y = \frac{3}{4}$ results in a true equation, $\frac{3}{4}$ is a solution to the equation $4y + 3 = 8y$.

> **TRY IT ::** 8.1   Is $y = \frac{2}{3}$ a solution for $9y + 2 = 6y$?

> **TRY IT ::** 8.2   Is $y = \frac{2}{5}$ a solution for $5y - 3 = 10y$?

We introduced the Subtraction and Addition Properties of Equality in Solving Equations Using the Subtraction and Addition Properties of Equality. In that section, we modeled how these properties work and then applied them to solving equations with whole numbers. We used these properties again each time we introduced a new system of numbers. Let's review those properties here.

Subtraction and Addition Properties of Equality

Subtraction Property of Equality

For all real numbers a, b, and c, if $a = b$, then $a - c = b - c$.

Addition Property of Equality

For all real numbers a, b, and c, if $a = b$, then $a + c = b + c$.

When you add or subtract the same quantity from both sides of an equation, you still have equality.

We introduced the Subtraction Property of Equality earlier by modeling equations with envelopes and counters. Figure 8.2 models the equation $x + 3 = 8$.

Figure 8.2

The goal is to isolate the variable on one side of the equation. So we 'took away' 3 from both sides of the equation and found the solution $x = 5$.

Some people picture a balance scale, as in Figure 8.3, when they solve equations.

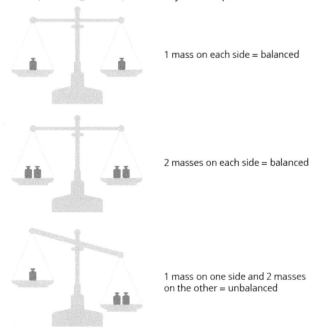

1 mass on each side = balanced

2 masses on each side = balanced

1 mass on one side and 2 masses on the other = unbalanced

Figure 8.3

The quantities on both sides of the equal sign in an equation are equal, or balanced. Just as with the balance scale, whatever you do to one side of the equation you must also do to the other to keep it balanced.

Let's review how to use Subtraction and Addition Properties of Equality to solve equations. We need to isolate the variable on one side of the equation. And we check our solutions by substituting the value into the equation to make sure we have a true statement.

EXAMPLE 8.2

Solve: $x + 11 = -3$.

⊘ **Solution**

To isolate x, we undo the addition of 11 by using the Subtraction Property of Equality.

$$x - 11 = -3$$

Subtract 11 from each side to "undo" the addition.	$x + 11 - 11 = -3 - 11$
Simplify.	$x = -14$
Check:	$x - 11 = -3$
Substitute $x = -14$.	$-14 + 11 \stackrel{?}{=} -3$
	$-3 = -3 \checkmark$

Since $x = -14$ makes $x + 11 = -3$ a true statement, we know that it is a solution to the equation.

> **TRY IT ::** 8.3   Solve: $x + 9 = -7$.

> **TRY IT ::** 8.4   Solve: $x + 16 = -4$.

In the original equation in the previous example, 11 was added to the x, so we subtracted 11 to 'undo' the addition. In the next example, we will need to 'undo' subtraction by using the Addition Property of Equality.

EXAMPLE 8.3

Solve: $m - 4 = -5$.

⊘ **Solution**

$$m + 4 = -5$$

Add 4 to each side to "undo" the subtraction.	$m + 4 - 4 = -5 - 4$
Simplify.	$m = -1$
Check:	$m + 4 = -5$
Substitute $m = -1$.	$-1 + 4 \stackrel{?}{=} -5$
	$-5 = -5 \checkmark$
	The solution to $m - 4 = -5$ is $m = -1$.

> **TRY IT ::** 8.5   Solve: $n - 6 = -7$.

> **TRY IT ::** 8.6   Solve: $x - 5 = -9$.

Now let's review solving equations with fractions.

EXAMPLE 8.4

Solve: $n - \frac{3}{8} = \frac{1}{2}$.

Solution

$$n - \frac{3}{8} = \frac{1}{2}$$

Use the Addition Property of Equality.

$$n - \frac{3}{8} + \frac{3}{8} = \frac{1}{2} + \frac{3}{8}$$

Find the LCD to add the fractions on the right.

$$n - \frac{3}{8} + \frac{3}{8} = \frac{4}{8} + \frac{3}{8}$$

Simplify

$$n = \frac{7}{8}$$

Check:

$$n - \frac{3}{8} = \frac{1}{2}$$

Substitute $n = \frac{7}{8}$.

$$\frac{7}{8} - \frac{3}{8} \overset{?}{=} \frac{1}{2}$$

Subtract.

$$\frac{4}{8} \overset{?}{=} \frac{1}{2}$$

Simplify.

$$\frac{1}{2} = \frac{1}{2} \checkmark$$

The solution checks.

> **TRY IT :: 8.7**   Solve: $p - \frac{1}{3} = \frac{5}{6}$.

> **TRY IT :: 8.8**   Solve: $q - \frac{1}{2} = \frac{1}{6}$.

In Solve Equations with Decimals, we solved equations that contained decimals. We'll review this next.

EXAMPLE 8.5

Solve $a - 3.7 = 4.3$.

Solution

$$a - 3.7 = 4.3$$

Use the Addition Property of Equality.

$$a - 3.7 + 3.7 = 4.3 + 3.7$$

Add.

$$a = 8$$

Check:

$$a - 3.7 = 4.3$$

Substitute $a = 8$.

$$8 - 3.7 \overset{?}{=} 4.3$$

Simplify.

$$4.3 = 4.3 \checkmark$$

The solution checks.

> **TRY IT :: 8.9**   Solve: $b - 2.8 = 3.6$.

> **TRY IT :: 8.10**   Solve: $c - 6.9 = 7.1$.

Solve Equations That Need to Be Simplified

In the examples up to this point, we have been able to isolate the variable with just one operation. Many of the equations we encounter in algebra will take more steps to solve. Usually, we will need to simplify one or both sides of an equation before using the Subtraction or Addition Properties of Equality. You should always simplify as much as possible before trying to isolate the variable.

Solve: $3x - 7 - 2x - 4 = 1$.

⊘ Solution

The left side of the equation has an expression that we should simplify before trying to isolate the variable.

	$3x - 7 - 2x - 4 = 1$
Rearrange the terms, using the Commutative Property of Addition.	$3x - 2x - 7 - 4 = 1$
Combine like terms.	$x - 11 = 1$
Add 11 to both sides to isolate x.	$x - 11 + 11 = 1 + 11$
Simplify.	$x = 12$

Check.
Substitute $x = 12$ into the original equation.

$$3x - 7 - 2x - 4 = 1$$
$$3(12) - 7 - 2(12) - 4 = 1$$
$$36 - 7 - 24 - 4 = 1$$
$$29 - 24 - 4 = 1$$
$$5 - 4 = 1$$
$$1 = 1 \checkmark$$

The solution checks.

> **TRY IT :: 8.11**   Solve: $8y - 4 - 7y - 7 = 4$.

> **TRY IT :: 8.12**   Solve: $6z + 5 - 5z - 4 = 3$.

Solve: $3(n - 4) - 2n = -3$.

⊘ Solution

The left side of the equation has an expression that we should simplify.

$$3(n-4)-2n=-3$$

Distribute on the left.	$3n-12-2n=-3$
Use the Commutative Property to rearrange terms.	$3n-2n-12=-3$
Combine like terms.	$n-12=-3$
Isolate n using the Addition Property of Equality.	$n-12+12=-3+12$
Simplify.	$n=9$

Check.
Substitute $n=9$ into the original equation.
$$3(n-4)-2n=-3$$
$$3(9-4)-2\cdot 9=-3$$
$$3(5)-18=-3$$
$$15-18=-3$$
$$-3=-3\ \checkmark$$

The solution checks.

> **TRY IT : :** 8.13   Solve: $5(p-3)-4p=-10$.

> **TRY IT : :** 8.14   Solve: $4(q+2)-3q=-8$.

EXAMPLE 8.8

Solve: $2(3k-1)-5k=-2-7$.

⊘ **Solution**

Both sides of the equation have expressions that we should simplify before we isolate the variable.

$$2(3k-1)-5k=-2-7$$

Distribute on the left, subtract on the right.	$6k-2-5k=-9$
Use the Commutative Property of Addition.	$6k-5k-2=-9$
Combine like terms.	$k-2=-9$
Undo subtraction by using the Addition Property of Equality.	$k-2+2=-9+2$
Simplify.	$k=-7$

Check.
Let $k=-7$.
$$2(3k-1)-5k=-2-7$$
$$2(3(-7)-1)-5(-7)=-2-7$$
$$2(-21-1)-5(-7)=-9$$
$$2(-22)+35=-9$$
$$-44+35=-9$$
$$-9=-9\ \checkmark$$

The solution checks.

> **TRY IT : :** 8.15   Solve: $4(2h - 3) - 7h = -6 - 7$.

> **TRY IT : :** 8.16   Solve: $2(5x + 2) - 9x = -2 + 7$.

Translate an Equation and Solve

In previous chapters, we translated word sentences into equations. The first step is to look for the word (or words) that translate(s) to the equal sign. Table 8.9 reminds us of some of the words that translate to the equal sign.

Equals (=)						
is	is equal to	is the same as	the result is	gives	was	will be

Table 8.9

Let's review the steps we used to translate a sentence into an equation.

   HOW TO : : TRANSLATE A WORD SENTENCE TO AN ALGEBRAIC EQUATION.

Step 1.   Locate the "equals" word(s). Translate to an equal sign.
Step 2.   Translate the words to the left of the "equals" word(s) into an algebraic expression.
Step 3.   Translate the words to the right of the "equals" word(s) into an algebraic expression.

Now we are ready to try an example.

EXAMPLE 8.9

Translate and solve: five more than x is equal to 26.

⊘ **Solution**

	Five more than x is equal to 26
Translate.	$x + 5$ $=$ 26
Subtract 5 from both sides.	$x + 5 - 5 = 26 - 5$
Simplify.	$x = 21$

Check:
Is 26 five more than 21?
$21 + 5 \overset{?}{=} 26$

$26 = 26$ ✓

The solution checks.

> **TRY IT : :** 8.17   Translate and solve: Eleven more than x is equal to 41.

> **TRY IT : :** 8.18   Translate and solve: Twelve less than y is equal to 51.

EXAMPLE 8.10

Translate and solve: The difference of $5p$ and $4p$ is 23.

⊘ Solution

	The difference of 5p and 4p	is	23
Translate.	$5p - 4p$	$=$	23
Simplify.		$p = 23$	

Check:

$$5p - 4p = 23$$

$$5(23) - 4(23) \overset{?}{=} 23$$

$$115 - 22 \overset{?}{=} 23$$

$$23 = 23 \checkmark$$

The solution checks.

> **TRY IT :: 8.19**   Translate and solve: The difference of $4x$ and $3x$ is 14.

> **TRY IT :: 8.20**   Translate and solve: The difference of $7a$ and $6a$ is -8.

Translate and Solve Applications

In most of the application problems we solved earlier, we were able to find the quantity we were looking for by simplifying an algebraic expression. Now we will be using equations to solve application problems. We'll start by restating the problem in just one sentence, assign a variable, and then translate the sentence into an equation to solve. When assigning a variable, choose a letter that reminds you of what you are looking for.

EXAMPLE 8.11

The Robles family has two dogs, Buster and Chandler. Together, they weigh 71 pounds.

Chandler weighs 28 pounds. How much does Buster weigh?

⊘ Solution

Read the problem carefully.	
Identify what you are asked to find, and choose a variable to represent it.	How much does Buster weigh? Let $b =$ Buster's weight
Write a sentence that gives the information to find it.	Buster's weight plus Chandler's weight equals 71 pounds.
We will restate the problem, and then include the given information.	Buster's weight plus 28 equals 71.
Translate the sentence into an equation, using the variable b.	$b + 28 = 71$
Solve the equation using good algebraic techniques.	$b + 28 - 28 = 71 - 28$ $b = 43$
Check the answer in the problem and make sure it makes sense.	
Is 43 pounds a reasonable weight for a dog? Yes. Does Buster's weight plus Chandler's weight equal 71 pounds? $$43 + 28 \overset{?}{=} 71$$ $$71 = 71 \checkmark$$	
Write a complete sentence that answers the question, "How much does Buster weigh?"	Buster weighs 43 pounds

---

> **TRY IT : :** 8.21

Translate into an algebraic equation and solve: The Pappas family has two cats, Zeus and Athena. Together, they weigh 13 pounds. Zeus weighs 6 pounds. How much does Athena weigh?

> **TRY IT : :** 8.22

Translate into an algebraic equation and solve: Sam and Henry are roommates. Together, they have 68 books. Sam has 26 books. How many books does Henry have?

HOW TO : : DEVISE A PROBLEM-SOLVING STRATEGY.

Step 1.   Read the problem. Make sure you understand all the words and ideas.
Step 2.   Identify what you are looking for.
Step 3.   Name what you are looking for. Choose a variable to represent that quantity.
Step 4.   Translate into an equation. It may be helpful to restate the problem in one sentence with all the important information. Then, translate the English sentence into an algebra equation.
Step 5.   Solve the equation using good algebra techniques.
Step 6.   Check the answer in the problem and make sure it makes sense.
Step 7.   Answer the question with a complete sentence.

EXAMPLE 8.12

Shayla paid $24,575 for her new car. This was $875 less than the sticker price. What was the sticker price of the car?

⊘ **Solution**

What are you asked to find?	"What was the sticker price of the car?"
Assign a variable.	Let $s =$ the sticker price of the car.
Write a sentence that gives the information to find it.	$24,575 is $875 less than the sticker price $24,575 is $875 less than s
Translate into an equation.	$24{,}575 = s - 875$
Solve.	$24{,}575 + 875 = s - 875 + 875$ $24{,}575 = s$

Check:

Is $875 less than $25,450 equal to $24,575?

$$25{,}450 - 875 \overset{?}{=} 24{,}575$$

$$24{,}575 = 24{,}575 \ ✓$$

Write a sentence that answers the question.	The sticker price was $25,450.

> **TRY IT : : 8.23**

Translate into an algebraic equation and solve: Eddie paid $19,875 for his new car. This was $1,025 less than the sticker price. What was the sticker price of the car?

> **TRY IT : : 8.24**

Translate into an algebraic equation and solve: The admission price for the movies during the day is $7.75. This is $3.25 less than the price at night. How much does the movie cost at night?

The *Links to Literacy* activity, "The 100-pound Problem", will provide you with another view of the topics covered in this section.

▶ **MEDIA : :** ACCESS ADDITIONAL ONLINE RESOURCES

- Solving One Step Equations By Addition and Subtraction (http://www.openstaxcollege.org/l/24Solveonestep)
- Solve One Step Equations By Add and Subtract Whole Numbers (Variable on Left) (http://www.openstaxcollege.org/l/24SolveByAdd)
- Solve One Step Equations By Add and Subtract Whole Numbers (Variable on Right) (http://www.openstaxcollege.org/l/24AddSubtrWhole)

8.1 EXERCISES

Practice Makes Perfect

Solve Equations Using the Subtraction and Addition Properties of Equality

In the following exercises, determine whether the given value is a solution to the equation.

1. Is $y = \frac{1}{3}$ a solution of $4y + 2 = 10y$?

2. Is $x = \frac{3}{4}$ a solution of $5x + 3 = 9x$?

3. Is $u = -\frac{1}{2}$ a solution of $8u - 1 = 6u$?

4. Is $v = -\frac{1}{3}$ a solution of $9v - 2 = 3v$?

In the following exercises, solve each equation.

5. $x + 7 = 12$

6. $y + 5 = -6$

7. $b + \frac{1}{4} = \frac{3}{4}$

8. $a + \frac{2}{5} = \frac{4}{5}$

9. $p + 2.4 = -9.3$

10. $m + 7.9 = 11.6$

11. $a - 3 = 7$

12. $m - 8 = -20$

13. $x - \frac{1}{3} = 2$

14. $x - \frac{1}{5} = 4$

15. $y - 3.8 = 10$

16. $y - 7.2 = 5$

17. $x - 15 = -42$

18. $z + 5.2 = -8.5$

19. $q + \frac{3}{4} = \frac{1}{2}$

20. $p - \frac{2}{5} = \frac{2}{3}$

21. $y - \frac{3}{4} = \frac{3}{5}$

Solve Equations that Need to be Simplified

In the following exercises, solve each equation.

22. $c + 3 - 10 = 18$

23. $m + 6 - 8 = 15$

24. $9x + 5 - 8x + 14 = 20$

25. $6x + 8 - 5x + 16 = 32$

26. $-6x - 11 + 7x - 5 = -16$

27. $-8n - 17 + 9n - 4 = -41$

28. $3(y - 5) - 2y = -7$

29. $4(y - 2) - 3y = -6$

30. $8(u + 1.5) - 7u = 4.9$

31. $5(w + 2.2) - 4w = 9.3$

32. $-5(y - 2) + 6y = -7 + 4$

33. $-8(x - 1) + 9x = -3 + 9$

34. $3(5n - 1) - 14n + 9 = 1 - 2$

35. $2(8m + 3) - 15m - 4 = 3 - 5$

36. $-(j + 2) + 2j - 1 = 5$

37. $-(k + 7) + 2k + 8 = 7$

38. $6a - 5(a - 2) + 9 = -11$

39. $8c - 7(c - 3) + 4 = -16$

40. $8(4x + 5) - 5(6x) - x = 53$

41. $6(9y - 1) - 10(5y) - 3y = 22$

Translate to an Equation and Solve

In the following exercises, translate to an equation and then solve.

42. Five more than x is equal to 21.

43. The sum of x and -5 is 33.

44. Ten less than m is -14.

45. Three less than y is -19.

46. The sum of y and -3 is 40.

47. Eight more than p is equal to 52.

48. The difference of $9x$ and $8x$ is 17.

49. The difference of $5c$ and $4c$ is 60.

50. The difference of n and $\frac{1}{6}$ is $\frac{1}{2}$.

51. The difference of f and $\frac{1}{3}$ is $\frac{1}{12}$.

52. The sum of $-4n$ and $5n$ is -32.

53. The sum of $-9m$ and $10m$ is -25.

Translate and Solve Applications

In the following exercises, translate into an equation and solve.

54. Pilar drove from home to school and then to her aunt's house, a total of 18 miles. The distance from Pilar's house to school is 7 miles. What is the distance from school to her aunt's house?

55. Jeff read a total of 54 pages in his English and Psychology textbooks. He read 41 pages in his English textbook. How many pages did he read in his Psychology textbook?

56. Pablo's father is 3 years older than his mother. Pablo's mother is 42 years old. How old is his father?

57. Eva's daughter is 5 years younger than her son. Eva's son is 12 years old. How old is her daughter?

58. Allie weighs 8 pounds less than her twin sister Lorrie. Allie weighs 124 pounds. How much does Lorrie weigh?

59. For a family birthday dinner, Celeste bought a turkey that weighed 5 pounds less than the one she bought for Thanksgiving. The birthday dinner turkey weighed 16 pounds. How much did the Thanksgiving turkey weigh?

60. The nurse reported that Tricia's daughter had gained 4.2 pounds since her last checkup and now weighs 31.6 pounds. How much did Tricia's daughter weigh at her last checkup?

61. Connor's temperature was 0.7 degrees higher this morning than it had been last night. His temperature this morning was 101.2 degrees. What was his temperature last night?

62. Melissa's math book cost $22.85 less than her art book cost. Her math book cost $93.75. How much did her art book cost?

63. Ron's paycheck this week was $17.43 less than his paycheck last week. His paycheck this week was $103.76. How much was Ron's paycheck last week?

Everyday Math

64. Baking Kelsey needs $\frac{2}{3}$ cup of sugar for the cookie recipe she wants to make. She only has $\frac{1}{4}$ cup of sugar and will borrow the rest from her neighbor. Let s equal the amount of sugar she will borrow. Solve the equation $\frac{1}{4} + s = \frac{2}{3}$ to find the amount of sugar she should ask to borrow.

65. Construction Miguel wants to drill a hole for a $\frac{5}{8}$-inch screw. The screw should be $\frac{1}{12}$ inch larger than the hole. Let d equal the size of the hole he should drill. Solve the equation $d + \frac{1}{12} = \frac{5}{8}$ to see what size the hole should be.

Writing Exercises

66. Is -18 a solution to the equation $3x = 16 - 5x$? How do you know?

67. Write a word sentence that translates the equation $y - 18 = 41$ and then make up an application that uses this equation in its solution.

Self Check

ⓐ After completing the exercises, use this checklist to evaluate your mastery of the objectives of this section.

I can...	Confidently	With some help	No-I don't get it!
solve equations using the Subtraction and Addition Properties of Equality.			
solve equations that need to be simplified.			
translate an equation and solve.			
translate and solve applications.			

ⓑ If most of your checks were:

...confidently. Congratulations! You have achieved the objectives in this section. Reflect on the study skills you used so that you can continue to use them. What did you do to become confident of your ability to do these things? Be specific.

...with some help. This must be addressed quickly because topics you do not master become potholes in your road to success. In math, every topic builds upon previous work. It is important to make sure you have a strong foundation before you move on. Who can you ask for help? Your fellow classmates and instructor are good resources. Is there a place on campus where math tutors are available? Can your study skills be improved?

...no—I don't get it! This is a warning sign and you must not ignore it. You should get help right away or you will quickly be overwhelmed. See your instructor as soon as you can to discuss your situation. Together you can come up with a plan to get you the help you need.

8.2 Solve Equations Using the Division and Multiplication Properties of Equality

Learning Objectives

By the end of this section, you will be able to:
- Solve equations using the Division and Multiplication Properties of Equality
- Solve equations that need to be simplified

Be Prepared!

Before you get started, take this readiness quiz.

1. Simplify: $-7\left(\frac{1}{-7}\right)$.
   If you missed this problem, review Example 4.28.

2. What is the reciprocal of $-\frac{3}{8}$?
   If you missed this problem, review Example 4.29.

3. Evaluate $9x + 2$ when $x = -3$.
   If you missed this problem, review Example 3.56.

Solve Equations Using the Division and Multiplication Properties of Equality

We introduced the Multiplication and Division Properties of Equality in Solve Equations Using Integers; The Division Property of Equality and Solve Equations with Fractions. We modeled how these properties worked using envelopes and counters and then applied them to solving equations (See Solve Equations Using Integers; The Division Property of Equality). We restate them again here as we prepare to use these properties again.

Division and Multiplication Properties of Equality

Division Property of Equality: For all real numbers a, b, c, and $c \neq 0$, if $a = b$, then $\frac{a}{c} = \frac{b}{c}$.

Multiplication Property of Equality: For all real numbers a, b, c, if $a = b$, then $ac = bc$.

When you divide or multiply both sides of an equation by the same quantity, you still have equality.

Let's review how these properties of equality can be applied in order to solve equations. Remember, the goal is to 'undo' the operation on the variable. In the example below the variable is multiplied by 4, so we will divide both sides by 4 to 'undo' the multiplication.

EXAMPLE 8.13

Solve: $4x = -28$.

 Solution

We use the Division Property of Equality to divide both sides by 4.

$$4x = -28$$

Divide both sides by 4 to undo the multiplication.	$\dfrac{4x}{4} = \dfrac{-28}{4}$
Simplify.	$x = -7$

Check your answer. Let $x = -7$.

$$4x = -28$$

$$4(-7) \overset{?}{=} -28$$

$$-28 = -28 \checkmark$$

Since this is a true statement, $x = -7$ is a solution to $4x = -28$.

> **TRY IT ::** 8.25   Solve: $3y = -48$.

> **TRY IT ::** 8.26   Solve: $4z = -52$.

In the previous example, to 'undo' multiplication, we divided. How do you think we 'undo' division?

EXAMPLE 8.14

Solve: $\dfrac{a}{-7} = -42$.

⊘ **Solution**

Here a is divided by -7. We can multiply both sides by -7 to isolate a.

$$\frac{a}{-7} = -42$$

$$-7\left(\frac{a}{-7}\right) = -7(-42)$$

Multiply both sides by -7.	
	$\dfrac{-7a}{-7} = 294$
Simplify.	$a = 294$

Check your answer. Let $a = 294$.

$$\frac{a}{-7} = -42$$

$$\frac{294}{-7} \overset{?}{=} -42$$

$$-42 = -42 \checkmark$$

> **TRY IT ::** 8.27   Solve: $\dfrac{b}{-6} = -24$.

> **TRY IT ::** 8.28   Solve: $\dfrac{c}{-8} = -16$.

EXAMPLE 8.15

Solve: $-r = 2$.

Solution

Remember $-r$ is equivalent to $-1r$.

$$-r = 2$$

Rewrite $-r$ as $-1r$.	$-1r = 2$
Divide both sides by -1.	$\dfrac{-1r}{-1} = \dfrac{2}{-1}$
	$r = -2$

Check.	$-r = 2$
Substitute $r = -2$	$-(-2) \overset{?}{=} 2$
Simplify.	$2 = 2 \checkmark$

In Solve Equations with Fractions, we saw that there are two other ways to solve $-r = 2$.

We could multiply both sides by -1.

We could take the opposite of both sides.

> **TRY IT :: 8.29**   Solve: $-k = 8$.

> **TRY IT :: 8.30**   Solve: $-g = 3$.

EXAMPLE 8.16

Solve: $\dfrac{2}{3}x = 18$.

Solution

Since the product of a number and its reciprocal is 1, our strategy will be to isolate x by multiplying by the reciprocal of $\dfrac{2}{3}$.

$$\frac{2}{3}x = 18$$

Multiply by the reciprocal of $\frac{2}{3}$.	$\frac{3}{2} \cdot \frac{2}{3}x = \frac{3}{2} \cdot 18$
Reciprocals multiply to one.	$1x = \frac{3}{2} \cdot \frac{18}{1}$
Multiply.	$x = 27$

Check your answer. Let $x = 27$

$$\frac{2}{3}x = 18$$

$$\frac{2}{3} \cdot 27 \overset{?}{=} 18$$

$$18 = 18 \checkmark$$

Notice that we could have divided both sides of the equation $\frac{2}{3}x = 18$ by $\frac{2}{3}$ to isolate x. While this would work, multiplying by the reciprocal requires fewer steps.

> **TRY IT : : 8.31**   Solve: $\frac{2}{5}n = 14$.

> **TRY IT : : 8.32**   Solve: $\frac{5}{6}y = 15$.

Solve Equations That Need to be Simplified

Many equations start out more complicated than the ones we've just solved. First, we need to simplify both sides of the equation as much as possible

EXAMPLE 8.17

Solve: $8x + 9x - 5x = -3 + 15$.

⊘ **Solution**

Start by combining like terms to simplify each side.

$$8x + 9x - 5x = -3 + 15$$

Combine like terms.	$12x = 12$
Divide both sides by 12 to isolate x.	$\frac{12x}{12} = \frac{12}{12}$
Simplify.	$x = 1$

Check your answer. Let $x = 1$

$$8x + 9x - 5x = -3 + 15$$

$$8 \cdot 1 + 9 \cdot 1 - 5 \cdot 1 \overset{?}{=} -3 + 15$$

$$8 + 9 - 5 \overset{?}{=} -3 + 15$$

$$12 = 12 \checkmark$$

> | **TRY IT ::** 8.33   Solve: $7x + 6x - 4x = -8 + 26$.

> | **TRY IT ::** 8.34   Solve: $11n - 3n - 6n = 7 - 17$.

EXAMPLE 8.18

Solve: $11 - 20 = 17y - 8y - 6y$.

⊘ **Solution**

Simplify each side by combining like terms.

$$11 - 20 = 17y - 8y - 6y$$

Simplify each side.	$-9 = 3y$
Divide both sides by 3 to isolate y.	$\dfrac{-9}{3} = \dfrac{3y}{3}$
Simplify.	$-3 = y$

Check your answer. Let $y = -3$

$$11 - 20 = 17y - 8y - 6y$$

$$11 - 20 \overset{?}{=} 17(-3) - 8(-3) - 6(-3)$$

$$11 - 20 \overset{?}{=} -51 + 24 + 18$$

$$-9 = -9 \checkmark$$

Notice that the variable ended up on the right side of the equal sign when we solved the equation. You may prefer to take one more step to write the solution with the variable on the left side of the equal sign.

> | **TRY IT ::** 8.35   Solve: $18 - 27 = 15c - 9c - 3c$.

> | **TRY IT ::** 8.36   Solve: $18 - 22 = 12x - x - 4x$.

EXAMPLE 8.19

Solve: $-3(n - 2) - 6 = 21$.

⊘ **Solution**

Remember—always simplify each side first.

$$-3(n-2)-6=21$$

Distribute.	$-3n+6-6=21$
Simplify.	$-3n=21$
Divide both sides by -3 to isolate n.	$\dfrac{-3n}{-3}=\dfrac{21}{-3}$ $n=-7$

Check your answer. Let $n=-7$.

$$-3(n-2)-6=21$$

$$-3(-7-2)-6\overset{?}{=}21$$

$$-3(-9)-6\overset{?}{=}21$$

$$27-6\overset{?}{=}21$$

$$21=21\ \checkmark$$

> **TRY IT : :** 8.37   Solve: $-4(n-2)-8=24$.

> **TRY IT : :** 8.38   Solve: $-6(n-2)-12=30$.

LINKS TO LITERACY

The *Links to Literacy* activity, "Everybody Wins" will provide you with another view of the topics covered in this section.

▶ **MEDIA : :** ACCESS ADDITIONAL ONLINE RESOURCES

- Solving One Step Equation by Mult/Div. Integers (Var on Left) (http://www.openstaxcollege.org/l/24OneStepMultiL)
- Solving One Step Equation by Mult/Div. Integers (Var on Right) (http://www.openstaxcollege.org/l/24OneStepMultiR)
- Solving One Step Equation in the Form: –x = –a (http://www.openstaxcollege.org/l/24xa)

8.2 EXERCISES

Practice Makes Perfect

Solve Equations Using the Division and Multiplication Properties of Equality

In the following exercises, solve each equation for the variable using the Division Property of Equality and check the solution.

68. $8x = 32$

69. $7p = 63$

70. $-5c = 55$

71. $-9x = -27$

72. $-90 = 6y$

73. $-72 = 12y$

74. $-16p = -64$

75. $-8m = -56$

76. $0.25z = 3.25$

77. $0.75a = 11.25$

78. $-3x = 0$

79. $4x = 0$

In the following exercises, solve each equation for the variable using the Multiplication Property of Equality and check the solution.

80. $\frac{x}{4} = 15$

81. $\frac{z}{2} = 14$

82. $-20 = \frac{q}{-5}$

83. $\frac{c}{-3} = -12$

84. $\frac{y}{9} = -6$

85. $\frac{q}{6} = -8$

86. $\frac{m}{-12} = 5$

87. $-4 = \frac{p}{-20}$

88. $\frac{2}{3}y = 18$

89. $\frac{3}{5}r = 15$

90. $-\frac{5}{8}w = 40$

91. $24 = -\frac{3}{4}x$

92. $-\frac{2}{5} = \frac{1}{10}a$

93. $-\frac{1}{3}q = -\frac{5}{6}$

Solve Equations That Need to be Simplified

In the following exercises, solve the equation.

94. $8a + 3a - 6a = -17 + 27$

95. $6y - 3y + 12y = -43 + 28$

96. $-9x - 9x + 2x = 50 - 2$

97. $-5m + 7m - 8m = -6 + 36$

98. $100 - 16 = 4p - 10p - p$

99. $-18 - 7 = 5t - 9t - 6t$

100. $\frac{7}{8}n - \frac{3}{4}n = 9 + 2$

101. $\frac{5}{12}q + \frac{1}{2}q = 25 - 3$

102. $0.25d + 0.10d = 6 - 0.75$

103. $0.05p - 0.01p = 2 + 0.24$

Everyday Math

104. Balloons Ramona bought 18 balloons for a party. She wants to make 3 equal bunches. Find the number of balloons in each bunch, b, by solving the equation $3b = 18$.

105. Teaching Connie's kindergarten class has 24 children. She wants them to get into 4 equal groups. Find the number of children in each group, g, by solving the equation $4g = 24$.

106. Ticket price Daria paid $36.25 for 5 children's tickets at the ice skating rink. Find the price of each ticket, p, by solving the equation $5p = 36.25$.

107. Unit price Nishant paid $12.96 for a pack of 12 juice bottles. Find the price of each bottle, b, by solving the equation $12b = 12.96$.

108. Fuel economy Tania's SUV gets half as many miles per gallon (mpg) as her husband's hybrid car. The SUV gets 18 mpg. Find the miles per gallons, m, of the hybrid car, by solving the equation $\frac{1}{2}m = 18$.

109. Fabric The drill team used 14 yards of fabric to make flags for one-third of the members. Find how much fabric, f, they would need to make flags for the whole team by solving the equation $\frac{1}{3}f = 14$.

Writing Exercises

110. Frida started to solve the equation $-3x = 36$ by adding 3 to both sides. Explain why Frida's method will result in the correct solution.

111. Emiliano thinks $x = 40$ is the solution to the equation $\frac{1}{2}x = 80$. Explain why he is wrong.

Self Check

ⓐ After completing the exercises, use this checklist to evaluate your mastery of the objectives of this section.

I can...	Confidently	With some help	No-I don't get it!
solve equations using the Division and Multiplication Properties of Equality.			
solve equations that need to be simplified.			

ⓑ After reviewing this checklist, what will you do to become confident for all objectives?

8.3 Solve Equations with Variables and Constants on Both Sides

Learning Objectives

By the end of this section, you will be able to:

- Solve an equation with constants on both sides
- Solve an equation with variables on both sides
- Solve an equation with variables and constants on both sides
- Solve equations using a general strategy

Be Prepared!

Before you get started, take this readiness quiz.

1. Simplify: $4y - 9 + 9$.

   If you missed this problem, review Example 2.22.

2. Solve: $y + 12 = 16$.

   If you missed this problem, review Example 2.31.

3. Solve: $-3y = 63$.

   If you missed this problem, review Example 3.65.

Solve an Equation with Constants on Both Sides

You may have noticed that in all the equations we have solved so far, all the variable terms were on only one side of the equation with the constants on the other side. This does not happen all the time—so now we'll see how to solve equations where the variable terms and/or constant terms are on both sides of the equation.

Our strategy will involve choosing one side of the equation to be the variable side, and the other side of the equation to be the constant side. Then, we will use the Subtraction and Addition Properties of Equality, step by step, to get all the variable terms together on one side of the equation and the constant terms together on the other side.

By doing this, we will transform the equation that started with variables and constants on both sides into the form $ax = b$. We already know how to solve equations of this form by using the Division or Multiplication Properties of Equality.

EXAMPLE 8.20

Solve: $4x + 6 = -14$.

 Solution

In this equation, the variable is only on the left side. It makes sense to call the left side the variable side. Therefore, the right side will be the constant side. We'll write the labels above the equation to help us remember what goes where.

$$\underset{\text{variable}}{} \quad \underset{\text{constant}}{}$$
$$4x + 6 = -14$$

Since the left side is the variable side, the 6 is out of place. We must "undo" adding 6 by subtracting 6, and to keep the equality we must subtract 6 from both sides. Use the Subtraction Property of Equality.	$4x + 6 - 6 = -14 - 6$
Simplify.	$4x = -20$

Now all the xs are on the left and the constant on the right.

Use the Division Property of Equality.	$\dfrac{4x}{4} = \dfrac{-20}{4}$
Simplify.	$x = -5$
Check:	$4x + 6 = -14$
Let $x = -5$.	$4(-5) + 6 = -14$
	$-20 + 6 = -14$
	$-14 = -14 \checkmark$

>	**TRY IT ::** 8.39	Solve: $3x + 4 = -8$.

>	**TRY IT ::** 8.40	Solve: $5a + 3 = -37$.

EXAMPLE 8.21

Solve: $2y - 7 = 15$.

⊘ **Solution**

Notice that the variable is only on the left side of the equation, so this will be the variable side and the right side will be the constant side. Since the left side is the variable side, the 7 is out of place. It is subtracted from the $2y$, so to 'undo' subtraction, add 7 to both sides.

$$\underset{\text{variable}}{} \quad \underset{\text{constant}}{}$$
$$2y - 7 = 15$$

Add 7 to both sides.	$2y - 7 + 7 = 15 + 7$
Simplify.	$2y = 22$

The variables are now on one side and the constants on the other.

Divide both sides by 2.	$\dfrac{2y}{2} = \dfrac{22}{2}$
Simplify.	$y = 11$
Check:	$2y - 7 = 15$
Substitute: $y = 11$.	$2 \cdot 11 - 7 \overset{?}{=} 15$
	$22 - 7 \overset{?}{=} 15$
	$15 = 15 \checkmark$

> **TRY IT : :** 8.41   Solve: $5y - 9 = 16$.

> **TRY IT : :** 8.42   Solve: $3m - 8 = 19$.

Solve an Equation with Variables on Both Sides

What if there are variables on both sides of the equation? We will start like we did above—choosing a variable side and a constant side, and then use the Subtraction and Addition Properties of Equality to collect all variables on one side and all constants on the other side. Remember, what you do to the left side of the equation, you must do to the right side too.

EXAMPLE 8.22

Solve: $5x = 4x + 7$.

⊘ **Solution**

Here the variable, x, is on both sides, but the constants appear only on the right side, so let's make the right side the "constant" side. Then the left side will be the "variable" side.

$$\underset{\text{variable}}{5x} = \underset{\text{constant}}{4x + 7}$$

We don't want any variables on the right, so subtract the $4x$.

$$5x - 4x = 4x - 4x + 7$$

Simplify.

$$x = 7$$

We have all the variables on one side and the constants on the other. We have solved the equation.

Check:

$$5x = 4x + 7$$

Substitute 7 for x.

$$5(7) \overset{?}{=} 4(7) + 7$$

$$35 \overset{?}{=} 28 + 7$$

$$35 = 35 \checkmark$$

> **TRY IT : :** 8.43   Solve: $6n = 5n + 10$.

> **TRY IT : :** 8.44   Solve: $-6c = -7c + 1$.

EXAMPLE 8.23

Solve: $5y - 8 = 7y$.

⊘ **Solution**

The only constant, -8, is on the left side of the equation and variable, y, is on both sides. Let's leave the constant on the left and collect the variables to the right.

	constant variable
	$5y - 8 = 7y$
Subtract $5y$ from both sides.	$5y - 5y - 8 = 7y - 5y$
Simplify.	$-8 = 2y$
We have the variables on the right and the constants on the left. Divide both sides by 2.	$\dfrac{-8}{2} = \dfrac{2y}{2}$
Simplify.	$-4 = y$
Rewrite with the variable on the left.	$y = -4$

Check: Let $y = -4$.

$$5y - 8 = 7y$$

$$5(-4) - 8 \stackrel{?}{=} 7(-4)$$

$$-20 - 8 \stackrel{?}{=} -28$$

$$-28 = -28 \checkmark$$

> **TRY IT : : 8.45**   Solve: $3p - 14 = 5p$.

> **TRY IT : : 8.46**   Solve: $8m + 9 = 5m$.

EXAMPLE 8.24

Solve: $7x = -x + 24$.

⊘ **Solution**

The only constant, 24, is on the right, so let the left side be the variable side.

	variable side constant side
	$7x = -x + 24$
Remove the $-x$ from the right side by adding x to both sides.	$7x + x = -x + x + 24$
Simplify.	$8x = 24$
All the variables are on the left and the constants are on the right. Divide both sides by 8.	$\dfrac{8x}{8} = \dfrac{24}{8}$
Simplify.	$x = 3$

Check: Substitute $x = 3$.

$$7x = -x + 24$$

$$7(3) \stackrel{?}{=} -(3) + 24$$

$$21 = 21 \checkmark$$

> **TRY IT : : 8.47**   Solve: $12j = -4j + 32$.

> | **TRY IT :: 8.48**   Solve: $8h = -4h + 12$.

Solve Equations with Variables and Constants on Both Sides

The next example will be the first to have variables *and* constants on both sides of the equation. As we did before, we'll collect the variable terms to one side and the constants to the other side.

EXAMPLE 8.25

Solve: $7x + 5 = 6x + 2$.

⊘ **Solution**

Start by choosing which side will be the variable side and which side will be the constant side. The variable terms are $7x$ and $6x$. Since 7 is greater than $6,$ make the left side the variable side and so the right side will be the constant side.

$$7x + 5 = 6x + 2$$

Collect the variable terms to the left side by subtracting $6x$ from both sides. $7x - 6x + 5 = 6x - 6x + 2$

Simplify. $x + 5 = 2$

Now, collect the constants to the right side by subtracting 5 from both sides. $x + 5 - 5 = 2 - 5$

Simplify. $x = -3$

The solution is $x = -3$.

Check: Let $x = -3$.

$$7x + 5 = 6x + 2$$
$$7(-3) + 5 \overset{?}{=} 6(-3) + 2$$
$$-21 + 5 \overset{?}{=} -18 + 2$$
$$-16 = -16 \checkmark$$

> | **TRY IT :: 8.49**   Solve: $12x + 8 = 6x + 2$.

> | **TRY IT :: 8.50**   Solve: $9y + 4 = 7y + 12$.

We'll summarize the steps we took so you can easily refer to them.

HOW TO :: SOLVE AN EQUATION WITH VARIABLES AND CONSTANTS ON BOTH SIDES.

Step 1.   Choose one side to be the variable side and then the other will be the constant side.

Step 2.   Collect the variable terms to the variable side, using the Addition or Subtraction Property of Equality.

Step 3.   Collect the constants to the other side, using the Addition or Subtraction Property of Equality.

Step 4.   Make the coefficient of the variable $1,$ using the Multiplication or Division Property of Equality.

Step 5.   Check the solution by substituting it into the original equation.

It is a good idea to make the variable side the one in which the variable has the larger coefficient. This usually makes the arithmetic easier.

EXAMPLE 8.26

Solve: $6n - 2 = -3n + 7$.

⊘ **Solution**

We have $6n$ on the left and $-3n$ on the right. Since $6 > -3$, make the left side the "variable" side.

	$6n - 2 = -3n + 7$
We don't want variables on the right side—add $3n$ to both sides to leave only constants on the right.	$6n + 3n - 2 = -3n + 3n + 7$
Combine like terms.	$9n - 2 = 7$
We don't want any constants on the left side, so add 2 to both sides.	$9n - 2 + 2 = 7 + 2$
Simplify.	$9n = 9$
The variable term is on the left and the constant term is on the right. To get the coefficient of n to be one, divide both sides by 9.	$\dfrac{9n}{9} = \dfrac{9}{9}$
Simplify.	$n = 1$

Check: Substitute 1 for n.

$$6n - 2 = -3n + 7$$
$$6(1) - 2 \overset{?}{=} -3(1) + 7$$
$$4 = 4 \checkmark$$

> **TRY IT ::** 8.51   Solve: $8q - 5 = -4q + 7$.

> **TRY IT ::** 8.52   Solve: $7n - 3 = n + 3$.

EXAMPLE 8.27

Solve: $2a - 7 = 5a + 8$.

⊘ **Solution**

This equation has $2a$ on the left and $5a$ on the right. Since $5 > 2$, make the right side the variable side and the left side the constant side.

	$2a - 7 = 5a + 8$
Subtract $2a$ from both sides to remove the variable term from the left.	$2a - 2a - 7 = 5a - 2a + 8$
Combine like terms.	$-7 = 3a + 8$
Subtract 8 from both sides to remove the constant from the right.	$-7 - 8 = 3a + 8 - 8$
Simplify.	$-15 = 3a$
Divide both sides by 3 to make 1 the coefficient of a.	$\dfrac{-15}{3} = \dfrac{3a}{3}$
Simplify.	$-5 = a$

Check: Let $a = -5$.

$$2a - 7 = 5a + 8$$
$$2(-5) - 7 \overset{?}{=} 5(-5) + 8$$
$$-10 - 7 \overset{?}{=} -25 + 8$$
$$-17 = -17 \checkmark$$

Note that we could have made the left side the variable side instead of the right side, but it would have led to a negative coefficient on the variable term. While we could work with the negative, there is less chance of error when working with positives. The strategy outlined above helps avoid the negatives!

> **TRY IT ::** 8.53   Solve: $2a - 2 = 6a + 18$.

> **TRY IT ::** 8.54   Solve: $4k - 1 = 7k + 17$.

To solve an equation with fractions, we still follow the same steps to get the solution.

EXAMPLE 8.28

Solve: $\frac{3}{2}x + 5 = \frac{1}{2}x - 3$.

⊘ **Solution**

Since $\frac{3}{2} > \frac{1}{2}$, make the left side the variable side and the right side the constant side.

$$\tfrac{3}{2}x + 5 = \tfrac{1}{2}x - 3$$

Subtract $\tfrac{1}{2}x$ from both sides.	$\tfrac{3}{2}x - \tfrac{1}{2}x + 5 = \tfrac{1}{2}x - \tfrac{1}{2}x - 3$
Combine like terms.	$x + 5 = -3$
Subtract 5 from both sides.	$x + 5 - 5 = -3 - 5$
Simplify.	$x = -8$
Check: Let $x = -8$.	

$$\tfrac{3}{2}x + 5 = \tfrac{1}{2}x - 3$$
$$\tfrac{3}{2}(-8) + 5 \stackrel{?}{=} \tfrac{1}{2}(-8) - 3$$
$$-12 + 5 \stackrel{?}{=} -4 - 3$$
$$-7 = -7 \checkmark$$

> **TRY IT ::** 8.55   Solve: $\tfrac{7}{8}x - 12 = -\tfrac{1}{8}x - 2$.

> **TRY IT ::** 8.56   Solve: $\tfrac{7}{6}y + 11 = \tfrac{1}{6}y + 8$.

We follow the same steps when the equation has decimals, too.

EXAMPLE 8.29

Solve: $3.4x + 4 = 1.6x - 5$.

Solution

Since $3.4 > 1.6$, make the left side the variable side and the right side the constant side.

$$3.4x + 4 = 1.6x - 5$$

Subtract $1.6x$ from both sides.	$3.4x - 1.6x + 4 = 1.6x - 1.6x - 5$
Combine like terms.	$1.8x + 4 = -5$
Subtract 4 from both sides.	$1.8x + 4 - 4 = -5 - 4$
Simplify.	$1.8x = -9$
Use the Division Property of Equality.	$\tfrac{1.8x}{1.8} = \tfrac{-9}{1.8}$
Simplify.	$x = -5$
Check: Let $x = -5$.	

$$3.4x + 4 = 1.6x - 5$$
$$3.4(-5) + 4 \stackrel{?}{=} 1.6(-5) - 5$$
$$-17 + 4 \stackrel{?}{=} -8 - 5$$
$$-13 = -13 \checkmark$$

TRY IT :: 8.57   Solve: $2.8x + 12 = -1.4x - 9$.

 TRY IT :: 8.58   Solve: $3.6y + 8 = 1.2y - 4$.

Solve Equations Using a General Strategy

Each of the first few sections of this chapter has dealt with solving one specific form of a linear equation. It's time now to lay out an overall strategy that can be used to solve *any* linear equation. We call this the *general strategy*. Some equations won't require all the steps to solve, but many will. Simplifying each side of the equation as much as possible first makes the rest of the steps easier.

> **HOW TO ::** USE A GENERAL STRATEGY FOR SOLVING LINEAR EQUATIONS.
>
> Step 1.   Simplify each side of the equation as much as possible. Use the Distributive Property to remove any parentheses. Combine like terms.
>
> Step 2.   Collect all the variable terms to one side of the equation. Use the Addition or Subtraction Property of Equality.
>
> Step 3.   Collect all the constant terms to the other side of the equation. Use the Addition or Subtraction Property of Equality.
>
> Step 4.   Make the coefficient of the variable term to equal to 1. Use the Multiplication or Division Property of Equality. State the solution to the equation.
>
> Step 5.   Check the solution. Substitute the solution into the original equation to make sure the result is a true statement.

EXAMPLE 8.30

Solve: $3(x + 2) = 18$.

⊘ **Solution**

$$3(x + 2) = 18$$

Simplify each side of the equation as much as possible.
Use the Distributive Property.

$$3x + 6 = 18$$

Collect all variable terms on one side of the equation—all x s are already on the left side.

Collect constant terms on the other side of the equation.
Subtract 6 from each side

$$3x + 6 - 6 = 18 - 6$$

Simplify.

$$3x = 12$$

Make the coefficient of the variable term equal to 1. Divide each side by 3.

$$\frac{3x}{3} = \frac{12}{3}$$

Simplify.

$$x = 4$$

Check: Let $x = 4$.

$$3(x + 2) = 18$$
$$3(4 + 2) \overset{?}{=} 18$$
$$3(6) \overset{?}{=} 18$$
$$18 = 18 \checkmark$$

> **TRY IT ::** 8.59   Solve: $5(x+3) = 35$.

> **TRY IT ::** 8.60   Solve: $6(y-4) = -18$.

EXAMPLE 8.31

Solve: $-(x+5) = 7$.

⊘ **Solution**

	$-(x+5)=7$
Simplify each side of the equation as much as possible by distributing. The only x term is on the left side, so all variable terms are on the left side of the equation.	$-x-5=7$
Add 5 to both sides to get all constant terms on the right side of the equation.	$-x-5+5=7+5$
Simplify.	$-x=12$
Make the coefficient of the variable term equal to 1 by multiplying both sides by -1.	$-1(-x)=-1(12)$
Simplify.	$x=-12$

Check: Let $x = -12$.

$$-(x+5)=7$$
$$-(-12+5)\overset{?}{=}7$$
$$-(-7)\overset{?}{=}7$$
$$7=7\checkmark$$

> **TRY IT ::** 8.61   Solve: $-(y+8) = -2$.

> **TRY IT ::** 8.62   Solve: $-(z+4) = -12$.

EXAMPLE 8.32

Solve: $4(x-2)+5 = -3$.

⊘ Solution

$$4(x - 2) + 5 = -3$$

Simplify each side of the equation as much as possible. Distribute.	$4x - 8 + 5 = -3$
Combine like terms	$4x - 3 = -3$
The only x is on the left side, so all variable terms are on one side of the equation.	
Add 3 to both sides to get all constant terms on the other side of the equation.	$4x - 3 + 3 = -3 + 3$
Simplify.	$4x = 0$
Make the coefficient of the variable term equal to 1 by dividing both sides by 4.	$\frac{4x}{4} = \frac{0}{4}$
Simplify.	$x = 0$

Check: Let $x = 0$.

$$4(x - 2) + 5 = -3$$
$$4(0 - 2) + 5 \overset{?}{=} -3$$
$$4(-2) + 5 \overset{?}{=} -3$$
$$-8 + 5 \overset{?}{=} -3$$
$$-3 = -3 \checkmark$$

> **TRY IT ::** 8.63   Solve: $2(a - 4) + 3 = -1$.

> **TRY IT ::** 8.64   Solve: $7(n - 3) - 8 = -15$.

EXAMPLE 8.33

Solve: $8 - 2(3y + 5) = 0$.

⊘ Solution

Be careful when distributing the negative.

	$8 - 2(3y + 5) = 0$
Simplify—use the Distributive Property.	$8 - 6y - 10 = 0$
Combine like terms.	$-6y - 2 = 0$
Add 2 to both sides to collect constants on the right.	$-6y - 2 + 2 = 0 + 2$
Simplify.	$-6y = 2$
Divide both sides by –6.	$\dfrac{-6y}{-6} = \dfrac{2}{-6}$
Simplify.	$y = -\dfrac{1}{3}$

Check: Let $y = -\dfrac{1}{3}$.

$$8 - 2(3y + 5) = 0$$
$$8 - 2\left[3\left(-\dfrac{1}{3}\right) + 5\right] = 0$$
$$8 - 2(-1 + 5) \stackrel{?}{=} 0$$
$$8 - 2(4) \stackrel{?}{=} 0$$
$$8 - 8 \stackrel{?}{=} 0$$
$$0 = 0 \checkmark$$

> **TRY IT :: 8.65**   Solve: $12 - 3(4j + 3) = -17$.

> **TRY IT :: 8.66**   Solve: $-6 - 8(k - 2) = -10$.

EXAMPLE 8.34

Solve: $3(x - 2) - 5 = 4(2x + 1) + 5$.

⊘ **Solution**

$$3(x-2)-5=4(2x+1)+5$$

Distribute.	$3x-6-5=8x+4+5$
Combine like terms.	$3x-11=8x+9$
Subtract $3x$ to get all the variables on the right since $8>3$.	$3x-3x-11=8x-3x+9$
Simplify.	$-11=5x+9$
Subtract 9 to get the constants on the left.	$-11-9=5x+9-9$
Simplify.	$-20=5x$
Divide by 5.	$\dfrac{-20}{5}=\dfrac{5x}{5}$
Simplify.	$-4=x$

Check: Substitute: $-4=x$.

$$3(x-2)-5=4(2x+1)+5$$
$$3(-4-2)-5\overset{?}{=}4[2(-4)+1]+5$$
$$3(-6)-5\overset{?}{=}4(-8+1)+5$$
$$-18-5\overset{?}{=}4(-7)+5$$
$$-23\overset{?}{=}-28+5$$
$$-23=-23\ \checkmark$$

> **TRY IT :: 8.67**   Solve: $6(p-3)-7=5(4p+3)-12$.

> **TRY IT :: 8.68**   Solve: $8(q+1)-5=3(2q-4)-1$.

EXAMPLE 8.35

Solve: $\dfrac{1}{2}(6x-2)=5-x$.

⊘ **Solution**

$$\frac{1}{2}(6x - 2) = 5 - x$$

Distribute.	$3x - 1 = 5 - x$
Add x to get all the variables on the left.	$3x - 1 + x = 5 - x + x$
Simplify.	$4x - 1 = 5$
Add 1 to get constants on the right.	$4x - 1 + 1 = 5 + 1$
Simplify.	$4x = 6$
Divide by 4.	$\dfrac{4x}{4} = \dfrac{6}{4}$
Simplify.	$x = \dfrac{3}{2}$
Check: Let $x = \dfrac{3}{2}$.	

$$\frac{1}{2}(6x - 2) = 5 - x$$

$$\frac{1}{2}\left(6 \cdot \frac{3}{2} - 2\right) \overset{?}{=} 5 - \frac{3}{2}$$

$$\frac{1}{2}(9 - 2) \overset{?}{=} \frac{10}{2} - \frac{3}{2}$$

$$\frac{1}{2}(7) \overset{?}{=} \frac{7}{2}$$

$$\frac{7}{2} = \frac{7}{2} \checkmark$$

> **TRY IT :: 8.69**   Solve: $\frac{1}{3}(6u + 3) = 7 - u$.

> **TRY IT :: 8.70**   Solve: $\frac{2}{3}(9x - 12) = 8 + 2x$.

In many applications, we will have to solve equations with decimals. The same general strategy will work for these equations.

EXAMPLE 8.36

Solve: $0.24(100x + 5) = 0.4(30x + 15)$.

⊘ **Solution**

$$0.24(100x + 5) = 0.4(30x + 15)$$

Distribute.

$$24x + 1.2 = 12x + 6$$

Subtract $12x$ to get all the x s to the left.

$$24x + 1.2 - 12x = 12x + 6 - 12x$$

Simplify.

$$12x + 1.2 = 6$$

Subtract 1.2 to get the constants to the right.

$$12x + 1.2 - 1.2 = 6 - 1.2$$

Simplify.

$$12x = 4.8$$

Divide.

$$\frac{12x}{12} = \frac{4.8}{12}$$

Simplify.

$$x = 0.4$$

Check: Let $x = 0.4$.

$$0.24(100x + 5) = 0.4(30x + 15)$$
$$0.24(100(0.4) + 5) \overset{?}{=} 0.4(30(0.4) + 15)$$
$$0.24(40 + 5) \overset{?}{=} 0.4(12 + 15)$$
$$0.24(45) \overset{?}{=} 0.4(27)$$
$$10.8 = 10.8 \checkmark$$

> **TRY IT :: 8.71**   Solve: $0.55(100n + 8) = 0.6(85n + 14)$.

> **TRY IT :: 8.72**   Solve: $0.15(40m - 120) = 0.5(60m + 12)$.

▶ **MEDIA ::** ACCESS ADDITIONAL ONLINE RESOURCES

- Solving Multi-Step Equations (http://www.openstaxcollege.org/l/24SolveMultStep)
- Solve an Equation with Variable Terms on Both Sides (http://www.openstaxcollege.org/l/24SolveEquatVar)
- Solving Multi-Step Equations (L5.4) (http://www.openstaxcollege.org/l/24MultiStepEqu)
- Solve an Equation with Variables and Parentheses on Both Sides (http://www.openstaxcollege.org/l/24EquVarParen)

8.3 EXERCISES

Practice Makes Perfect

Solve an Equation with Constants on Both Sides

In the following exercises, solve the equation for the variable.

112. $6x - 2 = 40$

113. $7x - 8 = 34$

114. $11w + 6 = 93$

115. $14y + 7 = 91$

116. $3a + 8 = -46$

117. $4m + 9 = -23$

118. $-50 = 7n - 1$

119. $-47 = 6b + 1$

120. $25 = -9y + 7$

121. $29 = -8x - 3$

122. $-12p - 3 = 15$

123. $-14q - 15 = 13$

Solve an Equation with Variables on Both Sides

In the following exercises, solve the equation for the variable.

124. $8z = 7z - 7$

125. $9k = 8k - 11$

126. $4x + 36 = 10x$

127. $6x + 27 = 9x$

128. $c = -3c - 20$

129. $b = -4b - 15$

130. $5q = 44 - 6q$

131. $7z = 39 - 6z$

132. $3y + \frac{1}{2} = 2y$

133. $8x + \frac{3}{4} = 7x$

134. $-12a - 8 = -16a$

135. $-15r - 8 = -11r$

Solve an Equation with Variables and Constants on Both Sides

In the following exercises, solve the equations for the variable.

136. $6x - 15 = 5x + 3$

137. $4x - 17 = 3x + 2$

138. $26 + 8d = 9d + 11$

139. $21 + 6f = 7f + 14$

140. $3p - 1 = 5p - 33$

141. $8q - 5 = 5q - 20$

142. $4a + 5 = -a - 40$

143. $9c + 7 = -2c - 37$

144. $8y - 30 = -2y + 30$

145. $12x - 17 = -3x + 13$

146. $2z - 4 = 23 - z$

147. $3y - 4 = 12 - y$

148. $\frac{5}{4}c - 3 = \frac{1}{4}c - 16$

149. $\frac{4}{3}m - 7 = \frac{1}{3}m - 13$

150. $8 - \frac{2}{5}q = \frac{3}{5}q + 6$

151. $11 - \frac{1}{4}a = \frac{3}{4}a + 4$

152. $\frac{4}{3}n + 9 = \frac{1}{3}n - 9$

153. $\frac{5}{4}a + 15 = \frac{3}{4}a - 5$

154. $\frac{1}{4}y + 7 = \frac{3}{4}y - 3$

155. $\frac{3}{5}p + 2 = \frac{4}{5}p - 1$

156. $14n + 8.25 = 9n + 19.60$

157. $13z + 6.45 = 8z + 23.75$

158. $2.4w - 100 = 0.8w + 28$

159. $2.7w - 80 = 1.2w + 10$

160. $5.6r + 13.1 = 3.5r + 57.2$

161. $6.6x - 18.9 = 3.4x + 54.7$

Solve an Equation Using the General Strategy

In the following exercises, solve the linear equation using the general strategy.

162. $5(x + 3) = 75$

163. $4(y + 7) = 64$

164. $8 = 4(x - 3)$

165. $9 = 3(x - 3)$

166. $20(y - 8) = -60$

167. $14(y - 6) = -42$

168. $-4(2n + 1) = 16$

169. $-7(3n + 4) = 14$

170. $3(10 + 5r) = 0$

171. $8(3 + 3p) = 0$

172. $\frac{2}{3}(9c - 3) = 22$

173. $\frac{3}{5}(10x - 5) = 27$

174. $5(1.2u - 4.8) = -12$

175. $4(2.5v - 0.6) = 7.6$

176. $0.2(30n + 50) = 28$

177. $0.5(16m + 34) = -15$

178. $-(w - 6) = 24$

179. $-(t - 8) = 17$

180. $9(3a + 5) + 9 = 54$

181. $8(6b - 7) + 23 = 63$

182. $10 + 3(z + 4) = 19$

183. $13 + 2(m - 4) = 17$

184. $7 + 5(4 - q) = 12$

185. $-9 + 6(5 - k) = 12$

186. $15 - (3r + 8) = 28$

187. $18 - (9r + 7) = -16$

188. $11 - 4(y - 8) = 43$

189. $18 - 2(y - 3) = 32$

190. $9(p - 1) = 6(2p - 1)$

191. $3(4n - 1) - 2 = 8n + 3$

192. $9(2m - 3) - 8 = 4m + 7$

193. $5(x - 4) - 4x = 14$

194. $8(x - 4) - 7x = 14$

195.
$5 + 6(3s - 5) = -3 + 2(8s - 1)$

196.
$-12 + 8(x - 5) = -4 + 3(5x - 2)$

197.
$4(x - 1) - 8 = 6(3x - 2) - 7$

198. $7(2x - 5) = 8(4x - 1) - 9$

Everyday Math

199. Making a fence Jovani has a fence around the rectangular garden in his backyard. The perimeter of the fence is 150 feet. The length is 15 feet more than the width. Find the width, w, by solving the equation $150 = 2(w + 15) + 2w$.

200. Concert tickets At a school concert, the total value of tickets sold was $\$1{,}506$. Student tickets sold for $\$6$ and adult tickets sold for $\$9$. The number of adult tickets sold was 5 less than 3 times the number of student tickets. Find the number of student tickets sold, s, by solving the equation $6s + 9(3s - 5) = 1506$.

201. Coins Rhonda has $\$1.90$ in nickels and dimes. The number of dimes is one less than twice the number of nickels. Find the number of nickels, n, by solving the equation $0.05n + 0.10(2n - 1) = 1.90$.

202. Fencing Micah has 74 feet of fencing to make a rectangular dog pen in his yard. He wants the length to be 25 feet more than the width. Find the length, L, by solving the equation $2L + 2(L - 25) = 74$.

Writing Exercises

203. When solving an equation with variables on both sides, why is it usually better to choose the side with the larger coefficient as the variable side?

204. Solve the equation $10x + 14 = -2x + 38$, explaining all the steps of your solution.

205. What is the first step you take when solving the equation $3 - 7(y - 4) = 38$? Explain why this is your first step.

206. Solve the equation $\frac{1}{4}(8x + 20) = 3x - 4$ explaining all the steps of your solution as in the examples in this section.

207. Using your own words, list the steps in the General Strategy for Solving Linear Equations.

208. Explain why you should simplify both sides of an equation as much as possible before collecting the variable terms to one side and the constant terms to the other side.

Self Check

ⓐ *After completing the exercises, use this checklist to evaluate your mastery of the objectives of this section.*

I can...	Confidently	With some help	No-I don't get it!
solve an equation with constants on both sides.			
solve an equation with variables on both sides.			
solve an equation with variables and constants on both sides.			

ⓑ *What does this checklist tell you about your mastery of this section? What steps will you take to improve?*

8.4 Solve Equations with Fraction or Decimal Coefficients

Learning Objectives

By the end of this section, you will be able to:

- Solve equations with fraction coefficients
- Solve equations with decimal coefficients

Be Prepared!

Before you get started, take this readiness quiz.

1. Multiply: $8 \cdot \frac{3}{8}$.

   If you missed this problem, review Example 4.28

2. Find the LCD of $\frac{5}{6}$ and $\frac{1}{4}$.

   If you missed this problem, review Example 4.63

3. Multiply: 4.78 by 100.

   If you missed this problem, review Example 5.18

Solve Equations with Fraction Coefficients

Let's use the General Strategy for Solving Linear Equations introduced earlier to solve the equation $\frac{1}{8}x + \frac{1}{2} = \frac{1}{4}$.

$$\frac{1}{8}x + \frac{1}{2} = \frac{1}{4}$$

To isolate the x term, subtract $\frac{1}{2}$ from both sides.	$\frac{1}{8}x + \frac{1}{2} - \frac{1}{2} = \frac{1}{4} - \frac{1}{2}$
Simplify the left side.	$\frac{1}{8}x = \frac{1}{4} - \frac{1}{2}$
Change the constants to equivalent fractions with the LCD.	$\frac{1}{8}x = \frac{1}{4} - \frac{2}{4}$
Subtract.	$\frac{1}{8}x = -\frac{1}{4}$
Multiply both sides by the reciprocal of $\frac{1}{8}$.	$\frac{8}{1} \cdot \frac{1}{8}x = \frac{8}{1}\left(-\frac{1}{4}\right)$
Simplify.	$x = -2$

This method worked fine, but many students don't feel very confident when they see all those fractions. So we are going to show an alternate method to solve equations with fractions. This alternate method eliminates the fractions.

We will apply the Multiplication Property of Equality and multiply both sides of an equation by the least common denominator of *all* the fractions in the equation. The result of this operation will be a new equation, equivalent to the first, but with no fractions. This process is called *clearing the equation of fractions*. Let's solve the same equation again, but this time use the method that clears the fractions.

EXAMPLE 8.37

Solve: $\frac{1}{8}x + \frac{1}{2} = \frac{1}{4}$.

⊘ **Solution**

Find the least common denominator of *all* the fractions in the equation.	$\frac{1}{8}x + \frac{1}{2} = \frac{1}{4}$ LCD = 8
Multiply both sides of the equation by that LCD, 8. This clears the fractions.	$8\left(\frac{1}{8}x + \frac{1}{2}\right) = 8\left(\frac{1}{4}\right)$
Use the Distributive Property.	$8 \cdot \frac{1}{8}x + 8 \cdot \frac{1}{2} = 8 \cdot \frac{1}{4}$
Simplify — and notice, no more fractions!	$x + 4 = 2$
Solve using the General Strategy for Solving Linear Equations.	$x + 4 - 4 = 2 - 4$
Simplify.	$x = -2$

Check: Let $x = -2$

$$\frac{1}{8}x + \frac{1}{2} = \frac{1}{4}$$

$$\frac{1}{8}(-2) + \frac{1}{2} \overset{?}{=} \frac{1}{4}$$

$$-\frac{2}{8} + \frac{1}{2} \overset{?}{=} \frac{1}{4}$$

$$-\frac{2}{8} + \frac{4}{8} \overset{?}{=} \frac{1}{4}$$

$$\frac{2}{4} \overset{?}{=} \frac{1}{4}$$

$$\frac{1}{4} = \frac{1}{4} \checkmark$$

> **TRY IT :: 8.73**   Solve: $\frac{1}{4}x + \frac{1}{2} = \frac{5}{8}$.

> **TRY IT :: 8.74**   Solve: $\frac{1}{6}y - \frac{1}{3} = \frac{1}{6}$.

Notice in Example 8.37 that once we cleared the equation of fractions, the equation was like those we solved earlier in this chapter. We changed the problem to one we already knew how to solve! We then used the General Strategy for Solving Linear Equations.

HOW TO :: SOLVE EQUATIONS WITH FRACTION COEFFICIENTS BY CLEARING THE FRACTIONS.

Step 1.   Find the least common denominator of *all* the fractions in the equation.

Step 2.   Multiply both sides of the equation by that LCD. This clears the fractions.

Step 3.   Solve using the General Strategy for Solving Linear Equations.

EXAMPLE 8.38

Solve: $7 = \frac{1}{2}x + \frac{3}{4}x - \frac{2}{3}x$.

⊘ **Solution**

We want to clear the fractions by multiplying both sides of the equation by the LCD of all the fractions in the equation.

Find the least common denominator of *all* the fractions in the equation.	$7 = \frac{1}{2}x + \frac{3}{4}x - \frac{2}{3}x$ LCD = 12
Multiply both sides of the equation by 12.	$12(7) = 12 \cdot \frac{1}{2}x + \frac{3}{4}x - \frac{2}{3}x$
Distribute.	$12(7) = 12 \cdot \frac{1}{2}x + 12 \cdot \frac{3}{4}x - 12 \cdot \frac{2}{3}x$
Simplify — and notice, no more fractions!	$84 = 6x + 9x - 8x$
Combine like terms.	$84 = 7x$
Divide by 7.	$\frac{84}{7} = \frac{7x}{7}$
Simplify.	$12 = x$

Check: Let $x = 12$.

$$7 = \frac{1}{2}x + \frac{3}{4}x - \frac{2}{3}x$$

$$7 \overset{?}{=} \frac{1}{2}(12) + \frac{3}{4}(12) - \frac{2}{3}(12)$$

$$7 \overset{?}{=} 6 + 9 - 8$$

$$7 = 7 \checkmark$$

> **TRY IT : : 8.75**   Solve: $6 = \frac{1}{2}v + \frac{2}{5}v - \frac{3}{4}v$.

> **TRY IT : : 8.76**   Solve: $-1 = \frac{1}{2}u + \frac{1}{4}u - \frac{2}{3}u$.

In the next example, we'll have variables and fractions on both sides of the equation.

EXAMPLE 8.39

Solve: $x + \frac{1}{3} = \frac{1}{6}x - \frac{1}{2}$.

⊘ Solution

Find the LCD of all the fractions in the equation.	$x + \frac{1}{3} = \frac{1}{6}x - \frac{1}{2},\ \text{LCD} = 6$
Multiply both sides by the LCD.	$6\left(x + \frac{1}{3}\right) = 6\left(\frac{1}{6}x - \frac{1}{2}\right)$
Distribute.	$6 \cdot x + 6 \cdot \frac{1}{3} = 6 \cdot \frac{1}{6}x - 6 \cdot \frac{1}{2}$
Simplify — no more fractions!	$6x + 2 = x - 3$
Subtract x from both sides.	$6x - x + 2 = x - x - 3$
Simplify.	$5x + 2 = -3$
Subtract 2 from both sides.	$5x + 2 - 2 = -3 - 2$
Simplify.	$5x = -5$
Divide by 5.	$\frac{5x}{5} = \frac{-5}{5}$
Simplify.	$x = -1$

Check: Substitute $x = -1$.

$$x + \frac{1}{3} = \frac{1}{6}x - \frac{1}{2}$$

$$(-1) + \frac{1}{3} \overset{?}{=} \frac{1}{6}(-1) - \frac{1}{2}$$

$$(-1) + \frac{1}{3} \overset{?}{=} -\frac{1}{6} - \frac{1}{2}$$

$$-\frac{3}{3} + \frac{1}{3} \overset{?}{=} -\frac{1}{6} - \frac{3}{6}$$

$$-\frac{2}{3} \overset{?}{=} -\frac{4}{6}$$

$$-\frac{2}{3} = -\frac{2}{3} \checkmark$$

> **TRY IT :: 8.77**   Solve: $a + \frac{3}{4} = \frac{3}{8}a - \frac{1}{2}$.

> **TRY IT :: 8.78**   Solve: $c + \frac{3}{4} = \frac{1}{2}c - \frac{1}{4}$.

In Example 8.40, we'll start by using the Distributive Property. This step will clear the fractions right away!

EXAMPLE 8.40

Solve: $1 = \frac{1}{2}(4x + 2)$.

⊘ **Solution**

$$1 = \frac{1}{2}(4x + 2)$$

Distribute.	$1 = \frac{1}{2} \cdot 4x + \frac{1}{2} \cdot 2$
Simplify. Now there are no fractions to clear!	$1 = 2x + 1$
Subtract 1 from both sides.	$1 - 1 = 2x + 1 - 1$
Simplify.	$0 = 2x$
Divide by 2.	$\frac{0}{2} = \frac{2x}{2}$
Simplify.	$0 = x$

Check: Let $x = 0$.

$1 = \frac{1}{2}(4x + 2)$

$1 \overset{?}{=} \frac{1}{2}(4(0) + 2)$

$1 \overset{?}{=} \frac{1}{2}(2)$

$1 \overset{?}{=} \frac{2}{2}$

$1 = 1 \checkmark$

> **TRY IT :: 8.79**   Solve: $-11 = \frac{1}{2}(6p + 2)$.

> **TRY IT :: 8.80**   Solve: $8 = \frac{1}{3}(9q + 6)$.

Many times, there will still be fractions, even after distributing.

EXAMPLE 8.41

Solve: $\frac{1}{2}(y - 5) = \frac{1}{4}(y - 1)$.

Solution

$$\tfrac{1}{2}(y-5)=\tfrac{1}{4}(y-1)$$

Distribute.	$\tfrac{1}{2}\cdot y - \tfrac{1}{2}\cdot 5 = \tfrac{1}{4}\cdot y - \tfrac{1}{4}\cdot 1$
Simplify.	$\tfrac{1}{2}y - \tfrac{5}{2} = \tfrac{1}{4}y - \tfrac{1}{4}$
Multiply by the LCD, 4.	$4\left(\tfrac{1}{2}y-\tfrac{5}{2}\right)=4\left(\tfrac{1}{4}y-\tfrac{1}{4}\right)$
Distribute.	$4\cdot\tfrac{1}{2}y - 4\cdot\tfrac{5}{2} = 4\cdot\tfrac{1}{4}y - 4\cdot\tfrac{1}{4}$
Simplify.	$2y-10=y-1$
Collect the y terms to the left.	$2y-10-y=y-1-y$
Simplify.	$y-10=-1$
Collect the constants to the right.	$y-10+10=-1+10$
Simplify.	$y=9$

Check: Substitute 9 for y.

$$\tfrac{1}{2}(y-5)=\tfrac{1}{4}(y-1)$$
$$\tfrac{1}{2}(9-5)\overset{?}{=}\tfrac{1}{4}(9-1)$$
$$\tfrac{1}{2}(4)\overset{?}{=}\tfrac{1}{4}(8)$$
$$2=2\checkmark$$

> **TRY IT :: 8.81** Solve: $\tfrac{1}{5}(n+3)=\tfrac{1}{4}(n+2)$.

> **TRY IT :: 8.82** Solve: $\tfrac{1}{2}(m-3)=\tfrac{1}{4}(m-7)$.

Solve Equations with Decimal Coefficients

Some equations have decimals in them. This kind of equation will occur when we solve problems dealing with money and percent. But decimals are really another way to represent fractions. For example, $0.3=\tfrac{3}{10}$ and $0.17=\tfrac{17}{100}$. So, when we have an equation with decimals, we can use the same process we used to clear fractions—multiply both sides of the equation by the least common denominator.

EXAMPLE 8.42

Solve: $0.8x-5=7$.

Solution

The only decimal in the equation is 0.8. Since $0.8=\tfrac{8}{10}$, the LCD is 10. We can multiply both sides by 10 to clear the decimal.

$$0.8x - 5 = 7$$

Multiply both sides by the LCD.	$10(0.8x - 5) = 10(7)$
Distribute.	$10(0.8x) - 10(5) = 10(7)$
Multiply, and notice, no more decimals!	$8x - 50 = 70$
Add 50 to get all constants to the right.	$8x - 50 + 50 = 70 + 50$
Simplify.	$8x = 120$
Divide both sides by 8.	$\dfrac{8x}{8} = \dfrac{120}{8}$
Simplify.	$x = 15$

Check: Let $x = 15$.

$$0.8(15) - 5 \overset{?}{=} 7$$
$$12 - 5 \overset{?}{=} 7$$
$$7 = 7 \checkmark$$

> **TRY IT :: 8.83**   Solve: $0.6x - 1 = 11$.

> **TRY IT :: 8.84**   Solve: $1.2x - 3 = 9$.

EXAMPLE 8.43

Solve: $0.06x + 0.02 = 0.25x - 1.5$.

⊘ **Solution**

Look at the decimals and think of the equivalent fractions.

$$0.06 = \frac{6}{100}, \quad 0.02 = \frac{2}{100}, \quad 0.25 = \frac{25}{100}, \quad 1.5 = 1\frac{5}{10}$$

Notice, the LCD is 100.

By multiplying by the LCD we will clear the decimals.

$$0.06x + 0.02 = 0.25x - 1.5$$

Multiply both sides by 100.	$100(0.06x + 0.02) = 100(0.25x - 1.5)$
Distribute.	$100(0.06x) + 100(0.02) = 100(0.25x) - 100(1.5)$
Multiply, and now no more decimals.	$6x + 2 = 25x - 150$
Collect the variables to the right.	$6x - 6x + 2 = 25x - 6x - 150$
Simplify.	$2 = 19x - 150$
Collect the constants to the left.	$2 + 150 = 19x - 150 + 150$
Simplify.	$152 = 19x$
Divide by 19.	$\dfrac{152}{19} = \dfrac{19x}{19}$
Simplify.	$8 = x$

Check: Let $x = 8$.

$$0.06(8) + 0.02 = 0.25(8) - 1.5$$
$$0.48 + 0.02 = 2.00 - 1.5$$
$$0.50 = 0.50 \checkmark$$

> **TRY IT :: 8.85**   Solve: $0.14h + 0.12 = 0.35h - 2.4$.

> **TRY IT :: 8.86**   Solve: $0.65k - 0.1 = 0.4k - 0.35$.

The next example uses an equation that is typical of the ones we will see in the money applications in the next chapter. Notice that we will distribute the decimal first before we clear all decimals in the equation.

EXAMPLE 8.44

Solve: $0.25x + 0.05(x + 3) = 2.85$.

⊘ **Solution**

$$0.25x + 0.05(x + 3) = 2.85$$

Distribute first. $0.25x + 0.05x + 0.15 = 2.85$

Combine like terms. $0.30x + 0.15 = 2.85$

To clear decimals, multiply by 100. $100(0.30x + 0.15) = 100(2.85)$

Distribute. $30x + 15 = 285$

Subtract 15 from both sides. $30x + 15 - 15 = 285 - 15$

Simplify. $30x = 270$

Divide by 30. $\dfrac{30x}{30} = \dfrac{270}{30}$

Simplify. $x = 9$

Check: Let $x = 9$.

$$0.25x + 0.05(x + 3) = 2.85$$
$$0.25(9) + 0.05(9 + 3) \overset{?}{=} 2.85$$
$$2.25 + 0.05(12) \overset{?}{=} 2.85$$
$$2.25 + 0.60 \overset{?}{=} 2.85$$
$$2.85 = 2.85 \checkmark$$

> **TRY IT :: 8.87** Solve: $0.25n + 0.05(n + 5) = 2.95$.

> **TRY IT :: 8.88** Solve: $0.10d + 0.05(d - 5) = 2.15$.

▶ **MEDIA ::** ACCESS ADDITIONAL ONLINE RESOURCES

- Solve an Equation with Fractions with Variable Terms on Both Sides (http://www.openstaxcollege.org/l/24FracVariTerm)

- Ex 1: Solve an Equation with Fractions with Variable Terms on Both Sides (http://www.openstaxcollege.org/l/24Ex1VariTerms)

- Ex 2: Solve an Equation with Fractions with Variable Terms on Both Sides (http://www.openstaxcollege.org/l/24Ex2VariTerms)

- Solving Multiple Step Equations Involving Decimals (http://www.openstaxcollege.org/l/24EquawithDec)

- Ex: Solve a Linear Equation With Decimals and Variables on Both Sides (http://www.openstaxcollege.org/l/24LinEquaDec)

- Ex: Solve an Equation with Decimals and Parentheses (http://www.openstaxcollege.org/l/24DecParens)

8.4 EXERCISES

Practice Makes Perfect

Solve equations with fraction coefficients

In the following exercises, solve the equation by clearing the fractions.

209. $\frac{1}{4}x - \frac{1}{2} = -\frac{3}{4}$

210. $\frac{3}{4}x - \frac{1}{2} = \frac{1}{4}$

211. $\frac{5}{6}y - \frac{2}{3} = -\frac{3}{2}$

212. $\frac{5}{6}y - \frac{1}{3} = -\frac{7}{6}$

213. $\frac{1}{2}a + \frac{3}{8} = \frac{3}{4}$

214. $\frac{5}{8}b + \frac{1}{2} = -\frac{3}{4}$

215. $2 = \frac{1}{3}x - \frac{1}{2}x + \frac{2}{3}x$

216. $2 = \frac{3}{5}x - \frac{1}{3}x + \frac{2}{5}x$

217. $\frac{1}{4}m - \frac{4}{5}m + \frac{1}{2}m = -1$

218. $\frac{5}{6}n - \frac{1}{4}n - \frac{1}{2}n = -2$

219. $x + \frac{1}{2} = \frac{2}{3}x - \frac{1}{2}$

220. $x + \frac{3}{4} = \frac{1}{2}x - \frac{5}{4}$

221. $\frac{1}{3}w + \frac{5}{4} = w - \frac{1}{4}$

222. $\frac{3}{2}z + \frac{1}{3} = z - \frac{2}{3}$

223. $\frac{1}{2}x - \frac{1}{4} = \frac{1}{12}x + \frac{1}{6}$

224. $\frac{1}{2}a - \frac{1}{4} = \frac{1}{6}a + \frac{1}{12}$

225. $\frac{1}{3}b + \frac{1}{5} = \frac{2}{5}b - \frac{3}{5}$

226. $\frac{1}{3}x + \frac{2}{5} = \frac{1}{5}x - \frac{2}{5}$

227. $1 = \frac{1}{6}(12x - 6)$

228. $1 = \frac{1}{5}(15x - 10)$

229. $\frac{1}{4}(p - 7) = \frac{1}{3}(p + 5)$

230. $\frac{1}{5}(q + 3) = \frac{1}{2}(q - 3)$

231. $\frac{1}{2}(x + 4) = \frac{3}{4}$

232. $\frac{1}{3}(x + 5) = \frac{5}{6}$

Solve Equations with Decimal Coefficients

In the following exercises, solve the equation by clearing the decimals.

233. $0.6y + 3 = 9$

234. $0.4y - 4 = 2$

235. $3.6j - 2 = 5.2$

236. $2.1k + 3 = 7.2$

237. $0.4x + 0.6 = 0.5x - 1.2$

238. $0.7x + 0.4 = 0.6x + 2.4$

239. $0.23x + 1.47 = 0.37x - 1.05$

240. $0.48x + 1.56 = 0.58x - 0.64$

241. $0.9x - 1.25 = 0.75x + 1.75$

242. $1.2x - 0.91 = 0.8x + 2.29$

243. $0.05n + 0.10(n + 8) = 2.15$

244. $0.05n + 0.10(n + 7) = 3.55$

245. $0.10d + 0.25(d + 5) = 4.05$

246. $0.10d + 0.25(d + 7) = 5.25$

247. $0.05(q - 5) + 0.25q = 3.05$

248. $0.05(q - 8) + 0.25q = 4.10$

Everyday Math

249. Coins Taylor has 2.00 in dimes and pennies. The number of pennies is 2 more than the number of dimes. Solve the equation $0.10d + 0.01(d + 2) = 2$ for d, the number of dimes.

250. Stamps Travis bought 9.45 worth of 49-cent stamps and 21-cent stamps. The number of 21-cent stamps was 5 less than the number of 49-cent stamps. Solve the equation $0.49s + 0.21(s - 5) = 9.45$ for s, to find the number of 49-cent stamps Travis bought.

Writing Exercises

251. Explain how to find the least common denominator of $\frac{3}{8}$, $\frac{1}{6}$, and $\frac{2}{3}$.

252. If an equation has several fractions, how does multiplying both sides by the LCD make it easier to solve?

253. If an equation has fractions only on one side, why do you have to multiply both sides of the equation by the LCD?

254. In the equation $0.35x + 2.1 = 3.85$, what is the LCD? How do you know?

Self Check

ⓐ *After completing the exercises, use this checklist to evaluate your mastery of the objectives of this section.*

I can...	Confidently	With some help	No-I don't get it!
solve equations using a general strategy.			
solve equations with fraction coefficients.			
solve equations with decimal coefficients.			

ⓑ *Overall, after looking at the checklist, do you think you are well-prepared for the next Chapter? Why or why not?*

CHAPTER 8 REVIEW

KEY TERMS

solution of an equation A solution of an equation is a value of a variable that makes a true statement when substituted into the equation.

KEY CONCEPTS

8.1 Solve Equations Using the Subtraction and Addition Properties of Equality

- **Determine whether a number is a solution to an equation.**

  Step 1. Substitute the number for the variable in the equation.

  Step 2. Simplify the expressions on both sides of the equation.

  Step 3. Determine whether the resulting equation is true.

  If it is true, the number is a solution.
  If it is not true, the number is not a solution.

- **Subtraction and Addition Properties of Equality**

  ○ **Subtraction Property of Equality**
    For all real numbers a, b, and c,
    if $a = b$ then $a - c = b - c$.

  ○ **Addition Property of Equality**
    For all real numbers a, b, and c,
    if $a = b$ then $a + c = b + c$.

- **Translate a word sentence to an algebraic equation.**

  Step 1. Locate the "equals" word(s). Translate to an equal sign.

  Step 2. Translate the words to the left of the "equals" word(s) into an algebraic expression.

  Step 3. Translate the words to the right of the "equals" word(s) into an algebraic expression.

- **Problem-solving strategy**

  Step 1. Read the problem. Make sure you understand all the words and ideas.

  Step 2. Identify what you are looking for.

  Step 3. Name what you are looking for. Choose a variable to represent that quantity.

  Step 4. Translate into an equation. It may be helpful to restate the problem in one sentence with all the important information. Then, translate the English sentence into an algebra equation.

  Step 5. Solve the equation using good algebra techniques.

  Step 6. Check the answer in the problem and make sure it makes sense.

  Step 7. Answer the question with a complete sentence.

8.2 Solve Equations Using the Division and Multiplication Properties of Equality

- **Division and Multiplication Properties of Equality**

  ○ **Division Property of Equality:** For all real numbers a, b, c, and $c \neq 0$, if $a = b$, then $ac = bc$.

  ○ **Multiplication Property of Equality:** For all real numbers a, b, c, if $a = b$, then $ac = bc$.

8.3 Solve Equations with Variables and Constants on Both Sides

- **Solve an equation with variables and constants on both sides**

  Step 1. Choose one side to be the variable side and then the other will be the constant side.

  Step 2. Collect the variable terms to the variable side, using the Addition or Subtraction Property of Equality.

  Step 3. Collect the constants to the other side, using the Addition or Subtraction Property of Equality.

  Step 4. Make the coefficient of the variable 1, using the Multiplication or Division Property of Equality.

  Step 5. Check the solution by substituting into the original equation.

- **General strategy for solving linear equations**

Step 1. Simplify each side of the equation as much as possible. Use the Distributive Property to remove any parentheses. Combine like terms.

Step 2. Collect all the variable terms to one side of the equation. Use the Addition or Subtraction Property of Equality.

Step 3. Collect all the constant terms to the other side of the equation. Use the Addition or Subtraction Property of Equality.

Step 4. Make the coefficient of the variable term to equal to 1. Use the Multiplication or Division Property of Equality. State the solution to the equation.

Step 5. Check the solution. Substitute the solution into the original equation to make sure the result is a true statement.

8.4 Solve Equations with Fraction or Decimal Coefficients

- **Solve equations with fraction coefficients by clearing the fractions.**

Step 1. Find the least common denominator of *all* the fractions in the equation.

Step 2. Multiply both sides of the equation by that LCD. This clears the fractions.

Step 3. Solve using the General Strategy for Solving Linear Equations.

REVIEW EXERCISES

8.1 Solve Equations using the Subtraction and Addition Properties of Equality

In the following exercises, determine whether the given number is a solution to the equation.

255. $x + 16 = 31$, $x = 15$

256. $w - 8 = 5$, $w = 3$

257. $-9n = 45$, $n = 54$

258. $4a = 72$, $a = 18$

In the following exercises, solve the equation using the Subtraction Property of Equality.

259. $x + 7 = 19$

260. $y + 2 = -6$

261. $a + \frac{1}{3} = \frac{5}{3}$

262. $n + 3.6 = 5.1$

In the following exercises, solve the equation using the Addition Property of Equality.

263. $u - 7 = 10$

264. $x - 9 = -4$

265. $c - \frac{3}{11} = \frac{9}{11}$

266. $p - 4.8 = 14$

In the following exercises, solve the equation.

267. $n - 12 = 32$

268. $y + 16 = -9$

269. $f + \frac{2}{3} = 4$

270. $d - 3.9 = 8.2$

271. $y + 8 - 15 = -3$

272. $7x + 10 - 6x + 3 = 5$

273. $6(n - 1) - 5n = -14$

274. $8(3p + 5) - 23(p - 1) = 35$

In the following exercises, translate each English sentence into an algebraic equation and then solve it.

275. The sum of -6 and m is 25.

276. Four less than n is 13.

In the following exercises, translate into an algebraic equation and solve.

277. Rochelle's daughter is 11 years old. Her son is 3 years younger. How old is her son?

278. Tan weighs 146 pounds. Minh weighs 15 pounds more than Tan. How much does Minh weigh?

279. Peter paid $9.75 to go to the movies, which was $46.25 less than he paid to go to a concert. How much did he pay for the concert?

280. Elissa earned $152.84 this week, which was $21.65 more than she earned last week. How much did she earn last week?

8.2 Solve Equations using the Division and Multiplication Properties of Equality

In the following exercises, solve each equation using the Division Property of Equality.

281. $8x = 72$

282. $13a = -65$

283. $0.25p = 5.25$

284. $-y = 4$

In the following exercises, solve each equation using the Multiplication Property of Equality.

285. $\frac{n}{6} = 18$

286. $\frac{y}{-10} = 30$

287. $36 = \frac{3}{4}x$

288. $\frac{5}{8}u = \frac{15}{16}$

In the following exercises, solve each equation.

289. $-18m = -72$

290. $\frac{c}{9} = 36$

291. $0.45x = 6.75$

292. $\frac{11}{12} = \frac{2}{3}y$

293. $5r - 3r + 9r = 35 - 2$

294. $24x + 8x - 11x = -7 - 14$

8.3 Solve Equations with Variables and Constants on Both Sides

In the following exercises, solve the equations with constants on both sides.

295. $8p + 7 = 47$

296. $10w - 5 = 65$

297. $3x + 19 = -47$

298. $32 = -4 - 9n$

In the following exercises, solve the equations with variables on both sides.

299. $7y = 6y - 13$

300. $5a + 21 = 2a$

301. $k = -6k - 35$

302. $4x - \frac{3}{8} = 3x$

In the following exercises, solve the equations with constants and variables on both sides.

303. $12x - 9 = 3x + 45$

304. $5n - 20 = -7n - 80$

305. $4u + 16 = -19 - u$

306. $\frac{5}{8}c - 4 = \frac{3}{8}c + 4$

In the following exercises, solve each linear equation using the general strategy.

307. $6(x + 6) = 24$

308. $9(2p - 5) = 72$

309. $-(s + 4) = 18$

310. $8 + 3(n - 9) = 17$

311. $23 - 3(y - 7) = 8$

312. $\frac{1}{3}(6m + 21) = m - 7$

313. $8(r - 2) = 6(r + 10)$

314.
$5 + 7(2 - 5x) = 2(9x + 1) - (13x - 57)$

315. $4(3.5y + 0.25) = 365$

316. $0.25(q - 8) = 0.1(q + 7)$

8.4 Solve Equations with Fraction or Decimal Coefficients

In the following exercises, solve each equation by clearing the fractions.

317. $\frac{2}{5}n - \frac{1}{10} = \frac{7}{10}$

318. $\frac{1}{3}x + \frac{1}{5}x = 8$

319. $\frac{3}{4}a - \frac{1}{3} = \frac{1}{2}a + \frac{5}{6}$

320. $\frac{1}{2}(k + 3) = \frac{1}{3}(k + 16)$

In the following exercises, solve each equation by clearing the decimals.

321. $0.8x - 0.3 = 0.7x + 0.2$

322. $0.36u + 2.55 = 0.41u + 6.8$

323. $0.6p - 1.9 = 0.78p + 1.7$

324. $0.10d + 0.05(d - 4) = 2.05$

PRACTICE TEST

325. Determine whether each number is a solution to the equation.
$3x + 5 = 23.$

ⓐ 6   ⓑ $\frac{23}{5}$

In the following exercises, solve each equation.

326. $n - 18 = 31$

327. $9c = 144$

328. $4y - 8 = 16$

329. $-8x - 15 + 9x - 1 = -21$

330. $-15a = 120$

331. $\frac{2}{3}x = 6$

332. $x + 3.8 = 8.2$

333. $10y = -5y + 60$

334. $8n + 2 = 6n + 12$

335. $9m - 2 - 4m + m = 42 - 8$

336. $-5(2x + 1) = 45$

337. $-(d + 9) = 23$

338. $\frac{1}{3}(6m + 21) = m - 7$

339. $2(6x + 5) - 8 = -22$

340.
$8(3a + 5) - 7(4a - 3) = 20 - 3a$

341. $\frac{1}{4}p + \frac{1}{3} = \frac{1}{2}$

342. $0.1d + 0.25(d + 8) = 4.1$

343. Translate and solve: The difference of twice x and 4 is 16.

344. Samuel paid $25.82 for gas this week, which was $3.47 less than he paid last week. How much did he pay last week?

Figure 9.1 Note the many individual shapes in this building. (credit: Bert Kaufmann, Flickr)

Chapter Outline

Introduction

We are surrounded by all sorts of geometry. Architects use geometry to design buildings. Artists create vivid images out of colorful geometric shapes. Street signs, automobiles, and product packaging all take advantage of geometric properties. In this chapter, we will begin by considering a formal approach to solving problems and use it to solve a variety of common problems, including making decisions about money. Then we will explore geometry and relate it to everyday situations, using the problem-solving strategy we develop.

9.1 | Use a Problem Solving Strategy

Learning Objectives

By the end of this section, you will be able to:

   Approach word problems with a positive attitude
   Use a problem solving strategy for word problems
   Solve number problems

Be Prepared!

Before you get started, take this readiness quiz.

1.   Translate "6 less than twice x" into an algebraic expression.
     If you missed this problem, review Example 2.25.

2.   Solve: $\frac{2}{3}x = 24$.
     If you missed this problem, review Example 8.16.

3.   Solve: $3x + 8 = 14$.
     If you missed this problem, review Example 8.20.

Approach Word Problems with a Positive Attitude

The world is full of word problems. How much money do I need to fill the car with gas? How much should I tip the server at a restaurant? How many socks should I pack for vacation? How big a turkey do I need to buy for Thanksgiving dinner, and what time do I need to put it in the oven? If my sister and I buy our mother a present, how much will each of us pay?

Now that we can solve equations, we are ready to apply our new skills to word problems. Do you know anyone who has had negative experiences in the past with word problems? Have you ever had thoughts like the student in Figure 9.2?

Figure 9.2 Negative thoughts about word problems can be barriers to success.

When we feel we have no control, and continue repeating negative thoughts, we set up barriers to success. We need to calm our fears and change our negative feelings.

Start with a fresh slate and begin to think positive thoughts like the student in Figure 9.3. Read the positive thoughts and say them out loud.

Figure 9.3 When it comes to word problems, a positive attitude is a big step toward success.

If we take control and believe we can be successful, we will be able to master word problems.

Think of something that you can do now but couldn't do three years ago. Whether it's driving a car, snowboarding, cooking a gourmet meal, or speaking a new language, you have been able to learn and master a new skill. Word problems are no different. Even if you have struggled with word problems in the past, you have acquired many new math skills that will help you succeed now!

Use a Problem-solving Strategy for Word Problems

In earlier chapters, you translated word phrases into algebraic expressions, using some basic mathematical vocabulary and symbols. Since then you've increased your math vocabulary as you learned about more algebraic procedures, and you've had more practice translating from words into algebra.

You have also translated word sentences into algebraic equations and solved some word problems. The word problems applied math to everyday situations. You had to restate the situation in one sentence, assign a variable, and then write an equation to solve. This method works as long as the situation is familiar to you and the math is not too complicated.

Now we'll develop a strategy you can use to solve any word problem. This strategy will help you become successful with word problems. We'll demonstrate the strategy as we solve the following problem.

EXAMPLE 9.1

Pete bought a shirt on sale for $18,$ which is one-half the original price. What was the original price of the shirt?

⊘ Solution

Step 1. Read the problem. Make sure you understand all the words and ideas. You may need to read the problem two or more times. If there are words you don't understand, look them up in a dictionary or on the Internet.
  • *In this problem, do you understand what is being discussed? Do you understand every word?*

Step 2. Identify what you are looking for. It's hard to find something if you are not sure what it is! Read the problem again and look for words that tell you what you are looking for!

  • *In this problem, the words "what was the original price of the shirt" tell you that what you are looking for: the original price of the shirt.*

Step 3. Name what you are looking for. Choose a variable to represent that quantity. You can use any letter for the variable, but it may help to choose one that helps you remember what it represents.

  • *Let* $p =$ *the original price of the shirt*

Step 4. Translate into an equation. It may help to first restate the problem in one sentence, with all the important information. Then translate the sentence into an equation.

$$\begin{array}{ccccc} 18 & \text{is} & \text{one-half} & \text{of} & \text{the original price .} \\ 18 & = & \dfrac{1}{2} & \cdot & p \end{array}$$

Step 5. Solve the equation using good algebra techniques. Even if you know the answer right away, using algebra will better prepare you to solve problems that do not have obvious answers.

Write the equation.	$18 = \dfrac{1}{2}p$
Multiply both sides by 2.	$2 \cdot 18 = 2 \cdot \dfrac{1}{2}p$
Simplify.	$36 = p$

Step 6. Check the answer in the problem and make sure it makes sense.

  • *We found that* $p = 36,$ *which means the original price was* $36.$ *Does* 36 *make sense in the problem? Yes, because* 18 *is one-half of* $36,$ *and the shirt was on sale at half the original price.*

Step 7. Answer the question with a complete sentence.

  • *The problem asked "What was the original price of the shirt?" The answer to the question is: "The original price of the shirt was* $36."$

If this were a homework exercise, our work might look like this:

Let p = the original price.

18 is one-half the original price.

$$18 = \frac{1}{2}p$$

$$2 \cdot 18 = 2 \cdot \frac{1}{2}p$$

$$36 = p$$

Check:
  Is $36 a reasonable price for a shirt? *Yes.*
  Is 18 one-half of 36? *Yes.*
The original price of the shirt was $36.

> **TRY IT : :** 9.1

Joaquin bought a bookcase on sale for $120, which was two-thirds the original price. What was the original price of the bookcase?

> **TRY IT : :** 9.2

Two-fifths of the people in the senior center dining room are men. If there are 16 men, what is the total number of people in the dining room?

We list the steps we took to solve the previous example.

Problem-Solving Strategy

Step 1.   **Read** the word problem. Make sure you understand all the words and ideas. You may need to read the problem two or more times. If there are words you don't understand, look them up in a dictionary or on the internet.

Step 2.   **Identify** what you are looking for.

Step 3.   **Name** what you are looking for. Choose a variable to represent that quantity.

Step 4.   **Translate** into an equation. It may be helpful to first restate the problem in one sentence before translating.

Step 5.   **Solve** the equation using good algebra techniques.

Step 6.   **Check** the answer in the problem. Make sure it makes sense.

Step 7.   **Answer** the question with a complete sentence.

Let's use this approach with another example.

EXAMPLE 9.2

Yash brought apples and bananas to a picnic. The number of apples was three more than twice the number of bananas. Yash brought 11 apples to the picnic. How many bananas did he bring?

⊘ **Solution**

Step 1. **Read** the problem.

Step 2. **Identify** what you are looking for.

How many bananas did he bring?

Step 3. **Name** what you are looking for.
Choose a variable to represent the number of bananas.

Let $b =$ number of bananas

Step 4. **Translate.** Restate the problem in one sentence with all the important information. Translate into an equation.

The number of apples	was	3	more than	twice the number of bananas	.
11	$=$	3	1	2b	

Step 5. **Solve** the equation.

$$11 = 2b + 3$$

Subtract 3 from each side.

$$11 - 3 = 2b + 3 - 3$$

Simplify.

$$8 = 2b$$

Divide each side by 2.

$$\frac{8}{2} = \frac{2b}{2}$$

Simplify.

$$4 = b$$

Step 6. **Check:** First, is our answer reasonable? Yes, bringing four bananas to a picnic seems reasonable. The problem says the number of apples was three more than twice the number of bananas. If there are four bananas, does that make eleven apples? Twice 4 bananas is 8. Three more than 8 is 11.

Step 7. **Answer** the question.

Yash brought 4 bananas to the picnic.

> **TRY IT :: 9.3**

> Guillermo bought textbooks and notebooks at the bookstore. The number of textbooks was 3 more than the number of notebooks. He bought 5 textbooks. How many notebooks did he buy?

> **TRY IT :: 9.4**

> Gerry worked Sudoku puzzles and crossword puzzles this week. The number of Sudoku puzzles he completed is seven more than the number of crossword puzzles. He completed 14 Sudoku puzzles. How many crossword puzzles did he complete?

In Solve Sales Tax, Commission, and Discount Applications, we learned how to translate and solve basic percent equations and used them to solve sales tax and commission applications. In the next example, we will apply our Problem Solving Strategy to more applications of percent.

EXAMPLE 9.3

Nga's car insurance premium increased by $60, which was 8% of the original cost. What was the original cost of the premium?

⊘ Solution

Step 1. **Read** the problem. Remember, if there are words you don't understand, look them up.	
Step 2. **Identify** what you are looking for.	the original cost of the premium
Step 3. **Name.** Choose a variable to represent the original cost of premium.	Let c = the original cost
Step 4. **Translate.** Restate as one sentence. Translate into an equation.	$\underbrace{\$60}$ $\underbrace{\text{was}}$ $\underbrace{8\%}$ $\underbrace{\text{of}}$ $\underbrace{\text{the original cost}}$. $60 \quad = \quad 0.08 \quad \cdot \quad c$
Step 5. **Solve** the equation.	$60 = 0.08c$
Divide both sides by 0.08.	$\dfrac{60}{0.08} = \dfrac{0.08c}{0.08}$
Simplify.	$c = 750$
Step 6. **Check:** Is our answer reasonable? Yes, a \$750 premium on auto insurance is reasonable. Now let's check our algebra. Is 8% of 750 equal to 60? $\qquad 750 = c$ $0.08(750) = 60$ $\qquad 60 = 60 \checkmark$	
Step 7. **Answer** the question.	The original cost of Nga's premium was \$750.

> **TRY IT : : 9.5**
>
> Pilar's rent increased by 4%. The increase was $\$38$. What was the original amount of Pilar's rent?

> **TRY IT : : 9.6**
>
> Steve saves 12% of his paycheck each month. If he saved $\$504$ last month, how much was his paycheck?

Solve Number Problems

Now we will translate and solve **number problems**. In number problems, you are given some clues about one or more numbers, and you use these clues to build an equation. Number problems don't usually arise on an everyday basis, but they provide a good introduction to practicing the Problem Solving Strategy. Remember to look for clue words such as *difference*, *of*, and *and*.

EXAMPLE 9.4

The difference of a number and six is 13. Find the number.

⊘ Solution

Step 1. **Read** the problem. Do you understand all the words?

Step 2. **Identify** what you are looking for.	the number
Step 3. **Name.** Choose a variable to represent the number.	Let $n =$ the number

Step 4. **Translate.** Restate as one sentence. Translate into an equation.

The difference of a number and 6 is 13.

$$n - 6 = 13$$

$$n - 6 = 13$$

Step 5. **Solve** the equation.
Add 6 to both sides.
Simplify.

$$n - 6 + 6 = 13 + 6$$

$$n = 19$$

Step 6. **Check:**
The difference of 19 and 6 is 13. It checks.

Step 7. **Answer** the question.	The number is 19.

> **TRY IT : : 9.7**   The difference of a number and eight is 17. Find the number.

> **TRY IT : : 9.8**   The difference of a number and eleven is −7. Find the number.

EXAMPLE 9.5

The sum of twice a number and seven is 15. Find the number.

⊘ Solution

Step 1. **Read** the problem.

Step 2. **Identify** what you are looking for.	the number
Step 3. **Name.** Choose a variable to represent the number.	Let $n =$ the number

Step 4. **Translate.** Restate the problem as one sentence.
Translate into an equation.

The sum of twice a number and 7 is 15.

$$2 \cdot n + 7 = 15$$

Step 5. **Solve** the equation.

$$2n + 7 = 15$$

Subtract 7 from each side and simplify.

$$2n = 8$$

Divide each side by 2 and simplify.

$$n = 4$$

Step 6. **Check:** is the sum of twice 4 and 7 equal to 15?

$$2 \cdot 4 + 7 = 15$$

$$8 + 7 = 15$$

$$15 = 15 \checkmark$$

Step 7. **Answer** the question.	The number is 4.

> **TRY IT ::** 9.9   The sum of four times a number and two is 14. Find the number.

> **TRY IT ::** 9.10   The sum of three times a number and seven is 25. Find the number.

Some number word problems ask you to find two or more numbers. It may be tempting to name them all with different variables, but so far we have only solved equations with one variable. We will define the numbers in terms of the same variable. Be sure to read the problem carefully to discover how all the numbers relate to each other.

EXAMPLE 9.6

One number is five more than another. The sum of the numbers is twenty-one. Find the numbers.

⊘ **Solution**

Step 1. **Read** the problem.	
Step 2. **Identify** what you are looking for.	You are looking for two numbers.
Step 3. **Name.** Choose a variable to represent the first number. What do you know about the second number? Translate.	Let $n = $ 1st number One number is five more than another. $x + 5 = 2^{nd}$ number
Step 4. **Translate.** Restate the problem as one sentence with all the important information. Translate into an equation. Substitute the variable expressions.	The sum of the numbers is 21. The sum of the 1st number and the 2nd number is 21. $\underbrace{1^{st}\text{ number}}_{n} + \underbrace{2^{nd}\text{ number}}_{n+5} = 21$ $n + n + 5 = 21$
Step 5. **Solve** the equation.	$n + n + 5 = 21$
Combine like terms.	$2n + 5 = 21$
Subtract five from both sides and simplify.	$2n = 16$
Divide by two and simplify.	$n = 8 \quad 1^{st}$ number
Find the second number too.	$n + 5 \quad 2^{nd}$ number
Substitute $n = 8$	$8 + 5$
	13
Step 6. **Check:**	
Do these numbers check in the problem? Is one number 5 more than the other? Is thirteen, 5 more than 8? Yes.	$13 \overset{?}{=} 8 + 5$ $13 = 13\ ✓$
Is the sum of the two numbers 21?	$8 + 13 \overset{?}{=} 21$ $21 = 21\ ✓$
Step 7. **Answer** the question.	The numbers are 8 and 13.

> **TRY IT :: 9.11**

One number is six more than another. The sum of the numbers is twenty-four. Find the numbers.

> **TRY IT :: 9.12**

The sum of two numbers is fifty-eight. One number is four more than the other. Find the numbers.

EXAMPLE 9.7

The sum of two numbers is negative fourteen. One number is four less than the other. Find the numbers.

⊘ **Solution**

Step 1. **Read** the problem.

Step 2. **Identify** what you are looking for.

two numbers

Step 3. **Name.** Choose a variable. What do you know about the second number? Translate.

Let n = 1st number
One number is 4 less than the other.
$n - 4$ = 2nd number

Step 4. **Translate.**
Write as one sentence.
Translate into an equation.
Substitute the variable expressions.

The sum of two numbers is negative fourteen.

$$\underset{n}{\underbrace{1^{st} \text{ number}}} + \underset{n-4}{\underbrace{2^{nd} \text{ number}}} = -14$$

Step 5. **Solve** the equation.

$$n + n - 4 = -14$$

Combine like terms.

$$2n - 4 = -14$$

Add 4 to each side and simplify.

$$2n = -10$$

Divide by 2.

$$n = -5 \quad 1^{st} \text{ number}$$

Substitute $n = -5$ to find the 2nd number.

$$n - 4 \quad 2^{nd} \text{ number}$$

$$-5 - 4$$

$$-9$$

Step 6. **Check:**

$$-5 - 4 \overset{?}{=} -9$$

Is −9 four less than −5?

$$-9 = -9 \checkmark$$

Is their sum −14?

$$-5 + (-9) \overset{?}{=} -14$$

$$-14 = -14 \checkmark$$

Step 7. **Answer** the question.

The numbers are −5 and −9.

> **TRY IT :: 9.13**

The sum of two numbers is negative twenty-three. One number is 7 less than the other. Find the numbers.

> **TRY IT : : 9.14**

The sum of two numbers is negative eighteen. One number is 40 more than the other. Find the numbers.

EXAMPLE 9.8

One number is ten more than twice another. Their sum is one. Find the numbers.

⊘ **Solution**

Step 1. **Read** the problem.	
Step 2. **Identify** what you are looking for.	two numbers
Step 3. **Name.** Choose a variable. One number is ten more than twice another.	Let x = 1st number $2x + 10$ = 2nd number
Step 4. **Translate.** Restate as one sentence.	Their sum is one.
Translate into an equation	The sum of the two numbers is 1. $$x + (2x + 10) \qquad = \quad 1$$
Step 5. **Solve** the equation.	$x + 2x + 10 = 1$
Combine like terms.	$3x + 10 = 1$
Subtract 10 from each side.	$3x = -9$
Divide each side by 3 to get the first number.	$x = -3$
Substitute to get the second number.	$2x + 10$ $2(-3) + 10$ 4

Step 6. **Check.**

$$2(-3) + 10 \stackrel{?}{=} 4$$

Is 4 ten more than twice −3?

$$-6 + 10 = 4$$
$$4 = 4 \checkmark$$

Is their sum 1?

$$-3 + 4 \stackrel{?}{=} 1$$
$$1 = 1 \checkmark$$

| Step 7. **Answer** the question. | The numbers are −3 and 4. |

> **TRY IT : : 9.15**   One number is eight more than twice another. Their sum is negative four. Find the numbers.

> **TRY IT : : 9.16**

One number is three more than three times another. Their sum is negative five. Find the numbers.

Consecutive integers are integers that immediately follow each other. Some examples of consecutive integers are:

$$...1, 2, 3, 4,...$$

$$...-10, -9, -8, -7,...$$

$$...150, 151, 152, 153,...$$

Notice that each number is one more than the number preceding it. So if we define the first integer as n, the next consecutive integer is $n + 1$. The one after that is one more than $n + 1$, so it is $n + 1 + 1$, or $n + 2$.

n	1st integer
$n + 1$	2nd consecutive integer
$n + 2$	3rd consecutive integer

EXAMPLE 9.9

The sum of two consecutive integers is 47. Find the numbers.

⊘ **Solution**

Step 1. **Read** the problem.	
Step 2. **Identify** what you are looking for.	two consecutive integers
Step 3. **Name.**	Let $n = 1^{st}$ integer $n + 1$ = next consecutive integer
Step 4. **Translate.** Restate as one sentence. Translate into an equation.	The sum of the integers is 47. $n + n + 1 \qquad = \quad 47$
Step 5. **Solve** the equation.	$n + n + 1 = 47$
Combine like terms.	$2n + 1 = 47$
Subtract 1 from each side.	$2n = 46$
Divide each side by 2.	$n = 23 \quad 1^{st}$ integer
Substitute to get the second number.	$n + 1 \quad 2^{nd}$ integer $23 + 1$ 24
Step 6. **Check:**	$23 + 24 \overset{?}{=} 47$ $47 = 47 \checkmark$
Step 7. **Answer** the question.	The two consecutive integers are 23 and 24.

> **TRY IT : : 9.17**   The sum of two consecutive integers is 95. Find the numbers.

> **TRY IT : : 9.18**   The sum of two consecutive integers is -31. Find the numbers.

EXAMPLE 9.10

Find three consecutive integers whose sum is 42.

⊘ **Solution**

Step 1. Read the problem.

Step 2. **Identify** what you are looking for.	three consecutive integers

Step 3. **Name.**	Let n = 1st integer $n + 1$ = 2nd consecutive integer $n + 2$ = 3rd consecutive integer

Step 4. **Translate.** Restate as one sentence. Translate into an equation.	The sum of the three integers is 42. $n + n + 1 + n + 2 = 42$

Step 5. **Solve** the equation.	$n + n + 1 + n + 2 = 42$
Combine like terms.	$3n + 3 = 42$
Subtract 3 from each side.	$3n = 39$
Divide each side by 3.	$n = 13$ 1st integer
Substitute to get the second number.	$n + 1$ 2nd integer
	$13 + 1$
	24
Substitute to get the third number.	$n + 2$ 3rd integer
	$13 + 2$
	15

Step 6. **Check:**	$13 + 14 + 15 \overset{?}{=} 42$ $42 = 42$ ✓

Step 7. **Answer** the question.	The three consecutive integers are 13, 14, and 15.

> **TRY IT :: 9.19**   Find three consecutive integers whose sum is 96.

> **TRY IT :: 9.20**   Find three consecutive integers whose sum is -36.

⊡ **LINKS TO LITERACY**

The Links to Literacy activities *Math Curse*, *Missing Mittens* and *Among the Odds and Evens* will provide you with another view of the topics covered in this section.

9.1 EXERCISES
Practice Makes Perfect

Use a Problem-solving Strategy for Word Problems

In the following exercises, use the problem-solving strategy for word problems to solve. Answer in complete sentences.

1. Two-thirds of the children in the fourth-grade class are girls. If there are 20 girls, what is the total number of children in the class?

2. Three-fifths of the members of the school choir are women. If there are 24 women, what is the total number of choir members?

3. Zachary has 25 country music CDs, which is one-fifth of his CD collection. How many CDs does Zachary have?

4. One-fourth of the candies in a bag of are red. If there are 23 red candies, how many candies are in the bag?

5. There are 16 girls in a school club. The number of girls is 4 more than twice the number of boys. Find the number of boys in the club.

6. There are 18 Cub Scouts in Troop 645. The number of scouts is 3 more than five times the number of adult leaders. Find the number of adult leaders.

7. Lee is emptying dishes and glasses from the dishwasher. The number of dishes is 8 less than the number of glasses. If there are 9 dishes, what is the number of glasses?

8. The number of puppies in the pet store window is twelve less than the number of dogs in the store. If there are 6 puppies in the window, what is the number of dogs in the store?

9. After 3 months on a diet, Lisa had lost 12% of her original weight. She lost 21 pounds. What was Lisa's original weight?

10. Tricia got a 6% raise on her weekly salary. The raise was $\$30$ per week. What was her original weekly salary?

11. Tim left a $\$9$ tip for a $\$50$ restaurant bill. What percent tip did he leave?

12. Rashid left a $\$15$ tip for a $\$75$ restaurant bill. What percent tip did he leave?

13. Yuki bought a dress on sale for $\$72$. The sale price was 60% of the original price. What was the original price of the dress?

14. Kim bought a pair of shoes on sale for $\$40.50$. The sale price was 45% of the original price. What was the original price of the shoes?

Solve Number Problems

In the following exercises, solve each number word problem.

15. The sum of a number and eight is 12. Find the number.

16. The sum of a number and nine is 17. Find the number.

17. The difference of a number and twelve is 3. Find the number.

18. The difference of a number and eight is 4. Find the number.

19. The sum of three times a number and eight is 23. Find the number.

20. The sum of twice a number and six is 14. Find the number.

21. The difference of twice a number and seven is 17. Find the number.

22. The difference of four times a number and seven is 21. Find the number.

23. Three times the sum of a number and nine is 12. Find the number.

24. Six times the sum of a number and eight is 30. Find the number.

25. One number is six more than the other. Their sum is forty-two. Find the numbers.

26. One number is five more than the other. Their sum is thirty-three. Find the numbers.

27. The sum of two numbers is twenty. One number is four less than the other. Find the numbers.

28. The sum of two numbers is twenty-seven. One number is seven less than the other. Find the numbers.

29. A number is one more than twice another number. Their sum is negative five. Find the numbers.

30. One number is six more than five times another. Their sum is six. Find the numbers.

31. The sum of two numbers is fourteen. One number is two less than three times the other. Find the numbers.

32. The sum of two numbers is zero. One number is nine less than twice the other. Find the numbers.

33. One number is fourteen less than another. If their sum is increased by seven, the result is 85. Find the numbers.

34. One number is eleven less than another. If their sum is increased by eight, the result is 71. Find the numbers.

35. The sum of two consecutive integers is 77. Find the integers.

36. The sum of two consecutive integers is 89. Find the integers.

37. The sum of two consecutive integers is −23. Find the integers.

38. The sum of two consecutive integers is −37. Find the integers.

39. The sum of three consecutive integers is 78. Find the integers.

40. The sum of three consecutive integers is 60. Find the integers.

41. Find three consecutive integers whose sum is −36.

42. Find three consecutive integers whose sum is −3.

Everyday Math

43. Shopping Patty paid $35 for a purse on sale for $10 off the original price. What was the original price of the purse?

44. Shopping Travis bought a pair of boots on sale for $25 off the original price. He paid $60 for the boots. What was the original price of the boots?

45. Shopping Minh spent $6.25 on 5 sticker books to give his nephews. Find the cost of each sticker book.

46. Shopping Alicia bought a package of 8 peaches for $3.20. Find the cost of each peach.

47. Shopping Tom paid $1,166.40 for a new refrigerator, including $86.40 tax. What was the price of the refrigerator before tax?

48. Shopping Kenji paid $2,279 for a new living room set, including $129 tax. What was the price of the living room set before tax?

Writing Exercises

49. Write a few sentences about your thoughts and opinions of word problems. Are these thoughts positive, negative, or neutral? If they are negative, how might you change your way of thinking in order to do better?

50. When you start to solve a word problem, how do you decide what to let the variable represent?

Self Check

ⓐ *After completing the exercises, use this checklist to evaluate your mastery of the objectives of this section.*

I can...	Confidently	With some help	No-I don't get it!
approach word problems with a positive attitude.			
use a problem solving strategy for word problems.			
solve number problems.			

ⓑ *If most of your checks were:*

...confidently. Congratulations! You have achieved the objectives in this section. Reflect on the study skills you used so that you can continue to use them. What did you do to become confident of your ability to do these things? Be specific.

...with some help. This must be addressed quickly because topics you do not master become potholes in your road to success.

In math, every topic builds upon previous work. It is important to make sure you have a strong foundation before you move on. Who can you ask for help? Your fellow classmates and instructor are good resources. Is there a place on campus where math tutors are available? Can your study skills be improved?

...no—I don't get it! This is a warning sign and you must not ignore it. You should get help right away or you will quickly be overwhelmed. See your instructor as soon as you can to discuss your situation. Together you can come up with a plan to get you the help you need.

9.2 Solve Money Applications

Learning Objectives

By the end of this section, you will be able to:

- Solve coin word problems
- Solve ticket and stamp word problems

Be Prepared!

Before you get started, take this readiness quiz.

1. Multiply: $14(0.25)$.

   If you missed this problem, review Example 5.15.

2. Simplify: $100(0.2 + 0.05n)$.

   If you missed this problem, review Example 7.22.

3. Solve: $0.25x + 0.10(x + 4) = 2.5$

   If you missed this problem, review Example 8.44.

Solve Coin Word Problems

Imagine taking a handful of coins from your pocket or purse and placing them on your desk. How would you determine the value of that pile of coins?

If you can form a step-by-step plan for finding the total value of the coins, it will help you as you begin solving coin word problems.

One way to bring some order to the mess of coins would be to separate the coins into stacks according to their value. Quarters would go with quarters, dimes with dimes, nickels with nickels, and so on. To get the total value of all the coins, you would add the total value of each pile.

Figure 9.4 To determine the total value of a stack of nickels, multiply the number of nickels times the value of one nickel.(Credit: Darren Hester via ppdigital)

How would you determine the value of each pile? Think about the dime pile—how much is it worth? If you count the number of dimes, you'll know how many you have—the *number* of dimes.

But this does not tell you the *value* of all the dimes. Say you counted 17 dimes, how much are they worth? Each dime is worth $0.10 —that is the *value* of one dime. To find the total value of the pile of 17 dimes, multiply 17 by $0.10 to get $1.70. This is the total value of all 17 dimes.

$$17 \cdot \$0.10 = \$1.70$$
$$\text{number} \cdot \text{value} = \text{total value}$$

Finding the Total Value for Coins of the Same Type

For coins of the same type, the total value can be found as follows:

$$number \cdot value = total\ value$$

where *number* is the number of coins, *value* is the value of each coin, and *total value* is the total value of all the coins.

You could continue this process for each type of coin, and then you would know the total value of each type of coin. To get the total value of *all* the coins, add the total value of each type of coin.

Let's look at a specific case. Suppose there are 14 quarters, 17 dimes, 21 nickels, and 39 pennies. We'll make a table to organize the information – the type of coin, the number of each, and the value.

Type	Number	Value ($)	Total Value ($)
Quarters	14	0.25	3.50
Dimes	17	0.10	1.70
Nickels	21	0.05	1.05
Pennies	39	0.01	0.39
			6.64

Table 9.11

The total value of all the coins is $6.64. Notice how Table 9.11 helped us organize all the information. Let's see how this method is used to solve a coin word problem.

EXAMPLE 9.11

Adalberto has $2.25 in dimes and nickels in his pocket. He has nine more nickels than dimes. How many of each type of coin does he have?

⊘ **Solution**

Step 1. **Read** the problem. Make sure you understand all the words and ideas.
  • Determine the types of coins involved.

Think about the strategy we used to find the value of the handful of coins. The first thing you need is to notice what types of coins are involved. Adalberto has dimes and nickels.

  • **Create a table** to organize the information.
    ◦ Label the columns 'type', 'number', 'value', 'total value'.
    ◦ List the types of coins.
    ◦ Write in the value of each type of coin.
    ◦ Write in the total value of all the coins.

We can work this problem all in cents or in dollars. Here we will do it in dollars and put in the dollar sign ($) in the table as a reminder.

The value of a dime is $0.10 and the value of a nickel is $0.05. The total value of all the coins is $2.25.

Type	Number	Value ($)	Total Value ($)
Dimes		0.10	
Nickels		0.05	
			2.25

Step 2. **Identify** what you are looking for.

- We are asked to find the number of dimes and nickels Adalberto has.

Step 3. **Name** what you are looking for.

- Use variable expressions to represent the number of each type of coin.
- Multiply the number times the value to get the total value of each type of coin.
In this problem you cannot count each type of coin—that is what you are looking for—but you have a clue. There are nine more nickels than dimes. The number of nickels is nine more than the number of dimes.

  Let d = number of dimes.

  $d + 9$ = number of nickels

Fill in the "number" column to help get everything organized.

Type	Number	Value ($)	Total Value ($)
Dimes	d	0.10	
Nickels	$d + 9$	0.05	
			2.25

Now we have all the information we need from the problem!

You multiply the number times the value to get the total value of each type of coin. While you do not know the actual number, you do have an expression to represent it.

And so now multiply $number \cdot value$ and write the results in the Total Value column.

Type	Number	Value ($)	Total Value ($)
Dimes	d	0.10	$0.10d$
Nickels	$d + 9$	0.05	$0.05(d + 9)$
			2.25

Step 4. **Translate** into an **equation**. Restate the problem in one sentence. Then translate into an equation.

$$\underbrace{\text{value of the dimes}} + \underbrace{\text{value of the nickels}} = \underbrace{\text{total value of the coins}}$$

$$0.10d + 0.05(d + 9) = 2.25$$

Step 5. **Solve** the equation using good algebra techniques.

Write the equation.	$0.10d + 0.05(d + 9) = 2.25$
Distribute.	$0.10d + 0.05d + 0.45 = 2.25$
Combine like terms.	$0.15d + 0.45 = 2.25$
Subtract 0.45 from each side.	$0.15d = 1.80$
Divide to find the number of dimes.	$d = 12$
The number of nickels is $d + 9$	$d + 9$ $12 + 9$ 21

Step 6. **Check.**

12 dimes: 12(0.10) = 1.20
21 nickels: 21(0.05) = 1.05
$2.25 ✓

Step 7. **Answer** the question.

Adalberto has twelve dimes and twenty-one nickels.

If this were a homework exercise, our work might look like this:

Adalberto has $2.25 in dimes and nickels in his pocket. He has nine more nickels than dimes. How many of each type does he have?

Type	Number • Value($)		= Total Value ($)
Dimes	d	0.10	0.10d
Nickels	d + 9	0.05	0.05(d + 9)
			2.25

$$0.10d + 0.05d + 0.45 = 2.25 \quad\quad d + 9$$
$$0.15d + 0.45 = 2.25 \quad\quad 12 + 9$$
$$0.15d = 1.80 \quad\quad 21 \text{ nickles}$$
$$d = 12 \text{ dimes}$$

Check:

12 dimes   12(0.10) = 1.20
21 nickels   21(0.05) = 1.05
$2.25

> **TRY IT :: 9.21**

Michaela has $2.05 in dimes and nickels in her change purse. She has seven more dimes than nickels. How many coins of each type does she have?

> **TRY IT :: 9.22**

Liliana has $2.10 in nickels and quarters in her backpack. She has 12 more nickels than quarters. How many coins of each type does she have?

HOW TO :: SOLVE A COIN WORD PROBLEM.

Step 1.   **Read** the problem. Make sure you understand all the words and ideas, and create a table to organize the information.

Step 2.   **Identify** what you are looking for.

Step 3.   **Name** what you are looking for. Choose a variable to represent that quantity.

   ◦   Use variable expressions to represent the number of each type of coin and write them in the table.

   ◦   Multiply the number times the value to get the total value of each type of coin.

Step 4.   **Translate** into an equation. Write the equation by adding the total values of all the types of coins.

Step 5.   **Solve** the equation using good algebra techniques.

Step 6.   **Check** the answer in the problem and make sure it makes sense.

Step 7.   **Answer** the question with a complete sentence.

   You may find it helpful to put all the numbers into the table to make sure they check.

Type	Number	Value ($)	Total Value

Table 9.16

EXAMPLE 9.12

Maria has $2.43 in quarters and pennies in her wallet. She has twice as many pennies as quarters. How many coins of each type does she have?

 Solution

Step 1. **Read** the problem.
   • Determine the types of coins involved.
      We know that Maria has quarters and pennies.
   • Create a table to organize the information.
      ◦ Label the columns type, number, value, total value.
      ◦ List the types of coins.
      ◦ Write in the value of each type of coin.
      ◦ Write in the total value of all the coins.

Type	Number	Value ($)	Total Value ($)
Quarters		0.25	
Pennies		0.01	
			2.43

Step 2. **Identify** what you are looking for.

   We are looking for the number of quarters and pennies.

Step 3. **Name:** Represent the number of quarters and pennies using variables.

We know Maria has twice as many pennies as quarters. The number of pennies is defined in terms of quarters.

Let q represent the number of quarters.

Then the number of pennies is $2q$.

Type	Number	Value ($)	Total Value ($)
Quarters	q	0.25	
Pennies	$2q$	0.01	
			2.43

Multiply the 'number' and the 'value' to get the 'total value' of each type of coin.

Type	Number	Value ($)	Total Value ($)
Quarters	q	0.25	$0.25q$
Pennies	$2q$	0.01	$0.01(2q)$
			2.43

Step 4. **Translate.** Write the equation by adding the 'total value' of all the types of coins.
Step 5. **Solve** the equation.

Write the equation. $\quad 0.25q + 0.01(2q) = 2.43$

Multiply. $\quad 0.25q + 0.02q = 2.43$

Combine like terms. $\quad 0.27q = 2.43$

Divide by 0.27. $\quad q = 9$ quarters

The number of pennies is $2q$.
$$2q$$
$$2 \cdot 9$$
$$18 \text{ pennies}$$

Step 6. **Check** the answer in the problem.

Maria has 9 quarters and 18 pennies. Does this make $2.43?

9 quarters $\quad 9(0.25) = 2.25$
18 pennies $\quad 18(0.01) = \underline{0.18}$
Total $\qquad\qquad\quad $2.43 ✓

Step 7. **Answer** the question. Maria has nine quarters and eighteen pennies.

> **TRY IT : :** 9.23

Sumanta has $4.20 in nickels and dimes in her desk drawer. She has twice as many nickels as dimes. How many coins of each type does she have?

> **TRY IT : : 9.24**

Alison has three times as many dimes as quarters in her purse. She has $9.35 altogether. How many coins of each type does she have?

In the next example, we'll show only the completed table—make sure you understand how to fill it in step by step.

EXAMPLE 9.13

Danny has $2.14 worth of pennies and nickels in his piggy bank. The number of nickels is two more than ten times the number of pennies. How many nickels and how many pennies does Danny have?

⊘ **Solution**

Step 1: **Read** the problem.

| Determine the types of coins involved. Create a table. | Pennies and nickels |

| Write in the value of each type of coin. | Pennies are worth $0.01. Nickels are worth $0.05. |

| Step 2: **Identify** what you are looking for. | the number of pennies and nickels |

| Step 3: **Name.** Represent the number of each type of coin using variables. The number of nickels is defined in terms of the number of pennies, so start with pennies. | Let p = number of pennies |

| The number of nickels is two more than then times the number of pennies. | $10p + 2$ = number of nickels |

Multiply the number and the value to get the total value of each type of coin.

Type	Number	Value ($)	Total Value ($)
pennies	p	0.01	$0.01p$
nickels	$10p + 2$	0.05	$0.05(10p + 2)$
			$2.14

Step 4. **Translate:** Write the equation by adding the total value of all the types of coins.
Step 5. **Solve** the equation.

$$0.01p + 0.50p + 0.10 = 2.14$$
$$0.51p + 0.10 = 2.14$$
$$0.51p = 2.04$$
$$p = 4 \text{ pennies}$$

How many nickels?	$10p + 2$
	$10(4) + 2$
	42 nickels

Step 6. **Check.** Is the total value of 4 pennies and 42 nickels equal to $2.14?

$$4(0.01) + 42(0.05) \overset{?}{=} 2.14$$
$$2.14 = 2.14 \checkmark$$

Step 7. **Answer** the question. Danny has 4 pennies and 42 nickels.

> **TRY IT :: 9.25**
>
> Jesse has $6.55 worth of quarters and nickels in his pocket. The number of nickels is five more than two times the number of quarters. How many nickels and how many quarters does Jesse have?

> **TRY IT :: 9.26**
>
> Elaine has $7.00 in dimes and nickels in her coin jar. The number of dimes that Elaine has is seven less than three times the number of nickels. How many of each coin does Elaine have?

Solve Ticket and Stamp Word Problems

The strategies we used for coin problems can be easily applied to some other kinds of problems too. Problems involving tickets or stamps are very similar to coin problems, for example. Like coins, tickets and stamps have different values; so we can organize the information in tables much like we did for coin problems.

EXAMPLE 9.14

At a school concert, the total value of tickets sold was $1,506. Student tickets sold for $6 each and adult tickets sold for $9 each. The number of adult tickets sold was 5 less than three times the number of student tickets sold. How many student tickets and how many adult tickets were sold?

⊘ **Solution**

Step 1: **Read the problem.**
- Determine the types of tickets involved.
  There are student tickets and adult tickets.
- Create a table to organize the information.

Type	Number	Value ($)	Total Value ($)
Student		6	
Adult		9	
			1,506

Step 2. **Identify** what you are looking for.

We are looking for the number of student and adult tickets.

Step 3. **Name.** Represent the number of each type of ticket using variables.

We know the number of adult tickets sold was 5 less than three times the number of student tickets sold.

Let s be the number of student tickets.

Then $3s - 5$ is the number of adult tickets.

Multiply the number times the value to get the total value of each type of ticket.

Type	Number	Value ($)	Total Value ($)
Student	s	6	$6s$
Adult	$3s - 5$	9	$9(3s - 5)$
			1,506

Step 4. Translate: Write the equation by adding the total values of each type of ticket.

$$6s + 9(3s - 5) = 1506$$

Step 5. Solve the equation.

$$6s + 27s - 45 = 1506$$
$$33s - 45 = 1506$$
$$33s = 1551$$
$$s = 47 \text{ students}$$

Substitute to find the number of adults.

$$3s - 5 = \text{number of adults}$$

$$3(47) - 5 = 136 \text{ adults}$$

Step 6. Check. There were 47 student tickets at $\$6$ each and 136 adult tickets at $\$9$ each. Is the total value $\$1506$? We find the total value of each type of ticket by multiplying the number of tickets times its value; we then add to get the total value of all the tickets sold.

$$47 \cdot 6 = 282$$
$$136 \cdot 9 = \underline{1224}$$
$$1506 \checkmark$$

Step 7. Answer the question. They sold 47 student tickets and 136 adult tickets.

> **TRY IT :: 9.27**
>
> The first day of a water polo tournament, the total value of tickets sold was $\$17,610$. One-day passes sold for $\$20$ and tournament passes sold for $\$30$. The number of tournament passes sold was 37 more than the number of day passes sold. How many day passes and how many tournament passes were sold?

> **TRY IT :: 9.28**
>
> At the movie theater, the total value of tickets sold was $\$2,612.50$. Adult tickets sold for $\$10$ each and senior/child tickets sold for $\$7.50$ each. The number of senior/child tickets sold was 25 less than twice the number of adult tickets sold. How many senior/child tickets and how many adult tickets were sold?

Now we'll do one where we fill in the table all at once.

EXAMPLE 9.15

Monica paid $\$10.44$ for stamps she needed to mail the invitations to her sister's baby shower. The number of 49-cent stamps was four more than twice the number of 8-cent stamps. How many 49-cent stamps and how many 8-cent stamps did Monica buy?

⊘ **Solution**

The type of stamps are 49-cent stamps and 8-cent stamps. Their names also give the value.

"The number of 49 cent stamps was four more than twice the number of 8 cent stamps."

Let x = number of 8-cent stamps

$2x + 4$ = number of 49-cent stamps

Type	Number	Value ($)	Total Value ($)
49-cent stamps	$2x + 4$	0.49	$0.49(2x + 4)$
8-cent stamps	x	0.08	$0.08x$
			10.44

Write the equation from the total values.

$0.49(2x + 4) + 0.08x = 10.44$

Solve the equation.

$0.98x + 1.96 + 0.08x = 10.44$
$1.06x + 1.96 = 10.44$
$1.06x = 8.48$
$x = 8$

Monica bought 8 eight-cent stamps.

Find the number of 49-cent stamps she bought by evaluating.

$2x + 4$ for $x = 8$.

$2x + 4$
$2 \cdot 8 + 4$
$16 + 4$
20

Check.

$8(0.08) + 20(0.49) \overset{?}{=} 10.44$

$0.64 + 9.80 \overset{?}{=} 10.44$
$10.44 = 10.44$ ✓

Monica bought eight 8-cent stamps and twenty 49-cent stamps.

> **TRY IT : :** 9.29

Eric paid $16.64 for stamps so he could mail thank you notes for his wedding gifts. The number of 49-cent stamps was eight more than twice the number of 8-cent stamps. How many 49-cent stamps and how many 8-cent stamps did Eric buy?

> **TRY IT : :** 9.30

Kailee paid $14.84 for stamps. The number of 49-cent stamps was four less than three times the number of 21-cent stamps. How many 49-cent stamps and how many 21-cent stamps did Kailee buy?

9.2 EXERCISES

Practice Makes Perfect

Solve Coin Word Problems

In the following exercises, solve the coin word problems.

51. Jaime has $2.60 in dimes and nickels. The number of dimes is 14 more than the number of nickels. How many of each coin does he have?

52. Lee has $1.75 in dimes and nickels. The number of nickels is 11 more than the number of dimes. How many of each coin does he have?

53. Ngo has a collection of dimes and quarters with a total value of $3.50. The number of dimes is 7 more than the number of quarters. How many of each coin does he have?

54. Connor has a collection of dimes and quarters with a total value of $6.30. The number of dimes is 14 more than the number of quarters. How many of each coin does he have?

55. Carolyn has $2.55 in her purse in nickels and dimes. The number of nickels is 9 less than three times the number of dimes. Find the number of each type of coin.

56. Julio has $2.75 in his pocket in nickels and dimes. The number of dimes is 10 less than twice the number of nickels. Find the number of each type of coin.

57. Chi has $11.30 in dimes and quarters. The number of dimes is 3 more than three times the number of quarters. How many dimes and nickels does Chi have?

58. Tyler has $9.70 in dimes and quarters. The number of quarters is 8 more than four times the number of dimes. How many of each coin does he have?

59. A cash box of $1 and $5 bills is worth $45. The number of $1 bills is 3 more than the number of $5 bills. How many of each bill does it contain?

60. Joe's wallet contains $1 and $5 bills worth $47. The number of $1 bills is 5 more than the number of $5 bills. How many of each bill does he have?

61. In a cash drawer there is $125 in $5 and $10 bills. The number of $10 bills is twice the number of $5 bills. How many of each are in the drawer?

62. John has $175 in $5 and $10 bills in his drawer. The number of $5 bills is three times the number of $10 bills. How many of each are in the drawer?

63. Mukul has $3.75 in quarters, dimes and nickels in his pocket. He has five more dimes than quarters and nine more nickels than quarters. How many of each coin are in his pocket?

64. Vina has $4.70 in quarters, dimes and nickels in her purse. She has eight more dimes than quarters and six more nickels than quarters. How many of each coin are in her purse?

Solve Ticket and Stamp Word Problems

In the following exercises, solve the ticket and stamp word problems.

65. The play took in $550 one night. The number of $8 adult tickets was 10 less than twice the number of $5 child tickets. How many of each ticket were sold?

66. If the number of $8 child tickets is seventeen less than three times the number of $12 adult tickets and the theater took in $584, how many of each ticket were sold?

67. The movie theater took in $1,220 one Monday night. The number of $7 child tickets was ten more than twice the number of $9 adult tickets. How many of each were sold?

68. The ball game took in $1,340 one Saturday. The number of $12 adult tickets was 15 more than twice the number of $5 child tickets. How many of each were sold?

69. Julie went to the post office and bought both $0.49 stamps and $0.34 postcards for her office's bills She spent $62.60. The number of stamps was 20 more than twice the number of postcards. How many of each did she buy?

70. Before he left for college out of state, Jason went to the post office and bought both $0.49 stamps and $0.34 postcards and spent $12.52. The number of stamps was 4 more than twice the number of postcards. How many of each did he buy?

71. Maria spent $16.80 at the post office. She bought three times as many $0.49 stamps as $0.21 stamps. How many of each did she buy?

72. Hector spent $43.40 at the post office. He bought four times as many $0.49 stamps as $0.21 stamps. How many of each did he buy?

73. Hilda has $210 worth of $10 and $12 stock shares. The numbers of $10 shares is 5 more than twice the number of $12 shares. How many of each does she have?

74. Mario invested $475 in $45 and $25 stock shares. The number of $25 shares was 5 less than three times the number of $45 shares. How many of each type of share did he buy?

Everyday Math

75. Parent Volunteer As the treasurer of her daughter's Girl Scout troop, Laney collected money for some girls and adults to go to a 3-day camp. Each girl paid $75 and each adult paid $30. The total amount of money collected for camp was $765. If the number of girls is three times the number of adults, how many girls and how many adults paid for camp?

76. Parent Volunteer Laurie was completing the treasurer's report for her son's Boy Scout troop at the end of the school year. She didn't remember how many boys had paid the $24 full-year registration fee and how many had paid a $16 partial-year fee. She knew that the number of boys who paid for a full-year was ten more than the number who paid for a partial-year. If $400 was collected for all the registrations, how many boys had paid the full-year fee and how many had paid the partial-year fee?

Writing Exercises

77. Suppose you have 6 quarters, 9 dimes, and 4 pennies. Explain how you find the total value of all the coins.

78. Do you find it helpful to use a table when solving coin problems? Why or why not?

79. In the table used to solve coin problems, one column is labeled "number" and another column is labeled '"value." What is the difference between the number and the value?

80. What similarities and differences did you see between solving the coin problems and the ticket and stamp problems?

Self Check

ⓐ After completing the exercises, use this checklist to evaluate your mastery of the objectives of this section.

I can...	Confidently	With some help	No-I don't get it!
solve coin word problems.			
solve ticket and stamp word problems.			

ⓑ *After reviewing this checklist, what will you do to become confident for all objectives?*

9.3 Use Properties of Angles, Triangles, and the Pythagorean Theorem

Learning Objectives

By the end of this section, you will be able to:

- Use the properties of angles
- Use the properties of triangles
- Use the Pythagorean Theorem

Be Prepared!

Before you get started, take this readiness quiz.

1. Solve: $x + 3 + 6 = 11$.
   If you missed this problem, review Example 8.6.

2. Solve: $\frac{a}{45} = \frac{4}{3}$.
   If you missed this problem, review Example 6.42.

3. Simplify: $\sqrt{36 + 64}$.
   If you missed this problem, review Example 5.72.

So far in this chapter, we have focused on solving word problems, which are similar to many real-world applications of algebra. In the next few sections, we will apply our problem-solving strategies to some common geometry problems.

Use the Properties of Angles

Are you familiar with the phrase 'do a 180'? It means to make a full turn so that you face the opposite direction. It comes from the fact that the measure of an angle that makes a straight line is 180 degrees. See Figure 9.5.

Figure 9.5

An **angle** is formed by two rays that share a common endpoint. Each ray is called a side of the angle and the common endpoint is called the **vertex**. An angle is named by its vertex. In Figure 9.6, $\angle A$ is the angle with vertex at point A. The measure of $\angle A$ is written $m\angle A$.

Figure 9.6 $\angle A$ is the angle with vertex at point A.

We measure angles in degrees, and use the symbol $^\circ$ to represent degrees. We use the abbreviation m to for the *measure* of an angle. So if $\angle A$ is $27°$, we would write $m\angle A = 27$.

If the sum of the measures of two angles is $180°$, then they are called **supplementary angles**. In Figure 9.7, each pair of angles is supplementary because their measures add to $180°$. Each angle is the *supplement* of the other.

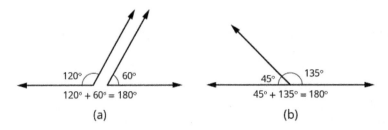

Figure 9.7 The sum of the measures of supplementary angles is $180°$.

If the sum of the measures of two angles is $90°$, then the angles are **complementary angles**. In Figure 9.8, each pair of angles is complementary, because their measures add to $90°$. Each angle is the *complement* of the other.

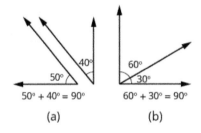

Figure 9.8 The sum of the measures of complementary angles is $90°$.

Supplementary and Complementary Angles

If the sum of the measures of two angles is $180°$, then the angles are supplementary.

If $\angle A$ and $\angle B$ are supplementary, then $m\angle A + m\angle B = 180°$.

If the sum of the measures of two angles is $90°$, then the angles are complementary.

If $\angle A$ and $\angle B$ are complementary, then $m\angle A + m\angle B = 90°$.

In this section and the next, you will be introduced to some common geometry formulas. We will adapt our Problem Solving Strategy for Geometry Applications. The geometry formula will name the variables and give us the equation to solve.

In addition, since these applications will all involve geometric shapes, it will be helpful to draw a figure and then label it with the information from the problem. We will include this step in the Problem Solving Strategy for Geometry Applications.

 HOW TO :: USE A PROBLEM SOLVING STRATEGY FOR GEOMETRY APPLICATIONS.

Step 1.   **Read** the problem and make sure you understand all the words and ideas. Draw a figure and label it with the given information.

Step 2.   **Identify** what you are looking for.

Step 3.   **Name** what you are looking for and choose a variable to represent it.

Step 4.   **Translate** into an equation by writing the appropriate formula or model for the situation. Substitute in the given information.

Step 5.   **Solve** the equation using good algebra techniques.

Step 6.   **Check** the answer in the problem and make sure it makes sense.

Step 7.   **Answer** the question with a complete sentence.

The next example will show how you can use the Problem Solving Strategy for Geometry Applications to answer questions about supplementary and complementary angles.

EXAMPLE 9.16

An angle measures $40°$. Find ⓐ its supplement, and ⓑ its complement.

✓ **Solution**

ⓐ

Step 1. **Read** the problem. Draw the figure and label it with the given information.

Step 2. **Identify** what you are looking for.

the supplement of a 40° angle.

Step 3. **Name.** Choose a variable to represent it.

let s = the measure of the supplement

Step 4. **Translate.**
Write the appropriate formula for the situation and substitute in the given information.

$$m\angle A + m\angle B = 180$$

$$s + 40 = 180$$

Step 5. **Solve** the equation.

$$s = 140$$

Step 6. **Check:**

$$140 + 40 \overset{?}{=} 180$$

$$180 = 180 \checkmark$$

Step 7. **Answer** the question.

The supplement of the 40° angle is 140°.

ⓑ

Step 1. **Read** the problem. Draw the figure and label it with the given information.

Step 2. **Identify** what you are looking for.

the complement of a 40° angle.

Step 3. **Name.** Choose a variable to represent it.

let c = the measure of the complement

Step 4. **Translate.**
Write the appropriate formula for the situation and substitute in the given information.

$$m\angle A + m\angle B = 90$$

$$c + 40 = 90$$

Step 5. **Solve** the equation.

$$c = 50$$

Step 6. **Check:**

$$50 + 40 \overset{?}{=} 90$$

$$90 = 90 \checkmark$$

Step 7. **Answer** the question.

The complement of the 40° angle is 50°.

> | **TRY IT ::** 9.31   An angle measures $25°$. Find its: ⓐ supplement ⓑ complement.

> | **TRY IT ::** 9.32   An angle measures $77°$. Find its: ⓐ supplement ⓑ complement.

Did you notice that the words complementary and supplementary are in alphabetical order just like 90 and 180 are in numerical order?

EXAMPLE 9.17

Two angles are supplementary. The larger angle is $30°$ more than the smaller angle. Find the measure of both angles.

⊘ **Solution**

Step 1. **Read** the problem. Draw the figure and label it with the given information.	
Step 2. **Identify** what you are looking for.	the measures of both angles
Step 3. **Name.** Choose a variable to represent it. The larger angle is 30° more than the smaller angle.	let a = measure of smaller angle $a + 30$ = measure of larger angle
Step 4. **Translate.** Write the appropriate formula and substitute.	$m\angle A + m\angle B = 180$
Step 5. **Solve** the equation.	$(a + 30) + a = 180$ $2a + 30 = 180$ $2a = 150$ $a = 75$ measure of smaller angle $a + 30$ measure of larger angle $75 + 30$ 105
Step 6. **Check:** $m\angle A + m\angle B = 180$ $75 + 105 \overset{?}{=} 180$ $180 = 180 ✓$	
Step 7. **Answer** the question.	The measures of the angles are 75° and 105°.

> | **TRY IT ::** 9.33

Two angles are supplementary. The larger angle is $100°$ more than the smaller angle. Find the measures of both angles.

> **TRY IT :: 9.34**

Two angles are complementary. The larger angle is $40°$ more than the smaller angle. Find the measures of both angles.

Use the Properties of Triangles

What do you already know about triangles? Triangle have three sides and three angles. Triangles are named by their vertices. The **triangle** in Figure 9.9 is called $\triangle ABC$, read 'triangle ABC'. We label each side with a lower case letter to match the upper case letter of the opposite vertex.

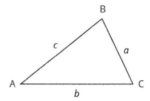

Figure 9.9 $\triangle ABC$ has vertices A, B, and C and sides a, b, and c.

The three angles of a triangle are related in a special way. The sum of their measures is $180°$.

$$m\angle A + m\angle B + m\angle C = 180°$$

Sum of the Measures of the Angles of a Triangle

For any $\triangle ABC$, the sum of the measures of the angles is $180°$.

$$m\angle A + m\angle B + m\angle C = 180°$$

EXAMPLE 9.18

The measures of two angles of a triangle are $55°$ and $82°$. Find the measure of the third angle.

⊘ **Solution**

Step 1. **Read** the problem. Draw the figure and label it with the given information.

Step 2. **Identify** what you are looking for.	the measure of the third angle in a triangle
Step 3. **Name.** Choose a variable to represent it.	let x = the measure of the angle
Step 4. **Translate.** Write the appropriate formula and substitute.	$m\angle A + m\angle B + m\angle C = 180$
Step 5. **Solve** the equation.	$55 + 82 + x = 180$
	$137 + x = 180$
	$x = 43$

Step 6. **Check:**

$55 + 82 + 43 \overset{?}{=} 180$

$180 = 180 \checkmark$

Step 7. **Answer** the question.	The measure of the third angle is 43 degrees.

> **TRY IT : :** 9.35

The measures of two angles of a triangle are $31°$ and $128°$. Find the measure of the third angle.

> **TRY IT : :** 9.36   A triangle has angles of $49°$ and $75°$. Find the measure of the third angle.

Right Triangles

Some triangles have special names. We will look first at the **right triangle**. A right triangle has one $90°$ angle, which is often marked with the symbol shown in Figure 9.10.

Figure 9.10

If we know that a triangle is a right triangle, we know that one angle measures $90°$ so we only need the measure of one of the other angles in order to determine the measure of the third angle.

EXAMPLE 9.19

One angle of a right triangle measures $28°$. What is the measure of the third angle?

⊘ Solution

Step 1. **Read** the problem. Draw the figure and label it with the given information.

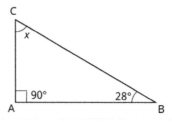

Step 2. **Identify** what you are looking for.   the measure of an angle

Step 3. **Name.** Choose a variable to represent it.   let x = the measure of the angle

Step 4. **Translate.**
Write the appropriate formula and substitute.

$$m\angle A + m\angle B + m\angle C = 180$$
$$x + 90 + 28 = 180$$

Step 5. **Solve** the equation.

$$x + 118 = 180$$
$$x = 62$$

Step 6. **Check:**

$$180 \overset{?}{=} 90 + 28 + 62$$
$$180 = 180 \checkmark$$

Step 7. **Answer** the question.   The measure of the third angle is 62°.

> **TRY IT : : 9.37**   One angle of a right triangle measures $56°$. What is the measure of the other angle?

> **TRY IT : : 9.38**   One angle of a right triangle measures $45°$. What is the measure of the other angle?

In the examples so far, we could draw a figure and label it directly after reading the problem. In the next example, we will have to define one angle in terms of another. So we will wait to draw the figure until we write expressions for all the angles we are looking for.

EXAMPLE 9.20

The measure of one angle of a right triangle is $20°$ more than the measure of the smallest angle. Find the measures of all three angles.

⊘ **Solution**

Step 1. **Read** the problem.

Step 2. **Identify** what you are looking for.	the measures of all three angles
Step 3. **Name.** Choose a variable to represent it.	Let $a = 1^{st}$ angle
Now draw the figure and label it with the given information.	$a + 20 = 2^{nd}$ angle
	$90 = 3^{rd}$ angle (the right angle)

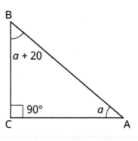

Step 4. **Translate.** Write the appropriate formula and substitute into the formula.	$m\angle A + m\angle B + m\angle C = 180$
	$a + (a + 20) + 90 = 180$
	$2a + 110 = 180$
	$2a = 70$
	$a = 35$ first angle
Step 5. **Solve** the equation.	$a + 20$ second angle
	$35 + 20$
	55
	90 third angle

Step 6. **Check:**
$$35 + 55 + 90 \overset{?}{=} 180$$
$$180 = 180 \checkmark$$

Step 7. **Answer** the question.	The three angles measure 35°, 55°, and 90°.

> ❯ **TRY IT : : 9.39**

The measure of one angle of a right triangle is $50°$ more than the measure of the smallest angle. Find the measures of all three angles.

> ❯ **TRY IT : : 9.40**

The measure of one angle of a right triangle is $30°$ more than the measure of the smallest angle. Find the measures of all three angles.

Similar Triangles

When we use a map to plan a trip, a sketch to build a bookcase, or a pattern to sew a dress, we are working with similar figures. In geometry, if two figures have exactly the same shape but different sizes, we say they are **similar figures**. One is a scale model of the other. The corresponding sides of the two figures have the same ratio, and all their corresponding angles are have the same measures.

The two triangles in Figure 9.11 are similar. Each side of $\triangle ABC$ is four times the length of the corresponding side of $\triangle XYZ$ and their corresponding angles have equal measures.

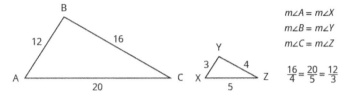

$$m\angle A = m\angle X$$
$$m\angle B = m\angle Y$$
$$m\angle C = m\angle Z$$

$$\frac{16}{4} = \frac{20}{5} = \frac{12}{3}$$

Figure 9.11 $\triangle ABC$ and $\triangle XYZ$ are similar triangles. Their corresponding sides have the same ratio and the corresponding angles have the same measure.

Properties of Similar Triangles

If two triangles are similar, then their corresponding angle measures are equal and their corresponding side lengths are in the same ratio.

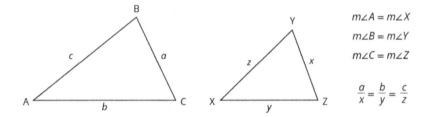

$$m\angle A = m\angle X$$
$$m\angle B = m\angle Y$$
$$m\angle C = m\angle Z$$

$$\frac{a}{x} = \frac{b}{y} = \frac{c}{z}$$

The length of a side of a triangle may be referred to by its endpoints, two vertices of the triangle. For example, in $\triangle ABC$:

the length a can also be written BC

the length b can also be written AC

the length c can also be written AB

We will often use this notation when we solve similar triangles because it will help us match up the corresponding side lengths.

EXAMPLE 9.21

$\triangle ABC$ and $\triangle XYZ$ are similar triangles. The lengths of two sides of each triangle are shown. Find the lengths of the third side of each triangle.

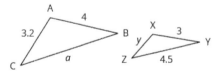

⊘ **Solution**

Step 1. **Read** the problem. Draw the figure and label it with the given information.	The figure is provided.
Step 2. **Identify** what you are looking for.	The length of the sides of similar triangles
Step 3. **Name.** Choose a variable to represent it.	Let a = length of the third side of $\triangle ABC$ y = length of the third side $\triangle XYZ$

Step 4. **Translate.**

The triangles are similar, so the corresponding sides are in the same ratio. So

$$\frac{AB}{XY} = \frac{BC}{YZ} = \frac{AC}{XZ}$$

Since the side $AB = 4$ corresponds to the side $XY = 3$, we will use the ratio $\frac{AB}{XY} = \frac{4}{3}$ to find the other sides.

Be careful to match up corresponding sides correctly.

	To find a:	To find y:
sides of large triangle ⟶	$\dfrac{AB}{XY} = \dfrac{BC}{YZ}$	$\dfrac{AB}{XY} = \dfrac{AC}{XZ}$
sides of small triangle ⟶	$\dfrac{4}{3} = \dfrac{a}{4.5}$	$\dfrac{4}{3} = \dfrac{3.2}{y}$

Step 5. **Solve** the equation.	$\begin{aligned} 3a &= 4(4.5) & \quad 4y &= 3(3.2) \\ 3a &= 18 & 4y &= 9.6 \\ a &= 6 & y &= 2.4 \end{aligned}$

Step 6. **Check:**

$$\frac{4}{3} \overset{?}{=} \frac{6}{4.5} \qquad \frac{4}{3} \overset{?}{=} \frac{3.2}{2.4}$$

$$4(4.5) \overset{?}{=} 6(3) \qquad 4(2.4) \overset{?}{=} 3.2(3)$$

$$18 = 18 \checkmark \qquad 9.6 = 9.6 \checkmark$$

Step 7. **Answer** the question.	The third side of $\triangle ABC$ is 6 and the third side of $\triangle XYZ$ is 2.4.

> **TRY IT :: 9.41** $\triangle ABC$ is similar to $\triangle XYZ$. Find a.

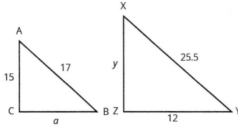

> **TRY IT ::** 9.42 $\triangle ABC$ is similar to $\triangle XYZ$. Find y.

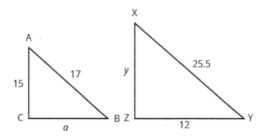

Use the Pythagorean Theorem

The **Pythagorean Theorem** is a special property of right triangles that has been used since ancient times. It is named after the Greek philosopher and mathematician Pythagoras who lived around 500 BCE.

Remember that a right triangle has a $90°$ angle, which we usually mark with a small square in the corner. The side of the triangle opposite the $90°$ angle is called the **hypotenuse**, and the other two sides are called the **legs**. See Figure 9.12.

Figure 9.12 In a right triangle, the side opposite the $90°$ angle is called the hypotenuse and each of the other sides is called a leg.

The Pythagorean Theorem tells how the lengths of the three sides of a right triangle relate to each other. It states that in any right triangle, the sum of the squares of the two legs equals the square of the hypotenuse.

The Pythagorean Theorem

In any right triangle $\triangle ABC$,

$$a^2 + b^2 = c^2$$

where c is the length of the hypotenuse a and b are the lengths of the legs.

To solve problems that use the Pythagorean Theorem, we will need to find square roots. In Simplify and Use Square Roots we introduced the notation $\sqrt{m}$ and defined it in this way:

$$\text{If } m = n^2, \text{ then } \sqrt{m} = n \text{ for } n \geq 0$$

For example, we found that $\sqrt{25}$ is 5 because $5^2 = 25$.

We will use this definition of square roots to solve for the length of a side in a right triangle.

EXAMPLE 9.22

Use the Pythagorean Theorem to find the length of the hypotenuse.

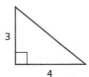

✓ **Solution**

Step 1. **Read** the problem.

Step 2. **Identify** what you are looking for.   the length of the hypotenuse of the triangle

Let c = the length of the hypotenuse

Step 3. **Name.** Choose a variable to represent it.

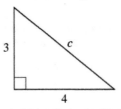

Step 4. **Translate.**
Write the appropriate formula. $a^2 + b^2 = c^2$
Substitute. $3^2 + 4^2 = c^2$

Step 5. **Solve** the equation. $9 + 16 = c^2$

$$25 = c^2$$
$$\sqrt{25} = c^2$$
$$5 = c$$

Step 6. **Check:**
$3^2 + 4^2 = 5^2$

$9 + 16 \overset{?}{=} 25$

$25 = 25 \checkmark$

Step 7. **Answer** the question.   The length of the hypotenuse is 5.

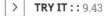 **TRY IT : : 9.43**   Use the Pythagorean Theorem to find the length of the hypotenuse.

> **TRY IT : : 9.44**   Use the Pythagorean Theorem to find the length of the hypotenuse.

EXAMPLE 9.23

Use the Pythagorean Theorem to find the length of the longer leg.

⊘ **Solution**

Step 1. **Read** the problem.

Step 2. **Identify** what you are looking for.

The length of the leg of the triangle

Step 3. **Name.** Choose a variable to represent it.

Let b = the leg of the triangle
Label side b

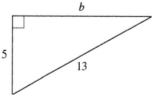

Step 4. **Translate.**
Write the appropriate formula. Substitute.

$a^2 + b^2 = c^2$
$5^2 + b^2 = 13^2$

Step 5. **Solve** the equation. Isolate the variable term. Use the definition of the square root.
Simplify.

$25 + b^2 = 169$
$b^2 = 144$
$b^2 = \sqrt{144}$
$b = 12$

Step 6. **Check:**
$5^2 + 12^2 \overset{?}{=} 13^2$
$25 + 144 \overset{?}{=} 169$
$169 = 169 \checkmark$

Step 7. **Answer** the question.

The length of the leg is 12.

> ❘ **TRY IT : :** 9.45   Use the Pythagorean Theorem to find the length of the leg.

> **TRY IT :: 9.46**   Use the Pythagorean Theorem to find the length of the leg.

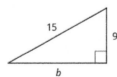

EXAMPLE 9.24

Kelvin is building a gazebo and wants to brace each corner by placing a 10-inch wooden bracket diagonally as shown. How far below the corner should he fasten the bracket if he wants the distances from the corner to each end of the bracket to be equal? Approximate to the nearest tenth of an inch.

⊘ **Solution**

Step 1. **Read** the problem.

Step 2. **Identify** what you are looking for.	the distance from the corner that the bracket should be attached

Step 3. **Name.** Choose a variable to represent it.	Let x = the distance from the corner

Step 4. **Translate.** Write the appropriate formula. Substitute.	$a^2 + b^2 = c^2$ $x^2 + x^2 = 10^2$

Step 5. **Solve** the equation. Isolate the variable. Use the definition of the square root. Simplify. Approximate to the nearest tenth.	$2x^2 = 100$ $x^2 = 50$ $x = \sqrt{50}$ $b \approx 7.1$

Step 6. **Check:**
$$a^2 + b^2 = c^2$$
$$(7.1)^2 + (7.1)^2 \overset{?}{\approx} 10^2$$

Yes.

Step 7. **Answer** the question.	Kelvin should fasten each piece of wood approximately 7.1" from the corner.

> **TRY IT : :** 9.47

John puts the base of a 13-ft ladder 5 feet from the wall of his house. How far up the wall does the ladder reach?

> **TRY IT : :** 9.48

Randy wants to attach a 17-ft string of lights to the top of the 15-ft mast of his sailboat. How far from the base of the mast should he attach the end of the light string?

▶ **MEDIA : :** ACCESS ADDITIONAL ONLINE RESOURCES

- Animation: The Sum of the Interior Angles of a Triangle (http://www.openstaxcollege.org/l/ 24sumintangles)

- Similar Polygons (http://www.openstaxcollege.org/l/24simpolygons)

- Example: Determine the Length of the Hypotenuse of a Right Triangle (http://www.openstaxcollege.org/l/24hyporighttri)

9.3 EXERCISES

Practice Makes Perfect

Use the Properties of Angles

In the following exercises, find ⓐ the supplement and ⓑ the complement of the given angle.

81. $53°$

82. $16°$

83. $29°$

84. $72°$

In the following exercises, use the properties of angles to solve.

85. Find the supplement of a $135°$ angle.

86. Find the complement of a $38°$ angle.

87. Find the complement of a $27.5°$ angle.

88. Find the supplement of a $109.5°$ angle.

89. Two angles are supplementary. The larger angle is $56°$ more than the smaller angle. Find the measures of both angles.

90. Two angles are supplementary. The smaller angle is $36°$ less than the larger angle. Find the measures of both angles.

91. Two angles are complementary. The smaller angle is $34°$ less than the larger angle. Find the measures of both angles.

92. Two angles are complementary. The larger angle is $52°$ more than the smaller angle. Find the measures of both angles.

Use the Properties of Triangles

In the following exercises, solve using properties of triangles.

93. The measures of two angles of a triangle are $26°$ and $98°$. Find the measure of the third angle.

94. The measures of two angles of a triangle are $61°$ and $84°$. Find the measure of the third angle.

95. The measures of two angles of a triangle are $105°$ and $31°$. Find the measure of the third angle.

96. The measures of two angles of a triangle are $47°$ and $72°$. Find the measure of the third angle.

97. One angle of a right triangle measures $33°$. What is the measure of the other angle?

98. One angle of a right triangle measures $51°$. What is the measure of the other angle?

99. One angle of a right triangle measures $22.5°$. What is the measure of the other angle?

100. One angle of a right triangle measures $36.5°$. What is the measure of the other angle?

101. The two smaller angles of a right triangle have equal measures. Find the measures of all three angles.

102. The measure of the smallest angle of a right triangle is $20°$ less than the measure of the other small angle. Find the measures of all three angles.

103. The angles in a triangle are such that the measure of one angle is twice the measure of the smallest angle, while the measure of the third angle is three times the measure of the smallest angle. Find the measures of all three angles.

104. The angles in a triangle are such that the measure of one angle is $20°$ more than the measure of the smallest angle, while the measure of the third angle is three times the measure of the smallest angle. Find the measures of all three angles.

Find the Length of the Missing Side

In the following exercises, ΔABC is similar to ΔXYZ. Find the length of the indicated side.

105. side b

106. side x

On a map, San Francisco, Las Vegas, and Los Angeles form a triangle whose sides are shown in the figure below. The actual distance from Los Angeles to Las Vegas is 270 miles.

107. Find the distance from Los Angeles to San Francisco.

108. Find the distance from San Francisco to Las Vegas.

Use the Pythagorean Theorem

In the following exercises, use the Pythagorean Theorem to find the length of the hypotenuse.

109.

110.

111.

112.

Find the Length of the Missing Side

In the following exercises, use the Pythagorean Theorem to find the length of the missing side. Round to the nearest tenth, if necessary.

113.

114.

115.

116.

117.

118.

119.

120.

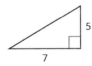

In the following exercises, solve. Approximate to the nearest tenth, if necessary.

121. A 13-foot string of lights will be attached to the top of a 12-foot pole for a holiday display. How far from the base of the pole should the end of the string of lights be anchored?

122. Pam wants to put a banner across her garage door to congratulate her son on his college graduation. The garage door is 12 feet high and 16 feet wide. How long should the banner be to fit the garage door?

123. Chi is planning to put a path of paving stones through her flower garden. The flower garden is a square with sides of 10 feet. What will the length of the path be?

124. Brian borrowed a 20-foot extension ladder to paint his house. If he sets the base of the ladder 6 feet from the house, how far up will the top of the ladder reach?

Everyday Math

125. Building a scale model Joe wants to build a doll house for his daughter. He wants the doll house to look just like his house. His house is 30 feet wide and 35 feet tall at the highest point of the roof. If the dollhouse will be 2.5 feet wide, how tall will its highest point be?

126. Measurement A city engineer plans to build a footbridge across a lake from point X to point Y, as shown in the picture below. To find the length of the footbridge, she draws a right triangle XYZ, with right angle at X. She measures the distance from X to Z, 800 feet, and from Y to Z, $1,000$ feet. How long will the bridge be?

Writing Exercises

127. Write three of the properties of triangles from this section and then explain each in your own words.

128. Explain how the figure below illustrates the Pythagorean Theorem for a triangle with legs of length 3 and 4.

Self Check

ⓐ After completing the exercises, use this checklist to evaluate your mastery of the objectives of this section.

I can...	Confidently	With some help	No-I don't get it!
use the properties of angles.			
use the properties of triangles.			
use the Pythagorean Theorem.			

ⓑ What does this checklist tell you about your mastery of this section? What steps will you take to improve?

9.4 | Use Properties of Rectangles, Triangles, and Trapezoids

Learning Objectives

By the end of this section, you will be able to:

> Understand linear, square, and cubic measure
> Use properties of rectangles
> Use properties of triangles
> Use properties of trapezoids

Be Prepared!

Before you get started, take this readiness quiz.

1. The length of a rectangle is 3 less than the width. Let w represent the width. Write an expression for the length of the rectangle.
   If you missed this problem, review Example 2.26.

2. Simplify: $\frac{1}{2}(6h)$.
   If you missed this problem, review Example 7.7.

3. Simplify: $\frac{5}{2}(10.3 - 7.9)$.
   If you missed this problem, review Example 5.36.

In this section, we'll continue working with geometry applications. We will add some more properties of triangles, and we'll learn about the properties of rectangles and trapezoids.

Understand Linear, Square, and Cubic Measure

When you measure your height or the length of a garden hose, you use a ruler or tape measure (Figure 9.13). A tape measure might remind you of a line—you use it for **linear measure**, which measures length. Inch, foot, yard, mile, centimeter and meter are units of linear measure.

Figure 9.13 This tape measure measures inches along the top and centimeters along the bottom.

When you want to know how much tile is needed to cover a floor, or the size of a wall to be painted, you need to know the **area**, a measure of the region needed to cover a surface. Area is measured is **square units**. We often use square inches, square feet, square centimeters, or square miles to measure area. A square centimeter is a square that is one centimeter (cm) on each side. A square inch is a square that is one inch on each side (Figure 9.14).

Figure 9.14 Square measures have sides that are each 1 unit in length.

Figure 9.15 shows a rectangular rug that is 2 feet long by 3 feet wide. Each square is 1 foot wide by 1 foot long, or 1 square foot. The rug is made of 6 squares. The area of the rug is 6 square feet.

Figure 9.15 The rug contains six squares of 1 square foot each, so the total area of the rug is 6 square feet.

When you measure how much it takes to fill a container, such as the amount of gasoline that can fit in a tank, or the amount of medicine in a syringe, you are measuring **volume**. Volume is measured in **cubic units** such as cubic inches or cubic centimeters. When measuring the volume of a rectangular solid, you measure how many cubes fill the container. We often use cubic centimeters, cubic inches, and cubic feet. A cubic centimeter is a cube that measures one centimeter on each side, while a cubic inch is a cube that measures one inch on each side (Figure 9.16).

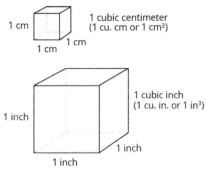

Figure 9.16 Cubic measures have sides that are 1 unit in length.

Suppose the cube in Figure 9.17 measures 3 inches on each side and is cut on the lines shown. How many little cubes does it contain? If we were to take the big cube apart, we would find 27 little cubes, with each one measuring one inch on all sides. So each little cube has a volume of 1 cubic inch, and the volume of the big cube is 27 cubic inches.

Figure 9.17 A cube that measures 3 inches on each side is made up of 27 one-inch cubes, or 27 cubic inches.

 MANIPULATIVE MATHEMATICS

Doing the Manipulative Mathematics activity Visualizing Area and Perimeter will help you develop a better understanding of the difference between the area of a figure and its perimeter.

EXAMPLE 9.25

For each item, state whether you would use linear, square, or cubic measure:

ⓐ amount of carpeting needed in a room

ⓑ extension cord length

ⓒ amount of sand in a sandbox

ⓓ length of a curtain rod

ⓔ amount of flour in a canister

ⓕ size of the roof of a doghouse.

⊘ **Solution**

ⓐ You are measuring how much surface the carpet covers, which is the area.	square measure
ⓑ You are measuring how long the extension cord is, which is the length.	linear measure
ⓒ You are measuring the volume of the sand.	cubic measure
ⓓ You are measuring the length of the curtain rod.	linear measure
ⓔ You are measuring the volume of the flour.	cubic measure
ⓕ You are measuring the area of the roof.	square measure

> **TRY IT :: 9.49**
>
> Determine whether you would use linear, square, or cubic measure for each item.
>
> ⓐ amount of paint in a can ⓑ height of a tree ⓒ floor of your bedroom ⓓ diameter of bike wheel ⓔ size of a piece of sod ⓕ amount of water in a swimming pool

> **TRY IT :: 9.50**
>
> Determine whether you would use linear, square, or cubic measure for each item.
>
> ⓐ volume of a packing box ⓑ size of patio ⓒ amount of medicine in a syringe ⓓ length of a piece of yarn ⓔ size of housing lot ⓕ height of a flagpole

Many geometry applications will involve finding the perimeter or the area of a figure. There are also many applications of perimeter and area in everyday life, so it is important to make sure you understand what they each mean.

Picture a room that needs new floor tiles. The tiles come in squares that are a foot on each side—one square foot. How many of those squares are needed to cover the floor? This is the area of the floor.

Next, think about putting new baseboard around the room, once the tiles have been laid. To figure out how many strips are needed, you must know the distance around the room. You would use a tape measure to measure the number of feet around the room. This distance is the perimeter.

Perimeter and Area

The **perimeter** is a measure of the distance around a figure.

The **area** is a measure of the surface covered by a figure.

Figure 9.18 shows a square tile that is 1 inch on each side. If an ant walked around the edge of the tile, it would walk 4 inches. This distance is the perimeter of the tile.

Since the tile is a square that is 1 inch on each side, its area is one square inch. The area of a shape is measured by determining how many square units cover the shape.

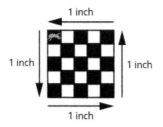

Figure 9.18

Perimeter = 4 inches
Area = 1 square inch

When the ant walks completely around the tile on its edge, it is tracing the perimeter of the tile. The area of the tile is 1 square inch.

 MANIPULATIVE MATHEMATICS

Doing the Manipulative Mathematics activity Measuring Area and Perimeter will help you develop a better understanding of how to measure the area and perimeter of a figure.

EXAMPLE 9.26

Each of two square tiles is 1 square inch. Two tiles are shown together.

ⓐ What is the perimeter of the figure?

ⓑ What is the area?

⊘ **Solution**

ⓐ The perimeter is the distance around the figure. The perimeter is 6 inches.

ⓑ The area is the surface covered by the figure. There are 2 square inch tiles so the area is 2 square inches.

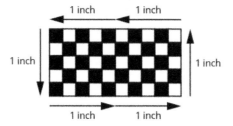

> **TRY IT : : 9.51**   Find the ⓐ perimeter and ⓑ area of the figure:

> **TRY IT : :** 9.52   Find the ⓐ perimeter and ⓑ area of the figure:

Use the Properties of Rectangles

A **rectangle** has four sides and four right angles. The opposite sides of a rectangle are the same length. We refer to one side of the rectangle as the length, L, and the adjacent side as the width, W. See Figure 9.19.

Figure 9.19 A rectangle has four sides, and four right angles. The sides are labeled L for length and W for width.

The perimeter, P, of the rectangle is the distance around the rectangle. If you started at one corner and walked around the rectangle, you would walk $L + W + L + W$ units, or two lengths and two widths. The perimeter then is

$$P = L + W + L + W$$
$$\text{or}$$
$$P = 2L + 2W$$

What about the area of a rectangle? Remember the rectangular rug from the beginning of this section. It was 2 feet long by 3 feet wide, and its area was 6 square feet. See Figure 9.20. Since $A = 2 \cdot 3$, we see that the area, A, is the length, L, times the width, W, so the area of a rectangle is $A = L \cdot W$.

Figure 9.20 The area of this rectangular rug is 6 square feet, its length times its width.

Properties of Rectangles

- Rectangles have four sides and four right $(90°)$ angles.

- The lengths of opposite sides are equal.

- The perimeter, P, of a rectangle is the sum of twice the length and twice the width. See Figure 9.19.

$$P = 2L + 2W$$

- The area, A, of a rectangle is the length times the width.

$$A = L \cdot W$$

For easy reference as we work the examples in this section, we will restate the Problem Solving Strategy for Geometry Applications here.

HOW TO :: USE A PROBLEM SOLVING STRATEGY FOR GEOMETRY APPLICATIONS

Step 1.   **Read** the problem and make sure you understand all the words and ideas. Draw the figure and label it with the given information.

Step 2.   **Identify** what you are looking for.

Step 3.   **Name** what you are looking for. Choose a variable to represent that quantity.

Step 4.   **Translate** into an equation by writing the appropriate formula or model for the situation. Substitute in the given information.

Step 5.   **Solve** the equation using good algebra techniques.

Step 6.   **Check** the answer in the problem and make sure it makes sense.

Step 7.   **Answer** the question with a complete sentence.

EXAMPLE 9.27

The length of a rectangle is 32 meters and the width is 20 meters. Find ⓐ the perimeter, and ⓑ the area.

Solution

ⓐ

Step 1. **Read** the problem. Draw the figure and label it with the given information.

Step 2. **Identify** what you are looking for.   the perimeter of a rectangle

Step 3. **Name.** Choose a variable to represent it.   Let P = the perimeter

Step 4. **Translate.**
Write the appropriate formula.
Substitute.

$$P \quad = \quad 2L \quad + \quad 2W$$
$$P \quad = \quad 2(32) \quad + \quad 2(20)$$

Step 5. **Solve** the equation.

$$P = 64 + 40$$
$$P = 104$$

Step 6. **Check:**

$$P \overset{?}{=} 104$$
$$20 + 32 + 20 + 32 \overset{?}{=} 104$$
$$104 = 104 \checkmark$$

Step 7. **Answer** the question.   The perimeter of the rectangle is 104 meters.

ⓑ

Step 1. **Read** the problem. Draw the figure and label it with the given information.	
Step 2. **Identify** what you are looking for.	the area of a rectangle
Step 3. **Name.** Choose a variable to represent it.	Let A = the area
Step 4. **Translate.** Write the appropriate formula. Substitute.	$A = L \cdot W$ $A = 32\,m \cdot 20\,m$
Step 5. **Solve** the equation.	$A = 640$
Step 6. **Check:** $A \overset{?}{=} 640$ $32 \cdot 20 \overset{?}{=} 640$ $640 = 640 \checkmark$	
Step 7. **Answer** the question.	The area of the rectangle is 60 square meters.

> **TRY IT : : 9.53**
>
> The length of a rectangle is 120 yards and the width is 50 yards. Find ⓐ the perimeter and ⓑ the area.

> **TRY IT : : 9.54**
>
> The length of a rectangle is 62 feet and the width is 48 feet. Find ⓐ the perimeter and ⓑ the area.

EXAMPLE 9.28

Find the length of a rectangle with perimeter 50 inches and width 10 inches.

⊘ Solution

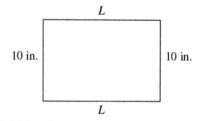

Step 1. **Read** the problem. Draw the figure and label it with the given information.

Step 2. **Identify** what you are looking for.

the length of the rectangle

Step 3. **Name.** Choose a variable to represent it.

Let L = the length

Step 4. **Translate.**
Write the appropriate formula.
Substitute.

$$P = 2L + 2W$$
$$50 = 2L + 2(10)$$

Step 5. **Solve** the equation.

$$50 - 20 = 2L + 20 - 20$$
$$30 = 2L$$
$$\frac{30}{2} = \frac{2L}{2}$$
$$15 = L$$

Step 6. **Check:**
$$P = 50$$
$$15 + 10 + 15 + 10 \overset{?}{=} 50$$
$$50 = 50 \checkmark$$

Step 7. **Answer** the question.

The length is 15 inches.

> **TRY IT :: 9.55**   Find the length of a rectangle with a perimeter of 80 inches and width of 25 inches.

> **TRY IT :: 9.56**   Find the length of a rectangle with a perimeter of 30 yards and width of 6 yards.

In the next example, the width is defined in terms of the length. We'll wait to draw the figure until we write an expression for the width so that we can label one side with that expression.

EXAMPLE 9.29

The width of a rectangle is two inches less than the length. The perimeter is 52 inches. Find the length and width.

⊘ **Solution**

Step 1. **Read** the problem.

Step 2. **Identify** what you are looking for.   the length and width of the rectangle

Since the width is defined in terms of the length, we let L = length. The width is two feet less that the length, so we let $L - 2$ = width

Step 3. **Name.** Choose a variable to represent it.

Now we can draw a figure using these expressions for the length and width.

$$L$$

$L - 2$ [rectangle] $L - 2$

$$L$$

Step 4.**Translate.**
Write the appropriate formula. The formula for the perimeter of a rectangle relates all the information.
Substitute in the given information.

P	=	2L	+	2W
52	=	2L	+	2(L − 2)

Step 5. **Solve** the equation. $52 = 2L + 2L - 4$

Combine like terms. $52 = 4L - 4$

Add 4 to each side. $56 = 4L$

Divide by 4. $\dfrac{56}{4} = \dfrac{4L}{4}$

                                             $14 = L$

                                             The length is 14 inches.

Now we need to find the width.

                                             $L - 2$
                                             $14 - 2$
The width is $L - 2$. 12

                                             The width is 12 inches.

Step 6. **Check:**
Since $14 + 12 + 14 + 12 = 52$, this works!

Step 7. **Answer** the question.   The length is 14 feet and the width is 12 feet.

> **TRY IT : : 9.57**

   The width of a rectangle is seven meters less than the length. The perimeter is 58 meters. Find the length and width.

> **TRY IT : : 9.58**

   The length of a rectangle is eight feet more than the width. The perimeter is 60 feet. Find the length and width.

EXAMPLE 9.30

The length of a rectangle is four centimeters more than twice the width. The perimeter is 32 centimeters. Find the length and width.

⊘ **Solution**

Step 1. **Read** the problem.

Step 2. **Identify** what you are looking for.

the length and width

Step 3. **Name.** Choose a variable to represent it.

let W = width
The length is four more than twice the width.
$2w + 4$ = length

Step 4. **Translate.**
Write the appropriate formula and substitute in the given information.

P	=	2L	+	2W
32	=	2(2w + 4)	+	2w

Step 5. **Solve** the equation.

$32 = 4w + 8 + 2w$

$32 = 6w + 8$

$24 = 6w$

$4 = w$ width

$2w + 4$ length

$2(4) + 4$

12 The length is 12 cm.

Step 6. **Check:**
$p = 2L + 2W$
$32 \overset{?}{=} 2 \cdot 12 + 2 \cdot 4$
$32 = 32$

Step 7. **Answer** the question.

The length is 12 cm and the width is 4 cm.

> **TRY IT :: 9.59**

The length of a rectangle is eight more than twice the width. The perimeter is 64 feet. Find the length and width.

> **TRY IT :: 9.60**

The width of a rectangle is six less than twice the length. The perimeter is 18 centimeters. Find the length and width.

EXAMPLE 9.31

The area of a rectangular room is 168 square feet. The length is 14 feet. What is the width?

⊘ **Solution**

Step 1. **Read** the problem.	
Step 2. **Identify** what you are looking for.	the width of a rectangular room
Step 3. **Name.** Choose a variable to represent it.	Let W = width
Step 4.**Translate.** Write the appropriate formula and substitute in the given information.	$A = LW$ $168 = 14W$
Step 5. **Solve** the equation.	$\dfrac{168}{14} = \dfrac{14W}{14}$ $12 = W$
Step 6. **Check:** $A = LW$ $168 \overset{?}{=} 14 \cdot 12$ $168 = 168 \checkmark$	
Step 7. **Answer** the question.	The width of the room is 12 feet.

> **TRY IT :: 9.61**   The area of a rectangle is 598 square feet. The length is 23 feet. What is the width?

> **TRY IT :: 9.62**   The width of a rectangle is 21 meters. The area is 609 square meters. What is the length?

EXAMPLE 9.32

The perimeter of a rectangular swimming pool is 150 feet. The length is 15 feet more than the width. Find the length and width.

Solution

Step 1. **Read** the problem. Draw the figure and label it with the given information.

W

$W + 15$
$P = 150\ ft$

Step 2. **Identify** what you are looking for.

the length and width of the pool

Step 3. **Name.** Choose a variable to represent it.
The length is 15 feet more than the width.

Let $W =$ width
$W + 15 =$ length

Step 4.**Translate.**
Write the appropriate formula and substitute.

$P \quad = \quad\quad 2L \quad + \quad 2W$

$150 \quad = \quad 2(w+15) \quad + \quad 2w$

Step 5. **Solve** the equation.

$150 = 2w + 30 + 2w$

$150 = 4w + 30$

$120 = 4w$

$30 = w$ the width of the pool

$w + 15$ the length of the pool

$30 + 15$

45

Step 6. **Check:**
$p = 2L + 2W$

$150 \overset{?}{=} 2(45) + 2(30)$

$150 = 150$

Step 7. **Answer** the question.

The length of the pool is 45 feet and the width is 30 feet.

> **TRY IT : :** 9.63

The perimeter of a rectangular swimming pool is 200 feet. The length is 40 feet more than the width. Find the length and width.

> **TRY IT : :** 9.64

The length of a rectangular garden is 30 yards more than the width. The perimeter is 300 yards. Find the length and width.

Use the Properties of Triangles

We now know how to find the area of a rectangle. We can use this fact to help us visualize the formula for the area of a triangle. In the rectangle in Figure 9.20, we've labeled the length b and the width h, so it's area is bh.

Figure 9.21 The area of a rectangle is the base, $b,$ times the height, $h.$

We can divide this rectangle into two **congruent** triangles (Figure 9.22). Triangles that are congruent have identical side lengths and angles, and so their areas are equal. The area of each triangle is one-half the area of the rectangle, or $\frac{1}{2}bh.$

This example helps us see why the formula for the area of a triangle is $A = \frac{1}{2}bh.$

Figure 9.22 A rectangle can be divided into two triangles of equal area. The area of each triangle is one-half the area of the rectangle.

The formula for the area of a triangle is $A = \frac{1}{2}bh,$ where b is the base and h is the height.

To find the area of the triangle, you need to know its base and height. The base is the length of one side of the triangle, usually the side at the bottom. The height is the length of the line that connects the base to the opposite vertex, and makes a $90°$ angle with the base. Figure 9.23 shows three triangles with the base and height of each marked.

Figure 9.23 The height h of a triangle is the length of a line segment that connects the the base to the opposite vertex and makes a $90°$ angle with the base.

Triangle Properties

For any triangle $\triangle ABC,$ the sum of the measures of the angles is $180°.$

$$m\angle A + m\angle B + m\angle C = 180°$$

The perimeter of a triangle is the sum of the lengths of the sides.

$$P = a + b + c$$

The area of a triangle is one-half the base, $b,$ times the height, $h.$

$$A = \frac{1}{2}bh$$

EXAMPLE 9.33

Find the area of a triangle whose base is 11 inches and whose height is 8 inches.

⊘ **Solution**

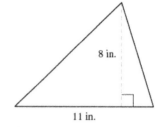

Step 1. **Read** the problem. Draw the figure and label it with the given information.

8 in.

11 in.

Step 2. **Identify** what you are looking for.

the area of the triangle

Step 3. **Name.** Choose a variable to represent it.

let A = area of the triangle

Step 4.**Translate.**
Write the appropriate formula.
Substitute.

$$A = \frac{1}{2} \cdot b \cdot h$$

$$A = \frac{1}{2} \cdot 11 \cdot 8$$

Step 5. **Solve** the equation.

$A = 44$ square inches

Step 6. **Check:**

$A = \frac{1}{2} bh$

$44 \overset{?}{=} \frac{1}{2}(11)8$

$44 = 44 \checkmark$

Step 7. **Answer** the question.

The area is 44 square inches.

> **TRY IT : : 9.65** Find the area of a triangle with base 13 inches and height 2 inches.

> **TRY IT : : 9.66** Find the area of a triangle with base 14 inches and height 7 inches.

EXAMPLE 9.34

The perimeter of a triangular garden is 24 feet. The lengths of two sides are 4 feet and 9 feet. How long is the third side?

⊘ **Solution**

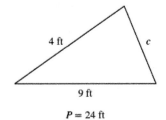

4 ft

c

9 ft

$P = 24$ ft

Step 1. **Read** the problem. Draw the figure and label it with the given information.

Step 2. **Identify** what you are looking for.	length of the third side of a triangle
Step 3. **Name.** Choose a variable to represent it.	Let c = the third side

Step 4.**Translate.**
Write the appropriate formula.
Substitute in the given information.

$$P = a + b + c$$
$$24 = 4 + 9 + c$$

Step 5. **Solve** the equation.

$$24 = 13 + c$$
$$11 = c$$

Step 6. **Check:**
$P = a + b + c$

$24 \overset{?}{=} 4 + 9 + 11$

$24 = 24 ✓$

Step 7. **Answer** the question.	The third side is 11 feet long.

> **TRY IT : :** 9.67

The perimeter of a triangular garden is 24 feet. The lengths of two sides are 18 feet and 22 feet. How long is the third side?

> **TRY IT : :** 9.68

The lengths of two sides of a triangular window are 7 feet and 5 feet. The perimeter is 18 feet. How long is the third side?

EXAMPLE 9.35

The area of a triangular church window is 90 square meters. The base of the window is 15 meters. What is the window's height?

⊘ **Solution**

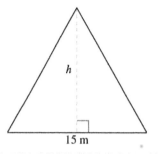

Step 1. **Read** the problem. Draw the figure and label it with the given information.

Step 2. **Identify** what you are looking for.   height of a triangle

Step 3. **Name.** Choose a variable to represent it.   Let h = the height

Step 4. **Translate.**
Write the appropriate formula.
Substitute in the given information.

$$A = \frac{1}{2} \cdot b \cdot h$$

$$90 = \frac{1}{2} \cdot 15 \cdot h$$

Step 5. **Solve** the equation.

$$90 = \frac{15}{2} h$$

$$12 = h$$

Step 6. **Check:**

$$A = \frac{1}{2}bh$$

$$90 \overset{?}{=} \frac{1}{2} \cdot 15 \cdot 12$$

$$90 = 90 \checkmark$$

Step 7. **Answer** the question.   The height of the triangle is 12 meters.

> **TRY IT : :** 9.69

The area of a triangular painting is 126 square inches. The base is 18 inches. What is the height?

> **TRY IT : :** 9.70   A triangular tent door has an area of 15 square feet. The height is 5 feet. What is the base?

Isosceles and Equilateral Triangles

Besides the right triangle, some other triangles have special names. A triangle with two sides of equal length is called an **isosceles triangle**. A triangle that has three sides of equal length is called an **equilateral triangle**. Figure 9.24 shows both types of triangles.

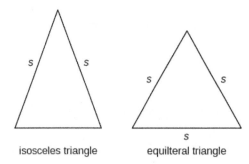

isosceles triangle   equilteral triangle

Figure 9.24 In an isosceles triangle, two sides have the same length, and the third side is the base. In an equilateral triangle, all three sides have the same length.

Isosceles and Equilateral Triangles

An **isosceles** triangle has two sides the same length.

An **equilateral** triangle has three sides of equal length.

EXAMPLE 9.36

The perimeter of an equilateral triangle is 93 inches. Find the length of each side.

Solution

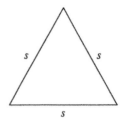

Step 1. **Read** the problem. Draw the figure and label it with the given information.

Perimeter = 93 in.

Step 2. **Identify** what you are looking for.

length of the sides of an equilateral triangle

Step 3. **Name.** Choose a variable to represent it.

Let s = length of each side

Step 4. **Translate.**
Write the appropriate formula.
Substitute.

$$P = a + b + c$$
$$93 = s + s + s$$

Step 5. **Solve** the equation.

$$93 = 3s$$
$$31 = s$$

Step 6. **Check:**

$$93 \stackrel{?}{=} 31 + 31 + 31$$
$$93 = 93 \checkmark$$

Step 7. **Answer** the question.

Each side is 31 inches.

> **TRY IT : : 9.71**   Find the length of each side of an equilateral triangle with perimeter 39 inches.

> **TRY IT : : 9.72**   Find the length of each side of an equilateral triangle with perimeter 51 centimeters.

EXAMPLE 9.37

Arianna has 156 inches of beading to use as trim around a scarf. The scarf will be an isosceles triangle with a base of 60 inches. How long can she make the two equal sides?

⊘ Solution

Step 1. **Read** the problem. Draw the figure and label it with the given information.	$P = 156$ in.
Step 2. **Identify** what you are looking for.	the lengths of the two equal sides
Step 3. **Name.** Choose a variable to represent it.	Let s = the length of each side
Step 4.**Translate.** Write the appropriate formula. Substitute in the given information.	$P = a + b + c$ $156 = s + 60 + s$
Step 5. **Solve** the equation.	$156 = 2s + 60$ $96 = 2s$ $48 = s$
Step 6. **Check:** $p = a + b + c$ $156 \stackrel{?}{=} 48 + 60 + 48$ $156 = 156 ✓$	
Step 7. **Answer** the question.	Arianna can make each of the two equal sides 48 inches long.

> **TRY IT : :** 9.73

> A backyard deck is in the shape of an isosceles triangle with a base of 20 feet. The perimeter of the deck is 48 feet. How long is each of the equal sides of the deck?

> **TRY IT : :** 9.74

> A boat's sail is an isosceles triangle with base of 8 meters. The perimeter is 22 meters. How long is each of the equal sides of the sail?

Use the Properties of Trapezoids

A **trapezoid** is four-sided figure, a *quadrilateral*, with two sides that are parallel and two sides that are not. The parallel sides are called the bases. We call the length of the smaller base b, and the length of the bigger base B. The height, h, of a trapezoid is the distance between the two bases as shown in Figure 9.25.

Figure 9.25 A trapezoid has a larger base, B, and a smaller base, b. The height h is the distance between the bases.

The formula for the area of a trapezoid is:

$$\text{Area}_{\text{trapezoid}} = \frac{1}{2}h(b + B)$$

Splitting the trapezoid into two triangles may help us understand the formula. The area of the trapezoid is the sum of the areas of the two triangles. See Figure 9.26.

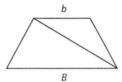

Figure 9.26 Splitting a trapezoid into two triangles may help you understand the formula for its area.

The height of the trapezoid is also the height of each of the two triangles. See Figure 9.27.

Figure 9.27

The formula for the area of a trapezoid is

$$\text{Area}_{\text{trapezoid}} = \frac{1}{2}h(b + B)$$

If we distribute, we get,

$$\text{Area}_{\text{trapezoid}} = \frac{1}{2}bh + \frac{1}{2}Bh$$

$$\text{Area}_{\text{trapezoid}} = A_{\text{blue}\triangle} + A_{\text{red}\triangle}$$

Properties of Trapezoids

- A trapezoid has four sides. See Figure 9.25.
- Two of its sides are parallel and two sides are not.
- The area, A, of a trapezoid is $A = \frac{1}{2}h(b + B)$.

EXAMPLE 9.38

Find the area of a trapezoid whose height is 6 inches and whose bases are 14 and 11 inches.

⊘ **Solution**

Step 1. **Read** the problem. Draw the figure and label it with the given information.

Step 2. **Identify** what you are looking for.   the area of the trapezoid

Step 3. **Name.** Choose a variable to represent it.   Let $A =$ the area

Step 4.**Translate.**
Write the appropriate formula.
Substitute.

$$A = \frac{1}{2} \cdot h \cdot (b + B)$$

$$A = \frac{1}{2} \cdot 6 \cdot (11 + 14)$$

Step 5. **Solve** the equation.

$$A = \frac{1}{2} \cdot 6(25)$$

$$A = 3(25)$$

$$A = 75 \text{ square inches}$$

Step 6. **Check:** Is this answer reasonable?

If we draw a rectangle around the trapezoid that has the same big base B and a height h, its area should be greater than that of the trapezoid.

If we draw a rectangle inside the trapezoid that has the same little base b and a height h, its area should be smaller than that of the trapezoid.

14 6 11	14 6 11	6
$A_{rectangle} = bh$	$A_{trapezoid} = \frac{1}{2}h(b + B)$	$A_{rectangle} = bh$
$A_{rectangle} = 14 \cdot 6$	$A_{trapezoid} = \frac{1}{2} \cdot 6(11 + 14)$	$A_{rectangle} = 11 \cdot 6$
$A_{rectangle} = 84$ sq. in.	$A_{trapezoid} = 75$ sq. in.	$A_{rectangle} = 66$ sq. in.

The area of the larger rectangle is 84 square inches and the area of the smaller rectangle is 66 square inches. So it makes sense that the area of the trapezoid is between 84 and 66 square inches

Step 7. **Answer** the question. The area of the trapezoid is 75 square inches.

> **TRY IT :: 9.75**   The height of a trapezoid is 14 yards and the bases are 7 and 16 yards. What is the area?

> **TRY IT :: 9.76**
The height of a trapezoid is 18 centimeters and the bases are 17 and 8 centimeters. What is the area?

EXAMPLE 9.39

Find the area of a trapezoid whose height is 5 feet and whose bases are 10.3 and 13.7 feet.

⊘ Solution

Step 1. **Read** the problem. Draw the figure and label it with the given information.

Step 2. **Identify** what you are looking for.

the area of the trapezoid

Step 3. **Name.** Choose a variable to represent it.

Let A = the area

Step 4.**Translate.**
Write the appropriate formula.
Substitute.

$$A = \frac{1}{2} \cdot h \cdot (b + B)$$

$$A = \frac{1}{2} \cdot 5 \cdot (10.3 + 13.7)$$

Step 5. **Solve** the equation.

$$A = \frac{1}{2} \cdot 5(24)$$

$$A = 12 \cdot 5$$

$$A = 60 \text{ square feet}$$

Step 6. **Check:** Is this answer reasonable?
The area of the trapezoid should be less than the area of a rectangle with base 13.7 and height 5, but more than the area of a rectangle with base 10.3 and height 5.

$$A_{rectangle} > A_{trapezoid} > A$$
$$68.5 \qquad 60 \qquad 51.5$$

Step 7. **Answer** the question.

The area of the trapezoid is 60 square feet.

> **TRY IT : : 9.77**

   The height of a trapezoid is 7 centimeters and the bases are 4.6 and 7.4 centimeters. What is the area?

> **TRY IT : : 9.78**

   The height of a trapezoid is 9 meters and the bases are 6.2 and 7.8 meters. What is the area?

EXAMPLE 9.40

Vinny has a garden that is shaped like a trapezoid. The trapezoid has a height of 3.4 yards and the bases are 8.2 and 5.6 yards. How many square yards will be available to plant?

⊘ Solution

Step 1. **Read** the problem. Draw the figure and label it with the given information.

5.6 yd.

3.4 yd.

8.2 yd.

Step 2. **Identify** what you are looking for. the area of a trapezoid

Step 3. **Name.** Choose a variable to represent it. Let A = the area

Step 4. **Translate.**
Write the appropriate formula.
Substitute.

$$A = \frac{1}{2} \cdot h \cdot (b + B)$$

$$A = \frac{1}{2} \cdot 3.4 \cdot (5.6 + 8.2)$$

Step 5. **Solve** the equation.

$$A = \frac{1}{2}(3.4)(13.8)$$

$$A = 23.46 \text{ square yards}$$

Step 6. **Check:** Is this answer reasonable?
Yes. The area of the trapezoid is less than the area of a rectangle with a base of 8.2 yd and height 3.4 yd, but more than the area of a rectangle with base 5.6 yd and height 3.4 yd.

$A_{rectangle} = Bh$	$A_{trapezoid} = \frac{1}{2}(3.4 \text{ yd})(5.6 = 8.2)$	$A_{rectangle} = bh$
= (8.2)(3.4)	= 23.46 yd²	= (5.6)(3.4)
= 27.88 yd²		= 19.04 yd²
$A_{rectangle} > A_{trapezoid} > A_{rectangle}$ 27.88 23.46 19.04		

Step 7. **Answer** the question. Vinny has 23.46 square yards in which he can plant.

> **TRY IT :: 9.79**

  Lin wants to sod his lawn, which is shaped like a trapezoid. The bases are 10.8 yards and 6.7 yards, and the height is 4.6 yards. How many square yards of sod does he need?

> **TRY IT :: 9.80**

  Kira wants cover his patio with concrete pavers. If the patio is shaped like a trapezoid whose bases are 18 feet and 14 feet and whose height is 15 feet, how many square feet of pavers will he need?

🗗 **LINKS TO LITERACY**

The Links to Literacy activity *Spaghetti and Meatballs for All* will provide you with another view of the topics covered in this section."

▶ **MEDIA : :** ACCESS ADDITIONAL ONLINE RESOURCES

- Perimeter of a Rectangle (http://www.openstaxcollege.org/l/24perirect)
- Area of a Rectangle (http://www.openstaxcollege.org/l/24arearect)
- Perimeter and Area Formulas (http://www.openstaxcollege.org/l/24periareaform)
- Area of a Triangle (http://www.openstaxcollege.org/l/24areatri)
- Area of a Triangle with Fractions (http://www.openstaxcollege.org/l/24areatrifract)
- Area of a Trapezoid (http://www.openstaxcollege.org/l/24areatrap)

9.4 EXERCISES

Practice Makes Perfect

Understand Linear, Square, and Cubic Measure

In the following exercises, determine whether you would measure each item using linear, square, or cubic units.

129. amount of water in a fish tank

130. length of dental floss

131. living area of an apartment

132. floor space of a bathroom tile

133. height of a doorway

134. capacity of a truck trailer

In the following exercises, find the ⓐ perimeter and ⓑ area of each figure. Assume each side of the square is 1 cm.

135.

136.

137.

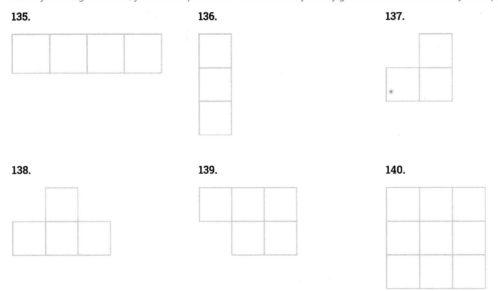

138.

139.

140.

Use the Properties of Rectangles

In the following exercises, find the ⓐ perimeter and ⓑ area of each rectangle.

141. The length of a rectangle is 85 feet and the width is 45 feet.

142. The length of a rectangle is 26 inches and the width is 58 inches.

143. A rectangular room is 15 feet wide by 14 feet long.

144. A driveway is in the shape of a rectangle 20 feet wide by 35 feet long.

In the following exercises, solve.

145. Find the length of a rectangle with perimeter 124 inches and width 38 inches.

146. Find the length of a rectangle with perimeter 20.2 yards and width of 7.8 yards.

147. Find the width of a rectangle with perimeter 92 meters and length 19 meters.

148. Find the width of a rectangle with perimeter 16.2 meters and length 3.2 meters.

149. The area of a rectangle is 414 square meters. The length is 18 meters. What is the width?

150. The area of a rectangle is 782 square centimeters. The width is 17 centimeters. What is the length?

151. The length of a rectangle is 9 inches more than the width. The perimeter is 46 inches. Find the length and the width.

152. The width of a rectangle is 8 inches more than the length. The perimeter is 52 inches. Find the length and the width.

153. The perimeter of a rectangle is 58 meters. The width of the rectangle is 5 meters less than the length. Find the length and the width of the rectangle.

154. The perimeter of a rectangle is 62 feet. The width is 7 feet less than the length. Find the length and the width.

155. The width of the rectangle is 0.7 meters less than the length. The perimeter of a rectangle is 52.6 meters. Find the dimensions of the rectangle.

156. The length of the rectangle is 1.1 meters less than the width. The perimeter of a rectangle is 49.4 meters. Find the dimensions of the rectangle.

157. The perimeter of a rectangle of 150 feet. The length of the rectangle is twice the width. Find the length and width of the rectangle.

158. The length of a rectangle is three times the width. The perimeter is 72 feet. Find the length and width of the rectangle.

159. The length of a rectangle is 3 meters less than twice the width. The perimeter is 36 meters. Find the length and width.

160. The length of a rectangle is 5 inches more than twice the width. The perimeter is 34 inches. Find the length and width.

161. The width of a rectangular window is 24 inches. The area is 624 square inches. What is the length?

162. The length of a rectangular poster is 28 inches. The area is 1316 square inches. What is the width?

163. The area of a rectangular roof is 2310 square meters. The length is 42 meters. What is the width?

164. The area of a rectangular tarp is 132 square feet. The width is 12 feet. What is the length?

165. The perimeter of a rectangular courtyard is 160 feet. The length is 10 feet more than the width. Find the length and the width.

166. The perimeter of a rectangular painting is 306 centimeters. The length is 17 centimeters more than the width. Find the length and the width.

167. The width of a rectangular window is 40 inches less than the height. The perimeter of the doorway is 224 inches. Find the length and the width.

168. The width of a rectangular playground is 7 meters less than the length. The perimeter of the playground is 46 meters. Find the length and the width.

Use the Properties of Triangles

In the following exercises, solve using the properties of triangles.

169. Find the area of a triangle with base 12 inches and height 5 inches.

170. Find the area of a triangle with base 45 centimeters and height 30 centimeters.

171. Find the area of a triangle with base 8.3 meters and height 6.1 meters.

172. Find the area of a triangle with base 24.2 feet and height 20.5 feet.

173. A triangular flag has base of 1 foot and height of 1.5 feet. What is its area?

174. A triangular window has base of 8 feet and height of 6 feet. What is its area?

175. If a triangle has sides of 6 feet and 9 feet and the perimeter is 23 feet, how long is the third side?

176. If a triangle has sides of 14 centimeters and 18 centimeters and the perimeter is 49 centimeters, how long is the third side?

177. What is the base of a triangle with an area of 207 square inches and height of 18 inches?

178. What is the height of a triangle with an area of 893 square inches and base of 38 inches?

179. The perimeter of a triangular reflecting pool is 36 yards. The lengths of two sides are 10 yards and 15 yards. How long is the third side?

180. A triangular courtyard has perimeter of 120 meters. The lengths of two sides are 30 meters and 50 meters. How long is the third side?

181. An isosceles triangle has a base of 20 centimeters. If the perimeter is 76 centimeters, find the length of each of the other sides.

182. An isosceles triangle has a base of 25 inches. If the perimeter is 95 inches, find the length of each of the other sides.

183. Find the length of each side of an equilateral triangle with a perimeter of 51 yards.

184. Find the length of each side of an equilateral triangle with a perimeter of 54 meters.

185. The perimeter of an equilateral triangle is 18 meters. Find the length of each side.

186. The perimeter of an equilateral triangle is 42 miles. Find the length of each side.

187. The perimeter of an isosceles triangle is 42 feet. The length of the shortest side is 12 feet. Find the length of the other two sides.

188. The perimeter of an isosceles triangle is 83 inches. The length of the shortest side is 24 inches. Find the length of the other two sides.

189. A dish is in the shape of an equilateral triangle. Each side is 8 inches long. Find the perimeter.

190. A floor tile is in the shape of an equilateral triangle. Each side is 1.5 feet long. Find the perimeter.

191. A road sign in the shape of an isosceles triangle has a base of 36 inches. If the perimeter is 91 inches, find the length of each of the other sides.

192. A scarf in the shape of an isosceles triangle has a base of 0.75 meters. If the perimeter is 2 meters, find the length of each of the other sides.

193. The perimeter of a triangle is 39 feet. One side of the triangle is 1 foot longer than the second side. The third side is 2 feet longer than the second side. Find the length of each side.

194. The perimeter of a triangle is 35 feet. One side of the triangle is 5 feet longer than the second side. The third side is 3 feet longer than the second side. Find the length of each side.

195. One side of a triangle is twice the smallest side. The third side is 5 feet more than the shortest side. The perimeter is 17 feet. Find the lengths of all three sides.

196. One side of a triangle is three times the smallest side. The third side is 3 feet more than the shortest side. The perimeter is 13 feet. Find the lengths of all three sides.

Use the Properties of Trapezoids

In the following exercises, solve using the properties of trapezoids.

197. The height of a trapezoid is 12 feet and the bases are 9 and 15 feet. What is the area?

198. The height of a trapezoid is 24 yards and the bases are 18 and 30 yards. What is the area?

199. Find the area of a trapezoid with a height of 51 meters and bases of 43 and 67 meters.

200. Find the area of a trapezoid with a height of 62 inches and bases of 58 and 75 inches.

201. The height of a trapezoid is 15 centimeters and the bases are 12.5 and 18.3 centimeters. What is the area?

202. The height of a trapezoid is 48 feet and the bases are 38.6 and 60.2 feet. What is the area?

203. Find the area of a trapezoid with a height of 4.2 meters and bases of 8.1 and 5.5 meters.

204. Find the area of a trapezoid with a height of 32.5 centimeters and bases of 54.6 and 41.4 centimeters.

205. Laurel is making a banner shaped like a trapezoid. The height of the banner is 3 feet and the bases are 4 and 5 feet. What is the area of the banner?

206. Niko wants to tile the floor of his bathroom. The floor is shaped like a trapezoid with width 5 feet and lengths 5 feet and 8 feet. What is the area of the floor?

207. Theresa needs a new top for her kitchen counter. The counter is shaped like a trapezoid with width 18.5 inches and lengths 62 and 50 inches. What is the area of the counter?

208. Elena is knitting a scarf. The scarf will be shaped like a trapezoid with width 8 inches and lengths 48.2 inches and 56.2 inches. What is the area of the scarf?

Everyday Math

209. Fence Jose just removed the children's playset from his back yard to make room for a rectangular garden. He wants to put a fence around the garden to keep out the dog. He has a 50 foot roll of fence in his garage that he plans to use. To fit in the backyard, the width of the garden must be 10 feet. How long can he make the other side if he wants to use the entire roll of fence?

210. Gardening Lupita wants to fence in her tomato garden. The garden is rectangular and the length is twice the width. It will take 48 feet of fencing to enclose the garden. Find the length and width of her garden.

211. Fence Christa wants to put a fence around her triangular flowerbed. The sides of the flowerbed are 6 feet, 8 feet, and 10 feet. The fence costs $\$10$ per foot. How much will it cost for Christa to fence in her flowerbed?

212. Painting Caleb wants to paint one wall of his attic. The wall is shaped like a trapezoid with height 8 feet and bases 20 feet and 12 feet. The cost of the painting one square foot of wall is about $\$0.05$. About how much will it cost for Caleb to paint the attic wall?

Writing Exercises

213. If you need to put tile on your kitchen floor, do you need to know the perimeter or the area of the kitchen? Explain your reasoning.

214. If you need to put a fence around your backyard, do you need to know the perimeter or the area of the backyard? Explain your reasoning.

215. Look at the two figures.

ⓐ Which figure looks like it has the larger area? Which looks like it has the larger perimeter?

ⓑ Now calculate the area and perimeter of each figure. Which has the larger area? Which has the larger perimeter?

216. The length of a rectangle is 5 feet more than the width. The area is 50 square feet. Find the length and the width.

ⓐ Write the equation you would use to solve the problem.

ⓑ Why can't you solve this equation with the methods you learned in the previous chapter?

Self Check

ⓐ *After completing the exercises, use this checklist to evaluate your mastery of the objectives of this section.*

I can...	Confidently	With some help	No-I don't get it!
understand linear, square, and cubic measure.			
use the properties of rectangles.			
use the properties of triangles.			
use the properties of trapezoids.			

ⓑ *On a scale of 1–10, how would you rate your mastery of this section in light of your responses on the checklist? How can you improve this?*

[9.5] Solve Geometry Applications: Circles and Irregular Figures

Learning Objectives

By the end of this section, you will be able to:

- Use the properties of circles
- Find the area of irregular figures

Be Prepared!

Before you get started, take this readiness quiz.

1. Evaluate x^2 when $x = 5$.
   If you missed this problem, review Example 2.15.

2. Using 3.14 for π, approximate the (a) circumference and (b) the area of a circle with radius 8 inches.
   If you missed this problem, review Example 5.39.

3. Simplify $\frac{22}{7}(0.25)^2$ and round to the nearest thousandth.

   If you missed this problem, review Example 5.36.

In this section, we'll continue working with geometry applications. We will add several new formulas to our collection of formulas. To help you as you do the examples and exercises in this section, we will show the Problem Solving Strategy for Geometry Applications here.

Problem Solving Strategy for Geometry Applications

Step 1. **Read** the problem and make sure you understand all the words and ideas. Draw the figure and label it with the given information.

Step 2. **Identify** what you are looking for.

Step 3. **Name** what you are looking for. Choose a variable to represent that quantity.

Step 4. **Translate** into an equation by writing the appropriate formula or model for the situation. Substitute in the given information.

Step 5. **Solve** the equation using good algebra techniques.

Step 6. **Check** the answer in the problem and make sure it makes sense.

Step 7. **Answer** the question with a complete sentence.

Use the Properties of Circles

Do you remember the properties of circles from Decimals and Fractions Together? We'll show them here again to refer to as we use them to solve applications.

Properties of Circles

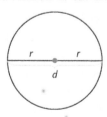

- r is the length of the radius

- d is the length of the diameter

- $d = 2r$

- Circumference is the perimeter of a circle. The formula for **circumference** is
$$C = 2\pi r$$

- The formula for area of a circle is

$$A = \pi r^2$$

Remember, that we approximate π with 3.14 or $\frac{22}{7}$ depending on whether the radius of the circle is given as a decimal or a fraction. If you use the π key on your calculator to do the calculations in this section, your answers will be slightly different from the answers shown. That is because the π key uses more than two decimal places.

EXAMPLE 9.41

A circular sandbox has a radius of 2.5 feet. Find the ⓐ circumference and ⓑ area of the sandbox.

⊘ **Solution**

ⓐ
Step 1. **Read** the problem. Draw the figure and label it with the given information.

Step 2. **Identify** what you are looking for.	the circumference of the circle
Step 3. **Name.** Choose a variable to represent it.	Let $c =$ circumference of the circle
Step 4. **Translate.** Write the appropriate formula Substitute	$C = 2\pi r$ $C = 2\pi(2.5)$
Step 5. **Solve** the equation.	$C \approx 2(3.14)(2.5)$ $C \approx 15\text{ft}$

Step 6. **Check.** Does this answer make sense?
Yes. If we draw a square around the circle, its sides would be 5 ft (twice the radius), so its perimeter would be 20 ft. This is slightly more than the circle's circumference, 15.7 ft.

Step 7. **Answer** the question.	The circumference of the sandbox is 15.7 feet.

ⓑ
Step 1. **Read** the problem. Draw the figure and label it with the given information.

Step 2. **Identify** what you are looking for.

the area of the circle

Step 3. **Name.** Choose a variable to represent it.

Let A = the area of the circle

Step 4. **Translate.**
Write the appropriate formula
Substitute

$A = \pi r^2$
$A = \pi (2.5)^2$

Step 5. **Solve** the equation.

$A \approx (3.14)(2.5)^2$
$A \approx 19.625$ sq. ft

Step 6. **Check.**

Yes. If we draw a square around the circle, its sides would be 5 ft, as shown in part ⓐ. So the area of the square would be 25 sq. ft. This is slightly more than the circle's area, 19.625 sq. ft.

Step 7. **Answer** the question.

The area of the circle is 19.625 square feet.

> **TRY IT : : 9.81**

A circular mirror has radius of 5 inches. Find the ⓐ circumference and ⓑ area of the mirror.

> **TRY IT : : 9.82**

A circular spa has radius of 4.5 feet. Find the ⓐ circumference and ⓑ area of the spa.

We usually see the formula for circumference in terms of the radius r of the circle:

$$C = 2\pi r$$

But since the diameter of a circle is two times the radius, we could write the formula for the circumference in terms of d.

$C = 2\,\pi\,r$
Using the commutative property, we get $C = \pi \cdot 2r$
Then substituting $d = 2r$ $C = \pi \cdot d$
So $C = \pi d$

We will use this form of the circumference when we're given the length of the diameter instead of the radius.

EXAMPLE 9.42

A circular table has a diameter of four feet. What is the circumference of the table?

⊘ **Solution**

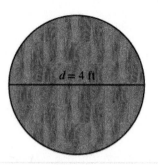

Step 1. **Read** the problem. Draw the figure and label it with the given
information.

Step 2. **Identify** what you are looking for.   the circumference of the table

Step 3. **Name.** Choose a variable to represent it.   Let c = the circumference of
                                                                  the table

Step 4. **Translate.**
Write the appropriate formula for the situation. $C = \pi d$
Substitute. $C = \pi(4)$

Step 5. **Solve** the equation, using 3.14 for π. $C \approx (3.14)(4)$
                                                                  $C \approx 12.56$ feet

Step 6. **Check:** If we put a square around the circle, its side would be 4.
The perimeter would be 16. It makes sense that the circumference of the
circle, 12.56, is a little less than 16.

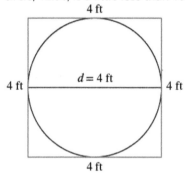

Step 7. **Answer** the question.   The diameter of the table is
                                                                 12.56 square feet.

> **TRY IT : : 9.83**   Find the circumference of a circular fire pit whose diameter is 5.5 feet.

> **TRY IT : : 9.84**   If the diameter of a circular trampoline is 12 feet, what is its circumference?

EXAMPLE 9.43

Find the diameter of a circle with a circumference of 47.1 centimeters.

Solution

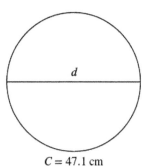

$$C = 47.1 \text{ cm}$$

Step 1. **Read** the problem. Draw the figure and label it with the given information.

Step 2. **Identify** what you are looking for.

the diameter of the circle

Step 3. **Name.** Choose a variable to represent it.

Let d = the diameter of the circle

Step 4. **Translate.**

Write the formula.
Substitute, using 3.14 to approximate π.

$$C = \pi d$$

$$47.1 \approx 3.14d$$

Step 5. **Solve.**

$$\frac{47.1}{3.14} \approx \frac{3.14d}{3.14}$$

$$15 \approx d$$

Step 6. **Check:**
$$C = \pi d$$

$$47.1 \overset{?}{=} (3.14)(15)$$
$$47.1 = 47.1 \checkmark$$

Step 7. **Answer the question.**

The diameter of the circle is approximately 15 centimeters.

> **TRY IT : :** 9.85   Find the diameter of a circle with circumference of 94.2 centimeters.

> **TRY IT : :** 9.86   Find the diameter of a circle with circumference of 345.4 feet.

Find the Area of Irregular Figures

So far, we have found area for rectangles, triangles, trapezoids, and circles. An **irregular figure** is a figure that is not a standard geometric shape. Its area cannot be calculated using any of the standard area formulas. But some irregular figures are made up of two or more standard geometric shapes. To find the area of one of these irregular figures, we can split it into figures whose formulas we know and then add the areas of the figures.

EXAMPLE 9.44

Find the area of the shaded region.

✓ Solution

The given figure is irregular, but we can break it into two rectangles. The area of the shaded region will be the sum of the areas of both rectangles.

$$A_{\text{figure}} = A_{\text{blue rectangle}} + A_{\text{red rectangle}}$$

The blue rectangle has a width of 12 and a length of 4. The red rectangle has a width of 2, but its length is not labeled.

The right side of the figure is the length of the red rectangle plus the length of the blue rectangle. Since the right side of the blue rectangle is 4 units long, the length of the red rectangle must be 6 units.

$$A_{\text{figure}} = A_{\text{rectangle}} + A_{\text{rectangle}}$$
$$A_{\text{figure}} = bh + bh$$
$$A_{\text{figure}} = 12 \cdot 4 + 2 \cdot 6$$
$$A_{\text{figure}} = 48 + 12$$
$$A_{\text{figure}} = 60$$

The area of the figure is 60 square units.

Is there another way to split this figure into two rectangles? Try it, and make sure you get the same area.

> **TRY IT : : 9.87**   Find the area of each shaded region:

> **TRY IT : : 9.88**   Find the area of each shaded region:

EXAMPLE 9.45

Find the area of the shaded region.

⊘ Solution

We can break this irregular figure into a triangle and rectangle. The area of the figure will be the sum of the areas of triangle and rectangle.

The rectangle has a length of 8 units and a width of 4 units.

We need to find the base and height of the triangle.

Since both sides of the rectangle are $4,$ the vertical side of the triangle is 3, which is $7 - 4$.

The length of the rectangle is $8,$ so the base of the triangle will be 3, which is $8 - 4$.

Now we can add the areas to find the area of the irregular figure.

$$A_{figure} = A_{rectangle} + A_{triangle}$$
$$A_{figure} = lw + \frac{1}{2}bh$$
$$A_{figure} = 8 \cdot 4 + \frac{1}{2} \cdot 3 \cdot 3$$
$$A_{figure} = 32 + 4.5$$
$$A_{figure} = 36.5 \text{ sq. units}$$

The area of the figure is 36.5 square units.

> **TRY IT :: 9.89**   Find the area of each shaded region.

> **TRY IT :: 9.90**   Find the area of each shaded region.

EXAMPLE 9.46

A high school track is shaped like a rectangle with a semi-circle (half a circle) on each end. The rectangle has length 105 meters and width 68 meters. Find the area enclosed by the track. Round your answer to the nearest hundredth.

⊘ Solution

We will break the figure into a rectangle and two semi-circles. The area of the figure will be the sum of the areas of the rectangle and the semicircles.

The rectangle has a length of 105 m and a width of 68 m. The semi-circles have a diameter of 68 m, so each has a radius of 34 m.

$$A_{\text{figure}} = A_{\text{rectangle}} + A_{\text{semicircles}}$$

$$A_{\text{figure}} = bh + 2\left(\frac{1}{2}\pi \cdot r^2\right)$$

$$A_{\text{figure}} \approx 105 \cdot 68 + 2\left(\frac{1}{2} \cdot 3.14 \cdot 34^2\right)$$

$$A_{\text{figure}} \approx 7140 + 3629.84$$

$$A_{\text{figure}} \approx 10{,}769.84 \text{ square meters}$$

> **TRY IT :: 9.91**   Find the area:

> **TRY IT :: 9.92**   Find the area:

▶ **MEDIA ::** ACCESS ADDITIONAL ONLINE RESOURCES

- Circumference of a Circle (http://www.openstaxcollege.org/l/24circumcircle)
- Area of a Circle (http://www.openstaxcollege.org/l/24areacircle)
- Area of an L-shaped polygon (http://www.openstaxcollege.org/l/24areaLpoly)
- Area of an L-shaped polygon with Decimals (http://www.openstaxcollege.org/l/24areaLpolyd)
- Perimeter Involving a Rectangle and Circle (http://www.openstaxcollege.org/l/24perirectcirc)
- Area Involving a Rectangle and Circle (http://www.openstaxcollege.org/l/24arearectcirc)

9.5 EXERCISES

Practice Makes Perfect

Use the Properties of Circles

In the following exercises, solve using the properties of circles.

217. The lid of a paint bucket is a circle with radius 7 inches. Find the ⓐ circumference and ⓑ area of the lid.

218. An extra-large pizza is a circle with radius 8 inches. Find the ⓐ circumference and ⓑ area of the pizza.

219. A farm sprinkler spreads water in a circle with radius of 8.5 feet. Find the ⓐ circumference and ⓑ area of the watered circle.

220. A circular rug has radius of 3.5 feet. Find the ⓐ circumference and ⓑ area of the rug.

221. A reflecting pool is in the shape of a circle with diameter of 20 feet. What is the circumference of the pool?

222. A turntable is a circle with diameter of 10 inches. What is the circumference of the turntable?

223. A circular saw has a diameter of 12 inches. What is the circumference of the saw?

224. A round coin has a diameter of 3 centimeters. What is the circumference of the coin?

225. A barbecue grill is a circle with a diameter of 2.2 feet. What is the circumference of the grill?

226. The top of a pie tin is a circle with a diameter of 9.5 inches. What is the circumference of the top?

227. A circle has a circumference of 163.28 inches. Find the diameter.

228. A circle has a circumference of 59.66 feet. Find the diameter.

229. A circle has a circumference of 17.27 meters. Find the diameter.

230. A circle has a circumference of 80.07 centimeters. Find the diameter.

In the following exercises, find the radius of the circle with given circumference.

231. A circle has a circumference of 150.72 feet.

232. A circle has a circumference of 251.2 centimeters.

233. A circle has a circumference of 40.82 miles.

234. A circle has a circumference of 78.5 inches.

Find the Area of Irregular Figures

In the following exercises, find the area of the irregular figure. Round your answers to the nearest hundredth.

235.

236.

237.

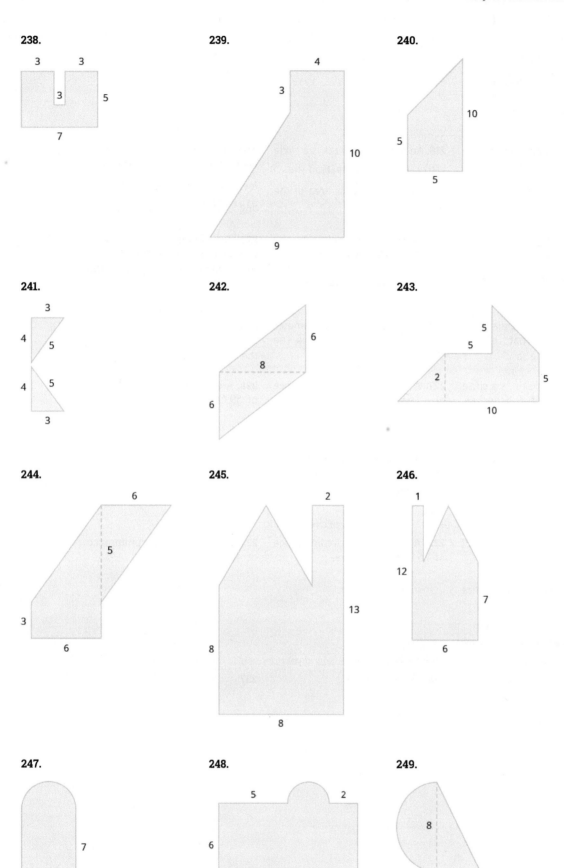

238.

239.

240.

241.

242.

243.

244.

245.

246.

247.

248.

249.

250.

251.

252.

253.

254.

In the following exercises, solve.

255. A city park covers one block plus parts of four more blocks, as shown. The block is a square with sides 250 feet long, and the triangles are isosceles right triangles. Find the area of the park.

256. A gift box will be made from a rectangular piece of cardboard measuring 12 inches by 20 inches, with squares cut out of the corners of the sides, as shown. The sides of the squares are 3 inches. Find the area of the cardboard after the corners are cut out.

257. Perry needs to put in a new lawn. His lot is a rectangle with a length of 120 feet and a width of 100 feet. The house is rectangular and measures 50 feet by 40 feet. His driveway is rectangular and measures 20 feet by 30 feet, as shown. Find the area of Perry's lawn.

258. Denise is planning to put a deck in her back yard. The deck will be a 20-ft by 12-ft rectangle with a semicircle of diameter 6 feet, as shown below. Find the area of the deck.

Everyday Math

259. Area of a Tabletop Yuki bought a drop-leaf kitchen table. The rectangular part of the table is a 1-ft by 3-ft rectangle with a semicircle at each end, as shown. ⓐ Find the area of the table with one leaf up. ⓑ Find the area of the table with both leaves up.

260. Painting Leora wants to paint the nursery in her house. The nursery is an 8-ft by 10-ft rectangle, and the ceiling is 8 feet tall. There is a 3-ft by 6.5-ft door on one wall, a 3-ft by 6.5-ft closet door on another wall, and one 4-ft by 3.5-ft window on the third wall. The fourth wall has no doors or windows. If she will only paint the four walls, and not the ceiling or doors, how many square feet will she need to paint?

Writing Exercises

261. Describe two different ways to find the area of this figure, and then show your work to make sure both ways give the same area.

262. A circle has a diameter of 14 feet. Find the area of the circle ⓐ using 3.14 for π ⓑ using $\frac{22}{7}$ for π. ⓒ Which calculation to do prefer? Why?

Self Check

ⓐ After completing the exercises, use this checklist to evaluate your mastery of the objectives of this section.

I can...	Confidently	With some help	No-I don't get it!
use the properties of circles.			
find the area of irregular figures.			

ⓑ After looking at the checklist, do you think you are well prepared for the next section? Why or why not?

9.6 | Solve Geometry Applications: Volume and Surface Area

Learning Objectives

By the end of this section, you will be able to:

- Find volume and surface area of rectangular solids
- Find volume and surface area of spheres
- Find volume and surface area of cylinders
- Find volume of cones

Be Prepared!

Before you get started, take this readiness quiz.

1. Evaluate x^3 when $x = 5$.
   If you missed this problem, review Example 2.15.

2. Evaluate 2^x when $x = 5$.
   If you missed this problem, review Example 2.16.

3. Find the area of a circle with radius $\frac{7}{2}$.

   If you missed this problem, review Example 5.39.

In this section, we will finish our study of geometry applications. We find the volume and surface area of some three-dimensional figures. Since we will be solving applications, we will once again show our Problem-Solving Strategy for Geometry Applications.

Problem Solving Strategy for Geometry Applications

Step 1. **Read** the problem and make sure you understand all the words and ideas. Draw the figure and label it with the given information.

Step 2. **Identify** what you are looking for.

Step 3. **Name** what you are looking for. Choose a variable to represent that quantity.

Step 4. **Translate** into an equation by writing the appropriate formula or model for the situation. Substitute in the given information.

Step 5. **Solve** the equation using good algebra techniques.

Step 6. **Check** the answer in the problem and make sure it makes sense.

Step 7. **Answer** the question with a complete sentence.

Find Volume and Surface Area of Rectangular Solids

A cheerleading coach is having the squad paint wooden crates with the school colors to stand on at the games. (See Figure 9.28). The amount of paint needed to cover the outside of each box is the **surface area**, a square measure of the total area of all the sides. The amount of space inside the crate is the volume, a cubic measure.

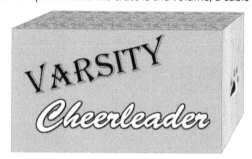

Figure 9.28 This wooden crate is in the shape of a rectangular solid.

Each crate is in the shape of a **rectangular solid**. Its dimensions are the length, width, and height. The rectangular solid shown in Figure 9.29 has length 4 units, width 2 units, and height 3 units. Can you tell how many cubic units there are altogether? Let's look layer by layer.

The top layer has 8 cubic units.

The middle layer has 8 cubic units.

The bottom layer has 8 cubic units.

Figure 9.29 Breaking a rectangular solid into layers makes it easier to visualize the number of cubic units it contains. This 4 by 2 by 3 rectangular solid has 24 cubic units.

Altogether there are 24 cubic units. Notice that 24 is the length $\times$ width $\times$ height.

$$V = L \cdot W \cdot H$$
$$24 = 4 \cdot 2 \cdot 3$$

The volume, V, of any rectangular solid is the product of the length, width, and height.

$$V = LWH$$

We could also write the formula for volume of a rectangular solid in terms of the area of the base. The area of the base, B, is equal to length$\times$width.

$$B = L \cdot W$$

We can substitute B for $L \cdot W$ in the volume formula to get another form of the volume formula.

$$V = L \cdot W \cdot H$$
$$V = (L \cdot W) \cdot H$$
$$V = Bh$$

We now have another version of the volume formula for rectangular solids. Let's see how this works with the $4 \times 2 \times 3$ rectangular solid we started with. See Figure 9.29.

$V = Bh$
$V = \text{Base} \times \text{height}$
$V = (4 \cdot 2) \times \text{height}$
$V = (4 \cdot 2) \times 3$
$V = 8 \times 3$
$V = 24$ cubic units

Figure 9.30

To find the *surface area* of a rectangular solid, think about finding the area of each of its faces. How many faces does the rectangular solid above have? You can see three of them.

$$A_{\text{front}} = L \times W \qquad A_{\text{side}} = L \times W \qquad A_{\text{top}} = L \times W$$
$$A_{\text{front}} = 4 \cdot 3 \qquad A_{\text{side}} = 2 \cdot 3 \qquad A_{\text{top}} = 4 \cdot 2$$
$$A_{\text{front}} = 12 \qquad A_{\text{side}} = 6 \qquad A_{\text{top}} = 8$$

Notice for each of the three faces you see, there is an identical opposite face that does not show.

$$S = (\text{front} + \text{back}) + (\text{left side} + \text{right side}) + (\text{top} + \text{bottom})$$
$$S = (2 \cdot \text{front}) + (2 \cdot \text{left side}) + (2 \cdot \text{top})$$
$$S = 2 \cdot 12 + 2 \cdot 6 + 2 \cdot 8$$
$$S = 24 + 12 + 16$$
$$S = 52 \text{ sq. units}$$

The surface area S of the rectangular solid shown in Figure 9.30 is 52 square units.

In general, to find the surface area of a rectangular solid, remember that each face is a rectangle, so its area is the product of its length and its width (see Figure 9.31). Find the area of each face that you see and then multiply each area by two to account for the face on the opposite side.

$$S = 2LH + 2LW + 2WH$$

Figure 9.31 For each face of the rectangular solid facing you, there is another face on the opposite side. There are 6 faces in all.

Volume and Surface Area of a Rectangular Solid

For a rectangular solid with length L, width W, and height H :

Volume: $V = LWH$

Surface Area: $S = 2LH + 2LW + 2WH$

 MANIPULATIVE MATHEMATICS

Doing the Manipulative Mathematics activity "Painted Cube" will help you develop a better understanding of volume and surface area.

EXAMPLE 9.47

For a rectangular solid with length 14 cm, height 17 cm, and width 9 cm, find the ⓐ volume and ⓑ surface area.

⊘ Solution

Step 1 is the same for both ⓐ and ⓑ, so we will show it just once.

Step 1. **Read** the problem. Draw the figure and label it with the given information.

ⓐ

Step 2. **Identify** what you are looking for.	the volume of the rectangular solid
Step 3. **Name.** Choose a variable to represent it.	Let V = volume
Step 4. **Translate.** Write the appropriate formula. Substitute.	$V = LWH$ $V = 14 \cdot 9 \cdot 17$
Step 5. **Solve** the equation.	$V = 2{,}142$
Step 6. **Check** We leave it to you to check your calculations.	
Step 7. **Answer** the question.	The surface area is $1{,}034$ square centimeters.

ⓑ

Step 2. **Identify** what you are looking for.	the surface area of the solid
Step 3. **Name.** Choose a variable to represent it.	Let S = surface area
Step 4. **Translate.** Write the appropriate formula. Substitute.	$S = 2LH + 2LW + 2WH$ $S = 2(14 \cdot 17) + 2(14 \cdot 9) + 2(9 \cdot 17)$
Step 5. **Solve the equation.**	$S = 1{,}034$
Step 6. **Check:** Double-check with a calculator.	
Step 7. **Answer** the question.	The surface area is 1,034 square centimeters.

> **TRY IT : :** 9.93
>
> Find the ⓐ volume and ⓑ surface area of rectangular solid with the: length 8 feet, width 9 feet, and height 11 feet.

> **TRY IT : :** 9.94
>
> Find the ⓐ volume and ⓑ surface area of rectangular solid with the: length 15 feet, width 12 feet, and height 8 feet.

EXAMPLE 9.48

A rectangular crate has a length of 30 inches, width of 25 inches, and height of 20 inches. Find its ⓐ volume and ⓑ surface area.

⊘ **Solution**

Step 1 is the same for both ⓐ and ⓑ, so we will show it just once.

Step 1. **Read** the problem. Draw the figure and label it with the given information.

ⓐ

Step 2. **Identify** what you are looking for.	the volume of the crate
Step 3. **Name.** Choose a variable to represent it.	let V = volume
Step 4. **Translate.** Write the appropriate formula. Substitute.	$V = LWH$ $V = 30 \cdot 25 \cdot 20$
Step 5. **Solve** the equation.	$V = 15,000$
Step 6. **Check:** Double check your math.	
Step 7. **Answer** the question.	The volume is 15,000 cubic inches.

ⓑ

Step 2. **Identify** what you are looking for.	the surface area of the crate
Step 3. **Name.** Choose a variable to represent it.	let S = surface area
Step 4. **Translate.** Write the appropriate formula. Substitute.	$S = 2LH + 2LW + 2WH$ $S = 2(30 \cdot 20) + 2(30 \cdot 25) + 2(25 \cdot 20)$
Step 5. **Solve** the equation.	$S = 3,700$
Step 6. **Check:** Check it yourself!	
Step 7. **Answer** the question.	The surface area is 3,700 square inches.

> **TRY IT ::** 9.95

  A rectangular box has length 9 feet, width 4 feet, and height 6 feet. Find its ⓐ volume and ⓑ surface area.

> **TRY IT ::** 9.96

  A rectangular suitcase has length 22 inches, width 14 inches, and height 9 inches. Find its ⓐ volume and ⓑ surface area.

Volume and Surface Area of a Cube

A **cube** is a rectangular solid whose length, width, and height are equal. See Volume and Surface Area of a Cube, below. Substituting, s for the length, width and height into the formulas for volume and surface area of a rectangular solid, we get:

$$V = LWH \qquad S = 2LH + 2LW + 2WH$$
$$V = s \cdot s \cdot s \qquad S = 2s \cdot s + 2s \cdot s + 2s \cdot s$$
$$V = s^3 \qquad\qquad S = 2s^2 + 2s^2 + 2s^2$$
$$\qquad\qquad\qquad\quad\; S = 6s^2$$

So for a cube, the formulas for volume and surface area are $V = s^3$ and $S = 6s^2$.

Volume and Surface Area of a Cube

For any cube with sides of length s,

Volume: $V = s^3$
Surface Area: $S = 6s^2$

EXAMPLE 9.49

A cube is 2.5 inches on each side. Find its ⓐ volume and ⓑ surface area.

⊘ **Solution**

Step 1 is the same for both ⓐ and ⓑ, so we will show it just once.

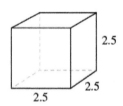

Step 1. **Read** the problem. Draw the figure and label it with the given information.

ⓐ

Step 2. **Identify** what you are looking for.	the volume of the cube
Step 3. **Name.** Choose a variable to represent it.	let V = volume
Step 4. **Translate.** Write the appropriate formula.	$V = s^3$
Step 5. **Solve.** Substitute and solve.	$V = (2.5)^3$ $V = 15.625$
Step 6. **Check:** Check your work.	
Step 7. **Answer** the question.	The volume is 15.625 cubic inches.

ⓑ

Step 2. **Identify** what you are looking for.	the surface area of the cube
Step 3. **Name.** Choose a variable to represent it.	let S = surface area
Step 4. **Translate.** Write the appropriate formula.	$S = 6s^2$
Step 5. **Solve.** Substitute and solve.	$S = 6 \cdot (2.5)^2$ $S = 37.5$
Step 6. **Check:** The check is left to you.	
Step 7. **Answer** the question.	The surface area is 37.5 square inches.

> **TRY IT : : 9.97**   For a cube with side 4.5 meters, find the ⓐ volume and ⓑ surface area of the cube.

> **TRY IT : : 9.98**   For a cube with side 7.3 yards, find the ⓐ volume and ⓑ surface area of the cube.

EXAMPLE 9.50

A notepad cube measures 2 inches on each side. Find its ⓐ volume and ⓑ surface area.

⊘ **Solution**

Step 1. **Read** the problem. Draw the figure and label it with the given information.	

ⓐ

Step 2. **Identify** what you are looking for.	the volume of the cube
Step 3. **Name.** Choose a variable to represent it.	let V = volume
Step 4. **Translate.** Write the appropriate formula.	$V = s^3$
Step 5. **Solve** the equation.	$V = 2^3$ $V = 8$
Step 6. **Check:** Check that you did the calculations correctly.	
Step 7. **Answer** the question.	The volume is 8 cubic inches.

Step 2. **Identify** what you are looking for.	the surface area of the cube
Step 3. **Name.** Choose a variable to represent it.	let S = surface area
Step 4. **Translate.** Write the appropriate formula.	$S = 6s^2$
Step 5. **Solve** the equation.	$S = 6 \cdot 2^2$ $S = 24$
Step 6. **Check:** The check is left to you.	
Step 7. **Answer** the question.	The surface area is 24 square inches.

> **TRY IT :: 9.99**
>
> A packing box is a cube measuring 4 feet on each side. Find its ⓐ volume and ⓑ surface area.

> **TRY IT :: 9.100**
>
> A wall is made up of cube-shaped bricks. Each cube is 16 inches on each side. Find the ⓐ volume and ⓑ surface area of each cube.

Find the Volume and Surface Area of Spheres

A **sphere** is the shape of a basketball, like a three-dimensional circle. Just like a circle, the size of a sphere is determined by its radius, which is the distance from the center of the sphere to any point on its surface. The formulas for the volume and surface area of a sphere are given below.

Showing where these formulas come from, like we did for a rectangular solid, is beyond the scope of this course. We will approximate π with 3.14.

Volume and Surface Area of a Sphere

For a sphere with radius r:

Volume: $V = \frac{4}{3}\pi r^3$
Surface Area: $S = 4\pi r^2$

EXAMPLE 9.51

A sphere has a radius 6 inches. Find its ⓐ volume and ⓑ surface area.

⊘ **Solution**

Step 1 is the same for both ⓐ and ⓑ, so we will show it just once.

Step 1. **Read** the problem. Draw the figure and label it with the given information.

ⓐ

Step 2. **Identify** what you are looking for.	the volume of the sphere
Step 3. **Name.** Choose a variable to represent it.	let V = volume
Step 4. **Translate.** Write the appropriate formula.	$V = \frac{4}{3}\pi r^3$
Step 5. **Solve.**	$V \approx \frac{4}{3}(3.14)6^3$ $V \approx 904.32$ cubic inches
Step 6. **Check:** Double-check your math on a calculator.	
Step 7. **Answer** the question.	The volume is approximately 904.32 cubic inches.

ⓑ

Step 2. **Identify** what you are looking for.	the surface area of the cube
Step 3. **Name.** Choose a variable to represent it.	let S = surface area
Step 4. **Translate.** Write the appropriate formula.	$S = 4\pi r^2$
Step 5. **Solve.**	$S \approx 4(3.14)6^2$ $S \approx 452.16$
Step 6. **Check:** Double-check your math on a calculator	
Step 7. **Answer** the question.	The surface area is approximately 452.16 square inches.

> **TRY IT : : 9.101**   Find the ⓐ volume and ⓑ surface area of a sphere with radius 3 centimeters.

> **TRY IT : : 9.102**   Find the ⓐ volume and ⓑ surface area of each sphere with a radius of 1 foot

EXAMPLE 9.52

A globe of Earth is in the shape of a sphere with radius 14 centimeters. Find its ⓐ volume and ⓑ surface area. Round the answer to the nearest hundredth.

⊘ **Solution**

Step 1. **Read** the problem. Draw a figure with the given information and label it.

ⓐ

Step 2. **Identify** what you are looking for.	the volume of the sphere
Step 3. **Name.** Choose a variable to represent it.	let V = volume
Step 4. **Translate.** Write the appropriate formula. Substitute. (Use 3.14 for π)	$V = \frac{4}{3}\pi r^3$ $V \approx \frac{4}{3}(3.14)14^3$
Step 5. **Solve.**	$V \approx 11{,}488.21$
Step 6. **Check:** We leave it to you to check your calculations.	
Step 7. **Answer** the question.	The volume is approximately 11,488.21 cubic inches.

ⓑ

Step 2. **Identify** what you are looking for.	the surface area of the sphere
Step 3. **Name.** Choose a variable to represent it.	let S = surface area
Step 4. **Translate.** Write the appropriate formula. Substitute. (Use 3.14 for π)	$S = 4\pi r^2$ $S \approx 4(3.14)14^2$
Step 5. **Solve.**	$S \approx 2461.76$
Step 6. **Check:** We leave it to you to check your calculations.	
Step 7. **Answer** the question.	The surface area is approximately 2461.76 square inches.

> | **TRY IT : :** 9.103

   A beach ball is in the shape of a sphere with radius of 9 inches. Find its ⓐ volume and ⓑ surface area.

> | **TRY IT : :** 9.104

   A Roman statue depicts Atlas holding a globe with radius of 1.5 feet. Find the ⓐ volume and ⓑ surface area of the globe.

Find the Volume and Surface Area of a Cylinder

If you have ever seen a can of soda, you know what a cylinder looks like. A **cylinder** is a solid figure with two parallel circles of the same size at the top and bottom. The top and bottom of a cylinder are called the bases. The height h of a cylinder is the distance between the two bases. For all the cylinders we will work with here, the sides and the height, h , will be perpendicular to the bases.

Figure 9.32 A cylinder has two circular bases of equal size. The height is the distance between the bases.

Rectangular solids and cylinders are somewhat similar because they both have two bases and a height. The formula for the volume of a rectangular solid, $V = Bh$, can also be used to find the volume of a cylinder.

For the rectangular solid, the area of the base, B , is the area of the rectangular base, length × width. For a cylinder, the area of the base, B, is the area of its circular base, πr^2. Figure 9.33 compares how the formula $V = Bh$ is used for rectangular solids and cylinders.

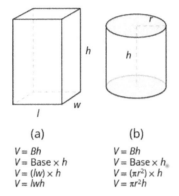

Figure 9.33 Seeing how a cylinder is similar to a rectangular solid may make it easier to understand the formula for the volume of a cylinder.

To understand the formula for the surface area of a cylinder, think of a can of vegetables. It has three surfaces: the top, the bottom, and the piece that forms the sides of the can. If you carefully cut the label off the side of the can and unroll it, you will see that it is a rectangle. See Figure 9.34.

Figure 9.34 By cutting and unrolling the label of a can of vegetables, we can see that the surface of a cylinder is a rectangle. The length of the rectangle is the circumference of the cylinder's base, and the width is the height of the cylinder.

The distance around the edge of the can is the **circumference** of the cylinder's base it is also the length L of the rectangular label. The height of the cylinder is the width W of the rectangular label. So the area of the label can be represented as

To find the total surface area of the cylinder, we add the areas of the two circles to the area of the rectangle.

$$S = A_{top\ circle} + A_{bottom\ circle} + A_{rectangle}$$
$$S = \pi r^2 + \pi r^2 + 2\pi r \cdot h$$
$$S = 2 \cdot \pi r^2 + 2\pi rh$$
$$S = 2\pi r^2 + 2\pi rh$$

The surface area of a cylinder with radius r and height h, is

$$S = 2\pi r^2 + 2\pi rh$$

Volume and Surface Area of a Cylinder

For a cylinder with radius r and height h:

Volume: $V = \pi r^2 h$ or $V = Bh$
Surface Area: $S = 2\pi r^2 + 2\pi rh$

EXAMPLE 9.53

A cylinder has height 5 centimeters and radius 3 centimeters. Find the ⓐ volume and ⓑ surface area.

⊘ **Solution**

Step 1. **Read** the problem. Draw the figure and label it with the given information.

ⓐ

Step 2. **Identify** what you are looking for.	the volume of the cylinder
Step 3. **Name.** Choose a variable to represent it.	let V = volume
Step 4. **Translate.** Write the appropriate formula. Substitute. (Use 3.14 for π)	$V = \pi r^2 h$ $V \approx (3.14)3^2 \cdot 5$
Step 5. **Solve.**	$V \approx 141.3$
Step 6. **Check:** We leave it to you to check your calculations.	
Step 7. **Answer** the question.	The volume is approximately 141.3 cubic inches.

ⓑ

Step 2. **Identify** what you are looking for.	the surface area of the cylinder
Step 3. **Name.** Choose a variable to represent it.	let S = surface area
Step 4. **Translate.** Write the appropriate formula. Substitute. (Use 3.14 for π)	$S = 2\pi r^2 + 2\pi rh$ $S \approx 2(3.14)3^2 + 2(3.14)(3)5$
Step 5. **Solve.**	$S \approx 150.72$
Step 6. **Check:** We leave it to you to check your calculations.	
Step 7. **Answer** the question.	The surface area is approximately 150.72 square inches.

> **TRY IT : : 9.105** Find the ⓐ volume and ⓑ surface area of the cylinder with radius 4 cm and height 7cm.

> **TRY IT : : 9.106** Find the ⓐ volume and ⓑ surface area of the cylinder with given radius 2 ft and height 8 ft.

EXAMPLE 9.54

Find the ⓐ volume and ⓑ surface area of a can of soda. The radius of the base is 4 centimeters and the height is 13 centimeters. Assume the can is shaped exactly like a cylinder.

⊘ **Solution**

Step 1. **Read** the problem. Draw the figure and label it with the given information.

ⓐ

Step 2. **Identify** what you are looking for.	the volume of the cylinder
Step 3. **Name.** Choose a variable to represent it.	let V = volume
Step 4. **Translate.** Write the appropriate formula. Substitute. (Use 3.14 for π)	$V = \pi r^2 h$ $V \approx (3.14)4^2 \cdot 13$
Step 5. **Solve.**	$V \approx 653.12$
Step 6. **Check:** We leave it to you to check.	
Step 7. **Answer** the question.	The volume is approximately 653.12 cubic centimeters.

ⓑ

Step 2. **Identify** what you are looking for.	the surface area of the cylinder
Step 3. **Name.** Choose a variable to represent it.	let S = surface area
Step 4. **Translate.** Write the appropriate formula. Substitute. (Use 3.14 for π)	$S = 2\pi r^2 + 2\pi rh$ $S \approx 2(3.14)4^2 + 2(3.14)(4)13$
Step 5. **Solve.**	$S \approx 427.04$
Step 6. **Check:** We leave it to you to check your calculations.	
Step 7. **Answer** the question.	The surface area is approximately 427.04 square centimeters.

> **TRY IT : :** 9.107

Find the ⓐ volume and ⓑ surface area of a can of paint with radius 8 centimeters and height 19 centimeters. Assume the can is shaped exactly like a cylinder.

> **TRY IT : :** 9.108

Find the ⓐ volume and ⓑ surface area of a cylindrical drum with radius 2.7 feet and height 4 feet. Assume the drum is shaped exactly like a cylinder.

Find the Volume of Cones

The first image that many of us have when we hear the word 'cone' is an ice cream cone. There are many other applications of cones (but most are not as tasty as ice cream cones). In this section, we will see how to find the volume of a cone.

In geometry, a **cone** is a solid figure with one circular base and a vertex. The height of a cone is the distance between its base and the vertex.The cones that we will look at in this section will always have the height perpendicular to the base. See Figure 9.35.

Figure 9.35 The height of a cone is the distance between its base and the vertex.

Earlier in this section, we saw that the volume of a cylinder is $V = \pi r^2 h$. We can think of a cone as part of a cylinder. Figure 9.36 shows a cone placed inside a cylinder with the same height and same base. If we compare the volume of the cone and the cylinder, we can see that the volume of the cone is less than that of the cylinder.

Figure 9.36 The volume of a cone is less than the volume of a cylinder with the same base and height.

In fact, the volume of a cone is exactly one-third of the volume of a cylinder with the same base and height. The volume of a cone is

$$V = \frac{1}{3} Bh$$

Since the base of a cone is a circle, we can substitute the formula of area of a circle, πr^2 , for B to get the formula for volume of a cone.

$$V = \frac{1}{3} \pi r^2 h$$

In this book, we will only find the volume of a cone, and not its surface area.

Volume of a Cone

For a cone with radius r and height h .

Volume: $V = \frac{1}{3} \pi r^2 h$

EXAMPLE 9.55

Find the volume of a cone with height 6 inches and radius of its base 2 inches.

⊘ **Solution**

Step 1. **Read** the problem. Draw the figure and label it
with the given information.

Step 2. **Identify** what you are looking for.	the volume of the cone
Step 3. **Name.** Choose a variable to represent it.	let V = volume
Step 4. **Translate.** Write the appropriate formula. Substitute. (Use 3.14 for π)	$V = \frac{1}{3}\ \pi\ \ \ r^2\ \ \ h$ $V \approx \frac{1}{3}\ \ 3.14\ \ (2)^2\ \ (6)$
Step 5. **Solve.**	$V \approx 25.12$
Step 6. **Check:** We leave it to you to check your calculations.	
Step 7. **Answer** the question.	The volume is approximately 25.12 cubic inches.

> | **TRY IT : :** 9.109   Find the volume of a cone with height 7 inches and radius 3 inches

> | **TRY IT : :** 9.110   Find the volume of a cone with height 9 centimeters and radius 5 centimeters

EXAMPLE 9.56

Marty's favorite gastro pub serves french fries in a paper wrap shaped like a cone. What is the volume of a conic wrap that
is 8 inches tall and 5 inches in diameter? Round the answer to the nearest hundredth.

⊘ **Solution**

Step 1. **Read** the problem. Draw the figure and label it with the given information. Notice here that the base is the circle at the top of the cone.

Step 2. **Identify** what you are looking for.

the volume of the cone

Step 3. **Name.** Choose a variable to represent it.

let V = volume

Step 4. **Translate.** Write the appropriate formula. Substitute. (Use 3.14 for π, and notice that we were given the distance across the circle, which is its diameter. The radius is 2.5 inches.)

$$V = \frac{1}{3} \pi \quad r^2 \quad h$$

$$V \approx \frac{1}{3} \; 3.14 \; (2.5)^2 \; (8)$$

Step 5. **Solve.**

$$V \approx 52.33$$

Step 6. **Check:** We leave it to you to check your calculations.

Step 7. **Answer** the question.

The volume of the wrap is approximately 52.33 cubic inches.

> **TRY IT : : 9.111**

How many cubic inches of candy will fit in a cone-shaped piñata that is 18 inches long and 12 inches across its base? Round the answer to the nearest hundredth.

> **TRY IT : : 9.112**

What is the volume of a cone-shaped party hat that is 10 inches tall and 7 inches across at the base? Round the answer to the nearest hundredth.

Summary of Geometry Formulas

The following charts summarize all of the formulas covered in this chapter.

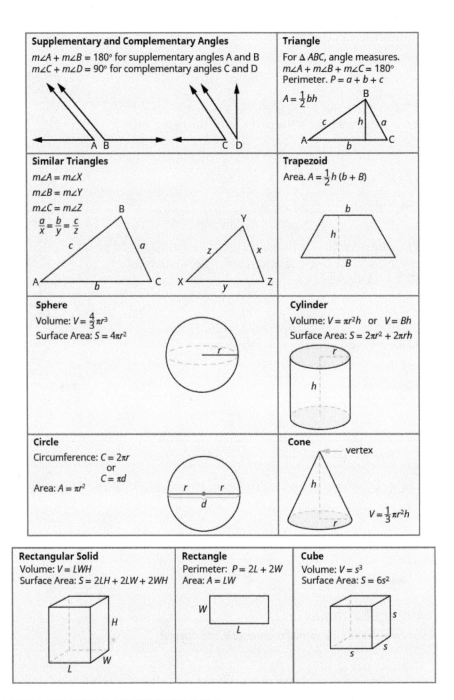

Supplementary and Complementary Angles
$m\angle A + m\angle B = 180°$ for supplementary angles A and B
$m\angle C + m\angle D = 90°$ for complementary angles C and D

Triangle
For $\triangle ABC$, angle measures.
$m\angle A + m\angle B + m\angle C = 180°$
Perimeter. $P = a + b + c$
$A = \frac{1}{2}bh$

Similar Triangles
$m\angle A = m\angle X$
$m\angle B = m\angle Y$
$m\angle C = m\angle Z$
$\frac{a}{x} = \frac{b}{y} = \frac{c}{z}$

Trapezoid
Area. $A = \frac{1}{2}h(b + B)$

Sphere
Volume: $V = \frac{4}{3}\pi r^3$
Surface Area: $S = 4\pi r^2$

Cylinder
Volume: $V = \pi r^2 h$ or $V = Bh$
Surface Area: $S = 2\pi r^2 + 2\pi rh$

Circle
Circumference: $C = 2\pi r$
or
$C = \pi d$
Area: $A = \pi r^2$

Cone
vertex
$V = \frac{1}{3}\pi r^2 h$

Rectangular Solid
Volume: $V = LWH$
Surface Area: $S = 2LH + 2LW + 2WH$

Rectangle
Perimeter: $P = 2L + 2W$
Area: $A = LW$

Cube
Volume: $V = s^3$
Surface Area: $S = 6s^2$

▶ **MEDIA : :** ACCESS ADDITIONAL ONLINE RESOURCES
   • **Volume of a Cone (http://openstaxcollege.org/l/24volcone)**

9.6 EXERCISES

Practice Makes Perfect

Find Volume and Surface Area of Rectangular Solids

In the following exercises, find ⓐ the volume and ⓑ the surface area of the rectangular solid with the given dimensions.

263. length 2 meters, width 1.5 meters, height 3 meters

264. length 5 feet, width 8 feet, height 2.5 feet

265. length 3.5 yards, width 2.1 yards, height 2.4 yards

266. length 8.8 centimeters, width 6.5 centimeters, height 4.2 centimeters

In the following exercises, solve.

267. Moving van A rectangular moving van has length 16 feet, width 8 feet, and height 8 feet. Find its ⓐ volume and ⓑ surface area.

268. Gift box A rectangular gift box has length 26 inches, width 16 inches, and height 4 inches. Find its ⓐ volume and ⓑ surface area.

269. Carton A rectangular carton has length 21.3 cm, width 24.2 cm, and height 6.5 cm. Find its ⓐ volume and ⓑ surface area.

270. Shipping container A rectangular shipping container has length 22.8 feet, width 8.5 feet, and height 8.2 feet. Find its ⓐ volume and ⓑ surface area.

In the following exercises, find ⓐ the volume and ⓑ the surface area of the cube with the given side length.

271. 5 centimeters

272. 6 inches

273. 10.4 feet

274. 12.5 meters

In the following exercises, solve.

275. Science center Each side of the cube at the Discovery Science Center in Santa Ana is 64 feet long. Find its ⓐ volume and ⓑ surface area.

276. Museum A cube-shaped museum has sides 45 meters long. Find its ⓐ volume and ⓑ surface area.

277. Base of statue The base of a statue is a cube with sides 2.8 meters long. Find its ⓐ volume and ⓑ surface area.

278. Tissue box A box of tissues is a cube with sides 4.5 inches long. Find its ⓐ volume and ⓑ surface area.

Find the Volume and Surface Area of Spheres

In the following exercises, find ⓐ the volume and ⓑ the surface area of the sphere with the given radius. Round answers to the nearest hundredth.

279. 3 centimeters

280. 9 inches

281. 7.5 feet

282. 2.1 yards

In the following exercises, solve. Round answers to the nearest hundredth.

283. Exercise ball An exercise ball has a radius of 15 inches. Find its ⓐ volume and ⓑ surface area.

284. Balloon ride The Great Park Balloon is a big orange sphere with a radius of 36 feet . Find its ⓐ volume and ⓑ surface area.

285. Golf ball A golf ball has a radius of 4.5 centimeters. Find its ⓐ volume and ⓑ surface area.

286. Baseball A baseball has a radius of 2.9 inches. Find its ⓐ volume and ⓑ surface area.

Find the Volume and Surface Area of a Cylinder

In the following exercises, find ⓐ the volume and ⓑ the surface area of the cylinder with the given radius and height. Round answers to the nearest hundredth.

287. radius 3 feet, height 9 feet

288. radius 5 centimeters, height 15 centimeters

289. radius 1.5 meters, height 4.2 meters

290. radius 1.3 yards, height 2.8 yards

In the following exercises, solve. Round answers to the nearest hundredth.

291. Coffee can A can of coffee has a radius of 5 cm and a height of 13 cm. Find its ⓐ volume and ⓑ surface area.

292. Snack pack A snack pack of cookies is shaped like a cylinder with radius 4 cm and height 3 cm. Find its ⓐ volume and ⓑ surface area.

293. Barber shop pole A cylindrical barber shop pole has a diameter of 6 inches and height of 24 inches. Find its ⓐ volume and ⓑ surface area.

294. Architecture A cylindrical column has a diameter of 8 feet and a height of 28 feet. Find its ⓐ volume and ⓑ surface area.

Find the Volume of Cones

In the following exercises, find the volume of the cone with the given dimensions. Round answers to the nearest hundredth.

295. height 9 feet and radius 2 feet

296. height 8 inches and radius 6 inches

297. height 12.4 centimeters and radius 5 cm

298. height 15.2 meters and radius 4 meters

In the following exercises, solve. Round answers to the nearest hundredth.

299. Teepee What is the volume of a cone-shaped teepee tent that is 10 feet tall and 10 feet across at the base?

300. Popcorn cup What is the volume of a cone-shaped popcorn cup that is 8 inches tall and 6 inches across at the base?

301. Silo What is the volume of a cone-shaped silo that is 50 feet tall and 70 feet across at the base?

302. Sand pile What is the volume of a cone-shaped pile of sand that is 12 meters tall and 30 meters across at the base?

Everyday Math

303. Street light post The post of a street light is shaped like a truncated cone, as shown in the picture below. It is a large cone minus a smaller top cone. The large cone is 30 feet tall with base radius 1 foot. The smaller cone is 10 feet tall with base radius of 0.5 feet. To the nearest tenth,

ⓐ find the volume of the large cone.

ⓑ find the volume of the small cone.

ⓒ find the volume of the post by subtracting the volume of the small cone from the volume of the large cone.

304. Ice cream cones A regular ice cream cone is 4 inches tall and has a diameter of 2.5 inches. A waffle cone is 7 inches tall and has a diameter of 3.25 inches. To the nearest hundredth,

ⓐ find the volume of the regular ice cream cone.

ⓑ find the volume of the waffle cone.

ⓒ how much more ice cream fits in the waffle cone compared to the regular cone?

Writing Exercises

305. The formulas for the volume of a cylinder and a cone are similar. Explain how you can remember which formula goes with which shape.

306. Which has a larger volume, a cube of sides of 8 feet or a sphere with a diameter of 8 feet? Explain your reasoning.

Self Check

ⓐ *After completing the exercises, use this checklist to evaluate your mastery of the objectives of this section.*

I can...	Confidently	With some help	No-I don't get it!
find volume and surface area of rectangular solids.			
find volume and surface area of spheres.			
find volume and surface area of cylinders.			
find volume of cones.			

ⓑ *After reviewing this checklist, what will you do to become confident for all objectives?*

9.7 # Solve a Formula for a Specific Variable

Learning Objectives

By the end of this section, you will be able to:
- Use the distance, rate, and time formula
- Solve a formula for a specific variable

Be Prepared!

Before you get started, take this readiness quiz.

1. Write 35 miles per gallon as a unit rate.
   If you missed this problem, review Example 5.65.
2. Solve $6x + 24 = 96$.
   If you missed this problem, review Example 8.20.
3. Find the simple interest earned after 5 years on $\$1,000$ at an interest rate of 4%.
   If you missed this problem, review Example 6.33.

Use the Distance, Rate, and Time Formula

One formula you'll use often in algebra and in everyday life is the formula for distance traveled by an object moving at a constant speed. The basic idea is probably already familiar to you. Do you know what distance you travel if you drove at a steady rate of 60 miles per hour for 2 hours? (This might happen if you use your car's cruise control while driving on the Interstate.) If you said 120 miles, you already know how to use this formula!

The math to calculate the distance might look like this:

$$\text{distance} = \left(\frac{60 \text{ miles}}{1 \text{ hour}}\right)(2 \text{ hours})$$

$$\text{distance} = 120 \text{ miles}$$

In general, the formula relating distance, rate, and time is

$$\text{distance} = \text{rate} \cdot \text{time}$$

Distance, Rate and Time

For an object moving in at a uniform (constant) rate, the distance traveled, the elapsed time, and the rate are related by the formula

$$d = rt$$

where $d =$ distance, $r =$ rate, and $t =$ time.

Notice that the units we used above for the rate were miles per hour, which we can write as a ratio $\frac{miles}{hour}$. Then when we multiplied by the time, in hours, the common units 'hour' divided out. The answer was in miles.

EXAMPLE 9.57

Jamal rides his bike at a uniform rate of 12 miles per hour for $3\frac{1}{2}$ hours. How much distance has he traveled?

⊘ **Solution**

	$d = ?$
Step 1. Read the problem. You may want to create a mini-chart to summarize the information in the problem.	$r = 12 \text{ mph}$ $t = 3\frac{1}{2} \text{ hours}$
Step 2. Identify what you are looking for.	distance traveled
Step 3. Name. Choose a variable to represent it.	let d = distance
Step 4. Translate. Write the appropriate formula for the situation. Substitute in the given information.	$d = rt$ $d = 12 \cdot 3\frac{1}{2}$
Step 5. Solve the equation.	$d = 42 \text{ miles}$

Step 6. Check: Does 42 miles make sense?
Jamal rides

12 miles in 1 hour,
24 miles in 2 hours,
36 miles in 3 hours,
48 miles in 4 hours,

42 miles in $3\frac{1}{2}$ hours is reasonable

Step 7. Answer the question with a complete sentence.   Jamal rode 42 miles.

> **TRY IT :: 9.113**   Lindsay drove for $5\frac{1}{2}$ hours at 60 miles per hour. How much distance did she travel?

> **TRY IT :: 9.114**   Trinh walked for $2\frac{1}{3}$ hours at 3 miles per hour. How far did she walk?

EXAMPLE 9.58

Rey is planning to drive from his house in San Diego to visit his grandmother in Sacramento, a distance of 520 miles. If he can drive at a steady rate of 65 miles per hour, how many hours will the trip take?

⊘ Solution

Step 1. **Read** the problem. Summarize the information in the problem.	$d = 520$ miles $r = 65$ mph $t = ?$
Step 2. **Identify** what you are looking for.	how many hours (time)
Step 3. **Name:** Choose a variable to represent it.	let t = time
Step 4. **Translate.** Write the appropriate formula. Substitute in the given information.	$d = rt$ $520 = 65t$
Step 5. **Solve** the equation.	$t = 8$

Step 6. **Check:**
Substitute the numbers into the formula and make sure
the result is a true statement.
$d = rt$

$520 \overset{?}{=} 65 \cdot 8$

$520 = 520> ✓$

Step 7. **Answer** the question with a complete sentence. We know the units of time will be hours because we divided miles by miles per hour.	Rey's trip will take 8 hours.

> **TRY IT :: 9.115**

> Lee wants to drive from Phoenix to his brother's apartment in San Francisco, a distance of 770 miles. If he drives at a steady rate of 70 miles per hour, how many hours will the trip take?

> **TRY IT :: 9.116**

> Yesenia is 168 miles from Chicago. If she needs to be in Chicago in 3 hours, at what rate does she need to drive?

Solve a Formula for a Specific Variable

In this chapter, you became familiar with some formulas used in geometry. Formulas are also very useful in the sciences and social sciences—fields such as chemistry, physics, biology, psychology, sociology, and criminal justice. Healthcare workers use formulas, too, even for something as routine as dispensing medicine. The widely used spreadsheet program Microsoft Excel™ relies on formulas to do its calculations. Many teachers use spreadsheets to apply formulas to compute student grades. It is important to be familiar with formulas and be able to manipulate them easily.

In Example 9.57 and Example 9.58, we used the formula $d = rt$. This formula gives the value of d when you substitute in the values of r and t. But in Example 9.58, we had to find the value of t. We substituted in values of d and r and then used algebra to solve to t. If you had to do this often, you might wonder why there isn't a formula that gives the value of t when you substitute in the values of d and r. We can get a formula like this by solving the formula $d = rt$ for t.

To solve a formula for a specific variable means to get that variable by itself with a coefficient of 1 on one side of the equation and all the other variables and constants on the other side. We will call this solving an equation for a specific variable *in general*. This process is also called *solving a literal equation*. The result is another formula, made up only of variables. The formula contains letters, or *literals*.

Let's try a few examples, starting with the distance, rate, and time formula we used above.

EXAMPLE 9.59

Solve the formula $d = rt$ for t:

      ⓐ when $d = 520$ and $r = 65$ ⓑ in general.

⊘ Solution

We'll write the solutions side-by-side so you can see that solving a formula in general uses the same steps as when we have numbers to substitute.

	ⓐ when $d = 520$ and $r = 65$	ⓑ in general
Write the forumla.	$d = rt$	$d = rt$
Substitute any given values.	$520 = 65t$	
Divide to isolate t.	$\dfrac{520}{65} = \dfrac{65t}{65}$	$\dfrac{d}{r} = \dfrac{rt}{r}$
Simplify.	$8 = t$ $t = 8$	$\dfrac{d}{r} = t$ $t = \dfrac{d}{r}$

Notice that the solution for ⓐ is the same as that in Example 9.58. We say the formula $t = \dfrac{d}{r}$ is solved for t. We can use this version of the formula anytime we are given the distance and rate and need to find the time.

> **TRY IT : : 9.117**   Solve the formula $d = rt$ for r:
>
>   ⓐ when $d = 180$ and $t = 4$ ⓐ in general

> **TRY IT : : 9.118**
>
> Solve the formula $d = rt$ for r:
>
>   ⓐ when $d = 780$ and $t = 12$ ⓑ in general

We used the formula $A = \dfrac{1}{2}bh$ in Use Properties of Rectangles, Triangles, and Trapezoids to find the area of a triangle when we were given the base and height. In the next example, we will solve this formula for the height.

EXAMPLE 9.60

The formula for area of a triangle is $A = \dfrac{1}{2}bh$. Solve this formula for h:

      ⓐ when $A = 90$ and $b = 15$ ⓑ in general

✓ **Solution**

	ⓐ when A = 90 and b = 15	ⓑ in general
Write the forumla.	$A = \frac{1}{2} bh$	$A = \frac{1}{2} bh$
Substitute any given values.	$90 = \frac{1}{2} \cdot 15 \cdot h$	
Clear the fractions.	$2 \cdot 90 = 2 \cdot \frac{1}{2} \cdot 15 \cdot h$	$2 \cdot A = 2 \cdot \frac{1}{2} \cdot b \cdot h$
Simplify.	$180 = 15h$	$2A = bh$
Solve for h.	$12 = h$	$\frac{2A}{b} = h$

We can now find the height of a triangle, if we know the area and the base, by using the formula

$$h = \frac{2A}{b}$$

> **TRY IT :: 9.119**   Use the formula $A = \frac{1}{2}bh$ to solve for h:

   ⓐ when $A = 170$ and $b = 17$ ⓑ in general

> **TRY IT :: 9.120**   Use the formula $A = \frac{1}{2}bh$ to solve for b:

   ⓐ when $A = 62$ and $h = 31$ ⓑ in general

In Solve Simple Interest Applications, we used the formula $I = Prt$ to calculate simple interest, where I is interest, P is principal, r is rate as a decimal, and t is time in years.

EXAMPLE 9.61

Solve the formula $I = Prt$ to find the principal, P:

   ⓐ when $I = \$5,600$, $r = 4\%$, $t = 7$ years   ⓑ in general

⊘ **Solution**

	$I = \$5600,\ r = 4\%,\ t = 7$ years	in general
Write the forumla.	$I = Prt$	$I = Prt$
Substitute any given values.	$5600 = P(0.04)(7)$	$I = Prt$
Multiply $r \cdot t$.	$5600 = P(0.28)$	$I = P(rt)$
Divide to isolate P.	$\dfrac{5600}{0.28} = \dfrac{P(0.28)}{0.28}$	$\dfrac{I}{rt} = \dfrac{P(rt)}{rt}$
Simplify.	$20{,}000 = P$	$\dfrac{I}{rt} = P$
State the answer.	The principal is $20,000.	$P = \dfrac{I}{rt}$

> **TRY IT : : 9.121**   Use the formula $I = Prt$.

   Find t: ⓐ when $I = \$2{,}160,\ r = 6\%,\ P = \$12{,}000$; ⓑ in general

> **TRY IT : : 9.122**   Use the formula $I = Prt$.

   Find r: ⓐ when $I = \$5{,}400,\ P = \$9{,}000,\ t = 5$ years ⓑ in general

Later in this class, and in future algebra classes, you'll encounter equations that relate two variables, usually x and y. You might be given an equation that is solved for y and need to solve it for x, or vice versa. In the following example, we're given an equation with both x and y on the same side and we'll solve it for y. To do this, we will follow the same steps that we used to solve a formula for a specific variable.

EXAMPLE 9.62

Solve the formula $3x + 2y = 18$ for y:

   ⓐ when $x = 4$ ⓑ in general

⊘ **Solution**

	when $x = 4$	in general
Write the equation.	$3x + 2y = 18$	$3x + 2y = 18$
Substitute any given values.	$3(4) + 2y = 18$	$3x + 2y = 18$
Simplify if possible.	$12 + 2y = 18$	$3x + 2y = 18$
Subtract to isolate the y-term.	$12 - 12 + 2y = 18 - 12$	$3x - 3x + 2y = 18 - 3x$
Simplify.	$2y = 6$	$2y = 18 - 3x$
Divide.	$\dfrac{2y}{2} = \dfrac{6}{2}$	$\dfrac{2y}{2} = \dfrac{18 - 3x}{2}$
Simplify.	$y = 3$	$y = \dfrac{18 - 3x}{2}$

> **TRY IT ::** 9.123   Solve the formula $3x + 4y = 10$ for y:

ⓐ when $x = 2$ ⓑ in general

> **TRY IT ::** 9.124   Solve the formula $5x + 2y = 18$ for y:

ⓐ when $x = 4$ ⓑ in general

In the previous examples, we used the numbers in part (a) as a guide to solving in general in part (b). Do you think you're ready to solve a formula in general without using numbers as a guide?

EXAMPLE 9.63

Solve the formula $P = a + b + c$ for a.

⊘ Solution

We will isolate a on one side of the equation.

We will isolate a on one side of the equation.

Write the equation.	$P = a + b + c$
Subtract b and c from both sides to isolate a.	$P - b - c = a + b + c - b - c$
Simplify.	$P - b - c = a$

So, $a = P - b - c$

> **TRY IT ::** 9.125   Solve the formula $P = a + b + c$ for b.

> **TRY IT ::** 9.126   Solve the formula $P = a + b + c$ for c.

EXAMPLE 9.64

Solve the equation $3x + y = 10$ for y.

⊘ Solution

We will isolate y on one side of the equation.

We will isolate y on one side of the equation.

Write the equation.	$3x + y = 10$
Subtract $3x$ from both sides to isolate y.	$3x - 3x + y = 10 - 3x$
Simplify.	$y = 10 - 3x$

> **TRY IT ::** 9.127   Solve the formula $7x + y = 11$ for y.

> **TRY IT ::** 9.128   Solve the formula $11x + y = 8$ for y.

EXAMPLE 9.65

Solve the equation $6x + 5y = 13$ for y.

⊘ Solution

We will isolate y on one side of the equation.

We will isolate *y* on one side of the equation.

Write the equation.	$6x + 5y = 13$
Subtract to isolate the term with *y*.	$6x + 5y - 6x = 13 - 6x$
Simplify.	$5y = 13 - 6x$
Divide 5 to make the coefficient 1.	$\dfrac{5y}{5} = \dfrac{13 - 6x}{5}$
Simplify.	$y = \dfrac{13 - 6x}{5}$

> **TRY IT :: 9.129**   Solve the formula $4x + 7y = 9$ for y.

> **TRY IT :: 9.130**   Solve the formula $5x + 8y = 1$ for y.

  LINKS TO LITERACY

The Links to Literacy activity *What's Faster than a Speeding Cheetah?* will provide you with another view of the topics covered in this section.

▶ | **MEDIA :: ACCESS ADDITIONAL ONLINE RESOURCES**
  - Distance=RatexTime (http://www.openstaxcollege.org/l/24distratextime)
  - Distance, Rate, Time (http://www.openstaxcollege.org/l/24distratetime)
  - Simple Interest (http://www.openstaxcollege.org/l/24simpinterest)
  - Solving a Formula for a Specific Variable (http://www.openstaxcollege.org/l/24solvespvari)
  - Solving a Formula for a Specific Variable (http://www.openstaxcollege.org/l/24solvespecivar)

9.7 EXERCISES

Practice Makes Perfect

Use the Distance, Rate, and Time Formula

In the following exercises, solve.

307. Steve drove for $8\frac{1}{2}$ hours at 72 miles per hour. How much distance did he travel?

308. Socorro drove for $4\frac{5}{6}$ hours at 60 miles per hour. How much distance did she travel?

309. Yuki walked for $1\frac{3}{4}$ hours at 4 miles per hour. How far did she walk?

310. Francie rode her bike for $2\frac{1}{2}$ hours at 12 miles per hour. How far did she ride?

311. Connor wants to drive from Tucson to the Grand Canyon, a distance of 338 miles. If he drives at a steady rate of 52 miles per hour, how many hours will the trip take?

312. Megan is taking the bus from New York City to Montreal. The distance is 384 miles and the bus travels at a steady rate of 64 miles per hour. How long will the bus ride be?

313. Aurelia is driving from Miami to Orlando at a rate of 65 miles per hour. The distance is 235 miles. To the nearest tenth of an hour, how long will the trip take?

314. Kareem wants to ride his bike from St. Louis, Missouri to Champaign, Illinois. The distance is 180 miles. If he rides at a steady rate of 16 miles per hour, how many hours will the trip take?

315. Javier is driving to Bangor, Maine, which is 240 miles away from his current location. If he needs to be in Bangor in 4 hours, at what rate does he need to drive?

316. Alejandra is driving to Cincinnati, Ohio, 450 miles away. If she wants to be there in 6 hours, at what rate does she need to drive?

317. Aisha took the train from Spokane to Seattle. The distance is 280 miles, and the trip took 3.5 hours. What was the speed of the train?

318. Philip got a ride with a friend from Denver to Las Vegas, a distance of 750 miles. If the trip took 10 hours, how fast was the friend driving?

Solve a Formula for a Specific Variable

In the following exercises, use the formula. $d = rt$.

319. Solve for t:

ⓐ when $d = 350$ and $r = 70$

ⓑ in general

320. Solve for t:

ⓐ when $d = 240$ and $r = 60$

ⓑ in general

321. Solve for t:

ⓐ when $d = 510$ and $r = 60$

ⓑ in general

322. Solve for t:

ⓐ when $d = 175$ and $r = 50$

ⓑ in general

323. Solve for r:

ⓐ when $d = 204$ and $t = 3$

ⓑ in general

324. Solve for r:

ⓐ when $d = 420$ and $t = 6$

ⓑ in general

325. Solve for r:

ⓐ when $d = 160$ and $t = 2.5$

ⓑ in general

326. Solve for r:

ⓐ when $d = 180$ and $t = 4.5$

ⓑ in general.

In the following exercises, use the formula $A = \frac{1}{2}bh$.

327. Solve for b:

ⓐ when $A = 126$ and $h = 18$

ⓑ in general

328. Solve for h:

ⓐ when $A = 176$ and $b = 22$

ⓑ in general

329. Solve for h:

ⓐ when $A = 375$ and $b = 25$

ⓑ in general

330. Solve for b:

ⓐ when $A = 65$ and $h = 13$

ⓑ in general

In the following exercises, use the formula $I = Prt$.

331. Solve for the principal, P for:

ⓐ $I = \$5{,}480$, $r = 4\%$, $t = 7$ years

ⓑ in general

332. Solve for the principal, P for:

ⓐ $I = \$3{,}950$, $r = 6\%$, $t = 5$ years

ⓑ in general

333. Solve for the time, t for:

ⓐ $I = \$2{,}376$, $P = \$9{,}000$, $r = 4.4\%$

ⓑ in general

334. Solve for the time, t for:

ⓐ $I = \$624$, $P = \$6{,}000$, $r = 5.2\%$

ⓑ in general

In the following exercises, solve.

335. Solve the formula $2x + 3y = 12$ for y:

ⓐ when $x = 3$

ⓑ in general

336. Solve the formula $5x + 2y = 10$ for y:

ⓐ when $x = 4$

ⓑ in general

337. Solve the formula $3x + y = 7$ for y:

ⓐ when $x = -2$

ⓑ in general

338. Solve the formula $4x + y = 5$ for y:

ⓐ when $x = -3$

ⓑ in general

339. Solve $a + b = 90$ for b.

340. Solve $a + b = 90$ for a.

341. Solve $180 = a + b + c$ for a.

342. Solve $180 = a + b + c$ for c.

343. Solve the formula $8x + y = 15$ for y.

344. Solve the formula $9x + y = 13$ for y.

345. Solve the formula $-4x + y = -6$ for y.

346. Solve the formula $-5x + y = -1$ for y.

347. Solve the formula $4x + 3y = 7$ for y.

348. Solve the formula $3x + 2y = 11$ for y.

349. Solve the formula $x - y = -4$ for y.

350. Solve the formula $x - y = -3$ for y.

351. Solve the formula $P = 2L + 2W$ for L.

352. Solve the formula $P = 2L + 2W$ for W.

353. Solve the formula $C = \pi d$ for d.

354. Solve the formula $C = \pi d$ for π.

355. Solve the formula $V = LWH$ for L.

356. Solve the formula $V = LWH$ for H.

Everyday Math

357. Converting temperature While on a tour in Greece, Tatyana saw that the temperature was $40°$ Celsius. Solve for F in the formula $C = \frac{5}{9}(F - 32)$ to find the temperature in Fahrenheit.

358. Converting temperature Yon was visiting the United States and he saw that the temperature in Seattle was $50°$ Fahrenheit. Solve for C in the formula $F = \frac{9}{5}C + 32$ to find the temperature in Celsius.

Writing Exercises

359. Solve the equation $2x + 3y = 6$ for y:

ⓐ when $x = -3$ ⓑ in general

ⓒ Which solution is easier for you? Explain why.

360. Solve the equation $5x - 2y = 10$ for x:

ⓐ when $y = 10$ ⓑ in general

ⓒ Which solution is easier for you? Explain why.

Self Check

ⓐ *After completing the exercises, use this checklist to evaluate your mastery of the objectives of this section.*

I can...	Confidently	With some help	No-I don't get it!
use the distance, rate, and time formula.			
solve a formula for a specific variable.			

ⓑ *Overall, after looking at the checklist, do you think you are well-prepared for the next Chapter? Why or why not?*

CHAPTER 9 REVIEW

KEY TERMS

angle An angle is formed by two rays that share a common endpoint. Each ray is called a side of the angle.

area The area is a measure of the surface covered by a figure.

complementary angles If the sum of the measures of two angles is $90°$, then they are called complementary angles.

cone A cone is a solid figure with one circular base and a vertex.

cube A cube is a rectangular solid whose length, width, and height are equal.

cylinder A cylinder is a solid figure with two parallel circles of the same size at the top and bottom.

equilateral triangle A triangle with all three sides of equal length is called an equilateral triangle.

hypotenuse The side of the triangle opposite the 90° angle is called the hypotenuse.

irregular figure An irregular figure is a figure that is not a standard geometric shape. Its area cannot be calculated using any of the standard area formulas.

isosceles triangle A triangle with two sides of equal length is called an isosceles triangle.

legs of a right triangle The sides of a right triangle adjacent to the right angle are called the legs.

perimeter The perimeter is a measure of the distance around a figure.

rectangle A rectangle is a geometric figure that has four sides and four right angles.

right triangle A right triangle is a triangle that has one $90°$ angle.

similar figures In geometry, if two figures have exactly the same shape but different sizes, we say they are similar figures.

supplementary angles If the sum of the measures of two angles is $180°$, then they are called supplementary angles.

trapezoid A trapezoid is four-sided figure, a quadrilateral, with two sides that are parallel and two sides that are not.

triangle A triangle is a geometric figure with three sides and three angles.

vertex of an angle When two rays meet to form an angle, the common endpoint is called the vertex of the angle.

KEY CONCEPTS

9.1 Use a Problem Solving Strategy

- **Problem Solving Strategy**

  Step 1. Read the word problem. Make sure you understand all the words and ideas. You may need to read the problem two or more times. If there are words you don't understand, look them up in a dictionary or on the internet.

  Step 2. Identify what you are looking for.

  Step 3. Name what you are looking for. Choose a variable to represent that quantity.

  Step 4. Translate into an equation. It may be helpful to first restate the problem in one sentence before translating.

  Step 5. Solve the equation using good algebra techniques.

  Step 6. Check the answer in the problem. Make sure it makes sense.

  Step 7. Answer the question with a complete sentence.

9.2 Solve Money Applications

- **Finding the Total Value for Coins of the Same Type**

  - For coins of the same type, the total value can be found as follows:
    number $\cdot$ value $=$ total value

    where number is the number of coins, value is the value of each coin, and total value is the total value of all the coins.

- **Solve a Coin Word Problem**

  Step 1. **Read** the problem. Make sure you understand all the words and ideas, and create a table to organize the information.

Step 2. **Identify** what you are looking for.

Step 3. **Name** what you are looking for. Choose a variable to represent that quantity.

  ▪ Use variable expressions to represent the number of each type of coin and write them in the table.

  ▪ Multiply the number times the value to get the total value of each type of coin.

Step 4. **Translate** into an equation. Write the equation by adding the total values of all the types of coins.

Step 5. **Solve** the equation using good algebra techniques.

Step 6. **Check** the answer in the problem and make sure it makes sense.

Step 7. **Answer** the question with a complete sentence.

Type	Number	Value ($)	Total Value ($)

9.3 Use Properties of Angles, Triangles, and the Pythagorean Theorem

- **Supplementary and Complementary Angles**
  - If the sum of the measures of two angles is 180°, then the angles are supplementary.
  - If $\angle A$ and $\angle B$ are supplementary, then $m\angle A + m\angle B = 180$.
  - If the sum of the measures of two angles is 90°, then the angles are complementary.
  - If $\angle A$ and $\angle B$ are complementary, then $m\angle A + m\angle B = 90$.

- **Solve Geometry Applications**

  Step 1. Read the problem and make sure you understand all the words and ideas. Draw a figure and label it with the given information.

  Step 2. Identify what you are looking for.

  Step 3. Name what you are looking for and choose a variable to represent it.

  Step 4. Translate into an equation by writing the appropriate formula or model for the situation. Substitute in the given information.

  Step 5. Solve the equation using good algebra techniques.

  Step 6. Check the answer in the problem and make sure it makes sense.

  Step 7. Answer the question with a complete sentence.

- **Sum of the Measures of the Angles of a Triangle**

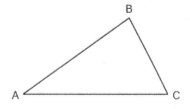

  - For any $\triangle ABC,$ the sum of the measures is 180°
  - $m\angle A + m\angle B = 180$

- **Right Triangle**

◦ A right triangle is a triangle that has one 90° angle, which is often marked with a ∟ symbol.

- **Properties of Similar Triangles**
  ◦ If two triangles are similar, then their corresponding angle measures are equal and their corresponding side lengths have the same ratio.

9.4 Use Properties of Rectangles, Triangles, and Trapezoids

- **Properties of Rectangles**
  ◦ Rectangles have four sides and four right (90°) angles.
  ◦ The lengths of opposite sides are equal.
  ◦ The perimeter, P, of a rectangle is the sum of twice the length and twice the width.
    - $P = 2L + 2W$
  ◦ The area, A, of a rectangle is the length times the width.
    - $A = L \cdot W$

- **Triangle Properties**
  ◦ For any triangle $\triangle ABC$, the sum of the measures of the angles is 180°.
    - $m \angle A + m \angle B + m \angle C = 180°$
  ◦ The perimeter of a triangle is the sum of the lengths of the sides.
    - $P = a + b + c$
  ◦ The area of a triangle is one-half the base, b, times the height, h.
    - $A = \frac{1}{2}bh$

9.5 Solve Geometry Applications: Circles and Irregular Figures

- **Problem Solving Strategy for Geometry Applications**

  Step 1. Read the problem and make sure you understand all the words and ideas. Draw the figure and label it with the given information.

  Step 2. Identify what you are looking for.

  Step 3. Name what you are looking for. Choose a variable to represent that quantity.

  Step 4. Translate into an equation by writing the appropriate formula or model for the situation. Substitute in the given information.

  Step 5. Solve the equation using good algebra techniques.

  Step 6. Check the answer in the problem and make sure it makes sense.

  Step 7. Answer the question with a complete sentence.

- **Properties of Circles**

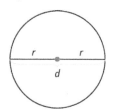

  ◦ $d = 2r$
  ◦ **Circumference:** $C = 2\pi r$ or $C = \pi d$
  ◦ **Area:** $A = \pi r^2$

9.6 Solve Geometry Applications: Volume and Surface Area

- **Volume and Surface Area of a Rectangular Solid**
  - $V = LWH$
  - $S = 2LH + 2LW + 2WH$
- **Volume and Surface Area of a Cube**
  - $V = s^3$
  - $S = 6s^2$
- **Volume and Surface Area of a Sphere**
  - $V = \frac{4}{3}\pi r^3$
  - $S = 4\pi r^2$
- **Volume and Surface Area of a Cylinder**
  - $V = \pi r^2 h$
  - $S = 2\pi r^2 + 2\pi rh$
- **Volume of a Cone**
  - For a cone with radius r and height h:
    Volume: $V = \frac{1}{3}\pi r^2 h$

9.7 Solve a Formula for a Specific Variable

- **Distance, Rate, and Time**
  - $d = rt$

REVIEW EXERCISES

9.1 Use a Problem Solving Strategy

Approach Word Problems with a Positive Attitude

In the following exercises, solve.

361. How has your attitude towards solving word problems changed as a result of working through this chapter? Explain.

362. Did the Problem Solving Strategy help you solve word problems in this chapter? Explain.

Use a Problem Solving Strategy for Word Problems

In the following exercises, solve using the problem-solving strategy for word problems. Remember to write a complete sentence to answer each question.

363. Three-fourths of the people at a concert are children. If there are 87 children, what is the total number of people at the concert?

364. There are 9 saxophone players in the band. The number of saxophone players is one less than twice the number of tuba players. Find the number of tuba players.

365. Reza was very sick and lost 15% of his original weight. He lost 27 pounds. What was his original weight?

366. Dolores bought a crib on sale for $\$350$. The sale price was 40% of the original price. What was the original price of the crib?

Solve Number Problems

In the following exercises, solve each number word problem.

367. The sum of a number and three is forty-one. Find the number.

368. Twice the difference of a number and ten is fifty-four. Find the number.

369. One number is nine less than another. Their sum is twenty-seven. Find the numbers.

370. The sum of two consecutive integers is -135. Find the numbers.

9.2 Solve Money Applications

Solve Coin Word Problems

In the following exercises, solve each coin word problem.

371. Francie has $4.35 in dimes and quarters. The number of dimes is 5 more than the number of quarters. How many of each coin does she have?

372. Scott has $0.39 in pennies and nickels. The number of pennies is 8 times the number of nickels. How many of each coin does he have?

373. Paulette has $140 in $5 and $10 bills. The number of $10 bills is one less than twice the number of $5 bills. How many of each does she have?

374. Lenny has $3.69 in pennies, dimes, and quarters. The number of pennies is 3 more than the number of dimes. The number of quarters is twice the number of dimes. How many of each coin does he have?

Solve Ticket and Stamp Word Problems

In the following exercises, solve each ticket or stamp word problem.

375. A church luncheon made $842. Adult tickets cost $10 each and children's tickets cost $6 each. The number of children was 12 more than twice the number of adults. How many of each ticket were sold?

376. Tickets for a basketball game cost $2 for students and $5 for adults. The number of students was 3 less than 10 times the number of adults. The total amount of money from ticket sales was $619. How many of each ticket were sold?

377. Ana spent $4.06 buying stamps. The number of $0.41 stamps she bought was 5 more than the number of $0.26 stamps. How many of each did she buy?

378. Yumi spent $34.15 buying stamps. The number of $0.56 stamps she bought was 10 less than 4 times the number of $0.41 stamps. How many of each did she buy?

9.3 Use Properties of Angles, Triangles, and the Pythagorean Theorem

Use Properties of Angles

In the following exercises, solve using properties of angles.

379. What is the supplement of a $48°$ angle?

380. What is the complement of a $61°$ angle?

381. Two angles are complementary. The smaller angle is $24°$ less than the larger angle. Find the measures of both angles.

382. Two angles are supplementary. The larger angle is $45°$ more than the smaller angle. Find the measures of both angles.

Use Properties of Triangles

In the following exercises, solve using properties of triangles.

383. The measures of two angles of a triangle are 22 and 85 degrees. Find the measure of the third angle.

384. One angle of a right triangle measures 41.5 degrees. What is the measure of the other small angle?

385. One angle of a triangle is $30°$ more than the smallest angle. The largest angle is the sum of the other angles. Find the measures of all three angles.

386. One angle of a triangle is twice the measure of the smallest angle. The third angle is $60°$ more than the measure of the smallest angle. Find the measures of all three angles.

In the following exercises, $\triangle ABC$ is similar to $\triangle XYZ$. Find the length of the indicated side.

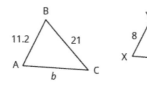

387. side x

388. side b

Use the Pythagorean Theorem

In the following exercises, use the Pythagorean Theorem to find the length of the missing side. Round to the nearest tenth, if necessary.

389.

390.

391.

392.

393.

394.

In the following exercises, solve. Approximate to the nearest tenth, if necessary.

395. Sergio needs to attach a wire to hold the antenna to the roof of his house, as shown in the figure. The antenna is 8 feet tall and Sergio has 10 feet of wire. How far from the base of the antenna can he attach the wire?

396. Seong is building shelving in his garage. The shelves are 36 inches wide and 15 inches tall. He wants to put a diagonal brace across the back to stabilize the shelves, as shown. How long should the brace be?

9.4 Use Properties of Rectangles, Triangles, and Trapezoids

Understand Linear, Square, Cubic Measure

In the following exercises, would you measure each item using linear, square, or cubic measure?

397. amount of sand in a sandbag

398. height of a tree

399. size of a patio

400. length of a highway

In the following exercises, find

ⓐ the perimeter ⓑ the area of each figure

401.

402.

Use Properties of Rectangles

In the following exercises, find the ⓐ perimeter ⓑ area of each rectangle

403. The length of a rectangle is 42 meters and the width is 28 meters.

404. The length of a rectangle is 36 feet and the width is 19 feet.

405. A sidewalk in front of Kathy's house is in the shape of a rectangle 4 feet wide by 45 feet long.

406. A rectangular room is 16 feet wide by 12 feet long.

In the following exercises, solve.

407. Find the length of a rectangle with perimeter of 220 centimeters and width of 85 centimeters.

408. Find the width of a rectangle with perimeter 39 and length 11.

409. The area of a rectangle is 2356 square meters. The length is 38 meters. What is the width?

410. The width of a rectangle is 45 centimeters. The area is 2700 square centimeters. What is the length?

411. The length of a rectangle is 12 centimeters more than the width. The perimeter is 74 centimeters. Find the length and the width.

412. The width of a rectangle is 3 more than twice the length. The perimeter is 96 inches. Find the length and the width.

Use Properties of Triangles

In the following exercises, solve using the properties of triangles.

413. Find the area of a triangle with base 18 inches and height 15 inches.

414. Find the area of a triangle with base 33 centimeters and height 21 centimeters.

415. A triangular road sign has base 30 inches and height 40 inches. What is its area?

416. If a triangular courtyard has sides 9 feet and 12 feet and the perimeter is 32 feet, how long is the third side?

417. A tile in the shape of an isosceles triangle has a base of 6 inches. If the perimeter is 20 inches, find the length of each of the other sides.

418. Find the length of each side of an equilateral triangle with perimeter of 81 yards.

419. The perimeter of a triangle is 59 feet. One side of the triangle is 3 feet longer than the shortest side. The third side is 5 feet longer than the shortest side. Find the length of each side.

420. One side of a triangle is three times the smallest side. The third side is 9 feet more than the shortest side. The perimeter is 39 feet. Find the lengths of all three sides.

Use Properties of Trapezoids

In the following exercises, solve using the properties of trapezoids.

421. The height of a trapezoid is 8 feet and the bases are 11 and 14 feet. What is the area?

422. The height of a trapezoid is 5 yards and the bases are 7 and 10 yards. What is the area?

423. Find the area of the trapezoid with height 25 meters and bases 32.5 and 21.5 meters.

424. A flag is shaped like a trapezoid with height 62 centimeters and the bases are 91.5 and 78.1 centimeters. What is the area of the flag?

9.5 Solve Geometry Applications: Circles and Irregular Figures

Use Properties of Circles

In the following exercises, solve using the properties of circles. Round answers to the nearest hundredth.

425. A circular mosaic has radius 3 meters. Find the

ⓐ circumference

ⓑ area of the mosaic

426. A circular fountain has radius 8 feet. Find the

ⓐ circumference

ⓑ area of the fountain

427. Find the diameter of a circle with circumference 150.72 inches.

428. Find the radius of a circle with circumference 345.4 centimeters

Find the Area of Irregular Figures

In the following exercises, find the area of each shaded region.

429.

430.

431.

432.

433.

434.

9.6 Solve Geometry Applications: Volume and Surface Area

Find Volume and Surface Area of Rectangular Solids

In the following exercises, find the

ⓐ volume   ⓑ surface area of the rectangular solid

435. a rectangular solid with length 14 centimeters, width 4.5 centimeters, and height 10 centimeters

436. a cube with sides that are 3 feet long

437. a cube of tofu with sides 2.5 inches

438. a rectangular carton with length 32 inches, width 18 inches, and height 10 inches

Find Volume and Surface Area of Spheres

In the following exercises, find the

ⓐ volume   ⓑ surface area of the sphere.

439. a sphere with radius 4 yards

440. a sphere with radius 12 meters

441. a baseball with radius 1.45 inches

442. a soccer ball with radius 22 centimeters

Find Volume and Surface Area of Cylinders

In the following exercises, find the

ⓐ volume   ⓑ surface area of the cylinder

443. a cylinder with radius 2 yards and height 6 yards

444. a cylinder with diameter 18 inches and height 40 inches

445. a juice can with diameter 8 centimeters and height 15 centimeters

446. a cylindrical pylon with diameter 0.8 feet and height 2.5 feet

Find Volume of Cones

In the following exercises, find the volume of the cone.

447. a cone with height 5 meters and radius 1 meter

448. a cone with height 24 feet and radius 8 feet

449. a cone-shaped water cup with diameter 2.6 inches and height 2.6 inches

450. a cone-shaped pile of gravel with diameter 6 yards and height 5 yards

9.7 Solve a Formula for a Specific Variable

Use the Distance, Rate, and Time Formula

In the following exercises, solve using the formula for distance, rate, and time.

451. A plane flew 4 hours at 380 miles per hour. What distance was covered?

452. Gus rode his bike for $1\frac{1}{2}$ hours at 8 miles per hour. How far did he ride?

453. Jack is driving from Bangor to Portland at a rate of 68 miles per hour. The distance is 107 miles. To the nearest tenth of an hour, how long will the trip take?

454. Jasmine took the bus from Pittsburgh to Philadelphia. The distance is 305 miles and the trip took 5 hours. What was the speed of the bus?

Solve a Formula for a Specific Variable

In the following exercises, use the formula $d = rt$.

455. Solve for t:

    ⓐ when $d = 403$ and $r = 65$

    ⓑ in general

456. Solve for r:

    ⓐ when $d = 750$ and $t = 15$

    ⓑ in general

In the following exercises, use the formula $A = \frac{1}{2}bh$.

457. Solve for b:

    ⓐ when $A = 416$ and $h = 32$

    ⓑ in general

458. Solve for h:

    ⓐ when $A = 48$ and $b = 8$

    ⓑ in general

In the following exercises, use the formula $I = Prt$.

459. Solve for the principal, P, for:

     ⓐ $I = \$720$, $r = 4\%$, $t = 3$ years

     ⓑ in general

460. Solve for the time, t for:

     ⓐ $I = \$3630$, $P = \$11,000$, $r = 5.5\%$

     ⓑ in general

In the following exercises, solve.

461. Solve the formula $6x + 5y = 20$ for y:

     ⓐ when $x = 0$

     ⓑ in general

462. Solve the formula $2x + y = 15$ for y:

     ⓐ when $x = -5$

     ⓑ in general

463. Solve $a + b = 90$ for a.

464. Solve $180 = a + b + c$ for a.

465. Solve the formula $4x + y = 17$ for y.

466. Solve the formula $-3x + y = -6$ for y.

467. Solve the formula $P = 2L + 2W$ for W.

468. Solve the formula $V = LWH$ for H.

469. Describe how you have used two topics from this chapter in your life outside of math class during the past month.

PRACTICE TEST

470. Four-fifths of the people on a hike are children. If there are 12 children, what is the total number of people on the hike?

471. The sum of 13 and twice a number is −19. Find the number.

472. One number is 3 less than another number. Their sum is 65. Find the numbers.

473. Bonita has $2.95 in dimes and quarters in her pocket. If she has 5 more dimes than quarters, how many of each coin does she have?

474. At a concert, $1600 in tickets were sold. Adult tickets were $9 each and children's tickets were $4 each. If the number of adult tickets was 30 fewer than twice the number of children's tickets, how many of each kind were sold?

475. Find the complement of a 52° angle.

476. The measure of one angle of a triangle is twice the measure of the smallest angle. The measure of the third angle is 14 more than the measure of the smallest angle. Find the measures of all three angles.

477. The perimeter of an equilateral triangle is 145 feet. Find the length of each side.

478. △ABC is similar to △XYZ. Find the length of side c.

479. Find the length of the missing side. Round to the nearest tenth, if necessary.

480. Find the length of the missing side. Round to the nearest tenth, if necessary.

481. A baseball diamond is shaped like a square with sides 90 feet long. How far is it from home plate to second base, as shown?

482. The length of a rectangle is 2 feet more than five times the width. The perimeter is 40 feet. Find the dimensions of the rectangle.

483. A triangular poster has base 80 centimeters and height 55 centimeters. Find the area of the poster.

484. A trapezoid has height 14 inches and bases 20 inches and 23 inches. Find the area of the trapezoid.

485. A circular pool has diameter 90 inches. What is its circumference? Round to the nearest *tenth.*

486. Find the area of the shaded region. Round to the nearest tenth.

487. Find the volume of a rectangular room with width 12 feet, length 15 feet, and height 8 feet.

488. A coffee can is shaped like a cylinder with height 7 inches and radius 5 inches. Find (a) the surface area and (b) the volume of the can. Round to the nearest tenth.

489. A traffic cone has height 75 centimeters. The radius of the base is 20 centimeters. Find the volume of the cone. Round to the nearest tenth.

490. Leon drove from his house in Cincinnati to his sister's house in Cleveland. He drove at a uniform rate of 63 miles per hour and the trip took 4 hours. What was the distance?

491. The Catalina Express takes $1\frac{1}{2}$ hours to travel from Long Beach to Catalina Island, a distance of 22 miles. To the nearest tenth, what is the speed of the boat?

492. Use the formula $I = Prt$ to solve for the principal, P, for:

ⓐ
$I = \$1380,\ r = 5\%,\ t = 3$ years

ⓑ in general

493. Solve the formula $A = \frac{1}{2}bh$ for h:

ⓐ when $A = 1716$ and $b = 66$

ⓑ in general

494. Solve $x + 5y = 14$ for y.

Figure 10.1 The paths of rockets are calculated using polynomials. (credit: NASA, Public Domain)

Chapter Outline

Introduction

Expressions known as polynomials are used widely in algebra. Applications of these expressions are essential to many careers, including economists, engineers, and scientists. In this chapter, we will find out what polynomials are and how to manipulate them through basic mathematical operations.

10.1 Add and Subtract Polynomials

Learning Objectives

By the end of this section, you will be able to:

- Identify polynomials, monomials, binomials, and trinomials
- Determine the degree of polynomials
- Add and subtract monomials
- Add and subtract polynomials
- Evaluate a polynomial for a given value

Be Prepared!

Before you get started, take this readiness quiz.

1. Simplify: $8x + 3x$.
   If you missed this problem, review Example 2.22.

2. Subtract: $(5n + 8) - (2n - 1)$.
   If you missed this problem, review Example 7.29.

3. Evaluate: $4y^2$ when $y = 5$
   If you missed this problem, review Example 2.18.

Identify Polynomials, Monomials, Binomials, and Trinomials

In Evaluate, Simplify, and Translate Expressions, you learned that a term is a constant or the product of a constant and one or more variables. When it is of the form ax^m, where a is a constant and m is a whole number, it is called a monomial. A monomial, or a sum and/or difference of monomials, is called a polynomial.

Polynomials
polynomial—A monomial, or two or more monomials, combined by addition or subtraction
monomial—A polynomial with exactly one term
binomial— A polynomial with exactly two terms
trinomial—A polynomial with exactly three terms

Notice the roots:

- *poly-* means many
- *mono-* means one
- *bi-* means two
- *tri-* means three

Here are some examples of polynomials:

Polynomial	$b+1$	$4y^2 - 7y + 2$	$5x^5 - 4x^4 + x^3 + 8x^2 - 9x + 1$
Monomial	5	$4b^2$	$-9x^3$
Binomial	$3a - 7$	$y^2 - 9$	$17x^3 + 14x^2$
Trinomial	$x^2 - 5x + 6$	$4y^2 - 7y + 2$	$5a^4 - 3a^3 + a$

Notice that every monomial, binomial, and trinomial is also a polynomial. They are special members of the family of polynomials and so they have special names. We use the words 'monomial', 'binomial', and 'trinomial' when referring to these special polynomials and just call all the rest 'polynomials'.

EXAMPLE 10.1

Determine whether each polynomial is a monomial, binomial, trinomial, or other polynomial:

    ⓐ $8x^2 - 7x - 9$ ⓑ $-5a^4$ ⓒ $x^4 - 7x^3 - 6x^2 + 5x + 2$ ⓓ $11 - 4y^3$ ⓔ n

⊘ Solution

	Polynomial	Number of terms	Type
ⓐ	$8x^2 - 7x - 9$	3	Trinomial
ⓑ	$-5a^4$	1	Monomial
ⓒ	$x^4 - 7x^3 - 6x^2 + 5x + 2$	5	Polynomial
ⓓ	$11 - 4y^3$	2	Binomial
ⓔ	n	1	Monomial

> **TRY IT :: 10.1**   Determine whether each polynomial is a monomial, binomial, trinomial, or other polynomial.

ⓐ z ⓑ $2x^3 - 4x^2 - x - 8$ ⓒ $6x^2 - 4x + 1$ ⓓ $9 - 4y^2$ ⓔ $3x^7$

> **TRY IT :: 10.2**   Determine whether each polynomial is a monomial, binomial, trinomial, or other polynomial.

ⓐ $y^3 - 8$ ⓑ $9x^3 - 5x^2 - x$ ⓒ $x^4 - 3x^2 - 4x - 7$ ⓓ $-y^4$ ⓔ w

Determine the Degree of Polynomials

In this section, we will work with polynomials that have only one variable in each term. The degree of a polynomial and the degree of its terms are determined by the exponents of the variable.

A monomial that has no variable, just a constant, is a special case. The degree of a constant is 0 —it has no variable.

Degree of a Polynomial

The **degree of a term** is the exponent of its variable.

The degree of a constant is 0.

The degree of a polynomial is the highest degree of all its terms.

Let's see how this works by looking at several polynomials. We'll take it step by step, starting with monomials, and then progressing to polynomials with more terms.

Remember: Any base written without an exponent has an implied exponent of 1.

Monomials	5	$4b^2$	$-9x^3$	-18
Degree	0	2	3	0

Binomial	$b+1$	$3a-7$	y^2-9	$17x^3+14x^2$
Degree of each term	1 0	1 0	2 0	3 2
Degree of polynomial	1	1	2	3

Trinomial	x^2-5x+6	$4y^2-7y+2$	$5a^4-3a^3+a$	x^4+2x^2-5
Degree of each term	2 1 0	2 1 0	4 3 1	4 2 0
Degree of polynomial	2	2	4	4

Polynomial	$b+1$	$4y^2-7y+2$	$4x^4+x^3+8x^2-9x+1$
Degree of each term	1 0	2 1 0	4 3 2 1 0
Degree of polynomial	1	2	4

EXAMPLE 10.2

Find the degree of the following polynomials:

ⓐ $4x$ ⓑ $3x^3 - 5x + 7$ ⓒ -11 ⓓ $-6x^2 + 9x - 3$ ⓔ $8x + 2$

Solution

ⓐ

$$4x$$

| The exponent of x is one. $x = x^1$ | The degree is 1. |

ⓑ

$$3x^3 - 5x + 7$$

| The highest degree of all the terms is 3. | The degree is 3 |

ⓒ

$$-11$$

| The degree of a constant is 0. | The degree is 0. |

ⓓ

$$-6x^2 + 9x - 3$$

| The highest degree of all the terms is 2. | The degree is 2. |

ⓔ

$$8x + 2$$

| The highest degree of all the terms is 1. | The degree is 1. |

> **TRY IT :: 10.3** Find the degree of the following polynomials:
>
> ⓐ $-6y$ ⓑ $4x - 1$ ⓒ $3x^4 + 4x^2 - 8$ ⓓ $2y^2 + 3y + 9$ ⓔ -18

> **TRY IT :: 10.4** Find the degree of the following polynomials:
>
> ⓐ 47 ⓑ $2x^2 - 8x + 2$ ⓒ $x^4 - 16$ ⓓ $y^5 - 5y^3 + y$ ⓔ $9a^3$

Working with polynomials is easier when you list the terms in descending order of degrees. When a polynomial is written this way, it is said to be in **standard form**. Look back at the polynomials in Example 10.2. Notice that they are all written in standard form. Get in the habit of writing the term with the highest degree first.

Add and Subtract Monomials

In The Language of Algebra, you simplified expressions by combining like terms. Adding and subtracting monomials is the same as combining like terms. Like terms must have the same variable with the same exponent. Recall that when combining like terms only the coefficients are combined, never the exponents.

EXAMPLE 10.3

Add: $17x^2 + 6x^2$.

Solution

$$17x^2 + 6x^2$$

| Combine like terms. | $23x^2$ |

> **TRY IT :: 10.5** Add: $12x^2 + 5x^2$.

> **TRY IT :: 10.6**   Add: $-11y^2 + 8y^2$.

EXAMPLE 10.4

Subtract: $11n - (-8n)$.

⊘ **Solution**

$$11n - (-8n)$$

Combine like terms. $19n$

> **TRY IT :: 10.7**   Subtract: $9n - (-5n)$.

> **TRY IT :: 10.8**   Subtract: $-7a^3 - \left(-5a^3\right)$.

EXAMPLE 10.5

Simplify: $a^2 + 4b^2 - 7a^2$.

⊘ **Solution**

$$a^2 + 4b^2 - 7a^2$$

Combine like terms. $-6a^2 + 4b^2$

Remember, $-6a^2$ and $4b^2$ are not like terms. The variables are not the same.

> **TRY IT :: 10.9**   Add: $3x^2 + 3y^2 - 5x^2$.

> **TRY IT :: 10.10**   Add: $2a^2 + b^2 - 4a^2$.

Add and Subtract Polynomials

Adding and subtracting polynomials can be thought of as just adding and subtracting like terms. Look for like terms—those with the same variables with the same exponent. The Commutative Property allows us to rearrange the terms to put like terms together. It may also be helpful to underline, circle, or box like terms.

EXAMPLE 10.6

Find the sum: $\left(4x^2 - 5x + 1\right) + \left(3x^2 - 8x - 9\right)$.

Solution

$$(4x^2 - 5x + 1) + (3x^2 - 8x - 9)$$

Identify like terms.	$\underline{4x^2} - \underline{5x} + \boxed{1} + \underline{3x^2} - \underline{8x} - \boxed{9}$
Rearrange to get the like terms together.	$\underline{4x^2 + 3x^2} - \underline{5x - 8x} + \boxed{1} - \boxed{9}$
Combine like terms.	$7x^2 - 13x - 8$

> **TRY IT : : 10.11**   Find the sum: $\left(3x^2 - 2x + 8\right) + \left(x^2 - 6x + 2\right)$.

> **TRY IT : : 10.12**   Find the sum: $\left(7y^2 + 4y - 6\right) + \left(4y^2 + 5y + 1\right)$.

Parentheses are grouping symbols. When we add polynomials as we did in Example 10.6, we can rewrite the expression without parentheses and then combine like terms. But when we subtract polynomials, we must be very careful with the signs.

EXAMPLE 10.7

Find the difference: $\left(7u^2 - 5u + 3\right) - \left(4u^2 - 2\right)$.

Solution

$$(7u^2 - 5u + 3) - (4u^2 - 2)$$

Distribute and identify like terms.	$\underline{7u^2} - \underline{5u} + \boxed{3} - \underline{4u^2} + \boxed{2}$
Rearrange the terms.	$\underline{7u^2 - 4u^2} - \underline{5u} + 3 + \boxed{2}$
Combine like terms.	$3u^2 - 5u + 5$

> **TRY IT : : 10.13**   Find the difference: $\left(6y^2 + 3y - 1\right) - \left(3y^2 - 4\right)$.

> **TRY IT : : 10.14**   Find the difference: $\left(8u^2 - 7u - 2\right) - \left(5u^2 - 6u - 4\right)$.

EXAMPLE 10.8

Subtract: $\left(m^2 - 3m + 8\right)$ from $\left(9m^2 - 7m + 4\right)$.

Solution

$$\text{Subtract } (m^2 - 3m + 8) \text{ from } (9m^2 - 7m + 4)$$

Distribute and identify like terms.	$\underline{9m^2} - \underline{7m} + \boxed{4} - \underline{m^2} + \underline{3m} - \boxed{8}$
Rearrange the terms.	$\underline{9m^2 - m^2} - \underline{7m + 3m} + \boxed{4} - \boxed{8}$
Combine like terms.	$8m^2 - 4m - 4$

> **TRY IT :: 10.15** Subtract: $\left(4n^2 - 7n - 3\right)$ from $\left(8n^2 + 5n - 3\right)$.

> **TRY IT :: 10.16** Subtract: $\left(a^2 - 4a - 9\right)$ from $\left(6a^2 + 4a - 1\right)$.

Evaluate a Polynomial for a Given Value

In The Language of Algebra we evaluated expressions. Since polynomials are expressions, we'll follow the same procedures to evaluate polynomials—substitute the given value for the variable into the polynomial, and then simplify.

EXAMPLE 10.9

Evaluate $3x^2 - 9x + 7$ when

ⓐ $x = 3$ ⓑ $x = -1$

⊘ **Solution**

ⓐ $x = 3$

$$3x^2 - 9x + 7$$

Substitute 3 for x	$3(3)^2 - 9(3) + 7$
Simplify the expression with the exponent.	$3 \cdot 9 - 9(3) + 7$
Multiply.	$27 - 27 + 7$
Simplify.	7

ⓑ $x = -1$

$$3x^2 - 9x + 7$$

Substitute –1 for x	$3(-1)^2 - 9(-1) + 7$
Simplify the expression with the exponent.	$3 \cdot 1 - 9(-1) + 7$
Multiply.	$3 + 9 + 7$
Simplify.	19

> **TRY IT :: 10.17** Evaluate: $2x^2 + 4x - 3$ when

ⓐ $x = 2$ ⓑ $x = -3$

> **TRY IT :: 10.18** Evaluate: $7y^2 - y - 2$ when

ⓐ $y = -4$ ⓑ $y = 0$

EXAMPLE 10.10

The polynomial $-16t^2 + 300$ gives the height of an object t seconds after it is dropped from a 300 foot tall bridge. Find the height after $t = 3$ seconds.

⊘ Solution

	$-16t^2 + 300$
Substitute 3 for t	$-16(3)^2 + 300$
Simplify the expression with the exponent.	$-16 \cdot 9 + 300$
Multiply.	$-144 + 300$
Simplify.	156

> **TRY IT : : 10.19**
>
> The polynomial $-8t^2 + 24t + 4$ gives the height, in feet, of a ball t seconds after it is tossed into the air, from an initial height of 4 feet. Find the height after $t = 3$ seconds.

> **TRY IT : : 10.20**
>
> The polynomial $-8t^2 + 24t + 4$ gives the height, in feet, of a ball x seconds after it is tossed into the air, from an initial height of 4 feet. Find the height after $t = 2$ seconds.

▶ **MEDIA : :** ACCESS ADDITIONAL ONLINE RESOURCES
  - Adding Polynomials (http://openstaxcollege.org/l/24addpolynomi)
  - Subtracting Polynomials (http://openstaxcollege.org/l/24subtractpoly)

10.1 EXERCISES

Practice Makes Perfect

Identify Polynomials, Monomials, Binomials and Trinomials

In the following exercises, determine if each of the polynomials is a monomial, binomial, trinomial, or other polynomial.

1. $5x + 2$

2. $z^2 - 5z - 6$

3. $a^2 + 9a + 18$

4. $-12p^4$

5. $y^3 - 8y^2 + 2y - 16$

6. $10 - 9x$

7. $23y^2$

8. $m^4 + 4m^3 + 6m^2 + 4m + 1$

Determine the Degree of Polynomials

In the following exercises, determine the degree of each polynomial.

9. $8a^5 - 2a^3 + 1$

10. $5c^3 + 11c^2 - c - 8$

11. $3x - 12$

12. $4y + 17$

13. -13

14. -22

Add and Subtract Monomials

In the following exercises, add or subtract the monomials.

15. $6x^2 + 9x^2$

16. $4y^3 + 6y^3$

17. $-12u + 4u$

18. $-3m + 9m$

19. $5a + 7b$

20. $8y + 6z$

21. Add: $4a, \ -3b, \ -8a$

22. Add: $4x, \ 3y, \ -3x$

23. $18x - 2x$

24. $13a - 3a$

25. Subtract $5x^6$ from $-12x^6$

26. Subtract $2p^4$ from $-7p^4$

Add and Subtract Polynomials

In the following exercises, add or subtract the polynomials.

27.
$(4y^2 + 10y + 3) + (8y^2 - 6y + 5)$

28.
$(7x^2 - 9x + 2) + (6x^2 - 4x + 3)$

29.
$(x^2 + 6x + 8) + (-4x^2 + 11x - 9)$

30.
$(y^2 + 9y + 4) + (-2y^2 - 5y - 1)$

31. $(3a^2 + 7) + (a^2 - 7a - 18)$

32. $(p^2 - 5p - 11) + (3p^2 + 9)$

33.
$(6m^2 - 9m - 3) - (2m^2 + m - 5)$

34.
$(3n^2 - 4n + 1) - (4n^2 - n - 2)$

35. $(z^2 + 8z + 9) - (z^2 - 3z + 1)$

36. $(z^2 - 7z + 5) - (z^2 - 8z + 6)$

37. $(12s^2 - 15s) - (s - 9)$

38. $(10r^2 - 20r) - (r - 8)$

39. Find the sum of $\left(2p^3 - 8\right)$ and $\left(p^2 + 9p + 18\right)$

40. Find the sum of $\left(q^2 + 4q + 13\right)$ and $\left(7q^3 - 3\right)$

41. Subtract $\left(7x^2 - 4x + 2\right)$ from $\left(8x^2 - x + 6\right)$

42. Subtract $\left(5x^2 - x + 12\right)$ from $\left(9x^2 - 6x - 20\right)$

43. Find the difference of $\left(w^2 + w - 42\right)$ and $\left(w^2 - 10w + 24\right)$

44. Find the difference of $\left(z^2 - 3z - 18\right)$ and $\left(z^2 + 5z - 20\right)$

Evaluate a Polynomial for a Given Value

In the following exercises, evaluate each polynomial for the given value.

45. Evaluate $8y^2 - 3y + 2$
ⓐ $y = 5$ ⓑ $y = -2$
ⓒ $y = 0$

46. Evaluate $5y^2 - y - 7$ when:
ⓐ $y = -4$ ⓑ $y = 1$
ⓒ $y = 0$

47. Evaluate $4 - 36x$ when:
ⓐ $x = 3$ ⓑ $x = 0$
ⓒ $x = -1$

48. Evaluate $16 - 36x^2$ when:
ⓐ $x = -1$ ⓑ $x = 0$
ⓒ $x = 2$

49. A window washer drops a squeegee from a platform 275 feet high. The polynomial $-16t^2 + 275$ gives the height of the squeegee t seconds after it was dropped. Find the height after $t = 4$ seconds.

50. A manufacturer of microwave ovens has found that the revenue received from selling microwaves at a cost of p dollars each is given by the polynomial $-5p^2 + 350p$. Find the revenue received when $p = 50$ dollars.

Everyday Math

51. Fuel Efficiency The fuel efficiency (in miles per gallon) of a bus going at a speed of x miles per hour is given by the polynomial $-\frac{1}{160}x^2 + \frac{1}{2}x$. Find the fuel efficiency when $x = 40$ mph.

52. Stopping Distance The number of feet it takes for a car traveling at x miles per hour to stop on dry, level concrete is given by the polynomial $0.06x^2 + 1.1x$. Find the stopping distance when $x = 60$ mph.

Writing Exercises

53. Using your own words, explain the difference between a monomial, a binomial, and a trinomial.

54. Eloise thinks the sum $5x^2 + 3x^4$ is $8x^6$. What is wrong with her reasoning?

Self Check

ⓐ *After completing the exercises, use this checklist to evaluate your mastery of the objectives of this section.*

I can...	Confidently	With some help	No-I don't get it!
identify polynomials, monomials, binomials, and trinomials.			
determine the degree of polynomials.			
add and subtract monomials.			
add and subtract polynomials.			
evaluate a polynomial for a given value.			

ⓑ *If most of your checks were:*

...confidently. Congratulations! You have achieved the objectives in this section. Reflect on the study skills you used so that you can continue to use them. What did you do to become confident of your ability to do these things? Be specific.

...with some help. This must be addressed quickly because topics you do not master become potholes in your road to success. In math, every topic builds upon previous work. It is important to make sure you have a strong foundation before you move on. Who can you ask for help? Your fellow classmates and instructor are good resources. Is there a place on campus where math

tutors are available? Can your study skills be improved?

...no—I don't get it! This is a warning sign and you must not ignore it. You should get help right away or you will quickly be overwhelmed. See your instructor as soon as you can to discuss your situation. Together you can come up with a plan to get you the help you need.

10.2 | Use Multiplication Properties of Exponents

Learning Objectives

By the end of this section, you will be able to:

- Simplify expressions with exponents
- Simplify expressions using the Product Property of Exponents
- Simplify expressions using the Power Property of Exponents
- Simplify expressions using the Product to a Power Property
- Simplify expressions by applying several properties
- Multiply monomials

Be Prepared!

Before you get started, take this readiness quiz.

1. Simplify: $\frac{3}{4} \cdot \frac{3}{4}$.
   If you missed the problem, review Example 4.25.

2. Simplify: $(-2)(-2)(-2)$.
   If you missed the problem, review Example 3.52.

Simplify Expressions with Exponents

Remember that an exponent indicates repeated multiplication of the same quantity. For example, 2^4 means to multiply four factors of 2, so 2^4 means $2 \cdot 2 \cdot 2 \cdot 2$. This format is known as **exponential notation**.

Exponential Notation

$$a^m \leftarrow \text{exponent}$$

$$\underset{\text{base}}{a}$$

a^m means multiply m factors of a

$$a^m = \underbrace{a \cdot a \cdot a \cdot \ldots \cdot a}_{m \text{ factors}}$$

This is read a to the mth power.

In the expression a^m, the exponent tells us how many times we use the base a as a factor.

$$7^3 \qquad\qquad (-8)^5$$

$$\underbrace{7 \cdot 7 \cdot 7}_{3 \text{ factors}} \qquad \underbrace{(-8)(-8)(-8)(-8)(-8)}_{5 \text{ factors}}$$

Before we begin working with variable expressions containing exponents, let's simplify a few expressions involving only numbers.

EXAMPLE 10.11

Simplify:

ⓐ 5^3 ⓑ 9^1

Solution

ⓐ

$$5^3$$

Multiply 3 factors of 5.	$5 \cdot 5 \cdot 5$
Simplify.	125

ⓑ

$$9^1$$

Multiply 1 factor of 9.	9

> **TRY IT : :** 10.21   Simplify:

ⓐ 4^3 ⓑ 11^1

> **TRY IT : :** 10.22   Simplify:

ⓐ 3^4 ⓑ 21^1

EXAMPLE 10.12

Simplify:

ⓐ $\left(\frac{7}{8}\right)^2$ ⓑ $(0.74)^2$

Solution

ⓐ

$$\left(\frac{7}{8}\right)^2$$

Multiply two factors.	$\left(\frac{7}{8}\right)\left(\frac{7}{8}\right)$
Simplify.	$\frac{49}{64}$

ⓑ

$$(0.74)^2$$

Multiply two factors.	$(0.74)(0.74)$
Simplify.	0.5476

> **TRY IT : :** 10.23   Simplify:

ⓐ $\left(\dfrac{5}{8}\right)^2$ ⓑ $(0.67)^2$

> **TRY IT : :** 10.24   Simplify:

ⓐ $\left(\dfrac{2}{5}\right)^3$ ⓑ $(0.127)^2$

EXAMPLE 10.13

Simplify:

ⓐ $(-3)^4$ ⓑ -3^4

✓ **Solution**

ⓐ

$$(-3)^4$$

Multiply four factors of –3.	$(-3)(-3)(-3)(-3)$
Simplify.	81

ⓑ

$$-3^4$$

Multiply two factors.	$-(3 \cdot 3 \cdot 3 \cdot 3)$
Simplify.	-81

Notice the similarities and differences in parts ⓐ and ⓑ. Why are the answers different? In part ⓐ the parentheses tell us to raise the (–3) to the 4th power. In part ⓑ we raise only the 3 to the 4th power and then find the opposite.

> **TRY IT : :** 10.25   Simplify:

ⓐ $(-2)^4$ ⓑ -2^4

> **TRY IT : : 10.26**   Simplify:

ⓐ $(-8)^2$ ⓑ -8^2

Simplify Expressions Using the Product Property of Exponents

You have seen that when you combine like terms by adding and subtracting, you need to have the same base with the same exponent. But when you multiply and divide, the exponents may be different, and sometimes the bases may be different, too. We'll derive the properties of exponents by looking for patterns in several examples. All the exponent properties hold true for any real numbers, but right now we will only use whole number exponents.

First, we will look at an example that leads to the Product Property.

$$x^2 \quad \cdot \quad x^3$$

What does this mean?

$$\underbrace{x \cdot x}_{2\ factors} \quad \cdot \quad \underbrace{x \cdot x \cdot x}_{3\ factors}$$

How many factors altogether?

$$5\ factors$$

So, we have

$$x^5$$

Notice that 5 is the sum of the exponents, 2 and 3.

$$x^2 \cdot x^3 \text{ is } x^{2+3}, \text{ or } x^5$$

We write:

$$x^2 \cdot x^3$$
$$x^{2+3}$$
$$x^5$$

The base stayed the same and we added the exponents. This leads to the Product Property for Exponents.

Product Property of Exponents

If a is a real number and m, n are counting numbers, then

$$a^m \cdot a^n = a^{m+n}$$

To multiply with like bases, add the exponents.

An example with numbers helps to verify this property.

$$2^2 \cdot 2^3 \overset{?}{=} 2^{2+3}$$
$$4 \cdot 8 \overset{?}{=} 2^5$$
$$32 = 32 \checkmark$$

EXAMPLE 10.14

Simplify: $x^5 \cdot x^7$.

 Solution

$$x^5 \cdot x^7$$

Use the product property, $a^m \cdot a^n = a^{m+n}$. x^{5+7}

Simplify. x^{12}

> **TRY IT : :** 10.27   Simplify: $x^7 \cdot x^8$.

> **TRY IT : :** 10.28   Simplify: $x^5 \cdot x^{11}$.

EXAMPLE 10.15

Simplify: $b^4 \cdot b$.

⊘ **Solution**

	$b^4 \cdot b$
Rewrite, $b = b^1$.	$b^4 \cdot b^1$
Use the product property, $a^m \cdot a^n = a^{m+n}$.	b^{4+1}
Simplify.	b^5

> **TRY IT : :** 10.29   Simplify: $p^9 \cdot p$.

> **TRY IT : :** 10.30   Simplify: $m \cdot m^7$.

EXAMPLE 10.16

Simplify: $2^7 \cdot 2^9$.

⊘ **Solution**

	$2^7 \cdot 2^9$
Use the product property, $a^m \cdot a^n = a^{m+n}$.	2^{7+9}
Simplify.	2^{16}

> **TRY IT : :** 10.31   Simplify: $6 \cdot 6^9$.

> **TRY IT : :** 10.32   Simplify: $9^6 \cdot 9^9$.

EXAMPLE 10.17

Simplify: $y^{17} \cdot y^{23}$.

⊘ **Solution**

$$y^{17} \cdot y^{23}$$

Notice, the bases are the same, so add the exponents. $\quad y^{17+23}$

Simplify. $\quad y^{40}$

> **TRY IT :: 10.33**   Simplify: $y^{24} \cdot y^{19}$.

> **TRY IT :: 10.34**   Simplify: $z^{15} \cdot z^{24}$.

We can extend the Product Property of Exponents to more than two factors.

EXAMPLE 10.18

Simplify: $x^3 \cdot x^4 \cdot x^2$.

⊘ **Solution**

$$x^3 \cdot x^4 \cdot x^2$$

Add the exponents, since the bases are the same. $\quad x^{3+4+2}$

Simplify. $\quad x^9$

> **TRY IT :: 10.35**   Simplify: $x^7 \cdot x^5 \cdot x^9$.

> **TRY IT :: 10.36**   Simplify: $y^3 \cdot y^8 \cdot y^4$.

Simplify Expressions Using the Power Property of Exponents

Now let's look at an exponential expression that contains a power raised to a power. See if you can discover a general property.

	$(x^2)^3$
	$x^2 \quad \cdot \quad x^2 \quad \cdot \quad x^2$
What does this mean?	$\underbrace{x \cdot x}_{2\ factors} \cdot \underbrace{x \cdot x}_{2\ factors} \cdot \underbrace{x \cdot x}_{2\ factors}$
How many factors altogether?	6 *factors*
So, we have	x^6
Notice that 6 is the product of the exponents, 2 and 3.	$(x^2)^3$ is $x^{2 \cdot 3}$ or x^6
We write:	$(x^2)^3$ $x^{2 \cdot 3}$ x^6

We multiplied the exponents. This leads to the Power Property for Exponents.

Power Property of Exponents

If a is a real number and m, n are whole numbers, then

$$(a^m)^n = a^{m \cdot n}$$

To raise a power to a power, multiply the exponents.

An example with numbers helps to verify this property.

$$(5^2)^3 \overset{?}{=} 5^{2 \cdot 3}$$
$$(25)^3 \overset{?}{=} 5^6$$
$$15{,}625 = 15{,}625 \checkmark$$

EXAMPLE 10.19

Simplify:

ⓐ $(x^5)^7$ ⓐ $(3^6)^8$

⊘ **Solution**

ⓐ

	$\left(x^5\right)^7$
Use the Power Property, $(a^m)^n = a^{m \cdot n}$.	$x^{5 \cdot 7}$
Simplify.	x^{35}

ⓑ

$$\left(3^6\right)^8$$

Use the Power Property, $(a^m)^n = a^{m \cdot n}$. $3^{6 \cdot 8}$

Simplify. 3^{48}

> **TRY IT :: 10.37**   Simplify:

ⓐ $\left(x^7\right)^4$ ⓑ $\left(7^4\right)^8$

> **TRY IT :: 10.38**   Simplify:

ⓐ $\left(x^6\right)^9$ ⓑ $\left(8^6\right)^7$

Simplify Expressions Using the Product to a Power Property

We will now look at an expression containing a product that is raised to a power. Look for a pattern.

$$(2x)^3$$

What does this mean? $2x \cdot 2x \cdot 2x$

We group the like factors together. $2 \cdot 2 \cdot 2 \cdot x \cdot x \cdot x$

How many factors of 2 and of x? $2^3 \cdot x^3$

Notice that each factor was raised to the power. $(2x)^3$ is $2^3 \cdot x^3$

We write: $(2x)^3$
$2^3 \cdot x^3$

The exponent applies to each of the factors. This leads to the Product to a Power Property for Exponents.

Product to a Power Property of Exponents

If a and b are real numbers and m is a whole number, then

$$(ab)^m = a^m b^m$$

To raise a product to a power, raise each factor to that power.

An example with numbers helps to verify this property:

$$(2 \cdot 3)^2 \overset{?}{=} 2^2 \cdot 3^2$$
$$6^2 \overset{?}{=} 4 \cdot 9$$
$$36 = 36 \checkmark$$

EXAMPLE 10.20

Simplify: $(-11x)^2$.

⊘ **Solution**

$$(-11x)^2$$

Use the Power of a Product Property, $(ab)^m = a^m b^m$.	$(-11)^2 x^2$
Simplify.	$121x^2$

> **TRY IT :: 10.39**   Simplify: $(-14x)^2$.

> **TRY IT :: 10.40**   Simplify: $(-12a)^2$.

EXAMPLE 10.21

Simplify: $(3xy)^3$.

⊘ **Solution**

$$(3xy)^3$$

Raise each factor to the third power.	$3^3 x^3 y^3$
Simplify.	$27x^3 y^3$

> **TRY IT :: 10.41**   Simplify: $(-4xy)^4$.

> **TRY IT :: 10.42**   Simplify: $(6xy)^3$.

Simplify Expressions by Applying Several Properties

We now have three properties for multiplying expressions with exponents. Let's summarize them and then we'll do some examples that use more than one of the properties.

Properties of Exponents

If a, b are real numbers and m, n are whole numbers, then

Product Property	$a^m \cdot a^n = a^{m+n}$
Power Property	$(a^m)^n = a^{m \cdot n}$
Product to a Power Property	$(ab)^m = a^m b^m$

EXAMPLE 10.22

Simplify: $(x^2)^6 (x^5)^4$.

✅ Solution

$$(x^2)^6 (x^5)^4$$

Use the Power Property. $\quad x^{12} \cdot x^{20}$

Add the exponents. $\quad\quad x^{32}$

> **TRY IT ::** 10.43   Simplify: $(x^4)^3 (x^7)^4$.

> **TRY IT ::** 10.44   Simplify: $(y^9)^2 (y^8)^3$.

EXAMPLE 10.23

Simplify: $(-7x^3 y^4)^2$.

✅ Solution

$$(-7x^3 y^4)^2$$

Take each factor to the second power. $\quad (-7)^2 (x^3)^2 (y^4)^2$

Use the Power Property. $\quad\quad 49x^6 y^8$

> **TRY IT ::** 10.45   Simplify: $(-8x^4 y^7)^3$.

> **TRY IT ::** 10.46   Simplify: $(-3a^5 b^6)^4$.

EXAMPLE 10.24

Simplify: $(6n)^2 (4n^3)$.

✅ Solution

$$(6n)^2 (4n^3)$$

Raise $6n$ to the second power. $\quad 6^2 n^2 \cdot 4n^3$

Simplify. $\quad\quad 36n^2 \cdot 4n^3$

Use the Commutative Property. $\quad 36 \cdot 4 \cdot n^2 \cdot n^3$

Multiply the constants and add the exponents. $\quad 144n^5$

Notice that in the first monomial, the exponent was outside the parentheses and it applied to both factors inside. In the second monomial, the exponent was inside the parentheses and so it only applied to the n.

> **TRY IT ::** 10.47   Simplify: $(7n)^2 (2n^{12})$.

> **TRY IT ::** 10.48   Simplify: $(4m)^2 (3m^3)$.

EXAMPLE 10.25

Simplify: $(3p^2 q)^4 (2pq^2)^3$.

⊘ **Solution**

$$(3p^2 q)^4 (2pq^2)^3$$

Use the Power of a Product Property.	$3^4 (p^2)^4 q^4 \cdot 2^3 p^3 (q^2)^3$
Use the Power Property.	$81 p^8 q^4 \cdot 8 p^3 q^6$
Use the Commutative Property.	$81 \cdot 8 \cdot p^8 \cdot p^3 \cdot q^4 \cdot q^6$
Multiply the constants and add the exponents for each variable.	$648 p^{11} q^{10}$

> **TRY IT ::** 10.49   Simplify: $(u^3 v^2)^5 (4uv^4)^3$.

> **TRY IT ::** 10.50   Simplify: $(5x^2 y^3)^2 (3xy^4)^3$.

Multiply Monomials

Since a monomial is an algebraic expression, we can use the properties for simplifying expressions with exponents to multiply the monomials.

EXAMPLE 10.26

Multiply: $(4x^2)(-5x^3)$.

⊘ **Solution**

$$(4x^2)(-5x^3)$$

Use the Commutative Property to rearrange the factors.	$4 \cdot (-5) \cdot x^2 \cdot x^3$
Multiply.	$-20x^5$

> **TRY IT ::** 10.51   Multiply: $(7x^7)(-8x^4)$.

> **TRY IT ::** 10.52   Multiply: $(-9y^4)(-6y^5)$.

EXAMPLE 10.27

Multiply: $\left(\frac{3}{4}c^3 d\right)(12cd^2)$.

⊘ **Solution**

$$\left(\frac{3}{4}c^3 d\right)(12cd^2)$$

Use the Commutative Property to rearrange the factors.

$$\frac{3}{4} \cdot 12 \cdot c^3 \cdot c \cdot d \cdot d^2$$

Multiply.

$$9c^4 d^3$$

> **TRY IT ::** 10.53   Multiply: $\left(\frac{4}{5}m^4 n^3\right)(15mn^3)$.

> **TRY IT ::** 10.54   Multiply: $\left(\frac{2}{3}p^5 q\right)(18p^6 q^7)$.

▶ **MEDIA ::** ACCESS ADDITIONAL ONLINE RESOURCES
- Exponent Properties (http://www.openstaxcollege.org/l/24expproperties)
- Exponent Properties 2 (http://www.openstaxcollege.org/l/expproperties2)

10.2 EXERCISES

Practice Makes Perfect

Simplify Expressions with Exponents

In the following exercises, simplify each expression with exponents.

55. 4^5

56. 10^3

57. $\left(\frac{1}{2}\right)^2$

58. $\left(\frac{3}{5}\right)^2$

59. $(0.2)^3$

60. $(0.4)^3$

61. $(-5)^4$

62. $(-3)^5$

63. -5^4

64. -3^5

65. -10^4

66. -2^6

67. $\left(-\frac{2}{3}\right)^3$

68. $\left(-\frac{1}{4}\right)^4$

69. -0.5^2

70. -0.1^4

Simplify Expressions Using the Product Property of Exponents

In the following exercises, simplify each expression using the Product Property of Exponents.

71. $x^3 \cdot x^6$

72. $m^4 \cdot m^2$

73. $a \cdot a^4$

74. $y^{12} \cdot y$

75. $3^5 \cdot 3^9$

76. $5^{10} \cdot 5^6$

77. $z \cdot z^2 \cdot z^3$

78. $a \cdot a^3 \cdot a^5$

79. $x^a \cdot x^2$

80. $y^p \cdot y^3$

81. $y^a \cdot y^b$

82. $x^p \cdot x^q$

Simplify Expressions Using the Power Property of Exponents

In the following exercises, simplify each expression using the Power Property of Exponents.

83. $(u^4)^2$

84. $(x^2)^7$

85. $(y^5)^4$

86. $(a^3)^2$

87. $(10^2)^6$

88. $(2^8)^3$

89. $(x^{15})^6$

90. $(y^{12})^8$

91. $(x^2)^y$

92. $(y^3)^x$

93. $(5^x)^y$

94. $(7^a)^b$

Simplify Expressions Using the Product to a Power Property

In the following exercises, simplify each expression using the Product to a Power Property.

95. $(5a)^2$

96. $(7x)^2$

97. $(-6m)^3$

98. $(-9n)^3$

99. $(4rs)^2$

100. $(5ab)^3$

101. $(4xyz)^4$

102. $(-5abc)^3$

Simplify Expressions by Applying Several Properties

In the following exercises, simplify each expression.

103. $(x^2)^4 \cdot (x^3)^2$

104. $(y^4)^3 \cdot (y^5)^2$

105. $(a^2)^6 \cdot (a^3)^8$

106. $(b^7)^5 \cdot (b^2)^6$

107. $(3x)^2(5x)$

108. $(2y)^3(6y)$

109. $(5a)^2(2a)^3$

110. $(4b)^2(3b)^3$

111. $(2m^6)^3$

112. $(3y^2)^4$

113. $(10x^2 y)^3$

114. $(2mn^4)^5$

115. $(-2a^3 b^2)^4$

116. $(-10u^2 v^4)^3$

117. $\left(\frac{2}{3}x^2 y\right)^3$

118. $\left(\frac{7}{9}pq^4\right)^2$

119. $(8a^3)^2 (2a)^4$

120. $(5r^2)^3 (3r)^2$

121. $(10p^4)^3 (5p^6)^2$

122. $(4x^3)^3 (2x^5)^4$

123. $\left(\frac{1}{2}x^2 y^3\right)^4 (4x^5 y^3)^2$

124. $\left(\frac{1}{3}m^3 n^2\right)^4 (9m^8 n^3)^2$

125. $(3m^2 n)^2 (2mn^5)^4$

126. $(2pq^4)^3 (5p^6 q)^2$

Multiply Monomials

In the following exercises, multiply the following monomials.

127. $(12x^2)(-5x^4)$

128. $(-10y^3)(7y^2)$

129. $(-8u^6)(-9u)$

130. $(-6c^4)(-12c)$

131. $\left(\frac{1}{5}r^8\right)(20r^3)$

132. $\left(\frac{1}{4}a^5\right)(36a^2)$

133. $(4a^3 b)(9a^2 b^6)$

134. $(6m^4 n^3)(7mn^5)$

135. $\left(\frac{4}{7}xy^2\right)(14xy^3)$

136. $\left(\frac{5}{8}u^3 v\right)(24u^5 v)$

137. $\left(\frac{2}{3}x^2 y\right)\left(\frac{3}{4}xy^2\right)$

138. $\left(\frac{3}{5}m^3 n^2\right)\left(\frac{5}{9}m^2 n^3\right)$

Everyday Math

139. Email Janet emails a joke to six of her friends and tells them to forward it to six of their friends, who forward it to six of their friends, and so on. The number of people who receive the email on the second round is 6^2, on the third round is 6^3, as shown in the table. How many people will receive the email on the eighth round? Simplify the expression to show the number of people who receive the email.

Round	Number of people
1	6
2	6^2
3	6^3
...	...
8	?

140. Salary Raul's boss gives him a 5% raise every year on his birthday. This means that each year, Raul's salary is 1.05 times his last year's salary. If his original salary was $\$40,000$, his salary after 1 year was $\$40,000(1.05)$, after 2 years was $\$40,000(1.05)^2$, after 3 years was $\$40,000(1.05)^3$, as shown in the table below. What will Raul's salary be after 10 years? Simplify the expression, to show Raul's salary in dollars.

Year	Salary
1	$\$40,000(1.05)$
2	$\$40,000(1.05)^2$
3	$\$40,000(1.05)^3$
...	...
10	?

Writing Exercises

141. Use the Product Property for Exponents to explain why $x \cdot x = x^2$.

142. Explain why $-5^3 = (-5)^3$ but $-5^4 \neq (-5)^4$.

143. Jorge thinks $\left(\frac{1}{2}\right)^2$ is 1. What is wrong with his reasoning?

144. Explain why $x^3 \cdot x^5$ is x^8, and not x^{15}.

Self Check

ⓐ After completing the exercises, use this checklist to evaluate your mastery of the objectives of this section.

I can...	Confidently	With some help	No-I don't get it!
simplify expressions with exponents.			
simplify expressions using the Product Property for Exponents.			
simplify expressions using the Power Property for Exponents.			
simplify expressions using the Product to a Power Property.			
simplify expressions by applying several properties.			
multiply monomials.			

ⓑ After reviewing this checklist, what will you do to become confident for all objectives?

10.3 Multiply Polynomials

Learning Objectives

By the end of this section, you will be able to:
- Multiply a polynomial by a monomial
- Multiply a binomial by a binomial
- Multiply a trinomial by a binomial

Be Prepared!

Before you get started, take this readiness quiz.

1. Distribute: $2(x + 3)$.
   If you missed the problem, review Example 7.17.

2. Distribute: $-11(4 - 3a)$.
   If you missed the problem, review Example 7.26.

3. Combine like terms: $x^2 + 9x + 7x + 63$.
   If you missed the problem, review Example 2.21.

Multiply a Polynomial by a Monomial

In Distributive Property you learned to use the Distributive Property to simplify expressions such as $2(x - 3)$. You multiplied both terms in the parentheses, x and 3, by 2, to get $2x - 6$. With this chapter's new vocabulary, you can say you were multiplying a binomial, $x - 3$, by a monomial, 2. Multiplying a binomial by a monomial is nothing new for you!

EXAMPLE 10.28

Multiply: $3(x + 7)$.

⊘ **Solution**

$$3(x + 7)$$

Distribute.

$$3 \cdot x + 3 \cdot 7$$

Simplify. $3x + 21$

> **TRY IT : : 10.55**   Multiply: $6(x + 8)$.

> **TRY IT : : 10.56**   Multiply: $2(y + 12)$.

EXAMPLE 10.29

Multiply: $x(x - 8)$.

✓ **Solution**

$$x(x - 8)$$

Distribute.

$$x(x - 8)$$

$$x^2 - 8x$$

Simplify.

$$x^2 - 8x$$

> **TRY IT : : 10.57**   Multiply: $y(y - 9)$.

> **TRY IT : : 10.58**   Multiply: $p(p - 13)$.

EXAMPLE 10.30

Multiply: $10x(4x + y)$.

✓ **Solution**

$$10x(4x + y)$$

Distribute.

$$10x(4x + y)$$

$$10x \cdot 4x + 10x \cdot y$$

Simplify.

$$40x^2 + 10xy$$

> **TRY IT : : 10.59**   Multiply: $8x(x + 3y)$.

> **TRY IT : : 10.60**   Multiply: $3r(6r + s)$.

Multiplying a monomial by a trinomial works in much the same way.

EXAMPLE 10.31

Multiply: $-2x(5x^2 + 7x - 3)$.

✓ **Solution**

$$-2x(5x^2 + 7x - 3)$$

Distribute.

$$-2x(5x^2 + 7x - 3)$$

$$-2x \cdot 5x^2 + \left(-2x\right) \cdot 7x - \left(-2x\right) \cdot 3$$

Simplify.

$$-10x^3 - 14x^2 + 6x$$

> **TRY IT ::** 10.61   Multiply: $-4y(8y^2 + 5y - 9)$.

> **TRY IT ::** 10.62   Multiply: $-6x(9x^2 + x - 1)$.

EXAMPLE 10.32

Multiply: $4y^3(y^2 - 8y + 1)$.

○ **Solution**

$$4y^3(y^2 - 8y + 1)$$

Distribute.

$$4y^3(y^2 - 8y + 1)$$

$$4y^3 \cdot y^2 - 4y^3 \cdot 8y + 4y^3 \cdot 1$$

Simplify. $4y^5 - 32y^4 + 4y^3$

> **TRY IT ::** 10.63   Multiply: $3x^2(4x^2 - 3x + 9)$.

> **TRY IT ::** 10.64   Multiply: $8y^2(3y^2 - 2y - 4)$.

Now we will have the monomial as the second factor.

EXAMPLE 10.33

Multiply: $(x + 3)p$.

○ **Solution**

$$(x + 3)p$$

Distribute.

$$(x + 3)p$$

$$x \cdot p + 3 \cdot p$$

Simplify. $xp + 3p$

> **TRY IT ::** 10.65   Multiply: $(x + 8)p$.

> **TRY IT ::** 10.66   Multiply: $(a + 4)p$.

Multiply a Binomial by a Binomial

Just like there are different ways to represent multiplication of numbers, there are several methods that can be used to multiply a binomial times a binomial.

Using the Distributive Property

We will start by using the Distributive Property. Look again at Example 10.33.

$$(x + 3)p$$

We distributed the p to get	$xp + 3p$
What if we have $(x + 7)$ instead of p? Think of the $(x + 7)$ as the p above.	$(x + 3)(x + 7)$
Distribute $(x + 7)$.	$x(x + 7) + 3(x + 7)$
Distribute again.	$x^2 + 7x + 3x + 21$
Combine like terms.	$x^2 + 10x + 21$

Notice that before combining like terms, we had four terms. We multiplied the two terms of the first binomial by the two terms of the second binomial—four multiplications.

Be careful to distinguish between a sum and a product.

Sum	**Product**
$x + x$	$x \cdot x$
$2x$	x^2
combine like terms	add exponents of like bases

EXAMPLE 10.34

Multiply: $(x + 6)(x + 8)$.

⊘ **Solution**

$$(x + 6)(x + 8)$$

	$(x + 6)(x + 8)$
Distribute $(x + 8)$.	$x(x + 8) + 6(x + 8)$
Distribute again.	$x^2 + 8x + 6x + 48$
Simplify.	$x^2 + 14x + 48$

> **TRY IT :: 10.67** Multiply: $(x + 8)(x + 9)$.

> **TRY IT :: 10.68** Multiply: $(a + 4)(a + 5)$.

Now we'll see how to multiply binomials where the variable has a coefficient.

EXAMPLE 10.35

Multiply: $(2x + 9)(3x + 4)$.

 Solution

$$(2x + 9)(3x + 4)$$

Distribute. $(3x + 4)$	$2x(3x + 4) + 9(3x + 4)$
Distribute again.	$6x^2 + 8x + 27x + 36$
Simplify.	$6x^2 + 35x + 36$

> **TRY IT : : 10.69** Multiply: $(5x + 9)(4x + 3)$.

> **TRY IT : : 10.70** Multiply: $(10m + 9)(8m + 7)$.

In the previous examples, the binomials were sums. When there are differences, we pay special attention to make sure the signs of the product are correct.

EXAMPLE 10.36

Multiply: $(4y + 3)(6y - 5)$.

 Solution

$$(4y + 3)(6y - 5)$$

Distribute.	$4y(6y - 5) + 3(6y - 5)$
Distribute again.	$24y^2 - 20y + 18y - 15$
Simplify.	$24y^2 - 2y - 15$

> **TRY IT : : 10.71** Multiply: $(7y + 1)(8y - 3)$.

> **TRY IT : : 10.72** Multiply: $(3x + 2)(5x - 8)$.

Up to this point, the product of two binomials has been a trinomial. This is not always the case.

EXAMPLE 10.37

Multiply: $(x + 2)(x - y)$.

⊘ **Solution**

$$(x + 2)(x - y)$$

Distribute.	$x(x - y) + 2(x - y)$
Distribute again.	$x^2 - xy + 2x - 2y$
Simplify.	There are no like terms to combine.

> **TRY IT ::** 10.73 Multiply: $(x + 5)(x - y)$.

> **TRY IT ::** 10.74 Multiply: $(x + 2y)(x - 1)$.

Using the FOIL Method

Remember that when you multiply a binomial by a binomial you get four terms. Sometimes you can combine like terms to get a trinomial, but sometimes there are no like terms to combine. Let's look at the last example again and pay particular attention to how we got the four terms.

$$(x + 2)(x - y)$$
$$x^2 - xy + 2x - 2y$$

Where did the first term, x^2, come from?

It is the product of x *and* x, the **first** terms in $(x + 2)$ and $(x - y)$.

First
$(x + 2)(x - y)$

The next term, $-xy$, is the product of x and $-y$, the two **outer** terms.

$(x + 2)(x - y)$
Outer

The third term, $+2x$, is the product of 2 and x, the two **inner** terms.

$(x + 2)(x - y)$
Inner

And the last term, $-2y$, came from multiplying the two **last** terms.

Last
$(x + 2)(x - y)$

We abbreviate "First, Outer, Inner, Last" as FOIL. The letters stand for 'First, Outer, Inner, Last'. The word FOIL is easy to remember and ensures we find all four products. We might say we use the FOIL method to multiply two binomials.

first last first last
$(a + b)$ $(c + d)$
inner
outer

Let's look at $(x + 3)(x + 7)$ again. Now we will work through an example where we use the FOIL pattern to multiply two binomials.

Distributive Property   FOIL

$(x + 3)(x + 7)$ $(x + 3)(x + 7)$

$x(x + 7) + 3(x + 7)$

$x^2 + 7x + 3x + 21$ $x^2 + 7x + 3x + 21$
F   O   I   L   F   O   I   L

$x^2 + 10x + 21$ $x^2 + 10x + 21$

EXAMPLE 10.38

Multiply using the FOIL method: $(x + 6)(x + 9)$.

⊘ Solution

Step 1: Multiply the **First** terms. $(x + 6)(x + 9)$ $x^2 + \_\_ + \_\_ + \_\_$
         F   O   I   L

Step 2: Multiply the **Outer** terms. $(x + 6)(x + 9)$ $x^2 + 9x + \_\_ + \_\_$
         F   O   I   L

Step 3: Multiply the **Inner** terms. $(x + 6)(x + 9)$ $x^2 + 9x + 6x + \_\_$
         F   O   I   L

Step 4: Multiply the **Last** terms. $(x + 6)(x + 9)$ $x^2 + 9x + 6x + 54$
         F   O   I   L

Step 5: Combine like terms, when possible. $x^2 + 15x + 54$

> **TRY IT : :** 10.75   Multiply using the FOIL method: $(x + 7)(x + 8)$.

> **TRY IT : :** 10.76   Multiply using the FOIL method: $(y + 14)(y + 2)$.

We summarize the steps of the FOIL method below. The FOIL method only applies to multiplying binomials, not other polynomials!

HOW TO :: USE THE FOIL METHOD FOR MULTIPLYING TWO BINOMIALS.

Step 1.   Multiply the **First** terms.
Step 2.   Multiply the **Outer** terms.
Step 3.   Multiply the **Inner** terms.
Step 4.   Multiply the **Last** terms.
Step 5.   Combine like terms, when possible.

$$\underbrace{(a+b)}_{} \quad \underbrace{(c+d)}_{}$$

first   last   first   last

inner

outer

EXAMPLE 10.39

Multiply: $(y - 8)(y + 6)$.

 Solution

Step 1: Multiply the **First** terms.	$(y - 8)(y + 6)$	$y^2 + \_\_ + \_\_ + \_\_$ $\ \ \ F \ \ \ O \ \ \ I \ \ \ L$
Step 2: Multiply the **Outer** terms.	$(y - 8)(y + 6)$	$y^2 + 6y + \_\_ + \_\_$ $\ \ \ F \ \ \ \ \ O \ \ \ I \ \ \ L$
Step 3: Multiply the **Inner** terms.	$(y - 8)(y + 6)$	$y^2 + 6y - 8y + \_\_$ $\ \ \ F \ \ \ \ \ O \ \ \ \ \ I \ \ \ \ L$
Step 4: Multiply the **Last** terms.	$(y - 8)(y + 6)$	$y^2 + 6y - 8y - 48$ $\ \ \ F \ \ \ \ \ O \ \ \ \ \ I \ \ \ \ \ L$
Step 5: Combine like terms		$y^2 - 2y - 48$

> **TRY IT :: 10.77**   Multiply: $(y - 3)(y + 8)$.

> **TRY IT :: 10.78**   Multiply: $(q - 4)(q + 5)$.

EXAMPLE 10.40

Multiply: $(2a + 3)(3a - 1)$.

Solution

$$(2a + 3)(3a - 1)$$

$$(2a + 3)(3a - 1)$$

Multiply the **First** terms.	$2a \cdot 3a$	$6a^2 + \underline{} + \underline{} + \underline{}$ $\quad\;\; F \quad\; O \quad\; I \quad\; L$
Multiply the **Outer** terms.	$2a \cdot (-1)$	$6a^2 - 2a + \underline{} + \underline{}$ $\quad\;\; F \quad\; O \quad\; I \quad\; L$
Multiply the **Inner** terms.	$3 \cdot 3a$	$6a^2 - 2a + 9a + \underline{}$ $\quad\;\; F \quad\; O \quad\; I \quad\; L$
Multiply the **Last** terms.	$3 \cdot (-1)$	$6a^2 - 2a + 9a - 3$ $\quad\;\; F \quad\; O \quad\; I \quad\; L$
Combine like terms.		$6a^2 + 7a - 3$

> **TRY IT : : 10.79**   Multiply: $(4a + 9)(5a - 2)$.

> **TRY IT : : 10.80**   Multiply: $(7x + 4)(7x - 8)$.

EXAMPLE 10.41

Multiply: $(5x - y)(2x - 7)$.

Solution

$$(5x - y)(2x - 7)$$

$$(5x - y)(2x - 7)$$

Multiply the **First** terms.	$10x^2 + \underline{} + \underline{} + \underline{}$ $\quad\;\; F \quad\; O \quad\; I \quad\; L$
Multiply the **Outer** terms.	$10x^2 - 35x + \underline{} + \underline{}$ $\quad\;\; F \quad\; O \quad\; I \quad\; L$
Multiply the **Inner** terms.	$10x^2 - 35x - 2xy + \underline{}$ $\quad\;\; F \quad\; O \quad\; I \quad\; L$
Multiply the **Last** terms.	$10x^2 - 35x - 2xy + 7y$ $\quad\;\; F \quad\; O \quad\; I \quad\; L$
Combine like terms. There are none.	$10x^2 - 35x - 2xy + 7y$

> **TRY IT : : 10.81**   Multiply: $(12x - y)(x - 5)$.

> **TRY IT : : 10.82**   Multiply: $(6a - b)(2a - 9)$.

Using the Vertical Method

The FOIL method is usually the quickest method for multiplying two binomials, but it works *only* for binomials. You can use the Distributive Property to find the product of any two polynomials. Another method that works for all polynomials is the Vertical Method. It is very much like the method you use to multiply whole numbers. Look carefully at this example of multiplying two-digit numbers.

$$\begin{array}{r} 23 \\ \times 46 \\ \hline 138 \\ 92 \\ \hline 1058 \end{array}$$

23
×46
138   partial product
92   partial product
1058   product

You start by multiplying 23 by 6 to get 138.

Then you multiply 23 by 4, lining up the partial product in the correct columns.

Last, you add the partial products.

Now we'll apply this same method to multiply two binomials.

EXAMPLE 10.42

Multiply using the vertical method: $(5x - 1)(2x - 7)$.

⊘ **Solution**

It does not matter which binomial goes on the top. Line up the columns when you multiply as we did when we multiplied $23(46)$.

$$\begin{array}{r} 2x - 7 \\ \times\; 5x - 1 \\ \hline \end{array}$$

Multiply $2x - 7$ by -1.	$-2x + 7$	partial product
Multiply $2x - 7$ by $5x$.	$10x^2 - 35x$	partial product
Add like terms.	$10x^2 - 37x + 7$	product

Notice the partial products are the same as the terms in the FOIL method.

$$(5x - 1)(2x - 7)$$
$$10x^2 - 35x - 2x + 7$$
$$10x^2 - 37x + 7$$

$$\begin{array}{r} 2x - 7 \\ \times\; 5x - 1 \\ \hline -2x + 7 \\ 10x^2 - 35x \\ \hline 10x^2 - 37x + 7 \end{array}$$

> **TRY IT : : 10.83**   Multiply using the vertical method: $(4m - 9)(3m - 7)$.

> **TRY IT : : 10.84**   Multiply using the vertical method: $(6n - 5)(7n - 2)$.

We have now used three methods for multiplying binomials. Be sure to practice each method, and try to decide which one you prefer. The three methods are listed here to help you remember them.

Multiplying Two Binomials

To multiply binomials, use the:

- Distributive Property
- FOIL Method
- Vertical Method

Remember, FOIL only works when multiplying two binomials.

Multiply a Trinomial by a Binomial

We have multiplied monomials by monomials, monomials by polynomials, and binomials by binomials. Now we're ready to multiply a trinomial by a binomial. Remember, the FOIL method will not work in this case, but we can use either the Distributive Property or the Vertical Method. We first look at an example using the Distributive Property.

EXAMPLE 10.43

Multiply using the Distributive Property: $(x + 3)(2x^2 - 5x + 8)$.

Solution

$$(x + 3)(2x^2 - 5x + 8)$$

Distribute. $\quad x(2x^2 - 5x + 8) + 3(2x^2 - 5x + 8)$

Multiply. $\quad 2x^3 - 5x^2 + 8x + 6x^2 - 15x + 24$

Combine like terms. $\quad 2x^3 + x^2 - 7x + 24$

> **TRY IT :: 10.85**   Multiply using the Distributive Property: $(y - 1)(y^2 - 7y + 2)$.

> **TRY IT :: 10.86**   Multiply using the Distributive Property: $(x + 2)(3x^2 - 4x + 5)$.

Now let's do this same multiplication using the Vertical Method.

EXAMPLE 10.44

Multiply using the Vertical Method: $(x + 3)(2x^2 - 5x + 8)$.

Solution

It is easier to put the polynomial with fewer terms on the bottom because we get fewer partial products this way.

$$2x^2 - 5x + 8$$
$$\underline{\times \qquad x + 3}$$

Multiply $(2x^2 - 5x + 8)$ by 3. $\quad 6x^2 - 15x + 24$

Multiply $(2x^2 - 5x + 8)$ by x. $\quad \underline{2x^3 - 5x^2 + 8x}$

Add like terms. $\quad 2x^3 + x^2 - 7x + 24$

> **TRY IT :: 10.87**   Multiply using the Vertical Method: $(y - 1)(y^2 - 7y + 2)$.

> **TRY IT :: 10.88**   Multiply using the Vertical Method: $(x + 2)(3x^2 - 4x + 5)$.

▶ | **MEDIA** : : ACCESS ADDITIONAL ONLINE RESOURCES

- Multiply Monomials (http://www.openstaxcollege.org/l/24multmonomials)
- Multiply Polynomials (http://www.openstaxcollege.org/l/24multpolyns)
- Multiply Polynomials 2 (http://www.openstaxcollege.org/l/24multpolyns2)
- Multiply Polynomials Review (http://www.openstaxcollege.org/l/24multpolynsrev)
- Multiply Polynomials Using the Distributive Property (http://www.openstaxcollege.org/l/24multpolynsdis)
- Multiply Binomials (http://www.openstaxcollege.org/l/24multbinomials)

10.3 EXERCISES

Practice Makes Perfect

Multiply a Polynomial by a Monomial

In the following exercises, multiply.

145. $4(x + 10)$

146. $6(y + 8)$

147. $15(r - 24)$

148. $12(v - 30)$

149. $-3(m + 11)$

150. $-4(p + 15)$

151. $-8(z - 5)$

152. $-3(x - 9)$

153. $u(u + 5)$

154. $q(q + 7)$

155. $n(n^2 - 3n)$

156. $s(s^2 - 6s)$

157. $12x(x - 10)$

158. $9m(m - 11)$

159. $-9a(3a + 5)$

160. $-4p(2p + 7)$

161. $6x(4x + y)$

162. $5a(9a + b)$

163. $5p(11p - 5q)$

164. $12u(3u - 4v)$

165. $3(v^2 + 10v + 25)$

166. $6(x^2 + 8x + 16)$

167. $2n(4n^2 - 4n + 1)$

168. $3r(2r^2 - 6r + 2)$

169. $-8y(y^2 + 2y - 15)$

170. $-5m(m^2 + 3m - 18)$

171. $5q^3(q^2 - 2q + 6)$

172. $9r^3(r^2 - 3r + 5)$

173. $-4z^2(3z^2 + 12z - 1)$

174. $-3x^2(7x^2 + 10x - 1)$

175. $(2y - 9)y$

176. $(8b - 1)b$

177. $(w - 6) \cdot 8$

178. $(k - 4) \cdot 5$

Multiply a Binomial by a Binomial

In the following exercises, multiply the following binomials using: ⓐ the Distributive Property ⓑ the FOIL method ⓒ the Vertical method

179. $(x + 4)(x + 6)$

180. $(u + 8)(u + 2)$

181. $(n + 12)(n - 3)$

182. $(y + 3)(y - 9)$

In the following exercises, multiply the following binomials. Use any method.

183. $(y + 8)(y + 3)$

184. $(x + 5)(x + 9)$

185. $(a + 6)(a + 16)$

186. $(q + 8)(q + 12)$

187. $(u - 5)(u - 9)$

188. $(r - 6)(r - 2)$

189. $(z - 10)(z - 22)$

190. $(b - 5)(b - 24)$

191. $(x - 4)(x + 7)$

192. $(s - 3)(s + 8)$

193. $(v + 12)(v - 5)$

194. $(d + 15)(d - 4)$

195. $(6n + 5)(n + 1)$

196. $(7y + 1)(y + 3)$

197. $(2m - 9)(10m + 1)$

198. $(5r - 4)(12r + 1)$

199. $(4c - 1)(4c + 1)$

200. $(8n - 1)(8n + 1)$

201. $(3u - 8)(5u - 14)$

202. $(2q - 5)(7q - 11)$

203. $(a + b)(2a + 3b)$

204. $(r + s)(3r + 2s)$

205. $(5x - y)(x - 4)$

206. $(4z - y)(z - 6)$

Multiply a Trinomial by a Binomial

In the following exercises, multiply using ⓐ the Distributive Property and ⓑ the Vertical Method.

207. $(u + 4)(u^2 + 3u + 2)$

208. $(x + 5)(x^2 + 8x + 3)$

209. $(a + 10)(3a^2 + a - 5)$

210. $(n + 8)(4n^2 + n - 7)$

In the following exercises, multiply. Use either method.

211. $(y - 6)(y^2 - 10y + 9)$

212. $(k - 3)(k^2 - 8k + 7)$

213. $(2x + 1)(x^2 - 5x - 6)$

214. $(5v + 1)(v^2 - 6v - 10)$

Everyday Math

215. Mental math You can use binomial multiplication to multiply numbers without a calculator. Say you need to multiply 13 times 15. Think of 13 as $10 + 3$ and 15 as $10 + 5$.

ⓐ Multiply $(10 + 3)(10 + 5)$ by the FOIL method.

ⓑ Multiply $13 \cdot 15$ without using a calculator.

ⓒ Which way is easier for you? Why?

216. Mental math You can use binomial multiplication to multiply numbers without a calculator. Say you need to multiply 18 times 17. Think of 18 as $20 - 2$ and 17 as $20 - 3$.

ⓐ Multiply $(20 - 2)(20 - 3)$ by the FOIL method.

ⓑ Multiply $18 \cdot 17$ without using a calculator.

ⓒ Which way is easier for you? Why?

Writing Exercises

217. Which method do you prefer to use when multiplying two binomials—the Distributive Property, the FOIL method, or the Vertical Method? Why?

218. Which method do you prefer to use when multiplying a trinomial by a binomial—the Distributive Property or the Vertical Method? Why?

Self Check

ⓐ *After completing the exercises, use this checklist to evaluate your mastery of the objectives of this section.*

I can...	Confidently	With some help	No-I don't get it!
multiply a polynomial by a monomial.			
multiply a binomial by a binomial.			
multiply a trinomial by a binomial.			

ⓑ *What does this checklist tell you about your mastery of this section? What steps will you take to improve?*

10.4 **Divide Monomials**

Learning Objectives

By the end of this section, you will be able to:
- Simplify expressions using the Quotient Property of Exponents
- Simplify expressions with zero exponents
- Simplify expressions using the Quotient to a Power Property
- Simplify expressions by applying several properties
- Divide monomials

Be Prepared!

Before you get started, take this readiness quiz.

1. Simplify: $\frac{8}{24}$.

   If you missed the problem, review Example 4.19.

2. Simplify: $\left(2m^3\right)^5$.

   If you missed the problem, review Example 10.23.

3. Simplify: $\frac{12x}{12y}$.

   If you missed the problem, review Example 4.23.

Simplify Expressions Using the Quotient Property of Exponents

Earlier in this chapter, we developed the properties of exponents for multiplication. We summarize these properties here.

Summary of Exponent Properties for Multiplication

If a, b are real numbers and m, n are whole numbers, then

$$\text{Product Property} \qquad a^m \cdot a^n = a^{m+n}$$
$$\text{Power Property} \qquad (a^m)^n = a^{m \cdot n}$$
$$\text{Product to a Power} \qquad (ab)^m = a^m b^m$$

Now we will look at the exponent properties for division. A quick memory refresher may help before we get started. In Fractions you learned that fractions may be simplified by dividing out common factors from the numerator and denominator using the Equivalent Fractions Property. This property will also help us work with algebraic fractions—which are also quotients.

Equivalent Fractions Property

If a, b, c are whole numbers where $b \neq 0$, $c \neq 0$, then

$$\frac{a}{b} = \frac{a \cdot c}{b \cdot c} \quad \text{and} \quad \frac{a \cdot c}{b \cdot c} = \frac{a}{b}$$

As before, we'll try to discover a property by looking at some examples.

Consider	$\dfrac{x^5}{x^2}$	and	$\dfrac{x^2}{x^3}$
What do they mean?	$\dfrac{x \cdot x \cdot x \cdot x \cdot x}{x \cdot x}$		$\dfrac{x \cdot x}{x \cdot x \cdot x}$
Use the Equivalent Fractions Property.	$\dfrac{\cancel{x} \cdot \cancel{x} \cdot x \cdot x \cdot x}{\cancel{x} \cdot \cancel{x} \cdot 1}$		$\dfrac{\cancel{x} \cdot \cancel{x} \cdot 1}{\cancel{x} \cdot \cancel{x} \cdot x}$
Simplify.	x^3		$\dfrac{1}{x}$

Notice that in each case the bases were the same and we subtracted the exponents.

- When the larger exponent was in the numerator, we were left with factors in the numerator and 1 in the denominator, which we simplified.

- When the larger exponent was in the denominator, we were left with factors in the denominator, and 1 in the numerator, which could not be simplified.

We write:

$$\frac{x^5}{x^2} \qquad\qquad \frac{x^2}{x^3}$$

$$x^{5-2} \qquad\qquad \frac{1}{x^{3-2}}$$

$$x^3 \qquad\qquad \frac{1}{x}$$

Quotient Property of Exponents

If a is a real number, $a \neq 0,$ and $m, \ n$ are whole numbers, then

$$\frac{a^m}{a^n} = a^{m-n}, \qquad m > n \qquad \text{and} \qquad \frac{a^m}{a^n} = \frac{1}{a^{n-m}}, \qquad n > m$$

A couple of examples with numbers may help to verify this property.

$$\frac{3^4}{3^2} \overset{?}{=} 3^{4-2} \qquad\qquad \frac{5^2}{5^3} \overset{?}{=} \frac{1}{5^{3-2}}$$

$$\frac{81}{9} \overset{?}{=} 3^2 \qquad\qquad \frac{25}{125} \overset{?}{=} \frac{1}{5^1}$$

$$9 = 9 \ \checkmark \qquad\qquad \frac{1}{5} = \frac{1}{5} \ \checkmark$$

When we work with numbers and the exponent is less than or equal to $3,$ we will apply the exponent. When the exponent is greater than 3, we leave the answer in exponential form.

EXAMPLE 10.45

Simplify:

ⓐ $\dfrac{x^{10}}{x^8}$ ⓑ $\dfrac{2^9}{2^2}$

✓ **Solution**

To simplify an expression with a quotient, we need to first compare the exponents in the numerator and denominator.

ⓐ

Since 10 > 8, there are more factors of x in the numerator.	$\dfrac{x^{10}}{x^8}$
Use the quotient property with $m > n$, $\dfrac{a^m}{a^n} = a^{m-n}$.	x^{10-8}
Simplify.	x^2

ⓑ

Since 9 > 2, there are more factors of 2 in the numerator.	$\dfrac{2^9}{2^2}$
Use the quotient property with $m > n$, $\dfrac{a^m}{a^n} = a^{m-n}$.	2^{9-2}
Simplify.	2^7

Notice that when the larger exponent is in the numerator, we are left with factors in the numerator.

> **TRY IT : : 10.89**   Simplify:

$$ⓐ \ \dfrac{x^{12}}{x^9} \qquad ⓑ \ \dfrac{7^{14}}{7^5}$$

> **TRY IT : : 10.90**   Simplify:

$$ⓐ \ \dfrac{y^{23}}{y^{17}} \qquad ⓑ \ \dfrac{8^{15}}{8^7}$$

EXAMPLE 10.46

Simplify:

$$ⓐ \ \dfrac{b^{10}}{b^{15}} \qquad ⓑ \ \dfrac{3^3}{3^5}$$

⊘ **Solution**

To simplify an expression with a quotient, we need to first compare the exponents in the numerator and denominator.

ⓐ

Since 15 > 10, there are more factors of b in the denominator.	$\dfrac{b^{10}}{b^{15}}$
Use the quotient property with $n > m$, $\dfrac{a^m}{a^n} = \dfrac{1}{a^{n-m}}$.	$\dfrac{1}{b^{15-10}}$
Simplify.	$\dfrac{1}{b^5}$

ⓑ

Since 5 > 3, there are more factors of 3 in the denominator.	$\dfrac{3^3}{3^5}$
Use the quotient property with $n > m$, $\dfrac{a^m}{a^n} = \dfrac{1}{a^{n-m}}$.	$\dfrac{1}{3^{5-3}}$
Simplify.	$\dfrac{1}{3^2}$
Apply the exponent.	$\dfrac{1}{9}$

Notice that when the larger exponent is in the denominator, we are left with factors in the denominator and 1 in the numerator.

> **TRY IT ∷** 10.91   Simplify:

ⓐ $\dfrac{x^8}{x^{15}}$ ⓑ $\dfrac{12^{11}}{12^{21}}$

> **TRY IT ∷** 10.92   Simplify:

ⓐ $\dfrac{m^{17}}{m^{26}}$ ⓑ $\dfrac{7^8}{7^{14}}$

EXAMPLE 10.47

Simplify:

ⓐ $\dfrac{a^5}{a^9}$ ⓑ $\dfrac{x^{11}}{x^7}$

⊘ **Solution**

ⓐ

Since 9 > 5, there are more a's in the denominator and so we will end up with factors in the denominator.	$\dfrac{a^5}{a^9}$
Use the Quotient Property for $n > m$, $\dfrac{a^m}{a^n} = \dfrac{1}{a^{n-m}}$.	$\dfrac{1}{a^{9-5}}$
Simplify.	$\dfrac{1}{a^4}$

ⓑ

Notice there are more factors of x in the numerator, since 11 > 7. So we will end up with factors in the numerator.	$\dfrac{x^{11}}{x^7}$
Use the Quotient Property for $m > n$, $\dfrac{a^m}{a^n} = a^{n-m}$.	x^{11-7}
Simplify.	x^4

> **TRY IT : :** 10.93   Simplify:

ⓐ $\dfrac{b^{19}}{b^{11}}$ ⓑ $\dfrac{z^5}{z^{11}}$

> **TRY IT : :** 10.94   Simplify:

ⓐ $\dfrac{p^9}{p^{17}}$ ⓑ $\dfrac{w^{13}}{w^9}$

Simplify Expressions with Zero Exponents

A special case of the Quotient Property is when the exponents of the numerator and denominator are equal, such as an expression like $\dfrac{a^m}{a^m}$. From earlier work with fractions, we know that

$$\frac{2}{2} = 1 \qquad \frac{17}{17} = 1 \qquad \frac{-43}{-43} = 1$$

In words, a number divided by itself is 1. So $\dfrac{x}{x} = 1$, for any x ($x \neq 0$), since any number divided by itself is 1.

The Quotient Property of Exponents shows us how to simplify $\dfrac{a^m}{a^n}$ when $m > n$ and when $n < m$ by subtracting exponents. What if $m = n$?

Now we will simplify $\dfrac{a^m}{a^m}$ in two ways to lead us to the definition of the **zero exponent**.

Consider first $\dfrac{8}{8}$, which we know is 1.

$$\frac{8}{8} = 1$$

Write 8 as 2^3.	$\dfrac{2^3}{2^3} = 1$
Subtract exponents.	$2^{3-3} = 1$
Simplify.	$2^0 = 1$

In general, for $a \neq 0$:

$$\frac{a^m}{a^m} \qquad \frac{a^m}{a^m}$$

$$a^{m-m} \qquad \frac{\overbrace{\cancel{a} \cdot \cancel{a} \cdot \,...\, \cdot \cancel{a}}^{m\ \text{factors}}}{\underbrace{\cancel{a} \cdot \cancel{a} \cdot \,...\, \cdot \cancel{a}}_{m\ \text{factors}}}$$

$$a^0 \qquad 1$$

We see $\dfrac{a^m}{a^n}$ simplifies to a a^0 and to 1. So $a^0 = 1$.

Zero Exponent

If a is a non-zero number, then $a^0 = 1$.

Any nonzero number raised to the zero power is 1.

In this text, we assume any variable that we raise to the zero power is not zero.

EXAMPLE 10.48

Simplify:

     ⓐ 12^0 ⓑ y^0

⊘ **Solution**

The definition says any non-zero number raised to the zero power is 1.

ⓐ

	12^0
Use the definition of the zero exponent.	1

ⓑ

	y^0
Use the definition of the zero exponent.	1

> **TRY IT :: 10.95**   Simplify:
>
>   ⓐ 17^0 ⓑ m^0

> **TRY IT :: 10.96**   Simplify:
>
>   ⓐ k^0 ⓑ 29^0

Now that we have defined the zero exponent, we can expand all the Properties of Exponents to include whole number exponents.

What about raising an expression to the zero power? Let's look at $(2x)^0$. We can use the product to a power rule to rewrite this expression.

$$(2x)^0$$

Use the Product to a Power Rule.	$2^0 x^0$
Use the Zero Exponent Property.	$1 \cdot 1$
Simplify.	1

This tells us that any non-zero expression raised to the zero power is one.

EXAMPLE 10.49

Simplify: $(7z)^0$.

⊘ **Solution**

$$(7z)^0$$

Use the definition of the zero exponent.	1

> **TRY IT :: 10.97**   Simplify: $(-4y)^0$.

> **TRY IT :: 10.98**   Simplify: $\left(\frac{2}{3}x\right)^0$.

EXAMPLE 10.50

Simplify:

ⓐ $\left(-3x^2 y\right)^0$ ⓑ $-3x^2 y^0$

⊘ **Solution**

ⓐ

The product is raised to the zero power.	$\left(-3x^2 y\right)^0$
Use the definition of the zero exponent.	1

ⓑ

Notice that only the variable y is being raised to the zero power.	$-3x^2 y^0$
Use the definition of the zero exponent.	$-3x^2 \cdot 1$
Simplify.	$-3x^2$

> **TRY IT : :** 10.99   Simplify:

$$ⓐ \left(7x^2 y\right)^0 \quad ⓑ 7x^2 y^0$$

> **TRY IT : :** 10.100   Simplify:

$$ⓐ -23x^2 y^0 \quad ⓑ \left(-23x^2 y\right)^0$$

Simplify Expressions Using the Quotient to a Power Property

Now we will look at an example that will lead us to the Quotient to a Power Property.

$$\left(\frac{x}{y}\right)^3$$

This means	$\frac{x}{y} \cdot \frac{x}{y} \cdot \frac{x}{y}$
Multiply the fractions.	$\frac{x \cdot x \cdot x}{y \cdot y \cdot y}$
Write with exponents.	$\frac{x^3}{y^3}$

Notice that the exponent applies to both the numerator and the denominator.

We see that $\left(\frac{x}{y}\right)^3$ is $\frac{x^3}{y^3}$.

We write: $\left(\frac{x}{y}\right)^3$

$\frac{x^3}{y^3}$

This leads to the Quotient to a Power Property for Exponents.

Quotient to a Power Property of Exponents

If a and b are real numbers, $b \neq 0$, and m is a counting number, then

$$\left(\frac{a}{b}\right)^m = \frac{a^m}{b^m}$$

To raise a fraction to a power, raise the numerator and denominator to that power.

An example with numbers may help you understand this property:

$$\left(\frac{2}{3}\right)^3 \overset{?}{=} \frac{2^3}{3^3}$$

$$\frac{2}{3} \cdot \frac{2}{3} \cdot \frac{2}{3} \overset{?}{=} \frac{8}{27}$$

$$\frac{8}{27} = \frac{8}{27} \checkmark$$

EXAMPLE 10.51

Simplify:

ⓐ $\left(\dfrac{5}{8}\right)^2$ ⓑ $\left(\dfrac{x}{3}\right)^4$ ⓒ $\left(\dfrac{y}{m}\right)^3$

✓ **Solution**

ⓐ

$$\left(\dfrac{5}{8}\right)^2$$

Use the Quotient to a Power Property, $\left(\dfrac{a}{b}\right)^m = \dfrac{a^m}{b^m}$. $\dfrac{5^2}{8^2}$

Simplify. $\dfrac{25}{64}$

ⓑ

$$\left(\dfrac{x}{3}\right)^4$$

Use the Quotient to a Power Property, $\left(\dfrac{a}{b}\right)^m = \dfrac{a^m}{b^m}$. $\dfrac{x^4}{3^4}$

Simplify. $\dfrac{x^4}{81}$

ⓒ

$$\left(\dfrac{y}{m}\right)^3$$

Raise the numerator and denominator to the third power. $\dfrac{y^3}{m^3}$

> **TRY IT :: 10.101**   Simplify:

ⓐ $\left(\dfrac{7}{9}\right)^2$ ⓑ $\left(\dfrac{y}{8}\right)^3$ ⓒ $\left(\dfrac{p}{q}\right)^6$

> **TRY IT :: 10.102**   Simplify:

ⓐ $\left(\dfrac{1}{8}\right)^2$ ⓑ $\left(\dfrac{-5}{m}\right)^3$ ⓒ $\left(\dfrac{r}{s}\right)^4$

Simplify Expressions by Applying Several Properties

We'll now summarize all the properties of exponents so they are all together to refer to as we simplify expressions using several properties. Notice that they are now defined for whole number exponents.

Summary of Exponent Properties

If a, b are real numbers and m, n are whole numbers, then

Product Property	$a^m \cdot a^n = a^{m+n}$
Power Property	$(a^m)^n = a^{m \cdot n}$
Product to a Power Property	$(ab)^m = a^m b^m$
Quotient Property	$\dfrac{a^m}{a^n} = a^{m-n}, \; a \neq 0, \; m > n$
	$\dfrac{a^m}{a^n} = \dfrac{1}{a^{n-m}}, \; a \neq 0, \; n > m$
Zero Exponent Definition	$a^0 = 1, \; a \neq 0$
Quotient to a Power Property	$\left(\dfrac{a}{b}\right)^m = \dfrac{a^m}{b^m}, \; b \neq 0$

EXAMPLE 10.52

Simplify: $\dfrac{(x^2)^3}{x^5}$.

⊘ **Solution**

$$\dfrac{(x^2)^3}{x^5}$$

Multiply the exponents in the numerator, using the Power Property.	$\dfrac{x^6}{x^5}$
Subtract the exponents.	x

> **TRY IT ::** 10.103   Simplify: $\dfrac{(a^4)^5}{a^9}$.

> **TRY IT ::** 10.104   Simplify: $\dfrac{(b^5)^6}{b^{11}}$.

EXAMPLE 10.53

Simplify: $\dfrac{m^8}{(m^2)^4}$.

⊘ **Solution**

$$\dfrac{m^8}{(m^2)^4}$$

Multiply the exponents in the numerator, using the Power Property.	$\dfrac{m^8}{m^8}$
Subtract the exponents.	m^0

> **TRY IT :: 10.105**

Simplify: $\dfrac{k^{11}}{(k^3)^3}$.

> **TRY IT :: 10.106**

Simplify: $\dfrac{d^{23}}{(d^4)^6}$.

EXAMPLE 10.54

Simplify: $\left(\dfrac{x^7}{x^3}\right)^2$.

⊘ **Solution**

$$\left(\dfrac{x^7}{x^3}\right)^2$$

Remember parentheses come before exponents, and the bases are the same so we can simplify inside the parentheses. Subtract the exponents.

$$\left(x^{7-3}\right)^2$$

Simplify.

$$\left(x^4\right)^2$$

Multiply the exponents.

$$x^8$$

> **TRY IT :: 10.107**

Simplify: $\left(\dfrac{f^{14}}{f^8}\right)^2$.

> **TRY IT :: 10.108**

Simplify: $\left(\dfrac{b^6}{b^{11}}\right)^2$.

EXAMPLE 10.55

Simplify: $\left(\dfrac{p^2}{q^5}\right)^3$.

⊘ **Solution**

Here we cannot simplify inside the parentheses first, since the bases are not the same.

$$\left(\frac{p^2}{q^5}\right)^3$$

Raise the numerator and denominator to the third power using the Quotient to a Power Property, $\left(\frac{a}{b}\right)^m = \frac{a^m}{b^m}$	$\frac{\left(p^2\right)^3}{\left(q^5\right)^3}$
Use the Power Property, $(a^m)^n = a^{m \cdot n}$.	$\frac{p^6}{q^{15}}$

> **TRY IT :: 10.109**
>
> Simplify: $\left(\frac{m^3}{n^8}\right)^5$.

> **TRY IT :: 10.110**
>
> Simplify: $\left(\frac{t^{10}}{u^7}\right)^2$.

EXAMPLE 10.56

Simplify: $\left(\frac{2x^3}{3y}\right)^4$.

⊘ **Solution**

$$\left(\frac{2x^3}{3y}\right)^4$$

Raise the numerator and denominator to the fourth power using the Quotient to a Power Property.	$\frac{\left(2x^3\right)^4}{(3y)^4}$
Raise each factor to the fourth power, using the Power to a Power Property.	$\frac{2^4\left(x^3\right)^4}{3^4 y^4}$
Use the Power Property and simplify.	$\frac{16x^2}{81y^4}$

> **TRY IT :: 10.111**
>
> Simplify: $\left(\frac{5b}{9c^3}\right)^2$.

> **TRY IT :: 10.112**
>
> Simplify: $\left(\frac{4p^4}{7q^5}\right)^3$.

EXAMPLE 10.57

Simplify: $\dfrac{(y^2)^3 (y^2)^4}{(y^5)^4}$.

⊘ **Solution**

$$\frac{(y^2)^3 (y^2)^4}{(y^5)^4}$$

Use the Power Property.

$$\frac{(y^6)(y^8)}{y^{20}}$$

Add the exponents in the numerator, using the Product Property.

$$\frac{y^{14}}{y^{20}}$$

Use the Quotient Property.

$$\frac{1}{y^6}$$

> **TRY IT :: 10.113**   Simplify: $\dfrac{(y^4)^4 (y^3)^5}{(y^7)^6}$.

> **TRY IT :: 10.114**   Simplify: $\dfrac{(3x^4)^2 (x^3)^4}{(x^5)^3}$.

Divide Monomials

We have now seen all the properties of exponents. We'll use them to divide monomials. Later, you'll use them to divide polynomials.

EXAMPLE 10.58

Find the quotient: $56x^5 \div 7x^2$.

⊘ **Solution**

$$56x^5 \div 7x^2$$

Rewrite as a fraction.

$$\frac{56x^5}{7x^2}$$

Use fraction multiplication to separate the number part from the variable part.

$$\frac{56}{7} \cdot \frac{x^5}{x^2}$$

Use the Quotient Property.

$$8x^3$$

> **TRY IT :: 10.115**   Find the quotient: $63x^8 \div 9x^4$.

> **TRY IT : :** 10.116   Find the quotient: $96y^{11} \div 6y^8$.

When we divide monomials with more than one variable, we write one fraction for each variable.

EXAMPLE 10.59

Find the quotient: $\dfrac{42x^2 y^3}{-7xy^5}$.

⊘ **Solution**

$$\frac{42x^2 y^3}{-7xy^5}$$

Use fraction multiplication.	$\dfrac{42}{-7} \cdot \dfrac{x^2}{x} \cdot \dfrac{y^3}{y^5}$
Simplify and use the Quotient Property.	$-6 \cdot x \cdot \dfrac{1}{y^2}$
Multiply.	$-\dfrac{6x}{y^2}$

> **TRY IT : :** 10.117   Find the quotient: $\dfrac{-84x^8 y^3}{7x^{10} y^2}$.

> **TRY IT : :** 10.118   Find the quotient: $\dfrac{-72a^4 b^5}{-8a^9 b^5}$.

EXAMPLE 10.60

Find the quotient: $\dfrac{24a^5 b^3}{48ab^4}$.

⊘ **Solution**

$$\frac{24a^5 b^3}{48ab^4}$$

Use fraction multiplication.	$\dfrac{24}{48} \cdot \dfrac{a^5}{a} \cdot \dfrac{b^3}{b^4}$
Simplify and use the Quotient Property.	$\dfrac{1}{2} \cdot a^4 \cdot \dfrac{1}{b}$
Multiply.	$\dfrac{a^4}{2b}$

> **TRY IT :: 10.119**   Find the quotient: $\dfrac{16a^7 b^6}{24ab^8}$.

> **TRY IT :: 10.120**   Find the quotient: $\dfrac{27p^4 q^7}{-45p^{12} q}$.

Once you become familiar with the process and have practiced it step by step several times, you may be able to simplify a fraction in one step.

EXAMPLE 10.61

Find the quotient: $\dfrac{14x^7 y^{12}}{21x^{11} y^6}$.

⊘ **Solution**

$$\frac{14x^7 y^{12}}{21x^{11} y^6}$$

Simplify and use the Quotient Property. $\dfrac{2y^6}{3x^4}$

Be very careful to simplify $\dfrac{14}{21}$ by dividing out a common factor, and to simplify the variables by subtracting their exponents.

> **TRY IT :: 10.121**   Find the quotient: $\dfrac{28x^5 y^{14}}{49x^9 y^{12}}$.

> **TRY IT :: 10.122**   Find the quotient: $\dfrac{30m^5 n^{11}}{48m^{10} n^{14}}$.

In all examples so far, there was no work to do in the numerator or denominator before simplifying the fraction. In the next example, we'll first find the product of two monomials in the numerator before we simplify the fraction.

EXAMPLE 10.62

Find the quotient: $\dfrac{(3x^3 y^2)(10x^2 y^3)}{6x^4 y^5}$.

⊘ **Solution**

Remember, the fraction bar is a grouping symbol. We will simplify the numerator first.

$$\frac{(3x^3 y^2)(10x^2 y^3)}{6x^4 y^5}$$

Simplify the numerator. $\dfrac{30x^5 y^5}{6x^4 y^5}$

Simplify, using the Quotient Rule. $5x$

> **TRY IT : :** 10.123

Find the quotient: $\dfrac{(3x^4 y^5)(8x^2 y^5)}{12x^5 y^8}$.

> **TRY IT : :** 10.124

Find the quotient: $\dfrac{(-6a^6 b^9)(-8a^5 b^8)}{-12a^{10} b^{12}}$.

▶ **MEDIA : :** ACCESS ADDITIONAL ONLINE RESOURCES

- Simplify a Quotient (http://openstaxcollege.org/l/24simpquot)
- Zero Exponent (http://openstaxcollege.org/l/zeroexponent)
- Quotient Rule (http://openstaxcollege.org/l/24quotientrule)
- Polynomial Division (http://openstaxcollege.org/l/24polyndivision)
- Polynomial Division 2 (http://openstaxcollege.org/l/24polydivision2)

10.4 EXERCISES

Practice Makes Perfect

Simplify Expressions Using the Quotient Property of Exponents

In the following exercises, simplify.

219. $\dfrac{4^8}{4^2}$

220. $\dfrac{3^{12}}{3^4}$

221. $\dfrac{x^{12}}{x^3}$

222. $\dfrac{u^9}{u^3}$

223. $\dfrac{r^5}{r}$

224. $\dfrac{y^4}{y}$

225. $\dfrac{y^4}{y^{20}}$

226. $\dfrac{x^{10}}{x^{30}}$

227. $\dfrac{10^3}{10^{15}}$

228. $\dfrac{r^2}{r^8}$

229. $\dfrac{a}{a^9}$

230. $\dfrac{2}{2^5}$

Simplify Expressions with Zero Exponents

In the following exercises, simplify.

231. 5^0

232. 10^0

233. a^0

234. x^0

235. -7^0

236. -4^0

237.
ⓐ $(10p)^0$ ⓑ $10p^0$

238.
ⓐ $(3a)^0$ ⓑ $3a^0$

239.
ⓐ $\left(-27x^5 y\right)^0$
ⓑ $-27x^5 y^0$

240.
ⓐ $\left(-92y^8 z\right)^0$
ⓑ $-92y^8 z^0$

241.
ⓐ 15^0 ⓑ 15^1

242.
ⓐ -6^0 ⓑ -6^1

243. $2 \cdot x^0 + 5 \cdot y^0$

244. $8 \cdot m^0 - 4 \cdot n^0$

Simplify Expressions Using the Quotient to a Power Property

In the following exercises, simplify.

245. $\left(\dfrac{3}{2}\right)^5$

246. $\left(\dfrac{4}{5}\right)^3$

247. $\left(\dfrac{m}{6}\right)^3$

248. $\left(\dfrac{p}{2}\right)^5$

249. $\left(\dfrac{x}{y}\right)^{10}$

250. $\left(\dfrac{a}{b}\right)^8$

251. $\left(\dfrac{a}{3b}\right)^2$

252. $\left(\dfrac{2x}{y}\right)^4$

Simplify Expressions by Applying Several Properties

In the following exercises, simplify.

253. $\dfrac{\left(x^2\right)^4}{x^5}$

254. $\dfrac{\left(y^4\right)^3}{y^7}$

255. $\dfrac{\left(u^3\right)^4}{u^{10}}$

256. $\dfrac{\left(y^2\right)^5}{y^6}$

257. $\dfrac{y^8}{\left(y^5\right)^2}$

258. $\dfrac{p^{11}}{\left(p^5\right)^3}$

259. $\dfrac{r^5}{r^4 \cdot r}$

260. $\dfrac{a^3 \cdot a^4}{a^7}$

261. $\left(\dfrac{x^2}{x^8}\right)^3$

262. $\left(\dfrac{u}{u^{10}}\right)^2$

263. $\left(\dfrac{a^4 \cdot a^6}{a^3}\right)^2$

264. $\left(\dfrac{x^3 \cdot x^8}{x^4}\right)^3$

265. $\dfrac{\left(y^3\right)^5}{\left(y^4\right)^3}$

266. $\dfrac{\left(z^6\right)^2}{\left(z^2\right)^4}$

267. $\dfrac{\left(x^3\right)^6}{\left(x^4\right)^7}$

268. $\dfrac{\left(x^4\right)^8}{\left(x^5\right)^7}$

269. $\left(\dfrac{2r^3}{5s}\right)^4$

270. $\left(\dfrac{3m^2}{4n}\right)^3$

271. $\left(\dfrac{3y^2 \cdot y^5}{y^{15} \cdot y^8}\right)^0$

272. $\left(\dfrac{15z^4 \cdot z^9}{0.3z^2}\right)^0$

273. $\dfrac{\left(r^2\right)^5 \left(r^4\right)^2}{\left(r^3\right)^7}$

274. $\dfrac{\left(p^4\right)^2 \left(p^3\right)^5}{\left(p^2\right)^9}$

275. $\dfrac{\left(3x^4\right)^3 \left(2x^3\right)^2}{\left(6x^5\right)^2}$

276. $\dfrac{\left(-2y^3\right)^4 \left(3y^4\right)^2}{\left(-6y^3\right)^2}$

Divide Monomials

In the following exercises, divide the monomials.

277. $48b^8 \div 6b^2$

278. $42a^{14} \div 6a^2$

279. $36x^3 \div \left(-2x^9\right)$

280. $20u^8 \div \left(-4u^6\right)$

281. $\dfrac{18x^3}{9x^2}$

282. $\dfrac{36y^9}{4y^7}$

283. $\dfrac{-35x^7}{-42x^{13}}$

284. $\dfrac{18x^5}{-27x^9}$

285. $\dfrac{18r^5 s}{3r^3 s^9}$

286. $\dfrac{24p^7 q}{6p^2 q^5}$

287. $\dfrac{8mn^{10}}{64mn^4}$

288. $\dfrac{10a^4 b}{50a^2 b^6}$

289. $\dfrac{-12x^4 y^9}{15x^6 y^3}$

290. $\dfrac{48x^{11} y^9 z^3}{36x^6 y^8 z^5}$

291. $\dfrac{64x^5 y^9 z^7}{48x^7 y^{12} z^6}$

292. $\dfrac{(10u^2 v)(4u^3 v^6)}{5u^9 v^2}$

293. $\dfrac{(6m^2 n)(5m^4 n^3)}{3m^{10} n^2}$

294. $\dfrac{(6a^4 b^3)(4ab^5)}{(12a^8 b)(a^3 b)}$

295. $\dfrac{(4u^5 v^4)(15u^8 v)}{(12u^3 v)(u^6 v)}$

Mixed Practice

296.
ⓐ $24a^5 + 2a^5$ ⓑ $24a^5 - 2a^5$ ⓒ $24a^5 \cdot 2a^5$ ⓓ $24a^5 \div 2a^5$

297.
ⓐ $15n^{10} + 3n^{10}$ ⓑ $15n^{10} - 3n^{10}$ ⓒ $15n^{10} \cdot 3n^{10}$ ⓓ $15n^{10} \div 3n^{10}$

298.
ⓐ $p^4 \cdot p^6$ ⓑ $\left(p^4\right)^6$

299.
ⓐ $q^5 \cdot q^3$ ⓑ $\left(q^5\right)^3$

300.
ⓐ $\dfrac{y^3}{y}$ ⓑ $\dfrac{y}{y^3}$

301.
ⓐ $\dfrac{z^6}{z^5}$ ⓑ $\dfrac{z^5}{z^6}$

302. $\left(8x^5\right)\left(9x\right) \div 6x^3$

303. $\left(4y^5\right)\left(12y^7\right) \div 8y^2$

304. $\dfrac{27a^7}{3a^3} + \dfrac{54a^9}{9a^5}$

305. $\dfrac{32c^{11}}{4c^5} + \dfrac{42c^9}{6c^3}$

306. $\dfrac{32y^5}{8y^2} - \dfrac{60y^{10}}{5y^7}$

307. $\dfrac{48x^6}{6x^4} - \dfrac{35x^9}{7x^7}$

308. $\dfrac{63r^6 s^3}{9r^4 s^2} - \dfrac{72r^2 s^2}{6s}$

309. $\dfrac{56y^4 z^5}{7y^3 z^3} - \dfrac{45y^2 z^2}{5y}$

Everyday Math

310. Memory One megabyte is approximately 10^6 bytes. One gigabyte is approximately 10^9 bytes. How many megabytes are in one gigabyte?

311. Memory One megabyte is approximately 10^6 bytes. One terabyte is approximately 10^{12} bytes. How many megabytes are in one terabyte?

Writing Exercises

312. Vic thinks the quotient $\dfrac{x^{20}}{x^4}$ simplifies to x^5. What is wrong with his reasoning?

313. Mai simplifies the quotient $\dfrac{y^3}{y}$ by writing $\dfrac{\cancel{y}^3}{\cancel{y}} = 3$. What is wrong with her reasoning?

314. When Dimple simplified -3^0 and $(-3)^0$ she got the same answer. Explain how using the Order of Operations correctly gives different answers.

315. Roxie thinks n^0 simplifies to 0. What would you say to convince Roxie she is wrong?

Self Check

ⓐ *After completing the exercises, use this checklist to evaluate your mastery of the objectives of this section.*

I can...	Confidently	With some help	No-I don't get it!
simplify expressions using the Quotient Property for Exponents.			
simplify expressions with zero exponents.			
simplify expressions using the Quotient to a Power Property.			
simplify expressions by applying several properties.			
divide monomials.			

ⓑ *On a scale of 1–10, how would you rate your mastery of this section in light of your responses on the checklist? How can you improve this?*

10.5 | Integer Exponents and Scientific Notation

Learning Objectives

By the end of this section, you will be able to:

- Use the definition of a negative exponent
- Simplify expressions with integer exponents
- Convert from decimal notation to scientific notation
- Convert scientific notation to decimal form
- Multiply and divide using scientific notation

Be Prepared!

Before you get started, take this readiness quiz.

1. What is the place value of the 6 in the number $64,891$?
   If you missed this problem, review Example 1.3.

2. Name the decimal 0.0012.
   If you missed this problem, review Exercise 5.0.

3. Subtract: $5 - (-3)$.
   If you missed this problem, review Example 3.37.

Use the Definition of a Negative Exponent

The Quotient Property of Exponents, introduced in Divide Monomials, had two forms depending on whether the exponent in the numerator or denominator was larger.

Quotient Property of Exponents

If a is a real number, $a \neq 0$, and m, n are whole numbers, then

$$\frac{a^m}{a^n} = a^{m-n}, \quad m > n \quad \text{and} \quad \frac{a^m}{a^n} = \frac{1}{a^{n-m}}, \quad n > m$$

What if we just subtract exponents, regardless of which is larger? Let's consider $\frac{x^2}{x^5}$.

We subtract the exponent in the denominator from the exponent in the numerator.

$$\frac{x^2}{x^5}$$
$$x^{2-5}$$
$$x^{-3}$$

We can also simplify $\frac{x^2}{x^5}$ by dividing out common factors: $\frac{x^2}{x^5}$.

$$\frac{\cancel{x} \cdot \cancel{x}}{\cancel{x} \cdot \cancel{x} \cdot x \cdot x \cdot x}$$
$$\frac{1}{x^3}$$

This implies that $x^{-3} = \frac{1}{x^3}$ and it leads us to the definition of a **negative exponent**.

Negative Exponent

If n is a positive integer and $a \neq 0$, then $a^{-n} = \frac{1}{a^n}$.

The negative exponent tells us to re-write the expression by taking the reciprocal of the base and then changing the sign of the exponent. Any expression that has negative exponents is not considered to be in simplest form. We will use the definition of a negative exponent and other properties of exponents to write an expression with only positive exponents.

EXAMPLE 10.63

Simplify:

       ⓐ 4^{-2} ⓑ 10^{-3}

✓ **Solution**

ⓐ

	4^{-2}
Use the definition of a negative exponent, $a^{-n} = \dfrac{1}{a^n}$.	$\dfrac{1}{4^2}$
Simplify.	$\dfrac{1}{16}$

ⓑ

	10^{-3}
Use the definition of a negative exponent, $a^{-n} = \dfrac{1}{a^n}$.	$\dfrac{1}{10^3}$
Simplify.	$\dfrac{1}{1000}$

> **TRY IT :: 10.125**   Simplify:

       ⓐ 2^{-3} ⓑ 10^{-2}

> **TRY IT :: 10.126**   Simplify:

       ⓐ 3^{-2} ⓑ 10^{-4}

When simplifying any expression with exponents, we must be careful to correctly identify the base that is raised to each exponent.

EXAMPLE 10.64

Simplify:

       ⓐ $(-3)^{-2}$ ⓑ -3^{-2}

✓ **Solution**

The negative in the exponent does not affect the sign of the base.

ⓐ

The exponent applies to the base, -3.	$(-3)^{-2}$
Take the reciprocal of the base and change the sign of the exponent.	$\dfrac{1}{(-3)^2}$
Simplify.	$\dfrac{1}{9}$

ⓑ

The expression -3^{-2} means "find the opposite of 3^{-2} ". The exponent applies only to the base, 3.	-3^{-2}
Rewrite as a product with –1.	$-1 \cdot 3^{-2}$
Take the reciprocal of the base and change the sign of the exponent.	$-1 \cdot \dfrac{1}{3^2}$
Simplify.	$-\dfrac{1}{9}$

> **TRY IT : :** 10.127   Simplify:

ⓐ $(-5)^{-2}$ ⓑ -5^{-2}

> **TRY IT : :** 10.128   Simplify:

ⓐ $(-2)^{-2}$ ⓑ -2^{-2}

We must be careful to follow the order of operations. In the next example, parts ⓐ and ⓑ look similar, but we get different results.

EXAMPLE 10.65

Simplify:

ⓐ $4 \cdot 2^{-1}$ ⓑ $(4 \cdot 2)^{-1}$

⊘ **Solution**

Remember to always follow the order of operations.

ⓐ

Do exponents before multiplication.	$4 \cdot 2^{-1}$
Use $a^{-n} = \dfrac{1}{a^n}$.	$4 \cdot \dfrac{1}{2^1}$
Simplify.	2

ⓑ

$$(4 \cdot 2)^{-1}$$

Simplify inside the parentheses first.	$(8)^{-1}$
Use $a^{-n} = \dfrac{1}{a^n}$.	$\dfrac{1}{8^1}$
Simplify.	$\dfrac{1}{8}$

> **TRY IT : :** 10.129 Simplify:

ⓐ $6 \cdot 3^{-1}$ ⓑ $(6 \cdot 3)^{-1}$

> **TRY IT : :** 10.130 Simplify:

ⓐ $8 \cdot 2^{-2}$ ⓑ $(8 \cdot 2)^{-2}$

When a variable is raised to a negative exponent, we apply the definition the same way we did with numbers.

EXAMPLE 10.66

Simplify: x^{-6}.

✓ **Solution**

$$x^{-6}$$

Use the definition of a negative exponent, $a^{-n} = \dfrac{1}{a^n}$.	$\dfrac{1}{x^6}$

> **TRY IT : :** 10.131 Simplify: y^{-7}.

> **TRY IT : :** 10.132 Simplify: z^{-8}.

When there is a product and an exponent we have to be careful to apply the exponent to the correct quantity. According to the order of operations, expressions in parentheses are simplified before exponents are applied. We'll see how this works in the next example.

EXAMPLE 10.67

Simplify:

ⓐ $5y^{-1}$ ⓑ $(5y)^{-1}$ ⓒ $(-5y)^{-1}$

⊘ **Solution**

ⓐ

Notice the exponent applies to just the base y.	$5y^{-1}$
Take the reciprocal of y and change the sign of the exponent.	$5 \cdot \dfrac{1}{y^1}$
Simplify.	$\dfrac{5}{y}$

ⓑ

Here the parentheses make the exponent apply to the base $5y$.	$(5y)^{-1}$
Take the reciprocal of $5y$ and change the sign of the exponent.	$\dfrac{1}{(5y)^1}$
Simplify.	$\dfrac{1}{5y}$

ⓒ

	$(-5y)^{-1}$
The base is $-5y$. Take the reciprocal of $-5y$ and change the sign of the exponent.	$\dfrac{1}{(-5y)^1}$
Simplify.	$\dfrac{1}{-5y}$
Use $\dfrac{a}{-b} = -\dfrac{a}{b}$.	$-\dfrac{1}{5y}$

> **TRY IT : : 10.133**   Simplify:
>
>   ⓐ $8p^{-1}$ ⓑ $(8p)^{-1}$ ⓒ $(-8p)^{-1}$

> **TRY IT : : 10.134**   Simplify:
>
>   ⓐ $11q^{-1}$ ⓑ $(11q)^{-1}$ ⓒ $(-11q)^{-1}$

Now that we have defined negative exponents, the Quotient Property of Exponents needs only one form, $\dfrac{a^m}{a^n} = a^{m-n}$, where $a \neq 0$ and m and n are integers.

When the exponent in the denominator is larger than the exponent in the numerator, the exponent of the quotient will be negative. If the result gives us a negative exponent, we will rewrite it by using the definition of negative exponents, $a^{-n} = \dfrac{1}{a^n}$.

Simplify Expressions with Integer Exponents

All the exponent properties we developed earlier in this chapter with whole number exponents apply to integer exponents, too. We restate them here for reference.

Summary of Exponent Properties

If a, b are real numbers and m, n are integers, then

Product Property	$a^m \cdot a^n = a^{m+n}$
Power Property	$(a^m)^n = a^{m \cdot n}$
Product to a Power Property	$(ab)^m = a^m b^m$
Quotient Property	$\dfrac{a^m}{a^n} = a^{m-n}, \ a \neq 0$
Zero Exponent Property	$a^0 = 1, \ a \neq 0$
Quotient to a Power Property	$\left(\dfrac{a}{b}\right)^m = \dfrac{a^m}{b^m}, \ b \neq 0$
Definition of Negative Exponent	$a^{-n} = \dfrac{1}{a^n}$

EXAMPLE 10.68

Simplify:

ⓐ $x^{-4} \cdot x^6$ ⓑ $y^{-6} \cdot y^4$ ⓒ $z^{-5} \cdot z^{-3}$

✓ Solution

ⓐ

	$x^{-4} \cdot x^6$
Use the Product Property, $a^m \cdot a^n = a^{m+n}$.	x^{-4+6}
Simplify.	x^2

ⓑ

	$y^{-6} \cdot y^4$
The bases are the same, so add the exponents.	y^{-6+4}
Simplify.	y^{-2}
Use the definition of a negative exponent, $a^{-n} = \dfrac{1}{a^n}$.	$\dfrac{1}{y^2}$

ⓒ

$$z^{-5} \cdot z^{-3}$$

The bases are the same, so add the exponents. $\qquad z^{-5-3}$

Simplify. $\qquad z^{-8}$

Use the definition of a negative exponent, $a^{-n} = \frac{1}{a^n}$. $\qquad \frac{1}{z^8}$

> **TRY IT : : 10.135**　　Simplify:

ⓐ $x^{-3} \cdot x^7$　ⓑ $y^{-7} \cdot y^2$　ⓒ $z^{-4} \cdot z^{-5}$

> **TRY IT : : 10.136**　　Simplify:

ⓐ $a^{-1} \cdot a^6$　ⓑ $b^{-8} \cdot b^4$　ⓒ $c^{-8} \cdot c^{-7}$

In the next two examples, we'll start by using the Commutative Property to group the same variables together. This makes it easier to identify the like bases before using the Product Property of Exponents.

EXAMPLE 10.69

Simplify: $(m^4 n^{-3})(m^{-5} n^{-2})$.

✓ **Solution**

$$(m^4 n^{-3})(m^{-5} n^{-2})$$

Use the Commutative Property to get like bases together. $\qquad m^4 m^{-5} \cdot n^{-2} n^{-3}$

Add the exponents for each base. $\qquad m^{-1} \cdot n^{-5}$

Take reciprocals and change the signs of the exponents. $\qquad \frac{1}{m^1} \cdot \frac{1}{n^5}$

Simplify. $\qquad \frac{1}{mn^5}$

> **TRY IT : : 10.137**　　Simplify: $(p^6 q^{-2})(p^{-9} q^{-1})$.

> **TRY IT : : 10.138**　　Simplify: $(r^5 s^{-3})(r^{-7} s^{-5})$.

If the monomials have numerical coefficients, we multiply the coefficients, just as we did in Integer Exponents and Scientific Notation.

EXAMPLE 10.70

Simplify: $(2x^{-6}y^8)(-5x^5y^{-3})$.

⊘ **Solution**

	$(2x^{-6}y^8)(-5x^5y^{-3})$
Rewrite with the like bases together.	$2(-5) \cdot (x^{-6}x^5) \cdot (y^8y^{-3})$
Simplify.	$-10 \cdot x^{-1} \cdot y^5$
Use the definition of a negative exponent, $a^{-n} = \frac{1}{a^n}$.	$-10 \cdot \frac{1}{x^1} \cdot y^5$
Simplify.	$\frac{-10y^5}{x}$

> **TRY IT :: 10.139**   Simplify: $(3u^{-5}v^7)(-4u^4v^{-2})$.

> **TRY IT :: 10.140**   Simplify: $(-6c^{-6}d^4)(-5c^{-2}d^{-1})$.

In the next two examples, we'll use the Power Property and the Product to a Power Property.

EXAMPLE 10.71

Simplify: $\left(k^3\right)^{-2}$.

⊘ **Solution**

	$\left(k^3\right)^{-2}$
Use the Product to a Power Property, $(ab)^m = a^m b^m$.	$k^{3(-2)}$
Simplify.	k^{-6}
Rewrite with a positive exponent.	$\frac{1}{k^6}$

> **TRY IT :: 10.141**   Simplify: $\left(x^4\right)^{-1}$.

> **TRY IT :: 10.142**   Simplify: $\left(y^2\right)^{-2}$.

EXAMPLE 10.72

Simplify: $\left(5x^{-3}\right)^2$.

⊘ Solution

$$\left(5x^{-3}\right)^2$$

Use the Product to a Power Property, $(ab)^m = a^m b^m$.	$5^2\left(x^{-3}\right)^2$
Simplify 5^2 and multiply the exponents of x using the Power Property, $(a^m)^n = a^{m \cdot n}$.	$25k^{-6}$
Rewrite x^{-6} by using the definition of a negative exponent, $a^{-n} = \frac{1}{a^n}$.	$25 \cdot \frac{1}{x^6}$
Simplify	$\frac{25}{x^6}$

> **TRY IT :: 10.143**
>
> Simplify: $\left(8a^{-4}\right)^2$.

> **TRY IT :: 10.144**
>
> Simplify: $\left(2c^{-4}\right)^3$.

To simplify a fraction, we use the Quotient Property.

EXAMPLE 10.73

Simplify: $\frac{r^5}{r^{-4}}$.

⊘ Solution

$$\frac{r^5}{r^{-4}}$$

Use the Quotient Property, $\frac{a^m}{a^n} = a^{m-n}$.	$r^{5-(-4)}$
Be careful to subtract $5 - (-4)$.	
Simplify.	r^9

> **TRY IT :: 10.145**
>
> Simplify: $\frac{x^8}{x^{-3}}$.

> **TRY IT :: 10.146**
>
> Simplify: $\frac{y^7}{y^{-6}}$.

Convert from Decimal Notation to Scientific Notation

Remember working with place value for whole numbers and decimals? Our number system is based on powers of 10. We use tens, hundreds, thousands, and so on. Our decimal numbers are also based on powers of tens—tenths, hundredths, thousandths, and so on.

Consider the numbers 4000 and $0.004.$ We know that 4000 means 4×1000 and 0.004 means $4 \times \frac{1}{1000}.$ If we write the 1000 as a power of ten in exponential form, we can rewrite these numbers in this way:

$$4000 \qquad\qquad 0.004$$
$$4 \times 1000 \qquad\qquad 4 \times \frac{1}{1000}$$
$$4 \times 10^3 \qquad\qquad 4 \times \frac{1}{10^3}$$
$$\qquad\qquad\qquad 4 \times 10^{-3}$$

When a number is written as a product of two numbers, where the first factor is a number greater than or equal to one but less than $10,$ and the second factor is a power of 10 written in exponential form, it is said to be in *scientific notation.*

Scientific Notation

A number is expressed in **scientific notation** when it is of the form

$$a \times 10^n$$

where $a \geq 1$ and $a < 10$ and n is an integer.

It is customary in scientific notation to use $\times$ as the multiplication sign, even though we avoid using this sign elsewhere in algebra.

Scientific notation is a useful way of writing very large or very small numbers. It is used often in the sciences to make calculations easier.

If we look at what happened to the decimal point, we can see a method to easily convert from decimal notation to scientific notation.

$$4000. = 4 \times 10^3 \qquad\qquad 0.004 = 4 \times 10^{-3}$$
$$4000. = 4 \times 10^3 \qquad\qquad 0.004 = 4 \times 10^{-3}$$

Moved the decimal point 3 places to the left.   Moved the decimal point 3 places to the right.

In both cases, the decimal was moved 3 places to get the first factor, $4,$ by itself.

- The power of 10 is positive when the number is larger than $1: 4000 = 4 \times 10^3.$

- The power of 10 is negative when the number is between 0 and $1: 0.004 = 4 \times 10^{-3}.$

EXAMPLE 10.74

Write $37,000$ in scientific notation.

⊘ Solution

Step 1: Move the decimal point so that the first factor is greater than or equal to 1 but less than 10.

37000.

Step 2: Count the number of decimal places, n, that the decimal point was moved.

3.70000
4 places

Step 3: Write the number as a product with a power of 10.

3.7×10^4

If the original number is:
- greater than 1, the power of 10 will be 10^n.
- between 0 and 1, the power of 10 will be 10^{-n}

Step 4: Check.

10^4 is 10,000 and 10,000 times 3.7 will be 37,000.

$$37{,}000 = 3.7 \times 10^4$$

> **TRY IT :: 10.147**   Write in scientific notation: $96{,}000$.

> **TRY IT :: 10.148**   Write in scientific notation: $48{,}300$.

HOW TO :: CONVERT FROM DECIMAL NOTATION TO SCIENTIFIC NOTATION.

Step 1.   Move the decimal point so that the first factor is greater than or equal to 1 but less than 10.

Step 2.   Count the number of decimal places, n, that the decimal point was moved.

Step 3.   Write the number as a product with a power of 10.

- If the original number is:
  - greater than 1, the power of 10 will be 10^n.
  - between 0 and 1, the power of 10 will be 10^{-n}.

Step 4.   Check.

EXAMPLE 10.75

Write in scientific notation: 0.0052.

⊘ **Solution**

	0.0052
Move the decimal point to get 5.2, a number between 1 and 10.	0.0052
Count the number of decimal places the point was moved.	3 places
Write as a product with a power of 10.	5.2×10^{-3}

Check your answer:

5.2×10^{-3}

$5.2 \times \dfrac{1}{10^3}$

$5.2 \times \dfrac{1}{1000}$

5.2×0.001

0.0052

$$0.0052 = 5.2 \times 10^{-3}$$

> **TRY IT : : 10.149**   Write in scientific notation: 0.0078.

> **TRY IT : : 10.150**   Write in scientific notation: 0.0129.

Convert Scientific Notation to Decimal Form

How can we convert from scientific notation to decimal form? Let's look at two numbers written in scientific notation and see.

$$9.12 \times 10^4 \qquad\qquad 9.12 \times 10^{-4}$$
$$9.12 \times 10,000 \qquad\qquad 9.12 \times 0.0001$$
$$91,200 \qquad\qquad\qquad 0.000912$$

If we look at the location of the decimal point, we can see an easy method to convert a number from scientific notation to decimal form.

$$9.12 \times 10^4 = 91,200 \qquad\qquad 9.12 \times 10^{-4} = 0.000912$$
$$9.12\_\_\times 10^4 = 91,200 \qquad\qquad \_\_\_9.12 \times 10^{-4} = 0.000912$$

In both cases the decimal point moved 4 places. When the exponent was positive, the decimal moved to the right. When the exponent was negative, the decimal point moved to the left.

EXAMPLE 10.76

Convert to decimal form: 6.2×10^3.

⊘ Solution

Step 1: Determine the exponent, n, on the factor 10.	6.2×10^3
Step 2: Move the decimal point n places, adding zeros if needed.	6,200,
• If the exponent is positive, move the decimal point n places to the right. • If the exponent is negative, move the decimal point $|n|$ places to the left.	6,200
Step 3: Check to see if your answer makes sense.	
10^3 is 1000 and 1000 times 6.2 will be 6,200.	$6.2 \times 10^3 = 6,200$

> **TRY IT :: 10.151**   Convert to decimal form: 1.3×10^3.

> **TRY IT :: 10.152**   Convert to decimal form: 9.25×10^4.

HOW TO :: CONVERT SCIENTIFIC NOTATION TO DECIMAL FORM.

Step 1.   Determine the exponent, n,   on the factor 10.

Step 2.   Move the decimal n places, adding zeros if needed.

  ◦ If the exponent is positive, move the decimal point n places to the right.

  ◦ If the exponent is negative, move the decimal point $|n|$ places to the left.

Step 3.   Check.

EXAMPLE 10.77

Convert to decimal form: 8.9×10^{-2}.

⊘ Solution

$$8.9 \times 10^{-2}$$

Determine the exponent n, on the factor 10.	The exponent is –2.
Move the decimal point 2 places to the left.	$.8.9$
Add zeros as needed for placeholders.	0.089
	$8.9 \times 10^{-2} = 0.089$

The Check is left to you.

> **TRY IT :: 10.153**   Convert to decimal form: 1.2×10^{-4}.

> **TRY IT :: 10.154**   Convert to decimal form: 7.5×10^{-2}.

Multiply and Divide Using Scientific Notation

We use the Properties of Exponents to multiply and divide numbers in scientific notation.

EXAMPLE 10.78

Multiply. Write answers in decimal form: $(4 \times 10^5)(2 \times 10^{-7})$.

⊘ **Solution**

	$(4 \times 10^5)(2 \times 10^{-7})$
Use the Commutative Property to rearrange the factors.	$4 \cdot 2 \cdot 10^5 \cdot 10^{-7}$
Multiply 4 by 2 and use the Product Property to multiply 10^5 by 10^{-7}.	8×10^{-2}
Change to decimal form by moving the decimal two places left.	0.08

> **TRY IT :: 10.155**   Multiply. Write answers in decimal form: $(3 \times 10^6)(2 \times 10^{-8})$.

> **TRY IT :: 10.156**   Multiply. Write answers in decimal form: $(3 \times 10^{-2})(3 \times 10^{-1})$.

EXAMPLE 10.79

Divide. Write answers in decimal form: $\dfrac{9 \times 10^3}{3 \times 10^{-2}}$.

⊘ **Solution**

	$\dfrac{9 \times 10^3}{3 \times 10^{-2}}$
Separate the factors.	$\dfrac{9}{3} \times \dfrac{10^3}{10^{-2}}$
Divide 9 by 3 and use the Quotient Property to divide 10^3 by 10^{-2}.	3×10^5
Change to decimal form by moving the decimal five places right.	300,000

> **TRY IT :: 10.157**   Divide. Write answers in decimal form: $\dfrac{8 \times 10^4}{2 \times 10^{-1}}$.

> **TRY IT :: 10.158**   Divide. Write answers in decimal form: $\dfrac{8 \times 10^2}{4 \times 10^{-2}}$.

▶ **MEDIA :: ACCESS ADDITIONAL ONLINE RESOURCES**

- Negative Exponents (http://www.openstaxcollege.org/l/24negexponents)
- Examples of Simplifying Expressions with Negative Exponents (http://www.openstaxcollege.org/l/24simpexprnegex)
- Scientific Notation (http://www.openstaxcollege.org/l/24scnotation)

10.5 EXERCISES
Practice Makes Perfect

Use the Definition of a Negative Exponent

In the following exercises, simplify.

316. 5^{-3}

317. 8^{-2}

318. 3^{-4}

319. 2^{-5}

320. 7^{-1}

321. 10^{-1}

322. $2^{-3} + 2^{-2}$

323. $3^{-2} + 3^{-1}$

324. $3^{-1} + 4^{-1}$

325. $10^{-1} + 2^{-1}$

326. $10^0 - 10^{-1} + 10^{-2}$

327. $2^0 - 2^{-1} + 2^{-2}$

328.
ⓐ $(-6)^{-2}$ ⓑ -6^{-2}

329.
ⓐ $(-8)^{-2}$ ⓑ -8^{-2}

330.
ⓐ $(-10)^{-4}$ ⓑ -10^{-4}

331.
ⓐ $(-4)^{-6}$ ⓑ -4^{-6}

332.
ⓐ $5 \cdot 2^{-1}$ ⓑ $(5 \cdot 2)^{-1}$

333.
ⓐ $10 \cdot 3^{-1}$ ⓑ $(10 \cdot 3)^{-1}$

334.
ⓐ $4 \cdot 10^{-3}$ ⓑ $(4 \cdot 10)^{-3}$

335.
ⓐ $3 \cdot 5^{-2}$ ⓑ $(3 \cdot 5)^{-2}$

336. n^{-4}

337. p^{-3}

338. c^{-10}

339. m^{-5}

340.
ⓐ $4x^{-1}$ ⓑ $(4x)^{-1}$
ⓒ $(-4x)^{-1}$

341.
ⓐ $3q^{-1}$ ⓑ $(3q)^{-1}$
ⓒ $(-3q)^{-1}$

342.
ⓐ $6m^{-1}$ ⓑ $(6m)^{-1}$
ⓒ $(-6m)^{-1}$

343.
ⓐ $10k^{-1}$ ⓑ $(10k)^{-1}$
ⓒ $(-10k)^{-1}$

Simplify Expressions with Integer Exponents

In the following exercises, simplify.

344. $p^{-4} \cdot p^8$

345. $r^{-2} \cdot r^5$

346. $n^{-10} \cdot n^2$

347. $q^{-8} \cdot q^3$

348. $k^{-3} \cdot k^{-2}$

349. $z^{-6} \cdot z^{-2}$

350. $a \cdot a^{-4}$

351. $m \cdot m^{-2}$

352. $p^5 \cdot p^{-2} \cdot p^{-4}$

353. $x^4 \cdot x^{-2} \cdot x^{-3}$

354. $a^3 b^{-3}$

355. $u^2 v^{-2}$

356. $\left(x^5 y^{-1}\right)\left(x^{-10} y^{-3}\right)$

357. $\left(a^3 b^{-3}\right)\left(a^{-5} b^{-1}\right)$

358. $\left(uv^{-2}\right)\left(u^{-5} v^{-4}\right)$

359. $\left(pq^{-4}\right)\left(p^{-6} q^{-3}\right)$

360. $\left(-2r^{-3} s^9\right)\left(6r^4 s^{-5}\right)$

361. $\left(-3p^{-5} q^8\right)\left(7p^2 q^{-3}\right)$

362. $\left(-6m^{-8}n^{-5}\right)\left(-9m^4n^2\right)$

363. $\left(-8a^{-5}b^{-4}\right)\left(-4a^2b^3\right)$

364. $\left(a^3\right)^{-3}$

365. $\left(q^{10}\right)^{-10}$

366. $\left(n^2\right)^{-1}$

367. $\left(x^4\right)^{-1}$

368. $\left(y^{-5}\right)^4$

369. $\left(p^{-3}\right)^2$

370. $\left(q^{-5}\right)^{-2}$

371. $\left(m^{-2}\right)^{-3}$

372. $\left(4y^{-3}\right)^2$

373. $\left(3q^{-5}\right)^2$

374. $\left(10p^{-2}\right)^{-5}$

375. $\left(2n^{-3}\right)^{-6}$

376. $\dfrac{u^9}{u^{-2}}$

377. $\dfrac{b^5}{b^{-3}}$

378. $\dfrac{x^{-6}}{x^4}$

379. $\dfrac{m^5}{m^{-2}}$

380. $\dfrac{q^3}{q^{12}}$

381. $\dfrac{r^6}{r^9}$

382. $\dfrac{n^{-4}}{n^{-10}}$

383. $\dfrac{p^{-3}}{p^{-6}}$

Convert from Decimal Notation to Scientific Notation

In the following exercises, write each number in scientific notation.

384. 45,000

385. 280,000

386. 8,750,000

387. 1,290,000

388. 0.036

389. 0.041

390. 0.00000924

391. 0.0000103

392. The population of the United States on July 4, 2010 was almost 310,000,000.

393. The population of the world on July 4, 2010 was more than 6,850,000,000.

394. The average width of a human hair is 0.0018 centimeters.

395. The probability of winning the 2010 Megamillions lottery is about 0.0000000057.

Convert Scientific Notation to Decimal Form

In the following exercises, convert each number to decimal form.

396. 4.1×10^2

397. 8.3×10^2

398. 5.5×10^8

399. 1.6×10^{10}

400. 3.5×10^{-2}

401. 2.8×10^{-2}

402. 1.93×10^{-5}

403. 6.15×10^{-8}

404. In 2010, the number of Facebook users each day who changed their status to 'engaged' was 2×10^4.

405. At the start of 2012, the US federal budget had a deficit of more than $\$1.5 \times 10^{13}$.

406. The concentration of carbon dioxide in the atmosphere is 3.9×10^{-4}.

407. The width of a proton is 1×10^{-5} of the width of an atom.

Multiply and Divide Using Scientific Notation

In the following exercises, multiply or divide and write your answer in decimal form.

408. $(2 \times 10^{5})(2 \times 10^{-9})$

409. $(3 \times 10^{2})(1 \times 10^{-5})$

410. $(1.6 \times 10^{-2})(5.2 \times 10^{-6})$

411. $(2.1 \times 10^{-4})(3.5 \times 10^{-2})$

412. $\dfrac{6 \times 10^{4}}{3 \times 10^{-2}}$

413. $\dfrac{8 \times 10^{6}}{4 \times 10^{-1}}$

414. $\dfrac{7 \times 10^{-2}}{1 \times 10^{-8}}$

415. $\dfrac{5 \times 10^{-3}}{1 \times 10^{-10}}$

Everyday Math

416. Calories In May 2010 the Food and Beverage Manufacturers pledged to reduce their products by 1.5 trillion calories by the end of 2015.

ⓐ Write 1.5 trillion in decimal notation.

ⓑ Write 1.5 trillion in scientific notation.

417. Length of a year The difference between the calendar year and the astronomical year is 0.000125 day.

ⓐ Write this number in scientific notation.

ⓑ How many years does it take for the difference to become 1 day?

418. Calculator display Many calculators automatically show answers in scientific notation if there are more digits than can fit in the calculator's display. To find the probability of getting a particular 5-card hand from a deck of cards, Mario divided 1 by 2,598,960 and saw the answer 3.848×10^{-7}. Write the number in decimal notation.

419. Calculator display Many calculators automatically show answers in scientific notation if there are more digits than can fit in the calculator's display. To find the number of ways Barbara could make a collage with 6 of her 50 favorite photographs, she multiplied $50 \cdot 49 \cdot 48 \cdot 47 \cdot 46 \cdot 45$. Her calculator gave the answer 1.1441304×10^{10}. Write the number in decimal notation.

Writing Exercises

420.

ⓐ Explain the meaning of the exponent in the expression 2^{3}.

ⓑ Explain the meaning of the exponent in the expression 2^{-3}

421. When you convert a number from decimal notation to scientific notation, how do you know if the exponent will be positive or negative?

Self Check

ⓐ *After completing the exercises, use this checklist to evaluate your mastery of the objectives of this section.*

I can...	Confidently	With some help	No-I don't get it!
use the definition of a negative exponent.			
simplify expressions with integer exponents.			
convert from decimal notation to scientific notation.			
convert scientific notation to decimal form.			
multiply and divide using scientific notation.			

ⓑ *After looking at the checklist, do you think you are well prepared for the next section? Why or why not?*

Introduction to Factoring Polynomials

10.6

Learning Objectives

By the end of this section, you will be able to:
- Find the greatest common factor of two or more expressions
- Factor the greatest common factor from a polynomial

Be Prepared!

Before you get started, take this readiness quiz.

1. Factor 56 into primes.
   If you missed this problem, review Example 2.48.

2. Multiply: $-3(6a + 11)$.
   If you missed this problem, review Example 7.25.

3. Multiply: $4x^2(x^2 + 3x - 1)$.
   If you missed this problem, review Example 10.32.

Find the Greatest Common Factor of Two or More Expressions

Earlier we multiplied factors together to get a product. Now, we will be reversing this process; we will start with a product and then break it down into its factors. Splitting a product into factors is called factoring.

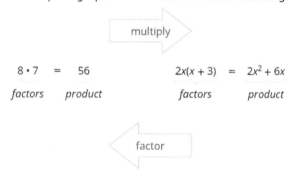

In The Language of Algebra we factored numbers to find the least common multiple (LCM) of two or more numbers. Now we will factor expressions and find the *greatest common factor* of two or more expressions. The method we use is similar to what we used to find the LCM.

Greatest Common Factor

The greatest common factor (GCF) of two or more expressions is the largest expression that is a factor of all the expressions.

First we will find the greatest common factor of two numbers.

EXAMPLE 10.80

Find the greatest common factor of 24 and 36.

⊘ **Solution**

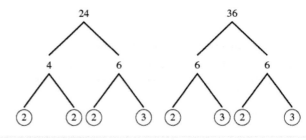

Step 1: Factor each coefficient into primes. Write all variables with exponents in expanded form.	Factor 24 and 36.	

Step 2: List all factors-- matching common factors in a column.

$$24 = 2 \cdot 2 \cdot 2 \cdot 3$$
$$36 = 2 \cdot 2 \cdot \quad 3 \cdot 3$$

In each column, circle the common factors.	Circle the 2, 2, and 3 that are shared by both numbers.	$24 = \boxed{2} \cdot \boxed{2} \cdot 2 \cdot \boxed{3}$ $36 = \boxed{2} \cdot \boxed{2} \cdot \quad \boxed{3} \cdot 3$ $\text{GCF} = 2 \cdot 2 \cdot \quad 3$ $\text{GCF} = 12$

Step 3: Bring down the common factors that all expressions share.	Bring down the 2, 2, 3 and then multiply.

Step 4: Multiply the factors.   The GCF of 24 and 36 is 12.

Notice that since the GCF is a factor of both numbers, 24 and 36 can be written as multiples of 12.

$$24 = 12 \cdot 2$$
$$36 = 12 \cdot 3$$

> **TRY IT : : 10.159**   Find the greatest common factor: 54, 36.

> **TRY IT : : 10.160**   Find the greatest common factor: 48, 80.

In the previous example, we found the greatest common factor of constants. The greatest common factor of an algebraic expression can contain variables raised to powers along with coefficients. We summarize the steps we use to find the greatest common factor.

HOW TO : : FIND THE GREATEST COMMON FACTOR.

Step 1.   Factor each coefficient into primes. Write all variables with exponents in expanded form.

Step 2.   List all factors—matching common factors in a column. In each column, circle the common factors.

Step 3.   Bring down the common factors that all expressions share.

Step 4.   Multiply the factors.

EXAMPLE 10.81

Find the greatest common factor of $5x$ and 15.

⊘ **Solution**

Factor each number into primes.
Circle the common factors in each column.
Bring down the common factors.

$$5x = \boxed{5} \cdot x$$
$$15 = 3 \cdot \boxed{5} \cdot$$
$$\overline{\text{GCF} = \quad 5}$$

The GCF of 5x and 15 is 5.

> **TRY IT : : 10.161**   Find the greatest common factor: $7y, \ 14.$

> **TRY IT : : 10.162**   Find the greatest common factor: $22, \ 11m.$

In the examples so far, the greatest common factor was a constant. In the next two examples we will get variables in the greatest common factor.

EXAMPLE 10.82

Find the greatest common factor of $12x^2$ and $18x^3$.

⊘ **Solution**

Factor each coefficient into primes and write
the variables with exponents in expanded form.
Circle the common factors in each column.
Bring down the common factors.
Multiply the factors.

$$12x^2 = \boxed{2} \cdot 2 \cdot \boxed{3} \cdot \quad \boxed{x} \cdot \boxed{x}$$
$$18x^3 = \boxed{2} \cdot \quad \boxed{3} \cdot 3 \cdot \boxed{x} \cdot \boxed{x} \cdot x$$
$$\overline{\text{GCF} = 2 \cdot \quad 3 \cdot \quad x \cdot x}$$
$$\text{GCF} = 6x^2$$

The GCF of $12x^2$ and $18x^3$ is $6x^2$

> **TRY IT : : 10.163**   Find the greatest common factor: $16x^2, \ 24x^3.$

> **TRY IT : : 10.164**   Find the greatest common factor: $27y^3, \ 18y^4.$

EXAMPLE 10.83

Find the greatest common factor of $14x^3, \ 8x^2, \ 10x.$

⊘ **Solution**

Factor each coefficient into primes and write
the variables with exponents in expanded form.
Circle the common factors in each column.
Bring down the common factors.
Multiply the factors.

$$14x^3 = \boxed{2} \cdot \qquad 7 \cdot \boxed{x} \cdot x \cdot x$$
$$8x^2 = \boxed{2} \cdot 2 \cdot 2 \cdot \quad \boxed{x} \cdot x$$
$$10x = \boxed{2} \cdot \qquad 5 \cdot \boxed{x}$$
$$\overline{\text{GCF} = 2 \cdot \qquad \qquad x}$$
$$\text{GCF} = 2x$$

The GCF of $14x^3$ and $8x^2$, and $10x$ is $2x$

> **TRY IT : : 10.165**   Find the greatest common factor: $21x^3, \ 9x^2, \ 15x.$

> **TRY IT ::** 10.166   Find the greatest common factor: $25m^4$, $35m^3$, $20m^2$.

Factor the Greatest Common Factor from a Polynomial

Just like in arithmetic, where it is sometimes useful to represent a number in factored form (for example, 12 as $2 \cdot 6$ or $3 \cdot 4$), in algebra it can be useful to represent a polynomial in factored form. One way to do this is by finding the greatest common factor of all the terms. Remember that you can multiply a polynomial by a monomial as follows:

$$2(x \ + \ 7) \text{ factors}$$
$$2 \cdot x \ + \ 2 \cdot 7$$
$$2x \ + \ 14 \text{ product}$$

Here, we will start with a product, like $2x + 14$, and end with its factors, $2(x + 7)$. To do this we apply the Distributive Property "in reverse".

Distributive Property

If a, b, c are real numbers, then

$$a(b + c) = ab + ac \qquad \text{and} \qquad ab + ac = a(b + c)$$

The form on the left is used to multiply. The form on the right is used to factor.

So how do we use the Distributive Property to factor a polynomial? We find the GCF of all the terms and write the polynomial as a product!

EXAMPLE 10.84

Factor: $2x + 14$.

⊘ **Solution**

Step 1: Find the GCF of all the terms of the polynomial.	Find the GCF of 2x and 14.	$2x = \boxed{2} \cdot \ x$ $14 = \boxed{2} \cdot 7$ ——————— $\text{GCF} = 2$
Step 2: Rewrite each term as a product using the GCF.	Rewrite 2x and 14 as products of their GCF, 2. $2x = 2 \cdot x$ $14 = 2 \cdot 7$	$2x + 14$ $2 \cdot x + 2 \cdot 7$
Step 3: Use the Distributive Property 'in reverse' to factor the expression.		$2(x + 7)$
Step 4: Check by multiplying the factors.		Check: $2(x + 7)$ $2 \cdot x + 2 \cdot 7$ $2x + 14$ ✓

> **TRY IT ::** 10.167   Factor: $4x + 12$.

> **TRY IT ::** 10.168   Factor: $6a + 24$.

Notice that in Example 10.84, we used the word *factor* as both a noun and a verb:

Noun	7 is a factor of 14
Verb	factor 2 from $2x + 14$

HOW TO :: FACTOR THE GREATEST COMMON FACTOR FROM A POLYNOMIAL.

Step 1.   Find the GCF of all the terms of the polynomial.

Step 2.   Rewrite each term as a product using the GCF.

Step 3.   Use the Distributive Property 'in reverse' to factor the expression.

Step 4.   Check by multiplying the factors.

EXAMPLE 10.85

Factor: $3a + 3$.

⊘ **Solution**

Find the GCF of $3a$, 3.

$$3a = 3 \cdot a$$
$$3 = 3$$
$$\overline{GCF = 3}$$

$$3a + 3$$

Rewrite each term as a product using the GCF. $3 \cdot a + 3 \cdot 1$

Use the Distributive Property 'in reverse' to factor the GCF. $3(a + 1)$

Check by multiplying the factors to get the original polynomial.

$3(a + 1)$
$3 \cdot a + 3 \cdot 1$
$3a + 3$ ✓

> **TRY IT :: 10.169**   Factor: $9a + 9$.

> **TRY IT :: 10.170**   Factor: $11x + 11$.

The expressions in the next example have several factors in common. Remember to write the GCF as the product of all the common factors.

EXAMPLE 10.86

Factor: $12x - 60$.

Solution

Find the GCF of 12x and 60.

$$12x = \boxed{2} \cdot \boxed{2} \cdot \boxed{3} \cdot \ x$$
$$60 = \boxed{2} \cdot \boxed{2} \cdot \boxed{3} \cdot 5$$
$$\text{GCF} = 2 \cdot 2 \cdot 3$$
$$\text{GCF} = 12$$

	$12x - 60$
Rewrite each term as a product using the GCF.	$12 \cdot x - 12 \cdot 5$
Factor the GCF.	$12(x - 5)$
Check by multiplying the factors.	

$$12(x - 5)$$
$$12 \cdot x - 12 \cdot 5$$
$$12x - 60 \checkmark$$

> **TRY IT :: 10.171**   Factor: $11x - 44$.

> **TRY IT :: 10.172**   Factor: $13y - 52$.

Now we'll factor the greatest common factor from a trinomial. We start by finding the GCF of all three terms.

EXAMPLE 10.87

Factor: $3y^2 + 6y + 9$.

Solution

Find the GCF of $3y^2$, 6y, and 9.

$$3y^2 = \qquad \boxed{3} \cdot \qquad y \cdot y$$
$$6y = 2 \cdot \boxed{3} \cdot \qquad y$$
$$9 = \qquad \boxed{3} \cdot 3$$
$$\text{GCF} = \qquad 3$$

	$3y^2 + 6y + 9$
Rewrite each term as a product using the GCF.	$3 \cdot y^2 + 3 \cdot 2y + 3 \cdot 3$
Factor the GCF.	$3(y^2 + 2y + 3)$
Check by multiplying.	

$$3(y^2 + 2y + 3)$$
$$3 \cdot y^2 + 3 \cdot 2y + 3 \cdot 3$$
$$3y^2 + 6y + 9 \checkmark$$

> **TRY IT :: 10.173**   Factor: $4y^2 + 8y + 12$.

> **TRY IT :: 10.174**   Factor: $6x^2 + 42x - 12$.

In the next example, we factor a variable from a binomial.

EXAMPLE 10.88

Factor: $6x^2 + 5x$.

⊘ Solution

$$6x^2 + 5x$$

Find the GCF of $6x^2$ and $5x$ and the math that goes with it.

$$6x^2 = 2 \cdot 3 \cdot \boxed{x} \cdot x$$
$$5x = \qquad 5 \cdot \boxed{x}$$
$$\overline{\text{GCF} = \qquad\qquad x}$$

Rewrite each term as a product.

$$x \cdot 6x + x \cdot 5$$

Factor the GCF.

$$x(6x + 5)$$

Check by multiplying.

$$x(6x + 5)$$
$$x \cdot 6x + x \cdot 5$$
$$6x^2 + 5x \checkmark$$

> **TRY IT ::** 10.175   Factor: $9x^2 + 7x$.

> **TRY IT ::** 10.176   Factor: $5a^2 - 12a$.

When there are several common factors, as we'll see in the next two examples, good organization and neat work helps!

EXAMPLE 10.89

Factor: $4x^3 - 20x^2$.

⊘ Solution

Find the GCF of $4x^3$ and $20x^2$.

$$4x^3 = \boxed{2} \cdot \boxed{2} \cdot \boxed{x} \cdot \boxed{x} \cdot x$$
$$20x^2 = \boxed{2} \cdot \boxed{2} \cdot 5 \cdot \boxed{x} \cdot \boxed{x}$$
$$\overline{\text{GCF} = 2 \cdot 2 \cdot \qquad x \cdot x}$$
$$\text{GCF} = 4x^2$$

$$4x^3 - 20x^2$$

Rewrite each term.

$$4x^2 \cdot x - 4x^2 \cdot 5$$

Factor the GCF.

$$4x^2(x - 5)$$

Check.

$$4x^2(x - 5)$$
$$4x^2 \cdot x - 4x^2 \cdot 5$$
$$4x^3 - 20x^2 \checkmark$$

> **TRY IT ::** 10.177   Factor: $2x^3 + 12x^2$.

> **TRY IT ::** 10.178   Factor: $6y^3 - 15y^2$.

EXAMPLE 10.90

Factor: $21y^2 + 35y$.

⊘ **Solution**

Find the GCF of $21y^2$ and $35y$	$21y^2 = 3 \cdot \boxed{7} \cdot \boxed{y} \cdot y$
	$35y = \quad 5 \cdot \boxed{7} \cdot \boxed{y} \cdot$
	$\overline{GCF = \qquad 7 \cdot y}$
	$GCF = 7y$

	$21y^2 + 35y$
Rewrite each term.	$7y \cdot 3y + 7y \cdot 5$
Factor the GCF.	$7y(3y + 5)$

> **TRY IT :: 10.179**   Factor: $18y^2 + 63y$.

> **TRY IT :: 10.180**   Factor: $32k^2 + 56k$.

EXAMPLE 10.91

Factor: $14x^3 + 8x^2 - 10x$.

⊘ **Solution**

Previously, we found the GCF of $14x^3$, $8x^2$, and $10x$ to be $2x$.

	$14x^3 + 8x^2 - 10x$
Rewrite each term using the GCF, 2x.	$2x \cdot 7x^2 + 2x \cdot 4x - 2x \cdot 5$
Factor the GCF.	$2x(7x^2 + 4x - 5)$

Check. $2x(7x^2 + 4x - 5)$
$2x \cdot 7x^2 + 2x \cdot 4x - 2x \cdot 5$
$14x^3 + 8x^2 - 10x$ ✓

> **TRY IT :: 10.181**   Factor: $18y^3 - 6y^2 - 24y$.

> **TRY IT :: 10.182**   Factor: $16x^3 + 8x^2 - 12x$.

When the leading coefficient, the coefficient of the first term, is negative, we factor the negative out as part of the GCF.

EXAMPLE 10.92

Factor: $-9y - 27$.

Solution

When the leading coefficient is negative, the GCF will be negative. Ignoring the signs of the terms, we first find the GCF of 9y and 27 is 9.

$$9y = \boxed{3} \cdot \boxed{3} \cdot \quad y$$
$$27 = \boxed{3} \cdot \boxed{3} \cdot 3$$
$$\text{GCF} = 3 \cdot 3$$
$$\text{GCF} = 9$$

Since the expression –9y–27 has a negative leading coefficient, we use –9 as the GCF.

$$-9y - 27$$

Rewrite each term using the GCF.

$$-9 \cdot y + (-9) \cdot 3$$

Factor the GCF.

$$-9(y + 3)$$

Check.
$$-9(y + 3)$$
$$-9 \cdot y + (-9) \cdot 3$$
$$-9y - 27 \checkmark$$

> **TRY IT ::** 10.183   Factor: $-5y - 35$.

> **TRY IT ::** 10.184   Factor: $-16z - 56$.

Pay close attention to the signs of the terms in the next example.

EXAMPLE 10.93

Factor: $-4a^2 + 16a$.

Solution

The leading coefficient is negative, so the GCF will be negative.

$$4a^2 = \boxed{2} \cdot \boxed{2} \cdot \quad \boxed{a} \cdot a$$
$$16a = \boxed{2} \cdot \boxed{2} \cdot 2 \cdot 2 \cdot \boxed{a}$$
$$\text{GCF} = 2 \cdot 2 \cdot \quad a$$
$$\text{GCF} = 4a$$

Since the leading coefficient is negative, the GCF is negative, –4a.

$$-4a^2 + 16a$$

Rewrite each term.

$$-4a \cdot a - (-4a) \cdot 4$$

Factor the GCF.

$$-4a(a - 4)$$

Check on your own by multiplying.

> **TRY IT ::** 10.185   Factor: $-7a^2 + 21a$.

> **TRY IT ::** 10.186   Factor: $-6x^2 + x$.

▶ | **MEDIA :** : ACCESS ADDITIONAL ONLINE RESOURCES
- Factor GCF (http://www.openstaxcollege.org/l/24factorgcf)
- Factor a Binomial (http://www.openstaxcollege.org/l/24factorbinomi)
- Identify GCF (http://www.openstaxcollege.org/l/24identifygcf)

10.6 EXERCISES

Practice Makes Perfect

Find the Greatest Common Factor of Two or More Expressions

In the following exercises, find the greatest common factor.

422. 40, 56

423. 45, 75

424. 72, 162

425. 150, 275

426. $3x$, 12

427. $4y$, 28

428. $10a$, 50

429. $5b$, 30

430. $16y$, $24y^2$

431. $9x$, $15x^2$

432. $18m^3$, $36m^2$

433. $12p^4$, $48p^3$

434. $10x$, $25x^2$, $15x^3$

435. $18a$, $6a^2$, $22a^3$

436. $24u$, $6u^2$, $30u^3$

437. $40y$, $10y^2$, $90y^3$

438. $15a^4$, $9a^5$, $21a^6$

439. $35x^3$, $10x^4$, $5x^5$

440. $27y^2$, $45y^3$, $9y^4$

441. $14b^2$, $35b^3$, $63b^4$

Factor the Greatest Common Factor from a Polynomial

In the following exercises, factor the greatest common factor from each polynomial.

442. $2x + 8$

443. $5y + 15$

444. $3a - 24$

445. $4b - 20$

446. $9y - 9$

447. $7x - 7$

448. $5m^2 + 20m + 35$

449. $3n^2 + 21n + 12$

450. $8p^2 + 32p + 48$

451. $6q^2 + 30q + 42$

452. $8q^2 + 15q$

453. $9c^2 + 22c$

454. $13k^2 + 5k$

455. $17x^2 + 7x$

456. $5c^2 + 9c$

457. $4q^2 + 7q$

458. $5p^2 + 25p$

459. $3r^2 + 27r$

460. $24q^2 - 12q$

461. $30u^2 - 10u$

462. $yz + 4z$

463. $ab + 8b$

464. $60x - 6x^3$

465. $55y - 11y^4$

466. $48r^4 - 12r^3$

467. $45c^3 - 15c^2$

468. $4a^3 - 4ab^2$

469. $6c^3 - 6cd^2$

470. $30u^3 + 80u^2$

471. $48x^3 + 72x^2$

472. $120y^6 + 48y^4$

473. $144a^6 + 90a^3$

474. $4q^2 + 24q + 28$

475. $10y^2 + 50y + 40$

476. $15z^2 - 30z - 90$

477. $12u^2 - 36u - 108$

478. $3a^4 - 24a^3 + 18a^2$

479. $5p^4 - 20p^3 - 15p^2$

480. $11x^6 + 44x^5 - 121x^4$

481. $8c^5 + 40c^4 - 56c^3$

482. $-3n - 24$

483. $-7p - 84$

484. $-15a^2 - 40a$

485. $-18b^2 - 66b$

486. $-10y^3 + 60y^2$

487. $-8a^3 + 32a^2$

488. $-4u^5 + 56u^3$

489. $-9b^5 + 63b^3$

Everyday Math

490. Revenue A manufacturer of microwave ovens has found that the revenue received from selling microwaves a cost of p dollars each is given by the polynomial $-5p^2 + 150p$. Factor the greatest common factor from this polynomial.

491. Height of a baseball The height of a baseball hit with velocity 80 feet/second at 4 feet above ground level is $-16t^2 + 80t + 4$, with $t =$ the number of seconds since it was hit. Factor the greatest common factor from this polynomial.

Writing Exercises

492. The greatest common factor of 36 and 60 is 12. Explain what this means.

493. What is the GCF of y^4, y^5, and y^{10}? Write a general rule that tells how to find the GCF of y^a, y^b, and y^c.

Self Check

ⓐ After completing the exercises, use this checklist to evaluate your mastery of the objectives of this section.

I can...	Confidently	With some help	No-I don't get it!
find the greatest common factor of two or more expressions.			
factor the greatest common factor from a polynomial.			

ⓑ Overall, after looking at the checklist, do you think you are well-prepared for the next Chapter? Why or why not?

CHAPTER 10 REVIEW

KEY TERMS

binomial A binomial is a polynomial with exactly two terms.

degree of a constant The degree of a constant is 0.

degree of a polynomial The degree of a polynomial is the highest degree of all its terms.

degree of a term The degree of a term of a polynomial is the exponent of its variable.

greatest common factor The greatest common factor (GCF) of two or more expressions is the largest expression that is a factor of all the expressions.

monomial A term of the form ax^m, where a is a constant and m is a whole number, is called a monomial.

negative exponent If n is a positive integer and $a \neq 0$, then $a^{-n} = \dfrac{1}{a^n}$.

polynomial A polynomial is a monomial, or two or more monomials, combined by addition or subtraction.

scientific notation A number expressed in scientific notation when it is of the form $a \times 10^n$, where $a \geq 1$ and $a < 10$, and n is an integer.

trinomial A trinomial is a polynomial with exactly three terms.

zero exponent If a is a non-zero number, then $a^0 = 1$. Any nonzero number raised to the zero power is 1.

KEY CONCEPTS

10.2 Use Multiplication Properties of Exponents

- **Exponential Notation**

$$a^{m} \leftarrow \text{exponent}$$
$$\uparrow \text{base}$$

a^m means multiply m factors of a

$a^m = a \cdot a \cdot a \cdot \ldots \cdot a$

m factors

This is read a to the mth power.

- **Product Property of Exponents**
  - If a is a real number and m, n are counting numbers, then

$$a^m \cdot a^n = a^{m+n}$$

  - To multiply with like bases, add the exponents.

- **Power Property for Exponents**
  - If a is a real number and m, n are counting numbers, then

$$(a^m)^n = a^{m \cdot n}$$

- **Product to a Power Property for Exponents**
  - If a and b are real numbers and m is a whole number, then

$$(ab)^m = a^m b^m$$

10.3 Multiply Polynomials

- **Use the FOIL method for multiplying two binomials.**

Step 1. Multiply the **First** terms.	
Step 2. Multiply the **Outer** terms.	$\begin{array}{cccc} first & last & first & last \\ (a+b) & & (c+d) \end{array}$
Step 3. Multiply the **Inner** terms.	*inner*
Step 4. Multiply the **Last** terms.	*outer*
Step 5. Combine like terms, when possible.	

- **Multiplying Two Binomials:** To multiply binomials, use the:
  - Distributive Property
  - FOIL Method
  - Vertical Method
- **Multiplying a Trinomial by a Binomial:** To multiply a trinomial by a binomial, use the:
  - Distributive Property
  - Vertical Method

10.4 Divide Monomials

- **Equivalent Fractions Property**
  - If a, b, c are whole numbers where $b \neq 0$, $c \neq 0$, then

  $$\frac{a}{b} = \frac{a \cdot c}{b \cdot c} \text{ and } \frac{a \cdot c}{b \cdot c} = \frac{a}{b}$$

- **Zero Exponent**
  - If a is a non-zero number, then $a^0 = 1$.
  - Any nonzero number raised to the zero power is 1.

- **Quotient Property for Exponents**
  - If a is a real number, $a \neq 0$, and m, n are whole numbers, then

  $$\frac{a^m}{a^n} = a^{m-n}, \qquad m > n \qquad \text{and} \qquad \frac{a^m}{a^n} = \frac{1}{a^{n-m}}, \qquad n > m$$

- **Quotient to a Power Property for Exponents**
  - If a and b are real numbers, $b \neq 0$, and m is a counting number, then

  $$\left(\frac{a}{b}\right)^m = \frac{a^m}{b^m}$$

  - To raise a fraction to a power, raise the numerator and denominator to that power.

10.5 Integer Exponents and Scientific Notation

- **Summary of Exponent Properties**
  - If a, b are real numbers and m, n are integers, then

Product Property	$a^m \cdot a^n = a^{m+n}$
Power Property	$(a^m)^n = a^{m \cdot n}$
Product to a Power Property	$(ab)^m = a^m b^m$
Quotient Property	$\dfrac{a^m}{a^n} = a^{m-n}, \ a \neq 0$
Zero Exponent Property	$a^0 = 1, \ a \neq 0$
Quotient to a Power Property	$\left(\dfrac{a}{b}\right)^m = \dfrac{a^m}{b^m}, \ b \neq 0$
Definition of Negative Exponent	$a^{-n} = \dfrac{1}{a^n}$

- **Convert from Decimal Notation to Scientific Notation:** To convert a decimal to scientific notation:

  Step 1. Move the decimal point so that the first factor is greater than or equal to 1 but less than 10.

  Step 2. Count the number of decimal places, n, that the decimal point was moved.

  Step 3. Write the number as a product with a power of 10.

    - If the original number is greater than 1, the power of 10 will be 10^n.

    - If the original number is between 0 and 1, the power of 10 will be 10^n.

  Step 4. Check.

- **Convert Scientific Notation to Decimal Form:** To convert scientific notation to decimal form:

  Step 1. Determine the exponent, n, on the factor 10.

  Step 2. Move the decimal n places, adding zeros if needed.

    - If the exponent is positive, move the decimal point n places to the right.

    - If the exponent is negative, move the decimal point $|n|$ places to the left.

  Step 3. Check.

10.6 Introduction to Factoring Polynomials

- **Find the greatest common factor.**

  Step 1. Factor each coefficient into primes. Write all variables with exponents in expanded form.

  Step 2. List all factors—matching common factors in a column. In each column, circle the common factors.

  Step 3. Bring down the common factors that all expressions share.

  Step 4. Multiply the factors.

- **Distributive Property**

    - If a, b, c are real numbers, then
    $a(b + c) = ab + ac$ and $ab + ac = a(b + c)$

- **Factor the greatest common factor from a polynomial.**

  Step 1. Find the GCF of all the terms of the polynomial.

  Step 2. Rewrite each term as a product using the GCF.

  Step 3. Use the Distributive Property 'in reverse' to factor the expression.

  Step 4. Check by multiplying the factors.

REVIEW EXERCISES

10.1 Add and Subtract Polynomials

Identify Polynomials, Monomials, Binomials and Trinomials

In the following exercises, determine if each of the following polynomials is a monomial, binomial, trinomial, or other polynomial.

494. $y^2 + 8y - 20$

495. $-6a^4$

496. $9x^3 - 1$

497. $n^3 - 3n^2 + 3n - 1$

Determine the Degree of Polynomials

In the following exercises, determine the degree of each polynomial.

498. $16x^2 - 40x - 25$

499. $5m + 9$

500. -15

501. $y^2 + 6y^3 + 9y^4$

Add and Subtract Monomials

In the following exercises, add or subtract the monomials.

502. $4p + 11p$

503. $-8y^3 - 5y^3$

504. Add $4n^5$, $-n^5$, $-6n^5$

505. Subtract $10x^2$ from $3x^2$

Add and Subtract Polynomials

In the following exercises, add or subtract the polynomials.

506.
$(4a^2 + 9a - 11) + (6a^2 - 5a + 10)$

507.
$(8m^2 + 12m - 5) - (2m^2 - 7m - 1)$

508. $(y^2 - 3y + 12) + (5y^2 - 9)$

509. $(5u^2 + 8u) - (4u - 7)$

510. Find the sum of $8q^3 - 27$ and $q^2 + 6q - 2$

511. Find the difference of $x^2 + 6x + 8$ and $x^2 - 8x + 15$

Evaluate a Polynomial for a Given Value of the Variable

In the following exercises, evaluate each polynomial for the given value.

512. $200x - \frac{1}{5}x^2$ when $x = 5$

513. $200x - \frac{1}{5}x^2$ when $x = 0$

514. $200x - \frac{1}{5}x^2$ when $x = 15$

515. $5 + 40x - \frac{1}{2}x^2$ when $x = 10$

516. $5 + 40x - \frac{1}{2}x^2$ when $x = -4$

517. $5 + 40x - \frac{1}{2}x^2$ when $x = 0$

518. A pair of glasses is dropped off a bridge 640 feet above a river. The polynomial $-16t^2 + 640$ gives the height of the glasses t seconds after they were dropped. Find the height of the glasses when $t = 6$.

519. The fuel efficiency (in miles per gallon) of a bus going at a speed of x miles per hour is given by the polynomial $-\frac{1}{160}x^2 + \frac{1}{2}x$. Find the fuel efficiency when $x = 20$ mph.

10.2 Use Multiplication Properties of Exponents

Simplify Expressions with Exponents

In the following exercises, simplify.

520. 6^3

521. $\left(\frac{1}{2}\right)^4$

522. $(-0.5)^2$

523. -3^2

Simplify Expressions Using the Product Property of Exponents

In the following exercises, simplify each expression.

524. $p^3 \cdot p^{10}$

525. $2 \cdot 2^6$

526. $a \cdot a^2 \cdot a^3$

527. $x \cdot x^8$

Simplify Expressions Using the Power Property of Exponents

In the following exercises, simplify each expression.

528. $(y^4)^3$

529. $(r^3)^2$

530. $(3^2)^5$

531. $(a^{10})^y$

Simplify Expressions Using the Product to a Power Property

In the following exercises, simplify each expression.

532. $(8n)^2$

533. $(-5x)^3$

534. $(2ab)^8$

535. $(-10mnp)^4$

Simplify Expressions by Applying Several Properties

In the following exercises, simplify each expression.

536. $(3a^5)^3$

537. $(4y)^2(8y)$

538. $(x^3)^5(x^2)^3$

539. $(5st^2)^3(2s^3t^4)^2$

Multiply Monomials

In the following exercises, multiply the monomials.

540. $(-6p^4)(9p)$

541. $\left(\frac{1}{3}c^2\right)(30c^8)$

542. $(8x^2y^5)(7xy^6)$

543. $\left(\frac{2}{3}m^3n^6\right)\left(\frac{1}{6}m^4n^4\right)$

10.3 Multiply Polynomials

Multiply a Polynomial by a Monomial

In the following exercises, multiply.

544. $7(10-x)$

545. $a^2(a^2-9a-36)$

546. $-5y(125y^3-1)$

547. $(4n-5)(2n^3)$

Multiply a Binomial by a Binomial

In the following exercises, multiply the binomials using various methods.

548. $(a+5)(a+2)$

549. $(y-4)(y+12)$

550. $(3x+1)(2x-7)$

551. $(6p-11)(3p-10)$

552. $(n+8)(n+1)$

553. $(k+6)(k-9)$

554. $(5u-3)(u+8)$

555. $(2y-9)(5y-7)$

556. $(p+4)(p+7)$

557. $(x-8)(x+9)$

558. $(3c+1)(9c-4)$

559. $(10a-1)(3a-3)$

Multiply a Trinomial by a Binomial

In the following exercises, multiply using any method.

560. $(x + 1)(x^2 - 3x - 21)$ **561.** $(5b - 2)(3b^2 + b - 9)$ **562.** $(m + 6)(m^2 - 7m - 30)$

563. $(4y - 1)(6y^2 - 12y + 5)$

10.4 Divide Monomials

Simplify Expressions Using the Quotient Property of Exponents

In the following exercises, simplify.

564. $\dfrac{2^8}{2^2}$ **565.** $\dfrac{a^6}{a}$ **566.** $\dfrac{n^3}{n^{12}}$

567. $\dfrac{x}{x^5}$

Simplify Expressions with Zero Exponents

In the following exercises, simplify.

568. 3^0 **569.** y^0 **570.** $(14t)^0$

571. $12a^0 - 15b^0$

Simplify Expressions Using the Quotient to a Power Property

In the following exercises, simplify.

572. $\left(\dfrac{3}{5}\right)^2$ **573.** $\left(\dfrac{x}{2}\right)^5$ **574.** $\left(\dfrac{5m}{n}\right)^3$

575. $\left(\dfrac{s}{10t}\right)^2$

Simplify Expressions by Applying Several Properties

In the following exercises, simplify.

576. $\dfrac{(a^3)^2}{a^4}$ **577.** $\dfrac{u^3}{u^2 \cdot u^4}$ **578.** $\left(\dfrac{x}{x^9}\right)^5$

579. $\left(\dfrac{p^4 \cdot p^5}{p^3}\right)^2$ **580.** $\dfrac{(n^5)^3}{(n^2)^8}$ **581.** $\left(\dfrac{5s^2}{4t}\right)^3$

Divide Monomials

In the following exercises, divide the monomials.

582. $72p^{12} \div 8p^3$ **583.** $-26a^8 \div (2a^2)$ **584.** $\dfrac{45y^6}{-15y^{10}}$

585. $\dfrac{-30x^8}{-36x^9}$ **586.** $\dfrac{28a^9 b}{7a^4 b^3}$ **587.** $\dfrac{11u^6 v^3}{55u^2 v^8}$

588. $\dfrac{\left(5m^9 n^3\right)\left(8m^3 n^2\right)}{\left(10mn^4\right)\left(m^2 n^5\right)}$

589. $\dfrac{42r^2 s^4}{6rs^3} - \dfrac{54rs^2}{9s}$

10.5 Integer Exponents and Scientific Notation

Use the Definition of a Negative Exponent

In the following exercises, simplify.

590. 6^{-2}

591. $(-10)^{-3}$

592. $5 \cdot 2^{-4}$

593. $(8n)^{-1}$

Simplify Expressions with Integer Exponents

In the following exercises, simplify.

594. $x^{-3} \cdot x^9$

595. $r^{-5} \cdot r^{-4}$

596. $\left(uv^{-3}\right)\left(u^{-4} v^{-2}\right)$

597. $\left(m^5\right)^{-1}$

598. $\left(k^{-2}\right)^{-3}$

599. $\dfrac{q^4}{q^{20}}$

600. $\dfrac{b^8}{b^{-2}}$

601. $\dfrac{n^{-3}}{n^{-5}}$

Convert from Decimal Notation to Scientific Notation

In the following exercises, write each number in scientific notation.

602. 5,300,000

603. 0.00814

604. The thickness of a piece of paper is about 0.097 millimeter.

605. According to www.cleanair.com, U.S. businesses use about 21,000,000 tons of paper per year.

Convert Scientific Notation to Decimal Form

In the following exercises, convert each number to decimal form.

606. 2.9×10^4

607. 1.5×10^8

608. 3.75×10^{-1}

609. 9.413×10^{-5}

Multiply and Divide Using Scientific Notation

In the following exercises, multiply and write your answer in decimal form.

610. $\left(3 \times 10^7\right)\left(2 \times 10^{-4}\right)$

611. $\left(1.5 \times 10^{-3}\right)\left(4.8 \times 10^{-1}\right)$

612. $\dfrac{6 \times 10^9}{2 \times 10^{-1}}$

613. $\dfrac{9 \times 10^{-3}}{1 \times 10^{-6}}$

10.6 Introduction to Factoring Polynomials

Find the Greatest Common Factor of Two or More Expressions

In the following exercises, find the greatest common factor.

614. $5n$, 45

615. $8a$, 72

616. $12x^2$, $20x^3$, $36x^4$

617. $9y^4$, $21y^5$, $15y^6$

Factor the Greatest Common Factor from a Polynomial

In the following exercises, factor the greatest common factor from each polynomial.

618. $16u - 24$

619. $15r + 35$

620. $6p^2 + 6p$

621. $10c^2 - 10c$

622. $-9a^5 - 9a^3$

623. $-7x^8 - 28x^3$

624. $5y^2 - 55y + 45$

625. $2q^5 - 16q^3 + 30q^2$

PRACTICE TEST

626. For the polynomial
$8y^4 - 3y^2 + 1$

ⓐ Is it a monomial, binomial, or trinomial?

ⓑ What is its degree?

In the following exercises, simplify each expression.

627.
$(5a^2 + 2a - 12) + (9a^2 + 8a - 4)$

628. $(10x^2 - 3x + 5) - (4x^2 - 6)$

629. $\left(-\frac{3}{4}\right)^3$

630. $n \cdot n^4$

631. $(10p^3 q^5)^2$

632. $(8xy^3)(-6x^4 y^6)$

633. $4u(u^2 - 9u + 1)$

634. $(s + 8)(s + 9)$

635. $(m + 3)(7m - 2)$

636. $(11a - 6)(5a - 1)$

637. $(n - 8)(n^2 - 4n + 11)$

638. $(4a + 9b)(6a - 5b)$

639. $\dfrac{5^6}{5^8}$

640. $\left(\dfrac{x^3 \cdot x^9}{x^5}\right)^2$

641. $(47a^{18} b^{23} c^5)^0$

642. $\dfrac{24r^3 s}{6r^2 s^7}$

643. $\dfrac{8y^2 - 16y + 20}{4y}$

644. $(15xy^3 - 35x^2 y) \div 5xy$

645. 4^{-1}

646. $(2y)^{-3}$

647. $p^{-3} \cdot p^{-8}$

648. $\dfrac{x^4}{x^{-5}}$

649. $\left(2.4 \times 10^8\right)\left(2 \times 10^{-5}\right)$

In the following exercises, factor the greatest common factor from each polynomial.

650. $80a^3 + 120a^2 + 40a$

651. $-6x^2 - 30x$

652. Convert 5.25×10^{-4} to decimal form.

In the following exercises, simplify, and write your answer in decimal form.

653. $\dfrac{9 \times 10^4}{3 \times 10^{-1}}$

654. A hiker drops a pebble from a bridge 240 feet above a canyon. The polynomial $-16t^2 + 240$ gives the height of the pebble t seconds a after it was dropped. Find the height when $t = 3$.

655. According to www.cleanair.org, the amount of trash generated in the US in one year averages out to 112,000 pounds of trash per person. Write this number in scientific notation.

Figure 11.1 Cyclists speed toward the finish line. (credit: ewan traveler, Flickr)

Chapter Outline

Introduction

Which cyclist will win the race? What will the winning time be? How many seconds will separate the winner from the runner-up? One way to summarize the information from the race is by creating a graph. In this chapter, we will discuss the basic concepts of graphing. The applications of graphing go far beyond races. They are used to present information in almost every field, including healthcare, business, and entertainment.

11.1 Use the Rectangular Coordinate System

Learning Objectives

By the end of this section, you will be able to:

- Plot points on a rectangular coordinate system
- Identify points on a graph
- Verify solutions to an equation in two variables
- Complete a table of solutions to a linear equation
- Find solutions to linear equations in two variables

Be Prepared!

Before you get started, take this readiness quiz.

1. Evaluate: $x + 3$ when $x = -1$.
   If you missed this problem, review Example 3.23.
2. Evaluate: $2x - 5y$ when $x = 3$, $y = -2$.
   If you missed this problem, review Example 3.56.
3. Solve for y: $40 - 4y = 20$.
   If you missed this problem, review Example 8.20.

Plot Points on a Rectangular Coordinate System

Many maps, such as the Campus Map shown in Figure 11.2, use a grid system to identify locations. Do you see the numbers 1, 2, 3, and 4 across the top and bottom of the map and the letters A, B, C, and D along the sides? Every location on the map can be identified by a number and a letter.

For example, the Student Center is in section 2B. It is located in the grid section above the number 2 and next to the letter B. In which grid section is the Stadium? The Stadium is in section 4D.

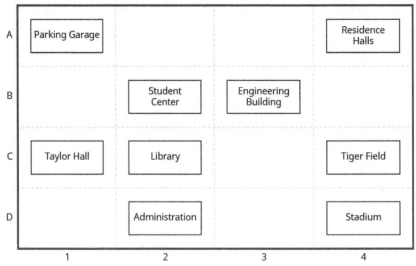

Figure 11.2

EXAMPLE 11.1

Use the map in Figure 11.2.

ⓐ Find the grid section of the Residence Halls.   ⓑ What is located in grid section 4C?

⊘ **Solution**

ⓐ Read the number below the Residence Halls, 4, and the letter to the side, A. So the Residence Halls are in grid section 4A.

ⓑ Find 4 across the bottom of the map and C along the side. Look below the 4 and next to the C. Tiger Field is in grid section 4C.

> **TRY IT :: 11.1**   Use the map in Figure 11.2.

ⓐ Find the grid section of Taylor Hall.   ⓑ What is located in section 3B?

> **TRY IT :: 11.2**   Use the map in Figure 11.2.

ⓐ Find the grid section of the Parking Garage.   ⓑ What is located in section 2C?

Just as maps use a grid system to identify locations, a grid system is used in algebra to show a relationship between two variables in a rectangular coordinate system. To create a rectangular coordinate system, start with a horizontal number line. Show both positive and negative numbers as you did before, using a convenient scale unit. This horizontal number line is called the **x-axis**.

Now, make a vertical number line passing through the x-axis at 0. Put the positive numbers above 0 and the negative numbers below 0. See Figure 11.3. This vertical line is called the **y-axis**.

Vertical grid lines pass through the integers marked on the x-axis. Horizontal grid lines pass through the integers marked on the y-axis. The resulting grid is the rectangular coordinate system.

The rectangular coordinate system is also called the x-y plane, the coordinate plane, or the Cartesian coordinate system

(since it was developed by a mathematician named René Descartes.)

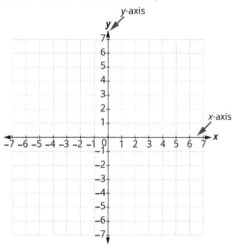

Figure 11.3 The rectangular coordinate system.

The x-axis and the y-axis form the rectangular coordinate system. These axes divide a plane into four areas, called **quadrants**. The quadrants are identified by Roman numerals, beginning on the upper right and proceeding counterclockwise. See Figure 11.4.

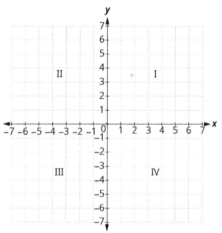

Figure 11.4 The four quadrants of the rectangular coordinate system

In the rectangular coordinate system, every point is represented by an **ordered pair**. The first number in the ordered pair is the x-coordinate of the point, and the second number is the y-coordinate of the point.

Ordered Pair

An ordered pair, (x, y) gives the coordinates of a point in a rectangular coordinate system.

The first number is the x-coordinate.
The second number is the y-coordinate.

So how do the coordinates of a point help you locate a point on the x-y plane?

Let's try locating the point $(2, 5)$. In this ordered pair, the x-coordinate is 2 and the y-coordinate is 5.

We start by locating the x value, 2, on the x-axis. Then we lightly sketch a vertical line through $x = 2$, as shown in Figure 11.5.

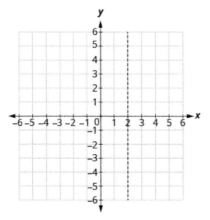

Figure 11.5

Now we locate the y value, 5, on the y-axis and sketch a horizontal line through $y = 5$. The point where these two lines meet is the point with coordinates $(2, 5)$. We plot the point there, as shown in Figure 11.6.

Figure 11.6

EXAMPLE 11.2

Plot $(1, 3)$ and $(3, 1)$ in the same rectangular coordinate system.

⊘ **Solution**

The coordinate values are the same for both points, but the x and y values are reversed. Let's begin with point $(1, 3)$. The x-coordinate is 1 so find 1 on the x-axis and sketch a vertical line through $x = 1$. The y-coordinate is 3 so we find 3 on the y-axis and sketch a horizontal line through $y = 3$. Where the two lines meet, we plot the point $(1, 3)$.

To plot the point $(3, 1)$, we start by locating 3 on the x-axis and sketch a vertical line through $x = 3$. Then we find 1 on the y-axis and sketch a horizontal line through $y = 1$. Where the two lines meet, we plot the point $(3, 1)$.

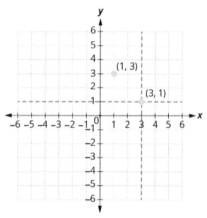

Notice that the order of the coordinates does matter, so, $(1, 3)$ is not the same point as $(3, 1)$.

> **TRY IT :: 11.3**   Plot each point on the same rectangular coordinate system: $(2, 5), (5, 2)$.

> **TRY IT :: 11.4**   Plot each point on the same rectangular coordinate system: $(4, 2), (2, 4)$.

EXAMPLE 11.3

Plot each point in the rectangular coordinate system and identify the quadrant in which the point is located:

ⓐ $(-1, 3)$ ⓑ $(-3, -4)$ ⓒ $(2, -3)$ ⓓ $\left(3, \frac{5}{2}\right)$

Solution

The first number of the coordinate pair is the x-coordinate, and the second number is the y-coordinate.

ⓐ Since $x = -1, y = 3$, the point $(-1, 3)$ is in Quadrant II.

ⓑ Since $x = -3, y = -4$, the point $(-3, -4)$ is in Quadrant III.

ⓒ Since $x = 2, y = -1$, the point $(2, -1)$ is in Quadrant IV.

ⓓ Since $x = 3, y = \frac{5}{2}$, the point $\left(3, \frac{5}{2}\right)$ is in Quadrant I. It may be helpful to write $\frac{5}{2}$ as the mixed number, $2\frac{1}{2}$, or decimal, 2.5. Then we know that the point is halfway between 2 and 3 on the y-axis.

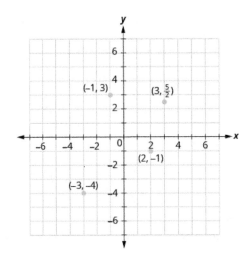

> **TRY IT :: 11.5**

Plot each point on a rectangular coordinate system and identify the quadrant in which the point is located:

ⓐ $(-2, 1)$ ⓑ $(-3, -1)$ ⓒ $(4, -4)$ ⓓ $\left(-4, \frac{3}{2}\right)$

> **TRY IT :: 11.6**

Plot each point on a rectangular coordinate system and identify the quadrant in which the point is located

ⓐ $(-4, 1)$ ⓑ $(-2, 3)$ ⓒ $(2, -5)$ ⓓ $\left(-3, \frac{5}{2}\right)$

How do the signs affect the location of the points?

EXAMPLE 11.4

Plot each point:

ⓐ $(-5, 2)$ ⓑ $(-5, -2)$ ⓒ $(5, 2)$ ⓓ $(5, -2)$

⊘ **Solution**

As we locate the x-coordinate and the y-coordinate, we must be careful with the signs.

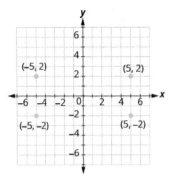

> **TRY IT :: 11.7**   Plot each point:

ⓐ $(4, -3)$ ⓑ $(4, 3)$ ⓒ $(-4, -3)$ ⓓ $(-4, 3)$

> **TRY IT : : 11.8**   Plot each point:

ⓐ $(-1, 4)$ ⓑ $(1, 4)$ ⓒ $(1, -4)$ ⓓ $(-1, -4)$

You may have noticed some patterns as you graphed the points in the two previous examples.

For each point in Quadrant IV, what do you notice about the signs of the coordinates?

What about the signs of the coordinates of the points in the third quadrant? The second quadrant? The first quadrant?

Can you tell just by looking at the coordinates in which quadrant the point $(-2, 5)$ is located? In which quadrant is $(2, -5)$ located?

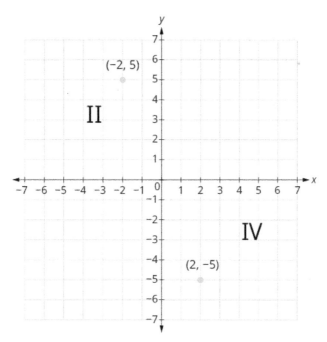

We can summarize sign patterns of the quadrants as follows. Also see Figure 11.7.

Quadrant I	Quadrant II	Quadrant III	Quadrant IV
(x,y)	(x,y)	(x,y)	(x,y)
$(+,+)$	$(-,+)$	$(-,-)$	$(+,-)$

Table 11.1

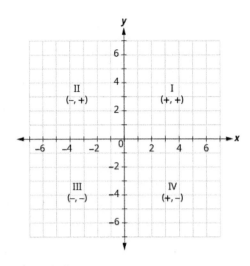

Figure 11.7

What if one coordinate is zero? Where is the point $(0, 4)$ located? Where is the point $(-2, 0)$ located? The point $(0, 4)$ is on the *y*-axis and the point $(-2, 0)$ is on the *x*-axis.

Points on the Axes

Points with a *y*-coordinate equal to 0 are on the *x*-axis, and have coordinates $(a, 0)$.

Points with an *x*-coordinate equal to 0 are on the *y*-axis, and have coordinates $(0, b)$.

What is the ordered pair of the point where the axes cross? At that point both coordinates are zero, so its ordered pair is $(0, 0)$. The point has a special name. It is called the *origin*.

The Origin

The point $(0, 0)$ is called the **origin**. It is the point where the *x*-axis and *y*-axis intersect.

EXAMPLE 11.5

Plot each point on a coordinate grid:

      ⓐ $(0, 5)$ ⓑ $(4, 0)$ ⓒ $(-3, 0)$ ⓓ $(0, 0)$ ⓔ $(0, -1)$

⊘ **Solution**

    ⓐ Since $x = 0,$ the point whose coordinates are $(0, 5)$ is on the *y*-axis.

    ⓑ Since $y = 0,$ the point whose coordinates are $(4, 0)$ is on the *x*-axis.

    ⓒ Since $y = 0,$ the point whose coordinates are $(-3, 0)$ is on the *x*-axis.

    ⓓ Since $x = 0$ and $y = 0,$ the point whose coordinates are $(0, 0)$ is the origin.

ⓔ Since $x = 0$, the point whose coordinates are $(0, -1)$ is on the y-axis.

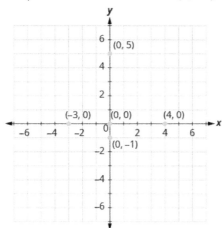

> **TRY IT : : 11.9**   Plot each point on a coordinate grid:

ⓐ $(4, 0)$ ⓑ $(-2, 0)$ ⓒ $(0, 0)$ ⓓ $(0, 2)$ ⓔ $(0, -3)$

> **TRY IT : : 11.10**   Plot each point on a coordinate grid:

ⓐ $(-5, 0)$ ⓑ $(3, 0)$ ⓒ $(0, 0)$ ⓓ $(0, -1)$ ⓔ $(0, 4)$

Identify Points on a Graph

In algebra, being able to identify the coordinates of a point shown on a graph is just as important as being able to plot points. To identify the x-coordinate of a point on a graph, read the number on the x-axis directly above or below the point. To identify the y-coordinate of a point, read the number on the y-axis directly to the left or right of the point. Remember, to write the ordered pair using the correct order (x, y).

EXAMPLE 11.6

Name the ordered pair of each point shown:

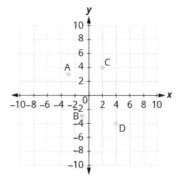

Ⓥ **Solution**

Point A is above -3 on the x-axis, so the x-coordinate of the point is -3. The point is to the left of 3 on the y-axis, so the y-coordinate of the point is 3. The coordinates of the point are $(-3, 3)$.

Point B is below -1 on the x-axis, so the x-coordinate of the point is -1. The point is to the left of -3 on the y-axis, so the y-coordinate of the point is -3. The coordinates of the point are $(-1, -3)$.

Point C is above 2 on the x-axis, so the x-coordinate of the point is 2. The point is to the right of 4 on the y-axis, so the y-coordinate of the point is 4. The coordinates of the point are $(2, 4)$.

Point D is below 4 on the x-axis, so the x-coordinate of the point is 4. The point is to the right of −4 on the y-axis, so the y-coordinate of the point is −4. The coordinates of the point are (4, −4).

> | **TRY IT : : 11.11**   Name the ordered pair of each point shown:

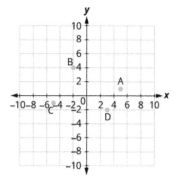

> | **TRY IT : : 11.12**   Name the ordered pair of each point shown:

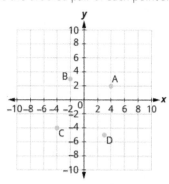

EXAMPLE 11.7

Name the ordered pair of each point shown:

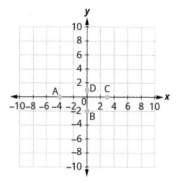

⊘ **Solution**

Point A is on the *x*-axis at $x = -4$.	The coordinates of point A are $(-4, 0)$.
Point B is on the *y*-axis at $y = -2$	The coordinates of point B are $(0, -2)$.
Point C is on the *x*-axis at $x = 3$.	The coordinates of point C are $(3, 0)$.
Point D is on the *y*-axis at $y = 1$.	The coordinates of point D are $(0, 1)$.

> **TRY IT : : 11.13**   Name the ordered pair of each point shown:

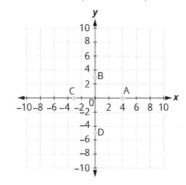

> **TRY IT : : 11.14**   Name the ordered pair of each point shown:

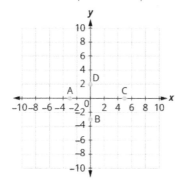

Verify Solutions to an Equation in Two Variables

All the equations we solved so far have been equations with one variable. In almost every case, when we solved the equation we got exactly one solution. The process of solving an equation ended with a statement such as $x = 4$. Then we checked the solution by substituting back into the equation.

Here's an example of a linear equation in one variable, and its one solution.

$$3x + 5 = 17$$
$$3x = 12$$
$$x = 4$$

But equations can have more than one variable. Equations with two variables can be written in the general form $Ax + By = C$. An equation of this form is called a linear equation in two variables.

Linear Equation

An equation of the form $Ax + By = C$, where A and B are not both zero, is called a linear equation in two variables.

Notice that the word "line" is in linear.

Here is an example of a linear equation in two variables, x and y:

$$Ax + By = C$$

$$x + 4y = 8$$

$$A = 1, B = 4, C = 8$$

Is $y = -5x + 1$ a linear equation? It does not appear to be in the form $Ax + By = C$. But we could rewrite it in this form.

$$y = -5x + 1$$

Add $5x$ to both sides.	$y + 5x = -5x + 1 + 5x$
Simplify.	$y + 5x = 1$
Use the Commutative Property to put it in $Ax + By = C$.	$Ax + By = C$ $5x + y = 1$

By rewriting $y = -5x + 1$ as $5x + y = 1$, we can see that it is a linear equation in two variables because it can be written in the form $Ax + By = C$.

Linear equations in two variables have infinitely many solutions. For every number that is substituted for x, there is a corresponding y value. This pair of values is a **solution to the linear equation** and is represented by the ordered pair (x, y). When we substitute these values of x and y into the equation, the result is a true statement because the value on the left side is equal to the value on the right side.

Solution to a Linear Equation in Two Variables

An ordered pair (x, y) is a solution to the linear equation $Ax + By = C$, if the equation is a true statement when the x- and y-values of the ordered pair are substituted into the equation.

EXAMPLE 11.8

Determine which ordered pairs are solutions of the equation $x + 4y = 8$:

ⓐ $(0, 2)$ ⓑ $(2, -4)$ ⓒ $(-4, 3)$

Solution

Substitute the x- and y-values from each ordered pair into the equation and determine if the result is a true statement.

ⓐ $(0, 2)$	ⓑ $(2, -4)$	ⓒ $(-4, 3)$
$x = 0, y = 2$	$x = 2, y = -4$	$x = -4, y = 3$
$x + 4y = 8$	$x + 4y = 8$	$x + 4y = 8$
$0 + 4 \cdot 2 \overset{?}{=} 8$	$2 + 4(-4) \overset{?}{=} 8$	$-4 + 4 \cdot 3 \overset{?}{=} 8$
$0 + 8 \overset{?}{=} 8$	$2 + (-16) \overset{?}{=} 8$	$-4 + 12 \overset{?}{=} 8$
$8 = 8\,\checkmark$	$-14 \neq 8$	$8 = 8\,\checkmark$
$(0, 2)$ is a solution.	$(2, -4)$ is not a solution.	$(-4, 3)$ is a solution.

> **TRY IT :: 11.15**   Determine which ordered pairs are solutions to the given equation: $2x + 3y = 6$

ⓐ $(3, 0)$ ⓑ $(2, 0)$ ⓒ $(6, -2)$

> **TRY IT :: 11.16**   Determine which ordered pairs are solutions to the given equation: $4x - y = 8$

ⓐ $(0, 8)$ ⓑ $(2, 0)$ ⓒ $(1, -4)$

EXAMPLE 11.9

Determine which ordered pairs are solutions of the equation. $y = 5x - 1$:

ⓐ $(0, -1)$ ⓑ $(1, 4)$ ⓒ $(-2, -7)$

⊘ Solution

Substitute the x- and y-values from each ordered pair into the equation and determine if it results in a true statement.

ⓐ $(0, -1)$

$x = 0, y = -1$
$y = 5x - 1$
$-1 \overset{?}{=} 5(0) - 1$
$-1 \overset{?}{=} 0 - 1$
$-1 = -1 ✓$

$(0, -1)$ is a solution.

ⓑ $(1, 4)$

$x = 1, y = 4$
$y = 5x - 1$
$4 \overset{?}{=} 5(1) - 1$
$4 \overset{?}{=} 5 - 1$
$4 = 4 ✓$

$(1, 4)$ is a solution.

ⓒ $(-2, -7)$

$x = -2, y = -7$
$y = 5x - 1$
$-7 \overset{?}{=} 5(-2) - 1$
$-7 \overset{?}{=} -10 - 1$
$-7 \neq -11$

$(-2, -7)$ is not a solution.

> **TRY IT :: 11.17**   Determine which ordered pairs are solutions of the given equation: $y = 4x - 3$

ⓐ $(0, 3)$ ⓑ $(1, 1)$ ⓒ $(1, 1)$

> **TRY IT :: 11.18**   Determine which ordered pairs are solutions of the given equation: $y = -2x + 6$

ⓐ $(0, 6)$ ⓑ $(1, 4)$ ⓒ $(-2, -2)$

Complete a Table of Solutions to a Linear Equation

In the previous examples, we substituted the x- and y-values of a given ordered pair to determine whether or not it was a solution to a linear equation. But how do we find the ordered pairs if they are not given? One way is to choose a value for x and then solve the equation for y. Or, choose a value for y and then solve for x.

We'll start by looking at the solutions to the equation $y = 5x - 1$ we found in Example 11.9. We can summarize this information in a table of solutions.

$y = 5x - 1$		
x	y	(x, y)
0	−1	$(0, -1)$
1	4	$(1, 4)$

To find a third solution, we'll let $x = 2$ and solve for y.

	$y = 5x - 1$
Substitute $x = 2$.	$y = 5(2) - 1$
Multiply.	$y = 10 - 1$
Simplify.	$y = 9$

The ordered pair is a solution to $y = 5x - 1$. We will add it to the table.

$y = 5x - 1$		
x	y	(x, y)
0	−1	$(0, -1)$
1	4	$(1, 4)$
2	9	$(2, 9)$

We can find more solutions to the equation by substituting any value of x or any value of y and solving the resulting equation to get another ordered pair that is a solution. There are an infinite number of solutions for this equation.

EXAMPLE 11.10

Complete the table to find three solutions to the equation $y = 4x - 2$:

$y = 4x - 2$		
x	y	(x, y)
0		
−1		
2		

Solution

Substitute $x = 0$, $x = -1$, and $x = 2$ into $y = 4x - 2$.

$x = 0$	$x = -1$	$x = 2$
$y = 4x - 2$	$y = 4x - 2$	$y = 4x - 2$
$y = 4 \cdot 0 - 2$	$y = 4(-1) - 2$	$y = 4 \cdot 2 - 2$
$y = 0 - 2$	$y = -4 - 2$	$y = 8 - 2$
$y = -2$	$y = -6$	$y = 6$
$(0, -2)$	$(-1, -6)$	$(2, 6)$

The results are summarized in the table.

$y = 4x - 2$		
x	y	(x, y)
0	-2	$(0, -2)$
-1	-6	$(-1, -6)$
2	6	$(2, 6)$

> **TRY IT : : 11.19**   Complete the table to find three solutions to the equation: $y = 3x - 1$.

$y = 3x - 1$		
x	y	(x, y)
0		
-1		
2		

> **TRY IT : : 11.20**   Complete the table to find three solutions to the equation: $y = 6x + 1$

$y = 6x + 1$		
x	y	(x, y)
0		
1		
-2		

EXAMPLE 11.11

Complete the table to find three solutions to the equation $5x - 4y = 20$:

$5x - 4y = 20$		
x	y	(x, y)
0		
	0	
	5	

⊘ **Solution**

$x = 0$	$y = 0$	$y = 5$
$5x - 4y = 20$	$5x - 4y = 20$	$5x - 4y = 20$
$5 \cdot 0 - 4y = 20$	$5x - 4 \cdot 0 = 20$	$5x - 4 \cdot 5 = 20$
$0 - 4y = 20$	$5x - 0 = 20$	$5x - 20 = 20$
$-4y = 20$	$5x = 20$	$5x = 40$
$y = -5$	$x = 4$	$x = 8$
$(0, -5)$	$(4, 0)$	$(8, 5)$

The results are summarized in the table.

$5x - 4y = 20$		
x	y	(x, y)
0	-5	$(0, -5)$
4	0	$(4, 0)$
8	5	$(8, 5)$

> **TRY IT :: 11.21**   Complete the table to find three solutions to the equation: $2x - 5y = 20$.

$2x - 5y = 20$		
x	y	(x, y)
0		
	0	
-5		

> **TRY IT :: 11.22**   Complete the table to find three solutions to the equation: $3x - 4y = 12$.

$3x - 4y = 12$		
x	y	(x, y)
0		
	0	
−4		

Find Solutions to Linear Equations in Two Variables

To find a solution to a linear equation, we can choose any number we want to substitute into the equation for either x or y. We could choose $1, 100, 1,000,$ or any other value we want. But it's a good idea to choose a number that's easy to work with. We'll usually choose 0 as one of our values.

EXAMPLE 11.12

Find a solution to the equation $3x + 2y = 6$.

⊘ **Solution**

Step 1: Choose any value for one of the variables in the equation.		We can substitute any value we want for x or any value for y.
		Let's pick $x = 0$.
		What is the value of y if $x = 0$?

Step 2: Substitute that value into the equation. Solve for the other variable.	Substitute 0 for x.	$3x + 2y = 6$
	Simplify.	$3 \cdot 0 + 2y = 6$
		$0 + 2y = 6$
	Divide both sides by 2.	$2y = 6$
		$y = 3$

| **Step 3:** Write the solution as an ordered pair. | So, when $x = 0$, $y = 3$. | This solution is represented by the ordered pair $(0, 3)$. |

Step 4: Check.	Substitute $x = 0, y = 3$ into the equation $3x + 2y = 6$.	$3x + 2y = 6$
		$3 \cdot 0 + 2 \cdot 3 \overset{?}{=} 6$
	Is the result a true equation? Yes!	$0 + 6 \overset{?}{=} 6$
		$6 = 6 \checkmark$

> **TRY IT :: 11.23**   Find a solution to the equation: $4x + 3y = 12$.

> **TRY IT :: 11.24**   Find a solution to the equation: $2x + 4y = 8$.

We said that linear equations in two variables have infinitely many solutions, and we've just found one of them. Let's find some other solutions to the equation $3x + 2y = 6$.

EXAMPLE 11.13

Find three more solutions to the equation $3x + 2y = 6$.

⊘ **Solution**

To find solutions to $3x + 2y = 6$, choose a value for x or y. Remember, we can choose any value we want for x or y. Here we chose 1 for x, and 0 and -3 for y.

	$y = 0$	$x = 1$	$y = -3$
	$3x + 2y = 6$	$3x + 2y = 6$	$3x + 2y = 6$
Substitute it into the equation.	$3x + 2(0) = 6$	$3(1) + 2y = 6$	$3x + 2(-3) = 6$
Simplify.	$3x + 0 = 6$	$3 + 2y = 6$	$3x - 6 = 6$
Solve.	$3x = 6$	$2y = 3$	$3x = 12$
	$x = 2$	$y = \dfrac{3}{2}$	$x = 4$
Write the ordered pair.	$(2, 0)$	$(1, \frac{3}{2})$	$(4, -3)$

Check your answers.

$(2, 0)$	$(1, \frac{3}{2})$	$(4, -3)$
$3x + 2y = 6$	$3x + 2y = 6$	$3x + 2y = 6$
$3 \cdot 2 + 2 \cdot 0 \overset{?}{=} 6$	$3 \cdot 1 + 2 \cdot \frac{3}{2} \overset{?}{=} 6$	$3 \cdot 4 + 2(-3) \overset{?}{=} 6$
$6 + 0 \overset{?}{=} 6$	$3 + 3 \overset{?}{=} 6$	$12 + (-6) \overset{?}{=} 6$
$6 = 6 ✓$	$6 = 6 ✓$	$6 = 6 ✓$

So $(2, 0)$, $\left(1, \frac{3}{2}\right)$ and $(4, -3)$ are all solutions to the equation $3x + 2y = 6$. In the previous example, we found that $(0, 3)$ is a solution, too. We can list these solutions in a table.

$3x + 2y = 6$		
x	y	(x, y)
0	3	$(0, 3)$
2	0	$(2, 0)$
1	$\frac{3}{2}$	$(1, \frac{3}{2})$
4	−3	$(4, -3)$

> **TRY IT : : 11.25**   Find three solutions to the equation: $2x + 3y = 6$.

> **TRY IT : : 11.26**   Find three solutions to the equation: $4x + 2y = 8$.

Let's find some solutions to another equation now.

EXAMPLE 11.14

Find three solutions to the equation $x - 4y = 8$.

⊘ **Solution**

	$x - 4y = 8$	$x - 4y = 8$	$x - 4y = 8$
Choose a value for x or y.	$x = 0$	$y = 0$	$y = 3$
Substitute it into the equation.	$0 - 4y = 8$	$x - 4 \cdot 0 = 8$	$x - 4 \cdot 3 = 8$
Solve.	$-4y = 8$ $y = -2$	$x - 0 = 8$ $x = 8$	$x - 12 = 8$ $x = 20$
Write the ordered pair.	$(0, -2)$	$(8, 0)$	$(20, 3)$

So $(0, -2)$, $(8, 0)$, and $(20, 3)$ are three solutions to the equation $x - 4y = 8$.

$x - 4y = 8$		
x	y	(x, y)
0	−2	$(0, -2)$
8	0	$(8, 0)$
20	3	$(20, 3)$

Remember, there are an infinite number of solutions to each linear equation. Any point you find is a solution if it makes the equation true.

> **TRY IT : : 11.27**   Find three solutions to the equation: $4x + y = 8$.

> **TRY IT : : 11.28**   Find three solutions to the equation: $x + 5y = 10$.

▶ **MEDIA : :** ACCESS ADDITIONAL ONLINE RESOURCES

- Plotting Points (http://openstaxcollege.org/l/24plotpoints)
- Identifying Quadrants (http://openstaxcollege.org/l/24quadrants)
- Verifying Solution to Linear Equation (http://openstaxcollege.org/l/24verlineq)

11.1 EXERCISES

Practice Makes Perfect

Plot Points on a Rectangular Coordinate System

In the following exercises, plot each point on a coordinate grid.

1. (3, 2)

2. (4, 1)

3. (1, 5)

4. (3, 4)

5. (4, 1), (1, 4)

6. (3, 2), (2, 3)

7. (3, 4), (4, 3)

In the following exercises, plot each point on a coordinate grid and identify the quadrant in which the point is located.

8.
ⓐ (−4, 2)   ⓑ (−1, −2)
ⓒ (3, −5)   ⓓ $\left(2, \frac{5}{2}\right)$

9.
ⓐ (−2, −3)   ⓑ (3, −3)
ⓒ (−4, 1)   ⓓ $\left(1, \frac{3}{2}\right)$

10.
ⓐ (−1, 1)   ⓑ (−2, −1)
ⓒ (1, −4)   ⓓ $\left(3, \frac{7}{2}\right)$

11.
ⓐ (3, -2)   ⓑ (−3, 2)
ⓒ (-3, −2)   ⓓ (3, 2)

12.
ⓐ (4, -1)   ⓑ (−4, 1)
ⓒ (-4, -1)   ⓓ (4, 1)

13.
ⓐ (−2, 0)
ⓑ (−3, 0)
ⓒ (0, 4)
ⓓ (0, 2)

Identify Points on a Graph

In the following exercises, name the ordered pair of each point shown.

14.

15.

16.

17.

18.

19.

20.

Verify Solutions to an Equation in Two Variables

In the following exercises, determine which ordered pairs are solutions to the given equation.

21. $2x + y = 6$

  ⓐ (1, 4) ⓑ (3, 0)

  ⓒ (2, 3)

22. $x + 3y = 9$

  ⓐ (0, 3) ⓑ (6, 1)

  ⓒ (-3, -3)

23. $4x - 2y = 8$

  ⓐ (3, 2) ⓑ (1, 4)

  ⓒ (0, -4)

24. $3x - 2y = 12$

  ⓐ (4, 0) ⓑ (2, -3)

  ⓒ (1, 6)

25. $y = 4x + 3$

  ⓐ (4, 3) ⓑ (-1, -1)

  ⓒ $(\frac{1}{2}, 5)$

26. $y = 2x - 5$

  ⓐ (0, -5) ⓑ (2, 1)

  ⓒ $(\frac{1}{2}, -4)$

27. $y = \frac{1}{2}x - 1$

  ⓐ (2, 0) ⓑ (-6, -4)

  ⓒ (-4, -1)

28. $y = \frac{1}{3}x + 1$

  ⓐ (-3, 0) ⓑ (9, 4)

  ⓒ (-6, -1)

Find Solutions to Linear Equations in Two Variables

In the following exercises, complete the table to find solutions to each linear equation.

29. $y = 2x - 4$

x	y	(x, y)
−1		
0		
2		

30. $y = 3x - 1$

x	y	(x, y)
−1		
0		
2		

31. $y = -x + 5$

x	y	(x, y)
−2		
0		
3		

32. $y = \frac{1}{3}x + 1$

x	y	(x, y)
0		
3		
6		

33. $y = -\frac{3}{2}x - 2$

x	y	(x, y)
−2		
0		
2		

34. $x + 2y = 8$

x	y	(x, y)
0		
4		
	0	

Everyday Math

35. Weight of a baby Mackenzie recorded her baby's weight every two months. The baby's age, in months, and weight, in pounds, are listed in the table, and shown as an ordered pair in the third column.

ⓐ Plot the points on a coordinate grid.

Age	Weight	(x, y)
0	7	(0, 7)
2	11	(2, 11)
4	15	(4, 15)
6	16	(6, 16)
8	19	(8, 19)
10	20	(10, 20)
12	21	(12, 21)

ⓑ Why is only Quadrant I needed?

36. Weight of a child Latresha recorded her son's height and weight every year. His height, in inches, and weight, in pounds, are listed in the table, and shown as an ordered pair in the third column.

ⓐ Plot the points on a coordinate grid.

Height x	Weight y	(x, y)
28	22	(28, 22)
31	27	(31, 27)
33	33	(33, 33)
37	35	(37, 35)
40	41	(40, 41)
42	45	(42, 45)

ⓑ Why is only Quadrant I needed?

Writing Exercises

37. Have you ever used a map with a rectangular coordinate system? Describe the map and how you used it.

38. How do you determine if an ordered pair is a solution to a given equation?

Self Check

ⓐ *After completing the exercises, use this checklist to evaluate your mastery of the objectives of this section.*

I can...	Confidently	With some help	No-I don't get it!
plot points on a rectangular coordinate system.			
identify points on a graph.			
verify solutions to an equation in two variables.			
complete a table of solutions to a linear equation.			
find solutions to linear equations in two variables.			

ⓑ *If most of your checks were:*

...confidently. Congratulations! You have achieved the objectives in this section. Reflect on the study skills you used so that you can continue to use them. What did you do to become confident of your ability to do these things? Be specific.

...with some help. This must be addressed quickly because topics you do not master become potholes in your road to success. In math, every topic builds upon previous work. It is important to make sure you have a strong foundation before you move on. Who can you ask for help? Your fellow classmates and instructor are good resources. Is there a place on campus where math tutors are available? Can your study skills be improved?

...no—I don't get it! This is a warning sign and you must not ignore it. You should get help right away or you will quickly be overwhelmed. See your instructor as soon as you can to discuss your situation. Together you can come up with a plan to get you the help you need.

Graphing Linear Equations

Learning Objectives

By the end of this section, you will be able to:
- Recognize the relation between the solutions of an equation and its graph
- Graph a linear equation by plotting points
- Graph vertical and horizontal lines

Be Prepared!

Before you get started, take this readiness quiz.

1. Evaluate: $3x + 2$ when $x = -1$.
   If you missed this problem, review Example 3.56.

2. Solve the formula: $5x + 2y = 20$ for y.
   If you missed this problem, review Example 9.62.

3. Simplify: $\frac{3}{8}(-24)$.
   If you missed this problem, review Example 4.28.

Recognize the Relation Between the Solutions of an Equation and its Graph

In Use the Rectangular Coordinate System, we found a few solutions to the equation $3x + 2y = 6$. They are listed in the table below. So, the ordered pairs $(0, 3)$, $(2, 0)$, $\left(1, \frac{3}{2}\right)$, $(4, -3)$, are some solutions to the equation $3x + 2y = 6$. We can plot these solutions in the rectangular coordinate system as shown on the graph at right.

$3x + 2y = 6$		
x	y	(x, y)
0	3	$(0, 3)$
2	0	$(2, 0)$
1	$\frac{3}{2}$	$\left(1, \frac{3}{2}\right)$
4	-3	$(4, -3)$

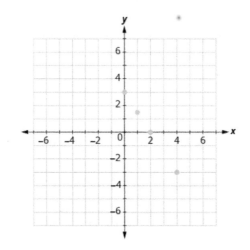

Notice how the points line up perfectly? We connect the points with a straight line to get the graph of the equation $3x + 2y = 6$. Notice the arrows on the ends of each side of the line. These arrows indicate the line continues.

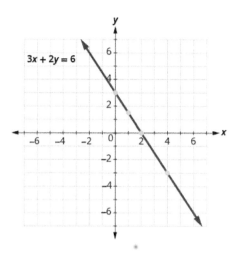

Every point on the line is a solution of the equation. Also, every solution of this equation is a point on this line. Points not on the line are *not* solutions!

Notice that the point whose coordinates are $(-2, 6)$ is on the line shown in Figure 11.8. If you substitute $x = -2$ and $y = 6$ into the equation, you find that it is a solution to the equation.

Test $(-2, 6)$:

$$3x + 2y = 6$$
$$3(-2) + 2(6) \overset{?}{=} 6$$
$$-6 + 12 \overset{?}{=} 6$$
$$6 = 6 \checkmark$$

So $(-2, 6)$ is a solution to the equation.

What about $(4, 1)$?

$$3x + 2y = 6$$
$$3 \cdot 4 + 2 \cdot 1 \overset{?}{=} 6$$
$$12 + 2 \overset{?}{=} 6$$
$$14 \neq 6$$

Figure 11.8

So $(4, 1)$ is not a solution to the equation $3x + 2y = 6$. Therefore the point $(4, 1)$ is not on the line.

This is an example of the saying," A picture is worth a thousand words." The line shows you all the solutions to the equation. Every point on the line is a solution of the equation. And, every solution of this equation is on this line. This line is called the *graph* of the equation $3x + 2y = 6$.

Graph of a Linear Equation

The graph of a linear equation $Ax + By = C$ is a straight line.

- Every point on the line is a solution of the equation.
- Every solution of this equation is a point on this line.

EXAMPLE 11.15

The graph of $y = 2x - 3$ is shown below.

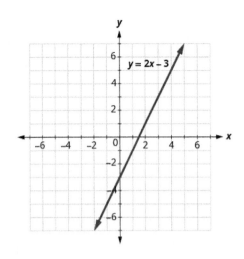

For each order pair decide

ⓐ Is the ordered pair a solution to the equation?   ⓑ Is the point on the line?

ⓐ $(0, 3)$ ⓑ $(3, -3)$ ⓒ $(2, -3)$ ⓓ $(-1, -5)$

✓ Solution

Substitute the x- and y-values into the equation to check if the ordered pair is a solution to the equation.

ⓐ

(a) $(0, -3)$	(b) $(3, 3)$	(c) $(2, -3)$	(d) $(-1, -5)$
$y = 2x - 3$	$y = 2x - 3$	$y = 2x - 3$	$y = 2x - 3$
$-3 \overset{?}{=} 2(0) - 3$	$3 \overset{?}{=} 2(3) - 3$	$-3 \overset{?}{=} 2(2) - 3$	$-5 \overset{?}{=} 2(-1) - 3$
$-3 = -3$ ✓	$3 = 3$ ✓	$-3 \neq 1$	$-5 = -5$ ✓
$(0, -3)$ is a solution.	$(3, 3)$ is a solution.	$(2, -3)$ is not a solution.	$(-1, -5)$ is a solution.

ⓑ Plot the points A: $(0, -3)$ B: $(3, 3)$ C: $(2, -3)$ and D: $(-1, -5)$.

The points $(0, -3)$, $(3, 3)$, and $(-1, -5)$ are on the line $y = 2x - 3$, and the point $(2, -3)$ is not on the line.

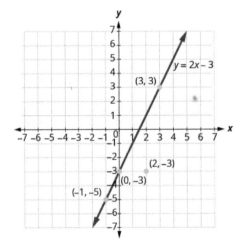

The points which are solutions to $y = 2x - 3$ are on the line, but the point which is not a solution is not on the line.

> **TRY IT : : 11.29**   The graph of $y = 3x - 1$ is shown.

For each ordered pair, decide

ⓐ is the ordered pair a solution to the equation?   ⓑ is the point on the line?

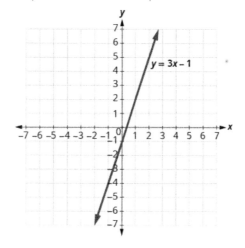

1. $(0, -1)$

2. $(2, 2)$

3. $(3, -1)$

4. $(-1, -4)$

Graph a Linear Equation by Plotting Points

There are several methods that can be used to graph a linear equation. The method we used at the start of this section to graph is called plotting points, or the Point-Plotting Method.

Let's graph the equation $y = 2x + 1$ by plotting points.

We start by finding three points that are solutions to the equation. We can choose any value for x or y, and then solve for the other variable.

Since y is isolated on the left side of the equation, it is easier to choose values for x. We will use $0, 1,$ and -2 for x for this example. We substitute each value of x into the equation and solve for y.

$x = -2$	$x = 0$	$x = 1$
$y = 2x + 1$	$y = 2x + 1$	$y = 2x + 1$
$y = 2(-2) + 1$	$y = 2(0) + 1$	$y = 2(1) + 1$
$y = -4 + 1$	$y = 0 + 1$	$y = 2 + 1$
$y = -3$	$y = 1$	$y = 3$
$(-2, -3)$	$(0, 1)$	$(1, 3)$

We can organize the solutions in a table. See Table 11.16.

$y = 2x + 1$		
x	y	(x, y)
0	1	(0, 1)
1	3	(1, 3)
−2	−3	(−2, −3)

Table 11.16

Now we plot the points on a rectangular coordinate system. Check that the points line up. If they did not line up, it would mean we made a mistake and should double-check all our work. See Figure 11.9.

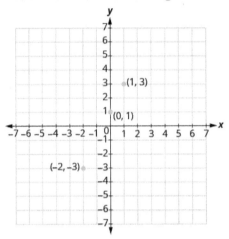

Figure 11.9

Draw the line through the three points. Extend the line to fill the grid and put arrows on both ends of the line. The line is the graph of $y = 2x + 1$.

Figure 11.10

HOW TO :: GRAPH A LINEAR EQUATION BY PLOTTING POINTS.

Step 1. Find three points whose coordinates are solutions to the equation. Organize them in a table.

Step 2. Plot the points on a rectangular coordinate system. Check that the points line up. If they do not, carefully check your work.

Step 3. Draw the line through the points. Extend the line to fill the grid and put arrows on both ends of the line.

It is true that it only takes two points to determine a line, but it is a good habit to use three points. If you plot only two points and one of them is incorrect, you can still draw a line but it will not represent the solutions to the equation. It will be the wrong line. If you use three points, and one is incorrect, the points will not line up. This tells you something is wrong and you need to check your work. See Figure 11.11.

(a)   (b)

Figure 11.11 Look at the difference between (a) and (b). All three points in (a) line up so we can draw one line through them. The three points in (b) do not line up. We cannot draw a single straight line through all three points.

EXAMPLE 11.16

Graph the equation $y = -3x$.

Solution

Find three points that are solutions to the equation. It's easier to choose values for $x,$ and solve for $y.$ Do you see why?

$x = 0$	$x = 1$	$x = -2$
$y = -3x$	$y = -3x$	$y = -3x$
$y = -3(0)$	$y = -3(\ )$	$y = -3(-2)$
$y = 0$	$y = -3$	$y = 6$
$(0, 0)$	$(1, 3)$	$(-2, 6)$

List the points in a table.

$y = -3x$		
x	y	(x, y)
0	0	$(0, 0)$
1	3	$(1, -3)$
-2	6	$(-2, 6)$

Plot the points, check that they line up, and draw the line as shown.

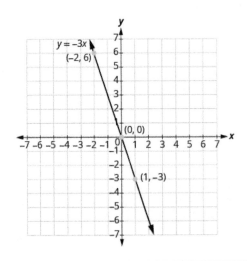

> **TRY IT : :** 11.30   Graph the equation by plotting points: $y = -4x$.

> **TRY IT : :** 11.31   Graph the equation by plotting points: $y = x$.

When an equation includes a fraction as the coefficient of x, we can substitute any numbers for x. But the math is easier if we make 'good' choices for the values of x. This way we will avoid fraction answers, which are hard to graph precisely.

EXAMPLE 11.17

Graph the equation $y = \frac{1}{2}x + 3$.

⊘ **Solution**

Find three points that are solutions to the equation. Since this equation has the fraction $\frac{1}{2}$ as a coefficient of x, we will choose values of x carefully. We will use zero as one choice and multiples of 2 for the other choices.

$x = 0$	$x = 2$	$x = 4$
$y = \frac{1}{2}x + 3$	$y = \frac{1}{2}x + 3$	$y = \frac{1}{2}x + 3$
$y = \frac{1}{2}(0) + 3$	$y = \frac{1}{2}(2) + 3$	$y = \frac{1}{2}(4) + 3$
$y = 3$	$y = 4$	$y = 5$
$(0, 3)$	$(2, 4)$	$(4, 5)$

The points are shown in the table.

$y = \frac{1}{2}x + 3$		
x	y	(x, y)
0	3	$(0, 3)$
2	4	$(2, 4)$
4	5	$(4, 5)$

Plot the points, check that they line up, and draw the line as shown.

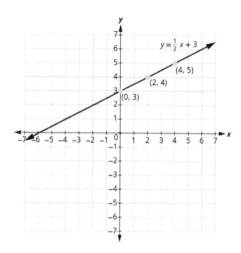

> **TRY IT : : 11.32**   Graph the equation: $y = \frac{1}{3}x - 1$.

> **TRY IT : : 11.33**   Graph the equation: $y = \frac{1}{4}x + 2$.

So far, all the equations we graphed had y given in terms of x. Now we'll graph an equation with x and y on the same side.

EXAMPLE 11.18

Graph the equation $x + y = 5$.

⊘ **Solution**

Find three points that are solutions to the equation. Remember, you can start with *any* value of x or y.

$x = 0$	$x = 1$	$x = 4$
$x + y = 5$	$x + y = 5$	$x + y = 5$
$0 + y = 5$	$1 + y = 5$	$4 + y = 5$
$y = 5$	$y = 4$	$y = 1$
$(0, 5)$	$(1, 4)$	$(4, 1)$

We list the points in a table.

$x + y = 5$		
x	y	(x, y)
0	5	$(0, 5)$
1	4	$(1, 4)$
4	1	$(4, 1)$

Then plot the points, check that they line up, and draw the line.

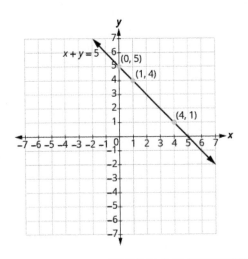

> | **TRY IT : :** 11.34   Graph the equation: $x + y = -2$.

> | **TRY IT : :** 11.35   Graph the equation: $x - y = 6$.

In the previous example, the three points we found were easy to graph. But this is not always the case. Let's see what happens in the equation $2x + y = 3$. If y is 0, what is the value of x?

$$2x + y = 3$$
$$2x + 0 = 3$$
$$2x = 3$$
$$x = \frac{3}{2}$$

The solution is the point $\left(\frac{3}{2}, 0\right)$. This point has a fraction for the x-coordinate. While we could graph this point, it is hard to be precise graphing fractions. Remember in the example $y = \frac{1}{2}x + 3$, we carefully chose values for x so as not to graph fractions at all. If we solve the equation $2x + y = 3$ for y, it will be easier to find three solutions to the equation.

$$2x + y = 3$$
$$y = -2x + 3$$

Now we can choose values for x that will give coordinates that are integers. The solutions for $x = 0$, $x = 1$, and $x = -1$ are shown.

$y = -2x + 3$		
x	y	(x, y)
0	5	$(-1, 5)$
1	3	$(0, 3)$
-1	1	$(1, 1)$

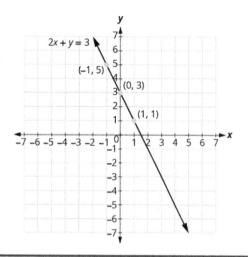

EXAMPLE 11.19

Graph the equation $3x + y = -1$.

⊘ Solution

Find three points that are solutions to the equation.

First, solve the equation for y.

$$3x + y = -1$$
$$y = -3x - 1$$

We'll let x be $0, 1,$ and -1 to find three points. The ordered pairs are shown in the table. Plot the points, check that they line up, and draw the line.

$y = -3x - 1$		
x	y	(x, y)
0	-1	$(0, -1)$
1	-4	$(1, -4)$
-1	2	$(-1, 2)$

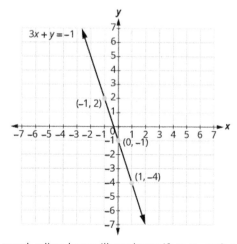

If you can choose any three points to graph a line, how will you know if your graph matches the one shown in the answers in the book? If the points where the graphs cross the x- and y-axes are the same, the graphs match.

> **TRY IT :: 11.36**   Graph each equation: $2x + y = 2$.

> **TRY IT :: 11.37**   Graph each equation: $4x + y = -3$.

Graph Vertical and Horizontal Lines

Can we graph an equation with only one variable? Just x and no y, or just y without an x? How will we make a table of values to get the points to plot?

Let's consider the equation $x = -3$. The equation says that x is always equal to -3, so its value does not depend on y. No matter what y is, the value of x is always -3.

To make a table of solutions, we write -3 for all the x values. Then choose any values for y. Since x does not depend on y, you can chose any numbers you like. But to fit the size of our coordinate graph, we'll use $1, 2,$ and 3 for the y-coordinates as shown in the table.

$x = -3$		
x	y	(x, y)
-3	1	$(-3, 1)$
-3	2	$(-3, 2)$
-3	3	$(-3, 3)$

Then plot the points and connect them with a straight line. Notice in Figure 11.12 that the graph is a **vertical line**.

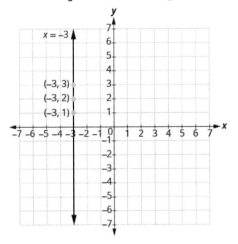

Figure 11.12

Vertical Line

A vertical line is the graph of an equation that can be written in the form $x = a$.

The line passes through the x-axis at $(a, 0)$.

EXAMPLE 11.20

Graph the equation $x = 2$. What type of line does it form?

⊘ **Solution**

The equation has only variable, x, and x is always equal to 2. We make a table where x is always 2 and we put in any values for y.

$x = 2$		
x	y	(x, y)
2	1	$(2, 1)$
2	2	$(2, 2)$
2	3	$(2, 3)$

Plot the points and connect them as shown.

The graph is a vertical line passing through the x-axis at 2.

> **TRY IT : : 11.38**   Graph the equation: $x = 5$.

> **TRY IT : : 11.39**   Graph the equation: $x = -2$.

What if the equation has y but no x? Let's graph the equation $y = 4$. This time the y-value is a constant, so in this equation y does not depend on x.

To make a table of solutions, write 4 for all the y values and then choose any values for x.

We'll use 0, 2, and 4 for the x-values.

y = 4		
x	y	(x, y)
0	4	(0, 4)
2	4	(2, 4)
4	4	(4, 4)

Plot the points and connect them, as shown in Figure 11.13. This graph is a **horizontal line** passing through the y-axis at 4.

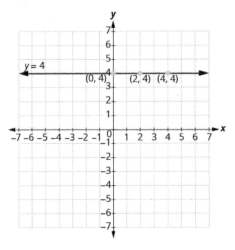

Figure 11.13

Horizontal Line

A horizontal line is the graph of an equation that can be written in the form $y = b$.

The line passes through the y-axis at $(0, b)$.

EXAMPLE 11.21

Graph the equation $y = -1$.

⊘ **Solution**

The equation $y = -1$ has only variable, y. The value of y is constant. All the ordered pairs in the table have the same y-coordinate, -1. We choose 0, 3, and -3 as values for x.

y = −1		
x	y	(x, y)
−3	−1	(−3, −1)
0	−1	(0, −1)
3	−1	(3, −1)

The graph is a horizontal line passing through the y-axis at -1 as shown.

> **TRY IT : : 11.40**   Graph the equation: $y = -4$.

> **TRY IT : : 11.41**   Graph the equation: $y = 3$.

The equations for vertical and horizontal lines look very similar to equations like $y = 4x$. What is the difference between the equations $y = 4x$ and $y = 4$?

The equation $y = 4x$ has both x and y. The value of y depends on the value of x. The y-coordinate changes according to the value of x.

The equation $y = 4$ has only one variable. The value of y is constant. The y-coordinate is always 4. It does not depend on the value of x.

y = 4x		
x	y	(x, y)
0	0	(0, 0)
1	4	(1, 4)
2	8	(2, 8)

y = 4		
x	y	(x, y)
0	4	(0, 4)
1	4	(1, 4)
2	4	(2, 4)

The graph shows both equations.

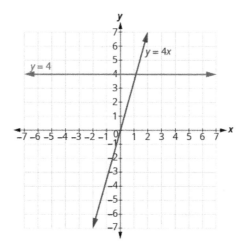

Notice that the equation $y = 4x$ gives a slanted line whereas $y = 4$ gives a horizontal line.

EXAMPLE 11.22

Graph $y = -3x$ and $y = -3$ in the same rectangular coordinate system.

⊘ Solution

Find three solutions for each equation. Notice that the first equation has the variable x, while the second does not. Solutions for both equations are listed.

$y = -3x$				$y = -3$		
x	y	(x, y)		x	y	(x, y)
0	0	(0, 0)		0	-3	(0, -3)
1	-3	(1, -3)		1	-3	(1, -3)
2	-6	(2, -6)		2	-3	(2, -3)

The graph shows both equations.

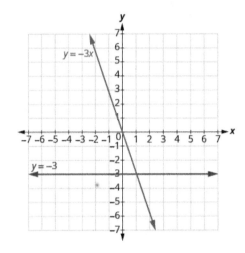

> **TRY IT :: 11.42**   Graph the equations in the same rectangular coordinate system: $y = -4x$ and $y = -4$.

> **TRY IT :: 11.43**   Graph the equations in the same rectangular coordinate system: $y = 3$ and $y = 3x$.

▶ **MEDIA :: ACCESS ADDITIONAL ONLINE RESOURCES**

- Use a Table of Values (http://www.openstaxcollege.org/l/24tabofval)
- Graph a Linear Equation Involving Fractions (http://www.openstaxcollege.org/l/24graphlineq)
- Graph Horizontal and Vertical Lines (http://www.openstaxcollege.org/l/24graphhorvert)

11.2 EXERCISES

Practice Makes Perfect

Recognize the Relation Between the Solutions of an Equation and its Graph

For each ordered pair, decide

ⓐ is the ordered pair a solution to the equation?   ⓑ is the point on the line?

39. $y = x + 2$
1. $(0, 2)$
2. $(1, 2)$
3. $(-1, 1)$
4. $(-3, 1)$

40. $y = x - 4$
1. $(0, -4)$
2. $(3, -1)$
3. $(2, 2)$
4. $(1, -5)$

41. $y = \frac{1}{2}x - 3$
1. $(0, -3)$
2. $(2, -2)$
3. $(-2, -4)$
4. $(4, 1)$

42. $y = \frac{1}{3}x + 2$
1. $(0, 2)$
2. $(3, 3)$
3. $(-3, 2)$
4. $(-6, 0)$

Graph a Linear Equation by Plotting Points

In the following exercises, graph by plotting points.

43. $y = 3x - 1$

44. $y = 2x + 3$

45. $y = -2x + 2$

46. $y = -3x + 1$

47. $y = x + 2$

48. $y = x - 3$

49. $y = -x - 3$

50. $y = -x - 2$

51. $y = 2x$

52. $y = 3x$

53. $y = -4x$

54. $y = -2x$

55. $y = \frac{1}{2}x + 2$

56. $y = \frac{1}{3}x - 1$

57. $y = \frac{4}{3}x - 5$

58. $y = \frac{3}{2}x - 3$

59. $y = -\frac{2}{5}x + 1$

60. $y = -\frac{4}{5}x - 1$

61. $y = -\frac{3}{2}x + 2$

62. $y = -\frac{5}{3}x + 4$

63. $x + y = 6$

64. $x + y = 4$

65. $x + y = -3$

66. $x + y = -2$

67. $x - y = 2$

68. $x - y = 1$

69. $x - y = -1$

70. $x - y = -3$

71. $-x + y = 4$

72. $-x + y = 3$

73. $-x - y = 5$

74. $-x - y = 1$

75. $3x + y = 7$

76. $5x + y = 6$

77. $2x + y = -3$

78. $4x + y = -5$

79. $2x + 3y = 12$

80. $3x - 4y = 12$

81. $\frac{1}{3}x + y = 2$

82. $\frac{1}{2}x + y = 3$

Graph Vertical and Horizontal lines

In the following exercises, graph the vertical and horizontal lines.

83. $x = 4$

84. $x = 3$

85. $x = -2$

86. $x = -5$

87. $y = 3$

88. $y = 1$

89. $y = -5$

90. $y = -2$

91. $x = \frac{7}{3}$

92. $x = \frac{5}{4}$

In the following exercises, graph each pair of equations in the same rectangular coordinate system.

93. $y = -\frac{1}{2}x$ and $y = -\frac{1}{2}$

94. $y = -\frac{1}{3}x$ and $y = -\frac{1}{3}$

95. $y = 2x$ and $y = 2$

96. $y = 5x$ and $y = 5$

Mixed Practice

In the following exercises, graph each equation.

97. $y = 4x$

98. $y = 2x$

99. $y = -\frac{1}{2}x + 3$

100. $y = \frac{1}{4}x - 2$

101. $y = -x$

102. $y = x$

103. $x - y = 3$

104. $x + y = -5$

105. $4x + y = 2$

106. $2x + y = 6$

107. $y = -1$

108. $y = 5$

109. $2x + 6y = 12$

110. $5x + 2y = 10$

111. $x = 3$

112. $x = -4$

Everyday Math

113. Motor home cost The Robinsons rented a motor home for one week to go on vacation. It cost them $594 plus $0.32 per mile to rent the motor home, so the linear equation $y = 594 + 0.32x$ gives the cost, y, for driving x miles. Calculate the rental cost for driving 400, 800, and 1,200 miles, and then graph the line.

114. Weekly earning At the art gallery where he works, Salvador gets paid $200 per week plus 15% of the sales he makes, so the equation $y = 200 + 0.15x$ gives the amount y he earns for selling x dollars of artwork. Calculate the amount Salvador earns for selling $900, $1,600, and $2,000, and then graph the line.

Writing Exercises

115. Explain how you would choose three x-values to make a table to graph the line $y = \frac{1}{5}x - 2$.

116. What is the difference between the equations of a vertical and a horizontal line?

Self Check

ⓐ *After completing the exercises, use this checklist to evaluate your mastery of the objectives of this section.*

I can...	Confidently	With some help	No-I don't get it!
graph a linear equation by plotting points.			
graph vertical and horizontal lines.			

ⓑ *After reviewing this checklist, what will you do to become confident for all objectives?*

11.3 **Graphing with Intercepts**

Learning Objectives

By the end of this section, you will be able to:
- Identify the intercepts on a graph
- Find the intercepts from an equation of a line
- Graph a line using the intercepts
- Choose the most convenient method to graph a line

Be Prepared!

Before you get started, take this readiness quiz.

1. Solve: $3x + 4y = -12$ for x when $y = 0$.
   If you missed this problem, review Example 9.62.

2. Is the point $(0, -5)$ on the x-axis or y-axis?
   If you missed this problem, review Example 11.5.

3. Which ordered pairs are solutions to the equation $2x - y = 6$?
   ⓐ $(6, 0)$ ⓑ $(0, -6)$ ⓒ $(4, -2)$.
   If you missed this problem, review Example 11.8.

Identify the Intercepts on a Graph

Every linear equation has a unique line that represents all the solutions of the equation. When graphing a line by plotting points, each person who graphs the line can choose any three points, so two people graphing the line might use different sets of points.

At first glance, their two lines might appear different since they would have different points labeled. But if all the work was done correctly, the lines will be exactly the same line. One way to recognize that they are indeed the same line is to focus on where the line crosses the axes. Each of these points is called an **intercept of the line**.

Intercepts of a Line

Each of the points at which a line crosses the x-axis and the y-axis is called an intercept of the line.

Let's look at the graph of the lines shown in Figure 11.14.

a) $2x + y = 6$

b) $3x - 4y = 12$

c) $x - y = 5$

d) $y = -2x$

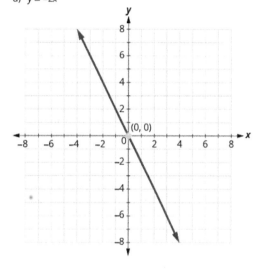

Figure 11.14

First, notice where each of these lines crosses the *x*- axis:

Figure:	The line crosses the x-axis at:	Ordered pair of this point
42	3	(3,0)
43	4	(4,0)
44	5	(5,0)
45	0	(0,0)

Table 11.23

Do you see a pattern?

For each row, the *y*- coordinate of the point where the line crosses the *x*- axis is zero. The point where the line crosses the *x*- axis has the form $(a, 0)$; and is called the *x-intercept* of the line. The **x-** intercept occurs when y is zero.

Now, let's look at the points where these lines cross the y-axis.

Figure:	The line crosses the y-axis at:	Ordered pair for this point
42	6	(0,6)
43	-3	(0,-3)
44	-5	(0,-5)
45	0	(0,0)

Table 11.24

x- intercept and y- intercept of a line

The x-intercept is the point, $(a, 0)$, where the graph crosses the x-axis. The x-intercept occurs when y is zero.

The y-intercept is the point, $(0, b)$, where the graph crosses the y-axis.

The y-intercept occurs when x is zero.

EXAMPLE 11.23

Find the x- and y-intercepts of each line:

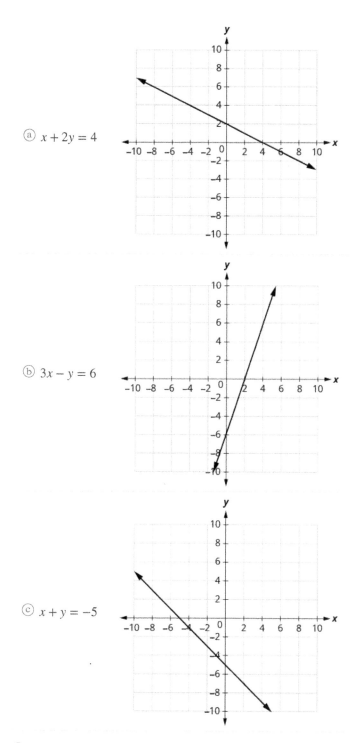

(a) $x + 2y = 4$

(b) $3x - y = 6$

(c) $x + y = -5$

✓ Solution

(a)

The graph crosses the x-axis at the point (4, 0).　　The x-intercept is (4, 0).

The graph crosses the y-axis at the point (0, 2).　　The x-intercept is (0, 2).

ⓑ

The graph crosses the x-axis at the point (2, 0).   The x-intercept is (2, 0)

The graph crosses the y-axis at the point (0, –6).   The y-intercept is (0, –6).

ⓒ

The graph crosses the x-axis at the point (–5, 0).   The x-intercept is (–5, 0).

The graph crosses the y-axis at the point (0, –5).   The y-intercept is (0, –5).

> **TRY IT :: 11.44**   Find the x- and y-intercepts of the graph: $x - y = 2$.

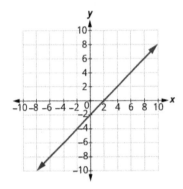

> **TRY IT :: 11.45**   Find the x- and y-intercepts of the graph: $2x + 3y = 6$.

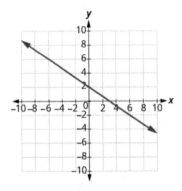

Find the Intercepts from an Equation of a Line

Recognizing that the x-intercept occurs when y is zero and that the y-intercept occurs when x is zero gives us a method to find the intercepts of a line from its equation. To find the x-intercept, let $y = 0$ and solve for x. To find the y-intercept, let $x = 0$ and solve for y.

Find the x and y from the Equation of a Line

Use the equation to find:

- the x-intercept of the line, let $y = 0$ and solve for x.

- the y-intercept of the line, let $x = 0$ and solve for y.

x	y
	0
0	

Table 11.29

 EXAMPLE 11.24

Find the intercepts of $2x + y = 6$

Solution

We'll fill in Figure 11.15.

$2x + y = 6$		
x	y	
	0	x-intercept
0		y-intercept

Figure 11.15

To find the x- intercept, let $y = 0$:

$$2x + y = 6$$

Substitute 0 for y.	$2x + 0 = 6$
Add.	$2x = 6$
Divide by 2.	$x = 3$

The x-intercept is (3, 0).

To find the y- intercept, let $x = 0$:

$$2x + y = 6$$

Substitute 0 for x.	$2 \cdot 0 + y = 6$
Multiply.	$0 + y = 6$
Add.	$y = 6$

The y-intercept is (0, 6).

$2x + y = 6$	
x	y
3	0
0	6

Figure 11.16

The intercepts are the points $(3, 0)$ and $(0, 6)$.

> **TRY IT :: 11.46** Find the intercepts: $3x + y = 12$

> **TRY IT :: 11.47** Find the intercepts: $x + 4y = 8$

EXAMPLE 11.25

Find the intercepts of $4x - 3y = 12$.

⊘ **Solution**

To find the x-intercept, let $y = 0$.

$$4x - 3y = 12$$

Substitute 0 for y.	$4x - 3 \cdot 0 = 12$
Multiply.	$4x - 0 = 12$
Subtract.	$4x = 12$
Divide by 4.	$x = 3$

The x-intercept is $(3, 0)$.

To find the y-intercept, let $x = 0$.

$$4x - 3y = 12$$

Substitute 0 for x.	$4 \cdot 0 - 3y = 12$
Multiply.	$0 - 3y = 12$
Simplify.	$-3y = 12$
Divide by -3.	$y = -4$

The y-intercept is $(0, -4)$.

The intercepts are the points $(-3, 0)$ and $(0, -4)$.

$4x-3y = 12$	
x	y
3	0
0	-4

> **TRY IT :: 11.48** Find the intercepts of the line: $3x - 4y = 12$.

> **TRY IT :: 11.49** Find the intercepts of the line: $2x - 4y = 8$.

Graph a Line Using the Intercepts

To graph a linear equation by plotting points, you can use the intercepts as two of your three points. Find the two intercepts, and then a third point to ensure accuracy, and draw the line. This method is often the quickest way to graph a line.

EXAMPLE 11.26

Graph $-x + 2y = 6$ using intercepts.

⊘ **Solution**

First, find the x-intercept. Let $y = 0$,

$$-x + 2y = 6$$
$$-x + 2(0) = 6$$
$$-x = 6$$
$$x = -6$$

The x-intercept is $(-6, 0)$.

Now find the y-intercept. Let $x = 0$.

$$-x + 2y = 6$$
$$-0 + 2y = 6$$
$$2y = 6$$
$$y = 3$$

The y-intercept is $(0, 3)$.

Find a third point. We'll use $x = 2$,

$$-x + 2y = 6$$
$$-2 + 2y = 6$$
$$2y = 8$$
$$y = 4$$

A third solution to the equation is $(2, 4)$.

Summarize the three points in a table and then plot them on a graph.

$-x + 2y = 6$		
x	y	(x,y)
−6	0	(−6, 0)
0	3	(0, 3)
2	4	(2, 4)

Do the points line up? Yes, so draw line through the points.

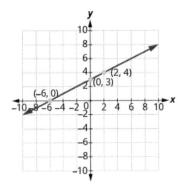

> **TRY IT :: 11.50**   Graph the line using the intercepts: $x - 2y = 4$.

> **TRY IT :: 11.51**   Graph the line using the intercepts: $-x + 3y = 6$.

 HOW TO :: GRAPH A LINE USING THE INTERCEPTS.

  Step 1.   Find the x - and y-intercepts of the line.

        ○ Let $y = 0$ and solve for x

        ○ Let $x = 0$ and solve for y.

  Step 2.   Find a third solution to the equation.

  Step 3.   Plot the three points and then check that they line up.

  Step 4.   Draw the line.

EXAMPLE 11.27

Graph $4x - 3y = 12$ using intercepts.

⊘ **Solution**

Find the intercepts and a third point.

x-intercept, let y = 0	y-intercept, let x = 0	third point, let y = 4
4x − 3y = 12	4x − 3y = 12	4x − 3y = 12
4x − 3(0) = 12	4(0) − 3y = 12	4x − 3(4) = 12
4x = 12	−3y = 12	4x − 12 = 12
x = 3	y = −4	4x = 24
		x = 6

We list the points and show the graph.

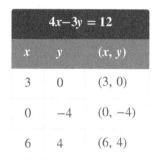

4x−3y = 12		
x	y	(x, y)
3	0	(3, 0)
0	−4	(0, −4)
6	4	(6, 4)

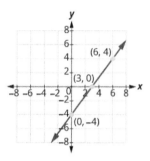

> **TRY IT : :** 11.52   Graph the line using the intercepts: $5x−2y = 10$.

> **TRY IT : :** 11.53   Graph the line using the intercepts: $3x−4y = 12$.

EXAMPLE 11.28

Graph $y = 5x$ using the intercepts.

⊘ **Solution**

x-intercept; Let y = 0.	y-intercept; Let x = 0.
y = 5x	y = 5x
0 = 5x	y = 5(0)
0 = x	y = 0
x = 0	The y-intercept is (0, 0).
The x-intercept is (0, 0).	

This line has only one intercept! It is the point $(0, 0)$.

To ensure accuracy, we need to plot three points. Since the intercepts are the same point, we need two more points to graph the line. As always, we can choose any values for x, so we'll let x be 1 and $−1$.

$$x = 1 \qquad x = -1$$
$$y = 5x \qquad y = 5x$$
$$y = 5(1) \quad y = 5(-1)$$
$$y = 5 \qquad y = -5$$
$$(1, 5) \qquad (-1, -5)$$

Organize the points in a table.

\multicolumn{3}{c}{$y = 5x$}		
x	y	(x, y)
0	0	$(0, 0)$
1	5	$(1, 5)$
-1	-5	$(-1, -5)$

Plot the three points, check that they line up, and draw the line.

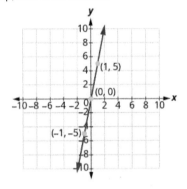

> **TRY IT : : 11.54**   Graph using the intercepts: $y = 3x$.

> **TRY IT : : 11.55**   Graph using the intercepts: $y = -x$.

Choose the Most Convenient Method to Graph a Line

While we could graph any linear equation by plotting points, it may not always be the most convenient method. This table shows six of equations we've graphed in this chapter, and the methods we used to graph them.

	Equation	Method
#1	$y = 2x + 1$	Plotting points
#2	$y = \frac{1}{2}x + 3$	Plotting points
#3	$x = -7$	Vertical line
#4	$y = 4$	Horizontal line
#5	$2x + y = 6$	Intercepts
#6	$4x - 3y = 12$	Intercepts

What is it about the form of equation that can help us choose the most convenient method to graph its line?

Notice that in equations #1 and #2, *y* is isolated on one side of the equation, and its coefficient is 1. We found points by substituting values for *x* on the right side of the equation and then simplifying to get the corresponding *y*- values.

Equations #3 and #4 each have just one variable. Remember, in this kind of equation the value of that one variable is constant; it does not depend on the value of the other variable. Equations of this form have graphs that are vertical or horizontal lines.

In equations #5 and #6, both *x* and *y* are on the same side of the equation. These two equations are of the form $Ax + By = C$. We substituted $y = 0$ and $x = 0$ to find the *x*- and *y*- intercepts, and then found a third point by choosing a value for *x* or *y*.

This leads to the following strategy for choosing the most convenient method to graph a line.

HOW TO :: CHOOSE THE MOST CONVENIENT METHOD TO GRAPH A LINE.

Step 1. If the equation has only one variable. It is a vertical or horizontal line.

- $x = a$ is a vertical line passing through the *x*-axis at *a*

- $y = b$ is a horizontal line passing through the *y*-axis at *b*.

Step 2. If *y* is isolated on one side of the equation. Graph by plotting points.

- Choose any three values for *x* and then solve for the corresponding *y*- values.

Step 3. If the equation is of the form $Ax + By = C$, find the intercepts.

- Find the *x*- and *y*- intercepts and then a third point.

EXAMPLE 11.29

Identify the most convenient method to graph each line:

ⓐ $y = -3$ ⓑ $4x - 6y = 12$ ⓒ $x = 2$ ⓓ $y = \frac{2}{5}x - 1$

Solution

ⓐ $y = -3$

This equation has only one variable, *y*. Its graph is a horizontal line crossing the *y*-axis at -3.

ⓑ $4x - 6y = 12$

This equation is of the form $Ax + By = C$. Find the intercepts and one more point.

ⓒ $x = 2$

There is only one variable, *x*. The graph is a vertical line crossing the *x*-axis at 2.

ⓓ $y = \frac{2}{5}x - 1$

Since *y* is isolated on the left side of the equation, it will be easiest to graph this line by plotting three points.

> **TRY IT :: 11.56**   Identify the most convenient method to graph each line:

ⓐ $3x + 2y = 12$ ⓑ $y = 4$ ⓒ $y = \frac{1}{5}x - 4$ ⓓ $x = -7$

> **TRY IT : : 11.57**   Identify the most convenient method to graph each line:

ⓐ $x = 6$ ⓑ $y = -\frac{3}{4}x + 1$ ⓒ $y = -8$ ⓓ $4x - 3y = -1$

▶ **MEDIA : :** ACCESS ADDITIONAL ONLINE RESOURCES

- Graph by Finding Intercepts (http://www.openstaxcollege.org/l/24findinter)
- Use Intercepts to Graph (http://www.openstaxcollege.org/l/24useintercept)
- State the Intercepts from a Graph (http://www.openstaxcollege.org/l/24statintercept)

11.3 EXERCISES

Practice Makes Perfect

Identify the Intercepts on a Graph

In the following exercises, find the x- and y- intercepts.

117.

118.

119.

120.

121.

122.

123.

124.

125.

126.

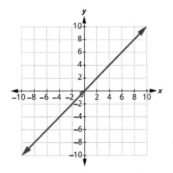

Find the x and y Intercepts from an Equation of a Line

In the following exercises, find the intercepts.

127. $x + y = 4$

128. $x + y = 3$

129. $x + y = -2$

130. $x + y = -5$

131. $x - y = 5$

132. $x - y = 1$

133. $x - y = -3$

134. $x - y = -4$

135. $x + 2y = 8$

136. $x + 2y = 10$

137. $3x + y = 6$

138. $3x + y = 9$

139. $x - 3y = 12$

140. $x - 2y = 8$

141. $4x - y = 8$

142. $5x - y = 5$

143. $2x + 5y = 10$

144. $2x + 3y = 6$

145. $3x - 2y = 12$

146. $3x - 5y = 30$

147. $y = \frac{1}{3}x - 1$

148. $y = \frac{1}{4}x - 1$

149. $y = \frac{1}{5}x + 2$

150. $y = \frac{1}{3}x + 4$

151. $y = 3x$

152. $y = -2x$

153. $y = -4x$

154. $y = 5x$

Graph a Line Using the Intercepts

In the following exercises, graph using the intercepts.

155. $-x + 5y = 10$

156. $-x + 4y = 8$

157. $x + 2y = 4$

158. $x + 2y = 6$

159. $x + y = 2$

160. $x + y = 5$

161. $x + y = -3$

162. $x + y = -1$

163. $x - y = 1$

164. $x - y = 2$

165. $x - y = -4$

166. $x - y = -3$

167. $4x + y = 4$

168. $3x + y = 3$

169. $3x - y = -6$

170. $2x - y = -8$

171. $2x + 4y = 12$

172. $3x + 2y = 12$

173. $3x-2y=6$

174. $5x-2y=10$

175. $2x-5y=-20$

176. $3x-4y=-12$

177. $y=-2x$

178. $y=-4x$

179. $y=x$

180. $y=3x$

Choose the Most Convenient Method to Graph a Line

In the following exercises, identify the most convenient method to graph each line.

181. $x=2$

182. $y=4$

183. $y=5$

184. $x=-3$

185. $y=-3x+4$

186. $y=-5x+2$

187. $x-y=5$

188. $x-y=1$

189. $y=\frac{2}{3}x-1$

190. $y=\frac{4}{5}x-3$

191. $y=-3$

192. $y=-1$

193. $3x-2y=-12$

194. $2x-5y=-10$

195. $y=-\frac{1}{4}x+3$

196. $y=-\frac{1}{3}x+5$

Everyday Math

197. Road trip Damien is driving from Chicago to Denver, a distance of $1,000$ miles. The x-axis on the graph below shows the time in hours since Damien left Chicago. The y-axis represents the distance he has left to drive.

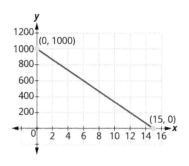

ⓐ Find the x- and y- intercepts

ⓑ Explain what the x- and y- intercepts mean for Damien.

198. Road trip Ozzie filled up the gas tank of his truck and went on a road trip. The x-axis on the graph shows the number of miles Ozzie drove since filling up. The y-axis represents the number of gallons of gas in the truck's gas tank.

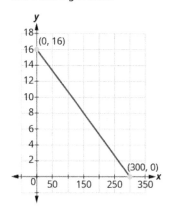

ⓐ Find the x- and y- intercepts.

ⓑ Explain what the x- and y- intercepts mean for Ozzie.

Writing Exercises

199. How do you find the x-intercept of the graph of $3x-2y=6$?

200. How do you find the y-intercept of the graph of $5x - y = 10$?

201. Do you prefer to graph the equation $4x + y = -4$ by plotting points or intercepts? Why?

202. Do you prefer to graph the equation $y = \frac{2}{3}x - 2$ by plotting points or intercepts? Why?

Self Check

ⓐ *After completing the exercises, use this checklist to evaluate your mastery of the objectives of this section.*

I can...	Confidently	With some help	No-I don't get it!
identify the intercepts on a graph.			
find the intercepts from an equation of a line.			
graph a line using the intercepts.			
choose the most convenient method to graph a line.			

ⓑ *What does this checklist tell you about your mastery of this section? What steps will you take to improve?*

Understand Slope of a Line

Learning Objectives

By the end of this section, you will be able to:

- Use geoboards to model slope
- Find the slope of a line from its graph
- Find the slope of horizontal and vertical lines
- Use the slope formula to find the slope of a line between two points
- Graph a line given a point and the slope
- Solve slope applications

Be Prepared!

Before you get started, take this readiness quiz.

1. Simplify: $\dfrac{1-4}{8-2}$.

   If you missed this problem, review Example 4.49.

2. Divide: $\dfrac{0}{4}$, $\dfrac{4}{0}$.

   If you missed this problem, review Example 7.37.

3. Simplify: $\dfrac{15}{-3}$, $\dfrac{-15}{3}$, $\dfrac{-15}{-3}$.

   If you missed this problem, review Example 4.47.

As we've been graphing linear equations, we've seen that some lines slant up as they go from left to right and some lines slant down. Some lines are very steep and some lines are flatter. What determines whether a line slants up or down, and if its slant is steep or flat?

The steepness of the slant of a line is called the **slope of the line**. The concept of slope has many applications in the real world. The pitch of a roof and the grade of a highway or wheelchair ramp are just some examples in which you literally see slopes. And when you ride a bicycle, you feel the slope as you pump uphill or coast downhill.

Use Geoboards to Model Slope

In this section, we will explore the concepts of slope.

Using rubber bands on a geoboard gives a concrete way to model lines on a coordinate grid. By stretching a rubber band between two pegs on a geoboard, we can discover how to find the slope of a line. And when you ride a bicycle, you <u>feel</u> the slope as you pump uphill or coast downhill.

 MANIPULATIVE MATHEMATICS

Doing the Manipulative Mathematics activity "Exploring Slope" will help you develop a better understanding of the slope of a line.

We'll start by stretching a rubber band between two pegs to make a line as shown in Figure 11.17.

Figure 11.17

Does it look like a line?

Now we stretch one part of the rubber band straight up from the left peg and around a third peg to make the sides of a right triangle as shown in Figure 11.18. We carefully make a $90°$ angle around the third peg, so that one side is vertical and the other is horizontal.

Figure 11.18

To find the slope of the line, we measure the distance along the vertical and horizontal legs of the triangle. The vertical distance is called the **rise** and the horizontal distance is called the **run**, as shown in Figure 11.19.

Figure 11.19

To help remember the terms, it may help to think of the images shown in Figure 11.20.

It goes straight up,
as if along the *y*-axis.
RISE ↕

A jogger runs straight across,
as if along the *x*-axis.
RUN ↔

Figure 11.20

On our geoboard, the rise is 2 units because the rubber band goes up 2 spaces on the vertical leg. See Figure 11.21.

What is the run? Be sure to count the spaces between the pegs rather than the pegs themselves! The rubber band goes across 3 spaces on the horizontal leg, so the run is 3 units.

Figure 11.21

The slope of a line is the ratio of the rise to the run. So the slope of our line is $\frac{2}{3}$. In mathematics, the slope is always represented by the letter m.

> **Slope of a line**
>
> The slope of a line is $m = \frac{\text{rise}}{\text{run}}$.
>
> The **rise** measures the vertical change and the **run** measures the horizontal change.

What is the slope of the line on the geoboard in Figure 11.21?

$$m = \frac{\text{rise}}{\text{run}}$$

$$m = \frac{2}{3}$$

The line has slope $\frac{2}{3}$.

When we work with geoboards, it is a good idea to get in the habit of starting at a peg on the left and connecting to a peg to the right. Then we stretch the rubber band to form a right triangle.

If we start by going up the rise is positive, and if we stretch it down the rise is negative. We will count the run from left to right, just like you read this paragraph, so the run will be positive.

Since the slope formula has rise over run, it may be easier to always count out the rise first and then the run.

EXAMPLE 11.30

What is the slope of the line on the geoboard shown?

⊘ **Solution**

Use the definition of slope.

$$m = \frac{\text{rise}}{\text{run}}$$

Start at the left peg and make a right triangle by stretching the rubber band up and to the right to reach the second peg. Count the rise and the run as shown.

The rise is 3 units. $m = \dfrac{3}{\text{run}}$

The run is 4 units. $m = \dfrac{3}{4}$

The slope is $\dfrac{3}{4}$.

> **TRY IT : : 11.58**   What is the slope of the line on the geoboard shown?

> **TRY IT : : 11.59**   What is the slope of the line on the geoboard shown?

EXAMPLE 11.31

What is the slope of the line on the geoboard shown?

⊘ **Solution**

Use the definition of slope.

$m = \dfrac{\text{rise}}{\text{run}}$

Start at the left peg and make a right triangle by stretching the rubber band to the peg on the right. This time we need to stretch the rubber band down to make the vertical leg, so the rise is negative.

The rise is −1. $m = \frac{-1}{\text{run}}$

The run is 3. $m = \frac{-1}{3}$

$m = -\frac{1}{3}$

The slope is $-\frac{1}{3}$.

> **TRY IT :: 11.60**   What is the slope of the line on the geoboard?

> **TRY IT :: 11.61**   What is the slope of the line on the geoboard?

Notice that in the first example, the slope is positive and in the second example the slope is negative. Do you notice any difference in the two lines shown in Figure 11.22.

A   B

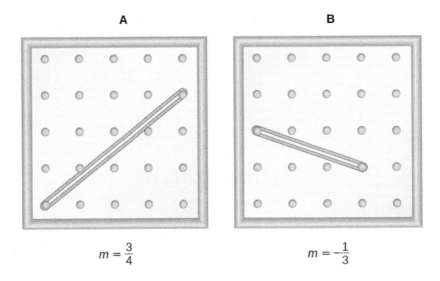

$$m = \frac{3}{4} \qquad\qquad\qquad\qquad m = -\frac{1}{3}$$

Figure 11.22

As you read from left to right, the line in Figure A, is going up; it has positive slope. The line Figure B is going down; it has negative slope.

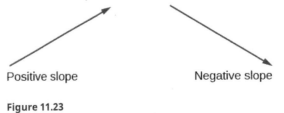

Positive slope   Negative slope

Figure 11.23

EXAMPLE 11.32

Use a geoboard to model a line with slope $\frac{1}{2}$.

⊘ **Solution**

To model a line with a specific slope on a geoboard, we need to know the rise and the run.

Use the slope formula.	$m = \frac{\text{rise}}{\text{run}}$
Replace m with $\frac{1}{2}$.	$\frac{1}{2} = \frac{\text{rise}}{\text{run}}$

So, the rise is 1 unit and the run is 2 units.

Start at a peg in the lower left of the geoboard. Stretch the rubber band up 1 unit, and then right 2 units.

The hypotenuse of the right triangle formed by the rubber band represents a line with a slope of $\frac{1}{2}$.

> **TRY IT : : 11.62**   Use a geoboard to model a line with the given slope: $m = \frac{1}{3}$.

> **TRY IT : : 11.63**   Use a geoboard to model a line with the given slope: $m = \frac{3}{2}$.

EXAMPLE 11.33

Use a geoboard to model a line with slope $\frac{-1}{4}$,

✓ **Solution**

Use the slope formula. $m = \frac{\text{rise}}{\text{run}}$

Replace m with $-\frac{1}{4}$. $-\frac{1}{4} = \frac{\text{rise}}{\text{run}}$

So, the rise is -1 and the run is 4.

Since the rise is negative, we choose a starting peg on the upper left that will give us room to count down. We stretch the rubber band down 1 unit, then to the right 4 units.

The hypotenuse of the right triangle formed by the rubber band represents a line whose slope is $-\frac{1}{4}$.

> **TRY IT : : 11.64**   Use a geoboard to model a line with the given slope: $m = \frac{-3}{2}$.

> **TRY IT : : 11.65**   Use a geoboard to model a line with the given slope: $m = \frac{-1}{3}$.

Find the Slope of a Line from its Graph

Now we'll look at some graphs on a coordinate grid to find their slopes. The method will be very similar to what we just modeled on our geoboards.

 MANIPULATIVE MATHEMATICS

Doing the Manipulative Mathematics activity "Slope of Lines Between Two Points" will help you develop a better understanding of how to find the slope of a line from its graph.

To find the slope, we must count out the rise and the run. But where do we start?

We locate any two points on the line. We try to choose points with coordinates that are integers to make our calculations easier. We then start with the point on the left and sketch a right triangle, so we can count the rise and run.

EXAMPLE 11.34

Find the slope of the line shown:

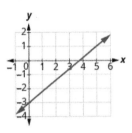

⊘ **Solution**

Locate two points on the graph, choosing points whose coordinates are integers. We will use $(0, -3)$ and $(5, 1)$.

Starting with the point on the left, $(0, -3),$ sketch a right triangle, going from the first point to the second point, $(5, 1)$.

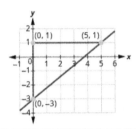

Count the rise on the vertical leg of the triangle.	The rise is 4 units.
Count the run on the horizontal leg.	The run is 5 units.
Use the slope formula.	$m = \dfrac{\text{rise}}{\text{run}}$
Substitute the values of the rise and run.	$m = \dfrac{4}{5}$
	The slope of the line is $\dfrac{4}{5}$.

Notice that the slope is positive since the line slants upward from left to right.

> **TRY IT ::** 11.66   Find the slope of the line:

TRY IT : : 11.67   Find the slope of the line:

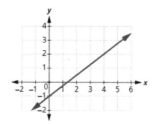

HOW TO : : FIND THE SLOPE FROM A GRAPH.

Step 1.   Locate two points on the line whose coordinates are integers.

Step 2.   Starting with the point on the left, sketch a right triangle, going from the first point to the second point.

Step 3.   Count the rise and the run on the legs of the triangle.

Step 4.   Take the ratio of rise to run to find the slope. $m = \dfrac{\text{rise}}{\text{run}}$

EXAMPLE 11.35

Find the slope of the line shown:

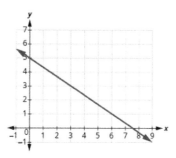

Solution

Locate two points on the graph. Look for points with coordinates that are integers. We can choose any points, but we will use (0, 5) and (3, 3). Starting with the point on the left, sketch a right triangle, going from the first point to the second point.

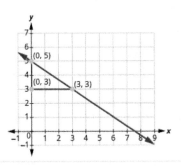

Count the rise – it is negative.	The rise is –2.
Count the run.	The run is 3.
Use the slope formula.	$m = \dfrac{\text{rise}}{\text{run}}$
Substitute the values of the rise and run.	$m = \dfrac{-2}{3}$
Simplify.	$m = -\dfrac{2}{3}$
	The slope of the line is $-\dfrac{2}{3}$.

Notice that the slope is negative since the line slants downward from left to right.

What if we had chosen different points? Let's find the slope of the line again, this time using different points. We will use the points $(-3, 7)$ and $(6, 1)$.

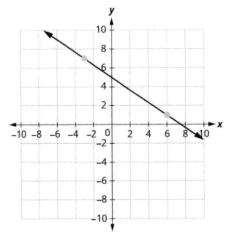

Starting at $(-3, 7)$, sketch a right triangle to $(6, 1)$.

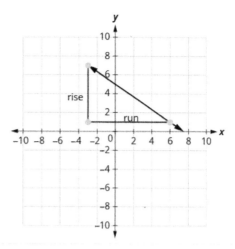

Count the rise.	The rise is −6.
Count the run.	The run is 9.
Use the slope formula.	$m = \frac{\text{rise}}{\text{run}}$
Substitute the values of the rise and run.	$m = \frac{-6}{9}$
Simplify the fraction.	$m = -\frac{2}{3}$

The slope of the line is $-\frac{2}{3}$.

It does not matter which points you use—the slope of the line is always the same. The slope of a line is constant!

> **TRY IT : :** 11.68   Find the slope of the line:

> **TRY IT : :** 11.69   Find the slope of the line:

The lines in the previous examples had y-intercepts with integer values, so it was convenient to use the y-intercept as one of the points we used to find the slope. In the next example, the y-intercept is a fraction. The calculations are easier if we use two points with integer coordinates.

EXAMPLE 11.36

Find the slope of the line shown:

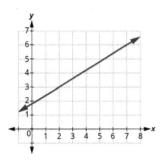

⊘ **Solution**

Locate two points on the graph whose coordinates are integers.	$(2, 3)$ and $(7, 6)$
Which point is on the left?	$(2, 3)$
Starting at $(2, 3)$, sketch a right angle to $(7, 6)$ as shown below.	

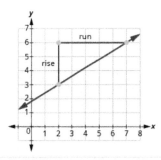

Count the rise.	The rise is 3.
Count the run.	The run is 5.
Use the slope formula.	$m = \dfrac{\text{rise}}{\text{run}}$
Substitute the values of the rise and run.	$m = \dfrac{3}{5}$
	The slope of the line is $\dfrac{3}{5}$.

> **TRY IT : : 11.70**   Find the slope of the line:

> **TRY IT : : 11.71**   Find the slope of the line:

Find the Slope of Horizontal and Vertical Lines

Do you remember what was special about horizontal and vertical lines? Their equations had just one variable.

- horizontal line $y = b$; all the y-coordinates are the same.

- vertical line $x = a$; all the x-coordinates are the same.

So how do we find the slope of the horizontal line $y = 4$? One approach would be to graph the horizontal line, find two points on it, and count the rise and the run. Let's see what happens in Figure 11.24. We'll use the two points $(0, \ 4)$ and $(3, \ 4)$ to count the rise and run.

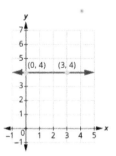

Figure 11.24

What is the rise?	The rise is 0.
What is the run?	The run is 3.
What is the slope?	$m = \dfrac{\text{rise}}{\text{run}}$
	$m = \dfrac{0}{3}$
	$m = 0$

The slope of the horizontal line $y = 4$ is 0.

All horizontal lines have slope 0. When the y-coordinates are the same, the rise is 0.

Slope of a Horizontal Line

The slope of a horizontal line, $y = b$,   is 0.

Now we'll consider a vertical line, such as the line $x = 3$, shown in Figure 11.25. We'll use the two points $(3, \ 0)$ and $(3, \ 2)$ to count the rise and run.

Figure 11.25

What is the rise?	The rise is 2.
What is the run?	The run is 0.
What is the slope?	$m = \dfrac{\text{rise}}{\text{run}}$
	$m = \dfrac{2}{0}$

But we can't divide by 0. Division by 0 is undefined. So we say that the slope of the vertical line $x = 3$ is undefined. The slope of all vertical lines is undefined, because the run is 0.

Slope of a Vertical Line

The slope of a vertical line, $x = a$,   is undefined.

EXAMPLE 11.37

Find the slope of each line:

ⓐ $x = 8$ ⓑ $y = -5$

⊘ **Solution**

ⓐ $x = 8$

This is a vertical line, so its slope is undefined.

ⓑ $y = -5$

This is a horizontal line, so its slope is 0.

> **TRY IT : : 11.72**   Find the slope of the line: $x = -4$.

> **TRY IT : : 11.73**   Find the slope of the line: $y = 7$.

Quick Guide to the Slopes of Lines

positive   negative   zero   undefined

Use the Slope Formula to find the Slope of a Line between Two Points

Sometimes we need to find the slope of a line between two points and we might not have a graph to count out the rise and the run. We could plot the points on grid paper, then count out the rise and the run, but there is a way to find the slope without graphing.

Before we get to it, we need to introduce some new algebraic notation. We have seen that an ordered pair (x, y) gives the coordinates of a point. But when we work with slopes, we use two points. How can the same symbol (x, y) be used to represent two different points?

Mathematicians use subscripts to distinguish between the points. A subscript is a small number written to the right of, and a little lower than, a variable.

  - (x_1, y_1) read x sub 1, y sub 1

  - (x_2, y_2) read x sub 2, y sub 2

We will use (x_1, y_1) to identify the first point and (x_2, y_2) to identify the second point. If we had more than two points, we could use (x_3, y_3), (x_4, y_4), and so on.

To see how the rise and run relate to the coordinates of the two points, let's take another look at the slope of the line between the points $(2, 3)$ and $(7, 6)$ in Figure 11.26.

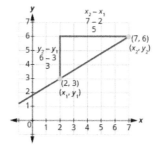

Figure 11.26

Since we have two points, we will use subscript notation.

$$\begin{array}{cc} x_1, y_1 & x_2, y_2 \\ (2, 3) & (7, 6) \end{array}$$

On the graph, we counted the rise of 3. The rise can also be found by subtracting the y-coordinates of the points.

$$y_2 - y_1$$
$$6 - 3$$
$$3$$

We counted a run of 5. The run can also be found by subtracting the x-coordinates.

$$x_2 - x_1$$
$$7 - 2$$
$$5$$

We know	$m = \dfrac{\text{rise}}{\text{run}}$
So	$m = \dfrac{3}{5}$
We rewrite the rise and run by putting in the coordinates.	$m = \dfrac{6 - 3}{7 - 2}$
But 6 is the y-coordinate of the second point, y_2 and 3 is the y-coordinate of the first point y_1. So we can rewrite the rise using subscript notation.	$m = \dfrac{y_2 - y_1}{7 - 2}$
Also 7 is the x-coordinate of the second point, x_2 and 2 is the x-coordinate of the first point x_2. So we rewrite the run using subscript notation.	$m = \dfrac{y_2 - y_1}{x_2 - x_1}$

We've shown that $m = \dfrac{y_2 - y_1}{x_2 - x_1}$ is really another version of $m = \dfrac{\text{rise}}{\text{run}}$. We can use this formula to find the slope of a line when we have two points on the line.

Slope Formula

The slope of the line between two points (x_1, y_1) and (x_2, y_2) is

$$m = \frac{y_2 - y_1}{x_2 - x_1}$$

Say the formula to yourself to help you remember it:

Slope is y of the second point minus y of the first point

over

x of the second point minus x of the first point.

 MANIPULATIVE MATHEMATICS

Doing the Manipulative Mathematics activity "Slope of Lines Between Two Points" will help you develop a better understanding of how to find the slope of a line between two points.

EXAMPLE 11.38

Find the slope of the line between the points $(1, 2)$ and $(4, 5)$.

⊘ **Solution**

We'll call $(1, 2)$ point #1 and $(4, 5)$ point #2.

$$\overset{x_1, \; y_1}{(1, \; 2)} \text{ and } \overset{x_2, \; y_2}{(4, \; 5)}$$

Use the slope formula.

$$m = \frac{y_2 - y_1}{x_2 - x_1}$$

Substitute the values in the slope formula:

y of the second point minus y of the first point

$$m = \frac{5 - 2}{x_2 - x_1}$$

x of the second point minus x of the first point

$$m = \frac{5 - 2}{4 - 1}$$

Simplify the numerator and the denominator.

$$m = \frac{3}{3}$$

$$m = 1$$

Let's confirm this by counting out the slope on the graph.

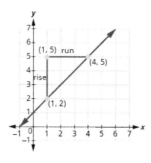

The rise is 3 and the run is 3, so

$$m = \frac{\text{rise}}{\text{run}}$$

$$m = \frac{3}{3}$$

$$m = 1$$

> **TRY IT :: 11.74**   Find the slope of the line through the given points: $(8, 5)$ and $(6, 3)$.

> **TRY IT :: 11.75**   Find the slope of the line through the given points: $(1, 5)$ and $(5, 9)$.

How do we know which point to call #1 and which to call #2? Let's find the slope again, this time switching the names of the points to see what happens. Since we will now be counting the run from right to left, it will be negative.

We'll call $(4,5)$ point #1 and $(1,2)$ point #2.	$\overset{x_1,\,y_1}{(4,\,5)}$ and $\overset{x_2,\,y_2}{(1,\,2)}$
Use the slope formula.	$m = \dfrac{y_2 - y_1}{x_2 - x_1}$
Substitute the values in the slope formula:	
y of the second point minus y of the first point	$m = \dfrac{2-5}{x_2 - x_1}$
x of the second point minus x of the first point	$m = \dfrac{2-5}{1-4}$
Simplify the numerator and the denominator.	$m = \dfrac{-3}{-3}$
	$m = 1$

The slope is the same no matter which order we use the points.

EXAMPLE 11.39

Find the slope of the line through the points $(-2, -3)$ and $(-7, 4)$.

⊘ **Solution**

We'll call $(-2, -3)$ point #1 and $(-7, 4)$ point #2.	$\overset{x_1,\,y_1}{(-2,\,-3)}$ and $\overset{x_2,\,y_2}{(-7,\,4)}$
Use the slope formula.	$m = \dfrac{y_2 - y_1}{x_2 - x_1}$
Substitute the values	
y of the second point minus y of the first point	$m = \dfrac{4 - (-3)}{x_2 - x_1}$
x of the second point minus x of the first point	$m = \dfrac{4 - (-3)}{-7 - (-2)}$
Simplify.	$m = \dfrac{7}{-5}$
	$m = -\dfrac{7}{5}$

Let's confirm this on the graph shown.

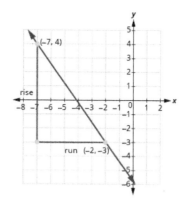

$$m = \frac{\text{rise}}{\text{run}}$$

$$m = \frac{-7}{5}$$

$$m = -\frac{7}{5}$$

> TRY IT :: 11.76   Find the slope of the line through the pair of points: $(-3, 4)$ and $(2, -1)$.

> TRY IT :: 11.77   Find the slope of the line through the pair of points: $(-2, 6)$ and $(-3, -4)$.

Graph a Line Given a Point and the Slope

In this chapter, we graphed lines by plotting points, by using intercepts, and by recognizing horizontal and vertical lines.

Another method we can use to graph lines is the point-slope method. Sometimes, we will be given one point and the slope of the line, instead of its equation. When this happens, we use the definition of slope to draw the graph of the line.

EXAMPLE 11.40

Graph the line passing through the point $(1, -1)$ whose slope is $m = \frac{3}{4}$.

⊘ **Solution**

Plot the given point, $(1, -1)$.

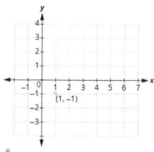

Use the slope formula $m = \frac{\text{rise}}{\text{run}}$ to identify the rise and the run.

$$m = \frac{3}{4}$$

$$\frac{\text{rise}}{\text{run}} = \frac{3}{4}$$

$$\text{rise} = 3$$
$$\text{run} = 4$$

Starting at the point we plotted, count out the rise and run to mark the second point. We count 3 units up and 4 units right.

Then we connect the points with a line and draw arrows at the ends to show it continues.

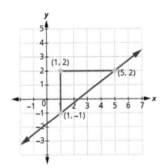

We can check our line by starting at any point and counting up 3 and to the right 4. We should get to another point on the line.

> **TRY IT ::** 11.78   Graph the line passing through the point with the given slope:

$(2, -2),\ m = \frac{4}{3}$

> **TRY IT ::** 11.79   Graph the line passing through the point with the given slope:

$(-2, 3),\ m = \frac{1}{4}$

 HOW TO :: GRAPH A LINE GIVEN A POINT AND A SLOPE.

Step 1.   Plot the given point.

Step 2.   Use the slope formula to identify the rise and the run.

Step 3.   Starting at the given point, count out the rise and run to mark the second point.

Step 4.   Connect the points with a line.

EXAMPLE 11.41

Graph the line with y-intercept $(0, 2)$ and slope $m = -\frac{2}{3}$.

⊘ **Solution**

Plot the given point, the y-intercept $(0, 2)$.

Use the slope formula $m = \frac{\text{rise}}{\text{run}}$ to identify the rise and the run.

$$m = -\frac{2}{3}$$

$$\frac{\text{rise}}{\text{run}} = \frac{-2}{3}$$

$$\text{rise} = -2$$
$$\text{run} = 3$$

Starting at $(0, 2)$, count the rise and the run and mark the second point.

Connect the points with a line.

> **TRY IT ::** 11.80   Graph the line with the given intercept and slope:

y-intercept 4, $m = -\dfrac{5}{2}$

> **TRY IT ::** 11.81   Graph the line with the given intercept and slope:

x-intercept -3, $m = -\dfrac{3}{4}$

EXAMPLE 11.42

Graph the line passing through the point $(-1, -3)$ whose slope is $m = 4$.

⊘ **Solution**

Plot the given point.

Identify the rise and the run.	$m = 4$
Write 4 as a fraction.	$\dfrac{\text{rise}}{\text{run}} = \dfrac{4}{1}$
	$\text{rise} = 4 \;\; \text{run} = 1$

Count the rise and run.

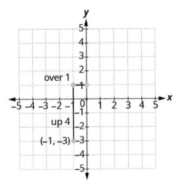

Mark the second point. Connect the two points with a line.

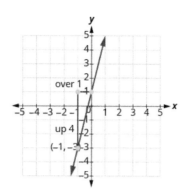

> **TRY IT : : 11.82**   Graph the line with the given intercept and slope: $(-2, 1)$, $m = 3$.

> **TRY IT : : 11.83**   Graph the line with the given intercept and slope: $(4, -2)$, $m = -2$.

Solve Slope Applications

At the beginning of this section, we said there are many applications of slope in the real world. Let's look at a few now.

EXAMPLE 11.43

The pitch of a building's roof is the slope of the roof. Knowing the pitch is important in climates where there is heavy snowfall. If the roof is too flat, the weight of the snow may cause it to collapse. What is the slope of the roof shown?

⊘ **Solution**

Use the slope formula. $m = \dfrac{\text{rise}}{\text{run}}$

Substitute the values for rise and run. $m = \dfrac{9 \text{ ft}}{18 \text{ ft}}$

Simplify. $m = \dfrac{1}{2}$

The slope of the roof is $\dfrac{1}{2}$.

> **TRY IT : : 11.84**   Find the slope given rise and run: A roof with a rise $= 14$ and run $= 24$.

> **TRY IT : : 11.85**   Find the slope given rise and run: A roof with a rise $= 15$ and run $= 36$.

Have you ever thought about the sewage pipes going from your house to the street? Their slope is an important factor in how they take waste away from your house.

EXAMPLE 11.44

Sewage pipes must slope down $\frac{1}{4}$ inch per foot in order to drain properly. What is the required slope?

⊘ **Solution**

Use the slope formula.	$m = \dfrac{\text{rise}}{\text{run}}$
	$m = \dfrac{-\frac{1}{4}\text{ in.}}{1\text{ ft}}$
	$m = \dfrac{-\frac{1}{4}\text{ in.}}{1\text{ ft}}$
Convert 1 foot to 12 inches.	$m = \dfrac{-\frac{1}{4}\text{ in.}}{12\text{ in.}}$
Simplify.	$m = -\dfrac{1}{48}$

The slope of the pipe is $-\dfrac{1}{48}$.

> **TRY IT : : 11.86**   Find the slope of the pipe: The pipe slopes down $\frac{1}{3}$ inch per foot.

> **TRY IT : : 11.87**   Find the slope of the pipe: The pipe slopes down $\frac{3}{4}$ inch per yard.

▶ **MEDIA : :** ACCESS ADDITIONAL ONLINE RESOURCES
  • Determine Positive slope from a Graph (http://www.openstaxcollege.org/l/24posslope)
  • Determine Negative slope from a Graph (http://www.openstaxcollege.org/l/24negslope)
  • Determine Slope from Two Points (http://www.openstaxcollege.org/l/24slopetwopts)

11.4 EXERCISES

Practice Makes Perfect

Use Geoboards to Model Slope

In the following exercises, find the slope modeled on each geoboard.

203.

204.

205.

206.

In the following exercises, model each slope. Draw a picture to show your results.

207. $\frac{2}{3}$

208. $\frac{3}{4}$

209. $\frac{1}{4}$

210. $\frac{4}{3}$

211. $-\frac{1}{2}$

212. $-\frac{3}{4}$

213. $-\frac{2}{3}$

214. $-\frac{3}{2}$

Find the Slope of a Line from its Graph

In the following exercises, find the slope of each line shown.

215.

216.

217.

218.

219.

220.

221.

222.

223.

224.

225.

226.

227.

228.

229.

230.

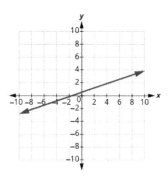

Find the Slope of Horizontal and Vertical Lines

In the following exercises, find the slope of each line.

231. $y = 3$

232. $y = 1$

233. $x = 4$

234. $x = 2$

235. $y = -2$

236. $y = -3$

237. $x = -5$

238. $x = -4$

Use the Slope Formula to find the Slope of a Line between Two Points

In the following exercises, use the slope formula to find the slope of the line between each pair of points.

239. $(1, 4), (3, 9)$

240. $(2, 3), (5, 7)$

241. $(0, 3), (4, 6)$

242. $(0, 1), (5, 4)$

243. $(2, 5), (4, 0)$

244. $(3, 6), (8, 0)$

245. $(-3, 3), (2, -5)$

246. $(-2, 4), (3, -1)$

247. $(-1, -2), (2, 5)$

248. $(-2, -1), (6, 5)$

249. $(4, -5), (1, -2)$

250. $(3, -6), (2, -2)$

Graph a Line Given a Point and the Slope

In the following exercises, graph the line given a point and the slope.

251. $(1, -2); m = \frac{3}{4}$

252. $(1, -1); m = \frac{1}{2}$

253. $(2, 5); m = -\frac{1}{3}$

254. $(1, 4); m = -\frac{1}{2}$

255. $(-3, 4); m = -\frac{3}{2}$

256. $(-2, 5); m = -\frac{5}{4}$

257. $(-1, -4)$; $m = \frac{4}{3}$ **258.** $(-3, -5)$; $m = \frac{3}{2}$ **259.** $(0, 3)$; $m = -\frac{2}{5}$

260. $(0, 5)$; $m = -\frac{4}{3}$ **261.** $(-2, 0)$; $m = \frac{3}{4}$ **262.** $(-1, 0)$; $m = \frac{1}{5}$

263. $(-3, 3)$; $m = 2$ **264.** $(-4, 2)$; $m = 4$ **265.** $(1, 5)$; $m = -3$

266. $(2, 3)$; $m = -1$

Solve Slope Applications

In the following exercises, solve these slope applications.

267. Slope of a roof A fairly easy way to determine the slope is to take a 12-inch level and set it on one end on the roof surface. Then take a tape measure or ruler, and measure from the other end of the level down to the roof surface. You can use these measurements to calculate the slope of the roof. What is the slope of the roof in this picture?

268. What is the slope of the roof shown?

269. Road grade A local road has a grade of 6%. The grade of a road is its slope expressed as a percent.

ⓐ Find the slope of the road as a fraction and then simplify the fraction.

ⓑ What rise and run would reflect this slope or grade?

270. Highway grade A local road rises 2 feet for every 50 feet of highway.

ⓐ What is the slope of the highway?

ⓑ The grade of a highway is its slope expressed as a percent. What is the grade of this highway?

Everyday Math

271. Wheelchair ramp The rules for wheelchair ramps require a maximum 1 inch rise for a 12 inch run.

ⓐ How long must the ramp be to accommodate a 24-inch rise to the door?

ⓑ Draw a model of this ramp.

272. Wheelchair ramp A 1-inch rise for a 16-inch run makes it easier for the wheelchair rider to ascend the ramp.

ⓐ How long must the ramp be to easily accommodate a 24-inch rise to the door?

ⓑ Draw a model of this ramp.

Writing Exercises

273. What does the sign of the slope tell you about a line?

274. How does the graph of a line with slope $m = \frac{1}{2}$ differ from the graph of a line with slope $m = 2$?

275. Why is the slope of a vertical line undefined?

276. Explain how you can graph a line given a point and its slope.

Self Check

ⓐ After completing the exercises, use this checklist to evaluate your mastery of the objectives of this section.

I can...	Confidently	With some help	No-I don't get it!
use geoboards to model slope.			
find the slope of a line from its graph.			
find the slope of horizontal and vertical lines.			
use the slope formula to find the slope of a line between two points.			
graph a line given a point and the slope.			
solve slope applications.			

ⓑ On a scale of 1–10, how would you rate your mastery of this section in light of your responses on the checklist? How can you improve this?

CHAPTER 11 REVIEW

KEY TERMS

horizontal line A horizontal line is the graph of an equation that can be written in the form $y = b$. The line passes through the y-axis at $(0, b)$.

intercepts of a line Each of the points at which a line crosses the x-axis and the y-axis is called an intercept of the line.

linear equation An equation of the form $Ax + By = C$, where A and B are not both zero, is called a linear equation in two variables.

ordered pair An ordered pair (x, y) gives the coordinates of a point in a rectangular coordinate system. The first number is the x-coordinate. The second number is the y-coordinate.

$$(x, y)$$
$$x\text{-coordinate, } y\text{-coordinate}$$

origin The point $(0, 0)$ is called the origin. It is the point where the the point where the x-axis and y-axis intersect.

quadrants The x-axis and y-axis divide a rectangular coordinate system into four areas, called quadrants.

slope of a line The slope of a line is $m = \frac{\text{rise}}{\text{run}}$. The rise measures the vertical change and the run measures the horizontal change.

solution to a linear equation in two variables An ordered pair (x, y) is a solution to the linear equation $Ax + By = C$, if the equation is a true statement when the x- and y-values of the ordered pair are substituted into the equation.

vertical line A vertical line is the graph of an equation that can be written in the form $x = a$. The line passes through the x-axis at $(a, 0)$.

x-axis The x-axis is the horizontal axis in a rectangular coordinate system.

y-axis The y-axis is the vertical axis on a rectangular coordinate system.

KEY CONCEPTS

11.1 Use the Rectangular Coordinate System

- **Sign Patterns of the Quadrants**

Quadrant I	Quadrant II	Quadrant III	Quadrant IV
(x,y)	(x,y)	(x,y)	(x,y)
$(+,+)$	$(-,+)$	$(-,-)$	$(+,-)$

- **Coordinates of Zero**
    - Points with a y-coordinate equal to 0 are on the x-axis, and have coordinates (a, 0).
    - Points with a x-coordinate equal to 0 are on the y-axis, and have coordinates (0, b).
    - The point (0, 0) is called the origin. It is the point where the x-axis and y-axis intersect.

11.2 Graphing Linear Equations

- **Graph a linear equation by plotting points.**
    Step 1. Find three points whose coordinates are solutions to the equation. Organize them in a table.
    Step 2. Plot the points on a rectangular coordinate system. Check that the points line up. If they do not, carefully check your work.
    Step 3. Draw the line through the points. Extend the line to fill the grid and put arrows on both ends of the line.
- **Graph of a Linear Equation:** The graph of a linear equation $ax + by = c$ is a straight line.

◦ Every point on the line is a solution of the equation.

◦ Every solution of this equation is a point on this line.

11.3 Graphing with Intercepts

- **Intercepts**
    ◦ The x-intercept is the point, $(a, 0)$, where the graph crosses the x-axis. The x-intercept occurs when y is zero.
    ◦ The y-intercept is the point, $(0, b)$, where the graph crosses the y-axis. The y-intercept occurs when y is zero.
    ◦ The x-intercept occurs when y is zero.
    ◦ The y-intercept occurs when x is zero.

- **Find the x and y intercepts from the equation of a line**
    ◦ To find the x-intercept of the line, let $y = 0$ and solve for x.

    ◦ To find the y-intercept of the line, let $x = 0$ and solve for y.

x	y
	0
0	

- **Graph a line using the intercepts**
    Step 1. Find the x- and y- intercepts of the line.

    - Let $y = 0$ and solve for x.

    - Let $x = 0$ and solve for y.

    Step 2. Find a third solution to the equation.

    Step 3. Plot the three points and then check that they line up.

    Step 4. Draw the line.

- **Choose the most convenient method to graph a line**
    Step 1. Determine if the equation has only one variable. Then it is a vertical or horizontal line.
    $x = a$ is a vertical line passing through the x-axis at a.
    $y = b$ is a vertical line passing through the y-axis at b.

    Step 2. Determine if y is isolated on one side of the equation. The graph by plotting points.
    Choose any three values for x and then solve for the corresponding y- values.

    Step 3. Determine if the equation is of the form $Ax + By = C$, find the intercepts.
    Find the x- and y- intercepts and then a third point.

11.4 Understand Slope of a Line

- **Find the slope from a graph**
    Step 1. Locate two points on the line whose coordinates are integers.

    Step 2. Starting with the point on the left, sketch a right triangle, going from the first point to the second point.

    Step 3. Count the rise and the run on the legs of the triangle.

    Step 4. Take the ratio of rise to run to find the slope, $m = \frac{\text{rise}}{\text{run}}$

- **Slope of a Horizontal Line**
    ◦ The slope of a horizontal line, $y = b$, is 0.

- **Slope of a Vertical Line**
    ◦ The slope of a vertical line, $x = a$, is undefined.

- **Slope Formula**
  - The slope of the line between two points (x_1, y_1) and (x_2, y_2) is $m = \dfrac{y_2 - y_1}{x_2 - x_1}$

- **Graph a line given a point and a slope.**

  Step 1. Plot the given point.

  Step 2. Use the slope formula to identify the rise and the run.

  Step 3. Starting at the given point, count out the rise and run to mark the second point.

  Step 4. Connect the points with a line.

REVIEW EXERCISES

11.1 Use the Rectangular Coordinate System

Plot Points in a Rectangular Coordinate System

In the following exercises, plot each point in a rectangular coordinate system.

277. $(1, 3), (3, 1)$ **278.** $(2, 5), (5, 2)$

In the following exercises, plot each point in a rectangular coordinate system and identify the quadrant in which the point is located.

279.

    ⓐ $(-1, -5)$

    ⓑ $(-3, 4)$

    ⓒ $(2, -3)$

    ⓓ $\left(1, \dfrac{5}{2}\right)$

280.

    ⓐ $(3, -2)$

    ⓑ $(-4, -1)$

    ⓒ $(-5, 4)$

    ⓓ $\left(2, \dfrac{10}{3}\right)$

Identify Points on a Graph

In the following exercises, name the ordered pair of each point shown in the rectangular coordinate system.

281.

282.

283.

284.

Verify Solutions to an Equation in Two Variables

In the following exercises, find the ordered pairs that are solutions to the given equation.

285. $5x + y = 10$

    ⓐ $(5, 1)$ ⓑ $(2, 0)$

    ⓒ $(4, -10)$

286. $y = 6x - 2$

    ⓐ $(1, 4)$ ⓑ $\left(\frac{1}{3}, 0\right)$

    ⓒ $(6, -2)$

Complete a Table of Solutions to a Linear Equation in Two Variables

In the following exercises, complete the table to find solutions to each linear equation.

287. $y = 4x - 1$

x	y	(x, y)
0		
1		
−2		

288. $y = -\frac{1}{2}x + 3$

x	y	(x, y)
0		
1		
−2		

289. $x + 2y = 5$

x	y	(x, y)
	0	
1		
−1		

290. $3x - 2y = 6$

x	y	(x, y)
0		
	0	
−2		

Find Solutions to a Linear Equation in Two Variables

In the following exercises, find three solutions to each linear equation.

291. $x + y = 3$

292. $x + y = -4$

293. $y = 3x + 1$

294. $y = -x - 1$

11.2 Graphing Linear Equations

Recognize the Relation Between the Solutions of an Equation and its Graph

In the following exercises, for each ordered pair, decide

    ⓐ if the ordered pair is a solution to the equation. ⓑ if the point is on the line.

295. $y = -x + 4$

    ⓐ $(0, 4)$ ⓑ $(-1, 3)$

    ⓒ $(2, 2)$ ⓓ $(-2, 6)$

296. $y = \frac{2}{3}x - 1$

    ⓐ $(0, -1)$ ⓑ $(3, 1)$

    ⓒ $(-3, -3)$

    ⓓ $(6, 4)$

Graph a Linear Equation by Plotting Points

In the following exercises, graph by plotting points.

297. $y = 4x - 3$

298. $y = -3x$

299. $2x + y = 7$

Graph Vertical and Horizontal lines

In the following exercises, graph the vertical or horizontal lines.

300. $y = -2$

301. $x = 3$

11.3 Graphing with Intercepts

Identify the Intercepts on a Graph

In the following exercises, find the x- and y-intercepts.

302.

303.

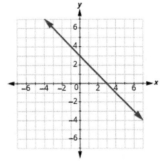

Find the Intercepts from an Equation of a Line

In the following exercises, find the intercepts.

304. $x + y = 5$

305. $x - y = -1$

306. $y = \frac{3}{4}x - 12$

307. $y = 3x$

Graph a Line Using the Intercepts

In the following exercises, graph using the intercepts.

308. $-x + 3y = 3$

309. $x + y = -2$

Choose the Most Convenient Method to Graph a Line

In the following exercises, identify the most convenient method to graph each line.

310. $x = 5$

311. $y = -3$

312. $2x + y = 5$

313. $x - y = 2$

314. $y = \frac{1}{2}x + 2$

315. $y = \frac{3}{4}x - 1$

11.4 Understand Slope of a Line

Use Geoboards to Model Slope

In the following exercises, find the slope modeled on each geoboard.

316.

317.

318.

319.

In the following exercises, model each slope. Draw a picture to show your results.

320. $\frac{1}{3}$

321. $\frac{3}{2}$

322. $-\frac{2}{3}$

323. $-\frac{1}{2}$

Find the Slope of a Line from its Graph

In the following exercises, find the slope of each line shown.

324.

325.

326.

327.

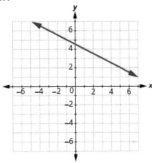

Find the Slope of Horizontal and Vertical Lines

In the following exercises, find the slope of each line.

328. $y = 2$

329. $x = 5$

330. $x = -3$

331. $y = -1$

Use the Slope Formula to find the Slope of a Line between Two Points

In the following exercises, use the slope formula to find the slope of the line between each pair of points.

332. $(2, 1), (4, 5)$

333. $(-1, -1), (0, -5)$

334. $(3, 5), (4, -1)$

335. $(-5, -2), (3, 2)$

Graph a Line Given a Point and the Slope

In the following exercises, graph the line given a point and the slope.

336. $(2, -2); m = \dfrac{5}{2}$

337. $(-3, 4); m = -\dfrac{1}{3}$

Solve Slope Applications

In the following exercise, solve the slope application.

338. A roof has rise 10 feet and run 15 feet. What is its slope?

PRACTICE TEST

339. Plot and label these points:

ⓐ $(2, 5)$

ⓑ $(-1, -3)$

ⓒ $(-4, 0)$

ⓓ $(3, -5)$

ⓔ $(-2, 1)$

340. Name the ordered pair for each point shown.

341. Find the x-intercept and y-intercept on the line shown.

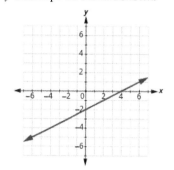

342. Find the x-intercept and y-intercept of the equation $3x - y = 6$.

343. Is $(1, 3)$ a solution to the equation $x + 4y = 12$? How do you know?

344. Complete the table to find four solutions to the equation $y = -x + 1$.

x	y	(x, y)
0		
1		
3		
-2		

345. Complete the table to find three solutions to the equation $4x + y = 8$

x	y	(x, y)
0		
	0	
3		

In the following exercises, find three solutions to each equation and then graph each line.

346. $y = -3x$

347. $2x + 3y = -6$

In the following exercises, find the slope of each line.

348.

349.

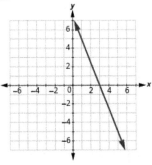

350. Use the slope formula to find the slope of the line between $(0, -4)$ and $(5, 2)$.

351. Find the slope of the line $y = 2$.

352. Graph the line passing through $(1, 1)$ with slope $m = \frac{3}{2}$.

353. A bicycle route climbs 20 feet for $1{,}000$ feet of horizontal distance. What is the slope of the route?

A | CUMULATIVE REVIEW

Note: Answers to the Cumulative Review can be found in the Supplemental Resources. Please visit http://openstaxcollege.org to view an updated list of the Learning Resources for this title and how to access them.

Chapter 1 Whole Numbers

No exercises.

Chapter 2 The Language of Algebra

Simplify:

1. $5(3 + 2 \cdot 6) - 8^2$

Solve:

2. $17 = y - 13$

3. $p + 14 = 23$

Translate into an algebraic expression.

4. 11 less than the product of 7 and x.

Translate into an algebraic equation and solve.

5. Twice the difference of y and 7 gives 84.

6. Find all the factors of 72.

7. Find the prime factorization of 132.

8. Find the least common multiple of 12 and 20.

Chapter 3 Integers

Simplify:

9. $|8 - 9| - |3 - 8|$

10. $-2 + 4(-3 + 7)$

11. $27 - (-4 - 7)$

12. $28 \div (-4) - 7$

Translate into an algebraic expression or equation.

13. The sum of -5 and 13, increased by 11.

14. The product of -11 and 8.

15. The quotient of 7 and the sum of -4 and m.

16. The product of -3 and is -51.

Solve:

17. $-6r = 24$

Chapter 4 Fractions

18. Locate the numbers on a number line. $\frac{7}{8}, \frac{5}{3}, 3\frac{1}{4}, 5$.

Simplify:

19. $\frac{21p}{57q}$

20. $\frac{3}{7} \cdot \left(-\frac{28}{45}\right)$

21. $-6\frac{3}{4} \div \frac{9}{2}$

22. $-3\frac{3}{5} \div 6$

23. $-4\frac{2}{3}\left(-\frac{6}{7}\right)$

24. $\dfrac{-2\frac{1}{4}}{-\frac{3}{8}}$

25. $\dfrac{7 \cdot 8 + 4(7 - 12)}{9 \cdot 6 - 2 \cdot 9}$

26. $-\frac{23}{36} + \frac{17}{20}$

27. $\dfrac{\frac{1}{2} + \frac{1}{3}}{\frac{3}{4} - \frac{1}{3}}$

28. $3\frac{5}{8} - 2\frac{1}{2}$

29. $-\frac{2}{3}r = 24$

Chapter 5 Decimals

Simplify:

30. $24.76 - 7.28$

31. $12.9 + 15.633$

32. $(-5.6)(0.25)$

33. $\$6.29 \div 12$

34. $\frac{3}{4}(13.44 - 9.6)$

35. $\sqrt{64} + \sqrt{225}$

36. $\sqrt{121x^2 y^2}$

37. Write in order from smallest to largest: $\frac{5}{8}$, 0.75, $\frac{8}{15}$

Solve:

38. $-8.6x = 34.4$

39. Using 3.14 as the estimate for pi, approximate the (a) circumference and (b) area of a circle whose radius is 8 inches.

40. Find the mean of the numbers, $18, 16, 20, 12$

41. Find the median of the numbers, $24, 29, 27, 28, 30$

42. Identify the mode of the numbers, $6, 4, 4, 5, 6, 6, 4, 4, 4, 3, 5$

43. Find the unit price of one t-shirt if they are sold at 3 for $\$28.97$.

Chapter 6 Percents

44. Convert 14.7% to (a) a fraction and (b) a decimal.

Translate and solve.

45. 63 is 35% of what number?

46. The nutrition label on a package of granola bars says that each granola bar has 180 calories, and 81 calories are from fat. What percent of the total calories is from fat?

47. Elliot received $\$510$ commission when he sold a $\$3,400$ painting at the art gallery where he works. What was the

rate of commission?

48. Nandita bought a set of towels on sale for $67.50. The original price of the towels was $90. What was the discount rate?

49. Alan invested $23,000 in a friend's business. In 5 years the friend paid him the $23,000 plus $9,200 interest. What was the rate of interest?

Solve:

50. $\frac{9}{p} = \frac{-6}{14}$

Chapter 7 The Properties of Real Numbers

51. List the (a) whole numbers, (b) integers, (c) rational numbers, (d) irrational numbers,

(e) real numbers $-5, -2\frac{1}{4}, -\sqrt{4}, 0.\overline{25}, \frac{13}{5}, 4$

Simplify:

52. $\left(\frac{8}{15} + \frac{4}{7}\right) + \frac{3}{7}$

53. $3(y + 3) - 8(y - 4)$

54. $\frac{8}{17} \cdot 49 \cdot \frac{17}{8}$

55. A playground is 55 feet wide. Convert the width to yards.

56. Every day last week Amit recorded the number of minutes he spent reading. The recorded number of minutes he read each day was 48, 26, 81, 54, 43, 62, 106. How many hours did Amit spend reading last week?

57. June walked 2.8 kilometers. Convert this length to miles knowing 1 mile is 1.61 kilometer.

Chapter 8 Solve Linear Equations

Solve:

58. $y + 13 = -8$

59. $p + \frac{2}{5} = \frac{8}{5}$

60. $48 = \frac{2}{3}x$

61. $4(a - 3) - 6a = -18$

62. $7q + 14 = -35$

63. $4v - 27 = 7v$

64. $\frac{7}{8}y - 6 = \frac{3}{8}y - 8$

65. $26 - 4(z - 2) = 6$

66. $\frac{3}{4}x - \frac{2}{3} = \frac{1}{2}x - \frac{5}{6}$

67. $0.7y + 4.8 = 0.84y - 5.3$

Translate and solve.

68. Four less than n is 13.

Chapter 9 Math Models and Geometry

69. One number is 8 less than another. Their sum is negative twenty-two. Find the numbers.

70. The sum of two consecutive integers is -95. Find the numbers.

71. Wilma has $3.65 in dimes and quarters. The number of dimes is 2 less than the number of quarters. How many of each coin does she have?

72. Two angles are supplementary. The larger angle is $24°$ more than the smaller angle. Find the measurements of both angles.

73. One angle of a triangle is $20°$ more than the smallest angle. The largest angle is the sum of the other angles. Find the measurements of all three angles.

74. Erik needs to attach a wire to hold the antenna to the roof of his house, as shown in the figure. The antenna is 12 feet tall and Erik has 15 feet of wire. How far from the base of the antenna can he attach the wire?

75. The width of a rectangle is 4 less than the length. The perimeter is 96 inches. Find the length and the width.

76. Find the (a) volume and (b) surface area of a rectangular carton with length 24 inches, width 18 inches, and height 6 inches.

Chapter 10 Polynomials

Simplify:

77. $\left(8m^2 + 12m - 5\right) - \left(2m^2 - 7m - 1\right)$

78. $p^3 \cdot p^{10}$

79. $\left(y^4\right)^3$

80. $\left(3a^5\right)^3$

81. $\left(x^3\right)^5 \left(x^2\right)^3$

82. $\left(\frac{2}{3}m^3 n^6\right)\left(\frac{1}{6}m^4 n^4\right)$

83. $(y - 4)(y + 12)$

84. $(3c + 1)(9c - 4)$

85. $(x - 1)\left(x^2 - 3x - 2\right)$

86. $(8x)^0$

87. $\dfrac{\left(x^3\right)^5}{\left(x^2\right)^4}$

88. $\dfrac{32a^7 b^2}{12a^3 b^6}$

89. $\left(ab^{-3}\right)\left(a^{-3} b^6\right)$

90. Write in scientific notation: (a) 4,800,000 (b) 0.00637

Factor the greatest common factor from the polynomial.

91. $3x^4 - 6x^3 - 18x^2$

Chapter 11 Graphs

Graph:

92. $y = 4x - 3$

93. $y = -3x$

94. $y = \frac{1}{2}x + 3$

95. $x - y = 6$

96. $y = -2$

97. Find the intercepts. $2x + 3y = 12$

Graph using the intercepts.

98. $2x - 4y = 8$

99. Find the slope of the line shown.

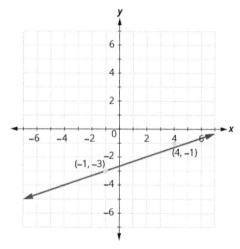

100. Use the slope formula to find the slope of the line between the points $(-5, -2)$, $(3, 2)$.

101. Graph the line passing through the point $(-3, 4)$ and with slope $m = -\frac{1}{3}$.

B POWERS AND ROOTS TABLES

n	n^2	$\sqrt{n}$	n^3	$\sqrt[3]{n}$
1	1	1	1	1
2	4	1.414214	8	1.259921
3	9	1.732051	27	1.442250
4	16	2	64	1.587401
5	25	2.236068	125	1.709976
6	36	2.449490	216	1.817121
7	49	2.645751	343	1.912931
8	64	2.828427	512	2
9	81	3	729	2.080084
10	100	3.162278	1,000	2.154435
11	121	3.316625	1,331	2.223980
12	144	3.464102	1,728	2.289428
13	169	3.605551	2,197	2.351335
14	196	3.741657	2,744	2.410142
15	225	3.872983	3,375	2.466212
16	256	4	4,096	2.519842
17	289	4.123106	4,913	2.571282
18	324	4.242641	5,832	2.620741
19	361	4.358899	6,859	2.668402
20	400	4.472136	8,000	2.714418
21	441	4.582576	9,261	2.758924
22	484	4.690416	10,648	2.802039
23	529	4.795832	12,167	2.843867
24	576	4.898979	13,824	2.884499
25	625	5	15,625	2.924018
26	676	5.099020	17,576	2.962496

Table B1

n	n^2	$\sqrt{n}$	n^3	$\sqrt[3]{n}$
27	729	5.196152	19,683	3
28	784	5.291503	21,952	3.036589
29	841	5.385165	24,389	3.072317
30	900	5.477226	27,000	3.107233
31	961	5.567764	29,791	3.141381
32	1,024	5.656854	32,768	3.174802
33	1,089	5.744563	35,937	3.207534
34	1,156	5.830952	39,304	3.239612
35	1,225	5.916080	42,875	3.271066
36	1,296	6	46,656	3.301927
37	1,369	6.082763	50653	3.332222
38	1,444	6.164414	54,872	3.361975
39	1,521	6.244998	59,319	3.391211
40	1,600	6.324555	64,000	3.419952
41	1,681	6.403124	68,921	3.448217
42	1,764	6.480741	74,088	3.476027
43	1,849	6.557439	79,507	3.503398
44	1,936	6.633250	85,184	3.530348
45	2,025	6.708204	91,125	3.556893
46	2,116	6.782330	97,336	3.583048
47	2,209	6.855655	103,823	3.608826
48	2,304	6.928203	110,592	3.634241
49	2,401	7	117,649	3.659306
50	2,500	7.071068	125,000	3.684031
51	2,601	7.141428	132,651	3.708430
52	2,704	7.211103	140,608	3.732511
53	2,809	7.280110	148,877	3.756286

Table B1

n	n^2	$\sqrt{n}$	n^3	$\sqrt[3]{n}$
54	2,916	7.348469	157,464	3.779763
55	3,025	7.416198	166,375	3.802952
56	3,136	7.483315	175,616	3.825862
57	3,249	7.549834	185,193	3.848501
58	3,364	7.615773	195,112	3.870877
59	3,481	7.681146	205,379	3.892996
60	3,600	7.745967	216,000	3.914868
61	3,721	7.810250	226,981	3.936497
62	3,844	7.874008	238,328	3.957892
63	3,969	7.937254	250,047	3.979057
64	4,096	8	262,144	4
65	4,225	8.062258	274,625	4.020726
66	4,356	8.124038	287,496	4.041240
67	4,489	8.185353	300,763	4.061548
68	4,624	8.246211	314,432	4.081655
69	4,761	8.306624	328,509	4.101566
70	4,900	8.366600	343,000	4.121285
71	5,041	8.426150	357,911	4.140818
72	5,184	8.485281	373,248	4.160168
73	5,329	8.544004	389,017	4.179339
74	5,476	8.602325	405,224	4.198336
75	5,625	8.660254	421,875	4.217163
76	5,776	8.717798	438,976	4.235824
77	5,929	8.774964	456,533	4.254321
78	6,084	8.831761	474,552	4.272659
79	6,241	8.888194	493,039	4.290840
80	6,400	8.944272	512,000	4.308869

Table B1

n	n^2	$\sqrt{n}$	n^3	$\sqrt[3]{n}$
81	6,561	9	531,441	4.326749
82	6,724	9.055385	551,368	4.344481
83	6,889	9.110434	571,787	4.362071
84	7,056	9.165151	592,704	4.379519
85	7,225	9.219544	614,125	4.396830
86	7,396	9.273618	636,056	4.414005
87	7,569	9.327379	658,503	4.431048
88	7,744	9.380832	681,472	4.447960
89	7,921	9.433981	704,969	4.464745
90	8,100	9.486833	729,000	4.481405
91	8,281	9.539392	753,571	4.497941
92	8,464	9.591663	778,688	4.514357
93	8,649	9.643651	804,357	4.530655
94	8,836	9.695360	830,584	4.546836
95	9,025	9.746794	857,375	4.562903
96	9,216	9.797959	884,736	4.578857
97	9,409	9.848858	912,673	4.594701
98	9,604	9.899495	941,192	4.610436
99	9,801	9.949874	970,299	4.626065
100	10,000	10	1,000,000	4.641589

Table B1

C | GEOMETRIC FORMULAS

Name	Shape	Formulas
Rectangle		Perimeter: $P = 2l + 2w$ Area: $A = lw$
Square		Perimeter: $P = 4s$ Area: $A = s^2$
Triangle		Perimeter: $P = a + b + c$ Area: $A = \frac{1}{2}bh$ Sum of Angles: $A + B + C = 180°$
Right Triangle		Pythagorean Theorem: $a^2 + b^2 = c^2$ Area: $A = \frac{1}{2}ab$
Circle		Circumference: $C = 2\pi r$ or $C = \pi d$ Area: $A = \pi r^2$
Parellelogram		Perimeter: $P = 2a + 2b$ Area: $A = bh$

Table C1 2 Dimensions

Name	Shape	Formulas
Trapezoid		Perimeter: $P = a + b + c + B$ Area: $A = \frac{1}{2}(B + b)h$

Table C1 2 Dimensions

Name	Shape	Formulas
Rectangular Solid		Volume: $V = lwh$ Surface Area: $SA = 2lw + 2wh + 2hl$
Cube		Volume: $V = s^3$ Surface Area: $SA = 6s^2$
Cone		Volume: $V = \frac{1}{3}\pi r^2 h$ Surface Area: $SA = \pi r^2 + \pi r \sqrt{h^2 + r^2}$
Sphere		Volume: $V = \frac{4}{3}\pi r^3$ Surface Area: $SA = 4\pi r^2$

Table C2 3 Dimensions

Name	Shape	Formulas
Right Circular Cylinder		Volume: $V = \pi r^2 h$ Surface Area: $SA = 2\pi r^2 + 2\pi rh$

Table C2 3 Dimensions

ANSWER KEY
Chapter 1

Try It

1.1.
ⓐ 2, 9, 241, 376

ⓑ 0, 2, 9, 241, 376

1.4. 237

1.2.
ⓐ 7, 13, 201

ⓑ 0, 7, 13, 201

1.5.
ⓐ ten millions

ⓑ tens

ⓒ hundred thousands

ⓓ millions

ⓔ ones

1.3. 176

1.6.
ⓐ billions

ⓑ ten thousands

ⓒ tens

ⓓ hundred thousands

ⓔ hundred millions

1.7. nine trillion, two hundred fifty-eight billion, one hundred thirty-seven million, nine hundred four thousand, sixty-one

1.10. thirty one million, five hundred thirty-six thousand

1.13. 34,000,000 miles

1.16. 880

1.19. 64,000

1.8. seventeen trillion, eight hundred sixty-four billion, three hundred twenty-five million, six hundred nineteen thousand, four

1.11. 53,809,051

1.14. 204,000,000 pounds

1.17. 17,900

1.20. 156,000

1.9. three hundred sixteen million, one hundred twenty-eight thousand, eight hundred thirty nine

1.12. 2,022,714,466

1.15. 160

1.18. 5,000

1.21.
ⓐ eight plus four; the sum of eight and four

ⓑ eighteen plus eleven; the sum of eighteen and eleven

1.22.
ⓐ twenty-one plus sixteen; the sum of twenty-one and sixteen

ⓑ one hundred plus two hundred; the sum of one hundred and two hundred

1.25.

$$5 + 7 = 12$$

1.23.

$$3 + 6 = 9$$

1.26.

$$6 + 8 = 14$$

1.24.

$$5 + 1 = 6$$

1.27.

$$15 + 27 = 42$$

1.28.

$$16 + 29 = 45$$

1.29.
ⓐ $0 + 19 = 19$

ⓑ $39 + 0 = 39$

1.30.
ⓐ $0 + 24 = 24$

ⓑ $57 + 0 = 57$

1.31. $9 + 7 = 16; 7 + 9 = 16$
1.34. $25 + 74 = 99$

1.32. $8 + 6 = 14; 6 + 8 = 14$
1.35. $35 + 98 = 133$

1.33. $32 + 54 = 86$
1.36. $72 + 89 = 161$

1.37. $456 + 376 = 832$
1.40. $5,837 + 695 = 6,532$

1.43. Translate: $17 + 26$; Simplify: 43
1.46. Translate $37 + 69$; Simplify 106
1.49. The perimeter is 30 inches.

1.38. $269 + 578 = 847$
1.41.
$46,195 + 397 + 6,281 = 52,873$
1.44. Translate: $28 + 14$; Simplify: 42
1.47. He rode 140 miles.

1.50. The perimeter is 36 inches.

1.39. $4,597 + 685 = 5,282$
1.42.
$53,762 + 196 + 7,458 = 61,416$
1.45. Translate: $29 + 76$; Simplify 105
1.48. The total number is 720 students.
1.51.
ⓐ twelve minus four; the difference of twelve and four
ⓑ twenty-nine minus eleven; the difference of twenty-nine and eleven

1.52.
ⓐ eleven minus two; the difference of eleven and two
ⓑ twenty-nine minus twelve; the difference of twenty-nine and twelve
1.55.

$12 - 7 = 5$

1.53.

$9 - 6 = 3$

1.56.

$14 - 8 = 6$

1.54.

$6 - 1 = 5$

1.57.

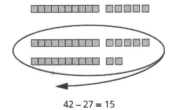

$42 - 27 = 15$

1.58.

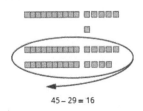

$45 - 29 = 16$

1.59. $7 - 0 = 7$; $7 + 0 = 7$

1.60. $6 - 2 = 4$; $2 + 4 = 6$

1.61. $86 - 54 = 32$ because $54 + 32 = 86$
1.64. $81 - 39 = 42$ because $42 + 39 = 81$
1.67. $832 - 376 = 456$ because $456 + 376 = 832$
1.70. $5,637 - 899 = 4,738$ because $4,738 + 899 = 5,637$

1.73. The difference is 19 degrees Fahrenheit.
1.76. The difference is $136.

1.62. $99 - 74 = 25$ because $74 + 25 = 99$
1.65. $439 - 52 = 387$ because $387 + 52 = 439$
1.68. $847 - 578 = 269$ because $269 + 578 = 847$
1.71.
ⓐ $14 - 9 = 5$ ⓑ $37 - 21 = 16$
1.74. The difference is 17 degrees Fahrenheit.
1.77.
ⓐ eight times seven ; the product of eight and seven
ⓑ eighteen times eleven ; the product of eighteen and eleven

1.63. $93 - 58 = 35$ because $58 + 35 = 93$
1.66. $318 - 75 = 243$ because $243 + 75 = 318$
1.69. $4,585 - 697 = 3,888$ because $3,888 + 697 = 4,585$
1.72.
ⓐ $11 - 6 = 5$ ⓑ $67 - 18 = 49$
1.75. The difference is $149.

1.78.
ⓐ thirteen times seven ; the product of thirteen and seven
ⓑ five times sixteen; the product of five and sixteen

1.79.

1.80.

1.81.
ⓐ 0 ⓑ 0

1.82.
ⓐ 0 ⓑ 0

1.85. 54 and 54; both are the same.

1.88. 342

1.91. 3,354

1.83.
ⓐ 19 ⓑ 39

1.86. 48 and 48; both are the same.

1.89. 1,735

1.92. 3,776

1.84.
ⓐ 24 ⓑ 57

1.87. 512

1.90. 3,234

1.93.
ⓐ 540 ⓑ 5,400

1.94.
ⓐ 750 ⓑ 7,500

1.97. 365,462

1.100. 47 · 14; 658

1.103. Valia donated 144 water bottles.

1.106. There are 36 women in the choir.

1.109. The area of the rug is 40 square feet.

1.95. 127,995

1.98. 504,108

1.101. 2(167); 334

1.104. Vanessa bought 80 hot dogs.

1.107. Jane needs 320 tiles.

1.110. The area of the driveway is 900 square feet

1.96. 653,462

1.99. 13 · 28; 364

1.102. 2(258); 516

1.105. Erin needs 28 dahlias.

1.108. Yousef needs 1,080 tiles.

1.111.

ⓐ eighty-four divided by seven; the quotient of eighty-four and seven

ⓑ eighteen divided by six; the quotient of eighteen and six.

ⓒ twenty-four divided by eight; the quotient of twenty-four and eight

1.112.

ⓐ seventy-two divided by nine; the quotient of seventy-two and nine

ⓑ twenty-one divided by three; the quotient of twenty-one and three

ⓒ fifty-four divided by six; the quotient of fifty-four and six

1.115. ⓐ 9 ⓑ 3

1.113.

1.116. ⓐ 4 ⓑ 5

1.114.

1.117.
ⓐ 1 ⓑ 27

1.118.
ⓐ 16 ⓑ 4

1.121. 659

1.124. 651

1.127. 476 with a remainder of 4

1.130. 121 R9

1.133. 91 ÷ 13; 7

1.136. Andrea can make 9 bows.

1.119. ⓐ 0 ⓑ undefined

1.122. 679

1.125. 704

1.128. 539 with a remainder of 7

1.131. 307 R49

1.134. 52 ÷ 13; 4

1.120. ⓐ 0 ⓑ undefined

1.123. 861

1.126. 809

1.129. 114 R11

1.132. 308 R77

1.135. Marcus can fill 15 cups.

Section Exercises

1.
ⓐ 0, 5, 125   ⓑ 0, 5, 125

7. 407

3.
ⓐ 50, 221   ⓑ 0, 50, 221

9.
ⓐ thousands   ⓑ hundreds
ⓒ tens   ⓓ ten thousands
ⓔ hundred thousands

5. 561

11.
ⓐ hundred thousands
ⓑ millions   ⓒ thousands
ⓓ tens   ⓔ ten thousands

13. One thousand, seventy-eight

15. Three hundred sixty-four thousand, five hundred ten

17. Five million, eight hundred forty-six thousand, one hundred three

19. Thirty seven million, eight hundred eighty-nine thousand, five

21. Fourteen thousand, four hundred ten

23. Six hundred thirteen thousand, two hundred

25. Two million, six hundred seventeen thousand, one hundred seventy-six

27. Twenty three million, eight hundred sixty-seven thousand

29. One billion, three hundred seventy-seven million, five hundred eighty-three thousand, one hundred fifty-six

31. 412
37. 3,226,512,017
43.
ⓐ 390   ⓑ 2,930
49.
ⓐ 64,000   ⓑ 63,900

33. 35,975
39. 7,173,000,000
45.
ⓐ 13,700   ⓑ 391,800
51. Twenty four thousand, four hundred ninety-three dollars

35. 11,044,167
41. 39,000,000,000,000
47.
ⓐ 1,490   ⓑ 1,500
53.
ⓐ $24,490   ⓑ $24,500
ⓒ $24,000   ⓓ $20,000

55.
ⓐ 1,000,000,000
ⓑ 1,400,000,000
ⓒ 1,356,000,000

57. Answers may vary. The whole numbers are the counting numbers with the inclusion of zero.

59. five plus two; the sum of 5 and 2.

61. thirteen plus eighteen; the sum of 13 and 18.

63. two hundred fourteen plus six hundred forty-two; the sum of 214 and 642

65.

$2 + 4 = 6$

67.

$8 + 4 = 12$

69.

$14 + 75 = 89$

71.

$16 + 25 = 41$

73.

+	0	1	2	3	4	5	6	7	8	9
0	0	1	2	3	4	5	6	7	8	9
1	1	2	3	4	5	6	7	8	9	10
2	2	3	4	5	6	7	8	9	10	11
3	3	4	5	6	7	8	9	10	11	12
4	4	5	6	7	8	9	10	11	12	13
5	5	6	7	8	9	10	11	12	13	14
6	6	7	8	9	10	11	12	13	14	15
7	7	8	9	10	11	12	13	14	15	16
8	8	9	10	11	12	13	14	15	16	17
9	9	10	11	12	13	14	15	16	17	18

75.

+	3	4	5	6	7	8	9
6	9	10	11	12	13	14	15
7	10	11	12	13	14	15	16
8	11	12	13	14	15	16	17
9	12	13	14	15	16	17	18

77.

+	5	6	7	8	9
5	10	11	12	13	14
6	11	12	13	14	15
7	12	13	14	15	16
8	13	14	15	16	17
9	14	15	16	17	18

79. (a) 13   (b) 13

81. (a) 11   (b) 11

83. 78

85. 99

87. 85

89. 142

91. 493

93. 861

95. 1,031

97. 6,850

99. 22,333

101. 1,104,860

103. 29,191

105. 101,531

107. $13 + 18 = 31$

109. $90 + 65 = 155$

111. $33 + 49 = 82$

113. $250 + 599 = 849$

115. $628 + 77 = 705$

117. $915 + 1,482 = 2,397$

119. The total cost was $1,875.

121. Ethan rode 138 miles.

123. The total square footage in the rooms is 1,167 square feet.

125. Natalie's total salary is $237,186.

127. The perimeter of the figure is 44 inches.

129. The perimeter of the figure is 56 meters.

131. The perimeter of the figure is 71 yards.

133. The perimeter of the figure is 62 feet.

135. The total number of calories was 640.

137. Yes, he scored 406 points.

139. Answers will vary.

141. fifteen minus nine; the difference of fifteen and nine

143. forty-two minus thirty-five; the difference of forty-two and thirty-five

145. hundred seventy-five minus three hundred fifty; the difference of six hundred seventy-five and three hundred fifty

147.

$5 - 2 = 3$

149.

$6 - 3 = 3$

151.

$18 - 5 = 13$

153.

$17 - 8 = 9$

155.

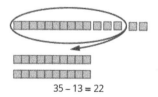

$35 - 13 = 22$

157.

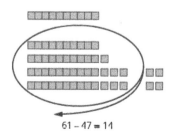

$61 - 47 = 14$

159. 5

161. 8

163. 22

165. 33

167. 123

169. 1,321

175. 346

181. 34,668

187. 9 – 6; 3

193. 92 – 67; 25

199. 29

205. 22

211. 100 – 76; 24

217. The difference between the regular price and sale price is $251.

223. Answers may vary.

229. ten times twenty-five; the product of ten and twenty-five

171. 28

177. 3,519

183. 10 – 3; 7

189. 75 – 28; 47

195. 16 – 12; 4

201. 72

207. 75 + 35; 110

213. The difference between the high and low temperature was 17 degrees

219. John needs to save $155 more.

225. four times seven; the product of four and seven

231. forty-two times thirty-three; the product of forty-two and thirty-three

173. 222

179. 1,186

185. 15 – 4; 11

191. 45 – 20; 25

197. 61 – 38; 23

203. 1,060

209. 41 – 13; 28

215. The difference between the third grade and second grade was 13 children.

221. 157 miles

227. five times twelve; the product of five and twelve

233.

$3 \times 6 = 18$

235.

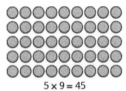

$5 \times 9 = 45$

237.

×	0	1	2	3	4	5	6	7	8	9
0	0	0	0	0	0	0	0	0	0	0
1	0	1	2	3	4	5	6	7	8	9
2	0	2	4	6	8	10	12	14	16	18
3	0	3	6	9	12	15	18	21	24	27
4	0	4	8	12	16	20	24	28	32	36
5	0	5	10	15	20	25	30	35	40	45
6	0	6	12	18	24	30	36	42	48	54
7	0	7	14	21	28	35	42	49	56	63
8	0	8	16	24	32	40	48	56	64	72
9	0	9	18	27	36	45	54	63	72	81

239.

×	3	4	5	6	7	8	9
4	12	16	20	24	28	32	36
5	15	20	25	30	35	40	45
6	18	24	30	36	42	48	54
7	21	28	35	42	49	56	63
8	24	32	40	48	56	64	72
9	27	36	45	54	63	72	81

241.

×	3	4	5	6	7	8	9
6	18	24	30	36	42	48	54
7	21	28	35	42	49	56	63
8	24	32	40	48	56	64	72
9	27	36	45	54	63	72	81

243.

×	5	6	7	8	9
5	25	30	35	40	45
6	30	36	42	48	54
7	35	42	49	56	63
8	40	48	56	64	72
9	45	54	63	72	81

245. 0

247. 0

253. 240,055

259. 1,650

265. 7,008

271. 360

277. 34,333

283. 26,624

289. 18 · 33; 594

295. 10(375); 3,750

301. 11,000

249. 43

255.

ⓐ 42   ⓑ 42

261. 23,947

267. 2,295

273. 88,000

279. 422,506

285. 245,340

291. 51(67); 3,417

297. 1,406

303. 11,424

251. 28

257. 395

263. 1,976

269. 230

275. 50,000,000

281. 804,285

287. 1,476,417

293. 2(249); 498

299. 148

305. 0

307. 15,383
313. 20 + 980; 1,000
319. 3,075 + 950; 4,025

325. There were 308 students.

331. There are 100 senators in the U.S. senate.
337. The area of the court is 4,700 square feet.
343. fifty-four divided by nine; the quotient of fifty-four and nine
349. sixty-three divided by seven; the quotient of sixty-three and seven

309. 50 – 18; 32
315. 12(875); 10,500
321. 814 – 366; 448

327. Rey donated 180 t-shirts.

333. The area of the wall is 117 square feet.
339. Javier's portfolio gained $3,600.
345. thirty-two divided by eight; the quotient of thirty-two and eight
351.

311. 2(35); 70
317. 89 – 74; 15
323. Tim brought 54 cans of soda to the party.
329. Stephanie should use 20 cups of fruit juice.
335. The area of the room is 1,428 square feet.
341. Answers will vary.

347. forty-eight divided by six; the quotient of forty-eight and six
353.

355.

357.

359. 9

361. 9
367. 9
373. 1
379. 0
385. 0
391. 93
397. 7,831
403. 704
409. 6,913 R1
415. 382 R5
421. 1,986 R17
427. 1,060
433. 288 ÷ 24; 12
439. Marta can wrap 16 cakes from 1 roll.
445. Bill hiked 50 miles

363. 7
369. 5
375. 23
381. undefined
387. 24
393. 132
399. 2,403
405. 10,209
411. 86,234 R4
417. 849
423. 3,060
429. 35
435. Ric can fill 32 bags.
441. The difference is 28 miles per gallon.
447. LaVonne treated 48 patients last week.

365. 9
371. 1
377. 19
383. undefined
389. 12
395. 871
401. 901
407. 352 R6
413. 43,338 R2
419. 96
425. 72
431. 45 ÷ 15; 3
437. There are 25 groups.
443. They will need 5 vans for the field trip
449. Answers may vary. Using multiplication facts can help you check your answers once you've finished division.

451. Jenna uses 26 pairs of contact lenses, but there is 1 day left over, so she needs 27 pairs for 365 days.

Review Exercises

453.

(a) 2, 99   (b) 0, 2, 99

455.

(a) 4, 90   (b) 0, 4, 90

457.

Place Value	Digit	Total Value
hundreds	2	200
tens	5	50
ones	8	8
		258

459.

(a) tens

(b) hundred thousands

(c) ones   (d) thousands

(e) ten thousands

466. 15,253
471. 3,560
477. four plus three; the sum of four and three

461. Five thousand two hundred eighty

467. 340,912,061
473. 39,000
479. five hundred seventy-one plus six hundred twenty-nine; the sum of five hundred seventy-one and six hundred twenty-nine

463. Five million twelve thousand five hundred eighty-two

469. 410
475. 81,500
481.

483.

+	0	1	2	3	4	5	6	7	8	9
0	0	1	2	3	4	5	6	7	8	9
1	1	2	3	4	5	6	7	8	9	10
2	2	3	4	5	6	7	8	9	10	11
3	3	4	5	6	7	8	9	10	11	12
4	4	5	6	7	8	9	10	11	12	13
5	5	6	7	8	9	10	11	12	13	14
6	6	7	8	9	10	11	12	13	14	15
7	7	8	9	10	11	12	13	14	15	16
8	8	9	10	11	12	13	14	15	16	17
9	9	10	11	12	13	14	15	16	17	18

485.

(a) 19   (b) 19

487.

(a) 13   (b) 13

489. 82
495. 30 + 12; 42
501. 46 feet

491. 154
497. 39 + 25; 64
503. fourteen minus five; the difference of fourteen and five

493. 19,827
499. $76
505. three hundred fifty-one minus two hundred forty-nine; the difference between three hundred fifty-one and two hundred forty-nine

507.

509. 3

511. 14

513. 23
519. 9,985
525. 58 degrees Fahrenheit

515. 322
521. 19 − 13; 6
527. eight times five the product of eight and five

517. 380
523. 74 − 8; 66
529. ten times ninety-five; the product of ten and ninety-five

531.

533.

×	0	1	2	3	4	5	6	7	8	9
0	0	0	0	0	0	0	0	0	0	0
1	0	1	2	3	4	5	6	7	8	9
2	0	2	4	6	8	10	12	14	16	18
3	0	3	6	9	12	15	18	21	24	27
4	0	4	8	12	16	20	24	28	32	36
5	0	5	10	15	20	25	30	35	40	45
6	0	6	12	18	24	30	36	42	48	54
7	0	7	14	21	28	35	42	49	56	63
8	0	8	16	24	32	40	48	56	64	72
9	0	9	18	27	36	45	54	63	72	81

535. 0

537. 99

539.
ⓐ 28   ⓑ 28

541. 27,783

543. 640
549. 15(28); 420
555. 1,800 seats

545. 79,866
551. 2(575); 1,150
557. fifty-four divided by nine; the quotient of fifty-four and nine
563. 7

547. 1,873,608
553. 48 marigolds
559. seventy-two divided by eight; the quotient of seventy-two and eight
565. 13

561.

567. 97
573. 300 R5

569. undefined
575. 64 ÷ 16; 4

571. 638
577. 9 baskets

Practice Test

579.
ⓐ 4, 87   ⓑ 0, 4, 8
585. 17
591. 0
597. 490
603. 16 + 58; 74
609. 300 − 50; 250

581.
ⓐ 613   ⓑ 55,208
587. 32
593. 66
599. 442
605. 32 − 18; 14
611. Stan had $344 left.

583. 68

589. 0
595. 3,325
601. 11
607. 2(524); 1,048
613. Clayton walked 30 blocks.

Chapter 2

Try It

2.1.
ⓐ 18 plus 11; the sum of eighteen and eleven
ⓑ 27 times 9; the product of twenty-seven and nine
ⓒ 84 divided by 7; the quotient of eighty-four and seven
ⓓ p minus q; the difference of p and q

2.2.
ⓐ 47 minus 19; the difference of forty-seven and nineteen
ⓑ 72 divided by 9; the quotient of seventy-two and nine
ⓒ m plus n; the sum of m and n
ⓓ 13 times 7; the product of thirteen and seven

2.3.
ⓐ fourteen is less than or equal to twenty-seven
ⓑ nineteen minus two is not equal to eight
ⓒ twelve is greater than four divided by two
ⓓ x minus seven is less than one

2.4.

ⓐ nineteen is greater than or equal to fifteen

ⓑ seven is equal to twelve minus five

ⓒ fifteen divided by three is less than eight

ⓓ y minus three is greater than six

2.7.

ⓐ equation   ⓑ expression

2.10. 7^9

2.13.

ⓐ 125   ⓑ 1

2.16.

ⓐ 35   ⓑ 99

2.19. 16

2.22. 1

2.25.

ⓐ 10   ⓑ 19

2.28.

ⓐ 8   ⓑ 16

2.31. 64

2.34. 10

2.37. The terms are $4x$, $3b$, and 2. The coefficients are 4, 3, and 2.

2.40. $4x^3$ and $6x^3$; $8x^2$ and $3x^2$; 19 and 24

2.43. $4x^2 + 14x$

2.46.

ⓐ 17 + 19   ⓑ $7x$

2.49.

ⓐ $4(p + q)$ ⓐ $4p + q$

2.52. $l + 2$

2.55. no

2.58. yes

2.61. $x = 13$

2.64. $y = 46$

2.67. $a = 37$

2.70. 8 + 6 = 14

2.73. $2(x - 5) = 30$

2.76. $y + 11 = 28$; $y = 17$

2.79.

ⓐ yes   ⓑ no

2.5.

ⓐ >   ⓑ >

2.8.

ⓐ expression   ⓑ equation

2.11.

ⓐ $4 \cdot 4 \cdot 4 \cdot 4 \cdot 4 \cdot 4 \cdot 4 \cdot 4$

ⓑ $a \cdot a \cdot a \cdot a \cdot a \cdot a \cdot a$

2.14.

ⓐ 49   ⓑ 0

2.17. 18

2.20. 23

2.23. 81

2.26.

ⓐ 4   ⓑ 12

2.29. 64

2.32. 81

2.35. 40

2.38. The terms are $9a$, $13a^2$, and a^3, The coefficients are 9, 13, and 1.

2.41. $16x + 17$

2.44. $12y^2 + 15y$

2.47.

ⓐ $x + 11$ ⓑ $11a - 14$

2.50.

ⓐ $2x - 8$ ⓑ $2(x - 8)$

2.53. $6q - 7$

2.56. yes

2.59. $x + 1 = 7$; $x = 6$

2.62. $x = 5$

2.65. $x = 22$

2.68. $n = 41$

2.71. $6 \cdot 9 = 54$

2.74. $2(y - 4) = 16$

2.77. $z - 17 = 37$; $z = 54$

2.80.

ⓐ no   ⓑ yes

2.6.

ⓐ <   ⓑ <

2.9. 41^5

2.12.

ⓐ $8 \cdot 8 \cdot 8 \cdot 8 \cdot 8 \cdot 8 \cdot 8 \cdot 8$

ⓑ $b \cdot b \cdot b \cdot b \cdot b \cdot b$

2.15.

ⓐ 2   ⓑ 14

2.18. 9

2.21. 86

2.24. 75

2.27.

ⓐ 13   ⓑ 5

2.30. 216

2.33. 33

2.36. 9

2.39. 9, 15; $2x^3$ and $8x^3$, y^2, and $11y^2$

2.42. $17y + 7$

2.45.

ⓐ 47 − 41   ⓑ $5x \div 2$

2.48.

ⓐ $j + 19$ ⓑ $2x - 21$

2.51. $w - 5$

2.54. $4n + 8$

2.57. yes

2.60. $x + 3 = 4$; $x = 1$

2.63. $y = 28$

2.66. $y = 4$

2.69. 7 + 6 = 13

2.72. $21 \cdot 3 = 63$

2.75. $x + 7 = 37$; $x = 30$

2.78. $x - 19 = 45$; $x = 64$

2.81.

ⓐ yes   ⓑ no

2.82.
ⓐ no ⓑ yes

2.83.
ⓐ no ⓑ yes

2.84.
ⓐ yes ⓑ no

2.85.
ⓐ yes ⓑ no

2.86.
ⓐ no ⓑ yes

2.87. Divisible by 2, 3, 5, and 10

2.88. Divisible by 2 and 3, not 5 or 10.

2.89. Divisible by 2, 3, not 5 or 10.

2.90. Divisible by 3 and 5.

2.91. 1, 2, 3, 4, 6, 8, 12, 16, 24, 32, 48, 96

2.92. 1, 2, 4, 5, 8, 10, 16, 20, 40, 80

2.93. composite

2.94. prime

2.95. $2 \cdot 2 \cdot 2 \cdot 2 \cdot 5$, or $2^4 \cdot 5$

2.96. $2 \cdot 2 \cdot 3 \cdot 5$, or $2^2 \cdot 3 \cdot 5$

2.97. $2 \cdot 3 \cdot 3 \cdot 7$, or $2 \cdot 3^2 \cdot 7$

2.98. $2 \cdot 3 \cdot 7 \cdot 7$, or $2 \cdot 3 \cdot 7^2$

2.99. $2 \cdot 2 \cdot 2 \cdot 2 \cdot 5$, or $2^4 \cdot 5$

2.100. $2 \cdot 2 \cdot 3 \cdot 5$, or $2^2 \cdot 3 \cdot 5$

2.101. $2 \cdot 3 \cdot 3 \cdot 7$, or $2 \cdot 3^2 \cdot 7$

2.102. $2 \cdot 3 \cdot 7 \cdot 7$, or $2 \cdot 3 \cdot 7^2$

2.103. 36

2.104. 72

2.105. 60

2.106. 105

2.107. 440

2.108. 360

Section Exercises

1. 16 minus 9, the difference of sixteen and nine

3. 5 times 6, the product of five and six

5. 28 divided by 4, the quotient of twenty-eight and four

7. x plus 8, the sum of x and eight

9. 2 times 7, the product of two and seven

11. fourteen is less than twenty-one

13. thirty-six is greater than or equal to nineteen

15. 3 times n equals 24, the product of three and n equals twenty-four

17. y minus 1 is greater than 6, the difference of y and one is greater than six

19. 2 is less than or equal to 18 divided by 6; 2 is less than or equal to the quotient of eighteen and six

21. a is not equal to 7 times 4, a is not equal to the product of seven and four

23. equation

25. expression

27. expression

29. equation

31. 3^7

33. x^5

35. 125

37. 256

39.
ⓐ 43 ⓑ 55

41. 5

43. 34

45. 58

47. 6

49. 13

51. 4

53. 35

55. 10

57. 41

59. 81

61. 149

63. 50

69. 22

71. 26

73. 144

75. 32

77. 27

79. 21

81. 41

83. 9

84. 225

85. 73

87. 54

89. $15x^2$, $6x$, 2

91. $10y^3$, y, 2

93. 8

95. 5

97. x^3, $8x^3$ and 14, 5

99. $16ab$ and $4ab$; $16b^2$ and $9b^2$

101. $13x$

103. $26a$

105. $7c$

107. $12x + 8$

109. $10u + 3$

111. $12p + 10$

113. $22a + 1$

115. $17x^2 + 20x + 16$

117. $8 + 12$

119. $14 - 9$

121. $9 \cdot 7$

123. $36 \div 9$

125. $x - 4$

127. $6y$

129. $8x + 3x$

131. $\frac{y}{3}$

133. $8(y - 9)$

135. $5(x + y)$

137. $b + 15$

139. $b - 4$

141. $2n - 7$

143. He will pay $750. His insurance company will pay $1350.

147.
ⓐ yes ⓑ no

149.
ⓐ no ⓑ yes

151.
ⓐ yes ⓑ no

153.
ⓐ no ⓑ yes

155.
ⓐ no ⓑ yes

157.
ⓐ no ⓑ yes

159. $x + 2 = 5$; $x = 3$

161. $x + 3 = 6$; $x = 3$

163. $a = 16$

165. $p = 5$

167. $r = 24$

169. $x = 7$

171. $p = 69$

173. $d = 67$

175. $y = 22$

177. $u = 30$

179. $f = 178$

181. $n = 32$

183. $p = 48$

185. $y = 467$

187. $8 + 9 = 17$

189. $23 - 19 = 4$

191. $3 \cdot 9 = 27$

193. $54 \div 6 = 9$

195. $2(n - 10) = 52$

197. $3y + 10 = 100$

199. $p + 5 = 21$; $p = 16$

201. $r + 18 = 73$; $r = 55$

203. $d - 30 = 52$; $d = 82$

205. $u - 12 = 89$; $u = 101$

207. $c - 325 = 799$; $c = 1124$

209. \$1300

211. \$460

215. 2, 4, 6, 8, 10 12, 14, 16, 18, 20, 22, 24, 26, 28, 30, 32, 34, 36, 38, 40, 42, 44, 46, 48

217. 4, 8, 12, 16, 20, 24, 28, 32, 36, 40, 44, 48

219. 6, 12, 18, 24, 30, 36, 42, 48

221. 8, 16, 24, 32, 40, 48

223. 10, 20, 30, 40

225. Divisible by 2, 3, 4, 6

227. Divisible by 3, 5

229. Divisible by 2, 3, 4, 6

231. Divisible by 2, 3, 4, 5, 6, 10

233. Divisible by 2, 4

235. Divisible by 3, 5

237. Divisible by 2, 5, 10

239. Divisible by 2, 5, 10

241. Divisible by 3, 5

243. 1, 2, 3, 4, 6, 9, 12, 18, 36

245. 1, 2, 3, 4, 5, 6, 10, 12, 15, 20, 30, 60

247. 1, 2, 3, 4, 6, 8, 12, 18, 24, 36, 48, 72,144

249. 1, 2, 3, 4, 6, 7, 12, 14, 21, 28, 42, 49, 84, 98, 147, 196, 294, 588

251. prime

253. composite

255. prime

257. composite

259. composite

261. composite

263.

Weeks after graduation	Total number of dollars Frank put in the account	Simplified Total
0	100	100
1	100 + 15	115
2	100 + 15 · 2	130
3	100 + 15 · 3	145
4	100 + 15 · 4	160
5	100 + 15 · 5	175
6	100 + 15 · 6	190
20	100 + 15 · 20	400
x	100 + 15 · x	$100 + 15x$

267. $2 \cdot 43$

269. $2 \cdot 2 \cdot 3 \cdot 11$

271. $3 \cdot 3 \cdot 7 \cdot 11$

273. $5 \cdot 23$

275. $3 \cdot 3 \cdot 5 \cdot 5 \cdot 11$

277. $2 \cdot 2 \cdot 2 \cdot 7$

279. $2 \cdot 2 \cdot 2 \cdot 3 \cdot 7$

281. $17 \cdot 23$

283. $2 \cdot 2 \cdot 2 \cdot 2 \cdot 3 \cdot 3 \cdot 3$

285. $2 \cdot 2 \cdot 2 \cdot 2 \cdot 3 \cdot 3 \cdot 3 \cdot 5$

287. $2 \cdot 3 \cdot 5 \cdot 5$

289. $3 \cdot 5 \cdot 5 \cdot 7$

291. $2 \cdot 2 \cdot 3 \cdot 3$

293. $2 \cdot 5 \cdot 5 \cdot 7$

295. 24

297. 30

299. 120

301. 300

303. 24

305. 120

307. 420

309. 42

311. 120

313. 40

Review Exercises

317. the product of 3 and 8

319. the quotient of 24 and 6

321. 50 is greater than or equal to 47

323. The sum of n and 4 is equal to 13

325. equation

327. expression

329. 2^3

331. x^6

333. $8 \cdot 8 \cdot 8 \cdot 8$

335. $y \cdot y \cdot y \cdot y \cdot y$

337. 81

339. 128

341. 20

343. 18

345. 74

347. 31

349. 58

351. 26

353. $12n^2, 3n, 1$

355. 6

357. 3, 4, and $3x$, x

359. $24a$

361. $14x$

363. $12n + 11$

365. $10y^2 + 2y + 3$

367. $x - 6$

369. $3n \cdot 9$

371. $5(y + 1)$

373. $c + 3$

375.
ⓐ yes   ⓑ no

377.
ⓐ yes   ⓑ no

379.
ⓐ no   ⓑ yes

381. $x + 3 = 5$; $x = 2$

383. 6

385. 11

387. 23

389. 34

391. $7 + 33 = 44$

393. $4 \cdot 8 = 32$

395. $2(n - 3) = 76$

397. $x + 8 = 35$; $x = 27$

399. $q - 18 = 57$; $q = 75$

401. $h = 42$

403. $z = 33$

405. $q = 8$

407. $v = 56$

409. 3, 6, 9, 12, 15, 18, 21, 24, 27, 30, 33, 36, 39, 42, 45, 48

411. 8, 16, 24, 32, 40, 48

413. 2, 3, 6

415. 2, 3, 5, 6, 10

417. 1, 2, 3, 5, 6, 10, 15, 30

419. 1, 2, 3, 4, 5, 6, 9, 10, 12, 15, 18, 20, 30, 36, 45, 60, 90, 180

421. prime

423. composite

425. $2 \cdot 2 \cdot 3 \cdot 7$

427. $2 \cdot 5 \cdot 5 \cdot 7$

429. 45

431. 350

433. Answers will vary

Practice Test

435. fifteen minus x

437. equation

439.
ⓐ n^6 ⓑ $3 \cdot 3 \cdot 3 \cdot 3 \cdot 3 = 243$

441. 36

443. 5

445. 45

447. 125

449. 36

451. $x + 5$

453. $3(a - b)$

455. $n = 31$

457. $y - 15 = 32$; $y = 47$

459. 4, 8, 12, 16, 20, 24, 28, 32, 36, 40, 44, 48

461. $2^3 \cdot 3^3 \cdot 5$

Chapter 3

Try It

3.1.

3.2.

3.3.
ⓐ >   ⓑ <   ⓒ >   ⓓ >

3.4.
ⓐ <   ⓑ >   ⓒ <   ⓓ >
3.7. 1

3.5.
ⓐ −4   ⓑ 3
3.8. 5

3.6.
ⓐ −8   ⓑ 5
3.9.
ⓐ −4   ⓑ 4

3.10.
ⓐ −11   ⓑ 11
3.13.
ⓐ 17   ⓑ 39   ⓒ −22
ⓓ −11
3.16.
ⓐ >   ⓑ =   ⓒ >   ⓓ <
3.19. 2
3.22. 9

3.11.
ⓐ 12   ⓑ −28
3.14.
ⓐ 23   ⓑ 21   ⓒ −37
ⓓ −49
3.17.
ⓐ 3   ⓑ 18
3.20. 3
3.23.
ⓐ −9   ⓑ 15   ⓒ −20
ⓓ 11−(−4)

3.12.
ⓐ 9   ⓑ −37
3.15.
ⓐ >   ⓑ >   ⓒ <   ⓓ =
3.18.
ⓐ 11   ⓑ 63
3.21. 16
3.24.
ⓐ 19   ⓑ −22   ⓒ −9
ⓓ −8−(−5)

3.25. 5 yards

3.26. -30 feet

3.27.

6

3.28.

7

3.29.

-6

3.30.

-7

3.31.

-2

3.32.

-3

3.33.

-2

3.34.

3

3.35.

ⓐ

ⓑ

ⓒ

ⓓ

3.36.

ⓐ

ⓑ

ⓒ

ⓓ

3.37.
ⓐ −17   ⓑ 57
3.40. -70
3.43.
ⓐ 2   ⓑ −12
3.46.
ⓐ −1   ⓑ 17
3.49. 196
3.52. −8 + (−6) = −14
3.55. 4 degrees Celsius
3.58. 37-yard line

3.38.
ⓐ −46   ⓑ 26
3.41. 13
3.44.
ⓐ 2   ⓑ −1
3.47. 9
3.50. 8
3.53. [9 + (−16)] + 4 = −3
3.56. -33 feet
3.59.

2

3.39. -50

3.42. 0
3.45.
ⓐ −6   ⓑ 10
3.48. 13

3.51. −7 + 4 = −3
3.54. [−8 + (−12)] + 7 = −13
3.57. 14-yard line
3.60.

3

3.61.

-2

3.62.

-3

3.63.

−10

3.64.

−11

3.67. (a)

(b)

(c)

(d)

3.70. (a)

−3

(b)

3

3.65.

10

3.68. (a)

(b)

(c)

(d)

3.71.

(a) 8, 8   (b) −18, −18

3.66.

11

3.69. (a)

−2

(b)

4

3.72.

(a) 8, 8   (b) −22, −22

3.73.

(a) 19, 19   (b) −4, −4

3.76. −26

3.79. −69

3.82.

(a) −2   (b) −7

3.85.

(a) −14 − (−23) = 37

(b) −17 − 21 = −38

3.88. 9 degrees Fahrenheit

3.74.

(a) 23, 23   (b) 3, 3

3.77. 3

3.80. −47

3.83.

(a) −2   (b) 36

3.86.

(a) 11 − (−19) = 30

(b) −11 − 18 = −29

3.89. 10,103 feet

3.75. −29

3.78. 13

3.81.

(a) −2   (b) −15

3.84.

(a) −19   (b) 9

3.87. 45 degrees Fahrenheit

3.90. 233 feet

3.91.
ⓐ $48 ⓑ –$2 ⓒ $18

3.92.
ⓐ –$54 ⓑ No, –$5

3.93.
ⓐ –48 ⓑ 28 ⓒ –63
ⓓ 60

3.94.
ⓐ –56
ⓑ 54
ⓒ –28
ⓓ 39

3.95.
ⓐ –9 ⓑ 17

3.96.
ⓐ –8 ⓑ 16

3.97.
ⓐ –7 ⓑ 39

3.98.
ⓐ –9 ⓑ 23

3.99.
ⓐ –6 ⓑ 36

3.100.
ⓐ –28 ⓑ 52

3.101. –63

3.102. –84

3.103.
ⓐ 81 ⓑ –81

3.104.
ⓐ 49 ⓑ –49

3.105. 29

3.106. 52
3.109. 21
3.112. 13
3.115. –5 (12) = –60
3.118. –72 ÷ –9 = 8

3.107. 4
3.110. 6
3.113. –8
3.116. 8 (–13) = –104
3.119.
ⓐ no ⓑ no ⓒ yes

3.108. 9
3.111. 39
3.114. 19
3.117. –63 ÷ –9 = 7
3.120.
ⓐ no ⓑ no ⓒ yes

3.121. –4
3.124. –4
3.127. 7
3.130. –9
3.133. $p - 2 = -4$; $p = -2$
3.136. $117 = -13z$; $z = -9$

3.122. –19
3.125. $4x = 12$; $x = 3$
3.128. 11
3.131. $x + 7 = -2$; $x = -9$
3.134. $q - 7 = -3$; $q = 4$

3.123. –6
3.126. $3x = 6$; $x = 2$
3.129. –12
3.132. $y + 11 = 2$; $y = -9$
3.135. $132 = -12y$; $y = -11$

Section Exercises

1.

3.

5.
ⓐ > ⓑ < ⓒ < ⓓ >

7.
ⓐ < ⓑ > ⓒ < ⓓ >
13. 4

9.
ⓐ –2 ⓑ 6
15. 15

11.
ⓐ 8 ⓑ –1
17.
ⓐ –3 ⓑ 3

19.
ⓐ –12; ⓑ 12
25.
ⓐ 28 ⓑ 15
31.
ⓐ > ⓑ >
37. 0
43.
ⓐ –8 ⓑ –(–6), or 6 ⓒ –3
ⓓ 4–(–3)
49. –40 feet

21.
ⓐ 7 ⓑ 25 ⓒ 0
27.
ⓐ –19 ⓑ –33
33. 4
39. 8
45.
ⓐ –20 ⓑ –(–5), or 5
ⓒ –12 ⓓ 18–(–7)
51. –12 yards

23.
ⓐ 32 ⓑ 18 ⓒ 16
29.
ⓐ < ⓑ =
35. 56
41. 80
47. –6 degrees

53. $3

55. +1

57.
ⓐ 20,320 feet   ⓑ −282 feet

59.
ⓐ $540 million

ⓑ −$27 billion

61. Sample answer: I have experienced negative temperatures.

63.

11

65.

−9

67.

−2

69.

1

71. −80

73. 32

75. −135

77. 0

79. −22

81. 108

83. −4

85. 29

87.
ⓐ −18   ⓑ −87

89.
ⓐ −47   ⓑ 16

91.
ⓐ −4   ⓑ 10

93.
ⓐ −13   ⓑ 5

95. −8

97. 10

99. 64

101. 121

103. −14 + 5 = −9

105. −2 + 8 = 6

107. −15 + (−10) = −25

109. [−1 + (−12)] + 6 = −7

111. [10 + (−19)] + 4 = −5

113. 7°F

115. −$118

117. −8 pounds

119. 25-yard line

121. 20 calories

123. −32

125. Sample answer: In the first case, there are more negatives so the sum is negative. In the second case, there are more positives so the sum is positive.

127.

6

129.

−4

131.

−9

133.

12

135.
ⓐ 9   ⓑ 9

137.
ⓐ 16   ⓑ 16

139.
ⓐ 17   ⓑ 17

141.
ⓐ 45   ⓑ 45

143. 27

145. 29

147. −39

149. −48

151. −42

153. −59

155. −51

157. 9

159. −2

161. −2

163. 22

165. 53

167. −20

169. 0

171. 4

173. 6

175. −8

177. −11

179.
ⓐ −3   ⓑ −9

181.
ⓐ 3   ⓑ 7

183. −8

185. −192

187.

ⓐ –3 – (–10) = 13

ⓑ 45 – (–20) = 65

193.

ⓐ 6 – 21 = –15

ⓑ –19 – 31 = –50

199. 21-yard line

205. $26

211. –32

217. –63

223. –4

229. –12

235. 43

241. –16

247. 9

253. –9

259.

ⓐ 1   ⓑ 33

265. 21

271. –3·15 = –45

277. –10 (p – q)

283. Sample answer: In one expression the base is positive and then we take the opposite, but in the other the base is negative.

289. –7

295. 6

301. 3x = 6; x = 2

307. –8

313. 20

319. 8 + p = –3; p = –11

325. f(–15) = 75; f = 5

331.

ⓐ 8   ⓑ 5

337. 7

343. 5

349. Sample answer: It is helpful because it shows how the counters can be divided among the envelopes.

189.

ⓐ –6 – 9 = –15

ⓑ –16 – (–12) = –4

195. –10°

201. $65

207. 13°

213. –35

219. –6

225. –8

231. –49

237. –125

243. 90

249. 41

255. –29

261.

ⓐ –5   ⓑ 25

267. 38

273. –60 ÷ (–20) = 3

279. –$3,600

285.

ⓐ no   ⓑ yes   ⓒ no

291. –17

297. –16

303. 2x = 8; x = 4

309. 3

315. 0

321. a – 3 = –14; a = –11

327. –6 + c = 4; c = 10

333.

ⓐ –9   ⓑ 30

339. –52

345. –42

351. Sample answer: The operation used in the equation is multiplication. The inverse of multiplication is division, not addition.

191.

ⓐ –17 – 8 = –25

ⓑ –24 – 37 = –61

197. 96°

203. –$40

209. Sample answer: On a number line, 9 is 15 units away from –6.

215. 36

221. 14

227. 13

233. –47

239. 64

245. –88

251. –5

257. 5

263. 8

269. –56

275. $\dfrac{-6}{a + b}$

281. Sample answer: Multiplying two integers with the same sign results in a positive product. Multiplying two integers with different signs results in a negative product.

287.

ⓐ no   ⓑ no   ⓒ yes

293. –4

299. –14

305. 9

311. –12

317. n + 4 = 1; n = –3

323. –42 = –7x; x = 6

329. m – 9 = –4; m = 5

335. 20

341. –9

347. 17 cookies

Review Exercises

353.

355.

357.

359. <
365. −6

361. >
367. 4

363. >
369.
ⓐ −8   ⓑ 8

371.
ⓐ −32   ⓑ 32

373. 21

375. 36

377. 0
383. <
389. 7
395. −16
401. 10
407. −50
413.
ⓐ 3   ⓑ −16
419. 10 + [−5 + (−6)] = −1

379. 14
385. =
391. 54
397. −3
403. 1
409. −1
415. −27

421. 16 degrees

381. −33
387. −55; −55
393. −1
399. −10°
405. 96
411. 21
417. −8 + 2 = −6

423.

5

425.

7
431. −58

427. 8

429. −38

433. −1

435.
ⓐ −2   ⓑ −11

437. 41
443. −36
449. −8
455. −81
461. −66
467.
ⓐ no   ⓑ yes   ⓒ no
471. −7
475. 9
481. $m + 4 = -48; m = -52$

439. −12 − 5 = −17
445. 121
451. −45
457. 54
463. −58
469. −12

472. −32
477. 4

441. −2 degrees
447. −7
453. −9
459. 4
465. −12(6) = −72
470. −6

473. $3x = 9; x = 3$>
479. $-6y = -42; y = 7$

Practice Test

485.
ⓐ <   ⓑ >
491. −27
497. −8
503. 34
509. $n = -1$

487.
ⓐ 7   ⓑ −8
493. 11
499. 22
505. −7 − (−4) = −3
511. $r = 6$

489. 5

495. 54
501. 39
507. 4°F
513. $y - 8 = -32; y = -24$

Chapter 4

Try It

4.1. ⓐ $\frac{3}{8}$ ⓑ $\frac{4}{9}$

4.2. ⓐ $\frac{3}{5}$ ⓑ $\frac{3}{4}$

4.3.

4.4.

4.5.

4.6.

4.7.

4.8.

4.9. $\frac{5}{3} = 1\frac{2}{3}$

4.10. $\frac{13}{8} = 1\frac{5}{8}$

4.11.

4.12.

4.13. $1\frac{2}{7}$

4.14. $1\frac{3}{4}$

4.15. $\frac{11}{8}$

4.16. $\frac{11}{6}$

4.17. $1\frac{6}{7}$.

4.18. $1\frac{5}{9}$

4.19. $3\frac{2}{7}$

4.20. $4\frac{4}{11}$

4.21. $\frac{26}{7}$

4.22. $\frac{23}{8}$

4.23. $\frac{50}{11}$

4.24. $\frac{34}{3}$

4.25. 2

4.26. 3

4.27. Correct answers include $\frac{6}{10}$, $\frac{9}{15}$, and $\frac{12}{20}$.

4.28. Correct answers include $\frac{8}{10}$, $\frac{12}{15}$, and $\frac{16}{20}$.

4.29. $\frac{18}{21}$

4.30. $\frac{30}{100}$

4.31.

4.32.

4.33.

4.34.

4.35.
(a) > (b) > (c) < (d) <

4.36.
(a) > (b) < (c) > (d) <

4.37. $\dfrac{2}{3}$

4.38. $\dfrac{3}{4}$

4.39. $-\dfrac{3}{4}$

4.40. $-\dfrac{2}{3}$

4.41. $-\dfrac{9}{7}$

4.42. $-\dfrac{9}{5}$

4.43. $\dfrac{23}{40}$

4.44. $\dfrac{5}{8}$

4.45. $\dfrac{x}{y}$

4.46. $\dfrac{a}{b}$

4.47. $\dfrac{3}{10}$

4.48. $\dfrac{5}{12}$

4.49. $\dfrac{2}{15}$

4.50. $\dfrac{21}{40}$

4.51. $\dfrac{5}{14}$

4.52. $\dfrac{14}{27}$

4.53. $-\dfrac{4}{21}$

4.54. $-\dfrac{3}{16}$

4.55.
(a) 9   (b) $-33a$

4.56.
(a) 24   (b) $\dfrac{44x}{3}$

4.57.
(a) $\dfrac{7}{5}$ (b) -8 (c) $-\dfrac{4}{11}$

(d) $\dfrac{1}{14}$

4.58.
(a) $\dfrac{7}{3}$ (b) -12 (c) $-\dfrac{9}{14}$

(d) $\dfrac{1}{21}$

4.59.

Number	Opposite	Absolute Value	Reciprocal
$-\dfrac{5}{8}$	$\dfrac{5}{8}$	$\dfrac{5}{8}$	$-\dfrac{8}{5}$
$\dfrac{1}{4}$	$-\dfrac{1}{4}$	$\dfrac{1}{4}$	4
$\dfrac{8}{3}$	$-\dfrac{8}{3}$	$\dfrac{8}{3}$	$\dfrac{3}{8}$
-8	8	8	$-\dfrac{1}{8}$

4.61.

4.62.

4.63.

4.64.

4.65. $-\dfrac{9}{14}$

4.66. $-\dfrac{10}{21}$

4.67. $\dfrac{21}{5p}$

4.68. $\dfrac{15}{8q}$

4.69. $\dfrac{4}{5}$

4.70. $\dfrac{5}{4}$

4.71. $\dfrac{4}{15}$

4.72. $\dfrac{2}{3}$

4.73. 2

4.74. $\dfrac{9}{4}$

4.75. -15

4.76. $-\dfrac{85}{6}$

4.77. $\dfrac{5}{8}$

4.78. $\dfrac{7}{8}$

4.79. 2

4.80. $\dfrac{5}{2}$

4.81. $\dfrac{9s}{14}$

4.82. $\dfrac{5y}{6}$

4.83. $\dfrac{a-b}{cd}$

4.84. $\dfrac{p+q}{r}$

4.85. $\dfrac{4}{5}$

4.86. $\dfrac{11}{14}$

4.87. $-\dfrac{2}{7}$

4.88. $-\dfrac{10}{3}$

4.89. $\dfrac{3}{4b}$

4.90. $\dfrac{4}{q}$

4.91. $\dfrac{25}{49}.$

4.92. $\dfrac{1}{2}$

4.93. $-\dfrac{3}{5}, \dfrac{3}{-5}$

4.94. $\dfrac{-2}{7}, \dfrac{2}{-7}$

4.95. $\dfrac{10}{9}$

4.96. $\dfrac{1}{2}$

4.97. $\dfrac{-3}{4}$

4.98. $-\dfrac{2}{3}$

4.99. $\dfrac{2}{9}$

4.100. $\dfrac{8}{5}$

4.101. 4

4.102. 2

4.103. $\frac{5}{8}$

4.104. $\frac{5}{6}$

4.105. $\frac{5}{6}$

4.106. 1

4.107. $\frac{x+3}{4}$

4.108. $\frac{y+5}{8}$

4.109. $\frac{1}{d}$

4.110. $\frac{3}{m}$

4.111. $\frac{9p}{8}$

4.112. $\frac{9q}{5}$

4.113. $-\frac{2}{3}$

4.114. $-\frac{2}{3}$

4.115. $\frac{3}{8}$, models may differ.

4.116. $\frac{1}{6}$, models may differ

4.117. $\frac{3}{7}$

4.118. $\frac{1}{2}$

4.119. $\frac{x-2}{7}$

4.120. $\frac{y-13}{14}$

4.121. $-\frac{16}{x}$

4.122. $-\frac{22}{a}$

4.123. -1

4.124. $-\frac{2}{3}$

4.125. 60

4.126. 15

4.127. 96

4.128. 224

4.129. $\frac{9}{12}, \frac{10}{12}$

4.130. $-\frac{35}{60}, \frac{44}{60}$

4.131. $\frac{52}{96}, \frac{51}{96}$

4.132. $\frac{72}{224}, \frac{189}{224}$

4.133. $\frac{7}{12}$

4.134. $\frac{7}{10}$

4.135. $\frac{5}{8}$

4.136. $\frac{1}{2}$

4.137. $\frac{79}{60}$

4.138. $\frac{103}{60}$

4.139. $\frac{1}{96}$

4.140. $\frac{75}{224}$

4.141. $\frac{37}{210}$

4.142. $-\frac{25}{96}$

4.143. $\frac{3y+14}{18}$

4.144. $\frac{5x+14}{30}$

4.145.
ⓐ $-\frac{11}{12}$ ⓑ $-\frac{1}{8}$

4.146.
ⓐ $-\frac{10}{3}$ ⓑ $\frac{13}{12}$

4.147.
ⓐ $\frac{27}{a}$ ⓑ $\frac{2}{a}$

4.148.
ⓐ $\frac{24}{k}$ ⓑ $\frac{24}{k}$

4.149. $\frac{1}{90}$

4.150. 272

4.151. 2

4.152. $\frac{2}{7}$

4.153.
ⓐ −1   ⓑ $-\frac{1}{2}$

4.154.
ⓐ $\frac{7}{6}$ ⓑ $-\frac{1}{4}$

4.155. $-\frac{3}{4}$

4.156. $-\frac{23}{8}$

4.157. $-\frac{1}{2}$

4.158. $\frac{2}{3}$

4.159. $-\frac{5}{2}$

4.160. $\frac{3}{2}$

4.161. 5

4.162. 5

4.163. $4\frac{2}{3}$

4.164. $3\frac{1}{2}$

4.165. $5\frac{6}{7}$

4.166. $7\frac{9}{11}$

4.167. $16\frac{1}{2}$

4.168. $15\frac{1}{3}$

4.169. $9\frac{1}{3}$

4.170. $6\frac{3}{5}$

4.171. $\frac{3}{4}$

4.172. $\frac{4}{5}$

4.173. $\frac{9}{5}$

4.174. $\frac{5}{3}$

4.175. $\frac{2}{3}$

4.176. $\frac{3}{4}$

4.177.

4.178.

4.179. $2\frac{2}{3}$

4.180. $1\frac{5}{7}$

4.181. $2\frac{2}{3}$

4.182. $1\frac{5}{7}$

4.183. $6\frac{7}{12}$

4.184. $12\frac{3}{10}$

4.185. $4\frac{7}{10}$

4.186. $2\frac{11}{12}$

4.187. $-\frac{41}{8}$

4.188. $-\frac{757}{63}$

4.189.
ⓐ no　ⓑ yes　ⓒ no

4.190.
ⓐ no　ⓑ no　ⓒ yes

4.191. $-\frac{1}{2}$

4.192. $-\frac{4}{15}$

4.193. -1

4.194. $-\frac{6}{7}$

4.195. $-\frac{19}{3}$

4.196. $\frac{23}{2}$

4.197. -125

4.198. -243

4.199. 245

4.200. 132

4.201. -48

4.202. 23

4.203. 35

4.204. 18

4.205. -91

4.206. -108

4.207. $\frac{n}{7} = -21; n = -147$

4.208. $\frac{n}{8} = -56; n = -448$

4.209. $\frac{q}{-8} = 72; q = -576$

4.210. $\frac{p}{-9} = 81; p = -729$

4.211. $\frac{2}{5}f = 16; f = 40$

4.212. $\frac{3}{4}f = 21; f = 28$

4.213. $\frac{n}{\frac{2}{3}} = \frac{5}{12}; n = \frac{5}{18}$

4.214. $\frac{c}{\frac{3}{8}} = \frac{4}{9}; c = \frac{1}{3}$

4.215. $\frac{5}{8} + x = \frac{1}{4}$; $x = -\frac{3}{8}$ **4.216.** $1\frac{3}{4} - x = \frac{5}{6}$; $x = \frac{11}{12}$

Section Exercises

1.
ⓐ $\frac{1}{4}$ ⓑ $\frac{3}{4}$ ⓒ $\frac{3}{8}$ ⓓ $\frac{5}{9}$

3.

5.

7.

9.

11.

13.

15.

17.
ⓐ $\frac{5}{4} = 1\frac{1}{4}$ ⓑ $\frac{7}{4} = 1\frac{3}{4}$
ⓒ $\frac{11}{8} = 1\frac{3}{8}$

19.
ⓐ $\frac{11}{4} = 2\frac{3}{4}$ ⓑ $\frac{19}{8} = 2\frac{3}{8}$

21.

23.

25.

27.

29. $1\frac{2}{3}$

31. $2\frac{3}{5}$ **33.** $3\frac{1}{9}$ **35.** $3\frac{2}{15}$

37. $\frac{7}{5}$ **39.** $\frac{17}{6}$ **41.** $\frac{19}{7}$

43. $\frac{32}{9}$ **45.** 4   **47.** 9

49. 9

51. Answers may vary. Correct answers include $\frac{2}{6}, \frac{3}{9}, \frac{4}{12}$.

53. Answers may vary. Correct answers include $\frac{10}{12}, \frac{15}{18}, \frac{20}{24}$.

55. Answers may vary. Correct answers include $\frac{10}{18}$, $\frac{15}{27}$, $\frac{20}{36}$.

57.

59.

61.

63.

65. <

67. >

69. <

71. <

73.
ⓐ 8   ⓑ 4

75. Answers will vary.

77. $\frac{1}{3}$

79. $\frac{3}{4}$

81. $-\frac{5}{11}$

83. $-\frac{12}{7}$

85. $\frac{10}{21}$

87. $-\frac{7}{8}$

89. $\frac{x}{y}$

91. $-\frac{x}{4y}$

93. $\frac{2x^2}{3y}$

95. $\frac{1}{3}$

97. $\frac{5}{18}$

99. $\frac{2}{15}$

101. $\frac{27}{40}$

103. $\frac{1}{4}$

105. $-\frac{1}{6}$

107. $-\frac{2}{9}$

109. $-\frac{21}{50}$

111. $\frac{11}{30}$

113. $\frac{20}{11}$

115. $9n$

117. $7p$

119. -34

121. $\frac{3}{8}$

123. $\frac{8}{27}$

125. $\frac{1296}{625}$

127. $\frac{4}{3}$

129. $-\frac{17}{5}$

131. $\frac{8}{11}$

133. $-\frac{1}{19}$

135. 1

137.

Number	Opposite	Absolute Value	Reciprocal
$-\frac{3}{13}$	$\frac{3}{13}$	$\frac{3}{13}$	$-\frac{13}{3}$
$\frac{9}{14}$	$-\frac{9}{14}$	$\frac{9}{14}$	$\frac{14}{9}$
$\frac{15}{7}$	$-\frac{15}{7}$	$\frac{15}{7}$	$\frac{7}{15}$
-9	9	9	$-\frac{1}{9}$

139. 4

141. 12

143. 4

145. $\frac{16}{15}$

147. $-\frac{5}{4}$

149. 1

151. $\frac{18}{5y}$

153. $\frac{25}{2c}$

155. $-\frac{3}{4}$

157. $\frac{2}{9}$

159. $\frac{14r}{15s}$

161. -12

163. $-\frac{1}{25}$

165. 9

167. $\frac{8}{7}$

169.
ⓐ $4\frac{2}{3} = \frac{8}{3} = 2\frac{2}{3}$

ⓑ Answers will vary.

171. $\frac{1}{8}$ yard

173. Answers will vary.

175. Answers will vary.

177. $\frac{44}{21}$

179. $\frac{35}{8}$

181. $-\frac{16}{3}$

183. $-\frac{63}{16}$

185. $\frac{3}{2}$

187. $-\frac{4}{3}$

189. 2

191. 5

193. $\frac{7v}{13}$

195. $\frac{a}{b}$

197. $\frac{A}{3-B}$

199. $\frac{3}{2}$

201. $-\frac{15}{22}$

203. $-\frac{3}{10}$

205. $\frac{1}{6}$

207. $\frac{3r}{5s}$

209. $\frac{9}{2y}$

211. 28

213. $-\frac{1}{18}$

215. $\frac{-4}{9},\ -\frac{4}{9}$

217. $\frac{13}{-6},\ \frac{-13}{6}$

219. $\frac{12}{7}$

221. $\frac{5}{2}$

223. $\frac{23}{4}$

225. $-\frac{1}{3}$

227. $\frac{4}{5}$

229. $-\frac{1}{2}$

231. 2

233. $\frac{5}{6}$

235. $\frac{26}{25}$

237. $\frac{11}{6}$

239. $\frac{5}{2}$

241. -10

243. -2

245. $\frac{51}{20}$

247. $\frac{18}{7}$

249.

ⓐ $\frac{4}{3} = 1\frac{1}{3}$ cups

ⓑ $\frac{80}{3} = 26\frac{2}{3}$ cups

251. Answers will vary.

253. Answers will vary.

255.

$\frac{7}{10}$

257.

$\frac{3}{4}$

259. $\frac{7}{9}$

261. $\frac{16}{15}$

263. $\frac{y+2}{3}$

265. $\frac{14}{q}$

267. $\frac{9a}{7}$

269. $\frac{-4x}{5}$

271. $-\frac{3}{4}$

273. $-\frac{7}{8}$

275. $\frac{8}{19}$

277. $-\frac{13}{12}$

279.

$\frac{1}{2}$

281. $\frac{1}{5}$

283. $\frac{5}{13}$

285. $\frac{1}{6}$

287. $-\frac{8}{3}$

289. $\frac{x-8}{19}$

291. $\frac{11z-8}{13}$

293. $-\frac{14}{c}$

295. $-\frac{55}{v}$

297. $\frac{3d}{11}$

299. $-\frac{14s}{3}$

301. $\frac{2}{7}$

303. $-\frac{3}{11}$

305. $-\frac{1}{8}$

307. $\frac{6-s}{11}$

309. $-\frac{2}{9}$

311. $\frac{49}{27}$

313. $\frac{1}{4}$ cup

315. Answers will vary.

317. 20

319. 48

325. 60

331. $\frac{33}{48}$, $-\frac{20}{48}$

337. $\frac{11}{24}$

343. $\frac{23}{20}$

349. $\frac{1}{24}$

355. $-\frac{53}{80}$

361. $\frac{11}{40}$

367. $\frac{3y+4}{6}$

373.
ⓐ $-\frac{37}{40}$ ⓑ $-\frac{1}{10}$

381. $\frac{11}{24}$

387. $\frac{-33-8x}{88}$

393. 32

399. $\frac{15}{2}$

405. -9

411. $\frac{5}{6}$

417.
ⓐ $\frac{1}{2}$ ⓑ -1

423.
ⓐ $\frac{1}{6}$ ⓑ $\frac{2}{3}$

429. -2

435. Answers will vary.

321. 240

327. $\frac{5}{20}$, $\frac{4}{20}$

333. $\frac{20}{60}$, $\frac{45}{60}$, $\frac{36}{60}$

339. $\frac{3}{8}$

345. $\frac{19}{24}$

351. $\frac{1}{12}$

357. $-\frac{291}{245}$

363. $\frac{11}{6}$

369. $\frac{4x-5}{20}$

375.
ⓐ $\frac{9a}{14}$ ⓑ $\frac{9a-14}{24}$

383. $\frac{7}{18}$

389. $\frac{16}{39}$

395. $\frac{36}{25}$

401. $\frac{3}{13}$

407. $\frac{91}{60}$

413. 1

419.
ⓐ 0   ⓑ $-\frac{1}{6}$

425. $\frac{4}{15}$

431. 3

437.

$3\frac{2}{3}$

443. 11

323. 245

329. $\frac{14}{24}$, $\frac{15}{24}$

335. $\frac{9}{20}$

341. $\frac{2}{3}$

347. $\frac{1}{48}$

353. $\frac{7}{60}$

359. $\frac{1}{20}$

365. $\frac{7}{10}$

371.
ⓐ $\frac{5}{6}$ ⓑ 4

377.
ⓐ $-\frac{4}{3q}$ ⓑ $\frac{12-25q}{45}$

385. $-\frac{2}{15}$

391. $\frac{1}{81}$

397. $\frac{60}{7}$

403. $\frac{19}{30}$

409. $\frac{11}{40}$

415. $\frac{22}{7}$

421.
ⓐ $\frac{1}{3}$ ⓑ -1

427. $-\frac{9}{16}$

433. She needs $2\frac{3}{8}$ cups

439.

$3\frac{2}{3}$

445. $11\frac{1}{3}$

447. $11\frac{1}{3}$

449.

$\frac{1}{2}$

451. $1\frac{1}{6}$

453. $6\frac{2}{5}$

455. $1\frac{7}{9}$

457. $\frac{5}{6}$

459. $7\frac{11}{12}$

461. $16\frac{1}{6}$

463. $5\frac{11}{20}$

465. $-1\frac{11}{24}$

467. $6\frac{17}{18}$

469. $\frac{7}{9}$

471. 23

473. $8\frac{3}{4}$

475. $\frac{4}{15}$

477. $5\frac{3}{5}$

479. $\frac{1}{16}$

481. $13\frac{1}{13}$

483. $7\frac{1}{30}$

485. $\frac{10}{27}$

487. $2\frac{7}{45}$

489. $\frac{17}{24}$

491. $\frac{7}{12}$ yards

493. $13\frac{1}{4}$ inches

495. Answers will vary.

497. Answers will vary.

499.
ⓐ no   ⓑ yes   ⓒ no

501.
ⓐ no   ⓑ yes   ⓒ no

503. $m = \frac{1}{2}$

505. $h = -\frac{2}{3}$

507. $c = -1$

509. $z = -1$

511. $p = \frac{37}{40}$

513. $k = -\frac{7}{15}$

515. $k = \frac{18}{7}$

517. $v = -\frac{11}{3}$

519. $b = -27$

521. $x = -256$

523. $q = 160$

525. $s = 45$

527. $y = -42$

529. $k = \frac{17}{20}$

531. $p = 100$

533. $m = -16$

535. $b = -21$

537. $v = 36$

539. $y = 0$

541. $g = \frac{1}{9}$

543. $q = -\frac{3}{4}$

545. $n = \frac{14}{5}$

547. $y = -\frac{25}{24}$

549. $d = -\frac{8}{15}$

551. $\frac{n}{6} = -24; n = -144$

553. $\frac{m}{-7} = -8; m = 56$

555. $\frac{f}{-4} = -20; f = 80$

557. $\frac{g}{9} = 14; g = 126$

559. $\frac{2}{5}q = 20; q = 50$

561. $\frac{4}{9}p = -28; p = -63$

563. $\frac{h}{2} = 43$

565. $\frac{a}{\frac{2}{3}} = \frac{3}{4}$

567. $\frac{3}{4} + x = \frac{1}{8}; x = -\frac{5}{8}$

569. $y - \frac{1}{3} = -\frac{1}{6}; y = \frac{1}{6}$

571. 30 inches

573. Answers will vary.

Review Exercises

575. $\frac{5}{9}$

577. $\frac{3}{2}$

579. $5\frac{8}{11}$

581. $\frac{49}{5}$

583. Answers may vary.

585.

587. >

589. $-\frac{3}{4}$

591. $-\frac{x}{y}$

593. $-\frac{4}{7}$

595. $\frac{24}{11}m$

597. 6

599. $\frac{4}{15}$

601. -4

603. 4

605. $\frac{4}{15}$

607. 8

609. $-\frac{268}{11}$

611. 8

613. $\frac{V}{h-6}$

615. $-\frac{2}{9}$

617. 22

619. $\frac{7}{36}$

621. $\frac{5}{8}$

623. $\frac{3}{5}$

625. $\frac{x+7}{10}$

627. $\frac{1}{2}$

629. $-\frac{19}{15}$

631. $\frac{8}{15}$

633. 15

635. 60

637. $\frac{9}{24}$ and $\frac{20}{24}$

639. $\frac{20}{60}$, $\frac{15}{60}$ and $\frac{48}{60}$

641. $\frac{1}{4}$

643. $-\frac{77}{90}$

645. $\frac{3y-10}{30}$

647. $\frac{14d}{11}$

649. $\frac{256}{225}$

651.
ⓐ $-\frac{8}{5}$ ⓑ $-\frac{11}{20}$

653. $13\frac{2}{3}$

655. $8\frac{1}{11}$

657. $5\frac{1}{10}$

659. $\frac{10}{3}$

661.
ⓐ no ⓑ yes ⓒ no

663. $n = -\frac{5}{11}$

665. $h = -\frac{51}{40}$

667. $z = -23$

669. $q - \frac{1}{10} = \frac{1}{2}$; $q = \frac{3}{5}$

671. $\frac{3}{8}y = 24$; $y = 64$

Practice Test

673. $\frac{23}{7}$

675. $\frac{1}{4}$

677. $\frac{1}{4}$

679. $16u$

681. -2

683. $\frac{12}{25}$

685. 5

687. $\frac{5p}{2q}$

689. 13

691. $-\frac{7}{13}$

693. -1

695. $-\frac{9}{4x}$

697. 3

699. $y = \frac{4}{5}$

701. $f = \frac{13}{12}$

703. $c = -27$

Chapter 5

Try It

5.1.
ⓐ six and seven tenths
ⓑ nineteen and fifty-eight hundredths
ⓒ eighteen thousandths
ⓓ negative two and fifty-three thousandths

5.2.
ⓐ five and eight tenths three and fifty-seven hundredths
ⓑ three and fifty-seven hundredths
ⓒ five thousandths
ⓓ negative thirteen and four hundred sixty-one thousandths

5.3. 13.68

5.4. 5.894

5.5. 0.058

5.6. 0.067

5.7.
ⓐ $5\frac{3}{10}$　ⓑ $6\frac{7}{100}$
ⓒ $-\frac{234}{1000}$

5.8.
ⓐ $8\frac{7}{10}$　ⓑ $1\frac{3}{100}$
ⓒ $-\frac{24}{1000}$

5.9.

5.10.

5.11.

5.12.

5.13.
ⓐ >　ⓑ >

5.14.
ⓐ <　ⓑ <

5.15. >

5.16. >

5.17. 1.05

5.18. 9.17

5.19.
ⓐ 6.58　ⓑ 6.6　ⓒ 7

5.20.
ⓐ 15.218　ⓑ 15.22　ⓒ 15.2

5.21. 17.6

5.22. 33.11

5.23. 16.49

5.24. 23.593

5.25. 0.42

5.26. 12.58

5.27. −1.53

5.28. −3.58

5.29. 27.4815

5.30. 87.6148

5.31. −13.427

5.32. 38.122

5.33. 0.00348

5.34. 0.00603

5.35.
ⓐ 25.8　ⓑ 258　ⓒ 2,580

5.36.
ⓐ 142　ⓑ 1,420　ⓒ 14,200

5.37. 0.07

5.38. 0.08

5.39. $0.19

5.40. $0.42

5.41. −0.39

5.42. −0.4

5.43. 587.3

5.44. 34.25

5.45. 200

5.46. 350

5.47. $16.52

5.48. $65.97

5.49. $41.28

5.50. $48.75

5.51. $15.47

5.52. $14.25

5.53. $5.97

5.54. $43.00

5.55. 0.25

5.56. 0.375

5.57. −2.25

5.58. −5.5

5.59. $2.\overline{45}$

5.60. $2.3\overline{18}$

5.61. 5.275

5.62. 6.35

5.63. >

5.64. <

5.65. <

5.66. >

5.67. $\frac{4}{5}$, 0.82, $\frac{7}{8}$

5.68. $\frac{3}{4}$, $\frac{13}{16}$, 0.835

5.69.
ⓐ −183.2　ⓑ 4.5

5.70.
ⓐ −776.25　ⓑ 2.2

5.71. 11.16

5.72. 1.51

5.73.
ⓐ 314 in.　ⓑ 7850 sq. in.

5.74.
ⓐ 628 ft.　ⓑ 31,400 sq. ft.

5.75.
ⓐ 325.304 cm
ⓑ 8425.3736 sq. cm

5.76.

ⓐ 165.792 m

ⓑ 2188.4544 sq. m

5.79.

ⓐ no ⓑ yes ⓒ no

5.82. $y = -8.4$

5.85. $b = -12$

5.88. $b = 6.48$

5.91. $-4.3x = 12.04$; $x = -2.8$

5.94. $\frac{r}{-2.6} = 2.5$; $r = -6.5$

5.97. 8.5

5.100. 10

5.103. 43

5.106. 20.5

5.109. 21

5.112.

ⓐ $\frac{1}{20}$ ⓑ 0.05

5.115.

ⓐ $\frac{3}{8}$ ⓑ $\frac{3}{2}$

5.118.

ⓐ $\frac{2}{9}$ ⓑ $\frac{5}{1}$

5.121. $\frac{37}{8}$

5.124. $\frac{2}{9}$

5.127. $18.00/hour

5.130. 28 mpg

5.133. Brand A costs $0.12 per bag. Brand B costs $0.13 per bag. Brand A is the better buy.

5.136.

ⓐ m mi/9 h

ⓑ x students/8 buses

ⓒ $y/40 h

5.139.

ⓐ −2 ⓑ −15

5.142.

ⓐ −7 ⓑ not a real number

5.145. $6 < \sqrt{38} < 7$

5.148. ≈ 3.61

5.151. $8x$

5.154. $-10p$

5.157. 19.2 feet

5.160. 3.5 seconds

5.77.

ⓐ $\frac{220}{147}$ m ⓑ $\frac{550}{3087}$ sq. m

5.80.

ⓐ yes ⓑ no ⓒ no

5.83. $a = 1.07$

5.86. $c = -8$

5.89. $y - 4.9 = 2.8$; $y = 7.7$

5.92. $-3.1m = 26.66$; $m = -8.6$

5.95. $j + 3.8 = 2.6$; $j = -1.2$

5.98. 9

5.101. $7.19

5.104. 30

5.107. 2

5.110. 5

5.113.

ⓐ $\frac{5}{8}$ ⓑ 0.625

5.116.

ⓐ $\frac{3}{8}$ ⓑ $\frac{3}{2}$

5.119. $\frac{2}{3}$

5.122. $\frac{102}{19}$

5.125. $\frac{123 \text{ miles}}{2 \text{ hours}}$

5.128. $19.00/hour

5.131. $0.29/box

5.134. Brand C costs $0.07 per ounce. Brand D costs $0.09 per ounce. Brand C is the better buy.

5.137.

ⓐ 6 ⓑ 13

5.140.

ⓐ −9 ⓑ −8

5.143.

ⓐ 7 ⓑ 5

5.146. $9 < \sqrt{84} < 10$

5.149. y

5.152. $13y$

5.155. $10ab$

5.158. 52 centimeters

5.161. 42.7 mph

5.78.

ⓐ $\frac{40}{21}$ in. ⓑ $\frac{200}{693}$ sq.in.

5.81. $y = -8$

5.84. $n = 0.83$

5.87. $c = 11.7$

5.90. $z - 5.7 = 3.4$; $z = 9.1$

5.93. $\frac{q}{-3.4} = 4.5$; $q = -15.3$

5.96. $k + 4.7 = 0.3$; $k = -4.4$

5.99. 21.5 years years

5.102. $39.62

5.105. 8.5

5.108. 5

5.111.

ⓐ $\frac{1}{10}$ ⓑ 0.1

5.114.

ⓐ $\frac{2}{8}$ ⓑ 0.25

5.117.

ⓐ $\frac{2}{5}$ ⓑ $\frac{10}{3}$

5.120. $\frac{9}{22}$

5.123. $\frac{8}{3}$

5.126. $\frac{121 \text{ miles}}{3 \text{ hours}}$

5.129. 23.5 mpg

5.132. $0.53/bottle

5.135.

ⓐ 689 mi/h hours

ⓑ y parents/22 students

ⓒ $d/9 min

5.138.

ⓐ 4 ⓑ 14

5.141.

ⓐ not a real number ⓑ −9

5.144.

ⓐ 17 ⓑ 23

5.147. ≈ 3.32

5.150. m

5.153. $-11y$

5.156. $15mn$

5.159. 9 seconds

5.162. 54.1 mph

Section Exercises

1. five and five tenths

3. five and one hundredth

5. eight and seventy-one hundredths

7. two thousandths

9. three hundred eighty-one thousandths

11. negative seventeen and nine tenths

13. 8.03
19. 0.001
25. 13.0395

15. 29.81
21. 0.029
27. $1\frac{99}{100}$

17. 0.7
23. -11.0009
29. $15\frac{7}{10}$

31. $\frac{239}{1000}$

33. $\frac{13}{100}$

35. $\frac{11}{1000}$

37. $-\frac{7}{100000}$

39. $6\frac{2}{5}$

41. $7\frac{1}{20}$

43. $4\frac{3}{500}$

45. $10\frac{1}{4}$

47. $1\frac{81}{250}$

49. $14\frac{1}{8}$

51.

53.

55.

57.

59. >

61. <
67. <
73. 2.8
79. 0.30

63. >
69. <
75. 0.85
81. 4.10

65. >
71. 0.7
77. 5.79
83.
ⓐ 5.78   ⓑ 5.8   ⓒ 6

85.
ⓐ 63.48   ⓑ 63.5   ⓒ 63

87.
ⓐ $58,966   ⓑ $59,000
ⓒ $60,000

89.
ⓐ $142.19   ⓑ $142

91. Answers will vary.

93. Tim had the faster time. 12.3 is less than 12.32, so Tim had the faster time.

95. 24.48

97. 170.88
103. -40.91
109. 35.8
115. 42.51
121. -4.89
127. 42.008
133. 337.8914
139. 92.4
145. 0.19
151. 3
157. 2.08
163. 19.2
169. $48.60
175. $17.80
181. $3.19
187. $296.00

99. -9.23
105. -7.22
111. -27.5
117. 102.212
123. 0.12
129. 26.7528
135. 2.2302
141. 55,200
147. $0.71
153. -4.8
159. 150
165. 12.09
171. 20
177. $24.89
183. 181.7 pounds
189. $12.75

101. 49.73
107. -13.5
113. 15.73
119. 51.31
125. 0.144
131. -11.653
137. 1.305
143. 0.03
149. $2.44
155. 35
161. 20
167. 32.706
173. 2
179. $29.06
185. $15.00
191.
ⓐ $3   ⓑ $2   ⓒ $1.50
ⓓ $1.20   ⓔ $1

193. $18.64

195. $259.45

197.
ⓐ $243.57   ⓑ $79.35

199. The difference: 0.03 seconds. Three hundredths of a second.

201. 0.4

203. -0.375

205. 0.85

207. 2.75

209. -12.4

211. $0.\overline{5}$

213. $1.\overline{36}$

215. $0.1\overline{35}$

217. 7

219. 3.025

221. 10.58

223. <

225. >

227. <

229. <

231. >

233. >

235. $0.55, \frac{9}{16}, \frac{3}{5}$

237. $\frac{5}{8}, \frac{13}{20}, 0.702$

239. $-\frac{7}{20}, -\frac{1}{3}, -0.3$

241. $-\frac{7}{9}, -\frac{3}{4}, -0.7$

243. -187

245. 295.12

247. 6.15

249. 20.2

251. 107.11

253. 449

255. 9.14

257. -0.23

259. -3.25

261. 16.29

263. 632.045

265. -5.742

267.
ⓐ 31.4 in   ⓑ 78.5 sq.in.

269.
ⓐ 56.52.ft.   ⓑ 254.34 sq.ft.

271.
ⓐ 288.88 cm

ⓑ 6644.24 sq.cm

273.
ⓐ 116.808 m

ⓑ 1086.3144 sq.m

275.
ⓐ $\frac{22}{5}$ mile   ⓑ $\frac{77}{50}$ sq.mile

277.
ⓐ $\frac{33}{14}$ yard   ⓑ $\frac{99}{224}$ sq.yard

279.
ⓐ $\frac{55}{21}$ m   ⓑ $\frac{275}{504}$ sq.m

281. $56.66

283. Answers will vary.

285.
ⓐ no   ⓑ no   ⓒ yes

287.
ⓐ no   ⓑ yes   ⓒ no

289. $y = 2.8$

291. $f = -0.85$

293. $a = -7.9$

295. $c = -4.65$

297. $n = 4.4$

299. $x = -3.5$

301. $j = -4.68$

303. $m = -1.42$

305. $x = 7$

307. $c = -5$

309. $p = 3$

311. $q = -80$

313. $x = 20$

315. $z = 2.7$

317. $a = -8$

319. $x = -0.28$

321. $p = 8.25$

323. $r = 7.2$

325. $x = -6$

327. $p = -10$

329. $m = 8$

331. $q = -\frac{3}{4}$

333. $m = \frac{4}{35}$

335. $y = -\frac{25}{24}$

337. $f = -\frac{11}{20}$

339. $a = -0.8$

341. $r = -1.45$

343. $h = 24$

345. $n - 1.9 = 3.4; 5.3$

347. $-6.2x = -4.96; 0.8$

349. $\frac{y}{-1.7} = -5; 8.5$

351. $n + (-7.3) = 2.4; 9.7$

353. $104

355. Answers will vary.

357. 4

359. 35

361. 245.5

363. 11.65

365. $18.84

367. 19.5 minutes

369. 0.329

371. 21

373. 45

375. 4.5

377. 99.65

379. $6.50

381. 40.5 months

383. 2

385. 22

387. 2 children

389. 11 units

391. $\frac{1}{20}, 0.05$

393. $\frac{1}{24}, 0.041\overline{6} \approx 0.042$

395. $\frac{4}{10}, 0.4$

397. $\frac{10}{14}, 0.\overline{714285} \approx 0.714$

399.
ⓐ $285.47   ⓑ $275.63

ⓒ $236.25

401. Answers will vary.

403. $\frac{5}{9}$

405. $\frac{7}{8}$

407. $\frac{7}{3}$

409. $\frac{7}{3}$

411. $\frac{1}{5}$

413. $\frac{10}{17}$

415. $\frac{5}{4}$

417. $\frac{2}{7}$

419. $\frac{11}{4}$

421. $\frac{1}{3}$

423. $\frac{6}{23}$

425. $\frac{82}{15}$

427. $\frac{35}{9}$

429. $\frac{9}{4}$

431. $\frac{35 \text{ calories}}{3 \text{ ounces}}$

433. $\frac{41 \text{ lbs}}{15 \text{ sq. in.}}$

435. $\frac{488 \text{ miles}}{7 \text{ hours}}$

437. $\frac{\$119}{8 \text{ hours}}$

439. 11.67 calories/ounce

441. 2.73 lbs./sq. in.

443. 69.71 mph

445. $14.88/hour

447. 32 mpg

449. 2.69 lbs./week

451. 92 beats/minute

453. 8,000

455. $1.09/bar

457. $1.33/pair

459. $0.48/pack

461. $0.60/disc

463. $1.29/box

465. The 50.7-ounce size costs $0.138 per ounce. The 33.8-ounce size costs $0.142 per ounce. The 50.7-ounce size is the better buy.

467. The 18-ounce size costs $0.222 per ounce. The 14-ounce size costs $0.235 per ounce. The 18-ounce size is a better buy.

469. The regular bottle costs $0.075 per ounce. The squeeze bottle costs $0.069 per ounce. The squeeze bottle is a better buy.

471. The half-pound block costs $6.78/lb, so the 1-lb. block is a better buy.

473. $\frac{793 \text{ miles}}{p \text{ hours}}$

475. $\frac{\$3}{0.5 \text{ lbs.}}$

477. $\frac{105 \text{ calories}}{x \text{ ounces}}$

479. $\frac{y}{5x}$

481. 15.2 students per teacher

483.

ⓐ 72 calories/ounce

ⓑ 3.87 grams of fat/ounce

ⓒ 5.73 grams carbs/once

ⓓ 3.33 grams protein/ounce

485. Answers will vary.

487. Answers will vary.

489. 6

491. 8

493. –2

495. –1

497. not a real number

499. not a real number

501. 5

503. 7

505. $8 < \sqrt{70} < 9$

507. $14 < \sqrt{200} < 15$

509. 4.36

511. 7.28

513. y

515. $7x$

517. $-8a$

519. $12xy$

521. 8.7 feet

523. 8 seconds

525. 15.8 seconds

527. 72 mph

529. 53.0 mph

531. 45 inches

533. Answers will vary. 9^2 reads: "nine squared" and means nine times itself. The expression $\sqrt{9}$ reads: "the square root of nine" which gives us the number such that if it were multiplied by itself would give you the number inside of the square root.

Review Exercises

535. three hundred seventy-five thousandths

537. five and twenty-four hundredths

539. negative four and nine hundredths

541. 0.09

543. 10.035

545. –0.05

547. $\frac{33}{40}$

549. $3\frac{16}{25}$

551. <

553. <

555.
ⓐ 12.53   ⓑ 12.5   ⓒ 13

557.
ⓐ 5.90   ⓑ 5.9   ⓒ 6

559. 24.67

561. 24.831

563. -2.37

565. -1.6

567. 15,400

569. 0.18

571. 4

573. 200

575. $28.22

577. $1.79

579. 0.875

581. -5.25

583. $0.\overline{54}$

585. >

587. >

589. >

591. $\frac{11}{15}$, 0.75, $\frac{7}{9}$

593. 6.03

595. 1.975

597. -0.22

599.
ⓐ 21.98 ft.   ⓑ 38.465 sq.ft.

601.
ⓐ 34.54 cm   ⓑ 379.94 sq.cm

603.
ⓐ no   ⓑ yes

605.
ⓐ no   ⓑ yes

607. $h = -3.51$

609. $p = 2.65$

611. $j = 3.72$

613. $x = -4$

615. $a = -7.2$

617. $s = 25$

619. $-5.9x = -3.54; x = 0.6$

621. $m + (-4.03) = 6.8; m = 0.83$

623. $269.10

625. $40.94

627. 24.5

629. 16 clients

631. 2

633. $\frac{1}{5}$; 0.2

635. $\frac{7}{4}$

637. $\frac{2}{3}$

639. $\frac{4}{9}$

641. $\frac{7}{9}$

643. $\frac{90 \text{ pounds}}{7.5 \text{ square inches}}$

645. $\frac{\$612.50}{35 \text{ hours}}$

647. 12 pounds/sq.in.

649. $17.50/hour

651. $0.42

653. $1.65

655. $0.11, $0.12; 60 tablets for $6.49

657. $\frac{a \text{ adults}}{45 \text{ children}}$

659. $\frac{19}{3 + n}$

661. 12

663. -9

665. not a real number

667. 17

669. $12 < \sqrt{155} < 13$

671. 7.55

673. $8b$

675. $15mn$

677. $7y$

679. $11cd$

681. 5.5 feet

683. 72 mph

Practice Test

685. $1\frac{73}{100}$

687.
ⓐ 16.7   ⓑ 16.75   ⓒ 17

689. 18.42

691. 0.192

693. -0.08

695. 2

697. 200

699. 1.975

701. -1.2

703. 8.8

705. $26.45

707.
ⓐ 59   ⓑ 51.5   ⓒ 55

709. 64 ounces for $10.99 is the better buy

711. $12n$

713. 15 feet

Chapter 6

Try It

6.1. $\frac{89}{100}$

6.2. $\frac{72}{100}$

6.3. $\frac{62}{100}$, 62%

6.4. $\frac{41}{100}$, 41%

6.5.
ⓐ $\frac{12}{25}$ ⓑ $\frac{11}{10}$

6.6.
ⓐ $\frac{16}{25}$ ⓑ $\frac{3}{2}$

6.7.
ⓐ $\frac{161}{250}$ ⓑ $\frac{2}{3}$

6.8.
ⓐ $\frac{113}{250}$ ⓑ $\frac{7}{80}$

6.9.
ⓐ 0.09   ⓑ 0.87

6.10.
ⓐ 0.03 ⓑ 0.91

6.11.
ⓐ 1.15 ⓑ 0.235

6.12.
ⓐ 1.23 ⓑ 0.168

6.13.
ⓐ $\frac{6}{25}$ ⓑ 0.24

6.14.
ⓐ $\frac{22}{50}$ ⓑ 0.44

6.15.
ⓐ $\frac{3}{10}$ ⓑ 0.3

6.16.
ⓐ $\frac{12.5}{100}$ ⓑ 0.125

6.17.
ⓐ 1% ⓑ 17%

6.18.
ⓐ 4% ⓑ 41%

6.19.
ⓐ 175% ⓑ 8.25%

6.20.
ⓐ 225% ⓑ 9.25%

6.21.
ⓐ 62.5% ⓑ 275% ⓒ 340%

6.22.
ⓐ 87.5% ⓑ 225% ⓒ 160%

6.23. 42.9%

6.24. 57.1%

6.25. $11.\bar{1}\%$, or $11\frac{1}{9}\%$

6.26. $16.\bar{6}\%$, or $16\frac{2}{3}\%$

6.27. 36

6.28. 33

6.29. 117

6.30. 126

6.31. 68

6.32. 64

6.33. $26

6.34. $36

6.35. 75%

6.36. 80%

6.37. 125%

6.38. 175%

6.39. $14.67

6.40. $2.16

6.41. 24.1 grams

6.42. 2,375 mg

6.43. 26%

6.44. 37%

6.45. 8.8%

6.46. 50%

6.47. 6.3%

6.48. 10%

6.49.
ⓐ $45.25 ⓑ $769.25

6.50.
ⓐ $20.50 ⓑ $270.50

6.51. 9%

6.52. 7.5%

6.53. $273

6.54. $394.20

6.55. 4%

6.56. 5.5%

6.57. $450

6.58. $82

6.59.
ⓐ $11.60 ⓑ $17.40

6.60.
ⓐ $256.75 ⓑ $138.25

6.61.
ⓐ $184.80 ⓑ 33%

6.62.
ⓐ $60 ⓑ 15%

6.63.
ⓐ 600% ⓑ $1,800

6.64.
ⓐ $2,975 ⓑ $11,475

6.65. $160

6.66. $56

6.67. $2,750

6.68. $3,560

6.69. 4.5%

6.70. 6.5%

6.71. $142.50

6.72. $7,020

6.73. 6%

6.74. 4%

6.75. $11,450

6.76. $9,600

6.77. $57.00

6.78. $143.50

6.79.
ⓐ $\frac{5}{9} = \frac{20}{36}$ ⓑ $\frac{7}{11} = \frac{28}{44}$
ⓒ $\frac{2.50}{8} = \frac{3.75}{12}$

6.80.
ⓐ $\frac{6}{7} = \frac{36}{42}$ ⓑ $\frac{8}{36} = \frac{12}{54}$
ⓒ $\frac{3.75}{6} = \frac{2.50}{4}$

6.81.
ⓐ no ⓑ yes

6.82.
ⓐ no ⓑ no

6.83. 77

6.84. 104

6.85. 65

6.86. 24

6.87. -7

6.88. -9

6.89. 12 ml

6.90. 180 mg

6.91. 300

6.92. 5

6.93. 590 Euros

6.94. 56,460 yen

6.95. $\frac{n}{105} = \frac{60}{100}$

6.96. $\frac{n}{85} = \frac{40}{100}$

6.97. $\frac{36}{n} = \frac{25}{100}$

6.98. $\frac{27}{n} = \frac{36}{100}$

6.99. $\frac{n}{100} = \frac{39}{52}$

6.100. $\frac{n}{100} = \frac{23}{92}$

6.101. 26

6.102. 34

6.103. 80

6.104. 147

6.105. 38

6.106. 64

6.107. 37.5%

6.108. 25%

Section Exercises

1. $\frac{6}{100}$

3. $\frac{32}{1000}$

5.
(a) $\frac{57}{100}$ (b) 57%

7.
(a) $\frac{42}{100}$ (b) 42%

9. $\frac{1}{25}$

11. $\frac{17}{100}$

13. $\frac{13}{25}$

15. $\frac{5}{4}$

17. $\frac{3}{8}$

19. $\frac{23}{125}$

21. $\frac{19}{200}$

23. $\frac{4}{75}$

25. 0.05

27. 0.01

29. 0.63

31. 0.4

33. 1.15

35. 1.5

37. 0.214

39. 0.078

41.
(a) $\frac{3}{200}$ (b) 0.015

43.
(a) $\frac{7023}{10,000}$ (b) 0.7023

45.
(a) $\frac{1}{4}$ (b) 0.25

47.
(a) $\frac{3}{5}$ (b) 0.6

49. 1%

51. 18%

53. 135%

55. 300%

57. 0.9%

59. 8.75%

61. 150%

63. 225.4%

65. 25%

67. 37.5%

69. 175%

71. 680%

73. 41.7%

75. $266.\overline{6}\%$

77. 42.9%

79. 55.6%

81. 25%

83. 35%

87.
(a) $\frac{1}{10}$

(b) approximately $9.50

90. $\frac{17}{20}$; 0.85

92. 80%; 0.8

94. $\frac{1}{4}$, $\frac{1}{2}$, $\frac{3}{4}$, 1.

96. The Szetos sold their home for five times what they paid 30 years ago.

98. 54

100. 26.88

102. 162.5

104. 18,000

106. 112

108. 108

110. $35

112. $940

114. 30%

116. 36%

118. 150%

120. 175%

122. $11.88

124. $259.80

126. 24.2 grams

128. 2,407 grams

130. 45%

132. 25%

134. 13.2%

136. 125%

138. 72.7%

140. 2.5%

142. 11%

144. 5.5%

146. 21.2%

148. The original number should be greater than 44.80% is less than 100%, so when 80% is converted to a decimal and multiplied to the base in the percent equation, the resulting amount of 44 is less. 44 is only the larger number in cases where the percent is greater than 100%.

150. Alex should have packed half as many shorts and twice as many shirts.

152.
(a) $4.20   (b) $$88.20

154.
(a) $9.68   (b) $138.68

156.
(a) $17.13   (b) $267.13

158.
(a) $61.45   (b) $1,260.45

160. 6.5%

162. 6.85%

164. $20.25

166. $975

168. $859.25

170. 3%

172. 16%

174. 15.5%

176. $139

177. $81

178. $125

180.
ⓐ $26.97   ⓑ $17.98

182.
ⓐ $128.37   ⓑ $260.63

184.
ⓐ $332.48   ⓑ $617.50

186.
ⓐ $576   ⓑ 30%

188.
ⓐ $53.25   ⓑ 15%

190.
ⓐ $370   ⓑ 43.5%

192.
ⓐ $7.20   ⓑ $23.20

194.
ⓐ $0.20   ⓑ 44.2%

196.
ⓐ $258.75   ⓑ $373.75

198.
ⓐ $131.25   ⓑ $126.25
ⓒ 25% off first, then $20 off

200.
ⓐ Priam is correct. The original price is 100%. Since the discount rate was 40%, the sale price was 60% of the original price.
ⓑ Yes.

202. $180

204. $14,000

206. 6.3%

208. $90

210. $579.96

212. $14,167

214. $3,280

216. $860

218. $24,679.91

220. 4%

222. 5.5%

224. $116

226. $4,836

228. 3%

230. 3.75%

232. $35,000

234. $3,345

236. $332.10

238. $195.00

240. Answers will vary.

242. Answers will vary.

244. $\frac{4}{15} = \frac{36}{135}$

246. $\frac{12}{5} = \frac{96}{40}$

248. $\frac{5}{7} = \frac{115}{161}$

250. $\frac{8}{1} = \frac{48}{6}$

252. $\frac{9.36}{18} = \frac{2.60}{5}$

254. $\frac{18.04}{11} = \frac{4.92}{3}$

256. yes

258. no

260. no

262. yes

264. 49

266. 7

268. 9

270. –11

272. 7

274. 2

276. 0.6

278. 4

280. 9 ml

282. 114, no

284. 159 cal

286. $\frac{3}{4}$ cup

288. $252.50

290. 1.25

292. 48 quarters

294. 19, $58.71

296. 12.8 hours

298. 4 bags

300. $\frac{n}{250} = \frac{35}{100}$

302. $\frac{n}{47} = \frac{110}{100}$

304. $\frac{45}{n} = \frac{30}{100}$

306. $\frac{90}{n} = \frac{150}{100}$

308. $\frac{17}{85} = \frac{p}{100}$

310. $\frac{340}{260} = \frac{p}{100}$

312. 117

313. 165

314. 16.56

316. 45.5

318. 1464

320. $45

322. $164

324. 25%

326. 12.5%

328. 20, 32

330. Answers will vary.

Review Exercises

332. $\frac{32}{100}$

334. $\frac{13}{100}$, 13%

336. $\frac{12}{25}$

338. $\frac{641}{1000}$

340. 0.06

342. 1.28

344.
ⓐ $\frac{27}{200}$ ⓑ 0.135

346.
ⓐ $\frac{1}{2}$ ⓑ 0.5

348. 4%

350. 282%
356. 362.5%
362. 240
368. $16.70
374.
ⓐ $45   ⓑ $795
380. 15%

352. 0.3%
358. 40%
364. 25
370. 28.4%
376. 7.25%

382. $45

354. 75%
360. 161
366. 68%
372. 4%
378. $11,400

384.
ⓐ $25.47   ⓑ $59.43

386.
ⓐ $13   ⓑ 26%
392. $4400
398. $\frac{3}{8} = \frac{12}{32}$
404. no
410. 12
416. $\frac{n}{395} = \frac{62}{100}$
422. $78

388.
ⓐ $0.48   ⓑ $1.28
394. $900
400. $\frac{1}{18} = \frac{23}{414}$
406. 20
412. 340
418. $\frac{15}{1000} = \frac{p}{100}$

390. $450

396. 2.5%
402. yes

408. 4
414. 13 gallons
420. 765

Practice Test

424. $0.24, \frac{6}{25}$

430. 25%
436. 4%
442. -52

426. $3.5, 3\frac{1}{2}$

432. 40
438. $50

428. 33.333%

434. 11.9%
440. 6.2%

Chapter 7

Try It

7.1.
ⓐ $\frac{-24}{1}$ ⓑ $\frac{357}{100}$

7.2.
ⓐ $\frac{-19}{1}$ ⓑ $\frac{841}{100}$

7.3.
ⓐ rational   ⓑ rational
ⓒ irrational

7.4.
ⓐ rational   ⓑ rational
ⓒ irrational

7.5.
ⓐ rational   ⓑ irrational

7.6.
ⓐ irrational   ⓑ rational

7.7.

Number	Whole	Integer	Rational
−3		✓	✓
−$\sqrt{2}$			
0.3			✓
$\sqrt{-49}$			
4	✓	✓	✓
$\frac{9}{5}$			✓

Number	Irrational	Real
−3		✓
−$\sqrt{2}$	✓	✓
0.3		✓
$\sqrt{-49}$		
4		✓
$\frac{9}{5}$		✓

7.8.

Number	Whole	Integer	Rational
−$\sqrt{25}$		✓	✓
−$\frac{3}{8}$			✓
−1		✓	✓
6	✓	✓	✓
$\sqrt{121}$	✓	✓	✓
2.041975...			

Number	Irrational	Real
−$\sqrt{25}$		✓
−$\frac{3}{8}$		✓
−1		✓
6		✓
$\sqrt{121}$		✓
2.041975...	✓	✓

7.9.
ⓐ −4 + 7 = 7 + (−4)
ⓑ 6 · 12 = 12 · 6

7.10.
ⓐ $14 + (-2) = -2 + 14$
ⓑ $3(-5) = (-5)3$

7.13. $32x$

7.16.
ⓐ 0.975 ⓑ 0.975

7.19. $-48a$

7.22. $\frac{11}{25}$

7.25. $15.58c$
7.28. 70.4
7.31. $32r - s$
7.34. $6x + 42$
7.37. $7x - 42$

7.40. $\frac{3}{7}u + 9$

7.43. $70 + 15p$
7.46. $yz - 8y$
7.49. $-18m - 15$
7.52. $-56 + 105y$
7.55. $-3x + 3$
7.58. $7x - 13$

7.61.
ⓐ 30 ⓑ 30

7.64.
ⓐ -45 ⓑ -45

7.67.
ⓐ -18 ⓑ $-\frac{7}{9}$ ⓒ -1.2

7.70.
ⓐ $\frac{1}{18}$ ⓑ $-\frac{5}{4}$ ⓒ $\frac{5}{3}$

7.73.
ⓐ 0 ⓑ 0 ⓒ 0

7.76.
ⓐ undefined   ⓑ undefined
ⓒ undefined

7.79. p
7.82. 0
7.85. $20y + 50$
7.88. 54 feet
7.91. $440,000,000$ yards
7.94. 48 teaspoons

7.11.
ⓐ
$(1 + 0.7) + 0.3 = 1 + (0.7 + 0.3)$
ⓑ $(-9 \cdot 8) \cdot \frac{3}{4} = -9\left(8 \cdot \frac{3}{4}\right)$

7.14. $-63y$

7.17.
ⓐ 24 ⓑ 24
7.20. $-92x$

7.23. $\frac{22}{15}$

7.26. $17.79d$
7.29. $24y$
7.32. $41m + 6n$
7.35. $27y + 72$
7.38. $8x - 40$

7.41. $5y + 3$

7.44. $4 + 35d$
7.47. $xp + 2p$
7.50. $-48n - 66$
7.53. $-z + 11$
7.56. $2x - 20$
7.59.
ⓐ 120 ⓑ 120

7.62.
ⓐ 3 ⓑ 3

7.65.
ⓐ identity property of addition
ⓑ identity property of
multiplication

7.68.
ⓐ -47 ⓑ $-\frac{7}{13}$ ⓒ -8.4

7.71.
ⓐ 0 ⓑ 0 ⓒ 0

7.74.
ⓐ 0 ⓑ 0 ⓒ 0

7.77. 9

7.80. r
7.83. undefined
7.86. $12z + 16$
7.89. 8600 pounds
7.92. $151,200$ minutes
7.95. 9 lbs. 8 oz

7.12.
ⓐ
$(4 + 0.6) + 0.4 = 4 + (0.6 + 0.4)$
ⓑ $(-2 \cdot 12) \cdot \frac{5}{6} = -2\left(12 \cdot \frac{5}{6}\right)$

7.15.
ⓐ 0.84 ⓑ 0.84

7.18.
ⓐ 15 ⓑ 15
7.21. $\frac{5}{49}$

7.24. $\frac{11}{9}$

7.27. 10.53
7.30. $60z$
7.33. $4x + 8$
7.36. $25w + 45$
7.39. $\frac{2}{5}p + 4$

7.42. $4n + 9$

7.45. $rs - 2r$
7.48. $yq + 4q$
7.51. $-10 + 15a$
7.54. $-x + 4$
7.57. $5x - 66$
7.60.
ⓐ 126 ⓑ 126

7.63.
ⓐ -32 ⓑ -32

7.66.
ⓐ identity property of
multiplication
ⓑ additive identity

7.69.
ⓐ $\frac{1}{5}$ ⓑ -7 ⓒ $\frac{10}{3}$

7.72.
ⓐ 0 ⓑ 0 ⓒ 0

7.75.
ⓐ undefined   ⓑ undefined
ⓒ undefined

7.78. -18

7.81. 0
7.84. undefined
7.87. 2.5 feet
7.90. $102,000,000$ pounds
7.93. 16 cups
7.96. 21 ft. 6 in.

7.97. 4 lbs. 8 oz.
7.98. 11 gal. 2 qts.
7.99. 5000 m
7.100. 250 cm
7.101. 2.8 kilograms
7.102. 4.5 kilograms
7.103.
7.104.
7.105. 83 cm
ⓐ 7250 kL   ⓑ 6300 mL
ⓐ 35,000 L   ⓑ 410 cL
7.106. 1.04 m
7.107. 2 L
7.108. 2.4 kg
7.109. 2.12 quarts
7.110. 3.8 liters
7.111. 19,328 ft
7.112. 3,470 mi
7.113. 15°C
7.114. 5°C
7.115. 59°F
7.116. 50°F

Section Exercises

1.
ⓐ $\frac{5}{1}$ ⓑ $\frac{319}{100}$

3.
ⓐ $\frac{-12}{1}$ ⓑ $\frac{9279}{1000}$

5. Rational: $0.75, 0.22\bar{3}$.
Irrational: $1.39174\ldots$

7. Rational: $0.\overline{45}$, 3.59 . Irrational:
$1.919293\ldots$

9.
ⓐ rational   ⓑ irrational

11.
ⓐ irrational   ⓑ rational

13.

Number	Whole	Integer	Rational
–8		✓	✓
0	✓	✓	✓
1.95286...			
$\frac{12}{5}$			✓
$\sqrt{36}$	✓	✓	✓
9	✓	✓	✓

Number	Irrational	Real
–8		✓
0		✓
1.95286...	✓	✓
$\frac{12}{5}$		✓
$\sqrt{36}$		✓
9		✓

15.

Number	Whole	Integer	Rational
$-\sqrt{100}$		✓	✓
–7		✓	✓
$-\frac{8}{5}$			✓
–1		✓	✓
0.77			✓
$3\frac{1}{4}$			✓

Number	Irrational	Real
$-\sqrt{100}$		✓
–7		✓
$-\frac{8}{5}$		✓
–1		✓
0.77		✓
$3\frac{1}{4}$		✓

17.
ⓐ 4

ⓑ Teachers cannot be divided

ⓒ It would result in a lower
number.

19. Answers will vary.
25. $(-12)(-18) = (-18)(-12)$
31. $-3m = m(-3)$
37. $(-2 + 6) + 7 = -2 + (6 + 7)$

43. $(17 + y) + 33 = 17 + (y + 33)$

21. $7 + 6 = 6 + 7$
27. $-15 + 7 = 7 + (-15)$
33. $(21 + 14) + 9 = 21 + (14 + 9)$
39. $\left(13 \cdot \frac{2}{3}\right) \cdot 18 = 13\left(\frac{2}{3} \cdot 18\right)$

45.
ⓐ 0.97   ⓑ 0.97

23. $7(-13) = (-13)7$
29. $y + 1 = 1 + y$
35. $(14 \cdot 6) \cdot 9 = 14(6 \cdot 9)$
41. $4(7x) = (4 \cdot 7)x$

47.
ⓐ 2.375   ⓑ 2.375

49.
ⓐ 21   ⓑ 21

55. $\frac{5}{12}$

61. –176

51.
ⓐ –8   ⓑ –8

57. $\frac{25}{7}$

63. $\frac{13}{12}$

53. 23

59. $\frac{65}{23}$

65. $\frac{23}{15}$

67. $9.89d$
73. $72w$
79. $42u + 30v$

85. $7.41m + 6.57n$

69. 36
75. $-46n$
81. $-57p + (-10q)$

87.
ⓐ $975   ⓑ $700   ⓒ $1675

ⓓ $185   ⓔ $270   ⓕ $1220

71. 29.193
77. $12q$
83. $a + \frac{6}{5}b$

89. Answers will vary.

91. $3a + 27$
97. $35u - 20$

93. $27w + 63$

99. $\frac{1}{3}u + 3$

95. $7y - 91$

101. $\frac{4}{5}m + 4$

103. $3x - 4$
109. $ax + 7x$
115. $-4q + 28$
121. $-5p + 4$
127. $-42n + 39$
133. $3y + 1$
139. $6n - 72$

105. $2 + 9s$
111. $-3a - 33$
117. $-42x + 48$
123. $8u + 4$
129. $-r + 15$
135. $47u + 60$
141. $17n + 76$

107. $uv - 10u$
113. $-81a - 36$
119. $-q - 11$
125. $-4x + 10$
131. $-c + 6$
137. $24x + 4$
143.
ⓐ 56   ⓑ 56

145.
ⓐ $\frac{9}{2}$ ⓑ $\frac{9}{2}$

147.
ⓐ -89 ⓑ -89

149.
ⓐ -525 ⓑ -525

151.
ⓐ 160   ⓑ 160

153.
ⓐ -1.03 ⓑ -1.03

155.
ⓐ $3(4 - 0.03) = 11.91$

ⓑ $1.42

159. identity property of multiplication

161. identity property of addition

163. $\frac{1}{14}$

165. $-\frac{1}{19}$

167. $\frac{13}{8}$

169. $-\frac{12}{5}$

171. $\frac{5}{2}$

173. -2

175. 0

177. 0
183. 0
189. $31s$
195. 0
201. undefined
207. $20q - 35$

179. undefined
185. undefined
191. p
197. 0
203. undefined
209. $225h + 360$

181. 0
187. 16
193. $2n$
199. 0
205. undefined
211.
ⓐ 8 hours   ⓑ 8

ⓒ associative property of multiplication

213. Answers will vary.
219. 58 inches
225. 300,000 pounds
231. 8100 seconds
237. 111 ounces
243. 5 weeks and 1 day
249. 8000 meters
255. 3000 milligrams
261. 0.3 liters
267. 16.8 grams
273. 8.2 meters
279. 33 pounds
285. $-10°C$
291. $77°F$
297. $60.8°F$

215. 24 inches
221. 90 feet
227. 110 tons
233. 256 tablespoons
239. 31.25 gallons
245. 9 ft 2 in
251. 245 centimeters
257. 25,000 milligrams
263. 65 centimeters
269. 42,000 milligrams
275. 41,500 kilograms
281. 30.4 liters
287. $-15.5°C$
293. $5°F$
299. 110 reflectors

217. 3.75 feet
223. 0.98 miles
229. 162 hours
235. 128 ounces
241. 4 lbs. 1 oz.
247. 8 yards
253. 10.911 kilometers
259. 3800 grams
265. 1.82 kilograms
271. 106.7 centimeters
277. 5.2 feet
283. $25°C$
289. $48.9°C$
295. $46.4°F$

Review Exercises

303. $\frac{-5}{1}$

305. $\frac{18}{10}$

307. $0.\overline{16},\ 1.95$

309.
ⓐ irrational   ⓑ rational

311.
ⓐ 4   ⓑ $-5, \ -\sqrt{4}, \ 4$

ⓒ
$-5, \ -2\frac{1}{4}, \ -\sqrt{4}, \ 0.\overline{25}, \ \frac{13}{5}, \ 4$

ⓓ none

ⓔ
$-5, \ -2\frac{1}{4}, \ -\sqrt{4}, \ 0.\overline{25}, \ \frac{13}{5}, \ 4$

313. $-14 \cdot 5 = 5(-14)$

315. $a + 8 = 8 + a$

317. $(22 + 7) + 3 = 22 + (7 + 3)$

319. $\frac{1}{2}(22y) = \left(\frac{1}{2} \cdot 22\right)y$

321.
ⓐ 5.39   ⓑ 5.39

323.
ⓐ 13   ⓑ 13

325. $\frac{11}{15}$

327. -60

329. 5.98 d

331. 25 q

333. $34\,m + (-25\,n)$

335. $9y - 36$

337. $56a + 96$

339. $yp + 10p$

341. $-4x + 68$

343.
ⓐ 9   ⓑ 9

345.
ⓐ 36   ⓑ 36

347. identity property of addition

349. identity property of multiplication

351. -19.4

353. $\frac{7}{15}$

355. $-\frac{1}{5}$

357. $-\frac{9}{4}$

359. 0

361. 0

363. $n + 7$

365. 34

367. $54x - 84$

369. 3.5 feet

371. 15 yards

373. 9000 pounds

375. 64 tablespoons

377. 1.9 gallons

379. 7 hours 10 minutes

381. 3 yards, 12 inches

383. 8.85 kilometers

385. 13,000 milligrams

387. 0.65 liters

389. 855 milliliters

391. 10,000 milligrams

393. 25.6 meters

395. 171.6 pounds

397. 11.4 kilograms

399. -5°C

401. 17.8°C

403. 23°F

405. 75.2°F

Practice Test

407.
$\sqrt{144} = 12$ therefore rational.

409. $x \cdot 14 = 14 \cdot x$

411. $(8 \cdot 2) \cdot 3 = 8 \cdot (2 \cdot 3)$

413.
ⓐ $-\frac{2}{5}$ ⓑ $\frac{5}{2}$

415. $15y$

417. $\frac{23}{15}$

419. $30y - 4z$

421. $30x - 24$

423. $2a + 3$

425. $66p - 2$

427. 0

429. 0

431. .276 grams

433. 9.317 miles

435. $95°F$

Chapter 8

Try It

8.1. no

8.2. no

8.3. $x = -16$

8.4. $x = -20$

8.5. -1

8.6. -4

8.7. $p = \frac{7}{6}$

8.8. $q = \frac{2}{3}$

8.9. $b = 6.4$

8.10. $c = 14$

8.11. $y = 15$

8.12. $z = 2$

8.13. $p = 5$

8.14. $q = -16$

8.15. $h = -1$

8.16. $x = 1$

8.17. $x + 11 = 41; x = 30$

8.18. $y - 12 = 51; y = 63$

8.19. $4x - 3x = 14$; $x = 14$

8.20. $7a - 6a = -8$; $a = -8$

8.21. $a + 6 = 13$; Athena weighs 7 pounds.

8.22. $26 + h = 68$; Henry has 42 books.

8.23. $19{,}875 = s - 1025$; the sticker price is $20,900.

8.24. $7.75 = n - 3.25$; the price at night is $11.00.

8.25. $y = -16$

8.26. $z = -13$

8.27. $b = 144$

8.28. $c = 128$

8.29. $k = -8$

8.30. $g = -3$

8.31. $n = 35$

8.32. $y = 18$

8.33. $x = 2$

8.34. $n = -5$

8.35. $c = -3$

8.36. $x = -\dfrac{4}{7}$

8.37. $n = -6$

8.38. $n = -5$

8.39. $x = -4$

8.40. $a = -8$

8.41. $y = 5$

8.42. $m = 9$

8.43. $n = 10$

8.44. $c = 1$

8.45. $p = -7$

8.46. $m = -3$

8.47. $j = 2$

8.48. $h = 1$

8.49. $x = -1$

8.50. $y = 4$

8.51. $q = 1$

8.52. $n = 1$

8.53. $a = -5$

8.54. $k = -6$

8.55. $x = 10$

8.56. $y = -3$

8.57. $x = -5$

8.58. $y = -5$

8.59. $x = 4$

8.60. $y = 1$

8.61. $y = -6$

8.62. $z = 8$

8.63. $a = 2$

8.64. $n = 2$

8.65. $j = \dfrac{5}{3}$

8.66. $k = \dfrac{5}{2}$

8.67. $p = -2$

8.68. $q = -8$

8.69. $u = 2$

8.70. $x = 4$

8.71. 1

8.72. -1

8.73. $x = \dfrac{1}{2}$

8.74. $y = 3$

8.75. $v = 40$

8.76. $u = -12$

8.77. $a = -2$

8.78. $c = -2$

8.79. $p = -4$

8.80. $q = 2$

8.81. $n = 2$

8.82. $m = -1$

8.83. $x = 20$

8.84. $x = 10$

8.85. $h = 12$

8.86. $k = -1$

8.87. $n = 9$

8.88. $d = 16$

Section Exercises

1. yes

3. no

5. $x = 5$

7. $b = \dfrac{1}{2}$

9. $p = -11.7$

11. $a = 10$

13. $x = \dfrac{7}{3}$

15. $y = 13.8$

17. $x = -27$

19. $q = -\dfrac{1}{4}$

21. $y = \dfrac{27}{20}$

23. 17

25. 8

27. -20

29. 2

31. 1.7

33. -2

35. -4

37. 6

39. -41

41. 28

43. $x + (-5) = 33$; $x = 38$

45. $y - 3 = -19$; $y = -16$

47. $p + 8 = 52$; $p = 44$

49. $5c - 4c = 60$; 60

51. $f - \dfrac{1}{3} = \dfrac{1}{12}$; $\dfrac{5}{12}$

53. $-9m + 10m = -25$; $m = -25$

55. Let p equal the number of pages read in the Psychology book $41 + p = 54$. Jeff read pages in his Psychology book.

57. Let d equal the daughter's age. $d = 12 - 5$. Eva's daughter's age is 7 years old.

59. 21 pounds

61. 100.5 degrees

63. $121.19

65. $d = \dfrac{13}{24}$

67. Answers will vary.

69. 9

71. 3

73. -7

75. 7

77. 15

79. 0

81. 28

83. 36

85. -48

87. 80

89. 25

91. -32

93. 5/2

95. $y = -1$

97. $m = -5$

99. $t = \dfrac{5}{2}$

101. $q = 24$

103. $p = 56$

105. 6 children

107. $1.08

109. 42 yards

111. Answer will vary.

113. 6

115. 6

117. -8

119. -8

121. -4

123. -2

125. -11

127. 9

129. -3

131. 3

133. -3/4

135. 2

137. 19

139. 7

141. -5

143. -4

145. 2

147. 4

149. 6

151. 7

153. -40

155. 3

157. 3.46

159. 60

161. 23

163. 9

165. 6

167. 3

169. -2

171. -1

173. 5

175. 0.52

177. 0.25

179. -9

181. 2

183. 6

185. 3/2

187. 3

189. -4

191. 2

193. 34

195. 10

197. 2

199. 30 feet

201. 8 nickels

203. Answers will vary.

205. Answers will vary.

207. Answers will vary.

209. $x = -1$

211. $y = -1$

213. $a = \frac{3}{4}$

215. $x = 4$

217. $m = 20$

219. $x = -3$

221. $w = \frac{9}{4}$

223. $x = 1$

225. $b = 12$

227. $x = 1$

229. $p = -41$

231. $x = -\frac{5}{2}$

233. $y = 10$

235. $j = 2$

237. $x = 18$

239. $x = 18$

241. $x = 20$

243. $n = 9$

245. $d = 8$

247. $q = 11$

249. $d = 18$

251. Answers will vary.

253. Answers will vary.

Review Exercises

255. yes

257. no

259. 12

261. $a = \frac{4}{3}$

263. $u = 17$

265. $c = \frac{12}{11}$

267. $n = 44$

269. $f = \frac{10}{3}$

271. $y = 4$

273. $n = -8$

275. $-6 + m = 25; m = 31$

277. $s = 11 - 3; 8$ years old

279. $c - 46.25 = 9.75; 56.00

281. $x = 9$

283. $p = 21$

285. $n = 108$

287. $x = 48$

289. $m = 4$

291. $x = 15$

293. $r = 3$

295. $p = 5$

297. $x = -22$

299. $y = -13$

301. $k = -5$

303. $x = 6$

305. $u = -7$

307. $x = -2$

309. $s = -22$

311. $y = 12$

313. $r = 38$

315. $y = 26$

317. $n = 2$

319. $a = \frac{14}{3}$

321. $x = 5$

323. $p = -20$

Practice Test

325.

ⓐ yes   ⓑ no

327. $c = 16$

329. $x = -5$

331. $x = 9$

333. $y = 4$

335. $m = 6$

337. $d = -32$

339. $x = -2$

341. $p = \frac{2}{3}$

343. $2x - 4 = 16; x = 10$

Chapter 9

Try It

9.1. $180
9.4. 7
9.7. 25
9.10. 6
9.13. −8, −15
9.16. −2, −3
9.19. 31, 32, 33
9.22. 17 nickels, 5 quarters
9.25. 41 nickels, 18 quarters

9.28. 112 adult tickets, 199 senior/child tickets
9.31.
ⓐ 155°   ⓑ 65°
9.34. 25°, 65°
9.37. 34°
9.40. 30°, 60°, 90°
9.43. 10
9.46. 12
9.49.
ⓐ cubic   ⓑ linear
ⓒ square   ⓓ linear
ⓔ square   ⓕ cubic
9.52.
ⓐ 8 centimeters
ⓑ 4 sq. centimeters
9.55. 15 in.
9.58. 11 ft , 19 ft
9.61. 26 ft
9.64. 60 yd, 90 yd
9.67. 8 ft
9.70. 6 ft
9.73. 14 ft
9.76. 225 sq. cm
9.79. 40.25 sq. yd

9.82.
ⓐ 28.26 ft   ⓑ 63.585 sq. ft
9.85. 30 cm
9.88. 110 sq. units
9.91. 103.2 sq. units

9.94.
ⓐ 1,440 cu. ft   ⓑ 792 sq. ft

9.2. 40
9.5. $950
9.8. 4
9.11. 9, 15
9.14. −29, 11
9.17. 47, 48
9.20. −11, −12, −13
9.23. 42 nickels, 21 dimes
9.26. 22 nickels, 59 dimes

9.29. 32 at 49 cents, 12 at 8 cents

9.32.
ⓐ 103°   ⓑ 13°
9.35. 21°
9.38. 45°
9.41. 8
9.44. 17
9.47. 12 feet
9.50.
ⓐ cubic   ⓑ square
ⓒ cubic   ⓓ linear
ⓔ square   ⓕ linear
9.53.
ⓐ 340 yd   ⓑ 6000 sq. yd
9.56. 9 yd
9.59. 8 ft, 24 ft
9.62. 29 m
9.65. 13 sq. in.
9.68. 6 ft
9.71. 13 in.
9.74. 7 m
9.77. 42 sq. cm
9.80. 240 sq. ft

9.83. 17.27 ft

9.86. 110 ft
9.89. 36.5 sq. units
9.92. 38.24 sq. units

9.95.
ⓐ 216 cu. ft   ⓑ 228 sq. ft

9.3. 2
9.6. $4,200
9.9. 3
9.12. 27, 31
9.15. −4, 0
9.18. −15, −16
9.21. 9 nickels, 16 dimes
9.24. 51 dimes, 17 quarters
9.27. 330 day passes, 367 tournament passes
9.30. 26 at 49 cents, 10 at 21 cents
9.33. 40°, 140°

9.36. 56°
9.39. 20°, 70°, 90°
9.42. 22.5
9.45. 8
9.48. 8 feet
9.51.
ⓐ 8 inches   ⓑ 3 sq. inches

9.54.
ⓐ 220 ft   ⓑ 2976 sq. ft
9.57. 18 m, 11 m
9.60. 5 cm, 4 cm
9.63. 30 ft, 70 ft
9.66. 49 sq. in.
9.69. 14 in.
9.72. 17 cm
9.75. 161 sq. yd
9.78. 63 sq. m
9.81.
ⓐ 31.4 in.   ⓑ 78.5 sq. in.

9.84. 37.68 ft

9.87. 28 sq. units
9.90. 70 sq. units
9.93.
ⓐ 792 cu. ft   ⓑ 518 sq. ft
9.96.
ⓐ 2,772 cu. in.
ⓑ 1,264 sq. in.

9.97.
ⓐ 91.125 cu. m
ⓑ 121.5 sq. m

9.98.
ⓐ 389.017 cu. yd.
ⓑ 319.74 sq. yd.

9.99.
ⓐ 64 cu. ft   ⓑ 96 sq. ft

9.100.
ⓐ 4,096 cu. in.
ⓑ 1536 sq. in.

9.101.
ⓐ 113.04 cu. cm
ⓑ 113.04 sq. cm

9.102.
ⓐ 4.19 cu. ft   ⓑ 12.56 sq. ft

9.103.
ⓐ 3052.08 cu. in.
ⓑ 1017.36 sq. in.

9.104.
ⓐ 14.13 cu. ft   ⓑ 28.26 sq. ft

9.105.
ⓐ 351.68 cu. cm
ⓑ 276.32 sq. cm

9.106.
ⓐ 100.48 cu. ft
ⓑ 125.6 sq. ft

9.109. 65.94 cu. in.
9.112. 128.2 cu. in.
9.115. 11 hours

9.107.
ⓐ 3,818.24 cu. cm
ⓑ 1,356.48 sq. cm

9.110. 235.5 cu. cm
9.113. 330 mi
9.116. 56 mph

9.108.
ⓐ 91.5624 cu. ft
ⓑ 113.6052 sq. ft

9.111. 678.24 cu. in.
9.114. 7 mi
9.117.
ⓐ $r = 45$ ⓑ $r = \dfrac{d}{t}$

9.118.
ⓐ $r = 65$ ⓑ $r = \dfrac{d}{t}$

9.119. ⓐ $h = 20$ ⓑ $h = \dfrac{2A}{b}$

9.120.
ⓐ $b = 4$ ⓑ $b = \dfrac{2A}{h}$

9.121.
ⓐ $t = 3$ years   ⓑ $t = \dfrac{I}{Pr}$

9.122.
ⓐ $r = 0.12 = 12\%$
ⓑ $r = \dfrac{I}{Pt}$

9.123.
ⓐ $y = 1$ ⓑ $y = \dfrac{10 - 3x}{4}$

9.124.
ⓐ $y = -1$ ⓑ $y = \dfrac{18 - 5x}{2}$

9.127. $y = 11 - 7x$

9.125. $b = P - a - c$

9.128. $y = 8 - 11x$

9.126. $c = P - a - b$

9.129. $y = \dfrac{9 - 4x}{7}$

9.130. $y = \dfrac{1 - 5x}{8}$

Section Exercises

1. There are 30 children in the class.

3. Zachary has 125 CDs.

5. There are 6 boys in the club.

7. There are 17 glasses.

9. Lisa's original weight was 175 pounds.

11. 18%

13. The original price was $120.
19. 5
25. 18, 24
31. 4, 10
37. −11, −12
43. The original price was $45.

15. 4
21. 12
27. 8, 12
33. 32, 46
39. 25, 26, 27
45. Each sticker book cost $1.25.

17. 15
23. −5
29. −2, −3
35. 38, 39
41. −11, −12, −13
47. The price of the refrigerator before tax was $1,080.

49. Answers will vary.
55. 12 dimes and 27 nickels

51. 8 nickels, 22 dimes
57. 63 dimes, 20 quarters

53. 15 dimes, 8 quarters
59. 10 of the $1 bills, 7 of the $5 bills

61. 10 of the $10 bills, 5 of the $5 bills
67. 110 child tickets, 50 adult tickets
73. 15 at $10 shares, 5 at $12 shares

63. 16 nickels, 12 dimes, 7 quarters
69. 40 postcards, 100 stamps
75. 9 girls, 3 adults

65. 30 child tickets, 50 adult tickets
71. 30 at 49 cents, 10 at 21 cents
77. Answers will vary.

79. Answers will vary.

85. 45°
91. 62°, 28°
97. 57°
103. 30°, 60°, 90°
109. 15
115. 12
121. 5 feet
127. Answers will vary.
133. linear

139.
ⓐ 10 cm   ⓑ 5 sq. cm
145. 24 inches
151. 7 in., 16 in.
157. 25 ft, 50 ft
163. 55 m
169. 60 sq. in.
175. 8 ft
181. 28 cm
187. 15 ft
193. 12 ft, 13 ft, 14 ft
199. 2805 sq. m
205. 13.5 sq. ft
211. $24
217.
ⓐ 43.96 in.   ⓑ 153.86 sq. in.
223. 37.68 in.
229. 5.5 m
235. 16 sq. units
241. 12 sq. units
247. 44.81 sq. units
253. 95.625 sq. units
259.
ⓐ 6.5325 sq. ft
ⓑ 10.065 sq. ft
265.
ⓐ 17.64 cu. yd.
ⓑ 41.58 sq. yd.
271.
ⓐ 125 cu. cm   ⓑ 150 sq. cm

277.
ⓐ 21.952 cu. m
ⓑ 47.04 sq. m
283.
ⓐ 14,130 cu. in.
ⓑ 2,826 sq. in.

81.
ⓐ 127°   ⓑ 37°
87. 62.5°
93. 56°
99. 67.5°
105. 12
111. 25
117. 10.2
123. 14.1 feet
129. cubic
135.
ⓐ 10 cm   ⓑ 4 sq. cm
141.
ⓐ 260 ft   ⓑ 3825 sq. ft
147. 27 meters
153. 17 m, 12 m
159. 7 m, 11 m
165. 35 ft, 45 ft
171. 25.315 sq. m
177. 23 in.
183. 17 ft
189. 24 in.
195. 3 ft, 6 ft, 8 ft
201. 231 sq. cm
207. 1036 sq. in.
213. Answers will vary.
219.
ⓐ 53.38 ft   ⓑ 226.865 sq. ft
225. 6.908 ft
231. 24 ft
237. 30 sq. units
243. 67.5 sq. units
249. 41.12 sq. units
255. 187,500 sq. ft
261. Answers will vary.

267.
ⓐ 1,024 cu. ft   ⓑ 640 sq. ft

273.
ⓐ 1124.864 cu. ft.
ⓑ 648.96 sq. ft
279.
ⓐ 113.04 cu. cm
ⓑ 113.04 sq. cm
285.
ⓐ 381.51 cu. cm
ⓑ 254.34 sq. cm

83.
ⓐ 151°   ⓑ 61°
89. 62°, 118°
95. 44°
101. 45°, 45°, 90°
107. 351 miles
113. 8
119. 8
125. 2.9 feet
131. square
137.
ⓐ 8 cm   ⓑ 3 sq. cm
143.
ⓐ 58 ft   ⓑ 210 sq. ft
149. 23 m
155. 13.5 m, 12.8 m
161. 26 in.
167. 76 in., 36 in.
173. 0.75 sq. ft
179. 11 ft
185. 6 m
191. 27.5 in.
197. 144 sq. ft
203. 28.56 sq. m
209. 15 ft
215. Answers will vary.
221. 62.8 ft

227. 52 in.
233. 6.5 mi
239. 57.5 sq. units
245. 89 sq. units
251. 35.13 sq. units
257. 9400 sq. ft
263.
ⓐ 9 cu. m   ⓑ 27 sq. m

269.
ⓐ 3,350.49 cu. cm
ⓑ 1,622.42 sq. cm
275.
ⓐ 262,144 cu. ft
ⓑ 24,576 sq. ft
281.
ⓐ 1,766.25 cu. ft
ⓑ 706.5 sq. ft
287.
ⓐ 254.34 cu. ft
ⓑ 226.08 sq. ft

289.

ⓐ 29.673 cu. m

ⓑ 53.694 sq. m

295. 37.68 cu. ft

301. 64,108.33 cu. ft

291.

ⓐ 1,020.5 cu. cm

ⓑ 565.2 sq. cm

297. 324.47 cu. cm

303.

ⓐ 31.4 cu. ft   ⓑ 2.6 cu. ft

ⓒ 28.8 cu. ft

293.

ⓐ 678.24 cu. in.

ⓑ 508.68 sq. in.

299. 261.67 cu. ft

305. Answers will vary.

307. 612 mi

313. 3.6 hours

319.

ⓐ $t = 5$ ⓑ $t = \dfrac{d}{r}$

325.

ⓐ $r = 64$ ⓑ $r = \dfrac{d}{t}$

331.

ⓐ $P = \$19,571.43$

ⓑ $P = \dfrac{I}{rt}$

337.

ⓐ $y = 13$ ⓑ $y = 7 - 3x$

343. $y = 15 - 8x$

349. $y = 4 + x$

355. $L = \dfrac{V}{WH}$

309. 7 mi

315. 60 mph

321.

ⓐ $t = 8.5$ ⓑ $t = \dfrac{d}{r}$

327.

ⓐ $b = 14$ ⓑ $b = \dfrac{2A}{h}$

333.

ⓐ $t = 6$ years   ⓑ $t = \dfrac{I}{Pr}$

339.

ⓐ $b = 90 - a$ ⓑ $a = 90 - b$

345. $y = -6 + 4x$

351. $L = \dfrac{P - 2W}{2}$

357. 104° F

311. 6.5 hours

317. 80 mph

323.

ⓐ $r = 68$ ⓑ $r = \dfrac{d}{t}$

329.

ⓐ $h = 30$ ⓑ $h = \dfrac{2A}{b}$

335.

ⓐ $y = 2$ ⓑ $y = \dfrac{12 - 2x}{3}$

341. $a = 180 - b - c$

347. $y = \dfrac{7 - 4x}{3}$

353. $d = \dfrac{C}{\pi}$

359. Answers will vary

Review Exercises

361. Answers will vary.

367. 38

373. 6 of $5 bills, 11 of $10 bills

379. 132°

385. 30°, 60°, 90°

391. 8

397. cubic

403.

ⓐ 140 m   ⓑ 1176 sq. m

409. 62 m

415. 600 sq. in.

421. 100 sq. ft.

427. 48 in.

433. 199.25 sq. units

363. There are 116 people at the concert.

369. 18, 9

375. 35 adults, 82 children

381. 33°, 57°

387. 15

393. 8.1

399. square

405.

ⓐ 98 ft.   ⓑ 180 sq. ft.

411. 24.5 in., 12.5 in.

417. 7 in., 7 in.

423. 675 sq. m

429. 30 sq. units

435.

ⓐ 630 cu. cm   ⓑ 496 sq. cm

365. His original weight was 180 pounds.

371. 16 dimes, 11 quarters

377. 3 of 26 -cent stamps, 8 of 41 -cent stamps

383. 73°

389. 26

395. 6 feet

401.

ⓐ 8 units   ⓑ 3 sq. units

407. 25 cm

413. 135 sq. in.

419. 17 ft., 20 ft., 22 ft.

425.

ⓐ 18.84 m   ⓑ 28.26 sq. m

431. 300 sq. units

437.

ⓐ 15.625 cu. in.

ⓑ 37.5 sq. in.

439.
ⓐ 267.95 cu. yd.

ⓑ 200.96 sq. yd.

445.
ⓐ 753.6 cu. cm

ⓑ 477.28 sq. cm

451. 1520 miles

441.
ⓐ 12.76 cu. in.

ⓑ 26.41 sq. in.

447. 5.233 cu. m

453. 1.6 hours

443.
ⓐ 75.36 cu. yd.

ⓑ 100.48 sq. yd.

449. 4.599 cu. in.

455.
ⓐ $t = 6.2$ ⓑ $t = \frac{d}{r}$

461.
ⓐ $y = 4$ ⓑ $y = \frac{20 - 6x}{5}$

467. $W = \frac{P - 2L}{2}$

457.
ⓐ $b = 26$ ⓑ $b = \frac{2A}{h}$

463. $a = 90 - b$

459.
ⓐ $P = \$6000$ ⓑ $P = \frac{I}{(r \cdot t)}$

465. $y = 17 - 4x$

Practice Test

471. −16
477. 48.3
483. 2200 square centimeters
489. 31,400 cubic inches

473. 7 quarters, 12 dimes
479. 10
485. 282.6 inches
491. 14.7 miles per hour

475. 38°
481. 127.3 ft
487. 1440
493.
ⓐ height = 52   ⓑ $h = \frac{2A}{b}$

Chapter 10

Try It

10.1.
ⓐ monomial   ⓑ polynomial

ⓒ trinomial   ⓓ binomial

ⓔ monomial

10.4.
ⓐ 0   ⓑ 2   ⓒ 4   ⓓ 5

ⓔ 3

10.7. $14n$
10.10. $-2a^2 + b^2$
10.13. $3y^2 + 3y + 3$
10.16. $5a^2 + 8a + 8$

10.19. 4 feet

10.22.
ⓐ 81   ⓐ 21

10.25.
ⓐ 16   ⓑ −16
10.28. x^{16}
10.31. 6^{10}
10.34. z^{39}
10.37.
ⓐ x^{28} ⓑ 7^{32}
10.40. $144a^2$

10.2.
ⓐ binomial   ⓑ trinomial

ⓒ polynomial   ⓓ monomial

ⓒ monomial

10.5. $17x^2$

10.8. $-2a^3$
10.11. $4x^2 - 8x + 10$
10.14. $3u^2 - u + 2$
10.17.
ⓐ 13   ⓑ 3

10.20. 20 feet

10.23.
ⓐ $\frac{25}{64}$ ⓑ 0.4489

10.26.
ⓐ 64   ⓑ −64
10.29. p^{10}
10.32. 9^{15}
10.35. x^{21}
10.38.
ⓐ y^{54} ⓑ 8^{42}
10.41. $256x^4 y^4$

10.3.
ⓐ 1   ⓑ 1   ⓒ 4   ⓓ 2

ⓔ 0

10.6. $-3y^2$

10.9. $-2x^2 + 3y^2$
10.12. $11y^2 + 9y - 5$
10.15. $4n^2 + 12n$
10.18.
ⓐ 114   ⓑ −2

10.21.
ⓐ 64   ⓑ 11

10.24.
ⓐ $\frac{8}{125}$ ⓑ 0.016129

10.27. x^{15}

10.30. m^8
10.33. y^{43}
10.36. y^{15}
10.39. $196x^2$

10.42. $216x^3 y^3$

10.43. x^{40}
10.46. $81a^{20}b^{24}$
10.49. $64u^{18}v^{22}$
10.52. $54y^9$
10.55. $6x + 48$
10.58. $p^2 - 13p$
10.61. $-32y^3 - 20y^2 + 36y$
10.64. $24y^4 - 16y^3 - 32y^2$
10.67. $x^2 + 17x + 72$
10.70. $80m^2 + 142m + 63$
10.73. $x^2 - xy + 5x - 5y$
10.76. $y^2 + 16y + 28$
10.79. $20a^2 + 37a - 18$
10.82. $12a^2 - 54a - 2ab + 9b$
10.85. $y^3 - 8y^2 + 9y - 2$
10.88. $3x^3 + 2x^2 - 3x + 10$

10.91.
ⓐ $\dfrac{1}{x^7}$ ⓑ $\dfrac{1}{12^{10}}$

10.94.
ⓐ $\dfrac{1}{p^8}$ ⓑ w^4

10.97. 1

10.100.
ⓐ $-23x^2$ ⓑ 1

10.103. a^{11}
10.106. $\dfrac{1}{d}$

10.109. $\dfrac{m^{15}}{n^{40}}$

10.112. $\dfrac{64p^{12}}{343q^{15}}$

10.115. $7x^4$

10.118. $\dfrac{9}{a^5}$

10.121. $\dfrac{4y^2}{7x^4}$

10.124. $-4ab^5$

10.127.
ⓐ $\dfrac{1}{25}$ ⓑ $-\dfrac{1}{25}$

10.130.
ⓐ 2   ⓑ $\dfrac{1}{16}$

10.44. y^{42}
10.47. $98n^{14}$
10.50. $675x^7y^{18}$
10.53. $12m^5n^6$
10.56. $2y + 24$
10.59. $8x^2 + 24xy$
10.62. $-54x^3 - 6x^2 + 6x$
10.65. $xp + 8p$
10.68. $a^2 + 9a + 20$
10.71. $56y^2 - 13y - 3$
10.74. $x^2 - x + 2xy - 2y$
10.77. $y^2 + 5y - 24$
10.80. $49x^2 - 28x - 32$
10.83. $12m^2 - 55m + 63$
10.86. $3x^3 + 2x^2 - 3x + 10$
10.89.
ⓐ x^3 ⓑ 7^9

10.92.
ⓐ $\dfrac{1}{m^9}$ ⓑ $\dfrac{1}{7^6}$

10.95.
ⓐ 1   ⓑ 1

10.98. 1

10.101.
ⓐ $\dfrac{49}{81}$ ⓑ $\dfrac{y^3}{512}$ ⓒ $\dfrac{p^6}{q^6}$

10.104. b^{19}
10.107. f^{42}

10.110. $\dfrac{t^{20}}{u^{14}}$

10.113. $\dfrac{1}{y^{11}}$

10.116. $16y^3$

10.119. $\dfrac{2a^6}{3b^2}$

10.122. $\dfrac{5}{8m^5n^3}$

10.125.
ⓐ $\dfrac{1}{8}$ ⓑ $\dfrac{1}{100}$

10.128.
ⓐ $\dfrac{1}{4}$ ⓑ $-\dfrac{1}{4}$

10.131. $\dfrac{1}{y^7}$

10.45. $-512x^{12}y^{21}$
10.48. $48m^5$
10.51. $-56x^{11}$
10.54. $12p^{11}q^8$
10.57. $y^2 - 9y$
10.60. $18r^2 + 3rs$
10.63. $12x^4 - 9x^3 + 27x^2$
10.66. $ap + 4p$
10.69. $20x^2 + 51x + 27$
10.72. $15x^2 - 14x - 16$
10.75. $x^2 + 15x + 56$
10.78. $q^2 + q - 20$
10.81. $12x^2 - 60x - xy + 5y$
10.84. $42n^2 - 47n + 10$
10.87. $y^3 - 8y^2 + 9y - 2$
10.90.
ⓐ y^6 ⓑ 8^8

10.93.
ⓐ b^8 ⓑ $\dfrac{1}{z^6}$

10.96.
ⓐ 1   ⓑ 1

10.99.
ⓐ 1   ⓑ $7x^2$ 1

10.102.
ⓐ $\dfrac{1}{64}$ ⓑ $-\dfrac{125}{m^3}$ ⓒ $\dfrac{r^4}{s^4}$

10.105. k^2
10.108. $\dfrac{1}{b^{10}}$

10.111. $\dfrac{25b^2}{81c^6}$

10.114. $9x^5$

10.117. $-\dfrac{12y}{x^2}$

10.120. $-\dfrac{3q^6}{5p^8}$

10.123. $2xy^2$

10.126.
ⓐ $\dfrac{1}{9}$ ⓑ $\dfrac{1}{10,000}$

10.129.
ⓐ 2   ⓑ $\dfrac{1}{18}$

10.132. $\dfrac{1}{z^8}$

10.133.
ⓐ $\frac{8}{p}$ ⓑ $\frac{1}{8p}$ ⓒ $-\frac{1}{8p}$

10.134.
ⓐ $\frac{11}{q}$ ⓑ $\frac{1}{11q}$ ⓒ $-\frac{1}{11q}$

10.135.
ⓐ x^4 ⓑ $\frac{1}{y^5}$ ⓒ $\frac{1}{z^9}$

10.136.
ⓐ a^5 ⓑ $\frac{1}{b^4}$ ⓒ $\frac{1}{c^{15}}$

10.137. $\dfrac{1}{p^3 q^3}$

10.138. $\dfrac{1}{r^2 s^8}$

10.139. $-\dfrac{12v^5}{u}$

10.140. $-\dfrac{30d^3}{c^8}$

10.141. $\dfrac{1}{x^4}$

10.142. $\dfrac{1}{y^4}$

10.143. $\dfrac{64}{a^8}$

10.144. $\dfrac{8}{c^{12}}$

10.145. x^{11}

10.146. y^{13}

10.147. 9.6×10^4

10.148. 4.83×10^4

10.149. 7.8×10^{-3}

10.150. 1.29×10^{-2}

10.151. 1,300

10.152. 92,500

10.153. 0.00012

10.154. 0.075

10.155. 0.06

10.156. 0.009

10.157. 400,000

10.158. 20,000

10.159. 18

10.160. 16

10.161. 7

10.162. 11

10.163. $8x^2$

10.164. $9y^3$

10.165. $3x$

10.166. $5m^2$

10.167. $4(x+3)$

10.168. $6(a+4)$

10.169. $9(a+1)$

10.170. $11(x+1)$

10.171. $11(x-4)$

10.172. $13(y-4)$

10.173. $4(y^2+2y+3)$

10.174. $6(x^2+7x-2)$

10.175. $x(9x+7)$

10.176. $a(5a-12)$

10.177. $2x^2(x+6)$

10.178. $3y^2(2y-5)$

10.179. $9y(2y+7)$

10.180. $8k(4k+7)$

10.181. $6y(3y^2-y-4)$

10.182. $4x(4x^2+2x-3)$

10.183. $-5(y+7)$

10.184. $-8(2z+7)$

10.185. $-7a(a-3)$

10.186. $-x(6x-1)$

Section Exercises

1. binomial

3. trinomial

5. polynomial

7. monomial

9. 5

11. 1

13. 0

15. $15x^2$

17. $-8u$

19. $5a+7b$

21. $-4a-3b$

23. $16x$

25. $-17x^6$

27. $12y^2+4y+8$

29. $-3x^2+17x-1$

31. $4a^2-7a-11$

33. $4m^2-10m+2$

35. $11z+8$

37. $12s^2-16s+9$

39. $2p^3+p^2+9p+10$

41. x^2+3x+4

43. $11w-66$

45.
ⓐ 187   ⓑ 40   ⓒ 2

47.
ⓐ -104 ⓑ 4   ⓒ 40

49. 19 feet

51. 10 mpg

53. Answers will vary.

55. 1,024

57. $\frac{1}{4}$

59. 0.008

61. 625

63. -625

65. $-10,000$

67. $-\dfrac{8}{27}$

69. $-.25$

71. x^9

73. a^5

75. 3^{14}

77. z^6

79. x^{a+2}

81. y^{a+b}

83. u^8

85. y^{20}

87. 10^{12}

89. x^{90}

91. x^{2y}

93. 5^{xy}

95. $25a^2$

97. $-216m^3$

99. $16r^2 s^2$

101. $256x^4 y^4 z^4$

103. x^{14}

105. a^{36}

107. $45x^3$

109. $200a^5$

111. $8m^{18}$

113. $1,000x^6 y^3$

115. $16a^{12}b^8$

117. $\dfrac{8}{27}x^6 y^3$

119. $1,024a^{10}$

121. $25,000p^{24}$

123. $x^{18}y^{18}$

125. $144m^8 n^{22}$

127. $-60x^6$

129. $72u^7$

131. $4r^{11}$

133. $36a^5 b^7$

135. $8x^2 y^5$

137. $\dfrac{1}{2}x^3 y^3$

139. 1,679,616

141. Answers will vary.

143. Answers will vary.

145. $4x + 40$
151. $-8z + 40$
157. $12x^2 - 120x$
163. $55p^2 - 25pq$
169. $-8y^3 - 16y^2 + 120y$
175. $2y^2 - 9y$
181. $n^2 + 9n - 36$
187. $u^2 - 14u + 45$
193. $v^2 + 7v - 60$
199. $16c^2 - 1$
205. $5x^2 - 20x - xy + 4y$
211. $y^3 - 16y^2 + 69y - 54$

147. $15r - 360$
153. $u^2 + 5u$
159. $-27a^2 - 45a$
165. $3v^2 + 30v + 75$
171. $5q^5 - 10q^4 + 30q^3$
177. $8w - 48$
183. $y^2 + 11y + 24$
189. $z^2 - 32z + 220$
195. $6n^2 + 11n + 5$
201. $15u^2 - 82u + 112$
207. $u^3 + 7u^2 + 14u + 8$
213. $2x^3 - 9x^2 - 17x - 6$

149. $-3m - 33$
155. $n^3 - 3n^2$
161. $24x^2 + 6xy$
167. $8n^3 - 8n^2 + 2n$
173. $-12z^4 - 48z^3 + 4z^2$
179. $x^2 + 10x + 24$
185. $a^2 + 22a + 96$
191. $x^2 + 3x - 28$
197. $20m^2 - 88m - 9$
203. $2a^2 + 5ab + 3b^2$
209. $3a^3 + 31a^2 + 5a - 50$
215.
ⓐ 195   ⓑ 195
ⓐ Answers will vary.

217. Answers will vary.
223. r^4

229. $\dfrac{1}{a^8}$

235. -1

241.
ⓐ 1   ⓑ 15
247. $\dfrac{m^3}{216}$

253. x^3

259. 1

265. y^3

271. 1

277. $8b^6$

283. $\dfrac{5}{6x^6}$

289. $-\dfrac{4y^6}{5x^2}$
295. $5u^4v^3$

301.
ⓐ z ⓑ $\dfrac{1}{z}$

307. $3x^2$
313. Answers will vary.

319. $\dfrac{1}{32}$

219. 4^6
225. $\dfrac{1}{y^{16}}$

231. 1

237.
ⓐ 1   ⓑ 10
239.
243. 7

249. $\dfrac{x^{10}}{y^{10}}$

255. u^2

261. $\dfrac{1}{x^{18}}$

267. $\dfrac{1}{x^{10}}$

273. $\dfrac{1}{r^3}$

279. $\dfrac{-18}{x^6}$

285. $\dfrac{6r^2}{s^8}$

291. $\dfrac{4z}{3x^2y^3}$

297.
ⓐ $18n^{10}$ ⓑ $12n^{10}$
ⓒ $45n^{20}$ ⓓ 5

303. $6y^6$

309. yz^2

315. Answers will vary.

321. $\dfrac{1}{10}$

221. x^9
227. $\dfrac{1}{10^{12}}$

233. 1

239.
ⓐ 1   ⓑ $-27x^5$
245. $\dfrac{243}{32}$

251. $\dfrac{a^2}{9b^2}$

257. $\dfrac{1}{y^2}$

263. a^{14}

269. $\dfrac{16r^{12}}{625s^4}$

275. $3x^8$

281. $2x$

287. $\dfrac{n^6}{8}$

293. $\dfrac{10n^2}{m^4}$

299.
ⓐ q^8 ⓑ q^{15}

305. $15c^6$

311. 1,000,000

317. $\dfrac{1}{64}$

323. $\dfrac{4}{9}$

325. $\frac{3}{5}$

327. $\frac{3}{4}$

329.
ⓐ $\frac{1}{64}$ ⓑ $-\frac{1}{64}$

331.
ⓐ $\frac{1}{4096}$ ⓑ $-\frac{1}{4096}$

333.
ⓐ $\frac{10}{3}$ ⓑ $\frac{1}{30}$

335.
ⓐ $\frac{3}{25}$ ⓑ $\frac{1}{225}$

337. $\frac{1}{p^3}$

339. $\frac{1}{m^5}$

341.
ⓐ $\frac{3}{q}$ ⓑ $\frac{1}{3q}$ ⓒ $-\frac{1}{3q}$

343.
ⓐ $\frac{10}{k}$ ⓑ $\frac{1}{10k}$ ⓒ $-\frac{1}{10k}$

345. r^3

347. $\frac{1}{q^5}$

349. $\frac{1}{z^8}$

351. $\frac{1}{m}$

353. $\frac{1}{x}$

355. $\frac{u^2}{v^2}$

357. $\frac{1}{a^2 b^4}$

359. $\frac{1}{p^5 q^7}$

361. $-\frac{21q^5}{p^3}$

363. $\frac{32}{a^3 b}$

365. $\frac{1}{q^{100}}$

367. $\frac{1}{x^4}$

369. $\frac{1}{y^6}$

371. m^6

373. $\frac{9}{q^{10}}$

375. $\frac{n^{18}}{64}$

377. b^8

379. m^7

381. $\frac{1}{r^3}$

383. p^3

385. 2.8×10^5
391. 1.03×10^{-5}
397. 830
403. 0.0000000615
409. 0.003
415. 50,000,000

387. 1.29×10^6
393. 6.85×10^9
399. 16,000,000,000
405. $15,000,000,000,000
411. 0.00000735
417.
ⓐ 1.25×10^{-4} ⓐ 8,000

389. 4.1×10^{-2}
395. 5.7×10^{-9}
401. 0.028
407. 0.00001
413. 200,000
419. 11,441,304,000

421. Answers will vary.
427. 4
433. $12p^3$
439. $5x^3$
445. $4(b - 5)$
451. $6(q^2 + 5q + 7)$
457. $q(4q + 7)$
463. $b(a + 8)$
469. $6c(c^2 - d^2)$
475. $10(y^2 + 5y + 4)$
481. $8c^3(c^2 + 5c - 7)$
487. $-8a^2(a - 4)$

423. 15
429. 5
435. $2a$
441. $7b^2$
447. $7(x - 1)$
453. $c(9c + 22)$
459. $3r(r + 9)$
465. $11y(5 - y^3)$
471. $24x^2(2x + 3)$
477. $12(u^2 - 3u - 9)$
483. $-7(p + 12)$
489. $-9b^3(b^2 - 7)$

425. 25
431. $3x$
437. $10y$
443. $5(y + 3)$
449. $3(n^2 + 7n + 4)$
455. $x(17x + 7)$
461. $10u(3u - 1)$
467. $15c^2(3c - 1)$
473. $18a^3(8a^3 + 5)$
479. $5p^2(p^2 - 4p - 3)$
485. $-6b(3b + 11)$
491. $-4(4t^2 - 20t - 1)$

Review Exercises

494. trinomial
500. 0
506. $10a^2 + 4a - 1$
512. 995
518. 64 feet
524. p^{13}
530. 3^{10}
536. $27a^{15}$
542. $56x^3 y^{11}$

496. binomial
502. $15p$
508. $6y^2 - 3y + 3$
514. 2,955
520. 216
526. a^6
532. $64n^2$
538. x^{21}
544. $70 - 7x$

498. 2
504. $-3n^5$
510. $8q^3 + q^2 + 6q - 29$
516. -163
522. 0.25
528. y^{12}
534. $256a^8 b^8$
540. $-54p^5$
546. $-625y^4 + 5y$

548. $a^2 + 7a + 10$

550. $6x^2 - 19x - 7$

552. $n^2 + 9n + 8$

554. $5u^2 + 37u - 24$

556. $p^2 + 11p + 28$

558. $27c^2 - 3c - 4$

560. $x^3 - 2x^2 - 24x - 21$

562. $m^3 - m^2 - 72m - 180$

564. 2^6 or 64

566. $\dfrac{1}{n^9}$

568. 1

570. 1

572. $\dfrac{9}{25}$

574. $\dfrac{125m^3}{n^3}$

576. a^2

578. $\dfrac{1}{x^{40}}$

580. $\dfrac{1}{n}$

582. $9p^9$

584. $-\dfrac{3}{y^4}$

586. $\dfrac{4a^5}{b^2}$

588. $\dfrac{4m^9}{n^4}$

590. $\dfrac{1}{36}$

592. $\dfrac{5}{16}$

594. x^6

596. $\dfrac{1}{u^3 v^5}$

598. k^6

600. b^{10}

602. 5.3×10^6

604. 9.7×10^{-2}

606. 29,000

608. 375

610. 6,000

612. 30,000,000,000

614. 5

616. $4x^2$

618. $8(2u - 3)$

620. $6p(p + 1)$

622. $-9a^3(a^2 + 1)$

624. $5(y^2 - 11y + 9)$

Practice Test

626.

ⓐ trinomial   ⓑ 4

628. $6x^2 - 3x + 11$

630. n^5

632. $-48x^5 y^9$

634. $s^2 + 17s + 72$

636. $55a^2 - 41a + 6$

638. $24a^2 + 34ab - 45b^2$

640. x^{14}

642. $\dfrac{4r}{s^6}$

644. $3y^2 - 7x$

646. $\dfrac{1}{2y}$

648. x^9

651. $-6x(x + 5)$

652. 0.000525

653. 3×10^5

Chapter 11

Try It

11.1.

ⓐ 1C

ⓑ Engineering Building

11.2.

ⓐ 1A   ⓑ Library

11.3.

11.4.

11.5.

11.6.

11.7.

11.8.

11.9.

11.10.

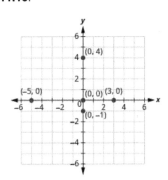

11.11.
1. A: (5,1)
2. B: (−2,4)
3. C: (−5,−1)
4. D: (3,−2)

11.12.
1. A: (4,2)
2. B: (−2,3)
3. C: (−4,−4)
4. D: (3,−5)

11.13.
1. A: (4,0)
2. B: (0,3)
3. C: (−3,0)
4. D: (0,−5)

11.14.
1. A: (−3,0)
2. B: (0,−3)
3. C: (5,0)
4. D: (0,2)

11.15. ⓐ, ⓒ

11.16. ⓑ, ⓒ

11.17. ⓑ

11.18. ⓐ, ⓑ

11.19.

$y = 3x - 1$		
x	y	(x, y)
0	−1	(0, −1)
−1	−4	(−1, −4)
2	5	(2, 5)

11.20.

$y = 6x + 1$		
x	y	(x, y)
0	1	(0, 1)
1	7	(1, 7)
−2	−11	(−2, −11)

11.21.

$2x - 5y = 20$		
x	y	(x, y)
0	−4	(0, −4)
10	0	(10, 0)
−5	−6	(−5, −6)

11.22.

3x − 4y = 12		
x	y	(x, y)
0	−3	(0, −3)
4	0	(4, 0)
−4	−6	(−4, −6)

11.23. Answers will vary.

11.24. Answers will vary.

11.25. Answers will vary.
11.28. Answers will vary.

11.26. Answers will vary.
11.29.
1. ⓐ yes ⓑ yes
2. ⓐ no ⓑ no
3. ⓐ no ⓑ no
4. ⓐ yes ⓑ yes

11.27. Answers will vary.
11.30.

11.31.

11.32.

11.33.

11.34.

11.35.

11.36.

11.37.

11.38.

11.39.

11.40.

11.41.

11.42.

11.43.

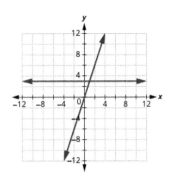

11.44. *x*-intercept (2,0);
y-intercept (0,−2)

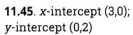

11.45. *x*-intercept (3,0);
y-intercept (0,2)

11.46. $(4, 0)$ and $(0, 12)$

11.47. $(8, 0)$ and $(0, 2)$

11.48. *x*-intercept (4,0);
y-intercept: (0,−3)

11.49. *x*-intercept (4,0);
y-intercept: (0,−2)

11.50.

11.51.

11.52.

11.53.

11.54.

11.55.

11.56.
ⓐ intercepts
ⓑ horizontal line
ⓒ plotting points
ⓓ vertical line

11.57.
ⓐ vertical line
ⓑ plotting points
ⓒ horizontal line
ⓓ intercepts

11.58. $\frac{4}{3}$

11.59. $\frac{1}{4}$

11.60. $-\frac{2}{3}$

11.61. $-\frac{4}{3}$

11.62.

11.63.

11.64.

11.65.

11.66. $\frac{2}{5}$

11.67. $\frac{3}{4}$

11.68. $-\frac{4}{3}$

11.69. $-\frac{3}{5}$

11.70. $\frac{5}{4}$

11.71. $\frac{3}{2}$

11.72. undefined

11.73. 0

11.74. 1

11.75. 1

11.76. −1   **11.77.** 10   **11.78.**

11.79.   **11.80.**   **11.81.**

11.82.   **11.83.**   **11.84.** $\frac{7}{12}$

11.85. $\frac{5}{12}$ **11.86.** $-\frac{1}{36}$ **11.87.** $-\frac{1}{48}$

Section Exercises

1.   **3.**   **5.**

7.

9.

11.

13.

21. (a), (b)

23. (a), (c)

25. (b), (c)

27. (a), (b)

29.

x	y	(x, y)
−1	−6	(−1, −6)
0	−4	(0, −4)
2	0	(2, 0)

31.

x	y	(x, y)
−2	7	(−2, 7)
0	5	(0, 5)
3	2	(3, 2)

33.

x	y	(x, y)
−2	1	(−2, 1)
0	−2	(0, −2)
2	−5	(2, −5)

35.

(a)

(b) Age and weight are only positive.

37. Answers may vary.

39.

ⓐ yes ⓑ yes   ⓐ no ⓑ no

ⓐ yes ⓑ yes   ⓐ yes ⓑyes

40.

1. ⓐ yes ⓑ yes

2. ⓐ yes ⓑ yes

3. ⓐ no ⓑ no

4. ⓐ no ⓑno

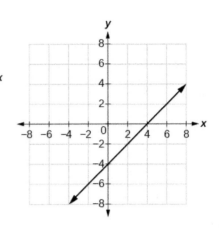

41.

ⓐ yes ⓑ yes   ⓐ yes ⓑ yes

ⓐ yes ⓑ yes   ⓐ no ⓑno

42.

ⓐ yes ⓑ yes   ⓐ yes ⓑ yes

ⓐ no ⓑ no   ⓐ yes ⓑyes

43.

45.

47.

49.

51.

53.

55.

57.

59.

61.

63.

65.

67.

69.

71.

73.

75.

77.

79.

81.

83.

85.

87.

89.

91.

93.

94.

95.

97.

98.

99.

100.

101.

102.

103.

104.

105.

106.

107.

108.

109.

110.

111.

112.

113.

$722, $850, $978

115. Answers will vary.

117. (3,0),(0,3)
123. (−1,0),(0,1)
129. (−2,0),(0,−2)
135. (8,0),(0,4)
141. (2,0),(0,−8)
147. (3,0),(0,−1)
153. (0,0)

119. (5,0),(0,−5)
125. (0,0)
131. (5,0),(0,−5)
137. (2,0),(0,6)
143. (5,0),(0,2)
149. (−10,0),(0,2)
155.

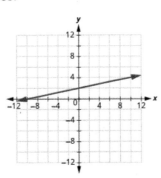

121. (−2,0),(0,−2)
127. (4,0),(0,4)
133. (−3,0),(0,3)
139. (12,0),(0,−4)
145. (4,0),(0,−6)
151. (0,0)
157.

159.

161.

163.

165.

167.

169.

171.

173.

175.

177.

179.

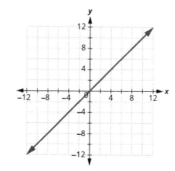

181. vertical line

183. horizontal line

189. plotting points

195. plotting points

185. plotting points

191. horizontal line

197. ⓐ (0,1,000),(15,0). ⓑ At (0,1,000) he left Chicago 0 hours ago and has 1,000 miles left to drive. At (15,0) he left Chicago 15 hours ago and has 0 miles left to drive.

187. intercepts

193. intercepts

199. Answers will vary.

201. Answers will vary.

203. $\frac{1}{4}$

205. $-\frac{3}{2}$

207.

209.

211.

213.

215. $\frac{2}{5}$

217. $\frac{5}{4}$

219. $-\frac{1}{3}$

221. $-\frac{3}{4}$

223. $\frac{3}{4}$

225. $-\frac{5}{2}$

227. $-\frac{2}{3}$

229. $\frac{1}{4}$

231. 0

233. undefined

235. 0

237. undefined

239. $\frac{5}{2}$

241. $\frac{3}{4}$

243. $-\frac{5}{2}$

245. $-\frac{8}{5}$

247. $\frac{7}{3}$

249. −1

251.

253.

255.

257.

259.

261.

263.

265.

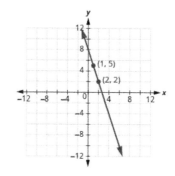

267. $\frac{1}{3}$

269. ⓐ $\frac{3}{50}$ ⓑ
rise = 3; run = 50

271.
ⓐ 288 inches (24 feet)
ⓑ Models will vary.

273. Answers will vary.

275. Answers will vary.

Review Exercises

277.

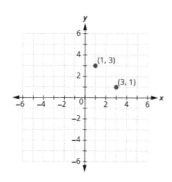

279.
ⓐ III ⓑ II ⓒ IV ⓐ I

281.
ⓐ (5,3) ⓑ (2,–1) ⓒ (–3,–2)
ⓓ (–1,4)

283.
ⓐ (2,0) ⓑ (0,–5) ⓒ (–4,0)
ⓓ (0,3)

285. ⓑ,ⓒ

287.

x	y	(x, y)
0	−1	(0, −1)
1	3	(1, 3)
−2	−9	(−2, −9)

289.

x	y	(x, y)
5	0	(5, 0)
1	2	(1, 2)
−1	3	(−1, 3)

291. Answers will vary.

293. Answers will vary.

295.
ⓐ yes ⓑ no ⓒ yes ⓓ yes
ⓐ yes ⓑ no ⓒ yes ⓓ yes

297.

299.

301.
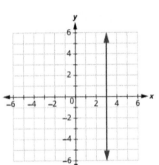

303. (0,3) (3,0)

305. (−1,0) (0,1)

307. (0,0)

309.

311. horizontal line

313. intercepts

315. plotting points

317. $\frac{4}{3}$

319. $-\frac{2}{3}$

321.

323.

325. 1

327. $-\frac{1}{2}$

329. undefined

331. 0

333. −4

335. $\frac{1}{2}$

337.

Practice Test

339.

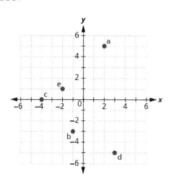

341. (4,0), (0,−2)

343. no; $1 + 4 \cdot 3 \neq 12$

345.

x	y	(x, y)
0	8	(0, 8)
2	0	(2, 0)
3	−4	(3, −4)

347.

349. $-\dfrac{5}{2}$

351. 0

353. $\dfrac{1}{50}$

INDEX